Nineteenth-Century
Literature Criticism

Guide to Gale Literary Criticism Series

For criticism on	Consult these Gale series
Authors now living or who died after December 31, 1959	*CONTEMPORARY LITERARY CRITICISM (CLC)*
Authors who died between 1900 and 1959	*TWENTIETH-CENTURY LITERARY CRITICISM (TCLC)*
Authors who died between 1800 and 1899	*NINETEENTH-CENTURY LITERATURE CRITICISM (NCLC)*
Authors who died between 1400 and 1799	*LITERATURE CRITICISM FROM 1400 TO 1800 (LC)* *SHAKESPEAREAN CRITICISM (SC)*
Authors who died before 1400	*CLASSICAL AND MEDIEVAL LITERATURE CRITICISM (CMLC)*
Authors of books for children and young adults	*CHILDREN'S LITERATURE REVIEW (CLR)*
Dramatists	*DRAMA CRITICISM (DC)*
Poets	*POETRY CRITICISM (PC)*
Short story writers	*SHORT STORY CRITICISM (SSC)*
Black writers of the past two hundred years	*BLACK LITERATURE CRITICISM (BLC)*
Hispanic writers of the late nineteenth and twentieth centuries	*HISPANIC LITERATURE CRITICISM (HLC)*
Native North American writers and orators of the eighteenth, nineteenth, and twentieth centuries	*NATIVE NORTH AMERICAN LITERATURE (NNAL)*
Major authors from the Renaissance to the present	*WORLD LITERATURE CRITICISM, 1500 TO THE PRESENT (WLC)*

ISSN 0732-1864

Volume 79

Nineteenth-Century Literature Criticism

Excerpts from Criticism of the
Works of Novelists, Poets, Playwrights,
Short Story Writers, Philosophers, and Other
Creative Writers Who Died between 1800
and 1899, from the First Published Critical
Appraisals to Current Evaluations

Suzanne Dewsbury
Editor

GALE GROUP

Detroit
San Francisco
London
Boston
Woodbridge, CT

STAFF

Suzanne Dewsbury, *Editor*
Gianna Barberi, *Associate Editor*
Tom Schoenberg, *Assistant Editor*
Janet Witalec, *Managing Editor*

Maria L. Franklin, *Permissions Manager*
Kimberly F. Smilay, *Permissions Specialist*
Kelly A. Quin, *Permissions Associate*
Erin Bealmear, Sandra K. Gore, *Permissions Assistants*

Victoria B. Cariappa, *Research Manager*
Cheryl Warnock, *Research Specialist*
Corrine Boland, Tamara C. Nott, Tracie A. Richardson, *Research Associates*
Phyllis Blackman, Timothy Lehnerer, *Research Assistants*

Dorothy Maki, *Manufacturing Manager*
Stacy Melson, *Buyer*

Gary Leach, *Graphic Artist*
Randy Bassett, *Image Database Supervisor*
Robert Duncan, Michael Logusz, *Imaging Specialists*
Pamela A. Reed, *Imaging Coordinator*

This book is printed on acid-free paper that meets the minimum requirements of American National Standard for Information Sciences—Permanence Paper for Printed Library Materials, ANSI Z39.48-1984.

Library of Congress Catalog Card Number 84-643008
ISBN 0-7876-3150-7
ISSN 0732-1864
Printed in the United States of America

10 9 8 7 6 5 4 3 2 1

Contents

Preface vii

Acknowledgments xi

Preface

Since its inception in 1981, *Nineteenth-Century Literature Criticism* has been a valuable resource for students and librarians seeking critical commentary on writers of this transitional period in world history. Designated an "Outstanding Reference Source" by the American Library Association with the publication of its first volume, *NCLC* has since been purchased by over 6,000 school, public, and university libraries. The series has covered more than 300 authors representing 29 nationalities and over 17,000 titles. No other reference source has surveyed the critical reaction to nineteenth-century authors and literature as thoroughly as *NCLC.*

Scope of the Series

NCLC is designed to introduce students and advanced readers to the authors of the nineteenth century, and to the most significant interpretations of these authors' works. The great poets, novelists, short story writers, playwrights, and philosophers of this period are frequently studied in high school and college literature courses. By organizing and reprinting commentary written on these authors, *NCLC* helps students develop valuable insight into literary history, promotes a better understanding of the texts, and sparks ideas for papers and assignments. Each entry in *NCLC* presents a comprehensive survey of an author's career or an individual work of literature and provides the user with a multiplicity of interpretations and assessments. Such variety allows students to pursue their own interests; furthermore, it fosters an awareness that literature is dynamic and responsive to many different opinions.

Every fourth volume of *NCLC* is devoted to literary topics that cannot be covered under the author approach used in the rest of the series. Such topics include literary movements, prominent themes in nineteenth-century literature, literary reaction to political and historical events, significant eras in literary history, prominent literary anniversaries, and the literatures of cultures that are often overlooked by English-speaking readers.

NCLC continues the survey of criticism of world literature begun by Gale's *Contemporary Literary Criticism (CLC)* and *Twentieth-Century Literary Criticism (TCLC),* both of which excerpt and reprint commentary on authors of the twentieth century. For additional information about *TCLC, CLC,* and Gale's other criticism series, users should consult the Guide to Gale Literary Criticism Series preceding the title page in this volume.

Coverage

Each volume of *NCLC* is carefully compiled to present:

- criticism of authors, or literary topics, representing a variety of genres and nationalities
- both major and lesser-known writers and literary works of the period
- 4-8 authors or 4-6 topics per volume
- individual entries that survey critical response to an author's work or a topic in literary history, including early criticism to reflect initial reactions, later criticism to represent any rise or decline in reputation, and current retrospective analyses.

Organization

An author entry consists of the following elements: author heading, biographical and critical introduction, list of principal works, excerpts of criticism (each preceded by a bibliographic citation and an annotation), and a bibliography of further reading.

- The **Author Heading** consists of the name under which the author most commonly wrote, followed by birth and death dates. If an author wrote consistently under a pseudonym, the pseudonym will be listed in the author heading and the real name given in parentheses on the first line of the biographical and critical introduction. Also located at the beginning of the introduction to the author entry are any name variations under which an author wrote, including transliterated forms for an author whose language uses a nonroman alphabet.

- The **Biographical and Critical Introduction** outlines the author's life and career, as well as the critical issues surrounding his or her work. References are provided to past volumes of *NCLC* in which further information about the author may be found.

- Most *NCLC* entries include a **Portrait** of the author. Many entries also contain reproductions of materials pertinent to an author's career, including manuscript pages, title pages, dust jackets, letters, and drawings, as well as photographs of important people, places, and events in an author's life.

- The list of **Principal Works** is chronological by date of first publication and identifies the genre of each work. In the case of foreign authors with both foreign-language publications and English translations, the English-language version is given in brackets. Unless otherwise indicated, dramas are dated by first performance, not first publication.

- **Criticism** in each author entry is arranged chronologically to provide a perspective on changes in critical evaluation over the years. All titles of works by the author featured in the entry are printed in boldface type to enable the user to easily locate discussion of particular works. Also for purposes of easier identification, the critic's name and the publication date of the essay are given at the beginning of each piece of criticism. Unsigned criticism is preceded by the title of the journal in which it appeared. Publication information (such as publisher names and book prices) and some parenthetical numerical references (such as page and line references to specific editions of works) have been deleted at the editors' discretion to provide smoother reading of the text. Footnotes that appear with previously published pieces of criticism are reprinted at the end of each essay or excerpt. In the case of excerpted criticism, only those footnotes that pertain to the excerpted text are included.

- A complete **Bibliographic Citation** provides original publication information for each piece of criticism.

- Critical excerpts are prefaced by **Annotations** providing the reader with a summary of the critical intent of the piece. Also included, when appropriate, is information about the critic's reputation, individual approach to literary criticism, and particular expertise in an author's works, as well as information about the relative importance of the critical excerpt. In some cases, the annotations cross-reference excerpts by critics who discuss each other's commentary.

- An annotated list of **Further Reading** appearing at the end of each entry suggests secondary sources on the author. In some cases it includes essays for which the editors could not obtain reprint rights.

Cumulative Indexes

■ Each volume of *NCLC* contains a cumulative **Author Index** listing all authors who have appeared in Gale's Literary Criticism Series, along with cross-references to such biographical series as *Contemporary Authors* and *Dictionary of Literary Biography*. Useful for locating authors within the various series, this index is particularly valuable for those authors who are identified with a certain period but who, because of their death dates, are placed in another, or for those authors whose careers span two periods. For example, Fyodor Dostoevsky is found in *NCLC,* yet Leo Tolstoy, another major nineteenth-century Russian novelist, is found in *TCLC* because he died after 1899.

■ Each *NCLC* volume includes a cumulative **Nationality Index** which lists all authors who have appeared in *NCLC*, arranged alphabetically under their respective nationalities.

■ Each new volume in Gale's Literary Criticism Series includes a cumulative **Topic Index**, which lists all literary topics treated in *NCLC, TCLC, LC 1400-1800*, and the *CLC* Yearbook.

■ Each new volume of *NCLC*, with the exception of the Topics volumes, contains a **Title Index** listing the titles of all literary works discussed in the volume. In response to numerous suggestions from librarians, Gale has also produced a **Special Paperbound Edition** of the *NCLC* title index. This annual cumulation lists all titles discussed in the series since its inception. Additional copies of the index are available on request. Librarians and patrons have welcomed this separate index: it saves shelf space, is easy to use, and is recyclable upon receipt of the following year's cumulation. Titles discussed in the Topics volume entries are not included in the *NCLC* cumulative index.

Citing *Nineteenth-Century Literature Criticism*

When writing papers, students who quote directly from any volume in Gale's Literary Criticism Series may use the following general forms to footnote reprinted criticism. The first example pertains to material drawn from periodicals, the second to material reprinted from books:

[1]Kim McQuaid, "William Apes, Pequot: An Indian Reformer in the Jackson Era," *The New England Quarterly*, 50 (December 1977), 605-25; excerpted and reprinted in *Nineteenth-Century Literature Criticism,* Vol. 73, ed. Janet Witalec (Farmington Hills, Mich.: The Gale Group, 1999), pp. 3-4.

[2]Richard Harter Fogle, *The Imagery of Keats and Shelley: A Comparative Study* (Archon Books, 1949); excerpted and reprinted in *Nineteenth-Century Literary Criticism,* Vol. 73, ed. Janet Witalec (Farmington Hills, Mich.: The Gale Group, 1999), pp. 157-69.

Suggestions Are Welcome

In response to suggestions, several features have been added to *NCLC* since the series began, including annotations to excerpted criticism, a cumulative index to authors in all Gale literary criticism series, entries devoted to criticism on a single work by a major author, more illustrations, and a title index listing all literary works discussed in the series.

Readers who wish to suggest authors, single works, or topics to appear in future volumes, or who have other suggestions, are cordially invited to write: The Editors, *Nineteenth-Century Literature Criticism,* The Gale Group, 27500 Drake Rd., Farmington Hills, MI 48331-3535; call toll-free at 1-800-347-GALE.

Acknowledgments

The editors wish to thank the copyright holders of the excerpted criticism included in this volume and the permissions managers of many book and magazine publishing companies for assisting us in securing reproduction rights. We are also grateful to the staffs of the Detroit Public Library, the Library of Congress, the University of Detroit Mercy Library, Wayne State University Purdy/Kresge Library Complex, and the University of Michigan Libraries for making their resources available to us. Following is a list of the copyright holders who have granted us permission to reproduce material in this volume of *NCLC*. Every effort has been made to trace copyright, but if omissions have been made, please let us know.

COPYRIGHTED EXCERPTS IN *NCLC*, VOLUME 79, WERE REPRODUCED FROM THE FOLLOWING PERIODICALS:

Bulletin of The John Rylands University Library of Manchester, v. 76, Autumn, 1994. Reproduced by permission of the Director and University Librarian, the John Rylands University Library of Manchester.—*Kansas Quarterly*, v. 16, Summer, 1984 for "Personal Fantasy in Andersen's *Fairy Tales*" by John Griffith. © Copyright 1984 by the *Kansas Quarterly*. Reproduced by permission of the publisher and the author.—*Literature and Psychology*, v. XVII, 1967. © Editor 1967. Reproduced by permission of the publisher.—*Modern Language Quarterly*, v. 49, December, 1988. © 1988 University of Washington. Reproduced by permission of Duke University Press.—*The New England Quarterly*, v. XLVI, September, 1973 for "'The Minister's Black Veil': Shrouded in a Blackness, Ten Times Black" by Robert E. Morsberger. Copyright 1973 by *The New England Quarterly*. Reproduced by permission of the publisher and the author.—*Nineteenth-Century Fiction*, v. 24, September, 1969 for "'The Minister's Black Veil': Symbol, Meaning, and the Context of Hawthorne's Art" by W. B. Carnochan; v. 31, December, 1976 for "The Autobiographical Nature of Disraeli's Early Fiction" by Robert O'Kell. © 1969, 1976 by the Regents of the University of California. Both reproduced by permission of the publisher and the respective authors.—*Novel: A Forum on Fiction*, v. 22, Spring, 1989. Copyright NOVEL Corp. © 1989. Reproduced with permission.—*PMLA*, v. 107, October, 1992. Copyright © 1992 by the Modern Language Association of America. Reproduced by permission of the Modern Language Association of America.—*Studies in Short Fiction*, v. IV, Winter, 1967; v. VIII, Fall, 1971. Copyright 1967, 1971 by Newberry College. Both reproduced by permission.—*The Victorian Newsletter*, no. 41, Spring, 1972 for "Tory Radicalism and 'The Two Nations' in Disraeli's *Sybil*" by Patrick Brantlinger. Copyright 1972 by New York University. Reproduced by permission of *The Victorian Newsletter* and the author.—*Victorian Periodicals Review*, v. XXV, Summer, 1992. © *Victorian Periodicals Review*. Reproduced by permission of the Research Society for Victorian Periodicals.—*Victorian Poetry*, v. 25, Summer, 1987 for "The Problem of Identity and the Grounds for Judgment in *The Ring and the Book*" by Adam Potkay; v. 27, Autumn-Winter, 1989 for "Browning's Murder Mystery: *The Ring and the Book* and Modern Theory" by W. David Shaw. © Copyright, West Virginia University, 1987, 1989. Both reproduced by permission of the respective authors.—*Victorian Studies*, v. 23, Autumn, 1979; v. 30, Winter, 1987. © The Trustees of Indiana University 1979, 1987. Both reproduced by permission of the Trustees of Indiana University.

COPYRIGHTED EXCERPTS IN NCLC, VOLUME 79, WERE REPRODUCED FROM THE FOLLOWING BOOKS:

Anderson, Celia Catlett. From "Andersen's Heroes and Heroines: Relinquishing the Reward" in *Triumphs of the Spirit in Children's Literature*. Edited by Francelia Butler and Richard Rotert. Library Professional Publications, 1986. Copyright 1986 Francelia Butler. All rights reserved. Reproduced by permission of The Shoe String Press, Inc.—Bloom, Harold. From an introduction to *Modern Critical Views: Robert Browning*. Edited by Harold Bloom. Chelsea House Publishers, 1985. Copyright © 1985 by Chelsea House Publishers, a division of Chelsea House Educational Communications, Inc. All rights reserved. Reproduced by permission.—Brask, Peter. From "Andersen on Love" in *The Nordic Mind: Current Trends in Scandinavian Literary Criticism*. Edited by Frank Egholm Andersen and John Weinstock. University Press of America, 1986. Copyright 1986 by University Press of America, Inc. All rights reserved. Reproduced by permission.—Bredsdorff, Elias. From *Hans Christian Andersen: The Story of His Life and Work 1905-75*. The Noonday Press, 1994. © 1977 by Elias Bredsdorff. All rights reserved. Reproduced by permission of Leonhardt & Hoier for the author.—Brumble, III, H. David. From *American Indian Autobiography*. University of California Press, 1988. Copyright © 1988 by The Regents of the University of California. © 1999 by H. David Brumble, III. Reproduced by permission of the author.—Cech, Jon. From *Touchstones: Reflections on the Best in Children's Literature, Volume Two: Fairy Tales, Fable, Myths, Legends, and Poetry.* Children's Literature Association, 1987. © ChLA Publishers. Reproduced by permission of the publisher.—Colacurcio, Michael J. From *The Province of Piety: Moral History in Hawthorne's Early Tales*. Harvard University Press, 1984. Copyright © 1984 by the President and Fellows of Harvard College. All rights reserved. Reproduced by permission of the author.—Doubleday, Neal Fran. From *Hawthorne's Early Tales, A Critical Study*. Duke University Press, 1972. © 1972, Duke University Press. Reproduced by permission of Duke University Press.—Dryden, Edgar A. From "Through a Glass Darkly: 'The Minister's Black Veil' as Parable" in *New Essays on Hawthorne's Major Tales*. Edited by Millicent Bell. Cambridge University Press, 1993. © Cambridge University Press 1993. Reproduced by permission of Cambridge University Press and the author.—Fogle, Richard Harter. From *Hawthorne's Fiction: The Light & The Dark*. University of Oklahoma Press, 1952. Copyright 1952 by the University of Oklahoma Press. Renewed 1980 by Richard Harter Fogel. Reproduced by permission.—Fowler, Catherine S. From "Sarah Winnemucca: Northern Paitute, ca. 1844-1891" in *American Indian Intellectuals*. Edited by Margot Liberty. West Publishing Co., 1976. Reproduced by permission.—Georgi-Findlay, Brigitte. From "The Frontiers of Native American Women's Writing: Sarah Winnemucca's Life Among the Piutes" in *New Voices in Native American Literary Criticism*. Edited by Arnold Krupat. Smithsonian Institution Press, 1993. © 1993 by the Smithsonian Institution. All rights reserved. Reproduced by permission.—Hazard, Paul. From "Superiority of the North Over the South: Hans Christian Andersen" in *Books, Children and Men, 5th edition*. Translated by Marguerite Mitchell. The Horn Book, Incorporated, 1983. Copyright © The Horn Book, Inc., 1983. All rights reserved. Reproduced by permission.—Hudson, Gertrude Reese. From *Robert Browning's Literary Life: From First Work to Masterpiece*. Eakin Press, 1992. Copyright © 1992 by Gertrude Reese Hudson.—Ingwersen, Niels. From "Being Stuck: The Subversive Andersen and His Audience" in *Studies in German and Scandinavian Literature after 1500: A Festschrift for George C. Schoolfield*. Edited by James A. Parente, Jr. and Richard Erich Schade. Camden House, 1993. Copyright © 1993 by Camden House, Inc. All rights reserved. Reproduced by permission of Boydell

Hans Christian Andersen

1805-1875

(Also wrote under the pseudonym Villiam Christian Walter.) Danish writer of fairy tales, poetry, short stories, novels, travel sketches, autobiographies, and dramas.

For further information on Andersen's works and career, see *NCLC,* Volume 7.

INTRODUCTION

Although he wrote in many genres, including novels, poems, plays, and travelogues, Hans Christian Andersen is remembered primarily as one of the most distinguished writers of fairy tales. Many of these—such as "The Ugly Duckling" (1843), "The Emperor's New Clothes" (1837), and "The Little Mermaid" (1837)—have become world famous. In all, Andersen wrote more than 150 tales, primarily between 1835 and 1874. Before this time, fairy tales had been part of the oral tradition of literature passed through generations and recorded in writing only for historical interest. Andersen revitalized and expanded the genre by merging the traditional folk tale with the more sophisticated literary tale. To this end he employed conversational language suitable for children, often provided sad rather than happy endings, combined an adult sensibility with a child-like simplicity, and blended into his tales aspects of his own personal life.

Biographical Information

Andersen was born into poverty in the town of Odense, Denmark. His father, a shoemaker, was an avid reader, and encouraged his son's intellectual and creative aspirations by reading to him tales from Danish folklore and from such works as *Arabian Nights*. The elder Andersen also built a marionette theatre for Hans, so the youngster could write and perform plays for the characters. When Hans was eleven, his father died, but the elder Andersen had already instilled a keen interest in literature in his son, who particularly enjoyed the works of Shakespeare and Sir Walter Scott. Desiring a career on stage as an actor, dancer, or singer, Andersen left home three years later in 1819, intent on joining Copenhagen's theater circle. Without references, though, he was denied admittance to the Royal Theater (many biographers have also stated that Andersen had neither the talent nor the appearance suitable for the theater). He was, nevertheless, taken under the wing of Jonas Collin, a director of

the Royal Theater and a prominent government official. Collin arranged for Andersen to obtain some basic schooling, including instruction at elite private schools during the mid-1820s, and by the late 1820s Andersen had passed the entrance exams for the University of Copenhagen. In the meantime, Collin had become a sort of surrogate father to Andersen, opening his home to the young man. Andersen never saw his own family again. Eventually, Andersen secured some work at the Royal Theater, appearing as an actor in minor roles and translating some French plays. Then in 1829 an original play of his was performed at the theatre: the farcical *Kjærlighed paa Nicolai Taarn, elle Hvad siger Parterret* (*Love on St. Nicholas Tower, or What Says the Pit*). That same year saw the publication of his mock travel book *Fodrejse fra Holmens Canal til Østpynten af Amager* (*Journey on Foot from Holmens Canal to the East Point of Amager*), which describes an imaginary walk through Copenhagen. But Andersen's first real success came after a more extended journey, a trip to Italy in 1833, which inspired his novel *Improvisatoren* (1835; *The*

1

Improvisatore), which is considered his literary break-through. Many scholars have contended that the trip marked a rebirth for Andersen, who turned from composing poetry to writing prose and fairy tales.

Andersen had begun his first fairy tales, published in the collection *Eventyr, Fortalte for Børn* (1835-42; *Fairy Tales Told for Children*), during his stay in Italy. Although he had originally intended the fairy tales for adults as well as children, he amended the title to "tales for children" after critics faulted the simplistic dialogue and style of the stories. Many of his early tales were adaptations of traditional folk tales, but he eventually concentrated on producing original stories: all but a dozen of his more than 150 tales are original creations. By 1837 and with the publication of his third novel, *Kun en Spillemand* (*Only a Fiddler*), Andersen began to be perceived as a European celebrity and was granted an annual stipend from Denmark for the remainder of his life. Thereafter Andersen continued his travels, visiting such countries as Germany, England, and Holland. Toward the end of his life, as his health began to fail, Denmark acknowledged him as its national author. He died in 1875 near Copenhagen.

Major Works

The tales most familiar to English-speaking readers are Andersen's early tales, written between 1835 and 1850. These include such stories as "The Princess on the Pea" (1835), "Thumbelina" (1835), "The Steadfast Tin Soldier" (1838), "The Snow Queen" (1844), "The Darning Needle" (1845), "The Little Match Girl" (1845), and "The Shirt Collar" (1848). Although some of his tales end happily, Andersen often deviated from the "happily ever after" conclusion of the traditional fairy tale; death, for example, is the primary motif in more than three-fourths of his tales. Andersen's heroes and heroines get consumed by fire or die of cold or have to renounce their love or their ambitions. They often suffer painful ordeals in an ugly or frightening world, and even if they succeed or are transformed in a positive way, like the ugly duckling, it is often not through their own doing, as in a traditional fairy tale, but through the workings of fate or some other external agency. Among Andersen's most popular and best loved fairy tales is "The Ugly Duckling," the story of a homely cygnet who becomes the most beautiful of all swans; many biographers have commented on the autobiographical elements in the tale. In another departure from the traditional fairy tale, Andersen's stories introduce the adult theme of the role of the artist, with an emphasis on the plight of neglected artistic genius. The stories also reflect a division in Andersen between sympathy with ordinary people and distrust of authority, and a desire to be accepted by authority. In general, the stories work on several levels, combining a child-like surface and simplicity of language with serious, adult themes.

Critical Reception

During his lifetime, Andersen became celebrated for his tales not only in Denmark, but throughout Europe and beyond. His tales have remained popular since his death, leading many critics to comment on the universality of his themes. Early scholars, including Paul Hazard, have pointed out the realism inherent in Andersen's tales. According to Hazard, the world Andersen witnessed—which encompassed sorrow, death, evil, and man's follies—is reflected in his tales. Discussing the essential "humanness" of Andersen's tales, Niels Kofoed has found that since they involve everyday-life themes of love, death, nature, injustice, suffering, and poverty, they appeal to all races, ideologies, classes, and genders. Critic Celia Catlett Anderson has also noted that the appeal of the stories is based on their intrinsic optimism, which typically prevails over pessimism. Anderson has contended that Andersen's tales reaffirm the strength of spirit of the protagonists, who prove themselves worthy of triumph.

In recent years, one major trend in Andersen criticism has involved psychoanalytic studies seeking to draw connections between the suffering depicted in Andersen's stories and the troubles of Andersen's own life, including his various psychological problems and his own unrequited love affairs. Throughout his life, as biographers have recorded, Andersen was ashamed of his working-class background and as such, they claim, was plagued by a sense of inferiority. John Griffith has speculated that Andersen turned to writing fantasies as an outlet for his own frustration and embarrassment over his poverty-stricken youth and the immorality of his background. Some critics have even maintained that Andersen retold his own life story over and over again in his stories—portraying his own self as triumphing over evil, persecution, poverty, and scorn.

There has also been interest among modern critics in Andersen's divided role as both an "insider" and an "outsider" in the upper reaches of society. Believing that Andersen's tales reveal the author's desire to be accepted by the upper classes, Jack Zipes has argued that the tales also depict the humiliation, pain, and suffering that "dominated" members of society must endure in order to prove their virtuosity and nobility. According to Zipes, Andersen, during his lifetime, "was obliged to act as a dominated subject within the dominant social circles despite his fame and recognition as a writer." This led Andersen to form an ambivalent attitude toward the aristocracy—at once he aspired to join the ranks of the higher classes, and at the same time he disdained them. Other critics have commented on this feeling of Andersen's of being "miscast" or of not belonging. Noting that although Andersen rose from the working-class ranks to join the upper classes, Niels Ingwersen has pointed out that Andersen never became their equal; instead, he served those who assisted him. Andersen's tales are subversive, then, toward the audience as well as toward Andersen himself, who often despised his own efforts to gain their approval. Critics have also paid some attention to Andersen's neglected plays as well as to his novels and travel writings, and it has been suggested that travel was an important motif in both Andersen's life and his works. But the critics, like the general public, still focus primarily on the fairy tales.

travel essays, novels, and poetry) 1876-80
*Levnedsbogen [The Book of My Life] (autobiography) 1926
The Complete Andersen. 6 vols. (fairy tales and short stories) 1942-48
The Complete Fairy Tales and Stories (fairy tales) 1974
The Diaries of Hans Christian Andersen (diaries) 1990

*Levnedsbogen was originally written in 1832.

PRINCIPAL WORKS

Ungdoms-Forsøg [as Villiam Christian Walter] (novel) 1822
Fodrejse fra Holmens Canal til Østpynten af Amager [Journey on Foot from Holmens Canal to the East Point of Amager] (travel essay) 1829
Kjærlighed paa Nicolai Taarn, elle Hvad siger Parterret [Love on St. Nicholas Tower, or What Says the Pit] (drama) 1829
Bruden fra Lammermoor [The Bride of Lammermoor] (libretto; adapted from Sir Walter Scott's novel of the same name) 1832
Improvisatoren [The Improvisatore] (novel) 1835
Eventyr, Fortalte for Børn [Fairy Tales Told for Children] (fairy tales) 1835-42
O.T. (novel) 1836
Kun en Spillemand [Only a Fiddler] (novel) 1837
De to Baronesser [The Two Baronesses] (novel) 1838
Den Usynlige paa Sprogø [The Invisible Man on Sprogø] (drama) 1839
Mulatten [The Mulatto] (drama) 1840
En Digters Bazar [A Poet's Bazaar] (poetry, short stories, and travel essays) 1842
Nye Eventyr [New Fairy Tales] (fairy tales) 1844-48
Den nye Barselstue [The New Maternity Ward] (drama) 1845
Liden Kirsten [Little Kirsten] (libretto) 1846
Das Märchen Meines Lebens ohne dichtung [The Story of My Life] (autobiography) 1847
Eventyr [Fairy Tales] (fairy tales) 1850
I Sverigg [Pictures of Sweden] (travel essays) 1851
Historier [Stories] (fairy tales) 1852-55
Mit Livs Eventyr [The Fairy Tale of My Life] (autobiography) 1855
At være eller ikke være [To Be or Not To Be?] (novel) 1857
Nye Eventyr og Historier [New Fairy Tales and Stories] (fairy tales) 1858-60
Nye Eventyr og Historier [New Fairy Tales and Stories] (fairy tales) 1861-66
I Spanien [In Spain] (travel essays) 1863
Et Besøg i Portugal [A Visit to Portugal] (travel essays) 1868
Samlede voerker. 15 vols. (fairy tales, short stories,

CRITICISM

William Makepeace Thackeray (essay date 1847)

SOURCE: "A Grumble about the Christmas Books," in *The Memoirs of Barry Lyndon, Esq. and the Miscellaneous Papers Written between 1843 and 1847*, edited by George Saintsbury, Oxford University Press, 1908, pp. 581-609.

[*The following was originally published by Thackeray under the name Michael Angelo Titmarsh and appeared in* Fraser's Magazine *in 1847. In the excerpt below, Thackeray praises Andersen for his wit and playfulness, calling him a "delicate and charming . . . genius."*]

I have, I trust, been tolerably ill-humoured hitherto; but what man can go on grumbling in the presence of such an angelical spirit as Hans Christian Andersen? Seeing him praised in the *Athenæum* journal, I was straight put away from reading a word of Hans's other works: and it was only last night, when going to bed, perfectly bored with the beef-fed English fairies, their hob-nailed gambols, and elephantine friskiness, his **Shoes of Fortune** and his **Wonderful Stories**[1] came under the eyes of your humble servant. Heaven bless Hans Christian! Here *are* fairies! Here *is* fancy, and graceful wit, and delicate humour, and sweet, naïve kindness, flowing from the heart! Here is frolic without any labour! Here is admirable fooling without any consciousness or degradation! Though we have no sort of respect for a great, hulking, whiskered, red-faced, middle-aged man, who dresses himself in a pinafore and affects to frolic like a baby, may we not be charmed by the play and prattle of a child? And Hans Christian Andersen so affects me.

Every page of the volumes sparkles with delightful grace and genial fancy. Hans and you are friends for life after an hour's talk with him. I shake thy hands, Hans Christian, thou kindly prattler and warbler! A happy Christmas to thee, thou happy-minded Christian! You smile, dear Miss Smith! When we become acquainted with so delicate and charming a genius, have we no right to be thankful? Yes: let us respect every one of those friends whom Heaven has sent us—those sweet Christian messengers of peace and goodwill. . . .

Notes

[1] *Wonderful Stories for Children.* By Hans Christian Andersen, Author of *The Improvisatore,* &c. Translated from the Danish by Mary Howitt. London, Chapman & Hall.

James O'Donnell Bennett (essay date 1927)

SOURCE: "Hans Andersen's Fairy Tales," in *Much Loved Books: Best Sellers of the Ages,* Boni and Liveright, 1927, pp. 291-96.

[*In the following excerpt, Bennett discusses the similarities between Andersen's personal life and the events in his well-known fairy tale* "The Ugly Duckling."]

"My life," said Hans Andersen in his serene old age, "is a lovely story, happy and full of incident. If, when I was a boy, and went forth into the world poor and friendless, a good fairy had met me and said, 'Choose now thine own course through life, and the object for which thou wilt strive, and then, according to the development of thy mind, and as reason requires, I will guide and defend thee to its attainment,' my fate could not, even then, have been directed more happily, more prudently, or better. The history of my life will say to the world what it says to me, 'There is a loving God, who directs all things for the best.'"

In its vicissitudes, its hardships, its triumphs that life was a fairy tale come true. The fourteen-year-old boy who came gawking into Copenhagen in 1819, clad in the confirmation suit that a small-town tailoress had made for him from his dead father's old overcoat, lived to be the man who could ride in the king's carriage when he wished to—once he made that wish known to his good-natured sovereign and it was granted—lived, also, to be the man whom almost every literary notable who visited Copenhagen during a period of forty years sought out and paid homage.

All that story this man wrote out in his old age in the most ingenuous and complacent spirit, and it is because of its spirit that his book is an authentic document among the world's masterpieces of autobiography. It has a right to a place on the shelf with the autobiographies of Benvenuto Cellini, Colley Cibber, Benjamin Franklin and Herbert Spencer. It is different from all those, lacking the excitement and shamelessness of Cellini's book, the spice of Cibber's, the pithiness of Franklin's and the wisdom of Mr. Spencer's, but it is an interesting narrative and important psychology because it is complete self-revelation by a man of

genius. Such documents are of great value and of the greatest entertainment, and when one outgrows Hans Andersen's fairy tales, one still does not lose touch with Hans Andersen. The guileless, candid old man of *The Story of My Life* remains a friend whom one likes to hear purling on—and on—and on.

Thus the book of the fairy tales of Hans Christian Andersen becomes one of the important lure-books. A child once introduced to the tales will soon come upon the lovely one called **"The Ugly Duckling,"** and if his reading is being guided by an elder who knows something about anything the child may be so fortunate as to learn that the tale of the ugly duckling is a parable on Hans Andersen's life, with pages of autobiography crowded into it. . . .

In the fifth line of **"The Ugly Duckling"** we are introduced in two and a half lines to the stork who "was walking around on his long red legs and talking Egyptian, because he had learned that language from his mother." When children grow old enough to be improved by prefaces they are not unlikely to be told that those two and a half lines about the stork and his talk are among the most characteristic of Hans Andersen's fleeting, unexpected touches by which, in a way that seems quite matter-of-fact but that is essentially poetic and delicate, he establishes poetic kinship between his readers and the creatures of his fancy.

Well, the stork was talking Egyptian, for the reason which you know now, and "the corn was yellow, the oats were green, the hay stood in stacks down in the green meadows, and . . . right in the sunshine lay an old manor, surrounded by deep canals, and from the wall down to the water grew big burdock leaves, so high that little children could stand upright under the tallest of them. It was just as wild there as in the thickest wood."

Children accept the first page of **"The Ugly Duckling"** as rather usual kind of writing, so easily does it move along, and so quietly does the picture it makes take shape before their eyes. No straining for an effect, no pretentiousness in it. But I suspect that such writing, with the wealth of soft color that it carries, is not easy, for if it were there would be more of it—the world so likes it and so treasures it.

Amid the sweet scene the Ugly Duckling was hatched—hatched into a world of trouble and snubs and unkind criticism, and of fun-making in which the source of the laughter was the pain it caused. Just such a world did Hans Andersen encounter when he, with ten Danish rigsdalers in a pocket of his confirmation suit, came to Copenhagen from the thriving manufacturing town of Odense, where in 1805 he was born.

"I think I will go out into the wide world," the Ugly Duckling had said. Hans Andersen had said that also.

The Ugly Duckling saw the swans—"had never before seen anything so beautiful . . . dazzlingly white, they uttered a very strange cry, spread their large splendid wings and . . . mounted so high that the ugly little Duckling had a very strange sensation."

That "very strange sensation" was the beautiful bird's (for he was no ugly duckling, nor ever had been) sudden consciousness of his kinship with the beautiful birds aloft, and mingled with that consciousness was the divine humility which is an attribute of heaven-dowered genius, as distinguished from the kind of genius that gets itself accepted by means of self-exploitation and self-assertion. . . .

Paul Hazard (essay date 1932)

SOURCE: "Superiority of the North over the South," in *Books, Children and Men,* 5th ed., translated by Marguerite Mitchell, The Horn Book, Inc., 1983, pp. 77-110.

[*In the following excerpt, originally written in 1932, Hazard celebrates the vitality and wisdom found in Andersen's tales, maintaining that the stories reflect the true meaning of life.*]

Supposing that, by some stretch of imagination, we were called upon to choose the very prince of all story writers for children, my vote would go, not to a Latin, but to Hans Christian Andersen. . . .

He is unexcelled because, within the slender framework of his tales, he brings in all the pageantry of the universe. It is never too much for children. You will find there not only Copenhagen and its brick houses, and its great reddish roofs and copper domes, and the golden cross of Notre-Dame that reflects the sun; Denmark with its marshes, its woods, its willows bent by the wind, its ever-present sea; Scandinavia, Iceland, snowy and frozen, but you will also find Germany, Switzerland, Spain flooded with sunshine, Portugal, Milan, Venice, Florence and Rome, Paris, city of the fine arts, city of revolutions. You will find there Egypt, Persia, China, the ocean to its very depths where the mermaids live; the sky where floats the whiteness of great wild swans.

It is a marvelous picture book that the moon makes in relating what she saw in the mountains, over the lakes, through the windows of human dwellings, in every place where her blue and melancholy light softly steals, plays and vanishes. If the present is not enough, evoke the past—Pompeian villas or the barbaric palaces of the Vikings. If reality is not enough, see magic scenes that the fairies build. If your eyes are not surfeited by nature's countless spectacles, close them; in your dreams will appear the luminous spirit of the truth, variable, ever changing, and more beautiful than the beauties of the waking day.

In these feasts of imagination, others will perhaps be capable of equalling him, but there are values he has revealed that are his very own sumptuous gift to children; enchanted scenes they will find only in him, the memory of which will charm them forever. Snow—Latin children hardly know it. Those at Naples or Granada never see it except from afar, way up high on the mountains. Scarcely does it appear before the eyes of small Parisians when it is changed into soot and mud. And where else would they get such another vision of icy vastness? Andersen opened up to them the fairylike domains of frost.

What strange beauty in his depiction of the glacial ocean where icebergs float like sea-faring monsters! What a sight is revealed to the fifth mermaid sister who becomes familiar with the world seen on the winter sea!

> Now came the turn of the fifth sister. Her birthday, it happened, was in winter, and so she saw what the others had not seen on their first visit. The sea was all green to look at, and round about there floated large icebergs, every one looking like a pearl, she said, and yet they were far bigger than the church towers that men built. They showed themselves in the strangest shapes and were like diamonds.

Winter over the town, placing curtains on the window panes that the children must clear away with their breath if they wish to see the house opposite. Winter that turns the fingers blue, that numbs the limbs of the little match-seller, that causes Knud, the lover, to pass from his dream into eternal sleep. Winter that makes the snow man grow proud, thinking that his mere glance suffices to make the sun hurry down behind the horizon. Winter on the dunes, that the tempest seems to push back still further inland, making waves of sand that cover up the village chapels. The Winter King, as he rules in Lapland, almost burying animals and men, lord of stark immensity. These are some of the spectacles that Andersen offers and lavishes on children.

Thanks to him, we have seen through our own eyes the Snow Queen all in ice, her eyes shining like bright stars. With little Kay, we fastened our sledge to her white one. She let us sit beside her. We glided over the soft surface and were lifted into the air. We passed over forests and lakes, land and seas. Below us blew a glacial wind, wolves howled, snow sparkled. Above black crows were flying, cawing. And away up above shone the moon, large and bright. Thus we arrived at the Queen's Palace.

> The walls of the Palace were made of drifting snow, and the windows and doors of biting winds. There were more than a hundred halls, shaped by the drifting of the snow. The largest of them stretched out for many miles, and all were lit up by the bright Northern Lights. These halls were tremendous—so

empty, so icy-cold, so dazzling. There was never any gaiety here, not even the smallest dance for the bears, at which the storm winds could make the music, and the polar bears walk on their hind legs and show off their good manners. There was never a party where they played at muzzle-slapping and paw-clapping, and never did the white fox-girls forgather to enjoy a bit of gossip over their coffee. Empty, vast, and icy-cold were the Snow Queen's halls. The Northern Lights glowed at such regular intervals that one could reckon exactly when they would be at their highest and lowest. In the midst of the immense empty snow hall was a frozen lake, cracked into a thousand pieces, and each piece so resembled all the others that it looked like a real work of art. When at home the Snow Queen sat in the very center, and then she said she was sitting on the "Mirror of Reason," which according to her was the only one that counted in this world.[1]

Fortunate indeed if in all this snow, our heart was not frozen as happened to little Kay:

> Little Kay was quite blue with the cold, indeed almost black, and his heart was practically a lump of ice. But he was not aware of it, because the Snow Queen had kissed away the icy chill. He was busy fitting together a few flat sharp-edged pieces of ice, and trying to shape them into some kind of pattern, for he wanted to make something out of them, just as we do when we make Chinese puzzles with little squares of wood. Kay was arranging patterns, and most intricate ones, in that game known as the "Puzzle of Ice-cold Reason." To him these figures appeared very remarkable and of the greatest importance because of the chip of glass in his eye. He put together patterns to form a written word, but he could never manage to spell out the one word he had in his mind—the word "Eternity."[1]

We should be fortunate indeed if, as in the tale, some little Gerda followed us to the end of the world, to the very palace of the Snow Queen, and with her warm tears made the block of ice melt. Fortunate if, through love, she permitted us to solve the puzzle and to recover the lost word.

Andersen is unique in his capacity for entering into the very soul of beings and of things.

That animals have an intelligible language, Andersen and children know better than anyone. When the cat says to little Rudy: "Come out on the roof; put one paw here, another a little higher; come on, hoist yourself up; see how I do it, nothing is easier," little Rudy understands perfectly. And the dog that, not satisfied with barking, expresses himself also with his eyes, his tail, and his whole body speaks a language that seems quite natural to the child. That plants talk is taken for granted also. After all, why should Mother Elder and Father Willow not exchange confidences

like everybody else? Leaves are very talkative; they murmur for no reason at all.

But what is rarer and finer is to see objects become animated and to hear their voices. Not only the toys, not only the porcelain dancer on the mantelpiece so full of airs and graces, not only the grotesque Chinese figure on the console who shakes his head when looking at you. This innumerable folk, that the indifferent call "things," stirs, moves, speaks and fills the air with its complaints or its songs. Everything is alive: the ray of sunshine that dances through the window, the branch of apple tree in its spring frock, the salon furniture, the gardener's tools, the kitchen utensils, the pail, the broom, the basket, the plates and even the matches, although they are a bit stiff. Of all the objects that you can imagine, there is not one that does not want to chat with its neighbors and make merry. At night, you believe there is no longer any life. On the contrary, it is the moment when silent ones feel free to speak; when the motionless ones feel their limbs itching and gambol about gaily. The arithmetic problem fidgets about on its slate, the letters grow restless in the copy book and complain at having been badly traced.

> When one is a child, and can hardly talk, one understands perfectly the language of the hens and ducks, dogs and cats. They speak to us as distinctly as father and mother. At that age we even hear grandfather's cane whinny; it has become our horse, and we see a head on it, legs and a tail. But once grown up this faculty is lost. However, there are children who keep it longer than others; we say of them that they remain big simpletons. . . .

Big simpletons or geniuses. On this latter count, let us thank Heaven that Andersen remained a child.

If others shrivel up everything they touch by analyzing and dissecting, Andersen, on the contrary, animates and vivifies. On the summit of mountains, on the highest peaks, he is hypnotized by Vertigo who tries to make him totter and fall headlong into the abyss. In the depths of the crevices lives the Queen of the glaciers. She is asking for her victims, and you hear her voice. Andersen is never alone. He is surrounded by a multitude of little lives, by countless beings who observe and watch him. He is only one of them, perhaps a little better endowed, in the vast comedy in which thousands of actors take part. All the others, the oak, the house, the butterfly, the wave, the stick of wood, the gravestone, rejoice or suffer with him. Hallucination that is perhaps not altogether voluntary nor altogether false, if it does nothing more than translate the mystery of being and the constant vibration of things.

How conscious we are in all this of the powerful imagination of the North, instinct with sensitiveness! How different it is from the imagination of the South which etches everything sharply under the direct brilliance of the sun! Beneath this sky laden with mists, where the light remains timid and gray even on the fairest days, we grasp the significance of doubts and confusions. There the sharpness of a too clear vision will not belie the man who sees grimacing faces in the tree roots, who peoples the sea with phantoms delicately traced on its grayish expanse. When he expresses himself, as the law of our nature demands, he does so with less pride and authority. He is never entirely sure that the tricks of his imagination are really nothing more than imagination. He likes to pretend that the questions, the appeals which he attributes to the universe, come actually from the universe and not from himself. Uncertain of himself, he respects the essential character of things as though by raising them to his own sphere he were finding friends on his lonely and colorless horizon. Feeling deference for every living thing, he promotes animals to his own level. Why should they not have the right to be themselves? The storks, in appearance all alike, clothed in white and black and wearing red stockings, why should they not have their own personality? The birds of woods or field, why should they not have different characters as they have different feathers?

And, by a transition from the external to the hidden life, why should we not try to discover the individual soul of each object? If it is nothing but a diversion, at least it is generous and merciful. That old lantern which has shared existence with humans, which was useful to them for keeping off the dangers of the night, seems to have will power. It persists in struggling against the wind, against the rain. It seems to have intelligence, for it is interested in the adventures of the passers-by to whom it lends its reflection. And a sensibility, for it suffers when it sees the misfortunes around it. Its ambition is to endure, to persist in its being. It has a horror of annihilation. And so on, continuing the dream, multiplying it to infinity. The starched collar is proud of its rigid splendor. The teapot looks disgusted and will sing only when it is warm. And the silver shilling, if we tell it that it is only a counterfeit piece, shivers with indignation.

When we finish reading the *Tales* we are not entirely the same as we were when we began them. We would gladly become, as Rimbaud says, *un opéra fabuleux.* The wheat that bends, what emotion makes it tremble? Where do the white clouds go that are passing over us? Do they go in light attire to some celestial festival in the palace of Prince Azur?

But of all Andersen's claims to supremacy, the finest and noblest claim is the wisdom inherent in his tales, their inner life. There is much sorrow in the world, Andersen believes. The woman you love does not love you. She says she would like to be your sister. It is not the same thing. She becomes a great singer, or goes abroad, or marries someone else. She forgets you. There

is also death, which is very badly planned. Parents die young and here are these little ones left alone; how they will suffer! We feel always insecure. Every second we are dying. Everything passes, the palaces of Caesar and the books of the poets. Animals are scarcely happier than we, and as the dog said when he was put on a chain, "Things are reasonably ordered neither for dogs nor for men."

If only one knew why, it would be a consolation, but the book of life is hard to read. The wise man may succeed in deciphering several chapters, but not the last that treats of the departure into the unknown. We would have to have the philosopher's stone to make the lines shine with a brighter light. Can we find such a stone? They tell us that all evil comes from the error of our first parents, but why should they have made any such mistake?

To all these doubts which work on your mind when you are taking a walk alone, or when you cannot sleep, is added the foolishness of man himself; for the number of fools is too great. Each one believes himself above his condition and swells with pride. The good old snow man, when evening comes, imagines, as we have said, that it is his imperious glance which has forced the sun to sink below the earth. The thistle claims descent from an illustrious Scottish family. The Portuguese duck believes herself of a superior species and despises those that are not Portuguese. The nettle proclaims that it is a distinguished plant since a delicate muslin is woven from it. And so forth, step by step, up to and including the fools who admire the Emperor's invisible clothes.

An excess of work not only makes hands callous, it may embitter the soul. Those who have no work to do risk becoming selfish and cruel. There are maidens, like the little Inger, who walk on bread to avoid soiling their slippers. **"The Marsh King's Daughter"** points out this double nature that is in us.

> Some magic power had a terrible hold over the little one. In the daytime she was as beautiful as any fairy, but had a bad, wicked temper. At night, on the other hand, she became a hideous toad, quiet and pathetic, with sad, mournful eyes. There were two natures in her both in soul and body continually shifting.

In short, all that would not be a very pleasant sight if we saw nothing else in it. In the words of the gingerbread merchant:

> I had two young gingerbread people in the window of my shop; one a man with a hat, the other a young lady without a hat. They had a human face only on one side and were not to be looked at from the other. What is more, men are like that and it is not kind to look at their wrong side.

That is what the storyteller in love with nature is think-ing about, the animater of things who has himself known pain. Andersen is not one of those saints who, shivering, insist that it is always warm on this earth. He knows the meaning of life. He states resolutely the problem of evil, the problem of existence. But far from being discouraged by the truth, he seeks to release it, to face it. Truth distresses us only when we have a half knowledge of it.

Pondering over existence, he understands that we are in a transitory state from which we cannot escape except through will, faith, love. The human world is only a pro-cess of evolution, a chance for us to meet the supreme realities that await us, or at least to prepare ourselves for them. Love, true love, is stronger than absence, stronger than sorrow; it accomplishes all miracles, even that of resurrection. It is the divine spark, symbol of eternal life. Through love, spells are broken. As foretold by the oracle, the King of Egypt, through the power of his daughter's love, came back to life. "Love produces life; from the most ardent love is born the noblest life. It is love only that can save the king's life." Through love, through total sacrifice, having almost given up hope, the little mermaid won immortality. The real evil is the sin against the spirit, the lack of kindness, of humanity. The real good is the aspiration to a higher state to which men of good will shall be admitted and the animals, yes, the animals themselves. "The animal is, like man, a creature of God, and, I believe firmly, no life will be lost, each creature will receive the hap-piness that it is capable of receiving."

Once there was a hideous toad with a splendid dia-mond set in its head; always he aspired towards the best.

> This precious stone, seek it in the sun, look at it if you can. You will not be able to, the light of the heavenly body is too bright. We have not yet the light that we need to recognize ourselves in the midst of the marvels that God has created. But we shall possess it some day. And then it will be the most beautiful of all the tales; it will be true.

It is this inner life that gives the **Tales** their deep qual-ity. From it also comes that exaltation which spreads through the soul of the readers. From it comes, finally, a marked quality of serenity. I know only one other author who, all differences taken into consideration, creates a similar impression. Manzoni, like Andersen, admitting only as a human weakness the confusion into which the fact of evil throws him, overcomes this state of doubt, and through faith arrives at serenity. Both, before the world spectacle, possess peace. They even allow themselves humor, gaiety, because they hold the secret: "Have faith and hope; they will not deceive you." Both turn by choice towards the humble, be-cause the hierarchy established in this transient world

is only an illusion destined to be replaced by a higher law of justice. "The love of the Creator is infinite and embraces equally everything that lives and moves in Him." "All creatures are equal before the infinite love of the Almighty and the same justice governs all the universe." One feels the same Biblical inspiration mov-ing through both Andersen and Manzoni.

The teller of tales stands at his window. He listens to the swallows and the storks that have returned to Denmark for the fine summer days. He listens to his friend the wind. Or, he mingles with the crowd and listens once more to what the gingerbread merchant is relating, to what the old eel fisherman is telling. He makes use of everything. He tells them again in his own way, these stories that provoke a smile or a tear. He gives them a lyrical style, dramatic and al-ways simple, a style of which he alone is master. He adorns them with brighter and more delicate colors; and, lending them wings, he sends them to the very limits of the world. But he fills them also with in-tense feeling and therein, without doubt, added to all the other qualities, lies the final attainment which explains their great power.

The children are not mistaken. In these beautiful tales they find not only pleasure, but the law of their being and the feeling of the great role they have to fill. They themselves have been subjected to sorrow. They sense evil confusedly around them, in them; but this vivid suffering is only transitory and not enough to trouble their serenity. Their mission is to bring to the world a renewal of faith and hope. What would become of the human spirit if it were not refreshed by this confident young strength? The new generation arrives to make the world beautiful once more. Everything grows green again. Life funds its reasons for enduring. Andersen, imbuing his tales with an invincible belief in a better future, communes with the soul of children, harmonizes himself with their deep nature, allies himself with their mission. He upholds, with them and through them, the ideal forces which save humanity from perishing. . . .

Notes

[1] As translated from the Danish by Paul Leyssac in *It's Perfectly True and Other Stories*. Harcourt, 1938.

Frederick J. Marker (essay date 1971)

SOURCE: "The Plays of H. C. Andersen," in *Hans Christian Andersen and the Romantic Theatre: A Study of Stage Practices in the Prenaturalistic Scandinavian Theatre*, University of Toronto Press, 1971, pp. 30-64.

[*In the excerpt below, Marker discusses Andersen's often-neglected dramatic works, focusing on Andersen's early dramatic influences and arguing that his works*

form part of a significant bridge between the roman-
ticism of the early part of the Century and the realism
that later followed.]

'In Denmark there is but one city and one theatre,'
wrote Kierkegaard in 1848,[1] and his characteristic
comment suggests the central place occupied by the
Royal Theatre in nineteenth-century Danish culture
and society. Architecturally as well as intellectually, it
dominated the daily life of Copenhagen; it was 'the
most important daily and nightly topic of conversation,'
Andersen declared, and it 'ranked among the finest in
Europe.'[2] It is no surprise, then, that Andersen's very
existence revolved around the imposing playhouse on
Kongens Nytorv. His lodgings were always within easy
walking distance of it. On most evenings he could be
found in the stalls together with the foremost figures of
the Danish Golden Age—Oehlenschläger, Thorvaldsen,
Heiberg, Kierkegaard—first as a young, promising author, eventually as the renowned mid-point of Scandinavian romanticism. As a dramatist, Andersen turned
eagerly and early to the theatre as the best source of
the personal admiration and financial support he so
desperately sought. He regarded his plays very seriously in comparison with his other work; the stage to
him was a 'mighty platform' from which it was possible to 'proclaim for hundreds what would hardly be
read by ten.'[3] As one of the most widely read novelists
in Europe and as a world-renowned writer of fairy-tales,
he continued to wage the struggle for acceptance and
recognition in the theatre that he had begun long before
as 'a musical servant' in *Nina*.

In Andersen's own pessimistic, persecuted view—although not in terms of production statistics or of theatrical history—his struggle ended in defeat. The Brandes
myth of Andersen as 'the hunted animal in Danish literature' has persisted, and posterity has had little to add
to this evaluation.[4] However, as a playwright Andersen
forms an important transition between two periods. He
belongs among the younger exponents of romanticism,
but at the same time points ahead toward the realism
which eventually triumphed in the 1870s. The production history of his plays provides a microcosm of the
exotic, historical, idyllic, and topical elements that were
the popular components of the colourful, romantic stage
picture. And it was to the Copenhagen theatre which
Andersen's plays reflect that a young apprentice was
sent from Bergen on a travelling scholarship in 1852
to learn his craft—an apprentice whose name was
Henrik Ibsen.

Andersen's early puerile efforts in the 'tragic' genre
were clearly bewildered products of his youthful encounters with the more sensational aspects of romantic
theatre. His first complete play, a 'tragedy in five acts'
entitled **The Forest Chapel / Skovcapellet,** was written
at the age of sixteen in the hope that it would provide
money with which he might continue his schooling.[5] It

is an example of hardboiled terror romanticism adapted
from a German short story published in C.N. Rosenkilde's
periodical *Brevduen* (nos 19 and 20, 1819); he was fortunately dissuaded from submitting it to the Royal Theatre. With his next effort, however, a 'patriotic tragedy' called **The Robbers of Vissenberg / Røverne i
Vissenberg,** Andersen became bolder. It was written
in two weeks and submitted anonymously to the Royal
Theatre in 1822, which reacted by replying in a letter
dated 16 June 1822 that it did not in future wish to
receive 'plays which to such a degree as this display
a lack of all elementary education.'[6] Although only a
single scene of this play, published in A.P. Liunge's
magazine *Harpen* (XXXII, 1822), survives, the melodramatic dialogue in the robbers' den gives ample evidence of
the drama's exaggerated *sturm und drang* tendencies. Yet
a third 'tragedy' was finished by Andersen in 1822, a
play entitled *Alfsol* which acquired its subject matter
from the historian P.F. Suhm's *Nordiske Noveller* (1783)
and its style from Oehlenschläger and the Danish novelist B.S. Ingemann. Although rejected for production,
Alfsol marked the turning point in its author's life since
it provided the impetus for the Royal Theatre's decision to support his further education. He expressed his
gratitude by dedicating his first book, published at his
own expense under the pseudonym William Christian
Walter (his own middle name plus his two favourite
authors, Shakespeare and Scott!) and containing *Alfsol*,
to the 'exalted Royal Theatre management.' The few
copies of the book still in existence belong among the
costliest rarities of Scandinavian literature.[7]

Although any of these early, youthful gothic tragedies
can be criticized on virtually every count, they nevertheless bear unmistakable evidence—as the Royal Theatre management also realized—of raw poetic talent. It
is noteworthy that when Andersen, having completed
his formal education, made his debut as a practising
dramatist in 1829, it was in a genre which directly
parodied the stiff, solemn, and sentimental style of these
first tragedies.

For the most part, however, Andersen's uncompleted
or unproduced plays have little bearing on his relation to the practical theatre of the nineteenth century. Similarly, four of his translations produced at the
Royal Theatre, including Scribe's *La quarantaine* (as
Skibet), Bayard's *La reine de seize ans* (as **Dronningen
paa 16 Aar**), Dorvigny's *La fête de campagne, ou
L'intendant comédien malgré lui* (as **En Comedie i
det Grønne**), and Meyerbeer's *Le pardon de Ploërmel*
(as **Dinorah**), are only indirectly relevant to his
personal artistic intentions as a playwright and assume only an incidental place in this discussion.
Nevertheless, despite these exclusions, original plays
and opera libretti by Andersen produced at the Royal
Theatre between 1829 and 1865 account for a total
of twenty-one works, embracing such widely diverse
forms as vaudeville, opera or singspiel, romantic

drama and fantasy, and romantic comedy. . . . Several of them were later performed at the private Casino Theatre, for which Andersen also wrote four additional dramatic fantasies, but no reliable production records of the Casino performances have survived.

Vaudeville

Andersen wrote for a theatre where musical genres played an extremely important role in the repertory. A large number of its performers were talented both as singers and as actors, and it possessed an excellent orchestra with distinguished traditions. Therefore it is not surprising to discover that vaudeville, opera, and singspiel are dominant forms in his dramaturgy. . . .

The successful production at the Royal Theatre in 1825 of Karl von Holtei's vaudeville-influenced 'musical farce' *Die Wiener in Berlin* led directly to the introduction of the Danish vaudeville with the performance in the same year of [J.L.] Heiberg's *King Solomon*. Andersen's enthusiastic discovery of the new genre has already been described, and he was not long in following Heiberg's example. In 1829 he made the first of several efforts in this genre with his vaudeville-parody, ***Love on St Nicholas Tower, or What Says the Pit / Kjærlighed paa Nicolai Taarn, eller Hvad siger Parterret.***

This short, delightful farce treats the star-crossed love affair of Ellen, daughter of the 'knight' (ie, watchman) of St Nicholas Tower, and the brave little tailor Søren Pind, about whom we learn:

> *A tailor is a rosebud here below,*
> *A butterfly that flutters to and fro,*
> *Too fragile, thin, and pale*
> *To withstand the wild and stormy gale.*[12]

Together this engaging pair battle the stormy gales of destiny, embodied in the person of Peer Hansen, a watchman from a neighbouring tower who also seeks Ellen's hand in marriage. The play is a characteristic student parody of the romantic tragedy of destiny, in which watchmen and tailors assume heroic poses and speak stilted verse. The farcical element in the action was further heightened by means of numerous topical points of reference in the setting, the music, and the dialogue. Satirical jibes at actual persons, especially Adam Oehlenschläger, proved particularly upsetting to the more conservative elements; reviews in *Maanedsskrift for Litteratur* (1, 1829, 543) and *Kjøbenhavnsposten* (22 May 1829) both reproached the young playwright for having parodied 'our finest tragedies.' Three years later, Andersen was ready to express appropriate contrition for having 'really believed at that time that parody of something excellent, or use of something truly moving, might be permitted in jest without thereby having a bad heart.'[13] *Mea culpa.*

The Royal Theatre readers' report of ***Love on St Nicholas Tower,*** which has not previously been printed, is so characteristic of contemporary opinion regarding vaudeville and parody that it deserves to be cited at some length:[14]

> That the vaudeville ***Love on St. Nicholas*** by no means corresponds to my ideas about the purpose and dignity of drama is hardly necessary to point out. Should it, however, despite my dissent, secure majority support, I must at least request that a fellow citizen is not mentioned on the stage in order to evoke a shameful laughter, as is the case on p. 35 and elsewhere.[15] It is high time to stop the boyish foolishness that more and more dominates our stage, and which naturally finds all-too-ready support from the crowd of boys in the house . . . Furthermore, I feel that the Theatre would act ignobly and unwisely to parody, by favouring such examples as this, some of the most beautiful situations and scenes which adorn our theatre.
>
> 31 Dec. 1828 RAHBEK

> If the author, as I do not doubt, observes with dutiful care the foregoing hints by my colleague, I do not believe that the present vaudeville should be rejected; the original turn at the end of the play, the fine, flowing verse, and the vigorous action throughout speak in its favour; at any rate I regard it as one of our best vaudevilles, and vote unconditionally for its acceptance.
>
> 5 Jan. 1829 G.H. OLSEN

Olsen, theatre manager, and Rahbek, author and critic, represented established, eighteenth-century conservatism; both were sixty-nine at this point, Olsen died the same year and Rahbek a year later. The conservative establishment triumphed, however. Despite the success of the play's unusual ending in which the audience is allowed to decide whether or not the tailor wins Ellen, its appearance at the close of the season, coupled with a heated controversy concerning the leading actress, resulted in a short run of only three performances.

Andersen's subsequent vaudevilles helped to shape the genre which Thomas Overskou later defined as 'a small, delicately drawn comedy stemming from local affairs, daily events, or piquant situations.'[16] The theme of the love affair threatened by circumstances remained the predominant one. In his later vaudevilles, however, Andersen abandoned almost entirely the satirical, burlesque tone for which ***Love*** had been criticized. Thus in writing ***Parting and Meeting,*** which takes for its background the visit of Spanish troops to Odense in 1808, his aim, as he hastened to assure an acquaintance in a letter dated 11 April 1831, was now a sentimental, rather than a satirical, vaudeville. 'Do not imagine,' he declared, 'that my new vaudeville will ridicule the dear town of my birth; no, the play is sentimental, very serious, written from the heart. I read some scenes for Heiberg recently, and they pleased him greatly because of the melancholy tone.'[17] Andersen benefited greatly in this vaudeville from the detailed, skilful dramaturgical hints on construction provided by Heiberg.[18] Following a sharp initial rejection by the Royal Theatre in 1833, a revised version of **Parting and Meeting** consisting of two short, separate but related plays was accepted for production in November 1835.[19] In the first playlet, **Spaniards in Odense / Spanierne i Odense,** Augusta falls in love with a dashing Spaniard, Francesco, who is stationed in Odense. However, her sense of duty persuades her to marry Ludvig, childhood sweetheart, as the Spanish troops march away in the distance. The sequel, **25 Years After / Fem og Tyve Aar derefter,** presents the same characters 'twenty-five years later' in Elsinore—a novelty to which the actors, in the opinion of the critic for *Dagen* (19 April 1836), proved unequal in their depiction of the age changes. The sentimental conclusion to this romance unites the daughter of the now–widowed Augusta, Louise, to Diego, the son of a Spanish ambassador who proves to be none other than Augusta's sometime soldier, Francesco.

Lovers' intrigues also provided the main themes in two other Andersen vaudevilles. **Mikkel's Parisian Love Stories / Mikkels Kjærlighheds Historier i Paris** is a brief vaudeville monologue composed for a benefit for the celebrated Danish comedian, Ludvig Phister, and performed twice in 1840. Mikkel, a character revived from an earlier Heiberg vaudeville, relates his amorous adventures in the French capital. In **The Bird in the Pear-Tree / Fuglen i Pæretrœet** the quarrel of two neighbours provides the comic background for the amorous intrigue of Herman and Henriette; here, too, love surmounts all obstacles, including a fence erected between the feuding neighbours' gardens and figuring prominently in the action. A high point in this atmospheric genre sketch is Andersen's rich characterization of Counsellor Arents, who in spite of his basically friendly nature becomes entangled in the neighbour dispute over the pear-tree. His outburst when he is finally compelled to recognize the fact that his daughter's heart has been captured by the son of the enemy suggests his nature:

> *Where is my daughter! Don't look at me like that!*
> *I know very well where she is! But it's a lie!*[20]

Following two successful summer performances in 1842, **The Bird in the Pear-Tree** was entered in the regular repertoire with Scandinavia's leading actress, Johanne Luise Heiberg, in the role of Henriette. Notwithstanding her services and the play's initial popularity, however, it was soon attacked by Andersen's opponents and, in the wake of polemical articles and hissing in the theatre, it was taken off the programme after four performances. 'For the past two weeks not a single sin has been commited in Denmark,' wrote *Corsaren* (11 Nov. 1842), one of the most vitriolic of the many polemically minded periodicals at this time; '**The Bird in the Pear-Tree** is no longer applauded, on the contrary it was hissed.' Heiberg, the authoritative voice of Danish culture and intellectual endeavour, succeeded in elegantly damning the play with faint praise: 'It belongs to that species of small creatures,' he commented in his influential *Intelligensblade* (XIX, 1842), 'whose inclusion in our theatre-menagerie it would be pedantic to oppose, since it can be said of them that if they do no good, neither do they do any harm; they are too small for that, too insignificant, and too innocuous.'[21] The bitterness caused by this hostility to his play pervades Andersen's diary entries for this period: one such entry notes that his depressed mood inspired him with the idea for his best-known fairy-tale, **The Ugly Duckling.**[22]

One of Andersen's most successful works for the stage, however, was the vaudeville farce **The Invisible Man on Sprogø / Den Usynlige paa Sprogø,** 'a dramatic jest in one act with chorus and songs' which he admittedly tailored to suit a particular landscape setting originally designed for Henrik Hertz's unsuccessful vaudeville, *Flight to Sprogø / Flugten til Sprogø.*[23] Following a summer performance in 1839 which became a personal triumph for the actor C.M. Foersom in the title role of Blomme, the gullible merchant who is made 'invisible,' the play went on to become a popular favourite at the Royal Theatre, where it ran for twenty-two performances, and at Casino and Odense Theatre. 'Gulling' was another common subject in vaudeville. In **The Bird in the Pear-Tree,** Arents is gulled at the end in order that the lovers can be united. In **The Invisible Man** the entire dramatic situation is based on the 'gulling' of the central character, the enthusiastically credulous Agent Blomme ('I am a Sunday-child, am I! / O, I see more than meets the eye!') who is stranded with his family on the island of Sprogø, and is made to believe that three drops of liquid in a glass of wine together with a magic incantation have the power to render him invisible. . . .

Despite Heiberg's relatively valid criticism that the songs in **Parting and Meeting** were undramatic, and the highly prejudiced criticism by Andersen's longtime adversary Christian Molbech that he 'under no circumstances understands how to write a *Danish* vaudeville such as we have become accustomed to that dramatic genre in Professor Heiberg's works,'[31] he obviously displayed both considerable wit and dramaturgical finesse in this genre. One of the better-known examples from his plays of a scene which succeeds perfectly in capturing the elusive 'vaudeville tone' is the celebrated *tour de force* by Theodor, man-of-the-world and matchmaker in **The Invisible Man,** in which he describes his international experience in affairs of the heart. 'It would be odd if I wasn't able to do for others what I have so often done for myself—reach the goal in the kingdom of love,' he boasts to the audience. 'But here it's a question of arranging a wedding—it's true I've never tried that, but the preliminaries . . . yes, in most countries I've made acquaintances!' An engaging, Maurice Chevalier lead-in is hereby provided for the international catalogue of amorous escapades which follows. Theodor describes the girls he has known in a witty medley of 'national' songs: 'Lovely Minka,' Weyse's 'Dannemark! Dannemark!,' a Swedish folksong, 'God Save the King,' 'La Parisienne,' 'Of Spanish Girls' from the comedy *Farinelli,* and a Tyrolese melody; the medley is framed by the untranslatably charming verse:

> *To all the world's four corners,*
> *My heart with me I brought,*
> *I left it with the lovely girls,*
> *You give them what you've got.*[32]

It was mainly in the 1830s that Andersen was occupied with the topical, lyrical vaudeville. A letter written from Leipzig and dated 3 July 1841 is indicative of his growing disinterest in this genre; 'this evening I was in the theatre,' he observed, 'to see the first and undoubtedly the only vaudeville . . . on my entire trip; I have almost forgotten this genre.'[33] The following year saw his final vaudeville effort produced at the Royal Theatre. By then, however, he had already contributed in large measure to popularizing in Denmark the form which Heiberg had succeeded in proving, by a specious application of Hegelian dialectics, was the most suitable type of dramatic art for the stage of the day. . . .

Romantic Drama and Fairy-Tale Fantasy

In the 1830s Andersen's concern as a playwright was chiefly with vaudevilles and with opera libretti featuring the gothic elements of Walter Scott romanticism. In the 1840s he took a new direction, as he consciously turned toward French romantic drama and the style of Victor Hugo. These two apparently found much in common on a personal basis as well. In March 1843 Andersen was a welcome guest of Hugo in Paris, attending *Les Burgraves* with the French dramatist only a few days after its tumultuous première.[56]

The strong interest during this period in local colour and ethnographic details spurred the popularity of 'exotic,' far-away environments and peoples on the stage. It is in direct relation to this theatrical convention that Andersen's two romantic verse dramas, **The Mulatto / Mulatten** and **The Moorish Girl / Maurerpigen,** must be seen. The increasing number of books which appeared on national customs, costumes, and mores served as an important stimulus for early nineteenth-century playwrights in presenting more convincing exotic surroundings and details in the theatre; Andersen's remark that in writing **The Mulatto** he 'swallowed all the available books on Africa and America' is characteristic. Moreover, in such dramas

music was frequently included as accompaniment or as background to strengthen and deepen the impact of the romantic pathos and picturesque localities depicted.

The Mulatto, which Andersen himself felt would mark an epoch in his career, quickly became his greatest scenic triumph when produced at the Royal Theatre in February 1840. Audiences greeted the play with a storm of enthusiasm, and five sold-out houses were registered in the course of the first eleven performances.[57] Much of this popular success was the result of the drama's piquant subject matter and the illusionistic presentation of its exotic milieu on the stage. The subject of **The Mulatto,** which Andersen clothed in lyrical rhymed verse 'in order to subjugate the theme to the music of language,'[58] is reminiscent of Hugo's French romanticism and of numerous popular romantic dramas of the time. The play was adapted from a story by Fanny Reybaud, 'Les épaves,' which the dramatist read in the *Revue de Paris* (Feb. 1838).[59] Both Eleonore and Cecilie, the wife and the ward of La Rebelliere, wealthy planter on Martinique, meet and fall in love with the young, cultivated mulatto, Horatio. However, La Rebelliere plots vengeance on the hero and, by unscrupulous means, has him imprisoned and offered for sale at a slave auction. Disaster seems imminent until a legal deus ex machina, in the form of Cecilie's declaration that she will marry Horatio, frees him from slavery and disgrace. Never far beneath the surface of the conflict is Andersen's perpetual preoccupation with the 'ugly duckling phenomenon,' his running apologia for the gifted but poor, persecuted, or 'different' individual, excluded from polite society but ultimately triumphant. The moral of *Cendrillon* [a stage adaptation of *Cinderella* in which Andersen had appeared as an actor] was carried forward by Andersen as a banner and a challenge.

Critical regard for **The Mulatto** was high. 'This widely admired author has,' wrote *Dagen* (4 Feb. 1840), 'again managed to grasp the tones which find response in the audience's breast.' In addition, fine acting by Johanne Luise Heiberg, for whom Andersen had written the role of Cecilie, and an exciting scenic representation of the exotic atmosphere, particularly in the dramatic juxtaposition of Horatio's dank prison with a glittering ballroom in the fourth act and in the sensational slave-auction scene of the last act, substantially aided the success of the play.

In marked contrast, generally wretched acting and apparent indifference toward the exotic Spanish setting in Andersen's romantic drama **The Moorish Girl** resulted in a disappointing run for this play of only three performances in December 1840.[60] Countless difficulties prior to the opening of **The Moorish Girl,** including Johanne Luise Heiberg's pointed refusal to play the 'masculine' leading role, led to an open breach between the playwright and the powerful House of

Heiberg. The apologia which the tormented author added as a preface to the play was particularly ill-timed. The 1840s marked the beginning of a new development in Danish theatrical criticism, characterized by the rise and eventual predominance of newspaper 'reviews' at the expense of the more sober evaluations of the critical journals. The domination of newspaper reporting in theatrical matters brought with it a wave of glib, slashing polemics, as publications like *Figaro* and *Corsaren* (The Corsair, which sported a Barbary marauder delivering a cannon salvo on its masthead!) spearheaded a reign of terror from which no dramatist or actor was safe. Seeking to vindicate **The Moorish Girl,** Andersen introduced it with a jeremiad which reproached such hostile treatment and which began: 'It is rather well known that I have suffered a miserable childhood, and even though the good God has since led me forward, I have, however, at each step had to survive many battles.'[61] This document, judiciously omitted from his collected works, bore its own punishment in the form of devastating ridicule in the columns of *Corsaren* (1 Jan. 1841) and other papers.

Separating evidence from outraged sensibilities, however, **The Moorish Girl** is clearly inferior to most of Andersen's other plays. Although the dramatist styled this five-act verse drama a 'tragedy,' its theme and use of background music composed by Hartmann bring it closer to the category of conventional melodrama. Raphaella, a Spanish Saint Joan-figure who wins the love of the King of Cordova after saving his life in a battle against the Moors but who flees from his proposal of marriage on patriotic grounds, is basically a stock melodramatic heroine with 'ugly duckling' overtones. Although Raphaella discovers that she is in reality the daughter of the enemy King of the Moors, the King of Cordova nevertheless renews his proposal. She pretends to agree, only to take her own life on rather vague grounds of honour and decency. The play should, however, be seen from a theatrical rather than a literary vantage point; 'all is and must be calculated for the stage, for performance, thus it must be judged,' Andersen insisted in his preface.[62] In this context, the picturesque exoticism in costuming, landscape, and architecture suggested in the text provided the concrete means by which the dramatist sought to invest the melodramatic story with an interesting and evocative atmosphere. His conference with the stage manager, the scene designer, and the costume designer which followed Heiberg's reading of the play in the greenroom on 20 Sept. 1840 was undoubtedly aimed at clarifying this objective.[63] Hence when the Royal Theatre succumbed to the negative attitude of the Heibergs and neglected to provide a suitable physical exoticism in the production, the disappointing result was a foregone conclusion.

After the florid exoticism of **The Mulatto** and **The Moorish Girl,** Andersen turned closer to home and explored the areas of Danish history and Danish folk material for romantic subjects. Moreover, following the failure of his ballad dramatization, **Agnete and the Merman,** he sought refuge in anonymity, a common practice in Denmark during this decade marked by the 'reign of terror' of the newspaper polemic. The first of Andersen's anonymous productions was the one-act romantic drama performed in 1844, **Dreams of the King,** which treats the historic imprisonment of King Christjern II in Sønderborg Castle. In many ways this short play ranks among Andersen's most interesting theatrical productions; in his critique as dramaturge Heiberg praised the work for its originality and inventiveness—causing Edvard Collin to remark: 'Anonymity already begins to have its interesting sides.'[64]

Dreams of the King is based on Samsøe's eighteenth-century historical tragedy, *Dyveke,* and on Andersen's own youthful studies of Christjern II conducted in connection with an unfinished historical novel.[65] The play depicts, by means of a 'flashback technique' which was effectively supported in production by Henrik Rung's dramatic music, Christjern's dreams of his mistress Dyveke, whom he meets in Bergen and subsequently allows to be poisoned in Copenhagen. The play's national-historical subject, verse treatment, and poetic-psychological contrast between the realms of fantasy and reality all make it a typical representative of the genre of romantic drama. The critical debate which greeted the production became essentially an aesthetic discussion of 'dramatic rules'; critics of the play's romanticism opposed its 'lack of dramatic action' and its violation of correct classical versification through an overabundance of caesura and hiatus.[66] It was Heiberg, meanwhile, who, in a brilliant review in his *Intelligensblade* (1 March 1844), cut through the foggy theoretical discussion to demonstrate the effective theatricality of the play's situation, and the visually striking manner in which the dreams become a part of reality. The scenic treatment of these dream transitions, foreshadowing more modern techniques, comprises the essential core of **Dreams of the King** as theatre.

The Blossom of Happiness / Lykkens Blomst, which appeared the following year and which Andersen designated a 'fairy-tale comedy,' similarly transfers the main character to two dream situations, thereby poetically contrasting the realms of fantasy and reality. Although the basic tones of **Dreams of the King** and **The Blossom of Happiness** are very different, the subject matter of the latter play is again national-historical. Henrik, a forester, 'becomes,' by means of an elf's magic pearls, first the eighteenth-century Danish poet Johannes Ewald and next the mediaeval Prince Buris at the castle of King Waldemar. However, once he discovers that 'wishing will make it so' and experiences the terrible sorrows of the poet and the torments of the prince, the forester of Andersen's fable is happy to find that true happiness—the 'blessed peace of mind' of the wise

Alidor in *Cendrillon*—is to be sought in his humble cottage together with his little family.

If the moral of the play was thus reminiscent of Andersen's own fairy-tales, its immediate theatrical model was most probably Heiberg's historical dream-play, *Day of the Seven Sleepers / Syvsoverdag,* first produced in 1840. In his role as the Royal Theatre's consultant, Heiberg charged (unjustly) that **The Blossom of Happiness** was a direct copy of the three spheres in his own play, the realistic as represented by Henrik and his wife Johanna, the fantastic as represented by the mischievous elf and the good fairy Kirsten Piil, and the ideal, depicted in the worlds of Johannes Ewald and King Waldemar. Heiberg found Andersen's unusual treatment of the material, particularly the fact that Henrik actually *becomes* Ewald and Prince Buris, 'absurd.'[67] Andersen studied and followed historical reality closely in the Ewald episode, and the actor who played the poet tried to achieve 'a portrait likeness,' thereby discarding the character of Henrik entirely.[68]

Although the play was finally accepted in spite of Heiberg's hostile attitude, the difficulties were thereby far from being overcome. Andersen's utter disregard for 'rules' of form and propriety distressed his contemporaries greatly. Bournonville refused on the grounds of decorum to choreograph a scene in which Kirsten, Prince Buris's sweetheart, is forced to dance herself to death.[69] Johanne Luise Heiberg temperamentally turned down the part of Kirsten; 'Fru Heiberg suggests that Kirsten's role be given to a dancer and not to her,' wrote Andersen in his diary on 10 Oct. 1844. 'In a furious rage! Would like to leave Denmark forever!' Finally, although the acting proved to be a strong point in the Royal Theatre's production in February 1845, the staging of the demanding poetic contrasts and transitions in this fantasy was beset by severe technical problems in performance.[70] 'The entire structure [of the play] conflicts with the existing and customary dramatic rules governing an ordinary (eg, Scribean) play,' declared the unimaginative reviewer for *Dansk Album* (23 Feb. 1845). While the play 'reveals a poetic genius' and 'a truly brilliant eye for scenic effect,' this critic advised Andersen to concentrate on a stricter and more 'well-made' construction.

In contrast to other prominent Danish authors such as Heiberg or Henrik Hertz, H.C. Andersen was immediately responsive when Casino Theatre, the first private theatre authorized in Copenhagen, opened in 1848 under the direction of W.H. Lange. Andersen was attracted from the outset by the idea of a smaller, popular theatre, and at Casino he found consolation for the unresponsiveness and high-handed treatment he was often forced to endure at the Royal Theatre. He became Casino's unofficial house dramatist, and for a time also functioned as its literary consultant and served on the board of directors. During the early 1850s he achieved considerable fame as a playwright at Casino with a series of fairy-tale fantasies similar in form to **The Blossom of Happiness.** His success in turn attracted other established dramatists to the new popular theatre and helped greatly to increase its prestige.

Following the production, five months after Casino's opening, of Andersen's one-act adaptation of Warin and Lefevre's *Une chambre à deux lits,* called **A Night in Roskilde / En Nat i Roskilde,** he turned for inspiration to the type of popular fairy-tale play perfected by the Austrian actor and dramatist Ferdinand Raimund, whose fantasies he later recommended for careful study to the young director Henrik Ibsen during his visit to Copenhagen in 1852.[71] During his first trip to Vienna in 1834 Andersen had had an opportunity to see the special Viennese *Zauberpossen* at first hand. He was particularly enthusiastic about Karl Meisl's *Das Gespenst auf der Bastei,* which he saw at the Theater an der Wien on 2 July, noting in his diary that 'the whole light fantastic humour delighted me,' especially Johann Nestroy as the ghost 'who very humorously haunts the Bastei.'[72] In 1838 Andersen tried unsuccessfully to secure a production at the Royal Theatre for his rather undistinguished translation of *Der Verschwender,* Raimund's saga of a reckless spendthrift. At Casino, however, he succeeded in capturing the unique style and flavour of the Viennese fairy-tale comedy. 'The talent which the world acknowledges in me as an author of fairy-tales must surely also bear some fruit in this direction,' he reasoned.[73] His prediction proved correct. His fairy-tale fantasy **More than Pearls and Gold / Meer end Perler og Guld,** produced for the first time at Casino on 3 October 1849, played to a succession of capacity audiences in the 2500-seat playhouse and enjoyed no fewer than 162 performances in the repertory until 1888. The play is an adaptation of Raimund's *Der Diamant des Geisterkönigs,* the story of a young man promised a statue of diamond if he can find a girl who has never told a lie. The technique is pure Raimund, presenting a fantastic mixture of realistic scenes from contemporary life and frankly unreal, supernatural situations in order to demonstrate the worth of good, honest, simple integrity. A sincere and honest girl is 'the finest diamond,' worth 'more than pearls and gold.' To Raimund's play Andersen added ideas from *The Arabian Nights* and a piquantly localized Copenhagen flavour. The audience was treated to a stream of topical details woven into the action: Tivoli with Lumbye's popular orchestra, the amazing wonders of the new railroad to Roskilde, a balloon ascent, the newly formed Parliament, and even Andersen's publisher were mentioned. . . .

In concluding his review of **More than Pearls and Gold,** the novelist and critic M.A. Goldschmidt remarked on Raimund's 'flirtation' with the notion of fantastic wealth: 'Many a spectator of such a folk-comedy perhaps goes home to his simple parlor and finds it poorer than before, is even more dissatisfied with life than before going to the theatre. We believe that H.C. Andersen, when he creates an original play, will offer the public healthier nourishment for its imagination.'[75] The play to which Goldschmidt alluded was *Ole Shuteye / Ole Lukøie,* which appeared at Casino five months later and became Andersen's most solid success in the genre of fairy-tale fantasy. It is based on one of his own fairy-tale characters, Ole Shuteye, the Nordic sandman or god of sleep. Its moral is that implied in Goldschmidt's remark and dramatized by Raimund in, for example, *Der Bauer als Millionär*—'health, good humour, and peace of mind' are worth more than the world's riches. The method used to demonstrate this optimistic message was, of course, the technique of the Viennese *Zauberpossen*—the free intermingling of topical reality and supernatural fantasy—presented with calculated naïveté and witty dialogue.

The specific literary influences in **Ole Shuteye** are many.[76] Raimund and Andersen's own fairy-tales have been mentioned. The basic dream structure of the play is clearly related to the framework of the powerful *Der Traum, ein Leben* by the Viennese dramatist Franz Grillparzer, a close friend of Andersen. In *Der Traum,* the Eastern hero dreams in such a way that his real life is influenced by what he has experienced when asleep. In **Ole Shuteye,** Christian, the honest but discontented chimney-sweep, wishfully dreams of acquiring limitless wealth—a dangerous fantasy in the fairy-tale genre! On Østergade in Copenhagen Christian encounters, in the dream which forms the play-within-the-play, the ghost of a vagabond 'dressed all in white with white cane and white cigar,' who allows the chimney-sweep the traditional three wishes. The genealogy of the figure in white is not difficult to discern: the very same character haunted the Bastei, the favourite promenade in old Vienna, in Meisl's *Das Gespenst auf der Bastei,* which Andersen had seen sixteen years earlier at the Theater an der Wien. Finally, Christian's plight closely resembles that of the charcoal-burner Peter Munk in Wilhelm Hauff's popular fairy-tale, *Das kalte Herz.* Both young heroes relinquish their hearts to the powers of evil in order to attain riches; the evil junk-dealer Blake replaces Christian's heartbeat with the tick of a costly gold watch. The ultimate moral of Hauff's tale is fully equivalent to the gospel of **Ole Shuteye:** 'Es ist doch besser, zufrieden sein mit wenigem, als Gold und Güter haben, und ein kaltes Herz' [Far better to be satisfied with little, than to have gold and goods and a cold heart].[77]

In the Viennese *Zauberpossen* the machinist was the dramatist's closest collaborator, and thus in **Ole Shuteye** spectacular theatricality played a major role. The audience was treated to surprising scene changes, lavish dance numbers, sudden transformations, and, not least, a scene of black magic in the second-hand shop of the wicked Blake, in which the furniture danced, portraits

moved, and the fireiron performed pirouettes! Although no production records have survived, Andersen found that his spectacular fantasy was staged 'as properly as possible' on the 'small, narrow, oppressive stage at Casino.'[78]

Least successful of Andersen's fairy-tale fantasies was his one-act dramatization of another of his own tales, **Mother Elder / Hyldemoer.** Its production at Casino in December 1851 convinced him that most Danes had 'little appreciation for the fantastic,' preferring 'to nourish themselves honestly on wretched dramatic recipes right out of the cookbook.'[79] Conservative critics found it difficult to accept Andersen's loosely structured and frankly impressionistic fantasy. 'The play lacks nearly all the conditions for being called a drama,' asserted *Berlingske Tidende* (2 Dec. 1851). 'Instead of a plot, the author gives us a series of isolated scenes which, since they lack all inherent connection, he has found necessary to paste together by means of "Phantasus," who at every turn must support poet and public with opinions and explanations.'

Comedy

In marked contrast to the complexities of his fairy-tale fantasies, Andersen's charming short comedy, **The New Maternity Ward / Den nye Barselstue,** provided the Royal Theatre with an uncomplicated and immediate success when first performed there anonymously in March 1845. The popularity of Andersen's best-known play has also been permanent, and to date it has been given a total of 116 performances in the Royal Theatre repertory. The inspiration for this comedy was undoubtedly a capricious little publication by Søren Kierkegaard entitled *Foreword / Forord,* which had appeared the previous June and which suggested that someone should write a new, literary version of Holberg's classic comedy, *The Maternity Ward / Barselstuen.*[80] Hence Andersen's comedy is a 'new' **Maternity Ward** in literary terms, written in the classical manner and presenting a cavalcade of amusing caricatures from the Copenhagen of Christian VIII. Its action follows Holberg's model. Doctor Wendel returns home after many years in America to find that his old friend Jespersen has just had a great success as the author of a comedy called *Love.* A group of foolish visitors therefore flocks to the 'maternity ward'—Jespersen's study—to pay homage to the new 'child.' Unlike Holberg's play, however, Jespersen is ironically *not* the father of the child, and it rapidly emerges that Doctor Wendel himself wrote the play as a poem of unrequited love for Jespersen's sister Christine, and gave it to his friend before going away. However, to the 'poet's' relief Wendel agrees to keep the secret, the latter decides to renew his suit to Christine, and the curtain falls on an ovation by the guests for the chastened Jespersen. If several of the comic portraits and coups de théâtre, such as Christine's opening speech about the guest list, were patterned directly on Holberg's play, Andersen's satire nevertheless had a sharp topical and contemporary edge. 'Taken from raw reality' was Heiberg's phrase, but this fact by no means hampered its sweeping popularity as he had implied it would.[81] The play's piquant salon tone represented a particular forte of the Royal Theatre personnel, led by its dominant spirit and chief artist Johanne Luise Heiberg, and the comic character portraits in the classical tradition afforded rewarding acting material.

Andersen's attempt a year later to reduplicate the witty tone, comic characterizations, and 'mistaken parenthood' intrigue of *The New Maternity Ward* in a comedy entitled *Herr Rasmussen* led, however, to his most resounding failure as a dramatist. *Herr Rasmussen* received a single, anonymous performance, after which it was, for very good reason, banished from the repertoire, ignored in Andersen's autobiography, and expunged from his collected works.[82] Reviews of the debacle are short and to the point; 'this evening the audience in the Royal Theatre was obliged to hiss a new play off the stage,' wrote the critic for *Kjøbenhavnsposten* (20 March 1846), 'which would never have been put on the stage if the Royal Theatre management was not—the Royal Theatre management.' It is no surprise to find that production records for this play are few and meagre. 'Everything functioned in the proper order. The play was completely hissed off,' recorded the Theatre's *Regiejournal* tersely.[83]

Apart from his libretti for *Wedding at Lake Como* and *The Nix,* and the short prologue play *The Bulwark of Art / Kunstens Dannevirke,* a patriotic panegyric of Danish arts and letters commissioned for the Royal Theatre centennial on 18 December 1848, eighteen years passed after *Herr Rasmussen* before Andersen was represented by another new play at the theatre on Kongens Nytorv. This was the romantic comedy *He is not well-born / Han er ikke født,* which was produced in April 1864. In that year the attention of Andersen and of the Danish nation was focussed on the war with Germany in Slesvig-Holstein rather than on the stage of the national theatre. Under the circumstances, however, the production was relatively successful, due largely to the acting of romantic idol Michael Wiehe, whose tragic death in October put an end to further performances of the play. Although he found the plot of this comedy 'very slender,' Bjørnstjerne Bjørnson regarded *He is not well-born* as 'a delightful little work,' written with 'elegance and psychological, adept refinement.'[84]

The play contrasts the nobility of blood, of money, and of intellect, a contrast effectively conveyed in the dialogue and the characterization. Gathered within a rather loose framework of mistaken parenthood, a gallery of amusing character portraits surrounds the two lovers, Frederik and Elisabeth. The topicality of this romantic comedy lent itself of effective realization on the stage.

Particularly the caricature of a sensitive and temperamental poet named Kluhd (Rag), author of an 'apocalyptic comedy in nine acts' entitled *Death and Damnation,* was drawn by Andersen with fine self-irony; 'they shall be all rotting in the ground when I am ripe fruit on the public tongue!' cries the vexed Kluhd vindictively, and when told that the company was concerned after he had rushed out in a rage he strikes an injured pose which epitomizes the Andersen whimsy: 'Let them worry! Let them torment themselves! Have they dragged for me in the canals?'

By this time Andersen's world renown had at last won him immunity from the vituperous domestic criticism that had previously dogged his steps as a dramatist. 'The public has realized,' wrote critic Erik Bøgh in *Folkets Avis* (29 April 1964), 'that although [Andersen] has never succeeded in forming a work for the stage according to the accepted rules of the art, he is a far greater poet than someone possessing the most complete talent for dramatic construction, and when he leaves his limitless realm in the world of the fairy-tale to visit the narrow stage with the slanting floor, upon which each step must be measured, he should be considered as a guest who brings rich gifts from another land, where art makes other demands.' In the eyes of the younger critics representing a new generation, Andersen's genius had already passed into legend. Yet their praise of his 'innocent–satirical, naïve-ingenious dialogue' tends somewhat to neglect his insights as a dramatist and the purely theatrical merits of his later comedies.

When the Spaniards were here / Da Spanierne var her, Andersen's last play, was a romantic comedy produced in April 1865 and written with his customary awareness of contemporary theatrical taste. Based on a rewriting of his vaudeville *Parting and Meeting,* the popular historical theme of the Spanish troops stationed in Odense in 1808 provided the scenic milieu. 'His picture has a large and brilliant ornamentation,' remarked the reviewer for *Berlingske Tidende* (7 April 1865), 'conveyed through scenic effect, the use of music, and the illumination of the spoken word. The scene is set in Middelfart and southern Jutland . . . the spectator has the Great Belt before him, where British warships cruise.' Andersen's diary entries for 15 and 16 June 1864 indicate that historical studies were made for the play, and the contemporary interest in historical 'accuracy' was also the basis for the rather pedantic objection, raised by the critic for *Tilskueren* (9 April 1865), that the Marseillaise heard at the end of the play had in reality been forbidden under Napoleon's emperorship from 1804 to 1814.

The Spanish element in this scenic environment was, however, projected through the ear rather than the eye: the sound of Spanish songs and castanets is heard but the Spaniards themselves are never shown, with the exception of three children dressed in uniform who appear at the close of the first scene. Unlike Francesco in **Parting and Meeting,** Hermania's Spanish soldier, Don Juan de Molina, never actually appears on stage; only his serenades are heard in the distance. Against this dim, idealized outline of the Spanish soldier, the character of the strong-willed and spirited Hermania stands out in yet bolder relief to dominate the action. Her attraction to and pursuit of the unseen Spanish lover assumes an added dimension and becomes in the play a flight towards a romanticized ideal which echoes the richest strains in Andersen's art:

> I need to cross the rolling water! I have the swan's nature—I won't stay in this stagnant pond, nice enough for geese and ducks to swim in.[85]

Hence the sharply etched character portraits, the love affairs, happy or otherwise, the intrigues of mistaken parenthood, the fairy-tale transformations, and the quests for a romantic ideal which pervade Andersen's dramaturgy received expression in a wide variety of styles and an assortment of dramatic forms that included vaudeville, opera, singspiel, romantic drama, fairy-tale fantasy, and comedy. This chapter [in *The Plays of H. C. Andersen*] has tried to suggest some of the more significant influences on Andersen's plays—the Heiberg vaudeville, Walter Scott romanticism, exoticism, Danish history, and folk material. In each of the genres he attempted, he registered popular successes—***The Invisible Man, The Mulatto, Dreams of the King, Little Kirsten, Ole Shuteye,*** and ***The New Maternity Ward,*** to mention the more obvious examples—although the myth of his totally fruitless career as a playwright prevails, nourished no doubt by his own misleading accounts. In reality, Andersen's plays were generally written with an acute awareness of the practical theatre of his time and a concrete image of that theatre constantly in mind. As such, they are remarkably informative reflections of the nineteenth-century theatrical context, the interplay of styles, methods, conventions, and techniques in staging, costuming, and acting which preceded the emergence of naturalism.

Notes

[1] Søren Kierkegaard, *Samlede Værker,* XIV (Copenhagen 1963), 118

[2] *Mit Livs Eventyr,* 1, 215

[3] *Ibid.,* 218

[4] See H. Topsøe-Jensen, *H.C. Andersen og andre Studier* [Odense 1966], p. 35

[5] The play is unpublished; the manuscript is in the Royal Library, Collinske Samling 18, 7, with corrections by Andersen's tutor.

[6] E. Collin, *H.C. Andersen [og det Collinske Huns,* (Copenhagen 1882)], p. xv

[7] See Cai M. Woel's facsimile edition of *Gjenfærdet ved Palnatokes Grav* (Copenhagen 1940)

. . . . .

[12] Andersen, *Samlede Skrifter,* XII, 6

[13] [H. Topsøe-Jensen (ed.),] *H.C. Andersens Levnedsbog* [*1805-1831* (Copenhagen 1962)], p. 190

[14] Loose sheet in the collection 'Det Kgl. Teater: Censurer 1821-29' (Rigsarkivet)

[15] The reference is to *Samlede Skrifter,* XII, 14: 'She sits often in a corner, Humming me a song by Bay,' *ie,* composer Rudolph Bay (1791-1856).

[16] [Thomas] Overskou, 'Johan Ludvig Heiberg og den danske Vaudeville,' *Danmarks ill. Almanak for 1861,* 90

[17] [C.St.A.] Bille and [N.] Bøgh, *Breve fra H.C. Andersen* [(Copenhagen 1878) 1, 89; cf *Mit Livs Eventyr,* 1, 109

[18] See Heiberg's letter to Jonas Collin dated 22 Nov. 1833 in Collin, *H.C. Andersen,* pp. 215-21; cf Bille and Bøgh, *Breve til H.C. Andersen* [(Copenhagen 1877)], pp. 109-10, and [H.] Topsøe-Jensen, *Brevveksling med Jonas Collin d. Ældre* [(Copenhagen 1945)], 1, 99-100

[19] The reader's report is reproduced in G. Hetsch, *H.C. Andersen og Musikken* [(Copenhagen 1930)], pp. 33-7

[20] *Samlede Skrifter,* XI, 192. [B.] Jensen, 'H.C. Andersens dramatiske Digtning og det moderne Teater,' [*Tilskueren* XLIV (August 1927), 120-9] has presented a good evaluation of this vaudeville, to which Rostand's *Les Romanesques* (better known as *The Fantasticks*) bears some resemblances.

[21] See [J.L.] Heiberg, *Prosaiske Skrifter* [(Copenhagen 1861-2)], VII, 287-90

[22] 4 July 1842, Collinske Samling 7, 1

[23] *Mit Livs Eventyr,* 1, 219

. . . . .

[31] Collin, *H.C. Andersen,* p. 218, and Hetsch, *H.C. Andersen,* pp. 50-1

[32] *Samlede Skrifter,* XI, 128-9

[33] Topsøe-Jensen, *Brevveksling med Jonas Collin,* 1, 185

. . . . .

[56] *Mit Livs Eventyr,* 1, 274

[57] Overskou, *Den danske Skueplads,* [*i dens Historie* (Copenhagen 1854-76)] v, 405

[58] *Mit Livs Eventyr,* 1, 219

[59] This provoked a hefty debate on originality in *Fædrelandet* (16 Feb. 1840); see P. Høybye, 'H.C. Andersen og Frankrig,' *Anderseniana,* ser. 2, 11 (1951-4), 146-7

[60] *Fædrelandet,* 28 Dec. 1840

[61] Topsøe-Jensen, *Omkring Levnedsbogen,* [(Copenhagen 1943)] p. 216

[62] *Ibid.,* p. 217

[63] Two and a half weeks before the actual reading rehearsal on 8 Oct.; see Andersen's letter of 16 Sept. in Topsøe-Jenson, *HCA og Henriette Wulff,* [(Odense 1954-60)] 1, 276, and his diary for 20 Sept. Heiberg was dramatic consultant for the Royal Theatre and also led the reading of new scripts for the actors. See [M.] Borup, *Johan Ludvig Heiberg,* [(Copenhagen 1947-49)] II, 163-4

[64] Bille and Bøgh, *Breve til H.C. Andersen,* p. 93

[65] Cf [T.] Høeg, *H.C. Andersens Ungdom,* [(Copenhagen 1934)] pp. 271-304

[66] For the various viewpoints see *Kjøbenhavnsposten* (15 Feb 1844), *Berlingske Tidende* (15 Feb.), *Fædrelandet* (17 Feb.), *Journal for Litteratur og Kunst* (1844), p. 129, and *Ny Portefeuille for 1844,* I, 187

[67] Heiberg's hostile report is reprinted in Topsøe-Jensen, *Brevveksling med Edvard og Henriette Collin,* [(Copenhagen 1933-37)] v, 116-17. For Andersen's description of the production of *Day of the Seven Sleepers* see Topsøe-Jensen, *H.C. Andersen og H. Wulff,* I, 274

[68] *Dansk Album,* 23 Feb. 1845. For the Ewald episode Andersen studied F.C. Olsen's 'Digteren Johannes Ewalds Liv og Forholdene i Aarene 1774-77,' published in 1835 in *Kjøbenhavns flyvende Post.*

[69] Bille and Bøgh, *Breve til H.C. Andersen,* p. 43

[70] *Berlingske Tidende,* 17 Feb. 1845

[71] [Robert] Neiiendam, *Gennem mange Aar,* [(Copenhagen 1950)] p. 99

[72] Topsøe-Jensen, *H.C. Andersen og andre Studier,* p. 169

[73] *Mit Livs Eventyr,* II, 111-12

. . . . .

[75] *Nord og Syd,* I (1849), 411

[76] Topsøe-Jensen presents a perceptive analysis of this play in *H.C. Andersen og andre Studier,* pp. 153-72.

[77] *Wilhelm Hauffs sämtliche Werke in sechs Bänden* (Stuttgart: Cottasche Bibliothek der Weltliteratur, nd), VI, 322

[78] *Mit Livs Eventyr,* II, 112

[79] *Ibid.,* 144

[80] [F.J.] Billeskov Jansen, *Danmarks Digtekunst* [(*Copenhagen* 1947-58)], III, 195

[81] Heiberg's official report appears in Collin, *H.C. Andersen,* p. 371.

[82] Edvard Agerholm first edited the play, with a short introduction describing its bizarre history, in 1913. It might be noted that Andersen earned only 70 Rdl. for his labours (*Theaterkassens Regnskaber,* 7 April 1846, Rigsarkivet).

[83] *Regiejournal Jan. 1837-April 1848,* 16 March 1846 (Royal Theatre library)

[84] Cf Bille and Bøgh, *Breve til H.C. Andersen,* p. 637

[85] *Samlede Skrifter,* XXXII, 46

Hans Mayer (essay date 1975)

SOURCE: "Alternatives in the Nineteenth Century," in *Outsiders: A Study in Life and Letters,* translated by Denis M. Sweet, MIT Press, 1982, pp. 191-222.

[*In the following excerpt, originally published in 1975, Mayer discusses Andersen's outsider status and sexual orientation as revealed in his novel* Only a Fiddler *and in his fairy tales.*]

In chapter 7 of *The Story of My Life,*[1] which deals with the period 1835-1837, Hans Christian Andersen reports a curious incident in his relations with Søren Kierkegaard. Andersen, born in 1805, was in his thirties. Kierkegaard, of the generation of 1813 along with Georg Büchner, Hebbel, and Richard Wagner, was still a student at the time, but he knew all manner of people in Copenhagen, among them the controversial Andersen, a child of poverty from the island of Fyn. Andersen had just published his third novel: *The Improvisatore* and *O. T.* were now followed by *Only a Fiddler.* This third novel (1837) in as many years was well known in Copenhagen to be filled with autobiographical detail.

Andersen reports the incident, looking back, of course, knowing exactly what had become of Kierkegaard or at least what had become of him in the eyes of the official circles of Danish church and crown. He says that his novel about the gifted and despised fiddler "made a strong impression for a short time on one of our country's young and highly gifted men, Søren Kierkegaard. Meeting him in the street, he told me that he would write a review of my book and that I should be more satisfied with that than I had been with the earlier, because, he said, they had misunderstood me!"[2]

Then some time went by, and Kierkegaard came to read the book anew, this time in a far less favorable light. "I must almost believe that the more seriously he examined the story, the more faults he found, and when the critique appeared it did not please me at all. It came out as a whole book, the first, I believe that Kierkegaard has written; and because of the Hegelian heaviness in the expression, it was very difficult to read, and people said in fun that only Kierkegaard and Andersen had read it through."

There is something of a patronizing tone when he then remarks of this work that it taught him he was no poet but himself a poetical figure that at some later date a real writer would be able to employ. In Andersen's constant striving to make no enemies, he provides the anecdote with a conciliatory finish: "Since that time I have had a better understanding with this author, who has always met me with kindness and discernment."

Did Andersen for a moment comprehend that Kierkegaard's book (it was, indeed, his first)[3] negated the foundations of his creative work by exposing and denouncing as lies its kind of transformation of a wretched life into edifying literature? One doubts it. Andersen scarcely possessed the intellectual and literary requisites for understanding the full scope of Kierkegaard's work, which was in fact difficult, if not ponderous, and studded with classical citations. What he did grasp was that this young philosopher took him and his novel seriously only as a symptom of other matters and disgustedly rejected the work as a poetic creation.

The success of the novel ***Only a Fiddler*** was, indeed, symptomatic for that era of *Weltschmerz*. Otherwise it would be incomprehensible how such a prescient writer and connoisseur of literature as Robert Schumann could write Andersen on October 1, 1842, that the ***Fiddler*** was charming, certainly the best thing in modern literature, and could only be compared to Immermann.[4]

Andersen's critics centering around Johan Ludvig Heiberg in Copenhagen, with whom Kierkegaard had associated himself, rejected the literary parvenu: the man without language and a solid education. Their judgment derived from bourgeois vanity. In Kierkegaard's Andersen polemic this provincial arrogance is entirely ignored. For

him a novel like ***Only a Fiddler*** represented an attempt by a writer to lie both to himself and the world—in an edifying and profitable way at that—that capitulation is fate, that failure to meet responsibilities is merely a bit of ill luck. Kierkegaard's work ("From the Papers of One Still Living. Published against His Will by S. Kierkegaard. About H. C. Andersen as a Novelist, with Special Reference to His Latest Work, *Only a Fiddler*") was a moral confrontation, not a literary one. Whoever sits down to read it today with Andersen's biography in mind finds all the moments already sketched out that make the case of Hans Christian Andersen an exemplary one: his attempt with the aid of seeming revelations to conceal the essential. And by that means he did, quite in fact, make himself over into a poetic figure time and time again: as the improvisatore lacking substance; as the musical genius doomed by circumstance; as the ugly duckling; as the little mermaid; as a miscast tin soldier. What did not quite succeed in the earlier novels came to life in the fairytales. It is not certain whether Kierkegaard recognized that. Nonetheless Kierkegaard's early criticism of an exemplary case of prevarication by means of literature is to this day the best means we have of unraveling Andersen and the make-believe constructions of his biographers.

This son of a mentally disabled shoemaker and an uneducated washerwoman seems all too willing to bare his insides. As the portraitist of his poverty and ugliness and the playstuff of his dreams, Andersen takes pleasure in portraying his defeats. How inclined he is to cry the tears of yesteryear all over again in the retelling! At the last, even, he makes allusions to the feminine elements of his nature. Writing of his lifetime friendship with Edvard Collin in **"The Fairytale of My Life,"** [**"Das Märchen meines Lebens,"** the commentary that Andersen wrote for the German edition of his writings (translator's note).], he says that "he was the antagonist to my almost girlish nature." When Collin decided to marry, Andersen wrote his famous fairytale, **"The Story of the Little Mermaid."** Nothing had ever moved him more in writing, he confessed later. Here he had not only dared to portray himself as outsider, but as a sexual outsider. Even a palliative biographer like Signe Toksvig, who tends to leave such matters undisclosed, can find no way to avoid the subject: "the little mermaid was himself—in her attempt to win the distant beloved mortal prince, though she was handicapped in every way; a foundling, a slave, an outsider. . . . She lost the prince, saw him wed another. . . . Rather a confession of weakness it was, this feminizing of himself."[5]

It was not a confession of weakness but one of the few documents of steadfast honesty, almost of an irrepressible urge to confess. Perhaps it was a mark of Andersen's true genius that he early recognized that his attempt to ward off scandal by dredging up everything in his past—except his revulsion at the female body and his love for young men—a tissue woven of lies and self-deception, could only endanger his life as a writer. That was exactly what Kierkegaard had said. The upshot was that Andersen created in his fairy stories the possibility of speaking about himself with a minimum of subterfuge; he had in them the opportunity to intimate that his loneliness was not the result of poverty, ugliness, low birth, lack of schooling, or even a self-isolating poetic genius, but that it had to do with an existential outsiderdom. Beings from another element, miscast, a swan among the ducks in the lake.

Andersen successfully attained a state of complete conformity in the nineteenth-century bourgeois social order. He can be compared only with the Jewish outsider Benjamin Disraeli in that. Toward the end of his life he had succeeded in establishing for public consumption a monumental stylization of his life—the authorized version, so to speak. Andersen was the author of fairytales, consequently a great friend of children, something that he actually was not. During his last illness, when he was concerned with plans for a monument to be erected in his honor, he forbade the addition of children's figures around his own. Even close friends took his tragicomic heart-throbbing intimations of love for women seriously, his feigned courting of Riborg Voigt or Louise Collin, which was wont to begin as soon as Andersen knew his lady was firmly committed to someone else. This women's courtier remained himself a virgin, as he is said to have confided in old age to a friend and physician. What was meant was a virgin in his relationships with women.

For the rest, this Danish child of poverty had discovered the possibilities of a double life. In Andersen it becomes a sundering of his existence into the moral and inconspicuous mode of life at home on the isle of Seeland, and the incessant erotic tours abroad of one always yearning to be on the move. And for Andersen too, as for Winckelmann, Platen, Tchaikovsky of the "Capriccio italien," the Englishmen who pilgrimage to Capri, the world of Italy becomes the landscape of happiness. Yet with the strange difference manifested in Andersen's letters, that he can see his fulfillment in the South only as a kind of substitute for the missing union with his friends in Denmark. Much complaint in his oftentimes whining letters home is stylized and subterfuge, meant to distract from the delights of being away. Behind his begging for letters, nonetheless, especially from Edvard Collin, there is a forlorn tornness seeking to unite the frustrating life in Denmark with the happiness of the South.

Andersen seems never to have been able to allay fears of discovery and scandal once he had embarked on his double life. From that comes his restless collecting of unimpeachable acquaintances and protectors, from ruling monarchs on down, which in the case of an actual scandal, as later was to be demonstrated with Oscar Wilde and Philipp, Prince of Eulenburg, would have been unavailing, perhaps even detrimental. Besides, he seems to have lived in a panicky anxiety of being taken for what he was, either by other homosexuals who were less constrained by total conformity or by strangers whom he was bound to fear as malicious spies. The sculptor Bertel Thorvaldsen belonged to the first group, who received Andersen, his young fellow countryman (as Andersen reports in a self-congratulatory manner), amid a round of hugs and kisses and very likely acquainted him with bohemian Rome. In his letters, however, you feel how Andersen, though clearly flattered by his acquaintance of such a celebrity, nonetheless carefully shuns any deeper community. His coldness is embarrassing in an obituary he wrote for a Hamburg newspaper the night after Thorvaldsen's sudden death during a theater performance. Andersen and others had had dinner with him and then accompanied him to the theater before going off on their own. He died there of a heart attack. Andersen described this last meeting coldly, almost as if relieved. It was not a friend who wrote the obituary notice.

It is curious that in his autobiography, among the gigantic collection of celebrities who were all claimed as his friends, above all in Paris although he scarcely comprehended French, there is to be found listed the name of Heinrich Heine. In his letters home, on the other hand, he reports how he anxiously guarded himself against Heine's visits. For what reason? Did he fear the Jewish outsider? Scarcely. More likely he feared the polemicist and adversary of Count Platen. Andersen was acquainted with Heine's *Baths of Lucca*.

The older he got, the less he was inclined to play the poor, rejected suitor forever chasing after the favors of women. More and more, young men begin to people his travel accounts; he cannot suppress the happiness they bring. In Madrid a festive dinner is given in his honor. "One of my young friends from Manila," is there who "seems to have taken quite a fancy to me."[6]

Even in his correspondence with H. E. Scudder, his American publisher, he feels obliged to mention the young friend he found in Vienna; what makes this acquaintance all the more precious is that he is the son of the novelist Bulwer, Lord Lytton.[7] On his sixty-fifth birthday he writes Scudder that he enjoys most the company of young people. This contradicts, of course, all the perorations of friendship in his letters to old friends, particularly old bosom friends like Signe Lässö, the mother of one of his boyhood chums, but is fully credible.

His Danish contemporaries were not deceived. The vehement attacks that Andersen experienced at the outset of his career were only mitigated by the worldwide fame of the fairytale composer; the tone of displeasure at so much stylization of life—stylization whereby the misogynist gives himself to appear as a praiser of women, the avaricious old man as a goodly benefactor, the egotistical hypochondriac as a friend of children—was always in the background. That he probably suffered a nervous shock as a boy in Rector Meisling's house in Copenhagen where he was supposed to make up for his missed schooling, a shock after repeated attempts to seduce him on the part of the mistress of the house and the parlor maid, is mentioned even in Elith Reumert's palliative biography, *Hans Andersen the Man.*[8]

Only with this in mind does it make any sense that when, in his older years, the high point of which doubtless was the ceremony making him an honorary citizen of Odense, he who was so much honored, he had an irrational fear before every ceremony that something would go awry. Even before the festival in Odense that concludes *The Story of My Life* and that he took to be evidence of a guiding providence, as he says at the start of his autobiography, the honored guest seems to have vividly anticipated the trauma of a sudden awakening in the midst of scandal. Signe Toksvig in her Andersen biography asserts that immediately after his "feminine" fairytale of the little mermaid, Andersen wrote a decidedly "masculine" and political fairytale, one of his most successful: **"The Emperor's New Clothes."**[9] But like **"The Ugly Duckling," "The Tin Soldier," "The Little Mermaid,"** this story too deals with the panic of conformity and being different. To be sure, the emperor parades his way amid pomp and honor; one could say he even goes back to Andersen's native Odense where they are going to memorialize him but where someone might suddenly say something, a child perhaps, allowing the truth to slip out so that everything will end in uncircumventable scandal.

In Denmark they awaited his passing away. Immediately thereafter the critic and dramatist Erik Bögh published an essay characterizing the man Andersen,[10] the public man Andersen at that, by underscoring the connection between Andersen's "feminine" nature, as Bögh calls it, and his political indifference, indeed even conservative bootlicking. In point of fact, one is flabbergasted reading the innumerable wooing letters from his travels. Whoever takes the trouble to read through this correspondence receives not the slightest inkling that their author was living in a time between two European revolutions, in an epoch when patronage by the ruling nobility meant less and less, when Denmark was twice involved in war with the Germans, which in 1864 led to a national catastrophe and in which several of the writer's close friends lost their lives. That was what Bögh demonstrated in his analysis, precipitating a flood of literature that swept over the seeming favorite and forced the Collin family to realign the memorial. Conformity had failed in the end. It happened as in the **"Emperor's New Clothes."**

Looking back at Andersen's life and works, at his means of skirting all the conflicts of the time by going over to the side of those who seemed mighty, it seems all of it had been anticipated in Kierkegaard's analysis of 1838. One has to assume that Kierkegaard from the first moment on had divined in that writer a moral and existential phenomenon, not a literary one.

Kierkegaard's main thesis posits that "Andersen's own realness, his own person, takes refuge in poetical works, so much so that one is really tempted in certain moments to view Andersen as a figure that has run off from a group some writer has invented and not yet finished; it is certainly indisputable that Andersen could become a most poetical figure in a story."[11] An object, then, not the creative subject of poetry. Yet the poetical figure that becomes delineated for Kierkegaard when reading and contemplating Andersen is that of a liar and self-deceiver.

"In consequence of the ill humor and unhappiness," as Kierkegaard writes in this first book of his, "which he feels in the real world, he seeks in the despondency of his own poetic creations a satisfaction as it were for his own despondency. Exactly like La Fontaine he sits there on that account and cries over his unhappy heroes who must perish, and why? Because Andersen is he who he is. The same joyless struggle that Andersen himself has to battle in life now repeats itself in his poetical works."[12] That is a perception of remarkable acuity. Kierkegaard was acquainted with Andersen in those days only as the author of poems, little prose pieces, and three for him unbearable novels. He had yet to make the acquaintance of the fairytale writer. On that account he somewhat condescendingly calls Andersen "an author not disadvantageously known through a fairly significant literary activity."[13] Nonetheless he compares him, surprisingly enough, with the fable writer La Fontaine. La Fontaine's heroes, however, over whom he ostensibly laments as he lets them fall to their doom, are above all figures of fable and appear in the form of animals. In a series of lectures on "The Five Temptations of La Fontaine," Jean Giraudoux relates how La Fontaine tried again and again to compete with the successful authors of his day in the lyric and verse epic, always unsuccessfully, until the animals came to him and he transformed himself into their darling and poet.[14]

Andersen, the author of what one must admit is the scarcely passable novel *Only a Fiddler,* against whom Kierkegaard mounted his attack, stood at the time at a crossroads—there where a mediocre and prodigious writer after so many lies to himself suddenly resolves to find a poetic form that admits some genuineness and honesty, and who then comes to his own identity as author of the fairytales—exactly as had La Fontaine thanks to the animals in his fables.

How that worked can be seen by comparing Andersen's typical fairytales with his novel about the poor tailor's apprentice and brilliant musician by the name of Christian who pitifully meets his ruin as "only a fiddler."[15] This novel is a psychoanalyst's delight. That it was packed with autobiographical detail, even obtrusively so, was known to the reading public throughout Copenhagen, hence Kierkegaard's transferring to the author his conclusions about the figure in the novel. Andersen was generally equated with the fiddler. Yet the novel is constructed as the contrast of two life stories, one male, the other female—the female's rising, yet unhappy, the male's waning, yet subjectively, as Andersen would have it, liberating. It is in the female figure of Naomi that the author has disclosed himself far more than in the fiddler. She is the illegitimate daughter of a Jewish girl and a wild adventurer. Her Jewish blood soon surfaces. She runs off with a gypsy trick rider named Ladislaus, disguises herself as a man, and becomes this virile outsider's lover. She lets herself be chastised with a riding crop, is then taken back to the aristocratic world of her adoptive parents, marries a marquess, and is consumed by desire for her gypsy.

The novelist has rid his Naomi of any and all inhibitions: she lives out what Andersen does not allow himself. Yet her social conformity leads away from her own identity. That identity was to be found in the one episode where social outsiderdom was lived to the fullest, in scandal both enjoyed and provoked. Jewishness, illegitimacy, gypsy life, transvestism. All thrown together without any particular concern for plausibility. Andersen has summed up the phenotypes of outsiderdom. That he identifies himself erotically with Naomi will scarcely escape the modern reader. He composed here the authentic fairytale of his life.

The fiddler Christian is meant, as Andersen later claimed in **"The Fairy Tale of My Life"** (1847), to exemplify another variation of providence: that of Hans Christian Andersen misfortunate and without protectors. One might also add: without lies and conformity as well.

It was precisely this that embittered Kierkegaard the more he read the mediocre work and the more exactly he came to reflect on it: the equation of unhappiness with fate, genius with failure. The result of that equation is a feeble and immoral complaisance in the conduct of one's life. Kierkegaard was at the time still self-sufficiently Hegelian and conceived genius as action and transformation. This is also the reason he gives no credence to Andersen's assertion that his fiddler Christian is a failed musical genius. "This conclusion of Andersen's," the critic Kierkegaard replies, "contains a basic misunderstanding of the power of genius and its relation to untoward circumstance (for genius is not a little wick of light that goes out in the first wind, but an inferno that the storm only whips on), and is grounded in the fact that Andersen does not show a genius in battle but more nearly a weakling, of whom it is said that he be a genius, and who has in common with genius only the fact that he suffers a couple of unpleasantnesses, to which he in fact succumbs."[16]

Between Kierkegaard's first reading of the novel and repeated later readings there falls a decisive religious turningpoint. Andersen probably reported correctly that the young student Kierkegaard had at first been filled with enthusiasm for the work and then later came to think (and write) of it in quite a different vein. At any event, this novel of Andersen's of an identity refused became for the reader Kierkegaard the occasion for the finding of an identity. And so Søren Kierkegaard's first book resulted out of it; the ephemeral occasion of Andersen was needed to enable Kierkegaard to speak of Kierkegaard.

Hans Christian Andersen had, after many mendacious attempts, to arrive at his identity as an author not by describing conditions of happiness and unhappiness but conditions of total and incurable outsiderdom—of the little mermaid, the miscast tin soldier, the swan in the duck pond who has to go on living in a pond where swans are not recognized as a higher category. So that scandal always awaits behind the scenes and can be called up by a child who sees the emperor naked. . . .

Notes

[1] Andersen's letters reveal with dismaying clarity not only the vanity that was the butt of his contemporaries' wit, but also a fawning servility that takes the words of the partner of the moment into its own mouth and presses itself upon high aristocrats, as the grand duke of Sachsen-Weimar-Eisenach, quite without conviction, always eager for equal status. See *Hans Christian Andersen's Correspondence,* ed. Frederick Crawford (London, 1891).

[2] Hans Christian Andersen, *The Story of My Life,* author's ed. (Boston, 1871), p. 136-7.

[3] "Af en endnu Levendes Papirer udgivet mod hans Villie af Søren Kierkegaard. Om Andersen som Romandigter med stadigt hensyn til hans sidste Vörk *Kum en Spillemand,"* *Samlede Vaerker,* vol. 1 (Copenhagen: Gyldendal, 1962), p. 11ff. ["From the Papers of One Still Living. Published against his will by S. Kierkegaard. About Andersen as a novelist with special reference to his last novel *Only a Fiddler.*"] German ed. Søren Kierkegaard, *Erstlingsschriften* (Düsseldorf: E. Diederichs, 1960), p. 41ff.; notes p. 176ff. See Emanuel Hirsch, *Kierkegaard-Studien* (Gütersloh: C. Bertelsmann, 1933), p. 13ff.

[4] *Andersen's Correspondence,* p. 155.

[5] Signe Toksvig, *The Life of Hans Christian Andersen* (New York: Harcourt, Brace, 1934), p. 185.

6 H. C. Andersen, *In Spain and a Visit to Portugal,* author's ed. (New York: Hurd & Houghton, 1870), p. 199.

7 *The Andersen-Scudder Letters,* ed. Jean Hershold and Waldemar Westergaard (Berkeley: University of California Press, 1949), pp. 59, 74.

8 Elith Reumert, *Hans Andersen the Man,* trans. Jessie Bröchner (London: Methuen, 1927), pp. 47-8.

9 Toksvig, *Hans Christian Andersen,* p. 186.

10 See the expositions in Reumert, *Hans Andersen the Man,* p. 15ff.

11 Kierkegaard, *Erstlingsschriften,* p. 62.

12 Ibid., p. 61.

13 Ibid., p. 55.

14 Jean Giraudoux, *Les Cinq tentations de Lafontaine* (Paris: Grasset, 1938).

15 An exact analysis of the novel, in connection with Kierkegaard's first publication, is provided in Hirsch's *Kierkegaard-Studien,* p. 26ff., and in his commentary in Kierkegaard, *Erstlingsschriften,* p. 177ff.

16 Kierkegaard, ibid., pp. 77-8. . . .

Elias Bredsdorff (essay date 1975)

SOURCE: "The Range of Andersen's Tales," in *Hans Christian Andersen: The Story of His Life and Work, 1805-75,* Phaidon, 1975, pp. 308-32.

[*In the following essay, Bredsdorff discusses the sources of some of Andersen's tales and proposes a system for grouping the tales.*]

Today Andersen's fame rests entirely on his fairy tales and stories. They have been translated into well over a hundred languages and are still being published and republished in millions of copies all over the world; but it is important to realize that when people speak of *Andersen's Fairy Tales* they are not necessarily speaking of the same tales.

The total number of tales published in Denmark during Andersen's lifetime under the title *Eventyr og Historier* is 156; but although they have all been translated,¹ many are unfamiliar in Denmark, and even fewer are well known abroad.

In the English-speaking world the early tales, those published between 1835 and 1850, are the ones best known. Judging by present-day editions the following thirty appear to be the most popular (the year of publication in Denmark being given in brackets): 'The Tinder Box', 'Little Claus and Big Claus', 'The Princess on the Pea',² 'Little Ida's Flowers', 'Thumbelina',³ 'The Travelling Companion' (1835); 'The Little Mermaid', 'The Emperor's New Clothes' (1837); 'The Steadfast Tin Soldier',⁴ 'The Wild Swans' (1838); 'The Garden of Eden', 'The Flying Trunk', 'The Storks' (1839); 'Willie Winkie' (Ole Lukøje),⁵ 'The Swineherd', 'The Buckwheat' (1841); 'The Nightingale', 'The Top and the Ball',⁶ 'The Ugly Duckling' (1843); 'The Fir Tree',⁷ 'The Snow Queen' (1844); 'The Darning Needle', 'The Elf Hill',⁸ 'The Red Shoes', 'The Shepherdess and the Chimney-Sweep', 'The Little Match Girl' (1845); 'The Shadow' (1847); 'The Old House', 'The Happy Family' and 'The Shirt Collar' (1848).

If I were asked to select the sixty tales which I considered most characteristic and representative, I would probably include most of these thirty, but I would certainly not regard them as adequately representative of the many different aspects of Andersen's genius.⁹

Andersen was a creative writer, not just a collector of folk tales. It is therefore wrong to bracket him, as is often done, with the brothers Jakob and Wilhelm Grimm, or with Asbjørnsen and Moe, the two Norwegian collectors of folk tales.

Nevertheless, a few of his tales, especially some of the early ones, were based on traditional Danish folk tales which he had heard as a child in Odense.¹⁰ Two months before the publication of his first four tales he wrote to Ingemann: 'I have given a few of the fairy tales I myself used to enjoy as a child and which I believe aren't well known. I have written them completely as I would have told them to a child.'

The inspiration for **'The Tinder Box'**, which is clearly in this category, appears to have come from two interdependent sources: partly from a Danish folk tale sometimes called 'The Spirit of the Candle', which again is based on the story of 'Aladdin and the Wonderful Lamp' in the *Arabian Nights,* and partly from Adam Oehlenschläger's famous Romantic play *Aladdin* (1805), a work greatly admired by Andersen, who liked to identify himself with Aladdin as Oehlenschläger saw him: the genius predestined to move along the road from poverty to greatness and fame. In writing the opening story in his first volume of fairy tales Andersen must have had in mind both the crude plot of the folk tale he had heard as a child, and the philosophy of Oehlenschläger's poetic masterpiece; but it was a matter of great importance to him not to appear to be imitating the latter. As Hans Brix puts it: 'In his first tale, **"The Tinder Box"**, he deliberately chooses the Aladdin story in·its popular form. The very fact that it is exactly the same theme [as Oehlenschläger's] forced him to be entirely original:

not a single detail must bear any resemblance. It is a true contest with Oehlenschläger.'

The three dogs appear to be Andersen's own invention—in the folk tale an 'iron man' (or a 'steel man') appears whenever the hero lights the candle, and the treasures in the cave are guarded by a sleeping troll. But the most important innovation was the style in which the tale was told, a narrative style, which was entirely Andersen's own, simple and straightforward, devoid of all the literary conventions of the time:

> Down the country-road a soldier came marching. Left, right! Left, right! He had his knapsack on his back and a sword at his side, for he had been at the war, and now he was on his way home. But then he met an old witch on the road. Oh! she was ugly—her lower lip hung right down on her chest. 'Good evening, soldier,' she said. 'What a nice sword you've got, and what a big knapsack! You're a proper soldier! Now I'll show you how to get as much money as you want.'—'Thank you very much, old witch!' said the soldier.

Little Claus, the hero of **'Little Claus and Big Claus'**, is another Aladdin character, certainly not a moral hero, but a cunning David who cannot help beating Goliath in the end. Andersen's story was taken from a Danish folk tale called 'Big Brother and Little Brother', recorded in several parts of the country. There are many similarities to the folk tale, but it is also obvious that Andersen has made a number of deliberate changes. Thus in the folk tale Big Brother actually kills Little Brother's grandmother (believing that it is Little Brother he is killing), but Andersen has seen to it that Little Claus's grandmother was already dead when Big Claus 'gave her a great clump on the forehead'. 'The unfaithful wife', a stock character in adult folk tales and *fabliaux,* did not seem to Andersen to belong to a nursery tale, and so he explains why the farmer's wife had to hide the parish clerk in the chest when her husband returned unexpectedly, by saying: 'the farmer had the strange failing that he never could bear the sight of a parish clerk'—an explanation completely satisfactory to a child.

The nearest known equivalent for **'The Princess on the Pea'** is a Swedish tale (related to Tieck's 'Puss in Boots') about a poor girl who goes out into the world accompanied by a cat (in some versions a dog), which advises her to present herself at the royal castle as a princess. Being suspicious the queen puts the alleged princess's sensitivity to the test by secretly placing some small objects (a bean, peas, a piece of straw) under her mattress; but on each occasion the cat (or dog) warns the girl so that next morning she can pretend to have slept very badly, thus proving her delicacy and sensitivity. In the Swedish version, therefore, the heroine wins by cheating, whereas in Andersen's version the heroine proves herself to be a real princess by actually being hypersensitive.

'The Travelling Companion' is based on a Danish folk tale called 'The Dead Man's Help', which contains all the basic features of Andersen's tale. As early as 1829 Andersen had used folk material for a story he called **'The Ghost'**, and it is interesting to compare it with 'The Travelling Companion'. In **'The Ghost'** the language is precious and abounds with hackneyed literary clichés; in **'The Travelling Companion'** this has been superseded by a much more directly spoken language—it is possible that Andersen tried out the story on children and found that it did not work in its first form.

In **'The Wild Swans'** Andersen again followed a traditional folk tale fairly closely, and in this case he had access to a printed version published in Matthias Winther's *Folkeeventyr* (1823) (the same theme also occurs in Grimm's 'Die sechs Schwäne'). In a letter dated 5 October 1838 Andersen wrote: 'Please read Matthias Winther's fairy tale of 'The Wild Swans' and tell me whether my rewriting of it is good or bad.' Unlike the folk tale Andersen refrains from inflicting cruel punishment on the villains, who are, in his version, the evil stepmother (a witch) and the archbishop (a kind of Grand Inquisitor). He has superimposed a religious element: at the end Elise is depicted as a saint, saved in the nick of time from being burnt at the stake, and while her eldest brother explains her innocence, 'a perfume as of a million roses spread around, because every faggot from the stake had taken root and put out branches, and a high sweet-smelling hedge stood there with crimson roses. Right at the top was a single flower of the purest white, glittering like a star.'

In an explanatory note to **'The Swineherd'** Andersen says that the tale on which it was based contained features, 'which could not decently be retold in the manner in which they were told to me as a child'. The folk tale in question, 'The Proud Maid', is the story of an arrogant girl who rejects her princely suitor, but ends by accepting him when he appears in the guise of a beggar whose possessions she happens to covet. In order to get hold of them she agrees to allow him to spend a night, first in her bed-chamber, and later in her bed. The tale is known internationally in a number of versions, but the part which Shakespeare used in *The Taming of the Shrew* has been omitted by Andersen, who discarded the happy ending. In **'The Swineherd'** the haughty princess, who scorns genuine beauty (the rose and the nightingale), but is prepared to degrade herself by kissing the stranger for the sake of his trivial mechanical gadgets, is eventually banished from her father's kingdom, and the prince, who has come to despise her, rejects her.

Andersen specifically refers to **'The Garden of Eden'** as being 'one of the many tales I heard related as a child'; he only wished it had been much longer, he says. The tale on which the first part is based is called

'The Isle of Bliss' and can be traced back to a story by Countess d'Aulnoy (1650-1705). It is about a prince, who loses his way and suddenly finds himself at the home of the four winds and their mother; one of the winds carries him to the beautiful fairy on the Isle of Bliss, where he stays for three centuries without noticing the passage of time; only on his return to his earthly home does it catch up with him. Further inspiration was the dramatic poem *Lycksalighetens ö* (1824-7) by the Swedish writer P. D. A. Atterbom, and some themes in the *Arabian Nights*.

'**Simple Simon**' is a humorous story without any fairy-tale element; it has various ancestors in folk-tale tradition. Simple Simon (by Andersen called Klods-Hans) is a kind of de-sentimentalized male Cinderella, and his two elder brothers, who are 'so clever that—well, the fact is they were too clever by half', correspond to the ugly sisters. While they ride off to propose to the princess on a coal-black and a milk-white horse respectively, Simple Simon rides on his billy-goat. Their useless knowledge does not help them win the princess, who cannot resist Simple Simon and admires his intrepid actions. Some of the objects the hero picked up on his way to the royal castle were such as could not be mentioned in decent company; so Andersen's hero collects less objectionable items, a dead crow, an old clog with the vamp missing, and mud straight out of the ditch. They all come in useful in his conversation with the princess, during which he is never at a loss for an answer.

This is how '**Dad's Always Right**' begins:

> Now listen! I'm going to tell you a story I heard when I was a boy. Since then the story seems to me to have become nicer every time I've thought about it. You see, stories are like a good many people—they get nicer as they grow older, and that is so pleasant.

The story which Andersen heard as a child is sometimes called 'The Praiseworthy Wife', because it is about a woman who always looks on the best side of her husband's bad bargains. In Andersen's story the husband, a poor Funen farmer, leaves home to sell his horse at the nearby market, but before getting to market he manages to swap the horse for a cow, the cow for a sheep, the sheep for a goose, the goose for a hen, and the hen for a bag of rotten apples. Having followed the folk tale thus far, Andersen then introduces two Englishmen. Now, what everybody knew about the English was that they were tremendously rich and fond of betting; so on hearing the farmer's story the two Englishmen were immediately prepared to bet a bushel of gold that the farmer's wife will be angry when he returns and tells her about his bargains; but the farmer insists that she will give him a kiss and say: 'Dad's always right!' which is, of course, exactly what she does.

Whereas the above nine tales were based on folk tales Andersen had heard, but (apart from a single case) never read, three of his others have literary sources.

'**The Naughty Boy**', Andersen's story about Cupid, who shoots his arrows into the hearts of innocent people (including the poet himself), is based, as Andersen openly admits, on a poem by Anacreon.

In his commentary to the 1862 edition of *Eventyr og Historier* Andersen states that '**The Emperor's New Clothes**' is of Spanish origin and mentions Prince don Juan Manuel as the author to whom he is indebted for the idea. Infante don Juan Manuel (1282-*c.*1349) is famous for his *Libro de Patronio* or *Conde Lucanor* (1328-35), a collection of fifty-one cautionary tales, based on Jewish and Arabic literature. Andersen did not know the Spanish work but had read one of the stories in a German translation entitled 'So ist der Lauf der Welt'. He took the main plot from this, while at the same time giving it a universality which the Spanish version did not have.

The Moorish king of the original has been changed into an emperor, whose empire could be nowhere and anywhere in this world, and the swindlers have been reduced from three to two. But the most important change is in the magic quality of the clothes made by the fraudulent weavers. In the Spanish story they claim that the material is invisible to any man who is not the son of his presumed father; in Andersen's story the swindlers claim that 'the clothes made from their material had the peculiarity of being invisible to anyone who wasn't fit for his post or was hopelessly stupid'. It is this which makes Andersen's story universally applicable, ridiculing the snobbery of people who pretend to understand or appreciate things they do not really understand or appreciate, in order not to be considered ignorant or stupid.

> 'What's this?' thought the emperor. 'I can't see anything this is appalling! Am I stupid? Am I not fit to be emperor? This is the most terrible thing that could happen to me. . . . Oh, it's quite wonderful,' he said to them; 'it has our most gracious approval.' And he gave a satisfied nod, as he looked at the empty loom; he wasn't going to say that he couldn't see anything.

In Andersen's original manuscript the story ends with everybody admiring the emperor's new clothes, the implied moral being that people willingly allow themselves to be deceived. *Mundus vult decipi.* The final paragraph ran as follows:

> 'I must put on that suit whenever I walk in a procession or appear before a gathering of people,' said the emperor, and the whole town talked about his wonderful new clothes.

Having sent the manuscript to the printer's Andersen had misgivings about this ending, and a few days later—on 25 May 1837—he wrote to Edvard Collin, who was responsible for the proof-reading:

> The story **'The Emperor's New Clothes'** ends with the following paragraph: 'I must put on that suit, etc.' I want this to be deleted completely and the following inserted instead, as it will give everything a more satirical appearance:
>
> 'But he hasn't got anything on!' said a little child.
>
> 'Goodness gracious, do you hear what the little innocent says?' cried the father; and the child's remark was whispered from one to the other.
>
> 'He hasn't got anything on! There's a little child saying he hasn't got anything on!'
>
> 'Well, but he hasn't got anything on!' the people all shouted at last. And the emperor felt most uncomfortable, for it seemed to him that the people were right. But somehow he thought to himself: 'I must go through with it now, procession and all.' And he drew himself up still more proudly, while his chamberlain walked after him carrying the train that wasn't there.

It was this ending—probably added after Andersen had read the original version to a child—which gave Andersen's masterpiece its final touch.

Finally, it should be mentioned that the *Rahmenerzählung* or 'narrative frame' of **'The Flying Trunk'** has been taken, with a few modifications and a complete change of style, from a story about Malek and Princess Shirine in *A Thousand and One Days* (1711-12) by Pétit de la Croix, which had been translated into Danish. The story within the story, however, is very much Andersen's own.

The remaining 144 tales are entirely his own invention, though this does not, of course, mean that he did not use themes or features from other sources.[11]

Andersen called his tales *Eventyr og Historier,* thus making a deliberate distinction between *Eventyr* (fairy tales, French *contes de fées,* German *Märchen*) and *Historier* (stories), the former with, the latter without a supernatural element in them. Thus **'The Little Mermaid'** is a fairy tale, **'The Emperor's New Clothes'** a story. But the dividing line is not always quite clear, nor is Andersen always consistent; in spite of its title **'The Story of a Mother'**, for instance, is not a 'story' but a 'fairy tale'; **'The Snow Queen'** has the sub-title **'A Fairy Tale in Seven Stories'**. He first used the term *Historier* in 1852; until then he had consistently used the term *Eventyr*. In **Mit Livs Eventyr** he explains that he had gradually come to regard the word *Historier*

as better covering his tales in their full range and nature: 'Popular language puts the simple tale and the most daring imaginative description together under this common designation; the nursery tale, the fable and the narrative are referred to by the child as well as by the peasant, among all common or garden people, by the short term: stories.'

In the following discussion of Andersen's tales (a word I use to include both 'fairy tales' and 'stories') I propose to divide them into seven groups: (1) fairy tales proper, in which the supernatural element is a dominating one, (2) tales mainly enacted in the natural world but containing an important element of magic, (3) tales in which the main characters belong to the animal world, (4) tales in which the main characters are trees or plants, (5) tales in which inanimate objects have become animated, (6) 'realistic' tales set in a fantasy world, and (7) realistic stories, anecdotes or *fabliaux* set in a real world.

Fairy tales proper

In his book *H. C. Andersens Eventyrverden* Bo Grønbech describes the geography of Andersen's poetic universe in these words:

> Our own geography has no validity. Immediately outside the typically Danish town in which Gerda grew up she arrives at 'the river'; during her wandering into the world she soon reaches a non-localized kingdom of the well-known fairy-tale type, and from there she goes to Lapland, whence she is again able to continue her wandering on foot to Spitzbergen. Travelling towards the East from human dwellings one reaches the Garden of Eden or to the splendid castle of the Sage. If one goes far enough through the wood one may end up at Death's hot-house. The mermaids and mermen live at the bottom of the sea, and the uncanny brewery of the marsh-woman is situated under the ground, as is the forecourt of hell. Heaven is the kingdom of God and the angels and not a cold and empty space.

In **'The Little Mermaid'** the human world only exists in so far as it relates to the dreams, the longings and the love of the little mermaid, and the only human being who has a clear identity is the prince. The main emphasis is on the 'sea people', especially the sea king, his mother and his six daughters. Living at the bottom of the sea as they do, their existence mirrors human existence: the sea king is a widower, looked after by his mother, who wears her status symbol, 'twelve oysters on her tail', while the rest of the nobility had to put up with only six'. The sea king's palace corresponds in splendour to a royal palace on dry land: 'It's walls are made of coral, and the long pointed windows of the clearest amber; but the roof is made of cockleshells that open and shut with the current.' Here little fishes fly in and out like swallows in a human dwelling, and outside the palace there is a lovely garden 'with trees of deep blue and fiery red'.

Just as the human world has its witches, so the world of the mermaids has its witch, living 'on the far side of the roaring whirlpools', and to get to her you have to pass over hot bubbling mud and go through a wood, whose trees and bushes are half animals, half plants. The sea witch sits in her house, built of the bones of shipwrecked humans, 'letting a toad feed out of her mouth, just as we might let a little canary come and peck sugar. She called the horrible fat water-snakes her little chicks and allowed them to sprawl about her great spongy bosom'.

Goodness and unselfish love also exist at the bottom of the sea, personified in the little mermaid who ultimately rejects the temptation to save her own life by stabbing the prince, whom she loves, with the knife, for which her sisters had paid the price of their beautiful hair. The main difference between the mermaid and the prince is that the latter has an immortal soul. By transforming the little mermaid in her dying moment into one of 'the daughters of the air', Andersen indicates that she may acquire an immortal soul in three hundred years time.

'**The Snow Queen**' has no clear dividing line between the natural and the supernatural world. The Snow Queen is first introduced as a fictional, fairy-tale character, but she materializes and takes Kay away to her kingdom of cold reason, because the splinter from the devil's glass had made him ripe for it. In his last, scared moment, before the Snow Queen's kisses make him forget everything, he wants to say the Lord's Prayer but can only remember the multiplication table.

Gerda preserves all the qualities of innocence and warmth which Kay has lost, and though she can be delayed in her search for Kay (by the old woman with the sun hat, by the mistaken identity of the prince, by the wild and spoilt little robber girl) nothing can prevent her from carrying on until she finds him. Having been carried by the reindeer to Lapland, Gerda continues to the Finmark, where she sees the Finn woman, who is so clever that she can tie up all the winds in the world with a thread of cotton and make a drink so potent that it would give Gerda the strength of twelve men; but that still won't be enough, the Finn woman says to the reindeer, explaining:

> 'I can't give her greater power than she has already. Don't you see how great it is? Don't you see how man and beast feel obliged to serve her, and how far she has come in the world in her bare feet? She mustn't learn of her power from us; it lies in her heart, in her being a dear innocent child. If she can't reach the Snow Queen and get rid of the glass from little Kay, then there's nothing we can do to help.'

In the end Gerda reaches the Snow Queen's palace. The walls are built of drifting snow, while the windows and doors are cutting winds. In the middle of the unending snow hall is a frozen lake called the Glass of Reason, where Kay is trying to make up the word ETERNITY out of flat pieces of ice. 'If you can find me that pattern, then you shall be your own master, and I'll make you a present of the whole world and a pair of new skates,' the Snow Queen had told him. Gerda's tears of joy when she finds Kay thaw out the lump of ice in his heart and dissolve the little bit of glass there, and Kay's own tears cause the splinter to trickle out of his eye. Such is their happiness that even the pieces of ice dance with delight and settle down to form the very word Kay had been unable to form.

While '**The Snow Queen**' has a pure entertainment value for small children and a deeper symbolic significance for their elders, '**The Story of a Mother**' may be called a purely allegorical fairy tale, or a poetic myth, with an appeal almost entirely for adults. Only the first paragraph describing the mother sitting by the bed of her dying child takes place in a recognizable world; from then on the allegory takes over. Disguised as an old man Death enters, and while the mother dozes off for a minute he vanishes with her child, and the clock stops—time ceases to exist. Then the desperate mother begins her search, which is entirely unlike Gerda's.

Out in the snow she meets Night, 'a woman in long black clothes', who requires her to sing all the songs she used to sing to her child as the price for telling her which way Death went with the child. Later, at a crossroads, a bramble bush 'with neither leaf nor blossom, for it was midwinter and the twigs were all frosted over', wants to be warmed at her breast before telling her which road to take. The thorns pierce her flesh, but 'the bramble shot out fresh green leaves and blossoms in the cold winter's night—such was the warmth from a sorrowing mother's heart'. At a lake she must weep out her eyes before being carried across 'to the great greenhouse where Death lives and looks after flowers and trees', and here the old woman who looks after the graves and the greenhouse reveals that 'every human being has his tree of life or his flower, each one according to his nature'; the old woman's price for her help is the mother's long black hair, in exchange for her own white hair.

Among millions the mother recognizes the heart-beat of her own child, 'a little blue crocus that stood there weakly and drooping'. Then Death arrives.

> 'How were you able to find your way?' asked Death. 'How could you get here more quickly than I did?'
>
> 'I am a mother,' she said.

In despair she threatens to pull up all the flowers unless Death gives her back her child; but then she realizes that she would make other mothers unhappy. Death gives her back her two eyes which he has fished out of the lake and shows her the future of two children, one whose life will be happy and one whose life will be miserable, and tells her that one of the two is her child. Terrified the mother asks Death to take away her child: ' "Forget about my tears—my pleading—all that I have said and done!" And Death went away with her child into the unknown land.'

I have dealt at some length with these three tales because I consider them the three greatest of Andersen's fairy tales.[12]

'The Elf Hill', one of Andersen's most amusing fairy tales, takes place entirely in a world of supernatural beings, the occasion being the Elf King's party in honour of some prominent guests, the Norwegian Dovre Troll and his two ill-mannered sons. Only very select guests are to be invited, not even ghosts will be admitted, says the Elf King's housekeeper, enumerating the guests:

> The merman and his daughters must first be invited, though I dare say they are not very keen on coming ashore; still I'll see that each of them gets a wet boulder or something better to sit on, so I rather fancy they won't say no this time. All old trolls of the first class with tails must be asked, and the river-sprite and the goblins; and then I don't see how we can leave out the grave-pig, the death-horse and the church-lamb. It's true that they really rank among the clergy, who don't belong to our people, but those are just their duties; they are nearly related to us, and they pay us regular calls.

The food is exquisite and suited to the occasion:

> The kitchen was crammed with frogs on the spit, snake-skins stuffed with little children's fingers and salads of toadstool seeds, moist mouse-noses and hemlock, beer from the marsh-woman's brewery, sparkling saltpeter wine from the burial vault—all very substantial. Rusty nails and bits of stained-glass window were for nibbling in the sweet course.

The natural world only comes into the story through the comments of the lizards and the earthworm. After sunrise, when the banquet is over, one lizard says to another:

> 'Oh, I *did* enjoy the old Norwegian Troll!'

> 'I prefer the boys,' said the earthworm, but then of course he couldn't see, poor creature.

Another fairy tale full of humour is **'Willie Winkie',** whose title character describes himself as an ancient heathen—'the Romans and Greeks call me the Dream God'. The fairy tale consists of seven stories which Willie Winkie tells a little boy called Hjalmar in his dreams during a whole week.

Nothing is impossible to Willie Winkie. He can turn flowers into trees, put Hjalmar's bad writing in the copybook through a drill, make the furniture talk and take Hjalmar on an excursion into the landscape picture on the wall. One night Hjalmar is out at sea, the next night at the wedding of two mice, for which he becomes so tiny that he can borrow a tin soldier's uniform and be transported to the party in his mother's thimble. Another night Hjalmar is taken to the wedding of his sister's two dolls, Herman and Bertha. The ceremony is performed by Willie Winkie, dressed in Hjalmar's granny's black petticoat, and they all sing a song, written by the pencil. On Saturday Willie Winkie explains that he must see to it that everything is ready for Sunday; for instance, all the stars must be taken down and given a thorough polish, with each star and the corresponding hole being numbered, so that they can find their right places again. At this point the portrait of Hjalmar's great-grandfather protests that Willie Winkie is muddling the boy with wrong ideas: 'A star is a globe, the same as the earth; that's just the beauty of it.' So next evening Willie Winkie takes the precaution of turning the portrait to the wall before continuing his stories.

In **'The Goblin at the Grocer's'** the main character is the Danish *nisse*, a kind of benevolent hobgoblin, whose loyalty is divided between the grocer and the student, i.e., between material and poetic values; he wisely decides to share himself between the two.

Unlike most of the other fairy tales **'The Marsh King's Daughter'** can be determined both in time and place. The time is the end of the Viking Age, the place partly North Jutland, partly Egypt. The commentators are a couple of storks who spend the summer in one place, the winter in the other. The title character is the daughter of the evil Danish Marsh King and an Egyptian princess; like another Thumbelina, she was found on the leaf of a water-lily, and the Viking's wife became her foster-mother. But because of the different character of her parents she is a beautiful girl with a wild and evil spirit during the day, and a toad with a kind though sad nature during the night—the Beauty and the Beast combined in one person. Eventually goodness conquers evil in her, and, finally united with her real mother, she flies back to Egypt, where she saves the life of the pharaoh. The ending is yet another version of the ancient legend about someone being allowed to spend three minutes in heaven—to find out on returning to earth that three hundred years have passed.

The time and place of **'The Ice Maiden'** can also be stated exactly; the place is Switzerland (with various locations given) and the time the middle of the nineteenth century (Rudy's death by drowning took place in 1856). Behind the love story of Rudy and the Miller's daughter is the underlying theme of the Ice Maiden, the Queen of the Glaciers, a dedicated enemy of man, who is constantly trying to give those who venture into her territory the kiss of death.

The Ice Maiden is Fate; what she is determined to get, she will eventually get. She lives at the bottom of the glacier, in a torrent of melted ice and snow; it is her laughter people hear when an avalanche is falling. 'If I move my palaces the roar is more deafening than the rolling thunder,' she says. This is how Andersen describes her:

> She, the slayer, the crusher, is partly the mighty ruler of the rivers, partly a child of the air. Thus it is that she can soar to the loftiest haunts of the chamois, to the towering summits of the snow-covered hills, where the boldest mountaineer had to cut footrests for himself in the ice; she sails on a light pine twig over the foaming river below and leaps lightly from one rock to another, with her long, snow-white hair fluttering about her, and her blue-green robe glittering like the water in the deep Swiss lakes.

Tales with an element of magic

This group of tales can hardly be described as fairy tales, for they include no supernatural beings. Their characteristic feature is that, at some crucial point in the tale, natural laws are broken.

'The Shadow', one of Andersen's most important tales, may serve as an example. The only violation of the laws of nature is that a man one day finds himself without a shadow; gradually, however, a new shadow grows out from his feet; 'the roots must still have been there'. The vanished shadow, which has become an independent being, turns up after several years, prosperous and well-dressed, at his former master's house and later invites his less prosperous master to a spa, where he pretends that the master is his shadow. By using the wisdom of the learned man (his former master) the shadow wins the heart of a beautiful princess, and when the former master refuses to act as the shadow's shadow he is executed on their wedding-day.

'The Shadow' begins in 'the hot countries', then moves back to a northern country and finally to an anonymous spa and to the anonymous kingdom of the princess. We are told that the learned man writes books about 'what is true and good and beautiful in the world' and in describing his reaction to having lost his shadow Andersen makes an oblique reference to Chamisso's *Peter Schlemihl:*

> He was very annoyed, not so much because the shadow had disappeared, but because he knew there was a story, well known to everybody at home in the cold countries, about a man without a shadow; and if he went back now and told them his own story, they would be sure to say that he was just an imitator, and that was the last thing he wanted.

When the shadow first presents himself again to his former master he tells him about the time he vanished in the south. The learned man had been fascinated by a strange house opposite in which music was heard but from which no human being ever emerged, except on one occasion when he had a brief vision of a young girl coming out on to the balcony—only to vanish again. It was into that house the shadow went, and in that house Poetry herself lived. 'I was there for three weeks,' says the shadow, 'and it meant as much as living for three thousand years and reading all that man has imagined and written down.' But pressed to explain what he experienced there, the shadow keeps on repeating: 'I have seen everything and I know everything.'

The knowledge the shadow has acquired over the years turns out to be of a special kind:

> 'I saw what none are supposed to know—but what all are dying to know—trouble in the house next door. . . . If I had edited a newspaper, it would have had plenty of readers! But I used to write direct to the person in question, and there was panic wherever I went. They were terribly afraid of me—and, oh! so fond of me. The professors made me a professor, the tailors gave me new clothes; I was well provided for. The master of the mint made me coins, and the women said I was handsome. And that's how I became the man I am.'

While the shadow prospers, the learned man is in despair because no one bothers about the things he writes about, the true, the good and the beautiful.

What first impresses the princess when she meets the shadow is that he is able to tell her much about her own country she did not know, for 'he had peeped in at the windows on every floor and seen all sorts of things through them'. When she wants to test his wisdom the shadow tells her that her questions are so elementary that even his shadow—as he pretends the learned man to be—can answer them. 'He has now been with me so many years, listening to me all the time—I should imagine he can.' Impressed with the learned man's conversation the princess reflects: 'What a man this must be when his mere shadow is as wise as that.'

As a contrast to this pessimistic story about the victory of the parasite, about people preferring the shadow to the substance, there is **'The Bell'**, which also belongs to this category; for though the bell and its sounds are described in tangible, realistic terms, as an object which people try to locate and identify, always in vain, it is not a bell in any realistic sense; it is a romantic philosophy, a way of life, and a way of looking at life.

There are for instance certain times when some people can hear this mystic bell:

> It was as though the sound came from a church in the very depths of the silent, fragrant wood; and people looked in that direction and became quite solemn.

In their search for the bell grown-ups are either distracted by cheap imitation bells, or are preoccupied with elaborate theories about the origin of its sounds. Then young people take over; boys and girls coming from the solemnity of Confirmation Sunday feel drawn to the ringing of the unknown bell; but they too drop out from the search one by one, distracted by a variety of other things. In the end only two boys are left, a prince and a pauper. The prince goes to the left, the poor boy to the right, and their search becomes more and more difficult and hazardous. At sunset the prince finds himself facing the open sea, the sinking sun like a great shining altar:

> Nature was a great holy cathedral, in which trees and hovering clouds were its columns, flowers and grass its altar-cloth of woven velvet, and the vault of heaven its mighty dome.

Here the poor boy meets the prince, for the road each of them has taken has led to the same goal:

> They ran to meet each other, taking each other by the hand there in the great cathedral of nature and poetry. And above them sounded the sacred invisible bell, while blessed spirits hovered about it in joyful praise to God.

The magic elements in **'Something to Write About'** are the spectacles and the ear-trumpet belonging to the wise woman, whom the young man, who wants to become a poet by Easter, consults. His trouble is that he cannot think of anything to write about, for it seems to him that every good idea has been used long before he came into the world. When the wise woman lends him her spectacles and her ear-trumpet he can see and hear all the prosaic everyday things telling their poetic tales, but when she takes back her glasses and her trumpet, he can no longer see or hear a thing.

> 'Very well, then you can't be a writer by Easter,' said the wise woman.
>
> 'No? But when can I?'
>
> 'Neither by Easter nor by Whitsuntide. You'll never learn to hit on anything.'

So the only thing left for him to do is to become a literary critic.

The trunk in **'The Flying Trunk'** was of a very special kind—as soon as the lock was pressed the trunk could fly. In 'The Swineherd' the gadgets invented by the disguised prince defy the laws of nature: the pot which has the peculiarity that if one holds one's finger in its steam, one can at once smell what is being cooked on every fire in the town, and the rattle which, when swung round, plays 'all the waltzes and jigs and polkas that anybody had ever heard of'.

'Everything in its Right Place' is a completely realistic story up to the point when the young tutor begins to play the flute he has cut out of a historic old willow tree, which symbolized the brutal way in which the old aristocracy had oppressed the poor. The flute suddenly transforms the whole social order in such a way that everybody finds his place in the social scale, not according to his title, rank or fortune, but according to his true human value.

Tales in which animals are the main characters

Andersen's use of animals as characters differs essentially from that of Aesop, La Fontaine and Lessing. His animal tales are not anecdotal and hardly ever teach a moral lesson; unlike the classical fables they certainly do not serve a rationalistic philosophy. Andersen's animals have a psychological make-up which is very much like that of certain humans, and their conversation and general behaviour mirrors that of human beings. Among his favourite animal characters are the inhabitants of the farmyard—cocks and hens, ducks and drakes, geese, ganders and turkeys, and they are usually selfish and narrow-minded. Other favourites are storks, usually with a broader outlook, being birds of the world. A variety of other creatures—cats and dogs, rats and mice, fishes, birds, snails, insects—play prominent parts in Andersen's tales.

The best example of these stories is **'The Ugly Duckling'**, which begins with 'the stork on his long red legs, chattering away in Egyptian, for he had learnt that language from his mother', and then moves on to the manor-house park, where a tame duck is sitting on her nest. Coming out of the eggs one by one the little ducklings are amazed at how big the world is; but their mother tells them that what they see is not the whole world: 'Why, it goes a long way past the other side of the garden, right into the parson's field; but I've never been as far as that.' The ugly duckling, whose egg broke later than the others, does not conform to the rules of the farmyard but commits the unforgivable sin of being different:

> 'Ugh! What a sight that duckling is! We can't possibly put up with him'—and one duck immediately flew at him and bit him in the neck.
>
> 'Leave him alone,' said the mother. 'He's doing no one harm.'
>
> 'Yes, but he's so gawky and peculiar,' said the one that had pecked him, 'so he'll have to be squashed.'

Pecked and jostled and teased by all the other inhabitants of the farmyard, even by his own brothers and sisters, the duckling runs away to the great marsh where the wild ducks live. 'What a scarecrow you are!' they say, 'but that won't matter to us, as long as you don't marry into our family.' The wild geese, on the other hand, being young and perky have a Bohemian attitude to life.

> 'Look here, my lad!' they began. 'You are so ugly that we quite like you. Will you come with us and migrate? Not far off, in another marsh, are some very nice young wild-geese, none of them married, who can quack beautifully. Here's chance for you to make a hit, ugly as you are.'

During the big shoot the ganders are killed, but even the retrievers won't touch the duckling.

Then, towards evening he comes to a poor little farm cottage—'it was so broken-down that it hardly knew which way to fall, and so it remained standing'. Inside the house lives an old woman with her cat and her hen.

> The cat, whom she called Sonny, could arch its back and purr; it could even give out sparks if you stroked its fur the wrong way. The hen had such short little legs that it was called Chickabiddy Shortlegs; it was a very good layer, and the woman loved it like her own child.

The house has its own social order and its strict conventions:

> Now, the cat was master in the house and the hen was mistress, and they always used to say 'We and the world', because they fancied that they made up half the world—what's more, much the superior half of it. The duckling thought there might be two opinions about that, but the hen wouldn't hear of it.
>
> 'Can you lay eggs?' she asked.
>
> 'No.'
>
> 'Well, then, hold your tongue, will you!'
>
> And the cat asked: 'Can you arch your back or purr or give out sparks?'
>
> 'No.'
>
> 'Well, then, your opinion's not wanted, when sensible people are talking.'

The duckling goes through all kinds of hardship until finally in the spring he sees some beautiful swans; bowing his head he expects to be killed by them—but then he sees a reflection of himself in the water, 'no longer a clumsy greyish bird, ugly and unattractive—no, he was himself a swan!' The moral of the tale, which has become proverbial, is that inborn qualities are more important than upbringing: 'It doesn't matter about being born in a duckyard, as long as you are hatched from a swan's egg.'

'**Thumbelina**' is full of animals, some of them nasty, others likable. On her way through life Thumbelina is first kidnapped by an ugly, slimy toad, who wants her son to marry her, then liberated by the fishes and the butterfly, and eventually caught by a cockchafer, whose family all find her ugly:

> 'Why, she's only got two legs,' they said. 'What a pitiable sight!' 'She hasn't any feelers,' they went on. 'She's so pinched in at the waist—ugh! she might almost be a human. Isn't she ugly!' exclaimed all the cockchafers.

'**It's Perfectly True!**' begins in a hen-house, where a hen preening herself causes a little feather to come out and flutter down. The news of this event, whispered from hen to hen, is passed on to the owls and picked up by the pigeons until finally it returns to the very hen-house where it originally took place. The story by this time is that 'five hens have all plucked out their feathers to show which of them had got thinnest for love of the cock. Then they pecked at each other till the blood came and they all fell down dead, to the shame and disgrace of their family and the serious loss of their owner'.

'**The Happy Family**' is about two old snails living among the burdock leaves in the park of an old manor-house; they are convinced that the forest of burdocks has been planted entirely for their benefit:

> They had never been outside it, though they realized that something else existed in the world called *The Manor,* where you got boiled and then turned black and were laid out on a silver dish; but what happened after that nobody knew. They couldn't anyhow imagine what it felt like to be boiled and to lie on a silver dish, but it must be delightful and very much the correct thing. Neither the cockchafer nor the toad nor the earthworm, when questioned, could reply; none of them had ever been boiled or laid on a silver dish.

The main characters in '**The High Jumpers**' are the flea, the grasshopper and the skipjack (a toy made from a wishbone), who compete to see which of them can jump the highest. The flea has perfect manners; 'he had of course gentle blood in his veins and was accustomed to mix only with mankind, and that does make such a difference'. The grasshopper is wearing his native green uniform and boasts of his old family in Egypt and of his ability to sing. When the skipjack wins by jumping into the princess's lap, the flea goes abroad on foreign service, 'where he is said to have been killed', and the grasshopper goes and sits in a ditch, pondering on the way of the world.

Concerning the idea behind **'The Beetle'** Andersen explained in 1862:

> In an issue of *Household Words* Charles Dickens had collected a number of Arabian proverbs and idioms; among them he emphasized this one: 'When the Emperor's horse was shod with gold shoes the beetle also put out his leg.' We suggest, Dickens says in a note, that Hans Christian Andersen should write a tale about this subject. I wanted to do so, but no tale came forth. Only nine years later, during a visit to the Danish manor of Basnæs, where I happened to read Dickens' words again, did the tale of **'The Beetle'** suddenly spring forth.

Deeply humiliated that the blacksmith refuses to give him gold shoes when the emperor's horse has got them, the beetle leaves the stable and on his way through the garden meets a variety of other creatures—some ladybirds, a caterpillar, two frogs, a couple of earwig families and some of his own relations. Self-important and arrogant as he is, the beetle despises the others for being different and therefore inferior. After having gone through various tribulations—being picked up by zoologists, caught by two children, who send him out sailing, tethered to the mast in an old broken clog—the beetle finally ends his journey by returning to the emperor's stable, where he finds himself sitting on the emperor's horse. And now he begins to understand: 'Why was the horse given gold shoes? He asked me that as well, the blacksmith did. Now I realize. It was because of me that the horse was given gold shoes.'

There is a paragraph at the beginning of **'The Ice Maiden'** which is worth quoting. Rudy, who is still a small boy, has been learning a great deal from his conversations with Ajola, a dog, and a tom cat, who first taught him to climb:

> 'Come up here on the roof,' the cat had said to him quite clearly, 'for when you're still a child and cannot yet talk you have no difficulty in understanding the language of hens and ducks, cats and dogs; they speak as plainly to children as their parents do if only the children are small enough; then even grandfather's walking-stick can neigh and become a horse with a head, legs and a mane. Some children lose this gift later than others, and then the grown-ups say that they are slow in developing and that they remain children for too long. Grown-ups say a lot of silly things.'

Andersen remained a child the whole of his life in that he never lost this understanding.

Tales in which trees and plants are the main characters

I shall choose **'The Fir Tree'** and **'Little Ida's Flowers'** as examples of this category.[13]

We follow the fate of the fir tree from its childhood in the wood to its death as a withered and discarded Christmas tree. In all its life it had never had a happy moment, for either it was looking forward to something better than the present, or it was thinking nostalgically of the past.

When it was small it was in a hurry to grow big, hated being called 'a dear little tree', and never felt able to enjoy the warmth of the sun or the sweetness of the air. It was envious of the big fir trees which were felled to make masts for splendid ships, and its impatience increased when it saw its friends being taken away before Christmas and heard the sparrows describing the glory and splendour in store for them as Christmas trees. But when its own turn came and it was the first to be felled, it had no thoughts of happiness, being 'so sad at parting from its home, from the place where it had grown up'.

The fir tree is taken into a house and decorated for the great event.

> 'Tonight,' they all said, 'tonight it's going to sparkle—you see!'

> 'Oh, if only tonight were here!' thought the tree. 'If only the candles were already lit! What happens then, I wonder? Do trees come from the woods to look at me? Will the sparrows fly to the window-panes? Shall I take root here and keep my decorations winter and summer?'

From sheer longing the tree gets barkache, 'and barkache is just as bad for a tree as headache is for the rest of us'. When the great moment comes and the candles are lit, the fir tree is so tense that it is unable to enjoy the moment but looks forward to a repetition the next night. Instead it is put up in the attic, where it entertains the mice with nostalgic memories of its early youth and retells the story of Humpty-Dumpty it heard on Christmas Eve. The rats, however, are less easy to please than the mice:

> 'Is that the only story you know?' asked the rats.

> 'Only that one,' replied the tree. 'I heard it on the happiest evening of my life, but I never realized then how happy I was.'

> 'It's a fearfully dull story. Don't you know any about pork and tallow candles? One about the larder?'

> 'No,' said the tree.

> 'Well, then, thank you for nothing,' answered the rats and went home again.

In the end the tree is taken out into the yard, all withered and yellow, and is trampled on by the children.

And the tree looked at the fresh beauty of the flowers in the garden and then at itself, and it wished it had stayed in that dark corner up in the attic. It thought of the fresh days of its youth in the wood, of that merry Christmas Eve, and of the little mice who had listened with such delight to the story of Humpty-Dumpty.

'All over!' said the poor tree, 'if only I had been happy while I could. All over!'

In **'Little Ida's Flowers'** it is the student, 'who knew the most lovely stories and could cut out such amusing pictures', who tells Ida that when the flowers hang their heads and look quite withered it is because they have been at a dance on the previous night. 'When it's dark and we are all asleep,' he explains, 'they go hopping round quite gaily; almost every night in the year they have a dance.' He also tells her how the flowers communicate with each other by signs: 'Surely you've noticed them when it's a bit windy—how the flowers keep nodding and fluttering their green leaves; that means as much to them as if they talked.' This annoys the grumpy old councillor. 'Fancy filling a child's head with such rubbish,' he says. 'All stuff and nonsense!'

One night Ida wakes up in the middle of the night, hears music coming from the next room, and when she peeps in, this is what she sees:

All the hyacinths and tulips were standing on the floor in two long rows; there wasn't one left in the window, where the pots stood empty. Down on the floor all the flowers were dancing round so nicely together, actually doing the Grand Chain, and holding each other by their long green leaves as they swung round. But over at the piano sat a tall yellow lily, which little Ida was sure she had seen last summer; for she remembered the student saying: 'Isn't it like Miss Lena!' Everybody had laughed at him, but now Ida, too, thought that the long yellow flower really was like Miss Lena. It had just the same way of sitting at the piano, and of turning its sallow oval face first to one side and then to the other, while it nodded time to the pretty music.

The climax of the evening is when suddenly the drawing-room door opens and a whole throng of beautiful flowers comes in:

Two lovely roses, wearing little crowns of gold, led the way; they were the king and queen. Next came the most charming stocks and carnations, bowing in every direction. There was a band playing, too—great poppies and peonies blowing away on pea-shells till they were purple in the face, and harebells and little white snowdrops tinkling away as if they had real bells. It was such funny music. After that came a lot of other flowers, and they all danced together—the blue violets and the red daisies, the ox-eyes and the

lilies-of-the-valley. And it was pretty to see how the flowers all kissed each other. At last they said good-night to one another, and little Ida also crept away to bed, where she dreamt of all she had seen.

Tales in which inanimate things become animated

Andersen's ability to give life to inanimate objects was one of the most striking innovations of the nursery tale. The following is a quotation from *Chambers's Journal,* 13 October 1855:

In many a nursery, the warlike 'tin-soldier' (now invariably a Russian, as he used to be a Frenchman), the top, the ball, and even Nurse's darning-needle, have all become so many deathless heroes of romance, through the magic touch of this gentle Scandinavian enchanter.

In an essay entitled 'Hamlet and the Danes'[14] G. K. Chesterton writes about Andersen:

His treatment of inanimate things as animate was not a cold and awkward allegory: it was a true sense of a dumb divinity in things that are. Through him a child did feel that the chair he sat on was something like a wooden horse. Through him children and the happier kind of men did feel themselves covered by a roof as by folded wings of some vast domestic fowl; and feel common doors like great mouths that opened to utter welcome. In the story of **'The Fir Tree'** he transplanted to England a living bush that can still blossom into candles. And in his tale of **'The Tin Soldier'** he uttered the true defence of romantic militarism against the prigs who would forbid it even as a toy for the nursery. He suggested, in the true tradition of the folk tales, that the dignity of the fighter is not in his largeness but rather in his smallness, in his still loyalty and heroic helplessness in the hands of larger and lower things.

The first tale in which Andersen gave life to inanimate objects was in fact **'The Steadfast Tin Soldier'**, again about someone who is different—unlike all the other tin soldiers he only has one leg. Whatever happens to him he always behaves with the decorum of a man in uniform. He falls in love with the little dancer cut out of paper, but does not betray his feelings, and when the search goes on for him in the street after he has fallen out of the window, he is still following the rules:

If only the tin soldier had called out 'Here I am!' they would have found him easily enough; but he didn't think it would be right to shout out, as he was in uniform.

He keeps a stiff upper lip even when faced with terrible dangers, as when the paper boat into which two street-boys have put him drifts from the gutter in under a broad culvert, where a water-rat asks for his passport and pursues him in raging fury. In the open sea he is swallowed by a large fish but is still shouldering arms while lying at full length inside the fish. The fish is caught, cut open, and out comes the tin soldier—back in the same house as before:

> There they were—the same children, the same toys on the table, the same beautiful castle with the pretty little dancer who still stood on one leg and kept the other one high in the air—she, too, had been steadfast. This touched the tin soldier, who could have wept tears of tin, only that would hardly have done!

Only in death is the tin soldier united with the dancer, in the glowing stove:

> The tin soldier was melted down to a lump and, when the maid cleared out the ashes next morning, she found him in the shape of a little tin heart; but all that was left of the dancer was her spangle, and that was burnt as black as coal.

Another famous example of this category[15] is **'The Darning Needle'**, about which tale Andersen wrote the following explanatory note in 1862:

> In the summer of 1846, during a fairly long visit to Nysø together with Thorvaldsen, who enjoyed **'The Top and the Ball'** and **'The Ugly Duckling'**, he said one day: 'Well, why don't you write us a new amusing tale? You're capable of writing even about a darning needle!'—and then I wrote **'The Darning Needle'**.

This explanation is amusing but cannot be quite true, for Thorvaldsen died in March 1844, and **'The Darning Needle'** was written at the manor of Bregentved in 1845 and published in 1846. The germ of it is to be found in **'Willie Winkie'** (1841), in which Hjalmar asks Willie Winkie to tell him 'the story about the darning needle who was so stuck-up that she fancied she was a sewing needle'—almost verbatim the opening of **'The Darning Needle'**: 'There was once a darning needle who was really so fine that she fancied she was a sewing needle.'

In spite of having warned the fingers (the only human element in the story) to handle her carefully the darning needle breaks when being forced to try to mend the cook's slippers. Put together with a drop of sealing-wax she is stuck in the front of a scarf.

> 'Look, now I'm a brooch,' said the darning needle. 'I was certain I should make my way in time. One who *is* something will always go far.' And she laughed inside her, for you can never tell from the outside whether a darning needle is laughing.

She talks to her neighbour, a pin, with a mixture of flattery and condescension, and holding herself up proudly she falls into the washtub and gets lost:

> 'I'm too fine for this world,' she said as she sat in the gutter. 'Still, my conscience is clear, and that's always a comfort.' And the darning needle held herself straight and kept up her spirits.

In the gutter all sorts of things go floating over her—sticks, straws, bits of newspaper, and she is appalled at their ego-centricity:

> 'Look at the way they go sailing along,' said the darning needle. 'Little do they realize what is at the bottom of it all. *I* am at the bottom here I sit. . . . Look, there goes a stick that thinks of nothing but "stick", and that's what he is. There goes a straw—see how he twists and turns! Don't think so much about yourself, or you'll bump into the kerb. . . . There goes a bit of newspaper - the news in it is all forgotten, and yet it still spreads itself. . . . I stay patient and quiet. I know what I am, and I shan't change.'

The title character in **'The Shirt Collar'** is a kind of male counterpart to the darning needle. The story begins:

> There was once a swell gentleman whose entire kit consisted of a bootjack and a comb—though he had the neatest shirt collar you ever saw, and it's about this collar that our story is to be.

Being old enough to think about getting married the collar first proposes to a garter he meets in the wash, but though he flatters her by calling her 'a girdle, a kind of understrap', she won't have anything to do with him. Next he proposes to a hot iron going over him:

> 'Madam,' said the collar, 'dear widow lady, I'm getting so hot, I shall soon be quite another person; I'm losing all my creases. Ugh! You're burning a hole in me—oh! will you marry me?'

> 'You rag!' said the iron, going disdainfully over the collar; for she fancied she was a steam-engine meant to draw trucks on the railway.

Being a bit frayed at the edges the collar has to be cut by the pair of scissors, to whom he next proposes, calling her a great *ballerina*. But the scissors give him such a jag that he has to be thrown away. Lastly the collar proposes to the comb—only to find that she is already engaged to the bootjack.

> 'Engaged,' sighed the collar. Now there was no one left to propose to, and so he came to despise the whole idea.

At last the collar finds himself in a bag at the paper-mill, together with a lot of other rags, to whom he brags about his past, turning all his defeats into conquests. His punishment is that he is made into paper, into that very bit of paper on which the story is printed.

One of Andersen's most sophisticated stories about inanimate objects has no title, for it is a story within a story: it is the tale told by the owner of the flying trunk to the King and Queen of Turkey to prove to them that he is worthy of marrying their daughter. It is a very amusing domestic conversation-piece which takes place in the kitchen. In order of appearance the characters are: a bundle of matches, the saucepan, the tinder box, the earthenware jar, the plates, the broom, the bucket, the tongs, the tea urn, an old quill pen, the tea kettle, and the market basket. The personality of each of the characters comes out in their contributions to the conversation, and they are all extremely human. This gem of a story is Andersen at his malicious best.

In an essay about Andersen in *Books and Authors,* 1922, Robert Lynd wrote:

> Andersen's genius as a narrator, as a grotesque inventor of incident and comic detail, saves his gospel from commonness. He may write a parable about a darning-needle alive, like a dog or a schoolboy. He endows everything he sees—china shepherdesses, tin soldiers, mice and flowers—with the similitude of life, action and conversation. He can make the inhabitants of one's mantelpiece capable of epic adventures, and has greater sense of possibilities in a pair of tongs or a door-knocker than most of us have in men and women. He is the creator of a thousand fancies.

Realistic tales set in a fantasy world

As the best example of this category I shall discuss **'The Nightingale'**, universally considered to be one of Andersen's masterpieces.[16]

Although this tale is set in China, it soon becomes clear that it is a fictitious and fantastic China. With the exception of the nightingale and Death towards the end of the tale, all the characters are very human, for better or worse.[17]

'The Nightingale' is basically the story of nature versus artificiality, and this conflict is illustrated not only by the contrast between the real nightingale and the mechanical bird, but also by the contrast between the ordinary Chinese people (represented by the fishermen and the poor kitchen-maid) on one hand, and by the Chinese imperial palace, its courtiers and civil servants, on the other. The difference is to be found even in the palace gardens; in the remote parts, where the inhabitants of the palace never go, there are deep lakes and glorious woods going right down to the sea; in the garden immediately outside the palace only rare and precious flowers, with silver bells attached in order to draw attention to them. Above

these differences sits the Chinese emperor himself, almost a prisoner of his surroundings, but with an appreciation of real values when he has a chance to see or hear them.

The remoteness of China allowed Andersen to invent a world full of *chinoiserie* and stiff, formal rules. The palace itself is made of porcelain, and on special occasions it is polished so that the china walls and floors glitter in the lights of thousands and thousands of gold lamps. The emperor sits in a gold chair when reading, and we are told that his gentleman-in-waiting 'was so grand that, whenever anyone of lower rank than himself ventures to speak to him or ask a question, he only answers "P!"—and that means nothing at all'. The punishment for a courtier who falls into disgrace is that he shall be punched in the stomach after supper, and the reward for the kitchen-maid for finding the nightingale is that she shall have a regular situation in the kitchen and be allowed to watch the emperor eat his dinner. The courtiers' ignorance of the natural world is such that when they hear a cow mooing or frogs croaking they believe these sounds to be the nightingale's song. When they first see the nightingale they are disappointed because she looks so ordinary. 'I expect she's off colour through having so many distinguished visitors,' the gentleman-in-waiting says.

A golden perch is provided for the nightingale, and the reward for her beautiful singing is the offer of a gold slipper to wear round her neck. The social order inside the palace is described: the court ladies show their approval by gurgling whenever anyone speaks to them; and at the bottom of the scale: 'Even the lackeys and lady's maids expressed their approval; and that's saying a good deal, for they are the most difficult of all to satisfy.'

Into this kind of artificiality the nightingale is supposed to fit:

> She was now to remain at court and have her own cage, with leave to go out for two walks in the daytime and one at night. She was given twelve attendants, who each held on tightly to a silk ribbon fastened round her leg. There was absolutely no fun in a walk like that.

The arrival of the artificial nightingale, covered all over with diamonds, rubies and sapphires, results in complete chaos, for the two birds cannot sing together. The Master of the Emperor's Music declares that it is not the fault of the artificial bird: 'It keeps perfect time and follows my methods exactly.' The real nightingale flies away and is regarded as being ungrateful and banished from the Chinese empire. The Master of Music explains why the artificial bird is preferable to the real one:

> 'You see, ladies and gentlemen and, above all, Your Imperial Majesty, with the real nightingale there's no telling what's going to happen. But with the artificial

bird everything is fixed beforehand. Such-and-such will be heard and no other. One can account for it all: one can open it up and show the cylinders, how they go round, and the way in which one thing follows from another!'

The artificial bird is promoted to be Chief Imperial Bedside Minstrel of the First Class on the Left, and the Master of Music writes a work in twenty-five volumes about it. 'It was very long and learned, full of the most difficult Chinese words, and everyone pretended they had read and understood it, or else of course they would have been thought stupid and got punched in the stomach.'

Then one evening the mechanism inside the bird goes wrong, the bearings being almost worn out, and from then on it is only allowed to sing once a year.

Five years later, as the emperor lies dying, longing for music to take his thoughts away from death, he appeals to the artificial bird, but in vain, and it is the real nightingale singing in the tree outside who wrestles with Death in an effort to save the emperor's life:

> She had heard of her emperor's distress and had therefore come to sing him consolation and hope; and as she sang, the shapes grew fainter and fainter, the blood in the emperor's weak limbs ran faster and faster, and Death himself listened and said, 'Go on, little nightingale, go on!'

The nightingale goes on, and for each song she sings Death gives up one of the treasures he had taken from the emperor until, longing for his garden, Death floats like a cold white mist out of the window.

Realistic stories set in a recognizable world

As a good example of this category I have chosen a story which is relatively little known internationally, **'The Gardener and the Squire'**.[18]

It is set in an old Danish manor house owned by a rich nobleman and his wife. To keep the large garden they employ a clever gardener, Mr Larsen, and it is a pleasure to see how nice and tidy he keeps it. Two big half-dead trees swarming with rooks and crows, who have built their nests in them, are an eyesore to the gardener, who wants to get rid of them; but to the squire and his wife both the trees and the birds represent the romantic past, and they will not hear of Larsen's suggestion that the old trees should be cut down to make way for something better:

> 'My dear Larsen, haven't you enough room already? With your flower-garden, glass-houses and kitchen garden?'

Yes, he had all these, and he tended and looked after them with great attention and skill. His master

and mistress admitted this, but they were afraid they had to tell him that at other people's houses they often ate fruit or saw flowers which were better than anything in their own garden. The gardener was sorry to hear this, for he did his best that the best should be done. He was good at heart and good at his job.

One day the squire tells Mr Larsen that in the house of some distinguished friends they had had some excellent fruit and suggests that Larsen should cultivate this particular species. When it emerges that in fact the fruit came from their own orchard, they refuse to believe it until Mr Larsen produces a written statement from the fruiterer.

> 'How very odd!' said the squire.

> And now every day at the manor huge bowls of these magnificent apples and pears from their own garden appeared on the table. Bushels and barrels of the fruit were sent to friends in and out of the town, and even abroad, bringing no end of pleasure. Still, they had to admit that of course there had been two unusually good summers for fruit trees; these had done well all over the country.

After the squire and his wife have dined at court they send for the gardener and tell him to get some melon seeds from their majesties' greenhouse, for they had such delicious melons at court. Again it turns out that the melons came from Larsen's greenhouse, and again he can produce a statement to that effect.

> This was indeed a surprise for the squire, and he made no secret of the incident, but showed people the certificate and even had melon seeds sent out far and wide just as previously the cuttings had been.

> Then news came back that the seeds were striking and setting admirably and the plant was called after the squire's manor, so that in this way its name could now be read in English, German and French. That was something never dreamed of before. 'I do hope the gardener won't begin to think too much of himself,' said the squire.

Mr Larsen's ambition, however, is to establish himself as one of the leading gardeners in the country, and he does produce some first-rate gardening.

> But, all the same, he often heard it said that his very first fruit, the apples and the pears, were really his best; all that came after was much inferior. The melons were no doubt extremely good, but they were of course something quite different. His strawberries might be called excellent, and yet no better than those to be found on other estates; and when one year the radishes were a failure, it was only the unfortunate radishes that they talked about and not

a word about anything else that turned out well. It was almost as though the squire felt relieved to be able to say, 'Well, Larsen, rather a poor year, eh?' They quite enjoyed saying, 'Rather a poor year.'

When Mr Larsen brings in beautifully arranged flowers he is told: 'You have taste, Larsen. That's a gift, not of your own, but of God.'

One day he brings in a big crystal bowl with a leaf of a water-lily and on top of this a brilliant blue flower, which the squire and his wife take to be an Indian water-lily. It is admired by everybody who sees it, including a princess. But the squire and his wife are appalled when they find out that the blue flower came from the kitchen garden, being the blossom of an artichoke.

> 'You should have told us that straight away,' said the squire. 'We couldn't help thinking it was a rare foreign flower. You've made us look ridiculous in the eyes of the young princess.'

But when they apologize to the princess and assure her that Mr Larsen has been told off, she says: 'How unfair! Why, he has opened our eyes to a splendid flower we had never noticed; he has shown us beauty where we never dreamed of looking.' So Mr Larsen may again bring a fresh artichoke blossom.

'It's really quite handsome,' the squire said; 'altogether remarkable.' And the gardener was praised.

'That's what Larsen enjoys,' said the squire. 'He's a spoilt child.'

An autumn gale blows down the two half-dead trees, and in their place Mr Larsen makes a most unusual and varied extension of the garden and puts up a flagstaff flying the Danish flag and nearby a pole, round which the hops twine their clusters in the summer and autumn and in winter a sheaf of oats is hung to feed the birds.

> 'Our good Larsen is getting sentimental in his old age,' said the squire. 'But he's faithful and devoted to us.'

With the New Year there appeared in one of the capital's illustrated papers a picture of the old manor house, showing the flagstaff and the sheaf of oats for the birds at Christmas, and emphasis was laid on the happy idea of keeping up a time-honoured custom in this way—an idea so very characteristic of the old place.

> 'They beat the big drum for every mortal thing that Larsen does,' said the squire.

> 'He's a lucky man. I suppose we ought almost to be proud of having him.'

But they weren't in the least proud of it. They felt that they were the master and mistress and could give Larsen a month's notice if they liked, but they didn't do that. They were kind people, and there are so many kind people of that sort. What a good thing that is for all the Larsens!

I have tried . . . to show the wide range of Andersen's ***Eventyr og Historier***. The grouping into seven identifiable categories is my own, and, admittedly, only one among several possible ways of looking at them. Another useful way might be to divide them into two groups: tales with a special appeal to children and tales with a special appeal to adults. The best of them, however, would fall into both categories: children will understand them in their way, and adults in theirs.

In 1861 Bjørnstjerne Bjørnson wrote in a letter to Jonas Collin junior:

> It is quite wrong to speak of what Andersen is writing now as 'fairy tales'. That was the name of his very first what you might call little bits of things, that could be put into a nutshell and then taken out again to span the world. Moreover, the form in which these tales were cast was quite perfect, concerned as it was solely with the very core of his subject. But now that Andersen has, often unjustly, been hustled out of the domain of the novel, of the drama and of philosophic narrative, the result has merely been that these thwarted suckers have thrust their own way out through the rock at some other point, and that he now has—God help us!—the novel, the drama and his philosophy all turning up in the fairy tale! That this is no longer a fairy tale, is obvious. It is something that is Andersenian, that is anyhow not generally dispensed by a literary pharmacist. . . . It is something that has no limits above or below, and so none in its shape—which, therefore, only a perfect genius can keep in hand. . . . But that freedom from all restraint—that assumption that all form and a whole world of tragic, comic, lyric and epic speculation, all singing, preaching, jesting, the animate and the inanimate, merge together as though in paradise—all this makes one tremble for the appearance of his next work. What secret is he going to solve? What journey must we make? And will it succeed or fail?

Notes

[1] The most recent English translation is Hans Christian Andersen, *The Complete Fairy Tales and Stories*. Translated from the Danish by Erik Christian Haugaard. (New York, foreword by Virginia Haviland, and London, foreword by Naomi Lewis, 1974).

[2] Sometimes called 'The Real Princess' or 'The Princess and the Pea'.

[3] In Haugaard's translation called 'Inchelina'.

[4] Sometimes called 'The Dauntless [or Constant or Staunch] Tin Soldier'.

[5] Having failed to realize that 'Ole' in the title 'Ole Lukøie' is a Christian name, some of the English translators have called this story 'Old Luke' or 'Old Luke, the Sandman'. In other versions the title is given as 'The Sandman' or 'The Little Sandman' or 'Ole Lucköie', or 'The Dustman'.

[6] Sometimes (as a correct translation of the Danish title, 'Kærestefolkene') called 'The Sweethearts' or 'The Lovers'.

[7] Sometimes called 'The Pine Tree'.

[8] Sometimes called 'The Hill of the Elves' or 'The Elfin Hill' or 'The Elfin Mound'.

[9] Among the tales I would include in such a collection would be 'The Naughty Boy' (1835), 'The Goloshes of Fortune' (or 'The Magic Galoshes') (1838), 'The Bell' (1845), 'The High Jumpers' (or 'The Leaping Match' or 'The Jumping Competition') (1845), 'The Drop of Water' (1848), 'The Story of a Mother' (1848), 'There's a Difference' (1851), 'It's Perfectly [or Quite or Absolutely] True!' (1852), 'A Good Temper' (or 'A Happy Disposition') (1852), 'Heartbreak' (or 'Grief') (1852), 'Everything in its Right Place' (1852), 'The Goblin at the Grocer's' (or 'The Pixy and the Grocer') (1852), 'In a Thousand Years Time' (or 'The Millenium') (1852), 'She was no good' (1852), 'Simple Simon' ('Klods-Hans') (or 'Clod-poll' or 'Clumsy Hans' or 'Clod Hans' or 'Numskull Jack') (1855), 'Soup from a Sausage-Stick' (or 'How to Cook Soup on a Sausage Pin') (1858), 'The Marsh King's [or Bog King's] Daughter' (1858), 'Pen and Inkpot' (1859), 'The Beetle' (or 'The Dung Beetle') (1861), 'Dad's Always Right' (or 'What the Old Man Does is Always Right' or 'Father Always Does What's Right') (1861), 'The Snow Man' (1861), 'The Ice Maiden' (1861), 'The Snail and the Rose Tree' (1861), 'The Storm Moves Signposts' (or 'How the Storm Changed the Signs') (1865), 'Auntie' (1866), 'The Rags' (1868), 'Something to Write About' (or 'What One Can Invent' or 'Hitting on an Idea' or 'A Question of Imagination') (1869), 'The Gardener and the Squire' (or 'The Gardener and his Master') (1872), 'Old Johanna's Tale' (or 'The Story Old Johanna Told') (1872), 'The Cripple' (1872), and 'Auntie Toothache' (1872).

[10] According to Andersen himself the tales in this category are 'The Tinder Box', 'Little Claus and Big Claus', 'The Princess on the Pea', 'The Travelling Companion', 'The Wild Swans', 'The Garden of Eden', 'The Swineherd', 'Simple Simon' and 'Dad's Always Right'.

The complicated question of Andersen's dependence on Danish folk tales has been dealt with in an important essay by Georg Christensen published in 1906. Since we are here dealing with an oral tradition it is not possible to know which particular versions Andersen heard as a child; we can only draw comparisons with versions recorded in other parts of Denmark.

[11] Themes from Danish legends are incorporated in several tales, e.g., 'Mother Elder', 'The Elf Hill', 'Holger the Dane', 'The Goblin at the Grocer's' and 'The Bishop of Børglum'. Elements from some of Hoffmann's tales (especially 'Nussknacker und Mäusekönig', 'Meister Floh' and 'Abenteuer eines Sylvesternacht') are to be found in 'Little Ida's Flowers', 'The Snow Queen' (the devil's looking-glass), 'The Shepherdess and the Chimney-Sweep' and 'The Shadow'. There are loans from Musäus and *Njáls Saga* in 'The Marsh King's Daughter'. Chamisso's *Peter Schlemihl* has had an influence on both 'The Goloshes of Fortune' and 'The Shadow'; one of the inspirations for 'The Little Mermaid' is de la Motte Fouqué's *Undine;* features borrowed from Grimm and Brentano may be found in 'The Red Shoes', and elements in other tales may be traced back to Boccaccio's *Decameron* and to the *Arabian Nights*.

[12] To the group of fairy tales proper also belong five of the tales previously mentioned, 'The Tinder Box', 'The Travelling Companion', 'The Wild Swans', 'The Naughty Boy' and 'The Garden of Eden', and such tales as 'The Elf of the Rose', the sentimental 'The Angel', and the strange and to me unpleasant and cruel story of vanity, punishment and atonement, 'The Red Shoes'.

[13] Others are: 'There's a Difference', a tale about class distinction in the plant world; the aristocratic apple blossom versus the despised dandelion; the message being that they are both beautiful but in different ways. 'Five Peas from one Pod' is the tale of five pea-siblings, one of which succeeds in bringing great happiness to a sick person. 'The Daisy' and 'The Flax' are stories of flowers whose attitude to life is exactly the opposite of that of the fir tree. The daisy enjoys every moment of its day and knows no envy. 'The sun shines upon me, and the wind kisses me. Oh! What gifts are given me!' The flax, too, is able to look on the best side of things in its transformation from a plant to linen which is woven and made into underwear, and finally discarded and burnt. 'The Buckwheat' is really a parable, and it could be said to illustrate one of the *Proverbs,* 'Pride goeth before destruction, and an haughty spirit before a fall.' (On 13 November 1845 Andersen noted in his diary that one of his acquaintances had drawn his attention to Jotham's parable of the trees in *The Old Testament* (Judges, IX): 'the only parable or what is similar to my fairy tales, the Greek *Einos'.*)

Trees and plants are also the main characters in 'The Last Dream of the Old Oak Tree', and 'What the Thistle Found Out'. The part flowers play in 'The Snow Queen' should be mentioned. While Gerda is staying with the old woman with the large sun hat, six flowers tell their stories—the tiger-lily, the convolvulus, the snow-drop, the hyacinth, the buttercup, and the narcissus. These six stories are really prose poems, in which Andersen has attempted to express in words the soul of each flower.

[14] Included in *The Crimes of England* (London 1915).

[15] For 'The Top and the Ball' see p. 162. 'The Shepherdess and the Chimney-Sweep' tells the story of how these two china figures elope, because an old nodding porcelain Chinaman who claimed to be the Shepherdess's guardian, wanted her to marry a carved satyr whom the children called 'Major-and-Minor-General-Company-Sergeant Billygoatlegs'. They escape to the top of the chimney but then return, and as he has been riveted after a fall the Old Chinaman is unable to nod his consent to the satyr any more, and so the two lovers are able to stay together.

A sad and lonely tin soldier is one of the main characters in 'The Old House'; unlike the other tin soldier this one does cry tin tears. The title character in 'The Snow Man' suffers from a longing for the warmth of the fireplace in the room into which he can see; and when he melts the reason is clear: there was a poker inside him, round which his snow body had been built. 'The Teapot' and 'The Rags' also belong to this category; the former being the reminiscences of a teapot who began her life as queen of the tea table and ended, her handle and spout broken off, as a flower-pot with a bulb in it. 'The Rags' records a dialogue between a Norwegian and a Danish rag, a witty satire on the presumed national characteristics of both nations. In 'Pen and Inkpot' the two characters quarrel about which of them is the real genius responsible for poetry being put on paper.

[16] To this category of tales set in a kind of real, yet fantastic world belong some of those discussed previously . . . 'The Princess on the Pea', 'The Emperor's New Clothes' and 'Simple Simon'. None of them contain any supernatural or magic elements, and they all take place in a human, though hardly in an ordinary or recognizable world.

'The Drop of Water' may also be regarded as belonging in this group, for though old Creepy-Crawley ('for that was his name') and his nameless colleague are both referred to as 'magicians', the point is, of course, that they are natural scientists, the drop of witch's blood ('the very finest kind at twopence a drop') a chemical substance, and the terrifying humans wrestling, wrangling, snapping and snarling which they see through the magnifying glass are in reality the kind of unicellular animals—the so-called animalcules—which could be seen at that time through a microscope.

'The Flea and the Professor' moves from Europe to Africa and back again, and however fantastic this amusing story is, it contains no elements which remove it from the real world.

Forty years before the invention of the first flying machines Andersen wrote the story he called 'In a Thousand Years Time', which must have appeared quite fantastic to his contemporaries, though in fact it fore-shadowed, with a surprising amount of precision, the invention of the aeroplane, which, as he predicted, has enabled Americans to 'see Europe in one week'.

[17] In spite of its title and the fact that the nightingale is capable of speaking (though its power lies in its singing) 'The Nightingale' certainly does not quite belong in the category of Andersen's animal tales. It would be possible to argue, on the other hand, that the appearance of Death as a character makes it into a fairy tale proper. However, it seems to me that the 'realistic' (though fantastic) elements in the tale are so important that in this, admittedly arbitrary, grouping of Andersen's tales I have found it reasonable to include this story here.

[18] Two of the *fabliaux* belonging to this category have already been mentioned as having their origin in Danish folk tales, 'Little Claus and Big Claus' and 'Dad's Always Right'; in both of these the milieu is that of a Danish farming community.

Another well-known example is the sentimental story 'The Little Match Girl'. Here a poor little match girl in the streets of Copenhagen on a cold New Year's Eve lights one by one three of the matches she could not sell. Every time she lights a match she has a dream-like vision, and with the last match she dies.

'A Good Temper' contains the quaint philosophy of a man whose favourite place for wondering about the strange ways of man is the churchyard; he has inherited his wonderful sense of humour from his father, whose profession was to drive a hearse. 'Heartbreak', a story in two parts, both of which are undoubtedly based on personal experience, contains a very Andersenian mixture of humour and genuine emotion in its sympathy for the outsider. 'She was no good' and 'Old Johanna's Tale' are both clearly based on memories of Andersen's childhood in Odense; the former is an attempt to show his mother in a better and probably truer light in a description of a washerwoman who became addicted to alcohol. 'Auntie' is an amusing story of a spinster who was mad about the theatre. It is a composite picture, to some extent based on the memory of people Andersen knew.

Two stories fall into a group of their own within this category, 'The Wind Tells the Story of Valdemar Daa and his Daughters' and 'Chicken-Grethe's Family', for apart from the fact that Andersen has chosen to use the wind as the narrator in the former, they both relate stories based on historical facts. Valdemar Daa was a Danish seventeenth-century nobleman and alchemist, who spent everything he owned in his vain search for gold, and Marie Grubbe, the chief character in 'Chicken-Grethe's Family', was a noble lady of about the same period, whose life also ended in poverty, if for other reasons.

'The Cripple', one of Andersen's last tales, may be seen as a tribute to the art in which he himself became the supreme master; for it is a book of fairy tales which is the indirect cause that enables Hans, the paralysed cripple, to walk again.

[19] Truisms with a humorous effect appear quite frequently in Andersen's tales, e.g., 'there were many people, and twice as many legs as heads'; 'when they travelled by train they went third class—that gets there just as quickly as first class'; 'two will-o'-the-wisps came hopping in, one faster than the other, and therefore he came in first'; ' "The sixth comes before the seventh," said the Elf King, for he could do arithmetic.'

[20] His own comments give some, if not reliable, information. He says 'Little Ida's Flowers' was written after telling the little Ida Thiele about the flowers in the Botanical Gardens and that her father suggested he write about a flute which could blow 'Everything in Its Right Place'. J. M. Thiele also gave the idea for 'The Bottleneck'.

Peter Brask (essay date 1979)

SOURCE: "Andersen on Love," in *The Nordic Mind: Current Trends in Scandinavian Literary Criticism*, edited by Frank Egholm Andersen and John Weinstock, translated by Turid Sverre, University Press of America, 1986, pp. 17-35.

[*In the following excerpt, originally presented on Radio Denmark in 1979, Brask discusses the obstacles in Andersen's tales to realizing true love.*]

"The Swineherd" ("Svindrengen") and **"The Shepherdess and the Chimney Sweep" ("Hyrdinden og Skorsteensfeiren")** are among Andersen's best-known fairy tales, and when we reread them, they seem so natural. They simply could not be different! Is it just habit, or is it because they are so well narrated, with such power and energy?

What does this mean? After all, they are sad stories; you'd have to look long and hard to find such embarrassing love stories. And yet, they are so funny! How can this be? If you were to ask why Andersen wrote them, there are so many possible answers. For example,

you could try to find out whether the poor man had recently been in love and whether, in that case, he had fared as badly as the men in the fairy tales. You will, of course, find that the poet *had* been unhappy in love, but this doesn't really tell us very much. The interesting thing, after all, is not that the poet fell in love and was unsuccessful in his love, but that he wrote the fairy tales. What actually happens in them? What is it that the poet does with his sad experiences in love when he uses them as a basis for his writing?

The fairy tales just mentioned were written five years apart, but when we hear them one after the other, we are struck by how closely they resemble each other. In a way we are being told the same story. This is true for a great number of tales written by Andersen during the same period, that is, within ten years' time: **"The Steadfast Tin Soldier" ("Den standhaftige Tinsoldat")** is from 1838, **"The Swineherd"** is from 1839, and **"The Shepherdess and the Chimney Sweep"** is from 1844. Between the latter two comes the long fairy tale **"The Nightingale" ("Nattergalen")**, which to a large degree is also "the same story" and which therefore also belongs to the group of stories we are trying to understand here.

After **"The Shepherdess and the Chimney Sweep"** we have **"The Bell" ("Klokken")** from 1845, **"The Shadow" ("Skyggen")** from 1846, and **"The Collars" ("Flipperne")** from 1848. Within the same ten-year period Andersen also wrote many other things, but there is a close connection between the fairy tales I have just mentioned. In their own way, they all work with the same story—the same problem of love, of woman, of sexuality, and of the importance of money in the game of love. We cannot deal with all of them here, but I will try to show some of their common features. I will also try to show that there is a gradual change in the situation. For although it is the same story that continues to be repeated, something happens to it—little by little, something changes.

If we try to determine *what* it is that changes and *how* it changes, then we are on our way toward learning why Andersen wrote these fairy tales. His negative experiences continue to play freely in his mind; they continue to torment and torture him until he gets them worked out and put into a meaningful context. The fairy tales are a direct expression of this dogged and ardent endeavor. When Andersen writes his fairy tales, he is laboring with his mind, working on and changing his consciousness. Naturally, this process also leads him to pass quite a few judgments on his surroundings, for his experiences do, after all, stem from his confrontations with these surroundings. Thus it is not so strange that the fairy tales are full of derision and biting satire toward the bourgeois world, to which he himself belonged but in which he never felt quite at home. He was a son of the proletariat as well as a refined man of the bourgeoisie; he knew poverty, but when he died, he was a millionaire with decorations and titles. Despite this, he never felt really accepted. He was grateful for his successes but always furious that, in spite of them, somehow he was not wholly recognized as the genius he was.

"The Swineherd" is full of scorching satirical remarks on life at the emperor's court—that is, among society's highest strata. And yet, this is not the main point. The core of the action is a story of revenge. Let's examine it more closely.

The court in **"The Swineherd"** is characterized by superficial mannerisms, power struggles, double standards, and class-determined tyranny. When the ladies-in-waiting speak French, each one worse than the other, when the princess's musical knowledge encompasses one melody and her performance at the piano is on the one-finger level, then these are signs of that same superficial mannerism that causes the court to prefer pot and rattle to rose and nightingale.

The emperor is tyrannized by the capricious princess; he will tolerate quite a lot before he gets so angry that *she* will feel the slipper. A power struggle, in other words. When the princess orders her ladies-in-waiting to kiss the swineherd, they resist, but the princess reminds them that she is their employer, after all. As swineherd, the prince must be content with a wretched little room by the pigsty. In other words, class difference and class tyranny.

When the lady-in-waiting will not repeat the naughty swineherd's price for the rattle, the princess says she may whisper it. The princess doesn't really mind paying the swineherd's exorbitant prices as long as no one finds out. "I am the emperor's daughter!" she actually says (p. 196).[1] In other words, a double standard. To be sure, the framework around all this is the code that Andersen got from the child's fairy tale, but he is only pretending—we must listen beyond the seemingly childish features and understand, among other things, that one hundred kisses from the princess is, within such a fairy tale, quite the same thing as going to bed with her outside the fairy tale, in adult reality.

This is the milieu, but what, then, is the plot? It is presented in the form of opposites: the princess's rejection of the prince opposite her acceptance of *his* opposite, the swineherd; her rejection of his offer of true love, the rose and the nightingale, opposite her acceptance of sexuality as something to be bought and sold; the rejected prince opposite the revenging prince; the arrogant princess opposite the humiliated princess; the henpecked emperor opposite the disciplining father. The central point of all these opposites in the action is where the prince disguises himself as a swineherd. This has its own

opposite in the scene at the very end, when he sheds his lowly disguise and again appears as the handsome prince that he is.

The whole world here is two-faced and divided. The two gifts that the prince sends to the princess when he proposes are the rose and the nightingale. The rose's opposite is the pot; the nightingale's opposite is the rattle. What does this mean? The remarkable thing about the prince and the princess is that *his* father is dead and *her* mother is dead. Perhaps this could be taken to mean that they should unite and together form a new father-mother pair. The prince got the rose from his father's grave—it stands for true love—and this is why it blooms so rarely, only once every five years. It can, however, perform miracles: its fragrance can make anyone who smells it forget all his sorrows and troubles. We don't learn very much about the nightingale, but it knows all the lovely melodies ever composed, as opposed to the princess, who knows only a single one. The rose and the nightingale are real and genuine, but the princess lives in a world of pretension and fads. To her, something is good when it is "interesting" and "artificial." This is why she plays children's games with the ladies-in-waiting, who of course don't really have anything to do, as opposed to the swineherd, who didn't let a day go by without accomplishing something. They play house; you leave the room and get all dressed up and come back and make yourself interesting by pretending to be someone you're not. What makes the game interesting is the piquancy and dishonesty, the thrill of merely acting out parts. When the prince's honest love is turned away, he seeks his revenge by acting the way the court does. He plays a part; he dresses as the opposite of what he is. He appears as his own shadow, so to speak.

These patterns are paralleled by the work given him by the emperor: tending the pigs. The pigs are symbols of drives in their base and misshapen forms. The emperor, poor man, says of the pigs: "We have such an awful lot of them" (p. 194). The emperor himself is not depraved, even though he is cowed by the infantile and demonic princess. When he hears the nightingale the prince has sent, he relives his feelings for his deceased wife, the dead queen, and he cries honest tears, or, in the language of fairy tales, he "cried like a baby" (p. 194). Since he is doing the crying, he cannot at the same time be used to inform the reader of why he is crying—he is too moved for that—but we do have very handy another old gentleman, "an old courtier," and he says that the nightingale reminds him of the late empress's music box. This is precisely where we can see how complex the fairy tales really are. On the one hand, the courtier is employed to express the emperor's feelings. On the other hand, satire creeps in here, too, for the fact that the courtier thinks that the living nightingale sounds like the artificial music box is, of course, a reflection of the stupidity of the court.

The difference between them will be elaborated on later in the fairy tale **"The Nightingale."**

What is ingenious and difficult in the fairy tale code is, generally, that it allows the presence of many different viewpoints all at once, even in one and the same sentence, in one and the same remark. Seen from the outside, the court is merely ridiculous, but for those inside and dependent upon it, it is not so amusing; to them, the stupid appears demonic, like a diabolical degradation of life's values. In short, it is like a piggish world, and if you care to get along in it, you must make yourself into a pig, or into a demon, like the shadow in the fairy tale that most directly deals with the demonic. In **"The Swineherd"** it is still one and the same person, the prince, who assumes both the positive and the negative figure; he is and remains a prince, a positive, "a prince whom everyone thought was a swineherd," the narrator assures us (p. 196).

In **"The Shadow"** they are, however, separated into the scholar, who perishes, and the shadow, who is successful—like Andersen himself, one might say. While the princess in **"The Swineherd"** is and remains a little pig, there are two aristocratic women in **"The Shadow"**—namely the positive, which is poetry, and the negative, a demonic princess who can so easily marry the shadow. They share the ability to see through the roles in the world around them and see all the bad and evil behind them, even in children. This is, however, all they can see. It is interesting that the scholar, whom they kill, is not presented as merely an innocent victim, for he is not entirely in the right. He knows a lot, but he understands far too little. Thus there is a giant leap from **"The Swineherd"** to **"The Shadow."** The former story is in total sympathy with the prince and puts the entire blame on the princess, who must in the end suffer the entire punishment: to be excluded from both the emperor's realm and from that of the prince. In the latter story no one is right, and there is nothing but disharmonious opposites. Between **"The Swineherd"** and **"The Shadow"** there are also almost ten years of literary activity.

One step along the way is **"The Shepherdess and the Chimney Sweep,"** and another and higher plateau is reached in **"The Nightingale."** The nightingale is the positive counterpart to the shadow. In **"The Nightingale,"** a remarkable thing happens: the positive forces—which in the previous fairy tales are associated with woman and which are so terribly difficult to release because woman is in turn bound by many other negative forces: above all, sexuality, economy, and the class difference—are separated from the feminine and presented in an entirely abstract form, namely as the nightingale itself. . . .

In **"The Shepherdess and the Chimney Sweep,"** this separation has not yet occurred, but the attitude toward it is already completely different from that of **"The Swineherd."** There are, as stated earlier, five years between them. In **"The Swineherd,"** the narrator simply sides with the prince throughout; everything is seen from the prince's perspective, at least where matters of judgment are concerned. In **"The Shepherdess and the Chimney Sweep,"** the narrator stands on the outside. He can do so because this fairy tale is staged in a world of things, not people. With incredible artistic economy, the things are equipped with exactly the qualities they must have in order to express some very definite human qualities, no more and no less.

In **"The Swineherd,"** we saw that the stupid world is a demonic world to those who are forced to live on its terms. The same is true for the world in **"The Shepherdess and the Chimney Sweep."** Here there are tyrants and authority figures, but their status is remarkably ambiguous. The main characters are the two young procelain people, who aren't *real* people yet but rather artificial. When they undertake the most daring expedition of their lives, out into reality, and the shepherdess is overwhelmed by it, she cries "so hard that the gold in her waistband began to chip" (p. 300). The artificial, the porcelain role, is beginning to fall off her. The chimney sweep, on the other hand, fares better from the beginning; this is evident from his profession as chimney sweep. He has the ladder, and he has the necessary courage for the dark, narrow road out into the real world.

But where do they really come from? What is it that they must escape from? Two forces are against them: the old Chinese mandarin and "Mr. Goat-legged Commanding-General-Private-War-Sergeant." Who are they? To begin with, they are typically characters who cannot move. The Chinese mandarin is rounded at the bottom, and the goat is carved in the wood of the old cabinet. Like the whole room, the cabinet is "an heirloom that had been in the family for four generations" (p. 297). This is the inherited world, the given society with all its roles and rules.

Within this world it is the Chinese mandarin who rules. He is quite cynical. The shepherdess doesn't want to marry the goat; she has heard that he has eleven porcelain wives in the cabinet already! The Chinese mandarin's justification for the marriage is purely economical: "You will have a husband who I am almost certain is made of mahogany" (p. 298). Mahogany was the preferred wood for fine furniture at that time, a sign of affluence, in other words. However, a mahogany man was—in the slang of those days—a dandy, a fop, a bon vivant, so it is probably correct that he has girls by the dozen. Here again, we see Andersen's artistic economy; in the world of human beings, the explanation for a total of twelve porcelain girls is, of course, found in the fact that you could buy such table decorations and knickknacks by the dozen, just like the silverware in the cabinet. Again, several worlds are layered on top of each other, so to speak.

Another example of economy is that the Chinese mandarin and the goat cannot go anywhere; they are completely bound to this world of convention in which young girls are married off for money and in which it is considered *comme il faut* that the rich man should keep a harem, hidden in the cabinet. When the shepherdess and the chimney sweep are on the run, they jump into the drawer by the window. At the window, we are told, there was a seat where you could sit with your sewing and have enough light for your work and look out on the street at the same time, and the empty space below had thriftily been filled with a drawer for the childrens' toys. Now we are in the world of toys, and plays are being performed. The audience is a deck of cards, and the knaves show that they have heads at both ends—again there is economy in the symbolism. It isn't so good to have a head in both ends, to turn love into economy rather than passion. The play being performed in the drawer is, of course, about love having to become tragedy in this world. The shepherdess cannot bear it, so they continue their flight.

It occurs to the chimney sweep that they might find refuge in the potpourri jar. It is full of salted, dried rose leaves, so they could lie on a bed of roses and throw salt in the eyes of the others. What does this mean? Perhaps it means that you will remain within the real world but relate to it ironically (i.e., the salt) and otherwise enjoy as best you can your lusts and passions—the rose leaves. However, the shepherdess knows there is a connection between the potpourri jar and the Chinese mandarin; they were once engaged, she says. The only solution is to make a complete break with this world, which they try to do but with no success. To be sure, the shepherdess manages the dangerous journey through the black stove and the chimney, but faced with the real, wide world, she cannot bear it any longer: "The world is much too big," she says, as if it isn't she who is too little (p. 300). The chimney sweep cannot help but feel a bit peeved, but her mind is made up and she even lies a little: "I followed you out into the wide world, now you must take me home, if you care for me at all" (p. 300). That isn't right; she was the one who first wanted to see the big wide world, and the chimney sweep had not felt too confident that she could handle it. He was right.

The love between them is also a bit questionable. Actually, their passion does not seem to be too fiery. The reason is said to be that "they had been standing close together, for that was the way they had always been placed; and so they thought it was natural that they be engaged" (p. 298). This is then followed by some bourgeois reasoning: they were both young and made from the same clay—that is, of the same class—but the narrator immediately manages to inject another point of view as well: they were "both breakable" (p. 298).

The Chinese mandarin really has no other power over the shepherdess than what she herself will grant him.

He has insisted that he is her grandfather, "although he couldn't really prove that he was related to her at all" (p. 298). She proves it to him when she, frightened by reality, finds her way back to the little table beneath the mirror, to that narrow world in which the mirror reflects only one's own role, one's outer costume. She proves it the moment she sees the Chinese mandarin lying on the floor. One should expect her to be happy to see the tyrant toppled, but her first thought is to have him riveted, and the next one is how much it might cost. She has a housewife's tone of voice already, and the lovers have their first row: "Don't carry on so," he says (p. 300). Coincidences keep them together now: the Chinese mandarin gets a rivet in his neck and can no longer nod to Mr. Goatlegged. So they stay together. But unlike the good old fairy tales in which the lovers live happily ever after, this one says that "they loved each other until they broke" (p. 301)—which is to say that they never became real people.

The Chinese mandarin represents society's norms, but what does the goat with the difficult name represent? The fairy tale does not say in so many words, for that is not possible in this language. However, it can still be conveyed in code language. The narrator shows disdain over the fact that Mr. Goat-legged is there. He describes him: he has horns on his forehead and the legs of a goat, and we learn that he keeps a harem "and is the most amazing figure in the central panel" (p. 297). Mr. Goat-legged is sexuality incarnate, that which remains when love becomes merchandise. Additional evidence of this interpretation is found in Andersen's draft, in which the "War-Sergeant" was initially called "the satyre."

Thus there are at least two things that will prevent true love from being realized. One is sexuality as naked, urgent drive, a War-Sergeant who will not be ignored—the drive is there, and somehow it must be included in the world, for one cannot be rid of it. The other hindrance is society's narrow rules and conventions, and these appear above all as money matters, as economy. In practice, these things are interwoven, for the realization of love in an acceptable manner would be synonymous with marriage. A precondition for marriage was, however, an acceptable economy and a steady income, and in order to provide himself with this, Andersen had to make himself a successful author first. Therefore the entire matter is woven into an almost Gordian knot; the precondition for success as an author was inspiration, and it, in turn, demanded an emotional life and thus a relationship to women. These are the interrelationships that the texts seek to untangle. . . .

Notes

[1] Page citations, unless otherwise indicated, are to Hans Christian Andersen, *The Complete Fairy Tales and Stories,* translated by Erik Christian Haugaard (New York: Doubleday, 1974).—TRANS.

Jack Zipes (essay date 1983)

SOURCE: "Hans Christian Andersen and the Discourse of the Dominated," in *Fairy Tales and the Art of Subversion: The Classical Genre for Children and the Process of Civilization,* Heinemann, 1983, pp. 71-96.

[*In the following essay, Zipes points to ambivalence in Andersen's tales, finding its roots in the conflict between Andersen's identification with the lower classes and his simultaneous efforts to legitimize Denmark's hierarchical social structure and particularly its powerful upper classes, which in essence controlled his literary success.*]

If the Grimm Brothers were the first writers in the nineteenth century to distinguish themselves by remolding oral folk tales explicitly for a bourgeois socialization process, then Hans Christian Andersen completed their mission so to speak and created a canon of literary fairy tales for children between 1835 and 1875 in praise of essentialist ideology. By infusing his tales with general notions of the Protestant Ethic and essentialist ideas of natural biological order, Andersen was able to receive the bourgeois seal of good housekeeping. From the dominant class point of view his tales were deemed useful and worthy enough for rearing children of all classes, and they became a literary staple in western culture. Fortunately for Andersen he appeared on the scene when the original middle-class prejudice against imaginative fairy tales was receding. In fact, there was gradual recognition that fantasy could be employed for the utilitarian needs of the bourgeoisie, and Andersen proved to be a most humble servant in this cause.

But what was at the heart of Andersen's mode of service? In what capacity did his tales serve children and adults in Europe and America? What is the connection between Andersen's achievement as a fairy-tale writer, his servile demeanour, and our cultural appreciation of his tales? It seems to me that these questions have to be posed even more critically if we are to understand the underlying reasons behind Andersen's rise to fame and general acceptance in the nineteenth century. In fact, they are crucial if we want to grasp the continual reception, service, and use of the tales in the twentieth century, particularly in regard to socialization through literature.

Despite the fact that Andersen wrote a great deal about himself and his tales and was followed by scholars who have investigated every nook and cranny of his life and work, there have been very few attempts to study his tales ideologically and to analyze their function in the acculturation process. This is all the more surprising when one considers that they were written with a plump didactic purpose and were overloaded with references to normative behavior and ideal political standards. Indeed, the discourse of his narratives has a distinct ideological bias peculiarly 'marred' by his ambivalent feelings toward his social origins and the dominant classes in Denmark that controlled his fortunes. It is this 'marred ambivalence' which is subsumed in his tales and lends them their dynamic tension. Desirous of indicating the way to salvation through emulation of the upper classes and of paying reverence to the Protestant Ethic, Andersen also showed that this path was filled with suffering, humiliation, and torture—and that it could even lead to crucifixion. It is because of his ambivalent attitude, particularly toward the dominance of essentialist ideology, that his tales have retained their basic appeal up through the present day. But before we re-evaluate this appeal as constituted by the socializing elements of the tales, we must first turn to reconsider Andersen in light of the class conflict and conditions of social assimilation in his day.

I

Son of a poor cobbler and a washerwoman, Andersen was embarrassed by his proletarian background and grew to insist on notions of natural nobility. Once he became a successful writer, he rarely mingled with the lower classes. If anything, the opposite was the case: he was known to kowtow to the upper classes throughout *all* of Europe—quite an achievement when one considers his fame! However, his success then and now cannot be attributed to his opportunism and conformism. That is, he cannot simply be dismissed as a class renegade who catered to the aesthetic and ideological interests of the dominant classes. His case is much more complex, for in many respects his tales were innovative narratives which explored the limits of assimilation in a closed social order to which he aspired. Despite all the recognition and acceptance by the nobility and bourgeoisie in the western world, Andersen never felt himself to be a fully fledged member of any group. He was the outsider, the loner, who constantly travelled in his mature years, and his wanderings were symptomatic (as the wanderers and birds in his tales) of a man who hated to be dominated though he loved the dominant class.

As Elias Bredsdorff, the leading contemporary biographer of Andersen, maintains:

> Speaking in modern terms Andersen was a man born in the 'Lumpenproletariat' but completely devoid of class 'consciousness'. In his novels and tales he often expresses an unambiguous sympathy for 'the underdog,' especially for people who have been deprived of their chance of success because of their humble origins, and he pours scorn on haughty people who pride themselves on their noble birth or their wealth and who despise others for belonging to, or having their origin in, the lower classes. But in his private life Andersen accepted the system of absolutism and its inherent class structure, regarded royalty with awe and admiration and found a special

pleasure in being accepted by and associating with kings, dukes and princes, and the nobility at home and abroad.[1]

Though Andersen's sympathy did lay with the downtrodden and disenfranchised in his tales, it was not as unambiguous as Bredsdorff would have us believe, for Andersen's fawning servility to the upper classes also manifested itself in his fiction. In fact, as I have maintained, the ambivalent feelings about both his origins and the nobility constitute the appeal of the tales. Andersen prided himself on his 'innate' gifts as poet (*Digter*), and he devoutly believed that certain biologically determined people were chosen by divine providence to rise above others. This belief was his rationalization for aspiring toward recognition and acceptance by the upper classes. And here an important distinction must be made. More than anything else Andersen sought the blessing and recognition of Jonas Collin and the other members of this respectable, wealthy, patriarchal family as well as other people from the educated bureaucratic class in Denmark like Henriette Wulff. In other words, Andersen endeavored to appeal to the Danish bourgeois elite, cultivated in the arts, adept at commerce and administration, and quick to replace the feudal caste of aristocrats as the leaders of Denmark.

The relationship to Jonas Collin was crucial in his development, for Collin took him in hand, when he came to Copenhagen, and practically adopted him as a son. At first he tried to make a respectable bourgeois citizen out of the ambitious 'poet' but gradually relented and supported Andersen's artistic undertakings. In due course Andersen's primary audience came to be the Collin family and people with similar attitudes. All his artistic efforts throughout his life were aimed at pleasing them. For instance, on Jonas Collin's birthday in 1845 he wrote the following:

> You know that my greatest vanity, or call it rather joy, consists in making you realize that I am worthy of you. All the kind of appreciation I get makes me think of you. I am truly popular, truly appreciated abroad, I am famous—all right, you're smiling. But the cream of the nations fly towards me, I find myself accepted in all families, the greatest compliments are paid to me by princes and by the most gifted of men. You should see the way people in so-called High Society gather round me. Oh, no one at home thinks of this among the many who entirely ignore me and might be happy to enjoy even a drop of the homage paid to me. My writings must have greater value than the Danes will allow for. Heiberg has been translated too, but no one speaks of his work, and it would have been strange if the Danes were the only ones to be able to make judgments in this world. You must know, you my beloved father must understand that you did not misjudge me when you accepted me as your son, when you helped and protected me.[2]

Just as important as his relationship to the father Collin was his relationship to his 'adopted' brother Edvard, who served as Andersen's super-ego and most severe critic. Not only did Edvard edit Andersen's manuscripts and scold him for writing too fast and too much to gain fame, but he set standards of propriety for the writer through his cool reserve, social composure, and business-like efficiency. In his person Edvard Collin, a Danish legal administrator like his father, represented everything Andersen desired to become, and Andersen developed a strong homo-erotic attachment to Edvard which remained visibly powerful during his life. In 1838 Andersen wrote a revealing letter which indicates just how deep his feelings for Edvard were:

> I'm longing for you, indeed, at this moment I'm longing for you as if you were a lovely Calabrian girl with dark blue eyes and a glance of passionate flames. I've never had a brother, but if I had I could not have loved him the way I love you, and yet—you do not reciprocate my feelings! This affects me painfully or maybe this is in fact what binds me even more firmly to you. My soul is proud, the soul of a prince cannot be prouder. I have clung to you, I have—*bastare!* which is a good Italian verb to be translated in Copenhagen as 'shut up!' . . . Oh, I wish to God that you were poor and I rich, distinguished, a nobleman. In that case I should initiate you into the mysteries, and you would appreciate me more than you do now. Oh! If there is an eternal life, as indeed there must be, then we shall truly understand and appreciate one another. Then I shall no longer be the poor person in need of kind interest and friends, then we shall be equal.[3]

The fact is that Andersen never felt himself equal to any of the Collins and that he measured his worth by the standards *they* set. Their letters to him prescribe humility, moderation, asceticism, decorum, economy of mind and soul, devotion to God, loyalty to Denmark. On the one hand, they provided Andersen with a home, and on the other, their criticism and sobriety made him feel insecure. They were too classical and refined, too 'grammatically' correct, and he knew he could never achieve full recognition as *Digter* in their minds. Yet that realization did not stop him from trying to prove his moral worth and aesthetic talents to them in his tales and novels. This is not to suggest that all the fairy tales are totally informed by Andersen's relationship to the Collins. However, to understand their vital aspect—the ideological formation in relationship to the linguistic and semantic discourse—it is important to grasp how Andersen approached and worked through notions of social domination.

Here Noëlle Bisseret's study, *Education, Class Language and Ideology,* is most useful for my purposes since she endeavors to understand the historical origins of essen-

"Fairy Tales" by Hans Christian Andersen

tialist ideology and concepts of natural aptitudes which figure prominently in Andersen's tales. According to her definition,

> essentialist ideology, which originates along with the establishment of those structures constituting class societies, is a denial of the *historical relations* of an economic, political, juridical and ideological order which preside over the establishment of labile power relationships. Essentialist ideology bases all social hierarchy on the transcendental principle of a natural biological order (which took over from a divine principle at the end of the eighteenth century). A difference in essence among human beings supposedly predetermines the diversity of a psychic and mental phenomena ('intelligence,' 'language,' etc.) and thus the place of individual in a social order considered as immutable.[4]

By analyzing how the concepts of aptitude and disposition were used to designate a contingent reality in the late feudal period, Bisseret is able to show a transformation in meaning to legitimize the emerging power of the bourgeoisie in the nineteenth century: aptitude becomes an *essential* hereditary feature and is employed to justify social inequalities. In other words, the principle of equality developed by the bourgeoisie was gradually employed as a socializing agent to demonstrate that there are certain select people in a free market system, people with innate talents who are destined to succeed and rule because they 'possess or own' the essential qualities of intelligence, diligence, and responsibility.

We must remember that the nineteenth century was the period in which the interest in biology, eugenics, and race became exceedingly strong.[5] Not only did Charles Darwin and Herbert Spencer elaborate their theories at this time, but Arthur de Gobincau wrote his *Essai sur l'inegalité des races humaines* (1852) and Francis Galton wrote *Hereditary Genius* (1869) to give a seemingly scientific veneer to the middle-class social selection process. Throughout the western world a more solidified bourgeois public sphere was establishing itself and replacing feudal systems, as was clearly the case in Denmark.[6] Along with the new institutions designed for rationalization and maximation of profit, a panoptic principle of control, discipline, and punishment was introduced into the institutions of socialization geared to enforce the interests and to guarantee the domination of the propertied classes. This is fully demonstrated in Michel Foucault's valuable study *Discipline and Punish,*[7] which supports Bisseret's thesis of how the ideological concept of attitudes became the 'scientific' warrant of a social organization which it justified.

> The ideology of natural inequalities conceived and promoted by a social class at a time when it took economic, and later on political, power gradually turned into a scientific truth, borrowing from craniometry, then from anthropometry, biology,

genetics, psychology, and sociology (the scientific practice of which it sometimes oriented); the elements enabling it to substantiate its assertions. And by this very means, it was able to impose itself upon all the social groups which believed in the values presiding over the birth of aptitude as an ideology: namely Progress and Science. It now appears that well beyond the controversies, which oppose the different established groups, this general ideology directs the whole conception of selection and educational guidance: the educational system aims at selecting and training an 'elite,' which by its competence, merit, and aptitude is destined for high functions, the responsibility of which entails certain social and economic advantages.[8]

If we look at the case of Andersen in light of Bisseret's thesis at this point, two factors are crucial for his personal conception of an essentialist ideology. First, Denmark was a tiny country with a tightly knit bureaucratic feudal structure which was rapidly undergoing a transformation into a bourgeois dominated society. There were less than 200,000 people in the country, and 120,000 in Copenhagen. Among the educated bourgeoisie and nobility everyone knew everyone else who was of importance, and, though the country depended on the bourgeois bureaucratic administrators and commercial investors, the king and his advisors made most of the significant decisions up until the early 1840s when constitutive assemblies representing the combined interests of industry, commerce, and agriculture began assuming more control. Essentially, as Bredsdorff has aptly stated, 'in Danish society of the early nineteenth century it was almost impossible to break through class barriers. Almost the only exceptions were a few individuals with unusual artistic gifts: Bertel Thorvaldsen, Fru Heiberg and Hans Christian Andersen. And even they had occasionally to be put in their place and reminded of their low origin.'[9] Here it is difficult to talk about a *real* breakthrough. Throughout his life Andersen was obliged to act as a dominated subject within the dominant social circles despite his fame and recognition as a writer.

Even to reach this point—and this is the second crucial factor—he had to be strictly supervised, for admission to the upper echelons had to be earned and constantly proved. And, Andersen appeared to be a 'security risk' at first. Thus, when he came to Copenhagen in 1819 from the lower-class and provincial milieu of Odense, he had to be corrected by his betters so that he could cultivate proper speech, behavior, and decorum. Then for polishing he was also sent to elite private schools in Slagelse and Helsingör at a late age from 1822 to 1827 to receive a thorough formal and classical education. The aim of this education was to curb and control Andersen, especially his flamboyant imagination, not to help him achieve a relative amount of autonomy.

> Jonas Collin's purpose in rescuing Andersen and sending him to a grammar school was not to make

a great writer out of him but to enable him to become a useful member of the community in a social class higher than the one into which he was born. The grammar-school system was devised to teach boys to learn property, to mould them into the desired finished products, to make them grow up to be like their fathers.[10]

As Bredsdorff remarks, the system was not so thorough that Andersen was completely broken. But it left its indelible marks. What Andersen was to entitle *The Fairy Tale of My Life*—his autobiography, a remarkable mythopoeic projection of his life[11]—was in actuality a process of self-denial which was cultivated as individualism. Andersen was ashamed of his family background and did his utmost to avoid talking or writing about it. When he did, he invariably distorted the truth. For him, home was the Collin family, but home, as Andersen knew quite well, was unattainable because of social differences.

It was through his writings and literary achievement that Andersen was able to veil his self-denial and present it as a form of individualism. At the beginning of the nineteenth century in Denmark there was a literary swing from the universality of classicism to the romantic cult of genius and individuality, and Andersen benefited from this greatly. As a voracious reader, Andersen consumed all the German romantic writers of fairy tales along with Shakespeare, Scott, Irving, and other writers who exemplified his ideal of individualism. Most important for his formation in Denmark, the romantic movement was

accompanied by what is known as the Aladdin motif, after the idea which Oehlenschläger expressed in his play Aladdin. This deals with the theory that certain people are chosen by nature, or God, or the gods, to achieve greatness, and that nothing can succeed in stopping them, however weak and ill-suited they may otherwise seem. . . . The twin themes of former national greatness and of the possibility of being chosen to be great, despite all appearances, assumed a special significance for Denmark after 1814. Romantic-patriotic drama dealing with the heroic past appealed to a population looking for an escape from the sordid present, and served as a source of inspiration for many years. At the same time the Aladdin conception also took on new proportions: it was not only of use as a literary theme, but it could be applied to individuals—Oehlenschläger felt that he himself exemplified it, as did Hans Christian Andersen—and it was also possible to apply it to a country.[12]

Andersen as Aladdin. Andersen's life as a fairy tale. There is something schizophrenic in pretending that one is a fairy-tale character in reality, and Andersen was indeed troubled by nervous disorders and psychic disturbances throughout his life. To justify his schizophrenic

existence, he adopted the Danish physicist Hans Christian Orsted's ideas from *The Spirit of Nature* and combined them with his animistic belief in Christianity.[13] Orsted believed that the laws of nature are the thoughts of God, and, as the spirit of nature becomes projected, reality assumes the form of a miracle. Moreover, Andersen felt that, if life is miraculous, then God protects 'His elect' and gives them the help they need. Such superstition—his mother was extraordinarily superstitious—only concealed Andersen's overwhelming desire to escape the poverty of his existence and his indefatigable efforts to gain fame as a writer. Certainly, if providence controlled the workings of the world, genius was a divine and natural gift and would be rewarded regardless of birth. Power was located in the hands of God, and only before Him did one have to bow. However, Andersen did in fact submit more to a temporal social system and had to rationalize this submission adequately enough so that he could live with himself. In doing so, he inserted himself into a socio-historical nexus of the dominated denying his origins and needs to receive applause, money, comfort, and space to write about social contradictions that he had difficulty resolving for himself. Such a situation meant a life of self-doubt and anxiety for Andersen.

Again Bisseret is useful in helping us understand the socio-psychological impact on such ego formation and perspectives:

Dominant in imagination (who am I?), dominated in reality (what am I?), the ego lacks cohesion, hence the contradiction and incoherence of the practices. Dominated-class children think in terms of aptitudes, tastes and interests because at each step in their education their success has progressively convinced them that they are not 'less than nothing' intellectually; but at the same time they profoundly doubt themselves. This doubt is certainly not unrelated to the split, discontinuous aspects of their orientations, as measured by the standards of a parsimonious and fleeting time. Their day-to-day projects which lead them into dead ends or which build up gaps in knowledge which are inhibitory for their educational future, reinforce their doubts as to their capacities.[14]

In the particular case of Andersen, the self-doubts were productive insofar as he constantly felt the need to prove himself, to show that his aptitude and disposition were noble and that he belonged to the elect. This is apparent in the referential system built into most of his tales which are discourses of the dominated. In analyzing such discourse, Bisseret makes the point that

the relationship to his social being simultaneously lived and conceived by each agent is based on unconscious knowledge. What is designated as the 'subject' (the 'I') in the social discourse is the social being of the dominant. Thus in defining his identity the dominated cannot polarize the comparison between the self/the others on his 'me' in the way the dominant does . . . There cannot be a cohesion except on the side of power. Perhaps the dominated ignore that less than the dominant, as is clear through their accounts. Indeed, the more the practices of the speaker are the practices of power, the more the situation in which he places himself in the conceptual field is the mythical place where power disappears to the benefit of a purely abstract creativity. On the other hand, the more the speaker is subjected to power, the more he situates himself to the very place where power is concretely exercised.[15]

Though Bisseret's ideas about the dominated and dominant in regard to essentialist ideology are concerned with linguistic forms in everyday speech, they also apply to modes of narration used by writers of fiction. For instance, Andersen mixed popular language or folk linguistic forms with formal classical speech in creating his tales, and this stylistic synthesis not only endowed the stories with an unusual tone but also reflected Andersen's efforts to unify an identity which dominant discourse kept dissociating. Andersen also endeavored to ennoble and synthesize folk motifs with the literary motifs of romantic fairy tales, particularly those of Hoffmann, Tieck, Chamisso, Eichendorff, and Fouqué. His stylization of lower-class folk motifs was similar to his personal attempt to rise in society: they were aimed at meeting the standards of 'high art' set by the middle classes. In sum, Andersen's linguistic forms and stylized motifs reveal the structure of relationships as they were being formed and solidified around emerging bourgeois domination in the nineteenth century.

With a few exceptions, most of the 156 fairy tales written by Andersen contain no 'I,' that is, the 'I' is sublimated through the third person, and the narrative discourse becomes dominated by constant reference to the location of power. The identification of the third-person narrator with the underdog or dominated in the tales is consequently misleading. On one level, this occurs, but the narrator's voice always seeks approval and identification with a higher force. Here, too, the figures representing dominance or nobility are not always at the seat of power. Submission to power beyond the aristocracy constituted and constitutes the real appeal of Andersen's tales for middle-class audiences: Andersen placed power in divine providence, which invariably acted in the name of bourgeois essentialist ideology. No other writer of literary fairy tales in the early nineteenth century introduced so many Christian notions of God, the Protestant Ethic, and bourgeois enterprise in his narratives as Andersen did. All his tales make explicit or implicit reference to a miraculous Christian power which rules firmly but justly over His subjects. Such patriarchal power would appear to represent a feudal organization but the dominant value system represented by providential action and the plots of the tales is thoroughly bourgeois and justifies essentialist notions of aptitude and disposition. Just as aristocratic

power was being transformed in Denmark, so Andersen reflected upon the meaning of such transformation in his tales.

There are also clear strains of social Darwinism in Andersen's tales mixed with the Aladdin motif. In fact, survival of the fittest is the message of the very first tale he wrote for the publication of his anthology—**"The Tinderbox."** However, the fittest is not always the strongest but the chosen protagonist who proves himself or herself worthy of serving a dominant value system. This does not mean that Andersen constantly preached one message in all his tales. As a whole, written from 1835 to 1875, they represent the creative process of a dominated ego endeavoring to establish a unified self while confronted with a dominant discourse which dissociated this identity. The fictional efforts are variations on a theme of how to achieve approbation, assimilation, and integration in a social system which does not allow for real acceptance or recognition if one comes from the lower classes. In many respects Andersen is like a Humpty-Dumpty figure who had a great fall when he realized as he grew up that entrance into the educated elite of Denmark did not mean acceptance and totality. Nor could all the king's men and horses put him back together when he was humiliated and perceived the inequalities. So his fairy tales are variegated and sublimated efforts to achieve wholeness, to gain vengeance, and to depict the reality of class struggle. The dominated voice, however, remains constant in its reference to real power.

Obviously there are other themes than power and domination in the tales and other valid approaches to them, but I believe that the widespread, continuous reception of Andersen's fairy tales in western culture can best be explained by understanding how the discourse of the dominated functions in the narratives. Ideologically speaking Andersen furthered bourgeois notions of the self-made man or the Horatio Alger myth, which was becoming so popular in America and elsewhere, while reinforcing a belief in the existing power structure that meant domination and exploitation of the lower classes. This is why we must look more closely at the tales to analyze how they embody the dreams of social rise and individual happiness which further a powerful, all-encompassing bourgeois selection process.

II

Bredsdorff notes that, among the 156 tales written by Andersen, there are 30 which have proven to be the most popular throughout the world.[16] My analysis will concentrate first on these tales in an effort to comprehend the factors which might constitute their popularity in reception. Since they form the kernel of Andersen's achievement, they can be considered the ultimate examples of how the dominated discourse can rationalize power in fairy tales written for children and adults as well. Aside from examining this aspect of these tales, I shall also analyze those features in other significant tales that reveal the tensions of a life which was far from the fairy tale Andersen wanted his readers to believe it was. Ironically, the fairy tales he wrote are more 'realistic' than his own autobiographies, when understood as discourses defined by dominance relationships in which the narrator defines what he would like to be according to definitions of a socially imposed identity.

Since there is no better starting point than the beginning, let us consider Andersen's very first tale "**The Tinderbox**" as an example of how his dominated discourse functions. As I have already mentioned, the basic philosophy of "**The Tinderbox**" corresponds to the principles of social Darwinism, but this is not sufficient enough to understand the elaboration of power relations and the underlying message of the tale. We must explore further.

As the tale unfolds, it is quite clear that the third-person narrative voice and providence are on the young soldier's side, for without any ostensible reason he is chosen by the witch to fetch a fortune. Using his talents, he not only gains a treasure but immense power, even if he must kill the witch to do so. Here the murder of the witch is not viewed as immoral since witches are evil *per se*. The major concern of Andersen is to present a young soldier who knows how to pull himself up by the bootstraps when fortune shines upon him to become a 'refined gentleman.'[17] The word refined has nothing to do with culture but more with money and power. The soldier learns this when he runs out of coins, is forgotten by fair-weather friends, and sinks in social status. Then he discovers the magic of the tinderbox and the power of the three dogs which means endless provision. Here Andersen subconsciously concocted a socio-political formula which was the keystone of bourgeois progress and success in the nineteenth century: use of talents for the acquisition of money, establish a system of continual recapitalization (tinderbox and three dogs) to guarantee income and power, employ money and power to achieve social and political hegemony. The soldier is justified in his use of power and money because he is *essentially* better than anyone else—chosen to rule. The king and queen are dethroned, and the soldier rises through the application of his innate talents and fortune to assume control of society.

Though it appears that the soldier is the hero of the story, there is a hidden referent of power in this dominated narrative discourse. Power does not reside in the soldier but in the 'magical' organization of social relations that allows him to pursue and realize his dreams. Of course, these social relations were not as magical as they appear since they were formed through actual class struggle to allow for the emergence of a middle class which set its own rules of the game and established those qualities necessary for leadership: cleverness, perseverence, cold calculation, respect for money and private property. Psychologically Andersen's hatred for his own class (his mother) and the Danish nobility (king and queen) are played out bluntly when the soldier kills the witch and has the king and queen eliminated by the dogs. The wedding celebration at the end is basically a celebration of the solidification of power by the bourgeois class in the nineteenth century: the unification of a middle-class soldier with a royal princess. In the end the humorous narrative voice appears to gain deep pleasure and satisfaction in having related this tale, as though it has been ordained from above.

In all the other tales published in 1835 there is a process of selection and proving one's worth according to the hidden referent of bourgeois power. In "**Little Claus and Big Claus**" the small farmer must first learn the lesson of humility before providence takes his side and guides him against the vengeful big farmer. Again, using his wits without remorse, an ordinary person virtually obliterates a rich arrogant landowner and amasses a small fortune. "**The Princess and the Pea**" is a simple story about the *essence* of true nobility. A *real* prince can only marry a *genuine* princess with the right sensitivity. This sensitivity is spelled out in different ways in the other tales of 1835: "**Little Ida's Flowers**," "**Thumbelina**," and "**The Travelling Companion**" portray 'small' or oppressed people who cultivate their special talents and struggle to realize their goals despite the forces of adversity. Ida retains and fulfills her dreams of flowers despite the crass professor's vicious attacks. Thumbelina survives many adventures to marry the king of the angels and become a queen. Johannes, the poor orphan, promises to be good so that God will protect him, and indeed his charitable deeds amount to a marriage with a princess. The *Taugenichts* who trusts in God will always be rewarded. All the gifted but disadvantaged characters, who are God-fearing, come into their own in Andersen's tales, but they never take possession of power which resides in the shifting social relations leading to bourgeois hegemony.

In all of these early tales Andersen focuses on lower-class or disenfranchised protagonists, who work their way up in society.[18] Their rise is predicated on their proper behavior which must correspond to a higher power that elects and tests the hero. Though respect is shown for feudal patriarchy, the correct normative behavior reflects the values of the bourgeoisie. If the hero comes from the lower classes, he or she must be humbled if not humiliated at one point to test obedience. Thereafter, the natural aptitude of a successful individual will be unveiled through diligence, perseverence, and adherence to an ethical system which legitimizes bourgeois domination. Let me be more specific by focusing on what I consider the major popular tales written after

1835: **"The Little Mermaid"** (1837), **"The Steadfast Tin Soldier"** (1838), **"The Swineherd"** (1841), **"The Nightingale"** (1843), **"The Ugly Duckling"** (1843), **"The Red Shoes"** (1845), and **"The Shadow"** (1847).

There are two important factors to bear in mind when considering the reception of these tales in the nineteenth century and the present in regard to the narrative discourse of the dominated. First, as a member of the dominated class, Andersen could only experience dissociation despite entrance into upper-class circles. Obviously this was because he measured his success as a person and artist by standards which were not of his own social group's making. That ultimate power which judged his efforts and the destiny of his heroes depended on the organization of hierarchical relations at a time of socio-political transformation which was to leave Denmark and most of Europe under the control of the bourgeoisie. This shift in power led Andersen to identify with the emerging middle-class elite, but he did not depict the poor and disenfranchised in a negative way. On the contrary, Andersen assumed a humble, philanthropic stance—the fortunate and gifted are obliged morally and ethically to help the less fortunate. The dominated voice of all his narratives does not condemn his former social class, rather Andersen loses contact with it by denying the rebellious urges of his class within himself and making compromises that affirmed the rightful domination of the middle-class ethic.

A second factor to consider is the fundamental ambiguity of the dominated discourse in Andersen's tales: this discourse cannot represent the interests of the dominated class; it can only rationalize the power of the dominant class so that this power becomes legitimate and acceptable to those who are powerless. As I have noted before, Andersen depersonalizes his tales by using the third-person stance which appears to universalize his voice. However, this self-denial is a recourse of the dominated, who always carry references and appeal to those forces which control their lives. In Andersen's case he mystifies power and makes it appear divine. It is striking, as I have already stressed, when one compares Andersen to other fairy-tale writers of his time, how he constantly appeals to God and the Protestant Ethic to justify and sanction the actions and results of his tales. Ironically, to have a soul in Andersen's tales one must sell one's soul either to the aristocracy or to the bourgeoisie. In either case it was the middle-class moral and social code which guaranteed the success of his protagonists, guaranteed his own social success, and ultimately has guaranteed the successful reception of the tales to the present.

Speaking about lost souls, then, let us turn to **"The Little Mermaid"** to grasp how the dominated seemingly gains 'happiness and fulfillment' while losing its voice and real power. This tale harks back to the folk stories of the water urchin who desires a soul so she

can marry a human being whom she loves. Andersen was certainly familiar with Goethe's *Melusine* and Fouqué's *Undine,* stories which ennobled the aspirations of pagan sprites, but his tale about the self-sacrificing mermaid is distinctly different from the narratives of Goethe and Fouqué, who were always part of the dominant class and punished upper-class men for forgetting their Christian manners. Andersen's perspective focuses more on the torture and suffering which a member of the dominated class must undergo to establish her true nobility and virtues. Characteristically, Andersen only allows the mermaid to rise out of the water and move in the air of royal circles after her tongue is removed and her tail is transformed into legs described as 'sword-like' when she walks or dances. Voiceless and tortured, deprived physically and psychologically, the mermaid serves a prince who never fully appreciates her worth. Twice she saves his life. The second time is most significant: instead of killing him to regain her identity and rejoin her sisters and grandmother, the mermaid forfeits her own life and becomes an ethereal figure, blessed by God. If she does good deeds for the next 300 years, she will be endowed with an immortal soul. As she is told, her divine mission will consist of flying through homes of human beings as an invisible spirit. If she finds a good child who makes his parents happy and deserves their love, her sentence will be shortened. A naughty and mean child can lengthen the 300 years she must serve in God's name.

However, the question is whether the mermaid is really acting in God's name. Her falling in love with royalty and all her future actions involve self-denial and a process of rationalizing self-denial. The mermaid's ego becomes dissociated because she is attracted to a class of people who will never accept her on her own terms. To join her 'superiors' she must practically cut her own throat, and, though she realizes that she can never express truthfully who she is and what her needs are, she is unwilling to return to her own species or dominated class. Thus she must somehow justify her existence to herself through abstinence and self-abnegation—values preached by the bourgeoisie and certainly not practiced by the nobility and upper classes. Paradoxically Andersen seems to be preaching that true virtue and self-realization can be obtained through self-denial. This message, however, is not so paradoxical since it comes from the voice of the dominated. In fact, it is based on Andersen's astute perception and his own experience as a lower-class clumsy youth who sought to cultivate himself: by becoming voiceless, walking with legs like knives, and denying one's needs, one (as a non-entity) gains divine recognition.

Andersen never tired of preaching self-abandonment and self-deprivation in the name of bourgeois laws. The reward was never power over one's life but security in adherence to power. For instance, in **"The Steadfast Tin Soldier,"** the soldier falls in love with a ballerina and remarks: 'She would be a perfect wife for me . . . but I am afraid she is above me. She has a castle, and I have only a box that I must share with twenty-four soldiers; that wouldn't do for her. Still, I would like to make her acquaintance.'[19] He must endure all sorts of hardships in pursuit of his love and is finally rewarded with fulfillment—but only after he and the ballerina are burned and melted in a stove. Again, happiness is predicated on a form of self-effacement.

This does not mean that Andersen was always self-denigrating in his tales. He often attacked greed and false pride. But what is interesting here is that vice is generally associated with the pretentious aristocracy and hardly ever with bourgeois characters. Generally speaking, Andersen punished overreachers, that is, the urge within himself to be rebellious. Decorum and balance became articles of faith in his philosophical scheme of things. In **"The Swineherd"** he delights in depicting the poor manners of a princess who has lost her sense of propriety. Andersen had already parodied the artificiality and pretentiousness of the nobility in **"The Tinderbox"** and **"The Emperor's Clothes."** Similar to the 'taming of the shrew' motif in the folk tale *King Thrushbeard,* Andersen now has the dominant figure of the fickle, proud princess humiliated by the dominated figure of the prince disguised as swineherd. However, there is no happy end here, for the humor assumes a deadly seriousness when the prince rejects the princess after accomplishing his aim: ' "I have come to despise you", said the prince, "You did not want an honest prince. You did not appreciate the rose or the nightingale, but you could kiss a swineherd for the sake of a toy. Farewell!" '[20]

The oppositions are clear: honesty vs. falseness, genuine beauty (rose/nightingale) vs. manufactured beauty (toys), nobility of the soul vs. soulless nobility. Indirectly Andersen argues that the nobility must adapt to the value system of the emerging bourgeoisie or be locked out of the kingdom of happiness. Without appreciating the beauty and power of genuine leaders—the prince is essentially middle-class—the monarchy will collapse.

This theme is at the heart of **"The Nightingale,"** which can also be considered a remarkable treatise about art, genius, and the role of the artist. The plot involves a series of transformations in power relations and service. First the Chinese Emperor, a benevolent patriarch, has the nightingale brought to his castle from the forest. When the chief courtier finds the nightingale, he exclaims: 'I had not imagined it would look like that. It looks so common! I think it has lost its color from shyness and out of embarrassment at seeing so many noble people at one time.'[21] Because the common-looking bird (an obvious reference to Andersen) possesses an inimitable artistic genius, he is engaged to serve the Emperor. The first phase of the dominant-dominated relationship based on bonded servitude is changed into neglect when the Emperor is given a jeweled mechanical bird that never tires of singing. So the nightingale escapes and returns to the forest, and eventually the mechanical bird breaks down. Five years later the Emperor falls sick and appears to be dying. Out of his own choice the nightingale returns to him and chases death from his window. Here the relationship of servitude is resumed with the exception that the nightingale has assumed a different market value: he agrees to be the emperor's songbird forever as long as he can come and go as he pleases. Feudalism has been replaced by a free market system; yet, the bird/artist is willing to serve loyally and keep the autocrat in power. 'And my song shall make you happy and make you thoughtful. I shall sing not only of the good and of the evil that happen around you, and yet are hidden from you. For a little songbird flies far. I visit the poor fisherman's cottages and the peasant's hut, far away from your palace and your court. I love your heart more than your crown, and I feel that the crown has a fragrance of something holy about it. I will come! I will sing for you!'[22]

As we know, Andersen depended on the patronage of the King of Denmark and other upper-class donors, but he never felt esteemed enough, and he disliked the strings which were attached to the money given to him. Instead of breaking with such patronage, however, the dominated voice of this discourse seeks to set new limits which continue servitude in marketable conditions more tolerable for the servant. Andersen reaffirms the essentialist ideology of this period and reveals how gifted 'common' individuals are the pillars of power—naturally in service to the state. Unfortunately, he never bothered to ask why 'genius' cannot stand on its own and perhaps unite with like-minded people.

In **"The Ugly Duckling"** genius also assumes a most awe-inspiring shape, but it cannot fly on its own. This tale has generally been interpreted as a parable of Andersen's own success story because the naturally gifted underdog survives a period of 'ugliness' to reveal its innate beauty. Yet, more attention should be placed on the *servility of genius.* Though Andersen continually located real power in social conditions which allowed for the emergence of bourgeois hegemony, he often argued—true to conditions in Denmark—that power was to be dispensed in servitude to appreciate rulers, and naturally these benevolent rulers were supposed to recognize the interests of the bourgeoisie. As we have seen in **"The Nightingale,"** the artist returns to serve royalty after he is neglected by the emperor. In **"The Ugly Duckling,"** the baby swan is literally chased by coarse lower-class animals from the henyard. His innate beauty cannot be recognized by such crude specimens, and only after he survives numerous ordeals, does he realize his essential greatness. But his self-realization is ambivalent, for right before he perceives his true nature, he wants to kill himself: 'I shall fly over to them, those royal birds! And they can hack me to death because I, who am so ugly, dare to approach them! What difference does it make! It is better to be killed by them than to be bitten by the other ducks, and pecked by the hens, and kicked by the girl who tends the henyard; or to suffer through the winter.'[23]

Andersen expresses a clear disdain for the common people's lot and explicitly states that to be humiliated by the upper class is worth more than the trials and tribulations one must suffer among the lower classes. And, again, Andersen espouses bourgeois essentialist philosophy when he saves the swan and declares as narrator: 'It does not matter that one has been born in the henyard as long as one has lain in a swan's egg.'[24] The fine line between eugenics and racism fades in this story where the once-upon-a-time dominated swan reveals himself to be a tame but noble member of a superior race. The swan does not return 'home' but lands in a beautiful garden where he is admired by children, adults, and nature. It appears as though the swan has finally come into his own, but, as usual, there is a hidden reference of power. The swan measures himself by the values and aesthetics set by the 'royal' swans and by the proper well-behaved children and people in the beautiful garden. The swans and the beautiful garden are placed in opposition to the ducks and the henyard. In appealing to the 'noble' sentiments of a refined audience and his readers, Andersen reflected a distinct class bias if not classical racist tendencies.

What happens, however, when one opposes the structures of the dominant class? Here Andersen can be merciless, just as merciless as the people who reprimanded and scolded him for overreaching himself. In **"The Red Shoes,"** Karen, a poor little orphan, mistakenly believes that she is adopted by a generous old woman because she wears red shoes, a symbol of vanity and sin. This red stigma is made clear as she is about to be baptized in church: 'When the bishop laid his hands on her head and spoke of the solemn promise she was about to make—of her convenant with God to be a good Christian—her mind was not on his words. The ritual music was played on the organ; the old cantor sang, and the sweet voices of the children could be heard, but Karen was thinking of her red shoes.'[25] Although she tries to abandon the red shoes, she cannot resist their red lure. So she must be taken to task and is visited by a stern angel who pronounces sentence upon her: ' "You shall dance," he said, "dance in your red shoes until you become red and thin. Dance till the skin on your face turns yellow and clings to your bones as if you were a skeleton. Dance you shall from door to door, and when you pass a house where proud and vain children live, there you shall knock on the door so they will see you and fear your fate." '[26]

The only way Karen can overcome the angel's curse is by requesting the municipal executioner to cut off her feet. Thereafter, she works diligently for the minister of the church. Upon her death, Karen's devout soul 'flew on a sunbeam up to God.'[27] This ghastly tale—reminiscent of the gory German pedagogical best-seller of this time, Heinrich Hoffmann's *Struwwelpeter* (1845)—is a realistic description of the punishment which awaited anyone who dared oppose the powers that be.

Though Andersen acknowledged the right of the Danish ruling class to exercise its power, he knew how painful it was to be at their mercy. The most telling tale about the excrutiating psychological effects of servility, the extreme frustration he felt from his own obsequious behavior, was **"The Shadow."** As many critics have noted, this haunting narrative is highly autobiographical; it stems from the humiliation that Andersen suffered when Edvard Collin adamantly rejected his proposal to use the 'familiar you' (*du*) in their discourse—and there was more than one rejection. By retaining the 'formal you' *(De)*, Collin was undoubtedly asserting his class superiority, and this distance was meant to remind Andersen of his humble origins. Though they had come to regard each other as brothers during their youth, Collin lorded his position over Andersen throughout their lives and appeared to administrate Andersen's life—something which the writer actually desired but feared. In **"The Shadow"** Andersen clearly sought to avenge himself through his tale about a philosopher's shadow who separates himself from his owner and becomes immensely rich and successful. When the shadow returns to visit the scholar, his former owner wants to know how he achieved such success. To which the shadow replies that he will reveal 'everything! And I'll tell you about it, but . . . it has nothing whatsoever to do with pride, but out of respect to my accomplishments, not to speak of my social position, I wish you wouldn't address me familiarly.'

'"Forgive me!" exclaimed the philosopher. "It is an old habit, and they are the hardest to get rid of. But you are quite right, and I'll try to remember."'[28]

Not only does the shadow/Andersen put the philosopher/Collin in his place, but he explains that it was *Poetry* which made a human being out of him and that he quickly came to understand his 'innermost nature, that part of me which can claim kinship to poetry.'[29] Human-like and powerful, the shadow can control other people because he can see their evil sides. His own sinister talents allow him to improve his fortunes, while the philosopher, who can only write about the beautiful and the good, becomes poor and neglected. Eventually, the philosopher is obliged to travel with his former shadow—the shadow now as master and the master as shadow. When the shadow deceives a princess to win her hand in marriage, the philosopher threatens to reveal the truth about him. The crafty shadow, however, convinces the princess that the old man himself is a deranged shadow, and she decides to have him killed to end his misery.

The reversal of fortunes and of power relations is not a process of liberation but one of revenge. Nor can one argue that the shadow possesses power, for power cannot be possessed in and of itself but is constituted by the organization of social classes and property. One can gain access to power and draw upon it, and this is what the shadow does. Aside from being Andersen's wish-fulfillment, the fantastic projection in this story is connected to the Hegelian notion of master/slave (*Herr/Knecht*). The shadow/slave, who is closer to material conditions, is able to take advantage of what he sees and experiences—the underpinnings of social life—to overthrow his master, whereas the master, who has only been able to experience reality through the mediation of his shadow, is too idealistic and cannot defend himself. In Andersen's tale it should be noted that the shadow does not act in the interests of the dominated class but rather *within* the framework of institutionalized power relationships. Therefore, he still remains servile and caters to the dominant class despite the reversal of his circumstances. In this regard Andersen's heroes, who rise in class, do not undergo a qualitative change in social existence but point more to manifold ways one can accede to power.

As we have seen, the major theme and its variations in Andersen's most popular tales pertain to the rise of a protagonist under conditions of servitude. Only if the chosen hero complies with a code based on the Protestant Ethic and reveres divine providence does he advance in society or reach salvation. Though this is not explicitly spelled out, the references to real power reveal that it resides in the social organization of relations affirming bourgeois hegemony of a patriarchal nature. Even the benevolent feudal kings cannot maintain power without obeying sacrosanct bourgeois moral laws. Obviously this applies to the members of the lower classes and circumscribes their rise in fortunes. Limits are placed on their position in acceptable society. In most of the other 126 tales, which are not as widely circulated as the best known Andersen narratives, the dominated voice remains basically the same: it humbly recognizes the bourgeois rules of the game, submits itself to them as loyal subject and has the fictional protagonists do the same.

III

What saves Andersen's tales from simply becoming sentimental homilies (which many of them are) was his extraordinary understanding of how class struggle affected the lives of people in his times, and some tales even contain a forthright criticism of abusive domination—though his critique was always balanced by admiration for the upper classes and a fear of poverty. For instance, there are some exceptional tales of the remaining 126 which suggest a more rebellious position. Such rebelliousness, perhaps, accounts for the fact that they are not among the 30 most popular. Indeed, the dominated discourse is not homogenous or univocal, though it constantly refers to bourgeois power and never seeks to defy it. In 1853, shortly after the revolutionary period of 1848-1850 in Europe, Andersen reflected upon the thwarted rebellions in a number of tales, and they are worth discussing because they show more clearly how Andersen wavered when he subjected himself to bourgeois and aristocratic domination.

In **"Everything in its Right Place"** (1853) the arrogant aristocratic owner of a manor takes pleasure in pushing a goose-girl off a bridge. The peddler, who watches this and saves the girl, curses the master by exclaiming 'everything in its right place.'[30] Sure enough, the aristocrat drinks and gambles away the manor in the next six years. The new owner is none other than the peddler, and, of course, he takes the goose girl for his bride and the Bible as his guide. The family prospers for the next hundred years with its motto 'everything in its right place.' At this point the narrator introduces us to a parson's son tutoring the humble daughter of the now wealthy enobled house. This idealistic tutor discusses the differences between the nobility and bourgeoisie and surprises the modest baronness by stating:

> 'I know it is the fashion of the day—and many a poet dances to that tune—to say that everything aristocratic is stupid and bad. They claim that only among the poor—and the lower you descend the better—does pure gold glitter. But that is not my opinion; I think it is wrong, absolutely false reasoning. Among the highest classes one can often observe the most elevated traits. . . . But where nobility has gone to a man's head and he behaves like an Arabian horse that rears and kicks, just because his blood is pure and he has a degree, there nobility has degenerated. When noblemen sniff the air in a room because a plain citizen has been there and say, "It smells of the street," why then Thespis should exhibit them to the just ridicule of satire.'[31]

This degradation is, indeed, what occurs. A cavalier tries to mock the tutor at a music soiree, and the tutor plays a melody on a simple willow flute which suddenly creates a storm with the wind howling 'everything in its right place!' In the house and throughout the countryside the wind tosses people about, and social class positions are reversed until the flute cracks and everyone returns to their former place. After this scare, Andersen still warns that 'eventually everything is put in its right place. Eternity is long, a lot longer than this story.'[32] Such a 'revolutionary' tone was uncharacteristic of Andersen, but given the mood of the times, he was prompted time and again in the early 1850s to voice his critique of the upper classes and question not only aristocratic but also bourgeois hegemony.

In **"The Pixy and the Grocer"** (1853) a little imp lives in a grocer's store and receives a free bowl of porridge and butter each Christmas. The grocer also rents out the garret to a poor student who would rather buy a book of poetry and eat bread for supper instead of cheese. The pixy visits the student in the garret to punish him for calling the grocer a boor with no feeling for poetry. Once in the garret, however, the pixy discovers the beauty and magic of poetry and almost decides to move in with the student. Almost, for he remembers that the student does not have much food, nor can he give him porridge with butter. So he continues to visit the garret from time to time. Then one night a fire on the street threatens to spread to the grocer's house. The grocer and his wife grab their gold and bonds and run out of the house. The student remains calm while the pixy tries to save the most valuable thing in the house—the book of poetry. 'Now he finally understood his heart's desire, where his loyalty belonged! But when the fire in the house across the street had been put out, then he thought about it again. "I will share myself between them," he said, "for I cannot leave the grocer altogether. I must stay there for the sake of the porridge." '[33] 'That was quite human,' the dominated narrator concludes, 'after all, we, too, go to the grocer for the porridge's sake.'[34]

This tale is much more ambivalent in its attitude toward domination than **"Everything in Its Right Place,"** which is open-ended and allows for the possibility of future revolutions. Here, Andersen writes more about himself and his own contradictions at the time of an impending upheaval (i.e., fire = revolution). Faced with a choice, the pixy/Andersen leans toward poetry or the lower classes and idealism. But, when the fire subsides, he makes his usual compromise, for he knows where his bread is buttered and power resides. The narrative discourse is ironic, somewhat self-critical but ultimately rationalizing. Since everyone falls in line with the forces that dominate and provide food, why not the pixy? Who is he to be courageous or different? Nothing more is said about the student, nor is there any mention of those who do not make compromises. Andersen makes it appear that servility is most human and understandable. Rarely does he suggest that it is just as human to rebel against inequality and injustice out of need as it is to bow to arbitrary domination.

The tales of 1853 demonstrate how Andersen was not unaware of possibilities for radical change and questioned the conditions of bourgeois/aristocratic hegemony. In one of his most remarkable tales **"The Gardner and His Master,"** written toward the very end of his life in 1871, he sums up his views on servitude, domination, and aptitude in his brilliantly succinct, ambivalent manner. The plot is simple and familiar. A haughty aristocrat has an excellent plain gardener who tends his estate outside of Copenhagen. The master, however, never trusts the advice of the gardener nor appreciates

what he produces. He and his wife believe that the fruits and flowers grown by other gardeners are better, and, when they constantly discover, to their chagrin, that their very own gardener's work is considered the best by the royal families, they hope he won't think too much of himself. Then, the storyteller Andersen comments, 'he didn't; but the fame was a spur, he wanted to be one of the best gardeners in the country. Every year he tried to improve some of the vegetables and fruits, and often he was successful. It was not always appreciated. He would be told that the pears and apples were good but not as good as the ones last year. The melons were excellent but not quite up to the standard of the first ones he had grown.'[35]

The gardener must constantly prove himself, and one of his great achievements is his use of an area to plant 'all the typical common plants of Denmark, gathered from forests and fields'[36] which flourish because of his nursing care and devotion. So, in the end, the owners of the castle must be proud of the gardener because the whole world beat the drums for his success. 'But they weren't really proud of it. They felt that they were the owners and that they could dismiss Larsen if they wanted to. They didn't, for they were decent people, and there are lots of their kind, which is fortunate for the Larsens.'[37]

In other words, Andersen himself had been fortunate, or, at least this was the way he ironically viewed his career at the end of his life. Yet, there is something pathetically sad about this story. The gardener Larsen is obviously the storyteller Andersen, and the garden with all its produce is the collection of fairy tales which he kept cultivating and improving throughout his life. The owners of the garden are Andersen's patrons and may be associated with the Collin family and other upper-class readers in Denmark. We must remember that it was generally known that the Collin family could never come to recognize Andersen as a *Digter* but thought of him as a fine popular writer. Andersen, whose vanity was immense and unquenchable, was extremely sensitive to criticism, and he petulantly and consistently complained that he felt unappreciated in Denmark while other European countries recognized his genius. Such treatment at home despite the fact he considered himself a most loyal servant, whether real or projected, became symbolized in this tale. The reference to the *common plants,* which the gardener cultivates, pertains to the folk motifs he employed and enriched so they would bloom aesthetically on their own soil. Andersen boasts that he, the garden has made Denmark famous, for pictures are taken of this garden and circulated throughout the world. Yet, it is within the confines of servitude and patronage that the gardener works, and the dominated voice of the narrator, even though ironic, rationalizes the humiliating ways in which his masters treat Larsen: they are 'decent' people. But, one must wonder—and the tension of the discourse compels us to do so—that, if the gardener is superb and brilliant, why doesn't he rebel and quit his job? Why does the gardener suffer such humiliation and domination?

Andersen pondered these questions often and presented them in many of his tales, but he rarely suggested alternatives or rebellion. Rather he placed safety before idealism and chose moral compromise over moral outrage, individual comfort and achievement over collective struggle and united goals. He aimed for identification with the power establishment that humiliates subjects rather than opposition to autocracy to put an end to exploitation through power. The defects in Andersen's ideological perspective are not enumerated here to insist that he should have learned to accept squalor and the disadvantages of poverty and struggle. They are important because they are the telling marks in the historical reception of his tales. Both the happy and sad endings of his narratives infer that there is an absolute or a divine, harmonious power, and that unity of the ego is possible under such power. Such a projection, however, was actually that of a frustrated and torn artist who was obliged to compensate for an existence which lacked harmonious proportions and a center of autonomy. Andersen's life was one based on servility, and his tales were endeavors to justify a false consciousness: literary exercises in the legitimation of a social order to which he subscribed.

Whether the discourse of such a dominated writer be a monologue with himself or dialogue with an audience who partakes of his ideology, he still can never feel at peace with himself. It is thus the restlessness and the dissatisfaction of the dominated artist which imbues his work ultimately with the qualitative substance of what he seeks to relate. Ironically, the power of Andersen's fairy tales for him and for his readers has very little to do with the power he respected. It emanates from the missing gaps, the lapses, which are felt when the compromises are made under compulsion, for Andersen always painted happiness as adjusting to domination no matter how chosen one was. Clearly, then, Andersen's genius, despite his servility, rested in his inability to prevent himself from loathing all that he admired.

Notes

[1] *Hans Christian Andersen. The Story of his Life Work* (London: Phaidon, 1975), p. 152.

[2] *Ibid.,* p. 179. Many more statements like this can be found in Andersen's letters and journals. See Hans Christian Andersen, *Das Märchen meines Lebens. Briefe. Tagebucher,* ed. by Erling Nielsen (Munich: Winkler, 1961). Unfortunately, the letters and journals have not been translated into English.

[3] *Ibid.,* pp. 132-3.

[4] London: Routledge & Kegan Paul, 1979, pp. 1-2.

[5] See Jeffrey M. Blum, *Pseudoscience and Mental Ability* (New York: Monthly Review Press, 1978) and Stephan L. Chorover, *From Genesis to Genocide: The Meaning of Human Nature and the Power of Behavior Control* (Cambridge: MIT Press, 1979).

[6] For the general development in Europe, see Jürgen Habermas, *Strukturwandel der Öffentlichkeit. Untersuchungen zu einer Kategorie der bürgerlichen Gesellschaft.* (Neuwied: Luchterhand, 1962) and Charles Morazé, *The Triumph of the Middle Classes. A Political and Social History of Europe in the Nineteenth Century* (London: Weidenfeld and Nicolson, 1966). For Denmark, see W. Glyn Jones, *Denmark* (New York: Praeger, 1970), pp. 17-129.

[7] New York: Pantheon, 1968.

[8] *Education, Class Language and Ideology,* p. 26.

[9] *Hans Christian Andersen,* p. 154.

[10] *Ibid.,* p. 69.

[11] Cf. *The Fairy Tale of My Life,* trans. by W. Glyn Jones (New York: British Book Centre, 1955.) Andersen wrote three major autobiographies during his life, and each one is filled with distortions and amplifications of fact.

[12] *Denmark,* pp. 66-7.

[13] Cf. Paul V. Rubow, 'Idea and form in Hans Christian Andersen's fairy tales,' in *A Book on the Danish Writer Hans Christian Andersen,* ed. by Svend Dahl and H.G. Topsoe-Jensen (Copenhagen: Det Berlingske Bogtrykkeri, 1955), pp. 97-136.

[14] *Education, Class Language and Ideology,* pp. 63-4.

[15] *Ibid.,* p. 65.

[16] *Hans Christian Andersen,* p. 308. They are as follows: *The Tinder Box, Little Claus and Big Claus, The Princess and the Pea, Little Ida's Flowers, Thumbelina, The Travelling Companion* (1835); *The Little Mermaid, The Emperor's New Clothes* (1837); *The Steadfast Tin Soldier, The Wild Swans* (1838); *The Garden of Eden, The Flying Trunk, The Storks* (1839); *Willie Winkie, The Swineherd, The Buckwheat* (1841); *The Nightingale, The Top and the Ball, The Ugly Duckling,* (1843); *The Fir Tree, The Snow Queen* (1844); *The Darning Needle, The Elf Hill, The Red Shoes, The Shepherdess and the Chimney-Sweep, The Little Match Girl* (1845); *The Shadow* (1847); *The Old House, The Happy Family, The Shirt Collar* (1848). Interestingly, the most popular tales are the earlier tales when Andersen

tended to be less critical of social conditions and wrote more expressly for children.

[17] Hans Christian Andersen, *The Complete Fairy Tales and Stories,* trans. by Erik Christian Haugaard (New York: Doubleday, 1974), p. 3.

[18] This is also true of the novels written during this time: *The Improvisatore* (1835), *O.T.* (1836), and *Only a Fiddler* (1837).

[19] *The Complete Fairy Tales and Stories,* p. 113.

[20] *Ibid.,* p. 197.

[21] *Ibid.,* p. 205.

[22] *Ibid.,* p. 211.

[23] *Ibid.,* pp. 223-4

[24] *Ibid.,* p. 224.

[25] *Ibid.,* p. 290.

[26] *Ibid.,* p. 292.

[27] *Ibid.,* p. 294.

[28] *Ibid.,* p. 339.

[29] *Ibid.*

[30] *Ibid.,* p. 417.

[31] *Ibid.,* pp. 420-1.

[32] *Ibid.,* p. 423.

[33] *Ibid.,* p. 427.

[34] *Ibid.*

[35] *Ibid.,* p. 1018.

[36] *Ibid.,* p. 1020.

[37] *Ibid.,* p. 1021.

John Griffith (essay date 1984)

SOURCE: "Personal Fantasy in Andersen's Fairy Tales," in *Kansas Quarterly,* Vol. 16, No. 3, Summer, 1984, pp. 81-88.

[*In the following essay, Griffith contends that Andersen depicted death as a welcome escape for the innocent from the frightening sexuality of the world.*]

"We can begin by saying that happy people never make fantasies, only unsatisfied ones," Freud wrote in his essay on the relation between imaginative writing and day-dreaming. "Unsatisfied wishes are the driving power behind fantasies; every separate fantasy contains the fulfillment of a wish, and improves on unsatisfactory reality. The impelling wishes may vary according to the sex, character and circumstances of the creator; they may be easily divided, however, into two principal groups. Either they are ambitious wishes, serving to exalt the person creating them, or they are erotic."[1]

There is little doubt that unsatisfied wishes inspired Hans Christian Andersen to write, and to write what he did. Neurotic, vain, skittish, inclined toward hysteria and melancholy, Andersen lived a life of yearning and self-denial, of awkward advances and embarrassed retreats. His fairy tales were an outlet for feelings of frustration that troubled him all his life.

His biographer Elias Bredsdorff summarizes the conditions of his earliest years this way: "In a candid letter to a friend who knew him better than most, Andersen once described himself as 'a swamp plant.' It is a valid description. Andersen's background was, from a social point of view, the lowest of the low: grinding poverty, slums, immorality and promiscuity. His grandmother was a pathological liar, his grandfather insane, his mother ended by becoming an alcoholic, his aunt ran a brothel in Copenhagen, and for years he was aware that somewhere a half-sister existed who might suddenly turn up and embarrass him in his new milieu—a thought which haunted his life and dreams."[2] From the beginning, Andersen turned to fantasy and make-believe to escape this reality. "I was a curiously dreamy child," he recalled. "As I walked about, I kept my eyes closed as often as not, so that people finally believed I had poor vision, despite the fact that this one of my senses was and is especially keen." He remembered being permitted to lie in his parents' bed for hours "in a waking dream, as if the actual world did not concern me."[3] He liked to sit at home alone, playing with the puppet-theater his father made him, sewing clothes for his dolls and making up stories about his dolls and himself. "I told the boys curious stories in which I was always the chief person," even though "I was sometimes rallied for that."[4] In particular, he recalled telling a little girl at school that he owned a castle, that he was a changeling child "of high birth, and that the angels of God came down and spoke to me."[5]

As a child, Andersen was squeamish about women, sex, and sensuality, and he never really outgrew that feeling. "I felt a strange dislike for grown-up girls, or for girls of more than twelve," he later wrote; "they really made me shudder; in fact, I used the expression about anything which I did not like touching that it was very 'girlish.'"[6] When he was 29, and his more worldly friends encouraged him to frequent houses of prostitution in Naples, Andersen wrote in his journal, "It made me very sensual and passionate, but I resisted the temptation all the same. If I get home without having lost my innocence I shall never lose it. . . . I am still innocent, but my blood is burning, in my dreams everything inside me is boiling. . . . I'm sure experienced people will laugh at my innocence, but it isn't really innocence, it is an abhorrence of this thing for which I have such a dislike."[7]

As did his feeling about sex, Andersen's fiction grew directly out of his childhood. Many of his stories are like free-form children's fantasies—improvised, unplanned, exaggerated, as free as dreams and as compulsive. And they serve many of the same psychological purposes that the child's fantasies serve, in that they talk of ambition and romance in narratives whose only rules are the requirements of wishes and fears.

But the stories Andersen wrote as a man are not free-hearted celebrations of ego and eros. They *begin* in normal desires for self-exaltation and love; they address themselves to those subjects, and they expand with an energy, a sheer force of invention that apparently comes from Andersen's deep feelings. But the stories are shot through, too, with the fears and aversions and inhibitions Andersen felt as a child. From the horror he first felt at the world of his childhood, and at the poor figure he himself cut in it, Andersen created dreams not of unfettered pride and passion but of their opposites, humility and chastity. Ordinary instincts for self-aggrandizement are present in his tales, but the tales themselves are devoted to censoring those instincts rather than fulfilling them. The heroes and heroines of his imaginings are brave fugitives from carnality—meek and humble adventurers who win by renouncing victory, lovers whose sensibilities are so untuned to crudity that their failing to find happiness becomes a mark of their superiority. In his tales, Andersen declared himself the champion of innocence and the enemy of pride, desire, and ambition.

He wrote love-stories by the dozen—**"The Little Mermaid," "Thumbelina," "The Steadfast Tin Soldier," "The Shepherdess and the Chimney Sweep," "The Sweethearts"** and **"The Bog King's Daughter"** are perhaps the most famous. Through them all runs one story, the basic Andersen fantasy. The central character is small, frail, more likely to be female than male—above all, *delicate,* an embodiment of that innocence which is harmlessness, that purity which is incapacity for lust. He/she is usually incapable of ordinary motion, physically unsuited to pursuit and consummation: the tin soldier has only one leg, the mermaid has no legs at all, Thumbelina is carried from place to place as if she were crippled. Andersen's imagination is much taken with *statues* as the emblem of chaste erotic feeling: the tin soldier and his ballerina are inanimate figurines, the shepherdess and the chimney sweep are made of porcelain, the little mermaid falls in love with a marble

statue before she ever sees the prince in the flesh. (It is fitting that Copenhagen has immortalized the little mermaid herself as a statue.) In another story, **"Psyche,"** the hero creates a statue of the girl he loves, the pristine symbol of his devotion. The girl herself rejects him.

Andersen's ideal lovers are often rejected. A few of the folk-tales he retold—such as **"The Tinderbox"**—end with the hero married and living happily ever after; but the stories he made up himself do not. Usually something prevents marriage—rejection, misunderstanding, snobbery, fate. At the end of **"The Bog King's Daughter,"** the heroine steps out onto a balcony on her wedding night and just disappears. Andersen doesn't care very much if love is satisfied in this world, since the conclusion his fantasy really works toward is splendid, mystical death—the launching out of the soul into the infinite, leaving troublesome flesh behind. "It is lovely to fly from love to love, from earth into heaven," says Andersen, describing the death of the hero in **"The Ice Maiden."** "A string snapped, a mournful tone was heard. Death's kiss of ice was victorious against corruption."[8] Similarly, the little mermaid leaves her body behind and becomes a daughter of the air. The tin soldier and the ballerina die together in flames, he melting into a tin heart and she reduced to a bright spangle. The shepherdess and the chimney sweep "loved each other until they broke" (301). Thumbelina dons white wings and flies away with her fairy-lover, who is "almost transparent, as if he were made of glass" (37). The bog king's daughter becomes "one single beautiful ray of light, that shot upward to God" (584).

Physical sensuality in these stories tends to be pictured as grasping, slimy, and disgusting. Thumbelina is coaxed, abducted, clutched at by a toad and her son, a fat black mole, and an ugly insect before she flies away to the fairy-king; the shepherdess is pursued by a satyr who had "a long beard, . . . little horns sticking out of his forehead and the legs of a goat" (297). The princess in **"The Bog King's Daughter"** is shudderingly embraced by an "ancient king; a mummy, black as pitch, glittering like the black slugs that creep in the forest" (574). Frequently the physical ordeal Andersen's lovers must go through in pursuit of transcendent love is a descent into dark, close, filthy places—the tin soldier floats down a gutter into a sewer and is swallowed by a fish; the shepherdess and the chimney sweep have to creep up and down a chimney flue; the ball and the top met in a garbage bin where "all kinds of things were lying: gravel, a cabbage stalk, dirt, dust, and lots of leaves that had fallen down from the gutter" (214).

Andersen's sharpest vision of sensual horror is in **"The Little Mermaid."** There the heroine, smitten with love for a human prince, sets out to find what she must do to make him love her in return. The grotesque ordeal Andersen contrives for her is a direct fantasy-enactment of the idea that, in order to be a wife, a girl must submit to rape. She must "divide her tail," and the experience is an excruciating one. She has to travel down to a terrible forest in the deepest part of the ocean, through polyps "like snakes with hundreds of heads," with "long slimy arms, and they had fingers as supple as worms" that reach out to grab her as she "held both her hands folded tightly across her breast" and hurries past (67, 68).

> At last she came to a great, slimy open place in the middle of the forest. Big fat eels played in the mud, showing their ugly yellow stomachs. . . . Here the witch . . . sat letting a big ugly toad eat out of her mouth, as human beings sometimes let a canary eat sugar candy out of theirs. The ugly eels she called her little chickens, and held them close to her spongy chest. (68)

The witch tells her that if the prince is to love her, she must lose her tail with a sensation of having her body pierced by a sword. "The little mermaid drank the potion, and it felt as if a sword were piercing her body. She fainted and lay as though she were dead." (70)

Nowhere else in classic children's literature is there so terrified a vision of sex, seen through the eyes of innocence. The scene in **"The Ice Maiden"** where Rudy accepts death as his lover is calm by comparison:

> He threw his arms around her and looked into her marvelous clear eyes for a second. Only for a second! And how is one to describe, to tell in words, what he saw in that fraction of a moment? What was it that overpowered him—a ghost? Or was it a bit of life that exists in death? Had he been lifted upward or had he been plunged into a deep, death-filled world of ice?

When she kisses him, "the eternal coldness penetrated his backbone and touched his forehead" (772). Here, as elsewhere, Andersen compresses into one scene the contradictory ideas that death is erotic, and that one can escape eroticism by dying. Something of that same paradox is present in another Andersen story, **"The Garden of Eden,"** which posits sex as original sin. A young prince falls from innocence by kissing the lips of a beautiful naked woman, and death is both the reward and punishment for his action.

> A fearful clap of thunder was heard, deeper, more frightening than any ever heard before. The fairy vanished and the garden of Eden sank into the earth: deep, deep down. The prince saw it disappear into the dark night like a far distant star. He felt a deathly coldness touch his limbs; his eyes closed, and he fell down as though he were dead. (143)

This troubled view of sex is important even in Andersen stories which are not explicitly about erotic subjects,

for it explains his obsession with innocence in many forms. *Innocence* is the watchword in Andersen's fantasies. No virtue rates so high with him as child-like purity, by which he means freedom from adult desire, ambition, and thought. He found inspiration of a sort in folk-tales, because they often begin with heroes who are simple, humble and childlike. But he had to change the folk-tale pattern in order to bring out his personal fantasies. The traditional folk-tale shows its protagonist's growth and happiness directly; he gets money, love and power—as for instance in Andersen's own re-telling of **"The Tinderbox,"** in which a soldier seizes a princess, kills her father, and ascends to the throne; or **"Little Claus and Big Claus,"** in which an underdog-hero kills his rival and gets rich. The stories that Andersen made up himself turn this pattern inside out. Like folk-tale heroes, Andersen's start poor—but his stories demonstrate that the poor in spirit are blessed. Like them, Andersen's heroes hurl themselves into life—but discover that they would do better to die and be with God. In an Andersen story, it is better to be the peasant girl who can hear the nightingale than the chamberlain who cannot (**"The Nightingale"**); better to be little Gerda, who trusts and believes and wants to stay at home than Kay, who "gets a piece of the Devil's glass in his eye" and questions and criticizes and explores (**"The Snow Queen"**).

In story after story, Andersen makes fun of and punishes people who care about money and power and artifice and prestige and critical judgment; he celebrates the humble and long-suffering and credulous and sentimental. His attitude belongs partly to Christian asceticism, and partly to nineteenth-century Romantic primitivism, sentimentalism, and anti-intellectualism, and no doubt takes many of its forms and phrases from those philosophies. But for Andersen personally the value of innocence is closely tied to his nightmarish view of sex, a fact which is easily discernible in several of his most famous stories. For him, to be innocent is, first and foremost, to expunge or repress one's sexual urges.

One especially graphic case in point here is his tale **"The Red Shoes,"** a story Andersen found to be a particular favorite in the Puritan strongholds of Scotland, Holland, and the United States. Read in the loosest, most abstract terms, the story is a parable on the idea that pride goeth before a fall: a pretty girl, preoccupied with beauty and finery, shows her vanity, is punished for it, and learns her lesson. But given the concrete details of Andersen's personal fantasy, the story vibrates with sexual panic, celebrating innocence that is won through the repression of sexuality.

Andersen records that **"The Red Shoes"** was inspired by a memory from his youth: "In *The Fairy Tale of My Life,* I have told how I received for my confirmation my first pair of boots; and how they squeaked as

I walked up the aisle of the church; this pleased me no end, for I felt that now the whole congregation must know that my boots are new. But at the same time my conscience bothered me terribly, for I was aware that I was thinking as much about my new boots as I was about our Lord."⁹ Out of that bothersome conscience came Andersen's story, with the new boots transformed to red shoes, and Andersen, the boy wearing them, transformed to a pretty girl named Karen.

What Andersen consciously thinks of as an emblem of pride and vanity, he unconsciously imbues with sexual significance in a number of ways. First, he gives his heroine the name of his scandalous half-sister, the one who disappeared into the red-light districts of Copenhagen and later embarrassed her brother by turning up with a common-law husband. Shoe and foot-symbolism tends to be sexual in many uses—the Old Testament and other folk-literatures often say "feet" as a euphemism for sexual organs, and foot-fetishism is a common neurotic device for expressing forbidden interest in the genitals. That **"The Red Shoes"** emanates from Andersen's memory of a ritual of puberty, and of his flaunting the new boots he had for that occasion, also helps to place it psychologically. Andersen emphasizes the sexual quality by making Karen's shoes red, the traditional color of unruly passion, and by making them dancing shoes, with a power to catch her up and carry her away against her conscious will: "Once she had begun, her feet would not stop. It was as if the shoes had taken command of them. . . . her will was not her own." (291) Giving herself over to their excitement, she faces the debility Andersen associated with sexual excess: "You shall dance in your red shoes until you become pale and thin. Dance till the skin on your face turns yellow and clings to your bones as if you were a skeleton." (292)

She must first acquire the red shoes against her mother's wishes; it is a man who sets them doing their fearful, orgiastic dancing, an old soldier with "a marvelously long beard that was red with touches of white in it" (291). When he touches them, they begin dancing.

The shoes "grow fast" to Karen's feet and will not come off—they are part of her body. The only way she can purge their evil is to cut off the offending members. "Do not cut off my head," she begs the executioner, "for then I would not be able to repent. But cut off my feet!" (293) He does as she asks, and she becomes like Andersen's other acceptable lovers: crippled. For a time thoughts of the lost sexuality still linger—she sees the red shoes dancing before her when she tries to go to church. Finally, in an agony of contrition and self-reproach, she wins God's mercy, and He sends His sunshine: "The sunshine filled Karen's heart till it so swelled with peace and happiness that it broke. Her soul flew on a sunbeam up to God; and up there no one asked her about the red shoes." (294)

"The Red Shoes" is a harrowing, gothic little tale, to be sure, and that may help explain its popularity. Actually, it doesn't succeed very well in advancing the dry moral idea that we should be humble and love God better than ourselves. What the solid events of the story convey is rather the idea that there is something we are tempted to do with our feet, but old ladies and ministers and angels don't want us to do it. If we refuse to listen to their warnings, a leering old man will touch our feet and set them working and we won't be able to stop. Then we'll be glad to have the grown-ups chop them off, and to be allowed to die and go to God. I suppose there is more than one way to say what that fantasy means; but any description which fails to account for the evocative image of the red-bearded man touching the girl's feet and setting them dancing uncontrollably has hardly done it justice.

Andersen himself was aware—at least partly—of the psychological links between his inhibited sexuality and his artistic creativity, his wish for fame as an artist, and his longing for death. The story **"Psyche"** shows clearly that he believed that his pursuit of ideal beauty and immortality through art and religion sprang from sexual longings that he could not allow himself to fulfill.

"Psyche" is the story of a young artist, poor and unknown, who strives for perfection in his art, but cannot produce anything that satisfies him. His worldly friends tell him he is too much the dreamer: "You have not tasted life. You ought to take a big healthy swallow and enjoy it." (786) They invite him to join them in their orgies and he is excited—"his blood ran swiftly through his body, his imagination was strong" (786). But he cannot bring himself to go with them—he feels "within himself a purity, a sense of piety" that stops him, and turns him toward working in clay and marble instead, as a superior alternative to physical lust. "What he wanted to describe [in his sculpture] was how his heart sought and sensed infinity, but how was he to do it?" (786)

The answer is that he sees a girl, just in passing, and falls in love. At first he makes no attempt to approach her; he turns his attention to a mental image he has of her, as she becomes "alive in his mind." He sets to work on a statue of her, made from marble he has to dig out from heaps of "broken glass," "discarded vegetables," "the tops of fennel and the rotten leaves of artichokes" (787). With these materials—a fantasy-image snatched from a passing glimpse of a beautiful girl, and white marble extracted from the filth of ordinary life—the artist constructs an image of perfect beauty.

He wants to believe that he now has what his friends have—only better. "Now I know what life is," he rejoices. "It is love! It is to be able to appreciate loveliness and to delight in beauty. And what my friends call 'life' is nothing but empty vanity, bubbles from the fermentation of the dregs, instead of the pure wine, drunk at the altar to consecrate life." (787) But despite this brave speech, he finds that his feelings for the statue are rooted in those "dregs" of erotic passion. He desires not just the idea of beauty, but the girl herself. "Soon both God and his tears were forgotten; instead he thought of his Psyche, who stood before him, looking as if she had been cut out of snow and blushing in the light of the dawn. He was going to see her: the living, breathing girl who stepped so lightly, as if she walked on air, the girl whose innocent words were music." (788)

His attempt to make love to the girl is a disaster. "He grabbed her hand and kissed it, and he thought it was softer than a rose petal and yet it inflamed him. He was so excited, so aroused, that he hardly knew what he was saying; words gushed out of his mouth and he could no more control their flow than the crater can stop the volcano from vomiting burning lava. He told her how much he loved her." (789) Contemptuously she spurns him.

His lust aroused, the young artist yields to his friends' coaxing and spends a riotous night with some beautiful peasant girls. Andersen's metaphors convey the sexual excitement, release, and disappointment he feels: "The flower of life . . . bloomed, bent its head, and withered. A strange, horrible smell of corruption blended itself with the odor of roses, it lamed his mind and blinded his sight. The fireworks of sensuality were over and darkness came." (791) Sickened with guilt, he buries the beautiful statue, enters a monastery, and begins a lifelong struggle to suppress the "unclean, evil thoughts" that spring up inside. "He punished his body, but the evil did not come from the surface but from deep within him" (793). He dies at last, his body and bones rot away, and the centuries pass over the unmarked grave of the statue which his love inspired him to make. At last, workmen digging a grave in a convent unearth the statue. No one knows the name of its creator. "But his gain, his profit from his struggle, and his search, the glory that proved the godliness within him, his Psyche, will never die. It will live beyond the name of its creator. His spark still shines here on earth and is admired, appreciated, and loved." (795)

What Andersen says in this elaborate parable is that the erotic hunger which other men feed with "a big healthy swallow of life"—"not only the bread, but the baker woman"—has for him been diverted to a hunger for ideal beauty and fame and spirituality. But he can find no satisfaction in these ideals; he goes to his grave cursing "the strange flames that seemed to set his body on fire." The statue he has made is beautiful, perfect, and his own, a product of his imagination inspired by passion. But there is no primary gratification to be had from it—only highly theoretical pleasure in the hope that this embodied fantasy would constitute a "gain, his profit from his struggle and his search, the glory that proved the godliness within him."

Andersen's stories are like the artist's statue—mined from the "dregs" and "filth" of ordinary life, with energy that might otherwise have been spent in sensual revels. Their substance is the stuff of desire, the drive for love and power; but the art that shapes them is self-doubt and anxiety and troubled conscience. So they become in the end monuments to chastity and innocence, a marble statue in a nun's grave: no abiding satisfaction to their creator, but still something to be admired by others, "his spark that still shines here on earth and is admired, appreciated, and loved." Thus, finally, and by a most circuitous route, is the desire for love and eminence to be fulfilled, for Andersen.

Notes

[1] Sigmund Freud, "On the Relation of the Poet to Day-Dreaming," trans. Joan Riviere, *et al.,* in *On Creativity and the Unconscious,* ed. Benjamin Nelson (New York: Harper & Row, 1958), 47.

[2] Elias Bredsdorff, *Hans Christian Andersen: The Story of His Life and Work 1805-1875* (New York; Scribner's, 1975), 16.

[3] Hans Christian Andersen, *The Fairy Tale of My Life: An Autobiography,* trans. Horace E. Scudder (1871; rpt. New York: Paddington, 1975), 8.

[4] *The Fairy Tale of My Life,* 21.

[5] *The Fairy Tale of My Life,* 9.

[6] Quoted by Bredsdorff, 20.

[7] Quoted by Bredsdorff, 281.

[8] Hans Christian Andersen, *The Complete Fairy Tales and Stories,* trans. Erik Christian Haugaard (New York: Doubleday, 1974), 772. All quotations from Andersen's stories are from this edition, with page numbers cited parenthetically in the text.

[9] Andersen's note on "The Red Shoes," *The Complete Fairy Tales and Stories,* 1075.

Celia Catlett Anderson (essay date 1986)

SOURCE: "Andersen's Heroes and Heroines: Relinquishing the Reward," in *Triumphs of the Spirit in Children's Literature,* edited by Francelia Butler and Richard Rotert, Library Professional Publications, 1986, pp. 122-26.

[In the following essay, Anderson argues that the endings of Andersen's fairy tales do not convey pessimism but that they instead express the "triumph of the Spirit" and the optimism and wisdom of remaining true to one's ideals and one's self.]

Hans Christian Andersen's fairy tales have sometimes been described as too adult or too pessimistic for children. For example, May Hill Arbuthnot in her classic *Children and Books,* although praising Andersen as an allegorist, notes that "because of the double meaning, the adult themes, and the sadness of many of these stories, the whole collection is usually not popular with children."[1] P. L. Travers found a "devitalizing element" of nostalgia in the tales.[2] Bruno Bettelheim has commented that the conclusions of some of Andersen's stories are discouraging in that "they do not convey the feeling of consolation characteristic of fairy tales," and Jack Zipes accuses Andersen of teaching lessons in servility to the young.[3] Andersen's tales continue, however to be published, read, discussed, and used as a basis for children's theater, and the most popular of them have an undeniable appeal for children. Furthermore, the most popular tales, such as **"The Ugly Duckling," "The Little Mermaid," "The Steadfast Tin Soldier," "The Little Fir Tree,"** and **"The Nightingale,"** include for the most part, those stories that were original with Andersen. His view of the world, then, the problems he poses and the solutions he offers must touch some nerve in us; there must be something more to them than simple pessimism, more than a servile call to compromise.

Andersen does indeed often deliberately undercut the facile happy ending that is the trademark of fairy tales, but are his many characters who fail to win a reward defeated in spirit? I would argue that they are not. Take the one that may be, perhaps, saddest of all his protagonists, the little fir tree (or pine tree as Erik Haugaard translates it).[4] The tree fails to appreciate its youth in the forest, is bewildered and frightened during its one glorious evening as a baubled Christmas tree, is exiled to an attic, and there is unable to hold an audience of mice who want to hear stories of "bacon or candle stumps" (232), not of "How Humpty-dumpty Fell Down the Stairs but Won the Princess Anyway" (229). Hauled out into the spring sunlight, the pine tree is forced to recognize that it is a dead thing among the green renewal of the season and achieves its one brief moment of wisdom: "If I only could have been happy while I had a chance to be" (233). Finally the poor tree is burned, sighing its sap away in shots, and "Every time the tree sighed, it thought of a summer day in the forest, or a winter night when the stars are brightest, and it remembered Christmas Eve and Humpty-dumpty: the only fairy tale it had ever heard and knew how to tell. Then it became ashes" (233). The tree dies unfulfilled, yes, but in one sense undefeated. It never loses its vision of the possibility of beauty in the world. Like King Lear, the tree is ennobled by wisdom that comes too late.

When we read this tale to our son, then eight years old, he had tears in his eyes and commented that it was the saddest story he had ever heard. Initially, I judged this as a negative reaction, a rejection of the story, but I was wrong. He returned to the story again and again. Like the small boy who rips the golden star from the tree's branch and pins it to his chest, our son took something shining from the story and, for all I know, wears it to this day.

Of course not all of Andersen's tales end sadly. Even considering only those stories that are not simply retellings of old folktales (and therefore with conventional conclusions), we can find several types of endings. There are some which express religious optimism, and some which reward the hero or heroine with acceptance and love. Stories in the first group are rather self-consciously overlaid with Christianity and conclude optimistically. To mention only one of these, consider **"The Old Oak Tree's Last Dream,"** a story quite different in tone and message from **"The Pine Tree."** The oak lives three hundred and sixty-five years, many of them as a landmark for sailors. It pities the mayflies and flowers for their short existences, but learns in a death dream of ascension into a joyous heaven that "Nothing has been forgotten, not the tiniest flower or the smallest bird" (548-49). The story concludes

> The tree itself lay stretched out on the snow-covered beach. From the ship came the sound of sailors singing a carol about the joyful season, when Christ was born to save mankind and give us eternal life. The sailors were singing of the same dream, the beautiful dream that the old oak tree had dreamed Christmas Eve: the last night of its life. (549)

At least for the believer, this conclusion is more encouraging than that which gives the pine tree only ashes of regret.

Another class of stories in Andersen does include more tangible rewards. In these, the protagonists win acceptance by remaining true to their natures and persisting in some quest or duty. **"The Ugly Duckling"** comes immediately to mind, but perhaps **"The Nightingale"** is an even better example. In that tale, the small bird is as plain and dull in plumage at the end as at the beginning, but its ability to remain natural, to sing a spontaneous, honest song finally wins it the respect of the emperor who has been saved by the power of its singing and now realizes the false choice he made in earlier preferring the bejewelled, mechanical bird who can sing only one song. Of all Andersen's stories, this may be the one in which the triumph of spirit over matter is most simply and directly presented.

Love is the ultimate form of acceptance, and the tale **"The Snow Queen"** most fully elaborates this theme. Bettelheim concedes that this tale belongs among the tales that console.[5] An allegory of reason versus love, **"The Snow Queen"** is, like all allegories, explicitly symbolic, and this very explicitness makes the story a good choice for analysis.

The childhood paradise of Gerda and Kai is blighted by Kai's growing away from Gerda into a cynical stage of adolescence (symbolized by the splinters of the mirror of reason that have entered his eyes and heart and by the numbing kisses of the Snow Queen who kidnaps him). Gerda, like the sister in Andersen's re-told folktale **"The Wild Swans,"** endures much suffering before she is able to restore Kai to his natural state as a warm-hearted, loving person. The story is a classic example of what Marie-Louise von Franz describes as the projection of anima—the suffering, brave woman as a projection of the man's problem with his feminine side. In this case the identification is very appropriately used since Gerda, in bringing about the union of intellect and emotion, is indeed a Sophia-like figure.

The story is one of Andersen's most successful blendings of Christian and folk elements. It contains not only many magical creatures (the Snow Queen herself, a talking raven, and a Finnish white witch), but also a hymn in place of the usual incantation, angels formed from the breath of prayers, and a wise old grandmother who knows both the language of ravens and that of the Bible. After Gerda, through her persistence, reaches the ice castle and frees Kai with her warm tears, the two retrace her steps and finally arrive back at the old grandmother's apartment. Andersen tells us that "as they stepped through the doorway they realized that they had grown: they were no longer children" (261). But the grandmother is reading "Whosoever shall not receive the Kingdom of Heaven as a little child shall not enter therein" (261). Kai and Gerda understand the lesson and "There they sat, the two of them grownups; and yet in their hearts children; and it was summer: a warm glorious summer day!" (261). In choosing that particular text from the New Testament, Andersen voices a central theme shared by Christian theologians and writers for children. For the child, and for all of us, the test of spirit is to grow into intellectual wisdom without losing the capacity for emotion, for love.

Certainly this is a central theme with Andersen himself. Elizabeth Cook holds that "two of his strongest themes are the plight of the outsider, and the primacy of Love over Reason."[6] We see these ideas combined in two tales where the endings are unhappy and love must be its own reward. In both **"The Little Mermaid"** and **"The Steadfast Tin Soldier"** the main characters persist and suffer and do not win. These stories, along with **"The Pine Tree," "The Little Match Girl,"** and that very complex Andersen tale **"The Shadow,"** are probably most responsible for the author's reputation for pessimism. The mermaid *is* promised eternal life at the last minute, but in this story the Christian promise is not as successfully woven into the plot as it is in some others (the tale always seems to me to end with the mermaid's dissolution into foam). Are these stories, then, about the defeat of the spirit? As I said earlier, I think not. Neither the mermaid nor the tin soldier turn aside from their goal, nor do they become bitter or vengeful. Through many trials they continue to be humane and loving. Many of Andersen's heroes and heroines, though they suffer greatly, remain true to their ideals. If not rewarded, neither are they defeated. And the true triumph of the spirit, after all, consists not in winning the prince or princess, the kingdom or riches, or even immortality, but in being worthy of the winning.

Much that is written for and about children springs from the premise that the young need the hope and encouragement provided by the success of the hero in the stories presented to them, and that they cannot cope with models of failure. This may be true for certain ages and types, but it is in many cases a condescending and even dishonest attitude. Hope can help develop a child, but false hope can absolutely devastate. Hans Christian Andersen knew that when Humpty-dumpty fell, he didn't win the princess anyway and that a storyteller who claims he did is a liar and, further, that an innocent, like the foolish pine tree, who believes the lie will reap much unhappiness.

The child who comes to Andersen for spiritual sustenance will learn that we must both test our dreams and be tested by them and that in this world some bright dreams have gray awakenings. Will this harm or strengthen a child? I think it strengthened our own children, that our son drank courage, not despair, from the tears he shed over the story of the pine tree. In Andersen's tale **"The Pixy and the Grocer"** the pixy peeks through the keyhole and sees the turbulent visions that the poor student enjoys while sitting under the magic tree of poetry. Before such splendor, the pixy "experienced greatness. . . . He cried without knowing why he cried, but found that in those tears happiness was hidden" (426). So art redeems us; as Tolkien put it so well in his famous essay on children and fairy stories, "It is one of the lessons of fairy stories (if we can speak of the lessons of things that do not lecture) that on callow, lumpish, and selfish youth peril, sorrow, and the shadow of death can bestow dignity and even sometimes wisdom."[7] Hans Christian Andersen gives us in his stories "peril, sorrow, and the shadow of death" but also "dignity" and "wisdom."

Notes

[1] May Hill Arbuthnot and Zena Sutherland, *Children and Books,* 4th ed. (Glenview, Ill.: Scott, Foresman, 1972), 313.

[2] P. L. Travers, "Only Connect," *Quarterly Journal of Acquisitions of the Library of Congress* (October 1967); repr. in *Only Connect: Readings on Children's Literature,* ed. Sheila Egoff, G. T. Stubbs, and L. F. Ashley (New York: Oxford University Press, 1969), p. 198.

3 Bruno Bettelheim, *The Uses of Enchantment: The Meaning and Importance of Fairy Tales* (New York: Knopf, 1976), 37; Jack Zipes, *Fairy Tales and the Art of Subversion: The Classical Genre for Children and the Process of Civilization* (New York: Wildman Press, 1983), 94.

4 Hans Christian Andersen, *The Complete Fairy Tales and Stories,* trans. Erik Haugaard (Garden City, N. Y.: Doubleday, 1983). Page numbers for quotes from this edition are given in the text.

5 Bettelheim, *Uses of Enchantment,* 37.

6 Elizabeth Cook, *The Ordinary and the Fabulous: An Introduction to Myths, Legends, and Fairy Tales for Teachers and Storytellers* (London: Cambridge University Press, 1971), 43.

7 J. R. R. Tolkien, "Children and Fairy Stories," from *Tree and Leaf,* in Sheila Egoff, G. T. Stubbs, and L. F. Ashley, *Only Connect,* New York: Oxford University Press, 1969, p. 120.

Jon Cech (essay date 1987)

SOURCE: "Hans Christian Andersen's Fairy Tales and Stories: Secrets, Swans and Shadows," in *Touchstones: Reflections on the Best in Children's Literature,* Vol. 2: *Fairy Tales, Fables, Myths, Legends, and Poetry,* Children's Literature Association, 1987, pp. 14-23.

[*In the essay following, Cech discusses the optimistic and pessimistic aspects of Andersen's fairy tales, relating them to the "competing sides of [Andersen's] nature."*]

Among the 156 "tales and stories" that Hans Christian Andersen wrote between 1835 and 1872, a dozen or so are among the best-known, most frequently anthologized and reprinted retellings of fairy tales or literary fairy tales of any canon. Indeed, such stories as **"The Ugly Duckling," "The Princess and the Pea,"** and **"The Emperor's New Clothes"** have been retold so often, and in so many different forms, that they have become part of the public domain of our oral folk tradition. Bo Grønbech claims that Anderson's tales have been translated into over a hundred languages; only the Bible and Shakespeare have been translated into more. Not long after the appearance of the first of Andersen's tales, one of his friends had quipped that Andersen's novels and plays might make him famous in Denmark, but his fairy tales would make him immortal. The friend's intuitive pronouncement has not been far off the mark.

This enormous success could not have been more unlikely, more unexpected than it was for Andersen, the son of a poor washerwoman and a melancholy cobbler from the Danish coastal town of Odense. When the fourteen-year-old Andersen left for Copenhagen in 1819, with thirteen thalers in his pocket and without an education, a trade or prospects, only two people in the world believed he would ever amount to anything: the local fortune-teller and Andersen himself. In *The Fairy Tale of My Life,* Andersen tells how, in her anxiety, his mother had consulted this "wise old woman," who had, after reading her cards and Andersen's coffee grounds, reassured her with the now famous prediction: "Your son will become a great man, and in honor of him Odense will one day be illuminated" (22). Andersen begged his mother to let him go to Copenhagen to seek his fortune there; he had dreamed that something wonderful would happen to him. "First one has to endure terrible adversity," he told his mother. "Then one becomes famous" (Stirling 53).

And suffer he had and did. The facts are well-documented in the numerous biographies of Andersen and in his diaries and *The Fairy Tale of My Life,* the autobiography which he revised frequently during his life. The grinding poverty of his childhood and youth, the desperate, depressing struggle for this lad from the wrong social class to climb the ladder of literary success, the unhappiness in his romantic life, the restless travelling, the hysteric phobias (of rabies, hotel fires, or being accidentally thought dead while asleep and buried alive), the "black" moods that swept over him—all are revealed by his biographers and more often than not by Andersen himself. He was, he informs us, the ugly duckling, the lowest in the town's pecking order—awkward, painfully sensitive, vulnerable—the brunt of crude jokes and coarse criticism. Famous as he later became, he never quite got over those early traumas, or the later scars. But they became the fuel of his fantasies and the substance of his stories. Reginald Spink quotes Andersen's own words to support that idea: "Most of what I have written is a reflection of myself. Every character is from life. I know and have known them all" (70). Spink observes:

> Andersen never stopped telling his own story; that was the way he abreacted. Sometimes he tells it in an idealized form, sometimes with self-revelatory candour. In tale after tale—**"The Tinder Box," "Little Claus and Big Claus," "The Steadfast Tin Soldier," "The Swineherd," "The Ugly Duckling"**—he is the hero who triumphs over poverty, persecution, and plain stupidity, and who sometimes, in reversal of the facts, marries the princess (**"Clodpoll"**) or scorns her (**"The Swineherd"**). (100)

For Andersen, the creative process was an act of remembering, of stating and then transforming biographical facts in order to somehow exorcise the demons that haunted him, those shadows that never quite stopped threatening to take over the poet and his identity.

But there are lives and there are lives. Not every *roman à clef* becomes a best-seller, let alone a classic; and not every reified life experience succeeds as a work of literature. In many of his fairy tales and stories, Andersen offered his readers a theme and its variations which was not only personal to him, but also had and continues to have a universal appeal: the rags-to-riches, duckling-to-swan theme. Every swineherd or common soldier is a potential prince, and every ugly duckling a swan, if they are true to their own good, decent nature. This idea, which appears with such frequency in Andersen's works, creates an immediate bond of identification and sympathy between Andersen and his readers, especially his younger readers who, like numerous heroes and heroines in Andersen, are struggling and are desperately in need of stories that frame the chaotic and conflicting emotions of this experience. In his tales Andersen is the champion of the underdogs, the downtrodden, the spurned, the impoverished—in short, those with every reason to hope for whatever transformations will lead to a better life.

Of course, this sense of hope, of a brighter and ultimately happy future (if one perseveres and remains good and kind in the process of enduring) is at the very core of the traditional fairy tale, as Bruno Bettelheim has pointed out in *The Uses of Enchantment.* Andersen had drawn his inspiration and the vehicle for expressing this theme from the traditional fairy tales that, he tells us in the notes he wrote to accompany his stories, he "had heard as a child, either in the spinning room or during the harvesting of the hops" (1071). Unlike other Romantic artists who also used the form and subject matter of the folk fairy tale, Andersen did not have to learn about his material second hand through study or from collecting trips in the countryside. He was steeped in its traditions; the world of the fairy tale "was his own world and had been so since birth" (Grønbech 95). This oral/aural sense of story, he felt, was important to capture, and he tried to do this, beginning with his first volume of stories which appeared in 1835. Of the four stories in this volume (**"The Tinder Box," "Little Claus and Big Claus," "The Princess and the Pea,"** and **"Little Ida's Flowers"**), only the last was an original creation. The others were based on tales from the oral tradition, but elaborated upon in Andersen's inimitable style. His life-long friend, Edvard Collin, remembers how Andersen, during visits to his house, would tell the Collin children

> stories which he partly made up on the spur of the moment, partly borrowed from well-known fairy tales; but whether the tale was his own or a retelling, the manner of telling it was entirely his own, and so full of life that the children were delighted. He, too, took delight in letting his humor run free. He spoke continually with plenty of phrases that children used, and gestures to match. Even the driest of sentences was given life. He didn't say, "The children got into the carriage and then drove away," but, "So they got into the carriage, good-bye Daddy, good-bye Mummy, the whip cracked, snick, snack, and away they went, giddy up!" People who later heard him reading aloud his tales would only be able to form a faint impression of the extraordinary vitality with which he told them to children. (Grønbech 89)

We hear this surging verbal energy in the swaggering first paragraph of Andersen's first published fairy tale—**"The Tinderbox."**:

> A soldier came marching down the road: Left . . . right! Left . . . right! He had a pack on his back and a sword at his side. He had been in the war and he was on his way home. Along the road he met a witch. She was a disgusting sight, with a lower lip that hung all the way down her chest.

Andersen wrote to a friend as he was finishing this first collection, which he called *Fairy Tales for Children,* to explain what he was doing: "I want to win the next generations, you see!" (Grønbech 89) But by 1843, he had changed the title of those little volumes, containing three or four stories each, to *Fairy Tales;* and, within another ten years, they became, simply, *Stories.* But it had not taken Andersen twenty years before he "found out how to write fairy tales." Within a few years of beginning the stories, he wrote to a friend to say: "Now I tell stories of my own accord, seize an idea for the adults—and then tell it for the children while still keeping in mind the fact that mother and father are often listening too, and they must have a little something for thought" (Grønbech 91-2).

We see Andersen's concern with reaching the adult listening to (or reading the tale) throughout the fairy tales and stories. Andersen can't resist such an "adult" touch in **"The Ugly Duckling,"** for example, when an old duck comes to call on the mother duck who has just hatched out her brood (except for the ugly duckling's egg). She brags to her guest that each of the new ducklings "looks exactly like their father." But then she quickly adds: "That scoundrel hasn't come to visit me once" (217). In **"The Nightingale,"** after the bird has been summoned to the emperor's palace and has made the monarch weep with his music, Andersen, with his tongue in his cheek, describes the trickle-down effects of the concert:

> "That was the most charming and elegant song we have ever heard," said all the ladies of the court. And from that time onward they filled their mouths with water, so they could make a clucking noise, whenever anyone spoke to them, because they thought that then they sounded like the nightingale. Even the chambermaids and the lackeys were satisfied; and that really meant something, for servants are the most difficult to please. Yes, the nightingale was a success. (207)

But there is more than just "a little something for thought" for the adults in many of the stories that Andersen began to include in these collections. Take, for instance, **"The Sweethearts,"** a tale about a wooden top and the leather ball with which he is in love. She rejects his attentions, telling him that "mother and father were a pair of morocco slippers, and . . . I have a cork inside me." The ball gets lost on her ninth bounce, but the top, still very much in love with her, stays on as a favored plaything in the house, eventually getting rewarded with a coat of gold paint. Years later when he, too, is lost one day, he winds up in the same trash can as the ball. Her years of exposure have left her unrecognizable, but she proudly announces herself as before. At that moment the maid finds the top and retrieves him from the trash, never noticing the ball. And Andersen leaves the reader with the biting (and male chauvinist) commentary about life and love: "You get over it when your beloved has lain in a gutter and oozed for five years. You never recognize her when you meet her in the garbage bin" (215).

Similarly, stories like **"The Shadow,"** have pushed beyond the boundaries of the literary fairy tale to become psychological fantasies directed toward an older reader. This story, one of Andersen's darkest and most enigmatic, examines what happens when a young scholar, an intellectual, sends his shadow across the street to the house of a beautiful woman, who turns out to be Poetry, while he himself remains aloof and detached, engrossed in his philosophical treatises and reveries on the other side of the street. Years pass, the scholar travels and writes, and the shadow, meanwhile, takes on a human form and a life of its own, becoming richly successful because it can peep into mankind's deepest secrets and because "he knew how to tell about some of what he had seen and how to hint at the rest, which was even more impressive" (342). Through an ironic reversal of events befitting a writer like Kafka, the philosopher becomes the shadow's shadow; the shadow goes on to marry the princess, and the philosopher, in the closing lines of the story, is executed. As the shadow has told the philosopher when he objects to the absurdity of becoming the shadow's servant, "that's the way of the world, and it isn't going to change" (341).

Andersen was criticized for writing such pessimistic and unfamiliar tales—such "philosophical" stories. He responded to his critics in the notes to his collected stories by arguing that "through the years . . . (he) tried to walk every radius, so to speak, in the circle of the fairy tale." The problem lay, Andersen felt, with some of those who had grown up with his earlier stories and thus expected a particular kind of tale from him. Somehow they had "lost the fresh spirit with which they once approached and absorbed literature (1087). To an extent, that is still true today. The popular notion of Andersen is that he is a writer or adapter of fairly traditional fairy tales; he has yet to receive the recognition he deserves as one of the pioneers and important innovators not only in the form of the literary fairy tale, but also in the forms of fantasy (what Andersen collectively referred to as the "wonder tale"). Tales like **"The Millennium"** (which begins: "They will home on wings of steam, the young citizens of America will fly through the air, across the great ocean, to visit old Europe.") are at the threshold of science fiction. **"Auntie Toothache,"** the last story that Andersen wrote, is a grotesquely absurd visit to a nineteenth century Twilight Zone, where a young poet is visited in his dream by the archetypal spirit of tooth problems. Andersen serves up the malaise to us in the form of an aunt who, in the waking world, has over-indulged the poet with sweets and with encouragement to keep writing his sentimental verse. In the young man's nightmare, though, "Auntie Toothache" treats him to an "Ode to Pain" on his wisdom teeth and forces him to admit that her power is "greater than poetry, mathematics, philosophy, and all the rest of the music . . . stronger and more penetrating than all other feeling that has been painted on canvas or carved in marble . . . older than all the others . . . born right outside the gates of paradise, where the wet winds blow and the toadstools grow" (1066). She leaves only when the poet, in a dental delirium, agrees to stop writing verse forever. Andersen wrote this sardonically witty story when he returned to Odense in December of 1867 to be made an honorary citizen of the town—the highest accolade that his neighbors could bestow on him—and to be feted at an evening banquet when, as the gypsy had predicted, the city would be illuminated to celebrate his accomplishments. On the day of the festivities, Andersen was suffering from an excruciating toothache, the victim of one of life's supreme poetic injustices. But as so often happened with Andersen, he transformed that bitter experience immediately into art.

Almost as often as Andersen allows his characters to triumph, it seems, he offers stories in which fortunes are frustrated (as above), love is unrequited, or at the farthest extreme, lives are lost. There are too many dead or dying children in Andersen to suit many modern tastes (see **"The Mother," "The Little Match Girl,"** and **"The Angel"**), and too many lovers who don't attain their heart's desire and are left in a kind of emotional limbo. Perhaps the most famous of these impossible loves is that of **"The Little Mermaid,"** whose sacrifices for the prince go unnoticed and unrewarded, and who is left, despite the objections of generations of readers and all the logical and emotional directions of the story, without the "love of a human being," "an immortal soul," and thus without a way to "God's kingdom"—at least not until she serves a three hundred year penance with the other "children of the air." But after condemning her, Andersen offers a kind of reprieve:

"You may be able to go there before that," whispered one of the others to her. "Invisibly, we fly through the homes of human beings. They can't see us, so they don't know when we are there; but if we find a good child, who makes his parents happy and deserves their love, we smile and God takes a year away from the time of our trial. But if there is a naughty and mean child in the house we come to, we cry; and for every tear we shed, God adds a day to the three hundred years we already must serve. (76)

This was not one of Andersen's better endings, and readers have often objected to its heavy-handed manipulation.

A similarly dispiriting story is **"The Little Fir Tree,"** often considered to be one of Andersen's most autobiographical fables. In this story Andersen creates a character (the little tree) who wants, in a sense, what every person—certainly every child wants—"to grow, to grow . . . to become tall and old; there's nothing in the world so marvelous" (226). And when it hears from the sparrows in the forest about Christmas and the special place of the tree in the festivities, it can't wait to be carted away to be decorated, even though the wind and the sunshine advise it to set aside these desires and "be happy with us . . . be glad you are young; enjoy your youth and your freedom, here in nature (227). Of course the tree is chosen the next year, plays its rather terrifying role in the celebration, and then is quickly removed to the attic, where it is stored for the winter. There it whiles away the days telling a story it heard on Christmas Eve to the mice who come to stay the winter in the house. But unlike the main character in the tree's story (ironically titled "How Humpty-dumpty Fell Down the Stairs but Won the Princess Anyway"), there is no ultimate triumph or happy ending for the little tree. As it is being consumed on a spring-cleaning bonfire, it thinks "of a summer day in the forest, or a winter night when stars are brightest, and it remembered Christmas Eve and Humpty-dumpty: the only fairy tale it had ever heard and knew how to tell. Then it became ashes" (233).

Andersen is commenting here on the vain, fleeting nature of fame, in contrast to the stability of an existence that is more accepting, modest, and rooted—a lesson he was having to deal with in his own rather itinerant, unsettled life, and in terms of the ups and downs of his literary fortunes, which often sent him into tantrums or depressions. He is clearly trying to tell another kind of "fairy tale"—one that expressed the other, dark side of his artistic vision. This pessimistic bleakness in Andersen, which sometimes seems so cruelly moralistic (as it does, say, in **"The Red Shoes"**) seems out of keeping with the sympathy that Andersen is so intent on creating for many of the other protagonists in his tales.

There are other contradictions, problems, and ambiguities in Andersen's work. One doesn't always know, for instance, why Andersen ridicules the pomposity and pretensions of the aristocracy on one page and then forgives them on the next. In **"The Nightingale,"** Andersen satirizes the ways of the Emperor of China's court and the Emperor's own shallow willingness to settle for the artificial nightingale's song. The nightingale, who is really the figure of the poet and the perceptive proletarian center of the story, tells the Emperor at the end: "I love your heart more than your crown." But then it adds: " . . . and yet I feel that the crown has a fragrance of something holy about it" (211). One explanation for this waffling is that Andersen himself was a son of the working class who aspired to be and ultimately became the darling of the salons and courts of Europe. In a sense, he was living the contradiction that he wrote about. These and other problematic contradictions arise throughout Andersen's stories to baffle or puzzle the reader because Andersen seems frequently less interested in maintaining a consistent point of view or tone than in letting loose mercurial impressions and almost free associations.

What, then, makes Andersen's tales "classics"? Why should they be considered "touchstones"? A very obvious reason is that many of Andersen's tales continue to be *read,* and to affect those who read them deeply. Regardless of how we might react to them individually, many of his stories are passed from generation to generation, through edition after edition, becoming household names and a part of our universal, literary vocabulary. Ursula Le Guin speaks for many when she writes that she "hated all the Andersen stories with unhappy endings. That didn't stop me from reading them, and rereading them. Or from remembering them" (104).

The secret to this success lies, perhaps, in the fact that Andersen was connecting with exactly that in his readers—secrets. On one level, Andersen was tapping the secret, emotional realms of his own troubled experience, often writing from his own despair out of what Keats might have called "negative capability." But Andersen succeeded in projecting these incidents onto a larger, more public screen, through forms and symbols ostensibly reserved for children but which Andersen was keenly aware would usually be introduced to children by adults. Ultimately, Andersen meant his stories to be for everyone, and to deal with the secrets that all of us keep in common but are unable or unwilling to tell. Etymologically speaking, the words for "secret" and "sacred" share the same Germanic roots: what is secret is also personally sacred to us, from those deepest yearnings to the most petty jealousies and vanities.

On the one hand, there is Andersen's composite hero, the duckling/swan, swineherd/prince, nightingale/poet, soldier/king. He frequently must undergo great suffering and trials but nevertheless remains steadfast and true to his principles and, thus, to his own inner nature and its humanity. This is the duckling's way, and the tin soldier's, and little Gerda's in **"The Snow Queen."**

Andersen is able to touch those chords of sympathy within his readers because, on some fundamental level, they, too, have shared these feelings and have hoped for the same optimistic resolution. Often this character is flawed, wounded, incomplete, but through his perserverance, kindness, and love he compensates for these inadequacies and becomes whole, metaphorically if not literally. At times this character is a poet, like the nightingale, whose songs "sing not only of those who are happy but also of those who suffer . . . of the good and of the evil that happen around you, and yet are hidden from you" (211). Sometimes she is disguised as a little child, whose stalwart love can melt the icy heart of her friend, a captive in the Snow Queen's palace. But whoever he or she is, this persona with dozens of faces expresses those profoundly human desires to love and be loved, and to seek a way to fulfill those feelings.

On the other hand, Andersen also explores those other, darker reaches of the psyche that we do not like to admit exist within ourselves. These shadowy realms appear in many of the tales, and they are Andersen's way of dealing with the dark side of his own soul. At its grimmest, in such tales as **"The Shadow,"** Andersen is wrestling with the need for the artist to be aware of the nether reaches of the psyche, even if these shadows may contain evil. To repress, to deny, to not confront these forces, as Ursula Le Guin argues, is to be ultimately ruled by them, to become their victim as an artist and as a human being.

> For the shadow [Le Guin insists] is not simply evil. It is inferior, primitive, awkward, animallike, childlike; powerful, vital, spontaneous. It's not weak and decent, like the learned young man from the north (in **"The Shadow"**); it's dark and hairy and unseemly; but, without it, the person is nothing. What is a body that casts no shadow? Nothing, a formlessness, two-dimensional, a comic-strip character. The person who denies his own profound relationship with evil denies his own reality. He cannot do, or make; he can only undo, unmake. (107)

Yet there is another dimension to Andersen's exploration of the shadow: humor. A finely tuned sense of humor gives many of Andersen's stories a vitality that holds them from the abyss of bitter gloom, despair or unrelieved seriousness. Andersen's humor can be very dark indeed, as in **"A Drop of Water,"** where he has his main characters, who are looking through a magnifying glass at a miniature but surprisingly vicious city they have discovered there, try to decide whether or not they are observing a microcosm of "Copenhagen or some other big city" or just plain "ditch water." In **"Big Claus and Little Claus"** the humor is deliciously macabre, when Big Claus ironically ties himself up in what will become his own shroud and violently demands that Little Claus push him into the river. In **"The Tinder Box"** Andersen's humor is suggestively risqué: when the soldier has the magic dog fetch the sleeping princess for him, he cannot resist kissing her, for "he was a soldier all over."

Finally, in **"The Emperor's New Clothes,"** Andersen provides us with the kind of humor that manages to touch everyone's pet vanities. No one knew better than Andersen about the serious side of this kind of public embarrassment; he had felt it keenly since he was an awkward child walking down the center aisle of the church in the squeaky new boots of which he was so proud. This particular story—one of Andersen's most famous—was also rooted in the facts of the writer's life. Haugaard retells the incident from Andersen's diaries:

> A foreign artist arrived in Copenhagen and announced in the newspapers that he had come to paint portraits of the most famous Danes, and he hoped that these great personages would come to the studio he had just rented. The very next morning who should appear at his door but Andersen and one of the actors from the Royal Theatre, a man known for his self-love and conceit. Andersen looked at the actor and could not help laughing, both at him and at himself. (74)

"To write the **'Emperor's New Clothes'**," Haugaard goes on, "one must be able to be as foolish as the emperor—although I admit that it is more important to be as wise as the child who saw that he was naked. But only the genius can be both at the same time and, therefore, be able to write the story."

P. M. Pickard writes that Andersen used "so much courage in displaying so much vulnerability" (78). This struggle of opposing elements within Andersen is at the paradoxical heart of his works—as it evidently was in his life. Throughout his works, Andersen tried to preserve a precarious balance between competing sides of his nature: the courtly and the colloquial, the exalted and the mundane, the realistic and the Romantic, the conservative and the iconoclast, the hopeful and the pessimistic. These and other dramatic oppositions give Andersen's stories their rich complexity and expressive range. Andersen took real emotional and artistic chances in his tales "for everyone." Because he did, Andersen was instrumental in creating a children's literature that could become a vehicle for carrying both traditional messages and values as well as an author's personal visions. Andersen wrote, as Keats puts it, "on the pulses," casting light on the shadows, telling his own, and our own, secrets, giving them a song and wings.

References

Andersen, Hans Christian. *The Complete Fairy Tales and Stories.* Trans. Erik Christian Haugaard. New York: Doubleday, 1974.

———. *The Fairy Tale of My Life.* 1868; rpr. New York: Paddington Press, 1975.

Grønech, Bo. *Hans Christian Andersen.* Boston: Twayne, 1982.

Haugaard, Erik Christian. "Portrait of a Poet: Hans Christian Andersen." *The Open-Hearted Audience: Ten Writers Talk about Writing for Children.* Ed. Virginia Haviland. Washington: Library of Congress, 1980.

Le Guin, Ursula. "The Child and the Shadow." *The Open-Hearted Audience.*

Pickard, P. M. *I Could a Tale Unfold: Violence, Horror and Sensationalism in Stories for Children.* New York: The Humanities Press, 1961.

Spink, Reginald. *hans Christian Andersen and His World.* New York: G. P. Putnam's, 1972.

Stirling, Monica. *The Wild Swan: The Life and Times of Hans Christian Andersen.* New York: Harcourt, Brace and World, 1965.

Niels Ingwersen (essay date 1993)

SOURCE: "Being Stuck: The Subversive Andersen and His Audience," in *Studies in German and Scandinavian Literature after 1500: A Festschrift for George C. Schoolfield,* edited by James A. Parente, Jr. and Richard Erich Schade, Camden House, 1993, pp. 166-80.

[*In the following excerpt, Ingwersen discusses the theme of the loss of freedom in Andersen's fairy tales, focusing particularly on those characters trapped by their social standing or by gender roles. Ingwersen also comments on the relationship between the artist and audience in Andersen's tales, finding Andersen concerned with the appreciation of art as well as the compromises an artist makes for his audience.*]

I

Hans Christian Andersen's butterfly (**"Sommerfuglen,"** [**"The Butterfly"**] 1862) flutters through life without finding anyone quite fit for marriage. When he finally proposes, he is firmly told by the desired object that too much time has passed to realize a marriage; friendship must suffice. As an old butterfly, he finds himself comfortably lodged in a parlor, but in spite of the warmth and protection of the locale, he passes judgment on his life by admitting that a butterfly ought to be outside enjoying the sunshine, the freedom, and the company of a little flower as a partner. . . . He deems his life to be wasted. At that point the inhabitants of the parlor notice him—presumably by his fluttering against the windowpane. They admire him, capture him, and stick a pin through him, and thus he becomes a decoration prominently displayed, an object to be seen by anyone who enters the room. He is "stuck," literally, in several senses.

There should be no need here to offer biographical comments on Andersen, who proposed to several women, more or less seriously, but who remained a bachelor and who, as he composed this particular tale, knew that he would remain single. Much criticism, be it biographical, psychological, sociological, or a mixture of these, has charted the relationship between Andersen's life and his art. One recent example of such an investigation can be said to be P. O. Enquist's play *Från regnormarnas liv* (1981). But even the reader who knows next to nothing about Andersen's life is bound to notice that the butterfly's experience of ending up "stuck" is one that occurs in a great many texts. That experience can, of course, take many different forms, but the general situation, that of being captured, of being trapped, of being in bondage, of being forced to do something against one's will—in sum, of being denied freedom—is one that is repeated with alarming and frightening frequency in Andersen's texts. One may recall the broken darning needle (**"Stoppenaalen,"** [**"The Darning Needle"**] 1847) that ends up stuck in the gutter, the bottle (**"Flaskehalsen,"** [**"The Bottle Neck"**] 1858) that is finally broken and turned upside down to become a waterdish for a bird, and the ball in (**"Kjærestefolkene,"** [**"The Top and Ball"**] 1844) whose final fate is to end up rotting away among other garbage.

Those situations are rendered in Andersen's fabulously poignant, whimsical language and, as Fredrik Böök has pointed out so well, with a wit that veers delightfully toward malice.[2] Andersen entertains marvellously and, at the same time, intimates with a sting and sadness that human beings are quite stuck and, at times, why they are so.

The butterfly offers some comments on his final situation that wittily and grimly suggest that being stuck is like being married. . . . Those comments reflect, of course, on the society that admired, captured, and literally pinned him down, for it is those people's mores and their marriages that the butterfly comments on. We are in that bourgeois or patrician parlor that Andersen knew so very intimately from his adult life in Copenhagen.

The butterfly resigns himself to the object role that society allots him . . . and thus he abandons any hope for a fulfilling life. By implication it is, however, quite clear that his captors are stuck as well. As he surrenders his earlier dreams of sunshine, freedom, and love, he is immediately taken to task by the potted plants. . . . In no uncertain terms he is told by the potted plants that his consolation is false, but since he is stuck, he cannot allow himself to accept their criticism. His reason for rejecting it suggests, so to speak by his own admission, that the potted plants know exactly what they are talking about. . . .

II

A full investigation of Andersen's tales in this light is beyond the scope of this essay, and only a handful of texts will be discussed in the following. The tales chosen, of course, all deal with being "stuck," but the selection of those that are given a fairly full treatment—although exhaustive analyses are not attempted—has been motivated by the hope that a new or sharpened reading of them can be given. First, I shall comment on Andersen's view that, no matter on which rung of the social ladder the members of the bourgeoisie are to be found, they are trapped by their own habitual thinking. The examples chosen to clarify that point deal mainly with Andersen's artistic analysis of the sex roles of his times, but some will pinpoint other forms of social or psychic entrapment. Secondly, those tales will be examined that chiefly capture Andersen's own feeling of being held in bondage, a claustrophobic experience that would nearly be inevitable for an artist who could not quite accept, adapt to, or adopt the values of his social world. Consequently, in many texts Andersen could hardly avoid depicting his audience, for it was, in a sense, his antagonist.

What complicates matters is that the proletarian youngster—to use Böök's term—realized that in his quest to become an artist who would conquer the world, he would have to "fit in" among the patricians who supported him and gave him an education. If he did not please them, he would have little chance of reaching his lofty goal, which he had obviously desired since his early youth. . . . Andersen, who wanted ardently to be up there and who enjoyed the benefits of being precisely up there to the hilt, nevertheless retained his proletarian consciousness and never quite found peace of mind as "a writer for those up there." Thus, he vacillated or fluctuated in his moods—as his journal shows—as well as from tale to tale or even within a single text.

Andersen was the outsider who was allowed inside and who, in many ways, was warmly welcomed within the patrician parlor; thus, it would be wrong to see him as the odd man out; rather he was the odd man in. Therefore, one can see the reason for those two languages that P. O. Enquist finds in Andersen's works. . . . [4] Andersen was, thus, both blessed and cursed with that keen insight and sharp perception that only the outsider on the inside can possess.

Maybe the image of people being trapped or victimized by the ideology of the times emerges most clearly when sex roles are considered. This view can best be demonstrated through a brief consideration of **"Tommelise"** [**"Thumbelina"**] (1835), **"Iisjomfruen"** [**"The Ice Maiden"**] (1862), **"Den lille Havfrue"** [**"The Little Mermaid"**] (1837), **"Den grimme Ælling"** [**"The Ugly Duckling"**] (1845)—and somewhat out of context—**"Dynd-Kongens Datter"** [**"The Marsh King's Daughter"**] (1858), **"Den standhaftige Tinsoldat"** [**"The Steadfast Tin Soldier"**] (1838), **"Hyrdinden og Skorsteensfeieren"** [**"The Shepherdness and The Sheep"**] (1845), and **"Svinedrengen"** [**"The Swineherd"**] (1842).

The tiny heroine of the first story is subjected to the pressure of a society that wants her to conform and to follow its seemingly sensible rules, and thus she is headed for one of those semi-arranged marriages that were not uncommon in the bourgeoisie of that time. If that marriage were to be realized, she would indeed be stuck. Her wealthy suitor, the mole, makes it clear that their marital life would exclude everything that brings joy to Tommelise's heart: open air, light, birdsong—the sunshine and freedom that the butterfly missed so bitterly—and, consequently, she will be walled up in the dark underground, a setting that to Tommelise must resemble a prison cell. The social pressures on Tommelise, as voiced by the kindly, but utterly conventional mouse, are tremendous, for she represents the persistent and authoritative voice of nineteenth-century bourgeois common sense.

It should be briefly mentioned here that Andersen elsewhere subtly compared a marriage undertaken for the wrong reasons to a prison cell. In **"Iisjomfruen,"** the hero Rudy, about to marry Babette, has left his beloved mountains for a tourist trip to Chillon, the setting of Byron's *The Prisoner of Chillon*. Whereas Babette and her relatives are wonderfully entertained by viewing the ruins, the remnants of the torture chamber and the prison cell strike Rudy with horror. Numerous signs in the text, especially that of the cell, indicate that Rudy's marriage to Babette would be a self-imprisonment that could only lead to unhappiness for both of them. In another scene in **"Iisjomfruen,"** Rudy, the wild and free hunter, performs a nearly impossible feat by climbing up to an eagle's nest to capture a young eaglet in order to gain Babette's father's acceptance. One might cheer the hero's audacity and success, but in reality Rudy is doing something that is foreign to him and wrong: he has become the stooge of society by imprisoning a wild bird that does not belong in a cage. In fact, one might see the captured eaglet as an ominous reflection of Rudy's potential fate.

Both Rudy and Tommelise are asked to give up what gives meaning to their lives and to fit in, and it is gratifying that they both escape the prison of marriage to the wrong partner. Tommelise is spirited away, meets a true partner, and assumes her true identity, which is signalled by her being renamed Maja. Smothering bondage is replaced by harmony. Rudy's escape route leads to death, but death is greeted with enthusiasm. . . .

As in **"Den lille Havfrue,"** which portrays the heroine's vehement quest not to be stuck in this world of the flesh, death is seen as a liberation.

These happy endings, however, deserve further scrutiny. Iona and Peter Opie in their *The Classic Fairy Tales* (1974) have remarked that Tommelise's final happiness seems to be conditioned by her having found one of her own kind.[5] She may, thus, actually have something in common with the May bug, who, after his initial infatuation, rejected her because she did not conform to his society's ideals of beauty. And even if Tommelise is too pure and innocent to be accused of prejudice, the text is not necessarily so. Many of Andersen's sentimental and, as a rule, popular stories tend to offer happy endings that, sweet and satisfying as they may be, upon scrutiny seem tainted by compromises—an integration process that allows the protagonists to live in a society that in reality traps them. In **"Den grimme Ælling,"** the wild bird becomes, as Georg Brandes has already noted, a tame pet, another object for admiration, one fed crumbs by the inhabitants of the manor.[6] Both Tommelise and the swan eventually seem to fit into a benevolent society, but that integration process may also be seen as their submission to society—on the part, of course, of the author as well. Such an underlying sadness, within the subtext and not immediately noticeable, is caused by the fact that the one who had seemed to liberate himself or herself has, nevertheless, ended up stuck in some other sense.

That, of course, cannot be said about Rudy in **"Iisjomfruen"** or about those of Andersen's other heroes and heroines who find liberation in death, such as the young princess in **"Dynd-Kongens Datter"** and the little mermaid. But that radical, frequent, and romantic solution to the experience of life as imprisonment may testify to Andersen's acknowledgment that it is nearly impossible to escape from being stuck. It is telling that death, particularly in **"Iisjomfruen,"** is often associated with brilliant beauty and that life within society is rendered as trivial. If in various ways, then, these stories confirm the butterfly's skeptical view of marriage as a condition of being stuck, others, like **"Tommelise,"** reveal that both sexes may yearn to be together in the here and now. Often, however, the sexual ideology of the epoch holds both woman and man hostage and prevents a union of the lovers.

A glaring example of people yearning for love, but being too passive to reach fulfillment, can be found in **"Den standhaftige Tinsoldat."** Among all the toys, the soldier and the ballerina are the only ones who do not *move* during the nightly party, and if love is to be realized one cannot, of course, remain immobile; their deficiencies have been analyzed perceptively by William Mishler, who employs a Freudian approach.[7] The soldier, in reality, follows the commands shouted to him by the nasty jack-in-the-box, who forbids him from laying his eyes on the ballerina. Even if the soldier steals fleeting glances at his heart's desire, he nevertheless obeys the orders given him by that restrictive voice of society and never approaches the ballerina.

Only in death are the lovers united, and the flames that envelop them in the end can perhaps be seen as the destructive fire of unfulfilled passion.

In the story **"Hyrdinden og Skorsteensfeieren,"** the couple does not make the mistake of obeying orders; thus, their chance of fulfillment in life seems more promising. When they *move* in order to escape from the bourgeois parlor, that world of immobility shakes with impotent rage against their daring. Their successful escape seems to prove that parental authority, as represented by the mandarin, has little power against those who dare to question its validity. But, sadly, their quest for freedom comes to nothing, for the shepherdess is so much a child of her society that the scary thought of unlimited freedom in an open world sends her fleeing back again to the prison she has just escaped. Although they return, some minor victory has been won, for she can now remain with the chimney sweep and will not be forced to marry one of the supposed pillars of society. But there seems to be no passion between the lovers, and their effort to become free human beings has ended in their assuming their former positions as immobile porcelain figures. They remain stuck in a world that they could not defeat, and it is telling and chilling that the only kiss exchanged between them is the one that she uses to convince him that they must go back home again.

The strength of the parlor mentality over the young is further emphasized by Andersen by his showing that the shepherdess clings to the safe man, the very clean chimney sweep—he is too clean, suggests Andersen—not because she loves him, but because she fears the sexuality of the arranged marriage. The banality of the relationship of the two, now completely immobilized figures is captured maliciously by Andersen in suggesting what they have in common. . . .

It would be utterly simplistic solely to blame the shepherdess for the couple's failure to escape, for the way in which she has been molded and trivialized by male authority directs her actions. In fact, upon their return, she feels deeply guilty over the distress she has caused the mandarin. Instilled guilt is an excellent means of keeping someone stuck in his or her place.

The molding of both sexes is also the main, if underlying, issue in **"Svinedrengen."** At first glance it seems to be a curious—and rather sexist—literary adaptation of a well-known *Schwankmärchen* about how a shrew is tamed. For example, in the Norwegian version of this story, "Haakon Borkenskjæg," the woman is allowed to shed her ignorance and arrogance through the male's educational scheming and become a human being worthy of marriage.[8] In **"Svinedrengen,"** however, she is left standing in the rain, rejected by both her father and her suitor, who informs her that he has come to despise her. . . .

The concluding statement with which the prince takes leave of the woman he once desired may cause modern readers consternation. It is unpleasant to imagine the liberal Andersen, who called himself "half feminine," composing a story that is more sexist than the folktale that may have inspired it.[9] But upon closer investigation of the subtext—one that was scarcely obvious to his contemporaries—"Svinedrengen" emerges as the exact opposite of a male chauvinist tale.

Even if the princess is a brat, it is those who have spoiled her who are to blame for her silly and thoughtless behavior and her lack of appreciation for the natural. It may be childish to reject nature's wonderful gifts and to desire the swineherd's mechanical gadgets, but she is a child. Since she has been formed to remain a child, she acts like an egocentric child who is used to getting what she wants. It is hardly laudable that she is willing to sell herself for those gadgets—a feature Andersen had to tone down in his literary adaptation of the folktale—but her punishment and the final, verbal verdict of the prince are hardly commensurate with her crime. Like the princess in "Haakon Borkenskjæg," she may very well need to be set straight, but by shortening the traditional narrative in his text, Andersen gives it—as Hans Brix cautiously intimates—a very brutal ending, leaving a dejected, cast-out princess, who is without any hope for the future and is utterly alone.[10]

Through this drastic revision of the folktale, Andersen lets the prince's final condemnation of the princess boomerang, so that the readers come to despise him for the cruel game he played with her. Here "Haakon Borkenskjæg" and "Svinedrengen" part ways, as they also likely do in the minds of the listeners and readers, for the prince in Andersen's story does not trick the princess to gain her hand but merely to take revenge. She emerges, thus, as the victim of those vindictive and manipulative tricks and ends up seduced and abandoned. She suffered her downfall because she was a product of a world that keeps women as children—she and her maids play the same silly game all day—and because she happened to wound a male ego. Having suffered humiliation, the male ego wants revenge and gets it. Both she and the prince are stuck in attitudes that separate the sexes from each other.

Even though Andersen often had to whitewash the folktales he adapted, their sting is retained—as is the case in both "Keiserens nye Klæder" ["The Emperor's New Clothes"] (1837) and "Lille Claus og Store Claus" ["Little Claus and Big Claus"] (1835). In "Svinedrengen," Andersen's radical revision of the folktale may well have occasioned a comparison between the attitudes of earlier, more tolerant times and those of his own day. If that is the case, the story is a stinging indictment of a society that makes women into children and men into self-righteous judges

of the women they have created. That it can be otherwise, Andersen shows in "Klods-Hans" ["Jack The Dullard"] (1855)—and in his earlier rendition of that story in "Sneedronningen" ["The Snow Queen"] (1845)—where the young people get together on equal terms because they are able to disregard habitual thinking about sex roles.

Maybe some readers of the above comments on "Svinedrengen" would balk and, as is not uncommon when ideology is taken to task, would protest against making a beloved, simple tale into a scathing criticism of the sexual politics of the bourgeois nineteenth century. To that criticism, it is possible to respond that there is nothing innocent about Hans Christian Andersen; he could skillfully feign innocence, but such stories as "Keiserens nye Klæder" and "Hun duede ikke" ["She was No Good"] (1855)—maybe Andersen's most politically radical text—demonstrate that he was not. It should also be recalled that quite early on Andersen wrote a wittily malicious text that is called "Det er Dig, Fabelen sigter til" ["This Fable Is Intended for You"] (1836). That Andersen knew the darkness and viciousness of the human heart—as well as how innocence can become self-destructive naiveté—is blatantly revealed in the chilling "Skyggen" ["The Shadow"] (1847). The fable in Andersen's works always alludes to the reader; but Andersen's contemporary reader may not have always been aware of that fact. Like Mark Twain, Andersen has been considered to be a rather harmless entertainer of children, but both Mark Twain and Andersen revolutionized the literary language of their countrymen by employing a stunning imitation of the vernacular, a feat they would hardly have achieved if they had been merely spinners of innocent tales for children.

III

It is tempting to continue for a moment this less than taxing search for people who are stuck in one way or another in Andersen's tales. The few texts mentioned above would suggest that the hierarchy of the class system traps people in terms of both their social standing and their attitudes. In "Keiserens nye Klæder," all the characters, high as well as low, are so concerned with preserving their image of not appearing stupid and incompetent, that they prove to be exactly that. The only exception is the little child, not yet brainwashed into realizing that lies are preferable to truths. "Hun duede ikke" makes clear that those in charge and with power over other people's lives are stuck in their own limited outlook, one that falsifies reality; those below them are trapped into accepting their social superiors as authorities of nearly divine standing. When the young servant woman is told that she should not marry her mistress's son, she immediately accepts whatever her mistress says as, literally, the gospel truth. . . .

But this wider investigation must, of necessity, be narrowed. In the following, I shall focus on those texts in which Andersen depicts the artist's relationship to his audience. That theme is, of course, one that Romantic poets everywhere have used quite often, and numerous texts pit *der Dichter* against the philistines. Since artists can only expect applause if they please, the artist who desires that gratification, as Andersen most certainly did, might have to compromise his convictions, as Andersen very likely did. Consequently, it is understandable that Andersen, like many of his colleagues, dreamt of the "dear reader" who is his or her soul mate, an ideal audience who will understand.

If, as is so often done, one can see **"Den grimme Ælling"** as Andersen's autobiography in the form of a tale, one finds a situation of bondage in which the poor misunderstood soul must repeatedly wail, as does the ugly duckling. . . . The story suggests that the swan, which has escaped from various kinds of duckyards, is finally among his peers, who will understand him, but—as mentioned earlier—that happy ending covertly suggests a compromise. The swan, in the future, must be the pretty pet, the ornament, the object to be admired—as the "stuck" butterfly is. How well did the admirers of the artist Hans Christian Andersen understand him—or how well did he feel understood? That is the underlying issue in many of his tales.

That topic is dealt with gently and generously in **"Nissen hos Spekhøkeren"** [**"The Goblin and the Huckster"**] (1853), in which the poor student saves a volume of poetry from being used as wrapping paper by the grocer. The grocer, his wife, and all the "servants" in the kitchen—inanimate objects given voices with Andersen's usual brilliance—have absolutely no use for poetry and probably will agree with the grocer that it is stupid to give up a tasty cheese for the sake of poetry. The discussion between the student and the grocer is, however, friendly banter, a point that the pixie misses entirely. Andersen thus benignly shows that one cannot ever expect everyone to grasp the beauty of art, but, as the ensuing transformation of the pixie demonstrates, some suddenly wake up to its wonder.

When the pixie ascends the stairs to take revenge on the student for insulting the grocer, he looks through the keyhole into the student's room and sees him reading the salvaged poetry. He is surrounded by an aura coming from the book that signifies the glory of his experience and the wonder and joy that art grants. The pixie, who had been completely satisfied with the grocer's world, suddenly understands that art opens a door to an unknown, marvelous beauty. If we see, then, in the student Andersen's conception of the ideal audience—the dear reader—the pixie becomes that part of the audience that has a potential to become one too.

It remains, however, only a possibility for the pixie, for even though, when a fire breaks out one night, he saves the volume of poetry and thus proves his heartfelt devotion to art, he soberly realizes that he needs the grocer's porridge too; he cannot, therefore, devote himself fully to art. To this sadly funny summation of the relationship between audience and art, it should be added that the pixie at no point enters the student's room, but always partakes in his experience by standing outside observing through the keyhole. Even positively inclined audiences are stuck too, for mundane demands in their daily lives keep them from fully giving art its due.

As a rule, however, Andersen's view of those whose "butterfly" or "handsome swan" he had become was less good-natured than in **"Nissen hos Spekhøkeren."** As critics Peer E. Sørensen and Finn Hauberg Mortensen have discussed, one reason for that hostility may well be that Andersen was angered and at times infuriated by being that trapped "butterfly" or tamed "swan." As a proletarian who had made it to the top, he always had an uneasy relationship to those who had helped him up the social ladder, and he served them uneasily.[11] But often he served them well, and anyone who served as well as Andersen did—and here one must remember the much less controversial part of his oeuvre—can stand accused of being a toady or a bootlicker. In Heinrich Heine's opinion, Andersen was just such a toady, and Andersen's good, but blunt friend Henriette Wulff chastised his glorying in being honored by empty-headed princes.[12]

It would, however, be more precise to compare Andersen with the court jester of yesteryear, the person who is called upon to perform and amuse those that feed him, but who at the same time has a position so unique that it gives him a certain restricted freedom to express unpleasant opinions and truths. **"Nattergalen"** [**"The Nightingale"**] (1844), **"Tante Tandpine"** [**"Auntie Toothache"**] (1872), **"Loppen og Professoren"** [**"The Professor and the Flea"**] (1870), and **"Den flyvende Kuffert"** [**"The Flying Trunk"**] (1839), among others, support this contention.

The audience in **"Nattergalen"** is surely not given much credit. Throughout the story it is quite obvious that the majority of the people at court will never grasp the beauty of the song of the nightingale, and that those who pretend to have taste prefer an imitation of art that can be explained intellectually. The emperor, of course, is a man with the potential for being the ideal audience—and eventually he realizes it—but, initially, he misunderstands completely the role that both art and the artist should have in his life. Andersen delivers a consummate image of the artist trapped by philistine society; the artist is shackled, denied freedom to move, and kept in a cage under lock and key—all under the pretense of being rewarded . . .

It is also not surprising that the emperor is a man who is stuck, for the majority of those who surround him and give him advice never have and never will gain any understanding of the existential function art can have in a person's life. The nightingale is reduced to a court jester who understandably longs to escape from bondage.

In this text, Andersen strikes that Romantic note that allots wisdom and true appreciation of art to the poor, for they intuitively grasp the qualitative difference in song between the real and the artificial nightingales. More significant, however, is the fact that after a deadly crisis, the emperor is reborn as a new man; through art he will become a real emperor who can rule his realm justly and wisely. The nightingale envisions his future role as an artist who will inform the emperor of everything that goes on in his realm, be it good and evil. Art thus grants moral knowledge and a better human existence for all.

As in the case of **"Den grimme Ælling,"** one cannot deny the ending of **"Nattergalen"** its grand triumph or its harmony, but if one first has gotten a piece of the devil's famous mirror from **"Sneedronningen"** in one's eye—and Andersen works hard to make that happen—it is difficult to ignore the underlying darkness of the subtext. This is not to say that all the happy endings are contradicted, but they are severely modified and undercut. When the nightingale asks the emperor, as they are about to part, not to tell anyone that his wisdom comes from a little bird, Andersen pinpoints once again the loneliness of the artist who can count on so few to understand him.

Andersen etched one of his sharpest portraits of his audience in **"Tante Tandpine"** (1872), the story with which he had concluded the last volume of tales he was ever to publish. The audience is embodied in the young artist's Aunt Mille, who refuses to see anything unpleasant in life. When her old suitor, Brewer Rasmussen, at one point suggests that friends can be false, she, who is normally kind and composed, lashes furiously out at him, for her perception of reality is threatened. She is, and wishes to be, stuck in a false reality, one that the poet-student captures when he depicts her claustrophobic room. . . . Hers is a place that is constructed to keep bothersome reality out. Such an audience makes certain demands, and undoubtedly many of contemporaries, for they wanted, as Auntie puts it, stories about unhappy people. Unhappiness, pain, and anguish are reduced to mere entertainment.

Two samples of the student's writing—and within the fiction of the text he is, of course, the author of the tale itself—suggest, however, that unlike his aunt he confronts harsh reality through art. Inspired by a fallen leaf on which an insect moves, he admits that human knowledge is severely limited and that all talk about God, the world, and eternity is mere conjecture. It

should be kept in mind that the dutiful Andersen, serving his audience, had written numerous texts in which he preached about all those great issues. Later the student depicts a sleepless night and reveals himself to be a hypersensitive, lonely man who just records his sense impressions without giving them any transcendental value. He does not write as a romantic, but Auntie, who likes romantic stories populated with unhappy human beings, completely misunderstands both texts; she has no comprehension—or will not admit to any such—of the pain and anguish of her nephew's art.

"Tante Tandpine," thus, gives another picture of an artist stuck in a world that leaves him misunderstood and lonely. In a way, he is appreciated, for Auntie tirelessly eggs him on to write what she wants to read, and in his somber attempts to write, she finds what is not there. Auntie sees only what she wants to see. It might be that situation that finally causes the student to denounce art and life; the frame of the story informs us laconically that the student is now dead. **"Tante Tandpine"** is also a somber farewell to a life and a vocation that Andersen, the old author, felt had given him much pain and isolation. Both in **"Tante Tandpine"** and in **"Hvad gamle Johanne fortalte"** [**"What old Johanne Told"**] (1872), which, as Topsøe-Jensen has shown, is the last story Andersen composed, the vision is bleak.[13]

It may be the very same vision that is covered up by gallows humor in the sprightly, sparkling **"Loppen og Professoren"** (1870). The professor, who is a flim-flam man, can be seen as one more of Andersen's many artists. And the flea, whose presence guarantees the professor a living, may well be seen as Andersen's less than respectful caricature of art. Fleas can jump, perform, and bite, and audiences fall in love with such creatures to the point that they hold the artist hostage.

If the picture of the artist and art is snide, the one of the audience is no less so. It is made up of what are called savages and cannibals. Earlier, in **"Vanddraaben"** [**"The Drop of Water"**] (1848), Andersen had cleverly managed to describe the inhabitants of Copenhagen as conformists who would furiously tear to pieces and eat anyone who did not fit in. In **"Loppen og Professoren,"** the audience captures both the flea and the professor; the artist's life is quite pleasant as long as he obeys the ruler of the realm, but he feels so stuck. There is surely heartfelt joy in those scenes in which the artist, utterly bored with his comfortable leisure, begins to scheme in order to free the flea and himself from the savages. He promises to provide them with "*det* man i Verdens største Lande kalder Dannelse!" (5:117). To savages it makes sense that "Dannelse" is a cannon that will make the earth tremble. The professor then constructs a balloon, but the savages remain steadfast in the belief that what is being built is a cannon, and thus the two escape from their bondage. To take off, the professor shouts: "'Slip Snorer og Toug! . . . 'Nu gaaer Ballonen!' De troede han sagde: Kanonen" (5:118). The audience not unexpectedly misunderstands, but that is something one, now and then, can turn to one's advantage—at least within a fictional world. Here, with marvellous, malicious humor, Andersen deflates not only his own vocation and its results but also his audience, the deserving victim of the con man/"artist."

Finally, in **"Den flyvende Kuffert,"** one again encounters not only the artist as con man, but also the audience as deserving victim of his conning. The rich man's spendthrift son finds himself with his flying machine in a land where storytelling is appreciated. He pretends to be divine—a nice jab at the Romantic notion of the elevated poet—and elbows his way into the home of the rulers, a king and queen, whose daughter he hopes to marry for the sake of convenience rather than love. To win her hand, he must tell a story that will amuse the king and satisfy the queen's wish for moral lessons. His story, the tale within the tale, is one of Andersen's joyous comedies in which inanimate objects come to life and mirror the life of the servants in the kitchen. As we, with the story's audience, listen to the voices of those servants, it becomes quite obvious that some of them, the matches in particular, predict that the end will come to absolute monarchies and that crowned heads may fall. This subversive message, as usual in Andersen's texts, is neatly and elegantly packaged among so many other seemingly harmless satirical or humorous points that one might excuse the audience for not understanding that an ominously, nasty prophecy is being aired. Besides, the king and the queen are very likely so stuck within their expectations about art that they—like Auntie in **"Tante Tandpine"**—hear only what they want to hear, and, like her, they are so stuck in their roles that they are deaf to any unpleasant truths.

The artist is fully accepted by the king and the queen and is just about to marry the princess when he loses his magical flying trunk. He wants to impress all with his power, so he starts a gigantic fireworks—a consummate metaphor for a grand performance—and a spark ignites the trunk. He thus loses the princess and now has to make a living telling stories that offer far fewer and lesser rewards. It is dangerous to make **"Den flyvende Kuffert"** too prophetic, but the text shows that the young Andersen, like the old man who wrote **"Loppen og Professoren,"** looked at his own vocation with a splinter of that devil's mirror in his eyes. From very early in his career, Andersen was subversive toward, and derogatory about, his own strivings—as well as toward and about those whom he wanted to applaud him.

IV

Enquist's aforementioned observation that Andersen uses two languages is astute, but the word *two* can be amended to *several* without losing Enquist's major

point. It needs to be modified, for the voices of the dutiful servant and of the subversive court jester—and of a number of voices in between these two poles—are to be found in the tales, and there are often subtle switches between them.

Whether and when sincerity and pretense can be separated, and where they may be found to overlap, presents a problem that no critic could or should hope to solve definitively. Andersen himself realized that the problem existed and, as usual, having encapsulated it within a larger narrative (**"Noget"** ["Something"] [1858]), he addressed it. In that text, one of the ambitious brothers, desirous of becoming an architect and joining the intelligentsia, agrees to serve, for the time required, as an apprentice to some carpenters. He knows very well that such service will result in some humiliation, but this he is willing to bear while masking his feelings and keeping his goal in mind. . . .

It is also revealing that the ambitious speaker uses the term "Maske-Frihed," [mask-freedom], for through the use of masks one is able to retain some measure of freedom and can avoid becoming completely stuck in a single role.

The impossible question that [**"Noget"**] raises is how conscious Andersen was of the dichotomies that so often marked his nearly yearly publication of a volume of tales. The question begs to be raised, for the tales included in any one volume can differ to a surprising degree. Were they merely a gathering together of the tales Andersen had produced since the last collection and had stored away, or were they carefully composed so that some were sure to please the audience, perceptive or not, whereas others were to send subversive messages to, and against, the very same audience? That separation into an either/or is, however, most likely naive, for even if the first assumption, for practical reasons, may be the case, the question still arises why Andersen would write tales that were so much at odds with one another.

A general and sweeping, if by necessity inconclusive, answer to that question has already been intimated above: Andersen lived both actually and artistically a double life. It may furthermore be conjectured that Andersen, the man who knew that masks had to be used, made sure that those comforting, harmonious stories, beloved then as now, were, as a rule, accompanied by others that questioned such harmony. The fluctuation in the choice of tale, probably both conscious and not, was consequently caused by Andersen's lifelong obsessive, contradictory relationship to his audience.

It may seem simplistic merely to speak of one audience, but at the time Andersen was publishing he was mainly concerned with that circle of patricians in Copenhagen to which he had come to belong. That fact, at least, can be gleaned from his journals. It may well be that, as Andersen wrote his tales, he thought of other, less prosperous audiences, but the sting of his major tales seems directed at a narrow patrician circle.

"Maske-Frihed" can also be detected in Andersen's small collections of tales. Only a selection of them can be discussed, and occasionally two or three of them, when published sequentially within a few years, are considered together. It is not possible to let all the voices speak, but some curious fluctuation or—what maybe should be called—authorial strategy is undeniably present.

First, it should be remembered that when Andersen published his first collection, *Eventyr, fortalte for Børn* (1835), he was slapped on the wrist by the reviewers. He was therefore most likely apprehensive when he issued further volumes. To be sure, some of those critics were right on target, for as stories such as **"Fyrtøjet,"** [**"The Tinder-Box"**] **"Den lille Idas Blomster,"** [**"Little Ida's Flowers"**] and particularly the darkly humorous **"Lille Claus og Store Claus"** [**"Little Claus and Big Claus"**] show . . . the reviewers recognized an author with strongly subversive leanings. The uproar was justified and very likely alerted Andersen to the fact that publishing tales might require the use of masks.

In the many volumes that followed, there were some tales that would placate and please the audience: a dosage of Romantic idealism; some mild satire that would hurt no one; some grotesque, but unthreatening, comedy; some weepy sentimentalism; some consoling Christianity (of various varieties); and, not to be forgotten, some grimly pietistic pieces that condemned wordly pleasures. Any member of the audience could find what she or he preferred. Andersen knew how to put on the right mask—even when he wanted to take his audience to task.

The second volume Andersen published, also in 1835, may appear quite harmless, but if **"Tommelise"** [**"Inchelina"**] and **"Reisekammeraten"** [**"The Travelling Companion"**] seem to promote the idea that providence and justice rule, the buoyantly humorous tale **"Den uartige Dreng"** reveals that love guarantees life to be unfair. In this volume there is hardly much subversion, but, it should be noted, different voices—with very different outlooks—are speaking.

If, for brevity's sake, the next three collections (1837, 1838, 1839), are viewed together, the presence of several voices is also evident. **"Den lille Havfrue"** and **"Keiserens nye Klæder"** were issued together and have little in common—but if one wants to be naive, that may be explained by Andersen's imitation of an age-old prose fabliau in the latter story. More significant, however, is the contrast between **"Den lille Havfrue"** and **"Paradisets Have"** [**"The Garden of Eden"**] (1839):

although the former lauds an ascetic ideal, the latter is boisterously sensual, as is **"Den standhaftige Tinsoldat."** Quite obviously, **"De vilde Svaner"** [**"The Wild Swans"**] (1838) is out-of-step with the radicalism and cynicism of **"Den flyvende Kuffert."**

In the first of the collections from 1845, the reader finds **"Sneedronningen"** and **"Grantræet"** side by side, but proclaiming widely different views of life. **"Sneedronningen"** speaks with a doctrinaire Christian voice, whereas **"Grantræet"** concludes with a view of death as nothingness; that contradiction was a lasting one within the oeuvre.

In the second collection from the same year, the humorous vision of the pleasure-loving creatures in **"Elverhøi"**—rather bourgeois Danes dressed up as folk figures—stands in sharp contrast to the grim and totally serious mood in **"De røde Sko,"** in which pleasure is shown to be the road to hell. Here one wonders whether the starkness of the protagonist's suffering somehow signifies Andersen's disapproval of the stern voice that promotes the dismissal of all pleasure.

The collection published in 1848 contained, among other texts, **"Historien om en Moder"** [**"The Story of a Mother"**] and **"Den lille Pige med Svovlstikkerne."** In the latter, the poor girl—whose abominable poverty can be contrasted with the sugarcoated view of poverty found in other texts, such as **"Nattergalen"** and much more blatantly in **"Lysene"** (1872)—is finally taken home to God; once again a Christian view is expressed. That also seems to be the case in **"Historien om en Moder,"** which superficially resembles the early poem **"Det døende Barn"** (written in 1826) and the later tale **"Barnet i Graven"** (1860). It should be noted, however, that the mother believes she has given her child to that God who will grant eternal bliss in Paradise, whereas Death consistently refers to the other side as "det ubekjendte Land" (2:164). With artistic mastery, Andersen lets that phrase conclude the tale. Although in some texts he is the doctrinaire Christian, or the Christian voicing acceptable views, in others he is the questioner or doubter. The voices cannot agree, and whereas one promotes order, the other appears to favor spiritual chaos.

The collections from 1852 and 1853 contain two very short texts, **"Et godt Humeur"** (1852) and **"Hjertesorg"** (1853). Among other topics, they ponder the costs of being an artist, for both texts suggest that the narrators take a lofty view of existence, one that prohibits an involvement in life. With their devastating self-irony, such meta-stories point backward to **"Den flyvende Kuffert"** and forward to **"Tante Tandpine"** and are told with very different voices than the other consoling stories to be found in the same volumes.

As Andersen's reputation grew, he might have felt less need to employ masks, but he may have had some trouble in letting them fall. In the late 1850s and early 1860s, he published nice Christian stories like **"Det gamle Egetræes sidste Drøm"** (1858), **"Pigen, som traadte paa Brødet"** (1859), **"Anne Lisbeth"** (1859), and **"Barnet i Graven"** (1860). But during the same period, he also published **"Vinden fortæller om Valdemar Daae og hans Døttre"** (1859), in which only the wind seems to have eternal life, and **"Taarnvægteren Ole"** (1859), in which Andersen, although he is twice removed as narrator, lets his main character voice opinions clearly suggesting that evolution, not religion, explains the world.

In 1868, Andersen once again included a story, **"Den onde Fyrste,"** dealing with Christianity. On the surface it depicts God's victory over an evil prince who had challenged him. The tale suggests, however, that the distant deity interferes only when he himself is threatened, not when human beings are being tormented by the powers of evil.

The other stories discussed above suggest that a tension always existed between the voices with which Andersen spoke. In the second volume, published in 1872, **"Krøblingen"** [**"The Cripple"**] gives art credit for curing the protagonist, whereas **"Tante Tandpine,"** as pointed out above, takes a much bleaker view of the powers of art. One cannot say that the two texts—or many other texts that are not in agreement—negate each other, for the reader is rarely provided with straightforward contradictions, but rather with a constant nagging questioning of any view held. As pure conjecture, it can be suggested that such a fluctuation may reflect an uneasy search for a story that would fully express a heartfelt opinion.

It can possibly be claimed that the tale, with its roots in several traditional subgenres, offered Andersen a unique opportunity to engage in that quest—an opportunity that the other literary genres he used could not grant him. The idea of imitating narrative folklore was fairly new at the time, and hence the composition of tales was not hindered by all those rules and regulations that, in spite of Romanticism, clung to the well-established literary genres. Thus, as Bo Hakon Jørgensen has argued, when Andersen resorted to tales, he was less restricted. . . . [14] Even if that opinion can be contested by showing how world views and morality differ between magic tales, prose fabliaux, and legends, the point is nevertheless well taken, for through Andersen's imitation and mixing of those subgenres, he fluctuates between their different styles and creates hybrid forms that can reflect any outlook.

In the short form of the tale, Andersen could breathe *fairly* freely. He could enjoy that "Maske-Frihed" that the ambitious brother mentioned as a means to avoid being stuck in **"Noget"** and thus deal with those problems that continued to nag him. The form of the tale,

a genre not taken very seriously at the time, allowed him a freedom to experiment, and that freedom resulted in a perplexing fluctuation, as different voices speak, blend, overcome, or silence one another. As one reads the oeuvre, the complexity of the author and his problems—be they personal, social, or artistic—stand out and suggest why this man, so stuck in so many ways, had to fight back and attempt to become, at least in his art, less stuck. In his best subversive tales, he succeeded.

Notes

. . . . .

[2] Fredrik Böök, *H. C. Andersen* (Stockholm: Bonniers, 1955), 235. The English wording used here is from George C. Schoolfield's translation of Böök, *Hans Christian Andersen: A Biography* (Norman, OK: University of Oklahoma Press, 1962), 203.

. . . . .

[4] P. O. Enquist, *Fra regnormenes liv: Et familiemaleri fra 1856,* trans. Frederik Dessau, ed. Claus Jensen, Aage Jørgensen, and Bendt Pedersen (Copenhagen: Dansklærerforeningen/Skov, 1981), 89-95. This Danish edition includes Enquist's commentary to his play.

[5] Iona and Peter Opie, comps., *The Classic Fairy Tales* (New York and Toronto: Oxford University Press, 1974), 228.

[6] Georg Brandes, *Samlede Skrifter,* vol. 2 (Copenhagen: Gyldendal, 1899), 112.

[7] William Mishler, "H. C. Andersen's 'Tin Soldier' in a Freudian Perspective," *Scandinavian Studies* 50 (1978): 389-95.

[8] P. Chr. Asbjørnsen and Jørgen Moe, *Samlede eventyr,* vol. 3 (Oslo: Gyldendal, 1965), 101-10.

[9] Lise Sørensen, "Bachelor Goes A-Wooing," *Danish Journal* (1975): 22.

[10] Hans Brix, *H. C. Andersen og hans eventyr* (Copenhagen: Schubotheske, 1907), 233.

[11] Peer E. Sørensen [*H.C. Andersen og herskabet Studier i borgerlig bevidsthed (Grenna GMT, 1973)*], 91-92; Finn Hauberg Mortensen, "H.C. Andersen og den litterære dannelse," in *H. C. Andersen og hans kunst i nyt lys,* ed. Jørgen Breitenstein, Mogens Brøndsted, et al. (Odense: Odense universitetsforlag, 1976), 68-71.

[12] Elias Bredsdorff, *Hans Christian Andersen: The Story of His Life and Work, 1805-75* (New York: Charles Scribner's Sons, 1975), 153; 234.

[13] H. Topsøe-Jensen, *Buket til Andersen: Bemærkninger til femogtyve eventyr* (Copenhagen: Gad, 1971), 307-16.

[14] Bo Hakon Jøgensen, "'At tænke i eventyr'," in *H. C. Andersen og hans kunst i nyt lys,* 55.

Hans Christian Andersen (essay date 1994)

SOURCE: "IIans Christian Andersen—The Journey of His Life," in *Bulletin of the John Rylands University Library of Manchester,* Vol. 76, No. 3, Autumn, 1994, pp. 127-43.

[*In the following essay, Andersen (a twentieth-century critic) discusses the motif of travel in Andersen's works, finding it connected with themes of restlessness, homelessness, and alienation, and maintaining that the idea of travel can be seen as a metaphor for Andersen's own life journey.*]

Hans Christian Andersen's delight in travel is well-known, as is his talent for describing his progress through Europe and, briefly, the Near East and North Africa. His very earliest works, and his earliest successful works, were travel books or fiction inspired by the experience of travel in the middle of the nineteenth century. They show him integrating fact and fiction seamlessly, so that the reader comes to experience the world through his mind, with his sensitive eye for the significant and the insignificant detail of life in those days.

This present work is indirectly inspired by research into Hans Christian Andersen's work for the stage, an aspect of his career that has to a great extent remained unseen in the work of critics. Among his thirty stage plays is one originally written for reading rather than for performance: ***Agnete and the merman*** (***Agnete og Havmanden,*** 1833). Written in Switzerland during his first long journey through Europe in 1833, it comes across as a strikingly personal and intense account of the nature of exile and the impossibility of making a proper return to one's homeland, once a decision has been made to leave it behind, even just temporarily.[1]

The student of Andersen's life and work soon becomes aware of the importance of travel and exile as themes both in the author's own career and in his written work. Both as a man and as an artist, Andersen was 'on the move' throughout his life, restlessly changing address both in real terms and metaphorically. There is, perhaps, nothing remarkable in this: it is in the nature of great men and women that they resist the temptation to settle, that they are constantly looking for new paths to travel. But in Andersen's case the significance is of a specific nature. He offers an opportunity to observe the artist's mind on the journey through the world.

Andersen is best known as the author of fairy tales for children, and his fame rests on a comparatively small number of the very best. In all, he wrote 157 and increasingly, as his career progressed, he changed the emphasis from children's tales to something much closer to the short story, which was gaining importance as a genre in nineteenth-century Denmark.[2] However, he never entirely let go of his young audience. After all, much of his fame in the later part of his career depended on it. This article will show that the travel motif acts as a guide through Andersen's career in much more general terms, and this can be taken as an indication of how important it was to Andersen's thinking.

A closer reading of his collected tales reveals that travel plays a part in almost twenty per cent of them.[3] This article will look at how the travel motif is developed in thirty-four of the tales, published between 1835 and 1874. It will also look at the different ways in which the travel motif is made to work for the story teller as he constructs the tales.

It soon becomes clear that it does so in a variety of ways. To a certain, limited extent it provides the plot for his stories. In this respect, the journey becomes a string of episodes, adding up into a full narrative. As in Homer's *Odyssey,* and as in countless folktales, the journey and its constituent parts are made significant for what they have to say both about the places where the travellers go and about the travellers themselves.

But more significant is the way in which Andersen uses the travel motif as part of the theme of a tale. Where this happens, it is possible to see how Andersen gradually moves away from an early reliance on folktale motifs to describe a pessimistic view of the life of the emotional and geographical exile, to a much more self-assured, realistic and cosmopolitan view of life, expressed in a more modern prose style.

At no time does he abandon the fairy tale entirely, in the sense that he continues to include elements of the irrational in many of his stories. This is part of Andersen's world view and fundamental to his art: everything under the heavens, be it animate or inanimate, has a voice, which the author hears and which informs his stories.

Travel feeds into the stories in different ways, sometimes simply by providing casual detail to the description of characters, at other times by providing the actual key to characterization or even the actual physical environment in which the characters move. Travel as such is rarely of great importance in the tales. Andersen is not using them to sell the idea of travel as an important part of the development in the individual. But they do suggest, by their example, why it is so important, and that is probably how they can contribute to the lives of their readers.

Andersen wrote several autobiographies, starting with the first, hand-written one from 1832, *Levnedsbogen*[4] (*The book of my life*), written when he was only twenty-seven years old and three years into his professional career as a writer. Here, for the first time, he puts the view that God has, as it were, written the script for his life, providing him with direction and, perhaps more to the point, offered this son of poor parents unexpected and almost miraculous opportunities in the middle-class world of literature. 'Day by day, my life becomes more and more like poetry', he writes: 'Poetry enters into my life and it seems to me that life itself is a great marvellous poetic work. I feel that an invisible, loving hand guides everything . . . '.[5] In later autobiographies, he was to update this image: 'My life is a beautiful fairy tale', he was to write, claiming that even a powerful fairy could not have guided him on the path of life with greater happiness and wisdom.[6]

There is no doubt that this is how he saw his life and it is certainly the metaphor which he, as a self-publicist, chose to use when presenting his life to his audience as a typical Romantic artist: the natural talent who had risen almost magically to international status as an artist. But the metaphor does not hold. Not only was magic obviously not involved: he earned his status by using his talent and he was given help by those of his contemporaries who could see that he deserved it.

A better metaphor for Andersen's life is that of the journey. Andersen remained single all his life and moved between a number of temporary addresses in Copenhagen until he settled in to his first real home in 1866, at the age of sixty-one years. The purchase of his first bed caused him great concern as he imagined that it would one day become his death bed. In fact, he died, still single, in the home of wealthy friends, some of the many who had invited him into their home for shorter or longer periods of his life; not because he was poor but because he was offered hospitality, often by top members of society, sometimes even by royalty.[7]

But somehow he remained 'homeless' in an existential sense. He left his poor background behind when he left for the Danish capital in 1819 and he never truly found another home of his own, except in the world of the arts. His relationship with the family of his benefactor, Jonas Collin, illustrates this excellently. Although Andersen saw a father figure in Jonas Collin and worked hard to get close to Collin's son, Edvard, he was never fully integrated into the family. Andersen accepted this: he was a public figure and he gradually came to accept that he had to live a public life, in other people's families.

Andersen travelled throughout his life. His first significant journey, significant because it changed his life, was the one that he made from his home town to the Danish capital in 1819. But he made many other journeys outside Denmark, from the first to the Harz Mountains in 1831 to his final journey in 1873, and he visited most of Europe. Andersen was not only a passionate traveller but also a professional one, and his experiences of foreign countries found their way not only into his fiction but also into actual travel descriptions. The earliest of these is *Skyggebilleder af en Rejse til Harzen og det sachsiske Schweiz* (1831, *Shadowy images of a journey to the Harz Mountains and Saxony*) where clear description of landscape mingles with humorous description of human behaviour.

His Grand Tour of 1833-34 resulted in a novel (*Improvisatoren* (*The improviser*), see below). His later, ten-month journey through Europe in 1840-41 inspired one of the great classics of nineteenth-century travel literature: *En Digters Bazar* (1842, *A poet's bazaar*), where the reader experiences all aspects of human nature of contemporary transport systems in a manner that still inspires the reader to follow in the footsteps of their guide.

The two journeys to Italy and beyond were the great formative events in the author's life. The first took him out of himself and away from the limited Danish intellectual environment, into a quite different world of unexpected natural beauty and intellectual challenge. Italy was the Mecca of Danish nineteenth-century artists from all art forms, and in Italy Andersen found himself included in an international artists' community. *Improvisatoren* is clear evidence of the impression which Italy made on Andersen, its artistic maturity reflects the maturity that Andersen himself was reaching, as a man and as an artist.

En Digters Bazar is no less indicative of his development. By the 1840s, Andersen was a seasoned traveller and writer who was no longer just observing but also much more directly absorbing and conquering the world around him. The down-side of this professional development is, perhaps, indicated by his final two travel descriptions: *I Spanien* (1863, *In Spain*) and *Et Besøg i Portugal* (1868, *A visit to Portugal*) have greater journalistic than artistic merit. Here, the experienced writer was drawing on his craft rather than innovating.

But it is not so much the 'straight' travel description that is of interest here. Even taking into account that Hans Christian Andersen was always imaginative in his approach to the objective truth of the world around him, some of his works use travel in a stylized manner which throws clearer light on the way in which travel plays a part in the fairy tale.

In 1829, having completed his school education, Andersen made his official debut on the Danish literary scene with *Fodrejse fra Holmens Kanal til østpynten af Amager* (*Journey on foot from Holmens Canal to the east point of Amager*). This fantastic description of an imaginary, dream-like trip on New Year's Eve of 1828 is not only interesting because of its grotesque, surreal atmosphere: the appearance of the supernatural prefigures the later fairy tales. It is also important because it shows Andersen submitting the real world almost completely to his own creative imagination. The reader is taken on a journey through a known location by the author, but it is a journey which could only be made with the author, through his imagination. This becomes particularly clear when, at the end of the novel, Andersen uses the Modernist technique of printing a short chapter consisting only of punctuation.[8] By instinct, this author was a surrealist rather than a realist, and the contemporary reading public immediately took to his idiosyncratic style.

Andersen was to use this mode—the synthesis of reality and the imagination—in several of his travel-inspired works, notably in *Improvisatoren* (1835) and *I Sverrig* (1851, *In Sweden*). The approach is different in both, and both are different from *Fodrejse.*

Improvisatoren is an autobiographical novel, an inspired blend of two of Andersen's favourite subjects: his own unusual career, and the world outside his own country. It gave him an international reputation as a novelist, in advance of his fame as a writer of fairy tales, or 'romances' as they were often called in the previous century. *Improvisatoren* tells the story of a young man who rises from humble beginnings to artistic fame. Its success relied—and relies—on the fact that it is told through the mind of the main character and that we witness the colourful Italy of the early nineteenth century through his eyes. He had seen that Italy himself on his Grand Tour in 1833-34 and he chose to present his impressions in fictional form.

The eyes through which the reader sees Italy are those of a talented traveller and fiction writer. To students of Andersen's work, the narrator's point-of-view is always of crucial importance. It often says something very directly about how close the reader is to Andersen's own experience.

I Sverrig is a very different kind of work, but it is also testimony to its author's ability to operate with a range of literary technique. Like *Improvisatoren,* it is the fruit of the actual travel experiences of its author.[9] But *I Sverrig* is no ordinary travel description, any more than *Improvisatoren* is. Rather, it is a collage of impressions of a country that was then not well known in Europe, at least by travellers. The structure is episodic, a collage made up of a variety of linguistic media, using straight prose interspersed with fairy tales[10] and lyrical poetry. Andersen does not restrict himself to straightforward description of what he sees, although such descriptions are included: he ranges from realism to philosophy, using his Scandinavian sister

nation as a springboard for all the many thoughts that travel may engender in a receptive mind.

What we have in these three works is evidence of Andersen's versatility and his ability to juggle narrative styles and levels of realism. They suggest that Andersen was not only crossing geographical borders on his way through Europe but also inhabiting a continent of the imagination, one without boundaries and with endless variety of landscape and experiences. It was this landscape which he was to travel in his fairy tales.

Andersen published his first fairy tales in 1835, in a small volume of *Eventyr fortalte for Børn,* 'fairy tales told for children'. He continued to write and publish them almost to the end of his life, the last collection being called *Eventyr og Historier,* 'fairy tales and stories'. The change in title to include the word 'stories' was deliberate and suggested Andersen's own changing priorities as a writer of short prose: he was increasingly seeing himself as a writer of short stories for adults, without leaving his young audience entirely behind. The truth is that audiences of all ages were always in the implied audience for his tales.

The four titles in the first volume included **"The tinder box"** and **"The princess and the pea."** Both of them make use of the travel motif, but at this point that motif plays only a simple part in straightforward plots: the soldier in **"The tinder box"** is marching home from war, apparently without aiming for any particular address, and is intercepted by his destiny, in the shape of money, power and love. This is an adaptation of the story about Aladdin from the *Arabian nights,* which Andersen had known since childhood, and as such it is a rare example of Andersen borrowing an idea from the existing folk tradition.

"The princess and the pea" shows a prince engaging in a futile journey to find a real princess. Only after his return does such a princess journey to his home, appearing mysteriously out of the blue and settling down as his Queen.

Both these stories have the ring of the true folk-tale about them, their characters are clearly acting without rational motivation and their plots progress in ways that suggest the interference of non-human powers. They represent a particular strand in the use of the travel motif: one that stems from the folk-tale, where the journey is a recurrent and purely functional plot element, offering opportunities for purely functional, one-dimensional characters to meet challenges and complete tasks set by agents of the non-human world.[11]

The earliest tale to illustrate this use of the motif is also one of Andersen's finest: **"The travelling companion"** (**"Rejsekammeraten,"** 1835).[12] **"Rejsekammeraten"** is, in the true sense of the word, a 'classical' tale. It shows a young man reaching a turning point in his life: his father dies, he himself is uprooted and sets out on a journey that will ultimately lead to a new equilibrium in his life, in the same way as happens in **"The tinder box"** and **"The princess and the pea."** To that extent, the plot of the tale is one that would be recognized by audiences and readers not only now or in Andersen's own time but as far back as ancient Greece, where the same plot is met in the *Odyssey* and in classical Greek drama. Throughout the story, the main character moves in a world that is only superficially like our own 'real' world: it is, in fact, suffused with the supernatural, in it witchcraft and magic both hinder and help the characters.

The final, happy end is contrived rather than probable in terms of modern realism, for this is story-telling as ritual, the plot is an acting-out of a transition from one stable condition to another. What Andersen has ultimately achieved with this tale is to show a young man undergoing the transition from boyhood to manhood, from living with his father to living, as an adult, with his own wife. He has been helped through this transition by a character with supernatural powers, and this character, the Travelling Companion, takes on the forces of darkness on his behalf.

Andersen is best known as a writer for children, but this is in reality also a tale of adolescence. For all that it involves the forces of evil, it also carries a comforting message: help is available, the main character does get through to the other side, stability will return.

The traditional tale is particularly characteristic of Andersen's early tales, from the 1830s, although it continues to appear into the 1850s and 1860s.[13] It is given a variety of uses, from providing the structure for stories with deep metaphysical significance such as **"The snow queen"** ("Snedronningen," 1845) to those that are much more straightforwardly amusing like **"Clod Hans"** ("Klods-Hans," 1855).

Although Andersen himself refers to the stories told to him in his own childhood,[14] he only relied on the actual oral folk-tale tradition to a limited extent, composing most of his stories independently of known literary or pre-literary models.[15] Although he is often mentioned in the same breath as the Brothers Grimm, he was no folklorist. Rather, he was an author of 'Kunstmärchen', a modern Romantic. It is therefore necessary to look immediately beyond the folk-tale as such, to see in what other way he makes the folk-tale work for him. Part of the answer lies in the way he develops as an author of short stories. But at this early point in his career, he appears to have drawn on the folk-tale for other things.

Most obviously Andersen makes travel provide him with *plot:* it offers a reason for stringing a series of events together, events that shape the life of the main character(s). Thus, in **"Inchelina"** ("Tommelise," 1835) the somewhat passive female main character passes through the hands of a series of potential husbands until she is carried off by the swallow to foreign parts. **"The ugly duckling"** ("Den grimme Ælling," 1844) gives a similar view of a character passively developing into a more mature character, as a hostile world passes by.

"The snow queen" and **"The story of a mother"** ("Historien om en Moder," 1848), by contrast, show two main characters making rather better use of their ability to travel, namely for a search for their loved ones. **"The snow queen"** and **"The story of a mother,"** like **"The travelling companion,"** are stories of human beings maturing, although in the case of **"The snow queen"** and **"The story of a mother,"** the process is intellectual or metaphysical rather than social or to do simply with ageing. It is not possible to say of stories such as these that they mainly exemplify a characteristic, conventional use of plot and character functions. These tales are far more sophisticated and their effect depends to a much greater extent on the use of symbolism. Although they *are* good stories, which work as entertainment at the surface, they invite interpretation that goes far beyond their story lines. At the story level, they have elements of the fairy tale, in that they include irrational and supernatural elements. But they also present themes of fundamental importance for human beings: the ability to love and, in the case of **"The story of a mother,"** the ability to let go of those we love.

At this point in his life, Andersen had made a reputation as a travel writer with *A poet's bazaar* (1842) and his experience as an observer of the world may explain why he was now capable of making better use of his plots. However, it is more likely that we are simply looking at a more mature writer in more general terms, for whom literature as such could be made to carry more meaning. Plot is now made to work harder, the individual events made to reveal more about the characters.

The use of travel as a means of structuring plot peters out in the 1850s along with the use of the folk-tale-like travel motif. It is likely that the two trends are linked. Andersen's tales were becoming increasingly realistic over the years and the focus moving increasingly away from plot structure to the reactions of the characters within the plots.

Andersen has rightly become renowned as a children's author, and the tales which most people now remember have become part of our collective unconscious, entering our cultural mythology. **"The emperor's new clothes,"** to mention just one obvious example, has provided countless public writers and speakers with ammunition for attacks on their opponents, and many of Andersen's tales have been published anonymously, adapted for children, proving that they are now themselves part of our narrative tradition, not even needing their author's name to survive.

Children are not naive and the universe which they inhabit is not one of simple, innocent bliss. Children know that and the most successful children's writers succeed by respecting that, as both Astrid Lindgren and Roald Dahl illustrate.[16] Andersen, too, reveals a complex and sometimes even frightening view of the world, both in his children's stories and in those intended for older audiences. The plots may lead us through landscapes peopled with devils and sprites before taking us up to the happy ending, and we do not forget that we had to see those landscapes as we travelled with the characters and that they are still there in the background as we learn that the main characters will live happily ever after.

"The little mermaid" (**"Den lille Havfrue,"** 1837) is a story of love that cannot succeed. That is, of course, not how it comes across in the recent animated version: Andersen's original tale commits the Mermaid to a fate of which the makers of modern mass entertainment dare not conceive.

Like its predecessor in Andersen's œuvre, **"Agnete and the merman"** (**"Agnete og Havmanden,"** 1834), it tells the story of a character who follows her heart in a decisive existential choice, thereby unwittingly committing herself to a life in loneliness and exile. The little mermaid, like Agnete, chooses a partner who is so fundamentally unlike herself that a real relationship is not possible, no matter how great a sacrifice she is prepared to make. The story, revolving around this decisive moment when the wrong step is taken, evolves like a Greek tragedy from hubris to eventual nemesis.

A number of Andersen's tales show characters unable to engage in harmonious relationships, men and women shipwrecked by life, and this motif recurs from the earliest tales, i.e. **"Inchelina"** (1835) to one of the latest, namely **"The wood nymph"** (**"Dryaden,"** 1868). **"The flying trunk"** (**"Den flyvende Koffert,"** 1839) provides a humorous example—the main character finds himself deservedly stranded abroad after an accident, but other examples leave little room for merriment. In **"The garden of Eden"** (**"Paradisets Have,"** 1839) the main character finds himself repeating the original biblical mistake, although without committing the original sin.

In **"Under the willow tree"** (**"Under Piletrœet,"** 1853) a man who emigrates in order to escape from the romantic disappointment of his youth encounters the love of his youth abroad and dies as he tries to escape in the opposite direction, travelling home. **"Ib and little Christina"** (**"Ib og lille Christine,"** 1855) shows a woman destroying herself as she travels away to partake of sophisticated city life rather than the simpler

and healthier provincial life which Ib could have offered her. And **"A story from the dunes"** (**"En Historie fra Klitterne,"** 1860) has a social misfit die, mad and alone, buried by the sanddunes in an abandoned church, after a life that starts and ends in shipwreck.

What is happening here? How does one account for this sombre aspect of Andersen's work? It is tempting to do what critics have so often done, namely to seek the reasons in Andersen's own life, and to a certain extent this makes good sense. Andersen was himself a 'misfit', he had left his poor childhood behind but he never truly seemed to arrive anywhere else, in spite of his international fame and comparative wealth. The fact that he never settled down in a love relationship, in spite of several involvements with various ladies, may have inspired his somewhat pessimistic view of love in the stories referred to here, where the characters are endlessly—and hopelessly—on the move.

One of the finest examples of how this motif is explored in the tales is **"The steadfast tin soldier"** (**"Den standhaftige Tinsoldat,"** 1838), whose main character only just has time to discover his love for the young ballerina before fate—or some other inexplicable force—casts him out into a hostile world from which he is miraculously and inexplicably saved, but only to be senselessly destroyed. What comes across in this story is that there is no sense to the universe, no apparent meaning or order, just casual and irrational changes of fate. Other stories in this group may not be quite so radical in their world view but they all share the feeling that we do not live in a safe universe.[17]

Andersen's treatment of the motif changes over the years, as he becomes more modern in his narrative style and can distance himself, perhaps, from his own personal experience. **"A story from the dunes"** shows tragic events in the lives of its characters, but they are the kind of events that you do tend to find in the nineteenth-century short story, where the sense of fate and of contrast between a person's young and old age is often what gives the short story its energy. In this particular story, Andersen moves close to the style of Steen Steensen Blicher, the father of the modern Danish short story. Like Blicher, Andersen gives his characters credibility by placing them in a recognizable universe, where events and people do, after all, seem probable even if their fate is extreme. In **"A story from the dunes,"** Andersen 'poses' as a nineteenth-century topographer, finding similarities between Arabia and Jutland.[18] There is still an element of the irrational in the story, but it has more to do with psychological irrationality than with the supernatural.

The homeless man, the exile who is out of his proper cultural environment, is still there but he is increasingly like a modern man. Characteristically, he still does not know what is hitting him, as is also seen in the case of the main character of **"The ice maiden"** (**"Isjomfruen,"** 1862). But by now the reader can see through the events and Andersen's technique is increasingly one of dramatic irony rather than the creation of alternative, 'parallel' worlds where nature and the supernatural interact.

At the same time as he was exploiting the existing thematic use of the journey in the traditional tale, he was also using it to express much more modern themes of alienation and exile. His inspiration may have come from his personal experience, but the real power of stories obviously depends on their reflection of a more general condition which his readers of all ages would be able to recognize and relate to, consciously or otherwise.

In about a dozen of his tales we thus meet characters who travel, perhaps because their instinct tells them to keep on the move, perhaps because fate hurls them along for no clear reason, perhaps because they are running away from their own anxieties or their own failure. But they do not escape: in Andersen's darker stories there is nowhere to hide, no home to go to.

To travel *is* to escape, perhaps from one's daily routine in order to go on holiday, perhaps to create a new life for oneself in new surroundings through emigration. There is, of course, that difference between the exile and the tourist—or the emigré—that the exile is not usually away from his home of his own free will. The exile is a refugee, unsettled, uprooted, only temporarily at his address, waiting for a chance to return. The tourist—and the explorer—engage in a more positive search for something different.

Andersen's later stories reveal a much more settled picture of the character away from home. Part of the change that happens in his narrative style is a greater emphasis on realistic details. Reality is always present in the fairy tales, whether through references to real locations or in details which more or less explicitly place the story in the reader's own universe. But in the later stories, reality becomes ever more obvious and in some cases the element of geographical and psychological realism brings Andersen's narrative close to the prose style of the short story writers of his own time.

This also suggests that the universe described in the stories—the world in which the characters 'live'—is becoming rather more manageable, because it is becoming easier to understand. This does not mean that the characters cope more easily with their world but that their problems are not always embodied in characters from another, metaphysical world. They are not necessarily any happier but they are more like 'real' people.

An example of a transitional story between 'exile' and the more realistic picture of the world abroad is **"The pepperman's nightcap"** (**"Pebersvendens Nathue,"** 1858), one of the best realistic stories among Andersen's many short tales. It tells the life story of a German merchant's representative, Anton, living in Copenhagen several centuries before Andersen's own time and making a living by selling spices (the 'pepper' of his title) on behalf of Lübeck and Hamburg merchants. The historical details of the story are interesting in themselves but the description of Anton's situation as an exile is more fascinating in this context.

Andersen takes his character's point of view, to the extent of describing German nature as being more attractive than Denmark's.[19] This may seem surprising to those who know Andersen as the author of some of the best-loved lyrical descriptions of the Danish countryside, but it is an indication of his cosmopolitan approach and it also says something about his ability to enter into the world of his characters. Andersen, after all, was also a playwright.

Because Anton is described with more psychological detail, his situation also calls to a greater extent on the reader's ability to observe and understand real events, and with Anton we move away from the well-known Andersen world of fairy tale to something that is closer to Andersen's contemporary Søren Kierkegaard. The focus is existential, the main character's problem cannot be solved by fairies or exacerbated by hostile trolls. His problem is one of living in a world that is in constant flux, one that changes constantly and which he is not equipped to understand. Andersen hints that modern nineteenth-century transport would have helped the character cope better with life away from home. At least now, in the 1850s, modern steam power has shrunk Europe to more manageable proportions.

Far from being an impoverishment of the tale, its existential emphasis becomes a sign of its author's versatility as well as, it may be assumed, some of his own experience of life. It is not a happy or desirable life, but as Andersen presents it, it does amount to a valid existence: the author is implicitly claiming to be presenting his reader with reality. Andersen describes his character's loneliness as seen through the character's mind: ' . . . he didn't understand himself, he didn't understand the others; but *we* understand! You can be in somebody's home, with the family, and yet you do not strike root, you converse in the way you might converse on a stage coach, you get to know each other in the way you get to know other passengers on a stage coach, you bother each other, you wish that you were somewhere else or that your good neighbour were'.[20]

Realism never entirely takes over the Andersen fairy tale, but it grows in importance as an element in his narrative style and in a way it brings him closer to our own century, helps us to see that his world view is not that different from our own as well as allowing him to bring his talents as a creative writer and a travel journalist together.

One may wonder, at reading **"The pepperman's night-cap,"** whether it is a reflection of Andersen's true experience of 'homelessness'. The answer would probably be both a 'yes' and a 'no'. He may well have felt what his character does: 'Bitter is the life of the stranger in a strange country! You are only noticed by others if you are in their way.'[21] What is more, the late twentieth-century reader easily recognizes the experience of living in a world in flux, where one's sense of belonging is constantly disturbed because modern technology keeps changing one's sense of what the world looks like. Feeling estranged has become one of the central experiences of life in our century and Andersen was ideally equipped to describe it well before it became commonly understood.

But at the same time he was also becoming used to it. The experience of homelessness, which he had had since childhood and which had become his both by choice and through necessity, had also become a strength. And so it is that late in life his attitude to rootless modern life begins to change. For one thing, foreign countries increasingly provide the setting for his tales or form part of the characters' world. Thus, **"The ice maiden"** (**"Iisjomfruen,"** 1862), **"Psyche"** (**"Psychen,"** 1862) and **"The wood nymph"** (**"Dryaden,"** 1868) are set outside Denmark. What is more, the author's attitude to life becomes increasingly cosmopolitan. His outlook, which is never narrow, becomes ever more worldly. He embraces, with enthusiasm, the concept of modern transport and he evidently understands that improved communication will also change the outlook of modern people. **"The muse of the new century"** (**"Det nye Aarhundredes Musa,"** 1861), **"The wood nymph"** (1862), **"The bird phoenix"** (**"Fugl Phønix,"** 1863) and **"The thorny path"** (**"Ærens Tornevei,"** 1863) are celebrations of life in a modern, cosmopolitan world. The 'Muse'—that of poetry—is a citizen of a world where, soon 'the Great Wall of China shall fall; the railways of Europe shall reach the closed cultural archives of Asia—two streams of culture shall meet and flow as one'.[22] **"The thorny path"** is an attempt to link the ancient Greek civilization with that of modern engineers, by listing some of the author's own heroes from world history. **"The phoenix"** is, again, creative writing as part of a timeless world-culture.

In **"The wood nymph,"** Andersen indulges in a description of the Paris World Exhibition of 1867 that combines his enthusiasm for the real, modern world with his fairy-tale style of writing. The story is described both through the eyes of the wood nymph, the dryad, who is granted twelve hours in human form, so that she can see modern Paris and the Exhibition; and through the eyes of Andersen himself and those of his readers: 'We are travelling to the Paris Exhibition. We are there! with speed, with a rush, entirely without witchcraft. We travelled on the wings of speed, at sea and on land. Ours is the age of fairy-tales. We are in the middle of Paris . . . '.[23] Once the wood nymph goes sightseeing in this modern Paris, we find that the author's enthusiasm has not blurred his vision: this is both a Paris of human tragedy and of modern sewers, a Paris where hotels are decorated with fresh flowers and where pollution kills the trees outside.

In a sense, **"The wood nymph"** brings this journey through Andersen's fairy tales full circle. From using the journey as a conventional folk-tale motif, Andersen had reached the point where the journey was part of the shared experience of modern Europeans, an experience which seemed likely to reach modern people everywhere, tying them together in a shared world with a shared culture.

In his autobiography Andersen describes the city where he grew up, Odense, as being in some senses unchanged since the Middle Ages. His own background, his childhood, was rooted in the past. Towards the end of his life, in 1872, he published a fairy tale in which an old man, **"Great-grandfather"** (**"Oldefader,"** 1872), appears. 'Great-grandfather' himself comes from Odense and remembers its old-fashioned culture. But now, in his old age, modern technology enables his grandson Frederik to travel to America (by steamship), and the same technological age has provided the means (the telegraph) whereby Frederik is able to stay in contact with 'Great-grandfather'.

Andersen had himself travelled from the world of the Middle Ages to that of Modernism, in both art and culture. In his fairy tales, travel remained a central motif. It played different parts in the tales at differnt stages of his artistic career and in that respect it reflects changes in his life and in his art. At an early age he set out on his life's journey, through an age of restless cultural, political and technological change. At the early stages, from 1835, travel was predominantly used in the way it happens in the folktale, as a conventional element in story-telling. But he soon began to explore travel at a more personal level in the tales, as a metaphor for homelessness and exile, reflecting his own dark vision of human life as a problematic journey.

But in the 1850s, a change takes place, a change which clearly reflects his own experience of travel and which may also reflect his own greater maturity as a man of the world: his outlook becomes increasingly cosmopolitan and his fascination grows for the technology of travel and foreign settings for his narratives.

He never loses track of the essential ingredient of the fairy-tale: its ability to merge the rational and irrational worlds. Nor does he ever forget that children are in the audience for the tales, after all writing tales specifically for children was one of his great achievements. But his view of the world changes and his readers—be they children or adults—are challenged to deal with ever more complex and advanced aspects of the world which they share with the author.

The great joy is that they have been allowed to go with him on his journey. Ivan Klima, remembering a school essay which he wrote in Theresienstadt, said that writing 'enables you to enter places inaccessible in real life, even the most forbidding spaces. More than that, it allows you to invite guests along'.[24] To this day, readers sense Andersen's generous invitation to go with him on that great journey of his life.

Notes

[1] Hans Christian Andersen, *H.C. Andersen and Thalia: love's labours lost?* (Odense: Odense University Press, 1992).

[2] Steen Steensen Blicher (1782-1848), clergyman, topographer and author, is the father of the Danish short story. Partly inspired by Sir Walter Scott, the Ossian tradition and folktales, he developed and perfected a style of pseudo-realistic narrative, often in regional Danish (Jutland) dialect. A number of stories are available in English translation (see Schroder, *A bibliography of Danish literature in English translation 1950-1980* (Copenhagen: The Danish Institute, 1982).

[3] This investigation covers 34 out of 157 printed in Gyldendal.

[4] Published in 1926. See H. Topsøe-Jensen: *Omkring Levnedsbogen* (1943).

[5] Hans Brix (ed.), *H.C. Andersens levnedsbog* (1971), 19.

[6] H.C. Andersen: *Mit eget eventyr uden digtning,* edited from the author's manuscript by H. Topsøe-Jensen (Copenhagen: Nyt Nordisk Forlag, 1942), 5. This is the Danish original of Andersen's first published autobiography, which appeared in German translation as *Das Märchen meines Lebens ohne Dichtung* (Leipzig: Carl B. Lorck, 1847). Andersen's second autobiography, *Mit Livs Eventyr* (1855), uses almost identical terms to the passage quoted.

[7] In 1857, he spent a month in Charles Dickens' home. See Elias Bredsdorff: *H.C. Andersen og Charles Dickens* (Copenhagen: Rosenkilde og Bagger, 1951). Andersen's many Copenhagen addresses are listed in B.H. Gjelten, *H.C. Andersen som teaterconnaisseur* (Copenhagen: Nyt Nordisk Forlag, 1982), 18.

[8] Andersen uses a similar device in his first stage play, *Kærlighed paa Nicolai Taarn* (1829, *Love on St Nicholas's tower*), which suddenly becomes 'interactive', when the author invites the audience to decide how the play should end.

[9] Andersen visited Sweden on several occasions, in 1837, 1838 and 1840. He spent three months in Sweden in 1849, before writing *I Sverrig.*

[10] E.g. *Fugl Phønix* and *Poesiens Californien.*

[11] See, for example, Terence Hawkes, *Structuralism and semiotics* (London: Methuen, 1977), 67 ff. V.I. Propp is the proponent of this functionalist or syntagmatic analysis of the fairytale in *Morphology of the folktale* (Russian edition 1928, English translation 1958, revised Austin and London: University of Texas Press, 1968).

[12] In fact, it is also his earliest fairy tale. He published the original version of this tale, *Dødningen* ('The dead man') in *Digte 1830* (*Poems 1830*). For the full text of *Dødningen,* see *H.C. Andersens eventyr,* ed. Erik Dal (Copenhagen: Det danske sprog- og litteraturselskab, 1963), 191 ff.

[13] In this category we also find *The little mermaid* (1837), *The wild swans* (1838), *The flying trunk* (1839), *The garden of Eden* (1839), *The ugly duckling* (1844), *The story of a mother* (1848), *How to cook soup up a sausage pin* (1858) and *The philosopher's stone* (1861). Note that in this investigation a tale may exemplify several uses of the travel theme and may therefore appear in different categories.

[14] See his preface from 1837, in *H.C. Andersens eventyr* (1963), i, 19ff.

[15] See Elias Bredsdorff, *Hans Christian Andersen: the story of his life and work* (London: Phaidon Press, 1975), 310 ff. On Andersen's use of the folk-tale see also Paul V. Rubow, *H.C. Andersens eventyr,* second edition, 1943 (Copenhagen: Gyldendal, 1967).

[16] See Alison Lurie, *Not in front of the grown-ups* (London: Sphere Books, 1991). For a discussion of Andersen and children, see e.g. Dot Pallis; 'H.C. Andersen's børneverden i eventyrene', *Anderseniana,* iv (1985-86), 297 ff.

[17] *The shadow* (*Skyggen,* 1847) depends on similarly irrational events, although in this instance the travel motif moves to the background of the story in favour of the drama that develops between the man and his shadow, as the latter to take over his identity.

[18] H.C. Andersen, *Samlede eventyr og historier* (Copenhagen: Gyldendal, 1972), ii, 386.

[19] After Denmark's defeat in 1864 in the war against Prussia, such a liberal gesture would have been much

less acceptable. The passage in question is the following: ' "Great is the beauty of the Danish beech forest!" they said, but to Anton the beeches at Warburg rose even more beautifully' (*Samlede eventyr og historier,* ii, 204.)

[20] *Samlede eventyr og historier,* iii, 208.

[21] Ibid.

[22] *Samlede eventyr og historier,* iii, 40.

[23] *Samlede eventyr og historier,* ii, 277.

[24] Ivan Klima, 'A childhood in Terezin' in *Granta,* (1993), no. 44, 200.

Niels Kofoed (essay date 1996)

SOURCE: "Hans Christian Andersen and the European Literary Tradition," in *Hans Christian Andersen: Danish Writer and Citizen of the World,* edited by Sven Hakon Rossel, Rodopi, 1996, pp. 209-56.

[*In the following excerpt, Kofoed discusses Andersen's sources and the double nature of his narrative voice, which expresses "the tension between the manners of the highly educated, adult person and the spontaneity of the child as a representative of unconscious life."*]

The sources of Andersen's tales and stories are manifold. First of all there is the anonymous folktale; next there is the German literary tale by writers such as Tieck, Arnim, Brentano, Chamisso, and Hoffmann, which had flourished throughout the romantic period; furthermore Andersen's own life story, and finally modern technology and natural science, a source pointed out by one of his closest friends, the physicist Hans Christian Ørsted. In his tales and stories Andersen exploits the entire treasure trove of motifs and themes to be found in European literature as well as in Greek and Roman antiquity, and he also found inspiration in Arabic, Persian, and Indian narrative.

One of the secrets behind Andersen's success may have been the fact that in his development as a writer he accomplished a transition from poetry to prose, from writing in verse for an educated reader to a modern narrative prose based on oral diction, addressing both children and adults. In the latter decades of romanticism, when popular and realistic tendencies made themselves felt together with an incipient political and social liberation from absolutist rule, prose writing came to the forefront in Danish as in European literature of the 1830s. 1827 was an epoch-making year in the history of literature: the year when Goethe proclaimed the existence of a new world literature in a letter to his assistant and close associate Johann Peter Eckermann,

when Hugo signed the preface to his romantic play *Cromwell* and Scott published his article on the supernatural in *Foreign Quarterly Review.*[67] A taste for the supernatural and the realistic at the same time demanded a new kind of prose. People with an extensive knowledge of folklore, such as Ingemann and Andersen in Denmark and the Grimm brothers in Germany, were able to draw on a large stock of popular legends and superstitions. That Andersen, within the compass of his literary work, had participated in a general development from eighteenth-century classicism to early nineteenth-century romanticism is clearly seen already in his first major work *A Walking Tour,* and in his first tale, **"Dødningen, et fyensk Folke-Eventyr" ("The Dead Man: A Folktale from Funen")**, which concludes his volume of *Poems* from 1830 and constitutes the first version of the tale **"Reisekammeraten"** (1835; **"The Traveling Companion"**). The witty and affected style Andersen used in his early, immature attempts was criticized by [his friend B.S.] Ingemann and his wife, who encouraged him to continue writing tales, but also to opt for a style with greater simplicity and seriousness. The rediscovery of a childlike universe in which also ordinary people take part would, according to Ingemann, be the true basis for a revival of story telling.

Andersen took notice of this bit of advice, but by preserving an adult undertone of irony and humor he managed to create his personal mode of double articulation. He felt himself naturally attracted to a childlike sphere and to the nearby world of children. He addressed himself directly to the child in the adult person by taking a short-cut to a world of fellowship and frankness shared by the storyteller and his public. A new interest in childhood with all its implications regarding faith and ideology was a characteristic of romantic literature in the 1830s. The child conceived as an ideological factor symbolized the true source of optimism and belief in the future, and this became an effective argument in polemics against the defenders of pure enlightenment and reason.[68] This fight against the hegemony of reason had begun with Jean-Jacques Rousseau, and had also appeared in Bernardin de Saint-Pierre's novel *Paul et Virginie* (1787), which in a dramatized version was the first play Andersen ever attended at the Royal Theater one of the first days in September 1819 after his arrival in Copenhagen. The notion of the child playing the part of an intermediary of imagination and feeling in literature was also accentuated by Novalis in Germany and Oehlenschläger and Grundtvig in Denmark.

By presenting children in literature as adults in disguise, the classicists of the enlightenment had kept any interest in childhood within narrow limits. To the rationalists of the eighteenth century, childhood seemed a period of waiting; to the romantics the world of children became the very center and culmination of life. It was not until the emergence of a new fairy tale literature that the child found a place in adult literature, and the tension between the manners of the highly educated, adult person and the spontaneity of the child as a representative of unconscious life is certainly at work in a sophisticated manner in many of Andersen's tales and stories. Tieck, who had been the first to renew the writing of short prose as a transitional form, was a master of the fairy tale. His *Volksmärchen von Peter Lebrecht* appeared already in 1795. Tieck had also given his fairy-tale play *Der gestiefelte Kater* (1797) the significant subtitle: "Ein Kindermärchen," and another fairy-tale play *Ritter Blaubart* (1797) he called "Ammenmärchen." Even a number of Hoffmann's and Chamisso's tales were told for children. On the whole the fairy tale seemed to constitute a genre *per se,* expressing the quintessence of imagination, the very canon of poetry. Hoffmann was strongly influenced by Carlo Gozzi, the Venetian playwright, who masterfully exploited folktale motifs in his comedies. The subjects of these tales have been handed down orally as well as in print and are frequently related to those in legends, myths and medieval ballads as well.

The romantics took over the themes and the material from the folktales in the same way as they used medieval ballads and epics as sources. The literary tale of German classicism and early romanticism as we know it from Goethe and Novalis, however, never seems to have been very popular in its mode and narrative technique. On the contrary, these tales were symbolic, complex and far from the simple folktale. It was not until the Grimm brothers began to reshape the folktale with their edition of *Kinderund Hausmärchen* (1812-15) that an oral narrative art came into fashion. It was by merging the folktale and the literary tale that Andersen succeeded in creating his works of excellence.[69]

The folktale is characterized by oral transmission, anonymous origin, formulaic structure and a general lack of style. The literary tale on the other hand is expressed in a sophisticated form in which the individual style of the author is apparent. Characters, setting and detailed descriptions of nature and surroundings play an important part. It is often allegorical and symbolic, as it reflects both a childlike universe and an adult world. It contains a considerable portion of realism, but preferably in a compound of the real and the imaginative.

The romantic literary tale developed in many directions. It was made up of motifs borrowed from comedies, anecdotes, short stories, symbolic stories, fables, and arabesques, among others, and thus it became a supple instrument for expressing the writer's personal philosophy of life. In the 1830s and during the later phases of the romantic movement, where popular and realistic tendencies took over the lead, this kind of short prose reached its height with writers such as

Nicolay Gogol, Gottfried Keller, Berthold Auerbach, Charles Baudelaire, and Edgar Allan Poe. In Denmark Oehlenschläger had tried already in 1805 to introduce the genre with *Vaulundurs Saga* (The Saga of Vaulundur), and in 1816 he had published two volumes of fairy tales, *Eventyr af forskiellige Digtere* (Fairy Tales by Various Authors), in which translations from Tieck, Motte Fouqué, Heinrich von Kleist, and Johann Musäus were represented. In 1820 Ingemann had published a volume of *Fairy Tales and Stories,* which had not aroused any attention. The reading public was not familiar with short prose of that kind and fairy tales were generally considered to belong in the nursery.

Only when Andersen at Ingemann's suggestion abandoned the sentimental and high-flown style of contemporary prose and replaced it with a colloquial language in which the narrator's own voice is heard and the presentation comes close to drama, did a real renewal take place. Andersen had read both Hoffmann, Tieck, Jean Paul, and Brentano since his early years. On his way back from Italy in 1834 he attended performances given by the children's ballet in Vienna, in which he may have found inspiration for two of his very first tales not based on folktales, **"Little Ida's Flowers"** and **"Hyrdinden og Skorstensfeieren"** (1845; **"The Shepherdess and the Chimney Sweep"**). Novalis' fragmentary novel *Heinrich von Ofterdingen* (1802) contains an allegory about Arcturus and Ginnistan telling how the realm of prose and reason is overthrown and poetry is set free. Arcturus's crystal palace reappears in Andersen's tale **"The Snow Queen."** Other lines can be drawn back to Goethe's *Die Leiden des jungen Werthers* (1774; The Sufferings of Young Werther) and *Faust* (1808), the poems of Schiller, and the comedies of Holberg. Numerous loans, parallels and traces of reading in European literature have already been pointed to in Andersen scholarship, for instance Andersen's dependence both on Motte Fouqué's *Undine* (1811)[70] and August Bournonville's ballet *Sylfiden* (1836; The Sylphide) for his own tale of **"The Little Mermaid."**

A certain shortness and clarity, a brisk action, a natural dialogue, humor and irony are essential ingredients in Andersen's narrative prose. However, his poetics of double articulation implies that a discourse that is childlike in the positive meaning of the word by appealing to the world of children and telling about it in their own words, has to be counterbalanced by some humor and irony in order to make another interpretation possible than the one based on lack of sophistication. This double articulation is not only part of a specific poetics, it is a new strategy as well, because it enables the writer to give a full expression of a world of experience resulting from a split in the adult mind.[71]

The literary fairy tale was a demanding genre revealing its possibilities only to a writer who in his personal development would measure up to its requirements.

All indications point to the fact that Andersen in the years just before his literary breakthrough in 1835, underwent a serious crisis that brought him maturity as a story teller. His social background, his strange vegetating as a young man in the Copenhagen slum, his moral strength and his first agonizing experiences as a writer had awakened a tremendous energy in him. His tales were not just a trio of folktales, romantic literary tales, and his autobiography. In fact, one can point to only about nine of his tales as being reproduced folktales. Andersen felt an urge to delve deeper into the anonymous layers of the history of civilization, which make up the common heritage of all humanity. It is easy to demonstrate that Andersen on the surface knew how to imitate the nuances, gestures and the diction of the Copenhagen bourgeoisie so masterly depicted in his tales and stories. But beneath this local and often humorous level there is a region taking us back to a prehistoric world.

As a storyteller Andersen was original, because he more or less deliberately kept in touch with the unconscious aspects of his soul. Beneath the personal experiences, which to a large extent reflect his own life story, we find the general and elementary conditions and conflicts that belong to all humanity. There is a common stock of experience and belief shared by all people, and if the solutions to the problems that arise cannot be explained in term of providence or fate, they tend to become meaningless. This tension between the belief in the wisdom of the people, a simple conviction of the possibility of being selected by fate, and a modern and adult knowledge about the absurdity of human existence, makes up the true high-voltage field in Andersen's writing. His strength does not lie as much in the delineation of the hero's individual character as in the description of his fate. It is the simple and strong emotions he depicts, the passions carrying life and death in them. Therefore the struggle for life and the pursuit of happiness are the main themes of his tales and stories. He never hesitates to pass beyond the borders of life and death in his desire to let his characters fulfill their lot. He even permits a few of them to ascend directly into Heaven.

Whether Andersen is treating his subject with a profound seriousness or a brilliant sense of humor, any human being regardless of race, sex, social class or religion will nod in recognition to the incidents or situations being described. Poverty, social struggle, childhood, love, human betrayal, and death constitute the central themes of Andersen's tales and stories. Without the rich harvest of German literary tales and the Grimm brothers' achievements these tales and stories would never have come into existence. However, Andersen's realism seems much more comprehensive than theirs, his humor more evident and his irony present everywhere as a double exposure of the motifs.

The folktale is unequivocal in its view of fate, because it is rooted in popular belief. It deals with the way fate does justice to the repudiated and the disowned. It elevates the humble hero and rewards the humiliated person. By bravely defying the way of the world, it creates a reality in which poetry and devoutness are crucial. But it is not the values and ideas of the folktales that permeate Andersen's creative work. A great many of his tales and stories approach the eighteenth-century rationalist approach to telling fairy tales, such as that proclaimed by Christoph Martin Wieland. According to Wieland the fairy tale should approach an expression of knowledge of the way of the world, should contain wit, satire and allegory expressed in any possible form. This definition, which has the fable as a literary model, suffices to explain the character of a large number of Andersen's tales and stories. In fact they have many sources. There is a romantic-religious group conveying the tradition of the folktale and the German literary tale, such as **"The Little Mermaid"** and **"De vilde Svaner"** (1838; **The Wild Swans**). There is also a second group of satires and allegories related to the classical fables, such as **"Keiserens nye Klæder"** (1837; **"The Emperor's New Clothes"**) with a motif borrowed from a Spanish collection of anecdotes from the fourteenth century, Juan Manuel's, *El Conde Lucanor,* or **"Den uartige Dreng"** (1835; **"The Naughty Boy"**) which is based on the Greek poet Anacreon. Finally there are examples of realistic short stories devoid of any supernatural element, such as **"En Historie fra Klitterne"** (1860; **"A Story from the Sand Dunes"**) and **"Hvad Fatter gjør, det er altid det Rigtige"** (1861; **"What the Old Man Does Is Always Right"**).

Generally speaking, the complex and highly sophisticated forms did not appeal to Andersen. He aimed deliberately at creating works of simplicity, truth and nature by conveying an atmosphere of intimacy. As a storyteller he acts like a phenomenalist philosopher grasping the characteristic details and trying to let the truth appear by glimpses of intuition. In accordance with the program of the earliest romantics, Andersen tried to develop his own mythology based on tradition. The essential characteristic of a great writer is that he has created types and characters more alive to the tradition than real human beings. Andersen not only succeeded in creating imperishable characters, he also invented creatures of a pure imaginative character like the heroes and heroines of the sagas and the myths; such are the title figures of **"The Snow Queen"** and **"The Ice Maiden."** It is a remarkable feature about Andersen's tales that the supernatural settings—populated with all kinds of fanciful figures—border directly on the bourgeois world of everyday life. Andersen's skill in linking the sphere of normal life to a supernatural or fabulous world by making these separate worlds function together with imperceptible transitions between them, is quite unique.

More and more Andersen felt the urge to specialize in writing short prose. The retold folktales and the fictitious fairy tales were after 1850 replaced by various kinds of tales and stories with the German author Berthold Auerbach's *Schwarzwälder Dorfgeschichten* (1843-54) as a model. Andersen tried to extend his small genre in all possible directions. One way of experimenting was by writing new tales and stories upon request. In 1846 he was asked by Thorvaldsen to write **"Stoppenaalen"** (1847; **"The Darning Needle"**), and several years later, following a suggestion by Dickens, he finished **"Skarnbassen"** (1861; **"The Dung Beetle"**). Just as some of Andersen's narratives are connected with European colleagues of his time—such as **"Det gamle Huus"** (1848; **"The Old House"**), which he wrote after a visit to the German author Julius Mosen, whose little son had presented him with a tin soldier at his departure, and **"Vanddraaben"** (1848; **"A Drop of Water"**), which he wrote for his close friend Ørsted—others are closely attached to definite geographic localities, such as **"The Ice Maiden,"** which is a genuine Swiss tale, **"Psychen"** (1861; **"The Psyche"**), which is set in Rome, **"Metalsvinet"** (1862; **"The Metallic Pig"**) in Florence and **"Venskabs-Pagten"** (1862; **"The Treaty of Friendship"**) in Greece.

In Andersen's writing a trend toward popular and realistic storytelling dominated the 1850s and 1860s. He seemed restless in his attempts at finding new modes of expression and went over his manuscripts again and again. His texts tended to increase in length and complexity. At the same time he came under the influence of the Swedish singer Jenny Lind . . . and went through a crisis of religious and philosophical scruples. Only about one-sixth of his 156 tales and stories are without any reference to death. In twenty-four of them death is the main theme and in another twenty-five death is part of the conclusion. Whereas Andersen avoids all descriptions of sexuality, since this topic found no place in the literature of the time, he confined himself to telling about illegitimate children and their life stories. He kept turning death over in his mind, because as a lifelong bachelor he had repressed his own sexuality. When all his attention turned on death, his descriptions approached the macabre. He liked to describe skulls, skeletons, burials, and cemeteries; however he could also spare the details and simply let death appear as an old man wrapped in a horse cloth as in **"Historien om en Moder"** (1847; **"The Story of a Mother"**).

Besides death described as the universal lot of all humans, we find Andersen's concept of immortality as a transcendental phenomenon. He held the view that man has a right to immortality because of all the injustice and sufferings the majority of people are subject to during their lifetime, and he proportioned this concept to his aesthetics, as expressed in his tale of **"Ærens Tornevei"** (1863; **"The Thorny Path of Honor"**): "Fairy tale and reality are so close to one another, but the fairy tale has a harmonious resolution on this earth. Reality removes it from our life on earth by relating it

to time and eternity." Andersen's later writings reveal a brooding and sometimes even overly scrupulous man occupied with new experiments. By taking his point of departure in the folktale and the romantic concepts of the child and the people as the main objectives of all poetry, Andersen deliberately tried to go beyond national borders and place himself as a poet for all humanity. He built his world from below, using the prose sketch and the child as simple models, letting the arabesque unify poetry and visual art, as proposed by Friedrich Schlegel . . . and combining in his own way the idea of a fanciful imagination and a light irony with an exuberant abundance of details. Precisely by insisting on the origin of the arabesque in pictorial art did Andersen succeed in creating a prose richly endowed with the colors and contours of a visual world. Reality and dream did not exist apart from each other as incompatible extremes. . . .

Notes

. . . . .

[67] See F. Baldensberger. ["La grande communion romantique de 1827 sous le signe de Walter Scott." *Revue de Littérature Comparée,* 7, 1926-27.]

[68] See H. Kind. *Das Kind in der Ideologie und der Dichtung der deutschen Romantik.* Dresden: Dittert, 1936.

[69] Niels Kofoed. *Studier i H. C. Andersens Fortællekunst.* Copenhagen: Munksgaard, 1967, p. 96. See also Richard Benz. *Märchendichtung der Romantiker.* Gotha: Perthes, 1908.

[70] See, for instance, Sven H. Rossel, "Undine-motivet hos Friedrich de la Motte Fouqué, H. C. Andersen og Jean Giraudoux." *Edda,* 70 (1970), 151-61.

[71] Søren Baggesen. "Dobbeltartikulationen i. H. C. Andersens eventyr." *Andersen og Verden.* Odense: Odense University Press, 1993, pp. 26-27.

FURTHER READING

Biography

Enquist, Per Olov. "The Hans Christian Andersen Saga." Translated by Joan Tate. First published, 1985. Reprinted in *Scandinavian Review* 74, 3 (Autumn 1986): 64-69.
    Brief discussion of Andersen's troubled, poverty-stricken ancestors and his own unstable personality.

Grønbech, Bo. *Hans Christian Andersen.* Boston, Mass.: Twayne, 1980, 171 p.
    An extensive study of Andersen's life and works.

Pickard, P. M. "Hans Christian Andersen: Success and Failure." In *I Could a Tale Unfold: Violence, Horror and Sensationalism in Stories for Children,* pp. 67-93. London: Tavistock, 1961.

Provides psychological analyses of Andersen and discusses his life and career.

Spink, Reginald. *Hans Christian Andersen and His World.* London: Thames and Hudson, 1972, 128 p.

Pictorial biography of Andersen, including caricatures, reproductions of title pages, and various other illustrations.

Stirling, Monica. *The Wild Swan: The Life and Times of Hans Christian Andersen.* London: Collins, 1965, 384 p.

Popular and authoritative biography of Andersen.

Toksvig, Signe. *The Life of Hans Christian Andersen.* New York: Harcourt, Brace, 1934, 289 p.

A personal approach to Andersen emphasizing his emotional growth throughout his career.

Criticism

Dahlerup, Pil and others. "Splash!: Six Views of 'The Little Mermaid'." *Scandinavian Studies* 63, 2 (Spring 1991): 141-63.

Presents various analyses of Andersen's well-known tale.

De la Mare, Walter. "Hans Christian Andersen." In *Pleasures and Speculations,* pp. 14-23. London: Faber, 1940.

Discusses the child-like nature of Andersen and his tales.

Haugaard, Erik Christian. "Portrait of a Poet: Hans Christian Andersen and His Fairy Tales." First published, 1973. Reprinted in *The Openhearted Audience: Ten Authors Talk about Writing for Children,* edited by Virginia Haviland, pp. 68-81. Washington: Library of Congress, 1980.

Haugaard briefly reviews how he went about translating Andersen; the critic also discusses Andersen's life and his views on artists and religion.

Malmkjœr, Kirsten. "Punctuation in Hans Christian Andersen's Stories and in Their Translations into English." In *Nonverbal Communication and Translation: New Perspectives and Challenges in Literature, Interpretation and the Media,* edited by Fernando Poyatos, pp. 151-62. Amsterdam: John Benjamins, 1997.

Analyzes the differences between the punctuation Andersen used in Danish and the punctuation that appears in the English translations of his stories.

Mudrick, Marvin. "The Ugly Duck." In *Books Are Not Life but Then What Is?,* pp. 87-97. New York: Oxford University Press, 1979.

Criticizes Andersen for sentimentality, finding the author "moony" and his stories full of "Victorian trash and tinsel." The critic also contends that "the best of the world's fairy tales have a symmetry and a cutting edge that are quite beyond even the best Andersen."

Nassaar, Christopher S. "Andersen's 'The Shadow' and Wilde's 'The Fisherman and His Soul': A Case of Influence." *Nineteenth-Century Literature* 50, 2 (September 1995): 217-24.

Sees Oscar Wilde's story "The Fisherman and His Soul" as a Christian response to the nihilistic vision in Andersen's "The Shadow."

Sanders, Karin. "Nemesis of Mimesis: The Problem of Representation in H. C. Andersen's 'Psychen'." *Scandinavian Studies* 64, 1 (Winter 1992): 1-25.

Studies narcissism and feminization as depicted in Andersen's tale "Psyche."

Robert Browning

1812-1889

English poet and dramatist. For further information on Browning's life and works, see *NCLC*, Volume 19.

INTRODUCTION

Though Browning was eventually considered a premier Victorian poet, his critical reputation was hard won. Throughout his career, he honed the dramatic monologue, elevating the form to a new level. His experimentation with versification and with language, combined with the diversity and scope of his subject matter, forced Browning's critics to realize that this poet could not be evaluated by conventional literary standards. Particularly devoted to dramatic characterization, Browning explored the human psychology through his characters and the dramatic situations he presented. Modern critics are concerned with Browning's poetic development, with the themes that unite the various poems in a particular volume, and with the unique elements of Browning's innovative style.

Biographical Information

Born in Camberwell, a borough in southeast London, Browning was raised in a relatively affluent environment. His father was a well-read clerk for the Bank of England, and his mother was a strict Congregationalist. While Browning read widely as a boy, his formal education was somewhat irregular. Beginning in the early 1820s he attended the nearby Peckam School, where he studied for four years. Because Browning had not been raised as an Anglican, he was unable to attend the major English universities, Oxford and Cambridge. Instead, in 1828 he entered the recently-founded London University but terminated his studies after less than one year. Browning decided to pursue a career as a poet and lived in his parents' home, supported by them, until 1846. He published his first poem, *Pauline: A Fragment of a Confession,* anonymously in 1833. Browning continued writing and publishing and experimenting with the dramatic monologue until 1845, when he fell in love with Elizabeth Barrett. The pair secretly married in 1846, then departed for Italy where they settled in Florence and wrote until Elizabeth's death in 1861. Browning then returned to England, and after a period of literary inactivity, he began writing again. He remained highly prolific throughout the rest of his life. Browning died in 1889 while visiting his son in Venice. Browning's body was returned to England and buried in the Poets' Corner of Westminster Abbey.

Major Works

After the anonymous publication of *Pauline*, which Browning later insisted was a dramatic piece, many readers speculated that the sentiments expressed were the poet's own. In his next work, *Paracelsus* (1835), Browning established the objective framework offered by a more dramatic form and was thus able to distance himself from the characters in the poem. The dramatic monologue is based on the life of the Renaissance chemist Paracelsus, and the work received largely positive critical reviews. Browning then published *Sordello* in 1840, also based on a Renaissance subject, but the poem was less than favorably received by the critics, many of whom found it obscure and affected. In 1841, Browning began publishing a series of poems and dramas under the title *Bells and Pomegranates*. The final volume appeared in 1846 and failed to restore Browning's reputation among critics. In 1855, with the publication of *Men and Women*, containing Browning's well-known love poems and dramatic monologues, Browning began to receive the respect of some of his critics, although popular success still eluded him. It was not until the 1860s, and in particular the publication of *Dramatis Personae* in 1864, that Browning achieved major critical and popular success. The volume was followed shortly thereafter by his masterpiece, *The Ring and the Book* (1868-69). A series of dramatic monologues spoken by different characters, the work was based on an Italian murder case. *The Ring and the Book* cemented Browning's reputation as one of the foremost poets of Victorian England.

Critical Reception

Contemporary critical acclaim evaded Browning for many years. Gertrude Reese Hudson observes that the poet's critics required regular and frequent exposure to his unique dramatic method in order to recognize the excellence of Browning's art. Hudson also notes that other factors contributed to Browning's winning over of his critics, including their changing opinion regarding the nature of poetry, as well as a growing appreciation for both the timeliness of Browning's writing, his intellect and originality, and the "totality of his achievement."

Browning's highly individualized style and his usage of dramatic monologue fascinate modern scholars as much as these elements troubled his early critics. John Woolford and Daniel Karlin demonstrate that in using the dramatic monologue format, Browning was primarily interested in the creation and development of dramatic speakers and dramatic situations. The two critics also analyze Browning's style, finding that his poetry, in its focus on the speaker, insists on being read aloud. Woolford and Karlin further argue that Browning develops two distinct voices in his poetry, voices Browning himself described as "saying" and "singing" voices and which the critics contend result from the influence of the Romantics on Browning's work. In a separate essay, Daniel Karlin examines Browning's use of binary oppositions, finding that "every Browning poem is oppositional in nature." Karlin studies in particular the opposition between love and hate, maintaining that Browning explores hate not simply as the opposite of love, but as a force with its own purpose, a force which can lead to love as well as self-realization.

Other critics review certain volumes of Browning's poetry as a whole, arguing that the individual poems support a larger theme or purpose. Clyde de L. Ryals studies Browning's *Dramatic Romances and Lyrics* (1845) with this in mind. Ryals stresses that the theme of loyalty unites the poems in this volume, and that this theme is often expressed in an ironic manner. Furthermore, Ryals argues that while the majority of the poems may concern national loyalties, the poems also explore other kinds of loyalties, including loyalty to one's self, to one's religion, and to one's beloved.

Similarly, Adam Roberts argues for the unity of the poems in Browning's *Men and Women* (1855), asserting that the volume demonstrates Browning's first successful attempt at balancing the subjective and objective impulses in his poetry. This synthesis is achieved, Roberts argues, through Browning's characterization. Roberts explains that compared to the idiosyncratic, often insane characters in the earlier *Dramatic Romances and Lyrics,* the personalities in *Men and Women*, though complex, "communicate on something approaching our own level," and thus engender empathy and understanding among readers. Roberts goes on to discuss how Browning's continued usage of "grotesque" style and imagery (including colloquial language, rough syntax, and precise but blunt forms of expression) helps to link the form of these poems to their content.

Considerable critical discussion of Browning's work pertains to his murder mystery, *The Ring and the Book.* The twelve dramatic monologues, delivered by different characters, have led critics to question which, if any, of these characters serves as the moral authority, or center, of the poem. Adam Potkay argues against assigning this position of moral authority to any one of the characters and instead considers the poem as a "decentered struggle of interpretations" in which the character of Guido leads the way in "decentering" the poem by questioning the very conception of identity. W. David Shaw likewise contends that there is no central viewpoint in *The Ring and the Book* and maintains that while Browning ranks the authority of the characters in the poem, the poet creates no central authority figure. Additionally, Shaw explores the way in which deconstructionism and hermeneutics pervade Browning's masterwork, finding the Pope aligned with hermeneutical criticism and Guido and Tertium Quid aligned with the deconstructionists.

PRINCIPAL WORKS

Pauline: A Fragment of a Confession [anonymous] (poetry) 1833
Paracelsus (poetry) 1835
Strafford (drama) 1837
Sordello (poetry) 1840
Pippa Passes (drama) 1841
Dramatic Lyrics (poetry) 1842
King Victor and King Charles (drama) 1842
A Blot in the 'Scutcheon (drama) 1843
The Return of the Druses (drama) 1843
Colombe's Birthday (drama) 1844
Dramatic Romances and Lyrics (poetry) 1845
Luria. A Soul's Tragedy (dramas) 1846
Christmas-Eve and Easter-Day (poetry) 1850
Men and Women (poetry) 1855

The Poetical Works, 3 vols. (poetry) 1863
Dramatis Personae (poetry) 1864
The Ring and the Book 4 vols. (poetry) 1868-69
Balaustion's Adventure, Including a Transcript from Euripedes (poetry) 1871
Prince Hohenstiel-Schwangau, Saviour of Society (poetry) 1871
Fifine at the Fair (poetry) 1872
Red Cotton Night-Cap Country; or, Turf and Towers (poetry) 1873
Aristophanes' Apology, Including a Transcript from Euripedes, Being the Last Adventure of Balaustion (poetry) 1875
The Inn Album (poetry) 1875
Pacchiarotto, and Other Poems (poetry) 1876
La Saisiaz (poetry) 1878
Two Poets of Croisic (poetry) 1878
Dramatic Idyls, first series (poetry) 1879
Dramatic Idyls, second series (poetry) 1880
Jocoseria (poetry) 1883
Ferishtah's Fancies (poetry) 1884
Parleyings with Certain People of Importance in Their Day, to Wit: Bernard de Mandeville, Daniel Bartoli, Christopher Smart, George Budd Doddington, Francis Furini, Gerard de Lairesse, and Charles Avison (poetry) 1887
**An Essay on Percy Bysshe Shelley* (essay) 1888
Poetical Works. 16 vols. (poetry) 1888-89
Asolando: Fancies and Facts (poetry) 1889
The Works of Robert Browning. 10 vols. (poetry, dramas, and translation) 1912
The Complete Poetical Works of Robert Browning (poetry) 1915
The Complete Works of Robert Browning. 5 vols. to date (poetry, dramas, and essays) 1969-
The Poetical Works of Robert Browning. 4 vols. to date (poetry) 1983-
The Brownings' Correspondence. 4 vols. to date (letters) 1984-

*This work was included in the series *Bells and Pomegranates*, published from 1841 to 1846. Dramatic works in this series are chronologized by date of publication rather than first performance.

**This work was first published in 1852 as an introductory essay to *Letters of Percy Bysshe Shelley.*

CRITICISM

Clyde de L. Ryals (essay date 1983)

SOURCE: "Dramatic Romances and Lyrics," in *Becoming Browning: The Poems and Plays of Robert Browning, 1833-1846*, Ohio State University Press, 1983, pp. 201-29.

[*In the following essay, Ryals maintains that the poems in Browning's 1845 volume,* Dramatic Romances and Lyrics, *are linked by the theme of loyalty, a theme which Ryals argues is often expressed ironically.*]

Several months after the publication of ***Colombe's Birthday,*** Browning wrote to his friend Domett enclosing a copy of his play: " . . . I feel myself so much stronger, if flattery not deceive, that I shall stop some things that were meant to follow, and begin again" (*Domett,* p. 106). The things meant to follow seem to have been plays, for although two more were soon to be published, neither was intended for stage production. Beginning again apparently meant returning to shorter pieces of the kind that had appeared in ***Dramatic Lyrics*** three years earlier. Yet before he could begin—"I really seem to have something fresh to say"—Browning felt himself in need of a change, a trip to southern Italy to complement his visit in 1838 to northern Italy, where he had found artistic renewal. After which, "I never took so earnestly to the craft as I think I shall—or may, for these things are with God" (*Domett,* p. 106).

The second journey to Italy made between August and December 1844, proved remarkably fruitful. He not only wrote verse on the way there and back but also was inspired by Italian scenes to compose a number of poems upon his return. Again in England, he began correspondence with Elizabeth Barrett in January 1845 and finally met her in person some four months later. She too may have inspired some of the short poems that Browning now wrote. She did, at any rate, see a number of them in manuscript and in page proof and made suggestions for changes in them.[1] The verses were published as ***Dramatic Romances and Lyrics,*** the seventh number of ***Bells and Pomegranates,*** in November 1845.

As he was completing ***Colombe's Birthday,*** Browning seems to have discovered that ironic romance was a more salutary mode for him than tragedy, certainly as far as playwriting was concerned. ***Dramatic Lyrics*** of 1842 had proved, in the words of John Forster in the *Examiner* for 26 November 1842, a "continued advance in the right direction"—lyrics for the most part dramatic that are "full of the quick turns of feelings, the local truth, and the picturesque force of expression, which the stage so much delights in" and that redeem his genius from "mere metaphysical abstraction." Where Browning excelled, said Richard Hengist Horne, was in "dramatic portraiture."[2] By 1844 Browning could have had no doubt that his genius was essentially ironic. For some years now he had been forcing his native gift into literary forms alien to it—namely, the dramatic tragedy, basically a closed-end form that gravitates toward judgment in favor of one particular side of a dilemma. Browning had struggled mightily with the form, attempting to provide it with the multiple perspectives, even in its closure, that his genius dictated.

But it was all wrong, for only with the greatest wrenching of the plot could he force it to yield the ironic possibilities of character portrayal—"dramatic portraiture"—that he found most congenial. Writing for the stage would simply no longer do. As he told Elizabeth Barrett, he would compose no more plays after the one he was currently working on (Kintner, 1:26).

We have already noted how the dramatic monologue—what Browning called the dramatic lyric—is a salutary form for an author who hangs between immanence and transcendence, involvement and detachment, the lyric and the dramatic. We have also noted how those dramatic lyrics in which an ironic conflict is most strongly felt are those that realize most fully the potentialities of the form. But what of poems in which ironic tensions are significantly diminished, as for example in those works where the conflict between love and power is concluded by the choosing of one and the suppression (or forgetting) of the other? We have seen in **Colombe's Birthday** how Valence and Colombe choose love and Berthold chooses power and how their decisions force the play into the mold of ironic romance. Shorter forms dealing with such subject matter would then also be romances. Irony would not cease to inform poems of this nature, but ironic tensions would be reduced. As a result the emphasis would lie more heavily on narrative than on revelation of character. Browning decided therefore to call such poems dramatic romances. One cannot be sure exactly which of the **Dramatic Romances and Lyrics** the poet had in mind as romances. In the edition of 1863, at any rate, six of the poems of this volume come under the head of "Dramatic Romances."[3]

Like **Dramatic Lyrics** this collection covers a wide range of subjects treated from many different points of view and expressed in highly varying meters and line lengths. Here as in the earlier volume, some of the poems were published under titles by which they are no longer known. The contents were as follows:

> **"How They Brought the Good News from Ghent to Aix."** (16—.)
> **"Pictor Ignotus."** Florence, 16—.
> **"Italy in England"** [later called **"The Italian in England"**]
> **"England in Italy."** (Piano di Sorrento.) [later called **"The Englishman in Italy"**]
> **"The Lost Leader"**
> **"The Lost Mistress"**
> **"Home Thoughts, from Abroad"**
> **"The Tomb at St. Praxed's"** (Rome, 15—.) [later called **"The Bishop Orders His Tomb at St. Praxed's Church"**]
> **"Garden Fancies"**
> I. **"The Flower's Name"**
> II. **"Sibrandus Schafnaburgensis"**
> **"France and Spain"**

> I. **"The Laboratory"** (Ancien Regime.)
> II. **"Spain—The Confessional"**
> **"The Flight of the Duchess"**
> **"Earth's Immortalities"**
> **"Song"** ["Nay, but you, who do not love her"]
> **"The Boy and the Angel"**
> **"Night and Morning"**
> I. **"Night"** [later called **"Meeting at Night"**]
> II. **"Morning"** [later called **"Parting at Morning"**]
> **"Claret and Tokay"** [later called **"Nationality in Drinks"**]
> **"Saul"** [the first nine sections only, at the end of which is printed "(End of Part the First.)"]
> **"Time's Revenges"**
> **"The Glove"** (Peter Ronsard *loquitur*)

It will be noted that a number of these poems are complementary but, with the exception of three instances, are not, as in **Dramatic Lyrics,** given joint titles. Why this should be so is unclear. It may be that Browning no longer felt the need to emphasize the dramatic (as opposed to the personal) nature of the verses; it may be that he felt the yoking under one title to be too obvious. But the fact remains that several of the poems are related and are enhanced, as I propose to demonstrate, by being considered together. Indeed, all the poems gain from examination of them as related pieces having a common theme, which more often than not is expressed ironically.

Like **Dramatic Lyrics** the volume begins with a lyric narrative of adventure in war and on horseback. The anapestic lines of **"How They Brought the Good News from Ghent to Aix"** carry us with the rider on an urgent journey to bring the news that alone could save Aix. The poem has an unusual perspective in that the narrator makes his horse, Roland, and not himself the protagonist of the story, this being emphasized by the meter that almost suggests that the tale is being told from the horse's point of view. In the end all the narrator remembers is the last of the town's wine being poured down the horse's throat, "which . . . / Was no more than his due who brought good news from Ghent." In the end, in fact, Roland becomes the hero—not "which" but "who" brought the goods news to Aix.

"How They Brought the Good News" was eventually classified as a dramatic lyric. We might even call it a low-level dramatic monologue in that the selfless character of the speaker in this instance is obliquely revealed by what he says. But the romance quality of the poem is evident in the narrative, which stresses not the result but the process. Thus the narrator remembers every detail of his journey—the departure, what his fellows said, what the landscape was like, what he wore—but of his goal he can remember nothing save the state of his horse, the means by which the journey was made.

Loyal praise of a brave animal is inverted in the next poem to self-praise, at least self-defense, by a cowardly painter—not how *he* triumphed but why *I* failed. **"Pictor Ignotus"** is the monologue of an unknown painter of the Florentine High Renaissance who explains why he has not achieved the fame of the youth, presumably Raphael, who seems everywhere to be praised.[4] He could have done all the youth had done: he had the necessary talent and insight, nothing barred his way. Yet a voice spoke forbidding him to paint for the kind of worldly collector portrayed in **"My Last Duchess."** If then he is bested and his pictures die because he has shrunk from the new naturalism now fashionable, at least he has been able to dictate the terms of his defeat, having consciously and determinedly chosen to paint in the old style and thereby keep his art unsullied by the marketplace.

On first hearing, the apologia sounds convincing enough. We are in fact impressed by the artist who turns from the materialism of the Medicis and preserves a religious concern for his art. If there is a note of self-pity in his plea, it serves all the more to elicit our sympathy for this man of enormous potential but limited achievement. Yet on reflection we begin to wonder about two matters—namely, was he as talented as he says, and whose was the voice deflecting him from the fame he wished? In other words, judgment sets in when sympathy of the moment fades.

Claiming a God-given ability to perceive truth in the heavens, on the earth, and in man, he also makes pretense to the talent that would permit him to translate this truth to canvas, showing

> Each face obedient to its passion's law,
>   Each passion clear proclaimed without a
>   tongue;
> Whether Hope rose at once in all the blood,
>   A-tiptoe for the blessing of embrace,
> Or Rapture drooped the eyes as when her
>   brood
>   Pull down the nesting dove's heart to its
>   place,
> Or Confidence lit swift the forehead up,
>   And locked the mouth fast, like a castle
>   braved.

We know from his descriptions that he would be showing these not embodied in real men and women but as personified abstractions in stylized form. And he too half faces up to his limitations when he asks, in the very next lines, "Men, women, children, hath it spilt, my cup? / What did ye give me that I have not saved?" The questions are not answered, but we see from the

metaphor that whatever artistic gifts he possesses he has hoarded without ever expending them in art.

He has dreamed of fame, of sending his pictures forth "through old streets named afresh" in honor of him, and then in death would "not go to heaven, but linger here," on earth. The thought was thrilling; but then it grew frightful, "'tis so wildly dear!" The expenditure of psychic energy would be simply too great: it would mean nothing less than becoming a new man, undergoing a rebirth. And is it worth it, after all? No, for "a voice changed it," this aspiration. The speaker does not tell us who spoke. He does not tell us for the very reason that he does not know. If he knew, then he could blame someone for his failure, and no apology to himself or to anybody else would be necessary. But he cannot seriously consider that the voice is his own because to do so would be tantamount to admitting to inadequacy.

Like so many of Browning's characters whom we have noticed, the painter attributes his limitations to fate, which in effect is the voice's authority. He was like a man looking through a door to the revels inside, the revels "of some strange House of Idols at its rites." Suddenly the world was changed for him. But he was afraid of what he saw, even afraid of himself. "Who summoned these cold faces which began / To press on me and judge me?" To enter would mean turning his back on the kind of art that he had perfected, doing violence to it and to himself. "They drew me forth," but "spite of me," like a nun "shrinking from the soldiery." Then the voice spoke and he went no farther. Fate intervened just in time. He can therefore urge that he did not transgress his own moral destiny: "they" drew him forth in spite of himself.

He and his pictures have been spared the "daily pettiness" of the collector who might purchase "our" work. Other artists may be willing to suffer the inanity of the material-minded virtuosos concerning "our pictures," but as for himself, "I chose my portion." If he is an unknown painter, it is because *he* has wanted to remain so. Fate, in the form of limitation of either skill or vision, has not barred the way; the responsibility, he says in a gesture of pride, is totally his: he has determined his own defeat.

The note of bravery wavers however: his heart "sinks" as he goes about his ordinary, "monotonous" business of painting the "endless cloisters and eternal aisles" with the "same" series of religious figures, all with "the same cold, calm, beautiful regard." In the end he poses as the pathetic but brave little soul who has consciously elected obscurity for himself and his art out of the highest principle. He knows his pictures will die, blackening and mouldering in the silence of the shrine, but at least he and they will be spared the merchant's traffic. Finally, he asks, is fame worth the debasement of principle and purity?

Throughout the monologue there are images of expansion and contraction, of blazing light and darkness, of expenditure and hoarding. Even the pictures he would paint reveal the same imagery: Hope rising to be embraced, Rapture drooping the eyes as when her brood pulls down the heart to its place, Confidence lighting up the forehead and locking the mouth. He paints, in other words, images of his own inhibiting will. Clearly every leaping up of his heart is checked by timidity and fear. Like his spiritual brother J. Alfred Prufrock, the unknown painter always settles down on the side of parsimony: "it" would not be worth the expenditure; the expense of spirit, whether in love or art, is lust in action.

The design of **"Pictor Ignotus"** is much like that of **"My Last Duchess."** The speaker inadvertently reveals his character by his utterance, which in this case is, as it is partially in the case of the earlier poem, a defense of, and apology for, himself. Where in the earlier monologue Browning employed rhymed couplets for a certain effect, he here uses alternative rhyme—*abab, bcbc* etc.—to suggest enclosure. Likewise, at the conclusion of the monologue, he introduces a further ironic note in a passage that epitomizes the speaker. Where the duke referred to Neptune taming a sea-horse, Pictor Ignotus asks: "Blown harshly, keeps the trump its golden cry? / Tastes sweet the water with such specks of earth?" These are of course the old Romantic questions: Is not the idea profaned when expressed in the imperfect medium of language? Is not the thought debased when translated into action? But here the questions, which the speaker intends as images of empty fame, are ironically expressed, as Herbert Tucker suggests,[5] in images of prophetic creativity. Gabriel's trumpet awakens the dead to new life; Shelley's west wind is to be a trumpet of prophecy. Moses strikes the rock to bring forth water from the earth; Browning himself uses the story in book three of **Sordello** to speak of the water of life that the multitude dispraises as dim oozings. By such means the poet himself intrudes, as it were, into his poem, to comment upon his creation, to make himself known, and to remind us that the monologue, for all its verisimilitude, is after all not life but art.

The same imagery of expansion and contraction is likewise used in the next two poems to yield an ironic effect. The first of the companion poems, **"Italy in England,"** is the monologue of an Italian patriot now in exile in England recounting how a loyal *contadina* helped him escape the Austrian police. For three days he had been hiding in a recessed aqueduct, when he managed to attract the attention of a girl passing by. He was going to lie to her concerning why he was there; but finding her so artless he tells her the truth, asks for food and drink, and requests her to carry a message into Padua. She does all this and thereby helps him elude capture. Now, safely in England, he looks back over his last days in Italy long ago, and in doing

so reveals how the intervening years have taken their toll of his youthful fervor and openness to spontaneous emotion.

During his long exile the monologist has become a professional patriot, so to speak, doing all those things, like raising money and eliciting statements of support, necessary for his cause. But in the process he has become a monomanic, has little "thought / Concerning—much less wished for—aught / Beside the good of Italy / For which I live and mean to die!" He is, in effect, dead to all save The Cause. He knows this, although he does not put it in exactly those terms and rationalizes it as the price one pays for such patriotism. Yet looking back over those few days just before he left Italy for good, he experiences something of the old emotion. For thinking what he might possibly wish for, if he pleased to spend three wishes on himself, he still turns to matters connected with The Cause for the first two, both of which, not unexpectedly, issue from hate: the bloody murder of Metternich and the slow death from a broken heart of his old friend Charles, who deserted The Cause. As for the third, he wishes to see the girl who rescued him, now grown into a married woman with children:

> know if yet that woman smiles
> With the calm smile—some little farm
> She lives in there, no doubt—what harm
> If I sat on the door-side bench,
> And, while her spindle made a trench
> Fantastically in the dust,
> Inquired of all her fortunes—just
> Her children's ages and their names,
> And what may be the husband's aims
> For each of them—I'd talk this out,
> And sit there, for an hour about,
> Then kiss her hand once more, and lay
> Mine on her head, and go my way.

Instead of such natural but homely joys that love can bring, he was wedded The Cause, which has sapped his soul's energy and made him dead to all natural joy. For an instant he is almost willing to admit that he wishes his life had been otherwise, but then the mania returns and in an *envoi* he says: "So much for idle wishing—how / It steals the time! To business now!"

Like Pictor Ignotus, the Italian in England refuses spiritual rebirth out of a mistaken sense of loyalty. And, as in the preceding monologue, Browning enters the poem, disguisedly, to try to make certain that we do not overlook what he intends. He does so here by infusing the poem with imagery of rebirth. The story takes place during Holy Week. The speaker is a man with a price on his head and has a friend who betrays him. The girl comes to him in his "crypt." He pictures her as Mary is frequently represented iconographically, her foot on a snake, and he asks her to be the mediatrix between himself and the help he seeks in the Duomo, where as a type of Our Lady of Peace she is to ask "whence comes peace?" to which she may expect the reply "From Christ and Freedom." At the end of seven days—that is, on Easter—help comes through her aid and he rises from his hiding place and departs from Italy by sea.[6] There is never any hint of passionate love between the two, only selfless devotion on her part to a man in need and, on the part of both, to a common cause. " . . . I could not choose," says the speaker, "But kiss her hand and lay my own / Upon her head," the same gestures he would make again were his third wish granted. By his imagery Browning would have us see that the possibility of rebirth still remains: what is necessary is that the patriot for a while forgo his "business" in favor of more ordinary and purely human relationships. The poem depicts concisely the monomania and the bitterness of long political exile.

The companion monologue, **"England in Italy,"** suffers from lengthiness and from the poet's lack of a clear conception of what he wanted it to be. Apparently Browning originally intended it as a description of the landscape around Naples, but then he added an ending concerning the Corn Laws, probably for two reasons: to give it a political slant so that it could more properly serve as a pendant to **"Italy in England"** and, secondly, to give the discursive stanzas a more pointed ending. Elizabeth Barrett wrote to the poet, after having seen first the manuscript and then the printer's proofs, that the ending "gives unity to the whole . . . just what the poem wanted" (Kintner, 1:244).

The monologue is addressed to a small peasant girl frightened by the scirocco that has brought a storm of rain. The Englishman tries to comfort her by describing his impressions of the past day: the dryness, the churning seas, the flapping birdnets, the wine-making, his ascent of a mountain to view the sea below and the clear sky above—all images suggestive of death and rebirth and clearer vision. The wind has now come, the storm has passed, the festive celebration will soon begin. All this is described in 285 lines, at which point the speaker says, doubtless sensing the child's boredom, "'Such trifles' you say?" On this very day in England, Parliament is debating the Corn Laws, whether abolishing them be "righteous and wise." Why, they might just as well debate whether the scirocco should vanish in black from the skies!

The sentiment is noble, and the poem has been read as expressive of Browning's own political liberalism. If it is no more than that—description of Neapolitan landscape followed by an ejaculation of political liberalism—then it can make no claim to being a dramatic monologue. We must, however, recall that the poem is presumably intended as a companion to **"Italy in England"** and that we are expected to note certain similarities. This means that, at the very least, we must

suspect an ironic intent. When we look carefully, we are puzzled by the speaker's claim to share Ulysses' secret: "He heard and he knew this life's secret / I hear and I know!" (227-28). Whatever the secret is—apparently it is that men should be free—the monologuist does little to help others realize it. Unlike the Italian in England, he is not forced into exile; on the contrary, he is a tourist fascinated by the quaint ways of Italian life and the oddity of the landscape. While "in my England at home, / Men meet gravely to-day" to debate the Corn Laws, he amuses himself with the "sensual and timorous beauty" (195) of southern Italy. Where the Italian exile has his country's freedom as his "business," the English tourist can give but a passing mention—and this to a child—of the most serious cause of starvation in England during the "hungry forties." The echo of Shelley's "Ode to the West Wind" that Browning so strongly intended is purely for ironic effect.

Loyalty to a cause is more forcefully the informing idea of the following poem, **"The Lost Leader."** The poet who was once in the glorious company of Shakespeare, Milton, Burns, and Shelley has broken from the vanguard and the freemen to sink to the rear and the slaves, although in the eyes of the world he is up front in the limelight for all to see. The apostate has gone and will never be welcomed back, being a "lost soul," the most serious charge Browning can make against anyone. But this Judas is lost only as a leader; his accomplished work remains and entitles him to be "pardoned in Heaven, the first by the throne!" It is not, I believe, so much Browning's devotion to the poetry of Wordsworth (who so obviously is the Lost Leader)[7] as his sense of irony that dictates the final turn in the poem.

"The Lost Mistress" is artificially linked to its companion by the adjective in the title. In tone it is entirely different. Where the speaker of the former poem was more than ready to shout invective and heap opprobrium upon the disloyal leader, the speaker of the second is more than gentle, making no charge against his unfaithful lady love. **"The Lost Mistress"** is a more interesting poem dramatically than its companion because here the speaker has a design upon his auditor, which is to elicit pity and show himself as the manly knight of infinite resignation. "All's over then . . ?" he asks. Surely this can hardly be, for his mistress's words of dismissal sound no bitterer than the sparrows' good-night twitter. Surely her farewell is but a signal for a slight transition in their relationship. She will not really send him away? He will appear as no more than a friend, claiming but ever so slightly more than mere friendship entitles him to.

We cannot know how the mistress interprets his pretty little speech, but we see that he enjoys his status as the rejected lover. In the first place, it is better to have loved and lost than never to have loved at all because in being the loser there are certain claims to distinction. In the second place, he enjoys playing the role of the martyr, enjoys abasing himself, enjoys the revel in self-pity: "Mere friends are we,—well, friends the merest / Keep much that I'll resign." The monologue is only twenty lines long but it manages to reveal the character of a rejected suitor who makes every effort to present himself in the most favorable light, to his auditor and to himself, as infinitely injured but eternally faithful. It is a sort of preliminary sketch of **"Andrea del Sarto."**

Loyalty of another kind is the theme of **"Home-Thoughts, from Abroad,"** which was originally composed of three separate lyrics instead of the two that we now know. The beauties praised in **"Oh, to be in England"** are those quiet ones alluded to in the **"The Lost Mistress."** We have often noted, from *Paracelsus* onward, how for Browning the present moment takes on meaning only when viewed in terms of the future, as being ever in the process of becoming. We may note the same in this lyric.

> Oh, to be in England
> Now that April's there,
> And who wakes in England
> Sees, some morning, unaware,
> That the lowest boughs and the brush-wood
>   sheaf
> Round the elm-tree bole are in tiny leaf,
> While the chaffinch sings on the orchard
>   bough
> In England—now!

The "some morning" turns out to be "now," and the lines that were growing longer under the promise of a future morning end in a final "In England—now," the shortest line of the strophe.

For most poets these beautiful lines would be poem enough. For Browning, however, they must be redeemed from their April nowness by the coming May. Or to put it another way, the lyric moment is to be incorporated into a dramatic movement.

> And after April, when May follows,
> And the whitethroat builds, and all the
>   swallows—
> Hark! where my blossomed pear-tree in the
>   hedge
> Leans to the field and scatters on the clover
> Blossoms and dewdrops—at the bent spray's
>   edge—
> That's the wise thrush; he signs each song
>   twice over
> Lest you should think he never could
>   recapture
> The first fine careless rapture!
> And though the fields are rough with hoary
>   dew,
> All will be gay when noontide wakes anew
> The buttercups, the little children's dower,
> —Far brighter than this gaudy melon-flower!

The April-becoming-May is a month of rapid movement. Where the boughs and sheaf *are* in tiny leaf in the first strophe, the pear tree *leans* and *scatters*. Where April's chaffinch sings, the thrush of anticipated May sings his song twice over. Like the bird the poet of this lyric sings twice over so as to recapture the first moment, to bind his days together, to redeem the past from its pastness, to put futurity into the present. All *will* be gay when April becomes May. And because April possesses this quality of becoming, the flowers of the future-in-the-present are far brighter than *this* southern gaudy melon-flower here and now. It is not that we pine for what is not or that unheard melodies are sweeter than tonal ditties—attitudes of Romantic poets; rather, it is the pregnancy of the present that makes it meaningful. This is why the English April landscape of dainty, quiet beauties about to be the blossoms of May makes dull by comparison the gaudy beauties of the south, which, in this spring month, are already fullblown.

The second lyric of **"Home-Thoughts"**—"Here's to Nelson's memory!"—is a drinking song that sounds more like Thomas Hood than Browning and that the poet may have included so as to give his volume a certain topicality.[8] In the third of **"Home-Thoughts,"** which takes place in the waters that inspired the preceding lyric, the speaker admonishes him who would help England to turn away from noisy earthly feats to silent prayer.

The irony is more pronounced in the next poem, **"The Tomb at St. Praxed's."** Officially a Christian, the speaker is actually an independent thinker who does not perceive that his speculations are often contrary to Christian doctrine. Like the soliloquizer of the Spanish cloister, he adheres to the outward forms of his religion but is almost totally oblivious to the meaning behind them. He begins his monologue with a quotation from Ecclesiastes—"Vanity, saith the preacher, vanity!"—which causes us to believe that we are about to hear a sermon on that text. But immediately we learn that the bishop, as the revised title of 1849 identifies him, is not in the pulpit but in bed. Yet in bed as in the pulpit, the bishop adopts a homiletic manner: "And as she died so must we die ourselves, / And thence ye may perceive the world's a dream. / Life, how and what is it?" The bishop is infected by a *déformation professionelle*: throughout his monologue he lapses into his homiletic style.

As he pleads with his sons for a magnificent tomb in which to be buried, he recalls his past (worldly) life, rehearses the recumbent posture of his effigy atop the desired tomb, and slips from time to time into his pulpit manner—all of which serve to point up the discrepancy between what as a Christian prelate he should be and what he actually is. Evidently unconcerned for the salvation of his soul, he is preoccupied with the tomb, which offers him a form of physical immortality. The most telling moral irony is expressed in the quotation from Job: "Swift as a weaver's shuttle fleet our years: / Man goeth to the grave, and where is he?" Where indeed? According to the bishop, in a beautiful tomb where he may gloat over his defeated rival. The bishop's greatest fear is not of the Last Judgment but of a cheap sepulcher.

As he continues to talk, his mind becomes muddled. At the beginning when he asked, "Do I live, am I dead?" he knew very well that, though dying, he was still very much alive and able, for perhaps the last time, to entreat his sons to bury him in proper fashion and to bargain with them concerning what they would be willing to give. At the end, however, when he asks the same question, he fancies himself already lying on his entablature atop the tomb, his sons' "ingratitude" having stabbed him to death.

In the case of the bishop of Saint Praxed's as in that of the Duke of Ferrara, the monologue serves no strategic prupose. The bishop knows that the more he talks, the less likely he is to get the tomb he wants. The sons have heard all this many times before and they whisper to Anselm that the old man's at it again. Why then does the bishop continue his monologue? For the same reason that the duke makes his indiscreet remarks to the envoy. The lyric impulse is so strong in each of them that they allow themselves to be carried away by the song of self, the song that they conceive not as condemning but as apologetic and justifying. In the bishop's own mind, he is an exemplary clergyman—"how I earned the prize!" He has met all the demands of religious formalism and been a Renaissance humanist to boot. What matter if he violated his priestly vow of celibacy or hated his brother clergyman? He has loved the blessed mutter of the Mass, felt the altar's candle flame, and tasted the strong incense smoke; he has lived with popes and cardinals and priests. What more could be expected of him? And now to crown his life, he must have a beautiful tomb as testimony not only to his Christian life but also to his superiority over his old rival, Gandolf. His sons may not give him what he deserves, but he wants to make clear that he has every right to it and is perfectly justified in whatever self-pity he may feel.

There is an obvious irony in all this. But the great irony is the poet's own intrusion into the monologue, an act that marks the monologue as a poem, calls attention to it as not merely the utterance of a Renaissance bishop but as a work of art. For Browning has designed the monologue as an exemplum, a sermon by example, on the text *Vanitas vanitatem,* the first line (in translation) of the monologue. **"The Tomb at St. Praxed's"** is thus a sermon unknowingly preached by the bishop; which is to say, the preacher proves his text by the revelation of his own character, and his plea for

sympathy becomes a literary form—a sermon—that stands in judgment of him. A poet can hardly go further in achieving so subtly those reflections of the work of art in the work of art itself that characterize Romantic Irony. In brief, **"The Bishop Orders His Tomb at St. Praxed's Church,"** the title by which it is now known, is a masterpiece. In future years Browning might add to the complexity of his dramatic monologues,[9] but he would never surpass the extraordinary ironic dimension of this poem.

The poems immediately following are of much smaller scale. **"Garden Fancies"** is composed of **"The Flower's Name"** and **"Sibrandus Schafnaburgensis,"** both about language. In the first the speaker's lady has given to an inconspicuous flower without any obvious beauty "its soft meandering Spanish name: / What a name! was it love, or praise? / Speech half-asleep, or song half-awake?" Where **"The Flower's Name"** deals with the preservative power of language, the second deals with the uncreating word. The speaker recognizes the book by the author named in the title as the work of a pedant that may well be cast away. He places it in the crevice of the crotch of a plum tree, where it meets with all sorts of teeming animal life that mock the lifeless words. Finding this unquiet grave unfit, the speaker then takes the book to be buried on a bookshelf under other dead books by "A," "B," and "C" to "dry-rot at ease till the Judgment-day!"

The next two poems, with the joint title **"France and Spain,"** are also concerned with language. In the first, **"The Laboratory,"** words disguise the horror of the action: if the lady describes the poison with which she would kill her rival as beautiful, then it cannot be so bad to administer it. The lady, in fact, attempts by language to make murder a fine art. She is an innocent concerning the means to do her deed: "Which is the poison to poison her, prithee?" "And yonder soft phial, . . . —is that poison too?" And it is her very innocence, the quality of the ingenue, that gives a passionate intensity to her monologue and the hatred that it expresses.

Throughout her visit to the laboratory, the lady—wearing a mask of glass to ward off the noxious fumes as well as a mask of language to filter reality—acts as though she were inspecting a flower garden, asking the name of each and admiring its pretty color. This is, however, but the *vorspiel* to the main play. "Let death be felt and the proof remain; / . . . He is sure to remember her dying face!" she says, preparing the enactment of the drama that she is concocting. And for the man who has put together the requisite properties, she offers, with all the innocence and cold-bloodedness of a diva acting an ingenue: "Now, take all my jewels, gorge gold to your fill, / You may kiss me, old man, on my mouth if you will!"

In contrast to the dramatic monologue to which it is linked, **"The Confessional"** is more nearly a romance, the monologue of an imprisoned young woman who was tricked into revealing the secrets of her lover, a political revolutionary. The poem turns on the verb "to lie," in both its physical and linguistic meanings. Having lain with her lover, the girl is shocked to discover that his lips have "kissed / My soul out in a burning mist." She feels guilty not so much for the act of fornication as for the fact that physical love has supplanted religious love. Confessing her sexual transgressions to a priest, she is informed that she can "turn this love . . . / To lawful love, almost divine"; even further, she can be an angel to save the soul of her lover. All she has to do is ask of her paramour, when he "lies" upon her breast, his plans for political action, then steal off and reveal them to her confessor, who may then act to purge the lover's soul. Because her father confessor seemed full of "love and truth," she does as he wishes: her lover tells all, as she "lay listening in such pride," and she next morning trips off to the confessional "to save his soul in his despite." The result is that the young man is hanged. As the girl discovers his distorted body on the scaffold, she sees also, "lo,—on high—the father's face!" Now in prison, she turns her back entirely on religion. Clearly the truth for her is the physical "lying" of passionate lovers, not the "lying" of the Church.

There is a slight revelation of character in this confession, but it results more from the story than from the manner in which the story is told. The same is likewise true of **"The Flight of the Duchess,"** which also shares the theme of loyalty. The poem seems to hesitate between the narrative and the dramatic modes. This was true of **"Waring"** of 1842, but as we saw, that poem finally comes down on the side of the dramatic. In the case of **"The Flight of the Duchess,"** a much longer monologue recounting a more elaborate story, we can never be sure whether the interest should lie in *what* the speaker sees or *how* he sees. All commentators refer to it as narrative,[10] yet it has a dramatic setting and a dramatically portrayed speaker.

The monologue takes place in what seems to be a country tavern and is addressed to a long-suffering auditor who sits through 915 lines without saying a word. The speaker begins the story in a tone of beery confidence to his "friend," apparently a man he has never seen before. Now it may be that he has a design upon his auditor, for two matters, besides the story of the duchess, are very much on his tongue: drink, which he mentions at least twenty times, and friendship, which he praises frequently and which, to my ear at any rate, he protests too much. It may be that he tells the story of the duchess in hope of a free drink. If so, his hope seems to be unrealized because at the end he speaks of "no further throwing / Pearls before swine that can't value them: Amen"—which utterance may be intended to apply to the listener as well as to the duke.

We can have no assurance that we are to read the poem in this (dramatic) way—and I offer this interpretation unconfidently—because the poet has not, so far as I can see, given us enough clues. If it is merely a dramatic monologue *manqué*, the fault is perhaps owing to the difference between the original conception and the actual composition of the poem at a later date. Browning said that the idea of the poem grew out of a snatch of song he heard a gypsy singing. Some time soon thereafter he sat down to work on it but was called upon by a visitor and then other interruptions occurred so that he forgot the plan of the poem (Hood, *Letters,* p. 217). He told Miss Barrett that of "the real conception . . . not a line is written"

> —tho' perhaps after all, what I am going to call the accessories in the story are real though indirect reflexes of the original idea, and so supersede properly enough the necessity of its personal appearance,—so to speak: but, as I conceived the poem, it consisted entirely of the gipsy's description of the life the Lady was to lead with her future gipsy lover—a *real* life, not an unreal one like that with the Duke—and as I meant to write it, all their wild adventures would have come out and the insignificance of the former vegetation have been deducible only—as the main subject has become now. . . . (Kintner, 1:135)

It would appear, therefore, that having the story told by a retainer of the duke's household was an afterthought, which may account for the imperfect dramatic realization of the speaker.

The story itself is one common enough in Browning's later works—a woman rescued from a stultifying marriage to pursue a freer life of emotional fulfillment—but this is its first major expression. Commentators have argued that the poem was a calculated move in the poet's courtship of Elizabeth Barrett,[11] but as we have seen, something of the same pattern of movement is reflected in **Colombe's Birthday,** written and published before he even met his wife-to-be. Something happened to cause Browning to decide that he would admit the dialectic struggle between power and love to be irresolvable and that he would declare in favor of love, but showing it to retreat in the face of power. **"The Flight of the Duchess"** is the retelling of **"My Last Duchess,"** the heroine this time, however, fleeing from the husband besotted by his family lineage. The gypsy woman who helps her escape assures her of "the thrill of the great deliverance," but such a life of love means to "retire apart" (671) from the ordinary world and all its responsibilities, as for Colombe and Valence it required retreat to flowery seclusion. In Browning's world love may no longer be a matter of pathology, but it is not one of healthy acceptance of the world. This is a point continually but unconsciously made by the narrator.

What the narrator proposes to recount is the duchess's tale "from beginning to end" (3). Yet it is the story of himself from start to almost finish. As far as the duchess is concerned, she does not even appear till line 133. The narrator then gives us a brief, straightforward, realistic account of the duke and of the duchess's unhappiness as his wife. But the realistic vein is soon transmuted as the old gypsy is metamorphosed from a crone into a stately woman who speaks with the sound of music and looks with beguiling eye to lend the duchess new life and transform her into a queen. Only at the end does the note of realism return, when he speaks of his dead wife and his duty to the duke. The world of the gypsies is but make-believe, one in which the fancied inhabitants live happily ever after, their story never coming to an end. The world of the huntsman, on the other hand, is all too real, lacking in picturesque adventure perhaps but not without its quiet pleasures, the domestic affections and loyalties that end (because being real they must end) only with death.[12] In romance the protagonist may depart into fancy to be a gypsy wanderer forever, but in the realistic tale, which is that of the huntsman, one "must stay till the end of the chapter" (861). In **"The Flight of the Duchess,"** therefore, we have two versions of love and loyalty—one enclosed and the other open-ended—both of which we are in effect invited to see as true.

Like earlier works **"The Flight of the Duchess"** portrays characters self-consciously playing roles and speaking in accord with what they believe the scripts for those roles to be. The narrator presents himself as the plain man ready to tell a tale in an artistic fashion, even in verse, but limited by his halting manner—"More fault of those who had the hammering / Of prosady into me and syntax" (699-700). The duke is a product of Gothic Revival: a "middle-age manners adapter" (861) who talks and acts according to how "old books showed the way of it" and "how taught old painters in their pictures" (228, 231). In the cast of his little play, he is *The Duke,* his retainers are *Serfs, Thralls, Venerers, Prickers,* and *Verderers.* In reality he is effete, artificial, and anachronistic, so frozen in his role (and in a stultifying past) that his duchess, craving for real life, as Browning put it, cannot bear to live with him. Only in **"Sibrandus Schafnaburgensis"** does Browning so blatantly make fun of one of the characters in this volume.

"The Flight of the Duchess," although it has some of the same charming improvised air as **"The Pied Piper,"** is not a successful poem because of its imperfectly realized narrator and because it is too long. It is, however, something of an experimental poem in that Browning employs in the opening lines a symbolic landscape.

> Ours is a great wild country;
> If you climb to our castle's top,
> I don't see where your eye can stop;
> For when you've pass'd the corn-field
>   country,
> Where vineyards leave off, flocks are pack'd,
> And sheep-range leads to cattle-tract,

> And cattle-tract to open-chase,
> And open-chase to the very base
> Of the mountain where, at a funeral pace,
> Round about, solemn and slow,
> One by one, row after row,
> Up and up the pine-trees go,
> So, like black priests up, and so
> Down the other side again
> To another greater, wilder country,
> That's one vast red drear burnt-up plain,
> Branch'd thro' and thro' with many a vein
> Whence iron's dug, and copper's dealt;
> Look right, look left, look straight before,
> Beneath they mine, above they smelt,
> Copper-ore and iron-ore,
> And forge and furnace mould and melt,
> And so on, more and ever more,
> Till, at the last, for a bounding belt,
> Comes the salt sand hoar of the great sea
>   shore,
> —And the whole is our Duke's country!

(6-31)

The mixing of the agricultural and the industrial, the high and the low, the light and the dark, the open and the enclosed—all suggest the course the poem is to follow. This lovely piece of landscape painting is admittedly more or less forced on the huntsman's tale, but it is worthy of remark in that it shows Browning experimenting with more sophisticated modes of narration.[13]

In the first lyric of **"Earth's Immortalities,"** the poet's grave—and by implication his reputation—"wants the freshness of its prime," the work of time having "softened down the crisp-cut name and date." In the second lyric the speaker, who may be the poet of the first, his initial line echoing the last word, "date," of the former,[14] notes how spring's garlands are severed by June's fever, which in turn is quenched in winter's snow—all in constant mockery of the words "Love me for ever!"[15] In **"Song"** ("Nay, but you, who do not love her"), the irony resides in a form of *praeterita.* In **"The Boy and the Angel,"** the irony of God's need for the human is set forth in a simple lyric reminiscent of the manner of Blake.

The first lyric of **"Night and Morning,"** now known as **"Meeting at Night,"** is in the present tense and describes the lover's coming to meet his beloved, the rhythm and imagery suggesting tension and anticipation until the final coming to rest with "two hearts beating each to each." In the lyric now known as **"Parting at Morning,"** which is one-third the length of the preceding one and which is related in the first person and in the past tense, there is no question of romantic love, as the speaker refuses to delude himself that rapture can sustain life: departing from the night's meeting, he declares "the need of a world of men."[16] **"Claret and Tokay"** are overly cute associations of certain wines with certain countries and are unworthy of mention save that they evince Browning's penchant for dramatizing everything, even bottles of claret and tokay.

"Saul" was printed as a fragment in 1845. It consisted of short half-lines instead of the anapestic pentameters with which we are now familiar, and it ended with the present section nine of the completed poem. These 102 lines, sung to the spiritually benumbed King Saul by the shepherd boy David, recall earth's beauties and bounties, great moments in Jewish history, his people's hymns of aspiration, the greatness of Saul's accomplishment—in short, all the things that Saul has to be thankful for. The matter and the manner of the song, largely a cataloguing of events and details, are doubtless borrowed from Christopher Smart, especially his "Song to David."[17] As it stands in 1845, the poem leaves us with the situation of a man who has everything to praise God for being unable to utter a word or even lift his eyes to heaven. Browning may not have been able to complete it either because after 102 lines he had exhausted the matter and manner of his model or because he had not in 1845 arrived at the stage of his religious development that would enable him to offer the Christian answer of the completed version.[18]

As a fragment (or even as a completed poem, for that matter), the monologue is generically unlike anything else in the 1845 volume. It is not a dramatic monologue because there is no revelation of character. It has a number of narrative elements, but clearly it is not primarily intended to tell a story. What it most nearly resembles is a Davidic psalm—and of course it would be very like Browning to have his David sing in the manner of the reputed author of Psalms.[19] In any case, the fragmentary "Saul" is a highly experimental poem, blending lyric, narrative, and dramatic elements in almost equal proportions. Browning recognized that some song of a different nature was required to bring Saul out of his lethargy and so complete the poem. The solution he eventually hit upon was to go beyond Psalms, as in the first nine sections he has gone beyond the Historical Books, to the Prophets; but that is a story for later telling, the completed poem not being published till 1855.

"Time's Revenges" deals with romantic love. On the one hand, the soliloquizer has a loyal friend who would go to any length of trouble for him but for whom he cares almost nothing. On the other hand, he has a ladylove who, although he has given up body and soul for her, not only would not help him in distress but would let him roast over a slow fire if this would procure her an invitation to a famous ball. In the end there is a balance of loyalties: his indifference to his friend is avenged by the indifference the lady shows toward him. Demanding obstacles to be erected and overcome so that he can prove himself "that sea / Of

passion" which he "needs must be," the soliloquizer reminds us that every romantic lover is engaged in playing a role.

"Time's Revenges" is like a prelude to the next and last poem in the volume, for its ironies of loyalty and disloyalty are developed at greater length and with greater complexity in "The Glove." The poem is a dramatic monologue spoken by the French poet Pierre Ronsard at the court of Francis I. Browning makes daring use of him, for he has Ronsard report, accurately enough, the details of the central story yet be himself a not totally sympathetic or even reliable narrator. His use of the speaker is, then, slightly different from that of earlier dramatic monologues, for the speaker here tells a story in which he was not involved other than as a spectator and thus has no need to defend or apologize for himself where the details of that story are concerned. It is only when the speaker refers to himself and others in relation to him that we must be wary and carefully scrutinize what he has to say. In terms of genre this means that "The Glove" is a dramatic monologue incorporating a narrative that is the main business of the monologue. It is truly a *dramatic* romance. All this may be obvious enough, but I do not recall having read any commentary that questions the total reliability of the speaker and thus reads the poem as anything other than a narrative monologue or romance.

We have noted frequently the number of times that Browning calls attention to language as a mask for deception. In "The Glove" he again cautions us, indirectly, to suspect ulterior meanings behind the words spoken by making rhetoric a dominant motif of the poem. Ronsard speaks as a buffoon, sounding like a cross between Samuel Butler and Thomas Hood; his words are rendered in fairly regular trimeter couplets all having feminine rhyme.[20] He accuses others of making "fine speeches like gold" (90), intending by the term to suggest the pretensions and triviality of the court. His harshest words, however, are reserved for the poet Clément Marot, whom he regards as a rival "whose experience of nature's but narrow, / And whose faculties move in no small mist" (46-47) and who is supposedly given to learned talk. Yet when the king asks for a verse, the best Ronsard can do is quote Ovid to the effect that "men are the merest Ixions" (14), whereupon the king interrupts to suggest that they go look at the lions. "Such," says Ronsard, "are the sorrowful chances / If you talk fine to King Francis" (17-18).[21] Further, he reports that when the lady departed after the glove episode, Marot stayed behind while he followed to ask "what it all meant" (119).[22] He goes up to her and says, "For I . . . am a Poet: / Human nature,—behooves that I know it!" (121-22). Surely such blatant posturizing (and such insipid rhymes) mark him as not much of a poet at all. Ronsard may not make "fine speeches like gold," but it may be because he is not capable of them. He may assume an ironic pose as a protest against the decadence of King Francis's court, but behind the pose there is little more than vacuity.

The lady's speech is rendered in somewhat irregular trimeter couplets all of male rhyme. Her speech sounds like human conversation instead of buffoonery. Although she holds views of mere words that seem to coincide with Ronsard's, we know that in her case they are not expressed simply for the benefit of others. The court is in fact depraved, from King Francis down. The talk is of superficialities or of views not truly held. Thus DeLorge wooed her with protestations of love and of his willingness to risk all danger for her sake. Too long she had heard "of the deed proved alone by the word" (124), so on the spur of the moment, as she reflected on what had been suffered by so many that the king might have a lion to look at as a sometime amusement, she decided to test DeLorge's words and threw the glove into the pit.

It is part of the irony of the tale that neither the lady nor Ronsard perceives that DeLorge's were not merely empty words. DeLorge had said that he would brave death if she commanded it, and when he leaps into the lion's pit to retrieve the glove she threw there, this is exactly what he does. The lady had thought to test his bravery or, rather, to discover the extent of his love by probing his courage. He proves his mettle, backs up word with deed, and does it, apparently, not only because the eyes of the court are upon him but also because of his regard for the lady and for the promises made to her. But her wanton disregard of his life causes him to question the object of that regard and, having fetched the glove, he gives public notice that he is through with her forever. The flinging of the glove into the lady's face is thus a symbolic act of praise and dispraise, of praise of himself for having endured the ordeal and dispraise of the one who forced such an ordeal upon him. As for the lady herself, she had every right to know whether her lover's protestations had any reality in deed. Yet from the trial she discovers his courage only to lose his love. It is worth noting that she makes no demands of her next lover to pass a similar test.

Objectively we have no reason to believe the lady more in the right than DeLorge. Most readers—all readers so far as I can find—see the right as belonging exclusively to the lady's side simply because the narrator says this is the way it should be. But as we have already noted, his is a flawed character, and we cannot accept what he says any more uncritically than we can accept what Browning's other narrators say. The king pronounces for the knight, saying, "'twas mere vanity, / Not love, set the task to humanity" (101-2). In a way his judgment is just as correct as Ronsard's, which is that the lady flung the glove so as "to know what she had *not* to trust to" (115). The fact that Marot does not go running after her the way Ronsard does also gives us

additional reason for not fully accepting the speaker's view of the situation. This is again a case where, in Thirlwall's words quoted earlier, "characters, motives, and principles are brought into hostile collision, in which good and evil are so inextricably blended on each side, that we are compelled to give an equal share of our sympathy to each. . . . "

The story of the subsequent marriages of DeLorge and the lady to other people does not help us to come down finally on the side of one or the other. Ronsard says that the lady carried her shame from the court and married a youth of lower social status. The court foresees unhappiness in this mixed marriage, but "to that marriage some happiness" Ronsard "dared augur" (169-70). We wonder whether we can trust his prophecy any more than the court's.

As for DeLorge, he married a renowned beauty, who eventually became King Francis's mistress for a week. DeLorge, now serving the king not as knight but as courtier, is frequently "honored" with the commission to fetch his wife's gloves from her chamber while the king is in conversation with her. When DeLorge appears with the gloves, the king always tells the story of this modern Daniel in the lion's den and his wife always says that nowadays he brings the gloves and "utters no murmur" (188). Obviously Ronsard includes this story to show how DeLorge has been placed in the ignominious position of assisting the king to enjoy his wife's favor and, further, been subjected to pleasantries upon his discomfiture. DeLorge's marital distress may be a fact, but does this in any way validate the lady's wanton demand that he enter a lion's cage to retrieve her glove?

As we have already seen, Browning frequently arranges the final lines of a dramatic monologue as a summation of a character or situation. Here in the last two lines of **"The Glove"** he does more or less the same thing. *"Venienti occurrite morbo! /* With which moral I drop my theorbo," says Ronsard in farewell. This piece of macaronic verse is a fitting summation of the character who has told us the story. First, it suggests the "fine" writer *manqué,* one retreating into doggerel and burlesque to show his contempt for what he cannot do but nevertheless employing the learned language that he makes fun of his rival Marot for using. Second, the Latin proverb offered as the moral is not a particularly felicitous one.[23] "Go to meet the approaching ill"? Far more apropos as a moral would have been the scriptural counsel *Sufficit diei malitia sua.* Third, the theorbo, the lute with two necks, suggests the two contending strains of the narrative that merge into the song, the dramatic lyric, which is **"The Glove."**[24]

As a dramatic monologue recounting a tale of opposing loyalties, **"The Glove"** fittingly brings the ***Dramatic Romances and Lyrics*** to a close. Thematically all the poems—with the possible exception of **"Claret and Tokay,"** which themselves may be about national loyalties—are concerned with many kinds of loyalties. In manner all are dramatic. In range of subject matter and prosody, they are enormously variegated. To this extent the 1845 poems bear a strong resemblance to the *Dramatic Lyrics* of 1842. The difference between the two volumes lies in the greater complexity of the *Dramatic Romances and Lyrics.* For here Browning makes his poems more allusive, more densely packed with different levels of meaning. In **"The Bishop Orders His Tomb,"** for example, there is not only a perfect evocation of what Ruskin called the Renaissance spirit but also an implied comment on contemporary Anglo-Catholic ritualism. Or, to take another instance, **"The Italian in England"** is not only a celebration of the patriot typified by Mazzini[25] but a study of the stultifying effect of exile for the political revolutionary. A large number of the poems in *Dramatic Romances and Lyrics* deal with contemporary matters—the Corn Laws, the hunger and poverty of the 1840s, Puseyism, the laureateship, Austrian domination of Italy—of general concern in 1845. In short, the poet was turning toward a sociocultural scene to make meaning. But he was not thereby forgoing irony. For he gives us an ironic reading of society and history embodied in a form that only superficially is a little less extravagant than that of *Sordello* and *Pippa Passes.*

In *Dramatic Romances and Lyrics,* Browning perfected the dramatic monologue. Though hereafter he was to write other exquisite monologues, they were formally to be but variations on those in this collection. Perceiving the quality of Browning's achievement, Walter Savage Landor wrote and published, in the *Morning Chronicle* for 22 November 1845, one of the most generous compliments ever paid by one poet to another.

> There is delight in singing, tho' none hear
> Beside the singer: and there is delight
> In praising, tho' the praiser sit alone
> And see the prais'd far off him, far above.
> Shakespeare is not our poet, but the world's,
> Therefore on him no speech! and brief for
>   thee,
> Browning! Since Chaucer was alive and hale,
> No man hath walkt along our road with step
> So active, so inquiring eye, or tongue
> So varied in discourse. But warmer climes
> Give brighter plumage, stronger wing: the
>   breeze
> Of Alpine highths thou playest with, borne on
> Beyond Sorrento and Amalfi, where
> The Siren waits thee, singing song for song.

Landor recognized that by 1845 his friend had become "Browning," a name to be listed, along with Shakespeare and Chaucer, among the greatest English poets.

Notes

Abbreviations

BIS Browning Institute Studies

CE College English

DeVane, *Handbook A Browning Handbook*

Domett Robert Browning and Alfred Domett

Griffin and Minchin *The Life of Robert Browning*

Hood, *Letters Letters of Robert Browning Collected by Thomas J. Wise*

Irvine and Honan *The Book, the Ring, & the Poet*

Kintner *The Letters of Robert Browning and Elizabeth Barrett Barrett, 1845-1846*

New Letters New Letters of Robert Browning

NLH New Literary History

Orr, *Handbook A Handbook of the Works of Robert Browning*

Orr, *Life Life and Letters of Robert Browning*

PBSA Publications of the Bibliographical Society of America

PQ Philological Quarterly

RES Review of English Studies

SBHC Studies in Browning and His Circle

SiR Studies in Romanticism

SP Studies in Philology

TSLL Texas Studies in Literature and Language

UTQ University of Toronto Quarterly

VNL Victorian Newsletter

VP Victorian Poetry

VS Victorian Studies

Yes Yearbook of English Studies

[1] Elizabeth Barrett's letters to Browning are full of remarks about the poems of the 1845 volume. In addition, she wrote fifty-six manuscript pages about them

and the two plays that were to follow. A somewhat inaccurate transcription is printed in *New Poems by Robert Browning and Elizabeth Barrett Browning,* and reprinted in the Macmillan Edition of Browning's works, *The Complete Poetical Works of Robert Browning, New Edition with Additional Poems First Published in 1914.* Eleven of the fifty-six pages were inexplicably omitted and have never been printed. See Kintner, 1: 134 n. 1.

[2] Richard Hengist Horne, *A New Spirit of the Age* (London: Smith, Elder, 1844), 2: 170.

[3] They are "The Italian in England," "The Englishman in Italy," "The Flight of the Duchess," "The Boy and the Angel," "Time's Revenges," and "The Glove." "Pictor Ignotus" and "The Bishop Orders His Tomb at St. Praxed's Church" were subsumed by the heading "Men and Women." The rest were classified as "Dramatic Lyrics."

[4] DeVane believes that the poem embodies a cultural-historical type: it is Browning's conception of how the unknown painters "of those pale, formal, monastic series—Virgin, Babe, and Saint—might defend themselves in the face of the great vogue for the newer, more vulgar, painters who depict the expressions of contemporary human beings" (*Handbook,* p. 155). This was first questioned by Paul F. Jamieson, "Browning's 'Pictor Ignotus, Florence, 15—,'" *Explicator* 11 (1952): item 8. Jamieson sees the speaker not as a type but as a failed painter who would have liked fame but found exposure to the crowd and to criticism unendurable. Jamieson suggests that "the youth" is Raphael. J. B. Bullen, "Browning's 'Pictor Ignotus' and Vasari's 'Life of Fra Bartolommeo di San Marco,'" *RES* 23 (1972): 313-19, identifies the speaker of the poem as Fra Bartolommeo, whose history Browning learned from Vasari's *Lives of the Painters* and who was a painter of great talent but limited achievement. Michael H. Bright, "Browning's Celebrated Pictor Ignotus," *ELN* 13 (1976): 192-94, argues that Bullen has missed "the central point Browning is making. The whole idea of the poem, as the title makes clear, is that the painter is unknown" (p. 194). In a later essay, "Browning's 'Pictor Ignotus': An Interpretation," *SBHC* 4 (1976): 53-61, Bright admits that the speaker could have done all he says but that the true reasons for his forswearing fame were his fear of idolatry and his less justifiable fear of unsympathetic criticism. In contrast to Bullen and Bright, Richard D. Altick, "'Andrea del Sarto': The Kingdom of Hell Is Within," in *Browning's Mind and Art,* ed. Clarence Tracy (Edinburgh: Oliver and Boyd, 1968), pp. 18, 24, maintains that the unknown painter's claim to artistic talent is unsupported and that the painter is thus rationalizing to his own satisfaction his refusal to compete.

[5] *Browning's Beginnings,* p. 170.

[6] I am endebted to Bernadine Brown, "Robert Browning's 'The Italian in England,'" *VP* 6 (1968): 179-83, for the suggestion of the religious overtones in the poem.

[7] See Hood, *Letters,* pp. 166-67; Orr, *Life and Letters,* p. 123; and DeVane, *Handbook,* pp. 159-62.

[8] James F. Loucks, "The Dating of Browning's 'Here's to Nelson's Memory,'" *SBHC* 4 (1976): 71-72, suggests that the poem was prompted by the recent donation of the coat Nelson wore when he was wounded at Trafalgar to the Greenwich Hospital. Loucks says that the poem could have been written so late as the autumn of 1845, when the poet was readying the volume for publication.

[9] Browning spoke of it as "just the thing for the time—what with the Oxford business, and Camden society and other embroilments" (*New Letters,* pp. 35-36), referring to the Tractarians and the concern over John Henry Newman's recent conversion to the Roman Catholic Church. Ruskin was of the opinion that there is "no other piece of modern English, prose or poetry, in which there is so much told, as in these lines of the Renaissance spirit,—its worldliness, inconsistency, pride, hypocrisy, ignorance of itself, love of art, of luxury, and of good Latin" (*Modern Painters,* vol. 4, chap. 20, in *The Works of John Ruskin,* ed. E. T. Cook and Alexander Wedderburn [London: George Allen, 1903-12], 6: 449). See Robert A. Greenberg, "Ruskin, Pugin, and the Contemporary Context of 'The Bishop Orders His Tomb,'" *PMLA* 84 (1969): 1588-94.

[10] See, for example, Robert Felgar, "Browning's Narrative Art," *SBHC* 3 (1975): 82, who says that Browning uses a dramatically imagined participant or onlooker in this poem to give the reader "a sense of immediacy, of almost being there."

[11] See Frederick Palmer and Edward Snyder, "New Light on the Brownings," *Quarterly Review* 269 (1937): 48-63, and DeVane, *Handbook,* pp. 175-76.

[12] Mrs. Orr, *Handbook,* p. 276, says of the narrator: "He is a jovial, matter-of-fact person, in spite of the vein of sentiment which runs through him; and the imaginative part of his narrative was more probably the result of a huntsman's breakfast which found its way into his brain." Here as elsewhere Mrs. Orr is more perspicacious than many of Browning's commentators who belittle her.

[13] The technique is reminiscent of Tennyson, particularly of such poems as "Oenone," in which the opening lines descriptive of the landscape prefigure, in their suggestive detail, the action of the poem. For Browning's love of Tennyson's early poems, see *Domett,* pp. 40-41, and the many references to Tennyson in Kintner.

[14] Mrs. Orr, *Handbook,* p. 293, also notes the close relationship of the two lyrics: "The words: 'love me for ever,' appeal to us from a tombstone which records how Spring garlands are severed by the hand of June. . . . "

[15] Browning said that he intended the refrain to be "a mournful comment on the short duration of the conventional 'For Ever'" (quoted in Macmillan Edition, p. 1350).

[16] Browning said that the man is the speaker in both parts of the poem and that "it is *his* confession of how fleeting is the belief (implied in the first part) that such raptures are self-sufficient and enduring—as for the time they appear" (quoted in Macmillan Edition, pp. 1350-51).

[17] See DeVane, *Handbook,* pp. 255-57.

[18] That the fragmentary nature of "Saul" is owing to an impasse in Browning's religious life is advanced by William Clyde DeVane, *Browning's Parleyings: The Autobiography of a Mind* (New Haven, Conn.: Yale University Press, 1927), pp. 116-18; A. W. Crawford, "Browning's *Saul,*" *Queen's Quarterly* 34 (1927): 448-54; and, later, Collins, *Robert Browning's Moral-Aesthetic Theory, 1833-1855,* pp. 91-92. Arguing that the first nine stanzas are as Christian in outlook as the stanzas of the second part completed seven years or so later are W. David Shaw, *The Dialectical Temper,* pp. 224-25; Ward Hellstrom, "Time and Type in Browning's 'Saul,'" *ELH* 33 (1966): 370-89; and Elizabeth Bieman, "The Ongoing Testament in Browning's 'Saul,'" *UTQ* 43 (1974): 151-68.

[19] J. S. McClatchey, "Browning's 'Saul' as a Davidic Psalm of the Praise of God: The Poetics of Prophecy," *SBHC* 4 (1976): 62-83, is, I believe, the first to note this as the genre of the poem.

[20] Cadbury, "Lyric and Anti-Lyric Forms: A Method for Judging Browning," p. 52, contends that the speaker of the poem "has no interest in lying to us, and so we can question what he says only by asking his relationship to it. Why, we ask, does he remain in a court, the depravity of which he sees so clearly? . . . He remains precisely because of the operation of the humorous irony which is the tone of the poem. His defence against depravity, his ironic wit, makes particularly vivid the necessity for less ironic souls to get out." David Sonstroem, "'Fine Speeches Like Gold,' in Browning's 'The Glove'," *VP* 15 (1977): 85-90, maintains that Ronsard's substitution of buffoonery for a lofty style is for the sake of deflation of the court, showing its pretensions and trivialities.

[21] Ronsard also sums up the moral of his story in a Latin tag.

[22] The historical Ronsard and Marot were bitterly divided on the subject of religion. During the religious wars Ronsard was committed to an extreme royalist and Catholic position. He was noted for attacking his opponents, especially in his *Discours,* whom he dismissed as traitors and hypocrites. Marot, on the other hand, was a Protestant who was imprisoned for his beliefs and who finally fled from France. If we apply this biographical information to the poem, then the action becomes doubly ironic.

[23] George Saintsbury, "Browning," reprinted in *The Browning Critics,* ed. Litzinger and Knickerbocker, p. 28, agrees that "the moral is mainly rubbish" and, in addition, that "Marot *was* a poet."

[24] Louise Schutz Boas, "Browning's 'The Glove'," *Explicator* 2 (1943): item 13, claims that by the theorbo Browning meant to refer to DeLorge's two actions in fetching the gloves for the two different ladies.

[25] Mrs. Orr, *Handbook,* p. 306 n., says that Mazzini told Browning how he had read the poem to his fellow exiles in England to show how an Englishman could sympathize with them.

Harold Bloom (essay date 1985)

SOURCE: Introduction to *Modern Critical Views: Robert Browning,* edited by Harold Bloom, Chelsea House Publishers, 1985, pp. 1-21.

[*In the following essay, Bloom explores the tendency of Browning's critics to misread the nature of the epiphanies and the "visions-of-failure" in Browning's poetry, noting that epiphanies are often wrongfully interpreted as negative events, while "visions-of-failure" are mistakenly read as celebrations.*]

One of the principles of interpretation that will arise out of the future study of the intricacies of poetic revisionism, and of the kinds of misreading that canon-formation engenders, is the realization that later poets and their critical followers tend to misread strong precursors by a fairly consistent mistaking of literal for figurative, and of figurative for literal. Browning misread the High Romantics, and particularly his prime precursor, Shelley, in this pattern, and through time's revenges most modern poets and critics have done and are doing the same to Browning. I am going to explore Browning, in this chapter, as the master of misprision he was, by attempting to show our tendency to read his epiphanies or "good moments" as ruinations or vastations of quest, and our parallel tendency to read his darkest visions-of-failure as if they were celebrations.

I will concentrate on a small group of Browning's poems including **"Cleon," "Master Hugues of Saxe-Gotha," "A Toccata of Galuppi's," "Abt Vogler,"** and **"Andrea del Sarto,"** but I cannot evade for long my own obsession with **"Childe Roland to the Dark Tower Came,"** and so it and its contrary chant, **"Thamuris Marching,"** will enter late into this discourse. Indeed, I want to end with a kind of critical self-analysis, and ask myself the question: why am I obsessed by the **"Childe Roland"** poem, or rather, what does it *mean* to be obsessed by that poem? How is it that I cannot conceive of an antithetical practical criticism of poetry without constantly being compelled to use **"Childe Roland"** as a test case, as though it were the modern poem proper, more even than say, *Tintern Abbey* or *Byzantium* or *The Idea of Order at Key West*? Is there a way to make these questions center upon critical analysis rather than upon psychic self-analysis?

In Browning's prose **"Essay on Shelley,"** there is an eloquent passage that idealizes poetic influence:

> There is a time when the general eye has, so to speak, absorbed its fill of the phenomena around it, whether spiritual or material, and desires rather to learn the exacter significance of what it possesses, than to receive any augmentation of what is possessed. Then is the opportunity for the poet of loftier vision, to lift his fellows. . . . The influence of such an achievement will not soon die out. A tribe of successors (Homerides) working more or less in the same spirit, dwell on his discoveries and reinforce his doctrine; till, at unawares, the world is found to be subsisting wholly on the shadow of a reality, on sentiments diluted from passions, on the tradition of a fact, the convention of a moral, the straw of last year's harvest.

Browning goes on to posit a mighty ladder of authentic poets, in an objective and subjective alternation, who will replace one another almost endlessly in succession, concerning which, "the world dares no longer doubt that its gradations ascend." Translated, this means: "Wordsworth to Shelley to Browning," in which Browning represents a triumph of what he calls the objective principle. Against Browning's prose idealization, I will set his attack upon the disciples of Keats in his poem **"Popularity":**

> And there's the extract, flasked and fine,
>   And priced and saleable at last!
> And Hobbs, Nobbs, Stokes and Nokes
>   combine
>   To paint the future from the past,
> Put blue into their line.

For "Hobbs, Nobbs, Stokes and Nokes" we might read Tennyson, Arnold, Rossetti, and whatever other contemporary Keatsian, whether voluntary or involuntary, that Browning wished to scorn. But the next stanza, the poem's last, would surely have cut against Browning himself if for "John Keats" we substituted "Percy Shelley":

> Hobbs hints blue,—straight he turtle eats:
>   Nobbs prints blue,—claret crowns his
>   cup:
> Nokes outdares Stokes in azure feats,—
>   Both gorge. Who fished the murex up?
> What porridge had John Keats?

The vegetarian Shelley, according to his friend Byron, tended to dine on air and water, not fit fare for the strenuously hearty Browning, who in his later years was to become London's leading diner-out. But though Browning seems not to have had the slightest *personal* consciousness of an anxiety of influence, he wrote the most powerful poem ever to be explicitly concerned with the problem. This is the dramatic monologue **"Cleon,"** in which the imaginary jack-of-all-arts, Cleon, is in my judgment a kind of version of Matthew Arnold, whose *Empedocles on Etna* Browning had been reading. Arnold's Empedocles keeps lamenting his own and the world's belatedness, a lament that becomes a curious kind of inauthentic overconfidence in Cleon's self-defense:

> I have not chanted verse like Homer, no—
> Nor swept string like Terpander, no—nor
>   carved
> And painted men like Phidias and his friend:
> I am not great as they are, point by point.
> But I have entered into sympathy
> With these four, running these into one soul,
> Who, separate, ignored each other's art.
> Say, is it nothing that I know them all?

Browning could enjoy the belatedness of Arnold or Rossetti, because no poet ever felt less belated than this exuberant daemon. We remember the malicious epithet applied to him by Hopkins: "Bouncing Browning." I think we can surmise that poetic belatedness as an affliction, whether conscious or unconscious, always rises in close alliance with ambivalence towards the prime precursor. Browning felt no ambivalence towards Shelley, such as Yeats had towards Shelley, or Shelley towards Wordsworth, or Wordsworth towards Milton. Browning loved Shelley unbrokenly and almost unreservedly from the age of fourteen, when he first read him, until his own death at the age of seventy-seven. But ambivalence is not the only matrix from which the anxiety of influence rises. There is perhaps a darker source in the guilt or shame of identifying the precursor with the ego-ideal, and then living on in the sense of having betrayed that identification by one's own failure to have become oneself, by a realization that the ephebe has betrayed his own integrity, and betrayed also the covenant that first bound him to the precursor. That guilt unmistakably was Browning's, as Betty Miller and others have shown, and so the burden of belatedness was replaced in Browning by a burden of dissimulation, a lying-against-the-self, rather than a lying-against-time.

But is not that kind of shame only another mask for the guilt-of-indebtedness, the only guilt that ever troubles a poet-as-poet? Certainly, Shelley for Browning was precisely the "numinous shadow" or ancestor-god whose baleful influence is stressed by Nietzsche. Rather than demonstrate this too obviously, whether by recourse to Browning's poem ***Pauline*** or by an examination of the unhappy episode in which the young Browning yielded to his stern mother's Evangelical will, I think it more interesting to seek out what is most difficult in Browning, which is the total contrast between his optimism, a quality both temperamental and theoretical, and the self-destructive peculiarities of his men and women. I want to start by puzzling over the grotesque and unique poem, **"Master Hugues of Saxe-Gotha,"** with its curious and central contrast between the charming organist who speaks the monologue and the heavy pseudo-Bachian composer, also invented by Browning, whose name is the poem's title. The relationship between performer and composer *is* the poem. This relationship is *not* a displaced form of the ambivalence between ephebe and precursor, because the performer's reading/misreading of the composer is very different from the later poet's interpretation of an earlier one, or anyone's reading/misreading of any poet. It is true that a performance is an interpretation, but a performance lacks the vital element of revisionism that makes for fresh creation. The charm of the poem **"Master Hugues of Saxe-Gotha,"** like the chill of the somewhat similar but greater poem, **"A Toccata of Galuppi's,"** is precisely that we are free of the burden of misprision and that the performer in each poem is more like a reciter of a text than he is like a critic of a text. Yet it remains true that you cannot recite any poem without giving some interpretation of it, though I would hazard the speculation that even the strongest recital, acting, or performance is at best a weak reading/misreading, in the technical antithetical senses of "weak" and "strong," for again there is no strength, poetic or critical, without the dialectics of revisionism coming into play.

The organist earnestly wants to understand Hugues without revising him, but evidently the world is right and the poor organist wrong, in that less is meant than meets the ear in Hugues' mountainous fugues. Hugues is a kind of involuntary musical nihilist, who in effect would rather have the void as purpose than be void of purpose. The organist is not only old-fashioned in his devotion to Hugues but, as we might say now, old-fashioned in his devotion to meaning. Yet skepticism, a suspicion concerning both meaning-in-Hugues and meaning-in-life, has begun to gain strength in the organist, despite himself. His quasi-desperate test-performance of Hugues, thematically racing the sacristan's putting-out of the light, moves from one sadly negative conclusion to a larger negation, from "But where's music, the dickens?" to:

> Is it your moral of Life?
> Such a web, simple and subtle,
> Weave we on earth here in impotent strife,
> Backward and forward each throwing his
>   shuttle,
> Death ending all with a knife?

The very reluctance of the organist's interpretation convinces us of its relevance to Hugues. Hugues will

not "say the word," despite the organist's plea, and the organist lacks the strength to break out on his revisionary own and do what he wants to do, which is "unstop the full-organ, / Blare out the *mode Palestrina,*" akin to the gentle simplicity of his own nature. Yet we must not take the organist too literally; after all, there is nothing whatsoever to prevent him from playing Palestrina to his own satisfaction in the moments of light that remain to him. But it is the problematical, cumbersome, absurdly intricate Hugues who obsesses him, whose secret or lack of a secret he is driven to solve. Despite himself, the organist is on an antithetical quest, like absolutely every other monologist in Browning. The luminous last line of the poem is to be answered, emphatically: "Yes!"

> While in the roof, if I'm right there,
> . . . Lo you, the wick in the socket!
> Hallo, you sacristan, show us a light there!
> Down it dips, gone like a rocket.
> What, you want, do you, to come unawares,
> Sweeping the church up for first
>   morning-prayers,
> And find a poor devil has ended his cares
> At the foot of your rotten-runged rat-riddled
>   stairs?
> Do I carry the moon in my pocket?

If the organist is right, then the gold in the gilt roof is a better emblem of a final reality than the spider web woven by Hugues. But fortunately the darkening of the light breaks in upon an uneasy affirmation, and leaves us instead with the realization that the organist is subject as well as object of his own quest for meaning. Hugues goes on weaving his intricate vacuities; the organist carries the moon in his pocket. Has the poem ended, however humorously, as a ruined quest or as a good moment? Does Browning make it possible for us to know the difference between the two? Or is it the particular achievement of his art that the difference cannot be known? Does the organist end by knowing he has been deceived, or does he end in the beautiful earliness of carrying imagination in his own pocket, in a transumptive allusion to the Second Spirit in one of Browning's favorite poems, Shelley's *The Two Spirits: An Allegory?* There the Second Spirit, overtly allegorizing desire, affirms that the "lamp of love," carried within, gives him the perpetual power to "make night day." Browning is more dialectical, and the final representation in his poem is deeply ambiguous. But that is a depth of repression that I want to stay with, and worry, for a space, if only because it bothers me that **"Master Hugues of Saxe-Gotha,"** like so many of Browning's poems, ends in an *aporia,* in the reader's uncertainty as to whether he is to read literally or figuratively. Browning personally, unlike Shelley, was anything but an intellectual skeptic, and that he should create figures that abide in our uncertainty is at once his most salient and his most challenging characteristic.

"**A Toccata of Galuppi's**" can be read as a reversal of this poem, since it appears to end in the performer's conscious admission of belatedness and defeat. But Browning was quite as multi-form a maker as poetic tradition affords, and the "**Toccata**" is as subtle a poem as ever he wrote. It invokes for us a grand Nietzschean question, from the Third Essay of *On the Genealogy of Morals:* "What does it mean when an artist leaps over into his opposite?" Nietzsche was thinking of Wagner, but Browning in the "**Toccata**" may be another instance. Nietzsche's ultimate answer to his own question prophesied late Freud, if we take the answer to be: "All great things bring about their own destruction through an act of self-overcoming." I think we can say rather safely that no one was less interested in *Selbstaufhebung* than Robert Browning; he was perfectly delighted to be at once subject and object of his own quest. Like Emerson, whom he resembles only in this single respect, he rejoiced always that there were so many of him, so many separate selves happily picnicking together in a single psyche. From a Nietzschean point of view, he must seem only an epitome of some of the most outrageous qualities of the British empirical and Evangelical minds, but he is actually more sublimely outrageous even than that. There are no dialectics that can subsume him, because he is not so much evasive as he is preternatural, wholly daemonic, with an astonishing alliance perpetual in him between an impish cunning and endless linguistic energy. I think we can surmise why he was so fascinated by poets like Christopher Smart and Thomas Lovell Beddoes, poets who represented the tradition of Dissenting Enthusiasm carried over into actual madness. With energies like Browning's, and self-confidence like Browning's, it took a mind as powerful as Browning's to avoid being carried by Enthusiasm into alienation, but perhaps the oddest of all Browning's endless oddities is that he was incurably sane, even as he imagined his gallery of pathological enthusiasts, monomaniacs, and marvelous charlatans.

There are at least four voices coldly leaping along in "**A Toccata of Galuppi's**," and only one of them is more or less Browning's, and we cannot be certain even of that. Let us break in for the poem's conclusion, as the monologist first addresses the composer whose "touch-piece" he is playing, and next the composer answers back, *but only through the monologist's performance,* and finally the speaker-performer acknowledges his defeat by the heartlessly brilliant Galuppi:

[Stanzas XI-XV have been deleted from text.]

The "swerve" *is* the Lucretian *clinamen,* and we might say that Galuppi, like Lucretius, assaults the monologist-performer with the full strength of the Epicurean argument. One possible interpretation is that Browning, as a fierce Transcendentalist of his own sect, a sect of one, is hammering at the Victorian spiritual compromise, which his cultivated speaker exemplifies. That interpretation would confirm the poem's serio-comic opening:

> Oh Galuppi, Baldassaro, this is very sad to
> find!
> I can hardly misconceive you; it would prove
> me deaf and blind;
> But although I take your meaning, 'tis with
> such a heavy mind!

Galuppi's triumph, on this reading, would be the dramatic one of shaking up this cultivated monologist, who first half-scoffs at Galuppi's nihilism, but who ends genuinely frightened by the lesson Galuppi has taught which is a lesson of mortality and consequent meaninglessness. But I think that is to underestimate the monologist, who is a more considerable temperament even than the organist who plays Hugues and can bear neither to give Hugues up nor accept Hugues' emptiness. Galuppi is no Hugues, but a powerfully sophisticated artist who gives what was wanted of him, but with a Dance-of-Death aspect playing against his audience's desires. And the speaker, who knows physics, some geology, a little mathematics, and will not quite abandon his Christian immortality, is at least as enigmatic as the organist, and for a parallel reason. Why cannot he let Galuppi alone? What does he quest for in seeing how well he can perform that spirited and elegant art? Far more even than Galuppi, or Galuppi's audience, or than Browning, the speaker is obsessed with mortality:

> Then they left you for their pleasure: till in
> due time, one by one,
> Some with lives that came to nothing, some
> with deeds as well undone,
> Death stepped tacitly and took them where
> they never see the sun.

One of the most moving elements in the poem is its erotic nostalgia, undoubtedly the single sphere of identity between the monologist and Browning himself. Eros crowds the poem, with an intensity and poignance almost Shakespearean in its strength. Nothing in the poem is at once so moving and so shocking as the monologist's final "Dear dead women, with such hair, too—," for this spiritual trimmer is very much a sensual man, like his robust creator. It is the cold Galuppi who is more the dualist, more the artist fulfilling the Nietzschean insight that the ascetic ideal is a defensive evasion by which art preserves itself against the truth. But where, as readers, does that leave us, since this time Browning elegantly has cleared himself away? His overt intention is pretty clear, and I think pretty irrelevant also. He wants us—unlike the monologist, unlike Galuppi, unlike Galuppi's hard-living men and women—to resort to his ferocious version of an antithetical Protestantism, which is I think ultimately his misprision of Shelley's antithetical humanism. Yet Browning's art has freed us of Browning, though paradoxically not of Shelley, or at least of the strong Lucretian element in Shelley. Has the monologist quested after Galuppi's truth, only to end up in a vastation of his own comforting evasions of the truth? That would be the canonical reading, but it would overliteralize a metaleptic figuration that knowingly has chosen not to attempt a reversal of time. When the speaker ends by feeling "chilly and grown old," then he has introjected Galuppi's world and Galuppi's music, and projected his own compromise formulations. But this is an *illusio,* a metaleptic figuration that is on the verge of becoming an opening irony or reaction-formation again, that is, rejoining the tone of jocular evasion that began the poem. Nothing has happened because nothing has changed, and the final grimness of Browning's eerie poem is that its speaker is caught in a repetition. He will pause awhile, and then play a toccata of Galuppi's again.

Let us try a third music-poem or improvisation, the still more formidable **"Abt Vogler,"** where the daemonic performer is also the momentary composer, inventing fitfully upon an instrument of his own invention, grandly solitary because there is nothing for him to interpret except his own interpretation of his own creation. The canonical readings available here are too weak to be interesting, since they actually represent the poem as being pious. The historical Vogler was regarded by some as a pious fraud, but Browning's Vogler is too complex to be regarded either as an impostor or as sincerely devout. What matters most is that he is primarily an extemporizer, rather than necessarily an artist, whether as performer or composer. The poem leaves open (whatever Browning's intentions) the problem of whether Vogler is a skilled illusionist, or something more than that. At the least, Vogler is self-deceived, but even the self-deception is most complex. It is worth knowing what I must assume that Browning knew: Vogler's self-invented instruments sounded splendid only when played by Vogler. Though the great temptation in reading this poem is to interpret it as a good moment precariously attained, and then lost, I think the stronger or antithetical reading here will show that this is very nearly as much a poem of ruined quest as **"Childe Roland"** or **"Andrea del Sarto"** is.

"Abt Vogler" is one of those poems that explain Yeats's remark to the effect that he feared Browning as a potentially dangerous influence upon him. If we could read **"Abt Vogler"** without interpretative suspicion (and I believe we cannot), then the poem would seem to be a way-station between the closing third of *Adonais* and Yeats's Byzantium poems. It establishes itself in a state of being that seems either to be beyond the antithesis of life and death, or else that seems to be the state of art itself. Yet, in the poem **"Abt Vogler,"**

I think we have neither, but something more puzzling, a willed phantasmagoria that is partly Browning's and partly an oddity, a purely visionary dramatic monologue.

Vogler, we ought to realize immediately, does not seek the purposes of art, which after all is hard work. Vogler is daydreaming, and is seeking a magical power over nature or supernature, as in the debased Kabbalist myth of Solomon's seal. Vogler is not so much playing his organ as enslaving it to his magical purposes, purposes that do not distinguish between angel and demon, heaven and hell. Vogler is no Blakean visionary; he seeks not to marry heaven and hell, but merely to achieve every power that he can. And yet he has a moving purpose, akin to Shelley's in *Prometheus Unbound,* which is to aid earth's mounting into heaven. But, is his vision proper something we can grant the prestige of vision, or is there not a dubious element in it?

Being made perfect, when the subject is someone like Vogler, is a somewhat chancy phenomenon. Unlike the sublimely crazy Johannes Agricola, in one of Browning's earliest and most frightening dramatic monologues, Vogler is not a genuine Enthusiast, certain of his own Election. Stanza VI has a touch of **"Cleon"** about it, and stanza VII is clearly *unheimlich,* despite the miraculous line: "That out of three sounds he frame, not a fourth sound, but a star." But with stanzas VIII and IX, which are this poem's *askesis* or sublimation, it is not so easy to distinguish Vogler from Browning, or one of the beings always bouncing around in Browning, anyway:

VIII

Well, it is gone at last, the palace of music I
  reared;
  Gone! and the good tears start, the praises
    that come too slow;
For one is assured at first, one scarce can say
  that he feared,
  That he even gave it a thought, the gone
    thing was to go.
Never to be again! But many more of the kind
  As good, nay, better perchance: is this your
    comfort to me?
To me, who must be saved because I cling
  with my mind
  To the same, same self, same love, same
    God: ay, what was, shall be.

IX

Therefore to whom turn I but to thee, the
  ineffable Name?
  Builder and maker, thou, of houses not made
    with hands!
What, have fear of change from thee who art
  ever the same?

Doubt that thy power can fill the heart that
  thy power expands?
There shall never be one lost good! What was,
  shall live as before;
The evil is null, is nought, is silence
  implying sound;
What was good shall be good, with, for evil,
  so much good more;
On the earth the broken arcs; in the heaven,
  a perfect round.

The poem, from here to the end, in the three final
stanzas, is suddenly as much Browning's Magnificat
as the *Song to David,* which is deliberately echoed in
the penultimate line, is Smart's. But what does that
mean, whether in this poem, or whether about Browning himself? Surely he would not acknowledge, openly,
that his is the art of the extemporizer, the illusionist
improvising? Probably not, but the poem may be acknowledging an anxiety that he possesses, to much
that effect. Whether this is so or not, to any degree,
how are we to read the final stanza?

Well, it is earth with me; silence resumes her
  reign:
I will be patient and proud, and soberly
  acquiesce.
Give me the keys. I feel for the common
  chord again,
Sliding by semitones, till I sink to the
  minor,—yes,
And I blunt it into a ninth, and I stand on
  alien ground,
Surveying awhile the heights I rolled from
  into the deep;
Which, hark, I have dared and done, for my
  resting-place is found,
The C Major of this life: so now I will try to
  sleep.

This descent to C Major separates Vogler totally from
Browning again, since of the many keys in which the
genuinely musical Browning composes, his resting
place is hardly a key without sharps or flats. Browning
has his direct imitation of Smart's *Song to David* in
his own overtly religious poem, **"Saul,"** and so we
can be reasonably certain that Vogler does not speak
for Browning when the improviser belatedly stands on
alien ground, surveying the Sublime he had attained,
and echoes Smart's final lines:

Thou at stupendous truth believ'd;—
And now the matchless deed's achiev'd,
  DETERMINED, DARED, and DONE.

What Vogler has dared and done is no more than to
have dreamed a belated dream; where Browning is, in
regard to that Promethean or Shelleyan a dream, is an
enigma, at least in this poem. What **"Abt Vogler,"** as

a text, appears to proclaim *is* the impossibility of our
reading it, insofar as reading means being able to govern the interplay of literal and figurative meanings in
a text. Canonically, in terms of all received readings,
this poem is almost an apocalyptic version of a
Browningesque "Good Moment," a time of privilege
or an epiphany, a sudden manifestation of highest vision. Yet the patterns of revisionary misprision are
clearly marked upon the poem, and they tend to indicate that the poem demands to be read figuratively
against its own letter, as another parable of ruined quest,
or confession or imaginative failure, or the shame of
knowing such failure.

I turn to **"Andrea del Sarto,"** which with **"Childe
Roland to the Dark Tower Came,"** and the meditation entitled **"The Pope"** in ***The Ring and the Book,***
seems to me to represent Browning at his greatest.
Here there would appear to be no question about the
main issue of interpretation, for the canonical readings
seem fairly close to the poem in its proclamation that this
artist's quest is ruined, that Andrea stands self-condemned
by his own monologue. Betty Miller has juxtaposed
the poem, brilliantly, with this troubled and troublesome passage in Browning's **"Essay on Shelley:"**

Although of such depths of failure there can be no
question here we must in every case betake ourselves
to the review of a poet's life ere we determine some
of the nicer questions concerning his poetry,—more
especially if the performance we seek to estimate aright,
has been obstructed and cut short of completion by
circumstances,—a disastrous youth or a premature
death. We may learn from the biography whether his
spirit invariably saw and spoke from the last height
to which it had attained. An absolute vision is not
for this world, but we are permitted a continual
approximation to it, every degree of which in the
individual, provided it exceed the attainment of the
masses, must procure him a clear advantage. Did
the poet ever attain to a higher platform than where
he rested and exhibited a result? Did he know more
than he spoke of?

On this juxtaposition, Andrea and Browning alike rested
on a level lower than the more absolute vision they
could have attained. Certainly Andrea tells us, perhaps
even shows us, that he knows more than he paints.
But Browning? If he was no Shelley, he was also no
Andrea, which in part is the burden of the poem. But
only in part, and whether there is some level of *apologia* in this monologue, in its patterning, rather than
its overt content, is presumably a question that a more
antithetical practical criticism ought to be capable of
exploring.

Does Andrea overrate his own potential? If he does,
then there is no poem, for unless his dubious gain-in-life
has paid for a genuine loss-in-art, then he is too
self-deceived to be interesting, even to himself.

Browning has complicated this matter, as he complicates everything. The poem's subtitle reminds us that Andrea was called "The Faultless Painter," and Vasari, Browning's source, credits Andrea with everything in execution but then faults him for lacking ambition, for not attempting the Sublime. Andrea, in the poem, persuades us of a wasted greatness not so much by his boasting ("At any rate 'tis easy, all of it! / No sketches first, no studies, that's long past: / I do what many dream of, all their lives . . ."), but by his frightening skill in sketching his own twilight-piece, by his showing us how "A common greyness silvers everything—." Clearly, this speaker knows loss, and clearly he is the antithesis of his uncanny creator, whose poetry never suffers from a lack of ambition, who is always Sublime where he is most Grotesque, and always Grotesque when he storms the Sublime. Andrea does not represent anything in Browning directly, not even the betrayed relationship of the heroic precursor, yet he does represent one of Browning's anxieties, an anxiety related to but not identical with the anxiety of influence. It is an anxiety of representation, or a fear of forbidden meanings, or in Freudian language precisely a fear of the return-of-the-repressed, even though such a return would cancel out a poem-as-poem, or is it *because* such a return would end poetry as such?

Recall that Freud's notion of repression speaks of an unconsciously *purposeful* forgetting, and remind yourself also that what Browning could never bear was a sense of *purposelessness.* It is purposelessness that haunts Childe Roland, and we remember again what may be Nietzsche's most powerful insight, which closes the great Third Essay of *On the Genealogy of Morals.* The ascetic ideal, Nietzsche said, by which he meant also the aesthetic ideal, was the only *meaning* yet found for human suffering, and mankind would rather have the void *for* purpose than be void *of* purpose. Browning's great fear, purposelessness, was related to the single quality that had moved and impressed him most in Shelley: the remorseless purposefulness of the Poet in *Alastor,* of Prometheus, and of Shelley himself questing for death in *Adonais.* Andrea, as an artist, is the absolute antithesis of the absolute idealist Shelley, and so Andrea is a representation of profound Browningesque anxiety.

But how is this an anxiety of representation? We enter again the dubious area of *belatedness,* which Browning is reluctant to represent, but is too strong and authentic a poet to avoid. Though Andrea uses another vocabulary, a defensively evasive one, to express his relationship to Michelangelo, Raphael, and Leonardo, he suffers the burden of the latecomer. His Lucrezia is the emblem of his belatedness, his planned excuse for his failure in strength, which he accurately diagnoses as a failure in will. And he ends in deliberate belatedness, and in his perverse need to be cuckolded:

What would one have?
In heaven, perhaps, new chances, one more
   chance—
Four great walls in the New Jerusalem,
Meted on each side by the angel's reed,
For Leonard, Rafael, Agnolo and me
To cover—the three first without a wife,
While I have mine! So—still they overcome
Because there's still Lucrezia,—as I choose.

Again the Cousin's whistle! Go, my Love.

Can we say that Andrea represents what Shelley dreaded to become, the extinguished hearth, an ash without embers? We know that Shelley need not have feared, yet the obsessive, hidden fear remains impressive. Browning at seventy-seven was as little burned out as Hardy at eighty-eight, Yeats at seventy-four, or Stevens at seventy-five, and his *Asolando,* his last book, fiercely prefigures Hardy's *Winter Words,* Yeats's *Last Poems,* and Stevens's *The Rock,* four astonishing last bursts of vitalism in four of the strongest modern poets. What allies the four volumes (*The Rock* is actually the last section of Stevens's *Collected Poems,* but he had planned it as a separate volume under the title *Autumn Umber*) is their overcoming of each poet's abiding anxiety of representation. "Representation," in poetry, ultimately means self-advocacy; as Hartman says: "You justify either the self or that which stands greatly against it: perhaps both at once." We could cite Nietzsche here on the poet's Will-to-Power, but the more orthodox Coleridge suffices, by reminding us that there can be no origination without discontinuity, and that only the Will can interrupt the repetition-compulsion that *is* nature. In the final phases of Browning, Hardy, Yeats, and Stevens, the poet's Will raises itself against Nature, and this antithetical spirit breaks through a final anxiety and dares to represent itself as what Coleridge called self-determining spirit. Whether Freud would have compounded this self-realizing instinct with his "detours towards death" I do not know, but I think it is probable. In this final phase, Browning and his followers (Hardy and Yeats were overtly influenced by Browning, and I would suggest a link between the extemporizing, improvising aspect of Stevens, and Browning) are substituting a transumptive representation for the still-abiding presence of Shelley, their common ancestor.

I want to illustrate this difficult point by reference to Browning's last book, particularly to its **"Prologue,"** and to the sequence called **"Bad Dreams."** My model, ultimately, is again the Lurianic Kabbalah, with its notion of *gilgul,* of lifting up a precursor's spark, provided that he is truly one's precursor, truly of one's own root. *Gilgul* is the ultimate *tikkun,* as far as an act of representation can go. What Browning does is fascinatingly like the pattern of *gilgul,* for at the end he takes up precisely Shelley's dispute with Shelley's prime precursor, Wordsworth. By doing for Shelley what Shelley could not do for himself, overcome Wordsworth, Browning lifts up or redeems Shelley's spark or ember, and renews the power celebrated in the *Ode to the West Wind* and Act IV of *Prometheus Unbound*. I will try to illustrate this complex pattern, after these glances at *Asolando,* by returning for a last time (I hope) to my personal obsession with **"Childe Roland to the Dark Tower Came,"** and then concluding this discourse by considering Browning's late reversal of **"Childe Roland"** in the highly Shelleyan celebration, **"Thamuris Marching."**

The **"Prologue"** to *Asolando* is another in that long series of revisions of the *Intimations* Ode that form so large a part of the history of nineteenth and twentieth-century British and American poetry. But Browning consciously gives a revision of a revision, compounding **"Alastor"** and the **"Hymn to Intellectual Beauty"** with the parent poem. What counts in Browning's poem is not the Wordsworthian gleam, called here, in the first stanza, an "alien glow," but the far more vivid Shelleyan fire, that Browning recalls seeing for the first time, some fifty years before:

> How many a year, my Asolo,
> Since—one step just from sea to land—
> I found you, loved yet feared you so—
> For natural objects seemed to stand
> Palpably fire-clothed! No—
>
> No mastery of mine o'er these!
> Terror with beauty, like the Bush
> Burning but unconsumed. Bend knees,
> Drop eyes to earthward! Language? Tush!
> Silence 'tis awe decrees.
>
> And now? The lambent flame is—where?
> Lost from the naked world: earth, sky,
> Hill, vale, tree, flower,—Italia's rare
> O'er-running beauty crowds the eye—
> But flame? The Bush is bare.

When Shelley abandoned the fire, then it was for the transumptive trumpet of a prophecy, or in *Adonais* for the same wind rising ("The breath whose might I have invoked in song / Descends on me") to carry him beyond voice as beyond sight. Browning, as an Evangelical Protestant, fuses the Shelleyan heritage with the Protestant God in a powerfully incongruous transumption:

> Hill, vale, tree, flower—they stand distinct,
> Nature to know and name. What then?
> A Voice spoke thence which straight unlinked
> Fancy from fact: see, all's in ken:
> Has once my eyelid winked?
>
> No, for the purged ear apprehends
> Earth's import, not the eye late dazed:

> The voice said 'Call my works thy friends!
> At Nature dost thou shrink amazed?
> God is it who transcends.'

This is an absolute logocentrism, and is almost more than any poem can bear, particularly at a time as late as 1889. Browning gets away with it partly by way of a purged ear, partly because his Protestantism condenses what High Romanticism normally displaces, the double-bind situation of the Protestant believer whose God simultaneously says "Be Like Me in My stance towards Nature" and "Do not presume to resemble Me in My stance towards nature." The sheer energy of the Browningesque demonic Sublime carries the poet past what ought to render him imaginatively schizoid.

But not for long, of course, as a glance at **"Bad Dreams"** will indicate, a glance that then will take us back to the greatest of Browning's nightmares, the demonic romance of **"Childe Roland." "Bad Dreams III"** is a poem in which the opposition between Nature and Art *has* been turned into a double-bind, with its contradictory injunctions:

> This was my dream! I saw a Forest
> Old as the earth, no track nor trace
> Of unmade man. Thou, Soul, explorest—
> Though in a trembling rapture—space
> Immeasurable! Shrubs, turned trees,
> Trees that touch heaven, support its frieze
> Studded with sun and moon and star:
> While—oh, the enormous growths that bar
> Mine eye from penetrating past
> Their tangled twine where lurks—nay, lives
> Royally lone, some brute-type cast
> In the rough, time cancels, man forgives.
>
> On, Soul! I saw a lucid City
> Of architectural device
> Every way perfect. Pause for pity,
> Lightning! Nor leave a cicatrice
> On those bright marbles, dome and spire,
> Structures palatial,—streets which mire
> Dares not defile, paved all too fine
> For human footstep's smirch, not thine—
> Proud solitary traverser,
> My Soul, of silent lengths of way—
> With what ecstatic dread, aver,
> Lest life start sanctioned by thy stay!
>
> Ah, but the last sight was the hideous!
> A city, yes,—a Forest, true,—
> But each devouring each. Perfidious
> Snake-plants had strangled what I knew
> Was a pavilion once: each oak
> Held on his horns some spoil he broke
> By surreptitiously beneath
> Upthrusting: pavements, as with teeth,
> Griped huge weed widening crack and split

In squares and circles stone-work erst.
Oh, Nature—good! Oh, Art—no whit
Less worthy! Both in one—accurst!

In the sequence of **"Bad Dreams,"** Browning himself, as interpreter of his own text, identifies Nature with the husband, Art with the wife, and the marriage of Art and Nature, man and woman—why, with Hell, and a sadomasochistic sexual Hell, at that. But the text can sustain very diverse interpretations, as the defensive intensity of repression here is enormously strong. The City is of Art, but like Yeats's Byzantium, which it prophesies, it is also a City of Death-in-Life, and the previous vision of the forest is one of a Nature that might be called Life-in-Death. Neither realm can bear the other, in both senses of "bear"—"bring forth" or "tolerate." Neither is the other's precursor, and each devours the other, if they are brought together. This is hardly the vision of the **"Prologue"** to *Asolando,* as there seems no room for either Browning or God in the world of the final stanza. Granted that this is nightmare, or severe repression partly making a return, it carries us back to Browning at his most problematic and Sublime, to his inverted vision of the Center, **"Childe Roland to the Dark Tower Came."**

As the author of two full-scale commentaries on this poem (in *The Ringers in the Tower,* 1971, and in *A Map of Misreading,* 1975) I reapproach the text with considerable wariness, fairly determined not only that I will not repeat myself, but also hopefully aiming not merely to uncover my own obsessional fixation upon so grandly grotesque a quest-romance. But I recur to the question I asked at the start of this discourse; is there an attainable *critical* knowledge to be gathered from this critical obsession?

Roland, though a Childe or ephebe on the road to a demonic version of the Scene of Instruction, is so consciously belated a quester that he seems at least as much an obsessive interpreter as anything else purposive that he might desire to become. He out-Nietzsches Nietzsche's Zarathustra in his compulsive will-to-power over the interpretation of his own text. It is difficult to conceive of a more belated hero, and I know of no more extreme literary instance of a quest emptying itself out. Borges accurately located in Browning one of the precursors of Kafka, and perhaps only Kafka's *The Castle* rivals **"Childe Roland"** as a Gnostic version of what was once romance. Nearly every figuration in the poem reduces to ruin, yet the poem, as all of us obscurely sense, appears to end in something like triumph, in a Good Moment carried through to a supreme representation:

There they stood, ranged along the hill-sides, met
To view the last of me, a living frame
For one more picture! in a sheet of flame

I saw them and I knew them all. And yet
Dauntless the slug-horn to my lips I set,
And blew, *'Childe Roland to the Dark Tower came.'*

Surely it is outrageous to call this a Supreme or even a Good Moment? The stanza just before ends with the sound of loss: "one moment knelled the woe of years." Wordsworth and Coleridge had viewed the Imagination as compensatory, as trading off experiential loss for poetic gain, a formula that we can begin to believe was an unmitigated calamity. It is the peculiar fascination of **"Childe Roland,"** as a poem, that it undoes every High Romantic formula, that it exposes the Romantic imagination as being merely an accumulative principle of repression. But such negation is itself simplistic, and evades what is deepest and most abiding in this poem, which is the representation of *power.* For here, I think, is the kernel of our critical quest, that Kabbalistic point which is at once *ayin,* or nothingness, and *ehyeh,* or the representation of Absolute Being, the rhetorical irony or *illusio* that always permits a belated poem to begin again in its quest for renewed strength. Signification has wandered away, and Roland is questing for lost and forgotten *meaning,* questing for *representation,* for a seconding or re-advocacy of his own self. Does he not succeed, far better than Tennyson's Ulysses and Percivale, and far better even than the Solitaries of the High Romantics, in this quest for representation? Let us grant him, and ourselves, that this is a substitute for his truly impossible original objective, for that was the *antithetical,* Shelleyan dream of rebegetting oneself, of breaking through the web of nature and so becoming one's own imaginative father. Substitution, as Roland shows, needs not be a sublimation, but can move from repression *through* sublimation to climax in a more complex act of defense.

Psychoanalysis has no single name for this act, unless we were willing (as we are not) to accept the pejorative one of paranoia for what is, from any point of view that transcends the analytic, a superbly valuable act of the will. Roland teaches us that what psychoanalysis calls "introjection" and "projection" are figurations for the spiritual processes of identification and apocalyptic rejection that exist at the outer borders of poetry. Roland learns, and we learn with him, that the representation of power *is* itself a power, and that this latter power or strength is the only purposiveness that we shall know. Roland, at the close, is re-inventing the self, but at the considerable expense of joining that self to a visionary company of loss, and loss means loss of *meaning* here. The endless fascination of his poem, for any critical reader nurtured upon Romantic tradition, is that the poem, more clearly than any other, nevertheless does precisely what any strong Romantic poem does, at once de-idealizes itself far more thoroughly than we can de-idealize it, yet points also beyond this self-deconstruction or limitation or reduction to the First Idea, on to a re-imagining, to a power-making that no other discursive mode affords. For Roland, as persuasively as any fictive being, warns us against the poisonous ravishments of truth itself. He and his reader have moved only through discourse together, and he and his reader are less certain about what they know than they were as the poem began, but both he and his reader have endured unto a representation of more strength than they had at the start, and such a representation indeed turns out to be a kind of restitution, a *tikkun* for repairing a fresh breaking-of-the-vessels. Meaning has been more curtailed than restored, but strength is revealed as antithetical to meaning.

I conclude with a great poem by Browning that is his conscious revision of **"Childe Roland:"** the marvelous late chant, **"Thamuris Marching,"** which is one of the finest unknown, unread poems by a major poet in the language. Twenty-two years after composing **"Childe Roland,"** Browning, not at the problematic age of thirty-nine, but now sixty-one, knows well that no spring has followed or flowered past meridian. But **"Childe Roland"** is a belated poem, except in its transumptive close, while all of **"Thamuris Marching"** accomplishes a metaleptic reversal, for how could a poem be more overwhelmingly early than this? And yet the situation of the quester is objectively terrible from the start of this poem, for Thamuris *knows* he is marching to an unequal contest, a poetic struggle of one heroic ephebe against the greatest of precursors, the Muses themselves. "Thamuris marching," the strong phrase repeated three times in the chant, expresses the *exuberance of purpose,* the Shelleyan remorseless joy in pure, self-destructive poetic quest, that Browning finally is able to grant himself.

Here is Browning's source, *Iliad* II, 594 ff:

> . . . and Dorion, where the Muses
> encountering Thamyris the Thracian stopped him from
> singing, as he came from Oichalia and Oichalian Eurytos;
> for he boasted that he would surpass, if the very Muses,
> daughters of Zeus who holds the aegis, were singing against him.
> and these in their anger struck him maimed, and the voice of wonder
> they took away, and made him a singer without memory;

                              (Lattimore version)

Homer does not say that Thamyris lost the contest, but rather that the infuriated Muses lost their divine temper, and unvoiced him by maiming his memory, without which no one can be a poet. Other sources, presumably

known to Browning, mention a contest decided in the Muses' favor by Apollo, after which those ungracious ladies blinded Thamyris, and removed his memory, so as to punish him for his presumption. Milton, in the invocation to light that opens Book III of *Paradise Lost,* exalted Thamyris by coupling him with Homer, and then associated his own ambitions with both poets:

> Nightly I visit: nor sometimes forget
> Those other two equall'd with me in Fate,
> So were I equall'd with them in renown,
> Blind Thamyris and blind Maemonides.

Milton presumably had read in Plutarch that Thamyris was credited with an epic about the war waged by the Titans against the Gods, the theme that Browning would associate with Shelley and with Keats. Browning's Thamuris marches to a Shelleyan *terza rima,* and marches through a visionary universe distinctly like Shelley's, and overtly proclaimed as being *early:* "From triumph on to triumph, mid a ray / Of early morn—." Laughing as he goes, yet knowing fully his own doom, Thamuris marches through a landscape of joy that is the deliberate point-by-point reversal of Childe Roland's self-made phantasmagoria of ordeal-by-landscape:

> Thamuris, marching, laughed 'Each flake of foam'
> (As sparkingly the ripple raced him by)
> 'Mocks slower clouds adrift in the blue dome!'
>
> For Autumn was the season; red the sky
> Held morn's conclusive signet of the sun
> To break the mists up, bid them blaze and die.
>
> Morn had the mastery as, one by one
> All pomps produced themselves along the tract
> From earth's far ending to near Heaven begun.
>
> Was there a ravaged tree? it laughed compact
> With gold, a leaf-ball crisp, high-brandished now,
> Tempting to onset frost which late attacked.
>
> Was there a wizened shrub, a starveling bough,
> A fleecy thistle filched from by the wind,
> A weed, Pan's trampling hoof would disallow?
>
> Each, with a glory and a rapture twined
> About it, joined the rush of air and light
> And force: the world was of one joyous mind.

                                    (19-36)

From Roland's reductive interpretations we have passed to the imagination's heightened expansions. And though this quest is necessarily for the fearful opposite of poetic divination, we confront, not ruin, but the Good Moment exalted and transfigured, as though for once Browning utterly could fuse literal and figurative:

> Say not the birds flew! they forebore their
> right—
> Swam, reveling onward in the roll of things.
> Say not the beasts' mirth bounded! that was
> flight—
>
> How could the creatures leap, no lift of
> wings?
> Such earth's community of purpose, such
> The ease of earth's fulfilled imaginings—
>
> So did the near and far appear to touch
> In the moment's transport—that an interchange
> Of function, far with near, seemed scarce too
> much;
>
>   (37-45)

Roland's band of failures has become the glorious band of precursors among whom Thamuris predominates. The Shelleyan west wind of imagination rises, Destroyer and Creater, as Thamuris, eternally early, stands as the true ephebe, "Earth's poet," against the Heavenly Muse:

> Therefore the morn-ray that enriched his face,
> If it gave lambent chill, took flame again
> From flush of pride; he saw, he knew the
> place.
>
> What wind arrived with all the rhythms from
> plain,
> Hill, dale, and that rough wildwood
> interspersed?
> Compounding these to one consummate strain,
>
> It reached him, music; but his own outburst
> Of victory concluded the account,
> And that grew song which was mere music
> erst.
>
> 'Be my Parnassos, thou Pangaian mount!
> And turn thee, river, nameless hitherto!
> Famed shalt thou vie with famed Pieria's
> fount!
>
> 'Here I await the end of this ado:
> Which wins—Earth's poet or the Heavenly
> Muse.'

There is the true triumph of Browning's art, for the ever-early Thamuris is Browning as he wished to have been, locked in a solitary struggle against the precursor-principle, but struggling *in* the visionary world of the precursor. Roland rode through a Gnostic universe in which the hidden God, Shelley, was repressed, a repression that gave Browning a negative triumph of the Sublime made Grotesque. In **"Thamuris Marching,"** the joyous struggle is joined overtly, and the repressed partly returns, to be repressed again into the true Sublime, as Browning lifts up the sparks of his own root, to invoke that great mixed metaphor of the Lurianic Kabbalah. There is a breaking-of-the-vessels, but the sparks are scattered again, and become Shelley's *and* Browning's words, mixed together, among mankind.

Adam Potkay (essay date 1987)

SOURCE: "The Problem of Identity and the Grounds for Judgment in *The Ring and the Book*," in *Victorian Poetry*, Vol. 25, No. 2, Summer, 1987, pp. 143-57.

[*In the following essay, Potkay suggests that contrary to the contentions of most modern critics,* The Ring and the Book *does not identify any character in the poem as the moral center or authority. Rather, the poem offers a "decentered struggle of interpretations," with the character of Guido taking on a decentering role which questions the very notion of identity.*]

Criticism of **The Ring and The Book,** with few exceptions, unites in assigning an infallible center of authority to the poem. Critics have attempted to transcend Browning's "text"—in which different interpretations of the Roman murder story converge and contend—in favor of an authoritatively unified "Book," obliquely promised by Browning in his title, but brought to light only through the auspices of humanist criticism.[1] Robert D. Altick and James F. Loucks, II, for example, devote their full-length study of **The Ring and the Book** to tracing the "basic movement" of the poem in "the coalescence of partial truths into a transcendent Truth."[2] The index to the transcendent Truth of the poem is, in practice, usually either Robert Browning in propria persona, the Pope as Browning's alter ego, or Pompilia as an authoritatively privileged figure of purity and sanctity. In "*Pompilia* and Pompilia," William Walker summarizes and criticizes contemporary critical efforts to attribute a transparent identity and absolute integrity to Pompilia, and consequently to designate Pompilia as the moral touchstone of the poem.[3] Similar critical efforts mark the Pope and the Robert Browning of Books I and XII as the intellectual and moral center of the poem.[4]

However, we cannot locate decisively a center of the poem because we cannot, preliminarily, attribute a definitive identity to a given character. The critic's gesture of assigning transparent identities to several characters in the text—notably to Robert Browning, the Pope, and Pompilia—is already "in play" within the text: anticipated by, mirrored in, and finally belied by the inutility of the crucial interpretive gestures of those very characters. As *The Ring and the Book* makes abundantly clear, all of our knowledge derives from acts of interested or relative interpretation, and the will to apodictic truth is merely symptomatic of the anxiety of misinterpretation.

To accept *The Ring and the Book* as a decentered struggle of interpretations has two conspicuous consequences for our evaluation of the characters in the poem. First, we emphasize Guido's archly decentering role in the poem. Guido, as the shifting self-presentations of his first and second monologues make clear, is not tied to a specific line of interpretation or to a specific construction of personal identity. Indeed, Guido throws the very notion of essential "identity" into question. Guido, as much as the structure of the poem itself, denies that the self can transcend public and normative interpretations.[5] Second, a decentered reading of *The Ring and the Book* disrupts the usual alignment of Robert Browning and the Pope; we are led, rather, to consider the affinities between Guido and the characterological or, to use Morse Peckham's phrase, the "compromised" Robert Browning of Books I and XII.[6]

I. The Identifying Mark

The wish to assign transparent identities to the characters of *The Ring and the Book,* and thereby sidestep or transcend the vagaries of interpretation, is not simply the response of an extraneous critical tradition. Rather, Pompilia and the Pope have already set this wish in play within the poem; their will to apodictic truth arises out of, and in reaction to, a fundamental concern with misinterpreting and being misinterpreted.

Pompilia is the first character to lament the absence of a transparent Truth in the poem. She refers us, instead, to "difference," a multeity of perspectives that resists integration:

> So we are made, such difference in minds,
> Such difference too in eyes that see the
>   minds!
> That man [Caponsacchi], you misinterpret and
>   misprise—
> The glory of his nature, I had thought,
> Shot itself out in white light, blazed the truth
> Through every atom of his act with me:
> Yet where I point you, through the chrystal
>   shrine,
> Purity in quintessence, one dew-drop,
> You all descry a spider in the midst.
> One says, 'The head of it is plain to see,'
> And one, 'They are the feet by which I
>   judge,'
> All say, 'Those films were spun by nothing
>   else.'

(VII, 918-929)[7]

Because of the necessary "difference" of perspectives, interpretation is inevitably and regrettably misinterpretation or misprision.[8] The inevitability of "difference," as Pompilia acknowledges it, does not assuage her indignation. The encompassing glory of Caponsacchi's nature should be self-evident, and Pompilia is outraged that it is not. Pompilia, in other words, is indignant at the very necessity of interpretation.

Pompilia's compensatory fantasy is to transcend interpretation altogether. Pompilia, in a passionately heightened moment of self-justification, imagines a "mark" placed upon her by God:

> I did think, do think, in the thought shall die,
> That to have Caponsacchi for my guide,
> Ever the face upturned to mine, the hand
> Holding my hand across the world,—a sense
> That reads, as only such can read, the mark
> God sets on woman, signifying so
> She should—shall peradventure—be divine;
> Yet 'ware, the while, how weakness mars the
>   print
> And makes confusion, leaves the thing men
>   see,
> —Not this man,—who from his own soul,
>   re-writes
> The obliterated charter,—love and strength
> Mending what's marred.

(VII, 1495-1506)

Pompilia praises Caponsacchi's ability to discern "the mark" she claims is upon her. This mark is oddly literal, a trace that God "sets" upon woman. Pompilia's invocation of the mark echoes the language of the archetypal marking of Cain: "And the Lord set a mark upon Cain, lest any finding him should kill him" (Genesis 4:15). Like Cain's mark, Pompilia's has a conspicuous, unequivocal, and universal meaning, "signifying so / She should—shall peradventure—be divine." The mark serves to consolidate the fluid self, subject to partial and unlimited interpretations, into a stable and limited identity. Thus, Caponsacchi does not need to interpret, that is, construct his own perspectival rendition of, Pompilia. He needs only to focus on—to "read" or at most "re-write"—the mark that is already written upon Pompilia, to know all that needs to be known about her character: that she "shall be" divine. The significance of the mark is perfectly apparent, if only to Caponsacchi and God.[9] Pompilia has progressed, in the course of her monologue, from deploring misinterpretation to imagining a "mark" that transcends the very necessity of interpretation.

Pompilia's desire to transcend interpretation is echoed in the monologue of the Pope. Commencing with a meditation on misinterpretation, the Pope comes to assert that character—here, the character of Guido—can be unmistakably identified. In the opening lines of his monologue, the Pope begins his daily ritual of reading "a History / . . . Of all my predecessors, Popes of Rome" (X,6). He professes to look in that History for an "example, rule of life" to guide him in his judgment of Guido (l. 21). He derives, however, no very specific guidance from his perusal of history. His narration of the succession of ninth-century Popes who alternately anathematized and canonized the corpse of Pope Formosus (ll. 24-149) suggests that judgment is provisional and, on the surface, strangely arbitrary. The Pope ends his narration not with conclusions, but with unanswerable questions:

> Which of the judgments was infallible?
> Which of my predecessors spoke for God?
> And what availed Formosus that this cursed,
> That blessed, and then this other cursed again?

> (ll. 150-153)

The "rule" supplied by this brief history is, ironically, that history provides no steadfast rule to guide our judgment. Accordingly, the Pope concludes that he "must give judgment on [his] own behoof" (l. 160). The Pope employs a brief parable to address this impasse between the necessity of "giving judgment" and the inherent fallibility of any judgment.

> Some surmise
> Perchance, that since man's wit is fallible,
> Mine may fail here? Suppose it so,—what then?
> Say,—Guido, I count guilty, there's no babe
> So guiltless, for I misconceive the man!
> What's in the chance should move me from my mind?
> If, as I walk in a rough country-side,
> Peasants of mine cry 'Thou art he can help,
> Lord of the land and counted wise to boot:
> Look at our brother, strangling in his foam,
> He fell so where we find him,—prove thy worth!'
> I may presume, pronounce, 'A frenzy-fit,
> A falling-sickness or a fever-stroke!
> Breathe a vein, copiously let blood at once!'
> So perishes the patient, and anon
> I hear my peasants—'All was error, lord!
> Our story, thy prescription: for there crawled
> In due time from our hapless brother's breast
> The serpent which had stung him: bleeding slew
> Whom a prompt cordial had restored to health.'
> What other should I say than 'God so willed:
> Mankind is ignorant, a man am I:
> Call ignorance my sorrow not my sin!'
> So and not otherwise, in after-time,
> If some acuter wit, fresh probing, sound

> This multifarious mass of words and deeds
> Deeper, and reach through guilt to innocence,
> I shall face Guido's ghost nor blench a jot.
> 'God who set me to judge thee, meted out
> So much of judging faculty, no more:
> Ask him if I was slack in use thereof!'

> (ll. 236-266)

The meaning of the parable is clear. Because of man's limited perspective, the interpretation of signs always carries with it the possibility of misinterpretation. Moreover, as in the case of the misdiagnosed peasant, misinterpretation may be disastrous. But since man is, nevertheless, called upon to interpret, it is his practical duty to suspend his wariness of misinterpretation and commit himself to his interpretive act. The Pope of necessity interprets, and he believes in his own interpretations. The Pope's avowed belief about Guido, stated early in the monologue, is that he is culpable:

> The case is over, judgment at an end,
> And all things done and irrevocable:
> A mere dead man is Franceschini here,
> Even as Formosus centuries ago.

> (ll. 207-210)

The sweeping cadence and dispassionate language of these lines connote an assured belief in Guido's guilt. Does, however, the Pope's belief fully allay his initial concern with misinterpretation? Once he begins his actual assessment of Guido, the Pope, far from embracing his interpretive belief on its own terms, imagines Guido as marked with a sign that needs no interpretation: "For I find this black mark impinge the man, / That he believes in just the vile of life" (ll. 510-511). The Pope imaginatively disengages himself from the sloppiness of interpretation through envisaging a "black mark impinge the man." The unsettling force of the verb "impinge" suggests that this mark, like the mark set upon Pompilia, is literally struck upon Guido. The mark, in turn, fixes the meaning of Guido. The mark identifies Guido as vile, just as the mark perceived by Pompilia identified her as divine. And, in both cases, the mark is the fantasy of the individual interpreter by whom it is assigned, not found.

The identifying mark remains a private fantasy, of course, because if there were publicly verifiable marks, there would be no Franceschini trial, no mystery, no "Old Yellow Book," no *The Ring and the Book.* There would not be "the struggle for truth" that the Pope himself comes to value later in his monologue (ll. 1850-1928). *The Ring and the Book* itself is both part of, and representative of, that interminable struggle. No one interpretation of the Roman murder story can claim absolute validity or transparent truth. Rather, *The Ring and the*

Book dramatizes the way in which interpretation works in an arena where no final truth is available. One rhetorically powerful strategy of interpretation, evinced in the conjuring of a "mark," is to deny that interpretation need occur at all.

The thesis that **The Ring and the Book** is a decentered struggle of interpretations invites an obvious ethical objection. A traditional humanist critic might ask: If we cannot legitimately assign an essential identity to any character in the poem, and hence cannot establish an authoritative center in the poem, then what can keep the critical enterprise from slouching toward ethical relativism, solipsism, nihilism, or worse? Let us approach this question negatively, by first examining the validity of Robert Langbaum's very conservative, and very well known, understanding of **The Ring and the Book.** Langbaum serves, at a moral level, to indemnify critics of **The Ring and the Book** against unbridled relativism. He proposes that as we read the interconnected monologues of **The Ring and the Book** our "judgment" transcends our dissipated Romantic "sympathy" and allies itself with Robert Browning and the Pope, the absolutely right critics of the Franceschini case. In the psychology of our response to the poem, what finally saves us from relativism, then, is the constraint of a timeless and universally shared "judgment." The impasse of Langbaum's psychological model is, however, precisely that the uniform concept of "judgment" Langbaum wants to preserve is already studiously deconstructed by the course of nineteenth-century experiential relativism as Langbaum propounds it (Langbaum, esp. pp. 38-74). The questions that emerge from this necessary rereading of Langbaum are: On what grounds can we judge the post-Romantic character? On what grounds do we ourselves stand? What, if anything, stands between us and an utterly solipsistic methodology?

II. Guido: The Communal Grounds for Judgment, and the Critique of Identity

The character in **The Ring and the Book** who openly addresses these questions is Guido Franceschini. Guido believes in no absolute ground for judgment. Rather, he submits his case to be judged by convention, ancient prejudice, and the arbitrary "rules of the game":

> I see my grandsire's hoof-prints,—point the
> spot
> Where he drew rein, slipped saddle, and
> stabbed knave
> For daring throw gibe—much less, stone—
> from pale,
> Then back, and on, and up with the cavalcade;
> Just so wend we, now canter, now converse,
> Till, 'mid the jauncing pride and jaunty port,
> Something of a sudden jerks at somebody—
> A dagger is out, a flashing cut and thrust,

> Because I play some prank my grandsire
> played,
> And here I sprawl: where is the company?
> Gone!
> A trot and a trample! only I lie trapped,
> Writhe in a certain novel springe just set
> By the good old Pope: I'm first prize. Warn
> me? Why?
> Apprize me that the law o' the game is
> changed?
> Enough that I'm a warning, as I writhe,
> To all and each my fellows of the file,
> And make law plain henceforward past
> mistake,
> 'For such a prank, death is the penalty!'

(XI, 103-120)

Later, Guido flips from sneering at his penalty to embracing it (from which he soon after flips back again); from this changed perspective, however, Guido still invokes the same notion of a social "pact" or "bond": "I broke bond, / And needs must pay price,—wherefore, here's my head, / Flung with a flourish!" (ll. 543-545). For Guido, judgment—be it for or against him—is always and only meaningful in context, and the pertinent context is always public and conventional. Guido does not believe in absolute rules of behavior, but only in what is permitted.

If we turn back to Guido's first monologue (Book V), we can see how thorough his appeal is to convention and public verification. His definition of the murder as "the irregular deed" (ll. 99, 113) denies any absolute value to the act; the murder has meaning only in relation to the sheerly normative standards of "regularity." Guido's entire narration makes no claims for transparent, self-evident truth, but instead acknowledges its own limited status as "interpretation" (l. 114), the validity of which is dependent on a communal verification: "Do your eyes here see with mine?" (l. 1064).

Guido's appeal to convention, as the case makes clear, would have succeeded in seventeenth-century Arezzo, where popular respect prevailed for the nobility and its ancient claims. As Guido himself claims, with a hyperbole that is not a little ironic, his privilege is as ancient as the "Etruscan, Aretine, / One sprung—your frigid Virgil's fieriest word,— / From fauns and nymphs, trunks and the heart of oak" (XI, 1919-21). Guido's appeal to ancient prejudice, but for the lights of the Pope, might even have succeeded in Rome. The historical "tragedy" of Guido is that his appeal, as Browning re-creates it, does not succeed in nineteenth-century England, or in the twentieth-century Anglo-American classroom. He is finally "reprehensible." What makes Guido such an oddly riveting and disconcerting character, however, is that his appeal to conventionality per se brings to light the bedrock of equally conventional assumptions and beliefs by which we judge him. The conventionality of our critical response to the character of Guido is evinced by the fact that that response changes in time, according to changing critical conventions. Hence, writing in 1987, I "condemn" Guido for his violent misogyny, but my condemnation does not extend to his flagrant atheism, which was reprehensible to Browning's Pope and would have doubtlessly been reprehensible to Browning's contemporaries, or to his putative "unmanliness," which formed the better part of the humanist critic's complaint against Guido. And although I can, in 1987, safely omit discussions of Guido's atheism and perhaps even of his manliness (or lack of it) within a "valid" interpretation of Guido's character, I cannot say just anything about Guido and still be heard. I cannot, for example, say that Guido's conception of women is essential to the preservation of a firm social order. I cannot say that Guido is a prefiguration of Mussolini. The reason is simply that my interpretation, in order to be heard at all, must operate within the constraints of the implicit codes of my own "interpretive community."[10] Like Guido, my appeal is always and only to a communal or institutional verification. Thus, Guido himself can be made to answer the anticipated ethical objection to a decentered text: there will never be an unbridled critical relativism or solipsism because our personal interpretations are always validated or invalidated by public, conventional norms of interpretation. The critic must ask of his own audience, "Do your eyes here see with mine?"

Finally, while I find Guido reprehensible at a moral level, the conventions of my interpretive community do allow me to appreciate Guido at a hermeneutical level. With due skepticism, Guido embraces and exploits the fact that our interested and imprecise interpretations of each other are all we can know. Thus, Guido subverts the notion of essential identity which is upheld by Pompilia, the Pope, and the critics who act as their apologists.

Guido's monologues offer an implicit critique of the identifying mark. Unlike the Pope or Pompilia, each of whom imagines a God-given "mark" that puts an end to interpretation, Guido imagines a mark that is publicly imagined. Guido first imputes the imagining of a mark to the court that reads his testimony:

> Would you not prophesy—'She [Pompilia] on
>   whose brow is stamped
> The note of imputation that we know,—
> Rightly or wrongly mothered with a whore,—
> Such an one, to disprove the frightful charge,
> What will she but exaggerate chastity.'

(V, 884-888)

Guido invokes the psychology of marking within quotation marks; the "stamp" upon Pompilia is part of the

public response Guido anticipates. Similarly, Guido conjures an image of Pompilia's child, who may or may not be his son, and imagines on its forehead the "brand" of public disgrace (ll. 1483-1531). In neither case does Guido actually refer to a "mark," a term whose theological connotations descend from Genesis. Rather, Guido invokes the public acts of "branding" and "stamping." A mark, according to this view, is the product of a public opinion. Guido's acknowledgement of the sheerly public significance of any marking serves as a counter to the Popean/Pompilian imagining of a "mark" whose meaning is independent of an audience.

A more profound (if inadvertent) critique of the identifying mark is found toward the end of Guido's second monologue. Commenting on his bad luck in not having caught Pompilia and Caponsacchi in flagrante delicto at the wayside inn, Guido concludes,

> Oh, why, why was it not ordained just so?
> Why fell not things out so nor otherwise?
> Ask that particular devil whose task it is
> To trip the all-but-at perfection . . .
>
> . . . . .
>
> Inscribes all human effort with one word,
> Artistry's haunting curse, the Incomplete!

(XI, 1551-59)

The passage offers a negative image of the identifying mark that, according to Pompilia and the Pope, God sets upon woman and upon Guido. In Guido's ironic version, a "devil" marks all human effort, not with positive identity but with negative potential, "the Incomplete." Applied broadly to Guido's monologues, the Incomplete can refer not only to Guido's endeavor but also to Guido's very self, which is not available for simple predication but is constantly changing according to shifting circumstances and being changed (as Guido rightfully laments) according to shifting interpretive conventions. Taken as a denial of the identity of the self, the Incomplete stands as the emblem for Guido's activity throughout the poem. As commentators have noted with some indignation, Guido has an extremely fluid sense of self-definition; he juggles motivations for his actions, causes for his effects.

Yet Guido's essential identity is routinely explicated by critics of *The Ring and the Book.* Critics, by the grace of Guido's last lines, would stamp Guido's character as complete. For that very reason, Guido's last lines are notorious:

> I am the Granduke's—no, I am the Pope's!
> Abate,—Cardinal,—Christ,—Maria,—God, . . .
> Pompilia, will you let them murder me?

(XI, 2423-25)

Taking these lines as an absolute revelation of character—the completion of our formerly incomplete picture of Guido—Morse Peckham writes that Guido "suddenly reveals" himself as "the jelly" he always was (p. 246). Langbaum writes, "When Guido finally speaks out of his *deepest instinct,* he recognizes in his own *absolute evil* and Pompilia's *absolute goodness* the reason for the fundamental antagonism between them" (Preface, emphasis mine).[11] The intransigence of these condemnations is in excess of any assertion about Guido that might be actually supported by the text. These condemnations are, in other words, in excess of interpretation.

The character of Guido is not so much critically judged at the end of his monologue as it is willfully marked or scapegoated. Guido must be marked so that the notion of verifiable identity and the corresponding possibility of a privileged judgment can be preserved. If we view Guido with critical sensitivity rather than with uncritical rancor, objections to his utter condemnation become apparent. How can we be sure that Guido's final lines are not said for a grand penitent effect? As Altick and Loucks point out, "normally it is difficult if not impossible to distinguish sincerity from show in [Guido's] wild speech" (pp. 71-72). Why exempt Guido's last lines from this "normal" condition of indeterminacy? Why decide that only Guido's last three lines, of a 2,425 line monologue, are unequivocally from the heart? In a move that fully reveals the mechanism of marking, Altick and Loucks turn, sharply and unexpectedly, from the judicious recognition that "it is impossible to distinguish fully" between fluctuating Guidos, to the identifying assertion that Guido "repeatedly likens himself to Jesus Christ but *in reality is* Satan" (p. 90, emphasis mine). In this move, as in all acts of marking in or of *The Ring and the Book,* the desire to positively identify a character as good or evil supersedes the interpreter's capacity to remain in uncertainty and doubt.

One possible justification of reading Guido's last three lines as absolutely revelatory of character is the argument for poetic closure: that is, for reading the end of a text (in this case, a monologue) as retrospectively and conclusively illuminating everything that has gone before in the text. The very structure of *The Ring and the Book,* however, militates against a closure argument. As Lee Erickson has most recently acknowledged, "The form [of *The Ring and the Book*] is almost frighteningly open-ended. As the trailing off of the reports in "The Book and the Ring" shows, there is always the possibility of considering yet another point of view" (p. 234). It is especially easy to imagine "yet another point of view" from a speaker like Guido who specializes in fabricating points of view. More than any of the other monologues in *The Ring and the Book* (except, perhaps, for the monologues of Robert Browning himself), Guido's two monologues resist closure; they do so by demonstrating that our sense of an ending is provisional and subject to the complications that may arise upon yet another beginning. As the ending of Guido's first monologue is, so the ending of his second monologue might be.

III. Robert Browning

For nearly all critics of *The Ring and the Book,* the firmest authority in the poem has been the Robert Browning of Books I and XII, who, despite Morse Peckham's caveat, is still identified rather routinely as the real, historical Robert Browning. Moreover, this real Robert Browning is somehow immediately knowable, if not through his monologues then through his letters, his biographically verifiable religious convictions, and his position in a humanist literary tradition. Whether the Robert Browning of Books I and XII is "real" (whatever that might mean) or characterological,[12] this Robert Browning has much more in common with the character of Guido than critics have recognized. Browning is similar to Guido, not in his moral convictions but in the grain of his interpretive assumptions. Robert Browning does not present us with unequivocal portraits of his characters but rather presents and re-presents characters according to his own shifting interpretations; and he is skeptical of his own ability to conjure up a transcendent "Truth" out of the sequential "facts" he presents, especially a Truth that could claim to transcend the final tribunal of public, communal verification.

Browning, in Book I, commits himself to three distinct tellings of the Franceschini case. The first telling (ll. 520-678) is Browning's Florentine "vision" of the murder story. Browning calls this rendition of the story "the tragic piece" (l. 523). It reads, more precisely, like a piece from the Grand Guignol. The narrative is condensed and melodramatic, laden with metaphors and a ponderous (even by Browning's standards) alliterative scheme. A feel for the style can be gathered from the following passage:

> Guido Franceschini took away
> Pompilia to be his for evermore,
> While [Pompilia's parents] sang 'Now let us depart in peace,
> Having beheld thy glory, Guido's wife!'
> I saw the star supposed, but fog o' the fen,
> Gilded star-fashion by a glint from hell;
> Having been heaved up, haled on its gross way,
> By hands unguessed before, invisible help
> From a dark brotherhood, and specially
> Two obscure goblin creatures, fox-faced this,
> Cat-clawed the other, called his next of kin
> By Guido the main monster,—cloaked and caped,
> Making as they were priests, to mock God more,—
> Abate Paul, Canon Girolamo.

(ll. 540-553)

Throughout the piece, the characters are defined in terms of absolutes that often teeter on the verge of comic overstatement. Guido is "the main monster" of "a dark brotherhood"; later, he is called a "wolf," a "werewolf," and "Lucifer." Meanwhile, Caponsacchi, "the young good beauteous priest," shines with the glory of "Saint George."

Browning's second telling of the story (ll. 780-823) issues, according to Browning, from his return to London. It is cast in the form of a brief and fairly impartial summary. It does not assume the viciousness of Guido, but merely states that in Arezzo Pompilia and Guido lived "Unhappy lives, whatever curse the cause."

Browning tells the story for a third and last time (ll. 838-1378) in his presentation of "the voices [that] presently shall sound / In due succession." In contrast to the cumbrous and impassioned melodrama of his early Florentine vision, the tone of this latter presentation is measured, distanced, and ironic. Browning's assessment of character is softened and is at times equivocal. For example, Caponsacchi, formerly "the young good beauteous priest," becomes "A courtly spiritual Cupid, squire of dames / By law of love, and mandate of the mode." Browning's tone, while affectionate, has become teasing and deflationary. On the other hand, by dwelling on the details of Guido's torture and digressing onto the topic of the religious sanctioning of torture (ll. 975-1015), Browning oddly elicits our sympathy for Guido's first monologue. This sympathy is not so much retracted as it is complicated when Browning reverts, in his synopsis of Guido's second monologue (ll. 1272-1329), to the language of the Grand Guignol. Guido again becomes "the part-man part-monster," attended this time by "the frightful Brotherhood of Death" that awaits his execution.

Browning's three divergent tellings of the Franceschini case do not necessarily converge in a kind of supertext, the ideal telling that critics refer to when they cite Browning's authoritative judgments in Book I. Instead, Book I offers a palimpsest of different interpretations, each telling remaining "visible" beside its subsequent re-telling. These different interpretations of a recurrent narrative event underline the very quality of interpretation involved in each telling, and thus highlight the relative, malleable nature of narrative "truth." Despite his predilection for certain characters, Browning makes no pretense of being able to identify authoritatively—to mark—any of the characters that he personifies in his text. His most emphatic (and little quoted) statement of the unavailability of "sentence absolute" comes near the end of Book I:

> See it for yourselves,
> This man's act, changeable because alive!
> Action now shrouds, now shows the informing thought;
> Man, like a glass ball with a spark a-top,
> Out of the magic fire that lurks inside,

> Shows one tint at a time to take the eye:
> Which, let a finger touch the silent sleep,
> Shifted a hair's-breadth shoots you dark for bright,
> Suffuses bright with dark, and baffles so
> Your sentence absolute for shine or shade.
> Once set such orbs,—white styled, black stigmatized,—
> A-rolling, see them once on the other side
> Your good men and your bad men every one,
> From Guido Franceschini to Guy Faux,
> Oft would you rub your eyes and change your names.

(ll. 1364-78)

Browning, in cautioning the reader against "stylizing" and "stigmatizing," provides the poem with its most eloquent critique of the mark.

Yet this lip-service paid to indeterminacy is at variance with Browning's predominant concern with getting at the Truth of the matter. Critics have written much on Browning's concern with Truth in Book I.[13] In brief, the criticism claims that Browning, through the happy analogy of the making of the Ring, successfully describes his own fabrication of a superior, unified "Truth" from the discrete "facts" of the Old Yellow Book. However, the relation of discrete "facts" to an overarching "Truth" is more slippery, as Browning expresses it, than critics have allowed. The following is frequently cited in traditional criticism of Browning's Ring-metaphor:

> Fancy with fact is just one fact the more;
> To-wit, that fancy has informed, transpierced,
> Thridded and so thrown fast the facts else free,
> As right through ring and ring runs the djereed
> And binds the loose, one bar without a break.

(ll. 464-468)

Critics usually interpret the passage along these lines: Browning's poem can claim not only the "truth" of the "facts" he works with, but the higher truth ("fact") of having given those facts a united, living form. This reading, then, can be supported by Browning's reiteration of his point: "Is fiction which makes fact alive, fact too?" (l. 705). What critics have failed to take into account is the tentativeness of Browning's claims for the truth of his Book. The latter "claim" takes the form of a question—"*Is* fiction which makes fact alive, fact too?"—which we have no reason to dismiss as a "rhetorical question." The former claim—"fancy with fact is just one fact the more"—is, in its flat way, even more noncommittal. The crucial ambiguities of the word "just" (does Browning mean "*no more than* one fact the more?") give Browning's claim an overtone of resignation. And what, at the outset, does "fact" mean for Browning? The Old Yellow Book does not, of course, present "facts" in an empirical sense, but the inscriptions of interpretive testimonies, which are already at a remove from the inscrutable historical phenomena of the case. Browning's use of the term "facts" underscores its etymological roots in the Latin *facta,* things that have been made. We can read Browning's claim—"fancy with fact is just one fact the more"—as an expression of despair at the inability to escape sheer enumeration, the piling up of facts which are always already interpretive acts. We can see Browning as arguing, as Guido argues, against the possibility of uniting the facts of an ongoing serialization into an essential and identifiable "Truth."

As Browning realized, *The Ring and the Book* is always open to yet another "one fact the more," the interpretive act of its readership. In anticipation of Guido's appeal, the final appeal of Browning's text is not to a transcendent Truth, but to a public, communal verification. Browning defers authority, acknowledging the tribunal of the "British Public" (ll. 410-412, ll. 1379-89). Indeed, Browning, in his third telling of the murder story, prefaces his sketch of the Pope with an acknowledgment of the superior authority of his readership: "Then comes the all but end, the ultimate / Judgment save yours" (ll. 1220-21).[14]

IV

In sum, the Robert Browning of Book I is closely related to Guido in his interpretive assumptions. Guido, accordingly, can claim to be at the epistemological heart of a decentered and decentering poem. There is no absolute knowledge or Truth in *The Ring and the Book,* but only a differential play of interpretations.

In his essay "On History" (1830), Thomas Carlyle writes,

> It is, in no case, the real historical Transaction, but only some more or less plausible scheme and theory of the Transaction, or the harmonized result of many such schemes, each varying from the other and all varying from the truth, that we can ever hope to behold.[15]

Carlyle asserts that our reading of history is always a balancing act of divergent interpretations of the past, a reading which finally retains a temporal perspective and remains as partial as the divergent interpretations it attempts to "harmonize." Yet a few paragraphs down, Carlyle confidently urges an artistic appreciation of "the Whole" of History, although he is vague about what such an appreciation might look like (Carlyle, p. 90). Carlyle turns dramatically from a purview of heterogeneous interpretations "all varying from the truth,"

to a wish for an aesthetically unified "Whole." A similar turn defines the conclusive moment in most criticism of *The Ring and the Book.* Thus Langbaum, at the end of his preface to *The Poetry of Experience,* succinctly tells us that the "moral" of the whole of *The Ring and the Book* lies in Fra Celestino's enunciation, "God is true / And every man a liar" (XII, 597-598). For Langbaum, the characters of Browning, the Pope, and Pompilia are miraculously like God, and therefore exempt from the implications of Celestino's verdict on "every man." Yet for a critic such as William Walker, for whom no character in *The Ring and the Book* is ontologically privileged over any other character, Fra Celestino's pronouncement can only be read as a paradox:

> But statements such as [Fra Celestino's] which explicitly assert the unreliability of all statement themselves are subject to the skepticism they voice and therefore allow for the possibility of reliable or true statement. Like some of Zeno's paradoxes, if they are assumed to be true they are false, and if assumed false they are true. There are, moreover, numerous affirmations in *The Ring and the Book* that, in spite of the limitations of individual statement, collective or aesthetic statement is capable of expressing true propositions. . . . As we are told in the summary to the work, "Art remains the one way possible / Of speaking truth, to mouths like mine, at least" (XII. 839-840); "Art may tell a truth / Obliquely" (XII. 855-856). Given these assertions, one might reasonably argue that in one way or another *The Ring and the Book* does articulate a knowledge of the Franceschini affair and its agents which could serve as a criterion for assessing the relationship between a character and his monologue. (pp. 62-63)

Walker tries, at the end of his essay, to gesture beyond the Cretan paradox of Fra Celestino's pronouncement toward a possible knowledge of *The Ring and the Book* as a whole. Yet Walker's description of how we might attain this knowledge—"in one way or another"—is the index to a moment of interpretive exasperation or exhaustion. Walker cannot, in good faith, get beyond the paradoxical structure of Fra Celestino's enunciation; no reader can. The paradox of Fra Celestino's "moral"—a paradox that calls upon us to exert, in Keats's phrase, our negative capability—remains the emblem of *The Ring and the Book.*

Notes

[1] Jacques Derrida draws the distinction between "text" and "book" in *Of Grammatology,* trans. Gayatri C. Spivak (Baltimore, 1976), pp. 10-18.

[2] *Browning's Roman Murder Story: A Reading of "The Ring and the Book"* (Chicago, 1968), p. 37.

[3] *VP,* 22 (1984), 47-63. Walker effectively challenges the critical notion that we can "know" Pompilia in a simple, unproblematic way and thereby decenters her narrative in *The Ring and the Book.*

[4] Robert Langbaum contends that Robert Browning's absolutely "*right* judgments" in Book I provide us with a "God's-eye view" of the poem, and outweigh the relative claims of most of the other monologists. "Precisely right judgments" are also attributed to the Pope and Fra Celestino. *The Poetry of Experience* (New York, rev. ed. 1971), Preface; see also pp. 109-136. Agreement with Langbaum is nearly universal. See, for example, William O. Raymond, "The Pope in *The Ring and the Book,*" *VP,* 6 (1968), 323-332; Altick and Loucks, p. 69. L. J. Swingle has discussed the problems that arise when the reader absolutely privileges Book I over the next eight Books. From an epistemological point of view the poem is no longer interesting: the revelation of absolute "truth" in Book I makes the rest of the monologues "anticlimactic," Swingle, however, sidesteps the problem he identifies by simply privileging the "ontology" of the poem over its epistemology. "Truth and *The Ring and the Book:* A Negative View," *VP,* 6 (1968), 259-269. Lee Erickson has recently revived Swingle's argument, with its ambiguities intact, in *Robert Browning: His Poetry and His Audiences* (Ithaca, 1984), pp. 234-237.

[5] My thinking about Guido is indebted to William Warner's Nietzschean reading of Richardson's Lovelace in *Reading* Clarissa (New Haven, 1979).

[6] Morse Peckham was the first critic to question the critical commonplace that Books I and XII are the unmediated expression of the historical Robert Browning. "The point," writes Peckham, "is that the carefully identified historical Robert Browning of Book I is fatally compromised by the very plan of the poem, for that plan puts Robert Browning in the same category as each of the other monologuists, including the two forms of Guido. . . . Hence the Robert Browning of Book I is to be conceived as interpreting the documents according to his own interests—necessarily and ineluctably." "Historiography and *The Ring and the Book,*" *VP,* 6 (1968), 246.

[7] All quotations of the poem are from *Robert Browning:* The Ring and the Book, ed. Richard D. Altick (New Haven, 1971); hereafter cited within the text.

[8] This particular interpreter's "eyes," for instance, lead him to "descry a spider" in the midst of Pompilia's narration itself: her claim for the purity of her relationship with Caponsacchi is compromised by the sexual imagery with which she formulates that relationship: "The glory of his nature . . . / Shot itself out in white light . . . / Through every atom of his act with me" (VII. 921-923).

[9] Neil Hertz has drawn attention to the psychology of "marking" in his essay "Two Extravagant Teachings," in *The End of the Line: Essays on Psychoanalysis and the Sublime* (New York, 1985), pp. 144-160.

[10] See Stanley Fish, *Is There a Text in this Class?: The Authority of Interpretive Communities* (Cambridge, Massachusetts, 1980), pp. 342-347.

[11] In a later essay, Langbaum pardons Guido precisely because Guido's ability to recognize his own absolute evil suggests his capacity for moral regeneration. See "Is Guido Saved? The Meaning of Browning's Conclusion to *The Ring and the Book,*" *VP,* 10 (1972), 289-305.

[12] In much of his early correspondence with E.B.B., Browning insists upon his inability to speak out directly. In a letter of January 13, 1845, Browning writes, "You speak out, *you,*—I only make men & women speak—give you truth broken into prismatic hues, and fear the pure white light, even if it is in me." A month later, Browning emphasizes his point: "First then,—what I have printed gives *no* knowledge of me—it evidences abilities of various kinds, if you will—and a dramatic sympathy with certain modifications of passion . . *that* I think: but I never have begun, even, what I hope I was born to begin and end,—'R.B. a poem.'" *The Letters of Robert Browning and Elizabeth Barrett Barrett, 1845-1846,* ed. Elvan Kintner (Cambridge, Massachusetts, 1969), I, 7, 17. While Browning's apparent desire for a lyric voice may be quite real, we are not warranted to casually assume that he attained that heretofore unattainable voice in the opening and closing books of *The Ring and the Book.* For a brief but suggestive discussion of these issues, see Herbert F. Tucker, "Dramatic Monologue and the Overhearing of Lyric," in *Lyric Poetry: Beyond New Criticism,* ed. Chaviva Hoek and Patricia Parker (Ithaca, 1985), p. 231.

[13] See, for example, Paul A. Cundiff, "The Clarity of Browning's Ring Metaphor," *PMLA,* 63 (1948), 1276-82; George R. Wasserman, "The Meaning of Browning's Ring-Figure," *MLN,* 76 (1961), 420-426.

[14] Langbaum's interpretation of this line privileges the Pope and the Pope's judgment of Guido: "The Pope is the most authoritative speaker in the poem. He delivers, Browning tells us in Book I, 'the ultimate / Judgment' . . . that should determine ours" (in "Is Guido Saved?" p. 295).

[15] In *Works* (New York, 1964), XXVII, 88. Altick and Loucks cite Carlyle's essay on pp. 26-28.

W. David Shaw (essay date 1989)

SOURCE: "Browning's Murder Mystery: *The Ring and the Book* and Modern Theory," in *Victorian Poetry,* Vol. 27, Nos. 3-4, Autumn-Winter, 1989, pp. 79-98.

[In the following essay, Shaw analyzes the way in which Browning makes use of critical theories—particularly deconstructionism and hermeneutics—in The Ring and the Book. *Shaw considers the main characters to be caricatures of various critical viewpoints and focuses on Tertium Quid and Guido specifically as the primary deconstructionists, and on the Pope as a representative of hermeneutical criticism.]*

Problems associated with contemporary deconstruction and hermeneutics were familiar to Browning and already understood by him in his Roman murder mystery, ***The Ring and the Book.*** This assertion may seem less contentious if we recall that critical theories, though rich in their accidental varieties, are poor in their essential types. Deconstruction, for example, was a favorite exercise of Victorians like Pater, who dismantled metaphysics in *Plato and Platonism,* and of the agnostic theologian H. L. Mansel, who dissolved the idea of God into logically contradictory concepts in *The Limits of Religious Thought.* Mansel takes the idea of the infinite, the idea of the absolute, and the idea of a first cause, and argues that they cannot all be predicated of God at one and the same time. As for hermeneutics, though critics sometimes claim it as an invention of Schleiermacher in the nineteenth century, it is surely as venerable a pursuit as patristic exegesis and as old as biblical commentary itself. Let me proceed at once to a definition of terms. By deconstruction I mean Browning's subversive use of double binds and antinomies; and by hermeneutics I mean his study of the simultaneous preservation and transformation of the original meaning of a text. In ***The Ring and the Book*** Browning comes to deconstruction via a hermeneutical dilemma. The more scrupulously he tries to transcribe the facts in his source-book—the facts in the Old Yellow Book—the stranger, more invented, they appear to be. The passage of events into history is not itself fictional. But every story an interpreter makes up about the past, especially if it is the story of a partisan or advocate, is precisely that: a historical fiction or a fictional history. The more Browning wrestles with this dilemma, the more double binds and contradictions of other kinds he discovers.

For example, a doctrine of historical continuity is developed by Browning's Pope, who discerns behind the literal events of the Roman murder story the lineaments of a biblical myth of rescue and deliverance. Opposed to his belief in a continuing bible or testament is the assumption of discontinuity favored by the skeptics, Tertium Quid and Guido. This opposition, which pervades the poem, starts to unravel, however (in a process critics have not so far discussed), when Browning shows how opposite critical methods unexpectedly converge. Thus, to accept the premise of Pompilia and Caponsacchi that truth is constant and that surface meanings do not deceive is to interpret events the way the skeptical exposer of discontinuity,

Guido, finally does. Guido insists that he is fiercely loyal to a single set of values. He is more consistent than his adversaries. If the Pope decides to play Higher critic and changes the rules halfway through the game, why should Guido be punished for being more consistent? Conversely, to argue like Guido that action and being are fatally at odds in the adulterous priest who masquerades as a deliverer and in the unfaithful wife who pretends to be undefiled and pure is also to interpret events the way Caponsacchi and Pompilia do. For it is to allow for 180 degree conversions and for the discovery of hidden moral and theological meanings in a story that means more than it appears to mean. Caponsacchi, after all, is what Kierkegaard would call "a knight of the hidden inwardness." He wears a mask or incognito: he is not the wordly cleric he seems to be. The same is true of Pompilia: she lives from a depth of inwardness that cannot be outwardly expressed. And so, as in many deconstructive readings, to interpret suspiciously or inconsistently like Guido is also to interpret consistently or in a spirit of faith, like Pompilia and Caponsacchi, and vice versa. There seems to be no way out of this double bind.

When Browning's narrator in Book XII asserts that human speech is naught and all testimony false (XII.834-835), he is laying claim to knowledge of the ultimate order of things—a knowledge for which his own theory of consistent skepticism makes no provision. Browning seems aware of this contradiction. How can his narrator deplore the general warping of critical insight and still maintain the fiction that his own superior mind is unaffected by the general distemper? His irony is necessarily a two-edged sword. There is no possibility of reserving enlightenment for the narrator and consigning all other interpreters to darkness. Any systematic school of suspicion includes the skeptic in its net. Though the discrepant testaments of ***The Ring and the Book*** and the endless progeny of critical commentary that such testaments breed are all problematic, all equally suspect, the pervasive skepticism of Browning's own narrator in Book XII obliquely elevates the subversion of standards into exactly such a standard—one that is miraculously true of every testimony it examines. The program of dismantling a center by leading us through a centerless labyrinth implies recognition of a center after all. Unlike modern deconstructionists, however, Browning finds such dismantling as riddled with contradiction as any theoretical position he tries to dismantle. The narrator in Book XII is no more exempt from Browning's irony than any other commentator. When criticism cannot become a systematic body of coherent premises, arguments, and conclusions, then it may degenerate into an effort by each commentator to impose his own ideas by sheer force of will.

The clash of judgments among the speakers of ***The Ring and the Book*** replicates itself in a clash of opinion among the readers of the poem. Carlyle thought that Pompilia was guilty; Judge J. M. Gest insisted that "Caponsacchi was a frivolous young fellow, . . . light in thought and unscrupulous in action"; and Morse Peckham has concluded that Browning never presumes to resolve the issue.[1] Such continuation of a critical quarrel that the poem itself initiates assimilates events of the narrative to events of reading in the most approved post-structuralist manner. Equally prophetic of some contemporary attitudes is the impatience of Tertium Quid, who despairs of criticism altogether. To both the ironists and the literalists Tertium Quid says in effect, "a plague on both your houses." He reminds us that double irony—the apparent endorsement of two opposite positions simultaneously—is evasive. The trick of presuming to understand both sides at once but rejecting (and so favoring) neither is liable to be unpopular in any historical period, not just among contemporary adversaries of deconstruction. As post-structuralist critics like to point out, the deeds of the characters are also the reverse of what we might expect from their nature. The Pope is sententious and reflective, yet in sentencing Guido on impulse he commits a violent act. What the sentencing of Guido means is undone by the way it means. The judgment and deliverance should be justified as instances of continuity between being and doing. But the way these acts are done affirms a discrepancy between being and doing that calls into question the principle affirmed.

As the deconstructionists of *The Ring and the Book,* Tertium Quid and Guido deserve brief separate treatment. Like some deconstructionists, Tertium Quid constructs aporias and antinomies with a facility that is mechanical and at times almost mindless. Forgetting that the mind's ability to lose facts unpredictably and to get relations wrong distinguishes it from an archival bank or computer, Tertium Quid tries to feed every fact through a grid of disjunctive propositions. He thwarts the intellect by contriving to trap it inside two alternatives that are made to exhaust the field of possibility. As in any disjunctive proposition, p and q cannot both be true, though there is no way of deciding which of the logically contradictory propositions is true and which is false. Tertium Quid is so wed to disjunction as an interpretive method that he even splits apart so undivided and spontaneous an act as Caponsacchi's decision to leap forth at once as Pompilia's champion. Tertium Quid must first invent a counter-speech for Caponsacchi, in which the priest counsels Pompilia to bear alone the heavy burden of her marriage, before inventing a speech pledging his service to her, which he then pronounces "best" (IV.826).

Tertium Quid realizes that if Caponsacchi makes the right choice, there is no way of knowing he makes it, since to "try" the "truth . . . by instinct" (IV.1006) is to dispense by definition with rational proof. Either Guido was jealous of Caponsacchi and tortured Pompilia because he suspected her of committing adultery (IV.914-915),

or else he was not jealous and wanted Pompilia to leave behind the dowry by eloping with the priest (IV.749-755). Since the two alternatives are in logical contradiction, one must be false. But since they exhaust the field of possibility—either Guido was jealous or he was not, either he plotted in cold blood or acted out of passion—one alternative must be true. Which that alternative is, however, Tertium Quid has no logical way of knowing. Tertium Quid realizes that either people are what they seem, or else being and action are in contradiction. But Guido, who avows consistency between his action and his being, ironically charges Caponsacchi, the priest whose incognito as an eloper hides his reserve of faith and inwardness, with the greater inconsistency in pretending to be what he is not. If Caponsacchi "must look to men more skilled / I' the reading hearts than ever was the world" (IV.1111-12), then he must seek an interpreter like Tertium Quid who can accept the principle of discontinuity without being immobilized by the uncertainty which results from any incessant use of disjunction and any incessant exposure of contradiction and deceit.

So much for Tertium Quid. What about Guido? Like some analytic philosophers of language, Guido is a reductive interpreter, a Benthamite, who is resolved to make comprehensible the great mystery words of his adversaries—faith, love, religion, truth—even if he must explain them away in the process. In Guido's two orations everything is subject to reductionist explanations except reductionism itself. Should a thoroughgoing reductionism like Guido's not be courageous enough to reduce and devalue even itself? Should Guido not perceive that he is debunking Pompilia and Caponsacchi out of a resentful envy of their values? In rooting out the concealed poetry in language, Guido even tries to revise downward the mystique attaching to his own social rank. He shows how simple supply and demand curves useful in economics can be made to quantify and give exact, non-inflationary meaning to a mystery word like "count," which he can then, like the Duke of Ferrara, barter on the market "with all other ware" (V.463).

To convince the court of his honest resolve to strip away all false pretense, Guido concedes that he forced Pompilia to trace over the letters he had written in her confession. But this admission of coercion is a more damaging concession than Guido seems to realize (V.846-847), since how can we reconcile Guido's exposure of deceit in his present oration with the general condition of deceit which must exist throughout the monologue if the exposure is true? If the confession of pervasive deceit is true, it would seem to follow it cannot be true. The only escape from this dilemma seems to be the axiom that an offhand admission of deceit like Guido's may have greater validity than direct testimony because, as Levi Hedge observes in his *Elements of Logick,* a book highly esteemed by Browning's father, "there is less reason" to apprehend in any act of casual self-incrimination a "deliberate intention to deceive."[2]

So far I have been concentrating on the exposure of double binds and contradictions appropriate to skeptics like Tertium Quid and Guido, the principal deconstructionists of the poem. Equally prophetic of modern theory is the hermeneutical criticism of Browning's Pope. Distinguishing between the Bible's essential meaning and the accidental significance it acquires for particular readers, the Pope asks how a sacred text can have both an original meaning and a new meaning for each successive generation. Faith in Christianity would seem to be faith in a historically grounded religion. But the Pope recognizes that this claim is paradoxical. For if faith is to be faith in history, as Dr. Thomas Arnold had insisted, then, as the skeptical W. G. Ward argued as early as 1841, in a review of Arnold's *Sermons,*[3] it must be faith in a fiction we make up about the past, or else faith in something that once happened but is now irrecoverable. Moreover, even if the past could be recovered, how could an adventurous knight of faith like Caponsacchi have faith in what is merely given? Such historical faith would not seem to qualify as faith at all, for like any proof that bludgeons its opponents, reducing them to silence, it leaves no room for free assent. Christianity is an historical faith only in an altered nineteenth-century sense of the word "historical," which equates history not with the antecedently given but with a self-constituting process of development through time. Truth that evolves historically in this second sense is not at first expressible, because it does not authentically exist until knights of faith like Caponsacchi will it into being. Though history as self-making would seem to be at odds with history as a synonym for the received and given, only some combination of these two easily confused and incompatible theories of history would seem to explain how both the transformation and preservation of biblical meaning is possible.

The object of the Pope's faith is the proclamation that Pompilia was delivered and saved. She has to be offered up to another world before her goodness deteriorates. In a sense, Guido is required to play the role of priest, sacrificing his wife so that she can die without blemish. Her great love for Caponsacchi, like Juliet's for Romeo, does not go wrong. It goes in the only way it can go—out of this world, which is also the way Christ's love went. The hermeneutical dilemma facing Browning's Pope is that his faith in the resurrected or redeemed Pompilia, which is his equivalent of the Gospel's proclaiming faith in the risen Christ, does not involve any assent to a verifiable proposition. It is not an assent to a scientific classification, nor is it grounded ultimately in the kind of historical or factual evidence admissible in a court of law. Such laws have only a negative function. They can tell us what cannot have happened, but can offer no proof of what did happen.

"Unless you introduce the resurrection," says Henry Melvill, the preacher who most influenced the young Browning, "you will not make intelligible 'the life.'"[4] As a continuing Bible, *The Ring and the Book* proclaims the importance of "resurrection experiences" that break through the barrier dividing life from death. The Pope distinguishes between the knight of faith and the historical Caponsacchi, between the hidden Word through whom God shows just sufficient of his "light / For us i' the dark to rise by" (VII.1844-45) and Caponsacchi, the public figure, who is half an embarrassment to the court, just as the historical Jesus was clearly an embarrassment to the establishment that had to deal with him. We begin to know God only when we know we know nothing about Him. The imminent deaths of Pompilia and the Pope invite us to discover the connection between death and the kind of goodness which must pass out of the world because, like Christ's goodness, that is where it already is.

An extraordinary experience, too good for this world, can break down the barriers, not just between life and death, but also between life as we live it now and life as it ought to be lived. We can experience new life when we allow our faith in someone like Pompilia or Caponsacchi to articulate a new understanding of human possibility. One does not first call Caponsacchi an exemplar of Christ and then experience an enlargement of life. It works the other way round. Grasping the significance of what redemption might be like enlarges and liberates the reader. Radical faith depends on an act of God which, though historical, is also curiously transhistorical. The Pope's belief seems to be both an object of historical knowledge and not such an object. But if faith has no historical content, it seems difficult to distinguish from Guido's formless faith, which is faith in nothing.

I associate "formless faith" with Paul Tillich's idea that faith cannot be identified with conscious assent to any truth. Faith is present whenever ultimate concern is expressed, and this concern—a theological equivalent of I. A. Richards' doctrine of "objectless beliefs"—is independent of any particular symbols or beliefs.[5] Though Browning refuses to embrace such a formless faith, he is equally critical of any form of historical faith. If history is the basis of saving faith, it would also seem to follow that it is not such a basis. For historical facts are never recoverable. Truths of faith are never identical with historical truths, anyway, and it is a disastrous distortion of faith to confuse them. The Higher Criticism cannot erode the grounds of saving faith. All it can subvert are the grounds of historical faith, which for Browning's Pope is never real faith at all.

Despite what the Pope says about correcting the portrait by the living face (X.1872), Browning knows that he can never get behind the pictures to encounter the historical Pompilia or the historical Mrs. Browning, any more than he can encounter the historical Jesus. And even if he could, it would not be necessary. For what kindles faith is not the original but the portrait, not the historical person but the picture. There must be analogies, not between portraits and real-life originals, but between pictures and other pictures, especially between portraits like Caponsacchi's and the portrait of Jesus, which expresses as no other portrait can the cruciform nature of faith. That faith is no more to be eroded by any perceived discrepancy between these pictures and their historical originals than the Gospels' picture of Christ can be invalidated by historical criticism of a figure called Jesus of Nazareth.

We might argue, however, that, though all pictures are selective, some are more imaginatively transformed than others. Pompilia's picture of Caponsacchi as a lesser savior-god, like St. John's picture of Christ, alters and transforms the tradition of deliverance found in Hebrew and classical sources, just as John's picture transforms the more historical selections of St. Mark. We can profitably speak of two kinds of interpretation: interpretation as selection, which is more inductive and judicial like the Pope's, and interpretation as imaginative transformation, which is more metaphorical like Pompilia's. Interpretation as selection, because it retains more trace of a historical referent, can incidentally provide a canon for criticizing both the selective interpretation itself and the more imaginative interpretations of a Pompilia or St. John. But this hermeneutical refinement does little to affect the relative unimportance of a real-life original. For more is at stake than some residual historical trace. Browning and Pompilia want to know if the last power can be trusted. Is God gracious? Or is He a mere vacancy and void? Is life significant in some sense that breaks through the barriers of ordinary experience and allows us to go outside the world? Because these are life-and-death issues, questions of faith, which no distinction between selective and imaginative interpretations can hope to settle, some new chasms will always open up to divide the objects of faith from their grounds.

Hermeneutics teaches either that faith can be dissociated from historical narrative or that it cannot be so dissociated. There is no third choice. In either case biblical criticism illuminates and is not discontinuous with any other mode of criticism. If it teaches that faith is historically grounded, then it abets the strictness of interpretive precision: critical freedom must then operate only within the boundaries prescribed by the author's text. Such is the theory of biblical interpretation advocated by Benjamin Jowett in his essay "On the Interpretation of Scripture" (1860). This essay exercises an important influence on Browning, especially on a poem like *Balaustion's Adventure* (1871), the most hermeneutical Greek poem in Browning's canon. As a classical scholar Jowett wants to interpret the Bible with the same scholarly rigor and critical

good sense that he brings to the study of Plato's *Dialogues*. Like Jowett, Browning seems to think that we should interpret the Bible as we interpret a work by Homer or Euripides. And if so, the converse is also true: we interpret secular literature as we interpret the Bible. But just as historical criticism can erode faith but cannot supply the grounds of it, so the text an author has supplied can invalidate a critical reading but cannot guarantee that any particular interpretation will begin to appropriate the full meaning of the text. Though the presentation of contradictory testimony requires the reader, like any member of a jury, to ask, "Is this what really happened?", readers must always project their own values, applying the warrants of their own beliefs as well as the warrants of history, logic, and the lawcourts. If Pompilia's deliverance were just another historical event, indistinguishable from other events like the marriage to Guido or the forgery of the love letters, then it could never be a true deliverance capable of shattering the boundaries of ordinary experience. An abnormal historical event would produce only the illusion of shattered boundaries. A real breakthrough must be a non-historical happening by which all other events in the story are bounded. To be fully meaningful, in other words, an event must be ungrounded, beyond history—and perhaps beyond truth or falsity—altogether.

Precisely this paradox keeps encompassing the Pope in contradictions. On the one hand, he has to refute the testimonies of Caponsacchi's critics, which are factual and historical, by making historical assertions about what Caponsacchi and Pompilia actually did. On the other hand, having made such assertions, he illogically claims that no historian, detective, or legal witness, has a right to assess them. One wonders whether an historical assertion that is incapable of being either refuted or confirmed is genuinely historical. If we want to claim the advantages of historical judgment, we must surely assume its risks. And if we want the warrants of faith, we have to assume a completely different set of risks. It is hard to have the faith without the loss of critical autonomy, and hard to enjoy the advantages of history without losing our beliefs.

Saving faith must see in an event a significance that revolutionizes the believer's self-understanding. But because of Browning's deep Protestant distrust of any continuity between faith and works, person and office, a character's motives tend to remain a mystery, even to the character himself. How can the Pope hope to read the hearts of Pompilia and Caponsacchi with any confidence when these characters cannot even read their own hearts? If a transformation of their self-understanding is to be the proper object of faith and the true meaning of correcting the portrait by the living face, on what a slender thread the whole enterprise is made to hang!

The leap involved in passing from historical to saving faith is the kind of leap envisaged by E. D. Hirsch in any transition from interpretation proper to the value-judgments of "criticism," by which he means the elucidation of significance as opposed to the examination of a given textual meaning. "It is not the meaning of the text which changes," he insists, "but its significance. *Meaning* is that which is represented by a text. . . . *Significance,* on the other hand, names a relationship between that meaning and a person."[6] Browning recognizes, however, that the distinction between criticism and interpretation, significance and meaning, is too simple, because the value-judgments of a critic may be just as much an antecedent fact as the events an historical interpreter tries to reconstruct. Like a contemporary commentator, Francis Sparshott, Browning also seems to doubt whether "the pure distinction between meaning and significance can be explicated or maintained in practice, except in cases where the significance is plainly idiosyncratic," as in the eccentric interpretations of the two advocates. "A meaning that is of no significance to anyone [else] is of no interest."[7] Moreover, is the distinction between significance and meaning a true-or-false proposition or a mere evaluative proposal? As a proposal of a critic rather than a discovery of the interpreter (as a "significant" claim, in Hirsch's sense, rather than a "meaningful" statement), it would seem to follow it cannot be true: it can be at best a proposal, a significant suggestion that is more or less felicitous or apt.

In the last book of his poem Browning caricatures a variety of critical positions, several of which have found favor in our own time. The Venetian visitor to Rome and Don Celestine (the first and fourth interpreters) are both to be commended for seeking self-enlightenment. But too detached from the events they interpret, the Venetian visitor degenerates into a dupe and Celestine into a proud Olympian. Mistaking Guido's execution for a Crucifixion, rather than the capital punishment of a criminal, the visitor assumes that every falsehood is so true that any truth must be false. Don Celestine makes the opposite mistake of taking every sign agnostically, as a mere empty signifier, which allows the true referent to escape through a hole at the center: "God is true / And every man a liar" (XII.600-601). Assuming that the truth is so true that any expression of it must be false, Celestine embodies the vice of all ideological critics (from the theologian or Hegelian commentator to the Marxist) for whom the study of art or history is never, like the pursuit of virtue, its own reward, an endotelic enterprise, but merely a means to some external end.

The second interpreter, Arcangeli, and the third interpreter, Bottinius, both subvert the Socratic premise of self-enlightenment by using knowledge, like the sophists, to gain power over others. Whereas Arcangeli resembles the untenured professor eager to secure his next commission, the bachelor Bottinius is the established critic, trying to convince himself that his reputation for insight is well deserved, and trying desperately to mask his obvious inferiority to rival critics. Arcangeli

is the interpreter as uncritical partisan, prepared to argue anything if it seems likely to influence a judge or client. Bottinius, the critic as jealous exhibitionist, who would rather lose an argument than invite the collaboration of some more gifted colleague who could make the case foolproof, glories in the relativist's axiom that every truth is so true that any truth must be false.

The commentator who intrudes at the end of the poem to assert that "human speech is naught" (XII.834) is the critic as disillusioned skeptic, who assumes that every interpretation is so false that no interpretation can be true. He is a precursor of some deconstructionists, who despair of reaching any consensus about the meaning of literature, except the consensus that no consensus can be reached. The skeptic shares the pessimism of the Augustinian monk, Don Celestine, the critic as proud Olympian. But if every man is a liar and only God is true (XII.600-601), how can we hope to learn this truth from a witness who, according to his own testimony, is a liar? The condition of falsehood which must prevail if the claim is true, the unreliability of all testimony, is incompatible with the claim that is made. Bottinius, a fame-seeker himself, is quick to spot a similar contradiction. The monk's claim that he seeks only obscurity cannot be allowed, for what else is his celebrated sermon on Pompilia's death if not a direct appeal for "just the fame he flouts?" (XII.645).

What is most subversive and unsettling about Browning's poem? The constant source of anxiety, I think, is Browning's repeated intimation that, even if Guido's suspicion about Pompilia's adulterous liaison with Caponsacchi were justified, even if the myth of deliverance and redemption turned out to be nothing more than stylized adultery, we still would not believe this suspicion was justified, and so we have no way of knowing that what Guido suspects is not true. The skeptic realizes that we could be living in a world conceptually identical to the one in which we think we are living, but in which everything we believe is false. Pompilia and Caponsacchi would then be as guilty as Guido says they are, and we would have no way of knowing this. Different worlds can lead to our having the same beliefs, just as different three-dimensional objects can have the same two-dimensional plane projection. Two worlds that produce identical beliefs can be different enough for everything believed in one world to be false in the other. The worlds inhabited by Second Half-Rome, Bottinius, and the Pope, for example, produce roughly identical beliefs. But could any worlds be more bizarrely different?

How, in retrospect, are we to identify the critical positions of the main speakers? I have argued that Tertium Quid and Guido are the deconstructionists of *The Ring and the Book.* Tertium Quid sets forth all the wrong ways of interpreting. He parodies the assumption of some of the more doctrinaire post-structuralists that there is a teachable method of deconstructing texts that will enable him to dismantle truth at will. His method is an uncritical, reflex demonstration that every truth is so true that any truth must be false. His indifference is a perversion of the skeptical critic's detachment, and his anxiety about ever reaching truth a perversion of the hermeneutical critic's concern. He is anxiously indifferent instead of disinterestedly concerned.

Guido, for his part, feels that the absence of standards turns critical judgment into a mystery exclusively controlled by the high priests of the Vatican. One might have thought that the Pope's scrupulous sifting and weighing of the testimony allows his own critical authority to be earned. But, as Guido reminds us, the Pope discovers that any critical theory, like any scientific theory, is "underdetermined" by the evidence: it is never tested proposition by proposition, but stands or falls by grids of other theories into which it is locked. Though the Pope keeps refining and exercising his interpretive capacities, they are ultimately of little use to him. At the end of his monologue an heroic leap to truth, followed by a self-congratulatory announcement that he has arrived safely on the far side of doubt, comes to the rescue of a theory of knowledge that has proved too unruly to be useful. But if judgments are reached by the use of some favorite code word like "the unknown God" or "the Genius of the Vatican" (XI.2028-29), as Guido charges, or by some ritual initiation into the mysteries guarded by the high priests of criticism, then no standards of evidence and no intentions would seem worth assessing.

One Victorian version of these priestly exercises is the typological criticism of Scripture advocated by John Keble in *Tract 89*—a theory of criticism vigorously attacked by Benjamin Jowett in his essay on "The Interpretation of Scripture" in *Essays and Reviews.* Jowett's critique applies with equal force to the secularized typologies of many structuralist critics today. In their hands the only setting in which the historicism of *The Ring and the Book* can survive is the verbal labyrinth, a literary haven for every historical phantom or ghostly abstraction that has lost its moorings in a world outside the maze. And yet, with its chain of commentary on commentary, stretching as it seems to infinity, *The Ring and the Book* often abets such an enterprise: the poem is curiously unincremental and exitless. Browning has little sympathy with Jowett's straightforward, demystifying view that the meaning of the Bible is its plain, historic sense. How are we to extract such a sense, assuming it exists? And how are we to identify or judge an author's intentions or the meaning these intentions had for his original audience? Indeed, once in the labyrinth of *The Ring,* it is difficult to find either an escape route or a center. And who in the poem is any longer capable of creating or initiating anything? Certainly not the poet. All Browning's narrator can do is play the role of ghostly resuscitator.

As a poetic Elisha breathing life into the dead facts, he may, if he is lucky, resuscitate a corpse (I.760-762), but genuine creation is beyond him.

Unlike Tertium Quid and Guido, the two deconstructionists, Caponsacchi and Pompilia are both myth critics. Their aim is not to classify texts or verbal propositions but to make metaphoric proposals. Their recommendation of projected values is the stabilizing principle that enables them to see life steadily, as the reenactment of some biblical or classical myth. And their empathy with other characters is the liberating principle that allows them to see life whole.

The Pope, by contrast, is a critical historian or judge, a surrogate for each reader, trying to infer what happened by harmonizing prior inferences about what happened. On the one hand, the interpreter must be certain that the witnesses brought the same consciousness to the past event as the interpreter would if he had been there. Only such an assumption allows him to empathize with the witness, to become the witness, by exercising negative capability. On the other hand, the interpreter must be critical of his witnesses: only by registering the differences between his own thought and that of a different historical time can his interpretation be an invention, a "coming upon" or a "finding," in both the constative and performative sense of that word.

Even when a prior event is unearthed, however, it has a way of turning out to be, not the first event in a series, but an imitation of earlier events. Browning is an oddly belated, even parasitic, poet, whose most authentic creations often seem a product of archival research or historical reconstruction. The most apparently original metaphor in the poem, the metaphor of the ring, proves not to be original with Browning at all. The poet who praised Elizabeth's "rare gold ring of verse" cannot have been Browning himself, because Browning is associated, like his dead wife, with "our England," while the phrase "his Italy" is reserved for the poet from whom Browning borrowed his metaphor:

> Might mine but lie outside thine, Lyric love,
> Thy rare gold ring of verse (the poet praised)
> Linking our England to his Italy!

> (XII.868-870)

What we wrongly took for an original metaphor—the rounding of "the rough ore . . . to a ring" (XII.865)—is only an instance of an instance, an example of a prior example.

What finally emerges, then, from the many caricatures of critical positions in *The Ring and the Book?* Positively, we may say that any single interpretation is provisional. What we say about a text or an event is for the time being. A second conclusion is the futility of trying to abase ourselves before any positivist model of historical research. Except in the mind of H. T. Buckle, such a model does not exist. As the Pope reminds us, a scientist's acoustical charts of the wrath of the sea are just as fictive a construction as a poet's description of the angry roar of the waves, even though the scientist looks for abiding cause-and-effect relations while the poetic interpreter tries to place himself at the center of energy, inside the waves themselves (X.1399-1402). Competing models of how sound waves work cannot be entirely adjudicated by theory-neutral rules and data. And even though choices are agent-relative, the rationality of science itself is never impaired. A final inference to be made is the importance of critical strategy. A resourceful interpreter will be able to capture and possess symbols like Molinism or rallying cries like "Quis est pro Domino?" (V.1549, X.2099), which the Pope effectively takes back from Guido, who thinks he has prematurely captured it from the Church. A critic's ability to demystify his adversaries' rhetoric, however, often prompts that critic to obfuscate or mystify language for his own ends. The strategies of obfuscation are universal and allow Browning to sharpen our own sense of irony by discriminating between critical positions like perspectivism, which partially ranks its views, and relativism, which holds all views equally deficient.

If there seems to be no center at the middle of Browning's ring, it is not because Browning knows the center of every ring is necessarily an empty space, like the hole in the middle of a doughnut. Browning works on the contrary assumption that his ring has a center. But the interpreters with the greatest claim to centrality are least prepared to press their claim. For they know that to declare any point of view central at the expense of other viewpoints has disastrous results. The so-called center then becomes a mere still center, like the superannuated symbols of a church which is all machinery without any vivifying soul. Browning's own position is not relativism, because his points of view are ranked. And yet no single view is adequate by itself. Though Browning writes monologues in order to step outside himself, he discovers that something of himself always remains behind the lens. Because something in the poet must continue to determine the resulting picture, Browning will have reason to doubt, whatever window he looks through, that he is really getting any closer to a detached view. As one commentator says, "The same ideas that make the pursuit of objectivity seem necessary for knowledge make both objectivity and knowledge seem, on reflection, unattainable."[8]

Browning and his speakers are involved in a contradictory enterprise. On the one hand, they are hard pressed to explain how critics can arrive at valid interpretations. On the other hand, they refuse to take refuge in the conclusion of some post-structuralist critics

that skepticism justifies a reluctance to interpret at all. They continue to criticize and comment even when they half recognize the futility of doing so. The alternative would be to offer interpretations that are merely "interesting." But who is to arbitrate disputes about intrinsic "interest"?

If no interpreter is infallible, perhaps a whole interpretive community devoted to accurate knowledge of texts can preserve the goals and values of historical scholarship. In the most enlightened speakers in *The Ring and the Book* Browning seeks his own hermeneutical equivalent of David Friedrich Strauss's community of believers. Instead of equating truth with Strauss's community of faith, Browning equates it with a community of experienced and devoted critics—some of them Higher Critics—committed to accurate knowledge of what is not, strictly speaking, knowable. Yet Browning's hermeneutical community is not to be confused with the "interpretive community" of a contemporary critic like Stanley Fish. How can a community of interpreters confer stable meaning on a text, when each individual reading is unstable?

The individual reader turns out to be the real hero of *The Ring and the Book.* He is invited to take some middle ground between the errant structuralism of the two advocates and the lunacies of Guido. Browning knows that prolonged study may rob the mind of its elasticity, and that erudition may make critics like the two advocates duller and sillier than they naturally are. Unless readers think for themselves, every truth they discover will adhere to them as a mere excrescence, as a false tooth or artificial limb. Beguiled by the a priori, like Swift's projectors in the Grand Academy of Lagado, the advocates begin at the roof and work downwards to the foundation. Their lack of method helps Browning dramatize a recurrent dilemma. If the biggest archive in the world is in disorder, it will be less useful than a small but well-organized library. The interpreter can organize only what he knows, but how can he know anything until he has organized it? If the facts are in perpetual disorder, then the biggest archive in the world will never produce organized thought. Schopenhauer says that "you can think about only what you know . . . ; on the other hand, you can know only what you have thought about."[10] Until original thinking has already taken place, it is difficult to imagine how it can ever get launched.

Browning shows that immersion in a text and its history is a reader's best antidote to slavery to fashion, and so his best hope of thinking originally for himself. I am not suggesting that Browning would advocate a return to historical criticism and research. He is saying, I think, that interpretive purity of any kind breeds self-destruction: a variety of critical modes is called for. Critics should recognize the limits of every single method of interpretation, and when one method threatens to become dominant they should endlessly advocate the restoration of disorder. To resist change and even strife in the name of methodological purity is a philosophical mistake. It is even a mistake to banish a new interpretive method because it seems wed, like some contemporary critical schools, to an uncongenial jargon. A jargon-ridden critic like Bottinius is the first to object to the jargon of the monk, whose discourse he rejects as mere "ampollosity" (XII.643). Someone else's critical jargon is the first refuge of ignorance, and the eternal refuge of disciples too stupid or fossilized to learn anything new.

Browning's Pope realizes that the surest way for the Church to commit institutional suicide is to try to stem the rising tide of skepticism. He tries instead to empathize with people experiencing new adventure—people like Caponsacchi, Pompilia, and presumably the much maligned Molinos. Conservative critics denounce Molinos in the name of morality and the authority of existing methods of interpretation. They frustrate reasoned argument and refuse to join in a critical debate that should be seized as an intellectual opportunity instead of denounced as a heresy. Browning's poem suggests that the cry of vested interests against interpreters who ask new, difficult, even embarrassing questions, and who then question the answers, has always been wrongheaded, whether it be the attack of theology on science in Victorian Britain or the attack of historical scholars on theorists or of theorists on historical scholars in our own time. Such rearguard attacks never succeed, it seems, in stemming the tide. Like Browning's "old Pope," who "totters" for a moment "on the verge o' the grave" (XII.38), all things sway forward on the dangerous flood of history. And the more we try to stay the tide, the more we find ourselves engulfed.

At the end of the poem Browning's narrator proclaims the existence of a latent meaning behind the manifest sense. He has written a book, he boasts, that "shall mean beyond the facts, / Suffice the eye and save the soul beside" (XII.862-863). Phrases like "Beyond mere imagery," "beyond the facts," "Deeper than ever the Andante dived" (XII.859-861), continue to intimate a hidden meaning. Inside the outer ring of the poem there is always some secret inner sense, which bears the same relation to the manifest meaning as the rougher ring of Browning's own commentary bears to Elizabeth's rarer inner "ring of verse" (XII.868-869). For all the boldness of these proclamations, however, the text is reticent to disclose its hidden sense. At the end of this inordinately long poem, it is as if Browning, like Guido at the end of his second long monologue, has spoken not "one word" "Out of the whole world of words [he] has to say" (XI.2415-16). What is Browning trying to deafen inside him with the fortissimo of his long declamations and fear of closure? We should remember that only with the publication of *Men and Women* in 1855 did

Browning become as popular a poet as his wife. Will the publication of *The Ring and the Book,* his first long poem since *Sordello,* consign him to obscurity for another twenty years? Is he afraid to face the verdict of his "British Public, ye who like me not, / (God love you!)" (I.410-411; 1379-80)? Moreover, what has been concluded that there is anything to conclude? Since the data are so hopelessly patient of all interpretations, they are an endless source of pleasure but also a necessary disappointment. Obscure order can be a blessing, but only because more definite order proves delusive.

After line 363 of the first book, the poem should conclude. "This is the bookful": all else is adulterating alloy added to untempered gold. Carlyle thought Browning's story could be told in ten lines and only wanted forgetting. Either the poem must end almost before it begins, or else it can never end at all. It becomes a book that is all beginning, without any end that is not imposed by an arbitrary stop rule. Like the Old Testament, the poem is in search of an ending, of a design that will fulfill it. But the ending is endlessly deferred. We cannot even satisfy our desire for an ending by regarding the concluding use of the ring metaphor (XII.869) as a synecdoche for the ending that is not there, the way we construe *"De te, fabula"* in "The Statue and the Bust" (l. 250). The ring parable simply returns us to the use of the same parable in Book I, and it intensifies our bafflement rather than eases it.

To think accurately about parables we have taken most completely for granted is always hardest. At the beginning of the poem Browning's fact-loving narrator is more adept at fashioning excessively precise descriptions of the ring than at explaining what they signify: "A thing's sign: now for the thing signified" (I.32). The narrator poses as a puzzled semiotician. Prejudging the referent by assuming it will be as material and thing-like as the ring, he gives the impression of stalling for time, trying to work out the exact meaning of his sign. It is as if his injunction to the errant reader—"beseech you, hold that figure fast!" (I.142)—were also a reminder to himself. Concluding that the gold in the ring is "Fanciless fact" (I.144), he is at a loss to say what the alloy is. If it is mere fancy, what use is it? Because the critic as positivist simply omits all reference to that part of his parable which resists analysis according to scientific methods, it remains for a second interpreter, the poet-critic, to assert that "Fancy with fact is just one fact the more" (I.464). Is that statement made as a fanciful interpretation of fact? Or is it offered as what his positivist adversary would call a "fanciless" fact? If it is a fanciful interpretation, then it is an interpretation of an interpretation, and the interpreted fact seems to recede farther and farther from view. Conversely, if the claim is offered as a fact, it would seem to follow it cannot be a fact. For the condition which must prevail if the claim is true—the union of "Fancy with fact"—is incompatible with the claim's being a "fanciless" fact. Moreover, the additive quality of the model—fancy superimposed on preexisting fact—precipitates a crisis in representation which puts at risk the more appropriate metaphor of the alloy's informing and transpiercing the gold until the two are no longer distinguishable.

The parable can support two contradictory interpretations, depending at what point in the process the alloy is examined. Early in the operation, the alloy is thoroughly mixed with the gold to make it malleable. Imaginative interpreters are drawn into the parable itself, as the alloy of the poet's own interpretation is drawn into the gold. And yet the second half of the parable reminds us of an unsettling truth: interpretation, though necessary, is bound to seem intrusive. Like the alloy that flies free after the acid is applied (I.24-25), interpreters may find themselves expelled from the parable by their very desire for access. They are free only in the sense that, like the alloy set free by the acid, they are free to stay outside the secret sense of the parable. Readers are dispossessed and excluded by the very parable that seemed at first to admit them. Because interpretation is always as obtrusive an act as the alloy's penetration of the slivers of gold, the illusion of being an insider is only a more elaborate way of being kept outside. It is as if Browning had written a parable about parables. For the more we seem to penetrate a parable, the more we are also kept on its periphery or edge: no great parable has ever been exhausted by our meditations.

Any theory of latent order in *The Ring and the Book* is put in question by the narrator's manifest playfulness. The "one lesson" to be learned, he says ironically at the end of the poem, is "that our human speech is naught, / Our human testimony false, our fame / And estimation words and wind" (XII.832, 834-836). If the text has a secret meaning, it is certainly not this "one lesson" half facetiously, half defensively extracted by the poet-narrator. Like some mysterious ur-text, Browning's hidden meanings are as obscure as a sunken object whose qualities we have laboriously to reconstruct from the splash made by the object as it sinks in the pool. The waves generated in the water then become "vibrations in the general mind," quite unable to fathom the "depth of deed already out of reach" (I.844-845). The phrase "depth of deed" focuses on both the inscrutability of human motives and on the very rapid removal of events from even the closest, most knowledgeable observers.

It is as if Browning were writing an ongoing testament or Bible, and that he does not yet know which germs in his mass of narrative detail exist merely in their own right, like some original covenant that is meaningful in itself without later typological "fulfillments" of its meaning, and which details are going to be fulfilled in some new testament, some new *Life of Jesus,* still to be revealed by a future David Friedrich Strauss. In *The Ring and the Book* we are puzzled, because we cannot tell which details resemble Mr. Candy's mysterious disappearance and return during the birthday dinner party in Wilkie Collins' novel *The Moonstone* (a detail that will grow immensely in importance later in that mystery fiction), and which details are merely gratuitous touches, a means of making the surface of the narrative more like the crowded surface of everyday life.

There are intermittent fulfillments in *The Ring and the Book,* but nothing sustained. The mystery poem is less like a book than an archive of newspapers, a cupboard of scrolls, which is the form Browning uses in the manuscript roll that both records and comments upon St. John's testament in **"A Death in the Desert."** Codexes promote figural designs; rolls discourage them. As Frank Kermode observes, "The Jews, upon whom the end of time had not come, whose prophecies of a Messiah were unfulfilled, kept the roll, but the Christians, having the desire to establish consonance between the end of the book and the beginning, needed the codex."[11] *The Ring and the Book* had the logic of a newspaper, and because nothing seems organized sequentially, quotations that stick in the throat of memory are often hard to find again in the text. Contributing to the enigmatic, scroll-like quality of the text is the fact that narrative in the source-book generates the character of agents in the poem and the character of commentators like Half-Rome, Other Half-Rome, and Tertium Quid, who keep interpreting the story recorded in the source. These characters generate new narratives, which often take their form from the narrative of the source-book, the way parts of Matthew's gospel are thought to be modeled on the narrative of Mark. And yet the total effect is less that of a Gospel codex than of an Old Testament roll because Browning's canon, unlike that of the New Testament, is never closed. Though the story in the Old Yellow Book is to the hidden or latent sense that Browning is continually trying to extract from it what the old covenant is to the new covenant in figural readings of Scripture, the typologies of the poem still require completion in the life and mind of each interpreter.

It is both important and unimportant that the source-book be historical, and for the same reason that it is both important and unimportant that the Old Testament be historical. It is unimportant because, in one sense, the whole historicity of the Jewish Bible is to be sacrificed to a validation of the historicity of the gospels. But historicity is also important, because the whole authority of an historical Jewish Bible is needed to establish the historicity of a figural reading of it. The more fictitious and typological Browning's narrative becomes, the more historical it must also claim to be, because typological readings always assume the historicity of the types they try to fulfill.

In interrogating the Old Yellow Book, Browning seems to be writing and reading simultaneously, like a Victorian

Derrida. Even in Browning's source-book, which recalls the midrash of accumulating commentary in **"A Death in the Desert,"** presumably only three-fifths of the book is a true source, for the rest is said to be "written supplement" (I.119). *The Ring and the Book* repeats this process by offering glosses on a work which, like Jennings' transcript of Candy's delirious testament in *The Moonstone,* already consists in part of marginal glosses. In Goethe's aphorism, "Alles factische ist schon Theorie." A fact is not even a fact without its interpretive supplement. The combination of F1S1 becomes a second fact, F2, only by adding a second supplement, S2. And F2S2 generates F3 only by adding S3, and so on. Even the interfilleting of cramped Latin with Italian streaks in the source-book replicates this seemingly endless regress of transcribed testaments and "written supplements." The only way to block an infinite regress of facts and supplements is to assume that one of the facts to be blocked is the fact that every fact requires an interpretive supplement. The "stooping" of the testament to "mother-tongue" (I.139) recalls the use of "stooping" in **"A Death in the Desert"** as a metaphor for Incarnation (l. 134). The "mother-tongue" is like the alloy of the ring: it gives the precepts and axioms a body. But it also suggests, in approved post-structuralist fashion, that figures of body and supplement, text and gloss, are easily reversed. The full-blooded Italian commentary may be more meaningful than the cramped and bloodless Latin axioms that seem at first to enjoy privileged status, just as the alloy may prove more important than the gold, which is the most prized but least useful of metals.

Browning's Roman murder mystery looks for mysteries and finds only Mystery. By "Mystery" I mean an ultimate principle that does not have an explanation. In this sense, God's treatment of Pompilia, like the laws of quantum mechanics, is a mystery. Equally mysterious is the way the world becomes intelligible in *The Ring and the Book* only as a nesting structure of sacred books, of commentaries on commentaries. Browning knows that there is no single sense or truth in the world, and that dreams of transparent meaning are at best consoling fictions. But he also knows that he must keep trying to entertain such fictions, because only by worshipping at the shrine of transparent sense, in a quest for some sacred ur-book or bible that "shall mean beyond the facts" (XII.862), can he discover the intermittent radiances, the moments of luminous seeing, that make the book and the book of the world an endless source of meaning.

Notes

[1] John Marshall Gest, *The Old Yellow Book* (Boston, 1925), p. 624. Morse Peckham, "Personality and the Mask of Knowledge," *Victorian Revolutionaries: Speculations on Some Heroes of a Culture Crisis* (New York, 1970), pp. 124-125: "There is no doubt that [Browning] believes he has found the truth of the story, the answer to the only real problem in it: Was Pompilia guilty of adultery with Caponsacchi? His answer is no, yet so well had he worked that Carlyle, for example, said it was obvious she was guilty. The argument over whether Browning had found the 'truth' of the matter, which has gone on for a hundred years, is quite beside the point. He does not assert that he has found what the truth really is, or even what it was, but only that he has found a 'truth' which is satisfactory to *him.*"

[2] Levi-Hedge, *Elements of Logick; Or, A Summary of the General Principles and Different Modes of Reasoning* (Cambridge, Massachusetts, 1816), p. 112. According to *The Browning Collections: A Reconstruction,* ed. Philip Kelley and Betty A. Coley (London, 1984), Browning owned a copy of this 1816 edition. It was inscribed by R.B. Sr. on the title page, and the father's annotations and underlining occur throughout.

[3] W.G. Ward asserts that "history by itself, if we knew it ten times better than we do, could prove little or nothing." "Review of Arnold's *Sermons,"* *British Critic and Quarterly Theological Review* 30 (1841): 318.

[4] Henry Melvill, *Sermons By Henry Melvill, B.D.,* ed. Rev. C. P. McIlvaine (New York, 1838), p. 111. Browning owned the 1833 London edition of Melvill's *Sermons.*

[5] Paul Tillich, *Systematic Theology* (Chicago, 1951), 1:11-15.

[6] E. D. Hirsch, Jr., *Validity in Interpretation* (New Haven, 1967), p. 8.

[7] Francis Sparshott, *The Theory of the Arts* (Princeton, 1982), p. 260.

[8] Thomas Nagel, *The View From Nowhere* (New York, 1986), p. 67.

[9] Stanley Fish, *Is There a Text in This Class? The Authority of Interpretive Communities* (Cambridge, Massachusetts, 1980), especially pp. 303-371.

[10] Arthur Schopenhauer, *Schopenhauer: Essays and Aphorisms,* ed. and trans. R. J. Hollingdale (Harmondsworth, 1970), p. 89.

[11] Frank Kermode, *The Genesis of Secrecy: On the Interpretation of Narrative* (Cambridge, Massachusetts, 1979), p. 88.

Herbert F. Tucker (essay date 1992)

SOURCE: "Epiphany and Browning: Character Made Manifest," in *PMLA,* Vol. 107, No. 5, October, 1992, pp. 1208-21.

[In the following essay, Tucker argues for the place of the concept of epiphany (or, "the moment of sudden illumination") in literary criticism, particularly in the analysis of character construction in Browning's poetry. Tucker contends that Browning explores the use of "epiphanic faith" as a measure of character.]

James Joyce minted a two-faced counter when he coined the term *epiphany* for literary use. "By an epiphany," he wrote of his alter ego, Stephen Dedalus, "he meant a sudden spiritual manifestation, whether in the vulgarity of speech or of gesture or in a memorable phase of the mind itself. It was for the man of letters to record these epiphanies with extreme care, seeing that they themselves are the most delicate and evanescent of moments" (221). Moment or record? Letter or spirit? On one side, a Joycean epiphany is the account of an *experience,* of a secular instant as sudden and complete as what was once called grace. Obversely, though, it is the *account* of an experience, the inspired composition of a moment of spiritual composure. *Epiphany* thus names something lived through, yet also something written down. At once empirical and documentary in character, it offers both a human image for recognition and a coded legend for interpretation.

Joyce's coinage probably has as wide a circulation as any other literary term now in use, and much of its currency seems due to the place it sustains between the world and the word. Its ambiguity lets readers hold in mutual solution their often conflicting desires for the intimation of a vitally imagined meaning and for the connoisseurship of an artistic feat. The double-sided Joycean epiphany extends the promise of a reading experience that is simultaneously appreciative and analytic: an indulgence in sympathy without deception, an exercise in discernment without alienation. To identify—and identify with—a literary epiphany is to claim what the modern reader has sought since Wordsworth: knowledge not purchased by the loss of power.[1]

This attractive claim has lately forfeited much of the prestige it used to enjoy. While the call of epiphany still makes itself felt in our lecture halls, writers' workshops, and book review columns, its appeal to scholarly inquiry and sophisticated criticism has grown faint. In graduate seminars and professional journals this once potent name is less confidently invoked now than it was during the heyday of the New Criticism, when it spread from Joyce scholarship into academic criticism at large and thence entered the general climate of informed literary discussion.[2] The divided fortunes of the term register more general divisions within literary discourse: a cultural disparity between academic criticism and informal discussion about books and, within academic criticism, a historical disparity between the leading orientations of today and those of a generation ago. At mid-century, epiphany achieved a thriving symbiosis with the highly influential, avowedly nonideological poetics and pedagogy of the New Criticism. But then, having prospered together during the 1950s and 1960s, together they fell, displaced first by structuralist emphases on differential linguistics and then by the deconstruction of symbolic meanings into allegories of reading. As a result, just when epiphany was irrigating a broader literary culture, its academic fonts were going dry.

Interest in epiphany may have evaporated at its source from the same cause that has kept it current elsewhere: the promise of ready commerce between the inner sanctum of writing and the greater world outside. Whether and how literature bears on the conduct of life are questions to which the academy has recently formulated a variety of sophisticated answers. Amid this variety, however, one common denominator is the conviction that the word and the world cannot share a magical identity, and to prevailing notions of epiphany such a conviction is poison. The late renascence of inquiry into the ideological configurations governing literary production has recalled scholarly criticism from exclusively rhetorical and textual concerns to a broader cultural pertinence. Although studies in this new-historicist mode might be expected to welcome the epiphanic bond between experience and writing, in methodological practice they are obliged to reject it. Indeed, the new historicism must distinguish between experience and writing before it can get on with its work. If it fails to discern and articulate the relation between empirical actuality and literary practice, it loses its disciplinary charter and practical agenda. *Epiphany* may have fallen under theoretical suspicion and into academic neglect because currently popular definitions violate the postulates of much advanced scholarship.

Acknowledging these developments need not deprive *epiphany* of descriptive and analytic value but may instead initiate its rehabilitation. Toward that end I would argue that the New Critical epiphany rested on an interpretive distortion compounded by historical oversight. The use the New Critics made of epiphany was essentialist and ahistorical; so was their sense of the literary background from which the term emerged in the modernist period. That they slighted Joyce's Romantic and Victorian antecedents is not surprising in view of their tilt against Romanticism. What is more curious, given the frequently Christian complexion of their work, is that they also slighted the scriptural tradition from which the term ultimately derives.

In attempting to redress these oversights, I proceed from remarks on Wordsworth and Joyce to more extended considerations of the Epiphany narrative in Matthew and the dynamics of character construction in Robert Browning's poetry. The texts I discuss show that epiphany, far from escaping ideology, is instinct with it. For its ablest and most traditionally scriptural exemplars, epiphany is not the hermetic phenomenon that a few turn-of-the-century experiments and many subsequent critical studies would suggest. It is instead one feature among many that conspire in the constitution of a written life. Major modern epiphanists use the device to represent character as an effect of culturally determined forces, even as they demonstrate that nothing more distinctly typifies modernity than the desire to elude such forces. In a culture where awakening from the nightmare of history is our common dream, the contradictions vested in epiphany continue to move us—and, perhaps, to keep us where we are. I examine them again in the hope that a fresh approach may revive *epiphany* for academic inquiry and in the belief that critical scholarship will not make much difference outside the academy until it can put to better use the literary terms that have already won general practical acceptance.

I

Scholars concerned with the continuity of the Romantic tradition have noted parallels between Joycean epiphanies and the "spots of time" Wordsworth wrote about a century earlier (*Prelude* 12.208; see Langbaum, "Epiphanic Mode"; Clayton; Nichols). Wordsworth's rich phrase captures a number of epiphanic features that are by now amply documented: the specificity of the privileged moment, its local-rooted ordinariness, and the tenacity of its spatiotemporal grip on the mind. Reading further in the same *Prelude* section that discusses the "spots of time," we observe an extra, particularly Joycean feature. For when Wordsworth says that the "efficacious spirit" of "renovating virtue" abides among certain "passages of life" (12.210-20), a gentle pun on "passages" (as pathways and as texts) implies that writing is the medium where otherwise volatile spirits stay put for contemplation. One of Wordsworth's deliberate raids across the line between spontaneous experience and tranquil recollection, the phrase "passages of life"—like the later "memorials" (12.287)—anticipates the duplicity of the Joycean epiphany; and it answers to a need, like Joyce's, to textualize life in the creation of a text that may live.

What keeps epiphanic time on the spot is textuality. Yet textuality, as poststructuralism reminds us, proves a slippery fixative at best. If the New Critical epiphany promised to dissolve the perennial (proverbial?) antagonism between the letter and the spirit, that solution left behind a residue, which has been extensively analyzed in subsequent debates over the relation between texts and referents. Yet the insistence, in such debates, on holding the theoretical line between experience and description suggests that this line tends to blur in literary practice. Wordsworth and Joyce in effect *read* an epiphanic experience as a passage of life: a text awaiting transcription by "the man of letters," the writer as innocent clerk. Equating the occurrence with the verbal account appears to finesse questions of mediation

by regarding language as a window on experience.[3] But the view through a window runs both ways, and the epiphanic equation is reversible: if we read it backward, the vitality of epiphany entails the textualization of life. The verbal record may reproduce the privileged moment and give to it, "as far as words may give, / Substance and life" (*Prelude* 12.283-84), only insofar as that moment is textually preempted on the spot.[4]

The literary epiphany thus represents a pretextualized phenomenon, as the autobiographical practice of Wordsworth and Joyce makes conveniently clear. Both authors place their seminal discussions of epiphany within extended accounts of personal change. *The Prelude* and *Portrait of the Artist as a Young Man* exploit the tension between a climactic moment and the temporal sweep within which this moment punctually meets the needs of narrative development. Composing a faithful and credible autobiographical record means negotiating epiphanic passages of life in ways that keep them intact but also embed them within a controlling story. The whole work becomes a whole precisely as its privileged moments exhibit affinities both with one another and with those little, nameless, underprivileged moments that mark a life's daily character and ultimate course.[5]

Instantaneous and incongruous, an epiphany appears to come out of nowhere, whether during the empirical past or, as Wordsworth attests, during the act of composition.[6] But then epiphanic writing overtakes that surprise by making it a device for developing portraiture. In semiotic terms, an epiphany seems underdetermined in origin and indeterminate in significance. It strikes the affected character—and, at first, probably the writer and reader too—as a moment glowing with genuine, though imprecise, meaning. Under analysis, however, a successful literary epiphany will seem adequately determined, even overdetermined, by the pattern of the life it illuminates. To the apprehending consciousness, an epiphany may intimate the meaning of life, but to the observer of that consciousness, an epiphany signifies the meaning of *a* life. And it is this charactered meaning that constitutes the epiphanic effect proper.

Epiphany as a textual effect, then, does not come out of nowhere. Neither does epiphany as a phenomenon of literary modernism, for Joyce's term gave a new name to a standard nineteenth-century practice. The situation of the literary historian thus resembles that of the creative writer: both seek to set a momentary luster within a larger design that will make it illustrative. Putting Joyce's upstart neologism in historical context admittedly entails some anachronism. When discussing epiphanies from the writings of Robert Browning (or John Ruskin, or George Eliot), we should bear in mind real differences in perspective between a lapsed latter-day Irish Catholic and a dissenting English Victorian.[7] Still, it is worth asking what epiphany might have meant in any case—upper or lower—to a mid-century figure like Browning. It meant something other, I submit, than the transcendental category postulated by Joyce's early critical followers: something truer to the reciprocal complexities of language, character, and society, something more entangled with a Victorian sense of history. In Browning's poetry epiphany involves conspicuous narrative and cultural dimensions, and a hard look at Browning here may make these dimensions easier to see in Wordsworth and Joyce as well. The way epiphany functions in a patently historicist poet like Browning suggests how, in the tradition exemplified by all three authors, epiphany arises at a major narrative juncture of modernity, the place where the story of the essential self meets the accidents of historical contingency.

II

Browning died in the decade of Joyce's birth, and neither *epiphany* nor any cognate term occurs throughout his lexically prolific oeuvre. But he was a staunch though idiosyncratic Christian who knew the Bible thoroughly, read it subtly, and alluded to it all the time. An attempt to plot Browning's use of epiphany might take bearings from the one text that he would surely have considered epiphanic, Matthew 2.1-12, the King James Version:

1 Now when Jesus was born in Bethlehem of Judaea, in the days of Herod the king, behold, there came wise men from the east to Jerusalem,

2 Saying, Where is he that is born King of the Jews? for we have seen his star in the east, and are come to worship him.

3 When Herod the king had heard *these things,* he was troubled, and all Jerusalem with him.

4 And when he had gathered all the chief priests and scribes of the people together, he demanded of them where Christ should be born.

5 And they said unto him, In Bethlehem of Judaea: for thus it is written by the prophet;

6 And thou Bethlehem, *in* the land of Juda, art not the least among the princes of Juda: for out of thee shall come a Governor, that shall rule my people Israel.

7 Then Herod, when he had privily called the wise men, inquired of them diligently what time the star appeared.

8 And he sent them to Bethlehem; and said, Go and search diligently for the young child; and when ye have found *him,* bring me word again, that I may come and worship him also.

9 When they had heard the king, they departed: and, lo, the star, which they saw in the east, went before them, till it came and stood over where the young child was.

10 When they saw the star, they rejoiced with exceeding great joy.

11 And when they were come into the house, they saw the young child with Mary his mother, and fell down, and worshipped him: and when they had opened their treasures, they presented unto him gifts; gold, and frankincense, and myrrh.

12 And being warned of God in a dream that they should not return to Herod they departed into their own country another way.

The charm of this vivid narrative, and much of its widespread iconographic appeal for the pictorial tradition in which Browning took so lively an interest, inheres in its promise that they who "search diligently" shall find the place of faith where seeing is believing. The direct *idou* 'lo and behold' that frames and punctuates the tale; the dramatic sighting of the star; and the beautifully understated revelation of child and mother—all highlight the visual accessibility of the Christian miracle to those who have eyes to see. In the Greek testament *epiphaneia* and its cognates connote a light to the gentiles, which remains the principal ecclesiastical meaning of Epiphany to this day.[8] Although Matthew does not use the term, the contrast he draws between the blindness of clerical insiders who know the prophecies cold and the warm trust of wise men from beyond the pale has led a crusading church to canonize his tale above all others as The Epiphany.

The invitation to belief issued by the Magi's example formed a staple in the exegesis of Matthew's Gospel across the nineteenth century (e.g., Henry and Scott 7-10; Sumner 15; Trench 68-71). Browning, as a Christian, almost certainly concurred in this interpretation. But, as a poet never given to simple commitments, he would have found imaginatively congenial several latent complications in the Mattheic Epiphany. For the plain tale of the Magi proves quite subtle from a semiotic viewpoint. The story turns on the interpretation of a set of ambiguous, enigmatically related signs. The first of these, the conspicuous star, is a physical phenomenon that portends something sufficiently extraordinary to motivate the journey of the Magi and sufficiently specific to guide it. Not only is the celestial appearance unusual (*tou phainomenou asteros* [v. 7]), it is also significant in the astrological system that wise men from the east are supposedly wise to. The Magi read the heavens, in other words, like a text. Whether they actually follow the star westward or only follow the directions encoded in its rising—as *en tēi anatolēi* (v. 2) strictly suggests (Brown 174)—their wisdom consists in interpreting the star's instructions and carrying them out. Those instructions are both necessary and insufficient: the Magi know that a new Jewish king has been born in the west, but they do not know just where. To focus their quest, they must supplement gentile science with the different, privileged authority of Hebrew scripture, which appears at verse 6 in a paraphrase of the prophecy in Micah 5.2. Their need for this supplement asserts the traditional authority of Scripture over nature and of God's chosen people over the gentiles. More broadly, and more pertinently to Browning's treatment of epiphany, it defines significance as essentially textual and underscores the concomitant importance of interpretation.[9]

In returning to Matthew's Epiphany, we return to the relation between experience and text that we also meet in the epiphanies of Joyce and Wordsworth. The Gospel's unapologetically miraculous story steers clear of the mystified phenomenality that attends modern critical conceptions of epiphany, and Matthew frankly prefers the order of interpretation to that of mere being.[10] He sees, moreover—with Wordsworth, Browning, and Joyce—how this preference bears on the cultural situation of interpretive acts. For while Matthew affirms the reign of grace over nature, his immediate concern is a related but distinct contrast between nature and culture. His entire Gospel draws energy from the tension between its ecumenical call to all believers and its focus on a target audience well versed in the Law and the Prophets. This tension produces in Matthew what might be called a primitive Christian anthropology.[11] The very exoticism of a visit by wise men from the east makes their story a study in cultural difference, a theme reinforced by Herod's application to the local custodians of cultural authority, the Jerusalem clerisy of chief priests and scribes.

Now it so happens that these *archiereis* and *grammateis* discharge their duty in verse 6 by garbling the prophecy they cite. This confusion of tongues has puzzled commentators since Jerome, who regarded the passage as a swipe at bad scholarship within a corrupt establishment.[12] For our purposes, though, the experts' official misquotation illustrates Matthew's evangelically anthropological agenda. His source reads, "But thou, Bethlehem Ephratah, *though* thou be little among the thousands of Judah, *yet* out of thee shall he come forth unto me *that is* to be ruler in Israel" (Micah 5.2). The most arresting difference between this text and Matthew 2.6 lies in the emphatic priestly contradiction of the prophetic diminutive: little Bethlehem, say the priests and scribes, is "not the least" (*oudamōs elachistē*). Why should these authorities violate the letter of Micah's text? In order, I think, to protect the spirit of his prophecy from misprision by uninitiated outsiders. From an intercultural perspective Matthew's misquotation seems the sort of rhetorical adjustment to circumstance that always caught Browning's fancy. It is an accommodation

that adepts in the arcana of a culture under imperial siege might offer to flatteringly curious strangers for the sake of clarity on the main point: appearances notwithstanding, little Bethlehem is a place big with meaning.

The incommensurability of appearances and meanings lies at the heart of the modern literary epiphany; it is also a major ingredient of biblical narrative.[13] Commentators have long agreed that Matthew expected learned readers to take his tale of gentile stargazers as a typological fulfillment of the prophecy of Balaam in Numbers 24.17: "There shall come a Star out of Jacob, and a Sceptre shall rise out of Israel."[14] Balaam in the Old Testament, like the Magi in the New, is an alien wise man—very nearly a wise guy, a folk trickster best known for his slapstick role in a fable about a speaking ass. It may have been a sense of the ironic potential in his materials that led Matthew to Balaam as a type of the gentile mage. For when Balaam is summoned by the wicked Moabite king Balak to curse Israel, he instead repeatedly testifies—to his own surprise—to God's grandeur and to the confusion of any earthly power that would suborn prophecy. If Balaam's outlandish exploits inform Matthew's conception of the Magi as outsiders who outwit bad King Herod, then the doctrine of accommodation I impute to the chief priests and scribes may have a further ironic point. Balaam's prophecy, like Micah's, highlights a familiar scriptural contrast between the humble and the mighty, between human appearances and divine purpose. This disparity, which is structurally essential both to biblical narrative and to the modern literary epiphany, is glossed over in the Jerusalem clerics' misquotation. As a result, the full weight of the incongruity falls on the fundamental point of Matthew's passage, of his Gospel, and indeed of the entire New Testament: the epiphanic manifestation of God in man, the revelation of Jesus as the Christ, the messiah who fulfills prophecy to the letter, yet enlarges its national spirit to global and transhistorical proportions.

This plenary evangel must remain implicit on the first page of the New Testament, where our story occurs. But Matthew borrows its force for a hushed climax: "And when they saw the star, they rejoiced with exceeding great joy. And when they were come into the house, they saw the young child with Mary his mother, and fell down, and worshipped him." Here a syntactic parallelism between verses draws out an epiphanic difference. By preceding the proper Epiphany of the second verse with the prevenient grace note of the first, Matthew heightens the contrast between the familiar joy of expectation confirmed and the uncanny wildness of surprise; between the star the Magi already know and the new king they instantly recognize despite his unprepossessing surroundings. The flat description of mother and child belies any standards of oriental majesty that the advice given the Magi in Jerusalem may have reinforced.[15] "They saw . . . and fell down": Matthew has set his wise men up for a fortunate fall that works, through an incongruity rooted in cultural difference, to lift ethnic barriers and enable the recognition of a sovereign mystery. Reserving comment on the quality of that mystery, Matthew does not say whether the Magi regard the goal of their quest as a Holy Family or wholly as a family. Instead, he sustains an ecumenical balance between divine and human truth, comparable to the balance between iconic and realistic portraiture in the Renaissance images of madonna and child that Browning most admired.[16]

III

That Browning likewise admired the narrative craft of the Epiphany text in Matthew must remain a matter for conjecture. His lifelong exposure to the Bible, biblical commentary, and preaching based on Scripture makes it certain that the episode of the Magi came regularly to his attention, and his interest was probably sharpened by an early fascination with magic and the figure of the sage. Still, in default of specific evidence, it will suffice here to educe a set of parallels between the Epiphany narrative and Browning's practice as a poet of character in the modern epiphanic line. Matthew's story concerns the interpretation of signs, an acculturated activity that culminates in the manifestation of personality. This manifestation occurs in two ways. The response of the Magi to the star, the effect the news has on the Jerusalem authorities, and the influence on the Magi of the vision of mother and child are all personal notes that animate the narrative with a local human interest. But the goal of the Magi's journey, the climax of the story and its doctrinal crux, is also the manifestation of personality: the revelation of deity in human form. These two sorts of personal manifestation—the texture of the Epiphany narrative and its point—converge in the question of scriptural incongruity. A sequence of imperfect interpretation, shortsighted accommodation, and defeated expectation (each a culturally induced event) leads the Magi to a surprising epiphany that fulfills the signs in unpredicted ways.

Browning's epiphanic poetry likewise aims to manifest personality through the interpretation of culturally specific signs. Like Matthew, Browning exhibits an interest in the historical insignia of manner, speech, and thought that differentiate characters and uses these limiting particulars to appeal to his readers' recognition of a fellowship that all souls share. But his epiphanies are as secular as the biblical Epiphany is theological, and his dramatic poetry reveals a personality resolutely human. This dramatic secularization of epiphany effaces the distinction between the incidental and the essential manifestations of personality. What I have called narrative texture and point in the Mattheic Epiphany—respectively, the culture-bound quest of the Magi and its culture-transcending goal—achieve identity in the economy of the dramatic monologue.

Where a text aims at revealing human personality rather than divine personhood, its texture is identical with its point, its empirical Joycean "evanescence" with its written Wordsworthian "memorial" or "passage of life."

In this respect Browning's practice typifies the modern literary epiphany, which deducts the biblical model's theological claims and reclaims them within a human story. The derivation of the secular epiphany from the religious original appears with particular clarity in Browning's works, where speakers often define themselves by their yearning for absolute ideals. These ideals, whether overtly theological or quasi-religious (a flawless art, a fulfilled love), serve as goals that Browning's dramatis personae postulate, seldom if ever attain, yet always strive for in characteristic ways. In straining after the absolute, the speakers attest to its hiddenness and undertake its imaginative recovery as an object of individual desire or an article of cultural faith. The abeyance of theophany—if not the disappearance of God, then God's failure to show up—draws forth the characteristic Browning miracle: the dramatic epiphany of the worded self.

The reader assists at this miracle, not despite the cultural differences that a poetics of sympathy may neutralize, but thanks to the cultural differences that a poetics of irony may exploit.[17] Browning's reader learns to note the symptomatic differentiae that set speakers off as historical subjects or objects of study. The speech of this Renaissance prelate or that Yankee spiritualist reproduces the assumptions, and the conflicts, of the cultural ambience that has produced him. But this ironic cognition of character entails a further recognition: historical contingencies also engulf the reader, asserting themselves in every judgment. The regularity with which Browning's speakers engage in interpretive acts that reveal character reinforces the specular structure of his dramatic epiphanies. If those acts manifest character, then so does the act of interpreting the poem. The way we read Browning's monologues characterizes us: recognizing the hermeneutic complicity that his texts both enact and exact, we disclose our investment in their epiphanic effectiveness.

Once dramatic irony turns back on the reader as ironist, the grounds of objectivity buckle to reveal, in their very historical and cultural distinctiveness, a common condition soliciting acknowledgment. And this solicitation constitutes in Browning a secular equivalent of the evangelical challenge that the Bible issues to its reader. *Idou* 'lo and behold': Matthew never imagines the reader as a passive spectator but always addresses a historical agent implicated by the Gospel. For Browning's generation faith in the factual authenticity of Scripture was fast eroding; yet in a newly skeptical historicism he found for modern literature the terms of an immediacy like Scripture's. "You of the virtue (we issue join) / How strive you? *De te, fabula*" (249-50). The Horatian tag here at the close of "The Statue and the Bust" (1855) expressly transmits the moral charge that Browning's art usually implies. *De te, fabula:* Reader, you're It.

Owning a common ground in the very fact of cultural difference, Browning's reader as *grammateus* 'scribal arbiter' turns *magos* 'wise man' and witnesses to mysteries of historically conditioned personality from which no reading is exempt. In this sense the Browningesque dramatic monologue is a paradigmatic modern genre: it recapitulates, and subjects to critique, structures of lyrical autonomy that we find in the age of Wordsworth; and it bequeaths its critical strategies to major lyrical and fictional forms practiced by the modernist generation of Joyce.[18] When opening the text of a Browning monologue, readers open their own analytic gifts to analysis. From such a transaction readers return, as they must, to their native place in cultural circumstance. But insofar as the transaction with the text has made them wiser—if only about that imperative return—like the Magi they go back into their own country another way.

IV

Epiphany is where you find it; and in Browning's poetry you find it everywhere. Yet in that poetry the moment of sudden illumination occurs far less often as an event than as a topic for discussion. When Browning scholars invoke the epiphanic doctrine of the "infinite moment" or "good minute," they are entering a conversation that Browning's speakers have already begun.[19] From the first his poetry centers on figures for whom epiphany is an article of faith rather than a matter of empirical record, and his career comprises a series of experiments in dramatic genres that assay epiphanic faith as an index of character. In *Paracelsus* (1835) and *Sordello* (1840), nothing short of an exhaustive drama or narrative will do the trick: last lines like "And this was Paracelsus!" (5.908) and "Who would has heard Sordello's story told" (6.886) send the nonplussed reader back to the entire work as a spheric manifestation of the eponymous poet-mage at its center. With *Pippa Passes* (1841), Browning shortens the attention span to a single scene: Each major episode of the play culminates in an epiphanic moment—the overhearing of Pippa's adventitious song—which redeems a tortured psyche in ways that the reader interprets as consistent with psychosocial determinants hidden from the character himself. Browning's early predilection for the psychological effect of epiphany, rather than for its ontological substance, culminates in his dramatic monologues. As a rule these poems find their plots not in the narrative of an epiphany but in a speaker's memory of or desire for a potentially epiphanic experience. Browning's monologists keep epiphany at art's length, picking it up on the reflective rebound; and the ways they cope with epiphany compose their lives and constitute their characters.

One instance especially germane here is that of Karshish, the Arab physician. A medical student doing fieldwork

in Palestine during the first century, Karshish is a belated gentile wise man from the east.[20] His situation parallels the Magi's, with the signal difference that his omen-ridden journey leads not to Jesus but to Lazarus, the man Jesus raised from the dead. Lazarus has been so touched by the presence of Jesus that his own presence touches Karshish in turn, but it touches him into literature rather than into conviction: "An itch I had, a sting to write, a tang!" (**"An Epistle . . . of Karshish"** [1855] 67). The distance between Karshish and the incarnate Christ creates, in the letter Karshish writes his friend Abib, the secular space of surmise, which is also the space of humane letters where the modern epiphany flourishes. "The madman saith He said so: it is strange" (312). From Jesus to Lazarus to Karshish to Abib to Browning to the reader—the medium transmitting this chain reaction of epiphanic contingency along a sequence of historically situated subjects is a discourse that incarnates meaning in personality.[21] Neither infidel nor enthusiast, Karshish signs off with the word *strange,* as good a word as any for what befalls in the Browningesque epiphany of character. The word signifies the outward differences that mark strangers; it also highlights the estrangement that is produced in Karshish, or in the time-traveling historicist reader, when encountering an uncanny presence that mines and riddles the cultural formations of personal identity.

Browning's humanist manifestation of character emerges further in two other poems from ***Men and Women*** (1855) that, like **"Karshish,"** translate into a secular context materials recalling the Mattheic Epiphany. The first of these is **"My Star"**:

> All that I know
>   Of a certain star
> Is, it can throw
>   (Like the angled spar)
> Now a dart of red,
>   Now a dart of blue;
> Till my friends have said
>   They would fain see, too,
> My star that dartles the red and the blue!
> Then it stops like a bird; like a flower, hangs
>   furled:
>   They must solace themselves with the Saturn
>   above it.
> What matter to me if their star is a world?
>   Mine has opened its soul to me; therefore I
>   love it.

This poem turns on a conceit that exploits a new nineteenth-century use of the word *star* to denote a celebrity, a personality endowed with the sort of charisma that Victorian readers had conferred on Elizabeth Barrett Browning, the presumptive subject of the poem, but had withheld from her husband.[22] Read as a reworking of the Mattheic Epiphany, the conceit of **"My Star"** conflates the astral with the human manifestation and presents in its speaker a magus with special gifts of insight. Even to this seer, however, the star reveals its soul only on the sly, by the chromatic way it "dartles the red and the blue," in contrast to the steadily shining planet Saturn. Even a sidereal language, it seems, deals in asides; like the "star," or main attraction, of a dramatic monologue, Browning's star declares itself not through what it is but through what it does, how it makes its characteristic mark.

The speaker, too, whether or not we accept his traditional identification as the poet, reveals himself as a modern familiar by his colloquial diction. Under an older dispensation the phrase "a certain star" would connote, as it would to Matthew's Magi, the transcendent fixity of the heavenly spheres. Here, though, it exhibits that blend of objective uncertainty and subjective certitude which typifies the modern spirit in its mid-Victorian phase. If a saturnine science has reduced the once ethereal stars to material worlds, "What matter to me?" The offhand idiom, like the dartling of the star, imparts a confidence in quirky beauty and private truth that is all the speaker knows on earth and all he needs to know. As sophisticated readers we need to know more, to be sure, and the advantage we seek consists in knowing the speaker—or, at least, in gauging the speaker's cultural position. If we deem his astral projection a typically Victorian bid to secure an intimate sphere of meaning against the public opinion and scientific materialism that threaten it, this judgment makes us epiphanic readers in Browning's sense. It illustrates the process whereby the privacy of epiphany helps create an external, historically placed, and publicly identifiable character: in short, a certain star.

"My Star" thus is something of a poetic manifesto. It both exemplifies the workings of the dramatic monologue and talks them over; and it does so through an image that has pronounced affinities with the Epiphany narrative in Matthew. Something similar may be said of "'**Transcendentalism: A Poem in Twelve Books,**'" a meta-poetic epilogue to *Men and Women* in which one Victorian poet counsels another on the function of poetry at the present time. That time being an age of thought, and the proper vehicle for thought being prose, the younger poet's composition of a philosophical epic on transcendentalism amounts to a generic category mistake: "Stop playing, poet! May a brother speak? / 'Tis you speak, that's your error. Song's our art" (1-2). In an era like the present it falls to poets to supply, not the prose of propositions, but a lyrical mode of "images and melody" that deliver the epiphanic sense of meaningfulness (17). We have purchased modern sophistication, the speaker complains, at the cost of our vital wonder at things in themselves:

> Then, who helps more, pray, to repair our loss—
> Another Boehme with a tougher book
> And subtler meanings of what roses say,—

> Or some stout Mage like him of Halberstadt,
> John, who made things Boehme wrote thoughts about?
> He with a "look you!" vents a brace of rhymes,
> And in there breaks the sudden rose herself,
> Over us, under, round us every side,
> Nay, in and out the tables and the chairs
> And musty volumes, Boehme's book and all,—
> Buries us with a glory, young once more,
> Pouring Heaven into this shut house of life.

(34-45)

Here is the promise of modern epiphany in full force, a force that I suspect owes much to the instance of Matthew's story. The age demands a poet who can show rather than tell, who overleaps textual discourse to make things happen, with the challenge of the New Testament *idou:* "look you!" The modern poet stands among the Magi, "some stout Mage like him of Halberstadt"—or them of Bethlehem—and testifies to a wonder that buries scribal industry, "musty volumes, Boehme's book and all," in a grammarian's funeral. The "sudden rose" that disrupts "this shut house of life," the miraculous image that bursts the coffin of the text, is a typological symbol of the Christian incarnation: not the "Star out of Jacob" from Balaam's prophecy, but its Old Testament analogue by the magic of New Testament hermeneutics, the everblooming rose sprung at winter midnight from Jesse's stem, out of the house of David.

I can think of no passage in Browning that is more Epiphanic. Yet the full Browningesque epiphany does not occur until the moment of privileged vision finds its secular place within the charactered pattern of a life:

> So, come, the harp back to your heart again!
> You are a poem, though your poem's naught.
> The best of all you showed before, believe,
> Was your own boy-face o'er the finer chords
> Bent, following the cherub at the top
> That points to God with his paired half-moon wings.

(46-51)

Ultimately the speaker reads his junior colleague's work as a "show" or manifestation of character, in a triumph of what amounts to psychological transcendentalism. To the speaker's expert eye, the promise of the earnest beginner rises above his unpromising topic, as his "boy-face" hovers over the instrument he harps on. This psychology lesson of the master, furthermore, teaches us to master the master in turn, through just the sort of character analysis to which he subjects his disciple. Even as the speaker vaunts a patronizing superiority, he takes his stand on an epiphanic poetics that soothes his cultured malaise a little too blandly for critical comfort. "By the time youth slips a stage or two / While reading prose," he confesses, "We shut the clasps and find life's summer past" (29-30, 33). As this musty whiff of Romantic nostalgia suggests, the magical epiphany sought by Browning's speaker flowers out of a mid-life crisis into a mid-century fantasy of rejuvenation.

The development of epiphanic writing across the turn of the century into the first modernist decades gives additional cause for skepticism about the critical doctrine of Browning's speaker. By now we can see how an epiphanic poetics very like the speaker's in **"'Transcendentalism'"** played into—and arguably played itself out in—certain symbolist and imagist works of Browning's successors. The young W. B. Yeats and Ezra Pound, two poets who acknowledged their debt to Browning, would appear to have taken the advice of his monologue to heart when versifying the epiphany of the theosophical rose or troping the apparition of metropolitan faces as "Petals on a wet, black bough." "The Secret Rose" (1897) and "In a Station of the Métro" (1916) are beautiful poems, but we have left the mystique of early modernism far enough behind to see how limited, and dated, their wan beauty appears beside Browning's robust copiousness. In retrospect his **"'Transcendentalism'"** looks like a proleptic critique of that naïveté of decontextualized vision, that escape from personality into the innocence of the eye, which constrains much modernist literature and theory.[23]

To an eye trained on Browning, epiphany in its rarefied symbolist or imagist form seems a diminished thing: the expression of a hunger for authenticity that craves isolated perceptions while it starves the perceiving self. Browning offers, in contrast to the impersonally streamlined epiphany of modern poetics, the ampler if messier model of character made manifest in the language and ideology of a conditioning time and place. Eventually modernism would ratify this model: it was to a contextualism like Browning's that Yeats returned in the great personal lyrics of his maturity, as did Pound in *The Pisan Cantos.* These masterpieces, along with Joyce's *Ulysses* and Eliot's *Four Quartets,* continue to apprehend in ordinary events extraordinary meanings, but meanings that arise from the design of a life. The luminous detail radiates in constellation: the rose pattern in the iron filings owes its significance, for the highest modernism, to its place in the larger pattern of a historically specific humanity.[24]

Although we may not credit the kind of epiphany the speaker in **"'Transcendentalism'"** advocates, the very skepticism his ideas awaken contributes to his own epiphany as a speaking self. Consider the title of the monologue, where nothing but a set of quotation marks distinguishes the urbane speaker's position from the zealous harper's. If to quote is to appropriate, the two

poets in this poem remain vulnerable to critical take-over, and vulnerable in the same way. Certainly neither of them meets the high standard of magical creativity set by John of Halberstadt, for both merely "speak" versified thought; their ultimately prosy ideas remain susceptible to the same cultural-psychological critique.

And so, at last, does that critique. The final lines of the poem describe a structure of stacked supervisory vantages: a harp under a face under a cherub under God. This structure, like the nested structures of interpersonal transference in **"Karshish"** and in many other poems by Browning, renders not a hierarchy of being but a progression toward the infinite. It corresponds to the potentially infinite regress that frames hermeneutic consciousness and to the rhetorical entanglements in which Browning's poetry involves its reader. What the psychologizing speaker says to his brother in the art—"You are a poem"—the reader learns to say in turn to the speaker, thus bringing this oddly titled monologue to charactered life and confirming its place in a collection called, not *Selected Poems,* but *Men and Women.* Just here, though, Browning gives us all the slip. For what the discerning reader says to the speaker, the poem says in haunting echo right back to the reader: You are a poem like me, a worded self, a cultural construct. **"'Transcendentalism'"** thus transcends the interpretation it prompts, as the reader too is read. Our instructed impulses to naturalize this Victorian poem by psychological means and to socialize it with reference to its cultural setting and afterlife can instruct us in turn about the constitution and situation of our critical practice now. What the interpretation of an epiphanic moment manifests, in the final analysis, is the character—psychological or formalist, deconstructive or historicist—of its interpreter. When all is said, the end of the text is the epiphany of the reader. *Idou, hypocrite lecteur: De te, fabula.*

Notes

[1] The ambiguous place of epiphany between self-accrediting vision and artificial construct is registered in the first critical treatment of the subject, Harry Levin's study of Joyce. Having done preliminary homage to epiphany as a "spiritual manifestation," Levin then calls it a "device," "a matter of literary technique" (28-31). For Booth, the double-sidedness of Joyce's epiphanic manifesto makes "the complications of distance become incalculable" (332). Like Donoghue, Booth decries in Joyce an abdication of authorial responsibility, a charge sometimes leveled against Browning as well.

[2] Introduced by Levin in 1941, the term *epiphany* acquired special cachet for Joyceans with the 1944 publication of *Stephen Hero.* Although Hendry extended its application in 1946, only during the 1950s was it widely adopted. It does not appear in the 1943 glossary to Brooks and Warren, but Brooks and Wimsatt's

1957 work refers in passing to the "now current Joycean word *epiphany*" (134). Writing in 1960, Levin called the term "a catchword of criticism" (230), and a decade later Abrams registered its promotion to canonical status: Joyce "affixed to the Moment what seems destined to become its standard name" (421). For an updated bibliographical survey, see Beja, "Epiphany."

[3] When Nichols writes that "the perceptual experience and its transformation into language *is* primary" (33; my emphasis), his grammar stumbles on the ideological crux of the New Critical epiphany. Beja gathers various modernist assertions of verbal art's fidelity to the preverbal moment (*Epiphany* 19).

[4] Frye holds that an epiphany is for Joyce "an actual event, brought into contact with the creative imagination, but untouched by it" and for Wordsworth "something observed but not essentially altered by the imagination" (158). Yet Frye himself casts imagination in a more formative role when he recognizes that epiphany is based not so much on "existential nature" as on "a *picture* of nature . . . something to be contemplated but not lived in" (161). Weiskel notes Wordsworth's "passages" pun (169) and goes on to show how the poet's "resistance to reading . . . as opposed to seeing" entails a "regression from the order of symbol to that of image" (173, 179).

[5] Abrams discusses Wordsworth's subordination of the spots of time to the plot of *The Prelude* (77, 419) and likens the "structural function" of the Snowdon vision from book 14 to Stephen's climactic epiphany in *Portrait* (422). Beja regards Joyce's epiphanies as fragments that are "transformed" into wholes by narrative contextualization (*Epiphany* 85-86) and comments on the crucial difference between Stephen's objectivist theory of epiphany and the psychological use to which Joyce's epiphanies are put (25, 78). The very theory, I would argue further, serves as a character note that dramatizes Stephen's need to drown subjectivity in the *quidditas* and *claritas* of things. See Bowen; S. Joyce 124.

[6] See, for example, *Prelude* 6.592-99. For Clayton this passage shows that a collision between "visionary power" and "the life of narrative"—antithetical forces "beyond the determination of the artist"—results in "a dislocation at a primary level of discourse, an alteration in narrative form that can neither be augmented nor suppressed without doing gross damage to the work's integrity" (14).

[7] Walzl reads *Dubliners* with reference to the "sub-cycle" of the liturgical year running from Epiphany to Candlemas. While such associations may inform the epiphanies of Hopkins, Matthew's text seems a likelier point of reference for Low Church Victorians like Browning.

[8] Some of the more striking New Testament occurrences of *epiphaneia* and its cognates are Luke 1.29, Acts 2.20, 2 Timothy 4.8, and Titus 2.11. For Victorian and contemporary ecumenical applications of the Epiphany see, respectively, Trench 68 and Prabhu 297. See also Beare 74.

[9] On the relation between scriptural authority and pagan science, contrast Patte 34 with Nolan 44, 78. The priority of Scripture to nature virtually becomes a plot event in verses 9-10, where the star departs from its westerly course and veers southward, forsaking a natural for a prophetic direction.

[10] Here Matthew differs sharply from those modern epiphanists for whom subjectivity is beside the point and interpretation a blot on *claritas*. For a strongly worded statement of this New Critical position, see Kenner 141-45; see also Nichols 17, 113. Conceptions closer to Matthew's—and Browning's—emerge from poststructuralist theory: "*manifestation* itself does not reveal a presence, it makes a sign" (Derrida 49); "The symbolic *manifestation* as a *thing* is a matrix of symbolic meanings as words. . . . The manifestation through the thing is like the condensation of an infinite discourse" (Ricoeur 11).

[11] The relation between an anthropological perspective and biblical hermeneutics lies at the heart of the Higher Criticism practiced in Browning's day. Strauss makes the analysis of Matthew 2.1-12 a set piece vindicating the Herderian "mythical" method of recuperating a collective mentality: "the mythus is founded not upon any individual conception, but upon the more elevated and general conception of a whole people" (78; see also 246). Even the insular commentator Horne recognized that Matthew wrote to a divided audience of Christians and Jews (230).

[12] Trench discusses Jerome's criticism (44). Horne attempts to harmonize the Testaments by adducing rare Greek and Syriac texts that translate Micah 5.2 as a rhetorical question. Strauss's astringent reading of this verse—the text means only that the Messiah will be a descendant of David—confers on the priests and scribes a yet more active hermeneutic role: "Thus allowing the magi to have been rightly directed by means of the rabbinical exegesis of the oracle, a false interpretation must have hit on the truth" (221).

[13] Beja's epiphanic criteria are "incongruity" and "insignificance" (*Epiphany* 16-17). Alter makes comparable points in his reading of the typologically germane Balaam narrative in Numbers (104-07).

[14] See Strauss 238-42; Trench 34; Farrar 1: 29; and, in modern times, Brown 190-96. The visual motif that Alter stresses in the book of Numbers is also present in the Epiphany narrative, as Trench maintains (68-73). Compare the obeisance of the Magi with the passage in Numbers where Balaam, his eyes newly opened to

the militant angel of the Lord, "bowed down his head, and fell flat on his face" (22.31). The comparative humility of Matthew's account might be read as an instance of the revisionary ratio that Bloom associates with homely repetition and calls, after the New Testament, *kenosis* (77-92).

[15] See Strauss: "One might wonder that there is no notice of the astonishment which it must have excited in these men to find, instead of the expected prince, a child in quite ordinary, perhaps indigent circumstances" (226). The way Strauss identifies the narrative issue at stake here, while entirely missing its affective point, helps us understand the ambivalence his work prompted in Browning, who caricatures him in "Christmas-Eve" (1850).

[16] *The Ring and the Book* (1868-69), for example, makes sustained use of the imagery of madonna and child. Caponsacchi compares Pompilia to a Rafael madonna (6.400-06, 909-15); representations of the Virgin Mary so inform Pompilia's identity that she likens Caponsacchi to the Mattheic "star" (7.1448-50).

[17] Langbaum regards epiphany and irony as "the alternate modes by which realistic notation achieves form and significance" ("Epiphanic Mode" 36). I contend, rather, that in Browning's monologues the "epiphany of character" (37), instead of setting off the ironic mode, incorporates it as a means of implicating the reader in the drama of interpretation. Guerra proposes a different reader-response theory of epiphany.

[18] See Langbaum, *Poetry;* Martin; Tucker; Nichols 5, 30-31. The influence of Browning on modernist fiction needs further investigation; the best recent study is Posnock's.

[19] At least since Chesterton identified "the doctrine of the great hour" (109), Browning scholars have been expounding that doctrine, in a torrent of studies that it would be as futile to itemize here as to divide into the aesthetic, ethical, and religious categories they fill. Suffice it to say that my approach to epiphany dissents from majority opinion (e.g., Whitla, Nichols), in which Browning's "good minute" or "infinite moment" constitutes a timeless transcendence of contingency.

[20] Browning's antiphon to "Karshish" in the 1855 *Men and Women* is "Cleon," an epistolary monologue whose blend of Christian polemic and cultural pathos Trench had strikingly anticipated five years before (72-73). The ethnological malaise behind "Karshish" may have helped inspire the most epiphanic of T. S. Eliot's dramatic monologues (in both biblical and Browningesque senses), the 1927 "Journey of the Magi": "no longer at ease here, in the old dispensation, / With an alien people clutching their gods" (41-42).

[21] Whitla contends that in Browning "the moment of vision is also the moment of Incarnation," which "gives significance to the whole poem" (17). But this standard formulation elides the role of interpretation in determining "significance." For an epiphanic poetics, opposed to an incarnational one, stress falls on the moment not of vision but of reading. See Weiskel 169-79.

[22] That Browning typically chose this poem for inscription in autograph albums does not make it any less a dramatic lyric. As in "One Word More" (1855), the "Epilogue" to *Dramatis Personae* (1864), and the introduction to *The Ring and the Book,* this poet in propria persona remains very much a persona.

[23] I have chiefly in mind the nuggets of pure image that adorn both sides of the fin de siècle in poetry and prose. As the major modernists grew into longer forms, of course, they adapted nineteenth-century arts of epiphanic contextualization to the demands of what Bornstein describes as a "continual tension between the public, prophetic stance and the private concern for lyrical moments" (*Poetic Remaking* 121). Still, as Bornstein suggests elsewhere, at first even the modernists' longer poems conformed to the standard of impersonality: Eliot's and Pound's associationist experiments in the dramatic monologue tend to dissolve character in privileged moments that come to the speaker only "as chance epiphanies, having nothing to do with his ordinary self" (*Transformations* 139).

[24] Christ sketches the line that extends through modernism to the tensional and persona-based poetics of the New Criticism (100).

Works Cited

Abrams, M. H. *Natural Supernaturalism: Tradition and Revolution in Romantic Literature.* New York: Norton, 1971.

Alter, Robert. *The Art of Biblical Narrative.* New York: Basic, 1981.

Beare, Francis W. *The Gospel according to Matthew.* Oxford: Blackwell, 1981.

Beja, Morris. "Epiphany and the Epiphanies." *A Companion to Joyce Studies.* Ed. Zack Bowen and James F. Carens. Westport: Greenwood, 1984. 707-25.

———. *Epiphany in the Modern Novel.* Seattle: U of Washington P, 1971.

Bloom, Harold. *The Anxiety of Influence.* New York: Oxford UP, 1973.

Booth, Wayne. *The Rhetoric of Fiction.* Chicago: U of Chicago P, 1961.

Bornstein, George. *Poetic Remaking: The Art of Browning, Yeats, and Pound.* University Park: Pennsylvania State UP, 1988.

———. *Transformations of Romanticism in Yeats, Eliot, and Stevens.* Chicago: U of Chicago P, 1976.

Bowen, Zack. "Joyce and the Epiphany Concept." *Journal of Modern Literature* 9 (1981-82): 103-14.

Brooks, Cleanth, and R. P. Warren. *Understanding Fiction.* New York: Crofts, 1943.

Brooks, Cleanth, and W. K. Wimsatt. *Literary Criticism: A Short History.* New York: Knopf, 1957.

Brown, Raymond E. *The Birth of the Messiah: A Commentary on the Infancy Narratives in Matthew and Luke.* Garden City: Doubleday, 1977.

Browning, Robert. *The Poems of Robert Browning.* Ed. John Pettigrew and Thomas J. Collins. 2 vols. New Haven: Yale UP, 1981.

———. *The Ring and the Book.* Ed. Richard Altick. New Haven: Yale UP, 1971.

Chesterton, G. K. *Robert Browning.* London: Macmillan, 1903.

Christ, Carol T. *Victorian and Modern Poetics.* Chicago: U of Chicago P, 1984.

Clayton, Jay. *Romantic Vision and the Novel.* Cambridge: Cambridge UP, 1987.

Derrida, Jacques. *Of Grammatology.* Trans. Gayatri Chakravorty Spivak. Baltimore: Johns Hopkins UP, 1976.

Donoghue, Denis. "Joyce and the Finite Order." *Sewanee Review* 68 (1960): 256-73.

Eliot, T. S. The Waste Land *and Other Poems.* 1930. New York: Harcourt, 1934.

Farrar, Frederic W. *The Life of Christ.* London: Cassell, 1874.

Frye, Northrop. *A Study of English Romanticism.* New York: Random, 1968.

Guerra, Lia. "Fragmentation in *Dubliners* and the Reader's Epiphany." *Myriadminded Man: Jottings on Joyce.* Ed. R. M. Bosinelli et al. Bologna: Cooperativa, 1986. 41-49.

Hendry, Irene. "Joyce's Epiphanies." *Sewanee Review* 54 (1946): 449-67.

Henry, Matthew, and Thomas Scott. *The Comprehensive Commentary on the Holy Bible.* Ed. William Jenks. Vol. 4. Brattleboro: Fessenden, 1834. 5 vols.

The Holy Bible. King James Version. Cleveland: World, n.d.

Horne, Thomas Hartwell. *An Introduction to the Critical Study and Knowledge of the Holy Scriptures.* 5th ed. Vol. 4. Philadelphia: Desilver, 1833. 4 vols.

Joyce, James. *Stephen Hero.* 1944. Rev. ed. New York: New Directions, 1955.

Joyce, Stanislaus. *My Brother's Keeper: James Joyce's Early Years.* New York: Viking, 1958.

Kenner, Hugh. *Dublin's Joyce.* London: Chatto, 1955.

Langbaum, Robert. "The Epiphanic Mode in Wordsworth and Modern Literature." *The Word from Below: Essays on Modern Literature and Culture.* Madison: U of Wisconsin P, 1987. 33-57.

———. *The Poetry of Experience: The Dramatic Monologue in Modern Literary Tradition.* 1957. Chicago: U of Chicago P, 1985.

Levin, Harry. *James Joyce: A Critical Introduction.* 1941. Rev. ed. New York: New Directions, 1960.

Martin, Loy D. *Browning's Dramatic Monologues and the Post-Romantic Subject.* Baltimore: Johns Hopkins UP, 1985.

Nichols, Ashton. *The Poetics of Epiphany: Nineteenth-Century Origins of the Modern Literary Moment.* Tuscaloosa: U of Alabama P, 1987.

Nolan, Brian M. *The Royal Son of God: The Christology of Matthew 1-2 in the Setting of the Gospel.* Göttingen: Vandenhoeck, 1979.

Novum Testamentum Graece. Ed. Alexander Souter. Oxford: Clarendon, 1910.

Patte, Daniel. *The Gospel according to Matthew: A Structural Commentary on Matthew's Faith.* Philadelphia: Fortress, 1987.

Posnock, Ross. *Henry James and the Problem of Robert Browning.* Athens: U of Georgia P, 1985.

Pound, Ezra. *Personae.* New York: New Directions, 1926.

Prabhu, George M. Soares. *The Formula Quotations in the Infancy Narrative of Matthew.* Rome: Biblical Inst., 1976.

Ricoeur, Paul. *The Symbolism of Evil.* Trans. Emerson Buchanan. New York: Harper, 1967.

Strauss, David Friedrich. *The Life of Jesus.* 4th ed. Trans. Marian Evans. Vol. 1. London: Chapman, 1846. 3 vols.

Sumner, John Bird. *Practical Exposition of the Gospels of St. Matthew and St. Mark.* London: Hatchard, 1838.

Trench, R. C. *The Star of the Wise Men: Being a Commentary on the Second Chapter of St. Matthew.* Philadelphia: Hooker, 1850.

Tucker, Herbert F. "Dramatic Monologue and the Overhearing of Lyric." *Lyric Poetry: Beyond New Criticism.* Ed. Chaviva Hošek and Patricia Parker. Ithaca: Cornell UP, 1985. 226-43.

Walzl, Florence L. "The Liturgy of the Epiphany Season and the Epiphanies of Joyce." *PMLA* 80 (1965): 436-50.

Weiskel, Thomas. *The Romantic Sublime: Studies in the Structure and Psychology of Transcendence.* Baltimore: Johns Hopkins UP, 1976.

Whitla, William. *The Central Truth: The Incarnation in Robert Browning's Poetry.* Toronto: U of Toronto P, 1963.

Wordsworth, William. *Poetical Works.* Ed. Thomas Hutchinson. Rev. Ernest de Selincourt. London: Oxford UP, 1969.

Gertrude Reese Hudson (essay date 1992)

SOURCE: "Overview," in *Robert Browning's Literary Life: From First Work to Masterpiece,* Eakin Press, 1992, pp. 548-62.

[*In the following essay, Hudson reviews Browning's critical reputation from 1833 through 1870, arguing that Browning's critical acclaim was slow in coming because the poet's critics refused for many years to realize that his unique and innovative poetry could not be judged by conventional literary standards.*]

The basic elements that determined Browning's reputation from 1833 to 1870 were of course his professional activities and the opinions of critics and others. To these should be added certain significant movements in the intellectual and spiritual milieu that encouraged relaxation of conventional poetic standards by widening the scope of subjects thought to be suitable to poetry and by liberalizing the manner of treatment. This was beneficial to Browning in the fifties and sixties and helped him advance to his position of security by 1870. The complexities of his career, present from the first, can hardly be reduced to simple statements and easy generalizations.

With considerable struggle Browning and his critics persevered in different ways until his reputation was established. Over a long period of time and with difficulty critics learned that they could not judge Browning's works by traditional standards. Repeated exposure to his individual dramatic method, a shift in their opinion of what constituted the province of poetry, an increasing awareness of the totality of his achievement, and a recognition of the timeliness of his work—these contributed to the process of growing acceptance and appreciation. Very early in his career Browning became aware of the gap between himself and the critics, who represented the poetry-reading public. Feeling that he had a sacred duty to attain his place as a poet, he was determined to protect the central force of his creative genius and at the same time narrow the existing gap. He was sensitive to whatever would help or hinder the achievement of his desired goal.

The highlights of the broad canvas with many details indicate the character and direction of the efforts of both Browning and his critics. In Browning's exercise of his innovative genius, his workshop habits, and the performance of the critics during the first period of his literary life (which ended with the publication of the collected edition of 1849) lie the clues for understanding the gradual progress that led to wide recognition. Browning's readers were frustrated in the beginning by his experimenting with genres. To recognize his movement toward the best medium of expression for his individual talent they would have needed superior judgment, with the ability to see beyond the early period of misleading efforts.

The four works after the unacknowledged *Pauline* included two that partook of the character of drama but were different from each other *(Paracelsus* and *Pippa Passes),* one play *(Strafford)* that was performed, and a poem that was primarily narrative *(Sordello).* All of them bore the mark of his originality and all were difficult for the critics to understand. In his continuing experiments in the forties Browning wrote six more plays, which seemed to type him as a dramatist. His interest in internal states and changes rather than external action kept his plays from being successful on the stage, though he wrote four out of the six to be performed. Best suited to his genius were the innovative *Pippa Passes* and such short poems as those in *Dramatic Lyrics* and *Dramatic Romances and Lyrics.* Unfortunately these were overshadowed by the sheer volume of works less indicative of his future accomplishments. The critics would need considerable exposure to his poetry to see the direction of his efforts.

Although they were not capable of adequately appreciating the value of Browning's efforts, early critics observed that he was better than the rank and file of poets. His interest in man and human behavior and his dramatic ability were noted, and qualities of his poetry that were later to be repeatedly praised were pointed out—intellect, originality, and power (variously called force, energy, or strength). In this awareness lay the bare rudiments of a better understanding. Though they recognized his poetic ability, even when they did not approve of the work they were reviewing, critics could not see that what they considered praiseworthy was involved in what they attacked. They were unable to relate lines of criticism. They perceived that Browning had originality, but their deeply ingrained conservatism impelled them to feel that he should follow conventional rules of art and avoid unwholesome or otherwise unacceptable subject matter for poetry. To them he seemed little concerned about the obscurity of his verse. Why not make an effort to be clear, pleasing, and easy to read? Since the critics thought that Browning could be better, they often indulged in irritable accusations of wilfulness. In their faultfinding they occasionally had a glimmer of his individual techniques without seeing their significance. These were years of frustration for both Browning and his critics.

Browning had confidence in his instinctive creative force, and he wanted others to understand his intentions. In an effort to guide readers and encourage acceptance he wrote introductory comments for three of his early works, but they did not serve the purpose he had in mind. He had not yet won over many readers when he made repeated but unsuccessful attempts to write plays for the stage, which provided an opportunity for attracting wide attention. After reviewers (and Macready) made clear the qualities necessary for a play to succeed, Browning tried in *A Blot* and *Colombe's Birthday* to tailor his creative ideas to the demands of critics, who represented the tastes of the general public. In spite of his failures in poetry and drama he was tireless in his efforts to advance his art as well as his reputation.

Browning paid attention to what critics and others said of his work. He was fully aware of the influence of reviews. The helping hand of explanation that he apparently extended to friends who were critics was intended to prepare the way for a better understanding of his artistic aims. He watched for reviews anxiously and took to heart particularly the important ones. Though at times he demonstrated rather noisily his sensitiveness to the detrimental effect of a review, at other times in general remarks he showed tolerance for shortsighted criticism. He expressed gratefulness for favorable reviews, even showing a remarkable appreciation for those by friends who wrote sympathetically but in some respects showed deficiencies in judgment. Alert to suggestions of ways to gain an audience, he not only

attempted to adapt his own ideas to standard notions of playwriting; he also wrote short pieces at the suggestion of his publisher Moxon and acted upon Fox's criticisms in his review of *Pauline.* He heeded professional advice for the best time to publish, and he gave up the compact appearance of his works as in *Bells and Pomegranates,* which he personally favored, after critics as well as other readers called attention to the cramped, ill-printed pamphlets in the series.

He took criticism seriously, and even sought well-intentioned suggestions. In fact, in the early part of his career he leaned on his friends to a great extent, though he had difficulty in seeing the problems that his work presented to others. He turned to Fox, Fanny Haworth, Domett, and Harriet Martineau as well as to others and later to Elizabeth, sometimes pressing them for suggestions. Most disturbing was the obscurity of his writing. He repeatedly assured others that he was working to eliminate it. Clarity in expression of thought was the "whole problem" of the artist, he wrote Elizabeth. His works as well as the reviews, indicated that his efforts resulted in improvement.

Contrary to the impression that he occasionally left on critics and others that he produced his works rapidly and did little or no revision, Browning put forth much effort in planning, writing, and revising his works. There is evidence that he withheld certain works, sometimes for a considerable period, so that he could better revise them, and then he examined them in proof for further revision. The early habits which he formed as a part of his literary life continued except as they had to be modified because of changes in his situation.

At the end of Browning's first period he was not satisfied. He looked upon his past efforts as experience that would result in better poetry. With a fundamentally optimistic nature, Browning sometimes suffered states of dejection that gave place to confidence in the future. The artistic ego that had prompted him to talk to Macready of his eventual celebrity, of *Sordello* with "obstinate faith" in it, and of the wisdom of putting his plays on the stage enabled him to continue his work. As strong as his ego, was a sense of humility in his dedication and his dependence on others for help.

After choosing a subject and deciding upon a plan for treating it, Browning applied his great energy and creative force to the task in hand, even before completing one work looking ahead to possible subjects and different genres. His unyielding application was not in vain. By the later forties signs of a departure from the earlier hidebound critical approach to his poetry began to appear. Indications of better understanding in the reception of the second collection of shorter dramatic poems continued through the criticism of the collected edition. Browning had drawn on his varied intellectual resources and critics were beginning to be impressed by the versatility of his genius and his interest in dramatic portrayal of character. In looking back on his total production, most of them were able to see the dramatic quality that characterized both poetry and plays. Instead of condemning the plays as unfit for the stage they were considering them as closet drama.

Complaints of the unwholesome and immoral were still present, but it is noteworthy that in religious periodicals, which were giving increasing attention to Browning, complaints were replaced by a marked duality of opinion. In both the sectarian and the nonsectarian press there were objections to the immoral and degrading. There also arose, with the recognition of Browning's intellectual range and interests, an awareness of the high seriousness with which he dramatically presented variety in life. These more definite perceptions of the qualities of Browning's poetry gave evidence of some attempt at drawing together hitherto separate lines of criticism with, in a few instances, clear and definite relations of lines. When the collected edition was published in 1849, the long poems, **Pippa Passes,** and the plays attracted most attention because they occupied the bulk of the two volumes. Since the shorter poems occupied less space the impression was given that they were of minor importance and hence they did not receive the recognition that the reviews of **Dramatic Romances and Lyrics** had promised.

The limitations of the critics when they were faced with unconventional writing had often contributed to their irritability. By the later forties Browning's manner of writing was not as disturbing as it had formerly been. Faultfinding because of obscurity had decreased. In fact, there was either acceptance of his manner or less emphasis on its shortcomings as attention was directed to the dramatic method and the subject matter. This and a very positive effort on the part of a few critics to explain the individuality of Browning's style and to persuade others that his poetry was worth the exertion needed to read it foreshadowed a critical position of the fifties and sixties.

The attitude of the critics toward Browning in the later forties seemed to predict an advance in the understanding of his genius upon the appearance of his next work. But instead of continuing his experiments with the dramatic revelation of character, which the critics had begun to appreciate, Browning, now living in Italy, wrote **Christmas-Eve and Easter-Day** (1850), which dealt with contemporary religious beliefs in a poem unlike any he had previously written. There was an outcry in the first of the reviews against the grotesque element and Hudibrastic style as unbefitting a religious poem. Passage of time could bring better understanding of a work of Browning's, as in the case of **Pippa Passes,** and now there was a shift in the appraisal after the major weeklies (with the exception of the *Examiner*) railed against **Christmas-Eve and Easter-Day.** In

the second month after publication, criticism of the style weakened as approval of the religious import began to appear in denominational periodicals, which had already given signs of seeing Browning as a poet of high seriousness. This shift in emphasis led to the view that Browning was a religious poet, which did much to shape his reputation. The realization that Browning, an intellectual poet, was concerned with contemporary religious questions took root in the fifties, when old beliefs of the Victorians were already being questioned.

In **Men and Women** (1855) Browning reverted to the mode of dramatic poetry that he had initiated in **Dramatic Lyrics** (1842) and continued in **Dramatic Romances and Lyrics** (1845). Instead of profiting by the gains which they had made in the late forties, many critics were overpowered by the wealth and number of original poems in the two volumes of 1855. Some were completely blind to the value of the great dramatic poems in this collection, and they as well as others who had a glimmer of light were so vociferous and querulous in their objections primarily to the style that it is difficult to see the progress that was in fact taking place. A cursory look at the reviews can easily result in a sweeping condemnation of the critics.

A more thorough examination shows that the lines of criticism favorable to Browning that began to emerge in the late forties, as well as new ones, received support in the fifties—even in the confusion, contradictions, and struggles that were present. These prepared the way for the effectiveness of critical appraisal in the sixties. Browning's employment of his wide range of knowledge and interest in the varied experience of man as shown by his dramatic revelation of character was impressive, and some critics called attention to his manner of projecting himself into the mind of the characters. The more liberal tolerance of different kinds of knowledge, characters, and mental states, especially those traditionally considered not fit for poetry, resulted in part from seeing Browning not only as an intellectual but also as a religious poet. Recognition of him as a poet of high intent went hand in hand with an awareness of the relevance of his poetry to the religious movements and spirit of his day, an awareness that had followed the publication of **Christmas-Eve and Easter-Day.** The critics' changing attitude toward remote and unusual subject matter was noticeable in their discussions of poems with moral or religious significance and of other poems as well.

The conventional attitude toward Browning's style that characterized many earlier reviews and a number of reviews of **Men and Women** was giving way in the more perceptive reviews. This was especially demonstrated in the discussion of obscurity. The discriminating critics spoke out in defense of Browning on that score, with the implication that too much emphasis had been placed on it. Though their understanding of his technique was limited, especially in the dramatic lyric, they appreciated the blank verse of his great dramatic monologues and a few seemed to realize that his poetry was not to be judged by ordinary standards. Objective and poised criticism characterized these reviews, which made up more than a third of the total number dealing with *Men and Women.* Other critics were querulous in a confusion of praise and blame while attempting to understand Browning, whose genius they recognized without clearly comprehending it. Guided by preconceived notions of poetry, the remaining were completely blind to Browning's merits and were blatantly impatient.

Browning could not see that the encouraging notes foreshadowed the advancements to be made in the sixties. What he did see was that the poems he and others had justifiably thought would bring recognition were received with much irritable condemnation. He wrote his publisher in strong language to express his anger with critics, who he thought were threatening his financial and professional success. As a result of the greatest professional disappointment of his life, Browning felt the futility of further attempts. Earlier he had been able to continue his efforts in spite of poor reception; now he wrote little and that little he pushed aside.

On his return to England after Elizabeth's death in 1861, following his fifteen years of married life in Italy, Browning ended his long period of nonproductivity as he again took up old professional habits. Following the earlier trials and errors in his attempts to gain an audience, the first publications could not have been better planned and presented as a means of advancing his reputation. The *Selections* (1863), arranged by friends to attract readers, and his *Poetical Works* (1863), published volume by volume with his most distinctive works first to emphasize their importance, achieved the desired effect. Browning further advanced and secured his reputation when he published two new works, successful because of their contemporary relevance and their position in the sequence of his works—*Dramatis Personae* (1864) and *The Ring and the Book* (1868-9).

After the publication of the *Poetical Works* and *Dramatis Personae* a new note appeared in the reviews. The critics were aware that Browning had gained sufficient recognition from readers to warrant the republication of his works and a second edition of *Dramatis Personae.* No longer, as after the publication of *Selections* (1863), did critics need to fear that readers failed to share their high opinion of Browning. The deterrent to their assertive recommendation was removed. There was another sign of forward-moving independence. Critics had already reproached other critics for their damagings reviews: in the forties blame was incidental and after the

publication of *Men and Women* it was more noticeable, usually either general or clearly directed against specific but unidentified reviews. After *Dramatis Personae* there were pronounced attacks. No less than four on the *Edinburgh Review* appeared, all effective in discrediting the identified offender.

Browning had not advanced in one area. His dramatic lyric failed to gain approval. He had first used the conventional lyric (in *Paracelsus*) as the result of Fox's advice. Later appeared the lyric that bore the stamp of his originality, but critics were too much blinded by their own traditional notion to accept Browning's individuality. Outspoken criticism began in the fifties and continued in the sixties. Except when they were discussing lyrics, the critics had grown less severe in their objections to style. In fact, there were encouraging signs in the reviews of the *Poetical Works* and *Dramatis Personae.* Among them was the continuation of recognition (which had appeared from time to time) that Browning's verse harmonized with the intended effect, that it could not be judged independently of the thought. Irritability had weakened as acceptance increased. Obscurity was no longer a main target. The attacks on it that had started with *Sordello* had lost force. When critics began opening their eyes in the forties, they realized that *Sordello* was not to be summarily rejected and in the sixties they discussed it on a new level.

The critics' opinion of what Browning said and how he said it should be examined with reference to the Victorian frame of thought. In the early sixties religious beliefs were being questioned in a climate of uncertainty. The second edition of *Dramatis Personae* was called for largely because of the attraction to the emphatic moral and religious pertinence of Browning's poetry. Changes in the intellectual milieu, such as the questioning of old assumptions and the appearance of new interests, contributed to the relaxing of hidebound standards of literary evaluation. Unusual or peculiar subjects, psychological probing, stylistic traits that made the poetry difficult—the general acceptance of these attested to the increasing appreciation of the range and employment of Browning's genius and at the same time to the intellectual forces at work. With more freedom in thinking came the acceptance of realism and the grotesque for serious purposes—both earlier denounced. The various dramatic presentations of a broad perspective of human behavior was welcome. Browning's projecting his mind into that of the characters provided not only the intellectual quality for better character revelation; it also allowed acceptable moral and spiritual values to emerge. In support of faith, the dramatic method was more effective than the subjective approach, said several critics of *Dramatis Personae.*

With *Dramatis Personae* out of the way and well received, Browning directed his energy to the great poem that he could now write and critics could appreciate. In

The Ring and the Book he turned the account of a murder, abhorrent in itself and remote in time and place, into an epic of human behavior with profound thought such as appealed to the Englishman of the time. He translated experience into moral and spiritual truths by going beyond the single monologue, which had already gained approval, to a series of related ones. The result was compatible with critical values, which had been undergoing changes not only as the result of the uprooting of settled religious beliefs and the search for new footings but also as the result of the shifting away from insularity, the intellectual stir in the study of history, and interest in the importance and complexities of the individual.

The general habits of thinking, expansive in the search for new outlooks, had already been reflected in the more liberal critical position. Browning had employed the ruminations of a brute in *Caliban* and the roguery of an imposter in *Mr. Sludge* to point up matters of contemporary moral and spiritual concern of special importance to Victorians. In *The Ring and the Book* he turned to a Roman murder story. Now instead of expressing a desire for a simple subject and inoffensive elementary human emotions for the sake of mere pleasure in reading as in earlier years, the great majority of critics did not object to the sordid story. It was the use made of the subject that had become the test for value, and the use of it involved the interrelation of the various aspects of Browning's poetry that critics had once considered separately. The continuing process of merging lines of criticism prompted them to see the whole of the poem in a better light.

Changing habits of thinking were further reflected in the criticism of Browning's manner of writing in *The Ring and the Book.* The earlier frequent cry, "We want poetry that is easy to read," challenged by relatively few, was now subdued. At first Browning's poetry had been considered too difficult; then appeared the notion that the poetry was difficult but worth the effort required for understanding it; then out of the new intellectual movements grew attitudes that further modified the early complaint. In the intellectual climate readers desired meaningful poetry, and many preferred poetry that brought before them serious topics in such a way as to exercise their thinking. The preference was for dramatic poetry, which—unlike subjective poetry with its restriction to the thought and feeling of the writer—extended to a great variety of human experiences. The process of analyzing the working of the mind of man in the totality of life—seeing reality as related to the ideal, the earthly to the divine—was welcome in a time when questions were being asked and values weighed.

That Browning was not completely orthodox and did not impose his judgments didactically upon his readers appealed to those who wanted the benefit of his thought but also the chance at the same time to follow through the process of arriving at a belief, an opinion, or a judgment. Critics of various faiths or no faith at all were receptive to Browning's poetry. They saw that searching for the truth and arriving at personal convictions was important. Browning's stress on the value of individualism was appropriate in a time when many had lost faith in orthodoxy. The shaping of his source material in *The Ring and the Book* made a special appeal; readers were involved in the conflicting evidence in the search for truth just as they were involved in the conflict of new knowledge and old convictions in their search for a solution to their problems in a changing world.

Critics were more interested in what Browning said in *The Ring and the Book* and the way he approached his subject than in his poetic line. In chiefly the unfavorable reviews there were severe complaints about the verse. In the rest there was, relatively speaking, a modicum of faultfinding, which was well controlled. In fact, what stands out in the criticism is that instead of isolating and exaggerating the faults the critics stressed the greatness of the poem. They had arrived at an attitude that Browning, in a letter to Isa Blagden had advocated for critics: "animadverting, if you please, on any blemishes, but doing justice on the whole to the real worth there."

Pertinent to the evaluation of a review was the character of the periodical in which it appeared—its life span, kind and extent of audience, and periodicity. Besides the value of each review according to the character of the periodical, important in a study of Browning's reputation is the effect of reviews in certain groups of periodicals. The first group consisted of weeklies falling between 1833 and 1845. The majority of reviews of Browning's works were published in them and they were generally unfavorable. To some extent the value of a review in a weekly was its immediacy after publication, but to prepare a review of Browning's poetry on short notice meant that the critic did not have enough time to cope with difficult and original writing. Most of the reviews in weeklies that were favorable as well as other receptive ones in nonweeklies were written by men who moved in Browning's social-professional circles, some of them close friends to whom he probably talked of his poetry.

The second significant group was composed of reviews in the sectarian periodicals of the late forties and the fifties. The nonweekly periodicals increased in number in the late forties, and among them were sectarian periodicals whose critics turned their attention to Browning as a poet of high seriousness. Then after *Christmas-Eve and Easter-Day* they saw him as a poet interested in religious beliefs. This awareness was significant because it gave direction to Browning's reputation.

Changes taking place in the multiplicity of periodicals of the sixties influenced the reception of Browning's poetry. For the first time he benefited by reviews in weeklies. Two of the long established weeklies that had formerly disapproved of him and ones reviewing him for the first time placed their stamp of approval on his works. Some of these commanded a wide readership, either general or literary, and others appealed to restricted audiences of different kinds. The most significant change came in reviews in monthlies making their first appearance. These monthlies manifested a lively interest in varied aspects of Victorian life and appealed to readers who were capable of appreciating Browning.

He profited by the high caliber of many critics of the sixties. In the widening vistas of thought, intellectual and openminded men were attracted to critical expression, including reviewing. Generally the critics of Browning no longer felt subservient to restrictive principles. Besides those who were receptive to new standards, though in some respects timidly rejecting the old, there were those who by virtue of training or profession (some were recognized in fields other than literature) had little difficulty in following their own critical dictates. The practice of signing articles, as it came into increasing use, was beneficial to Browning; his poetry had a head start when reviews favorable to him were signed by men from various areas of thinking whose names carried weight.

It is instructive to set the opinions of professional critics against the opinions of those who did not review Browning in the course of earning their livelihood. On the negative side they both denounced or lamented the obscurity and difficulty of his verse. Agreement existed in the praise of Browning's thought, originality, strength, and interest in human behavior and also in the conclusion that whatever might be the faults of **The Ring and the Book** its greatness assured Browning's place as a foremost poet. Some of both groups wished to serve as explicators and thus convince others that the poetry was worth the effort required to understand it. In both groups there were enthusiastic readers who, being members of the younger generation, welcomed Browning's individuality for its fresh departure from the conventionally acceptable. Two differences stand out. The irritable faultfinding that was prominent in the negative and unsympathetic reviews was the exception in the comments of the nonprofessionals who did not like Browning's poetry. The complaint of Browning's immorality and unwholesomeness was absent from private assessments, but it often appeared in the earlier professional criticism, which was influenced by public opinion. Taken all in all, there was considerable agreement between the professional and nonprofessional attitude toward Browning's poetry.

After Browning's early period of experimentation, criticism by both reviewers and friends continued to play an important part in his life. He turned to Fox,

Lytton, Kenyon, and Milsand for criticism of **Men and Women.** The surviving acknowledgments of his comments to Kenyon and other friends indicated that the most frequent complaints had to do with obscurity and difficulty. Since he could not escape the fact that his readers did have trouble, throughout his life he assured his friends that he made an effort to improve. There were times when he defended his manner of writing, but knowing that his friends had his interests at heart he was not indignant as he often was when he thought professionals were severe or obtuse.

Although after the forties Browning did not so openly show his desire to have his works reviewed—even to the point of soliciting reviews in earlier years—his letters to Conway indicated his willingness to help smooth a reviewer's path. After the publication of a work of his he continued to watch for reviews; that he felt their power is shown by his tenseness during the waiting period and his remarks after their appearance. When one was expected in an influential periodical and was delayed or did not appear at all he could be unduly disturbed. He was sometimes inclined to strike out against a critic who abused or misunderstood the work under consideration. His early frustration might be overcome temporarily and then, after going underground, reappear when activated by some reminder; harbored feelings gathered force and then erupted into an exaggerated account of what he considered an unfair or unjust reception. Unfortunately after the passage of years he could easily mix facts and fancies in defending his poetry. Throughout his life discordant notes tended to accompany the recall of a disappointing reception of one of his early efforts. Browning's reactions are best explained in the light of his strong impulse to foster his works and resist impediments to their acceptance.

Browning greatly appreciated those reviews that were written to further his cause and readily and generously gave credit where it was due. Long after the deed itself he was not forgetful of what others had done in his behalf. He acknowledged indebtiness to them in various ways and told others of the help he had received. A response that should be brought out as well as his gratefulness was his recognition, in the face of critical misunderstanding and inadequacy, of the difficult task of sympathetically inclined critics who could not, in a limited time, see his works as a whole. He also knew that they were sometimes subject to an editor who would diminish their degree of appreciation or otherwise alter their text for the worse. To his credit Browning maintained a high regard for Macready and Carlyle, who he felt had failed him professionally; he was capable of divorcing the lasting acute disappointment from the perpetrator of it, the professional pain from the friend.

Browning paid close attention to reviews and his consequent actions suggest their influence on him. He had turned from the confessional in **Pauline** after critics called attention to it and made changes in plays according to some of the complaints of his critics. He turned to contemporary English life in *Dramatis Personae* after objections to his use of the remote in time and place, especially Italy. The first part of *The Ring and the Book* was more than likely the consequence of repeated urging that to encourage ready understanding Browning should add an introductory explanation of what was to follow, and he said the simplicity of the story was an answer to the complaint of obscurity. His arrangements of the works in his collected editions of 1863 and 1868 were influenced by his desire to prevent critics from repeating mistaken evaluations made in the past and to guide them in the future. After the critics had difficulty as the result of coping in a limited time with the great wealth of subject matter and the individuality of poetic treatment in the two volumes of *Men and Women,* Browning published *Poetical Works* and *The Ring and the Book* in installments to allow time for understanding. And after being advised of the cramped effect of the pamphlet format of *Bells and Pomegranates* on his readers, he decided that the collection of 1868 should have six rather than fewer volumes, to make for easier reading and handling. Even after the failure of his early Prefaces, written to guide readers, he tried other means of forestalling misunderstanding, as in his lines at the end of *Christmas-Eve.*

Browning did not hesitate to talk of the means he used to attract readers. He talked to Allingham, Dante Gabriel Rossetti, George MacDonald, and others. During the years of his active professional life in England he talked with freedom of his writing and with enthusiasm for the finished product. He talked of his poetic life to one person or to a few in intimate gatherings in his ever-widening social life of the sixties. When serious discussion of his poetry was out of place, he was adept at making remarks to suit the occasion. Out of his social aplomb grew misconceptions of his attitude toward his works. A broad examination of his behavior shows that when communication was appropriate he did not hesitate to refer to his works, and he wrote to friends and sometimes to strangers of matters of importance to his poetry. He even went so far as to admit that socializing was beneficial to his writing.

In early years Browning revealed notions basic to his writing to Domett, Horne, Fanny Haworth, Macready, and Elizabeth, and later to Ruskin, Isa Blagden, W. W. Story, Julia Wedgwood, Kenyon, and Milsand as well as others. Besides stressing the importance of originality and clarity, he indicated his preference for conciseness and emphasized the worthiness of the study of the soul and the duty of the poet to teach, to advance truth, and to show evil as well as good in representing life and revealing spiritual insights. He admitted his sympathy with undesirable characters and his propensity for exploring dark corners of the soul. He talked of his aim to preserve the integrity of his art and of the responsibility of readers and audience. As a dramatic writer he talked of the degree of self-revelation that he sanctioned, of his principle of creating a central effect with subordinated details, and he called attention to the difference between the work of a dramatic poet and that of a narrative writer. He also indicated the change he had made in his prosody and his right to adapt verse to the rhythm of speech.

Both Browning and his critics, with frustration, confusion, and irritation throughout years of struggle, contributed to the gradual narrowing of the distance that lies between a great original poet and those who judge him. Browning followed and developed the bent of his creative impulse and observed critical response, and the critics by virtue of exposure and effort, supported by general changes in thinking, arrived at different standards of measurement. In *The Ring and the Book* Browning's genius—its integrity always safeguarded—reached a high level of expression, and his critics had attained a degree of appreciation that enabled them to recognize his achievement. Because of his confidence in his *daemon* and his determination to persevere, Browning produced poetry that in spirit and presentation contemporaries related to their time and in expression recognized as individual. He had attained a secure place as one of England's great poets.

Daniel Karlin (essay date 1993)

SOURCE: "Hatred's Double Face," in *Browning's Hatred,* Oxford at the Clarendon Press, 1993, pp. 169-92.

[*In the following essay, Karlin examines the binary oppositions in Browning's poetry, particularly the opposition between love and hate. Karlin asserts that the interplay between such contraries exists within all aspects of Browning's poetry and is especially fundamental to the poet's exploration of human relationships.*]

> Following Anaximander he [Heraclitus] conceived the universe as a ceaseless conflict of opposites regulated by an unchanging law, but he found in this law the proper object of understanding; it is the Logos which spans but could not exist without the cosmic process: 'people do not understand how what is at variance accords . . . with itself, an agreement in tension as with bow and lyre' . . . This Logos Heraclitus equated with transcendent wisdom and the elemental fire.
>
> (*Oxford Classical Dictionary,* 2nd edn., 1970)

> Without Contraries is no progression. Attraction and Repulsion, Reason and Energy, Love and Hate, are necessary to Human existence.
>
> (Blake)[1]

> the hateful siege
> Of contraries . . .
>
> (Milton)[2]

Browning's dualism has often been remarked upon. He is a writer obsessed as much as Blake (or Yeats, or Lawrence) with contraries, with binary opposites; and, like these writers, he sees such contraries as essential to human identity and behaviour, constitutive of each individual, of the relations between individuals, and of all the forms of social life. Contraries work through historical time (in the political struggle between progress and reaction, for example) and through personal time (in the moral conflicts that shape a life). It is not too much to say that Browning's poetry works, is driven by oppositions, at every level of structure, theme, and style. Sometimes these oppositions are enshrined in the titles of paired poems ("**Meeting at Night/Parting at Morning**", "**Love in a Life/Life in a Love**", "**One Way of Love/Another Way of Love**", "**Before/After**", etc.),[3] sometimes in the subtitles of individual works or volumes: *A Soul's Tragedy* ("**Part First, being what was called the Poetry of Chiappino's Life: and Part Second, its Prose**"), *Red Cotton Night-Cap Country* ("**Turf and Towers**"), and *Asolando* ("**Fancies and Facts**"). But more important than these formal gestures is the sense in which every Browning poem is oppositional in nature: both he and the characters he creates are seized with the passion of conflict and argument, whether with others or themselves. And these arguments come down to fundamental divisions, to radical and irreconcilable opposites: male and female, good and evil, soul and body; or at any rate to divisions that *seem* fundamental, to opposites that *start out* as fixed and unalterable, for the same poem which begins by taking them for granted may end up by calling them into question.

The opposition between love and hate, as I pointed out in the previous chapter, is among the most basic of all in Browning's work. Its importance can be measured by the frequency with which the two terms, or their cognates, are paired in single or adjoining lines. In the concordance I count at a glance over a hundred such pairings: take as an example the following, all from *The Ring and the Book:*

> Thus, two ways, does she love her love to the
>   end,
> And hate her hate,—death, hell is no such
>   price
> To pay for these,—lovers and haters hold.
>
>   (iv. 1473-5)

>   Too nakedly you hate
> Me whom you looked as if you loved once . . .
>
>   (v. 790-1)

> I am not ignorant,—know what I say,
> Declaring this is sought for hate, not love.
>
>   (vii. 805-6)

> 'Your husband dashes you against the stones;
> This man would place each fragment in a
>   shrine:
> You hate him, love your husband!
>
>   I returned,
> 'It is not'true I love my husband,—no,
> Nor hate this man.
>
>   (vii. 1160-5)[4]

> My babe nor was, nor is, nor yet shall be
> Count Guido Franceschini's child at all—
> Only his mother's, born of love not hate!
>
>   (vii. 1762-4)

> Give me my wife: how should I use my wife,
> Love her or hate her?
>
>   (xi. 961-2)

> What I call God's hand,—you, perhaps,—this
>   chance
> Of the true instinct of an old good man
> Who happens to hate darkness and love
>   light,—
>
>   (xii. 592-4)

All these examples have one thing in common: they assume an absolute and stable opposition between the two terms 'love' and 'hate', whatever *kind* of feeling or state these terms describe (in the first example sexual passion, in the second parental love, in the fifth spiritual symbolism, in the last moral allegiance). Duality is produced, of course, by division: the final example overtly alludes to the primary division of creation itself:

> And God said, Let there be light: and there was light. And God saw the light, that it was good: and God divided the light from the darkness. And God called the light Day, and the darkness he called Night. (Genesis 1: 3-5)

From this primary division all others flow: physical, metaphysical, moral. One of Browning's most extraordinary late poems, "**Pan and Luna**" (published in *Dramatic Idyls, Second Series,* 1880), itself a meditation on the duality of male and female, opens with a version of Genesis, in which the utter darkness of an Arcadian night abolishes the distinction between earth and sky ('the pines, / Mountains and vallies mingling made one mass / Of black with void black heaven', ll. 4-6), a distinction which is then restored, re-created by 'The naked Moon, full-orbed antagonist / Of night and dark' (ll. 20-1).

Such oppositions are productive—in the examples from *The Ring and the Book* productive of meaning, since without distinction the characters could not express ideas or emotions; productive of behaviour, too, since they lead to moral and other choices.[5] Oppositions play a dynamic and progressive role, as Bishop Blougram insists:

> No, when the fight begins within himself,
> A man's worth something. God stoops o'er his head,
> Satan looks up between his feet—both tug—
> He's left, himself, in the middle: the soul wakes
> And grows. Prolong that battle through his life!
> Never leave growing till the life to come!
>
> (ll. 693-8)

But the principle of division is not in itself a neutral one. It is light that God creates and finds good, not darkness; his division is also a judgement (as is the parable of the sheep and the goats, for that matter). In Blougram's tableau, after all, God is on top and Satan underneath (though with characteristic ambiguity God is stooping and Satan looking up). Christian dualism sets out to combat the Gnostic or Manichaean heresy that the principles of light and dark, good and evil are separate and equal forces, and of equal value in creation. Christian eschatology posits a struggle between opposites, but also, as Blougram acknowledges by alluding to 'the life to come', an apocalyptic end to the struggle, in which God triumphs over Satan, Heaven over Hell, the saved over the damned.

Even where the model is not explicitly Christian, it follows the same pattern: Juan, in *Fifine at the Fair,* imagines a progress of the soul towards ultimate truth whose prime requirement is that 'soul look up, not down, not hate but love, / As truth successively takes shape' (ll. 2172-3). In Carlyle's *Sartor Resartus* the 'Everlasting No' gives way to the 'Everlasting Yes': the dualistic division of the cosmos is ultimately progressive, as it operates both externally (in the political and social world) and within each individual. Moreover, Carlyle follows traditional Christian polemics (first formulated by Augustine, who drew on the work of Plotinus and other Neoplatonic sources) in his insistence that the negative side is all the time, however unwittingly and unwillingly, doing the work of the positive. When Teufelsdröckh is in the toils of negativity and doubt, 'perhaps at no era of his life was he more decisively the Servant of Goodness, the Servant of God' (chapter 7). Perhaps the fullest (if not the most straightforward) development of this idea in Browning comes in *Fifine at the Fair,* in Juan's vision of the carnival of souls: progressing from his initial impression of repulsive and apparently unredeemable evil, Juan comes to see that the vices of mankind are necessary and, indeed, praiseworthy:

> Are we not here to learn the good of peace through strife,
> Of love through hate, and reach knowledge by ignorance?
> Why, those are helps thereto, which late we eyed askance,
> And nicknamed unaware!
>
> (ll. 1768-71)

Following Augustinian logic, not only can the necessity of evil be demonstrated, but its very existence (as a substantive force in its own right) is called into question, since its operation is governed by divine providence, as part of an all-encompassing divine plan. In *Paradise Lost,* accordingly, when Satan raises himself from the burning lake he has only the illusion of heroic autonomy: in reality 'the will / And high permission of all-ruling heaven / Left him at large to his own dark designs' (i. 211-13), heaven's own design being to show 'How all his malice served but to bring forth / Infinite goodness' (ll. 216-17). It is this providential design of making hatred itself generate love which Adam perceives as his crowning consolation at the end of the poem:

> O goodness infinite, goodness immense!
> That all this good of evil shall produce,
> And evil turn to good; more wonderful
> Than that by which creation first brought forth
> Light out of darkness!
>
> (xii. 469-73)

According to this principle, one term of any pair is always subordinate to the other: light/dark, heat/cold, love/hate, each forms part of a vertical structure, a hierarchy of purpose and value. Good and evil co-operate, but only to produce good; equivalence of effort does not imply a balance in the outcome.

Browning's dualism is not, however, as orthodox or as optimistic as Milton's. Take, for example, its application to the political struggle between progressive and reactionary forces. Browning inherited from both Shelley and the tradition of radical Dissent a deep reverence for Milton's republicanism; but could anything be less Miltonic than Ogniben's emollient statement of the case in *A Soul's Tragedy?*

> you begin to perceive that, when all's done and said, both great parties in the state, the advocators of change in the present system of things, and the opponents of it, patriot and anti-patriot, are found working together for the common good, and that in the midst of their efforts for and against its progress, the world somehow or other still advances—to which result they contribute in equal proportions, those who spent their life in pushing it onward as those

who gave theirs to the business of pulling it back—now, if you found the world stand still between the opposite forces, and were glad, I should conceive you—but it steadily advances, you rejoice to see! (ii. 408-21)

What's wrong with this jovial view of things? Just what its tone suggests: that it is a burlesque, which the clever and manipulative papal legate is recommending to the political turncoat Chiappino as a means of justifying his betrayal of the popular revolution he has recently led, all the while intending to unmask him and restore the status quo. Ogniben offers Chiappino the argument that, since 'both great parties in the state' contribute equally to 'the common good', it doesn't matter which side he supports. Chiappino falls into the trap: he begins to slide into the comfortable position that good and evil not only co-operate with each other, but that in the course of their struggle they come to resemble each other, to turn into each other: 'the bitterest adversaries get to discover certain points of similarity between each other, common sympathies—do they not?' (ll. 433-5) Whereupon Ogniben pulls the rug from under him with sardonic relish:

> Ay, had the young David but sate first to dine on his cheeses with the Philistine, he had soon discovered an abundance of such common sympathies . . . but, for the sake of one broad antipathy that had existed from the beginning, David slung the stone, cut off the giant's head, made a spoil of it, and after ate his cheeses with the better appetite for all I can learn. My friend, as you, with a quickened eyesight, go on discovering much good on the worse side, remember that the same process should proportionably magnify and demonstrate to you the much more good on the better side . . . (ll. 436-50)[6]

So Ogniben would, after all, preserve the distinction between the two terms of every opposition, and if Chiappino had the wit to see it he would realize where the argument was leading. To support reform is honourable, and to support reaction is honourable; but to support both (or neither) is dishonourable, because it abolishes the moral distinction between them. The integrity of Chiappino's position is destroyed, and Ogniben will proceed with conscious irony to restore the 'present system of things'—not because he believes that reaction is superior to reform, but because Chiappino is a spurious reformer, a David who sits down to eat his cheeses with Goliath rather than holding to 'one broad antipathy that had existed from the beginning'.

Ogniben would agree with Blake that the reconciling of opposites is a treacherous ideal. In *The Marriage of Heaven and Hell*, Blake praises Christ for rejecting such a reconciliation. Referring to the division of humanity between the 'prolific' and the 'devouring', he writes:

> These two classes of men are always upon earth, & they should be enemies; whoever tries to reconcile them seeks to destroy existence.
>
> Religion is an endeavour to reconcile the two.
>
> Note. Jesus Christ did not wish to unite but to seperate them, as in the Parable of sheep and goats! & he says I came not to send Peace but a Sword.
>
> (plates 16-17)[7]

Where Ogniben would differ from Blake is in Blake's refusal to acknowledge hierarchy as well as difference. Blake cites the parable of the sheep and the goats without acknowledging that it relates to an eschatological division between the saved and the damned. Ogniben would argue that the Gnostic division of the world between equal, contending forces leads inevitably to the very reconciling which Blake purports to shun. Each is the mirror image of the other; each might as well be the other.

Sordello discovers (with, for a poet, an appropriate rhetorical flourish of parallelism and chiasmus) that the warring factions of the Guelfs and the Ghibellins are fundamentally identical, each degraded by self-interest and violence: 'men ranged with men, / And deed with deed, blaze, blood, with blood and blaze' (iv. 908-9). Or, in plainer language:

> Two parties take the world up, and allow
> No third, yet have one principle, subsist
> By the same method; whoso shall enlist
> With either, ranks with man's inveterate foes.
>
> (ll. 914-17)

Sordello tries to replace one dualism with another: instead of an illusory battle between two parties, one oppressive and the other liberal, there is a real battle between the two equally oppressive parties on the one hand, and the cause of mankind on the other. But this ideal dualism turns out to be itself illusory and impractical: setting up the cause of mankind outside existing conditions is either utopian foolishness or cowardly quietism, but in either case self-defeating. In the end, Sordello has to choose the less evil of the two existing parties, to convert equivalence (Guelf = Ghibellin) into hierarchy (Guelf > Ghibellin). He has to confer differing value where none apparently exists, or, more accurately, to perceive such value in a larger historical context. The Guelfs are part of the progressive movement of history, and must therefore be supported, even though their local behaviour is indistinguishable from that of their opponents. Moreover—like a supporter of Communism in the 1930s—Sordello confronts the unpalatable fact that the god of Humanity is worshipped with human sacrifice. For the sake of the future he must 'hate what Now [he] loved, / Love what [he] hated' (vi. 211-12). These human sympathies are in themselves aspects of a dualism, so that one opposition (between what is humanly lovable and hateful) has got tangled up with another (between what is politically good and bad).

Browning is both disturbed and exhilarated by the facility with which contraries can turn into each other, adopt each other's mask, employ each other's rhetoric. Seeking to express his unbounded admiration for Elizabeth Barrett's poetry, he wrote to her of a 'friend' who wanted to express his unbounded *dis*like of the efforts of 'a sonnet-writing somebody', and who was forced to coin 'a generous mintage of words to meet the sudden run on his epithets', from the simple 'bad, worse, worst' to 'worser, worserer, worserest . . . worster, worsterer, worsterest' and so on. At the end he commented: 'What an illustration of the law by which opposite ideas suggest opposite, and contrary images come together!' (Kintner: 11). Browning offers his homage to Elizabeth Barrett's 'affluent language' (as he called it in his first letter to her) by his own 'generous mintage of words', by sporting in the element of language for her delight and his own. The action of the 'law' is benign: love expresses itself by means of its contrary, with an added ingenuity, a spice of playfulness, as Aristophanes argues in *Aristophanes' Apology:*

> For come, concede me truth's in thing not
> word,
> Meaning not manner! Love smiles 'rogue' and
> 'wretch'
> When 'sweet' and 'dear' seem vapid; Hate
> adopts
> Love's 'sweet' and 'dear,' when 'rogue' and
> 'wretch' fall flat;
> Love, Hate—are truths, then, each in sense
> not sound.

> (ll. 2498-501)

But this attempt to divorce rhetoric from substance, to allow mobility in language without threatening the 'truths' that underlie it, can't be sustained either philosophically or practically. Meaning constantly threatens to collapse into manner: love represented by hate may be indistinguishable from hate itself (this is the argument Balaustion uses against Aristophanes himself).[8] In *Pippa Passes* the evil Lutwyche tells his enemy (or is it his beloved?) Jules that love and hate are 'the warders / Each of the other's borders' (ii. 168-9), and it is clear that in this relationship the very stability of the terms 'love' and 'hate' is in question.

In *The Ring and the Book,* Pompilia is threatened in Guido's house at Arezzo by just such a dissolving of categories, when Guido's brother (with Guido's connivance) tries to seduce her with 'love' which is 'worse than hate' (ii. 1291-2), a phrase which Pompilia herself repeats in her monologue, but modifies in her anxiety to separate name and thing: 'worse than husband's hate, I had to bear / The love,—soliciting to shame called love,— / Of his brother' (vii. 843-5). In such an atmosphere she pleads with her parents (in the letter which the sympathetic, but cowardly, friar agrees to write on her behalf but never sends):

> Even suppose you altered,—there's your hate,
> To ask for: hate of you two dearest ones
> I shall find liker love than love found here,
> If husbands love their wives. Take me away
> And hate me as you do the gnats and fleas,
> Even the scorpions!

> (vii. 1295-1300)

Pompilia's reflections extend back to her real mother, the prostitute who sold her to Violante Comparini: and here, too, she sees the conventional definitions cracking at the foundations:

> The rather do I understand her now,—
> From my experience of what hate calls
> love,—
> Much love might be in what their love called
> hate.

> (vii. 875-7)

Pompilia is striving to preserve the quality itself from the label which denominates it, since in her experience the labels have got mixed up. To Caponsacchi, no punishment for Guido seems more fitting than a nightmarish fusion of love and hate: in his fantasy of Guido's damnation he imagines him, 'at the doleful end' of hell, encountering and getting entangled with his soul-mate Judas Iscariot:

> The two are at one now! Let them love their
> love
> That bites and claws like hate, or hate their
> hate
> That mops and mows and makes as it were
> love!

> (vi. 1938-40)

The desire which underlies Caponsacchi's vision is for love and hate to be kept distinct, since an exchange of qualities threatens both their identity and the hierarchy of value in which they should be fixed. Caponsacchi cannot, in the nature of things, acknowledge that Guido's hatred is in any way *like* love, except as a perversion, a travesty. Even less can he acknowledge that such hatred might have an equal value in the moral universe, that it might be as truthful as love, that it might bear witness with the same integrity to a divine principle, a divine creativity (though Pompilia herself recognizes that hate is 'the truth' of Guido (vii. 1727)). He would agree with Browning's tiresome sage Ferishtah, who adjures his 'foolishest' student in **"A Pillar at Sebzevar"** to 'love the loveable':

'And what may be unloveable?'
                              'Why, hate!
If out of sand comes sand and nought but
    sand,
Affect not to be quaffing at mirage,
Nor nickname pain as pleasure.'

(ll. 116-19)

Again and again in Browning's writing this strenuous effort to maintain a division between absolutes proves unavailing. Ferishtah's injunction to love the lovable and hate the hateful is simplistic rather than simple. It cannot be obeyed, first because the energy which animates love and hate seems to come from the same source and to pour itself indifferently in either channel, and second because the opposition between the two terms is always on the point of collapse.

In **"A Forgiveness"**, the speaker wonders whether his wife might have been ready to admit her adultery because she was 'hungry for my hate . . . Eager to end an irksome lie, and taste / Our tingling true relation, hate embraced / By hate one naked moment' (ll. 62-5). This 'one naked moment' is no different in kind from the 'moment, one and infinite' of the lovers in **"By the Fire-Side"**. It turns out, as the speaker of **"A Forgiveness"** later realizes, that this was not what his wife had in mind at all: but he speaks truer than he knows, because hatred is indeed, in this instance, the mouthpiece of love. His wife declares:

I love him as I hate you. Kill me! Strike
At one blow both infinitudes alike
Out of existence—hate and love! Whence
    love?
That's safe inside my heart, nor will remove
For any searching of your steel, I think.
Whence hate? The secret lay on lip, at brink
Of speech, in one fierce tremble to escape,
At every form wherein your love took shape,
At each new provocation of your kiss.

(ll. 79-87)

The 'secret' couldn't be plainer, you would think: it reveals itself as an instinctive physical repulsion, similar to that which Pompilia, unlike the woman here, was never able to hide from Guido:

Deceive you for a second, if you may,
In presence of the child that so loves age,

Whose neck writhes, cords itself your kiss,
Whose hand you wring stark, rigid with
    despair!

(xi. 1017-20)

But later on in **"A Forgiveness"** the speaker's wife tells him that her outburst of sexual hatred had been a lie: that she had loved him all along, but had been jealous of his neglect of her. The 'love' she speaks of was indeed safe in her heart, but it was love for her husband, not her lover; the hatred she expressed was the inverse image of her desire for him. When the speaker hears this, he says:

                    your words retrieve
Importantly the past. No hate assumed
The mask of love at any time! There gloomed
A moment when love took hate's semblance,
    urged
By causes you declare; but love's self purged
Away a fancied wrong I did both loves
—Yours and my own: by no hate's help, it
    proves,
Purgation was attempted.

(ll. 354-61)

What matters to the speaker is the 'retrieval' of the past, the knowledge that his wife had concealed not her hatred of him but her love—that it was love masked as hate, and not hate masked as love, which motivated her actions. The hierarchy of love over hate reasserts itself, and allows the woman, in turn, to 'rise / High by how many a grade!' (ll. 361-2) in the speaker's estimation: his former contempt for her gives way to hatred, and hatred (after he has killed her) to love.[11]

But though the speaker may be relieved that his wife, like Bishop Blougram, had 'said true things but called them by wrong names', the reader may wonder whether it might not be put the other way round. The rhetoric of hatred in the poem—that of the speaker as well as his wife's—is more powerful and more convincing than the love of which it is supposed to be merely the disguise, and which we have to take on trust. The 'tingling true relation, hate embraced / By hate' has a stamp of Browningesque reality which the speaker's own hatefulness does nothing to diminish.

It is hard to keep separate the opposed terms of love and hate, to maintain them as 'pure' qualities in a hierarchy of value. At the very end of his visionary, deathbed speech, Paracelsus attempts to restore this hierarchy, to reinterpret his own bitter experience in terms of a Miltonic salvaging of good from evil, love from hate. But he cannot end there: he goes on in an attempt to resolve the duality itself, not by envisaging the eventual triumph of love over hate, but by finding a third term, a reconciling and 'temperate' state. He tells Festus that he learned from 'love's undoing', the tragedy of the poet Aprile's failure, 'the worth of love in man's estate, / And what proportion love should hold with power' (v. 841-3). Love, the desire for power, must always exceed the power actually available; the engine of human evolution is driven by *lack,* as human beings attempt to bridge (or leap) the gap between, to use Browning's own favourite terms, 'fancy' and 'fact', what can be imagined and what can be done. In Aprile's case, the gap had been too great: he failed, and perished, because love became an absolute for him; his desire to be a consummate artist overwhelmed his ability to be any sort of artist at all.

But Paracelsus does not fully understand the lesson of Aprile's fate. He is warned in time to engage with the world, to share some of his discoveries with mankind, and not to wait, like Aprile, for an ultimate revelation which will never come; but he preserves his vision of this ultimate revelation separate and intact, and despises those who cannot see beyond the immediate 'facts' to the consummate 'fancy':

> And thus, when men received with stupid
>   wonder
> My first revealings—would have worshipp'd
>   me— .
> And I despised and loathed their proffered
>   praise;
> When, with awaken'd eyes, they took revenge
> For past credulity in casting shame
> On my real knowledge—and I hated them—
> It was not strange I saw no good in man
>
> . . . . .
>
> In my own heart love had not been made wise
> To trace love's faint beginnings in mankind—
> To know even hate is but a mask of love's;
> To see a good in evil, and a hope
> In ill-success.
>
> . . . . .
>
> All this I knew not, and I fail'd; let men
> Regard me, and the poet dead long ago
> Who lov'd too rashly; and shape forth a third,
> And better temper'd spirit, warn'd by both;
> As from the over-radiant star too mad
> To drink the light-springs, beamless thence
>   itself—
> And the dark orb which borders the abyss,
> Ingulf'd in icy night, might have its course
> A temperate and equidistant world . . .

                                    (v. 849-80)

Paracelsus starts by suggesting that he ought to have overcome his hatred of mankind (for their ignorance

and malice towards him) by analogy with his own internal development. Just as he has been forced to acknowledge that perfection can only be attained by imperfect advances, so mankind's response to *him* was an imperfect, but not negative phenomenon: their hatred of him is a mask of love, in that their disappointment at his 'ill-success' measures the 'hope' they had of him. Seen in its right context, his rejection by mankind was not just inevitable, but cherishable.

Yet Paracelsus's vision does not culminate in this transformation of hate into love, or rather the subordination of hate into a means of love. What happens instead is that Paracelsus shifts his ground: he envisages a reconciling of opposites, and the production of a "'better temper'd spirit'. Although the opposition between Aprile and Paracelsus has been posed throughout the poem as that of 'Love' and 'Knowledge', Paracelsus's language here implies that it would be equally true to call it the opposition of love and hate, figured by a traditional imagery of heat and cold, light and dark, fire and ice, star and abyss.[12] Paracelsus's pursuit of knowledge has led him to hate and be hated, to the brink of 'the abyss, / Ingulf'd in icy night' (remember that in Dante's Inferno, it gets colder the lower down you go: and these are degrees of lovelessness, of distance from the divine 'love which moves the sun and the other stars'); Aprile's 'love', by contrast, acted like the gravitational pull of a black hole, absorbing creative energy into the ecstatic self, but giving nothing back. The notion of a 'temperate and equidistant world' between these two extremes is a way of evading an otherwise ineluctable dualism: for clearly the first solution, making hatred serve the purposes of love, is not tenable. Nor is the third term a transcendent and over-ruling force, such as that which operates in Wyatt's poem 'To cause accord':

> To cause accord or to agree
> Two contraries in one degree,
> And in one point, as seemeth me,
> To all man's wit it cannot be:
> It is impossible.
>
> . . . . .
>
> Yet Love, that all things doth subdue,
> Whose power there may no life eschew,
> Hath wrought in me that I may rue
> These miracles to be so true
> That are impossible.

Wyatt's 'Love' holds the opposition of contraries in a paradoxical suspension, so that the lover can both burn and freeze, live and die, but it does this by rhetorical *force majeure*. The 'better temper'd spirit' envisaged by Paracelsus is produced by an 'accord' of contraries some time in the future. And there lies the problem. It turns out, here and elsewhere in Browning, that the fusion of opposites is always being deferred to a future beyond the reach of the warring parties themselves. In his essay on Shelley, for example, the union of 'objective' and 'subjective' poetry is said to be theoretically possible, but also never to have occurred in practice:

> there [is no] reason why these two modes of poetic faculty may not issue hereafter from the same poet in successive perfect works, examples of which . . . we have hitherto possessed in distinct individuals only. A mere running-in of one faculty upon the other is, of course, the ordinary circumstance. Far more rarely it happens that either is found so decidedly prominent and superior, as to be pronounced comparatively pure: while of the perfect shield, with the gold and the silver side set up for all comers to challenge, there has as yet been no instance.[13]

Browning looks forward to two kinds of union between the contrary 'modes of poetic faculty', either their being jointly possessed by a single artist, who can produce purely objective or purely subjective works, or to their fusion in a single work, the 'perfect shield'. What he rejects is a false reconciliation, the 'mere running-in of one faculty upon the other', *con*fusion rather than fusion. But in any case it hasn't happened yet: it is a utopian fiction, similar to the one proposed by Balaustion in ***Aristophanes' Apology,*** and half-ironically accepted by her antagonist, of a poet who could reconcile the modes of comedy and tragedy:

> Had you, I dream . . .
>
> . . . . .
>
> Made Comedy and Tragedy combine,
> Prove some Both-yet-neither, all one bard,
> Euripides with Aristophanes
> Coöperant! this, reproducing Now
> As that gave Then existence: Life to-day,
> This, as that other—Life dead long ago!
> The mob decrees such feat no crown,
>   perchance,
> But—why call crowning the reward of quest?
> Tell him, my other poet,—where thou walk'st
> Some rarer world than e'er Ilissos washed!
>
> But dream goes idly in the air. To earth!
>
> (ll. 3430-45)

Aristophanes agrees with Balaustion as to the desirability of this 'Both-yet-neither', who can incorporate both the contemporary realism of comedy and the mythic truth of tragedy—and agrees with her as to its fancifulness:

> 　　　　　　as to your imaginary Third
> Who,—stationed (by mechanics past my
>   guess)
> So as to take in every side at once,
> And not successively,—may reconcile

> The High and Low in tragicomic verse,—
> He shall be hailed superior to us both
> When born—in the Tin-islands! Meantime,
>   here
> In bright Athenai, I contest the claim . . .
>
> (ll. 5134-41)[14]

Both Aristophanes and Balaustion deliberately bring themselves back 'to earth', to the here and now of 'bright Athenai', from the 'dream' of a reconciliation between contraries. We might say that the fulfilment of this dream, like Andrea del Sarto's heaven, is necessarily and beneficially out of reach: that the strife of contraries works towards a resolution which is perpetually deferred, and which thus guarantees continued progress—assuming, as Bishop Blougram does, such strife to be progressive in the first place. This idea depends, however, on each side of the opposition keeping its integrity, refusing, so to speak, to be influenced by the future. Aristophanes refuses to *try* to be 'the imaginary Third': 'Half-doing his work, leaving mine untouched , / That were the failure!' (ll. 5155-6).

It seems, then, that the very value of the 'temperate and equidistant world' foreseen by Paracelsus depends on the preservation of the radical opposition it is meant to resolve. Ten years after ***Paracelsus,*** Browning returned to the metaphor of fire and ice, once in a letter to Elizabeth Barrett (20 May 1845) and once in his play ***Luria*** (1846); and each time he did so in terms of *un*reconciled opposites. In ***Luria,*** Luria and his antagonist Braccio are emblems of love and hate: and Braccio claims that each has its function in the service of Florence to which both he and Luria are dedicated:

> Florence took up, turned all one way the soul
> Of Luria with its fires, and here he stands!
> She takes me out of all the world as him,
> Fixing my coldness till like ice it stays
> The fire! So, Braccio, Luria, which is best?
>
> (iii. 222-6)

Notice that Braccio specifically does not say that there is a 'temperate and equidistant' ground between himself and Luria, but that their conflict is governed by a Heraclitan 'Logos', a transcendent term, 'Florence'. In his letter to Elizabeth Barrett, Browning moves the conflict of ice and fire inside the psyche, so that identity itself becomes the transcendent term:

> To be grand in a simile, for every poor speck of a Vesuvius or a Stromboli in my microcosm there are huge layers of ice and pits of black cold water—and I make the most of my two or three fire-eyes, because I know by experience, alas, how these tend to extinction—and the ice grows & grows—still this last is true part of me, most characteristic part, *best* part perhaps, and I disown nothing—. (Kintner: 74)

Volcanoes are 'fire-eyes' because they resemble the Cyclops, the one-eyed artificers who, in classical mythology, labour in the forge of Vulcan, the god of fire, traditionally located beneath mount Aetna. The image generates as much light as heat, since the eye is the organ of perception (both physical and intellectual); together, light and fire make up an image of creativity, of sexual and artistic potency: we might say, an image of love. Against these 'fire-eyes' are set the 'huge layers of ice and pits of black cold water' which represent inhibition, impotence, hatred, and death. Moving the metaphorical ground from mythology to science, Browning then alludes to the theory that the earth was formed by processes of eruption and cooling, first advanced in James Hutton's *Theory of the Earth* (1795). He does so to emphasize that the forces of attraction and repulsion are equally 'natural', equally 'true' and 'characteristic' of his 'microcosm'; this microcosmic self is like 'Florence' in the passage from *Luria*, the 'Logos' which governs a strife of opposites. As Bishop Blougram puts it, man is 'left, himself, in the middle' of the struggle between God and Satan. The commas single out 'himself' like a spotlight: the self is the star of the show. Browning's letter gives the self an equally central role; but whereas Blougram, as I pointed out earlier, implicitly subscribes to the idea that God is also the director of the play, Browning's scientific metaphor implies the opposite: that, by a natural process, the divine fire 'tends to extinction' while 'the ice grows and grows'.[16] The self is bleakly neutral, certainly not allied to a transcendent and over-ruling value.

But Browning was unwilling to abandon the quest for such a value, for a 'Logos' which would govern the oppositions of human nature without collapsing them into each other. Yet this result perversely arises before the quester at every turn, as the Dark Tower arises before Childe Roland. At the end of his life, Sordello receives a final revelation, a 'closing-truth' which both sums up his experience and allows him to transcend it:

> he cast
> Himself quite thro' mere secondary states
> Of his soul's essence, little loves and hates,
> Into the mid vague yearnings overlaid
> By these; as who should pierce hill, plain,
>   grove, glade,
> And so into the very nucleus probe
> That first determined there exist a Globe:
> And as that's easiest half the globe dissolved,
> So seemed Sordello's closing-truth evolved
> In his flesh-half's break-up—the sudden swell
> Of his expanding soul showed Ill and Well,
> Sorrow and Joy, Beauty and Ugliness,
> Virtue and Vice, the Larger and the Less,
> All qualities, in fine, recorded here,
> Might be but Modes of Time and this one
>   Sphere,
> Urgent on these but not of force to bind
> As Time—Eternity, as Matter—Mind,

> If Mind, Eternity shall choose assert
> Their attributes within a Life . . .

> (vi. 456-74)[17]

All life's qualities are relative, defined only in relation to the conditions of human existence and identity, time, and matter; these conditions are 'urgent on' our life, that is they dictate its course, but are not 'of force to bind' what happens beyond their reach. The binary categories of human understanding collapse under the stress of an action which Browning represents as both radical, reaching to the 'very nucleus' of the world and the self, and transcendent, the self breaking through existing boundaries to a new kind of knowledge.

Sordello now sees his 'little loves and hates' as 'mere secondary states / Of his soul's essence', since that soul partakes (as do all human souls) of the absolute, the condition in which contraries are reconciled and the very principle of division is abolished. What he achieves is not absolute knowledge itself, but the projection of his self *into* 'vague yearnings', a state of desire whose object is the 'very nucleus' of life. What will this nucleus consist of? And what would happen to the self if it actually reached it? The 'probe/globe' rhyme takes us back to Book II of the poem, and to the platitudes of Naddo, Sordello's critic and hanger-on:

> Would you have your songs endure?
> Build on the human heart!—Why to be sure
> Yours is one sort of heart—but I mean theirs,
> Ours, every one's, the healthy heart one cares
> To build on! Central peace, mother of
>   strength,
> That's father of . . . nay, go yourself that
>   length,
> Ask those calm-hearted doers what they do
> When they have got their calm! Nay, is it true
> Fire rankles at the heart of every globe?
> Perhaps! But these are matters one may probe
> Too deeply for poetic purposes:
> Rather select a theory that . . . yes
> Laugh! what does that prove? . . . stations
>   you midway
> And saves some little o'er-refining.

> (ii. 798-810)[18]

Sordello is laughing at Naddo for offering a timid, compromised 'theory' of art, which rests in turn on a view of the self as stable and 'calm-hearted'. Naddo's language ('Central peace, mother of strength, / That's father of . . . ') may be clear as mud, but his argument is coherent enough: it can be found better expressed in Pope, not to mention Horace. His disagreement with Sordello can also be seen as a disagreement within Romanticism: Sordello defends Byronic individualism ('one sort of heart') against Naddo's espousal of Wordsworthian common humanity ('theirs, ours, every one's'). And true to his Byronic programme, Sordello sees not stability, but imbalance at the heart of the creative self. The word 'rankles' is especially sharp here: it is associated with an inward action of physical corruption or mental suffering, has no positive connotations that I can find in any dictionary,[19] and uncompromisingly expresses Sordello's belief that creative power is born of dissatisfaction and pain. Like the speaker of 'Two in the Campagna', he turns from 'Silence and passion, joy and peace' to ask the key question: 'Where does the fault lie? What the core / Of the wound, since wound must be?' (ll. 23, 39-40). To be stationed 'midway' is indeed to be saved the trouble of *ore refining,* of getting at what lies 'at the heart of every globe'. Alchemists (Browning's Paracelsus among them) believed that gold and other precious metals were deposits of fire:

> The centre-fire heaves underneath the earth,
> And the earth changes like a human face;
> The molten ore bursts up among the rocks—
> Winds into the stone's heart—outbranches
>   bright
> In hidden mines—

> (v. 638-42)

Might we say, then, that what Sordello is probing for at the end of his life is such a 'centre-fire', a hidden, volcanic source of energy and creation? Perhaps; but if the desire to reach this 'nucleus' is a desire for the intensest kind of life, it is also 'evolved' by, and directed towards, death.

The nearness of plenitude to nothingness is a philosophical commonplace, and a commonplace in Browning's poetry. 'What's come to perfection perishes', he writes in **"Old Pictures in Florence"** (l. 130); and in the idyllic landscape of **"Love Among the Ruins",** with its 'plenty and perfection . . . of grass', the bliss of sexual union is figured as annihilation:

> When I do come, she will speak not, she will
>   stand,
>   Either hand
> On my shoulder, give her eyes the first
>   embrace
>   Of my face,
> Ere we rush, ere we extinguish sight and
>   speech
>   Each on each.

> (ll. 67-72)

The extinction of sight and speech means the extinction of personality, of selfhood, of the capacity to discern and express *difference*. The closing of the eyes and stopping of the voice by a kiss reappear in the last lines of **"Now"** (published in *Asolando,* 1889): 'When ecstasy's utmost we clutch at the core / While cheeks burn, arms open, eyes shut and lips meet!' Here, moreover, the suppression of the lovers' personal identities in their 'moment eternal' of sexual bliss is figured by the grammatical suppression of the personal pronouns. Such a state of rapture, of the loss of self, is also a feature of the consummation of hatred in Browning's poems. In his first monologue in **The Ring and the Book,** Guido tells of his reaction when Violante Comparini opened the door of the villa:

> She the mock-mother, she that made the
>   match
> And married me to perdition, spring and
>   source
> O' the fire inside me that boiled up from heart
> To brain and hailed the Fury gave it birth,—
> Violante Comparini, she it was,
> With the old grin amid the wrinkles yet,
> Opened . . .
>
>   . . . . .
>
> Then was I rapt away by the impulse, one
> Immeasurable everlasting wave of a need
> To abolish that detested life.

> (v. 1651-63)

Guido's description of Violante as 'spring and source / O' the fire inside me' suggests that in abolishing her he is abolishing the principle of his own existence, the fire that rankles at the heart of his globe of self.

Hatred, like love, can precipitate the loss of self as well as the realization, the achievement of selfhood. In Part I of **Pippa Passes,** the murderer Sebald is drowned and reborn in the 'black, fiery sea' of his hatred (of Ottima, his accomplice, and of himself). Which is the 'true outcome', salvation or damnation? The poem doesn't tell. Similarly, at the end of his second monologue in **The Ring and the Book,** Guido defiantly refuses to 'unhate [his] hates': 'I use up my last strength to strike once more . . . ' (xi. 2399). Is he used up, or fulfilled? Perhaps the narrator, Browning, who follows hard on Guido's heels with the final book of the poem, can tell us:

> Here were the end, had anything an end:
> Thus, lit and launched, up and up roared and
>   soared
> A rocket, till the key o' the vault was
>   reached,
> And wide heaven held, a breathless
>   minute-space,
> In brilliant usurpature . . .
>
>   . . . . .
>
>   now decline must be.

> (xii. 1-8)

The phrase 'wide heaven' is Miltonic, and alerts us to the parallel between Guido and Satan, with his soaring ambition and 'immortal hate' (*Paradise Lost,* i. 107). But the difference is that, for a 'breathless minute-space', Guido's 'usurpature' of heaven succeeds. In **"Two in the Campagna"** the speaker has a similar upward-moving triumph, followed by a similar 'decline':

> I yearn upward—touch you close,
> Then stand away. I kiss your cheek,
> Catch your soul's warmth,—I pluck the rose,
> And love it more than tongue can speak—
> Then the good minute goes.

(ll. 46-50)

Just as Guido's 'usurpature' of heaven associates him with Satan, so the speaker's love associates him with divine rapture, with Dante's vision of the divine rose at the climax of the *Paradiso*. Dante, too, is able to grasp the full splendour of his vision only in a flash of perception, instantly followed by failure:

> la mia mente fu percossa
> da un fulgore, in che sua voglia venne.
> All' alta fantasia qui mancò possa;
> ma già volgeva il mio disiro e il *velle,*
> sì come rota ch' egualmente è mossa,
> l'amor che move il sole e l'altre stelle.

'(xxxiii. 140-5)[20]

It is the last qualifying *but* which is missing in **"Two in the Campagna"**: in Dante 'desire and will' are at one with divine love, even though consciousness fails to contain or express its fullness. Even Wordworth's sublime diminishment of Dante, at the end of 'A slumber did my spirit seal', where death and loss accomplish the work of love, and the great wheel of heaven is reduced to the inanimate movement of the earth ('No motion has she now, no force . . . Rolled round in earth's diurnal course')—even this is unavailable to Browning. The speaker of **"Two in the Campagna"** answers the speaker of **"Love Among the Ruins"** by refusing the rush to a death-like embrace, by 'standing away' from the kiss which seals up utterance; and he answers Sordello by refusing to 'cast / Himself quite thro' mere secondary states / Of his soul's essence', asserting instead the separation of the will from its object, the obstinate aloneness of the perceiving self and the grandeur of its negation: 'Only I discern— / Infinite passion, and the pain / Of finite hearts that yearn' (ll. 68-70). The lover's tragedy—or the hater's—is the writer's opportunity.

Notes

[1] *The Marriage of Heaven and Hell*, pl. 3.

[2] *Paradise Lost,* ix. 121-2.

[3] See Karlin 1981 for a discussion of Browning's paired poems.

[4] The first edition of *The Ring and the Book* (unusually for 19th-cent. verse) has line numbers, which I follow, and which count incomplete lines as wholes; hence 'I returned' counts here as l. 1163.

[5] In 'Pan and Luna' sexuality is produced by the division of light from dark, but in an odd, indirect, and disturbing way: the absolute contrast between the moon's brightness and the surrounding dark is figured as the moon's consciousness of nakedness, which impels her to take refuge in a cloud; the cloud turns out to be a disguise assumed by Pan.

[6] The 'cheeses' are those which David brought from his father Jesse as a present to the captain of the troop in which his older brothers were serving: see 1 Sam. 17.

[7] The spelling of 'separate' is authorial. The parable of the sheep and the goats is in Matt. 25: 31-46; 'I came not to send peace, but a sword' is in Matt. 10: 34.

[8] Browning may well have recalled Coleridge's lines at the end of *Christabel,* in which a father's love for his child is so intense 'that he at last / Must needs express his love's excess / With words of unmeant bitterness. / Perhaps 'tis pretty to force together / Thoughts so all unlike each other; / To mutter and mock a broken charm, / To dally with wrong that does no harm' (ll. 663-9). De Quincey quotes and comments on this passage in his 1839 essay on Wordsworth, agreeing that 'love in excess' is 'capable of prompting such appellations as that of "wretch" to the beloved objects' (p. 163). . . .

[11] I am not concerned here with the dramatic or psychological probability of this story, or indeed with its narrator's chilling and repugnant character, but with the specific terms of his response. . . .

[12] This imagery may be found in, for example, the poetry of courtly love, especially that of Petrarch and his imitators. Its origin is in Neoplatonic cosmology, which divided the elements and their qualities into the attractive (air, light, fire, warmth, lightness) and the repulsive (earth, dark, water, cold, heaviness).

[13] The essay was published in 1852 as the preface to a volume of Shelley's letters, which was withdrawn soon after publication when the letters were discovered to be forgeries; it is reprinted in Pettigrew and Collins: 1001-13. The passage quoted is on p. 1003.

[14] The 'Cassiterides' or 'Tin-islands' was the name given to Cornwall and the Scilly Islands in classical times, and here signifies (to the poem's readers) the

whole of Britain. The 'other poet' or 'imaginary Third' therefore 'really' arrived in time: he is Shakespeare, of whose 'mechanics' neither Balaustion nor Aristophanes can conceive. To them Shakespeare is a mythical projection; but it should be noted that, to Browning, Shakespeare was himself the type of the 'objective' poet, the supreme representative of one side of an opposition.

. . . .

[16] Since Browning goes on to speculate that the 'ice' might in fact be the 'best part' of his nature, it could be argued that Providence has rescued itself by an exchange of qualities between the two contraries; but this seems a desperate recourse to paradox.

[17] 'Mid' in l. 459 means 'midst of'; 'with' is understood after 'easiest' in l. 463, the sense being: 'And as this process [of probing into the nucleus] is easiest when the surface has been stripped away . . . '. The achievement of transcendental understanding is linked in both religious and philosophical tradition to the mind or soul freeing itself from the body.

[18] In l. 802, the sentence should be completed by something like 'the artist's works'; this is implied by what follows: 'nay, find out for yourself how full of energy are the works of those who are inwardly calm'. The passage is one of several prototypical dramatic monologues in *Sordello,* where the presence or utterance of an interlocutor (in this case Sordello himself) is inferred from what the speaker says.

[19] Dr Johnson is typically unequivocal: 'To fester; to breed corruption; to be inflamed in body or mind'.

[20] 'My mind was smitten by a flash wherein its will came to it. To the high fantasy here power failed; but already my desire and will were rolled—even as a wheel that moveth equally—by the Love that moves the sun and the other stars' (trans. Wicksteed, Temple Classics edn.).

John Woolford and Daniel Karlin (essay date 1996)

SOURCE: "Genre and Style," in *Robert Browning,* Longman Group Limited, 1996, pp. 38-73.

[In the following essay, Woolford and Karlin study Browning's use of the genre of dramatic monologue as well as elements of the poet's style. The critics argue that Browning's primary concern in his usage of dramatic monologue is the creation of dramatic speakers and situations. Additionally, Woolford and Karlin maintain that the style Browning employs is a vocal one—his poetry is meant to be spoken aloud—and

they define two distinct vocal styles in his poetry—a voice that "says" and a voice that "sings."]

Genre

Dramatic method

'O lyric Love!' begins one of the most famous passages of Browning's poetry, his invocation of EBB [Elizabeth Barrett Browning] in *The Ring and the Book.* But it is an unusual moment.[1] Browning is not a lyric poet. He never wrote an ode, disliked the sonnet-form, has a mere handful of solitary effusions or meditations.[2] **"Home-Thoughts, from Abroad"**, one of his best-known poems, is in this sense one of his least typical. His poetry is primarily dramatic: it consists of a few stage plays and a multitude of dramatic poems of one kind or another.[3] The titles of his shorter collections reflect this: ***Dramatic Lyrics, Dramatic Romances and Lyrics, Dramatis Personae, Dramatic Idyls.*** The most famous, ***Men and Women,*** does not have 'dramatic' in its title, but still implies a group of dramatic characters, a point which is made explicit in the 'extra' poem which concludes the volume, **"One Word More"**:

Love, you saw me gather men and women,
Live or dead or fashioned by my fancy,
Enter each and all, and use their service,
Speak from every mouth,—the speech, a
poem.

(ll. 129-32)[4]

The titles of individual poems often reflect this emphasis on character and dramatic speech: poems are named after their speakers (**"Fra Lippo Lippi"**, **"Andrea del Sarto,"** **"Cleon,"** **"Mr Sludge, 'the Medium'"**, **"Martin Relph"**), sometimes with a specific pointer to the dramatic situation (**"Soliloquy of the Spanish Cloister"**, **"Artemis Prologuizes"**, **"A Woman's Last Word"**, **"Any Wife to Any Husband"**, **"Bishop Blougram's Apology"**).[5] In **"A Light Woman"** Browning adopts a different tactic: the speaker reveals at the end that the person he has been confiding in is the poet himself:

Well, any how, here the story stays,
  So far at least as I understand;
And, Robert Browning, you writer of plays,
  Here's a subject made to your hand!

The poem cannot be 'Browning's', since it is spoken to him rather than by him. Indeed the text pretends not to be a poem at all, but a story told in conversation, which among other things illustrates the annoying habit that a writer's friends have of pressing their life-stories on him as suitable material; Browning's friend here hasn't even realised that Browning is no longer a 'writer of plays', having abandoned writing for the theatre ten years before.

Even when Browning declares that he is going to abjure the dramatic method for third-person narrative, as he does at the outset of **Sordello,** he cannot keep to the straight and narrow: the authorial voice keeps giving way to the voices of characters in the story or, even more significantly, splitting itself into more than one voice, staging a debate within the narrator-self which occupies half of book iii of the poem.[6] There are plenty of exciting stories in Browning, but most of them are told by participants and eye-witnesses, especially in his earlier work: "Count Gismond", "Incident of the French Camp", "How They Brought the Good News from Ghent to Aix", "The Flight of the Duchess", "Italy in England", "The Confessional", "The Glove", all dating from 1845 or before.[7] "Childe Roland to the Dark Tower Came" marks a crisis in this method, since Roland, who tells the story, ends up, like some of Edgar Allan Poe's narrators, in the apparently impossible position of surviving his own death in order to relate it. In later poems Browning experimented with narrative and dramatic frames: in "Clive" (**Dramatic Idyls, Second Series,** 1880), for example, the core of the poem is a story told by the great Lord Clive, but it is relayed, in a way which anticipates Conrad and Kipling, by an obscure acquaintance of Clive's, who is trying to justify to his son his own life's lack of adventure and achievement. But the greatest example of such framing is of course **The Ring and the Book,** ten of whose twelve books consist of monologues by participants in the story, while the first and last books comprise an authorial prologue and epilogue.[8]

Browning's dramatic method is varied, or rather he works with a number of dramatic methods; there is certainly no such thing as an archetypal dramatic monologue which dominates the field. The formal criteria for 'pure' dramatic monologue usually include the presence of an implied listener or interlocutor, a dramatic situation which is inferred from what the speaker says but not stated directly, and the poem beginning in the middle of its action. **"Andrea del Sarto",** for example, begins:

> But do not let us quarrel any more,
> No, my Lucrezia . . .

Immediately the reader picks up clues as to what is going on, and what has been going on before the beginning of a poem; Browning uses this technique in numerous poems, and he is especially fond of opening lines in which the speaker's desire to grab the listener's attention doubles as the poet's desire to grab the reader's; three poems open with the arresting word 'Stop':

> Stop playing, poet! may a brother speak?

> Stop, let me have the truth of that!

> Stop rowing![9]

All the features of 'pure' dramatic monologue occur many times in Browning's work, but a list of poems in which they all occur would comprise only a fraction of it. This fraction would admittedly contain some famous poems (**"My Last Duchess"**, **"Andrea del Sarto"**, and **"Mr Sludge, 'the Medium'"**, for example) but other, equally famous, poems would be left out: there is no implied listener in **"Childe Roland to the Dark Tower Came"**, the dramatic situation *is* stated in the opening lines of **"Caliban upon Setebos"** (rather clumsily, too, as though Browning couldn't trust his readers to work it out), and **"A Grammarian's Funeral"** opens with the start of a funeral procession and ends with its arrival at the cemetery. Even the commonest condition of all, that the poem should be *spoken,* is not universally fulfilled: **"An Epistle of Karshish"**, as its title implies, is a letter, and so is its companion-poem in **Men and Women** set in the early Christian period, **"Cleon; A Death in the Desert"** (**Dramatis Personae**) contains a long speech by St John, but it is a reported speech, transcribed in a parchment scroll.

The dramatic monologue cannot, then, be reduced to a set of generic rules; but it remains the case that Browning was principally concerned, as a poet, with the creation of dramatic speakers and dramatic situations. Many of his characters resemble him in this respect. Even where the speakers of poems are nominally alone, they often imagine an audience. The speaker of **"A Toccata of Galuppi's"** addresses the composer whose music he has been playing, as does the organist in **"Master Hugues of Saxe-Gotha"**; but these examples pale beside that of Prince Hohenstiel-Schwangau. When the poem of that name opens, the prince (a portrait of Napoleon III) is apparently in exile in London after the downfall of his political career. He tells the story of his life to a sympathising woman. Only when the poem nears its end (after nearly 2000 lines) do we learn that this whole scene has been a fantasy: the prince is on his own in his palace in Hohenstiel-Schwangau, his political career is not yet over, and he is in fact debating whether to send a certain letter which will decide his fate. But he could not bear to reason it out on his own. He had to project a time and place in which he could recast soliloquy as dramatic monologue. Similarly, when Bishop Blougram wants to discomfit his interlocutor, Gigadibs, he does so by constructing an imagined speech by Gigadibs, set at some point in the future:

> I well imagine you respect my place
> (Status, *entourage,* worldly circumstance)
> Quite to its value—very much indeed
> —Are up to the protesting eyes of you
> In pride at being seated here for once—
> You'll turn it to such capital account!

When somebody, through years and years to
   come,
Hints of the bishop,—names me—that's
   enough—
'Blougram? I knew him' (into it you slide)
'Dined with him once, a Corpus Christi Day,
All alone, we two—he's a clever man—
And after dinner,—why, the wine you
   know,—
Oh, there was wine, and good!—what with the
   wine . . .
'Faith, we began upon all sorts of talk!
He's no bad fellow, Blougram—he had seen
Something of mine he relished—some
   review—
He's quite above their humbug in his heart,
Half-said as much, indeed—the thing's his
   trade—
I warrant, Blougram's sceptical at times—
How otherwise? I liked him, I confess!'
Ché ch'é, my dear sir, as we say at Rome,
Don't you protest now! It's fair give and take;
You have had your turn and spoken your
   home-truths—
The hand's mine now, and here you follow
   suit.

                              (ll. 25-48)[10]

By projecting a monologue within his own monologue, Blougram gives Gigadibs a phantom voice
even as he effectively silences him on the occasion
of his own overbearing speech. It is a tactic which
fits Blougram's dramatic character, it matches the
combination of burly swagger and urbane irony with
which he treats Gigadibs throughout the poem, but
it is also compulsive on the *poet*'s part; that is,
Browning's poetry is filled with mimics, impersonat-
ors, ventriloquists, with characters whose speech
consists of putting words into other people's mouths,
for all the world as though they were poets or dramatists themselves. In **"Soliloquy of the Spanish Cloister"** the jealous monk satirises Brother Lawrence's
innocent prattle:

At the meal we sit together:
 Salve tibi! I must hear
Wise talk of the kind of weather,
 Sort of season, time of year:
*Not a plenteous cork-crop: scarcely
 Dare we hope oak-galls, I doubt:
 What's the Latin name for 'parsley'?*
What's the Greek name for Swine's Snout?

                              (ll. 9-16)

In *The Ring and the Book,* Guido is visited in his
death-cell by two old friends; he imagines them making capital of him after his execution:

I use my tongue: how glibly yours will run
At pleasant supper-time . . . God's curse! . . .
   to-night
When all the guests jump up, begin so brisk
'Welcome, his Eminence who shrived the
   wretch!
Now we shall have the Abate's story!'

                              (xi 138-42)

The thought of life continuing after his own death is
bound up for Guido with this social scene, with there
being speakers and storytellers. His antagonist, the
Pope, makes up his mind to confirm the death-sentence
after a monologue in which he 'listens' to other, imagined voices, some of which he allows their own dignity and integrity (the voice of Euripides, for example,
whose ghost challenges him from the classical past), others which he satirises and parodies, such as the collective
voice of civil society, the 'instinct of the world', which
demands that he spare Guido in the name of a false pity:

'Come, 'tis too much good breath we waste in
   words:
The pardon, Holy Father! Spare grimace,
Shrugs and reluctance! Are not we the world,
Bid thee, our Priam, let soft culture plead
Hecuba-like, *"non tali"* (Virgil serves)
"Auxilio", and the rest! Enough, it works!
The Pope relaxes, and the Prince is loth,
The father's bowels yearn, the man's will
   bends,
Reply is apt.'

                              (x 2084-92)

The Pope imagines himself bullied, patronised, and
taken for granted, but of course he has the last laugh:
Virgil will *not* serve here, after all. The quotation comes
from the *Aeneid:* as Troy falls, Hecuba persuades her
husband, the aged King Priam, not to go out to fight:
'It is not aid like that [non tali auxilio], nor any armed
defence, which is needed now' (ii 521-2). Priam would
do better, Hecuba says, to cling to the altar and hope
for mercy. It doesn't work: he's killed anyway. The
Pope imagines 'the world' casting him as this enfeebled,
weak-willed, and doomed old man, but by his very
imagining of its speech, he pre-empts it and demonstrates his own mastery. Unlike Priam, he still has the
authority and power to strike a blow; it is Guido who
clings to the altar and is not spared.

The tendency of Browning's characters to dramatize
the voices of others can make for a baffling complexity.[11] The most extreme example in a short poem is
"Dîs Aliter Visum" (*Dramatis Personae,* 1864). This
poem is spoken by a woman to a man who has just
informed her that, ten years before, he had been on the
point of proposing marriage to her, but had not done

so. Perhaps he uses the title phrase to her: 'to the gods it seemed otherwise', a tag from Virgil which is like a fatalistic shrug: 'it was not meant to be'; he is a famous and learned poet, after all. Her reaction is swift and bitter. It is not 'the gods'· who are to blame for missing an opportunity which might have proved their salvation, but his own emotional cowardice. She recalls not just the occasion, but what she now realises went through his mind as he hesitated and then failed to speak. Within *her* monologue, therefore, she projects *his* voice (the inner voice of his thoughts). But that is not all. The figure she projects—the man of ten years ago, debating within himself whether to ask her to marry him—is himself a dramatiser, who projects *her* voice, imagining what she would think if they did get married and it turned out badly; and, as though that were not enough . . . but here is the passage at its most complex:

'Then follows Paris and full time
 For both to reason: "Thus with us!"
She'll sigh, "Thus girls give body and soul
 At first word, think they gain the goal,
When 'tis the starting-place they climb!

' "My friend makes verse and gets renown;
 Have they all fifty years, his peers?
He knows the world, firm, quiet, and gay;
 Boys will become as much one day:
They're fools; he cheats, with beard less
  brown.

' "For boys say, *Love me or I die!*
 He did not say, *The truth is, youth
I want, who am old and know too much;
 I'd catch youth: lend me sight and touch!
Drop heart's blood where life's wheels grate
  dry!*

'While I should make rejoinder'—(then
 It was, no doubt, you ceased that least
Light pressure of my arm in yours)
 ' "I can conceive of cheaper cures
For a yawning-fit o'er books and men." '

(ll. 71-90)

She imagines him thinking that if they were to marry, they would both regret it (she because of his age, he because of her excessive emotional demands); the way she imagines him thinking this is by him imagining what she would say; and what she imagines him imagining her saying consists, in part, of her version of what *he* ought to have said had he been honest with her—at which point single and double quotation marks give out and the printers have to resort to italics. When the single quotation marks in l. 86 close and the parenthesis opens, it brings us back for a sharp instant to the 'present' in which the monologue is being spoken,

and to the woman who speaks it: she remembers how the pressure of his arm relaxed, but only now can she reconstruct the thoughts which influenced that small gesture and appreciate its fatefulness.

With **"Dîs Aliter Visum"** dramatic monologue reaches an apotheosis which is close to breakdown.[12] It is a sign that dramatic method, like civilisation, has its discontents. Browning had cultivated it since his earliest published poem, **Pauline,** but he did not do so with an express sense of pride or pleasure. On the contrary, he constantly described dramatic writing as *inferior* to lyric. Why should this have been so? The answer lies in the ideas about poetic creativity which govern Browning's work, ideas which, in turn, were generated by the pressure of his philosophical and political beliefs.[13]

So many Robert Brownings

Yet here comes one of those fatal ifs, the egoism of the man, and the pity of it. He cannot metempsychose with his creatures, they are so many Robert Brownings.

Eliza Flower's comment on **Pippa Passes** (cited Woolford and Karlin, ii, 17) is a familiar one in Browning criticism. Ruskin made exactly the same point, and about the same work, in a letter to Browning himself:

I entirely deny that a poet of your real dramatic power ought to let *himself* come up, as you constantly do, through all manner of characters, so that every now and then poor Pippa herself shall speak a long piece of Robert Browning. (Appendix B, pp. 255-6)

Ruskin's 'poor Pippa' puns on the idiom: poor Pippa to be forced to spout Browning, but especially so because Pippa is really, materially poor, a factory girl. The poet who asserted unequivocally that his poems were 'so many utterances of so many imaginary persons, not mine' ('Advertisement' to **Dramatic Lyrics,** 1842) stands accused of producing no more than 'so many Robert Brownings'. Compared to his vigorous rebuttals of Ruskin's other criticisms in this letter, Browning's reply on this point is curiously tentative:

The last charge I cannot answer, for you may be right in preferring it, however unwitting I am of the fact. I *may* put Robert Browning into Pippa and other men and maids. If so, *peccavi* [I have sinned]: but I don't see myself in them, at all events. (Appendix B, p. 258)

He was more robust with a later critic, Julia Wedgwood, though her criticism was more charitably expressed. She complained about a passage in **The Ring and the Book** which she found too learned for its speaker:

I should like to ask why you break down the dramatic framework so often in your characters? That passage about Justinian and the Pandects, for instance, is yours, and not Franceschini's. But you must have a distinct intention in this, and I can't help always enjoying it, it seems so characteristic of you—though it does seem to me an artistic defect. (Curle: 156)

Browning denied the particular charge and challenged Julia Wedgwood to substantiate the general one:

Why is the allusion to Justinian *mine* and not the man's I give it to? The whole of his speech, as I premise, is untrue—cant and cleverness . . . but he was quite able to cant, and also know something of the Pandects, which are the basis of actual Italian law. What are the other escapes from dramatic propriety into my own peculiar self—do tell me that! (p. 161)

But in one sense the charge is impossible to answer, because it is true: Julia Wedgwood is quite right to say that Guido's speech at this point is *characteristic,* in the sense that all Browning's characters sound like Browning; a Browning poem is instantly recognisable as itself, and for a writer with so much surface Browning is surprisingly hard to imitate. In **"Within a Budding Grove"**, Proust remarks of the painter, Elstir:

The particulars of life do not matter to the artist; they merely provide him with the opportunity to lay bare his genius. One feels unmistakably, when one sees side by side ten portraits of people painted by Elstir, that they are all, first and foremost, Elstirs. (Proust: i 910)

That Elstir is a fictitious painter makes the observation positively Browningesque; I imagine Browning enjoying the joke, but also taking it seriously. 'There they are, my fifty men and women', he tells EBB in 'One Word More'; there may be lots of them, but they are all *his:* 'Naming *me* the fifty poems finished' (ll. 1-2, my italics).[14] The multiplicity of Browning's characters are first and foremost characters in Browning; yet the multiplicity also matters, is in itself a formidable fact. There are two truths, then, about Browning's dramatic method, neither of which cancels the other out: that he is always himself, and that he is so in many guises: 'so many Robert Brownings'.

In his second letter to EBB, Browning was already keen to seize the low ground. 'Your poetry,' he declared, 'must be, cannot but be, infinitely more to me than mine to you' (13 Jan. 1845, Kelley: x 22). He was wrong, she replied:

Why shᵈ you deny the full measure of my delight & benefit from your writings? I could tell you why you should not. You have in your vision two worlds—or to use the language of the schools of the day, you are both subjective & objective in the

habits of your mind—You can deal both with abstract thought, & with human passion in the most passionate sense. (15 Jan. 1845, Kelley: x 26)

A month later, she repeated this praise of Browning's double vision, this time emphasising not subject matter but style:

You have taken a great range—from those high faint notes of the mystics which are beyond personality . . to dramatic impersonations, gruff with nature, 'gr-r- you swine' . . . (17 Feb. 1845, Kelley: x 79)[15]

The 'high faint notes of the mystics which are beyond personality' evidently belong to the 'subjective' world of 'abstract thought' while the 'dramatic impersonations, gruff with nature' belong to the 'objective' world of 'human passion'. Browning himself was later to deploy this opposition between subjective and objective poetry in the **Essay on Shelley,** but with a crucial variation in the meaning of the first term. In the **Essay,** the association of 'subjective' poetry with abstraction does not imply going 'beyond personality', but, on the contrary, the expression of pure personality, namely the poet's own:

Not with the combination of humanity in action, but with the primal elements of humanity he [the subjective poet] has to do; and he digs where he stands,—preferring to seek them in his own soul as the nearest reflex of that absolute Mind, according to the intuitions of which he desires to perceive and speak. . . . He is rather a seer, accordingly, than a fashioner, and what he produces will be less a work than an effluence. That effluence cannot be easily considered in abstraction from his personality,—being indeed the very radiance and aroma of his personality, projected from it but not separated. (Appendix A, p. 247)

Shelley, in Browning's view, was such a poet, and so was EBB; but he himself was not. In his letter to her of 13 January 1845, he goes on to explain why her poetry *must* mean more to him than his to her:

you *do* what I always wanted, hoped to do, and only seem now likely to do for the first time—you speak out, *you,*—I only make men & women speak,—give you truth broken into prismatic hues, and fear the pure white light, even if it is in me . . .

According to Browning, then, *all* his poetry consists of 'dramatic impersonations', including the 'high faint notes of the mystics'. None of it is the 'effluence' of his own personality, the 'pure white light' of self-consciousness; none of it is 'speaking out'. 'I never have begun, even, what I hope I was born to begin and end,—"R.B. a poem" ' (11 Feb. 1845, Kelley: x 69). EBB agreed: 'in fact, you have not written the R.B.

poem yet—your rays fall obliquely rather than directly straight' (17 Feb. 1845, Kelley: x 79).

The terms 'effluence', 'radiance' and 'pure white light' take us straight to the Platonic idea of knowledge or truth as *inwardly* generated which so influenced Browning's intellectual life. In Chapter 6 [of *Robert Browning*] we cite a passage of **Paracelsus** which directly bears on this point; and, as far as the opposition between dramatic and lyric forms is concerned, we can add the passage in his letter to EBB which immediately follows his declaration that he had not yet written 'R.B. a poem', and in which Browning describes the difficulty he feels he has in enabling his own 'imprison'd splendour' to 'dart forth':

> And, *next,* if I speak (and, God knows, feel) as if what you have read were sadly imperfect demonstrations of even mere ability, it is from no absurd vanity, tho' it might seem so—these scenes and song-scraps *are* such mere and very escapes of my inner power,—which lives in me like the light in those crazy Mediterranean phares I have watched at sea—wherein the light is ever revolving in a dark gallery, bright and alive, and only after a weary interval leaps out, for a moment, from the one narrow chink, and then goes on with the blind wall between it and you . . . the work has been *inside,* and not when, at stated times I held up my light to *you*—and, that there is no self-delusion here, I would prove to *you* . . . even by opening this desk I write on, and showing what stuff, in the way of wood, I *could* make a great bonfire with, if I might only knock the whole clumsy top off my tower! (11 Feb. 1845, Kelley: x 69-70)

The sense of imprisonment and frustration, of an almost physical bafflement, is palpable here; but there is also something odd about it, something which should alert us to a turn, a twist in the plot which the writer is unfolding. A lighthouse could not function with a steady, permanent beam; it would defeat the object, which is precisely to send out an intermittent, flashing signal. The conditions under which the light exists—the dark gallery, the weary interval, the narrow chink—are the only ones in which it can serve its purpose. And we should not forget what that purpose is: to illuminate, to warn, to save. These are not ignoble analogies for poetry.[16]

In the **Essay on Shelley** Browning wrote admiringly of Shelley's 'spheric poetical faculty', which had 'its own self-sufficing central light, radiating equally through immaturity and accomplishment, through many fragments and occasional completion' (Appendix A, p. 251). The word 'occasional' carries the sense of 'on occasion', but it can also mean 'accidental, not essential to the main purpose'. To perceive Shelley's greatness, in other words, is not to evaluate the works he actually produced, but to worship the 'self-sufficing central light' of his genius. The dualism fostered by Platonic thought, and expressed in the Gnostic divi-

sion of the cosmos into spiritual and material principles, results, when you apply it to poetry, in a contempt for actual poems (and the language of which they are composed), since these are the mere 'body' in which genius is forced reluctantly to clothe itself. But if genius, creative inspiration, 'radiate[s] equally through immaturity and accomplishment', why bother to accomplish anything at all?

The danger of poetic genius taking itself and its audience for granted can be articulated in the vocabulary of Platonic or Gnostic philosophy; it can also be articulated in another vocabulary equally close to Browning's experience, that of Protestant theology. Browning was well aware of extreme tendencies in Protestant thought: his father's library was filled with pamphlets, sermons, spiritual autobiographies, and histories of the religious controversies of the Reformation and beyond, which figure constantly in his work. One of his earliest dramatic monologues is spoken by a historical figure, Johannes Agricola, an early Protestant who founded the 'Antinomian' sect. Antinomianism is a perversely logical extension of Calvinist doctrine, and consists in the belief that the elect, those whom God has predestined for salvation, are exempt from the moral law: nothing they do or don't do can affect their ultimate salvation, since God has arbitrarily chosen them from all eternity. As Johannes says:

> I have God's warrant, could I blend
>   All hideous sins, as in a cup,—
> To drink the mingled venoms up,
> Secure my nature will convert
>   The draught to blossoming gladness fast . . .

(ll. 33-7)

However, Browning is not so interested in the licence which Johannes' theology gives him to commit sin without penalty, as in the malign consequences it has for his view of other people. In a passage of grotesque brilliance, Johannes imagines himself in heaven, 'smiled on, full fed / With unexhausted blessedness' (ll. 41-2), an infant eternally suckling but with a devil's relish:

> I gaze below on Hell's fierce bed,
>   And those its waves of flame oppress,
> Swarming in ghastly wretchedness,
> Whose life on earth aspired to be
>   One altar-smoke,—so pure!—to win
> If not love like God's love to me,
>   At least to keep his anger in . . .
> And all their striving turned to sin!
> Priest, doctor, hermit, monk grown white
>   With prayer: the broken-hearted nun,
> The martyr, the wan acolyte,
>   The incense-swinging child . . . undone
> Before God fashioned star or sun!

(ll. 43-55)

The damned are all, not surprisingly, Roman Catholic religious figures ('doctor' in l. 51 means 'doctor of the church', like Thomas Aquinas), but the point goes deeper than Johannes' local Protestant prejudice. His exalted belief in his own union with God has cut him off from humanity. Browning's satire on Antinominanism has a strong political edge: the poem was published in the *Monthly Repository* whose editor, Browning's 'literary father' W.J. Fox, was not only a Unitarian in religion but a radical in politics.[17] Egalitarian and democratic ideas, ideas of solidarity and community, depend crucially on empathy, on the willingness and ability to imagine other people. (This is especially true for those who, like Browning, come to such ideas from the privileged end of the social scale.) They also depend on the willingness to act, and to take responsibility for action. The 'striving' which Johannes scorns is one of Browning's talismanic words, summed up in the proverb he cites in the **"Epilogue"** to *Asolando,* 'Strive and thrive'.[18] But Johannes conceives of himself as blessed with divine inertia, divine irresponsibility:

> I lie—where I have always lain,
>   God smiles—as he has always smiled;—
> Ere suns and moons could wax and wane,
>   Ere stars were thundergirt, or piled
> The heavens . . . God thought on me his
>   child,
> Ordained a life for me—arrayed
>   Its circumstances, every one
> To the minutest . . .
>
>   (ll. 11-18)

This stasis of spirit, where nothing can 'wax and wane', where even the most majestic acts of creation are irrelevant, figures a poetry of utter self-absorption. Johannes is blazing away all right, without weary intervals or narrow chinks, but his 'self-sufficing central light' is, to use Milton's phrase, 'no light, but rather darkness visible'. Not surprisingly, therefore, Johannes is not speaking to anyone, except himself: he is his own dramatised listener.[19] Fear of becoming like Johannes, it might be argued, keeps Browning a dramatic poet, prevents him from yielding to the lyric self-expression he praised in the poetry of Shelley, of Tennyson, and of his wife. In the invocation to EBB from which I quoted at the beginning of this chapter, Browning pays his most intense and moving tribute to the faculty from which he had consciously alienated himself, but he makes it clear that he is not trying to emulate or adopt it. As against the image of the 'half-angel and half-bird', who 'braved the sun . . . And sang a kindred soul out to his face' (i 1391-5), an image which clearly links EBB to Shelley's skylark, is set the image of Browning himself as a 'wistful eagle' who dies with 'heaven, save by his heart, unreached'; and even that image sounds too grand, for Browning immediately adds: 'Yet heaven my fancy lifts to, ladder-like,— / As Jack reached, holpen of his beanstalk-rungs!' (i 1342-7). It

is an undignified image; but perhaps we should remember that the first thing Jack stole from the giant and brought back to earth was his golden harp.

Style: 'Is It Singing, Is It Saying?'[20]

Browning's style is vocal. His poems, like those of Donne, demand to be voiced: speakers predominate in Browning's work, pleading, hectoring, boasting, repenting, expiring. As we shall see, Browning's conception of voice is not uniform and does not follow a single creative pattern. There is a great division, a fault-line, running through Browning's poetics, a division which gives rise in his poetry to two voices, for which he himself used the terms 'saying' and 'singing'. But it is also the case that the voice for which Browning is best remembered is the first, the voice of 'saying', and we should begin by looking at how it works.

The voice of saying

In the poems written in this style, Browning makes verse imitate, as far as possible, the diction, idioms, and rhythms of human speech, the speech which consists of ordinary words in their natural order of utterance. He stretched the metrical forms with which he worked (both in blank verse and rhyme) to the limit in order to do this, though he never broke them and never showed any interest in 'free' verse or prose poetry.[21] This practice of making verse imitate speech does not depend on subject, mood, or occasion; the speakers concerned can be happy or sad, subdued or exclamatory, their utterances can be ten lines long or a thousand. Browning's poetic voice imposes itself on a multitude of differing dramatic situations and psychological states:

> Ah, did you once see Shelley plain,
>   And did he stop and speak to you?
>
> But do not let us quarrel any more,
> No, my Lucrezia . . .
>
> I will be quiet and talk with you,
>   And reason why you are wrong . . .
>
> Now, don't sir! Don't expose me! Just this
>   once!
>
> I am just seventeen years and five months old
>   . . . [22]

The purpose of this style is to give the impression that someone is 'simply' talking; the reader may not be taken in, but will be affected nonetheless, may even collude in the process, voicing the poem in such a way as to bring out its 'spoken' quality and subordinate its formal properties (rhyme, metre, structure, etc.). **"My**

Last Duchess" is written in couplets, and yet the
'natural' rhythm of the Duke's speech is at certain
moments so strong that it seems to over-ride and dissolve the poem's versification:

>   She had
> A heart . . how shall I say? . . too soon made
>   glad,
> Too easily impressed; she liked whate'er
> She looked on, and her looks went
>   everywhere.
>
>   . . . . .
>
>   She thanked men,—good; but
>   thanked
> Somehow . . I know not how . . as if she
>   ranked
> My gift of a nine hundred years old name
> With anybody's gift.
>
>   (ll. 21-24, 31-34)

A combination of enjambement and the Duke's colloquial hesitation makes the rhymes 'had/glad' and,
to a lesser extent, 'thanked/ranked' almost undetect-
able, certainly without rhetorical weight. The speaking voice in Browning is often modulated in this way
in order to disguise, or off-set, the effects of metre
and rhyme; not that rhyme and metre are unimportant, but that they are felt as pressure, as atmosphere,
rather than as constitutive of expression (the contrast
with Tennyson, again, is especially sharp). Such speakers seem to have fallen by accident into a metrical
stream, the force of whose current they alternately
acknowledge and resist.[23] And the current can be
strong, as strong as the swinging couplets of **"Up at
a Villa—Down in the City"**:

> But bless you, it's dear—it's dear! fowls,
>   wine, at double the rate.
> They have clapped a new tax upon salt, and
>   what oil pays passing the gate
> It's a horror to think of. And so, the villa for
>   me, not the city!
> Beggars can scarcely be choosers—but still—
>   ah, the pity, the pity!
>
>   (ll. 55-58)

or the jaunty quatrains of **"Soliloquy of the Spanish
Cloister"**:

> Oh, those melons! If he's able
>   We're to have a feast; so nice!
> One goes to the Abbot's table,
>   All of us get each a slice.
>
>   (ll. 41-44)

Both these poems are ostentatiously metrical, and
yet the speakers give the impression that, had they
not been in a poem by Browning, they would still
have spoken in the same way. For the speaker of the
'Soliloquy', in particular, the strongly marked rhymes
seem to be part of his colloquial energy and not at
all an external form imposed upon it. Browning is
equally capable of subordinating the rhythms of a
speaking voice to a metrical pattern, yet without
diminishing this sense that verse is second nature to
voice. Take, for example, these lines from **"Andrea
del Sarto"**:

> I dared not, do you know, leave home all day,
> For fear of chancing on the Paris lords.
> The best is when they pass and look aside;
> But they speak sometimes; I must bear it all.
>
>   (ll. 144-7)

Apart from the first phrase (which replaces 'I did not
dare, you know'), there is little to distinguish this from
prose as far as the word order is concerned; but the
rhythm is a different matter. Even written out as prose
the strong segmentation of the lines reveals itself:

> I dared not, do you know, leave home all day, for
> fear of chancing on the Paris lords. The best is when
> they pass and look aside; but they speak sometimes;
> I must bear it all.

End-stopping is the mark of Andrea's melancholy: there
are only a handful of true enjambements in the whole
poem, and most of the lines have the falling cadence
which suggests not merely Andrea's failure but the
pleasure he takes in it:

> There's the bell clinking from the chapel-top;
> That length of convent-wall across the way
> Holds the trees safer, huddled more inside;
> The last monk leaves the garden; days
>   decrease
> And autumn grows, autumn in everything.
>
>   (ll. 41-5)

The third line runs on syntactically from the second,
but the enjambement is notional: the strong stress on
'Holds' ensures that the self-containment of the line
is barely affected. Andrea's conversational phrasing
('There's the bell . . . That length of wall') is subordinated to a lyric self-absorption whose sign is
'the poetic' (alliteration, in this example, as well as
rhythm).[24] And yet these 'poetic' features seem not to
make Andrea's speech forced, but on the contrary to
form part of its naturalness.

In many poems the colloquial style predominates because it is itself of the essence of the speaker's dramatic

character.[25] Other examples (not coincidentally they are some of Browning's best-known works) include **"Fra Lippo Lippi"**, **"Bishop Blougram's Apology"**, and **"Mr Sludge, 'the Medium'"**. 'I was a baby when my mother died,' Lippi says, 'And father died and left me in the street' (ll. 81-2). He is rescued from the street, yet compulsively returns there: it is in the street that the watch finds him, and the street gives him his emotional and aesthetic language. His career as a painter begins in the margins of learned texts and sprawls outwards into the world:

> I drew men's faces on my copy-books,
> Scrawled them within the antiphonary's marge,
> Joined legs and arms to the long music-notes,
> Found nose and eyes and chin for A.s and
>   B.s,
> And made a string of pictures of the world
> Betwixt the ins and outs of verb and noun,
> On the wall, the bench, the door.

(ll. 129-35)

It is 'They, with their Latin' who denigrate his art (l. 242); Lippi's way of speaking, in its very vulgarity and matter-of-factness, is an intrinsic part of his protest at 'their' repressive learning and piety. Sludge, though a much less attractive character than Lippi, has the same linguistic grievance against his patrons and social superiors, expressed with a similar demotic relish. 'May I sit, sir?' he asks Hiram H. Horsefall, with mock-politeness, after agreeing to spill the beans about his career as a fraudulent medium:

> May I sit, sir? This dear old table, now!
> Please, sir, a parting egg-nogg and cigar!
> I've been so happy with you! Nice stuffed
>   chairs,
> And sympathetic sideboards; what an end
> To all the instructive evenings! (It's alight.)
> Well, nothing lasts, as Bacon came and said!
> Here goes,—but keep your temper, or I'll
>   scream!

(ll. 76-82)

These lines do more than mark Sludge's characteristic tone of odious familiarity; they show the edge of his intelligence and resentment, his ability to discomfit the very man who apparently has the power to ruin him. The 'dear old table' is the one which Sludge has been rapping in order to deceive Horsefall, whose bourgeois respectability and gullibility are figured in the 'Nice stuffed chairs / And sympathetic sideboards'. The parenthesis, which shows Horsefall ministering to Sludge instead of beating him, fixes the scene with a single dazzling stroke of the poet's art and the speaker's impudence. Bishop Blougram, too, is a master of conversational idiom, which in his case represents not impudence but condescension and the exercise of power, as when he interrupts his extended metaphor of the voyage of life to give Gigadibs a taste of how the metaphor works in practice:

> You peep up from your utterly naked boards
> Into some snug and well-appointed berth
> Like mine, for instance (try the cooler jug—
> Put back the other, but don't jog the ice)
> And mortified you mutter . . .

(ll. 130-4)

or when he disdains to remember the title of one of Verdi's operas:

> Like Verdi when, at his worst opera's end
> (The thing they gave at Florence,—what's its
>   name?)

(ll. 381-2)

or when he flicks a crumb of his intellect in Gigadibs' direction:

> Do you know, I have often had a dream
> (Work it up in your next month's article)

(ll. 780-1)

In all these examples, Blougram knows what he is doing; he is *using* idiomatic speech in the active sense, rather than using it because he always talks like that.[26] Yet such speech is also in the grain of the man, is characteristic and constitutive. Moreover Blougram's style, and that of Fra Lippo Lippi and Mr Sludge, is one aspect of a conflict between different ways of perceiving and interpreting the world.

All three of these speakers see themselves as realists, as down-to-earthlings, as partisans of the here-and-now against the untenable illusions and attempts at transcendence of their fellow-men, whether masters or dupes (in the case of Sludge, both). Lippi's painting is founded on the premise that

> This world's no blot for us,
> Nor blank—it means intensely, and means
>   good:
> To find its meaning is my meat and drink.

(ll. 313-15)

It was the 'admonitions from the hunger-pinch' which, Lippi says, taught him 'the look of things' in the first place (ll. 125-6); the idiom 'my meat and drink' comes naturally to him, he reads the world through an appetite for its surfaces, 'The shapes of things, their colours, lights and shades' (l. 284). Instructed by his superiors that his

business is not to catch men with
  show,
With homage to the perishable clay,
But lift them over it, ignore it all,
Make them forget there's such a thing as
  flesh . . .

              (ll. 179-82)

Lippi retorts:

          Now, is this sense, I ask?
A fine way to paint soul, by painting body
So ill, the eye can't stop there, must go
  further
And can't fare worse!

              (ll. 198-201)

So natural is the indignant exclamation in the first line that it takes a moment to realise the pun on 'sense', which means both 'common sense' and 'the faculty of physical sensation' (Lippi has already used 'sense' in opposition to 'soul' at l. 124). Lippi then takes the notion of elevation in art ('lift them over it') and, again using a popular turn of phrase, converts the vertical into a vulgar horizontal: 'must go further / And can't fare worse'.

For Blougram, too, plain speaking is the vehicle of a worldliness, a materialism, which he repeatedly launches against Gigadibs's unthinking idealism: 'your grand simple life, / Of which you will not realise one jot', as he puts it (ll. 82-3):

The common problem, yours, mine, every
  one's,
Is not to fancy what were fair in life
Provided it could be,—but, finding first
What may be, then find how to make it fair
Up to our means—a very different thing!
No abstract intellectual plan of life
Quite irrespective of life's plainest laws,
But one, a man, who is man and nothing
  more,
May lead within a world which (by your
  leave)
Is Rome or London—not Fool's-paradise.

             (ll. 87-96)

and again:

We speak of what is—not of what might be,
And how 'twere better if 'twere otherwise.
I am the man you see here plain enough . . .

             (ll. 346-8)

This 'common problem' is a problem *common* to all human beings, but also a commonplace; the epithet

threatens to become derogatory, if once the existence of a world which is *neither* 'Rome or London' *nor* 'Fool's-paradise' is acknowledged. And Blougram does acknowledge it; like Lippi and Sludge, he is haunted by what he has repudiated; on occasion he speaks in a different register, as when he argues that complete disbelief in God is as difficult to sustain as complete faith; but this 'high' speech is confused and flawed:

Just when we are safest, there's a
  sunset-touch,
A fancy from a flower-bell, some one's death,
A chorus-ending from Euripides,—
And that's enough for fifty hopes and fears
As old and new at once as Nature's self,
To rap and knock and enter in our soul,
Take hands and dance there, a fantastic ring,
Round the ancient idol, on his base again,—
The grand Perhaps!

             (ll. 182-90)

Romantic pathos governs the images in the first three lines, which speak of transience and closure in nature, human life, and art as though they were all alike and belonged in Keats's 'Ode on Melancholy'; then 'fifty hopes and fears', with Victorian briskness, 'rap and knock and enter in our soul', like spirits summoned by Sludge; finally the evocation of 'the ancient idol' shows that Blougram is abreast of current developments in religious anthropology which traced the links between Christianity and paganism.[27] The instability of the language here suggests that Blougram is more truly himself in the mask with which he confronts his opponent, that his declaration 'I am the man you see here plain enough' is truer than he would like to think.

Blougram's defence of living 'for this world now' is also a defence of the voice of 'saying', and is conducted in that voice; but it is not the voice that his interlocutor Gigadibs heeds. Blougram himself, as I pointed out earlier in this chapter, disappears from his own monologue, and it is Browning who, at the end of the poem, records that Gigadibs has emigrated to Australia, adding:

        there, I hope,
By this time he has tested his first plough,
And studied his last chapter of St. John.

             (ll. 1011-13)

The 'last chapter of St. John' may be either the last chapter of St John's gospel, or the last chapter of *Revelation,* both of them among Browning's favourite books of the Bible.[28] The last chapter of St John's Gospel concerns the third and final appearance of the risen Jesus to the disciples; the last chapter of *Revelation* tells of the 'river of water of life, clear as crystal, proceeding out of the throne of God and of the Lamb' (xxii 1). Neither in subject matter nor style are they concerned with 'this world now'. Gigadibs, we should note, has gone to Australia not to pursue a Utopian project but with 'settler's-implements' (l. 1010); his feet will be on the ground, but the spirit which guides him will nevertheless be exalted and apocalyptic. It is this spirit which governs the second voice of Browning's poetry, the voice of 'singing', dissident, devious, ineradicable; subversive of common speech, suggestive of transcendence. Without this radical opposition, Browning's colloquial style would lose half its force; but the opposition was there from the beginning, and Browning found the quarrel between singing and saying in the very roots of his poetic identity.

Genius and the common man

As with so much else in Browning's career as a writer, the conflict between 'saying' and 'singing', between the two voices of his poetry, derives from a conflict within Romanticism, in this case from the dispute over poetic language between Wordsworth and Coleridge. In the preface to *Lyrical Ballads,* Wordsworth argued

> that not only the language of a large portion of every good Poem, even of the most elevated character, must necessarily, except with reference to the metre, in no respect differ from that of good Prose, but likewise that some of the most interesting parts of the best Poems will be found to be strictly the language of Prose, when Prose is well written.[29]

This argument is not simply technical; in the next paragraph Wordsworth links it explicitly to a radical humanist aesthetic:

> I do not doubt that it may be safely affirmed, that there neither is, nor can be, any essential difference between the language of Prose and metrical composition. We are fond of tracing the resemblance between Poetry and Painting, and, accordingly, we call them sisters; but where shall we find bonds of connection sufficiently strict to typify the affinity betwixt metrical and Prose composition? They both speak by and to the same organs; the bodies in which both of them are clothed may be said to be of the same substance, their affections are kindred, and almost identical, not necessarily differing even in degree; Poetry sheds no tears 'such as Angels weep', but natural and human tears; she can boast of no celestial ichor that distinguishes her vital juices from those of Prose; the same human blood circulates through the veins of them both. (Mason: 68-9)

Wordsworth directs his allusions principally against Milton: it is Satan in *Paradise Lost* who sheds 'tears such as angels weep' (i 620), and when he is wounded 'A stream of nectarous humour issuing flowed / Sanguine,

such as celestial spirits may bleed' (vi 332-3).[30] And it is Milton who, in the invocation to book ix of the poem, seeks an 'answerable style' for his epic from his muse, Urania, his 'celestial patroness' (ll. 20-1). Wordsworth renounces a centuries-old tradition of the poet as *vates* or seer, uttering divinely-inspired oracles in an 'answerable style', a style whose first requirement is that it *differ* from 'natural and human' language. On the contrary, the poet is (in the preface's most famous phrase) 'a man speaking to men', and the word 'speaking' is not the least important part of this formula.

In *Biographia Literaria,* Coleridge ridicules Wordsworth's assertion that the language of poetry should be that of 'real life', and that a poem should sound as far as possible like someone (anyone, that is, but the divinely-inspired poet) talking.[31] And, citing a passage from 'The Thorn' as evidence that the best of Wordsworth's poetic language is in fact elevated and sublime even where it purports to be 'the language of ordinary men', Coleridge 'reflect[s] with delight how little a mere theory, though of his own workmanship, interferes with the processes of genuine imagination in a man of true poetic genius'. These phrases—'genuine imagination' and 'true poetic genius'—go to the heart of the matter; for Coleridge the poet is not 'a man speaking to men' but a philosopher or prophet, possessed of 'the highest and intuitive knowledge as distinguished from the discursive, or, in the language of Wordsworth, "The vision and the faculty divine" ' (ch. xii, Watson: 139).[32] Wordsworth would admit only differences of degree, not of kind, between the poet and the common run of humanity:

> the Poet is chiefly distinguished from other men by a greater promptness to think and feel without immediate external excitement, and a greater power in expressing such thoughts and feelings as are produced in him in that manner. But these passions and thoughts and feelings are the general passions and thoughts and feelings of men. And with what are they connected? Undoubtedly with our moral sentiments and animal sensations, and with the causes which excite these; with the operations of the elements and the appearances of the visible universe; with storm and sunshine, with the revolutions of the seasons, with cold and heat, with loss of friends and kindred, with injuries and resentments, gratitude and hope, with fear and sorrow. These, and the like, are the sensations and objects which the Poet describes, as they are the sensations of other men, and the objects which interest them. The Poet thinks and feels in the spirit of the passions of men. How, then, can his language differ in any material degree from that of all other men who feel vividly and see clearly? It might be *proved* that it is impossible. But supposing that this were not the case, the Poet might then be allowed to use a peculiar language when expressing his feelings for his own gratification, or that of men like himself. But Poets do not write for Poets alone, but for men. Unless therefore we are advocates for that admiration which depends upon

ignorance, and that pleasure which arises from hearing what we do not understand, the Poet must descend from this supposed height, and, in order to excite rational sympathy, he must express himself as other men express themselves. (Mason: 78-9)

It is hard to see that the object of a poem like 'Kubla Khan' is to 'excite rational sympathy'. Coleridge's poetics are based on the opposite principle to Wordsworth's: on the difference in kind between the poet and 'other men', on poetry as the product of 'the philosophic imagination, the sacred power of self-intuition' (ch. xii, Watson: 139). In an elaborate figure, which intentionally, I think, recalls a Wordsworthian landscape, Coleridge argues for the existence of a special and privileged class of beings, exactly the class to which Wordsworth denied that poets belonged:

> The first range of hills that encircles the scanty vale of human life is the horizon for the majority of its inhabitants. On its ridges the common sun is born and departs. From them the stars rise, and touching them they vanish. By the many even this range, the natural limit and bulwark of the vale, is but imperfectly known. Its higher ascents are too often hidden by mists and clouds from uncultivated swamps which few have courage or curiosity to penetrate. To the multitude below these vapors appear, now as the dark haunts of terrific agents on which none may intrude with impunity; and now all a-glow with colors not their own, they are gazed at as the splendid palaces of happiness and power. But in all ages there have been a few who, measuring and sounding the rivers of the vale at the feet of their furthest inaccessible falls, have learnt that the sources must be far higher and far inward; a few who even in the level streams have detected elements which neither the vale itself nor the surrounding mountains contained or could supply. (ch. xii, Watson: 137-8)

Coleridge's scorn for the 'common sun' which shines on 'the multitude below', and his corresponding exaltation of the 'few' who dare the 'higher ascents' translates into scorn of common language, the speech of ordinary people being as ill-adapted to transcendent vision as it is well-adapted to 'the general passions and thoughts and feelings of men'.[33]

Browning's poetic style is the product, not of a choice between these two opposed notions of poetry, but of a ceaseless and unstable conflict between them.[34] It figures in his poetry as a conflict between speech and song, associated respectively with Wordsworth and Coleridge. As 'a man speaking to men', the poet uses not just the vocabulary and syntax of common language, but its form as well, which is one reason why there are so many speakers in Browning's poetry. Speech is the medium of 'men and women' (Browning's most famous collection is not called 'ladies and gentlemen') and suggests the poet's appeal, with all the word implies of

humility and fellowship, to 'the general passions and thoughts and feelings of men'. But song is the most ancient form of poetry: poets began as singers, as bards, and the figure persisted long after poetry ceased literally to be sung or chanted. By Browning's time the 'singer' was either very high and famous (the prophetic bard with his lyre) or very low and anonymous (the ballad-monger), but in either case could claim a prestige which was specifically denied to colloquial speech, the middle class of literary language. Not surprisingly, therefore, though Browning's poetry is famous for its speakers, the first poet in his work, the narrator of *Pauline,* consistently describes himself as a singer,[35] the second, Sordello, is a minstrel who sings his own compositions, and the pattern continues throughout his work. Its most potent manifestation comes towards the end of *Aristophanes' Apology* (ll. 5182-258) in a poem recited (or chanted) by Aristophanes, which is known to Browning critics by its first two words, 'Thamuris marching'.[36] Thamyris was a legendary Thracian bard who boasted that he could defeat the Muses in a singing-contest, for which they blinded him and took away his gift of song. Homer tells his story briefly in the *Iliad* (ii 594-600), and Milton also names him with honour in *Paradise Lost* (iii 35). In 'Thamuris marching', the bard is represented as advancing, confident of victory, towards his fatal contest with the Muses, through a landscape of incandescent beauty, his perception of it matched by his lyric power. The poem is written in the same *terza rima* as Shelley's *The Triumph of Life,* with a comparable intensity of vision and utterance. There is nothing like it in Browning except **"Childe Roland to the Dark Tower Came"**, of which it is undoubtedly, as Harold Bloom remarks, a 'conscious revision', its 'landscape of joy' a 'deliberate point-by-point reversal of Childe Roland's self-made phantasmagoria of ordeal-by-landscape' (Bloom and Munich: 144-5). But Bloom is wrong, I think, to read the poem in isolation from its context. It is true that Browning wrote it separately and pasted it into its position in the manuscript of **Aristophanes' Apology;** but after all, that is what he did with it. Unlike the beautiful **'Spring Song'** ('Dance, yellows and whites and reds') which was originally published as a separate poem and subsequently incorporated into **"Parleying with Gerard de Lairesse"** (ll. 426-34), **"Thamuris marching"** was never published separately, and indeed never finished as a complete poem in itself. It resembles *The Triumph of Life* not only in form and rhetorical energy, but in being a fragment; it resembles **"Childe Roland"** in breaking off just before a moment of defeat which may also be read as a moment of triumph; but it resembles neither Shelley's poem nor Browning's own in being *performed* by a dramatic speaker. Aristophanes tells the story as an apologia for his *own* art, which is deliberately not that of the transcendent singer. The intensity of the verse is rhetorical in this sense: it represents Aristophanes' desire for the kind of creative power which he attributes to Thamuris, and simultaneously suggests that this power carries too high a price. A speaker enfolds and encloses the song, and the figure of the singer, in a gesture of yearning but also of renunciation. Thamuris reaches and grasps his heaven, in which the qualities of the world exchange themselves in blissful abandon:

> Say not the birds flew! they forbore their
>   right—
> Swam, revelling onward in the roll of things.
> Say not the beasts' mirth bounded! that was
>   flight—
>
> How could the creatures leap, no lift of
>   wings?
> Such earth's community of purpose, such
> The ease of earth's fulfilled imaginings,—
>
> So did the near and far appear to touch
> I' the moment's transport,—that an
>   interchange
> Of function, far with near, seemed scarce too
>   much . . .

> (ll. 5218-26)

But it *is* too much, and this is what Aristophanes knows. He shows Thamuris attaining an unfathomably ironic immortality, struck blind and dumb in a pose of inspiration:

> Thamuris, marching, let no fancy slip
> Born of the fiery transport; lyre and song
> Were his, to smite with hand and launch from
>   lip—
> Peerless recorded, since the list grew long
> Of poets (saith Homeros) free to stand
> Pedestaled mid the Muses' temple-throng,
>
> A statued service, laureled, lyre in hand,
> (Ay, for we see them)—Thamuris of Thrace
> Predominating foremost of the band.

> (ll. 5236-44)[37]

The 'moment's transport' and the 'fiery transport' both figure the poet's daemonic energy, which expresses itself in motion ('Thamuris *marching*') and in the *mobility* of the natural world, so that fixed properties are loosened and freed, and the barriers of separate identity are dissolved. But how does Thamuris end up? His 'transport' is imaged as fixity, as ultimate stasis; with cruel wit Aristophanes says that he is 'free to stand / Pedestaled'; he epitomises the violent overthrow of poets who 'smite with hand and launch from lip'. Aristophanes concludes his recital with Thamuris's 'outburst / Of victory' (ll. 5251-2), but breaks off before he can be implicated in the terrible reply to the bard's challenge:

> Here I await the end of this ado:
> Which wins—Earth's poet or the Heavenly
>   Muse. . . .
>
> But song broke up in laughter. 'Tell the rest,
> Who may! *I* have not spurned the common
>   life,
> Nor vaunted mine a lyre to match the Muse
> Who sings for gods, not men! Accordingly,
> I shall not decorate her vestibule—
> Mute marble, blind the eyes and quenched the
>   brain,
> Loose in the hand a bright, a broken lyre!
> —Not Thamuris but Aristophanes![']

> (ll. 5257-66)

It would be too simple to say that Browning sees himself here as Aristophanes/Wordsworth, embracing 'the common life' and its poetic language; what he has done is to stage the conflict between this Wordsworthian impulse and the transcendent or Coleridgean side of his poetry, its claim to divine origin and warrant, to special insights and privileges, its lofty attitude towards its readers. Twenty years before *Aristophanes' Apology* Browning had written to Ruskin: 'A poet's affair is with God, to whom he is accountable, and of whom is his reward; look elsewhere, and you find misery enough' (Appendix B, p. 258). After all he, too, 'sings for gods, not men'.

In writing thus to Ruskin Browning was paraphrasing the description of the poet in **"How It Strikes a Contemporary"** (recently published in *Men and Women*):

> Did the man love his office? frowned our
>   Lord,
> Exhorting when none heard—'Beseech me
>   not!
> Too far above my people,—beneath Me!
> I set the watch,—how should the people
>   know?
> Forget them, keep Me all the more in mind!'
> Was some such understanding 'twixt the Two?

> (ll. 66-71)

The poet's 'contemporary', who claims he 'could never write a verse' (l. 114), is the speaker of the poem, one of the most 'colloquial' in Browning (in fact, it would be a good candidate for the poem least like 'Thamuris marching' in all his work). The speaker represents the poet as the reverse of poetic or even bohemian in appearance and habits, and he does this in language which implies that he, himself, is a plain man using plain speech. Yet what this plain man speaks is verse. **"How It Strikes a Contemporary"** is song masked as speech; its speaker passionately affirms the poet's transcendent status and destiny, in language which apparently denies it. The speaker describes the poet as an acute observer of life in terms which have nothing Coleridgean about them:

> He stood and watched the cobbler at his trade,
> The man who slices lemons into drink,
> The coffee-roaster's brazier, and the boys
> That volunteer to help him turn its winch.
> He glanced o'er books on stalls with half an
>   eye,
> And fly-leaf ballads on the vendor's string,
> And broad-edge bold-print posters by the wall.
> He took such cognisance of men and things,
> If any beat a horse, you felt he saw;
> If any cursed a woman, he took note;
> Yet stared at nobody,—they stared at him,
> And found, less to their pleasure than surprise,
> He seemed to know them and expect as much.

(ll. 23-35)[38]

Why should the artist here be a poet rather than a novelist or a painter? The speaker's own language is as prosaic as Wordsworth could wish, devoid of a single figure of speech; the syntax, with the sole exception of line 34, is utterly plain.[39] Yet the speaker has not done with the theme of watching. At the end of the poem the poet-observer becomes the subject of the speaker's speculative gaze:

> I'd like now, yet had haply been afraid,
> To have just looked, when this man came to
>   die,
> And seen who lined the clean gay garret's
>   sides
> And stood about the neat low truckle-bed,
> With the heavenly manner of relieving guard.

(ll. 99-103)

The poet watching 'the cobbler at his trade' has become a poet who dies watched over by angels, or by the spirits of other great poets, in a transformation of the scene of mourning in Shelley's *Adonais*; watched also by the supposedly unpoetic speaker, whose poetic imagination in fact creates this scene of triumph and transcendence.[40]

Wordsworth at Coleridge's service? The poem's colloquial style may carry a message of divine provenance, but the irony cuts both ways; the message has to be smuggled in, disguised as its opposite, because if it appeared in its own guise it would not be accepted. It might be rejected, or ridiculed, or simply not believed, as the speaker does not believe reports of the poet's hidden wealth:

> I found no truth in one report at least—
> That if you tracked him to his home, down
>   lanes
> Beyond the Jewry, and as clean to pace,
> You found he ate his supper in a room

> Blazing with lights, four Titians on the wall,
> And twenty naked girls to change his plate!
> Poor man, he lived another kind of life
> In that new, stuccoed, third house by the
>   bridge,
> Fresh-painted, rather smart than otherwise!

(ll. 72-80)

In one sense the speaker misses the point here. He is wrong to find 'no truth' in the 'report', if the 'truth' be understood metaphorically; the poet may indeed conceal, beneath his respectable bourgeois exterior, just such a life of luxury and erotic excess, the life of the imagination; if you 'tracked him to his home', the place of his inner being, you might find the singer of *Pauline* who 'ne'er sung / But as one entering bright halls, where all / Will rise and shout for him' (ll. 77-9). But the poet lives his daily, visible life in the house of speech. So does Browning. What we *hear* in **"How It Strikes a Contemporary"** is the speaker's urbane, worldly chat; like Molière's Monsieur Jourdain in reverse, he speaks verse without knowing it.[41]

Notes

[1] Only 9 of his poems begin with 'O' or 'Oh'; Shelley has 17, Tennyson 30, EBB 23.

[2] Of Browning's 11 sonnets he included only 3 in his published volumes, the three slight 'illustrations' of Rabbinical legend which follow 'Jochanan Hakkadosh' (*Jocoseria*, 1883). He did not collect his best sonnets, notably 'The Names'. Among Browning's major works, I would count only 'Johannes Agricola' ['Johannes Agricola in Meditation'], 'Abt Vogler' and the 'Prologue' to *Asolando* as meditative lyrics, and 'Caliban upon Setebos' as a genuine soliloquy (a debate with the self).

[3] Browning himself never used the term 'dramatic monologue'. The term seems to have been first used by George W. Thornbury in a collection of poems published in 1857 (Culler: 366) and first applied to Browning's poetry in William Stigand's review of *Dramatis Personae* in the *Edinburgh Review,* Oct 1864 (not, as Culler says, in a review of *The Ring and the Book* in 1869). Browning did distinguish between 'dramatic lyric' and 'dramatic romance', the former presenting an emotional or psychological state (e.g. 'The Laboratory', 'Two in the Campagna', 'A Toccata of Galuppi's') and the latter telling a story of action (e.g. 'Incident of the French Camp', 'The Flight of the Duchess', 'Childe Roland'). The two categories are present as 'Lyrics' and 'Romances' in his *Poetical Works* of 1863, and as 'Dramatic Lyrics' and 'Dramatic Romances' in the *Poetical Works* of 1868 and 1888-9. See Woolford and Karlin: ii, Appendix A (pp.

463-9). Some of the poems included in either category don't fit ('How They Brought the Good News from Ghent to Aix' and 'The Confessional' are 'lyrics', while 'Time's Revenges' is a 'romance'), and the boundary between the two categories is in any case blurred by such poems as 'By the Fire-Side', 'Saul', 'Waring', 'The Last Ride Together', and 'A Grammarian's Funeral' (the first two are 'lyrics', the others are 'romances'). Browning defined the 'idyl' of *Dramatic Idyls* as 'a succinct little story complete in itself' (letter of 7 Oct. 1889, cited in Pettigrew and Collins: ii 1067).

[4] If 'each and all' means what it says, then it includes the speakers of poems which have traditionally been regarded as strongly autobiographical—for example 'By the Fire-Side', 'The Guardian-Angel', and 'Two in the Campagna'. The case of 'The Guardian-Angel' is especially puzzling, since in the three concluding stanzas Browning all but names himself and his wife and does in fact name his close friend, Alfred Domett. Perhaps he is using *himself* as a persona, to whose feelings and ideas he is not (as a *poet*) committed; but this seems a rather desperate expedient, and I think it more likely that Browning wanted to insist on the uniqueness of 'One Word More' and was prepared to cut corners. . . .

[5] This is probably the reason why Browning changed some of his titles from their first-edition forms: 'The Tomb at St Praxed's', for example, became 'The Bishop Orders His Tomb at Saint Praxed's Church', which gives much more of a stage-direction to the reader.

[6] See the notes to *Sordello* iii 574-994 in Woolford and Karlin: i 562-93.

[7] There are exceptions, of course: 'The Statue and the Bust' in *Men and Women,* for example, 'Gold Hair' in *Dramatis Personae,* a number of the *Parleyings* (1887), for example the 'Parleying with Daniel Bartoli', and 'Beatrice Signorini' in Browning's last volume, *Asolando* (1889). These stories are all told by a narrator who is so close to the poet as scarcely to be distinguished from him except in purely formal terms. *Asolando* also has a cluster of short, anecdotal poems: 'Which?', 'The Cardinal and the Dog', 'The Pope and the Net', 'The Bean-Feast', 'Muckle-Mouth Meg'. Of the book-length poems, only *Red Cotton Night-Cap Country* (1873) and *The Two Poets of Croisic* (1878) would qualify as stories told by the poet as omniscient narrator, and in both cases the telling of the story is staged in a narrative frame. Dialogue-poems are even rarer in Browning: 'In a Gondola' (Dramatic *Lyrics,* 1842) is the only example before the appearance in a long poem, *La Saisiaz* (1878) of a dialogue between 'Reason' and 'Fancy' (ll. 405-524); then there is nothing before *Asolando,* which has the only other examples: 'Arcades Ambo', 'The Lady and the Painter', and 'Flute-Music, with an Accompaniment'. See also Chapter 4, p. 131 and n. 14 [of Woolford and Karlin's *Robert Browning*].

[8] Even in book xii there are several interpolations by characters in the story, some of whom we have met before (the two lawyers, for example), others of whom make cameo appearances (a Venetian envoy, the friar who gave Pompilia absolution).

[9] 'Transcendentalism' (*Men and Women*), 'Dîs Aliter Visum' (*Dramatis Personae*), 'Ponte dell' Angelo, Venice' (*Asolando*). To these we might add the opening of 'Popularity' (*Men and Women*): 'Stand still, true poet that you are.'

[10] This passage is finely analysed by Hugh Sykes Davies (pp. 12-14) from the point of view of its 'representing the fluidity of a man's most intimate colloquy'; see my discussion of Browning's style in the second section of this chapter.

[11] The complexity occasionally defeated his printers even before it affected his readers: there is a brain-bewildering example in *Sordello* iii 617-25 (see notes in Woolford and Karlin: i 567-9).

[12] In *Fifine at the Fair* (1872) the form does in fact break down, and, for the first time in Browning's work, the interlocutor in a monologue breaks the convention and speaks (first at l. 199, then ll. 254-6 and other places).

[13] For more detail on some of these ideas, to which brief reference will be made in the next section of this chapter, see Chapter 6 [of Woolford and Karlin's *Robert Browning*].

[14] The syntax of ll. 1-2 is ambiguous; it allows this reading, but does not prescribe it.

[15] EBB quotes the last line of 'Soliloquy of the Spanish Cloister'; the 'high faint notes of the mystic' probably refer to *Paracelsus,* especially Paracelsus's deathbed speech beginning at v 582.

[16] For other images of imprisoned creativity, see Chapter 4, pp. 143-4 [of Woolford and Karlin's *Robert Browning*].

[17] Unitarians rejected the doctrines of the trinity and of the divinity of Christ, and were sceptical about the doctrines of original sin and eternal punishment. Their rationalism and belief in the goodness of human nature made them natural exponents of political reform. See also Chapter 5, pp. 160-1 [of Woolford and Karlin's *Robert Browning*].

[18] The words 'strive' and 'strife' occur 139 times in 55 poems by Browning. The eponymous speaker of 'Ixion' (*Jocoseria,* 1883) is representative: 'Strive, my kind, though strife endure thro' endless obstruction, / Stage after stage, each rise marred by as certain

a fall!' (ll. 97-8). In the *Poetical Works* of 1888-9 Browning revised 'my kind' to 'mankind'.

[19] Browning emphasised this point when he revised the title in the *Poems* of 1849 to 'Johannes Agricola in Meditation'.

[20] The phrase is adapted from 'The Flight of the Duchess', l. 512. See the note on this line in Woolford and Karlin: ii 318.

[21] The closest Browning comes to an irregular metre is his occasional use of variable stress in, e.g., the Gypsy's speech in 'The Flight of the Duchess' (ll. 567-689), where the influence of Coleridge is prominent: see Chapter 1, p. 10 [of Woolford and Karlin's *Robert Browning*].

[22] The openings of 'Memorabilia', 'Andrea del Sarto', 'Mr Sludge, "the Medium" ', part iv of 'James Lee' ('Along the Beach'), and book vii of *The Ring and the Book*.

[23] See, for example, the moment in 'Mr Sludge, "the Medium" ', which is written in blank verse, when Sludge perpetrates an 'inadvertent' rhyme and comments: 'Bless us, I'm turning poet!' (l. 1184).

[24] 'There's the bell' and 'That length of wall' are also characteristic of Andrea's use of demonstratives: 'There's what we painters call our harmony . . . This chamber for example— . . . that cartoon, the second from the door . . . Yonder's a work, now . . . That arm is wrongly put' (ll. 34, 53, 57, 103, 110). He points to things, to landscapes, to the actions of his wife and himself: 'To paint a little thing like that you smeared . . . My works are nearer heaven, but I sit here' (ll. 74, 87). The word 'here' brings together a general condition ('earthbound') and a particular situation ('here, in this room with you'). A similar combination is active, but to a quite different effect, in the passage from 'Bishop Blougram's Apology' discussed earlier (p. 43). Where Andrea stages a drama of defeated narcissism, Blougram uses 'here' to point towards the future, to control his interlocutor's own demonstrations: 'here, / I well imagine you respect my place . . . Are up to the protesting eyes of you / In pride at being seated here for once . . . The hand's mine now, and here you follow suit'.

[25] The same reason would account for Browning's extensive use of technical vocabulary and professional jargon (e.g. medicine, music, law); but it is also true that Browning (like Kipling) delighted in such language for its own sake, as his comment on a particularly ripe legal document in *The Ring and the Book* shows: 'I like and shall translate the eloquence / Of nearly the worst Latin ever writ . . . ' (xii 794-5).

[26] The effectiveness of Blougram's conversational asides may be judged by comparing them with their lacklustre equivalents in *Prince Hohenstiel-Schwangau* (e.g. ll. 255-61).

[27] Browning returned to this image in later poems, after he began spending his summer holidays in Brittany, where traces still remained of pre-Christian fertility rituals: see *Fifine at the Fair*, 2022 ff. and *The Two Poets of Croisic*, 89 ff.

[28] The full title of *Revelation* is *The Revelation of St John the Divine*. The traditional identification of John the author of *Revelation* with the John who wrote the fourth gospel was already being questioned by biblical scholarship in Browning's day, but Browning accepted it, at any rate for poetic purposes: see 'A Death in the Desert' (*Dramatis Personae*, 1864).

[29] The text is that of the 1805 edition (Mason: 67).

[30] The word 'ichor' glances at Homer as well as Milton; Satan's wound is modelled on that of Ares, the god of war, in *Iliad* v 339.

[31] Coleridge takes the first lines of 'The Last of the Flock' as a 'chance' example: 'In distant countries I have been, / And yet I have not often seen / A healthy man, a man full grown, / Weep in the public roads, alone', and rewrites them as they would really have been spoken by a 'rustic' narrator: ' "I have been in a many parts far and near, and I don't know that I ever saw before a man crying by himself in the public road; a grown man I mean, that was neither sick nor hurt," etc. etc.'

[32] The quotation is from *The Excursion* i 79. Coleridge uses it again, with even more ironic force, in the passage from ch. xviii just quoted.

[33] 'A Grammarian's Funeral' takes up the theme of genius and the imagery of ascent, and is purportedly chanted by a chorus of students.

[34] It is arguable that this conflict is in fact present in both Wordsworth's and Coleridge's own poetry, but this does not affect the argument here.

[35] See, for example, ll. 17, 77, 126, 252, 258, 376.

[36] The name is more usually Thamyris; Browning's spelling of Greek names attempts a more phonetic rendering than the traditional forms; for his defence of this practice, see his Preface to the *Agamemnon* (1877).

[37] The phrase 'foremost of the band' may well allude to Wordsworth—a poet who also marched through a good deal of landscape in his day, and who would figure here not as 'a man speaking to men' but as the exponent of what Keats called the 'egotistical sublime'. 'Foremost of the band' occurs twice in the 1850 text

of *The Prelude,* which Browning certainly read: once in book x (l. 570), when Wordsworth meets a group of travellers and the 'foremost of the band' tells him the thrilling news of Robespierre's death; and once, even more significantly, in book xiv, when Wordsworth describes climbing Snowdon with a companion and their guide, 'And I, as chanced, the foremost of the band' (l. 34); the great vision of the moonlit 'sea of hoary mist' immediately follows. If Wordsworth is saved, in Browning's eyes, from Thamuris's fate (and it is not certain that he is saved) it may be because his vision is itself followed by *reflection.* But this is too complex a topic to pursue here.

[38] The poet's observant eye here is both like and unlike that of Fra Lippo Lippi (see ll. 112-26) and the Roman police spy described by Sludge (ll. 519-43). The passage also uncannily foreshadows Browning's discovery of the Old Yellow Book on a market-stall in Florence (see *The Ring and the Book* i 33 ff.).

[39] Even the omission of 'that' before 'If' in lines 31 and 32 and 'He' in line 35 (nominally required by 'such' in line 30) is more of a colloquial feature than a poetic device.

[40] Compare the poets whom Aprile sees in a vision at the point of death (*Paracelsus* ii 594-90), and the 'lost adventurers', the 'peers' whom Childe Roland similarly sees gathered to witness his death (ll. 194-201).

[41] *Le Bourgeois Gentilhomme* II iv: '[M. Jourdain:] What? when I say: "Nicole, bring me my slippers, and give me my night-cap," is that prose? [Philosophy Teacher:] Yes, Sir. [M. Jourdain:] Good heavens! For more than forty years I have been speaking prose without knowing it.'

John Maynard (essay date 1998)

SOURCE: "The Decade's Work in Browning Studies," in *Browning Re-viewed: Review Essays, 1980-1995,* Peter Lang, 1998, pp. 127-57.

[*In the following essay, Maynard reviews the critical issues concerning Browning's poetry which were debated throughout the 1980s. Maynard also traces the roots of such issues, noting the dependence of modern criticism on the work of earlier scholars.*]

When I was volunteered to write a summary of the decade's work in Browning criticism and scholarship for *Victorian Poetry,* this did not seem a too much larger task than the year's evaluations I have been turning out for most of this decade—only one-thousand percent. It was, in any event, not the entirely appropriate, but far too ambitious, task of a summary and evaluation of the century's work. The common wisdom is

that criticism, and even editing practices, have (as you like it) finally come of age/gone entirely crazy or to the dogs of late so that recent critical history should, in any event, stand alone, case unparalleled.

In fact, I find now that I am not so sure that the subject easily stands alone. The more I think about what we have said and learned about Browning recently, the more I am seeing patterns that go right back to the century of criticism—so much of it seemingly outdated and overworn—since Browning's death. I should not be so surprised: one of the many things we have been learning by relearning is the dependence of all cultural products, including our own genteel work of criticism, on the work that preceded it and on which it necessarily feeds—feeds much more than we like to admit, with our Romantic and overreaching faith in the originality of critical genius. As modern theoretical criticism has tended to diminish belief in the absolute originality of creative genius, it has seemed only to leave critical originality, by vanity or courtesy, still standing as a hopeful exception. All the recent work in criticism, so new and original, looked at again, seems at least firmly rooted in the past. By the same token our residual Romantic faith in a few Promethean and determining new critical approaches and individual critical movers and shakers bumps up against a growing sense that an invisible hand of critical history has moved us all along a few heavily channeled critical canals. Doubtless certain critical barges catch our attention far more than others, blazoned with sharp thinking, festooned with wit and excellent writing. But the more I assemble the pieces of the picture, the more I begin to see the preoccupations that create our critical culture, that indeed give us as firm critical horizons as those of any other age and make true originality, except as small moments of innovation on the current drift, unimaginable. What will criticism of Browning look like at the bicentenary? We can't know or we would be there already. All we can know is that the scene then will have great historical sap roots in our own—though what now seem the major elements to my eye in 1989 may look like so many irrelevant miscellanea put in one of those time capsules to the desperate reviewer of 2089 who—God love you—should take an interest in what we thought of our contribution at the time.

Perhaps I dare say that the future historian of the reception of Browning in the 1980s will be likely to say very much what we all always say of Victorian culture: it was a time of change and a time of continuity, a time that thought it was undergoing major changes and achieving major conservations. (And of course it thought it was the best of critical times and the worst of critical times.) The sense of great change, great conservation, momentous consequences hanging on the resolution, was nowhere more evident, or strident, than in the set of critical issues turning on the current debates variously labeled deconstruction, post-structuralism, or more broadly, post-modernism. And here the historian, like ourselves, may see the intense disagreements of the time as often more apparent than real, concealing by their shrill opposition the tacit agreement about what issues are central and worth discussing.

Certainly this is the area of Browning studies, as of literary study in general, where there has been the most action—and most lively discussion. I hope I will be forgiven if I begin, like the author of **Sordello,** by summoning up a worthy from the past to focus this discussion and suggest how deeply seated it is in perennial preoccupations of Browning criticism: I call as undeconstructive a figure as G. K. Chesterton himself—a pre-postmodern, pre-modern, indeed by preference medieval man. Yet his mature fictions, no less than his early tortured drawings, were haunted by a vision of a world in which nothing exists beneath appearance, all things fall apart, noses, as in *The Man Who Was Thursday,* keep deconstructing. In fear of such a postmodern world he of course called up a ruddy solid man, a kind of Yeatsian fisherman of poetry, the good Robert, English as old ale, creating a super-solid neo-Chaucerian world of fictional people. Never mind that many are villains, fast-talkers, or self-deceivers: they are at least real fictions, with no complexities of difference between art and life, from an age when writers' hearts beat hard and their brains ticked high-blooded. If Chesterton could shore up a vision of Browning's unified sensibility against the ruin promised by the coming century, Santayana, of course, saw him not as the solution but the problem, a force of barbarous emotional chaos threatening to overwhelm organization and order. Browning's position as a contested case—a figure of either reassuring solidity or disturbing disintegration—has persisted through the rage of modernism for order and into the rage of post-modernism at order. The issue could of course be traced back to Browning's own confused vacillations between an objective and subjective role for the poet and these conceptions have also persisted in the debate. Those seeing Browning as a creator of objective and hence "real" characters have focused on explaining their genesis or on the moral issues that naturally come to the fore when we imagine fictional characters as people much like those who live in real Valladolid. Jacob Korg's *Browning and Italy* (1983) continued this tradition in focusing on the relation between Browning's life (in Italy) and his works (Italian scenes—though mostly from literature not life) and in arguing for the influence of Italy in leading Browning to an objective poetry based on a substantial world of real men and women. Or William Buckler, working in a close analytical and in itself somewhat skeptical tradition associated with the New Criticism in his *Poetry and Truth in Robert Browning's* The Ring and the Book (1985), nonetheless emphasized moral issues in evaluating Browning's characters, on the presumption that an essentially mimetic art demands an evaluative and moral criticism: how lifelike and convincing are they? what does one say about their values and actions? Or, in an apparently different mode of criticism, Samuel L. Chell in *The Dynamic Self: Browning's Poetry of Duration* (1984) used Bergson (and not Poulet) to stress the coherence of internal experience and internal time in Browning's rendition of the consciousness of time of a lifetime compressed into a dramatic monologue (and we remember that stream of consciousness itself could function either as an extreme of realism or as its subversion). The combination in Chell of a substantial and referential view of the nature of Browning's art (creating coherent consciousnesses) with an argument stressing Browning's belief in immersion in the destructive element of time and defending Browning against Santayana only suggests on how many different levels of criticism these issues played out their oppositions.

On the level of character, the most obvious and most recurrent arena for debate in Browning criticism, the case for insubstantiality and deconstruction was made most emphatically by E. Warwick Slinn in his *Browning and the Fictions of Identity* (1982). Here again, far from creating a totally new approach to Browning, Slinn had distinguished predecessors, for instance in J. Hillis Miller's early phenomenological criticism, *The Disappearance of God,* which stressed a common experience in Browning characters rather than their solid individuality, or in W. David Shaw's focus on argumentation, which created not so much a vision of substantial identity as Kierkegaardian levels of being in character (*The Dialectical Temper*). Drawing on the full-blown poststructuralist dogmas of the necessary fictive non-referentiality of language, Slinn subjected Browning to a rigorous reading on a "dramatically based model of man as artifice." As in Leo Bersani's seminal study of character in fiction, *A Future for Astyanax,* substantial characters, all those men and women, are dissolved not merely into dramatis personae but a "shifting series of dramatic hypotheses, unified only by a self-perpetuating consciousness." Each monologue deconstructs its own appearance of creating coherent identity. Slinn has somewhat moderated his views in later, interesting articles (e.g., *BSN* 15:1-9: *VP* 25:67-81) but his position, in its extreme deconstructionist first form, found echoes in later criticism, for instance Adam Potkay's somewhat reductive reading of **The Ring and the Book** (*VP* 25:143-157). A less influential work, in some respects less challenging in its approaches to individual poems, Constance Hassett's *The Elusive Self in the Poetry of Robert Browning* (1982) is also a more useful approach to the broad issue of substantiality of character. Hassett in effect argued for discriminating between constructivist sheep, known by the experience of conversion that creates a coherent personality within, and incoherent goats, who, like Guido, are mere artifices of their own will to persuade or perform. She allowed us to see Browning's presentations of character historically, set in a moment (though perhaps it is one of those historical moments that keeps recurring) when the notion of character is in crisis between creation and decreation and thus problematic.

Two finer works of criticism, by Herbert F. Tucker, Jr., and Clyde de L. Ryals, and a suggestive one by Loy D. Martin, with many parallels, took these issues to a different level of critical discourse. Tucker's justly celebrated *Browning's Beginnings: The Art of Disclosure* (1980) looked less at the idea of character than at the way in which Browning's language and poetry works. As such his explicitly Derridean investigation of difference in Browning as a process of avoiding closure picked up much of the strength of the New Critical focus on careful analysis of verbal structures. (Tucker's model explication of Cleon's too well-wrought urn perhaps exemplified the liaisons as well as contrasts between Yale past and more recent.) Starting with an elegant restatement of Browning's convoluted relation to Shelley—differing from whom, he learned to always be differing even from himself—continuing with a thorough rereading of that gateway to Browning monologues, *Sordello,* Tucker elegantly unrolled the process of Browning's poetry in which renewal and new beginnings displace each movement toward artistic finish or completion, thus both enacting and creating modern poetry.

Some of the excitement of Tucker's work—in which we felt a new critical mode really offering a new experience of the work—was repeated in Martin's eclectic, fitfully brilliant and opaque work, *Browning's Dramatic Monologues and the Post-Romantic Subject* (1985). His notion of processive experience paralleled and drew strength from Slinn and Hassett on Browning's characters, from Tucker on the structure of the poems. To this he added the conceptual schemes of Bakhtin and Kristeva (also suggested by Susan Blalock, *BIS* 11:39-50) as a way of recognizing the openness and freedom of Browning's poetic world: rather than direct and control his characters he enables them to create a complex system of communication, combining voices of author and speaker, reaching out from the isolated individual to a community of language, everywhere allowing in the monologue a dialogue of social values and of ways of representing reality.

Ryals' work, *Becoming Browning: The Poems and Plays of Robert Browning, 1833-1846* (1983), comes closest to Tucker's in giving us an entire way to reread Browning. Apparently something of a glutton for punishment, Ryals moved from his earlier studies of difficult late Browning to the early difficult (or sometimes tedious) work. What he found there is a different, though often compatible model to Tucker's, more rhetorical than deconstructive, for Browning's ceaseless rewritings of himself. If in Tucker's view Browning is always beginning over again, in Ryals' he is always becoming, moving to position himself at a

higher level of being or consciousness. Ryals labeled the process Romantic Irony and stressed the way in which greater breadth of consciousness is always paid for by ironic self-awareness, often both of the limitedness of everyday life and matters and also of the insufficiency of any mythic fabrication of one's becomings into higher intellectual and spiritual states. Such an approach, here focused on the overall strategy of Browning's art, whether in his early long poems, his attempts at drama, or his first monologues, parallels Hassett's to character in that it leaves room for deconstruction and construction, working simultaneously to offer, take back, offer again. The pattern is a familiar one in **Paracelsus** with its ironies of aspiration, attainment, failure, aspiration in failure, and of course in the essential mode of narrative creation/destruction in **Sordello.** Like Tucker, Ryals was especially good in opening up Browning's long deplored early masterwork as the critical entrée to his poetics that it is. Also like Tucker, he was somewhat less impressive when he turned to the fruit of that poetics, the early success of the **Bells and Pomegranates** monologues—though both are excellent on **Pippa.**

If the postmodern, poststructuralist controversy enacted itself in Browning criticism as a restatement in new terms of issues central to Browning since his own distinction between objective and subjective poetry, the equally current and vivid feminist movement in criticism found voice through new articulations of equally old issues: namely the issue, beginning in the 1840s, between Robert and Elizabeth. Who dares judge between a wife and her husband? the traditional wisdom asks. "I," said Victorian critics, who of course regularly preferred Elizabeth and, later, saw Robert as an obstacle to their curiosity about her. "I," said Besier, DeVane, and also so many male and female sentimentalists in and out of Browning societies who fixated their gaze on the rescue of poor Andromeda Elizabeth from dragon Edward Barrett by Perseus Robert—a Caponsacchi determined on rescuing his Pompilia and having her too. And "I," have of course said feminist critics of all persuasions who regularly begin with a view of the marriage of the poets and, from that, fabricate their reading of the works. Here, while there has been important work on the long neglected Elizabeth herself, one must begin by saying that there has been far less important work on Robert than that promoted by deconstruction. Feminist approaches to male writers are a relatively late phase in the rapid evolution of feminist criticism since the mid seventies; the first explicitly feminist booklength study of Robert appeared only this year. The most seminal work, also perhaps the most extreme, was an article by Nina Auerbach, "Robert Browning's Last Word" (*VP* 22:161-173), whose general approach has been followed, with equal wit and panache, by Adrienne Munich (*BIS* 15:69-78). Beginning by deconstructing the idyll of rescue and happy Victorian marriage, they saw the conflict between two types of poets, two sexes, worked out in the poems, especially *The Ring and the Book,* where Browning's final one word more, after his spouse's death, serves to appropriate (or, in Munich's adaption of the ring metaphor, encircle and enclose) Elizabeth. If Auerbach's argument led her to understate the strength of Browning's treatment of women, especially the relatively great truth spoken by Pompilia, other approaches to Browning's treatment of women, focusing on the same issues, somewhat overstated both Browning's "feminism" and the place of Pompilia in the poem. Buckler's study of *The Ring and the Book* virtually excepted Pompilia from the careful scrutiny of the limits of human truth in words that he brought to bear on the other speakers. Ann P. Brady's recent *Pompilia* (1988) followed U.C. Knoepflmacher's argument for Browning's anti-patriarchal feminism (*VP* 22:139-159) with some illuminating detail on Guido's very specifically sexual tyranny. The work romanticizes both Pompilia and Caponsacchi as saintly discoverers of pure love. The tendency to turn Robert into either a husband devil or a writer of feminist saints' lives was usefully corrected by Ashby Crowder's summary of Browning's perplexed and perplexing attitudes to women (*SBHC* 14:91-134) and William Walker's look at Pompilia's rhetorical strategies (*VP* 22:47-63).

Perhaps the most significant work on Browning and women has been free of direct feminist intent but also centrally focused on the Brownings' relation. Lee Erickson's *Robert Browning: His Poetry and His Audiences* (1984) traced Robert's movement toward writing for an audience of one, his spouse, though this study of a very special reception situation was weakened by his failure to acknowledge the differences and conflicts Auerbach stressed. Daniel Karlin's *The Courtship of Robert Browning and Elizabeth Barrett* (1985), one of the more original works on both poets of the past decade, drew on Elvan Kintner's splendid edition of the love letters to provide a striking analysis of both the psychodynamics and mythopoesis involved in this marriage of true, and very complicated, minds. His analysis of the necessary mythmaking in the damnation of Edward Barrett and the inevitable mutual misprision of poet and lover by poet and lover gives a firmer base on which to develop future stories, whether biographical or critical, of the two poets.

Another major field of critical activity of the past decade, what the New Criticism called the affective fallacy and we have come to call reader-response criticism, has also been a steady area of activity in Browning studies. And like feminism and deconstruction, it has very substantial roots in Browning criticism, along with the coordinate reception studies that also emanate from Germany's critical school of Constance. Study of Browning's reception, before we knew it by that name, featured serious evaluation of the aims and limitations of Browning's age in William Peterson's book on the Browning Society, *Interrogating the Oracle* (1968).

Robert Langbaum's classic study of the dramatic monologue in many ways derived its importance from the recasting of traditional genre studies into what we would now call a reader-response mold. Experience in *The Poetry of Experience* is not only the subject of the poem but an action in the reader, who evaluates the poem on that somewhat restricted response coordinates of sympathy and judgment. Langbaum's relative success in speaking excitingly about Browning at a time when the New Criticism signally failed with him, might have suggested the productivity of this approach, under its new name and theoretical formulations, in the eighties.

Erickson's book, mentioned above, was the closest thing to recent full study of Browning's reception. His approach, with its interesting summaries of information concerning Browning's critical fortunes among his contemporaries, opened up a number of subjects but was also marred by its diffuseness and lack of critical self-definition. His shift to an author-centered criticism to propose the rather strained thesis that Browning moved from writing to people generally to an ever narrower target, first Elizabeth and God, then finally God alone, drew his attention away from the full and rigorous study of the context in which Browning's works were received that we need. John Woolford's recent *Browning the Revisionary* (1988) also contained useful information on Browning's critical reception, especially the shocking failure of *Men and Women.* But his main focus in a critically syncretic study was also reader-centered, on Browning's reactions to his contemporary readers' responses—in his next work, where he revised his prior work in a careful response. The dialectic of author and contemporary readers was productive of new approaches to Browning—for instance Woolford's focus on the "structured collections" of monologues in the 1863 reordering of poems, in *Dramatis Personae,* and in *The Ring and the Book.* Woolford's definition of a Browning sequence of poems as a strategy to bring the reader into active work of interpretation often left me in doubt whether he was uncovering Browning's structure or merely providing his own response to (that is, his interpretation of) the themes he found in the group of poems. But as an approach that tried to define Browning's relation to his Victorian audience from his point of view—the critical terms here are strategy or response—it was more convincing than Erickson's. Finally, David DeLaura, in a subtle study of interrelations and to some extent intertextuality between Browning and Ruskin (in *Victorian Perspectives,* ed. John Clubbe and Jerome Meckier, 1989), used Browning's famous comments to Ruskin describing reading as a form of skipping over glaciers as a starting point for fine observations on Browning's demanding, sometimes teasing relation to his reader. He saw Browning positioning himself between the removed classicism of Arnold and the blunt moralism demanded by many

Victorian readers—indeed, where Ruskin would have the artist, though he failed sadly to appreciate it in Browning.

Woolford's study, especially the good sections on the political attitudes implicit in Browning's strategy to involve the reader in the poems of the 1830s, can profitably be set beside the more specifically reader-oriented work of David E. Latané, Jr., *Browning's* Sordello *and the Aesthetics of Difficulty* (1987). Latané usefully located Browning's strategy toward the reader in contemporary attitudes, stemming from the Romantics, about the necessary challenge to the reader made by serious works of literature and he provided a just summary of basic theoretical issues in reader-response criticism. His work was especially helpful in unwinding the mummy's sheet of *Sordello* by showing us both the thematics of reader issues in the poem (the many readers it conjures up, including ourselves) and in offering a model reading by the active reader. Christine Froula, "Browning's *Sordello* and the Parables of Modernist Poetics" (*ELH* 52:965-992) also intelligently discussed readers in *Sordello*. The dramatic monologues, where reader-text interrelations are most productively at play in Browning, have received less attention. Dorothy Mermin's *The Audience in the Poem: Five Victorian Poets* (1984) looked specifically at the varieties of listeners in the poems and their relations to the speakers. Herbert F. Tucker, Jr. (in a contribution to *Lyric Poetry: Beyond New Criticism,* ed. Chaviva Hošek and Parker, 1985, pp. 226-243), drew upon Ralph Rader's concise generic taxonomy of 1976 (*CI* 3:131-151) to tease out the conflict in the reader's experience of a dramatic monologue between rhetorical, dramatic communication, and lyric utterance. My own article (*BIS* 15:105-112) attempted to configure and calculate the dynamics among speaker, listener, and the reader conceived as an overhearer. Perhaps it is worth stressing the reader-oriented approach implicit in so much traditional Browning criticism. Those "new views" of familiar speakers of major monologues that were so common a product of the New Critical emphasis on interpretation of individual poems paradoxically forced us to transcend all single perspectives by displaying the variety of plausible interpretations available to successive readers. If clever special pleaders and devil's advocates, those attractive/despicable wits of the Browning critical world, have been less prominent recently it is perhaps because a more theoretical decade asks for broader views rather than interpretive tours de force alone. Still I enjoyed many briefer articles that forced us to see another side of a monologue we knew thoroughly and had settled in one pattern or a few: for instance, Joseph A. Dupras' (*BIS* 15:113-122) and Russell M. Goldfarb's (*SBHC* 13:59-65) reversal of our usual sympathetic response to that genial and worldly imprecision and genius Fra Lippo Lippi. Andrea as a Rabelaisian carnival figure anyone? She or he

who should be tired of critical one word mores (as I confess I sometimes am) would be tired of criticism itself.

Studies of influences and sources, a preoccupation in Browning criticism since the days of the first Browning Society, have been themselves heavily influenced by the large critical shadow of Harold Bloom who has, of course, generally been at the center of thinking about tradition and intertextuality. Although Bloom himself has never written extensively on Browning, he has given him a central place as a major poet in the tradition and the first strong successor who had to grapple with Shelley's influence. Indeed this central agon of the imagination was already very present at Yale, through the work of Pottle and DeVane, as a model case for Bloom's rethinking of influence in psychoanalytic terms. Bloom's reading of Childe Roland as antithetical quester, a Romantic reading of a Victorian poet with which we have, most of us, been uncomfortable, has been among the most influential, and provocative, rereadings of Browning since the New Criticism. In his introductory essay for his Chelsea *Robert Browning* (1985), otherwise not a particularly representative or useful selection of contemporary essays on Browning, Bloom eloquently revisited this central critical preoccupation. His importance has been felt more emphatically in the work of his students, especially Tucker's elegant restatement of the Shelley-Browning relation, not to mention productive parleyings with his view in Erickson's, Martin's, and my own study of the early Browning. Important as Shelley's influence obviously was, I argued that we must also see Browning in a broader relation to central English and continental traditions. Two articles on Browning and Keats, U. C. Knoepflmacher on Keats and Browning's feminism mentioned above, and Martin Bidney on "Madhouse Cells" (*SEL* 24:671-681) have at least begun to fill in the picture of Browning's broader romantic heritage. John Coates reached back to Cervantes to interpret "How It Strikes a Contemporary" (*SBHC* 11:41-46) and I argued for Donne's formative influence on Browning's development of the dramatic monologue (*John Donne Journal* 4:253-257). Two full books and one booklet filled in Browning's relations with Italian, French, and Russian literature. Korg's book, mentioned above, was a compendium of source work on the poems with an Italian setting, especially those on art, though less helpful on Browning's relations to serious Italian writers, classical or contemporary. Other complementary studies of Italian sources were made by Mary Louise Albrecht (*SBHC* 11:47-60) and Allan Dooley (*MP* 81:38-46). Roy Gridley, *The Brownings and France* (1982) was exceptionally useful in detailing Browning's reading in and enthusiasm for French writers, especially contemporaries such as Balzac (his favorite), Stendhal, and Flaubert. Mark Siegchrist's *Rough in Brutal Print* (1981) thoroughly presented the lurid French legal sources for *Red Cotton Night-Cap*

Country, showing Browning's distortions and changes without denying him his creative rights, as so many commentators on *The Ring and the Book* have, to lie in the service of imaginative truth. Finally, Patrick Waddington's little book, *Browning and Russia* (1985) provided a detailed account of what little Browning did know of Russian writers (on a personal level, mainly a not very cordial relation with Turgenev) and examined sources of "Iván Ivànovitch." Browning's problematic relation with Arnold was reexamined in two good articles, John Coates's "Two Versions of the Problem of the Modern Intellectual" (*MLR* 79:769-788) and Jane A. McCusker's study of Arnold and *Aristophanes' Apology* (*MLR* 79:783-796). DeLaura, in the study mentioned above, drew upon both articles to position Browning in opposition to Arnold but in fundamental agreement with Ruskin. The article, using the letters DeLaura previously published, was important for its fuller view of Browning's debt to Ruskin in his poetics—a big improvement over the endless retelling of Ruskin's gracious recognition of "The Bishop Orders His Tomb." It also offered an interesting appendix on Browning's distrusting use of Arnold's key term, "culture."

The investigation of Browning's own influence on contemporaries and successors, also a topic with a long pedigree in Browning studies, found fertile, largely untilled soil, in a nonpoet modern, Henry James. Ross Posnock's *Henry James and the Problem of Robert Browning* (1985) again showed the influence on influence studies of Bloom: his elegant argument from both biography and textual comparison suggested that Browning was a central and troubling figure of potency to James. (**Men and Women** was a forbidden and therefore dangerously attractive book to the young James.) In Posnock's original formulation James created a myth of Browning to overcome his influence, much as Browning did of Shelley and, again like Browning with Shelley, he proceeded to encompass and to rewrite Browning's work in his own fiction. The study was a good critical approach to both writers, with interesting ideas about the development of the theatrical self, as opposed to the sincere self of the Romantics, and the use of perspectivism. I was less persuaded by the comparative readings and somewhat unsure of the cross discussions from biography and society to the works: like New Historicist studies that it resembles, there was both originality and a certain degree of idiosyncrasy.

The relation to Pound continued a valued old chestnut in discussion of Browning and modernism. George Bornstein (in his edition of *Ezra Pound Among the Poets,* 1985), offered a full review of Pound's Browning, emphasizing the way in which Pound's renovative relation to past writers allowed him to learn from Browning and build on him without the distortions and displacements of Bloomian anxiety. Jonathan Ward (*BSN* 15:10-27) focused more narrowly on Pound's recasting of historical poetry as he worked through

and then away from Browning and, in his penultimate chapter, Loy Martin interestingly underlined the difference in sensibility and relation to the past that led Pound, and even Eliot, to transform totally, and finally abandon, the dramatic monologue. Finally, Bornstein also looked at Browning's relation to Yeats (*Yeats Annual* 1:114-132) and here we end back in Bloom's main-traveled road with Yeats reacting to, and attempting to swerve away from merely following, Browning and Tennyson's first generation reaction to and swerve from Romanticism.

Many major topics in Browning studies over the years have found contemporary critical restatement, though often less satisfactorily and thoroughly than one would wish. There is the old one of Browning and religion, the issue that moved the Browning Society—those pale, unsatisfied ones in their quest for another answer to the crisis of faith of their time—they being unsatisfied by the Tennysonian turbulence that had contented an earlier generation. Vincent P. Anderson's serviceable *Robert Browning as a Religious Poet: An Annotated Bibliography of Criticism* (1984), with excerpts and summaries, served to remind us how regularly Browning has been reread to fit each generation's religious preoccupations. We have had heretical Brownings, skeptical Brownings, Brownings very sure of God and pessimist Brownings, existential Brownings, Brownings preoccupied with a central Truth of Incarnation, and Brownings swimming in phenomena, Brownings for whom God is love, and Brownings for whom he refuses to come. Woolford's book restated Whitla's emphasis on the Truth of Incarnation. Hassett's study of how Browning adapted ideas of conversion and apocalypse in his presentation of character offered a more original study of Browning's particular moment—putting to secular use major aspects of religious tradition. The same was true of Glenn Everett's "Typological Structures in Browning's 'Saul'" (*VP* 23:267-279), which followed generally the work of George Landow and also Linda Peterson's excellent summary, "Biblical Typology and the Self-Portrait of the Poet in Robert Browning" (in *Approaches to Victorian Autobiography,* ed. Landow, 1979). Everett rightly raised questions about the implications of such a traditional mode of interpretation, here again consciously and perhaps also historically used, in an essentially secular literary form. Peterson's more recent article, "Rereading *Christmas-Eve,* Rereading Browning" (*VP* 26:363-380), provided an important reflection on Browning's awareness of hermeneutic problems arising in religious issues and spilling over to all forms of interpretation. Her elegant interpretation of **Christmas-Eve** saw it as an enactment and demonstration of the problems of religious interpretation, whether typological, based on historical tradition, or rational and mythological. In her persuasive view, we are driven to accept the impossibility of privileging any one interpretive stance; hence Browning's poems employing typology necessarily question and historicize the biblical interpretive structures they offer. I was less persuaded by her special pleading for the poem as a turning point in unleashing Browning's reader to multiple interpretations of monologues (the history of criticism of **"My Last Duchess"** alone says the moment was far earlier).

Other good interpretive articles have focused on religious issues: Blair Ross on progressive mythology in **"Apollo and the Fates,"** a typological poem outside the Christian system (*VP* 22:15-30); Michael Berens, on **"Karshish"** (*SBHC* 12:41-53), also concerned with religion as universal myth-making; and John Lammers and Jeff Karr (*SBHC* 12:94-119; 13:37-46) on **"Caliban Upon Setebos."** Lammers read the poem as a mini-divine comedy ready for his allegorical interpretation; Karr noted parallels to Paley in order to read the poem as a version of natural theology in a Darwinian world; both were helpful, neither fully persuasive.

This relatively weak addition to thinking and knowledge on the topic of religion found a parallel in the even weaker record of studies on two other great issues, politics and science. Here the earlier critical history itself is less rich, except in regular complaints (such as this one) over the failure to explore such obvious subjects. Yet on first sight the failure seems to have been also Browning's, especially in science. His apparent interest in evolution in *Paracelsus* yielded to uninformed positions later in his career. Only George Myerson, in an article on the science of Browning's *Paracelsus* (*BSN* 15:20-47), returned to this apparently barren field. Drawing on Kuhn's paradigm for the emergence of modern science, he interestingly plotted Paracelsus' growth as one toward scientific as well as moral awareness. Browning endorses the modern scientific view of the world as open, objective, and infinite, though he draws back from a totally secular vision of the universe. We need other studies that similarly examine the implied, if often confused, attitudes of Browning toward the emerging scientific disciplines, hard and soft, of his century.

Politics was a more conscious and habitual theme of Browning's, though we look in vain, as we do in so much nineteenth-century British literature, for the central work overtly about politics. Here three studies have at least raised the discussion to interesting levels of discourse. John Woolford, in an article (*BSN* 14:1-20) substantially repeated in his recent book, offered a thoughtful analysis of Browning's early liberalism as an author's position. Browning's ideal of power, stemming from what Woolford called Puritan anarchism, made him reject the author's authority over the reader, an elegant way of explaining the embarrassed attempts at sharing authorship in *Sordello.* In somewhat parallel terms to the early study by Lawrence Poston (*PMLA* 88:260-270) of Browning's political skepticism as an ironic view of the relation between nobility and power, Woolford interestingly reviewed the themes of renunciation and abdication of power so clear in some of the plays. Robert Viscusi (*BIS* 12:1-28) found a different, also intriguing, way of unmasking the political positions of the apparently apolitical professed liberal. His study of imperialism in Browning's celebration of Italy avoided the simplicities of classic Marxist imperialist theory by its sensitivity to the positive side of Browning's liberal culture, his ability to balance and hold in suspension various views of a subject, here both the Italy of classical Rome and that of Dante. In this decade of renewed and highly abstract Marxist cultural/literary theory Loy Martin's formulations of a social drive for an event in literary history—the production of the dramatic monologue—were predictably abstract and unfortunately lacking in specific social context. His thesis of a crisis in bourgeois Cartesian individualism leading to a work (of art) alienated from its producer (the author, who cedes authority, here not in the first instance to the reader but to the indeterminable dialogic subjects of the dramatic monologue), leans heavily, almost certainly too heavily, on a single long interpretation of "Pictor Ignotus." It is a way of thinking about the relation between a literary form and a cultural-economic context (superstructure and infrastructure) useful enough in itself but much too speculative in form. Obviously we badly need more comprehensive and fully worked out approaches to both Browning's own discourse on politics and society and his larger place in a rapidly changing Victorian world.

The coordinate subject of history was of course much more directly a concern of the poet and has elicited regular critical comment since, from the only somewhat useful research into the real history behind Browning's poems, undertaken with the rather naive aim of seeing how true Browning's poetry was to history, to the sophisticated historiographical comments of Morse Peckham. There have not been many persons writing about Browning and history in the last decade, but fortunately there was one good article and a substantial, well-developed book. Lee Baker (*VP* 24:31-46) drew on Hayden White's rhetorical approach to history writing as necessarily a form of fiction making to contrast Browning and Carlyle. He found Carlyle a romantic ironist (as Ryals has found Browning) but Browning an unselfconscious mythmaker. From this analysis he criticized Peckham's view of Browning as an historical relativist, aware of the limits of all positions, including his own. Mary Ellis Gibson's *History and the Prism of Art* (1987) was a much larger and more impressive approach to the complexities of this major subject in Browning. She cast a wider net, avoiding reductive descriptions of Browning's involvement with history. Her overall position on Browning's historiography was closer to that of Peckham than Baker. She emphasized Browning's affinities to Carlyle as relativist and ironist: she rightly stressed the concern with history Browning learned in his family, from father and half-brothers. She accepted the influence of Ranke and his school in Browning's concern with sources and accurate evidence but saw this as compatible with a perspective on history that stressed context, cultural history, and the relativism of perspectivism. Clearly there is still an issue that will not go away, as Baker rightly insisted, in Browning's countervailing push—let us call it a force of desire against its own skepticism—to have the record mean something and mean for good. Yet it is Browning's persisting relativism and even skepticism, as Gibson competently showed in her good discussions of the rhetoric of the poems on historical issues, that creates the objective plenitude of his art against the reductive mythmaking of his heart. Better, perhaps, to see the tension between the two historicisms, romantic/prophetic and relativist/skeptical as the determining site of the poems. Gibson makes a case for affinities between Browning's historicism and that of twentieth-century writers; but again, this should be balanced against other points of view, especially Ward's article and the section in Martin's book, both mentioned above, on the differences between Browning and Pound's historicism, which take better account of the radically antihistorical vision of much high modernist art.

A complementary, interesting, and relatively unexplored topic, Browning's relation to the heart of darkness in man's prehistory and in his psyche at least found one able analysis in Dorothy Mermin's "Browning and the Primitive" (*VP* 20:211-237). Here again Browning is surprisingly in touch with the newer historical—here anthropological—work of students such as Edward Tyler, who saw primitive cultures as the origins, not degradations, of civilized societies. And here again, as Mermin ably showed, Browning counters his own expanding, implicitly relativist vision with his heart's need to impose a Christian mythological pattern—albeit a very sophisticated progressive one—on the span of human history. As interesting was Mermin's sense of Browning's preoccupation in his later works especially, with primitive urges, sexuality, violence, religious ritual, often revealed through dreams and other unconscious phenomena. In this she followed Samuel B. Southwell's *Quest for Eros: Browning and "Fifine"* (1980). Southwell explored a similar terrain of intellectual history, relating Browning's use of the term "soul" to the emerging concept of the unconscious as outlined by Lancelot Whyte's *The Unconscious Before Freud*. Like Mermin, he generally saw Browning involved in the fertile discussion of myth, anthropology, primitivism, and sexuality that led both to modern anthropology and Freud. His provocative analysis of *Fifine at the Fair* seemed more problematic, just because his argument wanted to show what Browning wished to say but dared not. Such an author-, or biography-, centered reading was naturally more effective in suggesting external influences on the poem—the

presence of Browning's complicated feelings for the dead Elizabeth, for example—than in fully proving his thesis, that Browning's hidden meaning, the meaning whose name he dared not speak, was a vision of cultural unity built on acceptance of the sexual drive as a central life force. Yet his approach rightly reminded us how very much this poem, which we have tended to treat as a casuistic or metaphysical sport, was involved in the new ideas of woman, sexuality, and primitivism. This area of Browning should not be romanticized into a confrontation between Mr. Browning and the dark gods. Mermin especially sets us on the right track by seeing the emergence of these modern myths of myth, sexuality, and primitivism in Browning as a part of a general intellectual movement in his culture to which, unlike developments in the natural sciences, Browning was rather precisely attuned.

I might end this summary of criticism by daring ourselves to look directly sometimes at the white light that Browning himself mostly avoided: the poetics stated or implicit in his work. What theoretical statement can we find in Browning or create from our reading of his works that might seem somewhat to suffice as an explanation of his unique imagination? Of course answers exist everywhere in all these special studies of aspects of Browning's work. We have been less ready, despite the heady theoretical dialogue of our day, and despite some heavy theoretical statements about Browning, to try a direct art of Browning's poesy. Despite his reticence as a self-explainer, Browning's own statements are not irrelevant. **"The Essay on Shelley,"** as Thomas J. Collins well showed some years ago, offers an elliptic but often stunningly useful system of criticism for speaking of his work. **"The Essay on Chatterton,"** too, as Donald Smalley and I have emphasized, provides ways of talking about Browning's poetic argumentation and his sense of his own development. We have recently had added to this Browning's rather wonderful letter of August 1837 to his French friend, Count Amédée de Ripert-Monclar, in which he sketches his history of his own growth as a poet. In the study of Browning and Ruskin mentioned above, DeLaura, who gave us the unusually self-reflexive Ruskin letters, well used them to define precisely the similarities between Browning and Ruskin's poetics. Christine Froula's article, also mentioned above, has called our attention to the poetics that are somewhat more than half stated in *Sordello.* Her useful discussion in effect completed the statements of *Sordello* as a poem about the nature of poetry, seeing Browning advocating a turn from a Shelleyan poetics of inspiration to an exploratory and open-ended engagement with experience, in which the reader is involved in the process of making the poem. Her more direct attempt to formulate a poetics from Browning's agonizing self-inquiry into his art in *Sordello* built upon, or had clear parallels to, the excellent reading of the project of the early Browning that we have had especially in the books by Tucker, Ryals, and Latané.

Perhaps most important, Daniel Karlin's study of the letters of Robert and Elizabeth has amply shown what a helpful ring of keys they are to unlock both poets' poetics as well as their hearts. The problem was of course following their private, allusive, and especially elliptic (indeed filled with actual ellipses) way of discussing their ideas and aspirations for their poetry. Karlin saw Robert creating Elizabeth to take the place of the Shelleyan poet and then using this formulation to reestablish his own view of himself as different from this romantic idea of a poet who is the poetry he speaks.

By contrast, Browning is almost morbidly aware that he speaks not as the linnets sing but through the forms of poetry and the cultural artifice of words. Since Rader's 1976 article, mentioned above, there has been little work directly on issues of genre in Browning, nothing to compare with the earlier work of Donald S. Hair in *Browning's Experiments with Genre* (1972). Exceptions might be Martin's book, which as I noted brought various theoretical perspectives to bear in explaining the production and nature of the dramatic monologue, or the genre discussions implicit in reader-response approaches to the dramatic monologue. There have been few works—William Butts on Menippean satire in Caliban (*SBHC* 13:24-36) and Allan Dooley on **The Ring and the Book** as epic and anti-epic (*BIS* 15:137-150) are two exceptions—that look directly at Browning's parodic genius in recasting and replaying traditional genres with seemingly effortless dexterity and unlimited resourcefulness. John Woolford's recent book called attention to a special kind of genre in Browning, which he called the structured collection of groups of dramatic monologues.

There has also been nothing on the varieties of resources in language in Browning to compare with Park Honan's 1961 *Browning's Characters*. With some success, both Martin and Gibson risked making their already somewhat prolix books too diffuse in order to include chapters linking their general topics to analysis of style and diction. Gibson saw Browning's commitment to the objective detail of recorded history and to accepting life lived through history finding its parallel in a language filled with colloquial speech, hard, knotty, and difficult style, and the resistant "clayey soil" of specific words for real things, people, places. She then suggested a system of variation from this standard diction by which characters are satirized through grandiloquent speech or elevated by sincere lyric. This was useful for certain poems but, unlike Honan's study, it tended to reduce Browning's infinite variety too much to one plain song—that indeed of an essentially prose Browning. In a chapter on "The Being Written" Martin used a linguistic analysis, primarily of progressive verb forms, to show on a local level how Browning finds a way of communicating open-ended process rather than closed and complete being. As he acknowledged, this was a systematically formulated parallel to

the similar analyses of processive effect in Tucker's readings of Browning's poems. Oddly, the analysis of individual poems is more persuasive, because it seems clearly to hold true for the poem in question. Martin's broader description of "typical" Browning linguistic effects left me uneasily aware of its unscientific form and uneasy about the intimidating computer studies, comparing Browning's usages to norms in other poets (or average great poets!) that could back a proper linguistic study.

Objective scholarship will always be with us—and indeed we have great reason to be thankful for the painstaking and careful labors in the vineyards of a number of biographical scholars and editors. The emphasis for the eighties should be on the fine work of editors. In biography there have been no full-length studies to succeed Irving and Honan's 1974 *The Book, the Ring and the Poet* or, if I do say so myself, my own 1977 study of the formative period and culture, *Browning's Youth*. Donald Thomas' survey biography, *Robert Browning: A Life Within a Life* (1982), merely retold others' tales, often without even using the latest scholarship. Gridley's study of the Brownings in France provided important new information and a gracious account of the Brownings' infatuation with France, Paris, and all things French. Korg's study of Browning and Italy, with less new information and a far less surprising story to tell, did recount gracefully Browning's once lyric, later somewhat tired love affair with Italy. The much briefer fling with Russia was carefully reported, with some important new detail, in Waddington's study. Perhaps most important, Daniel Karlin's reading of those perplexing and voluminous love letters from the Cherokee, also noted above, provided the best plotting and psychological analysis of the real courtship years that we have. We should be grateful for a number of other special studies in biography, John Coulter's (*BSN* 15, nos. 2-3:3-19) identification of the Brownings' residence at New Cross from work in local records; Richard Purdy's (*YULG* 61:143-153) gracious summary of the relation with Ripert-Monclar, now available in the record of the letters as well; and Meredith's Raymond (*SBHC* 14:32-62) well-researched and well-presented account of the Brownings' magnificent Maecenas, John Kenyon. These most illuminating stabs into the relative dark of Browning's biography suggest how much more could be accomplished through determined biographical research. Honan's treatment of the late Browning, my own of the early life and culture, and many of these specialized studies rightly begin with the assumption that the biography of Browning is not complete in detail, is filled with traditional myths and pieties that need critical examination, and is, like criticism, and despite its dependence on the good gold of fact, finally a matter of individual fabrication and interpretation—and thus always beginning over again with each new student of the poet and his life.

This survey of the decade's work in Browning studies, which seems to me to be reporting in fact some substantial new strengths, if also some relative weaknesses, in our contemporary current of ideas about Browning, is structured to end in any case on an upbeat. I have been suggesting how much more than we may like to think our critical approaches to Browning have grown out of and built on the tradition of discourse about him and his work. In the record of editing this is more obvious. The work of generations in assembling and editing the full record of Browning works and letters has been coming to remarkable fruition. The achievement of the last decade was striking. From its position as one of the weakest (and indeed even rather ridiculed) areas of basic scholarship in Victorian literature, Browning studies now stand fair to be one of the best and most sophisticated. And, as often, sophistication here has come in the maturing theoretical study of editing to mean both great knowledge and also a willingness to live in awareness of diversity and differences of opinion. Oddly, it was more lack of knowledge than of sophistication that brought Browning editing efforts in the 1970s into disrepute. The now notorious first four volumes of the Ohio Browning foundered especially over the ignorance of the entire Browning world about Browning's own writing, editing, and publishing practices and the location and even existence of certain manuscripts and revises. That lack has been and is still being rather massively corrected. Part of the problem was the incredible dispersion of Browning family letters, manuscripts, and books at the great Sotheby sale in 1913, at which the entire remains of the poet's literary life were sold off in large lots, often to other booksellers who kept breaking them down and dispersing them to buyers throughout the world.

Philip Kelley and Ronald Hudson, lately assisted in part of their work by Betty Coley, have done us all a truly major benefit in tracking down as many of these materials as they could and cataloging them carefully in two essential works of reference: *The Brownings' Correspondence: A Checklist,* published by Kelley and Hudson in 1978, and *The Browning Collections: A Reconstruction* (1984), compiled by Kelley and Coley. The latter completed this great task of reassembling the collection in catalog form in a magnificent way. It gave Browning students—both those of Robert and Elizabeth—a single invaluable source for locating manuscripts, proofs, revises, corrected copies, notebooks, diaries, address books, memoranda, and even all the known copies of *Pauline.* 2519 books of Browning or his family were identified—albeit some, here, as in other parts of the *Reconstruction,* only by booksellers' references—as well as presentation copies, association copies and manuscripts, and even lists of likenesses and photos, works of art, and household and personal effects, including 37 known locks of hair of the Brownings! We are now far more in control of

the primary information available on Browning than on most other Victorian writers: a major, foundational achievement.

Kelley and Hudson, whose grasp seems surprisingly well suited to their bold reach, have added to this great work with the very solid beginnings of another—publication of *The Brownings' Correspondence.* There have now appeared seven volumes. All, certainly including the most recent (1989), maintained impressively high standards not only of comprehension and editorial accuracy—which we expected—but also of scholarship and annotation, where Hudson's work splendidly complemented Kelley's assembling and editing. The publication, a cost-efficient operation through Kelley's Wedgestone Press, has also been splendid: handsome, spacious, beautifully illustrated volumes that recall fine academic editions of an earlier decade. The generous inclusion of reprints of all contemporary reviews of the time period at the end of each volume has been a bonus that has already proven of great value in critical and reception studies, where we can all substitute our own appraisal of what the critics of the age said for the inherited, usually reductive and anecdotal, wisdom about Robert's reception.

With all this, the student of Robert may be nonetheless not a little disappointed to find how little of him has appeared in the seven volumes so far, where he is outwritten by his spouse-to-be far more than seven to one (volumes 6 and 7, June 1842 to October 1843 have, respectively, 19 and 7 letters to and from Robert and 147 and 225 to and from Elizabeth). Doubtless the Robert Browning scholar would have been better served for the early period, before the convergence of the twain, by one separate (and rather slim) volume, though already in volumes 6 and 7 some references to each other and different perspectives on contemporary events—for instance, Elizabeth's interesting comments on Macready's damning Robert's new play *A Blot*—show the eventual advantage of full combined publication when they do couple. On the face of it, there were also few major additions to Browning's record for this period, perhaps mainly the letters to Ripert-Monclar that had been in Professor Purdy's private collection. Browning has been on the whole very successful in covering his early tracks. Yet just because of the scarcity of information on his early life, we should be doubly appreciative of the comprehensive method that has presumably brought virtually every scrap there is to proper publication. To take the most recent volumes again as examples, 9 of the 16 by Robert in volume 6, and 3 of the 6 in volume 7 were previously unpublished. If most of the new letters are, as typically with Robert, brief, unrevealing, embarrassed, or all three, they also often provide important new details for what are otherwise entirely blank months in the record or, sometimes, offer new perspectives—as the letter in volume 6 showing Robert asking Macready to help him divide *A Blot* into three acts from five and planning to revise the play "while the printers have it in hand"! The editors' inclusion of a further section of supporting documents is also helpful, but here probably they will find their record less definitive; I also thought the biographical sketches, often of well-known folk, usually unnecessary, though they might interest the casual reader, if there are any, of these volumes.

Complementary to this excellent, ongoing work have been Ian Jack's collection of letters to James T. Fields, Browning's American publisher (*HLQ* 45:185-199), and Michael Meredith's handsome book, *More Than Friend* (1985), publishing the letters to his affluent American Friend in his autumn years, Katharine de Kay Bronson. Meredith annotated these interesting letters carefully and also provided a graceful and informative introduction; I must say I was skeptical of his attractive thesis, that an autumn friendship was also more: an Indian Summer passion. The mystery of Browning's late romantic life would seem to be other than we naturally think: not who was he with after Elizabeth but why was he generally still with her (love, guilt, convenience, habit?). Daniel Karlin's edition of Robert and Elizabeth's *Courtship Correspondence* (1989) is an attractive selection, about one half of the letters in the full, monumental Elvan Kintner edition and a good deal less than that in bulk. It is a reader's edition, focusing on the love tale to the exclusion of much of the literary and other gossip. I am not sure why the text had to be re-edited: annotation is itself useful, giving the common reader much of the helpful perspective and analysis provided in Karlin's earlier fine book on the letters. Finally, Mark Samuels Lasner (*BIS* 15:79-88) ably provided the context for his discovery of Browning's interesting first letter to Rossetti in William Allingham's commonplace book.

As for manuscripts other than letters, Craig Turner well edited the odd journal of Browning's envious and rather untrustworthy cousin in *The Poet Robert Browning and his Kinsfolk by his Cousin Cyrus Mason* (1983). Turner impressively eschewed overplaying his material, giving us an objective and critical view of this document which, brought out otherwise, could have generated any number of new Browning myths, those hydra things. Another odd but interesting set of documents, the acting versions of *Strafford, A Blot in the 'Scutcheon,* and *Colombe's Birthday,* published in facsimile, without apparatus, and too quietly in a Salzburg series by James Hogg (from the Lord Chamberlain's collection in the British Library), is now available from Longwood (U.S.A.) along with Hogg's companion volume summarizing criticism of Browning's plays. The edition complements Anneliese Meidl's (*BIS* 12:163-188) report of the *Strafford* text.

So much new information, very much including investigation in the 1970s of two separate records of Browning's

revisions of the first ten volumes of his 1888-1889 *The Poetical Works* (the Dykes Campbell copies in the British Library and a list for volumes 4-10 at Brown) and useful commentary on Browning's publishing practices by Ian Jack (*BIS* 15:161-175) and Michael Meredith (*SBHC* 13:97-107), have improved, or are still improving, all three new editions of Browning's work. After the fiasco of the first four volumes of the Ohio Browning we have had a rare corroboration of Milton's faith that truth would not be put to the worse in a fair grapple with falsehood. We now have three acceptable versions of truth about texts of Browning's works and a fourth announced as on its way. The only completed text was that in the Penguin/Yale series of *The Poems* (1981) begun by John Pettigrew and finished by Thomas J. Collins. The two-volume text, which has already become accepted as the current usable scholarly edition for classes and most students, accepted Browning's last wishes as known by the volumes of *The Poetical Works* emended by his authoritative corrections for the second impression of the first ten volumes. The editors have implicitly followed Morse Peckham's persuasive argument, made by his edition of *Sordello* (1977), that editors must scrutinize the final text for printers' errors introduced in successive editions or even the poet's own repeated mistakes. There are corrections indicated, though perhaps fewer than one would suspect to be there. Annotation was a particular strength, with Pettigrew's pithy and often witty definitions throwing added salt in the wounds the original Ohio volumes received in reviews of their long, pedantic notes or identifications of Venice. The weakness of this edition was mainly outside the editors' control: Penguin/Yale had already issued Richard Altick's *The Ring and the Book* in the series; Altick's interesting reprint of the first edition is not compatible with the editorial principles of the Collins-Pettigrew edition nor does it pretend to full annotation. Penguin/Yale also did not find room for the plays; as part of plans to base a concordance on the edition, the plays now have appeared in a separate volume published by Garland (1988) and edited by Collins and Richard J. Shroyer. This is a compatible scholarly text, though again one suspects more errors than are found (Oxford found eleven needing emendation to Collins and Shroyer's six). They have not used some manuscript variants for *A Blot* and *Colombe's Birthday* on the view that these are not in direct descent; but Oxford does use them profitably. The annotation was competent, though neither as full or incisive as Penguin/Yale. The brief history of criticism of the plays is a helpful summary essay. The edition will serve its immediate purpose but is not likely to have the practical use of the Penguin/Yale text, which rightly has been having its day while the two editions in progress are slowly appearing.

Ohio has in fact got its act together and come out with a competent volume 5 (1981) of its *Complete Works* as well as two very useful volumes, 7 (1985) and 8 (1988) of three planned on *The Ring and the Book,* which has no other full modern edition. (Volume 6, despite some notices to the contrary, has not yet appeared.) Ohio now incorporates manuscript variants and has a good argument for its only slightly different choice of copy-text. (They use the second, 1889, impression of *The Poetical Works* for volumes 1-10 rather than 1888 as Penguin/Yale and Oxford, with the updated rationale that Browning's actual changes may amount to more than the two records of changes Penguin/Yale and Oxford use and that the later text is reliable because the plates were changed only where Browning called for changes.) They are now especially suspicious of the copy-text as one that may carry forward or create error. Volume 8 emends the text in twenty-two places and restores lost line breaks accurately. The texts in my examinations were very accurate, unlike the earlier volumes, and annotation was far better focused than before and yet often generous and well researched.

The special value of the Ohio text was in fact one of its features that first provoked most vehement criticism. By providing a record of all the variants, now from manuscript through earlier collected editions to final copy-text, Ohio gave each reader a way of establishing Browning's text at any point in its, and his, career. The implicit challenge to notions of an author as a solid thing existing at only one point in time, when his definitive text was created by his fiat for all time, so troubling in the early 1970s, now seems reasonable enough (*pace,* Professor Crowder). For different critical purposes we require or prefer different texts. Browning did not generally rewrite his texts as remarkably as a Wordsworth or a Yeats; but he did continuously innovate (as the original Ohio editors rightly noted). For our practical purposes we may have good reason to prefer the earlier *Pauline* or the manuscript of *Paracelsus,* the first edition of *Dramatic Lyrics* (as George Bornstein has argued in an essay in *Poems in Their Place: The Intertextuality and Order of Poetic Collections,* ed. Neil Fraistat, 1986), or, as John Woolford's recent book interestingly suggests, even to go back to the reordering Browning himself imposed on his dramatic monologues when he collected his works in the 1860s. Ohio gives us the kit to build the text we need: guarantee not valid if not used cautiously and wisely.

The Ohio editors plan—someday—to return to those early volumes and correct. Meanwhile Ian Jack and his associates have published three of the excellent volumes in his projected *The Poetical Works.* The copy-text was the same as that chosen by Penguin/Yale and it has been especially carefully scrutinized for errors by comparison to manuscripts and revises, wherever available, as well as earlier editions. Jack did not give full variants but he usefully indicated those

that seem most important and clearly marked his own emendations. In the case of *Pauline* and *Paracelsus,* he published the earlier versions (*Pauline,* 1833, and the manuscript of *Paracelsus*). We were not given everything we might want or need; rather, and this is true throughout Jack's edition, we were given the editor's personal but well-seasoned and judicious choices of what seems especially important. (I might say I would have welcomed more parallel texts, say of the first *Dramatic Lyrics* or *Pippa Passes,* in volume 3.) Oxford's glory has been its scholarly introductions and annotations. Here Jack has made especially good use of the full biographical record available in the letters, published and unpublished. The introductions really update and replace DeVane on most issues relating to the works published. The notes are especially strong in providing a literary context for Browning, a particularly difficult task for a poet so concerned not to sound like his predecessors. And Jack has not been afraid to befriend the reader and help him through cruxes in meaning, especially in his fine notes on *Sordello.* Each of the three editions of Browning has notes with different emphases worth consulting. Jack's are, however, generally fuller than Penguin/Yale and better focused than Ohio.

In sum, I think we have great reason to be pleased with the development of all three editions. Penguin/Yale is already available as a very respectable text for the serious student, a great improvement over what we had in general use before, with sharp and lively notes. Ohio, back on its feet, offers an acceptable scholarly text, full annotation, and a unique library-in-one of Browning's different texts. Its *The Ring and the Book* is immediately useful as the only scholarly text. Oxford is on its way to being the most authoritative and reliable single text, the choice for critical work and the most helpful compilation of information on a poem. If this were not plenty already, we have plans announced by Woolford and Karlin for another text, in the Longman's Annotated English Poets series, that will feature publication of poems in their first printed form, a rival text, in effect, to that of all three other editions.

On this note, with such plenty of good editions on or in hand and promise of a rejuvenated, younger Browning to come, I will end this review. With all the controversy in our current critical, and even editing, worlds Browning has not been neglected. Our criticism has shown him as an especially interesting test case for many of the current critical approaches, or for their opponents. The good of this is of course that we are taking the problem of reading and understanding Browning seriously; we are challenging former readings and approaches, which go dead in any case with mere repetition; or we are being challenged to defend our positions, exhibiting the rationale behind our customary procedures. Major work in editing Browning has both made important new information and texts available and helped us to rethink more carefully our relation to those texts. Put all this in the time capsule and see what it will look like—important or minor—another centenary from now. The level of activity, even the amount of disagreement and excitement over it, assures me that Browning at least will survive for another hundred years.

Abbreviated Journal Titles

AUMLA—Journal of the Australasian Universities Language and Literature Association

BIS—Browning Institute Studies (later *VLC*)

BSN—Browning Society Notes

CI—Critical Inquiry

ELH—English Literary History

HLQ—Huntington Library Quarterly

JNT—Journal of Narrative Technique

MLR—Modern Language Review

MP—Modern Philology

SBHC—Studies in Browning and His Circle

SEL—Studies in English Literature, 1500-1900

TLS—Times Literary Supplement

VLC—Victorian Literature and Culture (formerly *BIS*)

VP—Victorian Poetry

VS—Victorian Studies

YULG—Yale University Library Gazette

FURTHER READING

Biography

Ryals, Clyde de L. *The Life of Robert Browning: A Critical Biography.* Oxford, UK: Blackwell, 1993, 291 p.

> Studies the poetical development of Browning, observing that Browning's poetry is informed both by Browning's "biographical presence" and his "biographical absence."

Criticism

Armstrong, Isobel. "Browning in the 1850s and After: New Experiments in Radical Poetry and the Grotesque." In *Victorian Poetry: Poetry, Poetics and Politics*, pp. 284-317. London: Routledge, 1993.

> Explores the development of Browning's poetry following his 1846 marriage and the subsequent 1855 publication of *Men and Women*, examining in particular the poet's experiments with language and form.

Bristow, Joseph. *Robert Browning.* Harvester New Readings. Hertfordshire, England: Harvester Wheatsheaf, 1991, 178 p.

> Provides a critical introduction to Browning's poetry, focusing on Browning's desire and struggle to impart his views regarding the "divine necessity of cultural change."

Buckler, William E. *Poetry and Truth in Robert Browning's The Ring and the Book.* New York: New York University Press, 1985, 293 p.

> Book-length study of *The Ring and the Book*, focusing on the "poetry" and the "imagination" of the text rather than on the "learning" and "erudition" of it. Buckler maintains that Browning intended the poem to be "a course in critical-creative reading."

DeLaura, David J. "The Context of Browning's Painter Poems: Aesthetics, Polemics, Historics." *PMLA* 95, No. 3 (May 1980): 367-88.

> Argues that Alexis François Rio's influential 1836 book on the depiction of Christian devotion in paintings provides the backdrop against which Browning's painter poems may be understood.

Gibson, Mary Ellis, ed. *Critical Essays on Robert Browning.* New York: G. K. Hall, 1992, 275 p.

> Collection of contemporary essays analyzing the structure, style, and themes of Browning's poems.

Jack, Ian and Margaret Smith, eds. *The Poetical Works of Robert Browning*, Vols. I, II, III (edited by Ian Jack and Rowena Fowler), and IV (edited by Ian Jack, Rowena Fowler, and Margaret Smith). Oxford: Clarendon Press, 1983, 1984, 1988, and 1991.

> These volumes contain critical introductions to *Pauline* and *Paracelsus* (Vol. I); *Strafford* and *Sordello* (Vol. II); and the individual poems contained in the *Bells and Pomegranates* series (Vols. III and IV). Volume IV also contains a critical introduction to *Christmas-Eve and Easter-Day*.

O'Neill, Patricia. *Robert Browning and Twentieth-Century Criticism.* Columbia, S.C.: Camden House, 1995, 157 p.

> Discusses the history of Browning criticism, from the time of the poet's death in 1889 through the critical debates of the 1970s, 1980s and beyond.

Roberts, Adam. "Men and Women, 1855," in *Robert Browning Revisited.* New York: Twayne, 1996, pp. 57-74.

Argues for the unity of Browning's _Men and Women_.

———"Using Myth: Browning's _Fifine at the Fair_." _Browning Society Notes_ 20, No. 1 (1990): 12-30.
Studies the mythological allusions in the poem to determine whether or not they are logically connected with one another. The critic also contends that classical mythic reference "underlies the broader message of the poem."

Slinn, E. Warwick. _Browning and the Fictions of Identity_. London: The Macmillan Press, Ltd., 1982, 173 p.
Explores Browning's conception of human psychology and personality as exemplified in the poet's dramatic monologues.

Tucker, Herbert F., Jr. _Browning's Beginnings: The Art of Disclosure_. Minneapolis: University of Minnesota Press, 1980, 257 p.
Examines Browning's fascination with "the fatal, frightening, yet necessary muse of closure," maintaining that it is this interest of Browning's which motivates his "open-ended" poetry.

Woolford, John. _Browning the Revisionary_. London: The Macmillan Press Ltd., 1988, 233 p.
Argues that Browning's desire to achieve popular success colored the first thirty-six years of the poet's career, and that this ambition drove Browning's "self-revision," or "the practical application of his revision of Romantic aesthetics."

Additional coverage of Browning's life and works can be found in the following sources published by The Gale Group: _Poetry Criticism_, **Vol. 2;** _World Literature Criticism, 1500 to the Present, Second Edition_; **and** _Dictionary of Literary Biography_, **Vols. 32 and 163.**

Benjamin Disraeli

1804-1881

English novelist, essayist, poet, dramatist, and short story writer. For additional information on Disraeli's life and works, see *NCLC,* Volumes 2 and 39.

INTRODUCTION

Acknowledged as the originator of the political novel, Disraeli was also a unique and remarkable politician in Victorian England. In spite of numerous obstacles, including prevalent anti-Semitism and a bias on the part of aristocrats against members of the middle class, Disraeli ascended to the highest social and political circles, his career culminating in his election as prime minister in 1868. As a literary figure, Disraeli is best known for his political trilogy of the 1840s—comprising the novels *Coningsby, Sybil,* and *Tancred,* and often referred to as the Young England trilogy—which celebrates England's aristocracy while also recounting the social ills brought on by the Industrial Revolution.

Biographical Information

Disraeli was born to Maria and Isaac D'Israeli in a middle-class London neighborhood. Although the family was of Jewish descent, Disraeli's father broke with Judaism and had his children baptized as Anglicans; however, throughout his life Disraeli maintained an interest in a number of religions, finding his Jewish heritage in particular to be a source of spiritual value. He grew up in a home filled with literary activity—the family library was extensive, and his father was a respected and well-liked author and critic. Disraeli's formal education was brief: he went to private schools for a time, but then his father decided to instruct him at home, hoping to prepare him for a career in law. Although he developed political aspirations at an early age, Disraeli showed no affinity for law, preferring instead to pursue his interest in literature. As a young man, he invested in several ambitious projects designed to secure him fame and fortune but that instead resulted in the accumulation of enormous debts that plagued him for years. In an attempt to alleviate these debts, Disraeli wrote his first novel, *Vivian Grey,* which portrays the manners and mores of upper-class English society. Published anonymously, the work caused an immediate sensation and was quite popular. When it was disclosed that the author was not actually a member of the aristocracy, but a middle-class citizen of Jewish descent, Disraeli became the object of bitter attacks from London literary figures. After the *Vivian Grey* controversy, Disraeli was befriended by fellow novelist Edward Bulwer-Lytton, who helped him gain entrance to the fash-

ionable society that had previously despised him. Disraeli, operating under the maxim that "affectation is better than wit," earned a reputation as a dandy with his unusual behavior and flamboyant appearance. While his eccentricity proved entertaining in London's social circles, it did not assist him in realizing his political ambitions, and he soon began to modify his conduct.

In 1837, Disraeli was elected to Parliament and soon thereafter assumed leadership of the Young England movement. This group, which advocated a new direction for the conservative Tory party, espoused the preservation of the monarchy and the privileged class, compassion for the poor, and a return to the religious devotion of ages past. During the next decade, Disraeli incorporated these tenets into his *Coningsby, Sybil,* and *Tancred.* In 1847, he was chosen as leader of the Tory party in the House of Commons, a position he retained for over 20 years. He served as prime minister for a short time in 1868 and was elected to that position again in 1874. For most of this time, Disraeli devoted himself solely to politics, publishing no fiction after the Young England trilogy until *Lothair* in 1870. He retired from public life in 1880 and published his last novel, *Endymion,* that same year. He had completed only a few chapters of a novel that parodied the life of his political nemesis, William Gladstone, when he died in 1881.

Major Works

Disraeli began writing fiction at a time when England was experiencing increased social mobility; an influx of money and acquisition of land was helping middle-class citizens become landed gentry. Living amidst these developments, Disraeli experimented with a fashionable literary genre known as the "silver fork" novel, which featured highly romantic depictions of aristocratic life and which served as social guidebooks for parvenus. Frequently these novels, like Disraeli's *Vivian Grey* (1826) and *The Young Duke* (1831), contained character sketches of well-known public figures and required keys to decipher the characters' real-life counterparts. Disraeli also experimented with a number of other genres, including poetry and drama. Robert Blake, an eminent Disraeli biographer, has commented that Disraeli "produced an epic poem, unbelievably bad, and a five-act blank verse tragedy, if possible worse."

With *Coningsby; or, The New Generation* (1844), Disraeli infused the novel genre with political sensibility, espousing the belief that England's future as a world power depended not on the complacent old guard, but on youthful, idealistic politicians. This novel was followed by *Sybil; or, The Two Nations* (1845), which was less idealistic than *Coningsby* in its examination of the vast economic and social disparity between the privileged and working classes. Completing Disraeli's political novel trilogy was *Tancred; or, The New Crusade* (1847), in which the author advocated the restoration of the Anglican Church to a position of spiritual preeminence in England. Disraeli rounded out his literary career with *Lothair* and *Endymion,* the former a novel of political life and a commentary on the Roman Catholic Church, and the latter a concluding statement of his economic and political policies.

Critical Reception

Although critics have acknowledged that Romantic elements can be found in all of Disraeli's works, his early novels particularly reflect that influence. Daniel Schwarz has suggested that "as an outsider, as a man who savoured his own feelings and sought unusual sensations, the youthful Disraeli saw himself as an heir to Byron and Shelley." The young heroes of his novels frequently travel to mysterious lands in search of adventure and romance, and they often consult an older man whose wisdom is of a prophetic, even mystical, nature. Commentators have also discussed how Disraeli's political philosophy heavily influenced his novels, observing that while the early works reflect a youthful idealism, the later ones show evidence of more mature and humanitarian concerns. The cumulative

effect of these insights, critics have maintained, make Disraeli's novels exceptionally valuable both as highly original works of art and as important reflections of the social changes that took place during the Victorian age.

Commentators have also argued that stylistically Disraeli's prose reveals a sparkling wit and colorful imagination, as well as a skillful use of irony, deft psychological analysis, and the creative depiction of aristocratic mores and fashions. However, supporters and detractors alike have acknowledged that certain stylistic flaws cannot be ignored. They cite clumsy prose and poorly constructed plots as particularly weak elements of Disraeli's novels and point out his failure to convey emotions sincerely and to describe working-class life and poverty convincingly. Furthermore, while Disraeli has been censured for what some scholars consider the unwieldy, rambling nature of his novels, Schwarz has defended the author by asserting that "reading Disraeli's novels . . . is more like moving from room to room in a large museum than studying a single painting for hours."

PRINCIPAL WORKS

Vivian Grey (novel) 1826
The Voyage of Captain Popanilla (satire) 1828
The Young Duke (novel) 1831
Contarini Fleming: A Psychological Autobiography (novel) 1832
The Wondrous Tale of Alroy. The Rise of Iskander (novel and short story) 1832
The Revolutionary Epick (poem) 1834
A Year at Hartlebury; or, The Election [published with his sister Sarah, under the pseudonyms Cherry and Fair Star] (novel) 1834
Henrietta Temple: A Love Story (novel) 1836
Venetia; or, The Poet's Daughter (novel) 1837
The Tragedy of Count Alarcos (drama) 1839
Coningsby; or, The New Generation (novel) 1844
Sybil; or, The Two Nations (novel) 1845
Tancred; or, The New Crusade (novel) 1847
Lothair (novel) 1870
Endymion (novel) 1880
Whigs and Whiggism: Political Writings (essays) 1913

CRITICISM

Patrick Brantlinger (essay date 1972)

SOURCE: "Tory Radicalism and 'The Two Nations' in Disraeli's *Sybil,*" *The Victorian Newsletter,* No. 41, Spring, 1972, pp. 13-17.

[In the following essay, Brantlinger explores the political theory expressed in Sybil, *focusing on Disraeli's Tory-Radicalism and analyzing his purported acceptance of the "two-nations" theory of the Chartists.]*

Despite F. R. Leavis' praise of Disraeli's neglected maturity in a footnote to *The Great Tradition,* there has been no revival of interest in his novels. And rightly so, if only because Disraeli's three most important novels, **Coningsby, Sybil,** and **Tancred,** espoused a cause that was more laughed at than respected even in the 1840s. "Young Hengland," as Thackeray's C. Jeames De La Pluche called it, was an attempt to bring people and aristocracy together under a single "Tory-Radical" banner; it was therefore open to censure by Tories, by Radicals, and of course also by Whigs. As Marx and Engles put it, the "feudal socialism" of Young England was "half lamentation, half lampoon," not to be taken seriously as a political theory.[1] Defending Disraeli against charges of slipperiness, egoism, and superficiality would be a thankless task. But even his weaknesses as a political thinker and as a novelist merit study, because they illuminate an age and the literature of "feudal socialism" generally, including the attitudes of Carlyle.

It was in **Sybil** that Disraeli went farthest in his attempt to weld Toryism and Radicalism together, for it was there that he focused on "the condition of the people" and recommended a political union of the working classes and the aristocracy against the middle classes. This union he tried to symbolize by the standard Victorian fictional strategy of an interclass marriage, joining his aristocratic hero, Egremont, with his working-class heroine, Sybil Gerard. As some of Disraeli's first readers noted, however, this symbolic union of "the two nations" of rich and poor turns into tommyrot when it is learned that Sybil isn't a working-class girl at all but an aristocrat. An equivalent turn of the screw, one imagines, might be changing Blake's tiger into Mehitabel. Monckton Milnes, himself associated with Young England, thought Sybil's metamorphosis was contradictory, and because of it John Lucas concludes that **Sybil** is "a mostly unintelligent, because badly muddled, piece of work."[2]

Without disputing Lucas' condemnation of a typically histrionic lapse of logic on Disraeli's part, it is important to consider what he was getting at when he so marred his symbolic union of classes. Disraeli is contradictory, but he isn't stupid, and if Sybil is transmogrified from a Chartist working-class girl into a fine lady, it can't be in total violation of reason. Sybil's metamorphosis, in fact, is matched by a series of historical digressions that reveal Egremont's family to be less aristocratic than it claims. The antiquarian revelations that prove Sybil to be of noble ancestry are paralleled by Disraeli's accounts of the modern, felonious origins of the great Whig families. Of Egremont's family, Disraeli tells

us that "the founder . . . had been a confidential domestic of one of the favourites of Henry VIII, and had contrived to be appointed one of the commissioners for 'visiting and taking the surrenders of divers religious houses'" (pp. 10-11).[3] Upon the basis of property pirated from the Church, "honest Baldwin Greymount" boosted his descendants into the peerage. Such are the histories, Disraeli tells us, of most of the "ancient" families who make up the "Venetian oligarchy" of the Whigs and the "pseudo-Tories" (that is, the Peelites). And such, too, is one basis for the Tory-Radical version of history that runs throughout Disraeli's novels and speeches, for the Church was the first victim of "the spirit of utility" and upon her former property modern liberalism sprang up, wresting power from the Stuarts along the way. By the same process of spoliation and fraud, the poor were losing their rights. Sybil claims that "the people" have been "driven from the soil" (p. 95) and Philip Warner, the handloom weaver, that he and the rest of the poor "have lost our estates" (p. 134). Although it seems to get Disraeli out of a jam, Sybil's metamorphosis also symbolizes the restoration of the rights and estates of the lower classes, many of whom are more truly aristocratic than the modern nobility. Not only is the family tree of Egremont and Lord Marney of dubious and recent origin but so are those of Lord de Mowbray (pp. 88-93), the Duke of Fitz-Aquitaine (pp. 146-47), and Lord Deloraine (pp. 239-40). On the other hand, as Millbank says in **Coningsby:**

> The real old families of this country are to be found among the peasantry; the gentry, too, may lay some claim to old blood. I can point you out Saxon families in this country who can trace their pedigrees beyond the Conquest. (p. 169)

Walter Gerard, Mr. Trafford, Aubrey St. Lys, and even Sybil's bloodhound, Harold, are "of the ancient breed" (p. 139). Through the shoddy machinations of Baptist Hatton, the powerful quack antiquarian who "has made more peers of the realm than our gracious Sovereign" (p. 273) and who elevates Sybil to a station of doubtful value, Disraeli ridicules the whole concept of the hereditary nobility. "There is no longer in fact an aristocracy in England, for the superiority of the animal man is an essential quality of aristocracy" (p. 123). To think in terms of class at all, an apparently Radical Disraeli implies, is nowadays absurd, for blue blood has become thin blood. A person ought to be judged by his talents and not by his birth—look at Disraeli as an example.

The trouble is that having satirized the hereditary basis of the class structure, Disraeli still insists on giving Sybil aristocratic status. Furthermore, while he is ridiculing the modern aristocracy out of one side of his mouth, out of the other issues nothing like the sympathy for the poor we expect from someone who claims to champion them. On the contrary, while Disraeli satirizes the Whigs and the Pseudo-Tories, he also satirizes the Radicals, the Chartists, and, perhaps unintentionally, the poor as a "nation." Parallel to the history of upperclass politics since 1832 that forms the subject of the whole Young England trilogy, *Sybil* contains a history of Chartism from its beginnings in 1838 through the Plug Plot riots in the summer of 1842. When the first Chartist petition was presented to the House of Commons in 1839, Disraeli had made a speech that, while arguing *against* its official consideration, argued *for* a sympathetic rejection of it.[4] It is typical of the wily ambiguities that appear in *Sybil.* This speech is echoed in *Sybil,* for the heroine discovers one day that the Charter has been defended in Parliament by an aristocrat:

> Yes! there was one voice that had sounded in that proud Parliament, that, free from the slang of faction, had dared to express immortal truths: the voice of a noble, who without being a demagogue, had upheld the popular cause. . . . With . . . eyes suffused with tears, Sybil read the speech of Egremont. She ceased. . . . Before her stood the orator himself. (p. 337)

besides this noteworthy piece of egotism, Disraeli's history of Chartism in *Sybil* shows its decline from the early, glowing idealism of Walter Gerard and his daughter through the failure of the first petition, the encroachments of factional strife, and the fiascoes of "physical force"—the riots in the Birmingham Bullring, the Newport Rising of 1839, and the Plug Plot violence of 1842. As Sybil sadly tells Stephen Morley, "I believed that we had on our side God and Truth."

> "They know neither of them in the National Convention," said Morley. "Our career will be a vulgar caricature of the bad passions and the low intrigues, the factions and the failures, of our oppressors." (p. 289-90)

Walter Gerard's "moral force" idealism succumbs to the influence of "the party of violence," and this is seen as the tragedy of Chartism as a whole. Gerard takes part in a conspiracy aiming at a national insurrection, but this leads only to the abortive Newport Rising of 1839 and to his arrest along with numerous other leaders of the movement. By revealing the bankruptcy of both Chartism and Whiggery, of both the Radical and the Liberal political alternatives, Disraeli tries to demonstrate the need for a third alternative—the Tory-Radicalism of Young England.

But while Disraeli's presentation of Chartism is unsympathetic, his presentation of the nation of the poor generally is so riddled with irony that it is difficult to think of him as even approximately their champion. The failure of logic that leads to Sybil's transformation

reveals itself again in the fact that there are two distinct kinds of poor people in the novel—the good ones (who are aristocrats anyway in the case of the Gerards), and the riffraff. Thus, while Gerard and his daughter both seem noble and are noble, the mobs of miners and mechanics who fill the background of the tale are hardly idealized. Like Oliver Twist in the clutches of Sikes and Fagin, the angelic Sybil is constantly forced to rub elbows with lower-class villains. At least as important symbolically as the union of Egremont and Sybil is the fact that Egremont snatches Sybil from the grasp of a lower-class mob during the Plug Plot riots:

> One ruffian had grasped the arm of Sybil, another had clenched her garments, when an officer, covered with dust and gore, sabre in hand, jumped from the terrace, and hurried to the rescue. He cut down one man, thrust away another, and, placing his left arm round Sybil, he defended her with his sword. . . . Her assailants were routed, they made a staggering flight! The officer turned round and pressed Sybil to his heart.

> "We will never part again," said Egremont.

> "Never," murmured Sybil. (p. 484)

It is scenes like this that led Arnold Kettle to describe *Sybil* as "operatic"; he might have added that Disraeli, not Sybil, is the prima donna.[5] At any rate, if Sybil is presented to us as a "daughter of the people" who turns out to be blue-blooded, she is also brought into rough contact with "the people" at several points in the novel. Her terrifying venture into Seven Dials in search of her father presents us with a contrast between her unconscious gentility and the violence of the slum dwellers (pp. 362-66), and her nightmare after her arrest continues the pattern:

> She woke . . . in terror from a dream in which she had been dragged through a mob, and carried before a tribunal. The coarse jeers, the brutal threats, still echoed in her ear. (pp. 382-83)

Before uniting Egremont and Sybil, Disraeli weans her from her "moral force" Chartism by showing her just how degraded, ignorant, and violent "the people" can be, giving her doses of revolutionary chaos and of the lower depths in order to teach her that the tenants in the social cellar need governors and not that they need to govern themselves.

Disraeli is not much interested in making us feel sorry for the poor; he is much more intent on proving the poor to be mistaken. Thus, the two chief factory workers in *Sybil,* Dandy Mick and Devilsdust, are shown to be adolescent malcontents with only the negligence of their superiors as a real motive for rebellion. They are well paid enough to entertain two girl friends with drinks and hot sausages in that swank gin palace, "The Cat and the Fiddle." Further, in sketching in their backgrounds, Disraeli avoids evidence that would support Lord Ashley's Ten Hours Bill, even though he voted for it in 1847. The story of Devilsdust's childhood does not present us with arguments for saving children from the horrors of the mill by passing the Ten Hours Bill, and in fact it weighs against that Bill. Abandoned by his mother and cared for only by a brutal "nurse" who sends him "out in the street to 'play,' in order to be run over," Devilsdust survives partly by miracle and partly by tenacity. Neglect is what almost kills him, and opposed to neglect is the order and the security of the factory system. His salvation comes when good luck guides him, still only an infant, through the gates of a factory and into a job. "A child was wanting in the Wadding Hole. . . . The nameless one was preferred to the vacant post, received even a salary, more than that, a name; for as he had none, he was christened on the spot DEVILSDUST" (p. 114). "Fortune had guided him." Disraeli suggests that the factories afford protection to children who would otherwise be neglected and abused by their working-class parents, an idea often expressed by the defenders of child labor.

The most startling scene among the poor occurs when the Owenite, Stephen Morley, travels to Wodgate in search of the antiquarian, Mr. Hatton. There he discovers Hatton's brother, who is the "Bishop" or head man of a town that, though a slough of filth and degradation, is an entirely independent community run by the workers themselves—proletarian blacksmiths and their apprentices.[6] The inhabitants of Wodgate are the most brutalized and violent characters whom Disraeli describes. From an apprentice, Thomas, Morley learns about the "Bishop" and at the same time he learns how illiterate and deprived some of the citizens of England are, for Thomas' fiancée believes in "our Lord and Saviour Pontius Pilate, who was crucified to save our sins" (pp. 192-93). Backward as the Wodgate metalworkers are, they are also, Disraeli stresses, free, for they are under the control of neither laissez-faire government nor upperclass capitalists but of masters like the Bishop who belong to their own class. They form a natural society, and they present Morley with two possible lessons, although he comes away from Wodgate as staunchly socialistic as ever. First, Morley might learn that the workers, if left to govern themselves, would increase rather than diminish their degradation. Disraeli exposes the neglect from which the poor suffer, but he also exposes their unfitness to manage their own affairs. Secondly, Morley might learn that, if left alone, the workers would form a government along aristocratic rather than democratic lines, for Wodgate is ruled by an aristocracy "by no means so unpopular as the aristocracy of most other places."

> . . . it is a real aristocracy; it is privileged, but it does something for its privileges. It is distinguished from the main body not merely by name. It is the most knowing class at Wodgate; it possesses indeed in its way complete knowledge; and it imparts in its manner a certain quantity of it to those whom it guides. Thus it is an aristocracy that leads, and therefore a fact. (p. 188)

Between the misrule of Bishop Hatton and the misrule of Lord Marney, Disraeli sees a damnable similarity. Between either of these and an aristocracy as it ought to be—as Young England would make it or even as the "Captains of Industry" should make it—there is no similarity.

In the Wodgate episode, Disraeli's satire is both consistent and well-expressed. His first task all along has been to show the bankruptcy of all potential sources of governmental authority save one—a revitalized aristocracy led by Young England. By exposing the absurdity of Bishop Hatton's rule, he simultaneously exposes the neglect of the Church and of the governing classes. Chartism and trade unionism are also failures, but their very existence is symptomatic of the bungling of the Whigs and the pseudo-Tories. Having pointed out the inadequacy of all current political programs, Disraeli would suggest that there is a group of idealistic young social saviors waiting in the wings, led by an inscrutable Oriental prophet named Disraeli. The program of this saving remnant, however, remains cloudy, for instead of containing a pattern of genuine paradoxes leading to "Tory-Radicalism" as a climactic oxymoron *Sybil* contains only a skein of contradictions, growing out of its conflicting plots of the educations of hero and heroine.

Sybil describes the disillusionment of its Chartist characters at the same time that it describes the introduction of Egremont to "the condition of England question." Even more than the discovery of Sybil's aristocratic lineage, it is this double plot that stirs up contradictions and causes consternation in its readers. As Egremont is acquiring some sympathy for the poor, Sybil is losing part of hers, and the Tory-Radical compromise that should exist between them does not materialize. Contradiction, in fact, arises where there should be compromise, and the most glaring instance is what happens to the central theme of the novel. This theme is that Queen Victoria rules over "two nations," "the rich and the poor." As Monypenny says, Disraeli's main purpose is to show the difference "between riches and poverty, luxury and suffering."[7] As a description of *Sybil,* this is perfectly reasonable as far as it goes, but it does not go far enough, for Disraeli's other main purpose is to show that the difference "between riches and poverty, luxury and suffering" is blown out of all proportion by Chartists and Radicals. The idea that the Queen rules over two distinct nations with a great gulf fixed between is one of Disraeli's arguments, but it is also an erroneous belief of Sybil's that she loses during the process of her disillusionment. It is significant that the idea of "the two nations" is first presented to Egremont and the reader, in the most famous "operatic" set-piece of the novel (pp. 76-77), by Stephen Morley, a godless socialist who later tries to murder Egremont out of jealousy. Disraeli treats the "two nations" theme as a paradox he hopes will startle his readers into some awareness of the problems of the poor, but he also treats it as a dangerous illusion and a cliché of radicals like Morley.

The idea of "the two nations" comes as a revelation to Egremont; it is the beginning of his acceptance of social responsibility as an aristocrat. On the other hand, the idea of "the two nations" is also an illusion from which Sybil must be won before she can find Egremont acceptable as a suitor. When Egremont undergoes his pastoral education in the humble abode of the Gerards, he conceals his social rank and adopts the democratic alias, "Mr. Franklin." He quickly discovers that disguise is necessary, for so thoroughly is Sybil a "daughter of the people" and a Chartist that, when she discovers who he is, she spurns him:

> "The brother of Lord Marney!" repeated Sybil, with an air almost of stupor.

> "Yes," said Egremont; "a member of that family of sacrilege, of those oppressors of the people, whom you have denounced to me with such withering scorn." (p. 284)

When Egremont pleads with Sybil not to cast him off because he is an aristocrat, she says, "haughtily": "I am one of those who believe the gulf is impassable. Yes . . . utterly impassable."

Disraeli's Prince cleans the hearth while Cinderella snubs him. It is a situation similar to one in *Coningsby*, wherein that young aristocrat falls in love with the daughter of the rich manufacturer Millbank, whose dislike for the "factitious" nobility makes marriage unthinkable. But just as Millbank eventually abandons his class prejudice, so Sybil learns that the gulf between rich and poor is not "impassable." Disraeli's irony is clever but also superficial, because it has never made sense to tell the oppressed (in this case, Chartist workers) that they should be more tolerant and less tyrannical toward their oppressors. That, however, is the lesson Disraeli teaches Sybil, while he is also making Egremont aware of the existence of the poor.

Sybil had led a sheltered and privileged life, and nothing has taught her to abandon the illusion of the "impassable gulf" between "the two nations" until she encounters two very different forces—handsome Egremont and working-class violence. "Educated in solitude and exchanging thoughts only with individuals of the same sympathies," Sybil has reached the view "that the world was divided only between the oppressors and the oppressed."

> With her, to be one of the people was to be miserable and innocent; one of the privileged, a luxurious tyrant. In the cloister, in her garden . . . she had raised up two phantoms which with her represented human nature.

> But the experience of the last few months had operated a great change in these impressions. She had seen enough to suspect that the world was a more complicated system than she had preconceived. . . . The characters were more various, the motives more mixed, the classes more blended, the elements of each more subtle and diversified, than she had imagined. (p. 335)

The two nations then, are no more than "two phantoms" of Sybil's imagination that do not describe society realistically, and Egremont is right when he taxes her with being "prejudiced" (p. 318).

Disraeli's contradictory attitude toward his theme affects the structure of his novel in at least two ways. First, it keeps him from offering a straightforward contrast between rich and poor and leads him instead into a series of ambiguous contrasts between a multiplicity of classes, in which factory workers and miners and farm laborers are juxtaposed, while manufacturers disagree with landlords and Chartists disagree with each other. And second, it causes him to make odd, ambiguous assertions about each of the social groups he describes, like Millbank's claim that many of the poor have noble blood in their veins. Working perhaps more from blue books than from personal knowledge, Disraeli describes conditions among miners, farm workers, cotton operatives, handloom weavers, metalworkers, and the Irish poor of London, and he shows with some sympathy and much colorful detail the roots of social rebellion in those conditions. But in the process he demonstrates that the poor are not at all a unified "nation" confronting the rich. The poor are rather a congeries of quarreling factions, and the same is true of the rich, who split up into at least two major groups, landlords and manufacturers. And while it is true that there may be various classes in a society that is nevertheless divided between the haves and the have-nots, Disraeli points to the diversity of the class system as a refutation of "the two nations" theory held by his Chartist characters.

Disraeli's social panorama is remarkable for its range and its vividness; he often makes the dead bones of the blue books come to life. But it is marred repeatedly by spurious paradoxes and flashy riddles, and it is finally perhaps necessary to regard it as only a colorful "muddle," to use Stephen Blackpool's word. Walter Bagehot said of Disraeli that "nothing has really impeded his progress more than his efforts after originality," and this is exactly the trouble with **Sybil**.[8] Disraeli is so in love with irony that he allows it to undermine the central thesis of **Sybil**. He mocks even his own Young England comrades, as when Lord Everingham laughs at Lord Henry Sidney in **Coningsby** for his notion that "the people are to be fed by dancing round a Maypole." Disraeli offers the standard Burkean arguments about custom and faith as opposed to theory and reason and about society as an organism, and this gives his rhetoric a prophetic ring. But his portrait of social England reveals so many complexities and shatters so many clichés—not least of which is "the two nations" idea—that finally the only logical program appears to be the one described by the heroine:

> "It sometimes seems to me," said Sybil despondingly, "that nothing short of the descent of angels can save the people of this kingdom." (p. 199)

When Disraeli beat Peel on the Corn Law issue and irreparably broke the old Tory party, one wonders how many astonished and grateful Saxons realized that the first of the angels had arrived among them.

Notes

[1] "Manifesto of the Communist Party," in Marx and Engels, *Basic Writings on Politics and Philosophy,* ed. Lewis S. Feuer (New York, 1959), p. 30.

[2] Richard Monckton Milnes, "The Emancipation of the Jews," *Edinburgh Review* (July 1847), p. 75. John Lucas, "Mrs. Gaskell and Brotherhood," *Tradition and Tolerance in Nineteenth-Century Fiction,* ed. Howard, Lucas, and Goode (New York, 1967), p. 154.

[3] Quotations from *Coningsby* and *Sybil* are from the Hughenden Edition (London, 1881), IX and VII. Page numbers are given in parentheses.

[4] *Hansard's Debates,* June 12, 1839, cols. 246-52.

[5] Arnold Kettle, "The Early Victorian Social-Problem Novel," in *From Dickens to Hardy,* ed. Boris Ford (Baltimore, 1968), p. 176.

[6] For the significance of the scene as well as its factual basis, see Sheila M. Smith, "Willenhall and Wodgate: Disraeli's Use of Blue Book Evidence," *RES,* XIII (November 1962), 368-84.

[7] William F. Monypenny and G. E. Buckle, *The Life of Benjamin Disraeli* (London, 1929), I, 651.

[8] "Mr. Disraeli," in *Walter Bagehot,* ed. Norman St. John-Stevas (Bloomington, Ind., 1959), p. 411.

Robert O'Kell (essay date 1976)

SOURCE: "The Autobiographical Nature of Disraeli's Early Fiction," *Nineteenth-Century Fiction,* Vol. 31, No. 3, December, 1976, pp. 253-84.

[*In the essay that follows, O'Kell discusses how Disraeli's early novels reflect his attempt to forge a public identity. According to O'Kell, these early works represent Disraeli's struggle to combine a desire for public recognition with an acute sense of his marginalization as a writer of Jewish descent.*]

Extant biographical material suggests that the young Disraeli held two opposing senses of himself that were manifested in contradictory desires for recognition of very different sorts. Although he gloried in the ambitious egotism of his own genius and constantly sought expedient means of demonstrating its power in the pursuit of "success," Disraeli also clung to a sense of the innate superiority of another identity, one related to an awareness of his alien Jewish heritage and a need to claim an altruistic innocence or "purity" of heart. The tension between these psychic forces found expression in virtually every dimension of Disraeli's life—emotional involvements, intellectual development, aesthetic perceptions, and religious attitudes—but nowhere more consistently than in the imaginative shaping of his political career and the fantasy structure upon which his novels rest. The intention here is not to supplant the traditional interpretations of Disraeli's life and work with a reductionist psychological one. Clearly the novelist had aesthetic motives and the politician practical incentives, and neither can safely be ignored. In Disraeli's case, though, it can be argued that beyond these considerations the early fiction, however consciously organized, represents an embodiment of his fantasies about himself.

Vivian Grey (1826) was instantly successful because its readers took it to be a disguised account of *The Representative*[1] affair and the recent intrigues in John Murray's circle. They delighted in attempting to discover the identities of both the author and the characters. But this literalist attempt to relate the work to specific events and people is of little more than curiosity value. The book, however, is worth study of a different kind to those interested in the development of Disraeli's career for it confirms and develops the emotional pattern of his involvement in the events surrounding the publication of Murray's newspaper. The writing of it provided Disraeli with an opportunity for compensatory self-justification by enabling him to reconstruct imaginatively the immediate past and project it upon the future. Somewhat ironically the success of the work in some measure transcended the collapse of the power fantasy it described. The fame or notoriety Disraeli acquired as "the author of *Vivian Grey*" was not the perfect fulfillment of his desire for recognition, but, for the moment at least, it did seem to validate his conception of how he could demonstrate his remarkable talents.

The imaginative content of the novel itself, however, reflects no such validation, and, indeed, is true to the author's central ambivalence beneath his alternatively seeking success through a demonstration of his genius and claiming recognition of an innate, unquestioned superiority, the public model of which was the English aristocracy. Vivian Grey is a hero with neither noble birth nor fortune to distinguish him. But the young, bold, somewhat deliberately Byronic protagonist, sure of his extraordinary power but frustrated by the restraints of established persons, finally resorting to desperate maneuver to achieve his revenge and effect his escape from the consequences of his ultimate failure to manipulate those whom he would surpass, is prototypical of many of the early Disraelian heroes. Chapter 7 of *Vivian Grey* begins with the implied author discoursing upon the subject of success: "In England, personal distinction is the only passport to the society of the great. Whether this distinction arise from fortune, family, or talent, is immaterial; but certain it is, to enter into high society, a man must either have blood, a million, or a genius."[2] Then Vivian's interest in politics and the engagement of his genius in the ambitious manipulation of the Marquess of Carabas and others swiftly develop into the major theme of the novel. The most striking characteristic of this manipulation is the self-conscious detachment with which it is carried out. Not only is the reader given the benefit of the narrator's awareness, but also of the hero's: "He was already a cunning reader of human hearts; and felt conscious that his was a tongue which was born to guide human beings" (18). Another example of this same technique also gives away some of the insecurity underneath the repeated assertion of the hero's "sang-froid": "how many a powerful noble wants only wit to be a Minister; and what wants Vivian Grey to attain the same end? That noble's influence. . . . There wants but one thing more: courage, pure, perfect courage; and does Vivian Grey know fear? He laughed an answer of bitterest derision" (20). But despite the implicit passivity, the dominant tone at the surface of the narrative is one of Vivian's condescending confidence in his ability to lead the Marquess into giving him the name and influence with which he can take upon himself "the whole organisation of the Carabas party" (38). The cynical progress of Vivian's political career is entertaining stuff, even today, but when, finally, he can no longer control events and becomes the victim of people he once thought he influenced, his fantasy of attaining power collapses in a patently melodramatic end-

ing to an increasingly improbable plot which admits of no further development. Part I closes with the hero recuperating from a loss of consciousness under the sheltering auspices of his doting parents, and with the escape of a European tour.

This summary ignores many nuances within the novel's theme, but it is important to see the central pattern in which the protagonist attempts to manipulate people in the context of events which will establish his own brilliant career and demonstrate his superiority to all around him. Accordingly, the most significant elements of Disraeli's fantasy are Vivian's contempt for the Marquess, whose wealth and position he admires; his winning to his cause of Cleveland, whose talents and accomplishments he would outstrip; and his failure through the deceit of a siren, Mrs. Felix Lorraine, whose heart he fancies is captive, first by charm and then by fear. Furthermore, the novelist does not dwell upon his hero's extravagances in proclaiming the moral of the story to lie in the effects of his miseducation, but rather, he absolves Vivian of the responsibility for failure by means of a romanticized plot of revenge and escape.

George Augustus Frederick, Duke of St. James, the protagonist of Disraeli's second novel, is an orphan whose patrimony gives him an annual income of over two hundred thousand pounds. The central theme of *The Young Duke* (1831) concerns his overcoming the effects of an indulgent miseducation which almost allows his egotism and selfishness to ruin him financially and morally. The reversals of fortune by which the hero's conscience is fully developed constitute a more interesting novel than might at first seem likely. The plot of the novel is "hardly less improbable" than is *Vivian Grey*'s and the style is "artificial."[3] But despite this, the book has a kind of excitement that keeps the reader skimming forward. This is because the fantasy it embodies offers the author so much more security than does that of *Vivian Grey* that he can confront much more honestly and directly the hero's weaknesses and follies. Despite its superficial removal from reality, the novel has a momentum derived from a plausible internal conflict that is entirely convincing; and because the novel is superficially less autobiographical it is in a sense ultimately more so. The secure position from which the hero begins his growth to maturity is not just a matter of his nobility and wealth, though these are important. Nor is it simply a matter of self-asserted superiority. The most important element of this position is the acceptance of the young Duke of England's most distinguished social circle, an acceptance based upon his innate nobility. Among the disagreeable shocks to the young nobleman's initial complacency—the rejection of his amorous proposals by the heroine, May Dacre, the indebtedness incurred through extravagance and gambling, or the hovering scandal of his affair with Lady Aphrodite—none evades the issue of his own responsibility. And in the end, it is his willingness to accept Mr. Dacre's good advice on financial matters, and his responsible and generous response to the social and political issues of the Catholic Question, that redeem his unthinking, egotistical selfishness. Ultimately, however, this transformation of character is presented less as a result of agonizing self-appraisal than as the inevitable blossoming of his latent nobility. The close of the novel, in which the young Duke is united in marriage with the beautiful May Dacre and spends his life "in the agreeable discharge of all the important duties of his exalted station" (350), is, perhaps, for modern taste, too simply a case of virtue rewarded, but it acts as a final sanction of the premise upon which the fantasy it embodies is built: that it is impossible that a hero of such "personal distinction," noble, wealthy, handsome, and charming, could have a career "anything but the most brilliant" (*Vivian Grey,* 17, 47).

Respectively troubled and triumphant, these two fictions obviously represent Disraeli's fantasies about finding suitable recognition for the dichotomous identities or senses of himself that he felt. In *Vivian Grey* the hero's attempt to demonstrate his superiority is ultimately overwhelmed by the political circumstances and he is forced to retreat to the secure claim of essential purity of heart inherent in his parents' loving solicitude. In *The Young Duke* the hero's innate superiority is established in his nobility, and when that superiority is combined with a regained purity and innocence of true love Disraeli can imagine for him a personal, social, and political recognition of his distinction.

The next novel, *Contarini Fleming* (1832), contains all of the elements of these psychological patterns that exist in Disraeli's earliest political venture and first two novels. Moreover, it contains a quite explicit thematic development of the nature of the ambivalence Disraeli felt about the alternative forms of recognition he sought and the conflicting awarenesses of himself that underlay them. Here the ambivalence of the author represents not just a struggle between two opposite identities, but rather a conflict within the conception of each one. In other words, Disraeli's senses of himself were locked in hostile symbiosis. Further, the thematic development of *Contarini Fleming* suggests that while this hostility might conceivably be transcended in future transformations of the related fantasies, the dependency itself could never be dissolved. In *Contarini Fleming,* then, the hero's struggle for success is entangled in guilt over what he feels is his betrayal of his pure, innocent self. Contarini's political success is portrayed as necessitating a hypocritical abandonment of his childhood dream of being loved and admired simply for what he is by nature. Similarly, his search for fulfillment in a private sense, which is imagined in terms of a romance that is clearly a substitute for a childhood deprivation of maternal love, is conceived to involve a rejection of the very values of social and political success and a catastrophic exile from the realm in which it could be obtained.

In this novel there are two quite distinct thematic levels of the hero's consciousness, one overt, the other latent. The explicit theme concerns the formation of the implied author's, that is, Contarini's, character: "an ideal and complete picture of the development of the poet" (Preface, 1845, p. ix). The protagonist, we are told, was conceived as a person "whose position in life" is "at variance, and, as it were, in constant conflict with his temperament" (p. x). This conflict is established in terms of Contarini's unhappiness with the social realities of his family, his education, and the forms of success to which he is presumed to aspire. But what merit the novel has, as such, comes from the tension between Contarini's self-assertiveness and his anxieties. While it purports to be based on the hero's conscious awareness of his own development, most of the book is about his by no means necessarily conscious search for affection and security. And the implicit theme that one derives from this material concerns the discrepancy between the implied author's potential as a hero and his performance as one. The story, in fact, is a rationalization of this discrepancy.

In *Contarini Fleming* the dark, Byronic hero's quest for a realm in which he could gain recognition of his "poetic" character remains unfulfilled. This is so because the explicit struggle between the hero's "position in life" and his "temperament" is in fact a contest between two mutually exclusive desires, about both of which Contarini feels ambivalent. The desire to find a private recognition of his innate, childlike purity and innocence through romantic absorption in the figure of the substitute mother (represented overtly by both Christiana, his first childhood and adolescent object of adoration, and Alcesté, his cousin bride who bears an astonishing resemblance to his deceased mother) precludes the exercise of his ambition. When at the very height of his considerable social and political success, without which he confesses he should find life intolerable, Contarini again meets Christiana as a mature and married woman who now appears to him as the even more beautiful embodiment of an innocence and a love he has lost, her presence is a sharp reminder that he has become an ignorant and selfish "beast" quite unworthy of the harmony of love and sympathy he really desires:

> the presence of this woman . . . amid my corrupt and heartless and artificial life, of so much innocence, and so much love, and so much simplicity, they fell upon my callous heart like the first rains upon a Syrian soil. . . . I recoiled with disgust from the thought of my present life; I flew back with rapture to my old aspirations. . . . and when I remembered what I was, I buried my face in my hands and wept. (162)

Imaginatively the search for that affection is shown to be possible only in exile; Contarini abandons his political and poetic ambitions to visit Venice, the city of his maternal ancestors. Further, that search is frustrated at the culminating moment by a fate (the death of his magdalen-cousin-wife in childbirth) that reflects both the protagonist's feelings of anxiety and guilt about pursuing that desire and his sense of its inadequacy to complete fulfillment. But, as the quotation also shows, the desire to find a public recognition of his demonstrable superiority in the realm of society and politics involves a denial of his maternal heritage and "true" self. Imaginatively such success necessitates a hypocritical use of power that precludes the possibility of Contarini finding acceptance in terms of his nostalgic ideal. *Vivian Grey* is clearly a troubled embodiment of Disraeli's essential power fantasy, for in it the hero's ambitious desire to find a recognition of his demonstrable talents is thwarted by his ultimate inability to control the people and events necessary to his success. *The Young Duke,* on the other hand, embodies a fantasy of acceptance. The hero's innate nobility in the end transcends the selfishly indulgent corruption of his pure heart that threatens to mar his happiness. The young Duke's aristocratic heritage is so preeminent that the social and romantic acceptance he seeks requires no demonstration of superiority on his part beyond the expression of his natural character. In *Contarini Fleming,* however, the dark hero's heritage is dichotomous. The Protestant, northern realm of his father's life offers the opportunity of fulfilling his social and political ambitions by means of suitable demonstrations of his genius, but it is the Catholic, Venetian realm of his deceased mother that offers the personal fulfillment of unquestioning love. Significantly, in this third novel, the two worlds are conceived to be mutually exclusive. Consequently, Contarini's desire for both kinds of fulfillment becomes the source of his ambivalence about the recognition that either the struggle for "success" or the struggle for "purity" can supply. In effect this ambivalence is a conflict between two opposing senses of himself; his father's son, committed to a worldly success in terms of public recognition of the legitimacy of his ambitions; or his mother's child, committed to a personal happiness in terms of an all-absorbing love that in effect is a recognition of his heart's innate innocence and purity.

The religious dimension of Contarini's ambivalence is by no means incidental. The conflicting potentials of the Protestant and Catholic worlds as realms of fulfillment are shown to be an integral part of his identity confusion. Indeed, the tension between the protagonist's religion by birth and his religion by choice is central to the structure of many of Disraeli's novels. Disraeli had first publicly used this motif of religious allegiance as a defining characteristic of his protagonist in *The Young Duke.* In that novel,

written at the height of the Catholic Emancipation debate in 1829, his hero is a Protestant by birth whose eventual happiness comes in part as a result of his redeeming advocacy of the Catholic cause and his subsequent marriage to the Catholic heroine. It is clear now that Disraeli found in the issue of Catholic Emancipation not just a topical setting to exploit, but a disguise for his own ambiguous feelings about his Jewish heritage. He had, in fact, abandoned the manuscript of *The Wondrous Tale of Alroy* (1833) in order to write *The Young Duke* in 1829, and this is strong circumstantial evidence that his Jewish heritage was at least at that time a preoccupation directly linked in his thinking to the Catholic question. It is, however, a comparison between *Alroy* (which Disraeli completed after his defeat in the second Wycombe election, marked by overt anti-Semitism) and *Contarini Fleming* that confirms the importance of religious allegiance to the problem of personal identity in the life and in the fiction. Both novels, for example, reflect an initial isolation of the hero, a sense of expectancy with which his maturity is anticipated, and a sense of guilt which his actions create. But in *Alroy* it is not very helpful to attempt to make the distinction between explicit and implicit themes that illuminates *Contarini Fleming,* for it is clear throughout that the central theme is the ambiguity and conflict in the hero's character. In that regard *Alroy* is the product of a greater degree of conscious awareness of himself on the part of the author. While in its fantasy structure the novel confirms the pattern of early conflict and tension in the author's personality, it also proves that Disraeli was undertaking a reassessment of his behavior which led him to renewed attempts, in his fiction and in his political life, to establish his sincerity.[4]

In the person of the emotionally autobiographical David Alroy, Disraeli creates a hero who is an ideal, noble, and divinely chosen savior of his people and who essentially represents a personal defiance of reality parallel to the public postures his creator had recently adopted on the hustings. But, just as there is a deep insecurity underneath the bravado of Disraeli's early political campaigns, there is a fear of failure within the imaginative projection of the ideal. Even before he is fully possessed of the supernatural power of the messiah to free the Jewish people, Alroy is twice tempted to abandon that pure identity. The first entirely materialistic suggestion, that he be disguised and pass as Lord Honain's son and so acquire great social success and power in the Moslem world, he rejects to pursue the "eternal glory" of his religious quest. But when, at the emotional climax of the novel, disguised as a deaf-mute eunuch he meets the daughter of the Caliph, the Princess Schirene, whose mother was a Christian, Alroy's feverish and agitated response reveals the complexity of his character. Suddenly, seizing the rosary given to him by the Princess and pressing it to his lips, he soliloquizes:

"The Spirit of my dreams, she comes at last; the form for which I have sighed and wept; the form which rose upon my radiant vision when I shut my eyes against the jarring shadows of this gloomy world.

"Schirene! Schirene! here in this solitude I pour to thee the passion long stored up: the passion of my life, no common life, a life full of deep feeling and creative thought. O beautiful! O more than beautiful! for thou to me art as a dream unbroken: why art thou not mine? why lose a moment in our glorious lives, and balk our destiny of half its bliss?

"Fool, fool, hast thou forgotten? The rapture of a prisoner in his cell, whose wild fancy for a moment belies his fetters! The daughter of the Caliph and a Jew!

"Give me my father's sceptre.

"A plague on talismans! Oh! I need no inspiration but her memory, no magic but her name. By heavens! I will enter this glorious city a conqueror, or die.

"Why, what is Life? for meditation mingles ever with my passion. . . . Throw accidents to the dogs, and tear off the painted mask of false society! Here am I a hero; with a mind that can devise all things, and a heart of superhuman daring, with youth, with vigour, with a glorious lineage, with a form that has made full many a lovely maiden of our tribe droop her fair head . . . and I am, nothing.

"Out on Society! 'twas not made for me. I'll form my own, and be the deity I sometimes feel." (74-75)

This passage is the true climax of the novel not simply because it reflects most intensely the violent ambivalence in the hero's mind about himself and his situation, although it certainly does that. The opening confession of a long felt need for erotic fulfillment quickly gives way to an expression of social alienation and failure which is then immediately followed by a declaration of his talent and uniqueness. But this too is an unstable mood quickly dissipated by the remembrance of the racial stigma under which he lives with a sense of degrading captivity. The frustration engendered by this thought creates the impulse toward action: "Give me my father's sceptre." But the romantic confidence is subverted by the fear of failure implicit in the alternative of dying rather than conquering, and the initial defiance turns to despair at being "nothing." This conviction reflects the social impotence of the Jew so aptly expressed in the metaphor of the captive and the disguise of the eunuch. Thus the disparity between the knowledge of innate superiority and the lack of recognition breeds the final defiance of sublime egotism.

All of this pattern suggests that the fascinating correlation with events in Disraeli's social and political career

is justified and that *Alroy* is indeed part of the secret history of his feelings.[5] The most important point in the analysis of this particular passage, however, concerns Alroy's and, by implication, Disraeli's motivations. Significantly, the soliloquy occurs after Alroy has found in the beauty of Schirene and the magnificence of the Caliph's palace concrete temptations more persuasive than Honain's abstractions. The tale at this point embodies both literally and metaphorically the impotence of the hero. Admittedly in the former case it is a matter of disguise, but that fact in itself has thematic significance. Disguise of the hero enters the novel in three places. In the first, on the journey to Bagdad, it is a matter of denying the fact that he is a Jew, which ironically is a fact that would seem to endanger his life, but actually saves him in two separate encounters. The second incident is the visit to Schirene, the significance of which has already been shown. The third action in disguise is also a visit to the Princess, after Alroy has conquered the "glorious city," in which she discovers that Honain's slave is in fact a noble and powerful prince. The act of disguise is thus associated with the racial stigma and the impotence of Alroy's position at the moment of temptation, and the fantasy structure works toward the revelation of his ideal, truly heroic identity, as formulated in the penultimate paragraph of this passage. The defiant resolutions thus show that this "true" identity is for him no longer that of the altruistic mystical messiah and that his deepest wish fulfillment would be a worldly recognition of his personal power.

The remainder of *Alroy* is a dramatization of the conflict within the hero's character as to which identity is the stronger: the Prince of the Captivity on a messianic mission to free his people, or the worldly prince of "superhuman daring" in search of an empire and its tribute and willing, if necessary, to adopt the Romantic hubris of making himself a deity. The symbiotic relationship between these identities is, however, the most interesting aspect of that dramatization. When Alroy at the height of his messianic power has completely conquered the Moslem world Lord Honain comes to deliver formally the city of Bagdad into his hands:

"we must bow to your decree with the humility that recognises superior force. Yet we are not without hope. We cannot forget that it is our good fortune not to be addressing a barbarous chieftain, unable to sympathise with the claims of civilisation, the creations of art, and the finer impulses of humanity. We acknowledge your irresistible power, but we dare to hope everything from a prince whose genius all acknowledge and admire, who has spared some portion of his youth from the cares of government and the pursuits of arms to the ennobling claims of learning, whose morality has been moulded by a pure and sublime faith, and who draws his lineage from a sacred and celebrated race, the unrivalled antiquity of which even the Prophet acknowledges." (140)

This is obviously an exhilarating fantasy for Disraeli as he lived through the frustrations of political defeat in the summer of 1832, for it clearly represents a transformation of the hero's most humiliating captivity into a seemingly limitless victory. Interestingly, it blends the purity of the religious role with a wordly recognition. But significantly, although Honain (representing the city's inhabitants) has been forced to recognize Alroy's position by an overwhelming demonstration of the latter's superiority, his words of submission stress the qualities of innate genius which bring forth the admiration for the King's nobility, manifested in learning, morality, and the appreciation of the arts of civilization. The sensitive reader can see, however, that the fantasy is not the complete victory it might seem. The concluding references to Alroy's "pure and sublime faith" and "sacred and celebrated race" only serve to show how completely those attributes have come to subserve the glorification of the hero's genius. That Disraeli clearly perceives his hero's sin of pride is, of course, borne out by the remaining plot.

The marriage of the King and the daughter of the Caliph represents the dramatic climax of the novel. Although his fall from grace has already been prefigured astrologically, Alroy is now at the height of his fortunes, and, as the lovers retire to consummate the marriage, the author intrudes to point the moral: "Now what a glorious man was David Alroy, lord of the mightiest empire in the world, and wedded to the most beautiful princess, surrounded by a prosperous and obedient people, guarded by invincible armies, one on whom Earth showered all its fortune, and Heaven all its favour; and all by the power of his own genius!" (177). The abandonment of any pretense at performing Hebrew rituals, the rumor of Alroy's attendance at a mosque, his alliance with his former enemies, and, finally, his assumption of the title, "Caliph," and his public display of effete decadence eventually provoke the faithful into a conspiracy against the life of "this haughty stripling" (181, 183); Alroy's empire is quickly consumed by rebellion and he becomes the captive of his rival. In narrating these events Disraeli's chief concern is the portrayal of the hero's consciousness of what he has done. Indeed, the conflict between Alroy's two symbiotic selves and their respective commitments to his sister, Miriam, and to the Princess Schirene (and all they represent: altruism, innocence, religious and sexual purity versus expediency, hypocrisy, religious betrayal, and self-glorification) is the subject of his thoughts as, alternately despairing and defiant, he awaits his fate in his dungeon cell. Significantly, it is the question of Alroy's Jewish faith and race that leads to his ultimate act of defiance. For when Honain reveals the conditions for Alroy's release, that he should plead guilty to the charge of having had "intercourse with the infernal powers," that he should confess to having "won the Caliph's daughter by an irresistible spell" which at last is broken, and

that he should deny his "Divine mission" in order "to settle the public mind," the captive raises no objections. But when Honain adds the final condition of "form," that he will be expected to "publicly affect to renounce our faith, and bow before their Prophet," Alroy leaps into indignation: "Get thee behind me, tempter! Never, never, never! . . . I'll not yield a jot. Were my doom one everlasting torture, I'd spurn thy terms! Is this thy high contempt of our poor kind, to outrage my God! to prove myself the vilest of the vile, and baser than the basest?" (244). The explicit irony, that he has already done this in the service of his own exalted egotism, only serves to prove the complete dichotomy of Alroy's sense of his own identity. In the strength of his reemergent purity he can immediately again assert his own glory and resolve to die a hero for Schirene's sake (245). But this momentary attempt to join the glorification of his God and the glorification of himself into one destiny cannot succeed; he falls into a trance and is saved from his final temptation by the ghost of the faithful priest, Jabaster. In the denouement Alroy finds consolation in the presence of his pure and holy sister and defies his conqueror's threats of torture even as the sword flashes down to behead him.

In some sense the ending of his life is a triumph for Alroy. He dies forgiven by his God for his sin of pride, comforted by his sister, and secure in the belief that he is ultimately true to his real and primary identity. At the same time, however, it is obviously a Pyrrhic victory in that his divine mission to free his people has come to nought, and in that he dies after having completely fallen from the heights of glory. It is not necessary to doubt the hero's sincerity of his return to innocence to recognize that it is an escape from the consequences of a personal failure. But it is important to recognize the final act of defiance as an attempt to turn defeat into victory without ever having consciously to admit that defeat. Consequently that defiance, even though supported with a sense of righteous purity, leaves the central conflict between Alroy's two senses of his own identity unresolved.

Looking at **Alroy** as an embodiment of a fantasy structure created by Disraeli, it is reasonable to conclude that the author felt within himself the need both to deny and to affirm his Jewishness, and by implication, the innocence and purity that characterize his hero. The many striking parallels between the author and his hero—between Disraeli's desire to liberate the Conservative Party and Alroy's desire to liberate his people, between Disraeli's recognition that hypocrisy is a necessary ingredient of worldly success and Alroy's betrayal of his faith, between Disraeli's confidential attachment to his sister, Sarah, and Alroy's reliance upon Miriam's recognition of his purest self, and finally between Disraeli's defiant response to political defeat and Alroy's defiant mockery of his conqueror—

all suggest that Disraeli did indeed feel in his own early career similar tensions to those he attributes to his hero and that his struggle for "purity" in the context of personal distinction remained an unresolved issue in 1832. Clearly, though, Disraeli's fictions do not simply serve as an escape through fantasy from the unpleasant social and political realities of his early career. *Alroy,* for example, is a medium for exploring imaginatively the ambivalence Disraeli felt about both of his senses of himself and an imaginative assessment of the costs of choosing either of those identities. But, nevertheless, it is a less than satisfactory fantasy because in its attempt to accommodate the conflicting goals of purity and success within the characterization of a less than perfect hero, it cannot permit a complete wish fulfillment and remain honest. The unsatisfactory conclusion of the fantasy did, however, provide Disraeli with the impetus to return in subsequent novels to the subject of his ambivalence about his racial heritage in the disguised form of his heroes' concern with Catholicism.[6]

Henrietta Temple: A Love Story (1836) is an interesting and significant illustration of this theme, for again in this work the hero's essential problem is to find an answer to the question, "What Is He?"[7] In this case the conflicting possibilities are dramatized in terms of the implications of defining his pure, innocent self in different ways. Although in 1836 Disraeli had achieved considerable fame or notoriety for his **"Letters of Runnymede,"** which were marked by a continuation of the violent anti-Catholicism of his *Morning Post* articles of the previous year, *Henrietta Temple* begins with a sympathetic and elaborate, if bizarre, delineation of the protagonist's family's Catholicism. This emphasis is so strong that the reader is prepared to see Ferdinand Armine's struggle for happiness ultimately connected with the issue of his faith. Once the Protestant heroine of the novel is introduced, however, the story veers sharply in another direction and the hero's Catholicism is clearly subordinated to what seems to be the larger issue of his filial devotion.

The apparent central plot established in the early portion of the novel, begun in 1833, concerns the hero's endeavor to revive the Armine family's fortunes, and the ostensible element of conflict suggested is his disappointed expectations of being heir to the family fortune of his maternal grandfather, Lord Grandison. The development of this conflict depends, however, on an inheritance of a different sort, one that accounts for the early emphasis upon the family's Catholicism. For the second remarkable feature of the first portion of the story is the explicit description of potential ambivalence within the hero's character, which makes any reader familiar with the earlier novels immediately aware that the struggle for purity is not yet exhausted as a theme. From his devoted, pious, and virtuous parents and tutor, young Ferdinand learns "to be sincere, dutiful, charitable, and just; and to have a deep sense of the great account hereafter to be delivered to his Creator," which combined with "great gifts of nature, with lively and highly cultivated talents, and a most affectionate and disciplined temper" make him "idolised" and "adored" by all who know him. But the narrator, implied author, is quick to interject, "But for his character, what was that? . . . Custom blunts the fineness of psychological study. . . . Nor is it, indeed, marvellous, that for a long time temperament should be disguised" (22, 23). The answer, suggestive of the novel's true thematic concern, is quickly supplied by next describing Ferdinand's fascination for the family portrait of his reckless and flamboyant paternal grandfather, Sir Ferdinand, and by intruding to ask, "Did the fiery imagination and the terrible passions of that extraordinary man lurk in the innocent heart and the placid mien of his young descendant?" (24).

The dramatization of this ambivalence is begun upon the eve of the hero's leaving home to take up his commission as Ensign in the Royal Fusileers.

> Lady Armine, without speaking, knelt down by his bedside and took him in her arms. She buried her face in his breast. He felt her tears upon his heart. He could not move; he could not speak. At length he sobbed aloud.
>
> "May our Father that is in heaven bless you, my darling child; . . . I would have spared you this, my darling. . . . But I knew not the strength of a mother's love. Alas! what mother has a child like thee? O! Ferdinand, my first, my only-born: child of love and joy and happiness . . . so kind, so gentle, and so dutiful! must we, oh! must we indeed part?"
>
> "It is too cruel," continued Lady Armine, kissing with a thousand kisses her weeping child. "What have I done to deserve such misery as this? . . . beloved Ferdinand, I shall die."
>
> "I will not go, mother, I will not go," wildly exclaimed the boy. . . . "Mother, I cannot go. No, no, it never can be good to leave a home like this. . . . "
>
> "My own, own mother, what shall I say? what shall I do? I love you, mother, with all my heart and soul and spirit's strength: I love you, mother. There is no mother loved as you are loved!"
>
> "'Tis that that makes me mad. I know it. Oh! why are you not like other children, Ferdinand?" (47)

Although the rationale for the separation is momentarily regained when he says, "think, dearest mother, how much I have to do. All now depends on me. . . . I must restore our house," the continuation of this scene emphasizes the innocence demanded of Ferdinand in the maternal relationship and links his filial and religious devotion. Somewhat consoled by her son's promise to write to her by every ship and to send her an emblematic pet gazelle, Lady Armine extracts a final avowal of innocence, "If I forget thee . . . dear mother, may God indeed forget me," and reminds him of her solicitude, "Mind, you have eight packages. . . . And take the greatest care of old Sir Ferdinand's sword" (48, 49-50). This scene, only a small portion of which is quoted here, establishes in two different ways that the struggle for "purity" is indeed the author's chief concern. The mission to restore the fortunes of Ferdinand's house, the invocation of God's witness to his familial and religious loyalty, the mention of the gazelle, and the introduction of the magical phallic sword as the instrument of power, all bring to mind *The Wondrous Tale of Alroy,* which is Disraeli's most explicit and direct treatment of that theme, and which had just recently been published in March 1833.

Moreover, the whole scene itself, in its sentimentality and infantilism, is an idealization of the maternal relationship in which the almost seventeen-year-old hero is literally and figuratively made a "child." It is interestingly very close in quality to the scene in *Contarini Fleming* where Christiana smothers the child hero with compensatory maternal affection (11, 15). And the extent to which this scene is a wish-fulfillment fantasy, an idealization of the past, can in part be judged by contrasting it with a poem the adolescent Disraeli wrote and recorded in an early notebook:

> The steps within my father's hall, her voice
> Sounds in the chambers of my early youth,
> The voice of one whose tones my heart
> rejoice,
> Mine & not mine, a melancholy truth!
> Ah! thought of woe, ah! memory of sadness
> The bitter drop, the very serpent's tooth
> Gnawing my highest joy to very madness
> And turning my existence which in sooth
> Might be the sweet repose of perfect love
> Into an anxious & a quivering dream,—
> Away with these dread fancies! yon dark
> grove
> Sends forth a being brighter than the beam
> That plays upon the terraced walks above
> And gilds my Myrrha with its golden gleam.[8]

This is a lament for the incomplete fulfillment he finds in his relationship with his mother. The bitter drop is the knowledge of her divided loyalty, as wife as well as mother, which denies him total ab-

sorption. Significantly, it is the realm of fantasy which provides release from the insecurity which in its intensity turns reality into the madness of a nightmare. The scene in *Henrietta Temple,* however, does provide Ferdinand with total immersion in maternal love. Further, he is recognized as different from other children and loved the more for being so. The depth of Lady Armine's misery is the measure of her affection, an emotion which not only permits but encourages her son's expressions of his love in terms of childlike purity. Thus, given Disraeli's sense of alienation from his own mother, attested to by the poem quoted above, the content of his earlier novels, and the search for a substitute mother so evident in the affair with Lady Henrietta Sykes and his later courtship of Mary Anne Wyndham Lewis,[9] it is reasonable to see this scene as a wish-fulfillment fantasy which establishes his hero's essential, or at least original, purity and his need to be loved for simply being himself. The first portion of the novel that became *Henrietta Temple,* however, does no more than suggest that in 1833 Disraeli was beginning a story which, like its predecessor *Alroy,* would embody the theme of purity betrayed and perhaps recovered.

In the 1836 continuation of this little more than embryonic novel the hero's debts become the agent of his corruption. At Malta, Ferdinand's innately superior qualities and almost magically acquired accomplishments are immediately recognized, and he instantly becomes the most popular person in the garrison. With his vanity flattered and his expectations of being Lord Grandison's heir increased by a visit to England, he is soon immersed in a life of unwarranted extravagance. The significance of this characterization, however, derives less from the facts of Disraeli's own reception on his Mediterranean tour of 1830-31 or his ruinously expensive social life than from the implied author's *self*-indulgence even as he melodramatically moralizes on the "fatal misery" of debt, that "prolific mother of folly and crime . . . which taints the course of life in all its dreams":

> there are few things more gloomy than the recollection of a youth that has not been enjoyed. What prosperity of manhood, what splendour of old age, can compensate for it? Wealth is power; and in youth . . . we require power. . . . What, then, is to be done? I leave the question to the schoolmen, because I am convinced that to moralise with the inexperienced availeth nothing. (61)

This intrusion, while it might seem to be a distressing artistic flaw in its combination of high seriousness and flippancy, is in fact highly significant, for it establishes a pattern of authorial ambivalence—which is often implicit in characterization and plot—with respect to the hero that is in a sense the essence of the novel.

In *Henrietta Temple,* as in *Alroy,* the hero corrupts the mission of his "true" self by indulging his exalted egotism. When Ferdinand learns that his cousin Katherine has inherited the Grandison fortune he determines to marry her, though he feels no love for her. And with no difficulty he succeeds in making the "poor inexperienced, innocent" Katherine love him. Their engagement settled, we are told, "he called for a tumbler of champagne, and secretly drank his own health, as the luckiest fellow of his acquaintance, with a pretty, amiable, and highbred wife, with all his debts paid, and the house of Armine restored" (65, 66). But it is, of course, obvious that the noble and heroic purpose of restoring the Armines' estates and honor, a purpose directly associated with his pure, filial love, comes to subserve the interests of Ferdinand's insincere, "false" self. This change is noticed by the narrator who immediately intrudes to comment upon the "not . . . favourable" difference in his "character and conduct," but it is also recognized in the form of nostalgia by Ferdinand himself: "he could not but feel that a great change had come over his spirit since the days he was wont to ramble in this old haunt of his boyhood. *His innocence was gone. Life was no longer that deep unbroken trance of duty and of love from which he had been roused* to so much care; and if not remorse, at least to so much compunction" (70; italics mine). This third-person passage effectively represents Ferdinand's stream of consciousness, a technique Disraeli frequently uses to link the narrator's and hero's awareness. Significantly, the passive voice evades the weight of responsibility for his (Ferdinand's) compromise, placing it upon the inevitability of lost innocence rather than upon his own vanity. The same desire to avoid self-indictment is reflected in the almost immediately following tentative denial of the now threatening (because in its contrast it implies guilt) past: "there are moments I almost wish that I had no father and no mother; . . . and that Armine were sunk into the very centre of the earth. If I stood alone in the world methinks I might find the place that suits me; now everything seems ordained for me. . . . My spirit has had no play" (71). Clearly here the hero finds both of his previous worlds insufficient, and what he longs for is a realm in which the claims of "sympathy" and success can be reconciled. And the development of the novel from this point on is essentially an elaboration of a fantasy structure related to that end.

The dramatic potential of the hero's rhetorical passivity is established by his rationalizations (which are in effect fantasies) about his identity. He first finds a "wonderful. . . . providential dispensation" (73) in his fallen circumstances which have led to the "destiny" of being the family's restorer. There is considerable vanity in this claim to innate superiority as one of God's chosen. But the assumption of such significance is an evasion of responsibility which runs counter to the Byronic role he also imagines.

"Conceal it as I will," he exclaimed, "I am a victim; disguise them as I may, all the considerations are worldly. There is, there must be, something better in this world than power and wealth and rank; and surely there must be felicity more rapturous even than securing the happiness of a parent. . . . Is love indeed a delusion, or am I marked out from men alone to be exempted from its delicious bondage?" (74)

The sharp reversal of values, in which the divinely sanctioned restorative mission of the true self, originating in filial and religious purity, is transformed into an acquisition of "power and wealth and rank," seems to represent both a recognition of his own corruption and a denial of responsibility for it. The exclamation is appropriately the voice of the "devil" because it expresses the inadequacy of the former pure ideal and a desire for a substitute better than the original. Interestingly, as a "victim" of worldly considerations, "marked out" and "exempted" from "rapturous" felicity, Ferdinand is completely passive. And significantly, his conception of the love he longs for is a "delicious bondage," that of the child held transfixed by the mother's love (cf. 47).

Ferdinand then postulates that his "wild and restless" grandfather, "while the world . . . marvelled and moralised at his wanton life, and . . . his heartless selfishness . . . was sighing for some soft bosom whereon to pour his overwhelming passion" (75). Given the devout Glastonbury's devotion to Lady Barbara and her son Ratcliffe (Bk. I, ch. 3), a devotion so strong that he considers retreating to a monastery when she dies, and his justification of his purchase of her grandson's army commission by invoking the memory of "that blessed and saintly being" (42), Ferdinand's identification with Sir Ferdinand and the implication of a want of love in his grandfather's marriage thus becomes a denial of the values of the family and their religion. The rhetorical structure and diction of the spasmodic climax of the exclamation quoted above reveal Disraeli's thematic intentions in this reversal of values: "O Nature! why art thou beautiful? My heart requires not, imagination cannot paint, a sweeter or a fairer scene. . . . This azure vault of heaven, this golden sunshine, this deep and blending shade, these rare and fragrant shrubs, yon grove of green and tallest pines, and the bright gliding of this swan-crowned lake; my soul is charmed with all this beauty and this sweetness" (75). Debased Romanticism has scarcely received a more regrettable expression. But the archaic phrasing of the ultimately theological question completes the invocation of "Nature" as an embodiment of the divine and sanctifies the "beauty" which charms the "soul." The "poetic" and spontaneous expression of love of beauty becomes a form of worship. And through such love lies the individual's salvation. The love of beauty in Nature is, however, but a paradigm of holiness and purity.

Both the hero's rationale of his essential purity of heart and the narrative *self*-indulgence of the novel's fantasy structure are confirmed in the lengthy authorial intrusion immediately preceding the introduction of the dazzling, beautiful heroine, Henrietta Temple (Bk. II, ch. 4). Love at first sight is defined as "the transcendent and surpassing offspring of sheer and unpolluted sympathy," while "all other is the illegitimate result of observation, of reflection, of compromise, of comparison, of expediency." Apart from the purity of spontaneous love the narrator invokes two additional elements of this emotion, the lover's dependence on the loved one—her beauty is overwhelming and it is her responses, "her joy . . . her sigh of love" and "her smile of fondness" which create his "bliss"—and the power of love, the very birth of which (to use the author's metaphor) comes "amid the gloom and travail of existence," to replace the lover's "flaunty ambition." The chief ostensible conflict of the novel is established as "this mighty passion," which makes "revolutions of empire, changes of creed, mutations of opinion . . . but the clouds and meteors of a stormy sky," and which rages in Ferdinand's heart when he first sees the "ravishing vision" of Henrietta in the park at Armine (76, 77, 78). For even as he exclaims his "overwhelming . . . absorbing . . . burning passion" for this "exquisite, enchanting, adored being" (87, 86), he remembers that his parents and cousin are expected home within a week.

> "Beautiful Henrietta! . . . what wild, what maddening words are these? Am I not Ferdinand Armine, the betrothed, the victim? . . . I'll cast to the winds all ties and duties; I will not be dragged to the altar, a miserable sacrifice, to redeem, by my forfeited felicity, the worldly fortunes of my race. . . . But this woman: I am bound to her. Bound? The word makes me tremble. I shiver: I hear the clank of my fetters. Am I indeed bound? Ay! in honour. Honour and love! A contest! Pah! The Idol must yield to the Divinity!" (87)

As the rapid alterations of mood suggest, the hero's essential struggle is to find an identity compatible with his "dearest desires." Here the alternative to being the romantic "victim" is the role of Byronic defiance so conveniently anticipated in the author's definition of love. The exaggerated language constitutes both a denial of the past and a justification of the future. Since the purity of love transcends all conventions of honor, he is free, though engaged to Katherine, to fall into an "intense delirium of absorbing love" for Henrietta (106).

Disraeli then establishes dramatically that his hero's denial of his past and justifications of the present are rationalizations of his ambivalent feelings about himself. One night Ferdinand's dream of Henrietta turns into a nightmare of Katherine's presence so powerful that it continues as hallucination after waking. Significantly, the reverie-transforming guilt manifests itself not in any recognition of why Katherine might

appear "sad and reproachful," but rather in speculation about the "angelic" Henrietta which can only be termed a loss of love fantasy: "what were her slumbers? Were they wild as his own, or sweet and innocent as herself? . . . Bore any one to her the same relation as Katherine Grandison to him?" Letters from his mother and his cousin soon replace this imaginatively projected threat to his love with the "dreadful reality" of his actual situation, and images of "his melancholy father, his fond and confiding mother, the devoted Glastonbury," and "all the mortifying circumstances of his illustrious race" rise before him "in painful succession" (107, 108, 109). Although this threat is momentarily fended off with the recurrent wish to be "alone in the world, to struggle with his fate and mould his fortunes," there is no longer defiance in Ferdinand's renewed denial of his family: "He felt himself a slave and a sacrifice. He cursed Armine, his ancient house, and his broken fortunes." Indeed, the appropriateness of the heroic Byronic role with its potential for despair as well as defiance is shown through Ferdinand's ensuing passivity and the confusion of values it reflects. There is in the reference to the "gratification of his own wild fancies" (109) the suggestion that Ferdinand's self-knowledge could eventually embrace his own responsibility for his situation. But that potential is quickly dissipated as he tells Henrietta that he is "the victim of family profligacy and family pride" (111). In this passivity there is no conviction that love conquers all. Indeed, the hero feels helpless because he lacks the worldly considerations he was so recently willing to forego.

This summary of the first third of the novel establishes that there is both an ambivalence of mood and an ambivalence of values within the character of the hero. Behind his dilemma, of being engaged to one woman and in love with another, and behind the reversals of mood and values it occasions, lies a basic crisis of identity. There is a conflict between two opposing images of the self which he holds; between what he *is* by upbringing and what he *is* by nature, between the fair child of duty and filial love and the dark progeny of passionate imagination. Further examination of Ferdinand's passivity confirms the conclusion that with this story Disraeli was creating yet another fictional version of his own struggle for an identity comprising purity *and* success. For his hero the claims of both filial duty and profligate success are enslaving. And neither his defiance nor his self-pity seems capable of altering this. The inescapable imaginative fact is that Ferdinand is an Armine and whichever way he chooses to define his pure, true self, as devoted son or heroic romantic, he incurs the stigma of their poverty. The specific imagery describing Ferdinand's despair is significant: "Bound? The word makes me tremble. I shiver: I hear the clank of my fetters" (87). And later the narrator, in describing the hero's thoughts, says, "Nor could he forget his own wretched follies and that fatal visit to Bath, of which the consequences clanked upon his memory like degrading and disgraceful fetters" (109). The image is quite striking in its own right, but it is not the first time Disraeli had used it. His response to O'Connell's anti-Semitic attack on him at the time of the Taunton by-election—"I admire your scurrilous allusions to my origin. It is quite clear that the 'hereditary bondsman' has already forgotten the clank of his fetter"[10]—shows in comparison that in *Henrietta Temple* Disraeli is indeed again employing the Catholic disguise of the Jewish question in another attempt to create a fantasy which resolves satisfactorily the struggle for purity that still bedevils him.

Disraeli's hero does not, however, simply remain caught between the rationalizations of his dilemma. Accompanying Henrietta on her round of cottage charity, Ferdinand is struck by the "sweet simplicity" of her maternal care and sympathy for the peasants and he is overcome with nostalgia for "the time when he was a happy boy at his innocent home; his mother's boy, the child she so loved and looked after." With a sense of irrevocable isolation from that "sylvan paradise" he reflects upon "his dissipation, his vanity, his desperate folly, his hollow worldliness" and concludes that he cannot admit his beautiful companion into the "sweet and serene society" of that "unpolluted home," not because of "the profligacy of his ancestor," and not because of "the pride of his family," but because of "his own culpable and heartless career!" (114, 115). That Ferdinand's self-knowledge finally comes in the context of so much nostalgia for lost innocence is a measure of how much his passion is a function of his need for solicitude comparable to that which Henrietta has lavished upon the cottagers. Thus, the setting Disraeli has chosen is entirely appropriate, for the idealization of the cottagers' life is a function of the absolute trust implicit in the paternalistic tenant society.

That trust is the most important element of the love Ferdinand experiences is readily apparent from the rhetoric of the romantic scenes. The explicit fear of rejection and its attendant helplessness that overwhelms his declaration of passion recalls to mind the scene in *Contarini Fleming* where the hero slips from the fictional recitation of his desperate heroics into a confession of love for Christiana, the now married object of his childhood search for a substitute mother (10-16). That episode ends in Contarini's rage, confusion, "shame" and "irritation" when his passion is rejected and his proposal, that she share his destiny of glory, liberty, and love as an Aegean pirate, elicits only "blank astonishment" and alarm. The imaginative connection is further suggested by one of Ferdinand's earlier moods of Byronic defiance in which he imagines himself "winning Henrietta" and becoming a soldier of fortune: "Why might he not free Greece, or revolutionise Spain, or conquer the Brazils?"

(129). In both scenes the extravagant imagery of exile confirms that the crucial issue is the heroine's acceptance or rejection of her suitor. But in *Henrietta Temple* the happy resolution of the anxiety is made possible by the hero's passivity. The significance of Ferdinand's fears is shown by the imagery used to describe his newly found resolution. Once having accepted him Henrietta becomes "the light in the Pharos, amid all his stormy fortunes." The "contest," really between past and future, honor and guilt, guilt and honor, can apparently be abandoned for "the ravishing and absorbing present" of requited love (146-47). The essence of that love is trust and purity, as is reflected by the anxiety of the confession itself—"if you but knew how I have fed but upon . . . one sacred image of absorbing life" (144)—and by the implicit regression of Ferdinand's thoughts as he retires for the night.

> Ferdinand is within his little chamber, that little chamber where his mother had bid him so passionate a farewell. Ah! he loves another woman better than his mother now. Nay, even a feeling of embarrassment and pain is associated with the recollection of that fond and elegant being, that he had recognised once as the model of all feminine perfection, and who had been to him so gentle and so devoted. He drives his mother from his thoughts. It is of another voice that he now muses. (147)

In its thematic bearings this passage is complex, for, even as it works to establish the purity of the new love through infantilism, it recalls the guilt associated with the original betrayal. This is confirmed by the implied loss-of-loved-one fantasies contained both in the authorial intrusion which immediately follows, "All nature seems to bear an intimate relation to the being we adore; and as to us life would now appear intolerable . . . without this transcendent sympathy, so we cannot help fancying that were its sweet and subtle origin herself to quit this inspired scene, the universe itself would not be unconscious of its deprivation" (148), and in the dramatization of it within Ferdinand's thoughts in a subsequent chapter as he conjures up "a crowd of unfortunate incidents" ("what if this night she died? . . . Perhaps she was ill") (162, 160, 162) in her absence. The obvious insecurities of these fantasies reveal the fragility of the hero's new identity drawn from his love for Henrietta. Since that identity, with all its felicity rests upon deceit of his cousin, family, and lover herself, it is not surprising that guilt compounds Ferdinand's insecurities:

> were he to dare to reveal the truth. . . . Would she not look upon him as the unresisting libertine of the hour, engaging in levity her heart as he had already trifled with another's? For that absorbing and overwhelming passion, pure, primitive, and profound, to which she now responded with an

enthusiasm as fresh, as ardent, and as immaculate, she would only recognise the fleeting fancy of a vain and worldly spirit. (163)

This makes the hero's struggle perfectly clear; however real their consequences, the vanity and egotism which have led to his predicament must be denied as false in order to maintain the purity of the true self for which alone Ferdinand longs to be adored. This is the essence of the illusions of victimization in which he indulges and of the infantilism of his characterization at crucial moments. Indeed, these forms of passivity are essential to the evasion of responsibility for the continued deceits which, paradoxically, he must practice to maintain the innocence of his love. But the limits of this characterization are quickly reached when Ferdinand engages in the climactic deceit of involving his lover in a secret betrothal.

At this moment, the end of Book III, the novel breaks rather sharply in two. The second half, as Robert Blake points out, is very different in tone from the passionate lyricism of the first part; it is, on the whole, "an urbane comedy of manners."[11] Ferdinand's deceit is accidentally discovered by Henrietta, the lovers are separated, she becomes engaged to another nobleman, Ferdinand is arrested for his debts, and then the interests of true love are served by the generosity of friends and Ferdinand is reunited with Henrietta, who in the meantime has been discovered to be "one of the richest heiresses in England" (298). Despite the rapidly accumulating improbabilities of plot, this second half of *Henrietta Temple* is by far the best part of the novel and in some respects matches the best of all Disraeli's fiction. In the continuation the theme of sincerity and hypocrisy is absorbed into the new material. Ferdinand at first repeats the rationalizations of the victimized lover that reflect his continuing ambivalence of having both pride in and hatred of his heritage. This is, of course, sustained by the ironic fact that it is the dark, romantic qualities of his character, exemplified by his likeness to his grandfather's portrait hanging at Armine, to which Henrietta has been attracted but which now have destroyed his hopes of requited love. Consequently, while the ambivalence accounts most satisfactorily for the hero's procrastinations before the inexorable force of time, it admits of no further character development short of the hero's choosing a true self embodying one or the other, but not both, definitions of purity already established. Rather than have his protagonist make this choice Disraeli turns to the exigencies of plot to resolve the artistic and emotional dichotomies. Interestingly, the passivity which previously embodied his ambivalence is now used to begin the resolution or negation of the hero's emotional dilemma. Having in exhaustion and despair verging on madness confessed to the pious Glastonbury that his "heart and resolution have

never for an instant faltered" in his love for the "innocent, so truly virtuous" Henrietta (232), Ferdinand collapses. But to the priest's offer of his bed Ferdinand replies in "a faint voice," "No! let me go to my own room. . . . where my mother said the day would come, oh! . . . Would there were only mother's love, and then I should not be here or thus!" (235). And after the necessary arrangements, we are told, "Glastonbury and the stout serving-man bore him to his chamber, relieved him from his wet garments, and placed him in his earliest bed. . . . Ferdinand . . . did not speak; and it was remarkable, that while he passively submitted to their undressing him, and seemed incapable of affording them the slightest aid, yet he thrust forth his hand to guard a lock of dark hair that was placed next to his heart" (236). In this scene the two identities, involving the purities of filial devotion and passionate romance, become one; the exhaustion of the desperate lover is absorbed by the regression to innocent childhood.

The task Disraeli sets himself in the second half of the novel is to establish this unity in the context of the hero's happiness as a dramatic actuality for him rather than simply an imaginative conception. To this end Ferdinand undergoes the purification of a nearly fatal fever which the attending physician can only attribute to psychic rather than bodily cause. His mother's love for him is reestablished in the care lavished upon him during his illness. His cousin generously releases him from his engagement to her when she learns of his love for Henrietta. Katherine and Lord Montfort, Henrietta's considerate fiancé, nobly conspire with Lady Bellair and Glastonbury to reunite the original lovers, and when Ferdinand's arrest for debts prevents that from happening, it turns out to be "the luckiest incident in the world" (433). Lord Montfort finds he is really in love with Katherine, and Count Mirabel proves himself the best of friends by offering to loan Ferdinand the money he has just won at gambling, something which is made unnecessary by the receipt of a similar amount from his cousin. Finally, Lord Montfort offers to win Mr. Temple over to the lovers' cause, and the families are united in benevolent approval of it.

In this marvelous conclusion Ferdinand's early extravagances are "but the consequences of his fiery youth," his debts prove trivial before the immense fortunes of the Grandisons and the Temples, and his deceits are but insignificant means to a greater end. Significantly, the tension in the novel's fantasy structure is completely dissolved in the satisfaction of the implied author: "Ferdinand had been faithful to Henrietta. His constancy to her was now rewarded. . . . Ferdinand Armine had great tenderness of disposition, and somewhat of a meditative mind; schooled by adversity, there was little doubt that his coming career would justify his favourable destiny" (436-37). From this the second half of *Henrietta Temple* may seem distressingly contrived, but it is in fact not so. When Disraeli abandons the hostile symbiosis of Ferdinand's characterization, he frees himself and his hero from the extravagant perturbations of self-absorption and with a completely passive protagonist writes a better novel: Childe Harold becomes Don Juan. The hero's providential destiny is unfolded in brilliantly depicted settings, varying from the drawing rooms of the aristocracy to the depressing surroundings of the sponging-house, and every "improbable" event is founded securely upon realistic characterization, from the compassion, charm, and generosity of the dandy, de Mirabel (modeled upon D'Orsay), to the buoyant optimism of the deferential gaoler. Even more impressive is the deft blend of sympathy and satire inherent in the narrative presentation.

What is remarkable, then, about this shift in tone is the extent to which the author has gained control over his material. The stability, which is reflected in the distance between narrator and hero of the authorial intrusions as well as in the elements of plot, characterization, and setting, suggests that the escape from passionate lyricism, manifest in the change from the world of Armine to the world of London, is as much an artistic as an autobiographical one. Compared with those of *Contarini Fleming* and *Alroy,* the other novels in which the struggle for purity is the dominant theme, the conclusion of *Henrietta Temple* represents a complete reversal. Contarini is left in desolation and exile with a vague hope in his future destiny. Alroy is killed for his defiance in the face of defeat. Since it is surely not accidental that Disraeli imagines in the end a blissful Ferdinand Armine as a Member of Parliament with the good sense to support a "national" administration, it is reasonable to suggest that the change in this novel reflects a new sense of potential fulfillment in its author. In this regard the nature of the relation between the life and the fiction is important. At the time Disraeli wrote the conclusion in which his hero finds himself with a "beautiful bride . . . whom he loved with intense passion" and a "noble fortune, which would permit him to redeem his inheritance," he was probably aware that his love affair with the real Henrietta was finished. Their last recorded meeting was in mid-August of 1836 and the entry of the Mutilated Diary for that year says in part, "Returned to Bradenham at the latter end of August; concluded *Henrietta Temple,*" and the one for the following year specifies that "During the election [of 1837, held in July] occurred the terrible catastrophe of Henrietta [exposed for adultery with Daniel Maclise] exactly one year after we had parted."[12] On the other hand, Disraeli had found in the affair with Henrietta Sykes a kind of acceptance on which his imagination could feed, as witnessed to by the similarity of role he chose in courting Mrs. Lewis some years later. Beyond this, the success of the *Morning Post* articles, the *Vindication of the English Constitution,*

and the **"Letters of Runnymede"** had placed Disraeli at the very center of Lord Lyndhurst's ultra-Tory circle and brought him some acceptance in the Conservative party at large. He writes in the Mutilated Diary for 1836, for example, "Establish my character as a great political writer by the *Letters of Runnymede.* Resume my acquaintance with Sir Robert Peel. My influence greatly increases from the perfect confidence of L. and my success as a political writer."[13] Disraeli's fame or notoriety largely resulted from his extravagant invective. But, nevertheless, Peel did recognize the genuine merit of the *Vindication* and was undoubtedly flattered by the glorification of himself in Letter V of the Runnymede series as St. George, in whose "chivalry alone" lay England's hope of not being devoured by the dragon of Whiggism, and by Disraeli's dedication to him of the collected series when it appeared in July.[14] Peel's response was to invite the author "to dine with a party . . . of the late Government at the Carlton,"[15] so Disraeli's estimation of his newly won acceptance, if not influence, is not unwarranted.

Previous critics have resisted an autobiographical reading of *Henrietta Temple.* While Blake admits the original inspiration of the novel to have been Disraeli's affair with Lady Sykes, and describes its "authentic ring of personal passion," he finds that the discrepancies between reality and fiction establish that "Armine bears no resemblance whatever to Disraeli."[16] This is also the view expressed earlier by Jerman: "Except that his heroine takes on the Christian name of his mistress and that Lady Sykes' pet name for him, Amin, is transposed into the family name of his hero, there is, alas, little—too little— autobiography here. Ferdinand Armine in nowise resembles Benjamin Disraeli."[17] But clearly these readings are too literalist in their definition of autobiography. *Henrietta Temple* is indeed an autobiographical novel, not in the sense that historical matter from the author's life gets directly into the fiction, but rather in the sense that the same pattern runs through the life and the fiction displaying there the same needs and motives. As such this novel embodies a fantasy in which Disraeli again returns to the fundamental problem of defining his identity. Here, once again, he adopts the Catholic disguise of his Jewish heritage for the purpose of establishing in his fiction the issue of his ambivalence about himself. The emphasis upon the hero's guilt about betraying his heritage and upon his need to reestablish his essential purity of heart is in effect a return to the fundamental issue of *Alroy.* In both novels that need is the basis for the rationalization of ambivalent behavior and values which characterizes the psychic conflict at the heart of the story. In the first half of *Henrietta Temple* that rationalization of the hero's past and present deceits by means of the exaltation of transcendent love, a process in which both he and the implied author engage, fails to overcome his basic insecurity. This is clearly shown by the loss-of-love fantasies manifest in both Ferdinand's thoughts and the author's intrusions. To the question of his identity the inescapable answer at first seems to be, "a Catholic," the fact of which binds him either to the twin inheritance of poverty and profligacy or to the guilt of self-denial. Disraeli's way out of this two-fold emotional and artistic dilemma is a fantasy of acceptance that negates the hero's emotional ambivalence by means of his regression to childlike innocence and escapes the artistic conflict (which definition of the hero's true self to choose) by means of his completely passive role in a comedy of manners.

Perhaps paradoxically this resolution of the struggle for "purity" and "success" reflects Disraeli's new confidence in eventually being able to transcend the conflicting senses of his own identity. Even as wish fulfillment this fantasy of acceptance is a confident response on Disraeli's part to the question. "What Is He?"[18] The fictional answer, in its simplest form, is that the hero is lovable—so lovable that all his friends, his mother, his cousin, and Henrietta want to ensure his happiness. Further, the character of the love he wishes for—the maternal, unquestioning adoration—comes true for him. As a result Ferdinand's compelling need to insist upon his "purity" of heart is sanctioned by other people's responses to him. For, while he is a completely passive hero amidst the events that lead to his finally being accepted as Henrietta's husband, that resolution entails a destiny of power, wealth, and, by virtue of his wife's nobility, a position among the nation's Protestant aristocracy. Since the corollaries of Disraeli's fundamental doubts about his identity are the questions of whether he will succeed and whether he will be accepted among England's social and political elite, both the tone and content of the concluding fantasy in **Henrietta Temple** show that at least an imaginative confidence pervades his hope, undoubtedly strengthened by the Sykes affair and the recent political recognition, that he can achieve success and be loved for himself at the same time.

Thus while the characterizations, plot, and setting in the concluding portion of **Henrietta Temple** are only superficially autobiographical in a literal sense, the theme of that ending is profoundly so in an imaginative one. And by looking at this novel in the context of his earlier ones, it is possible to see the significance of Disraeli's use of this autobiographical mode of fiction. As both the structure of the fantasies within the characterizations of the heroes and the fantasy structure of the plots themselves show, in embodying the ambivalences of his senses of his own identity in these early novels, Disraeli was able to explore imaginatively the possibilities of various roles and so to some extent make the fiction serve the function of self-

realization. Readers of Disraeli's deservedly better-known novels, the political trilogy of **Coningsby, Sybil,** and **Tancred,** and the later ones, **Lothair** and **Endymion,** are aware that from the 1840's on his fiction came to serve other overt political purposes. Yet it can be shown that even as Disraeli attempted to use fiction as a medium for discussing the nature of political parties, the state of the nation, or the role of the Church, he was in significant ways still concerned with both the public and private dimensions of his own identity, indeed, perhaps more compellingly so as the heroic role became realizable in fact as well as fancy. It would not seem to be an extravagant claim, therefore, that a convincing assessment of the artistic quality and significance of his more important novels cannot be made without some awareness of the relation between his continuing use of the autobiographical mode of fiction and the political concerns those works reflect.[19]

Notes

[1] Robert Blake provides an excellent account of the founding of this newspaper in his biography, *Disraeli* (London: Eyre and Spottiswoode, 1966). A detailed assessment of Disraeli's relationship with John Murray, the publisher, and the other principals is also contained in my dissertation, "The Psychological Romance: Disraeli's Early Fiction and Political Apprenticeship," DAI 35:11 (7264A), Diss. Indiana University, 1974.

[2] Benjamin Disraeli, *Vivian Grey,* Vol. I of *The Novels and Tales of Benjamin Disraeli,* ed. Philip Guedalla, Bradenham ed., 12 vols. (New York: Knopf, 1927-29), p. 17. Page references to Disraeli's novels are to this edition and appear parenthetically in the text.

[3] Blake, pp. 57-58.

[4] The extent to which charges of inconsistency, insincerity, hypocrisy, and expediency affected Disraeli can be gauged by reading his political pamphlets, *"What Is He?"* (1833) and *The Crisis Examined* (1834), as well as his satires, "Ixion in Heaven" and "The Infernal Marriage."

[5] "In Vivian Grey I have portrayed my active and real ambition. In Alroy, my ideal ambition. The P.R. [*Contarini Fleming*] is a develop. of my poetic character. This trilogy is the secret history of my feelings. I shall write no more about myself." Mutilated Diary, Disraeli Papers, Box 11/A/III/C/21-22.

[6] I have also argued that this ambivalence is manifested in Disraeli's shifting attitude toward Catholicism amid the political events of the 1830's. "The Psychological Romance" provides a detailed account of Disraeli's violent anti-Catholic prejudice at the time of the Municipal Corporations Reform Bill (1835) and assesses this prejudice in the context of Disraeli's

involvement with the Ultra-Tory faction of the Conservative party and his campaign in the Taunton by-election.

[7] *"What Is He?"*, Published in April 1833, was one of Disraeli's first attempts to rationalize the apparent political inconsistency and expediency with which he was charged by his political opponents. The pamphlet is reprinted in *Whigs and Whiggism,* ed. William Hutcheon (London: Murray, 1913), pp. 16-22.

[8] Early Notebook, Disraeli Papers, Box 11/A/III/E/1.

[9] Disraeli's letters to Mrs. Lewis during the period of their courtship reveal that he cast her in a maternal role in much the same way that he had done with Henrietta Sykes. Disraeli Papers, Box 1/A/I/A/34b, 44.

[10] A public letter to Daniel O'Connell, May 1835, inserted in the press; quoted by W. F. Monypenny and G. E. Buckle, *The Life of Benjamin Disraeli,* new and rev. ed., 2 vols. (New York: Macmillan, 1929), I, 295.

[11] Blake, pp. 143-44.

[12] Blake, p. 137; Disraeli Papers, Box 11/A/III/C/49; 53-54.

[13] Disraeli Papers, Box 11/A/III/C/44.

[14] "To Sir Robert Peel" ("The Letters of Runnymede," V), *Times* (London), 26 January 1836; rpt. in *Whigs and Whiggism,* pp. 256 ff.

[15] Disraeli to William Pyne, July 1836, quoted by Blake, p. 134.

[16] Blake, p. 143.

[17] B. R. Jerman, *The Young Disraeli* (Princeton: Princeton Univ. Press, 1960), pp. 277-78.

[18] The pamphlet was subtitled, "By the Author of Vivian Grey," a testimony to the fact that Disraeli's political identity was at this time seen by the voting public as an extension of his authorial persona.

[19] I wish to thank the officers of the National Trust for making the Disraeli Papers at Hughenden so readily available to me in a spirit of courtesy and cooperation. Mr. R. W. Stewart's handlist of those papers from which the form of citation is drawn must also be acknowledged as invaluable.

Robert O'Kell (essay date 1979)

SOURCE: "Disraeli's *Coningsby:* Political Manifesto or Psychological Romance?," *Victorian Studies,* Vol. 23, No. 1, Autumn, 1979, pp. 57-78.

[*In the following essay, O'Kell interprets* Coningsby *as an attempt by Disraeli to clarify his developing Tory ideology by "replacing the actuality of his struggle to transcend his alienation from the establishment . . . with ideal versions of the past as it should have been."*]

Coningsby; or, the New Generation, written in the autumn and winter of 1843-44, has traditionally been seen as the first example of a subgenre, the political novel, and, as such, part of a trilogy that is overtly propagandist in conception. Further, most critics, of whom Robert Blake is the most eloquent and representative, have agreed that Benjamin Disraeli's trilogy made up by *Coningsby, Sybil,* and *Tancred* "is quite different from anything he had written before" and that "a wide gulf separates them from his silver fork novels and historical romances of the 'twenties and 'thirties."[1] This view has been largely derived from Disraeli's retrospective statements of intention, first in his preface to the fifth edition of *Coningsby* in 1849 and later in the general preface to the 1870 collected edition of his novels, wherein he claims to have adopted "the form of fiction as the instrument to scatter his suggestions" about the "derivation and character of political parties; the condition of the people which had been the consequence of them; and the duties of the Church as a main remedial agency."[2] There is, of course, some validity for this post hoc authorial perspective. The world of Tadpole and Taper clearly reflects Disraeli's disenchantment with the Conservative party of the 1840s, and the portrayal of Young England's characters and ideas in *Coningsby* at least partially reflects his involvement in that movement.

But *Coningsby,* which is significantly subtitled: by the "author of 'Contarini Fleming,'" also reflects the relation between Disraeli's private and public lives and is, I think, more concerned with the development of a compensatory, ideal, heroic, political identity than it is with the contemporary state of political parties. The structure of the novel confirms this claim, for the careful reader can see that although *Coningsby* is, in fact, part fiction and part tract, the portion of it that takes the form of political essays is very much subordinate to the *bildungsroman* in which Harry Coningsby, Esq. finds the sources of his fulfillment. Yet, in resolutely attempting to elucidate the message of the *roman à thèse* which they take the novel to be, most critics have rested heavily upon those essays—chapters 1 and 7 of Book I, chapters 1 and 5 of Book II, and, to a lesser extent, chapter 4 of Book V. The message is, of course, there. But the reason it becomes a critical synecdoche is perhaps that few readers of *Coningsby* have read all or even some of Disraeli's early novels and that most have an imperfect understanding of his political thinking in the 1830s. Because there seems to be no appreciable distance between the authorial voice and Disraeli's own, it is easy to conclude that the novel is indeed little more than a "manifesto of Young England."[3] The difficulty with this argument, however, is that, as the novel progresses, the voice of the essayist is increasingly subsumed in the romance of Coningsby's private *and* public self-fulfillment. Far from the implicit assumption of most previous critics, that the romance is merely an illustrative embellishment of the narrator's political philosophy, the essays seem, rather, to form a context for the romance, which, once established, carries on with its own momentum in Books VI through IX. Thus, to overcome one's reluctance to treat the work as fiction is to be forced to the conclusion that there is a strong continuity between it and Disraeli's earlier works, from *Vivian Grey* and *The Young Duke* through *Contarini Fleming, Alroy,* and *Henrietta Temple*.[4]

For all the emphasis upon the duties of the "New Generation," *Coningsby* is in essence a fiction that looks retrospectively upon the period of the formation of Disraeli's Tory ideology in the 1830s, replacing the actuality of his struggle to transcend his alienation from the establishment—the basic terms of which were his racial heritage, his literary improprieties, and his reputation for insincerity—with ideal versions of the past as it should have been. As much as anything else, it is a romance of fictional wish fulfillment, so purified that elements of the author's internal conflicts are projected upon characters other than his nominal hero rather than embodied in him as had been the case with Vivian Grey, Contarini Fleming, David Alroy, and Ferdinand Armine. This is the most plausible explanation of the insipid and almost completely passive character of Coningsby and of the bizarre projection of supernatural powers on to his alter-ego, Sidonia. Lest this notion seem extreme, it should be pointed out that the fictional split personality is also a feature of two of Disraeli's other works, **"The Rise of Iskander"** and *Tancred,* and that the central theme of both is also the conflict between principle and expediency, or altruism and betrayal.

While the discussion of politics in *Coningsby* is an expression of this theme, it might be said to serve four aesthetic functions. First, it creates a topicality designed to enhance the matter of the actual fiction. Second, and more importantly, it creates the vacuum that Disraeli's hero is ultimately to fill: "No one had arisen," we are told, "either in Parliament, the Universities, or the Press, to lead the public mind to the investigation of principle; and not to mistake, in their reformations, the corruption of practice for fundamental ideas" (Bk. II, chap. 4). Third, both in satirical and expository terms, the political analysis helps to define by contrast Coningsby's true nature. Fourth, the political ideology itself works to shape the thematic impact of the romance's controlling fantasy. The first two of these functions are quite obvious and require

little comment, but both the matter of characterization and that of the fantasy seem more complex.

I

Coningsby is initially presented in terms similar in some respects to those which describe both the Duke of St. James and David Alroy. Like them he is an orphan, and his situation is given a melodramatic cast. He is clearly in the clutches of the "sinister," "dishonest," and "innately" vulgar Rigby (Bk. I, chap. 1); Lord Monmouth's tyranny has occasioned Mrs. Coningsby's cruel fate of estrangement and death; and the moral is explicit in the narrator's intrusion: "the altars of Nemesis are beneath every outraged roof, and the death of this unhappy lady, apparently without an earthly friend or an earthly hope, desolate and deserted, and dying in an obscure poverty, was not forgotten" (Bk. I, chap. 2). But in thus establishing the exemplum of poetic justice, the implied author is led a step beyond the limits of his heroic conception. For, when Coningsby's tears fail to impress his grandfather in their first interview, the authorial voice intrudes once more:

> How often in the nursery does the genius count as a dunce because he is pensive. . . . The school-boy, above all others, is not the simple being the world imagines. In that young bosom are often stirring passions as strong as our own, desires not less violent, a volition not less supreme. In that young bosom what burning love, what intense ambition, what avarice, what lust of power; envy that fiends might emulate, hate that man might fear.

> (Bk. I, chap. 3)

It does not take an astute critic to realize that this passage, with its increasing intensity and emotional violence, quickly becomes tangential to the characterization of Coningsby. In so doing, it casts an autobiographical reflection, given what we know of Disraeli's adolescence, that collapses whatever aesthetic distance might have been presumed to exist between the author and his narrator and that suggests the nature of the creative inspiration which shapes the novel. Interestingly, Coningsby, who is, of course, devoid of "avarice," "lust of power," "envy," and "hate," finds an early recognition, as Disraeli did not, of his preeminence and nobility in the form of adulation from his schoolboy peers following his heroism in saving Oswald Millbank's life. But what is equally striking is that at the time of his initiation into the realm of social and political action (in Book III), the narrator describes Coningsby's feelings in terms virtually identical to those of the internal struggle that characterizes the protagonists of *Contarini Fleming* (1832) and *Henrietta Temple* (1836).

Coningsby's "pure and innocent" heart, we are told, "notwithstanding all his high resolves and daring thoughts, was blessed with that tenderness of soul which is sometimes linked with an ardent imagination and a strong will" (Bk. III, chap. 1). And, although his "noble aim" demands "absolute, not relative distinction," he feels in his isolation the need for a companion for his heart as well as for his intellect (Bk. III, chap. 1). In short, he longs for a heroic role in which the struggle for "purity" and the struggle for "success" are blended and the two made manifest by the recognition of his own genius.[5] For example, immediately following the delineation of the hero's aspirations, the author turns to an account of Rigby's feeblemindedness ("he told Coningsby that want of religious Faith was solely occasioned by want of Churches"). This suggests that Disraeli's satirical portraits are primarily designed to define by contrast his protagonist's character: "His deep and pious spirit recoiled with disgust and horror from such lax, chance-medley maxims" (Bk. III, chap. 2). Similarly, the point of the portrait of life at Coningsby Castle is to establish the hero's true sensibility. The other guests, however distinguished and graceful, are caught up in an artificial world of questionable motives, dubious propriety, and studied effects the very opposite of his innocent spontaneity and tender affection.

It is important to recognize that Coningsby, rather like the Duke of St. James in *The Young Duke* and Ferdinand Armine in *Henrietta Temple,* is ultimately accepted as a hero because of his innate, natural superiority. Action on his part is superfluous and unnecessary, as is, indeed, stressed by the fact that the only active demonstrations of his heroic sensibility occur when he saves Oswald Millbank from drowning at Eton and when he solaces the actress, Flora. The point of the fantasy is that he is accepted for what he is—noble and pure of heart—and not for what he does. That is why his rewards of political preferment, marriage to his true love, and enormous wealth have the miraculous quality of wish fulfillment. It is also why Disraeli's characterization, with its emphasis upon the youth's nobility, innocence, virtue, and sensibility, can justly be seen in part as a compensatory version of the potential political protagonist. The very traditional quality of the ideal—grandson of a marquis, hero of Eton, Cambridge undergraduate—was for the author, however, a denial of a large part of his imaginative self.

The other side of Disraeli's ambivalence is embodied in the characterization of Sidonia, which in psychological terms might be said to represent the projected ideal of his other, alienated self. As a member of the Jewish race, Sidonia, too, is innately superior, but his acceptance among the social and political elite is based upon his demonstrated superiority. Ultimately, it is not just his enormous wealth or his dazzling intellect but rather his power and success in exerting political control over the whole of Europe that gains him his welcome. It has been suggested that Sidonia is modelled upon Baron Solomon de Rothschild, with whom Disraeli had become familiarly acquainted during his marvellous visit to Paris in the fall of 1842.[6] But there is no real similarity, other than their Jewishness and wealth, between Sidonia and his alleged model, so it is more sensible to argue that de Rothschild was merely the match that set Disraeli's imagination on fire. Sidonia was "descended from a very ancient and noble family of Arragon," who, "strange as it may sound, . . . secretly adhered to the ancient faith and ceremonies of their fathers—a Belief in the unity of the God of Sinai, and the rites and observances of the laws of Moses" (Bk. IV, chap. 10). Interestingly, Disraeli maintained that his own ancestors on his father's side of the family were aristocratic secret Jews expelled from Spain in 1492, and he included this highly romantic but false account of his origins in the memoir with which he prefaced his father's collected works in 1849.[7] Moreover, the theme of a secret religious allegiance is an important feature of both *Alroy* and **"The Rise of Iskander,"** and what I have termed "the Catholic disguise of his Jewish heritage" is embodied in *The Young Duke, Contarini Fleming,* and *Henrietta Temple.*[8] Significantly, too, Sidonia constantly speaks with Disraeli's voice. Virtually all of his political opinions are taken, often word for word, from Disraeli's earlier expressions of his creed in the *Morning Post* articles of 1835, his early pamphlets, **"A Vindication of the English Constitution,"** and **"The Revolutionary Epick."** For example, Sidonia tells Coningsby that: "'It is not the Reform Bill that has shaken the aristocracy of this country, but the means by which that Bill was carried'" (Bk. IV, chap. 11). By 1844 this may have become something of a Tory cliché, but in **"What Is He?"** (April 1833) Disraeli had written: "The aristocratic principle has been destroyed in this country, not by the Reform Act, but by the means by which the Reform Act was passed."[9] Further, Sidonia's elaborate justifications of Hebrew superiority were to be repeated both in *Tancred* and in Disraeli's anomalous chapter on the Jewish Question in his political "biography" of Lord George Bentinck in 1852.[10]

Despite the obvious sincerity of the latter statement of Disraeli's views, some critics would argue that the extravagant characterization of Sidonia is satirical. But it seems as much mistaken to judge the absurdity of his accomplishments by the test of verisimilitude as to restrict oneself to a literal definition of autobiography. It is clear that the two-fold essence of Sidonia's character, in both respects contrasting sharply with that of Coningsby, is that he is an outsider and that he is powerful. Consequently, he should be interpreted as an equally idealized counterassertion. Perhaps the conclusive proof of this ambivalence is the allegorical steeplechase in Book IV, chapter 14, where Coningsby, mounted on the best of his grandfather's stud, aptly called "Sir Robert," comes in second behind Sidonia on his gorgeous Arab "of pure race," again symbolically named "The Daughter of the Star" (Bk. III, chap. 1 and Bk. IV, chap. 14). In showing that the outsider, the alienated Jew, is equally "pure" and, indeed, superior to his nominal protagonist, Disraeli adopts an imaginative posture of defiance rather similar to that of taking up *Alroy* immediately after his defeat in the second Wycombe campaign of 1832, a campaign in which he was the victim of marked anti-Semitism. The most important aspects of Sidonia's characterization, however, go well beyond such obvious compensation and confirm my claim that Disraeli's identity confusion manifested itself not only as a tension between conflicting views of himself but also as ambivalence within each one (O'Kell, "Psychological Romance," p. 35).

The ostensible political lesson that Sidonia teaches his youthful protégé concerns the inspirational potency of heroic individualism. Coningsby is, of course, an apt pupil, for, as an adolescent, he had indulged in "visions of personal distinction, of future celebrity, perhaps even of enduring fame." Thus Sidonia preaches to the converted when, in discoursing upon "the Spirit of the Age," he extols the "'influence of individual character'" (Bk. III, chap. 1). It is a doctrine of elegant simplicity. Power residing in institutions, whether nobility, monarchy, Church, or Parliament, brings opprobrium upon them (Bk. IV, chap. 13), but truly "great men, . . . prophets, . . . legislators, . . . conquerors," can control or create "a vast public opinion" and are "Divine" (Bk. III, chap. 1). For the present the "'age does not believe in great men, because it does not possess any,'" but the "'Spirit of the Age is the very thing that a great man changes.'" According to Coningsby's alter ego, the function of institutions is subsidiary: "'From the throne to the hovel all call for a guide. You give monarchs constitutions to teach them sovereignty, and nations Sunday-schools to inspire them with faith'" (Bk. III, chap. 1). The hope of "'an age of social disorganisation'" is in "'what is more powerful than laws and institutions,'" in the regeneration of a sense of "community" based on "national character" and "public virtue" (Bk. IV, chap. 13). Perhaps most importantly, such a reconstruction of society can occur not from "'any new disposition of political power,'" nor "'on a purely rational basis'":

> "A political institution is a machine; the motive power is the national character. . . . There has been an attempt to reconstruct society on a basis of material motives and calculations. It has failed. . . . Man is only truly great when he acts from the passions; never irresistable but when he appeals to the imagination. . . . Man is made to adore and obey: but if you will not command him, if you give him nothing to worship, he will fashion his own divinities, and find a chieftain in his own passions."
>
> (Bk. IV, chap. 13)

This statement, with its division between mechanical and organic theories of society, its rejection of materialism, its doctrine of hero worship, and its fear of unregulated human nature, is so obviously resonant with the ideas of Carlyle that critics have often surmised that Disraeli was here borrowing directly from him. There is, however, no conclusive evidence that Disraeli had read Carlyle's works. When one recognizes that all of the elements of this political theory had found expression in *The Revolutionary Epick*, published in 1834 (considerably earlier than Carlyle's major works), the most sensible conclusion would seem to be that such ideas were, as much as their antithesis, a part of the spirit of the age, which found its most forceful expression in Carlyle's prose.

The ultimate simplicity and attraction of Sidonia's political theory resides in its seemingly magical quality. Among the most enchanting things he tells Coningsby are his convictions that "'Great men never want experience'" and that "'To believe in the heroic makes heroes'" (Bk. III, chap. 1). Such notions recall to mind *The Wondrous Tale of Alroy* in which the youthful, indeed adolescent, protagonist, empowered by his altruistic faith in his role as the spiritual leader of the Hebrew people, finds that his exertions result in almost miraculous conquests. But the point of such a comparison is not just a matter of the inherent egocentricity. The implicit assertion of Hebrew superiority in *Alroy* is matched in *Coningsby* by Sidonia's similar belief (given the sanction of "fact" by the implied author) that the Hebrews, along "with the Saxons and the Greeks," are "in the first and superior class" of the human species and as an "unmixed race of a first-rate organisation are the *aristocracy of Nature*" (italics mine, Bk. IV, chap. 10). Perhaps the intrusion of the authorial voice here is significant, for *Alroy*, though begun in 1829, was completed in 1833, only a year before Disraeli's first explicit advocacy of a natural aristocracy in *The Revolutionary Epick*. Thus, Sidonia's simple notion, however circular, of faith in one's own destiny as the motivating and creative source of the heroic sensibility, might be said to confirm the suspicion that there was a more than casual connection between Disraeli's egocentricity and the Ultra-Tory, paternalistic ideology he formulated in the 1830s from his understanding of Lord Bolingbroke's ideas.[11] In any case, Sidonia's ideas, when seen in the context of their first expression, confirm that Disraeli was drawing his inspiration for *Coningsby* as much from his experiences in the 1830s as from his circumstances in the 1840s.

As the collapse of the heroic fantasy in *Alroy* establishes, the imaginative links between Disraeli's egocentricity and his ideology were the issues of altruism and sincerity. In this respect Sidonia is also important, for the characterization suggests that the tension between "purity" and "success," between altruism and expediency, that distinguished David Alroy continued ten years later to be an ambivalence within the expression of the political ideal expressed by Sidonia and espoused by Coningsby. Although Sidonia's political theory embraces a nobility of character and an altruistic vision of an organic community, his political practice is a sanction of very different values. For one thing, his true self remains largely hidden; though he is, we are told, "affable and gracious," it is "impossible to penetrate him," and the dichotomy between his surface candor and underlying secrecy is expressed in explicit terms. Moreover, juxtaposed to Sidonia's sense of himself as the alienated outsider, looking upon life "with a glance rather of curiosity than content" and perceiving himself as "a lone being," are the compensatory gratifications of clandestine power.

> No Minister of State had such communications with secret agents and political spies as Sidonia. He held relations with all the clever outcasts of the world. The catalogue of his acquaintance in the shape of Greeks, Armenians, Moors, secret Jews, Tartars, Gypsies, wandering Poles and Carbonari, would throw a curious light on those subterranean agencies of which the world in general knows so little, but which exercise so great an influence on public events. . . . The secret history of the world was his pastime. His great pleasure was to contrast the hidden motive, with the public pretext, of transactions.
>
> (Bk. IV, chap. 10)

The content of this fantasy, in contrast to the ideals of Young England, is obviously manipulative and subversive, but it is the implied author's subordinate reference to "subterranean agencies" that suggests the imaginatively autobiographical links.

Perhaps more substantial than the contrasting gratifications of alienation from society and of engagement in its affairs is Sidonia's inconsistency on the Jewish Question. For, however much he believes in the superiority of the Jewish race as a "fact," he puts the argument against anti-Semitic prejudice and discrimination in purely pragmatic and expedient terms. When Coningsby suggests that it would be easy to repeal any law embodying "so illiberal" a conception, Sidonia replies:

> "Oh! as for illiberality, I have no objection to it if it be an element of power. Eschew political sentimentalism. What I contend is, that if you permit men to accumulate property, and they use that permission to a great extent, power is inseparable from that property, and it is in the last degree impolitic to make it the interest of any powerful class to oppose the institutions under which they live."
>
> (Bk. IV, chap. 15)

He then goes on to assure his protégé that the Jews "'are essentially Tories'" and "'Toryism . . . but copied

from the mightly prototype which has fashioned Europe.'" This opinion is supported by a very egocentric account of the way in which the intellectual and political affairs of Russia, Spain, France, and Prussia are all interconnected through his financial manipulations and by the narcissistic conclusion that "'the world is governed by very different personages from what is imagined by those who are not behind the scenes'" (Bk. IV, chap. 15). To fully explore the implications of this vision for Disraeli's later political career, especially his involvement in foreign affairs, is well beyond the scope of this essay. But it is important to recognize that the characterization of Sidonia does contain a conspiratorial theory of politics that gives a legitimacy to the kind of secret manipulation and intrigue that is the antithesis of the ideals Disraeli has traditionally been thought to have been propounding in this "manifesto of Young England."

On the other hand, however extravagant a creature, Sidonia also represents, through the conception of his "natural aristocracy" *and* his demonstrated success, an attempt to blend the conflicting claims of altruism and expediency. While the justification of his identity rests upon his undeniable genius, the rationalization of his conduct rests upon his indisputable power. For this reason Sidonia, as much as Coningsby himself, can be seen as part of the heroic fantasy of wish fulfillment, the content and scope of which, in comparison with those of **Alroy** and **Henrietta Temple,** reflects Disraeli's increasing confidence in his sense of himself.

II

To fully appreciate the continuity of Disraeli's fiction, it is essential to examine the way in which politics in an ideological sense supports **Coningsby**'s central theme of heroic individualism. In **Contarini Fleming,** the conflicting worlds of the hero's public and private fulfillment are conceived to be mutually exclusive. Contarini finds erotic fulfillment of his purest feelings in the love of his cousin Alcesté, who is explicitly portrayed as a mother substitute. But this expression of the true self necessitates an exile from the realm of political success in his father's world and from what he feels is the hypocritical behavior essential to it. Importantly, the contrast between the two worlds is presented as a dichotomy between Catholic and Protestant cultures in such a marked manner that the use of the religious motif must be seen as a reflection of the author's ambivalence about his racial heritage. With this in mind, it is interesting to notice that Sidonia, the exemplum of demonstrated success, is an exile from the possibility of erotic or romantic involvement. Indeed, his emotional impotence confirms that the tension between "purity" and "success" which is the essence of the earlier work continues to exist in Disraeli's imaginative shaping of **Coningsby.** For, though it is true that this characterization partially resolves the political expression of that tension by means of the notion of natural aristocracy, it is also true that the unsatisfactory explanation of Sidonia's emotional aridity is that he "notoriously would never diminish by marriage the purity of his race" (Bk. VI, chap. 2). But the fact that the religious dimension of Sidonia's character is both part of the attempted resolution of the conflict between altruism and expediency and part of the renewed expression of that tension's power is suggestive of the continuing complexity of Disraeli's own attitudes toward his Jewish heritage, essentially a hostile symbiosis capable of producing both pride and despair.

The passage describing Sidonia's emotional deprivation is in the voice of the implied author. The conception of romantic love it contains is, not surprisingly, perfectly consistent with that inherent in the earlier fictions and with what we know of the emotional currents of Disraeli's own involvement with Henrietta Sykes and with his wife Mary Anne. Clearly, the disconcertingly strong emphasis upon the consolatory nature of love—with its "profound sympathy," softening of "sorrows," counseling in "cares," and support in "perils"—is a vision in which "the lot the most precious to man" is to find in unquestioning acceptance the antidote to frustrated genius and fear of failure (Bk. IV, chap. 10). With respect to Sidonia, the effect of the passage is to deny any such vulnerability, a denial that is later confirmed in the plot by his immunity to the passionate advances of the Princess Lucretia and his purely avuncular affection for Edith Millbank. The Princess Lucretia, who later marries Lord Monmouth and conspires to cheat Coningsby of his inheritance, is an interesting character, rather like Mrs. Felix Lorraine in *Vivian Grey*. In their treachery, both seem to display the dangers of unromanticized sexual passion. But the main point is that, through the portrayal of Sidonia, the imaginative conflict between love and power that was the mainspring of the plot in *Contarini Fleming* continues to exist in *Coningsby*.

The alternative, a vision in which love and power are blended, was for Disraeli an equally compelling fantasy. It finds its expression in the almost miraculous unfolding of Coningsby's destiny, and, not surprisingly, that expression bears comparison with the earlier novels. When, for example, Coningsby first visits Millbank, he is fascinated by a portrait of a beautiful young woman. He later finds out, upon opening a box of his father's papers held in trust for him and discovering there a locket containing the same likeness, that this woman is his deceased mother. This use of the portrait-locket-mother detail, while admittedly a romance convention, is clearly a repetition of that in *Contarini Fleming* where at the conclusion the hero discovers in the same way that his magdalen-cousin-bride was physically identical to his deceased mother. Moreover, in *Coningsby*, Edith Millbank, while not literally the

hero's sister, is, as the daughter of the man who first loved his mother, nevertheless an imaginative variant of Miriam in *Alroy*, whose devotion to her brother is the emblem of his purity of motive. The variations of the fantasy elements are, of course, important in that they ultimately permit the marriage of Edith and Coningsby, but the similarities are equally so in that they imaginatively confirm the purity of that union.

The structure and diction of the story make much the same point. When Coningsby realizes at the ball given by the Baroness S. de R-d. in Paris that the beautiful young woman he has fallen in love with is none other than the girl who had so charmed him at Millbank, we are told she had "a face of sunshine amid all that artificial light." His conversation with her recalls the "high, and pure" ideas which bind him in friendship to her brother. Yet, juxtaposed to this scene is a long passage that reiterates Sidonia's indifference to the heart's affections as "one of those men . . . who shrink . . . from an adventure of gallantry" with "neither time nor temper for sentimental circumlocutions," and who "detested the diplomacy of passion" and found its "studied hypocrisies . . . wearisome" (Bk. VI, chap. 2). This sharply contrasting vision of love as a social game strongly reflects precisely the sort of ambivalence the subject occasions in Disraeli's earlier fiction, the more so since the following chapter begins with Coningsby's "agitated slumber" in which he is "haunted" by dreams of a "beautiful countenance that was alternately the face of the mysterious picture, and then that of Edith" and from which he awakes "little refreshed; restless, and yet sensible of some secret joy" (Bk. VI, chap. 3).

The presence of the mother-motif, soon elaborated as "fanciful speculations which connected Edith and the mysterious portrait of his mother," is sufficient to establish this development of the plot as an extension of the imaginative shaping not only of *Contarini Fleming* but also of *Henrietta Temple* in which Ferdinand Armine is similarly haunted in dreams by the apparently conflicting claims of his pure, filial devotion to his mother, associated with the family's restoration, and his equally pure passion for Henrietta. The depth of the imaginative connection between *Henrietta Temple* and *Coningsby* is also suggested, however, by the voice of the narrator, who intrudes at this point in the latter work to philosophize upon love: "Ah! what is that ambition that haunts our youth, that thirst for power or that lust of fame that forces us from obscurity into the sunblaze of the world, what are these sentiments so high, so vehement, so enobling? They vanish, and in an instant, before the glance of a woman!" (Bk. VI, chap. 3). This passage has a strikingly similar theme to that in Book II, chapter 4, of *Henrietta Temple* where the narrator intrudes to say that to behold a beautiful being and sense the bliss of love is "to feel our flaunty ambition fade away like a shrivelled gourd before her vision; to feel fame a juggle and posterity a lie." The difference in language between the two would seem to reflect that as a protagonist, Coningsby embodies none of the guilt occasioned by hypocritical or calculating motives that characterizes Ferdinand. Yet, despite this purification of the hero in *Coningsby,* the most convincing evidence of the close imaginative affinity with *Henrietta Temple* can be found in the very much related characterizations and plots.

Among the obvious instances of such similarity are Coningsby's alternations between a sense of his innate helplessness and a resolution to confront his destiny with Byronic defiance (Bk. VIII, chap. 4). His changes of affect are less reckless, but in despair at thinking Sidonia is his rival for Edith's love, he, very much like Ferdinand Armine (and David Alroy, too), confesses, "'I am nothing.'"[12] Also, like Ferdinand, he sees himself as a victim of his hereditary position, thwarted in love by his grandfather's actions.[13] Further, Coningsby responds to the threat of failure, just as does Ferdinand, by denying the reality of his circumstances and living for the pleasures of the enchanting moment. In Edith's presence, he wishes that the party should never end: "All mysteries, all difficulties, were driven from his recollection; he lived only in the exciting and enjoyable present."[14] Just as Ferdinand procrastinates leaving Henrietta to return to Bath, so Coningsby postpones his departure for Cambridge.[15]

All of these relatively minor details suggest the true nature of Coningsby's imaginative ancestry. But perhaps more convincing evidence of the affinity between the two works is the plot contrivance in both whereby the lovers are separated by rumors of their respective engagements to others—Coningsby to Lady Theresa Sydney, Edith to Lord Beaumanoir, Ferdinand to his cousin Katherine, and Henrietta to Lord Montfort. Moreover, in both novels the hero is then shown to be completely altruistic and lovable, and the disentanglement of the romantic complication is occasioned by the intervention of a circle of his friends who gladly conspire to remove all obstacles to his felicity. Interestingly, both Coningsby and Ferdinand are completely passive protagonists in the unfolding of these events. This is not to argue that this plot mechanism is more than the hackneyed convention of the comedy of manners, but that it is significant that the pattern of wish fulfillment in the two works is identical.

III

Having recognized the parallels between *Henrietta Temple* and the first volume of Disraeli's "trilogy," it is instructive to look again at the relation between the politics and the romance in *Coningsby.* The argument that the political ideology serves to define an ideal identity or role of heroic individualism can best be sustained by citing the passage which de-

scribes Coningsby's aspirations at the moment he moves from adolescence to manhood.

> It was that noble ambition, the highest and the best, that must be born in the heart and organised in the brain, which will not let a man be content, unless his intellectual power is recognised by his race, and desires that it should contribute to their welfare. It is the heroic feeling; the feeling that in old days produced demi-gods; . . . without which political institutions are meat without salt; the Crown a bauble, the Church an establishment, Parliaments debating clubs, and Civilisation itself but a fitful and transient dream.
>
> (Bk. V, chap. 1)

This is strong stuff; but, as the rhetorical flourish of the passage implies, a full appreciation of Disraeli's use of the political theme requires further analysis of the ideology itself. In this respect, the ambivalence of Disraeli's role in the Young England movement is worth noticing. George Smythe, the most wordly of the *partie carrée* composed also of Lord John Manners and Alexander Baillie-Cochrane, instinctively understood Disraeli better than the others, and he was not really disconcerted by the possibility that their leader might have ulterior political motives.[16] Cochrane, on the other hand, was much disturbed by Disraeli's performance in Paris during the parliamentary recess of 1842, by his "self-aggrandisement" and the "phantasmagoria of politique legerdemain" in which he pictured himself "the founder of some new dynasty with his Manfred love-locks stamped on the current coin of the realm" (Whibley, I, 148-149). Even the gentle and unsuspicious Manners confided to his diary: "Could I only satisfy myself that D'Israeli believed all that he said, I should be more happy: his historical views are quite mine, but does he believe them?" (Whibley, I, 149). The full extent of Disraeli's ambivalence is revealed, however, in his own words. Seizing the opportunity of an audience with Louis Phillipe, he wrote the King a lengthy memorandum in which he embodied his plans for an Anglo-French alliance. He proposed to initiate a Commons debate on the subject which would see his voice "echo in every Cabinet in Europe," to organize a party of Conservative members who "full of youth and energy and constant in their seats, must exercise an irresistable control over the tone of the Minister" and "dictate the character of his foreign" policy, and, finally, to coordinate the "Press of England in favour of the . . . alliance" and make "the ideas of a single man . . . the voice of the nation." (Monypenny and Buckle, II, 409-413). This is more than the euphoric posturing of a naive egotist; for all its sublime egotism, the memorandum is really a fantasy embodying Disraeli's conception of his own potential, though it certainly confirms Cochrane's worst fears of his manipulative intentions. But to assert this is not to deny that Disraeli was equally and genuinely attracted by the purity and nobility of Young England's motives and ideals and, in particular, that he shared the others' conception of patriotism as the antidote to the battle of warring factions that early nineteenth-century society seemed to them to have become.

Indeed, the essence of Coningby's new Toryism, derived largely from Bolingbroke's *On the Spirit of Patriotism* and *The Idea of a Patriot King,* is trust.[17] The vision that compels Coningsby is that of the necessity of undertaking the heroic struggle to restore the ancient solidarity of the governed and the governing classes. Most of the elements of that vision Disraeli had expressed as early as 1834 in **The Revolutionary Epick.** But the struggle now requires a modern "demigod" because in the current state of affairs all of the political institutions, monarchy, Church, Lords, and Commons, have become debased by either the Whigs' "Destructive Creed" or the Conservatives' "Political Infidelity." Indeed, the only weapons that the ideal political protagonist has at his command are the conviction of his own genius and the power to influence public opinion. Here Disraeli steps beyond the Tory orthodoxy of the *Vindication,* where he had argued that Parliament was the constitutional representative of the estate of the Commons and the monarchy and Church the representatives of the people. For Coningsby, echoing Sidonia, tells Oswald Millbank:

> "Representation is not necessarily, or even in a principal sense, Parliamentary. . . . a principle of government is reserved for our days. . . . Opinion is now supreme, and Opinion speaks in print. The representation of the Press is far more complete than the representation of Parliament. Parliamentary representation was the happy device of a ruder age . . . but it exhibits many symptoms of desuetude. It is controlled by a system of representation more vigorous and comprehensive; which absorbs its duties and fulfills them more efficiently."
>
> (Bk. VII, chap. 2)

This "polity" is, Coningsby argues, "'capable of great ends and appealing to high sentiments.'" The means by which it is to "'render government an object of national affection'" is the symbolic restoration of the power of the sovereign, who is both to lead and yet be restrained from arbitrary action by public opinion (Bk. VII, chap. 2).

As a political theory, this argument is based entirely upon subjective qualities. When Oswald Millbank objects that "'public opinion may be indifferent. A nation may be misled, may be corrupt,'" Coningsby urges in reply a faith in the "national character." He then goes on to justify that conception in terms of individual nobility: "'If a nation be led to aim at the good and the great, depend upon it, whatever be its form, the government

will respond to its convictions and its sentiments.'" In short, the political ideology Coningsby advocates depends for its efficacy entirely on the integrity or the purity of the hero. Interestingly, too, there is in this conception a noticeable detachment from the constitutional focus of government. Coningsby goes on to assure Oswald that "'true wisdom lies in the policy that would effect its ends by the influence of opinion, and yet by the means of existing forms'" (Bk. VII, chap. 2). The idea that these "forms," the monarchy, the Church, and Parliament, are but "means" to the "ends" of "the good and the great" throws an entirely new light upon both the consistency of Disraeli's later political practice and the satirical portrait of the Conservative party's expediency. Indeed, from such a perspective, the latter has a cogency very much related to Coningsby's destiny.

What I am arguing is that Disraeli's satirical treatment of the Conservatives' "Political Infidelity" in abandoning the constitutional forms that should support the cause of true Toryism is not implicitly a defense of those institutions for their own sake. It is their symbolic power to effect the heroic vision that interests Coningsby and, by implication, Disraeli. Thus, at the climax of the novel, Book VIII, chapter 3, the central issue is Coningsby's purity. At this point, his political ideology and his love for Edith are blended into one theme. The essence of the climax is Coningsby's resolution to defy his grandfather and to refuse to be the family's Conservative candidate at Darlford. Lord Monmouth's aim in returning Coningsby to Parliament is overtly selfish; he believes that such expedient support of the Conservative cause will result in a dukedom for himself and the revival of a family barony in his grandson's name. Coningsby, however, confesses that he has "'for a long time looked upon the Conservative party as a body who have betrayed their trust; more from ignorance . . . than from design; yet clearly a body of individuals totally unequal to the exigencies of the epoch, and . . . unconscious of its real character'" (Bk. VIII, chap. 3). In contradicting his grandfather's pragmatic cynicism by demanding political "faith," he does, admittedly, seem to shift the basis of his thinking and refer to the "rights and privileges" of the Crown, the Church, and the House of Lords as if they were political ends in themselves. But his final words in this scene revert to the conception of trust, or social harmony, at the center of his ideology.

> "What we want, sir, is . . . to establish great principles which may maintain the realm and secure the happiness of the people. Let me see authority once more honoured; a solemn reverence again the habit of our lives; let me see property acknowledging, as in the old days of faith, that labour is his twin brother, and that the essence of all tenure is the performance of duty."
>
> (Bk. VIII, chap. 3)

The blending of this nostalgic ideal with the rather practical assessment of the new social conditions under which a political leader must operate is by no means the least significant aspect of Coningsby's thinking. It not only embodies the ambivalence of Disraeli's role in Young England but also foreshadows the most controversial aspects of his later career. For this reason, it deserves more respect in our analyses of the Victorian political dilemma than it has received. But equally important to this study is the linking of the hero's public and private fulfillments.

Coningsby's first reaction to his grandfather's news is a vision of the strife and anguish that his rival candidacy to Millbank's would cause him: "The countenance of Edith . . . rose to him again. He saw her canvassing for her father, and against him. Madness!" (Bk. VIII, chap. 3). In other words, the fantasy is so constructed that the abandonment of his political faith would entail an alienation of his love. In this respect, Disraeli's choice of words is important. Near the end of the previous chapter, when Edith has just heard the rumor that Coningsby is engaged to marry Lady Theresa Sydney, the implied author summarizes Coningsby's feelings occasioned by the resultant change in his true love's demeanor:

> he passed a sleepless night, agitated and distracted by the manner in which she had received him. To say that her appearance had revived all his passionate affection for her would convey an unjust impression of the nature of his feelings. His affection had never for a moment swerved; it was profound and firm. . . . whatever were the barriers which the circumstances of life placed against their union, they were partakers of the solemn sacrament of an unpolluted heart.
>
> (Bk. VIII, chap. 2)

Quite apart from the fact that this passage closely resembles a description of Ferdinand's love for Henrietta, the phrase "an unpolluted heart" suggests the true motivating power and the ultimate shape of Disraeli's romance. For, when in double despair that both his political prospects and his personal happiness have been irrevocably damaged, Coningsby is suddenly seized with a heroic conception of his identity. Having compared himself to Caesar,

> He thought of Edith in her hours of fondness; he thought of the pure and solemn moments when to mingle his name with the heroes of humanity was his aspiration, and to achieve immortal fame the inspiring purpose of his life. What were the tawdry accidents of vulgar ambition to him? No domestic despot could deprive him of his intellect, his knowledge, the sustaining power of an unpolluted conscience.
>
> (Bk. VIII, chap. 4)

The language is indicative of the theme. From this it is obvious that the defining quality of the ideal political identity embodied in the characterization of Coningsby is purity of heart, conscience, and ambition. The shape of the fantasy is a testimony to the fact that such purity, at least in the realm of this romance which is indisputably the realm of the author's imagination, guarantees a transcendant success. The plot is, however, not without further complications. Before Coningsby finds himself possessed of that success, he is temporarily disinherited and plunged once more into profound gloom. At this moment, the implied author's language in describing his hero's thoughts has an anomalous extravagance that dissolves the screen of fiction and confirms again the imaginatively autobiographical nature of the romance:

> Nothing is great but the personal. . . . The power of man, his greatness and his glory, depend on essential qualities. Brains every day become more precious than blood. . . .

> This conviction of power in the midst of despair was a revelation of intrinsic strength. . . . He felt that he must be prepared for great sacrifices, for infinite suffering; that there must devolve on him a bitter inheritance of obscurity, struggle, envy, and hatred, vulgar prejudice, base criticism, petty hostilities, but the dawn would break, and the hour arrive, when the welcome morning hymn of his success and his fame would sound and be re-echoed.
>
> (Bk. IX, chap. 4)

Just as in the authorial intrusion in Book I, chapter 3, this reference to "a bitter inheritance" of "obscurity," "struggle," "envy," "hatred," "prejudice," "criticism," and "hostilities" steps beyond the limits of Disraeli's characterization of his hero. But the real significance of the passage lies in both its explicit and contextual egocentricity, for it is clear that here the issues of party ideology are absorbed in the destiny of the heroic role. Thus, Coningsby's election to Parliament *in absentia,* his reunion with Edith accompanied by the tangible blessing of Millbank's generosity, and his ultimate inheritance of his grandfather's fortune from the grateful Flora can legitimately be seen as the completion of the fiction's central fantasy of acceptance, one in which the melodramatic delight of revenge in destroying Rigby's venomous, self-serving career is combined with the gratifications of otherwise universal recognition of the hero's genius. In the end, the links between purity and power, love and success, sustain the argument that ***Coningsby,*** very much like Disraeli's earlier fictions, is chiefly concerned with his conflicts of identity; that politics, while an integral part of the work, is essentially a motif within the genre of the "psychological romance"; and, that "romance," however quixotic the struggles of Young England, was to be a shaping force in Victorian politics.

This analysis inevitably disturbs our assumptions about Disraeli's subsequent novels, particularly *Sybil* (1845) and *Tancred* (1847), which have been widely thought to complete a "trilogy" of sociopolitical themes. If the relationship between *Coningsby* and the earlier fiction is so much closer than has been previously granted, it is possible that Disraeli's later novels might also embody in significant ways a tension between public statement and private fantasy that cannot be understood as simply literal autobiography or *roman à thèse*.

In the "General Preface" of 1870, Disraeli says that he intended, when he began *Coningsby,* to treat all three of the "trilogy's" principal topics—the character of political parties, the condition of the people, and the duties of the Church—but found that "they were too vast for the space . . . allotted," so that only the first was adequately dealt with. Indeed, the favorable reception of *Coningsby* reflected a widespread conviction that he had produced a "manifesto of Young England" and, not so incidentally, a treatise upon the shortcomings of Peel's Conservatism. So, although the less flattering conclusion—that Disraeli found his "romance" had run off with his theme—seems valid, he undoubtedly set out to develop the implications of that theme in *Sybil,* his second "political" novel. Seeing, as he clearly did, the character of political parties, the condition of the people, and the duties of the Church as aspects of "the same subject" ("General Preface," p. x) and feeling that *Coningsby*'s ostensible message did not need more than a resonant echo in his new work, Disraeli intended *Sybil* to be an illustration of the symbiotic nature of his thematic trinity. The success of the novel, however, reflected his readers' much narrower and more literal understanding of the story—a widespread failure to see that Disraeli's prime concern is the *moral* condition of parties, people, and Church and that he views the degradation of the people as a result of moral and spiritual inadequacy, not as a first cause of social unrest. Criticism of the novel, even to the present day, has often concerned itself with tracking down the author's many sources, with the historical inaccuracies of his treatment of economic distress, and with the aesthetic flaw of the culminating marriage of Sybil and Egremont. With few exceptions, critics have ignored the devastating conscious ironies that pervade the work.[18]

It is this neglect, perhaps more than our excessive concern for the matter of his assimilation of his secondary sources, that has shaped the critical distortion by which we have come to assume *Sybil* to be Disraeli's most typical fiction. Rather, it would seem that in writing *Sybil,* his reaction to *Coningsby*'s fame as a "political" novel, his reliance upon printed sources, and his haste (the novel was finished in less than a year, despite a very hectic political and social life) combined to free Disraeli to a considerable extent from the imaginatively autobiographical mode of fiction and to establish a greater aesthetic distance between himself and his characters. Thus it is that Disraeli's best and most widely read novel is the one least typical of his canon.

By the time he completed *Sybil,* Disraeli knew that he would need the space of a third novel to elucidate fully the themes begun in *Coningsby,* or so *Sybil*'s narrator implies in the denouement. The best explication to date of the next novel, *Tancred; or, the New Crusade,* is undoubtedly Richard Levine's.[19] The key to the novel, he suggests, is the theoretical basis of Disraeli's religious philosophy and its embodiment in Tancred's quest for the divine law that retrospectively sanctions the political creed and social message of *Coningsby* and *Sybil.* But, however clearly one extracts Disraeli's prophecy of the Hebraeo-Christian destiny, most readers find the relevance of the great Asian mystery to British politics obscure, the motivation of the characters implausible, and the exigencies of the plot baffling. Hence, the view that *Tancred* reflects a discontinuity in the trilogy would seem to be on good ground.[20]

The present view of *Coningsby* and the obvious revival in the "New Crusade" of Sidonia's theory of Hebrew superiority suggest, however, that an analysis of the exotic fantasy structure in *Tancred* would confirm that the novel is a significant extension of Disraeli's use of the imaginatively autobiographical mode of fiction. Whether this is also true of his last two completed novels, *Lothair* (1870) and *Endymion* (1880), is an intriguing question. But, insofar as they embody ambivalence about the costs of such political success as their author had achieved, or still sought, they too would be works within the genre of the "psychological romance." As his speeches, letters, diaries, and actions show, romance also shapes, as well as reflects, Disraeli's political career. The fiction is not simply a gloss on the politics, nor the politics an explanation of the fiction. Both are enactments of the same urgencies and purposes. The political career, like the fiction, is an invention, and seen in the light of their common imaginative patterns, the novels and the political career will provoke a fuller understanding of Disraeli's achievements.

Notes

[1] Robert Blake, *Disraeli* (London: Eyre & Spottiswoode, 1966), p. 190. Cf. Bernard Langdon-Davies, Introduction to *Coningsby,* by Benjamin Disraeli (New York: Capricorn, 1961), p. xxviii: "Disraeli has created a new type. The novel is essentially political, written to expound a political creed."

[2] Both prefaces are cited by Blake, pp. 193-194. *Coningsby* was published by Henry Colburn; the collected edition was published by Longmans & Co.

[3] W. F. Monypenny and G. E. Buckle, *The Life of Benjamin Disraeli,* 6 vols. (London: Murray, 1910-20), II, 199.

[4] Chapter references in parentheses are to *The Bradenham Edition of the Novels and Tales of Benjamin Disraeli, 1st Earl of Beaconsfield,* 12 vols. (London: Peter Davies, 1927; New York: Knopf, 1927-29).

[5] See Robert O'Kell, "The Autobiographical Nature of Disraeli's Early Fiction," *Nineteenth-Century Fiction,* 31 (1976), 253-284.

[6] For a brief account of the visit and its importance to the formation of the Young England movement, see Blake, pp. 173-175. Disraeli first met the baron's nephew, Antony de Rothschild, several years earlier at a dinner party in London.

[7] Isaac D'Israeli, *Curiosities of Literature with a View of the Life and Writings of the Author by his Son,* 3 vols., 14th ed. (London: Moxon, 1849), I, xx-xxi.

[8] See Robert O'Kell, "The Psychological Romance: Disraeli's Early Fiction and Political Apprenticeship," (Ph.D. dissertation, Indiana University, 1974).

[9] "What Is He?" is reprinted in *Whigs and Whiggism,* ed. William Hutcheon (London: Murray, 1913), pp. 16-22. This quotation is from p. 19.

[10] Benjamin Disraeli, *Lord George Bentinck: A Political Biography* (London: Colbum, 1852), chap. 24.

[11] See Robert O'Kell, "*The Revolutionary Epick:* Tory Democracy or Radical Gallomania?" *Disraeli Newsletter,* II, No. 1 (1977), 24-42. Chapter 5 of O'Kell, "Psychological Romance" also provides a detailed discussion of the development of Disraeli's political ideas in the 1830s.

[12] *Coningsby,* Bk. VI, chap. 7 and *Henrietta Temple,* Bk. II, chaps. 5 and 9. Cf. *The Wondrous Tale of Alroy,* Pt. V, chap. 6.

[13] *Coningsby,* Bk. VI, chap. 8 and Bk. VII, chap. 1; *Henrietta Temple,* Bk. II, chap. 9.

[14] *Coningsby,* Bk. VI, chap. 8; *Henrietta Temple,* Bk. II, chaps. 11 and 13.

[15] *Coningsby,* Bk. VI, chap. 8; *Henrietta Temple,* Bk. III, chap. 1.

[16] Charles Whibley, *Lord John Manners and His Friends,* 2 vols. (London: Blackwood, 1925), I, 143-144.

[17] See Richard Faber, *Beaconsfield and Bolingbroke* (London: Faber, 1961). In chap. 8 of "Psychological Romance," I argue that Disraeli's identification with Bolingbroke also involved a perception of their similar political roles.

[18] The best discussion of irony in *Sybil* is Patrick Brantlinger's in *The Spirit of Reform: British Literature and Politics, 1832-1867* (Cambridge, Massachusetts and London: Harvard University Press, 1977).

[19] Richard A. Levine, *Benjamin Disraeli* (New York: Twayne, 1968), pp. 114-134.

[20] Daniel R. Schwarz, "Progressive Dubiety: The Discontinuity of Disraeli's Political Trilogy," *Victorian Newsletter,* No. 47 (1975), 12-19.

Daniel R. Schwarz (essay date 1979)

SOURCE: "From Immersion to Reflection: Romance and Realism in *Henrietta Temple* and *Venetia*" in *Disraeli's Fiction,* Macmillan, 1979, pp. 55-77.

[*In the following excerpt, Schwarz defends* Henrietta Temple *and* Venetia *against charges that the novels lack aesthetic value and are discontinuous with Disraeli's other works.*]

I

The only book-length critical study of Disraeli's novels, Richard A. Levine's *Benjamin Disraeli,* criticises *Henrietta Temple* (1836) and *Venetia* (1837) because of their supposed objectivity:

> In the final analysis, however, [*Henrietta Temple*] is neither typical nor meaningful in Disraeli's canon; for it carries within it few ideas or authorial observations, and Disraeli's fundamental interests for us are as a novelist of ideas and as a writer of personal involvement and observation. In *Henrietta Temple* and *Venetia,* Disraeli stands at some distance from his creations and produces two relatively impersonal works. His effectiveness for us is thereby lessened.[1]

My argument in this chapter will take issue with Levine's statement on a number of grounds: (i) *Venetia* and *Henrietta Temple* have important continuities with Disraeli's other work; (ii) the novels have thematic interest and aesthetic appeal apart from Disraeli's ideas; (iii) these middle novels do not suffer from the author having created more objective characters; and (iv) finally, although Disraeli does move, to recall Price's phrase, from immersion to reflection, these novels are hardly impersonal.

The family is the essential focus of Disraeli's middle period, particularly the way a child relates to his family history. The eighteenth-century novel's focus on the plight of orphans and disowned children may have provided Disraeli with a model. The early English novel is preoccupied with the relationship between fathers and sons, with the search of parents for real or putative children and vice versa, and with the plight of the homeless, rejected child. As political ideology and religious institutions failed to provide certainties, the English novel intensified its concern with nuances of family relationships, a concern which continues in Woolf, Lawrence and Joyce. One reason for the primacy of family relationships in the eighteenth- and nineteenth-century English novel may be the gradual diminishment of the English monarchy. Certainly nineteenth-century England's perception of the royal family as a kind of paradigmatic domestic institution gradually replaced the Renaissance concept that the king was God's representative on earth. Family values became an alternative to the primacy of church and Monarchy in the lives of individuals. As Walter Houghton has written in his chapter on 'Love' in *The Victorian Frame of Mind,* 'the sanctification of love and woman could rescue a worried Victorian from sliding into disbelief by reassuring him of a divine world, manifested here in the flesh, so to speak'.[2]

Throughout his career, Disraeli required private relations to balance his ambition. Once he attained office it was essential for him to go to Hughenden for rest and renewal. It may be that the emotional security of a womblike retreat to his wife and home was not only an alternative to political turmoil, but also compensation both for ambiguous national identity and for his apparently unsatisfactory relationship with his mother. As Blake notes, 'All his life he seems to be searching for a substitute for the mother who was somehow missing. His wife, his mistresses, his friends were almost always older women who could, or he hoped they could, supply that need'.[3] His quest for older, maternal women culminated in his marrying Mary Anne Lewis, a woman eleven years his senior.

In these novels, written during and subsequent to his affairs with older women, most notably Henrietta Sykes, Disraeli dramatises several variations of the relationship between parent and child. At this time, he was anxious to wrench himself free from financial dependence upon his father. Until he married in 1839, his father provided him with a centre of stability at crucial periods in his life, although neither his father nor his wife seems to have been a strong dominating figure. In the memoir which Disraeli prefaced to the 1848 edition of his father's *Curiosities of Literature,* he wrote: 'The philosophic sweetness of his disposition, the serenity of his lot, and the elevating nature of his pursuits, combined to enable him to pass through life without an evil act, almost without an evil thought'.[4] In *Venetia,* his narrator comments on the supremacy of parental love:

All other intimacies, however ardent, are liable to cool; all other confidences, however unlimited, to be violated. . . . Love is a dream, and friendship a delusion. No wonder we grow callous; for how few have the opportunity of returning to the hearth which they have quitted in levity or thoughtless weariness, yet which alone is faithful to them; whose sweet affections require not the stimulus of prosperity or fame, the lure of accomplishments, or the tribute of flattery; but which are constant to us in distress, and console us even in disgrace. (I, xvii, p. 90)

Even if the passage was written at a time of disappointment with his former friend Benjamin Austen for haunting him about an unpaid debt, and with Henrietta Sykes for betraying his love, the passage accurately reflects Disraeli's views.[5]

A brief look at the plots of these novels will illustrate Disraeli's focus on family responsibility and heterosexual relationships. The historical sweep of the opening chapters may represent an unsuccessful attempt to make Ferdinand Armine's social and economic history typical of the history of the Catholic nobility in England. But the real subject is the redemptive possibilities of heterosexual passion for a potentially talented, but immature and irresponsible young man. As *Henrietta Temple* opens, Ferdinand Armine is the only child of parents whose family fortune is in decline. He had been educated by the family priest Glastonbury who obtains a commission for him in Malta. As the favourite of his maternal grandfather, Ferdinand expects to be heir to a considerable estate and on the basis of his expectations lives extravagantly. But when his grandfather dies, the fortune is left to the granddaughter, Katherine Grandison. To redeem the family fortune, Ferdinand becomes engaged to Katherine, but after he returns home, he discovers the beautiful and gifted Henrietta Temple with whom he falls in love at first sight. Ferdinand asks her to keep their love a secret until he informs his parents, who are at Bath; Henrietta reluctantly agrees not to tell her father of their engagement until he returns. Of course, Ferdinand does not tell her that he is in fact engaged to two women. After three weeks, the Temples learn that Ferdinand has betrayed their trust and is engaged to Katherine.

Upon learning of Ferdinand's duplicity, Henrietta has a nervous collapse and goes to Italy to recover. There she meets and eventually becomes engaged to Lord Montfort, whose decorum and tact are in striking contrast to Ferdinand's passion. Ferdinand is befriended by Count Mirabel (a character based on Count D'Orsay, the famous dandy and a close friend of Disraeli) who helps Ferdinand woo and win Henrietta. Mirabel consoles Ferdinand when he suffers the ignominy of a sponging-house—and even raises the necessary funds to pay Ferdinand's debts, although by then Katherine has already learned of his plight and paid his release. When Montfort and Katherine discover their temperamental compatability, the obstacles to the marriage of Henrietta and Ferdinand dissolve. The novel concludes with both couples happily married.

Disraeli was in desperate financial straits when he wrote *Venetia,* in part because *Henrietta Temple,* although his most successful novel since *Vivian Grey,* did not produce anything like the revenue he required to pay his debts. He chose for his subjects England's most unconventional recent poetic geniuses, Shelley and Byron, because they gave him an opportunity to embody in fiction his pique that major artists, like himself, were unappreciated if not ostracised. Disraeli saw himself as heir to the tradition of genius which those figures represented to him. By creating fictional versions of Byron and Shelley, he was reaffirming his ties to the Romantic tradition. Because Shelley and Byron were both regarded as disreputable and immoral geniuses by the early Victorian establishment, his choice of subject was both a ploy to attract a voyeuristic audience and a statement about the kind of imaginative and personal life that intrigued him. His major figures, Lord Cadurcis and Marmion Herbert, are modelled respectively on Byron and Shelley. (In the novel Shelley is a generation older, although he was actually three years younger.) The novel fuses the melodrama of the Gothic plot with Disraeli's intensifying interest in the inner workings of the psyche.

Deserted by her husband and living in self-imposed seclusion in Cherbury, Lady Annabel Herbert (modelled on Byron's wife who was called Annabelle) devotes her life to her child, Venetia. Cadurcis and his mother come to live at the nearby Abbey. Because his mother is emotionally erratic if not mentally ill, Cadurcis becomes increasingly dependent on the affection of Lady Annabel and Venetia. When his mother abuses him without provocation, he runs away, and during his flight, his mother dies of heart failure. Subsequently Cadurcis leaves the Abbey to continue his education. Only the local vicar, Dr Masham, knows the secret of Venetia's paternity or the reasons for her mother's seclusion. One day Venetia discovers that a closed-off room contains her father's portrait and his poems which she reads. In true Gothic fashion, she becomes ill; while delirious, she reveals to her mother what she has seen.

After a long absence and years without correspondence, Cadurcis returns and after renewing his acquintance with Venetia, proclaims his love. But Venetia refuses, because she feels Cadurcis is not the equal to her father, whom she has apotheosised. After Venetia rejects him because of her devotion to her father and tells him that she would only 'unite [her] fate' with 'a great man; one with whose name the world rung; perhaps, like my father, a genius and a poet' (III, vii, p. 201), Cadurcis begins to emulate the career of her father as a social rebel and as a poet. He becomes a famous poet who is lionised by London society. He woos Venetia by praising her father in a poem, but Lady Annabel, fearing that her daughter will also be deserted by a poet who has become a public figure, now opposes the relationship. After Cadurcis fights a duel with the man with whose wife he has had an affair, he becomes a notorious character. No sooner does he write a volume which won him sympathy than 'he left his native shores in a blaze of glory, but with the accents of scorn still quivering on his lip' (IV, xix, 331). The scene shifts to Europe where not only Venetia and Cadurcis, but also Marmion and Lady Annabel are reunited. After a short period of bliss, Herbert and Cadurcis drown in a boating accident. Venetia returns to Cherbury, but eventually rejects the former celibate existence of her mother and marries Cadurcis's loyal if unexciting cousin, George.

In *Henrietta Temple* and *Venetia* Disraeli is not only more interested than he once was in the subtleties of private lives, and the way that the child is father to the man, but also in observing complex psychological problems. In contrast to his early novels, he is no longer preoccupied with projecting his own radically vacillating emotions into the psychological pattern of the protagonists. He understands how binding the maternal tie can be on a fatherless boy. In *Venetia,* Lord Cadurcis is profoundly affected by the death of his mother, no doubt in part because his departure, after she struck him, was the catalytic event that caused her death, but also because he instinctively understands that his mother's abusive behaviour was at odds with her intent. With a good deal of childish wisdom he understands that 'A mother is your friend as long as she lives; she cannot help being your friend' (I, xviii, p. 91). Yet such is his emotional need that he responds to Lady Annabel's surrogate mother role even while he regrets the loss of his own mother. Ferdinand Armine is torn between his family commitment and his personal emotional needs. The memory of his emotional separation from his mother when he joined the army has oedipal overtones. After he realises that he is passionately in love with Henrietta, he feels he has betrayed his mother by displacing her: 'Ah! he loves another woman better than his mother now. Nay, even a feeling of embarrassment and pain is associated with the recollection of that fond and elegant being, that he had recognised once as the model of all feminine perfection, and who had been to him so gentle and so devoted. He drives his mother from his thoughts' (III, i, p. 150). Ironically, his emotion is similar to Henrietta's guilt for loving someone other than her father. True, she feels bad that she cannot share her feelings with him, but her complex emotions seem to be a response to an incipient awareness that she plays more than a mere daughter's role in his life. Mr Temple wants to direct her choice, and when he does so he chooses a man who authenticates him, a man who is a younger version of himself, Lord Montfort, and who offers Henrietta the polish and elegance that she had found in her father. But Henrietta is drawn to Ferdinand's passion and spontaneity, qualities that her father lacks. She recollects her father in terms which recreate her astonishment and excitement, and which illustrate her unsuccessful effort to view her new emotions with detachment: 'She who had moved in the world so variously, who had received so much homage, and been accustomed from her childhood to all that is considered accomplished and fascinating in man, and had passed through the ordeal with a calm, clear spirit; behold, she is no longer the mistress of her thoughts and feelings; she had fallen before a glance, and yielded in an instant to a burning word!' (III, ii, p. 154). The last phrases underline the difference from her father's cool elegance. Venetia, like Ferdinand, must overcome a physical illness caused by emotional problems.

In these novels Disraeli becomes a defter psychologist which relates to his ability to maintain a clear distinction between himself and his characters. He is now concerned with the intricacies of behaviour in the world beyond himself. Such an instance is his striking portrait of the severely disturbed, although well-meaning mother of Cadurcis. Mrs Cadurcis is a character whose behaviour is controlled by atavistic passions and unacknowledged impulses that she cannot understand. When we realise that in 1836 Dickens had only just begun to publish *Pickwick Papers* and Emily Brontë was not to publish *Wuthering Heights* for a decade, we have some idea of the originality of Disraeli's achievements. Mrs Cadurcis cannot control her erratic behaviour; she provokes Cadurcis into the fatal rebellion that ultimately causes her death when she orders his fire to be put out so that he will be forced to be with her; she is jealous of Lady Annabel even while she knows intellectually that the latter does not in any way wish to interfere with her relation with her son. Unable to bring her contrary impulses into a coherent personality, Mrs Cadurcis's frustration finds an outlet in irrational jealousy of Lady Annabel's composure and judgment, and of the efficacious results such a temperament has on Lady Annabel's relationship with Venetia and her own son.

II

That Disraeli does try to constrain his propensity for writing disguised autobiography and for using his fiction as a means of creating an heroic mask affects every aspect of his art, including structure, narrative technique and tone. In his earlier novels, Disraeli's protagonists provided an outlet for his Promethean fantasies; the energy of those fantasies shaped the plot from within, sometimes almost as if the narrator and author were not in full control. If the plots of the earlier novels derived from the central characters' actions, emotions and moods (which were often thinly disguised versions of Disraeli's actions, emotions and moods), in these novels the plot tends at times to seem arbitrarily

imposed by the author and to be extraneous to the characters' actions. Events that are neither determined nor controlled by force of character play a more prominent role than in Disraeli's earlier fiction. The elaborately contrived plot of the middle novels would have been at odds with one central premise of the earlier ones: that a strong character and a dynamic personality are values in themselves. In *Henrietta Temple* and *Venetia,* the narrator (but less frequently the author) for the most part maintains his distance and control; perhaps Disraeli's choice of female title characters was in part an effort to separate his inner life from the text. But despite the titles, Venetia and Henrietta Temple are not independent women in their own right; Venetia depends upon her quest for a father and husband to define her, and Henrietta is a kind of allegorical reward that awaits Ferdinand if he can settle his personal affairs. She has little vitality or control over her destiny. Both novels have reductive conclusions which ignore the complex issues previously raised. When Mr Temple inherits a fortune, the putative and oft postponed marriage between Ferdinand and Henrietta can take place. *Venetia* dispenses with Cadurcis and Herbert by means of the boating accident; the novel's focus suddenly shifts to Venetia's and her mother's mourning, and soon comes to rest on Venetia's marriage to Cadurcis's cousin, George.

As we shall see in the next two chapters, learning how to use increased objectivity was essential to the political trilogy where Disraeli's focus shifts from an interest in a grammar of personal motives to a vision of historical, political and economic cause and effect. In *Henrietta Temple* and *Venetia,* the central characters do mime some *aspects* of Disraeli's life but they are not larger-than-life depictions of his personal activities, as in *Vivian Grey,* or of his fantasies and imaginative life, as in *Contarini Fleming.* Although these two novels have women as the title figures, the male characters are the ones who embody Disraeli's values, experiences and goals. Yet he does not use Ferdinand or Marmion Herbert or Cadurcis to shape his identity as he had used the protagonists in his earlier novels. In the middle thirties he had begun to achieve a little of the recognition and success that he craved (although he was a long way from fulfilling his insatiable ambition). On the threshhold of election to Parliament, he knew that he needed to modify his public image as a dandy and eccentric in order to woo his constituency and to succeed once he entered the House of Commons.

In these novels, more conventional artistic control and more consistent point of view are achieved at the sacrifice of the double focus upon the teller as well as the tale that was so prominent a feature of the early novels. The influence of Byron, particularly *Don Juan* with its undisciplined and extravagant speaker and impulsive and uninhibited energy, virtually disappears (although that influence had played a much lesser role in

Contarini Fleming and *Alroy* than in *Vivian Grey* and *The Young Duke*). In these middle novels Disraeli wanted his narrator to assume the stance of worldliness and urbanity that he now thought appropriate for tales of aristocratic manners and passions. Such a stance contrasts with the passionate excesses of Lord Cadurcis, Marmion Herbert and Ferdinand Armine, and of course implicitly comments on their extravagant behaviour until each of these characters is modified by experience to conform to the narrator's values. On occasion, Disraeli's former propensity to present himself in his novels as a dramatised personality and performer overwhelms the ironic detachment that he sought. In the 1853 edition of *Henrietta Temple* Disraeli slightly restrains this propensity by omitting a few passages in which the narrator dramatises himself. But the original edition of *Henrietta Temple* clearly shows more balance and maturity than his earlier novels.[6] Disraeli successfully creates a sympathetic but controlled speaker who plays a role akin to Fielding's narrator-host in *Tom Jones;* the speaker refers to Ferdinand, Henrietta and Mr Temple as they walk in the park of Armine as 'our party', and later when Ferdinand visits the Temples, he refers to them as 'our friends' (II, v, p. 88; II, vi, p. 101). Or, recalling for us the good-natured hospitality of Fielding's host, he entitles a chapter in which Ferdinand's and Henrietta's love continues to develop rapidly, 'Which I hope May Prove as Agreeable to the Reader as to Our Hero' (II, ix, p. 110). But at times the speaker abruptly shifts to a more subjective vein as when he concludes a glorious evening with a response that might have been voiced by either lover rather than the voice, 'Oh! why did this night ever have an end!' (II, x, p. 121).

Venetia shows even more consistent control of tone and voice. The following passage in *Venetia* begins as if the speaker were the performer who often intrudes into the original versions of *The Young Duke* and *Vivian Grey,* but soon the voice becomes a conventional omniscient narrator who sympathises with Lord Cadurcis, both as a unique individual and as an abstract victim:

> It has been well observed, that no spectacle is so ridiculous as the British public in one of its periodical fits of morality. . . . We must teach libertines that the English people appreciate the importance of domestic ties. Accordingly, some unfortunate man, in no respect more depraved than hundreds whose offenses have been treated with lenity, is singled out as an expiatory sacrifice. . . . He is, in truth, a sort of whipping boy, by whose vicarious agonies all the other transgressors of the same class are, it is supposed, sufficiently chastised. (IV, xvii, p. 320)

As surely as an eighteenth-century satirist, Disraeli uses his narrator to uphold the standards of civilisation. His logical, restrained and balanced prose comments on the folly of singling out a chosen victim and implicitly compares such a practice to primitive sacrificial rites.

In the mid-1830s Disraeli moved from rewriting Byron in prose to more traditional concepts of prose fiction. Disraeli was influenced by the eighteenth-century novel with its uneasy balance between romance and realism, between comedy and tragedy, between seriousness and burlesque, between satire and sentimentalism. What Leslie Stephen has called Disraeli's 'ambiguous hovering between two meanings. . . . the ironical and the serious' derives from this mixed mode of romance and realism, but in these middle novels, unlike the earlier ones, Disraeli is usually in deft control of his genre mix and his tone.[7] Recent criticism of the Victorian novel has accustomed us to different *kinds* of mimesis within the same novels. Disraeli's technique depends upon his perceptions that in life and in fiction, fantasy and realism not only exist side by side, but are sometimes incongruously superimposed upon one another like a double-exposure negative.

Disraeli deliberately evokes Richardson's tragedy *Clarissa* to raise the possibility that Ferdinand is capable of duplicity and immoral conduct. Henrietta is betrayed by a man who, as soon as he declares his love for her, appears to be something of a rake. For when Henrietta discovers that Ferdinand is betrothed to another, the subsequent shock to both her and her father culminates in his denunciation of Ferdinand as 'unworthy' of his daughter. The epistolary section, in which Henrietta becomes more desperate for his return and, finally, even for promises of his affection, inevitably suggests the form and content of Richardson's novel. The reader shares Henrietta's fears of betrayal and desertion, when, following his reply to her first letter, she apparently writes seventeen letters without receiving a response. (In his role of editor, Disraeli omits letters thirteen to seventeen in IV, ii.) Her cry at the close of the final letter teases the reader into expecting the worst: 'All my happy life I have never had a secret from my father; and now I am involved in a private engagement and a clandestine correspondence' (IV, ii, p. 212). While Henrietta is not really threatened with rape, Disraeli has cleverly raised the rhetorical stakes to the point where, by the end of the series of letters, the reader is prepared to consider the merest peccadillo on the part of Ferdinand as the ultimate outrage. Part of the reason is that Ferdinand had seemed so sensitive and delicate, if not oversentimental, when he engaged in frequent weeping before they parted. Both Ferdinand's and Henrietta's exaggerated emotions and rapid oscillations from one emotion to another seem to owe something to the Gothic tradition as well as the sentimentalism of Richardson, Sterne, Smollett, and especially Mackenzie. Indeed, what seems to redeem Ferdinand for Disraeli is that, whatever else, he is always a man of feeling. However, in the 1853 edition, Disraeli somewhat subdued a few of Henrietta's gushier moments. If in *Henrietta Temple* he wishes at times to create the tragic density of *Clarissa,* in *Venetia* he uses the model of the eighteenth-century comic novel to lighten the novel's texture by inter-weaving humorous characters and farcical scenes into his melodramatic plot. Mrs Pauncefort (a play on Pounce-for-it, an apt name for her verbally aggressive and opportunistic personality) would not be out of place in a Fielding novel, and the incompetent magistrate Squire Mountmeadow clearly derives from the good-natured but biting social satire of Smollett. The idyll of Book VI, after the lovers are reunited, belongs to the pastoral vision of a Golden Age.

Venetia also owes some of its more intense moments to earlier forms of fiction. The sentimental scenes in which lovers dissolve in tears owe much to eighteenth-century sentimentalism. Lady Annabel's hermetic retreat, and the Herbert family secret enclosed in a locked room, derive from the mysterious, bizarre world of Gothic novels. But the illness of Henrietta and the complex portraits of the private emotions and the inner lives of Venetia, her mother and Cadurcis, belong to the world of nineteenth-century realism. At times the mixture of realism and romance works brilliantly. For example, when Cadurcis's mother's eccentricity and instability are revealed as madness within the fairy-tale world that Lady Annabel has created, the reader feels the ironic tension that implies both the impossibility and desirability of romance. Or, Plantagenet Cadurcis retreats to the world of comic romance—complete with gypsies and the stereotype cartoon figure, Squire Mountmeadow—which points up the claustrophobic and repressed nature of the world in which Plantagenet has been raised.

The two crucial biographical sources for *Henrietta Temple* are Disraeli's debts and his relationship with Henrietta Sykes. While Ferdinand Armine embodies crucial aspects of Disraeli's experience, he is not simply another of Disraeli's masks. Like Ferdinand, Disraeli was hounded by debts. In fact, Disraeli was deeply in debt throughout his life. As late as 1857, he was faced with one member of the Bentinck family calling in a large loan that he had never expected to have to repay. Jerman's study makes clear how these debts came to dominate his life and how at times 'visions of sponging houses haunted Disraeli.'[8] Disraeli knew how financial difficulty could weave itself into the very texture of a person's psyche and dominate his every thought. Despite his impetuous nature, Ferdinand has a very strong sense of family, and wants to redeem the family's financial situation and relieve his parents' anxiety. Yet, on the other hand, he is a man of passion like his grandfather and cannot, in contrast to Montfort, let his libido *follow* his self-interest. Disraeli might have perceived his own love for Henrietta Sykes in the terms Glastonbury uses to describe Ferdinand's love: 'Ferdinand is the most impetuous of human beings. His passions are a whirlwind; his volition more violent than becomes a suffering mortal' (V, ix, p. 346).

Disraeli wrote all but Books I and II of *Henrietta* after his final break with Henrietta. Interestingly, in September of 1833, the year he published *Alroy* and *Iskander,* and after he had begun *Henrietta Temple* in the full flush of his passion, he remarked on the effects of love—and he undoubtedly had Henrietta in mind—on his 'awful ambition and fiery passions'.[9] It may be that the reliance upon friends and family to complete Ferdinand's happiness reflects Disraeli's awareness that passionate love can be no more than part of one's existence. In the books of *Henrietta Temple* written in 1836, Disraeli is quite ambivalent about the 'all for love' implications of the relationship between Henrietta and Ferdinand which causes them to abandon their personal and family responsibilities. When Ferdinand turns from his commitment to Katherine, the novel displays him in an attractive light. *Henrietta Temple* celebrates both passionate love and rational merger between two complementary temperaments. If Henrietta's ardour for Ferdinand begins by celebrating the 'all for love' philosophy that dominated Disraeli's dalliance with Henrietta Sykes, the final marriage between Katherine and Montfort anticipates his practical and economically intelligent marriage to Mary Anne Lewis, an older widow who adored him and always placed his interest first.[10] Even the complications that Ferdinand must overcome before marriage to Henrietta reflect Disraeli's maturing vision of sexual love and his understanding that passion is not enough for a lasting adult relationship.

Ferdinand's erratic oscillation between guilt and self-righteousness may indicate Disraeli's state of mind towards his own adulterous relationship. In the following soliloquy, Disraeli's ironic stance seems to dissolve and be replaced by complete empathy, even though Ferdinand is manifestly unjust to Henrietta:

> When he recollected how he had loved this woman, what he had sacrificed for her, and what misery he had in consequence entailed upon himself and all those dear to him; when he contrasted his present perilous situation with her triumphant prosperity, and remembered that while he had devoted himself to love which proved false, she who had deserted him was, by a caprice of fortune, absolutely rewarded for her fickleness; he was enraged, he was disgusted, he despised himself for having been her slave; he began even to hate her. Terrible moment when we first dare to view with feelings of repugnance the being that our soul has long idolised! It is the most awful of revelations. We start back in horror, as if in the act of profanation. (V, x, p. 349)

In the above passage, Disraeli's rendering of the way that Ferdinand's intensifying resentment gives way to self-pity and self-consuming wrath, shows how his sentences can reveal the human psyche. The shift to the first person gains its validity from our having participated in the thoughts of Ferdinand. Disraeli's use of the first-person plural to generalise Ferdinand's response is especially revealing if we recall the finality of an entry in his diary: 'Autumn 1836—Parted forever from Henrietta'.[11] While his empathy with Ferdinand's passionate resentment occasionally disrupts his efforts to maintain distance, the novel is the livelier for it. As has been pointed out, Armine is a version of Amin, Henrietta Syke's pet name for Disraeli.[12]

Ferdinand's resilience echoes that of Disraeli, who was increasingly able to put behind him melancholy, disappointment and humiliation. Dramatising Ferdinand's regaining of his reputation may have been a psychological necessity for Disraeli whose reputation for, as Blake puts it, 'cynicism, double-dealing, recklessness and insincerity' haunted him throughout the thirties.[13] More than Disraeli's prior protagonists, Ferdinand has the ability to dispel gloom and despair no matter how severe the circumstances. No sooner had he despaired of his engagement and the family debts, than his imagination retrieves him from gloom:

> Could sorrow ever enter [Ducie, the Temple home]? Was it possible that these bright halls and odorous bowers could be polluted by the miserable considerations that reigned too often supreme in his unhappy breast? An enchanted scene had suddenly risen from the earth for his delight and fascination. . . . All the troubles of the world were folly here; this was fairy-land, and he some knight who had fallen from a gloomy globe upon some starry region flashing with perennial lustre. (II, x, p. 119)

But Disraeli reveals the essence of Ferdinand's perpetual adolescence and shows how Ferdinand displaces actual circumstances with fantasies of a blissful future. For Ferdinand, as for Contarini, dreams are just as real as waking life. In a memorable dream, occuring immediately after he has met Henrietta, Katherine displaces Henrietta as he is about to pluck a flower, and the flowers are replaced by an altar from which fire shoots. Undoubtedly, such a dream reflects Ferdinand's conscience which recoils at his disloyalty towards, and putative betrayal of, Katherine. Ferdinand can temporarily exclude reality and live in the world of his own imagination, as when he becomes engaged to Henrietta. Yet in assertive, balanced, self-contained, independent clauses, Disraeli ironically mimes Ferdinand's egoism and mocks his self-inflated solipsism:

> He loved Henrietta Temple. She should be his. Who could prevent him: Was he not an Armine? Was he not the near descendant of that bold man who passed his whole life in the voluptuous indulgence of unrestrained volition! . . . He was born to follow his own pleasure; it was supreme; it was absolute; he was a despot; he set everything and everybody at defiance; and, filling a huge tumbler to the health of the great Sir Ferdinand, he retired, glorious as an emperor. (II, xiii, p. 131)

Lord Montfort and Ferdinand represent two facets of Disraeli in the mid-1830s. Disraeli knew that before he could play a political role, the impetuous, extravagant part of his character would have to be constrained, if only for appearances. Ferdinand is at times like the passionate and impulsive young man who created the early novels and involved himself in risky publishing and financial ventures. Lord Montfort is the shrewd, controlled, rational man that Disraeli knew he had to become to fulfil his ambition:

> Lord Montfort was a man of deep emotions, and of a very fastidious taste. He was a man of as romantic a temperament as Ferdinand Armine; but with Lord Montfort, life was the romance of reason; with Ferdinand, the romance of imagination. He observed finely, he calculated nicely, and his result was generally happiness. Ferdinand, on the contrary, neither observed nor calculated. His imagination created fantasies, and his impetuous passions struggled to realize them. (V, vi, p. 297)

The novel's ending is a significant indication of the direction of Disraeli's fiction. The marriages are not only important for the private lives of the four major figures, but, at least in Ferdinand's case, they prepare him for a public life in the House of Commons. Private bliss is interrelated with the fulfilment of public responsibilities; Ferdinand's character has been honed for larger responsibilities. The reformation of Ferdinand's character may be Disraeli's way of assuring his audience—and, possibly, himself— that he has overcome a profligate past and can be depended upon. That the outsiders, the Catholics, are now permitted to play a prominent role in the realm may for Disraeli be a means of illustrating to his audience the folly of excluding anyone for racial and religious reasons. It is clear that the calm, judicious Lord Montfort and the polished, tactful Mr Temple (who, however, is capable of selfish and even boorish conduct when his domination of his daughter is challenged) could not be more able men; yet they had been excluded from Parliament merely because they were Catholics.

Although written under the pressure of financial crises for the purpose of alleviating Disraeli's debts, ***Henrietta Temple*** shows a new sophistication in his management of point of view. Blake may overstate the change that ensues after the first two books written in 1833, when he remarks, 'From a story of passionate romance, the novel has become an urbane comedy of manners'.[14] But the novel is the better for its sophisticated awareness of the complexities of heterosexual relationships. Disraeli perceives that both Henrietta and Ferdinand are hampered in their psychosexual development by strong parental ties. Ferdinand feels guilty about his debts, but he is also resentful that his family [has] dissipated their estate. On one hand, he feels he deserves to marry whomever he pleases, but, on the other, he is not oblivious to his responsibilities to his family and Katherine. In this novel, Disraeli is more objective and presents a more balanced perspective that takes ·account of the complexities of human character. To be sure, Books One and Two of *Henrietta Temple* certainly present a simplified view of the characters; but Monypenny's complaint that in the later books the images of Ferdinand and Henrietta are both in some degree defaced ignores one of Disraeli's merits, namely, his determination to show that characters are fundamentally changed by the people they meet, the environment in which they live, and the experiences to which they are exposed.[15] It is an indication of Disraeli's maturation as an artist that he enables the reader to take a complex view of his characters. *Henrietta Temple* is satisfying in part because we cannot be comfortable with a pat judgment of either major character. Disraeli realises that circumstances define an action and what looks like heinous conduct from one perspective may be excused by subsequent revelation of extenuating circumstances. Far more than in the early novels, his presentation of characters is dynamic and evolving so that the reader is not permitted to have a set image of a complex character.

The subtlety of *Henrietta Temple* derives from Disraeli's evolving tone towards his imaginative hero. He shows how difficult it is for his hero to grow beyond emotional self-indulgence and to look at himself objectively. By moving at crucial points back and forth between the perspective of the protagonist and that of the heroine, he illustrates the validity of both characters' views of the broken engagement. In Book IV, chapter viii, he brilliantly restores our confidence in Ferdinand after several chapters in which he has been depicted unfavourably—because the narrator was rendering Henrietta's gradual discovery that she has been duped. In a sense, Disraeli has tested not only the heroine but the reader. Because Glastonbury notices that Ferdinand is ill, the reader suspends his moral judgment. Ferdinand's illness wins our sympathy as we realise that even if he is imprudent, he is not insincere. Even before that, his affirmation of his love for Henrietta and his confession of his debts make him a far more sympathetic character than would have seemed possible at the time Henrietta learned of the behaviour of Captain Armine at Bath and of his forthcoming marriage to Katherine.

III

Excepting the political trilogy, students of English literature tend to think of Disraeli's work, when they think of it at all, as that of an extravagant performer, a kind of Emperor of Ice Cream. But in truth he deserves to stand in the company of Dickens as a psychologist of children, adolescents and young adults, particularly members of these groups who are caught in emotionally claustrophobic circumstances. Since the search for a missing father is always lurking in the shadows of Disraeli's early novels, and becomes even more dominant in *Henrietta Temple,* it is hardly surprising that in *Venetia* the search for the missing parent should become the central element of the dramatic plot. The focus on fathers and children (surrogate and real) may derive from Disraeli's desire to acknowledge his father's significance to him. It may not be too much to see both Cadurcis's intellectual recognition of Marmion's worth and Venetia's emotional reconciliation with her father as indications of Disraeli's own increasing appreciation of his father. Venetia's search for her father shapes her entire life; had she not lacked a father, she would not have made the following bizarre statement to Cadurcis: 'I cannot love you as a husband should be loved. I· can never love you as I love my father' (III, vii, p. 200). Despite the incestuous overtones of this statement, she is in love with an idealised and spiritualised image that she has invented. Disraeli understands how the lack of one parent and the dominance of the other can seriously distort the personality. Lady Annabel's proud self-control and desire to dominate her daughter Venetia derive from the disruption of her marriage. She has two unconscious and quite contradictory goals: to regain her husband and to revenge herself on him by destroying every trace of his paternity within their daughter.

Disraeli is never a more acute psychologist than when he writes about the loss of one or both parents. (It may be that Dickens knew *Venetia* and the title character's obsessive search for her father when he wrote of Esther Summerson's quest for her mother.) Venetia's recurrent illness is a response to being deprived of her father. She suffers physically and psychologically from not having known her father. Yet her mother's severely formal manner causes her to repress her curiosity about her father, and that repression is related to her recurring illness. Lady Annabel's attitude makes her feel that her need for a father is a betrayal of her mother. Disraeli's rendering of Venetia's inner confusion is deft. Because he does not use the psychological jargon to which we are accustomed, we may underestimate the subtlety with which he renders Venetia's self-indictment for the emotional disharmony that she feels beneath the surface of the home she shares with her mother: '[Venetia] sat mute and motionless . . . as if she were conscious of having committed some act of shame, as if she had been detected in some base and degrading deed' (II, ii, p. 110). Those who fault Disraeli for stylistic extravagance are not familiar with passages such as the one above where precise, lean phrasing conveys Venetia's inarticulate sense of moral disgrace. Disraeli's delicate artistry reveals how Venetia awakens to mystery and guilt. In a careful linear progression, the following sentence rises to a controlled climax that mimes her movement from emotional equilibrium to a conviction of her unworthiness: 'as she grew older, [she] could not refrain at times from yielding to the irresistible belief that her existence was enveloped in some mystery. Mystery too often presupposes guilt. Guilt! Who was guilty?' (II, i, p. 107). Like Esther, misery envelopes her very existence, but, unlike Dickens's heroine, she does not find an emotional outlet in compensating ties or in the routine of work and responsibility. Her uncertainty and dubiety are all the more excruciating because of the perpetual presence of her proud, self-controlled, and unyielding mother.

Isolated from normal social development, Venetia tends to worship her mother. The narrator's gentle but shrewd irony depicts Venetia's idolatry of her mother, who represents to her not only a paradigm, but an apotheosis of Goodness:

> Yet while Venetia loved her mother, she could not but also respect and revere the superior being whose knowledge was her guide on all subjects, and whose various accomplishments deprived her secluded education of all its disadvantages; and when she felt that one so gifted had devoted her life to the benefit of her child, and that this beautiful and peerless lady had no other ambition but to be her guardian and attendant spirit; gratitude, fervent and profound, mingled with admiring reverence and passionate affection, and together formed a spell that encircled the mind of Venetia with talismanic sway. (II, iii, pp. 116-17)

The prose depicts the way that her mother has temporarily succeeded in creating an emotional island from which shame and guilt are banished. The problem is that as Venetia matures, she wants to be an archipelago and reach out to the world. And despite her apparent self-sufficiency, her mother also regrets her isolation. When Lady Annabel is restored to Marmion, she seems completely dominated by his intellect and personality. Like her mother, Venetia turns to God as an alternative to her emotional frustration. Later, after Dr Masham warns her that she would jeopardise her mother's health, if not her life, were she to mention her father to her, Venetia becomes obsessed with reuniting her parents because that would absolve her of the nameless guilt she feels. Her recurring illness appears whenever she feels a sense of unworthiness and incompleteness. As a fiction, her father not only plays the same role as God the Father plays for her mother, but becomes for her interchangeable with Him.

Venetia longs for the kind of marriage that eludes her mother and, perhaps unconsciously, a triumph over the mother who has deprived her of a father. Surely, Venetia's stipulation that her husband *must* be a great man—a mirror of Disraeli's compulsion that he be a great man—derives from her father's being absent and being replaced by a mythical figure that seems to her to have a larger than life stature. Venetia feels that if she were to marry a great poet, she would offer sufficient attraction to keep him. One reason for Lady Annabel's fervent objections to Cadurcis is her unconscious fear (perhaps not unmixed with unconscious envy) lest her daughter be correct. Yet her conscious motives are her daughter's interest and her fear that her daughter's future will replicate her past.

Lady Annabel has an obsession that Cadurcis will desert her daughter as Herbert has deserted her. Subscribing to conventions and accepted social standards, she stands for a tradition of aristocratic manners and mores that is the polar opposite of Cadurcis and Herbert. As one whose life has been based on self-restraint and self-sacrifice, she regards Cadurcis's behaviour as a personal defiance of her standards which she as a surrogate mother taught him: 'And what is he now? The most lawless of the wild; casting to the winds every salutary principle of restraint and social discipline, and glorying only in the abandoned energy of self' (IV, xiv, p. 297). She is certain that were Venetia to marry Cadurcis, he would treat her daughter in the same way that Marmion did herself. Because she has failed to control Herbert or Cadurcis, whom she once regarded as a surrogate son, she is all the more determined to control her daughter's conduct. Lady Annabel makes the case against the man of imagination when she equates imagination with emotional self-indulgence. Speaking of Cadurcis, but with Herbert in mind, she says: 'Spirits like him are heartless. It is another impulse that sways their existence. It is imagination; it is vanity; it is self, disguised with glittering qualities that dazzle our weak senses, but selfishness, the most entire, the most concentrated' (IV, xiv, p. 296).

But Book VI undermines her effort to equate imagination with heartlessness. Imagination rescues the family from unhappiness. Indeed, had Herbert not been imaginative in pursuing his wife and daughter, had he not at the risk of his life zealously pursued them to Italy, and engaged the holy man to present his letter, Herbert and Lady Annabel, and the younger couple, Cadurcis and Venetia, would not have had their period of bliss. Herbert has been sufficiently modified by his experience to fulfil the role of ideal father and son. He has made the transformation, to use the terms proposed in *Henrietta Temple,* from a romantic of the imagination, to a romantic of reason. Cadurcis now seems no less suitable than Herbert for family life. Disraeli may have been proving to himself as well as to others that one who had a reputation as a dandy and an eccentric, one who had been involved in an adulterous relationship as he had with Henrietta Sykes, need not be disqualified from fulfilling the roles of father and parent.

In the guise of his fictional counterparts, Herbert and Cadurcis, Disraeli presents both Shelley and Byron as sympathetic figures and extenuates their unconventional conduct. Of course, by giving them other names, Disraeli could have it both ways; Herbert and Cadurcis do not parallel Shelley and Byron, except in the broad outlines of their careers.[16] While it adds a dimension to the novel, it is doubtful whether a modern reader requires the identification to find the novel interesting. While Herbert is nominally Shelley after he finally emerges late in the novel, his energies are rather reduced. He becomes both the typical Disraeli wisdom figure and the surrogate father who fulfils the emotional needs of Cadurcis. Cadurcis may be based on Byron, but he is also a recognisable successor to the tempestuous, impulsive, passionate hero of the prior novels, the man whose energies are never fully controlled and threaten to undermine their possessor; I am thinking of Contarini, Alroy, Vivian Grey, and even Ferdinand. Shelley and Byron provide Disraeli with models of the rebellious over-reacher to whom he was attracted, without exposing him to possible criticism for creating dissatisfied social misfits. They do so at a time when he was gaining increasing political recognition and when he knew that he was close finally to gaining the seat in Parliament that he had so frequently sought.[17] These poets dramatise the direction that he was turning his back upon. Herbert and Cadurcis are the literary and imaginative *ubermenschen* of his imagination. Their lives are ways that Disraeli tests the premise articulated by Annabel's sister-in-law: "Everything is allowed, you know, to a genius!' (IV, vii, p. 248).

Disraeli's heroes are often forced by circumstances to retirement and travel. Retreat and exile were anathemas to Disraeli the political figure, but they represented an attractive alternative to the private man haunted by debts. While providing a necessary outlet for Disraeli from frustrated ambition, the travelogue which occurs in virtually every one of Disraeli's first six novels is at times barely related to the action. (Even the young Duke travels about England, stopping at various castles.) Undoubtedly one reason that Disraeli took his protagonist on tour was to extend the length of the novels to three, full, separately issued volumes. But dramatising memories of his past travels, travels undertaken to relieve disappointment and ill health, was restorative for himself as well as the characters he created. The pastoral scenes in the Apennines are typical of Disraeli's use of place to create a state of mind.

Both the younger Herbert and Lord Cadurcis, prior to meeting Herbert, represent the self that Disraeli, rather reluctantly but quite consciously, is in the process of putting behind him, while the mature Herbert represents the idealised philosophic, mature man that Disraeli is trying to become. After the most tumultuous, unconventional life, Herbert discovers that human happiness resides in family ties. The dialogue between Disraeli's two surrogates, Cadurcis

and Herbert, is really a dialogue between two aspects of himself. Cadurcis's iconoclastic view, that 'men have always been fools and slaves, and fools and slaves they always will be' (VI, iv, [p.] 415), parallels one strand of Disraeli's own thinking. Yet, like his character, Disraeli had experienced the erratic fluctuation of public opinion and knew what it was to be in public disfavour (for example, when *Vivian Grey* was ridiculed and lampooned). Herbert, the man who carried individualism to an extreme, renounces his Byronic quest and speaks for Disraeli's commitment to community values: 'Love . . . is an universal thirst for a communion, not merely of the senses, but of our whole nature, intellectual, imaginative and sensitive. He who finds his antitype, enjoys a love perfect and enduring; time cannot change it, distance cannot remove it; the sympathy is complete' (VI, vi, p. 429).

Disraeli wrote of the modification and maturation of two men of genius when he wished to convince both an electorate that kept rejecting him, and those party leaders who selected candidates for Parliament, of his suitability for office. He wanted his readers to identify him with prophetic figures such as Shelley and Byron but also he wanted to show them that these figures could mature and embrace socially acceptable philosophic views. The novel gradually establishes the authority of Herbert and discards Cadurcis's cynicism. Herbert is the philosopher of a kind of optimistic upward evolution with which his fellow Tories could feel comfortable. That both Cadurcis and his cousin George fulfil their public responsibilities in Parliament, while Herbert has helped lead a revolution, shows that Disraeli retains an interest in the public world even when writing about family relationships.

Herbert's theoretical optimism reflects the utopian and prophetic strand in Disraeli's thinking which places him as well as his character within the Visionary Company of which we spoke in the last chapter. While Disraeli rejected utilitarianism and the mid-nineteenth-century faith in progress and the perfectibility of man, he believed the most profound questions might be answered by the mind of man. Herbert's utopian ideal that 'the principle of life' may be discovered and that man may attain earthly immortality anticipates the search for spiritual truth in *Tancred:* 'The annihilation of death . . . will . . . be produced by some vast and silent and continuous operation of nature, gradually effecting some profound and comprehensive alteration in her order' (VI, iv, pp. 416-17).

The ambitiousness of Herbert's vision, if not its profundity, testifies to the kind of cosmic and prophetic view to which Disraeli aspired in the 1830s. If the younger and unseen Herbert is Shelley, the rebel and iconoclast, the mature Herbert gives us an insight into the visionary and imaginative pretensions of Disraeli's mind at this time. Like the descent of the angel in *Tancred,* the actual details are unimportant as predictions, but illustrative of the kind of fantasy that Disraeli could articulate and temporarily believe. Yet, as Blake writes, Disraeli was 'one of those actors who enter so deeply into their role that for the time being they suspend disbelief and really live the part which they enact.'[18]

Disraeli's father had inquired after learning that he was writing **Henrietta Temple:** 'How . . . will the fictionist assort with the politician? Most deeply am I regretting that you will find it necessary to return to drink of the old waters'.[19] *Venetia* is in part a response to that inquiry. It is extremely significant that Disraeli has the mature Marmion Herbert quote Shelley's famous statement that 'poets are the unacknowledged legislators of the world' (VI, viii, p. 438). Self-conscious about his failure to make any mark as a poet, after the first three books of **The Revolutionary Epick** (1834) had been unenthusiastically received, Disraeli wished to establish the legitimacy of his novels. His original preface to **Alroy** in 1832, which boasted of an innovative merging of prose and poetry based on the use of rhyme and rhythm in his romance, reflected his desire that he be taken seriously as an artist, even though he was writing in prose.[20] Disraeli evokes Shelley's words to convince both his father and himself of the importance of his creative endeavours. When Herbert says of Cervantes's work, '[Cervantes] is the same to this age as if he had absolutely wandered over the plains of Castile and watched in the Sierra Morena', he is applying Shelley's words that only a poem is 'universal, and contains within itself the germ of a relation to whatever motives or actions have place in the possible varieties of human nature' (IV, i, p. 394).[21] Through his character, Disraeli is claiming the same position for prose as Shelley did for poetry.[22] When Herbert quotes Shelley, Disraeli the novelist includes himself in the vast claims for imaginative literature implied by the invocation of Shelley's spirit. Nor is it accidental that Herbert is moved, not by a poet's, but by a novelist's vision of the golden age. It is Disraeli's position that the *imaginative writer,* not merely the poet, combines the roles of legislator and prophet.[23]

Notes

Page references throughout the text refer to the readily accessible Hughenden Edition (London: Longmans & Green & Co., 1882). Book (or Part) and chapter number, indicated respectively by upper and lower case Roman numerals are standard for every edition. My source for the original edition of *Vivian Grey* and *The Young Duke* is the less accessible but authoritative Centenary Edition, ed. Lucian Wolf (London: Alexander Moring, Ltd., 1904-5). Unfortunately only two volumes ever appeared in this edition. . . .

[1] Richard A. Levine, *Benjamin Disraeli* (New York: Twayne, 1968), p. 58.

[2] Walter E. Houghton, *The Victorian Frame of Mind* (New Haven: Yale University Press, 1957), p. 392.

[3] [Robert Blake, *Disraeli* (London: Eyre & Spottiswoode, 1966),] p. 16; see also p. 154.

[4] Quoted in James Ogden, *Isaac D'Israeli* (Oxford: The Clarendon Press, 1969), p. 190.

[5] See [B.R. Jerman, *The Young Disraeli* (Princeton: Princeton University Press), 1960,] for an account of Disraeli's relationship with the Austens and Henrietta Sykes, especially Chapters 6 to 8.

[6] While the original edition has a slightly more exuberant voice and an occasionally more effusive and silly Henrietta, Blake's implication that it has been bowdlerised in a manner similar to *Vivian Grey* and *The Young Duke* is somewhat misleading. See Blake, p. 37n.

[7] Leslie Stephen, *Hours in a Library,* Vol. II (London: Smith, Eldes & Co., 1892), p. 108.

[8] Jerman, p. 286; see Blake, p. 422.

[9] 'The Mutilated Diary', Hughenden Papers, A/III/C. See Jerman, p. 190, for the entire passage.

[10] See Blake, pp. 150-65.

[11] 'The Mutilated Diary', Hughenden Papers, A/III/C. See Blake, pp. 136-40.

[12] Jerman, p. 277; but I disagree with Jerman's contention that 'Ferdinand Armine in nowise resembles Benjamin Disraeli'.

[13] Blake, p. 48.

[14] Blake, p. 144.

[15] [William F. Monypenny and George E. Buckle, *The Life of Benjamin Disraeli, Earl of Beaconsfield,* 6 vols. (London: John Murray, 1910-20),] I, p. 342.

[16] The novel was originally entitled *Venetia or the Poet's Daughter;* for more on the Byron and Shelley parallel, see Monypenny and Buckle, I, pp. 360-4.

[17] After several tries, he was elected in 1837.

[18] Blake, p. 288.

[19] Quoted in Monypenny and Buckle, I, p. 338.

[20] With characteristic immodesty, he speaks of the 'artists's' difficulty in using such a style: '[This] style . . . is a delicate and difficult instrument for an artist to handle. . . . He must alike beware the turgid and the bombastic, the meagre and the mean. He must be easy in his robes of state, and a degree of elegance and dignity must accompany him even in the camp and the market house. The language must rise gradually with the rising passions of the speakers and subside in harmonious unison with their sinking emotions'. Quoted in Monypenny and Buckle, I, p. 198. This preface was omitted in later editions.

[21] *Shelley,* ed. A. S. B. Glover (London: The Nonesuch Press, 1951), p. 1030.

[22] Nevertheless, Disraeli probably appreciated the review of *Henrietta Temple* in the *New Monthly Magazine* which observed: 'In any other age than the present, or even now, had he lived less in society, Mr. Disraeli would have been a poet. He has essentially the poetic temperament—the intense self-consciousness, the impetuosity, and the eye for the beautiful'. Quoted in R. W. Stewart, *Disraeli's Novels Reviewed, 1836*-1968 (Metuchen, N.J.: The Scarecrow Press, 1975), p. 155.

[23] He would certainly have insisted on the inclusion of novelists in the following statement that Shelley made of poets in *A Defence of Poetry:* 'For he not only beholds intensely the present as it is, and discovers those laws according to which present things ought to be ordered, but he beholds the future in the present, and his thoughts are the germs of the flower and the fruit of latest time'. *Shelley,* pp. 1026-7.

Robert O'Kell (essay date 1987)

SOURCE: "Two Nations, or One?: Disraeli's Allegorical Romance," *Victorian Studies,* Vol. 30, No. 2, Winter, 1987, pp. 211-34.

[*In this essay, O'Kell examines* Sybil *in terms of its political, religious, and allegorical content, distinguishing it from the psychological romances typical of Disraeli's early work.*]

The popularity of *Coningsby: Or The New Generation* when it first appeared in May 1844 was undoubtedly part of what prompted Disraeli to begin immediately writing another "political" novel. But part of his motive must also have been his realization that the enormous success of *Coningsby* derived less from any appreciation of his reflexive attempt to define the proper contemporary role of heroic sensibility than from the widespread conviction that he had produced a "manifesto of Young England" and, not so incidentally, another sensational roman à clef.[1] Disraeli knew, however, that in *Coningsby* his "romance" had run away with his theme before he had fully developed the social implications of his political views.[2] And while it was true that in part the work could still be seen as a satirical treatise on the short-comings of Sir Robert Peel's conservatism, Disraeli's intention in writing *Coningsby* had been much broader and deeper than such notoriety acknowledged. The writing of another novel thus became a pressing matter: *Sybil: or the Two Nations* was completed and published within a year (May 1845), despite the author's hectic political and social life.

Perhaps because of its prominence in the subgenre known as the social-problem novel, *Sybil* has attracted more serious critical comment than the rest of Disraeli's fiction. But this commentary has often reflected equally serious misreadings, for *Sybil* has generally been assumed to be Disraeli's most typical novel when there are important respects in which it is his least typical work.[3] And only when these differences between *Sybil* and the other novels are perceived can the force of Disraeli's social vision in the 1840s be fully understood.

What is missing from *Sybil* and present in almost every other of Disraeli's novels except his last, *Endymion* (1880), is the central, imaginatively autobiographical fantasy about the ambivalent nature of his protagonist. For the moment, though, in 1844 that recurring fantasy embodying a conflict between altruism and expediency had reached a most satisfactory fictional resolution in *Coningsby* with the romance of Harry Coningsby and Edith Millbank. And in Disraeli's private life it had also temporarily lost some of its urgency. As the leader of the Young England coterie, as the confidant of the King of France, as a successful orator in the House of Commons, and as a popular novelist, Disraeli had in his own eyes gained a considerable measure of acceptance and recognition among England's social and political elite.

Sybil also differs from most of the other novels in that so much of it is derived from a variety of printed materials.[4] His debts to the Children's Employment Commission's Blue Books (1842-43), Thomas Tancred's *First Report from the Midland Mining Commissioners, South Staffordshire* (1843), William Dodd's *The Factory System* (1842), Edwin Chadwick's *Report of the Sanitary Condition of the Labouring Population of Great Britain, 1842,* William Cobbett's *A History of the Protestant Reformation in England and Ireland* (1824), Bishop Gilbert Burnet's *History of my own Times* (1724-34), and Isaac D'Israeli's *Commentaries on the Life and Reign of Charles I* (1828-30) are significant discoveries that illuminate Disraeli's artistic methods, in particular the ways in which he seemed careless of factual detail and often conflated material from several sources to augment the emotional impact of his story. But the scholarly interest in Disraeli's numerous sources for *Sybil* has proved to be a mixed blessing, for the efforts to show that the descriptions of such things as the effects of the New Poor Law or the rick-burning incidents are inaccurate only reinforce the notion, far too prevalent, that social-problem novels are themselves merely historical documents, if somewhat unreliable ones. Indeed, the question of Disraeli's accuracy in conveying the "historical truth" is largely irrelevant to a critical appreciation of his purposes as a politician and novelist. However much he intended to propagate the knowledge of social conditions he had obtained from his reading of Parliamentary Papers and from his travels to England's industrial regions, in writing *Sybil* Disraeli was much more importantly attempting to write propaganda in the form of an allegorical romance.[5] And the second charge often laid against Disraeli—that in *Sybil* he has no sensible solution for the social problems he exposes—needs to be re-examined in the light of that allegorical romance's meaning.

I

In the "General Preface" to the 1870 collected edition of his novels, Disraeli maintains that *Coningsby, Sybil,* and *Tancred* form "a real trilogy" because they treat the same subject: "The origin and character of our political parties, their influence on the condition of the people of this country, some picture of the moral and physical condition of that people, and some intimation of the means by which it might be elevated and improved, were themes which had long engaged my meditation."[6] He said as well that in beginning *Coningsby* he intended to treat all of these principal topics—the character of political parties, the condition of the people, and the duties of the Church—but found "they were too vast for the space . . . allotted," so that only the first was adequately dealt with in that work ("General Preface," p. xiv). This has led most critics to assume that this "trilogy" is the result of careful planning in which each volume deliberately treats a separate topic, and that *Sybil* is primarily concerned with the second of Disraeli's avowed interests, the condition of the people. Accordingly, his artistic and political purpose has been judged to be transparently that of exposing the discrepancies between the lives of the Two Nations, the Rich and the Poor. And his success as a social novelist has been qualified not only by citing the inaccuracies of factual detail already mentioned, but by interpreting the marriage of Egremont and Sybil as a symbolic failure because the revelation of her nobility destroys the reconciliation of the classes that their union is supposed to represent. In this light Disraeli stands convicted of imaginative "tommyrot" (Brantlinger, p. 97).

Much more cogent is Patrick Brantlinger's argument that *Sybil* is pervaded by ironies, not the least of which

is that the idea of the "Two Nations" is a "dangerous illusion," and clearly seen to be so by Disraeli. Although it is an idea that startles Egremont out of his complacency and edges him toward responsible political thought, it is worth remembering that the concept of the "Two Nations" is expressed by the atheist and utopian radical, Stephen Morley, and it is ultimately exposed and discredited by Egremont as a "false doctrine" which only sustains the heroine's prejudice. However sharp the contrast between the scenes of luxury and the scenes of destitution— those at Mowbray Castle versus those in the room of Warner, the handloom weaver—it is not unwitting ambiguity that informs Disraeli's demonstration that the poor are "not at all a united nation confronting the rich," but "rather a congeries of quarreling factions" (Brantlinger, p. 104). Brantlinger is quite right when he says that "Disraeli points to the diversity of the class system as a refutation of the two-nations theory held by his Chartist characters" (p. 104). Indeed, the ironies and satire in *Sybil,* which encompass both the rich and the poor and demonstrate on the one hand the recent "felonious origins" of the "Venetian oligarchy" and on the other the naiveté of working-class political and social consciousness, are quite deliberate. And the conclusion that Disraeli simply fails in "his attempt to weld Toryism and radicalism together" (Brantlinger, p. 97) would seem to be a reading that misinterprets Disraeli's compassion for the face of distress as a radical political sympathy, and mistakes his Tory social conscience for a reformist ideology.

Such a confusion seems to rest primarily upon the novel's central paradox that the "symbolic" marriage of the "working-class girl" and the aristocratic hero is unconvincing in the light of her revealed nobility. However, the truth is that though Disraeli fully acknowledges the legitimacy of the people's grievances in his "social" novel, he has no "political" sympathy with their cause whatever. *Sybil,* in fact, reflects his actual position in the House of Commons debates on the Chartist petitions.[7] This is also consistent with the theory of the "mixed constitution," which he had advocated publicly since 1835.[8] Accordingly, he considered the proper political representation of "the People" to be the duty of the aristocracy and the Church. And he argued that the true interests of the aristocracy and the true interests of the people are identical and demand a social harmony based upon mutual trust and the acceptance of their respective positions and duties within society. Thus the error of looking for a Tory-Radical compromise where none was intended is in part based upon our Whiggish assumptions about what the work as a realistic social novel ought to be arguing, and upon our limited sympathy for Disraeli's rather primitive Toryism.[9]

While it is ultimately true that Disraeli is less interested "in making us feel sorry for the poor" than in proving them "to be mistaken" (Brantlinger, p. 100), the connection between his melodramatic evocation of pathos among the working class and his rejection of Chartism is both stronger than has yet been granted and by no means the antithesis usually implied. Disraeli's illustration of the "condition of the people" goes, and is intended to go, beyond the quality of their material existence. In the "General Preface" of 1870, he writes that in 1845 he had been attempting "some picture of the moral and physical condition" of the country's people and "some intimation of the means by which it might be elevated" (p. x). His claim that this improvement had "long engaged" his meditation is borne out by the fact that as early as 1833, in an election address to the electors of the borough of Marylebone, he had stressed the need for an elevation of the moral condition of the people. Moreover, in *Sybil* the "condition" that Disraeli is trying to illustrate is "the degradation of the multitude," both physical and moral, a process that was, he felt, the result of the oligarchic Whigs' addiction to "the triple blessings of Venetian politics, Dutch finance, and French wars."[10] The short revisionist and conspiratorial "history" of England in book I, chapter 3, makes his concerns explicit: the principle of Dutch finance "to mortgage industry in order to protect property"[11]:

> has ended in the degradation of a fettered and burthened multitude. . . . Nor have the demoralizing consequences . . . on the more favoured classes been less decided. . . . It has introduced a loose, inexact, haphazard, and dishonest spirit . . . ruthless of consequences and yet shrinking from responsibility. . . . It has so over-stimulated the energies of the population to maintain the material engagements of the state, and of society at large, that the moral condition of the people has been entirely lost sight of.

(Bk. I, chap. 3, 45)

Such a passage makes it clear that Disraeli saw the physical distress of the working population as intimately related to their moral and spiritual condition. And it is also clear from this passage that he saw both of these aspects as in turn closely connected to the lack of proper leadership among their social superiors. It is thus hardly surprising that Disraeli's intimation of how "the moral and physical condition" of the people could be elevated involved a regeneration of not only concrete political and social responsibility, but also a spirit whose essence is religious.

Oddly, perhaps the least-satisfactorily discussed aspect of *Sybil* is Disraeli's very obvious yet important use of a religious motif.[12] This is the more surprising given the presence of the allegorical "Baptist" and "Bishop" Hatton brothers presiding respectively over

the secular Heaven and Hell of the novel. It seems that in the haste to decry the inefficacy of the supposedly interclass marriage of Charles Egremont and Sybil, critics have forgotten that Disraeli would have recognized from the outset that she was not a representative working-class heroine. Indeed, since the plot works from the beginning to deny the simplicities of polarized class antagonism and to reveal Sybil's aristocratic ancestry, it is surely more plausible to argue that Disraeli attached a rather different symbolic value to the concluding marriage: the wedding of sensitive but secular leadership to the spirit of piety and devotion that provides a divine sanction for the political settlement of true Toryism.

At the moment of her first appearance, at twilight amid the ruins of Marney Abbey where she sings "the evening hymn to the Virgin," Sybil is dressed in "the habit of a Religious," though the revelation of her physical beauty suggests that she is not in fact a nun. Significantly, Egremont's first glimpse of her "countenance . . . impressed with a character of almost divine majesty" comes soon after his discussion with the stranger (Sybil's father, Walter Gerard) about the spirit of community and the moral commitment that had marked the administration of the monasteries prior to their dissolution. But it also comes immediately after Stephen Morley's pronouncement of the existence of the two nations, "THE RICH AND THE POOR." The juxtaposition of Morley's bitter claim and Sybil's seraphic presence is so theatrical as to be clearly intended as an epiphany. In other words, the ultimate inadequacy of the secular class dichotomy and the religious nature of Disraeli's alternative are surely embodied in Egremont's response to Sybil's piety and beauty (Bk. II, chap. 5, 96-97). His "conversion" from the aristocratic life of idle hedonism, which is brilliantly portrayed with all its decadent complacency in the opening "Derby" chapters, to an existence imbued with conscientious compassion for the less fortunate, is in part a matter of his innate character: "A physiologist would hardly have inferred from the countenance and structure of Egremont the career he had pursued, or the character which attached to him. The general cast and expression of his features when in repose was pensive: an air of refinement distinguished his well-moulded brow; his mouth breathed sympathy, and his rich brown eye gleamed with tenderness. The sweetness of his voice in speaking was in harmony with this organization" (Bk. I, chap. 5, 58). But Disraeli's concern is equally to establish Egremont's need of a vocation. His "native generosity of heart," we are told, is matched by a mind "worth opening" and "conscious that he wanted an object, . . . ever musing over action, though as yet ignorant how to act" (Bk. I, chap. 5, 60-61).

The process of Egremont's conversion is, however, initiated by means of a series of schematic contrasts in the first few chapters of book II. His intelligence, sensitivity, and compassion, for example, are enlarged by his encounters with the "iron selfishness," the greed, and the cruelty of his elder brother, Lord Marney, and with the obsessive stupidities of Sir Vasavour Firebrace. Lord Marney is a petty domestic tyrant whose only idea of public policy is to suppress all discontent with stringency and severity. His "brother magistrate," the absurd Sir Vasavour, imagines that the salvation of the country depends entirely on the restoration of baronets' rituals and privileges. Equally striking is the contrast of settings provided in chapter 3. The rural town of Marney is situated amidst a "merry prospect" in "a spreading dale, contiguous to the margin of a clear and lively stream, surrounded by meadows and gardens, and backed by lofty hills, undulating and richly wooded" (p. 80). This "beautiful illusion" is juxtaposed to the ugly vision of the town itself, mostly "wretched tenements" and "squalid hovels" surrounded by filthy open drains and putrid dung-heaps, where "penury and disease fed upon the vitals of a miserable population" (pp. 80-81). Such a generalized description at this point in the novel ensures that the reader too can begin the process of conversion, from the simple delight in the malicious satire of the *beau-monde* to sober reflection on what appears to be another nation. Significantly, it is here that the narrator tells us that the "Holy Church at Marney had forgotten her sacred mission" and that the "harrowed souls of a Saxon peasantry" found religious consolation instead in "conventicles" bearing names such as Sion, Bethel, and Bethesda— "names of a distant land, and the language of a persecuted and ancient race" (pp. 82-83).

For the moment his remark about the "mysterious power" of these Judaic allusions may seem to be only one of Disraeli's idiosyncracies. But the narrator's reference to "Holy Church" is picked up in the next chapter as Egremont wanders over the ruins of Marney Abbey, musing upon the causes of rick-burning, an instance of which had occurred the previous night at the Abbey farm. The details of the ruins are lovingly described by the narrator as he nostalgically evokes the time of the monks' lives there with its true hospitality, profound devotion, and sacred charity (Bk. II, chap. 4, 86-88). It is this reverie of past and present, implicitly Egremont's as well, with its sense of impending social calamity, that is disturbed by the dramatic encounter in the graveyard with the mysterious strangers—the one, frank, manly, and vigorous; the other, pale, pox-marked, and intellectual. Disraeli's thematic assertion of the need for a religious revival is thus amply established before the moment of Egremont's epiphany, when he sees the radiant "Religious . . . with a character of almost divine majesty" singing the hymn to the Virgin in the Lady's Chapel (Bk. II, chap. 5, 96-97).

II

In the ensuing chapters of book II, the unfolding of the two strands of the plot, those of secular temptation and moral obligation, gives the attentive reader some important hints about Disraeli's allegorical romance. On the one hand, Lord Marney's calculated plan to marry his younger brother to an heiress, the eldest daughter of the earl de Mowbray, is clearly undercut from the outset by Egremont's thoughts about the strangers he had met at the Abbey ruins, who were also from Mowbray, and especially by his feelings of "sweet perplexity" about the identity of the "beautiful Religious" with which chapter 6 ends. Much more obvious is the narrator's exposure of Lord Mowbray's shoddy family history, which reveals that in the space of seventy years Mowbray's father, John Warren, rose from being a club waiter and valet to the ranks of the nobility by means of speculation, sharp financial practice, marriage, and borough-mongering. This account of the earl's plebian origins and false Norman pedigree is juxtaposed with the revelations in chapter 8 about the identities of the mysterious strangers, who, though apparently of humble yeoman stock, are attempting to regain their lost lands. In the best tradition of gothic romances, this sudden clarification is accompanied by further mystery. The reader learns that Walter Gerard's name is the same as that of the martyred last lay abbot of Marney Abbey from whom the "holy trust" of these lands was apparently seized. And, as the reader remembers from chapter 3, this plunder was perpetrated by Egremont's and Lord Marney's ancestor, Baldwin Greymount, who, much as John Warren had latterly done, rose by despicable means from being a confidential domestic servant to a peer of the realm apparently of Norman descent. In contrast, Gerard implicitly claims a more honest pedigree when he tells his young companion, Stephen Morley, "my fathers fought at Agincourt," and when his daughter refers to their name as that of "the good old faith" (Bk. II, chap. 8, 115). At the same time Gerard reveals that, with the aid of a mysterious man named Hatton, his father had once obtained a "writ of right" to the lost lands, but that it had disappeared along with Hatton in the confusion of affairs at his death. This chapter concludes with their return to Mowbray, where Sybil lives in a convent, and with the indication in their farewells that Morley is in love with her although he has no religious faith.

Given the emphasis placed on the corrupt genealogies of Lord Marney and the earl of Mowbray,[13] and given the details of Walter Gerard's claim to be the heir to the lost estates of an ancient family, probably of Saxon roots, it is difficult to see why the theme of dispossession is not recognized more widely as the structural framework of the novel. And given the limits of Sybil's characterization, confined initially almost entirely to her tedious religiosity, her striking beauty, and her filial devotion, it is equally difficult to imagine that Disraeli intended her to be a representative, that is, typical working-class heroine. Part of such a reading may come from Gerard's active role among the Chartists and from his and Sybil's talk about restoring "the people to the land" (Bk. II, chap. 8, 114), but most of it derives from the sheer vitality of the working-class world Disraeli does depict, and from the mediating role Sybil plays amidst scenes of working-class misery and popular agitation. She certainly sees herself as a moral representative of the people. But even readers who see the emblematic quality of Sybil's character often fail to recognize the intent of the allegory of which she is a part. Daniel Schwarz, for example, describes Sybil as "an *emblem,* within the novel's dialectic, for the potential of the Church," and he recognizes that Disraeli wishes her "to represent the spiritual values that England requires" (Schwarz, pp. 111, 114), but he does not take his own insight seriously enough to overcome his assumptions that the novel is an exposure of the Two Nations, and that the concluding marriage is a failed attempt to bridge the "schism between rich and poor" (Schwarz, p. 120).

To understand the full meaning of Sybil's emblematic role, it is essential to see the significance of other characters in the larger allegorical romance. And inevitably this brings one to Disraeli's peculiar ideas about Christianity and Judaism, and to his feelings about Roman Catholicism. One such emblematic figure is Aubrey St. Lys, the new vicar of Mowbray Church. His name literally embodies his true nobility, saintliness, and purity—the lily, of course, having a rich symbolic value within both Catholic and Anglican liturgies of the Resurrection and the Annunciation, as well as heraldic resonance with French royalty and nobility.[14] But the pronunciation of his name, clearly "sín-less" (on the precedent of Disraeli's favourite Tory philosopher, Henry St. John, Viscount Bolingbroke), also makes it clear that he is more than a character within a realistic social context. Disraeli presents St. Lys as a man who has accepted a divine mission, although his talents would have justified a richer ecclesiastical or secular preferment. Prior to his arrival the narrator says, "the frigid spell of Erastian self-complacency fatally prevailed" in the magnificant and beautiful church built centuries earlier by the monks of Mowbray. Indeed, although the building is so glorious as to be appropriate as an episcopal seat, the congregation has dwindled almost to "zero." And so, instead of a bishop, Mowbray received "a humble vicar . . . who came among a hundred thousand heathens to preach 'the Unknown God'" (Bk. II, chap. 11, 142).

Part of St. Lys's mission is to be an agent of divine consolation, charity, and mercy for the destitute and dying. This is effectively dramatized in his conversations with Lord Marney about the cruelly low wages paid to his agricultural workers, and in the piteous scenes in the room of Warner, the handloom weaver. There his timely intervention adds both a spiritual sanction to Warner's honesty in the face of starvation and an institutional corroboration of Sybil's private charity. But the most interesting aspect of St. Lys's presence in *Sybil* is his theological influence on Egremont's thinking. Their conversation, recorded at the end of book II, chapter 12, begins with St. Lys blaming only the Church for "all that has occurred," claiming that the Church deserted the people, thus degrading them and endangering itself. His lament at first passes for a typical piece of Tractarian or Young England nostalgia for the mediaeval past:

> Formerly religion undertook to satisfy the noble wants of human nature, and by its festivals relieved the painful weariness of toil. The day of rest was consecrated, if not always to elevated thought, at least to sweet and noble sentiments. The Church convened to its solemnities under its splendid and almost celestial roofs amid the finest monuments of art that human hands have raised, the whole Christian population; for there, in the presence of God, all were brethren. It shared equally among all its prayer, its incense, and its music; its sacred instructions, and the highest enjoyments that the arts could afford.
>
> (Bk. II, chap. 12, 146)

Certainly the emphasis in this passage upon the "essentially spiritual" existence of all art would have sounded an alarmingly Puseyite tone in the ears of Disraeli's readers (p. 146). Before addressing that issue, however, it is important to see that St. Lys's exaltation of a community based upon the union of all people under God and made literally harmonious by religious forms and ceremonies, is a direct alternative to the secular community of human purpose based upon "co-operation" and "association," which was advocated by Stephen Morley, the author of the Two Nations paradox (Bk. II, chap. 5).

Disraeli's admiration for St. Lys's Tractarian mystical aesthetics is, no doubt, genuine, but he is well aware (as who was not in 1845, a few months before Newman's formal defection) of the political dangers of Tractarian ideas. Thus Egremont directly addresses the Romish tendencies when he protests that the people of England associate such forms and ceremonies "with an enthralling superstition and a foreign dominion" (Bk. II, chap. 12, 146). St. Lys's response is crucial to our reading of Disraeli's allegorical intentions, for it not only defuses the paranoia about the "Romish system," but also provides the theological basis for the concluding marriage of a Protestant hero and a Catholic heroine. St. Lys argues that, "as the only Hebraeo-christian church extant," the Church of Rome must be respected, for even its intervening excesses should not "make us forget its early and apostolic character, when it was fresh from Palestine and as it were fragrant from Paradise" (p. 146). Palestine and Paradise are in apposition because the Judaic and Christian religions are one, the latter form being the fulfillment of the former. St. Lys points out that the apostles succeeded the prophets and that "Our Master announced himself as the last of the prophets" who were in turn "the heirs of the patriarchs." Consequently, St. Lys argues, the rituals they have been discussing are the products of a continuity far older than the establishment of the Church of Rome: "The second Testament is avowedly only a supplement. . . . Christianity is completed Judaism, or it is nothing. . . . The order of our priesthood comes directly from Jehovah; and the forms and ceremonies of His church are the regulations of His supreme intelligence. . . . I recognize in the church an institution thoroughly, sincerely catholic: adapted to all climes and to all ages" (p. 147). These claims are interesting because they bear a close relation to Sidonia's emphasis upon the genius of the Jews in *Coningsby* and because they are an anticipation of the great Asian mystery which is the putative climax of Disraeli's next novel, *Tancred: or the New Crusade.*

But the most interesting feature of these ideas is that St. Lys clearly speaks for his author—Disraeli used almost identical arguments both in speaking in the House of Commons on the subject of Jewish disabilities and in his biography, *Lord George Bentinck* (1852): "Who can deny that Jesus of Nazareth, the Incarnate Son of the Most High God, is the eternal glory of the Jewish race?"[15] The lesson that Egremont thus learns is that a recognition of the true "Hebraeo-christian" catholicity of the Church renders the distinction between Protestant and Catholic merely perversely political. And thus *Sybil* embodies a very old Disraelian theme, for the marriage of Protestant and Catholic protagonists is a central feature of *Henrietta Temple* (1836), *Contarini Fleming* (1832), and *The Young Duke* (1831). Elsewhere I have argued that in his fiction Disraeli disguised his ambivalence about his Jewish heritage in this recurring Catholic motif, partly because the Catholic issue was of much stronger public interest than the matter of Jewish disabilities.[16] What is interesting about its use in *Sybil* is that Disraeli is here able to integrate the reality and the disguise so that the individual question of religious identity comes to serve his vision of an ideal relation between religion and politics, between Church and State. In other words, in *Sybil,* to a degree greater than in his earlier works, the realm of private fantasy embodied in the romance of Egremont's pursuit of Sybil is successfully integrated with the realm of public debate about the condition of England.

III

Like Carlyle, Disraeli sees the social and economic crisis of the 1840s as a symptom of a moral collapse. This view expresses itself in the very structuring of *Sybil.* Many critics have remarked upon the juxtapositions of scenes of aristocratic wealth and working-class poverty. But the structuring is more complex and ideational than that formula of simple contrasts suggests. For example, immediately after Egremont's conversation with St. Lys, Disraeli presents the pathetic scene in Warner's room, where the weaver is struggling valiantly to finish a task which may bring the price of a meal for his ill and starving family on the verge of eviction. Here the theme of dispossession is renewed in Warner's reverie about why workers like himself were driven from their "innocent and happy homes" and "country cottages" to face life in cellars and squalid lairs "without even the common necessaries of existence" (Bk. II, chap. 13, 151). It is perfectly clear, even to him, that the laissez-faire argument that "the interests of Capital and of Labour are identical" does not address the moral issue in the fate of "the race whose only property is labour," and who, though "innocent," have lost their "estates." Even though the metaphor lies in Warner's nostalgic imagination, the linking of his sense of dispossession to Walter Gerard's leaves Disraeli open to the charge of mangling the factual truth. But perhaps he is not so guilty of distorting the psychological one, for victims of other people's greed or indifference no doubt felt the truth of such metaphors as much in the 1840s as at any time before or since. In any case, Disraeli's purpose here is also to create the first meeting between Egremont and Sybil in a moment of mutual charity that Egremont later describes as a "mission of grace" (Bk. III, chap. 5, 212), and then to complicate his romantic desire with her disgust for the owners of Marney Abbey.

The stagecraft involved in making his hero's identity a central concern of both the plot and theme is typical of the method in romantic novels in general and Disraeli's in particular. But, significantly, Egremont lacks the intense ambivalence about himself that is characteristic of virtually all of Disraeli's earlier protagonists from Vivian Grey to Harry Coningsby. In *Sybil* Disraeli makes the question of identity one of public vocation, just as he attempted to do in *Coningsby.* In the earlier novel, however, the conflict between altruism and expediency is partly projected outward onto other characters such as Sidonia, and partly subsumed by the magic and purity of Coningsby's reciprocated love for Edith Millbank. In *Sybil,* by contrast, Egremont's ambitions are completely dissolved in his duty; and his political career emerges with the unassailable sanction of being a religious vocation.[17]

The first evidence that Egremont conceives of his political career as a "mission of grace" is a small but intrusive detail. When (he having returned to London and taken up his seat in Parliament) his mother asks him to accept a birthday present from among her possessions, Egremont chooses a picture that reminds him of Sybil and the "portrait of a female saint" which she had placed "over the mantle-piece" of her father's cottage. His choice is "the portrait of a saint by Allori: the face of a beautiful young girl, radiant and yet solemn, with rich tresses of golden brown hair, and large eyes dark as night, fringed with ebon lashes that hung upon the glowing cheek" (Bk. IV, chap. 2, 257). Then, three chapters later, when Gerard and Morley arrive at his rooms as Chartist delegates in their canvass of M.P.s, the portrait is mentioned again in a way that indicates its real symbolic importance, not just as an icon of romantic memory, but also as one of guiding spiritual force:[18]

> The servant opened a mahogany folding-door which he shut after him and announced to his master the arrival of the delegates. Egremont was seated in his library, at a round table covered with writing materials, books, and letters. On another table were arranged his parliamentary papers and piles of blue books. The room was classically furnished. On the mantlepiece were some ancient vases, which he had brought from Italy, standing on each side of that picture of Allori of which we have spoken.

(Bk. IV, chap. 5, 279)

This description is meant to confirm for the reader the transformation that Egremont has undergone, from being a languorous aristocrat who stood for Parliament "at the instigation of the family" and from "no feeling of his own" (Bk. III, chap. 2, 192), to an energetic representative of the people's interests, who in his new vigor can only mock those of his own class who think of politics as a game of social intrigue, where all the "power, patronage, and pay" are reserved for a small circle of self-indulgent, vapid, noble society. An example of this is his forthright attack on Lady St. Julians and Lady Firebrace:

> 'This is a lesson for you fine ladies, who think you can govern the world by what you call your social influences: asking people once or twice a-year to an inconvenient crowd in your house; now haughtily smirking, and now impertinently staring, at them; and flattering yourselves all this time, that to have the occasional privilege of entering your saloons and the periodical experience of your insolent recognition, is to be a reward for great exertions, or if necessary an inducement to infamous tergiversation.'

(Bk. IV, chap. 3, 261-264)

This transformation, which is actually a realization of his innate character, takes place during the period of his earlier sojourn (in disguise as Mr. Franklin) as a neighbour of Gerard and his daughter in Mowedale. Central to Egremont's new understanding of "the condition of the people" is his visit to Trafford's model factory. Here the true "baronial principle" has been revived in the practice of industrial feudalism to create an idyllic village where the moral and physical well-

being of the whole population is the result of the proprietor's paternal, loving concern. At the center of this community, whose every detail has been designed to foster the "domestic virtues," lies a "gothic church," which "Mr. Trafford, though a Roman Catholic, had raised and endowed" (Bk. III, chap. 8, 225-226). Significantly, it is to this church that Egremont pays a visit when Lord de Mowbray and his entourage suddenly arrive to inspect Trafford's factory. The symbolism of the action is clear, for any other retirement would just as easily have preserved his incognito. But clearly Egremont wishes specifically to deny his association with the spirit of secular grandeur and the unwarranted differentiation of rank embodied in the "pretension," "pride," and "condescension" of the de Mowbrays (Bk. III, chap. 8, 227-234).

At the same time Disraeli reinforces the previous strong hints in his theme of dispossession. First, the narrator comments that after his tour of the works, Lord de Mowbray was "profuse of praise and compliments. . . . His lordship was apt to be too civil. The breed would come out sometimes. Today he was quite the coffee-house waiter. he praised everything: the machinery, the workmen, the cotton manufactured and the raw cotton, even the smoke" (Bk. III, chap. 8, 228). A moment later, as the conversation of the luncheon party turns to the subject of Sybil's beauty, Lady Maud de Mowbray is so astonished to learn that Sybil is Gerard's daughter that she twice in one sentence refers to him as that "so very aristocratic-looking . . . person" she had seen in the factory (Bk. III, chap. 8, 229). Finally, after the de Mowbrays' departure, Gerard tells Egremont (Franklin):

> "A year ago this earl had a son—an only son, and then his daughters were not great heiresses. But the son died and now it's their turn. And perhaps some day it will be somebody else's turn. If you want to understand the ups and downs of life, there's nothing like the parchmounts of an estate. Now master, now man! He who served in the hall now lords in it; and very often the base born change their liveries for coronets, while gentle blood has nothing left but—dreams; eh, master Franklin?"

(Bk. III, chap. 8, 231-232)

The chapter in which this passage occurs follows immediately upon those in which Morley, in quest of Gerard's lost family documents, tracks down the brother of the mysterious Hatton at Wodgate. And it immediately precedes that in which Gerard remarks to Morley upon the strangeness of his meeting Lord de Mowbray face to face: "'He offered me money when it was over. . . . I would not look at it. Though to be sure, they were perhaps my own rents, eh?'" (Bk. III, chap. 9, 237). It is a fine point, but Disraeli seems to use the habitual colloquial interjection as a verbal echo to link this conversation to the earlier one with Egremont, for it has previously been used sparingly. In any case, it is clear that only by ignoring her obvious symptoms of good breeding and neglecting the more intrusive elements of the dispossession theme can a reader interpret Sybil to be a working-class heroine, or be truly surprised at the revelation, or rather, confirmation of her nobility.

Just as important to an understanding of Disraeli's intentions in the first half of the novel is an awareness of how Stephen Morley's ideas are undercut. Apart from the several references to his lack of religious faith, there are some dramatic incidents which demonstrate that within the larger allegorical romance his ideas are a foil for Disraeli's main thesis. On the way to Wodgate he stops in a colliery village where, in the local pub, he explains his "principle of association" and the advantages of cooperative living and collective action to the miners grumbling about tommy shops. But Mr. Nixon's pithy comment, "'Sir, . . . you speak like a book,'" in conjunction with the narrator's summary of abuses of children's employment in the mines and the specific grievances of the men, is a devastating, contemptuous retort to Morley's assertions of the people's "rights" and "power" (Bk. III, chap. 1, 183). Morley seems more sensitive when next he intervenes at Diggs's tommy shop to assist the young boy injured in the brutal crush (Bk. III, chap. 3, 200-201). He does this by threatening to expose Diggs and his son in the *Mowbray Phalanx* as "oppressors of the people," unless they carry the boy to a warm bed in their house. But such sympathy is, perhaps, suspect, for it is arguably a hollow victory for a radical journalist to buy a moment of forced kindness with his silence.

Disraeli is much less ambiguous when he has Morley reject as "unnatural" the example of Trafford's altruistic concern for his workers' domestic virtue:

> "The domestic principle has fulfilled its purpose. The irresistable law of progress demands that another should be developed. It will come. . . . It will work out like the development of organic nature. In the present state of civilization and with the scientific means of happiness at our command, the notion of home should be obsolete. Home is a barbarous idea; the method of a rude age; home is isolation; therefore antisocial. What we want is Community."

(Bk. III, chap. 9, 238)

Apart from the fact that Gerard and Sybil both disagree with Morley, the reader is also guided by the narrator's previous endorsement of Trafford's views: he had "imbibed" a "correct conception of the relations that should subsist between the employer and the employed" (Bk. III, chap. 8, 224) and, having "deeply . . . pondered" upon his possible influence, he "knew well that the domestic virtues are dependent on the existence of a home" (Bk. III, chap. 8,

225). The results of Trafford's efforts speak for themselves; in his village there is cleanliness and order, crime and drunkenness are unknown, the people are well-clad and the "moral condition of the softer sex" has been "proportionately elevated" (Bk. III, chap. 8, 226). Finally, Morley's claim to the reader's intellectual sympathies is completely destroyed in the last chapter of book III. Here Disraeli descends to comic pathos in using the affections of Sybil's "Saxon" bloodhound, Harold, to indicate both her fondness for the still-disguised Egremont and Morley's violent intentions. But in having the utopian, secular rationalist driven to attempted murder by his sexual jealousy, Disraeli is undermining all of the ideas, including that of the Two Nations, which that utilitarian frame of mind has produced.[19] In effect, Morley is shown not to be wicked, but perverse, for he has developed a materialist conception of human nature which ignores the very aspects of it that Disraeli sees as fundamental to humanity's morality and happiness.

IV

The development of Disraeli's religious allegory does not depend solely upon the overtly sincere emblematic elements of his romantic plot. It also comprises parodic elements, which in effect are illustrations of the antithetical, or Satanic, view of society. The most obvious of these parodies are the scenes in Wodgate and the investiture of Dandy Mick into a Trades Union. In the former, "Bishop" Hatton presides over a secular Hell in which all of the principles of Christian civilization have been inverted. Wodgate has no Church, no government, no magistrate, no schools; and the working population of this "most hideous burgh" exists amid "gutters of abomination" and "pools of filth," in a state of complete degradation and "savage instinct."[20] Ironically, in Wodgate, "Labour reigns supreme," for the manufacture of ironmongery is carried on in the form of a pre-industrial guild. And equally so, the masters form a "real aristocracy" which earns its privileges. As the very name of the town indicates, Disraeli intends here to illustrate the perverse consequences of such forms when inspired by pagan rather than Christian values. This is also the function of the Satanic sacrament of marriage in which the Bishop, Tummas tells Morley, "'sprinkled some salt over a gridiron, read "Our Father" backwards, and wrote our name in a book'" (Bk. III, chap. 4, 207). Equally obvious in its purpose is Sue's statement of their creed: "'He believes now in our Lord and Saviour Pontius Pilate who was crucified to save our sins; and in Moses, Goliath, and the rest of the Apostles'" (Bk. III, chap. 4, 208). Disraeli's wit, it should be noted, is deadly serious, for embodied in the Dantesque infernal scenes of grotesque physical deformities, horrifying punishments, and the incessantly compelled motion of the files is the central vision of life governed not by love and charity, but by fear and violence.

The same inversion of religious values is the most salient characteristic of Dandy Mick's induction into a Trades Union. The torchlit procession in "mystic robes" and "secret masks," the blindfolding before being thrust kneeling into the presence of the *"Seven,"* the skeleton, the marshalls with swords and battle-axes, and the mystic rhymes are all kin to the diabolic rituals in gothic fiction. Further, the demonic impact of the scene is enhanced by the use of such religious language as "prayer," "Hymn," "neophyte," and "sacred volume"; for what Mick Radley is required to swear in the name of "Almighty God" is his willingness to "execute with zeal and alacrity" whatever "chastisement, . . . assassination . . . and demolition" is imposed as his task. Disraeli thus satirizes the notion that such unholy "Brethren" could be furthering the "common welfare" (Bk. IV, chap. 4, 270).

Again it is worth noticing that Disraeli's control of the episodic structure continually reinforces the central religious allegory. The Trades Union initiation is followed by the chapter in which Egremont is at work in his study beneath the inspiring picture of the saint by Allori discussed above. Then immediately following is the symbolic, seemingly chance meeting between Egremont and Sybil in Westminster Abbey. That scene begins with the narrator discoursing on the general purifying and elevating influence of sacred buildings and then protesting the "mean discipline and sordid arrangements," which "injure and impair the holy genius" of the Abbey by confining the public to small portions of the building. Although on his first visit Egremont had felt "as if the Abbey were in a state of siege" and had been outraged to find "iron gates shutting him out from the solemn nave and the shadowy aisles," it has become his favourite habit to retreat there from the "dull" debates in Parliament to listen to the "celestial symphony" of the organ. A similar delight, the narrator suggests, brings Sybil to stand just before the Poet's Corner, against "the iron grating that shut her out from the body of the church," looking "wistfully down the long dim perspective of the beautiful southern aisle" (Bk. IV, chap. 6, 282-283). Just as Egremont comes forth from the choir his eye catches, but does not immediately recognize, "the symmetry of her shape and the picturesque position which she gracefully occupied; still gazing through that gate, while the light pouring forth through the western window, suffused the body of the church with a soft radiance, just touching the head of the unknown with a kind of halo" (Bk. IV, chap. 6, 283-284). Because of its representation of a national Church in need of reclamation, and of a figure of saintly piety excluded from the centre of that Church—albeit in part from her own prejudice and naiveté—this scene ought to be recognized as the core of Disraeli's allegorical romance of secular politics and spiritual devotion.

But many readers focus instead upon the ostensible realism of class distinction in Sybil's rejection of Egremont, once she learns his true identity: "'the gulf is impassable . . . utterly impassable'" (Bk. IV, chap. 8, 300). To do so is to mistake the contrivance of plot for thematic concern. The narrator, who can be taken as a reliable guide to Disraeli's views, describes Egremont's momentary despair in terms of Sybil's "prejudices and convictions more impassable than all the mere consequences of class" (Bk. IV, chap. 8, 300). This contrasting comparison suggests that what Sybil must give up in recognizing and accepting Egremont's true nobility and moral vocation is not only her false dichotomy of the Two Nations, but also the fanatical exclusivity of her "old faith." This is the reason that within the allegory both Trafford and "Baptist" Hatton are Catholics, the former a model of ecumenical charity, the latter a master of deceit, who profanely rationalizes his own scheming fantasy of marrying Sybil and producing a noble son as a "glorious vision" of restoring an old Catholic family to its former greatness (Bk. IV, chap. 10, 307-310).

"Baptist" Hatton's acknowledgement to Gerard that "'on every principle of justice . . . Mowbray Castle is as much yours as the house that is built by the tenant on the lord's land'" (Bk. IV, chap. 10, 305), his courtesy to "Lady Sybil," his reflection that he has deprived her of "a principality," and his fantasy of restoring her to "the rank she would honour," and thus assuaging the "sharp pangs of conscience" and achieving through marriage to her "the secret ambition" of his life (Bk. IV, chap. 10, 309) all cast an ironic light on Sybil's subsequent claims to be "a daughter of the people" (Bk. IV, chap. 15, 336). The point of such irony is not, however, to undermine her moral identification with "the people," but to show that her conception of them is as mistaken as are her notions of the aristocracy. It does this in part by making it clear that the accidents of her humble birth and education are as confining as those of Egremont's nobility. The shape of the allegorical romance is, therefore, that of their mutual transcendence of these limitations through their reciprocal powers of inspiration. Just as Egremont admits that her beauty has been the master of his spirit, so Sybil comes to acknowledge that his love determines her fate.

Unfortunately, the simplicity of this romance tempts the reader to over-simplify Disraeli's depiction of social class.[21] The process of Sybil's reeducation discredits the view that Disraeli intends merely to expose the social reality of the Two Nations. Egremont calls her idealistic notions of the People's strength and integrity, "fallacious fancies," and he insists that her dualistic "phantoms," the oppressors and the oppressed, are not an accurate representation of either human nature or society. Further, he predicts that the ideals of the Chartist Convention will end in factions, betrayal, and violence. Of course, Sybil's experiences in London soon confirm these lessons:

> She had seen enough to suspect that the world was a more complicated system than she had preconceived. . . . The characters were more various, the motives more mixed, the classes more blended, the elements of each more subtle and diversified, than she had imagined. The People she found was not that pure embodiment of unity of feeling, of interest, and of purpose, which she had pictured in her abstractions. . . . Nor could she resist the belief that the feeling of the rich toward the poor was not that sentiment of unmingled hate and scorn which she associated with Norman conquerors and feudal laws. She would ascribe rather the want of sympathy that unquestionably exists between Wealth and Work in England, to mutual ignorance between the classes which possess these two great elements of national prosperity.

> (Bk. V, chap. 1, 349-350)

It is in this frame of mind that she reads Egremont's speech from the debate on the National Petition and begins to realize the power of moral commitment wedded to secular position: "Yes, there was one voice that . . . had dared to express immortal truths: the voice of a noble, who without being a demagogue, had upheld the popular cause; had pronounced his conviction that the rights of labour were as sacred as those of property; . . . who had declared that the social happiness of the millions should be the first object of a statesman" (Bk. V, chap. 1, 350). It is with these convictions to support her that Sybil learns that her father has become entangled in a conspiracy against the State. At the same time she finds that Morley, the utilitarian idealist and advocate of moral power, has been reduced by the exigencies of his "indecent" passion for her to the "pollution" of slander, blackmail, and blasphemy (Bk, V, chap. 4, 363-369).

The implications of such knowledge are dramatized in the ensuing search for her father through the slums of Seven Dials, which is both literally and figuratively a descent to the underworld. The full impact of Disraeli's ironic use of class in the novel is felt here, for although the narrator describes the houses, population, costume, manners, and language of this district as "of a different state and nation to those with which the dwellers in the dainty quarters of this city are acquainted," the emphasis is not upon poverty. Indeed, the impression conveyed of the life in the streets is one of vulgar, but fascinating vitality:

> They were plunged into a labyrinth of lanes teeming with life, and where the dog-stealer and the pickpocket, the burglar and the assassin, found comrades for every enterprise; and a market for every booty. . . . A multitude were sauntering in the mild though tainted air; bargaining, blaspheming, drinking, wrangling; and varying their business and their potations, their fierce strife and their impious irreverence, with flashes of rich humour, gleams of native wit, and racy phrases of idiomatic slang.

> (Bk. V, chap. 6, 376)

Disraeli's point is that this is a world of complete moral depravity; so much so that he knows he is challenging the middle-class boundaries of innocence and purity (and even the limits of what is acceptable in fiction) by having Sybil traverse it. After all, she is not only confronted by thieves and a half-naked, drunken woman with "brutality stamped on every feature," she is "overwhelmed with shame and terror" when she finds herself invited to enter a brothel (Bk. V, chap. 6, 377, 379). That such a descent into humanity is an integral part of Disraeli's allegorical theme is shown by the way she is protected from the entirely plausible fate worse than death.

In chapter 4 of book V when Morley, having already sneered at the power of "the Holy Virgin," nevertheless attempts to force Sybil to foreswear her love for Egremont in the name of the Holy Virgin, by all the saints, and by her hope of heaven, she "became white as the marble saint of some sacred niche" (Bk. V, chap, 4, 368-369). But when she faltered, "a burning brightness suffused the cheek of Sybil," causing Morley to rush out frantically and abandon her in the extermity of her fears for her father's safety. She then sets out upon her search, which takes her into the criminal underworld, with the courage and faith inspired by prayer and with "a conviction of celestial aid" (Bk. V, chap. 5, 371). That celestial aid appears in the form of the good and presumably sober Irishman who hears her cry of alarm, "'O! holy Virgin aid me!'" and who, replying "'that's a blessed word to hear in this heathen land,'" undertakes to guide "a sister in Christ" to her true destination (Bk. V, chap. 6, 379).

In this paradigmatic encounter Sybil is both a victim rescued and an agent of redemption. In a small way this episode reveals as well as any in the book how Disraeli furthers his political allegory by blending the conventions of realism and romance. Much the same point can be made about the often remarked upon shifts from the scenes of poverty to scenes of wealth. But in juxtaposing the incidents in Seven Dials to the grand ball at Deloraine House, Disraeli is as much interested in the moral comparison as the theatrical contrast. This is made explicit by the double perspective. The members of the *beau-monde* are shown to be every bit as morally depraved as are the denizens of the criminal slums, both by the selfish intrigues that consume their thoughts and by the conversations of the destitute and homeless vagrants lying in the darkness of the park opposite the brilliantly lit mansion, of whom the noble guests are of course completely unaware. By such means Disraeli is constantly making the point that "the degradation of the people" is the result, not of economic circumstances, but of immoral leadership. In other words, his social and political satire of both upper and lower classes is an integral part of his illustration that the lamentable "condition of England" is a symptom, not a cause, of moral depravity.

V

Readers who are dissatisfied with the conclusion of *Sybil* have good grounds for their discontent, even though Disraeli cannot justifiably be convicted of the imaginative "tommyrot" of converting his "daughter of the People" into an aristocrat. As this essay has shown, Sybil's identification with the People is largely a moral one. And the theme of Gerard's dispossession is so strong throughout that there is a constant ironic light cast upon her naiveté about social class. Nevertheless, the conclusion seems unsatisfactory because the exigencies of the romance plot become too intrusive. Rather like the wish-fulfillment fantasies of some fairytales, the climactic scenes of the riot at Mowbray Castle dispose of all the characters who stand in the way of the symbolic consummation Disraeli has in mind. Lord Marney, Walter Gerard (who was convicted and gaoled for his Chartist conspiracy), and Stephen Morley ("the Apostle of Community") are all dispatched in violent deaths which are the consequences of their moral errors. Disraeli thereby denounces the selfish indifference of the aristocracy, the temptation to use violent means for the redress of grievances, and the distortion of love in the motives of abstractly rational utopian thought. But in so abandoning the balance of genres that has characterized his novel thus far, he disappoints the reader intent on realism by seeming to undermine the public significance of the symbolic union he has laboured to create.

Seen as the completion of a religious allegorical romance, however, the conclusion of *Sybil* is less troubling. Disraeli's view of the Chartist movement, for example, is revealed by the delightful irony that the "Chartist Apostle," Field, succeeds in converting the illiterate "Bishop" Simon Hatton to the belief that, by leading an insurrection of the "Hell-Cats," he will be the liberator of the people (Bk. VI, chap. 6, 442-444). But as such he is really a parodic disciple of the Anti-Christ:

> The march of Bishop Hatton at the head of the Hell-Cats into the mining districts was perhaps the most striking popular movement since the Pilgrimage of Grace. Mounted on a white mule, wall-eyed and of hideous form, the Bishop brandished a huge hammer with which he announced he would destroy the enemies of the people. . . . Some thousand Hell-Cats followed him brandishing bludgeons, or armed with bars of iron, pickhandles, and hammers. On each side of the Bishop, on a donkey, was one of his little sons, as demure and earnest as if he

> were handling his file. A flowing standard of silk inscribed with the Charter, and which had been presented to him by the delegate, was born before him like the oriflamme. Never was such a gaunt, grim crew.

> (Bk. VI, chap. 6, 443)

In the end the "Utopia of Toil" brings destruction to every place he visits. Disraeli turns the "Bishop" into a ridiculous figure, clamouring for fire with which to destroy Trafford's idyllic factory, but he is finally consumed in the flames of the conflagration of Mowbray Castle ("the funeral pile of the children of Woden," Bk. VI, chap. 12, 491) that his own besotted followers set.

It is significant, too, that St. Lys reappears and is described as a check to Chartist violence as he uses every opportunity to preach sermons on the theme of "Fear God and honour the King" (Bk. V, chap. 10, 404; Bk. VI, chap. 9, 460-461). In the midst of the riot at Mowbray Castle, St. Lys rallies the honest workmen of Mowbray "in the name of God," and he combines with Sybil to rescue Lady de Mowbray and her daughters from the murderous mob and its "deed of darkness" (Bk. VI, chap. 12, 484).

The extensive ironic use of religious epithets and allusions ("Bishop *Simon*," "Baptist," "Apostle," "Hell-Cats") in contrast to the saintly imagery of the devout struggles of Egremont, Sybil, and St. Lys, indicates that Disraeli wishes to represent the consequence of conceiving England to be Two Nations as an infernal version of the Gospel. And given this inversion, the climactic and penultimate episode must also be read symbolically. When Egremont, in command of a troop of yeomen, arrives to rout the mob, his valorous, melodramatic rescue of Sybil, literally from the hands of a band of drunken ruffians, is, in effect, the deliverance of the Church from the imminent moment of its desecration:

> Suddenly a band of drunken ruffians, with shouts and oaths, surrounded her; she shrieked in frantic terror; Harold sprung at the throat of the foremost. . . . The brave dog did wonders, but the odds were fearful; and the men had bludgeons, were enraged, and had already wounded him. One ruffian had grasped the arm of Sybil, another had clenched her garments, when an officer covered with dust and gore, sabre in hand, jumped from the terrace, and hurried to the rescue. He cut down one man, thrust away another, and placing his left arm around Sybil, he defended her with his sword. . . . Her assailants were routed, they made a staggering flight; the officer turned round and pressed Sybil to his heart.

> "We will never part again," said Egremont.

> "Never," murmured Sybil.

> (Bk. VI, chap. 12, 491-492).

Disraeli's resolution of the dichotomy of the Two Nations is, thus, to wed the compassionate secular leadership of true nobility to the spirit of piety and devotion in a pure Christian faith.

The political implications of this resolution are suggested in the denouement, when, after the marriage of Egremont and Sybil, both of whom have succeeded to their titles, the narrator endorses the allegory's harmonious vision of One Nation: "There is a whisper rising in this country that Loyalty is not a phrase, Faith not a delusion, and Popular Liberty something more diffusive and substantial than the profane exercise of the sacred rights of sovereignty by political classes" (Bk. VI, chap. 13, 497). Clearly, a society based on common loyalty, faith, and liberty would subsume the potentially divisive distinctions of wealth, class, and religious practice, which would then cease to corrupt the aristocracy and degrade the people.

The vision of society expressed in *Sybil* is thus consistent with the ideals of Young England embodied in *Coningsby* and with the characteristic ideas of Disraeli's ideological commitment in the 1830s to the theory of the mixed constitution, wherein in a society conceived as organic in nature, the true representatives of the people are the aristocracy and the Church.[22] *Sybil* is, however, very different from *Coningsby* and Disraeli's earlier novels because there is an allegorical rather than a psychological romance blended with the sympathetic and satirical material derived from his own "observation" of life.[23] The reader of *Sybil* who notices the religious intent of that allegorical romance cannot but conclude that Disraeli achieved his later stated purpose of examining both "the condition of the people" and "the duties of the Church as a main remedial agency."[24] But the contemporary response to the novel, like much recent criticism, did not focus on the latter intention as often as the author might have wished. This may in part be because the exigencies of the allegorical romance are often in conflict with the claims of plausibility and truth which are supposed to inform the social-problem novel. On those grounds it might be better to conclude that because its religious theme strikes the social realist as unworldly and impractical *Sybil,* not *Coningsby,* should be considered Disraeli's "manifesto of Young England."[25]

Notes

[1] *Coningsby,* like *Vivian Grey,* inspired the publication of unofficial "Keys," intended to inform those not in the know about the real identities of the various characters.

[2] For a fuller discussion of *Coningsby,* see Robert O'Kell, "Disraeli's *Coningsby:* Political Manifesto or Psychological Romance?," *Victorian Studies* 23 (1979), 57-78. Disraeli published retrospective statements of his intentions in the "Preface" to the 5th edition of *Coningsby* in 1849 and in the "General Preface" to the collected edition of his novels in 1870. See Robert Blake, *Disraeli* (London: Eyre and Spottiswoode, 1966), which gives the best account of the context in which the trilogy of the 1840s was written.

[3] O'Kell, "Disraeli's *Coningsby,*" p. 77. Among the best discussions of *Sybil* are Richard A. Levine, *Benjamin Disraeli* (New York: Twayne, 1968); Patrick Brantlinger, *The Spirit of Reform: British Literature and Politics, 1832-1867* (Cambridge, MA: Harvard University Press, 1977); Daniel Schwarz, *Disraeli's Fiction* (New York: Barnes and Noble, 1979); and Thom Braun, *Disraeli the Novelist* (London: Allen and Unwin, 1981). Donald Stone, *The Romantic Impulse in Victorian Fiction* (Cambridge, MA: Harvard University Press, 1980), though it contains only a brief discussion of *Sybil,* has a good essay on "Benjamin Disraeli and the Romance of the Will."

[4] A good deal of work has been done to uncover Disraeli's sources. Among the best are Sheila M. Smith, "Willenhall and Wodgate: Disraeli's Use of Blue Book Evidence," *Review of English Studies* n.s. 13 (1962), 368-384; and Martin Fido, "'From His Own Observation': Sources of Working Class Passages in Disraeli's *Sybil,*" *Modern Language Review* 72 (1977), 268-284.

[5] Disraeli subtitled *Contarini Fleming* "A Psychological Romance." I use the term in much the same sense he did, and, accordingly, an allegorical romance in this case is a love story whose plot and characters can be seen to embody the struggle of various social, political, and religious values within Victorian society.

[6] "General Preface" to the collected edition of the novels (London: Longmans, 1870); reprinted in *The Bradenham Edition of the Novels and Tales of Benjamin Disraeli, 1st Earl of Beaconsfield,* 12 vols. (London: Peter Davies, 1926-27; New York: Alfred Knopf, 1934), I (*Vivian Grey*), p. x. A more convenient citation is Blake, *Disraeli,* pp. 193-194.

[7] In his speeches in 1839 and 1840 Disraeli criticized the centralization of relief inherent in the New Poor Law, advocating instead the traditional system of local responsibility for the poor. He also voted against a bill advancing money for a police force in Birmingham and he spoke against the harsh sentences given to Chartist leaders convicted of felonies. See Blake, *Disraeli,* pp. 161-162. Disraeli was, in fact, sympathetic to individual Chartists and their grievances without ever endorsing essentially democratic ideas.

[8] For a discussion of Disraeli's political ideas in the 1830s, see Robert O'Kell, "The Psychological Ro-

mance: Disraeli's Early Fiction and Political Apprenticeship" (Ph.D. dissertation, Indiana University, 1974).

[9] The subject of Disraeli's early Toryism and his concept of the "natural aristocracy" is treated in Robert O'Kell, "*The Revolutionary Epick:* Tory Democracy or Radical Gallomania?," *Disraeli Newsletter* 2:1 (Spring, 1977), 24-42.

[10] Benjamin Disraeli, *Sybil: or the Two Nations,* ed. Thom Braun (Harmondsworth: Penguin, 1980), Bk. I, chap. 6, 64; Bk. I, chap. 3, 46.

[11] "Industry" in this context means "the spirit of labour"; see the *Oxford English Dictionary.*

[12] The best previous treatments of religion in *Sybil* are Levine, pp. 107-114, and Schwarz, pp. 111-114.

[13] See the notes by Thom Braun to the Penguin edition of *Sybil,* pp. 505-509, 514-515.

[14] Lilies are often associated with the Virgin Mary and appear symbolically in many paintings of the period. In the Tate Gallery's catalogue of *The Pre-Raphaelites* (London: Penguin, 1984), for example, the notes to Dante Gabriel Rossetti's *Ecce Ancilla Domini!* (1850) read in part: "the dove, symbolising the Holy Spirit, and the lily, with one bud still to break, . . . are the instruments of conception" (p. 73). See Charles Allston Collins's "Convent Thoughts" (1850-51) in the same catalogue: "The inscription at the top of the frame, 'Sicut Lilium,' is from the Song of Solomon 2.2, 'Sicut lilium inter spinas' ('As the lily among thorns'), an image applied frequently to the Virgin Mary" (p. 87).

[15] Disraeli, *Lord George Bentinck: A Political Biography* (London: Colburn, 1852), p. 507. Lord John Russell's motion to remove the Jewish disabilities was made on 16 December 1847. Disraeli's unorthodox views gave consternation to his friends, who preferred to argue the case on the basis of tolerance.

[16] Robert O'Kell, "The Autobiographical Nature of Disraeli's Early Fiction," *Nineteenth Century Fiction* 31 (1976), 253-284.

[17] Not the least curious feature of this development in *Sybil* is the underlying similarity it suggests between Disraeli's ideas on the ideal relation between politics and religion and Gladstone's. Of course, the differences between the two men are many and obvious. While Disraeli's Young England ideas were laced with Byronic recklessness, Gladstone's Tractarian sympathies were well diluted with Evangelical probity. And Disraeli was increasingly estranged from the Conservatism of Sir Robert Peel which Gladstone idolized. Further, Gladstone would have found Disraeli's claims of Hebrew superiority repugnant, even though he shared

the strong sense of continuity in the historical development of Judaic-Christian theology. In light of such comparisons, it is interesting to speculate on what the conception of *Falconet* might have shown about Disraeli's awareness of the similarity. The protagonist, Joseph Toplady Falconet, is clearly a caricature of Gladstone.

[18] Surrogate portraits with both romantic and spiritual associations are also used in *Contarini Fleming* and *Coningsby.*

[19] Brantlinger recognizes that Disraeli puts the theory of Two Nations in the mouth of "a godless Owenite," but sees that as part of a genuine paradox (p. 102). Schwarz also describes the author of the Two Nations concept as Egremont's "amoral, agnostic, and paranoid rival," but concludes that this is merely "a curiosity of *Sybil*" (p. 120).

[20] Bk. III, chap. 4, 202-208. Disraeli's exaggeration of some of the conditions at Willenhall is discussed by Sheila M. Smith in "Willenhall and Wodgate." Thom Braun summarizes her points in *Disraeli the Novelist,* p. 98.

[21] The best previous discussion of social class and irony in *Sybil* is that of Brantlinger, pp. 96-107.

[22] Disraeli's political ideology in the 1830s and 1840s is largely derived from his reading of the works of Henry St. John, Viscount Bolingbroke. For a discussion of the specific influences at work see O'Kell, "The Psychological Romance: Disraeli's Early Fiction and Political Apprenticeship," pp. 307-340.

[23] Disraeli, "Advertisement," to *Sybil,* May 1845 (London: Colburn, 1845).

[24] "General Preface" to the Bradenham edition of the novels, p. xiii. Quoted by Blake, *Disraeli,* pp. 193-194.

[25] After the triumph of Young England at the meeting of the Manchester Athenaeum on 3 October 1844, Disraeli and his wife made an extended round of visits in the north of England to the homes of friends and sympathizers. While visiting the Ferrands at Bingley, Disraeli made a speech which outlines his political ideas at the time he was writing *Sybil:* "We are asked sometimes what we want. We want in the first place to impress upon society that there is such a thing as duty. We don't do that in any spirit of conceit or arrogance; we don't pretend that we are better than others, but we are anxious to do our duty, and, if so, we think we have a right to call on others, whether rich or poor, to do theirs. If that principle of duty had not been lost sight of for the last fifty years, you would never have heard of the classes into which England is divided" (W. F. Monypenny and G. E. Buckle, *The Life of Benjamin Disraeli,* 6 vols. [London: John Murray,

1910-1920], II, 247-248). It is only presumptive evidence that Disraeli had one, not two nations in mind when he began to work on *Sybil,* but in *The Croker Papers* Louis J. Jennings describes the Young Englanders' speeches at the Manchester Athenaeum: "They went to Manchester (in 1844) and attended meetings of the operatives, and Mr. Disraeli showed how strongly he held the opinions which he afterwards developed in 'Sybil, or the New Nation,' as the book was at first called, the sub-title being afterwards changed to 'The Two Nations.'" (Louis J. Jennings, ed., *The Croker Papers: The Correspondence and Diaries of the Late Right Honourable John Wilson Croker,* 3 vols. [London: John Murray, 1884], III, 9). Although *Sybil* was never published with such a sub-title, it fits with the earlier work, *Coningsby: or the New Generation,* and the the later, *Tancred: or the New Crusade.*

Gary Handwerk (essay date 1988)

SOURCE: "Behind *Sybil*'s Veil: Disraeli's Mix of Ideological Messages," *Modern Language Quarterly,* Vol. 49, No. 4, December, 1988, pp. 321-41.

[*In the following essay, Handwerk analyzes Disraeli's rhetorical and political aims in* Sybil, *contending that despite the tension among the various strands of the novel, Disraeli actually put forward a coherent ideology.*]

The status accorded Benjamin Disraeli's fiction has begun to shift significantly of late as critics have started to reestimate the interest and complexity of his novels. Those texts were long considered to be of secondary or merely historical value as novels of ideas whose aesthetic possibilities fell prey to their all-too-blatant (and often idiosyncratic or hazy) polemical political intentions. More recent readings, by critics such as Patrick Brantlinger, Catherine Gallagher, and Rosemarie Bodenheimer, have brought the kind of sophisticated attention to these texts that allows us to recognize the intricate, often ironic ideological structures of Disraeli's narratives.[1]

For most critics, *Sybil* remains the focal text for Disraeli's career and the programmatic centerpiece of his Young England trilogy, despite Robert O'Kell's valid reservation that it may well be his "least typical work."[2] Yet its multiple, even divergent, aims explain its attraction for critics interested in Disraeli's own fictional purposes and the general ideological mechanisms of narrative. Despite the apparent allegorical simplicity of this novel and its many points of connection to Young England's romantic, regressive ideology, we must begin by perceiving that the various narrative layers of *Sybil* do not mesh neatly. Nor are these layers simply inconsistent and mutually contradictory. Instead, they constitute fragments of a general ideological argument whose coherence may be obscured because it moves first on one level and then on another, with no overriding narrative voice to cover the resultant gaps in the logic of any single thread.[3] Only by separating out the force and prospective audience of each thread can we expect to define the full range of ideological purposes that shapes Disraeli's fiction.

My argument ultimately focuses on two ambiguous "hero" figures in *Sybil,* as the basis for the claim that the text's underlying theme is that politics revolves around persons rather than principles, and is more attuned to pragmatic issues of persuasion and power than to abstract political concepts. To set up the framework for that discussion, I begin by distinguishing three textual levels within *Sybil.* The first division is between rhetorical and narrative levels. The former comprises the theoretical and didactic aspects of the novel insofar as they are presented in explicitly argumentative form. Besides the narrator's interpolations on political history and institutions, this level also includes other elements such as minor characters embodying political virtues or vices (a Tadpole or a Taper) as well as the often detachable political set speeches by individual characters. The narrative level, less overtly shaped by the narrator's rhetoric, is composed of the central characters and those plot events relevant to their personal lives, i.e., the dramatic threads of the text. Here, though, a further separation of political plot and domestic plot is helpful, for these two strands do not always move in parallel or even mutually consistent ways. The pursuit of political success and the growth of personal relationships often intersect, to be sure, but not always in complementary ways.

Sybil is an intriguing case for narrative analysis because of the intricate interplay of its textual levels. The progress of its central ideological argument occurs sporadically through direct rhetorical presentation, political events, or personal circumstances, shifting in the course of the novel from one level to another while leaving gaps that can give the reader the impression that the text is finally only inconsistent. Just as a discussion or a speech can displace or advance the narrative situation in subtle or indirect ways (as well as in direct ones), so can events alter the significance of ideas not brought into direct juxtaposition with them. The complex nature of its construction demonstrates that *Sybil* is far more than a simplistic use of allegory to validate doctrine. Exploring this complexity restores to the text its genuine aesthetic interest as a mediator of ideological values and problems.

This critical perspective also fits the Disraeli we know as politician far better than does the image of him as a naïvely self-expressive, technically uneven, uncritically romantic writer.[4] He may well have been a romantic, but only if one understands this term to include those ironic and self-reflective elements that get lost when it becomes a convenient categorizing tag. Admittedly, Disraeli's novels can ill support the programmatic weight that their rhetoric seems to claim for them; that political rhetoric itself often appears overstated, contrived, or simplistic. Yet attributing such structural incongruities to carelessness, superficiality, or personal obsession might cause us to misapprehend the force of the author's cryptically complex rhetorical strategy. *Sybil*'s messages are decidedly mixed, yet for that very reason they reveal more fully the multiple aims of a political novel trying to speak to diverse audiences. If confused or inconsistent at points, the novel is still more likely to betray the Machiavellian parliamentary politician than an aesthetic dilettante or a naïve theorist.

On one level, *Sybil* presents itself as a factual depiction of British society, whose ills Disraeli attributes to the policies of a Whig administration grown administratively mechanical and socially indifferent. More a brief for social change than a precise program of possible reforms, it does nonetheless place that social distress within a causal framework, in which exploitative economic activities such as the destruction of cottages or the tommy system are identified as direct sources of the workers' miseries. Disraeli adds urgency to his call for reform by suggesting that conditions are progressively worsening and that pressures such as population growth are likely to increase tensions within British society.[5]

The criticisms of that society voiced by various characters in the text take on systematic dimensions. Aubrey St. Lys, vicar of Mowbray, attacks the economic system that makes a decent life impossible for underpaid laborers and shatters the family structure. Philip Warner, a displaced weaver, places the blame for his plight directly on the capitalist system:

> "It is that the Capitalist has found a slave that has supplanted the labour and ingenuity of man. Once he was an artisan: at the best, he now only watches machines; and even that occupation slips from his grasp to the woman and the child. The capitalist flourishes, he amasses immense wealth; we sink, lower and lower." (p. 134)

Warner goes on to deduce from the situation a general doctrine of social responsibility: "If a society that has been created by labour suddenly becomes independent of it, that society is bound to maintain the race whose only property is labour, out of the proceeds of that other property, which has not ceased to be productive." Radical words for the novel, especially when endorsed emphatically and repeatedly by the narrator, who states that "power has only one duty: to secure the social welfare of the PEOPLE" (p. 318). Disraeli's desire to create through *Sybil* an awareness of social problems and a will to solve them is indisputable. The

novel's overt subordination of political power to social welfare promises a solution for social ills that is practical as well as theoretical.

Yet for many critics *Sybil*'s resolutions seem problematic or contrived. Scholars have noted the questionable premises behind the use of factual description, as in Disraeli's equation of Wodgate's anarchy with worker self-government.[6] Disraeli is demonstrably unfair to certain ideological positions, such as Stephen Morley's communalism or Walter Gerard's Chartism, and cavalier in his use of various characters, as when he sacrifices Gerard and Marney to the needs of the plot. Yet even though the text seems blatantly manipulative in the service of ideology, any simple coherence among its levels cannot easily be found. The narrative resolution of the political plot not only remains in tension with the rhetorical solution that it seems it should parallel but contradicts aspects of the domestic plot as well. To understand *Sybil,* we must first define its broad purposes within the programmatic Young England trilogy.

In contrast with *Coningsby,* in which the primary concern is political leadership and identifying and training the hero, *Sybil*'s main interest is political legitimacy as reached by a process of consensus. Where *Coningsby* sought to define Young England's ideals theoretically, Disraeli here wants to show how they might be made legitimate for the nation as a whole. The multiple demands on any theory of political legitimacy form the basis of Gallagher's outstanding reading of *Sybil.* Her analysis provides a valuable starting point for any critique of the novel because she seeks to explain the text's contradictions as evidence of the divergent aims of its ideology.[7]

According to Gallagher, Disraeli's text displays a tension between two fundamentally contradictory purposes—one descriptive, the other prescriptive—that finally undercuts the ideological claims of the novel. Disraeli wants to restore a historically legitimate aristocracy, one that would represent the higher traits and purposes of the nation. His narrative description of English society, however, deconstructs precisely those distinctions crucial to such a hierarchical order. The pervasive parallelism between rich and poor, designed to highlight the irresponsibility of the aristocracy, ultimately collapses all difference between the classes. As Gallagher notes, "In *Sybil* both typical aristocrats and workers are not so much representatives of their own classes as ironic representatives of the opposite class" (p. 203).[8] Gallagher further argues that Disraeli's ironic destabilizing of the aristocracy's pretensions through such parallelism and the uncovering of the recent and fraudulent origins of "noble" families finally undermines the hierarchical order completely: "History, therefore, collapses the class differences, showing the fact of an aristocratic title to be fictional and thus meaningless" (p. 205). The rise of every aristocratic clan in *Sybil* is tied to usurpation and plunder: the Greymount-Egremonts, Warren-Fitz-Warenes, even the Duke of Fitz-Aquitaine prove to be recent, illegitimate upstarts. The essential, stable historical origin for aristocratic legitimacy is nowhere to be found.

Gallagher locates the text's fundamental tension between Disraeli's desire for a transcendent realm of political values grounded in symbolic representation (along the lines of Samuel Taylor Coleridge's tautegorical symbols) and his recognition of the inevitable submergence of such symbols in a pattern of ironic representation (Thomas Carlyle's theory of symbols) subject to the displacements of history. She notes that "whenever [Disraeli] begins portraying true political representation, he starts sketching an autonomous political realm, but an autonomous political realm would threaten what Disraeli called the 'territorial constitution,' the very thing that Tory Democracy is designed to perpetuate" (p. 209). Disraeli's commitment to a territorial constitution, necessary for his own parliamentary career, thus entangles his political ideal in ironic instability. It finally renders that ideal unrepresentable, since any concrete locating of political authority would subject it to pervasive and destabilizing historical displacements. The only possible solution would be to step outside of history entirely, as Disraeli does in portraying Sybil. As Gallagher points out, "There is no gap in her between origin and being, fact and value, for she has been displaced from the displacements of history" (p. 214). Raised in a convent, untouched by riot, Sybil provides a prescriptive resolution for Disraeli's text only by negating its sociohistorical analysis. Yet her marriage to Egremont offers only an illusory political option, for it severs the social from the sacred, the historically grounded from the divinely inspired legitimacy of the political order.

Gallagher's analysis of the metaphoric shifts of "representation" demonstrates how suspiciously one must read Disraeli. Yet I would argue that Disraeli's ironies reach even deeper, for his narrative plot ultimately highlights the functional, rhetorical nature of all political abstractions such as "representation." Behind the veil of political theory, Disraeli depicts a Machiavellian political dynamic, whose heroes are not the central, symbolically representative figures of Egremont and Sybil but instead the paired agents Morley and Baptist Hatton. Disraeli's text represents, and itself enacts, the dialectic of persuasion and power that determines the success of any political philosophy. It concedes that historical legitimacy is properly secondary to popular legitimacy, that the former is meaningless unless grounded upon the latter. Hence the novel can abandon history without regret, or more precisely, can personalize and mythologize it. Significantly, Disraeli's prologue portrayal of Victoria's corona-

tion culminates not in an overview of her imperial territories but in the personal relation between queen and people, "a nation nearer her footstool, and which at this moment looks to her with anxiety, with affection, perhaps with hope. . . . Will it be her proud destiny at length to bear relief to suffering millions?" (p. 48). Present acts, or at least present dispositions, matter more than history to Disraeli. Power and property are justified primarily by use, not by origin or length of possession.[9]

Historical questions of origin and lineage matter little to this political outsider, as one can see from his favorable portrayal of Deloraine's rise to the aristocracy (p. 242). Deloraine differs most from other upstart aristocracy, such as the Marneys and the Mowbrays, in what he is likely to do with his acquired power. Disraeli readily satirizes pretensions to ancient lineage unsupported by accomplishments, but his only inherent objection to the *nouveaux riches* is that they are too likely to direct their ambition at narrowly personal or familial ends. Sybil's elevation to (or recovery of) aristocratic status therefore has an emblematic role more than an instrumental one. It follows upon her de facto engagement to Egremont and serves the same sort of mythic function as her parallel to Queen Victoria. The historical legitimacy of her reestablishment counts for far less than the fact that she merits her position. Her representative willingness to transcend class boundaries, born of native sympathy and fostered by Egremont's arguments, makes her worthy of her aristocratic inheritance.

So the domestic plot seems to carry much of the burden of Disraeli's ideological arguments, with the relation of Sybil and Egremont containing allegorically the apparent political core of the text. At this textual level, the normative political act is persuasion. Disraeli wants to convince his readers that persuasion precedes and grounds all questions of representation, for he concedes that legitimacy in the modern era depends essentially upon public opinion. Disraeli sees persuasion as unifying the political theory of the text's rhetorical level and its political plot. His text first asks whether the political system can thus absorb or channel the social forces whose potential for conflict he portrays.

The privileged political action in *Sybil* is speech, in both its public (Parliamentary, mass meeting) and conversational forms. Disraeli seeks above all to defend the effectiveness of discussion as a political mechanism.[10] Virtually every political situation recurs to the issue of establishing channels of communication. To demonstrate the efficacy of speech in resolving conflict, Disraeli both discredits alternative political strategies and shows how serious discussion between classes inevitably produces sympathy and cooperation.

The problem of persuasion is central to the two-nations theme, first articulated by Morley. He argues that there are "two nations; between whom there is no intercourse and no sympathy; who are as ignorant of each other's habits, thoughts, and feelings, as if they were dwellers in different zones, or inhabitants of different planets" (p. 77). Disraeli elsewhere depicts the economic causes of the gap between rich and poor but here has Morley present it as a problem of communication that results from an inevitable mutual ignorance given the lack of regular, direct contact between the classes.[11]

The novel's key plot events test whether the political dialogue that would heal this split can be established. Not only Egremont's stay in disguise as a journalist in Mowbray but the whole Chartist movement becomes an expression of this theme. We see the Chartists most closely in their series of visits to various members of Parliament, whose general indifference and refusal to speak to the delegates bring about the subsequent recourse to violence. The Chartists' list of demands begins with the limited assertion that "all that the people desired was a respectful discussion of their claims" (p. 261). The narrator later elaborates on the purposes pursued by the majority in the first phase of Chartist agitation:

> The National Petition, and the belief that, although its objects would not at present be obtained, yet a solemn and prolonged debate on its prayer would at least hold out to the working-classes the hope, that their rights might from that date rank among the acknowledged subjects of parliamentary discussion, and ultimately, by the force of discussion, be recognised, as other rights of other portions of the people once equally disputed. (p. 330)

This adherence to the principles of discussion and persuasion matters far more than any specific claims, as Disraeli neatly glides past possible differences about just what "rights" might be in question.

Coningsby already had posited the predominance of public opinion, seeing the press as its primary organ. As Coningsby puts it,

> "Opinion is now supreme, and Opinion speaks in print. The representation of the Press is far more complete than the representation of Parliament. Parliamentary representation was the happy device of a ruder age. . . . It is controlled by a system of representation more vigorous and comprehensive; which absorbs its duties and fulfils them more efficiently, and in which discussion is pursued on fairer terms, and often with more depth and information." (8:374-75)

In *Sybil*, Morley is a journalist and Egremont plays the part of one. Gerard dominates as a speaker to popular assemblies; Egremont takes up the same themes in Parliament. Even the Reform Bill, so often disparaged by

Disraeli's narrator, does have the benefit of contributing to the growth of political discussion and consciousness ("It set men a-thinking; it enlarged the horizon of political experience . . . and insensibly it created and prepared a popular intelligence to which one can appeal, no longer helplessly" [p. 36]). Egremont's growth in political awareness and eloquence parallels that of the country as a whole.

Oddly, Disraeli chose to work out the problem of political persuasion not primarily at the rhetorical level of the text but at the level of domestic plot, in the romantic involvement of Sybil and Egremont. The domestic plot revolves around a contest between Egremont and Morley for Sybil's mind.[12] She represents the stake of this political debate, both as an individual and as a symbol of the neutral mass of workers and aristocrats whom Disraeli would like to convince of the efficacy of dialogue. She begins as Morley's adherent, insisting that the gulf between the rich and poor cannot be bridged. She initially conceives the problem in terms of personal ethics, attributing the oppression of the workers to the insensibility of aristocratic families like the Marneys: "Nor do I think there is any other cause for their misery, than the hard hearts of the family that have got the lands" (p. 144). As the cause of economic exploitation lies in moral failure, so does its cure lie in a moral transformation. "I will believe that moral power is irresistible," says Sybil, "or where are we to look for hope?" (p. 197). Agreeing with Morley, her view is not that real social unity could arise—that the gap between the classes might be bridged—but that the rich might at least be made aware of their moral responsibilities. More guilty in mind, they might be less coercive in practice and allow the poor to go their own way, to create the socialist communities that Morley envisages.

Egremont instead insists upon the need to bridge a gap whose origin he locates in the absence of social interaction. As he gradually convinces Sybil, overcoming ignorance seems even to erase the underlying causes of economic exploitation, carefully projected by Disraeli into a distant past:

> She would ascribe . . . the want of sympathy that unquestionably exists between Wealth and Work in England, to mutual ignorance between the classes . . . and though the source of that ignorance was to be sought in antecedent circumstances of violence and oppression, the consequences perhaps had outlived the causes, as customs survive opinions. (p. 338)

Egremont promotes patience, supplemented by an affectionate sympathy that stretches across class lines, as the ideal political virtue for the working classes. Thus prepared, Sybil's accidental visit to Mowbray Castle prompts her symbolic pardon of all those who had disinherited her class. She is said to have "regretted the harsh thoughts that irresistible circumstances had forced her to cherish respecting persons who . . . had apparently many qualities to conciliate and to charm" (p. 471).

Egremont's persuasion of Sybil makes plausible an understanding between the classes; their marriage provides a prophetic evocation of a possible future. Disraeli thus presents the theme of political sympathy in terms of romantic affection. Given that he devotes scant attention to wider political changes, the domestic plot must carry the full weight of the political argument. The marriage has to serve as an index of broader political success, an emblem of political integration. It provides a strictly symbolic resolution similar to that which cuts short the first debate between Egremont, Morley, and Gerard. Sybil's song, emerging from the ruined abbey, harmonizes their class-determined conflict of perspectives and terminates the unresolved discussion as sovereignly as her marriage terminates the text. Critical dissatisfaction with Disraeli stems in part from such evasive, if adroit, shifting of levels at key points of rhetorical stress.

Disraeli's support of persuasion as a means of resolving conflict is undercut not only by this reliance on the symbolic force of the domestic plot but also by contrary currents in the text that undermine its surface commitment to dialogue. In the text's political plot, persuasion is often associated with manipulation and deception and serves as a tool of self-interest.[13] Disraeli's sardonic picture of Peel disseminating contrary interpretations of protectionism to two rival delegations captures this rhetorical duplicity perfectly. As his "gentleman in Downing Street" says, "'frank and explicit' . . . is the right line to take when you wish to conceal your own mind and to confuse the minds of others" (p. 406). It would be wrong to assume that Disraeli is merely satiric here, that he does not intend some measure of admiration for Peel's cunning. Disraeli was well aware of the power of persuasive distortion, as his Young England project of historical reinterpretation illustrates. The crucial question is whether Egremont's full speech can be differentiated from the text's prevalent deceptive discourse.

The novel's rhetoric does seek to ally us with Egremont, but in practical terms his persuasive powers seem singularly ineffectual. Just as Coningsby's wonted heroism spawns no heroic action, so Egremont's oratory has minimal effect. His only convert is Sybil, and even she cannot be convinced by dint of his persuasion alone to marry him or to believe that class lines can be transcended. Elsewhere, as in Parliament, Egremont meets incomprehension. After his pro-Chartist speech, one M.P. sums him up in terms that splendidly illustrate Disraeli's ironic relation to his own text: "I should say [he] made a great impression, though no one knew exactly what

he was after" (p. 328). Egremont's persuasive powers are thus absorbed by the domestic plot. His conversion of Sybil validates at most the possibility of intermittent class contact, not its imminent or widespread realization.

One suspects, finally, that the rhetoric of persuasion has a limited purpose and a particular audience, that it is directed to those masses—middle class and working class alike—outside the inner circles of political decision making. The real motive energies of the political plot lie elsewhere, leaving an ideological remainder that cannot be factored into the neat calculations of the text's overt symbolism. Neither private persuasion nor appeal to public opinion affects the outcome of the text as significantly as do outside events—those unpredictable circumstances that imprint personal destiny and public fortune alike. Such events crucially alter the sum of the text and call for a reshaping of the question of what constitutes political legitimacy.

The novel's first chapter evokes the power of events, there displaced from politics to betting on the upcoming Derby. As for the politician, what matters most here is whether events or the fortune that controls them can be anticipated or shaped by human agency. Disraeli's portrayal of the feverish calculations of aristocratic horsemen is, like so many of his images, strongly ironic. On the one hand, the race is a degraded correlate for political contests such as elections or Parliamentary maneuvering. Yet it also provides a valid analogy, with valuable lessons visible in the parallel. For betting on horses requires knowledge of facts and persons much like that essential for any politician. Egremont's betting errors, born of insufficient knowledge, are recounted in the first two chapters and are juxtaposed in chapter three with the Disraelian history of recent events, in which Wellington's political mistakes are said to derive from a lack of knowledge of the country. The ominous message at the end of the first chapter thereby acquires a deeper symbolic resonance. As the betting proceeds, a flash of lightning and a grumble of thunder remind us how unpredictable natural events can upset the most careful calculations. The thunder echoes the "growl of reform" (p. 27) that will soon rumble in Wellington's slightly deaf ears.

Events, far more than Egremont's words, contribute to Sybil's change of mind. Brantlinger points out how contrived the plot seems in its attempt to provide a moral lesson for Sybil:

> Disraeli weans her from her "moral force" Chartism by showing her just how degraded, ignorant, and violent "the people" can be, giving her doses of revolutionary chaos and of the lower depths in order to teach her that the tenants in the social cellar need governors and not that they need to govern themselves. (p. 15)

The plot does indeed bypass the rhetorical stalemate between Egremont and Morley. Yet this strategy is not simply a contrivance, for it accords with the general narrative logic of a text intent on demonstrating the causal complexity of events, a complexity that finally distances them from the power of persuasion. Sybil learns from experience that moral polarities of good and evil are inadequate to explain the world: "She had seen enough to suspect that the world was a more complicated system than she had preconceived. . . . The characters were more various, the motives more mixed, the [plots] more blended, the elements of each more subtle and diversified, than she had imagined" (p. 337). A useful, even unarguable, lesson in its own terms, but what conclusions does Disraeli draw from it? If moral calculations cannot explain this world's structure, what accounts for the important events of the text?

The political plot initially seems to be driven by the social forces analyzed by the narrator and to parallel his assertions at the rhetorical level. Yet those political forces are curiously emptied out, detached from the historical specificity that would give them substance, and reduced to symbolic abstraction.[14] Disraeli also employs mythic parallels that rival or even undercut the socioeconomic causality by inscribing it within larger cosmological patterns. For example, "Wodgate . . . was a district that in old days had been consecrated to Woden, and which appeared destined through successive ages to retain its heathen character" (p. 187). Finally, Disraeli displaces causality from social forces to individuals, a process that I will analyze more closely after reviewing the structure of the plot.

Sybil's political events in some measure do fit neatly into the logic of persuasion set up at the rhetorical level. The violent, destabilizing events in the narrative, from the early rick burning through the Chartist conspiracy and the miners' rebellion, are in fact unleashed by a refusal to engage in dialogue. Furthermore, their outcomes reinforce the primacy given to persuasion. The text repeatedly enacts the self-destruction inherent in recourse to violence. In *Sybil*'s climactic scene, the uprising of the lower class resolves itself with a fire that incarnates the madness of the event and destroys the rioters: "Whether from heedlessness or from insane intention, for the deed sealed their own doom, the drunken Hell-cats, brandishing their torches, while they rifled the cellars and examined every closet and corner of the offices, had set fire to the lower part of the building" (p. 485). Not only the violent workers' movement but also the individual advocates of force perish in the final conflict, as Bishop Hatton, Marney, and even Gerard are expeditiously removed from the scene.[15] The brutal response of Marney's aristocratic regiment is rebuked just as clearly as is the violent re-

bellion. With force discredited, the field is left by default to the advocates of persuasion.

This conservative repudiation of force seems straightforward, even contrived in the way it denigrates every alternative to persuasion. Yet that surface reading, which the text's rhetoric sustains and reinforces, bypasses much of the intricacy of the novel. For the effect of violence is not exhausted in the apocalyptic conflagration, i.e., at the level of the political plot; the tumultuous events have significant consequences for the domestic plot as well. Chartism and the miners' rebellion bring Sybil and Egremont together, allowing them to defy a separation that social convention, if not their own attitudes, would force upon them. Likewise, these forces make both of them heirs, facilitating their marriage and raising them to positions where their personal alliance could have widespread social results. There is a fairy-tale quality about the story's outcome; the political plot seems to exist for the sake of the domestic plot. Yet even as the domestic plot reabsorbs disturbing social forces, this crossing of levels creates tensions that alter the ideological force of the text's overt rhetoric.

The domestic plot amplifies as well as absorbs the resonances of the political events. Disraeli's persistent parallelism gives wider significance to almost every event in the novel, making the domestic resolution both prophetic and admonitory. Sybil's elevation parallels that of Queen Victoria at the end of Book 1; Egremont's return from the exclusion of a younger son prefigures the return of true conservatism from political exile. This parallelism, however, conceals and evades a residual ambiguity. The means to all of these laudable, promising ends involve, by necessity and not by accident, that same violence and force that the text's rhetoric sought to discredit. The rebellion and riot permit the domestic resolution of Egremont and Sybil's marriage to have the force of a political solution, through Sybil's restoration and inheritance. The text couples a rhetorical renunciation of force with a narrative justification of its consequences. Force brings about the wider reform that persuasion seems unable to achieve. It alone generates change on a basis broader than that of personal affection, for only when restored to ownership of the Mowbray estates could Sybil alter the relation between the governors and the governed.

Behind this anomaly, and behind the surface structures of Disraeli's text, lies the influential force of character. Disraeli evokes this often, as in his explanation of the Wodgate uprising. "But all this had been brought about, as most of the great events of history, by the unexpected and unobserved influence of individual character" (p. 435). This eulogy of individual character creates tensions in the text by undermining the carefully presented analysis of systems, rendering social forces and public rhetoric alike largely irrelevant. Only here, then, can we expect to find a full explanation for *Sybil's* narrative resolutions.[16]

Sybil's restoration remains extremely ambiguous because of this overall context. Her recovery of the Mowbray estates is essential for the theoretical argument; it establishes her historically legitimate claim to social power. Yet Sybil's reestablishment occurs through violence and force—through the planned diversion of the riotous workers to Mowbray Castle, where their violence is fueled in order to enable Morley to steal the document that will prove her claim. However just her restoration, Sybil requires and benefits from force at the same time she remains aloof from it herself. Likewise Baptist Hatton, the ultimate agent behind these events, remains apart from the violence, whereas Morley is killed after seizing the crucial documents, and Dandy Mick, who conveys them to Sybil, is rewarded by Egremont and Sybil for what they have to know was an illegal act. Here, in Disraeli's portrayal of these few, exceptional agents of change, the ambiguities and tensions of *Sybil* find their focus.

The fate of Morley is especially telling, for his views represent the only real political alternative in the novel to Disraeli's pragmatic conservatism. He decries the existence of the "two nations" in Britain, since "it is a community of purpose that constitutes society" (p. 75). Yet his agenda of vague Owenite socialism (though perhaps no vaguer than Disraeli's own vision) is dismissed by Gerard as some "joint-stock felicity" (p. 346). He accepts the division of classes as inevitable, deducing from it the need for the people to have their own leaders and organizations. This communitarian bent marks his sharpest divergence from Disraeli, although they are both in a theoretical sense advocates of moral force and its persuasive powers. If Morley falls short of this ideal in practice, so too does Disraeli in manipulating persons and events to produce a desirable outcome for his text. Morley's opposition to Disraeli's cherished individualist ideology, though, is fundamental. As Morley says, "It is not individual influence that can renovate society; it is some new principle that must reconstruct it. . . . home is isolation; therefore antisocial. What we want is Community" (p. 225).

Disraeli does not explicitly dispute Morley's position. In a novel supposedly of ideas, there is in fact little real debate about principles—no rhetorical confrontation, for example, between Egremont and Morley. Disraeli often settles for a witty retort such as Gerard's response to Morley's attack on the home: "I dare say you are right, Stephen; but I like stretching my feet on my own hearth" (p. 225). Morley is instead discredited through his actions, as he engages in attempted murder, betrayal, blackmail, and encouragement to riot. Not content to rely on logical persua-

sion here, Disraeli exerts his narrative control to undercut Morley's stance as the "votary of Moral Power" (pp. 484-85). The aim is obvious—to discredit political agitation in general while attributing its failure, as in the case of the fire, to the self-destructiveness of the working class. Sybil rebukes Morley in exactly these terms when he tries to force her to marry him as the price for saving her father from arrest: "This is the first time that a child of the people has been so assailed by one of her own class. . . . It is bitter; bitter for me and mine; but for you, pollution" (p. 357). With only this basis, Disraeli's ideological attack flounders. He relies solely on arbitrary, personal failings rather than on necessary political ones to discredit Morley.

Morley actually shifts uneasily between his roles in the different layers of the narrative, as ideological theorist, political agent, and domestic villain. Disraeli never depicts him from the inside so that we might see how, or if, these anomalous parts fit together. Nor are the shifts well prepared narratively. Morley's attack on Egremont and his blackmail attempt spring suddenly and incongruously from the political texture of the novel, as Gothic irruptions of pure evil into a very different kind of text. Yet these personal weaknesses, rooted in an insane jealousy of Egremont and love for Sybil, form the only basis for his political devaluation. Disraeli makes certain Morley will be discredited politically even within the text by making the political plot the means for punishing his undiscovered private crimes. By having Morley use the riot as an occasion to steal the document that can restore Sybil's heritage, Disraeli guarantees that the character will be remembered as the betrayer of moral power.

Morley should not be seen within a one-dimensional ideological framework, however, merely as a victim of Disraeli's narrative despotism. His function and significance for the novel's meaning are broader. Paradoxical and polluted though he may be, he does act as the agent of Sybil's restoration. He succeeds where Gerard does not, where Hatton cannot, where Egremont has no clue at all. Almost alone, he is responsible for the political promise of the end of the novel, for its restoration of legitimacy and sympathetic openness to British politics. Not quite alone, though, for he becomes effective only through his cooperation with Baptist Hatton, an alliance of the working class and aristocracy whose importance for the political plot is much greater than the marriage of Sybil and Egremont. Indeed, behind almost all of the significant events of this text one can glimpse the mysterious, rather neglected figure of Hatton.

To penetrate *Sybil's* rhetorical veil, we must recognize how central Baptist Hatton is to the novel's narrative mechanism and ideological message.[17] His role within the plot corresponds to that of the narrator at the rhetorical level. He is an entrepreneur of status and titles, an unmatched purveyor of social information, a maker of identities. As Morley's journalist friend describes him,

> "He is an heraldic antiquary; a discoverer, inventor, framer, arranger of pedigrees; profound in the mysteries of genealogies; an authority I believe unrivalled in everything that concerns the constitution and elements of the House of Lords; consulted by lawyers, though not professing the law; and startling and alarming the noblest families in the country by claiming the ancient baronies which they have often assumed without authority, for obscure pretenders, many of whom he has succeeded in seating in the parliament of his country." (p. 275)

He is the actual creator of the aristocracy so central to Disraeli's political program, the center of power in this text. Disraeli concerns himself little with the specifics of his trade or with the plausibility of one man possessing such extensive influence; it suffices to paint the existence of one like Hatton.[18] He alone can control social forces, people, fortune itself. "There is a combination for every case," says Hatton, "Ponder and it comes" (p. 400). So speaks the father of circumstance, the master of events.

His characterization includes nothing in the way of scruples. As the narrator puts it, "Hatton always believed that everything desirable must happen if a man had energy and watched circumstances. He had confidence too in the influence of his really insinuating manner, his fine taste, his tender tone, his ready sympathy, all which masked his daring courage and absolute recklessness of means" (p. 429). He, rather than Egremont, confronts Morley with a philosophy opposed to moral-force populism:

> "Now listen, good friend Morley; moral force is a fine thing, especially in speculation, and so is a community of goods, especially when a man has no property, but when you have lived as long as I have, and have tasted of the world's delights, you'll comprehend the rapture of acquisition, and learn that it is generally secured by very coarse means." (pp. 399-400)

To judge by the narrative, Disraeli had lived quite long enough to perceive Hatton's point. In his zeal to aid Sybil, Hatton proposes burglary and then a full-scale riot.

Hatton is the Sidonia figure in *Sybil,* with a few instructive additions about what the use of such mysterious power entails. Hatton resembles his brother, the master of Wodgate, and suggests the value of refined over brute force. When he meets his brother, Hatton does not hesitate to divert, to Sybil's private advantage, the "destruction and rapine" (p. 457) of the rebellion led by his sibling. There is, the text implies, no alternative to force in such cases.

Hatton emerges as a hero of conservatism who channels and controls those forces that might otherwise rend the fabric of society. By providing an alternative target for social violence, he permits its release at the same time he achieves the socially useful end of Sybil's restoration. He can do all of this from behind the scenes. Never implicated in the riot he instigated, he vanishes from the narrative and even from critical interpretations of it, in which his role has been consistently underplayed or ignored. Yet he is motivated by personal reasons; he never considers the political implications of his actions in light of any particular principles. The neatness of the narrative resolution therefore depends on coincidence—the fortuitous combination of his affectionate association with the Gerards and the providential outbreak of social rebellion. It does not respond to political necessity or political philosophy but rather to the requirements and dynamics of the domestic plot. Hence the resolution wobbles beneath the symbolic weight Disraeli attempts to place upon it.

One senses, though, that Hatton's lesson of political pragmatism has not gone unnoticed by Egremont. How else can one explain the latter's cunning in rewarding those leaders who could threaten him personally or politically by recounting the tale of Sybil's document or by stirring up social discontent? The narrator explains:

> Dandy Mick was rewarded for all the dangers he had encountered in the service of Sybil, and what he conceived was the vindication of popular rights. Lord Marney established him in business, and Mick took Devilsdust for a partner. . . . The firm of Radley, Mowbray, and Co. is a rising one; and will probably furnish in time a crop of members of Parliament and peers of the realm. (pp. 489-90)

Egremont's seed has been well sown. These are hardly self-made capitalists, but rather aspirants to a self-sustaining political oligarchy that can absorb the social stresses of heroism or revolution. The message for such real or aspiring leaders is not to trust in the rhetoric of persuasion but to seek out and become allied with those centers of power and influence, like Hatton, that already exist.

To call Disraeli maladroit because of the tension between this message of expediency and the support of persuasion at the rhetorical level would be to underestimate his subtlety and pragmatism. *Sybil*'s success lies in how well the author mixes its messages, in the mingling of a surface insistence on dialogue directed to society at large with a Machiavellian justification of whatever works and a manual for political control. The historical and practical dimensions lacking in Sybil herself are not absent but displaced into the active agency of Hatton. Not quite hero of this political novel, he knows that heroism and persuasion are servants of circumstances that are never quite as accidental as they may appear. That air of accident, however, can be useful, as can the deft concealment of practical politics beneath an ideology of consensus. As the literary embodiment of Disraeli's narrative strategies, Baptist Hatton provides the indispensable key to *Sybil*'s many messages.

Notes

[1] One can date the significant revival in critical interest to the appearance of Robert Blake's outstanding biography, *Disraeli* (New York: St. Martin's Press, 1967), and Richard A. Levine's *Benjamin Disraeli,* Twayne's English Authors, 68 (New York: Twayne, 1968). Both authors, however, generally assume an unmediated connection between man and works that underestimates the ideological complexity of narrative fiction. Levine asserts, for instance, "In his novels, therefore, we can often perceive the ideologically uncompromised Disraeli" (p. 28). Besides ignoring the ironic stance characteristic of Disraeli, this perspective also leads to critical condescension toward the novels' aesthetic flaws that interferes with rigorous examination of their ideological structures. Remarks such as the following, while valid to a certain degree, can too easily deflect critics from significant issues of interpretation: "Modern apologists sometimes ignore [Disraeli's liveliness] in an effort to construct theories of coherence and artistic integrity in his works. The fact remains that Disraeli's writings were often slipshod" (Thom Braun, *Disraeli the Novelist* [London: George Allen & Unwin, 1981], p. 66). Daniel R. Schwarz, *Disraeli's Fiction* (New York: Barnes & Noble, 1979), provides a perceptive analysis of how aesthetic "flaws" contribute even to the literary appeal of Disraeli's fiction.

[2] "Two Nations, or One?: Disraeli's Allegorical Romance," *VS,* 30 (Winter 1987): 211-12. With its stress on religious imagery, the theme of spiritual regeneration, and the romance logic of *Sybil,* O'Kell's article has opened up a further dimension of Disraeli's text but one tangential to my focus here.

[3] Daniel R. Schwarz, "Art and Argument in Disraeli's *Sybil,*" *JNT,* 4 (1974): 19-31, acutely analyzes some such elements in *Sybil.* Although he reads the political message of the novel as more direct and less ironic than I would (as on p. 22), his sense of how narrative devices, such as the juxtaposition of scenes (p. 24), function as rhetorical arguments contains a fundamental insight into how we should read Disraeli, an insight on which most recent critics have relied.

[4] Blake has best captured the theatrical aspect of Disraeli's political persona: "Where Disraeli excelled was in the art of presentation. He was an impresario and an actor manager. He was a superb parliamentarian, one

of the half dozen greatest in our history. He knew how much depends upon impression, style, colour; and how small a part is played in politics by logic, cool reason, calm appraisal of alternatives. . . . [Politicians] know how much of the art of politics lies in concealing behind a facade of rigid adherence to immutable principle those deviations or reversals which events and responsibility so often force upon governments" (p. 764).

[5] The decline of Mistress Carey's fourtunes in the course of the novel provides one instance of this for laborers in Mowbray (*Sybil, or The Two Nations,* The Bradenham Edition of the Novels and Tales of Benjamin Disraeli, 12 vols. [London: Peter Davies, 1926-1927], 9:100, 391, 410; unless otherwise noted, all quotations from Disraeli's works are from this edition). Gerard repudiates the argument that the workers are better off than before, insisting that poverty can be measured only by comparing the contemporary conditions of the rich and poor: "At any rate, the condition of classes must be judged of by the age, and by their relation with each other" (p. 200). Even if the workers' condition had improved in recent years, which he denies, their relative decline would suffice to indict the economic system.

[6] For a detailed study of Disraeli's use of factual material, see Sheila M. Smith, "Willenhall and Wodgate: Disraeli's Use of Blue Book Evidence," *RES,* n.s., 13 (1962): 368-84, and "Blue Books and Victorian Novelists," *RES,* n.s., 21 (1970): 23-40. More probing in its assessment of the ideological consequences of Disraeli's compositional methods is Patrick Brantlinger's "Tory-Radicalism and 'The Two Nations' in Disraeli's *Sybil,*" *VN,* 41 (1972): 13-17.

[7] *The Industrial Reformation of English Fiction* (Chicago: University of Chicago Press, 1985). Brantlinger's article anticipates some of the crucial points made by Gallagher while stressing Disraeli's polemically condescending view of the working class. Rosemarie Bodenheimer, *The Politics of Story in Victorian Social Fiction* (Ithaca: Cornell University Press, 1988), pp. 169-88, sets up a sharp dichotomy between historical continuity and politics (or honest storytelling and false fictions) that I am disinclined to see as characteristic of Disraeli's thought; nonetheless, she presents an insightful reading of the novel. All of these studies have contributed to an increasingly sophisticated understanding of *Sybil* because they take into account the ironic complexity of Disraeli's narrative gestures. My focus on the mechanism of events in the novel (especially those surrounding Morley and Baptist Hatton) rather than on the novel's allcegorical surface shows how Disraeli's philosophy of political pragmatism dominates even the seemingly didactic or doctrinaire layers of the text. Disraeli, that is, had himself already seen through the rhetorical veils

that current critics have begun to demystify but saw therein no reason to discard them.

[8] Disraeli would concede this much, seeing here a cause of Britain's problems. As Gerard says, "[The people] no longer believe in any innate difference between the governing and the governed classes of this country" (p. 264).

[9] Gerard does waver a bit between the notions of inherent property rights and rights justified by use when he describes the dispossession of the Catholic church. He tells Egremont that "you had no right to deprive men of their property, and property moreover which, under their administration, so mainly contributed to the welfare of the community" (p. 75).

[10] In *Endymion,* the hero's father also depends upon this ability for his rise in politics. His demise suggests Disraeli's more prudent reassessment of the notion that it is sufficient in itself for political success (12:9).

[11] The miners who eventually form the backbone of the social uprising similarly attribute their ills to the refusal of the owners to speak to them directly. Master Nixon says that "it's as easy for a miner to speak to a main-master, as it is for me to pick coal with this here clay. Sir, there's a gulf atween 'em. . . . Atween the poor man and the gentleman there never was no connection, and that's the wital mischief of this country" (pp. 167-68).

[12] That neither Sybil nor any other female figure in the novel has an active or public role is typical of Disraeli's restriction of female figures to the private or domestic sphere (to which *Tancred* provides some exceptions). Yet Disraeli sees this arena as significant enough to determine key political actions. In *Endymion,* for example, the important figure is not Lady Firebrace, with her inflated notion of her own political maneuverings, but Endymion's sister, who is the driving force behind his rise to prominence.

[13] Taking a more cynical approach, the young Disraeli links rhetoric to mob appeal, where its effectiveness is seen to be in direct proportion to its incomprehensibility: "But the fact is no people relish eloquence of the highest order so much as the lowest mob. They understand or seem to understand everything. Allusion to History which they have never read, metaphorical expressions drawn from sources of which they have no experience—with all they sympathise," says the narrator in Benjamin and Sarah Disraeli, *A Year at Hartlebury or The Election* (London: John Murray, 1983), p. 114.

[14] For one example among many, the return of Gerard after his arrest for conspiracy leads to a procession whose political significance is wholly caught up in the ritual, ceremonial forms in which it is described: "All hurried, yet spontaneous and certain, indications how mankind, under the influence of high and earnest feelings, recur instantly to ceremony and form" (p. 395). Bodenheimer has valuable comments on many of these parallels (see esp. pp. 174-80).

[15] Although Gerard's death may seem unjustified, in discussions with Morley, with Lord Valentine, and with the Chartist conspirators he has repeatedly shown sympathy for the old-fashioned test of force or arms. So Disraeli does attach some symbolic plausibility to his expeditious removal of a potential obstacle to Sybil's union with Egremont.

[16] William Stafford, "Romantic Elitism in the Thought of Benjamin Disraeli," *L&H,* 6 (1980): 43-58, ably demonstrates how romantic aesthetics contribute to and justify an elitist political doctrine. What he sees as flaws in the novels' heroes (p. 56), however, seem to me to be ideologically functional elements. Disraeli's romantic heroes are already reined in by a pragmatic conservatism and can use the rhetoric of heroism without fully believing or embodying it.

[17] Bodenheimer finds in Morley and Baptist Hatton a double illustration of the general "incompatibility of action and theory" (pp. 183-85). She was the first to recognize the great significance of Hatton's likeness to Disraeli but sees in his behavior (as in the whole relation of the novel to history) an unresolved ideological contradiction. *Sybil* seems to me to gain force when seen as a remarkably frank depiction by Disraeli of the Machiavellian power that he sees behind political forms. Although he is willing to deploy such forms, at the same time he is cognizant of their limits.

[18] Disraeli seems genuinely to have believed in the enormous power wielded by individuals and secret societies. Sidonia, his Machiavellian figure in *Coningsby,* derives his power from just such connections: "To these sources [those subterranean agencies of which the world in general knows so little] he owed that knowledge of strange and hidden things which often startled those who listened to him. . . . The secret history of the world was his pastime" (8:231). In *Sybil,* Disraeli attributes a power to the workers' union apparently as extensive in its sphere as is Hatton's in his, though he never develops the point (p. 256). That he carried this belief into his political practice as well arouses the ire even of the generally approving and restrained Blake: "Presumably Disraeli believed in this farrago, but it can only be regarded by the historian as a sign of his complete failure to understand the realities of Slav nationalism and Turkish misrule" (p. 602).

Daniel Bivona (essay date 1989)

SOURCE: "Disraeli's Political Trilogy and the Antinomic Structure of Imperial Desire," *Novel: A Forum on Fiction,* Vol. 22, No. 3, Spring, 1989, pp. 305-25.

[*In the following essay, Bivona argues that Disraeli's political trilogy was written in order to reinvigorate the Tory party and, particularly, to give him "a forum in which to ally ideological argument with imperial fantasy" through his portrayal of the government's expansion to include the middle and working classes.*]

Recent history provides few examples of successful political careers founded on literary careers. When politicians turn to letters, they usually do so after leaving the political wars to beguile the hours of retirement by constructing overly-detailed, self-aggrandizing memoirs. Benjamin Disraeli's career is unique in this respect. The son of a collector of literary curiosities who was admired by Byron, Disraeli forced his way into "society" and thence into the House of Commons at least partly by cultivating a reputation as a somewhat unscrupulous literary figure. The notoriety which descended on him after he was revealed as the author of the *roman à clef* **Vivian Grey,** much discussed in London in the late 1820s, helped provide him with entrance to important literary and political circles, although it is no doubt also true that the controversial way in which Disraeli's publisher promoted the book (it was "puffed" as the work of an anonymous society insider with access to the highest circles) hurt him by cementing in the minds of some influential people the feeling that he was a ruthless, untrustworthy, "bounder."[1] Nevertheless, one token of Disraeli's modernity is the way he was able throughout his career to use "publicity" of any kind, whether positive or negative, to promote his own interests. Being notorious was for him simply another and sometimes more effective way of being known.

Disraeli continued to write novels throughout his political career, completing his last—*Endymion*—in 1880 after six years of service as prime minister. The publication of the three books of the so-called "political trilogy" of the 1840s coincided roughly with his greatest Parliamentary successes: his defeat of Peel over the Corn Law issue and his subsequent recognition as titular head of the Tory party in the Commons. This "coincidence" of Disraeli's rise to political preeminence and his writing of the three books—*Coningsby, Sybil,* and *Tancred*—by which he is chiefly known as a novelist by posterity, is, I submit, no coincidence at all but rather a demonstration of the importance of Disraeli's novels in positioning him ideologically on certain prominent political questions of the 1840s. To Disraeli, novel-writing was a very expedient act of political ambition which, like the artificially curled hairlock adorning his forehead and the black velvet waistcoat which he wore early in his career, set him visibly apart from the sober landed aristocrats in the Commons to whose ideological beliefs he had pledged public allegiance.

Beyond merely marking his difference, however, his novels, and especially his "political trilogy," were written to establish the "emotional" basis for a new Conservative ideology with which he hoped to reinvigorate the Tory party in the era after the downfall of Peel. The fact that this ideology is logically flawed is not necessarily an argument against its persuasiveness. Most ideologies reveal their fissures when subjected to close examination. What Disraeli accomplished in his trilogy, however, was a wish-fulfilling realignment of political debate: one which resolves, in a fantastically grand imperial synthesis, the pressing domestic social questions about the role of middle and working classes in governing nineteenth-century Britain. In a literary gesture which anticipates the late nineteenth-century stress on imperialism in the politics of Lord Salisbury and Joseph Chamberlain, Disraeli's trilogy, read as a unit, promotes the expansion of England as the inevitable extension of the governing structure of the country to include the middle and working classes. His novels, in short, gave him a forum in which to ally ideological argument with imperial fantasy, and to do so in a way which expediently insulated Disraeli the politician from the full implications of this alignment.

The trilogy develops its imperial metanarrative in a peculiarly Disraelian way. Disraeli conceives of history as structured like a spiral, permitting progress or displacement forward provided it is conceptualized so as to evoke the hallowed past.[2] In the charged political atmosphere of the 1840s, with middle class reformers complaining heatedly that the Whig-inspired Reform Bill of 1832 did not go far enough in enfranchising the middle classes while, in the streets, Chartist mobs were pressing for a widening of the franchise to include the working class, it was becoming clear that a new Tory ideology with staying power would have to address the very insistent call for domestic political change. How to clothe this necessary social change in the garb of ancient English precedent is the ideological project Disraeli sets for himself in the trilogy. Moreover, during a decade when England's "imperial" policy was being fashioned in a decentralized way and for baldly private economic and bureaucratic motives—largely by the East India Company—Disraeli set out, in *Tancred,* to establish a "moral" and emotional justification for imperial expansion which would set the stage for the late century celebration of a more "public" ideal—the "white man's burden." However, there were limits to how far this political "bounder" could push the Conservative squires who were his political allies. Disraeli felt he could only square the idea of the systematic geographical expansion of England with an inherited conservative ideology which privileged "Little England" if he could justify imperialism as an attempt to re-store an ancient unity disrupted in the modern era. In short, as only the trilogy reveals, Disraeli saw the mission to colonize alien cultures as an impera-tive of the same form as the mission to "colonize" the middle and working classes in England. England's duty is defined as one of expanding by appropriating and reshaping the alien to suit its purposes, but it must do so under the guise of restoring an ancient unity. Thus, *Tancred,* the final book of the trilogy, an Orientalist lark which Disraeli prized over all his other novels,[3] is also the logical culmination of the trilogy for it carries the *mission civilisatrice* of *Coningsby* and *Sybil* beyond the domestic sphere into the imperial field of the Middle East. The Middle East which is remade in the imagination of the would-be crusader Tancred de Montacute is dif-ferent in degree but not in kind from the aristo-cratic-dominated utopia which emerges from the ashes of English civilization at the end of *Sybil.*

Disraeli's emphasis on the appropriation of the alien in his trilogy is rooted in a quasi-Hegelian epistemology. In discussing the "aims of knowledge" in his *Logic,* Hegel casts the attempt to appropriate the objective as subjective, to "overcome" the "non-ego," in terms of a kind of "domestication" or "taming" of that which is outside of, and therefore opposed to, the subject. As he argues: "The aim of knowledge is to divest the objec-tive world that stands opposed to us of its strangeness, and, as the phrase is, to find ourselves at home in it: which means no more than to trace the objective world back to the notion—to our innermost self."[4] This re-duces to the idea that cognition—knowing—is really a process of "reappropriation," of discovering the sub-ject in the object, of finding the self in the world, of reducing the strangeness of what is alien to us by uncovering the reality of its familiarity. As Alan Sandison asserts in *The Wheel of Empire:*

> the development of the Romantic antinomy leads to a moral imperialism, by which is meant literally the expansion and aggrandisement of self, where, in the classic Hegelian manner, the subject wages a continuous war of conquest against the alien object. And the principal weapon is the thoroughly Hegelian one of cognition.[5]

This implicitly "imperial" appropriation of the unfa-miliar by the knowing subject receives perhaps its most interesting formulation in English prose in Carlyle's advice to his reader, through Teufelsdröckh, to "Feed" on the "Not-Me" in order to cure the disease of self-consciousness.[6] But it was Nietzsche who was first to note the implicitly "imperialistic" emphasis in this epistemological stance:

> The spirit's power to appropriate the foreign stands revealed in its inclination to assimilate the new to the old, to simplify the manifold, and to overlook or repulse whatever is totally contradictory—just as it involuntarily emphasizes certain features and lines in what is foreign, in every piece of the "external world," retouching and falsifying the whole to suit itself. Its intent in all this is to incorporate new "experiences," to file new things in old files—growth, in a word—or, more precisely, the feeling of growth, the feeling of increased power.[7]

In Nietzsche's terms, Disraeli's novels can be said to be novels of "digestion" and "growth." In a general sense, the three novels of the trilogy are tied together by a common thread with imperial implications: a con-cern with defining or determining something which lies outside the subject and which at least initially repre-sents a threat to the subject, a threat which is only removed when the non-subject's unfamiliar mask is removed and it is discovered always already to have been a part of the subject. The result of this process is a displacement: the unfamiliar is revealed as familiar and the subject "grows" in the Nietzschean sense—sometimes in power, mastery, spiritual awareness, so-cial fulfillment, geographical extension, or the mere "feeling" of mastery. In political terms, the trilogy embodies Disraeli's political metanarrative, charging England with the mission of incorporating first the middle classes into the polity (in *Coningsby*), then the laboring classes (in *Sybil*), and, finally, alien cultures (in *Tancred*). In this respect, *Tancred's* imperial set-ting (in England's "legitimate sphere of influence") is crucial: when the Montacutes arrive in Jerusalem at the end of that book, they complete a cycle of ex-pansive incorporation begun in the first book with Coningsby's symbolic merger of the aristocracy and the manufacturing class. By reuniting the Montacute family in Jerusalem, Disraeli forecasts that England is to become what he would have it "eat."

II

Coningsby, the first book of the trilogy, marks the high point of the influence of the "Young England" movement on Disraeli. The aristocratic hero of the novel is patterned, in a highly inflated way, after George Smythe, a younger colleague of Disraeli's in the "Young England" group in the Commons. Coningsby's even-tual recovery of his lost inheritance, through a round-about route, from his grandfather Lord Monmouth and his eventual marriage to Edith Millbank, is intended to mark both the metaphorical passage of landed wealth from a decadent Regency aristocracy to a youthful but serious and reform-minded Victorian one. More importantly, it marks a symbolic merger of the manufacturing class with the landed aristocracy: a fantasy empowerment here imagined as a taming process which softens and "civilizes" the unpol-ished manners of the middle classes as it appropri-ates their world-historical energies.

However, Disraeli attached to the fifth edition of this book (published in 1849) a seemingly irrelevant preface in which he reminds his English readers of the importance of Asia to Europe. Picking up a theme which at times seems to take an inordinate amount of space in many of his novels (as well as, irrelevantly, in Chapter 24 of his biography of Lord George Bentinck), he argues for the importance of the Jewish origins of the Christian Church. Although a familiar theme with Disraeli, he casts it here in terms intended to shock his readers: "the Church is a sacred corporation for the promulgation and maintenance in Europe of certain Asian principles, which, although local in their birth, are of divine origin, and of universal and eternal application."[8] Leaving aside for the moment the question of its relevance to the thematic material of the novel, one must concede that this passage has a decentering effect on common prejudices: is not Europe the center of Christianity? The term "Asian," one suspects, is deceptive, cloaking a heterogeneity in the guise of a singular entity. Written after the completion of *Tancred* in 1847, this preface suggests a latter day attempt on Disraeli's part to give renewed emphasis to this theme in the trilogy's first book so as to link it more closely to *Sybil* and *Tancred,* especially to the latter book's projection of Judaism as the privileged origin of Christianity—the "mother," if you will, of European civilization.

In this insistence on the Jewish origins of Christianity, both in this preface and in each of the books of the trilogy, Disraeli reveals very clearly an allegiance to "essentialist" notions of race as well as a commitment to a Burkean account of history as that which softens barbarous behavior by reminding men of the truth which lies at the origin. To assert, for instance, that a Jew was the founder of the Christian Churches of Asia is to refuse the common designation of an early Christian as precisely one who has refused Judaism; yet Disraeli insisted throughout his career on the "Jewishness" of the Church fathers. To Disraeli, what is seen as exterior is originally interior and remains so: it is the role of historical knowledge to erase false boundaries, revealing a unity underlying the appearance of diversity.

To argue, as he does, that a knowledge of the past can itself help to reunify what has been dispersed over the course of time—for a reversal of the *Diaspora* is the key to Disraeli's historical imagination—is to run counter to the main impetus of the Romantic notions of history on which he is also relying. For, as Geoffrey Hartman argues, it is the Romantic discovery that a knowledge of history reveals the past existence of "immediate experience" only at the price of barring the subject from ever reexperiencing it. The Romantic is acutely conscious of the gap between subject and object, man and nature, but only his living in this divided world enables him to glimpse the world of immediate experience from which he is barred.[9] What

Disraeli offers, on the other hand, is a wish-fulfilling "restoration" of the object to the subject by a reappropriation of the former by the latter, a dissolving of the barrier which divides them by the revelation that the barrier is ephemeral. In this respect, Sidonia's seemingly authoritative claim in *Tancred,* "All is race," is a disguised oxymoron: the Disraelian notion of "race," while seeming to suggest a principle of differentiation, merely cloaks an underlying sameness, a sameness revealed by a thorough knowledge of history.[10] If one defines history in this light as the serial succession of novelty or difference,[11] one can assert that Disraeli advocates a return to a time before history, before differentiation and dispersal, and advocates it as a lesson which history itself—paradoxically—teaches. The complicated contradictory logic of this position structures all three books of the trilogy, revealing a singular ambivalence at work shaping his views of empire, his racial theories, and his "Tory Democratic" interest in justice for the lower and middle classes.

This contradictory logic of Disraeli's "racial" ideas is precisely what relates Sidonia's "digressions" on the importance of "racial purity" to Jews to the dynastic and sexual themes of *Coningsby.* Coningsby is an orphan (more or less), yet an orphan blessed with a name for which there is already a matching manorial seat—Coningsby Castle, the home of his grandfather Lord Monmouth. His first visit to Coningsby Castle, thus, is already a return, a return underlined by a familiar greeting he is accorded by the servants when he arrives. Yet this "return" merely suggests the key structural pattern of the book: all forays into the unfamiliar are in some sense uncanny returns in this novel. Coningsby's plot is a repetition of his father's in basic form: first embraced and welcomed by the imperious Monmouth, he later alienates his affections and finds himself disinherited. In fact, it is Millbank (Coningsby's eventual "father-in-law," the representative of industrial capitalism in the book) who first explicitly notes the parallels between Coningsby and his natural father when, in rejecting Coningsby's request to marry his daughter Edith, he reminds him that in seeking her hand he would be repeating his father's primal mistake—the error that led to his disinheritance—of choosing a wife from the lower classes. However, the words Millbank uses to warn Coningsby ("You are in the same position as your father; you meditate the same act" [C XIII, 103]) manage to reinforce a suggestion of incest while simultaneously criticizing his planned exogamy. The ambiguity of "same" here reveals the author's hand intruding to taint Edith who, the novel hints, may well be closely related to Coningsby's mysterious Spanish (Sephardic?) mother.

This incest threat is forecast much earlier in a staged love scene at Coningsby Castle between Villebecque and his titular daughter Flora (C XII, 260). Although the suggestion of incest turns out to be misleading (we discover eventually that Monmouth is Flora's real father), the scene does insinuate that it constitutes the pattern for the other love-making in the novel. Thus, when Coningsby notices what seems to be a portrait of his long-dead mother hanging on the wall of the Millbanks' dining room and later discovers the uncanny resemblance between Edith and his mother (as well as both women's unspecified connection with Spain), his pursuit of Edith for a wife is certainly tainted by what appear to be incestuous motives.

That Coningsby would seek a replacement for the missing mother he idealizes, and find her in Edith who resembles her physically, is certainly not an odd plot event in Victorian fiction, given its preoccupation with incest (or the threat of incest), for which a "Freudian" explanation might now account: because one is denied the opportunity of reestablishing an (invented) originary relationship with one's mother, one seeks to master the attendant frustration by establishing a relationship with a new object who resembles her. Thus, marriage is a substitute for life at the breast because of the analogical or metaphorical relationship between the woman one marries and the mother one misses. Leaving aside for a moment the difficulties raised by the fact that the "mother" herself is already a substitute,[12] one ought nevertheless to note that the resolution of the plot in *Coningsby* implicitly acknowledges that actual "restoration" of the "original" is interdicted: in Disraeli, "restoration" requires a displacement in order to achieve legitimacy.

More importantly, however, Disraeli's attempt to incorporate the alien under the guise of the original or familiar, while explicable in terms of psychological motives, also serves a dynastic and political function. Like the authors of the Old Testament who sought to "mediate" between conflicting political demands in constructing their accounts of the disparate origins of Solomon's wives,[13] Disraeli needs to bestow an anomalous origin on Edith to render her eventual marriage to Coningsby as simultaneously endogamous and exogamous: Coningsby needs a wife drawn from his own class on whose values he can count, as well as one from the manufacturing class who can also help to reinvigorate the tired blood of the aristocracy (best exemplified here by the dissolute Lord Monmouth). Like Jane Austen's Fanny Price in *Mansfield Park,* Edith Millbank is an outsider whose attractiveness lies in her paradoxical familiarity. As the daughter of Coningsby's erstwhile father Millbank, the spokesman in this novel for the "essential aristocracy" that is the manufacturing class, her merit is guaranteed, and her brief appearance in *Tancred* (T XV, 131) underlines the fact that she becomes a witty drawing room ornament after marrying Coningsby. But her resemblance to Coningsby's mother and her never fully-explained connection with Sidonia and his privileged site of origin—Spain—also reinforces her dual nature: exotic and "homey," alien and familiar, sexualized and innocent, middle class but also—secretly—aristocratic. Her marriage to Coningsby refounds the Coningsby line as a more inclusive whole, merging the aristocracy and trade, Coningsby and Hellingsley, the "formal" and "essential" aristocracies.

The marriage with Edith, who is associated with a number of heterogeneous historical and psychological elements—the maternal, the Jews of the *Diaspora,* and the English manufacturing class—brings Coningsby (metonymically, "Young England") into anomalous alliance with world-historical forces which, in Disraeli's imagination, are projections of a privileged and fructifying origin. The plot assumes a spiral shape, as Coningsby's pursuit of the seemingly alien—the prohibited Edith—returns him somehow to the familiar and original—to Judaism as the origin of Christianity, and to the mother he never knew. Yet the origin to which he returns inevitably recedes before him as he removes the mask to reveal it as merely a substitute for an anterior point. For instance, the repetitive structure of the plot which enacts this spiralling movement is mirrored in the parallelism of institutions here: Parliament becomes the public school writ large; hence, Coningsby's ascendancy among the Young England group in the Commons late in the book is but the natural fulfillment of the promise of leadership made by his earlier ascendancy at Eton. In fact, his parliamentary cohorts—Oswald Millbank, Buckhurst, and Henry Sydney—are the same figures who lionize him as a public school boy. The narrator even credits Coningsby's school experience, along with his inherent disposition, as the origin of the emotional qualities which stand him in such good stead later in his career; but at the same time he insists that Eton merely substitutes for the primal experience of tenderness that was denied him:

> The sweet sedulousness of a mother's love, a sister's mystical affection, had not cultivated his early susceptibility. No soft pathos of expression had appealed to his childish ear. He was alone, among strangers calmly and coldly kind. It must indeed have been a truly gentle disposition that could have withstood such hard neglect. All that he knew of the power of the softer passions might be found in the fanciful and romantic annals of schoolboy friendship. (C XII, 150)

The "first great separation of life," as Disraeli's narrator disingenuously terms Coningsby's departure from Eton, is already a substitute, a "repetition" of an earlier separation from his mother which the novel takes for granted and which it calls on to motivate his search for his mother in Edith Millbank. No sooner does the narrator identify an origin than he denies that origin's "originality" by marking it as a substitute for one that is always deferred. School here functions like a Derridean "supplement": an experience both primal and secondary simultaneously, both the source of special feelings which later experiences will recall or repeat and a compensation for a missing primal experience; in fact, an event which falls outside the binary logic of absence and presence although it must be recovered within the terms of this logic.[14] Thus, the narrator treats it as both origin and repetition. In fact, origins are never truly originating in Disraeli, whether they are identified with public school values, the maternal, feudal social ties, or the founding principles of the Disraelian brand of "Toryism."

Nevertheless, Coningsby's response to Lord Monmouth's request that he stand for Parliament on the Conservative side underlines Disraeli's need to establish something that is worthy of reverence because grounded in an "original" state of social relations:

> Let me see authority once more honoured; a solemn reverence again the habit of our lives; let me see property acknowledging, as in the old days of faith, that labour is his twin brother, and that the essence of all tenure is the performance of duty; let results such as these be brought about, and let me participate, however feebly, in the great fulfilment, and public life then indeed becomes a noble career, and a seat in Parliament an enviable distinction. (C XIII, 139)

Not surprisingly, the "authority" which Coningsby wishes to see reestablished here is the authority of "history," or rather, of a peculiar romanticized view of the history of the Middle Ages that characterized the political theology of Young England.[15] One could say that Disraeli is essentially attempting to re-legitimize traditional lines of descent and inherited privilege by establishing the need for them to be refounded (or, in Millbank's terms, "earned") by each new generation. As Young England was founded to re-purify and re-monarchize the Tory Party, so Coningsby's inheritance of his grandfather's estate through Flora re-legitimizes an otherwise traditional (albeit roundabout) chain of inheritance: by receiving the estate as an unasked-for-gift from the generous Flora, Coningsby experiences the emotion of gratitude otherwise alien to those who come to riches as a matter of right. Thus, he is placed in a position analogous to that of Eustace Lyle's tenants: suitably humbled by the experience of having received something for which he has not asked and which he has no "right" to expect. The central mythic problem the book sets out to solve then—how to marry bourgeois ambition and talent to aristocratic legitimacy so that the state can prevent revolution and refound itself as a more inclusive, although still hierarchically-organized whole—is merely one form of a more general, implicitly "imperialistic," task: how to incorporate the exterior into the interior while legitimizing that incorporation as the merger of two spheres imagined as always already one.

III

Sybil, or The Two Nations, Disraeli's fictional attempt to come to terms with Chartism and the larger "Condition of England" question, hints in its very title that the problem involved in incorporating the lower classes into the English polity stems from the fact that upper and lower classes are separated by a gulf so wide they can be said to live in different nations. As Stephen Morley tells Egremont early on, the two groups live by completely different social rules:

> Two nations; between whom there is no intercourse and no sympathy; who are as ignorant of each other's habits, thoughts, and feelings, as if they were dwellers in different zones, or inhabitants of different planets; who are formed by a different breeding, are fed by a different food, are ordered by different manners, and are not governed by the same laws.[16]

What this implies is that any reunification of the two "nations" will involve the subjection of one to the other, although the "medievalizing" outlook of Young England, which to a certain extent still shapes Disraeli's political vision at the time of writing this novel, guarantees that that subjection will be imagined as a benevolent one—a new paternalist order much like that of Eustace Lyle's estate, wherein the different and unequal but complementary rights of lord and serf are harmonized. Like the implied new society of which Coningsby forecasts the emergence, the new society that the ending of *Sybil* promises will coalesce out of the ashes of ruined Mowbray Manor will be a society that is still hierarchically organized, still ruled by a landed aristocracy, albeit one which has earned what it has inherited and which has demonstrated through its benevolence its right to preeminent position. *Sybil* sets out initially to demonstrate that England is two nations, only to awaken the reader finally to the same realization as Sybil and Egremont at the end: that the two nations are really one.

Locating the seeds of radical Chartism in the "unjust" Whig-inspired Reform Act of 1832 (just one of countless gestures of partisan ideological positioning in which Disraeli engages through his novels), Disraeli argues that this legislation nevertheless accomplished one good thing: it encouraged men "to pry into the beginnings of some social anomalies, which, they found, were not so ancient as they had been led to believe, and which had their origin in causes very different from what they had been educated to credit" (S XIV, 44). Thus, the task of the hero in *Sybil* becomes to "pry into the beginnings," to apply the corrosive test of historical precedence to the social arrangements of the present so as to determine what is in need of changing. In charging his hero with the task of questioning the "beginnings" of "social anomalies," Disraeli means to establish this medievalized ideal as a center which will ground the process of questioning: henceforth, one questions in order to measure the distance England has fallen from this "community"; that this "community" did once exist is not in question. While this project marks this novel for its radical questioning of the early Victorian social order, Disraeli's attempt to arrest the "questioning" at an arbitrarily chosen point in his idealized Middle Ages reveals the conservative ideologue desperately attempting to sandbag his own radical social criticism, designed to challenge the bases of class privilege in industrial society, before it floods the edifice of landed wealth.[17]

The gesture Disraeli makes to forestall this erosion of authority is as old as conservatism itself: a version of the "Great Chain of Being" mythology which justifies class differentiation and hierarchy within human societies because they recapitulate the hierarchical structure of the cosmos. Despite the "Whiggish" origin of his hero Egremont and the association of his family with the despoilation of the Church in the time of Henry VIII (the historical "crime" to which Disraeli traces the origins of the great Whig fortunes), Egremont, a "second son" of the nobility, is also described as having an affinity with the sixteenth-century monks whose lands were confiscated at that time as well as with the larger "Yeoman" class to which Disraeli assimilates them. Like the monks of old (themselves mainly "second sons" of the aristocracy) and the "squires" of a slightly later time, Egremont is implicitly assigned the task of legitimizing the hierarchization of English social life by demonstrating in his own person that what is wrong with Britain in the nineteenth century is not the fact that it is governed by an aristocracy, but rather, the fact that that aristocracy has wrongheadedly labored for hundreds of years to abolish the mediating class, to reduce English life to the vicious simplicity of master and slaves. As Sybil's father Gerard tells Egremont:

> All agree that the monastics were easy landlords; their rents were low; they granted leases in those days. Their tenants, too, might renew their term before their tenure ran out: so they were men of spirit and property. There were yeomen then, sir: the country was not divided into two classes, masters and slaves; there was some resting-place between luxury and misery. (S XIV, 87)

What Disraeli condemns here is not hierarchy or differentiation but simple division in two: a social organization founded on the distinction between the interior and the exterior, a division which turns the lower classes into a restive alien realm, threatening to social peace and upper class privilege. Thus, the novel promotes social mediation as the principle means of reinforcing the legitimacy of the traditional class structure.[18]

In this respect, Disraeli's representation of the "Saxon" lower classes in *Sybil* is governed by a dual purpose:

they must appear alien because they have been historically marginalized, and, as such, constitute a threat to the aristocratic "interior" of English life;[19] but they must also bear the traces of an "original" inferiority which guarantees that they are always already truly English. Both master and slave need each other for reasons that Nietzsche underscores: mastery is established only in opposition to slavery; the master is "essentially" nothing more than he who subjugates (Nietzsche 215). Thus, the "Norman" aristocracy which Egremont represents is dependent on its opposition to the "Saxon" lower classes for its very self-definition. However, the consequences of this view—one close to the views of the most extreme Chartists in the novel—are insupportable to Disraeli because they would strip away the civilized veneer covering aristocratic authority, revealing it as but the pure exercise of power for its own sake—a consequence that would eventually threaten the exercise of that authority. Thus, in staging a metaphorical marriage of upper and lower classes through the love affair of Sybil and Egremont (although even this is anomalous: as we later discover, Sybil is a dispossessed aristocrat), that is, in having these lovers rise above the Norman/Saxon opposition, Disraeli must land them in a seemingly new but really old mediating class—the yeoman class. There is an unintended irony, then, in Egremont's passionately attempting to dispel the mists of democracy that cloud Sybil's judgment, at one point, by chasing them with some new Disraelian "mists" of his own—the "new generation," implicitly a revival of the yeoman class in Victorian England:

> The people are not strong; the people never can be strong. Their attempts at self-vindication will end only in their suffering and confusion. It is civilisation that has effected, that is effecting, this change. It is that increased knowledge of themselves that teaches the educated their social duties. There is a dayspring in the history of this nation, which perhaps those only who are on the mountain tops can as yet recognise. You deem you are in darkness, and I see a dawn. The new generation of the aristocracy of England are not tyrants, not oppressors, Sybil, as you persist in believing. . . . their hearts are open to the responsibility of their position. But the work that is before them is no holiday-work. It is not the fever of superficial impulse that can remove the deep-fixed barriers of centuries of ignorance and crime. Enough that their sympathies are awakened; time and thought will bring the rest. They are the natural leaders of the people, Sybil; believe me, they are the only ones. (S XIV, 400-401)

The mystifying function of the "new generation" is nowhere better revealed than here. Not only does Egremont reaffirm the Disraelian doctrine of the inevitability of hierarchy but he unequivocally rejects the claim that the activities of the Chartist lower classes can be an actual stimulus to the reformation of English political life. The "new generation" cannot be shaped by the opposition of a "Saxon multitude"; it is self-defined, and will change with its own "increased knowledge of" itself. Although intended to mark a promise that Saxon slavery will soon end, this claim to self-sufficiency of a new master class is enabled only by the crystallization of a new (but really time-worn) opposition—the opposition of "civilization" and "barbarism," which informs the first four lines of Egremont's speech here. Henceforth, the goal of the "new generation" must be to restore the exteriorized "Saxon" multitude to the interior of English political and social life, but such a gesture cannot dispense with the opposition of exterior and interior. Thus, the lower classes must retain a threatening aspect that, in Disraeli's view, justifies the continued hierarchization of classes. The invasion of Mowbray Manor at the close of the novel, then, not only justifies Egremont's "yeoman" rescue as a mission to save civilization from the threat of barbarian hordes (as a parallel to this, Disraeli's depiction of the social hierarchy of "Bishop" Hatton's mob both parodies the English class structure and drives home the ideological point that hierarchy—and rule by either the best or the worst—is a human universal), but it precipitates also a new symbolic "sorting out" of exterior from interior, barbarian from civilized, the truly alien from those who only temporarily appear so, "Bishop" Hatton from Dandy Mick. The storming of Mowbray Manor at the end of the book can thus be seen as a purification rite meant to separate those who were always already truly English from those who are tarred with foreign association. Although the rioters evoke all the home-grown rebellions of English history, from Wat Tyler and the Levellers to the Luddites, this riot is led by a man of undeniably "heathenish" antecedents, which Disraeli signals by describing the burning castles as the "funeral pyre of the children of Woden" (S XV, 184) and having the "Liberator" strut the stage as a grotesque but unmistakable parody of Napoleon returned from Elba.

The book ends with Disraeli's offering a wish-fulfilling resolution to an essentially irresolvable social and psychological contradiction. Egremont's putting the truly unassimilable members of "Bishop" Hatton's mob to the sword metaphorically purifies the lower classes, rendering the remainder fit for assuming their rightful if lowly place in English society—at the cost of his repeating the historical crime by which the usurping Norman crosses the Channel to enslave the original Saxon. And, the marriage which symbolizes the new incorporation of the working classes into the mainstream of English life—the union of Egremont and Sybil—is rendered anomalous by Disraeli's revelation of Sybil's secret aristocratic lineage. The tension which is left unresolved in *Coningsby* between the imperative to incorporate the alien—the exogamous necessity—and the contrary demand for racial and class purity—the

endogamous ideal—remains likewise to fissure *Sybil.* The social critique which Disraeli initiates in *Sybil,* the project of returning to origins to question the foundation of the present, leads Disraeli (unwittingly perhaps) to pursue an origin whose authority recedes before him. Ultimately, the quest to achieve a political synthesis of upper and lower classes under the guise of a restoration of a Medieval moment founders where all such schemes must founder: one cannot both privilege an arbitrary point of origin and, simultaneously, promulgate the doctrine that a knowledge of history will offer knowledge of that origin. Historical precedence is corrosive of all authority; history never offers a center without undermining its centrality.

What becomes clear by the end of *Sybil* is that Disraeli really has nowhere to go but in the direction of further literalization of his romantic historical schemes. Where the ancient Hebrew race serves purely as an analogy for the erection of a vital English aristocracy in *Coningsby, Sybil* traces a nineteenth-century class conflict which is not so much analogous to earlier conflicts as it is the actual fruit of unresolved class tensions persisting from the sixteenth century and earlier. Thus, the notion of Roman Catholicism as completed Judaism, the idea for which the "Norman" vicar Aubrey St. Lys is the spokesman, is introduced to sanctify the role of the Roman Church as the center of a medievalizing dream in *Sybil.*[20] This religious theme which serves a relatively minor novelistic function in *Sybil,* nevertheless links the book with *Tancred* and thus prepares its readers for Tancred's "spiritual" quest to restore "direct" communication with the divine in the only land where such a restoration is said to be possible—the Middle East. Not surprisingly, miscegenation and religio-imperial appropriation become the goals of English aristocratic youth in the final novel of the trilogy. The pursuit of an absolute origin must draw one back, eventually, to the site where history began and to the deed—simultaneously incestuous and exogamous—that lies at the origin of human history, viewed genetically.

IV

Tancred, or The New Crusade, published in 1847, has been described by Phillip Guedalla as the "strangest book ever written on the front bench."[21] Written during the years 1845 and 1846 and thus after Disraeli's successful Parliamentary rebellion against Peel over the Corn Law issue, *Tancred* has been thought by a number of critics to be an attempt by Disraeli to place some distance between himself (now one of the leaders of the Conservative Party) and his former allies in the Young England movement (which had already died an unremarked death anyway). Certainly, Tancred's repudiation of the value of a career in Parliament in favor of adventurer in the Middle East is hardly the kind of sentiment one expects from a leader of the Conservative Party in the Commons. Yet, for all its exotic strangeness, the book's foreign setting and romantic quest make it a comparatively "safe" vehicle for the expression of Disraeli's imperial myth at a crucial point in his career.

Tancred is the mythic culmination of Disraeli's trilogy. By transporting his surprisingly passive aristocratic hero away from his overly-close English family, depositing him in the imperial field of the Middle East, and restoring his family to him at Jerusalem at the end of the narrative, Disraeli once again performs the conjuror's trick of confronting the alien, unmasking it as familar, taming it, and displacing "England" in the process. When the Duke and Duchess of Montacute move to the Middle East, the final step in the process of incorporation and displacement has occurred. Henceforth, for reasons that *Tancred* implies, England's sphere of political operation, its field for the exercise of its aspirations, will be in the East; the thrust of English political energies must be directed outward geographically, even though the literal pursuit of such an enterprise ultimately entails a loss of "racial purity," a gradual erasure of the difference which distinguishes Christian from Jew, aristocrat from commoner, Englishman from foreigner.

Tancred is a Disraelian hero in many ways like Coningsby. He too comes of age at a time when young men of his class were channeled into Parliament, but more forcefully and successfully than Coningsby, he resists that channeling. He meets Sidonia and is impressed with his ideas on the Hebræo-Christian Church, finally adopting him as his most important mentor. However, his plot life does not conform neatly to the model of the progressive spiral. Where Coningsby's plot begins in lack (of home and mother) and ends in his having to accept metaphorical substitutes which are associated with those original objects of desire, Tancred's plot life begins not in lack but in what looks like satisfaction. The Montacutes dote on him. As Disraeli says,

> From the moment of his birth, the very existence of his parents seemed identified with his welfare. The duke and his wife mutually assumed to each other a secondary position, in comparison with that occupied by their offspring. From the hour of his birth to the moment when this history opens, and when he was about to complete his majority, never had such solicitude been lavished on a human being as had been continuously devoted to the life of the young Lord Montacute. (T XV, 22)

Indeed, so solicitous are the parents that they even arrange for Tancred to marry his first cousin Kate—an exact parallel to their own situation, for both the Duke and the Duchess are also first cousins. Moreover, as the Duchess reminds Tancred, this arrangement will involve a virtually painless renunciation on his part: "She is my perfect image, my very self . . . in disposition, as well as face and form" (T XV, 33). Thus,

Disraeli begins the novel by suggesting a psychological situation just the opposite of Coningsby's: Tancred's plot life could be an almost perfect circle—the Oedipal boy who must renounce the mother nevertheless is provided by his parents with a substitute who is virtually identical; marriage is not a painful imposition of difference but a delightful return of the same.

In rejecting both his parents' marriage plans for him and his father's wish that he enter Parliament, Tancred reinforces the novel's suggestion that parents and son have a relationship almost close enough to be called a *ménage à trois:* as he pointedly tells them, "we should for a time separate" (T XV, 63). *Tancred,* in fact, is about the generation of lack out of satisfaction, and thus, provides the key to the imperial metanarrative of the trilogy. To seek a need for Tancred to explore the Middle East one need go no further than to look at his satisfaction: Tancred's motive "exceeds" the alternative of presence and absence, satisfaction and lack.[22] In rejecting his parents' marriage plans for him, Tancred seeks to escape the cyclical return of the same in favor of an irruption into history and the play of difference. That he casts his plans in terms of a repetition of his ancestor's crusade, however, suggests that he must discover an ancient claim of right in the foreign field, that the alien world is assimilable only under the guise of a re-appropriation or re-claiming of what is always already his own, ultimately, that the alien world holds secrets that are at base his own. Like the past that has never been present in *Sybil* (the moment when Church, poor, and nobility were one) the privileged moment of the past which Tancred seeks to repeat—the moment when his crusading ancestor Tancred de Montacute experienced his "direct" communication with God—is, at least initially, intended to function as a center grounding the play of repetitions here. However, it is quickly superseded by two more ancient "moments," the creation and the promised redemption of the human race as revealed in Genesis and the New Testament. As Tancred explains to his startled father:

> When I remember that the Creator, since light sprang out of darkness, has deigned to reveal Himself to His creature only in one land, that in that land He assumed a manly form, and met a human death, I feel persuaded that the country sanctified by such intercourse and such events must be endowed with marvellous and peculiar qualities, which many may not in all ages be competent to penetrate, but which, nevertheless, at all times exercise an irresistible influence upon his destiny. It is these qualities that many times drew Europe to Asia during the middle centuries. Our castle has before this sent forth a De Montacute to Palestine. For three days and three nights he knelt at the tomb of his Redeemer. Six centuries and more have elapsed since that great enterprise. It is time to restore and renovate our communications with the Most High. I, by the Holy hills and sacred groves of Jerusalem, would relieve

my spirit from the bale that bows it down; would lift up my voice to heaven, and ask, What is duty, and what is faith? What ought I to do, and what ought I to believe? (T XV, 70)

Given Disraeli's historical premises, Tancred's pursuit of the historical original draws him necessarily to the Jews, the originary race in Disraeli's myth, and to a "moment" necessarily anterior to the Medieval moment of the Crusades—the beginnings of human history as revealed in Genesis. Tancred's quest ultimately becomes a quest to arrest and recapture, mythically, the original ontogenetic and phylogenetic moments, for these "moments" are called into being by Disraeli's diachronic premises—the dynastic assumption that the beginning of the "line" is the beginning of a history as well as the genetic assumption that human history must have been initiated by an original moment of sexual congress between aboriginal parents. Disraeli's genetic viewpoint presupposes a beginning point to human history, an Adam to fertilize an Eve who is also, somehow, his sister-self. In many ways, one can see this as a recapitulation of Disraeli's already familiar romantic pursuit of the mystery of diversity: how does unity produce diversity or difference? How can the one generate the many? Both of these questions are already implicitly raised by the "supplementary" nature of Tancred's imperial quest: how can satisfaction or repletion generate lack or desire?

Thus, when Tancred experiences his crucial "vision" on Mount Sinai, the incident which energizes his "mission," the angel charges him with restoring a state of unity, a unity of all the gods—necessarily a unity of cultures as well as a collapsing of a chain of metonymies into a "unitary" experience. As the angel informs him:

> The equality of man can only be accomplished by the sovereignty of God. The longing for fraternity can never be satisfied but under the sway of a common father. The relations between Jehovah and his creatures can be neither too numerous nor too near. In the increased distance between God and man have grown up all those developments that have made life mournful. Cease, then, to seek in a vain philosophy the solution of the social problem that perplexes you. Announce the sublime and solacing doctrine of theocratic equality. (T XVI, 158)

This pronouncement forecasts the pattern for Tancred's subsequent adventures: he is to embark on a syncretizing mission that is also an historical and personal return. Hence, when Sheikh Amelek sees him off with the traditional farewell—"There is but one God"—he seals his mission as one to prove the truth of that Arab greeting. The rest of the book will see Tancred sampling, Rasselas-style, the representative cultures of the Middle East, a passage which is really a mythic return through the ages of time back to the absolute

point of historical origin, identified here as a Jewish one. Tancred also undergoes, parallel to this, a concomitant psychological return, capped by his reunion with his family in Jerusalem on the last page of the novel. The impulse, of course, behind this desire to restore a once-existent unity—both a political one and a personal or psychological one; in fact, an attempt to bridge the fissure between the personal and the political—is the dream of restoring "presence," the absolute presence of God to man, the closing of the gap between subject and object, signifier and signified, a gesture which will abolish language, difference, history. However, the dream of restoring "immediate" communication is the dream of abolishing communication. The notion of returning through history to a time before history is itself an anti-historical notion. The fantasy of reunifying the races of humanity in a theologico-imperial synthesis is ultimately a fantasy of abolishing the distinction between ruler and ruled, a distinction which is, nevertheless, held elsewhere by Disraeli to be the necessary precondition for such a reunification. Moreover, the dream of abolishing the interior/exterior dichotomy by uncovering the exterior as always already interior is the dream of obliterating all distinctions, including that between the metaphorical and the literal.

The rest of the novel, then, takes Tancred to three significant places: to the patriarchal "totem feast" of Fakredeen's Canobia, where he enjoys a lordly banquet meant to be read as a recapitulation of his own coming of age in England, described earlier in the novel; to the lost Greek theocratic matriarchy of the Ansarey, where he not only proves his mettle in battle with the Turks but must fight off the sexual temptation of the Queen-goddess to preserve his knightly virginity; and, finally, back to Jerusalem, where he first passes a night of portentous dreams which merge all the important female characters in his life, and then visits Eva the Rose of Sharon in her garden at Bethany to propose marriage to her. Tancred's final adventures trace a familiar if confusing Disraelian pattern that is the expression of his own ambivalent imperial desire.

Returning to a Jerusalem which has now become his home, Tancred passes a night of "agitating dreams": he imagines himself in a Bellamont castle ruled by Fakredeen and, when he "rushed forward to embrace his mother, she assumed the form of the Syrian goddess, and yet the face was the face of Eva" (T XVI, 409). The dream sequence reinforces the repetitive structure of Tancred's plot: not only is Canobia a recapitulation of Bellamont, but, more importantly, the available but undesirable Astarte (the Queen-goddess of the Ansarey) is imaginatively merged with the interdicted but desirable mother as well as with the enigmatic and racially interdicted—although not legally prohibited—Eva. When Tancred "returns" to the "Garden" at Bethany to confront Eva with the full extent of his passion for her, the Sidonian ideal of "desert purity," the practice of which, Tancred claims, is the anomalous key to regeneration, is threatened with suspension in favor of his desire for sexual congress with all women, represented here by the mother of all—Eva. The claim that barrenness and sexual abstinence are the source of fertility, the renunciatory Sidonian ideal which imposes an impossible psychological burden, is implicitly abandoned in Tancred's gesture toward Eva, although Disraeli the author has too great a stake in it to surrender it at this point.

When the Duke and Duchess of Bellamont arrive at Jerusalem, interrupting and suspending for all time the moment when Eva would either have to accept or to reject Tancred's suit in the garden at Bethany, the scene has been set. Tancred's suit for the heart of Eva—the historical original by virtue of her privileged link with the chosen people and a name which marks her as the source of the human race—is interrupted by the arrival of his mother—the psychological original. The once unified "woman," shattered into a number of shards in a primeval *Diaspora,* had been provisionally reconstituted into a momentary psychological whole in Tancred's dream through the momentary suspension of interdictions. However, the abrupt rhetorical jolt that the subsequent announcement of the Bellamonts' arrival engenders (the servant's announcement of their arrival are the last words of the text) is occasioned by the fact that outside of the dream is the reality of fragmentation and interdiction: placing the two women in physical proximity occasions a reversal of the historically "primal scene" with which Disraeli plays—Adam and his "Eva" as (suddenly) children are interrupted in the act by the parents. One could say that the humor introduced by the awkward intrusion of Tancred's parents at just this point springs from the fact that they constitute an unwelcome reminder of the fact that Adam and Eve are not supposed to have parents, that, in other words, to "begin again" is impossible because one cannot discard history in order to renew it.

Disraeli is thus left in a quandary occasioned by his insistence on closing the cycle of Tancred's life by reuniting his parents with him in the East—implicitly, by his attempt to displace England in an East already domesticated and prepared for their arrival and assumption of power. Although the imperial metanarrative of the trilogy, the historical dynamic for which Sidonia is the best spokesman, requires that "England" be displaced in the East to enact the incorporative gesture that will fertilize English civilization with the world historical energies of the privileged Jewish race, the ending of *Tancred* abruptly throws into relief the contradictions which ground such a view through the medium of what has been called Disraeli's "undecidable tone." If miscegenation (and empire) is a gesture of cultural reinvigoration and revitalization—

if the marriage of Eva and Tancred is to inaugurate a theologico-imperial merger of creeds and cultures—then it must take place regardless of the fact that it undermines the very Sidonian ideal of racial purity which is offered to Tancred as a model for the English aristocracy to follow. However, Tancred's suit for Eva's hand is also child's play here—a flirtation with miscegenation, a game of "naughty" children—and this interpretation reinstitutes the Sidonian ideal at the cost of calling the "seriousness" of most of Tancred's adventure into question. That Disraeli is dangling both of these incompatible interpretive possibilities in front of his readers is clear from the abrupt ending and the tone throughout. Disraeli finally offers us the choice of either taking him seriously or treating the novel as a harmless *jeu d'esprit.*

Ultimately, this justly famous "undecidable tone" is but the literary expression of an ambivalent imperial desire which informs all three books of the trilogy. The political implications of such a dual vision must have been clear to Disraeli on some level: thus, the "undecidable tone" and the exotic setting of *Tancred*—ostensibly removing it from any direct relation to the hot political issues being debated in Parliament in the late 1840s—ironically plunge it into the center of what would become a growing argument over England's imperial mission, a debate about to heat up in the deliberations over the "Don Pacifico Affair." As Tancred's Jerusalem dream merges exotic and familiar in a soup which is notable for its suspension of psychological interdictions—domesticating the exotic while sexually charging the familiar and forbidden—so the imperial mission, conceived as a process of reducing the strangeness of the alien by appropriating it to English categories and English political desires, ultimately, subjecting it to the dictates of English political will, runs head-on into the rock of its own incoherence: the East made available for imperial appropriation is inevitably made "too" available, inevitably remodeled on the lines of an original which never was originating but which nevertheless still bears the signs of interdiction—both a spur to desire and a sign of the impossibility of satisfaction and complete assimilation.

While *Tancred*'s lines of literary affiliation run backward to the Oriental Gothic of Beckford and ahead to the Ethnological Romance of such writers as Haggard and Ballantyne, this novel does serve the important literary-political function of locating orientalist fantasy in something resembling an actual Middle East whose politics are being appropriated to English political categories.[23] In that sense, it anticipates Haggard's mythic inflation of "Darkest Africa" into a recumbent, inviting female body awaiting penetration by the phallic hero as imperial adventurer: ethnological fantasy set in an actual geographic locale which is the locus of real British imperial desire in the late nineteenth century.

Moreover, despite its incoherence, *Tancred* as imperial fantasy is surprisingly compelling, at least in part because of Disraeli's translation of the symbology of the Judæo-Christian tradition into an imperial project. The Victorian fans of this tale included, among others, Isabel Arundell, the well-born Evangelical wife of the Victorian explorer "Dirty Dick" Burton, who was apparently quite moved by the tale, so much so that she claimed it inspired her efforts over many years' duration to procure for her husband the British consulship in Damascus.

Ultimately, however, Disraeli wished his readers to see *Tancred* as the culmination of the political trilogy, the work that lends purpose and direction to the whole mythic project. As we have demonstrated, his imperial metanarrative does give the trilogy a direction as a unit, despite the inconsistencies which fissure all three texts. The image of the noble aristocratic crusader, stepping boldly into an alien land to reclaim a legacy and affect a benevolent reunification of world cultures, was a resonant one in the 1840s, the decade of Puseyism, Young England, and the Carlylean Hero. Although Disraeli as political leader paid little attention to political imperialism until much later in his Parliamentary career, when he did come to the issue he put his individual stamp on it by trying to tap romantic impulses he sensed were latent in the middle class ideology of "self-help." In his famous "Crystal Palace" speech of 1872, he seeks to garner middle class support for a more aggressive imperial policy by speaking of the significance of empire to those who wish to see their sons rise in the world. Reversing the Livingstonian "moralistic" perspective on empire, an important ideological framework for middle class perceptions of the imperial project in the 1870s, one which emphasized the selfless use of imperial power to bring the benefits of "Christianity and commerce" to brighten the lives of the heathen,[24] Disraeli in this speech promotes empire not for the benefits it offers the benighted heathen, but for what it holds for the middle class Englishman:

> England will have to decide between national and cosmopolitan principles. This issue is not a mean one. It is whether you will be content to be a comfortable England, modelled and moulded upon continental principles and meeting in due course an inevitable fate, or whether you will be a great country—an imperial country—a country where your sons, when they rise, rise to paramount positions, and obtain not merely the esteem of their countrymen, but command the respect of the world.[25]

One can read out of this not only a traditional aristocratic disdain for a set of values that are purely "commercial" or "self-serving," but also a conjuring into existence of a "higher duty," or at least a "higher significance," that necessarily, so Disraeli implies, attaches itself to actions of world-historical importance. In this respect, the later Disraeli is offering an updated version of the romantic religio-imperial myth which informs *Tancred.* If the rhetorical appeal of this speech lies in its pitch to the "self-help" ideology of the Victorian middle classes, the meaning of empire-building, so he implies, lies beyond the ken of a merely utilitarian code of ethics. There is, in short, something inadequate, something which does not touch the human spirit, in a life dedicated purely to commercial gain, and all the citizens of an imperial country ought to be grateful for the chance to participate in the grand world-historical process which is empire building.

Despite the fact that Disraeli's tenure as Prime Minister in the 1870s was marked more by adroit political management (the purchase of the Suez Canal, the facing down of Bismarck at the Berlin Conference, the propping up of the "Sick Man of Europe") and a lavish show of imperial grandeur (the crowning of Victoria as Empress of India) rather than by much of anything one might trace to an aggressive imperial policy to match the aggressive rhetoric, nevertheless, it is as an ideologist of imperialism that Disraeli left his mark. The influence of the trilogy is to be seen in its linking the improvement of social class relations within England to a project which implies imperial incorporation, for this ideological linkage is perhaps Disraeli's most enduring legacy. It is not by accident that the Prime Minister who was best able to articulate the emotional bases of England's sense of its imperial mission was also the Prime Minister who introduced the first comprehensive social welfare legislation in English history up to that time (1875). Both projects were intended to strengthen Tory support among newly enfranchised voters from the middle and working classes, and it is this political linkage, for which the trilogy was the literary rehearsal, that undergirded later Tory projects to tie together home and empire more closely (for instance, as in Joseph Chamberlain's imperial federation scheme at the turn of the century).

All this is not to make exaggerated claims for the political impact of flawed literary works such as the books of the political trilogy indubitably are. However, all of Disraeli's novels were political acts comparable in form if not in public impact with his public speeches, and one can see in these works the crystallization of a fundamentally imperial ideology which Disraeli was to articulate in a different form later in his career and which was to have an important historical impact. The contradictions which afflict this ideology, moreover, were to remain unresolved and irresolvable for they are the expressions of powerful desires in perpetual conflict.

Notes

[1] As Lord Blake describes its impact: "*Vivian Grey* had an instant *succès de scandale*. It was discussed in

society. There was much speculation about the identity of the characters—and above all about that of the author. Some people were delighted and some furious, but few were bored." Robert Blake, *Disraeli* (London: Eyre and Spottiswoode, 1966), p. 40.

[2] Richard A. Levine, *Benjamin Disraeli* (New York: Twayne, 1968), p. 90.

[3] Levine, p. 114.

[4] Quoted in Alan Sandison, *The Wheel of Empire* (New York: St. Martin's, 1967), p. 57.

[5] Sandison, p. 61.

[6] Thomas Carlyle, *Sartor Resartus* (New York: Doubleday, 1937), p. 170. Certainly Disraeli would have had every opportunity to read Carlyle, although there is no conclusive evidence that he ever did. Cf. Blake, p. 192.

[7] Friedrich Nietzsche, *Beyond Good and Evil,* trans. Walter Kaufmann (New York: Vintage, 1966), p. 160.

[8] Benjamin Disraeli, *Coningsby,* Vols. XII and XIII, *The Works of Benjamin Disraeli, Earl of Beaconsfield* (New York: Walter Dunne, 1904), xvi, hereafter cited as "C."

[9] Geoffrey H. Hartman, "Romanticism and Antiselfconsciousness," in *Romanticism: Points of View,* ed. Robert F. Gleckner and Gerald E. Enscoe, 2nd ed. (Detroit: Wayne State, 1975), p. 290.

[10] Benjamin Disraeli, *Tancred, or The New Crusade,* Vol. XVI, *The Works of Benjamin Disraeli, Earl of Beaconsfield* (New York: Walter Dunne, 1904), p. 191, hereafter cited as "T."

[11] This is essentially what Jeffrey Mehlman does in his book *Revolution and Repetition* (Berkeley: University of California Press, 1977), p. 12, where he argues that repetition collapses history because history is nothing but the "serial ordering of the novel."

[12] See Laplanche's argument here that the mother merely comes to stand for the breast—the favored "partial object" of the infant. Jean Laplanche, *Life and Death in Psychoanalysis,* trans. Jeffrey Mehlman (Baltimore: Johns Hopkins University Press, 1976), p. 20.

[13] Edmund Leach, "The Legitimacy of Solomon," in *Introduction to Structuralism,* ed. Michael Lane (New York: Basic, 1970), p. 252.

[14] For Coningsby, school is both the source or ground of his experience of separation and a recapitulation, a reflection, of an earlier experience. The paradox this creates is part of a more general paradox that besets all

representation conceived in terms of ocular metaphors. As Derrida states it: "In this play of representation, the point of origin becomes ungraspable. There are things, like reflecting pools, and images, an infinite reference from one to the other, but no longer a source, a spring. There is no longer a simple origin. For what is reflected is split *in itself* and not only as an addition to itself of its image. The reflection, the image, the double, splits what it doubles. The origin of the speculation becomes a difference. What can look at itself is not one; and the law of the addition of the origin to its representation, of the thing to its image, is that one plus one makes at least three." Jacques Derrida, *Of Grammatology,* trans. G. Chakravorty Spivak (Baltimore: Johns Hopkins, 1976), pp. 36-37.

[15] See Lord Blake: "Young England was the Oxford Movement translated by Cambridge from religion into politics," a revulsion from "Liberal utilitarianism," Blake, p. 171.

[16] Benjamin Disraeli, *Sybil, or The Two Nations,* Vols. XIV and XV, *The Works of Banjamin Disraeli, Earl of Beaconsfield* (New York: Walter Dunne, 1904), hereafter cited as "S."

[17] Cf. Patrick Brantlinger's argument that *Sybil* is only a "skein of contradictions," not a pattern of "paradoxes" to be resolved by "Young England," in his "Tory Radicalism and 'The Two Nations' in Disraeli's *Sybil,*" *VN* 41 (Spring 1972): 15, hereafter cited as "Brantlinger."

[18] This is essentially what Brantlinger claims when he argues that Disraeli seeks to èstablish the illusory nature of the "two nations" theory by having his protagonists discover the diversity of the class system in England. Brantlinger, p. 16. If there is a difference between us on this point it lies in emphasis: I am emphasizing the way in which Disraeli's mediating classes are not so much "found" in history as they are constructed by his ideological discourse.

[19] Compare Nietzsche's assertion that all "moralities" spring from the opposition of exterior and interior, "we" and "they." The function of the dangerous exteriorized class is to give one a focus for projecting feelings of "power" and "dangerousness." As he argues in *Beyond Good and Evil:* "into evil one's feelings project power and dangerousness, a certain terribleness, subtlety, and strength that does not permit contempt to develop. According to slave morality, those who are 'evil' thus inspire fear; according to master morality it is precisely those who are 'good' that inspire, and wish to inspire, fear, while the 'bad' are felt to be contemptible." Nietzsche, p. 207.

[20] "The Church of Rome is to be respected as the only Hebraeo-Christian Church extant; all other churches established by the Hebrew apostles have disappeared,

but Rome remains; and we must never permit the exaggerated position which it assumed in the middle centuries to make us forget its early and apostolical character, when it was fresh from Palestine, and as it were, fragrant from Paradise." (S XIV, 160). Thus, the Roman Church derives its special privilege from the criterion of historical precedence. The Church is not the original but it helps "complete" the original: it is a metonymical substitute for the "real" thing. As St. Lys argues: "Christianity is completed Judaism, or it is nothing" (S XIV, 161).

21 Quoted in Cecil Roth, *Benjamin Disraeli, Earl of Beaconsfield* (New York: Philosophical Library, 1952), p. 64.

22 Cf. Jacques Derrida, *Margins of Philosophy,* trans. Alan Bass (Chicago: University of Chicago Press, 1982), p. 20.

23 Edward Said says of *Tancred* that it is "not merely an Oriental lark but an exercise in the astute political management of actual forces on actual territories." *Orientalism* (New York: Vintage, 1979), p. 169. While one might wish to temper such a claim with the reminder that Tancred is mired in a Middle East of a peculiarly Disraelian sort, nevertheless, Said does imply that *Tancred* is imperial fantasy of a new type: one in which the machinery of romantic fantasy (angels, and so forth) is grafted onto the verisimilitude of the political novel. Fakredeen's manipulation of the various Lebanese factions which constitute his political base would not be out of place on the pages of *Coningsby,* although Disraeli achieves this "political" verisimilitude only by assimilating Lebanese politics to English Parliamentary politics—a rather long leap indeed.

24 A.P. Thornton, *The Imperial Idea and Its Enemies* (London: Macmillan, 1959), p. 15.

25 Benjamin Disraeli, "Crystal Palace Speech" (June 24, 1872), in *Selected Speeches,* ed. T.E. Kebbel (London: Longmans, 1882), p. 534. As Thornton argues, Disraeli as political leader was best not as an imperial leader but as an imperial ideologist, a florid speaker who could evoke unblushingly the "majesty of power" in terms that contained just the right "admixture of Romance and Reality." Thornton, p. xiii.

John Vincent (essay date 1990)

SOURCE: "The Earlier Writings" in *Disraeli,* Oxford University Press, 1990, pp. 57-80.

[*In this excerpt, Vincent surveys Disraeli's early novels, concluding that they have little literary value.*]

Disraeli's novels have never lacked intelligent, if unlikely, admirers, The great Victorian critic Sir Leslie

Stephen, inventor of muscular atheism, warmly approved. The equally austere Dr Leavis, in the least damnatory footnote in *The Great Tradition,* singled out Disraeli as a supreme intelligence. In youth, Disraeli was saluted by Heine; in age, Henry James wrote in his defence. The reviewer and Labour leader Michael Foot (who called his dog Dizzy) has argued brilliantly that Disraeli's novels were a magnificent denunciation of the cold, dull, purposeless, unimaginative Tory world. Only Trollope, a Liberal and a keen partisan of Thackeray (so maliciously attacked in *Endymion*), jealously denounced Disraeli's novels as flashy frippery.

Yet Disraeli wrote much trash, and much of his trash is bad trash: that is, it fails even to entertain or to give passing pleasure. His later works all succeed, or succeed in patches, but they are in the minority: *Coningsby* (1844), *Sybil* (1845), *Tancred* (1847), *Lord George Bentinck* (1852), *Lothair* (1870), and *Endymion* (1880), all written in the intervals of a busy political career. Even here there is much unevenness, a readiness to revert to type when pressed for time or when bored. The latter part of *Tancred* is inconsequential, religiose, and, as a story, absurd; the second part of *Lothair* is a ludicrous melodrama-cum-travelogue which fits ill with the acute social comedy of the first part. Disraeli never relinquished his gift for absurdity and bathos, for mixing incompatible genres within one cover. But it is the early works, now very much the preserve of Disraeli enthusiasts and hobbyists, which neither could nor should be revived. Their biographical, psychological, and political interest is considerable; as literature, they are slight.

Disraeli published sixteen titles before his Young England phase: that is, his seventeenth book was his first good one. There were reasons for this, quite apart from youth, haste, and financial pressure. Two books were co-authored: *Gallomania* (1832) and *Hartlebury* (1834). Two were in verse: *The Revolutionary Epick* (1834) and *Count Alarcos* (1839), both bad of their kind. None, save *The Wondrous Tale of Alroy* (1833), had the Jewish motif that was to become so remarkable once Sidonia had made his first appearance in *Coningsby. Henrietta Temple* (1837) and *Venetia* (1837) were, as romantic novels, moderately good of their kind, but their pretensions were romantic, not intellectual or social. *Gallomania* (1832), the *Vindication* (1836), the *Letters of Runnymede* (1836), and the ephemera posthumously published as *Whigs and Whiggism* were political works, looking forward at times to the Young England Toryism of the next decade, but defaced by immediate polemical purpose, often of the crudest kind. Throughout these earlier writings religion is nowhere a preoccupation, and social questions are conspicuously absent. (A possible exception is the anti-utilitarianism of the skit *Popanilla*

(1828) and of the semi-philosophic *Vindication.*) Sometimes, as with *The Young Duke* (1831), Disraeli's motive in writing was narrowly financial: literary prostitution, as he called it. Had Disraeli written none of these works, his reputation would stand higher today.

Vivian Grey (1826-7) is a young man's book. In its hopes, its gaucheries, its despairs, it is perhaps the youngest young man's book ever to attain wide fame. It is an account of society—high society and high politics—by an untutored middle-class town boy who had never experienced either. Despite that, it took society by storm; even after its early exposure, it attracted readers and was for a long time the book by which Disraeli was best known. Its very audacity breathes genius. From internal evidence, the great scholar Lucien Wolf suggests that its 80,000 words were written in about three weeks: an amazing feat. 'As hot and hurried a sketch as ever yet was penned', is how Disraeli describes it (*VG* i.236). Its story is as fascinated and half-horrified a self-exposure as any in romantic literature.

Vivian Grey, who outwardly resembles Disraeli at 21, finds out early that he is of no common clay. 'Mankind, then, is my great game.' (*VG* i. 26.) As his all-wise father, a tender portrait of Isaac D'Israeli, observes: 'Vivian, you are a juggler' (*VG* i. 182). Vivian's flair for manipulation encounters a corrupt adult world: he was 'a young and tender plant in a moral hot-house. His character was developing itself too soon.' (*VG* i. 24.) School barely over, he conquers society; but finding that he 'had all the desires of a matured mind—of an experienced man, but without maturity and experience', his thoughts turn to power. Encountering a *passé* statesman, the Marquess of Carabas, he persuades him and others in the great world that England sighs for a Carabas party—with Vivian Grey making the arrangements. With callous dexterity and supreme contempt for those he manipulates, Vivian Grey assembles a great national party, only to find it fall apart amid bitter recriminations. The story ought to end here, with Vivian Grey a ruined boy. It ought to, but unfortunately it does not. It continues for several hundred pages, with Vivian Grey, now penitent, wandering misanthropically round the Rhineland. This sequel is so entirely different in mood and style, not to say merit, that mankind has universally disregarded the second volume. It contains crumbs of evidence about Disraeli's state of mind; but it is not talented, and therefore it is not Disraelian.

Too much attention has always been focused on the circumstances surrounding the publication of *Vivian Grey,* and too little on its contents. The book, not the background, is the thing; and though he disavowed it as early as 1829 as a 'juvenile indiscretion', Disraeli's portrait of the superficiality of the high society he had never entered showed the power to create a coherent imaginary world. At 21, Disraeli had decided that the

eminent and established were to be seen through. With few exceptions, he never changed his opinion.

But *Vivian Grey* was not a work of self-glorification. On the contrary, it was the record of the humbling of 'early vices and early follies'; it was, as Lucien Wolf writes, 'a retrospect, not an anticipation'. Grey is built up in order that he be knocked down. Above all, Disraeli is *not* Vivian Grey. As Wolf says: 'there is a narrator as well as a hero, and the philosophy of one is not the philosophy of the other' (*VG* i, p. xxxvii). 'Of the vices of Vivian Grey', writes Disraeli, 'no one is perhaps more sensible than their author.' (ibid.) The novelist of 1826 was looking back in remorse on the unlucky adventurer of 1825. That was the year in which Disraeli had tried to effect a great combination among his elders; but it was a middle-class affair, an attempt to induce the great publisher John Murray, who is Carabas, to set up a new daily paper. It is a long story, and still by no means a clear one; but nobody doubts that *Vivian Grey* is disguised autobiography, the record of hopeless, and probably final, failure. 'I have seen too much of politics', says Vivian Grey, 'ever to want to meddle with them again.' (*VG* ii. 89.) For the 'literary vices' of the novel, which indeed at points resembled Daisy Ashford's *The Young Visiters*, Disraeli apologized; but, he added, 'there is nothing written in it of which I am morally ashamed', meaning that it was a salutary tale—as indeed it is.

Two incidental points may be noticed. In Stapylton Toad, the forerunner of the immortal Tadpole in *Coningsby,* we see Disraeli's genius for creating minor characters. The unlovable Toad, moreover, anticipates Disraeli's own role in 1846 of being a hired gun in the defence of the Corn Laws: all in the way of business, of course. Also worth noting is the Tristram Shandyish chapter, 'The Development of the Plot' (*VG* i. 201-6), where Disraeli writes, and writes well, about the composition of *Vivian Grey,* mimicking in his sentences the actual discontinuities and interruptions in an author's thought. This reminds us that Disraeli, even in his first novel, was not just a fluent and intense writer, but also an experimental one, interested in redrawing the boundaries of literary genre.

Was *Vivian Grey* the production of a charlatan or of a boy? The question is idle. His portrait of political nature was right in its essentials, wrong in the inessentials. The charlatanism was only skin-deep. Vanity, egotism, the wish for attention; in all these, he demonstrated, the senate resembled the nursery. This great truth had not previously been set out with such uncompromising force in a political novel. *Vivian Grey* is no youthful error; it lays the ground for all that follows. And it is fun.

Popanilla (1828), a product of Disraeli's years of nervous breakdown, is a quaint, disrespectful, semi-radical, not very funny or biting satire on British society. For literary models, it used Voltaire's *Candide,* Johnson's *Rasselas,* and Thomas Love Peacock's recent novels of philosophic comedy: all hard acts to follow. The hero, Popanilla, a handsome youth, 'the delight of society and the especial favourite of the women', lived happily on a hedonistic tropical isle until stirred to rationality by the chance shipwreck of some utilitarian tracts. Roused to seriousness, he travelled to Vraibleusia (Britain), a country whose motto is 'something will turn up'. There he looks at national institutions (currency, law, trade, aristocracy) through utilitarian spectacles.

Utility itself is Disraeli's main object of ridicule, but there are others: in particular the Corn Laws. One conceit relates to a monopolist proprietor whose acres produced the only corn of the country, and who made the islanders purchase only from him: he 'swore it was the constitution of the country . . . He then clearly proved to them that, if ever they had the imprudence to change any of their old laws, they would necessarily never have more than one meal a day as long as they lived. Finally he recalled to their recollection that he made the island what it was . . . ' (*P* 410-11). Such a mockery of the stock protectionist arguments made Disraeli the first literary Cobdenite—the more so as the anti-protectionism first hinted at in *Vivian Grey* was to appear in stronger form in *Coningsby* and *Sybil.* In another passage a 'total revolution was occasioned by the prohibition of foreign pineapples. What an argument in favour of free trade!' (*P* 469). *Popanilla* is too long for a skit, too lacking in direction for a satire. It is a readable, boyish experiment which offers only a few clues to the invention of the Tory Disraeli.

The Young Duke (1831) was a novel of fashionable life, written, with tongue in cheek, to provide funds for Disraeli's Mediterranean travels of 1830-1: 'I fear I must hack for it. A literary prostitute I have never yet been . . . '; 'I am confident that it will complete the corruption of the public taste.' Disraeli disliked it in retrospect, and regretted having written it. He drastically expurgated it in the 1853 edition of his works, and in his General Preface of 1870 he mentions it not at all. In this he was almost, but not quite, right. *The Young Duke* is a mechanical production, a typical 'silver fork' novel produced almost to a formula. As a whole, the best case that can be made for it is that it is enjoyable light reading.

This was inevitable. Disraeli at this time knew neither high society nor women; the novel was about little else, and Disraeli had nothing to say about either. 'What does Ben know about Dukes?', asked his father. It was a fair question to ask about an unemployed middle-class youth in his third year of nervous breakdown. But intelligence will out—even though writing with the express intention of not being himself, and of distancing

himself and his hero from the creed of the amoral superboy celebrated in *Vivian Grey* (his subtitle is *A Moral Tale, though Gay*). Disraeli did not entirely confine himself to 'the fleeting manners of a somewhat frivolous age'. 'Let me die eating ortolans to the sound of soft music!' (*YD* 33.) This recalls Sydney Smith's undatable remark about heaven being eating pâté de foie gras to the sound of trumpets. Who, if anyone, plagiarized whom? We do not know. Radicals seized on this view of life, characteristic of much of *The Young Duke,* as sybaritic, 'très snob', and void of meaning. In fact, it was a search for meaning, for redemption by intensity; as Disraeli continues: 'At no time of his life had the Duke felt existence so intense.' From Disraeli's dandyism to the solemn aestheticism of Baudelaire and Pater is no long step.

Only in the final stages of *The Young Duke* does Disraeli turn to flexing his literary muscles. He gives us fleeting sketches of statesmen, including a disdainful one of Peel (*YD* 287). We see a prototype of George Eliot's Mrs Poyser (*YD* 270-2), a forerunner of Dickens's Mr Gradgrind (*YD* 289-97), and even a cockney soldier from India on the Kipling model (*YD* 293-6). As in *Popanilla,* the utilitarians are mocked, no doubt echoing Thomas Love Peacock, master of the genre; but it reminds us that Disraeli was anti-utilitarian long before he was a party Tory.

Disraeli's own Byronic unhappiness at this time breaks through in passages of unusual feeling:

> For genius to be conscious that its supernatural energies might die away without creating their miracles: can the wheel or the rack rival the tortures of such a suspicion? . . . View the obscure Napoleon starving in the streets of Paris! What was St. Helena to the bitterness of such existence? (*YD* 82)

> Bitter are hope deferred, and self-reproach, and power unrecognised . . . But bitterer far than this, than these, than all, is waking from our first delusion! For then we first feel the nothingness of self: that hell of sanguine spirits. All is dreary, blank and cold. (*YD* 117-18)

Disraeli, as *The Young Duke* shows, could have turned his pen to demotic social comedy, or analysed the nature of depression; but there was no demand for a Dickens, so he did the market's bidding.

Contarini Fleming, A Psychological Romance (1832) invites peremptory judgement. As psychology it lives; as romance it is insipid; as autobiography, tantalizing. Where childhood, youth, and family are concerned it is intense; where passion or the ways of man are involved it is a pot-boiler. Yet Heine, no mean critic, praised it warmly. Disraeli certainly intended it as a serious contribution to literature, and for that reason it is perhaps the best of his early works. Or would have been, had he not fallen foul of the grim requirement to fill three volumes, as publishers then demanded. Even Disraeli could not make examination of his own ego extend beyond two volumes, and so the novel collapses in the last hundred pages. It ceases to be a novel, and becomes a Mediterranean travelogue instead. ('The Spanish women are very interesting'.) Of Switzerland we learn, 'there is something magical in the mountain air' (*CF* 192-5); of a Turkish bath, that it is the most delightful thing in the world (*CF* 245). Commonplaces indeed! Albania, Athens, Jerusalem, Venice, Spain—Disraeli unblushingly retraced his recent tour, and locality did duty for character.

Disraeli's inimitable gift for bathos emerged in the ending. His hero, having seen and suffered all, retires to the Bay of Naples to build a 'Saracenic' palace for his art treasures, with a sphinx at each end of the terrace, and a tower 150 feet high. 'This tower I shall dedicate to the Future, and I intend that it shall be my tomb.' Disraeli was not good at endings. That apart, **Contarini Fleming** (first published anonymously) is about the development of the poetic character, the growth of identity in youth, the 'individual experience of self-formation'—a theme central to Disraeli's early work. By poetic character we should not understand just the character of a man who writes poetry: the poet is the man with an intellectual and political vocation. The discovery of vocation, often miscalled ambition, in youth is what still resounds in **Contarini Fleming**.

The novel takes place as much within the self as outside it, hence the necessity for an autobiographical form. 'In the earlier stages . . . the self-discoverer seemed an indispensable agent. What narrative by a third person could sufficiently paint the melancholy and brooding childhood, the first indications of the predisposition, the growing consciousness of power, the reveries, the loneliness, the doubts, the moody misery, the ignorance of art, the failures, the despair?' (*CF*, p. vi.) The story is simple. Young Contarini, son of a Swedish nobleman and Foreign Secretary, grows up in his northern land, uneasily aware that his true nature comes from his mother, the daughter of a great Venetian family, who died at his birth. He felt alien: 'I knew not why, but I was unhappy.' He felt remote from his stepmother and his two stepbrothers: 'There was no similitude between us.' Race played a part in this: the stepbrothers were 'my white brethren'.

As in **Venetia**, it is the mother-son relationship which queers the pitch, and from which all else arises. 'She was cold and I was repulsive' (*CF* 6). He develops 'a loathing for the government of women', and 'a contempt for the chatter of women' (*CF* 8, 16). Only when fleeing to his father's embrace did matters improve:

'For the first time in my life I felt happy, because, for the first time in my life, I felt loved' (*CF* 7). From disinheritance came depression:

> I know not how it was, but the fit came upon me in an instant, and often when least counted on. A star, a sunset, a tree, a note of music, the sound of the wind, a fair face flitting by me in unknown beauty, and I was lost. All seemed vapid, dull, spiritless, and flat. Life had no object and no beauty; and I slunk to some solitary corner, where I was content to lie down and die. These were moments of agony . . . At last I had such a lengthened fit that it attracted universal attention. I would scarcely move, or speak, or eat for days. . . . Now that I can analyse my past feelings, these dark humours arose only from the want of being loved. (*CF* 18)

At school he remained the outsider. For a time the passion of schoolboy friendship, described in a classic passage, absorbed his mind: 'I lavished upon him all the fanciful love that I had long stored up' (*CF* 26). Then his father 'talked to me for an unusual time upon the subject of school friendships, and his conversation, which was rare, made an impression' (*CF* 32). The objection was that Contarini's friend was a bumpkin. Contarini dropped his friend, provoking the anger of his school, and ran away, another episode paralleled in **Venetia**. Thus does Contarini explain himself at the end of his school life: 'But I have ever been unhappy, because I am perplexed about myself. I feel that I am not like other persons . . . ' (*CF* 52).

From early deprivation grew his passion to excel, whether in literature or in politics. At school 'I perceived only beings I was determined to control.' Later 'I entertained . . . a deep conviction that life must be intolerable unless I were the greatest of men' (*CF* 29). At 18 or so, told by his wise and loving father that 'with words we govern men', Contarini still harks back to early sorrows: 'I am always unhappy . . . There is no one who loves me . . . Life is intolerable to me, and I wish to die . . . What is the Baroness to me? Always this wretched nursery view of life, always considered an insignificant, unmeaning child!' (*CF* 102-3). Thereafter Contarini's adventures lose inner content. He goes to university, wins a learned prize, discovers Voltaire, founds a Secret Union for the Amelioration of Society, and absconds to form a robber band. Then, despite 'my natural impatience of control and hatred of responsibility', he returns to act as private secretary to his father, to write a satirical novel (**Vivian Grey**), states that 'Fame, although not posthumous fame, is necessary to my felicity', and runs off, inconsequentially, to Venice, a tragic marriage, and some even more inconsequential Mediterranean travels.

Some Disraelian crumbs may be noted. 'There is no character in the world higher bred than a Turk of rank', he wrote (*CF* 320). He formulated a revolutionary system of poetics based on his objection to poetry being 'natural feelings in unnatural language' (*CF* 269-71). And he recalls that 'when a boy . . . I believed I had a predisposition for conspiracies' (*CF* 208). Three passages stand out as having a meaning that extends beyond the pages of the novel: 'Truly may I say that on the plains of Syria I parted for ever with my ambition. The calm enjoyment of existence appeared to me, as it now does, the highest attainable felicity . . . ' (*CF* 343). Then come two political texts which could have fallen from the lips of a congenital radical: 'Bitter jest, that the most civilised portion of the globe should be considered incapable of self-government! When I examine the state of European society with the unimpassioned spirit which the philosopher can alone command, I perceive that it is in a state of transition from feudal to federal principles' (*CF* 372). Whatever that meant, it was not traditional Toryism.

> Yet if I am to be remembered, let me be remembered as one who, in a sad night of gloomy ignorance and savage bigotry was prescient of the flaming morning-break of bright philosophy, as one who deeply sympathises with his fellow-men, and felt a proud and profound conviction of their perfectibility; as one who devoted himself to the amelioration of his kind, by the destruction of error and the propagation of truth. (*CF* 373)

Behind the literary flourishes, Disraeli is saying that he is a reformer, a man of 1832; as indeed he was (and as Gladstone was not). Disraeli the Tory hero is hard to find in the self-absorbed romanticism of *Contarini Fleming;* while the Disraeli who, in his diary, claimed to have 'a revolutionary mind' is fitfully present, restrained only by an almost undue reverence for an idealized father.

But there is a twist in the tail. Consider the novel as a whole, especially the early parts. If politics start in the struggles of the nursery; if the nursery is the most intense part of life; if life is an aesthetic exercise in self-realization and self-creation; if all is subjectivity—then what becomes of the Enlightenment values of rational liberalism? *Contarini Fleming* was far ahead of its time not exactly in its politics, but in its portrayal of the way politics can grow out of a son's hatred for his mother. No other novelist before Lawrence attempted such a theme.

Most modern critics, writes Lord Blake, would attribute no merit whatever to *The Wondrous Tale of Alroy* (1833), 'which is written in a deplorable sort of prose-poetry and is perhaps the most unreadable of his romances' (B 108). Schwarz calls *Alroy* 'Disraeli's ultimate heroic fantasy' (Schw. 42); important for the author, though less so for his readers, because the book was not as unsuccessful as its predecessor *Contarini*

Fleming, earning Disraeli £300 against *Fleming*'s £18. It proved, however, that Disraeli was never likely to be a popular success again so long as he said what he thought or wrote in the way he wanted. The public did not want Disraeli neat; *Alroy* was a landmark in the retreat towards the conventional story-telling of *Henrietta Temple* and *Venetia.*

At first sight, *Alroy* is poor man's Sir Walter Scott, with a touch of poor man's Byron. It is a historical novel, in full period costume. David Alroy, a medieval prince of the Jewish captivity, overthrows his Muslim masters and sets up a Jewish empire of Asia, based on Baghdad, before he is then overthrown. He dies a Jewish martyr, preferring death to apostasy. Its stage effects require no comment. There is much cleaving of skulls, flashing of scimitars, and use of magic talismans. The din of battles resounds. If tales of adventure are unreadable, then *Alroy* is unreadable. The psychology is equally predictable. Alroy is the standard Byronic hero, 'a mind to whose supreme volition the fortunes of the world would bow like fate' (*A* 187). Subjectively, he has a troubled mind: 'I know not what I feel, yet what I feel is madness' (Schw. 43). He cannot sleep, yet seeks 'glory, eternal glory', and finds the necessary therapy for his *mal du siècle* in action. 'Say what they like, man is made for action', is his doctrine (*A* 166)—and perhaps the author's too, for Disraeli later wrote that Alroy represented his 'ideal ambition'. The connection between mental disturbance, even weakness, and human greatness is just beneath the surface.

Alroy is important because of its Jewishness. Of Disraeli's first seventeen or so titles (those before *Coningsby,* with its Jewish sage Sidonia), it is the only one with significant Jewish content. To Disraeli its merit lay in its being 'the celebration of a gorgeous incident in the annals of that sacred and romantic people from whom I derive my blood'. He conveyed a true sense of Jewish lowliness: 'in Jerusalem, our people speak only in a whisper' (*A* 101). Do not blame Muslim oppression, he adds; Christian (or Jewish) intolerance, Disraeli makes clear, would have been worse: 'A Turk is a brute, but a Christian is a demon. (*A* 101). There was nothing anti-Muslim in Disraeli's revivalism.

Hope unfulfilled is at the heart of Disraeli's Judaism, as it was also of his personal affairs when, as a young man at a loose end, he produced *Alroy.* When he wrote: 'if thou were greeted only with the cuff and the curse; if thou dist rise each morning only to feel existence to be dishonour, and to find thyself marked out among surrounding men as something foul and fatal; if it were thy lot . . . at best to drag on a mean and dull career, hopeless and aimless . . . and this all too with a keen sense of thy intrinsic worth, and a deep conviction of superior race' (*A* 78), Disraeli could be speaking either of his youthful débâcles or of the lot of the Jew everywhere. The two experiences, psychological and social, merge.

Disraeli's Jews are 'a proud and stiff-necked race, ever prone to rebellion' (*A* 130). They are warlike. They scoff at long rabbinical treatises. Disraeli's ideal of Jewish regeneration is decidedly military and is assisted by 'agents in every court, and camp, and cabinet' (*A* 157). (Would Disraeli have been so drawn to Jewishness had he not seen it as a vehicle for his beloved talent for conspiracy?) The drama of *Alroy* lies in the struggle of Jew against Jew. The victorious Alroy is a multiculturalist, as it were. He wishes to found a powerful Middle Eastern state in which Arab and Jew can live at ease with each other. To this end, he marries a Muslim princess, swears four Muslim nobles into his Council, and generally sets himself up as a liberal figure. 'Universal empire', he declares, 'must not be founded on sectarian prejudices and exclusive rights' (*A* 187).

Such rationalism, however magnanimous, hardly pleases the Jewish fundamentalists. Alroy wishes 'Baghdad to be my Sion'; he sneers at the thought of being 'the decent patriarch of a pastoral horde' (*A* 187) in impoverished Palestine. Theocracy in Israel, or empire in Baghdad; the rebuilding of the Temple, or military rejuvenation—these were not difficult alternatives on which to decide.

But Alroy fails, because he is no fanatic. He represents power unsupported by imagination. Against Alroy's imperial dream, his opponent the High Priest urges: 'You ask me what I wish: my answer is, a national existence' (*A* 204). *Alroy* is Disraeli's anti-imperialist novel.

Which side was Disraeli on? It is hard to know, perhaps because he changed his mind half-way through. At first there seems no doubt. Alroy's secular realism is good; the High Priest's brooding intensity is sinister. Alroy is a boyish hero, a knight in shining armour. Yet by the end of the book the dying Alroy speaks in traditionalist, not latitudinarian, terms of Jewish destiny: 'My people stand apart from other nations, and ever will' (*A* 329). Here, surely, it is Alroy, the liberal figure, who has come round to the High Priest's unshakeable belief: 'We cannot mingle with them and yet be true to Him. We must exist alone. To preserve that loneliness, is the great end and essence of our law' (*A* 207). Besides struggle and spiritual purity, Disraeli offered, not without approval, a third form of Jewish redemption: upward social mobility based on uncompromising accommodation with existing power: 'Take my experience, child, and save yourself much sorrow . . . Freedom and honour are mine, but I was my own messiah' (*A* 78-9). So says the apostate court physician, confidant of the mighty, a calmly wise

forerunner of Sidonia. Apostasy can be more than a Jewish vocation; it can itself be Messianic.

In *Alroy* Disraeli stated three predicaments: that of an oppressed race; that of a frustrated ambitious young man; and that of Jewish exclusiveness and the accommodation of Arabs (or indeed, political reality of any kind). All such questions are still with us. Disraeli had no solutions; but to find the West Bank in a light romance of 1833 is certainly curious.

Disraeli's prose poetry does not work, they say. Be that as it may, Disraeli wrote *Alroy* as a modernist in revolt against literary convention, and in the belief that he was a literary genius. His attempt to break the bounds of the customary language of fiction was ahead of its time. It would never do to forget that Disraeli was as ambitious in literature as he was in politics.

'The Rise of Iskander' (1833), a colourful adventure story, was published with *Alroy,* which it somewhat resembles. Both are romances of national liberation. *Alroy* concerns Jewish revolt against Islam; Iskander, or Scanderbeg, a medieval Albanian national hero, freed his people from the Turks. Though Iskander was mainly intent on abducting a Christian princess from the Turkish seraglio, there was at least a whiff of proto-Zionism to be found between the lines. Otherwise, guile and courage are the supreme human qualities, and none can withstand them: that is Disraeli's text.

'Ixion in Heaven,' a short magazine piece, is seen by admirers as a 'sparkling trifle'. Ixion, a peccant king on earth, is invited by Jove to Olympus, where the moral tone of the inhabitants curiously resembles that of London society. If it is a study in anything, it is in social climbing. Two gods talk thus of Ixion: '"Not three days back an outcast among his own wretched species!" "and now commanding everybody in Heaven."' Ixion does not lack confidence: 'These worthy Immortals required their minds to be opened, and I trust I have effectively performed the necessary operation . . . To make your way in Heaven you must command. These exclusives sink under the audacious invention of an aspiring mind. . . . I am a prime favourite.' Prime favourite indeed: Ixion ends up in the embrace of Juno. The cad will always win. 'Ixion' is a metaphor for social ascent; its message, as in *Vivian Grey* or *Hartlebury,* is 'The Importance of Being Disraeli'.

'The Infernal Marriage,' published as a magazine piece in July-October 1834, is in the same vein as 'Ixion.' As Lord Blake says, judged as 'light satires, modelled on Lucian, they have a freshness, wit and daring which still charm. Isaac [D'Israeli] considered them to be his son's most original contribution to literature' (*B* 86). The apparatus is purely classical. Proserpine marries Pluto, King of Hades, hence the title; but we also pay visits to Olympus and Elysium. The gods, as in '**Ixion,**' have their origins in London society, but not so much so as to spoil the fable. The topical allusions, to Brougham and others, have faded; the classicism remains. (Apollo appears as the editor of a daily journal; Jupiter remarks: 'for my part I should only be too happy to extinguish the *Sun* and every other newspaper were it only in my power'.)

Slight though each is, '**Iskander,**' '**Ixion,**' and '**The Infernal Marriage**' can be used as evidence that Disraeli had the ease and inventiveness of the natural bellelettrist, the pure man of letters, writing from no intellectual or political motive, but seeking only to give passing amusement. Had circumstances required it, he could have carved a niche as a literary entertainer. A passage at the end of '**The Infernal Marriage**' gives some notion of how he saw felicity:

> To wander in the green shade of secret woods and whisper our affection; to float on the sunny waters of some gentle stream, and listen to a serenade; to canter with a light-hearted cavalcade over breezy downs, or cool our panting chargers in the summer stillness of winding and woody lanes; to banquet with the beautiful and the witty; to send care to the devil, and indulge the whim of the moment; the priest, the warrior, and the statesman may frown and struggle as they like; but this is existence, and this, this is Elysium!

The sensuality of relaxation is more than a pose of Home Counties ruralism. It was so often stated, both publicly and privately, that it must have been an inner necessity. 'The green shade of woods' was a large part of the Disraelian ideology, and can be taken in two ways: either as contempt for public bustle, an assertion of the private; or as a characteristically conservative statement that politics are not the most important thing in life.

In 1979 the Canadian editors of Disraeli's letters discovered a long-forgotten novel, *Hartlebury, or The Election,* published pseudonymously in 1834. Most of it was written by Disraeli's sister Sarah; he contributed only an episode of fifty pages describing a borough election. Though Victorian novels are not short of election scenes set in country towns, *Hartlebury* is good of its kind: rattling, lively, and true to its period. Its main importance, however, lies in its portrayal of its brilliant hero, Mr Bohun, a thinly disguised version of Disraeli, and of his political ideas.

Mr Bohun, the local magnate, has (like Disraeli) just returned from the East. He combines a fine poetical temperament with a love of action. To women he was irresistible: 'God bless his curly locks', they cry. As an orator he combined 'inexhaustible sarcasm' with perorations of 'elaborate gorgeousness'. Bohun's motives

owed more to Byron than to Burke. Politics was an extension of personality: 'This is life, this is excitement, and that is all I care about. I feel I live. For the rest, if I live I *must* be a great man.' This, surely, is Disraeli in the confessional.

Bohun's political method was modern. 'Agitate', he cried, 'agitate, agitate. That magic word is the essence of all political success.' All this, remember, was written half a decade before the Anti-Corn Law League. Because he was writing anonymously, Disraeli could be frank in presenting the Tory party as a vehicle for clever adventurers to ride mockingly for 'excitement'. Because gentry Toryism was moribund (or seemed so in 1834), its only chance lay in taking the side of 'the people' against the Whigs and their local oligarchy of sectarian high-street tradesmen. Though still only 'the Alcibiades of an obscure country town', Bohun wanted to see the formation of a new party, with himself at its head, on a truly national basis. Disraeli's answer to the débâcle of 1832 was to root Toryism as firmly in mass politics as Whiggism was among the shallower soil of the shopkeepers.

Hartlebury is Disraeli's *Mein Kampf:* it foreshadows, albeit patchily, much that lay ahead. The outmanoeuvring of the Whigs; a popular franchise; a social policy for the poor; the relation between individual genius and mass politics; and an anti-Whig sociology—all these can be traced there. It owes much to local events. Hartlebury is Bradenham, then the home of the Disraeli family, and the election takes place in neighbouring High Wycombe, which Disraeli had just lost, on a Radical-Tory platform, to the son of the Whig Prime Minister, Grey. From this trivial local episode, Disraeli proclaims the need to transform Toryism from an upper-class party of resistance to a broadly based popular party of national solidarity. The fictional message of *Hartlebury* coincides with the political theory of the *Vindication:* the Tories must become the party of the many.

The sole distinction of *The Revolutionary Epick* (1834), happily a work that was never completed, lay in its being the only epic ever written at Southend. Its lack of modesty was total. As Disraeli's original preface remarks, Greece, Rome, Florence, and Milton's England had all produced epics: 'And the spirit of my Time shall it alone be uncelebrated? . . . Is Napoleon a less interesting character than Achilles? For me remains the Revolutionary Epick.' The first two books comprise the pleadings before a heavenly judge of two rival genii, one putting the case for the aristocratic principle, the other for the egalitarian or republican. Each scans history from antiquity to the present day. The third book, by an abrupt transition, jumps to Napoleon's Italian campaign; and there the project stops. The table of contents is promising at points (e.g. 'The State sacred: even its faults to be viewed with reverence'), but dissolves in a mechanical facility for versification.

Henrietta Temple: A Love Story (1836) and ***Venetia*** (1837) showed that Disraeli could produce readable middle-brow fiction more or less to order. It was fortunate that he could, for his finances were never more embarrassed than they were in these two years. Arrest for debt seemed imminent. A city deal had gone awry; and this was probably the reason for Disraeli's sudden need, in the latter part of 1836, to complete and publish ***Henrietta Temple,*** which he had begun three years earlier. The necessity to produce saleable fiction ended equally suddenly, a few months after the publication of ***Venetia,*** when in July 1837 he entered Parliament as MP for Maidstone. This gave him security from his creditors; marriage to a fairly rich widow in 1839 enhanced his position, though his debts remained intermittently troublesome. Certainly, if it had not been for the electors of Maidstone, Disraeli would have had little choice but to continue his steady and mechanical production of what the literary market wanted. As it was, he published no prose in the years 1837 to 1844; between the ages of 32 and 39.

Henrietta Temple was a success, Disraeli's greatest hit with the public since ***Vivian Grey.*** It succeeded largely because it was so un-Disraelian. It contained no ideological baggage, no social message, no Jewishness, no religion, and no Toryism. Indeed, the hero was a Whig (though Disraeli by this time was an active Tory) who, though a member of the old Catholic gentry, never attends mass or makes confession, as one editor, Anthony Hern, points out. His Catholicism is an aesthetic stage prop, not a motif. 'We have no theatre for action', the hero complains, referring to the exclusion of Catholics from public life, but in fact he behaves like any other young man about town. Unlike Vivian Grey, Alroy, Ixion, Contarini Fleming, and Bohun, the young hero Ferdinand Armine is no Byronic genius born to conquer. Like Disraeli, he is an outsider (being Catholic), he is deeply indebted and in the clutches of the Jews (here unflatteringly portrayed), and he is a cad in need of redemption—in Armine's case, by love, entry into Parliament, and a lucky win of £15,000 at Crockford's by a generous friend. He has Disraeli's problems without Disraeli's talent.

Armine's difficulty, on which the story turns, is that he is engaged twice over: once to a rich cousin, heiress to the family estates, and a second time to Henrietta Temple, the love of his life. Henrietta finds out, retires to Italy, and seeks solace in an engagement to Lord Montfort. This obliging fellow, however, duly becomes attached to the rich cousin, leaving Ferdinand and Henrietta free to resume love at first sight. Of such stuff is romantic fiction made. But ***Henrietta Temple: A Love Story*** is not exactly what the title implies. There is one obvious reason for this. Books 1-2 were written in 1833, when Disraeli was in love. They were then put in a drawer, and Books 3-6 were added, with 'a very terrible exertion', after Disraeli had put passion behind him. Thus, as with ***Vivian Grey, Tancred,*** and ***Lothair,*** an original impulse is resumed in a sequel that is written in a very different mood.

At first, love is all; but as the novel proceeds, love becomes one part, and a fairly subordinate part, of life's rich tapestry. We are after all in high society, where all agree 'that the man who permitted himself a moment's uneasiness about a woman was a fool' (*HT* 326). Disraeli presents such a view for our derision; but in the soberer part of the novel, he will only go so far as to offer this passionless dictum: 'A female friend, amicable, clever, and devoted, is a possession more valuable than parks and palaces; and without such a muse, few men can succeed in life, none be content' (*HT* 160). In fact, the novel is not story-telling pure and simple. It is about 'scrapes' (its key word): male scrapes. Of these the principal is passion, followed closely by debts. The answer to scrapes may in theory be the love of a good woman; but in practice, as ***Henrietta Temple***'s later chapters show, the most effective remedy consists of a few choice male spirits sticking together. For a love story, there is a great deal of male bonding going on. We feel that the author, if asked to choose between perfect passion and having Count Mirabel as a chum, might be hard put to it. Mirabel, or D'Orsay, the great dandy to whom the book was dedicated, quite stole Henrietta's show.

Both as romance and West End social comedy, ***Henrietta Temple*** is a competent work by a practised hand. It is as free from intellectual ambition as a Trollope pot-boiler. But even so, there are two unremarked-upon passages where Disraeli's pen ran away with him. Both are declarations of a creed. Both are speeches of challenge and assertion. One, by Count Mirabel, the true hero of the novel and a partial forerunner of Sidonia, states his belief:

> Existence is a pleasure, and the greatest. The world cannot rob us of that; and if it is better to live than to die, it is better to live in a good humour than a bad one. If a man be convinced that existence is the greatest pleasure, his happiness may be increased by good fortune, but it will be essentially independent of it. He who feels that the greatest source of pleasure always remains to him ought never to be miserable. (*HT* 328-9)

Such was the philosophy of the adventurer; of the man, too, whom Disraeli always most admired as a great human being. A more Disraelian utterance comes in a set speech from a quite minor character, a former prize-fighter who has risen to vast, if dubious, wealth:

My position is difficult. I have risen by pursuits which the world does not consider reputable, yet if I had not recourse to them, I should be less than nothing. My mind, I think, is equal to my fortune: I am still young, and I would now avail myself of my power and establish myself in the land, a recognized member of society. But this cannot be. Society shrinks from an obscure foundling . . . Debarred therefore from a fair theatre for my energy and capital, I am forced to occupy, perhaps exhaust, myself in multiplied speculations . . . But I would gladly emancipate myself . . . Count Mirabel sympathizes with my situation. I believe he does not think, because a man has risen from an origin the most ignoble and obscure to a powerful position, by great courage and dexterity, and let me add also, by some profound thought, by struggling too, be it remembered, with a class of society as little scrupulous, though not so skilful as himself, that he is necessarily an infamous character. What if, at eighteen years of age, without a friend in the world . . . I flung myself into the ring? Who should be a gladiator if I were not? (*HT* 331-2)

This apologia surely comes from the heart.

Was Disraeli feeling the strain of incipient respectability? *Venetia, or the Poet's Daughter* (1837), dedicated to the far from respectable Tory ex-Lord Chancellor Lord Lyndhurst, provided an answer of sorts. Lord Blake sees the novel as 'an awkward and artificial work, fatally marred by its whole concept—a fictionalized account of Byron and Shelley put back in the period of the American War of Independence' (*B* 146). As such, Blake, summarizing the views of Professor Jerman, calls it 'Disraeli's last tribute to the Byronic myth, a final protest against the respectable world'. There is much in this. Byron and Shelley were, in Tory eyes, men of the left. Moreover, their private lives were hardly conventional. To write about them was only to advertise to the world, and especially to the Tory world, all that was suspect about Disraeli. Where Armine had debts, Marmion Herbert (Shelley) had a mistress. Disraeli had had both; but why draw attention to the fact? Yet in his introduction Disraeli boldly commended Shelley and Byron as 'two of the most renowned and refined spirits that have adorned these, our latter days'.

While writing *Venetia,* Disraeli was in 'savagely gay' mood. He feared being 'nabbed' for debt, while hoping that William IV's failing health would shortly precipitate a general election. Disraeli had ideas of standing for Buckinghamshire, his home county and very much a gentry county; yet he intruded into *Venetia* a stock caricature of the rural magistrate, Squire Mountmeadow. On the face of it, prudence was not his dominant consideration. Yet, considering the possibilities of the subject (about which Disraeli had much inside knowledge), protest against convention is conspicuous by its absence. If in

younger days Byron and Shelley set society by the ears, they were but the victims of misconception and priggishness. By the end of the story Shelley has settled down as a good family man: the perfect father and husband. We rub our eyes. Byron, too, though preaching the lower worldliness, does so while bathing in an innocent solitariness that is presented as his true self. The point being made here is not concerned with protest; it is that all scrapes pass in the end. As with *Henrietta Temple,* rehabilitation is the central preoccupation.

But again, have we not missed the central oddity of the novel? Namely, that this is a novel about Byron and Shelley in which Byron and Shelley play a surprisingly small part. To be exact, Shelley is firmly off-stage until page 212. He then, disconcertingly but without amplification, becomes a United States general on page 223; and finally emerges as a Venetian monk on page 381, ready to be a good father. This is all the stranger, as Disraeli chooses to make Shelley and his higher nonsense prevail over Byron's knowingness. Byron appears more as a schoolboy than anything else; it is not until page 229 that he emerges as a poet. To us today the two poets must be the focus of comment; but as the title states, this is a book about the poet's daughter, not the poet; about children and families, and especially about broken families. As Schwarz says, this is a novel about children; Disraeli's true preoccupation lay in being 'a psychologist of children, adolescents, and young adults, particularly members of those groups who are caught in emotionally claustrophobic circumstances' (Schw. 70).

In *Venetia* Disraeli was not doing himself any good politically. But he was not protesting either. He was celebrating the innate beauty of childhood and of the English countryside, and doing so with naturalness and authority. We cannot fit this into our picture of Disraeli the novelist of ideas, and we therefore push *Venetia* impatiently aside; but had it come from the pen of, say, Mark Rutherford or Trollope, it might be better regarded.

Count Alarcos (1839), a five-act blank-verse drama, is perhaps Disraeli's deadest work. Lord Blake calls it 'almost as destitute of literary merit as *The Revolutionary Epick*' (B 153). Intended as 'an attempt to contribute to the revival of English tragedy', it is an imitation of Shakespeare. If to write bad Shakespeare constitutes success, then it achieved success: the verse is springy, well-paced, and fluent. If nothing else, its archaic diction helps to link the modern romantic motive and the story set in a medieval Spanish court—Alarcos being 'the brightest knight, that ever waved a lance in Old Castille'. Alarcos had a problem; he had married the wrong woman, a woman he did not love. For Disraeli to take this as his theme in the year he made his own strange marriage was at least curious.

Very bad plays, and very bad verse, were normal in Victorian literature; Disraeli was far from being alone. It is puzzling, though, that he was pleased with his failure: 'Strange that I never wrote anything that was more talked of in society, and yet it has never been noticed by the scribbling critics,' Disraeli wrote. Nowhere is there the least trace of irony or thought, nor any hint that Disraeli was capable of a masterpiece in his next book. No route leads from **Count Alarcos** to **Coningsby.** Disraeli, at the ripe age of 35 and in the year of the Chartist Convention and revolt, had nothing to say.

Abbreviations

A   *Alroy* (Bodley Head, 1906).

B   Blake, *Disraeli* (Eyre and Spottiswoode, 1966).

C   *Coningsby* (The World's Classics; OUP 1982).

CF   *Contarini Fleming* (Hughenden edn.; Longmans, 1881).

DR   *Disraeli's Reminiscences,* ed. H. M. and M. Swartz (Macmillan, 1975).

E   *Endymion* (Hughenden edn.)

F   Sir William Fraser, Baronet, *Disraeli and his Day* (Kegan Paul, 1891).

GP   General Preface to the Novels (Longmans, 1870).

HT   *Henrietta Temple* (Panther, 1969).

L   *Lothair* (Longmans, 1870).

LGB   *Lord George Bentinck* (Routledge, 1858 edn.).

M&B   Monypenny and Buckle, *Life of Disraeli* (John Murray, 1910-20).

P   *Popanilla* (Hughenden edn.).

R   *Letters of Runnymede* (John Macrone, 1836).

S   *Sybil* (The World's Classics; OUP 1981).

Schw.   Schwarz, *Disraeli's Fiction* (Macmillan, 1979).

T   *Tancred* (Hughenden edn.).

V   *Vindication of the English Constitution* (Saunders and Otley, 1835).

VG   *Vivian Grey* (Centenary edn.; Moring, 1904).

YD   *The Young Duke* (Highenden edn.).

Mary S. Millar and M. G. Wiebe (essay date 1992)

SOURCE: "'This power so vast . . . & so generally misunderstood': Disraeli and the Press in the 1840s," *Victorian Periodicals Review,* Vol. XXV, No. 2, Summer, 1992, pp. 79-85.

[*In the essay that follows, Millar and Wiebe discuss ways in which Disraeli used his writing for newspapers as a means to transmit his political views, and conclude that his "management of the press" contributed significantly to his political success.*]

In October of 1849, Disraeli wrote to G. Lathom Browne, the editor of his local newspaper, *The Bucks Herald:* "No newspaper is important as far as its advocacy. The importance of newspapers is to circulate your opinions, and a good report of a speech is better than 10,000 articles."[1] It is not, as we shall see, that in his dealings with the press Disraeli scorned either advocacy or articles. He practised the one and wrote many of the other. In the 1840s, however, his prime interest in the newspapers was as a means of transmitting—quickly and accurately—his own political ideas to a national, and even international audience.

The 1840s were crucial to Disraeli's career. These were the years when he made himself. He began on the back-benches, with a reputation to live down—as a philanderer, gambler, dandy and not-quite-respectable novelist (the closest contemporary political parallel is probably someone like Jeffrey Archer). By the end of the decade in 1849 he made himself into a brilliant parliamentary speaker and formidable political opponent; he had succeeded in ousting Sir Robert Peel, leader of the Conservative party, and he had become himself leader of the Protectionist faction in the Commons.

And the shift in public perception which recognised his achievement was, in large part, due to his management of the press during those years.

One of the many exciting things which comes out of working on Disraeli's letters on the kind of comprehensive basis that we are able to do (as opposed to the fragmentary, inaccurate, versions which were all that was previously available) is the finding of patterns which were not evident before. In the years we are discussing, one such striking pattern emerges from the number of references he makes during the Parliamentary sessions to the coverage of his speeches by the newspapers.

"I have sent you the 'Morning Chronicle' . . . it is the best report tho' many fine hits are lost" [1156 (May 1841)]; "There is a précis of the speech in the Times, a report in the Herald, even in the Chronicle; & this morning a leading article in the Post" [1307 (May 1843)]; "The Chronicle is often, perhaps usually, the best Reporter, but I have fallen lately, . . . on short-hand writers of the 'Times,' who suit me to a t. The Chronicle report of my speech . . . appeared to me, as I glanced over it, very good; but the Times report was short hand until the last twenty lines or so, when the pen changed, & the peroration, if you can call it such, is more accurate in the Chronicle." [1399A (Apr. 1845)]; or (to be quite direct): "Was it in the Times about me?" [15 Apr. 1849].

This obsessive interest was not (as his detractors might suppose) mere egotism. The *Letters* show that it was part of a strategy, the use of the press to make the ideas in his speeches known to the public. He was not, of course, the only 19th-century politician with active press connections. The whole history of the mid-Victorian press is one of what is euphemistically called "influence" and "control." But he himself was very familiar with what could, and could not, be done. He had already, in 1825 (before he was 21), tried (and failed) with the *Representative,* a paper intended to rival *The Times.* In the 1830s, before he entered Parliament, he had been a writer for both *The Times* and *The Morning Post.* Later, in the 1850s, after he had held office for the first time, he would begin his own paper, which he called, simply, *The Press.*

At the end of 1842 he outlined his plan in a written memorandum which he drew up for the then King of France, Louis Philippe. This memorandum marks the point at which Disraeli the politician began definitively to move on his own. He had begun the parliamentary session of 1842 as a follower of Peel; he ended it convinced of the inadequacy of current Conservative policies to solve the most urgent national problems: the plight of the poor, the country's finances, the difficulties of farmers and landowners, free trade versus protectionism. The press was the means by which, from 1842, he would make his views have an effect on the voters and parliamentarians of Britain.

He described the press thus in his memorandum: "This power so vast but the management of [which] is so frequently neglected, & so generally misunderstood even by English ministers is of itself if skillfully conducted capable of effecting great things; but whenever it has chanced to be combined with a parliamentary power its influence has invariably been irresistible" [IV app III]. The remark about "English ministers" who do *not* understand how to manage the press is probably a shot at Peel himself. As a recent study has shown, Peel was very much aware of the effect of the press on public perceptions of him, but he strenuously avoided personal involvement.[2] Disraeli's own approach was the opposite.

In brief, he used the press much as a politician would use the media now, and he built upon his strengths. In the first place, he had already begun in 1842 to establish a reputation as a parliamentary speaker—provocative and fiery, and one whom the papers would *want* to report—he continued from 1843 on to make speeches whose brilliance caught the attention, even of readers who might not otherwise have considered the ideas in them. Secondly, he already had connections from his writing for the newspapers; all through the 1840s, he kept them up with a barrage of signed letters to the papers (even political poems), backed up by anonymous leaders and articles expressing his opinions (and, masked by that anonymity, was, on occasion, thus even able to comment on his own speeches!). Thirdly, he was already a best-selling novelist, with his sensational novels of the 1830s (such as *Vivian Grey* or *Henrietta Temple*); in the autumn of 1843, he set about writing a trilogy of further best-sellers—*Coningsby, Sybil,* and *Tancred*—on the national topics which concerned him most. And he wrote them in a deliberately controversial way, which would get them talked about and well reviewed.

As an offshoot of all three of these procedures, he also encouraged his followers. These were particularly the splinter-group of young Members of Parliament known as "Young England," otherwise known as the "Diz-Union," among them George Smythe (the original for *Coningsby*) and Lord John Manners. Thanks to Disraeli's coaching, they both emulated their leader in speeches, books, and writing for periodicals and newspapers, all of which spread the group's ideas.

In all of these fields, Disraeli's approach was what we would call a "hands-on" management. He knew perfectly well the potential for error—he would later complain on one occasion: "I never went to Manchester, though the newspaper gave an account of my visit." [16 September 1857] He also knew how much the accuracy of a report going to the nation depended on the diligence of the paper's shorthand reporters in the Gallery and the letters frequently record his disappointment at mistakes made by a tired reporter, or at omissions when a change-over was not slick enough. Thus, his own methods involved beforehand alerting the editor when he was due to speak, even down to indicating the likely hour. Afterwards, he was even willing to supervise personally the paper's printing of a speech.[3] It was this kind of involvement that he meant when in his memorandum he distinguished his own approach from that of politicians who "neglected" and "misunderstood" the management of the press.

In the memorandum, he made it plain that his methods would not involve the use of a single paper as a party organ. In 1840, he turned down an offer of *The Courier* as just such an organ [1056X (17 Apr. 1840)]; and in 1845 he would be considerably vexed (publicly, at least) at the effrontery of a short-lived weekly, *Young England,* which tried to capitalise on the renown of his own group of that name. [1399 (5 Apr. 1845)] There were severe limitations in credibility and authority attached to a paper known to be only a mouthpiece, and what he had in mind was much broader and more far-reaching. "The monitor that counsels the people of England . . . must speak in journals of every school of politics & sound in every district. It is with a machinery of this description that the ideas of a single man . . . soon become the voice of a nation." [IV app III]

Just how wide a net he cast can be seen by the number of publications we have had to make reference to in our work on the *Letters* for these years—over 100. Space does not allow for a detailed discussion here, but in brief they involve most of the London dailies (where the bulk of each issue was devoted to Parliamentary news), the London-based periodicals, including the literary magazines which ran articles on his skill as a speaker, or which reviewed the novels, and the satirical ones, like *Punch* and *The Satirist,* whose attentions were often offensive but were nevertheless a form of national exposure. Then there are the provincial newspapers, which reprinted reports from the London papers for country readers, but whose own reports of local events (such as speeches at constituency meetings) would, in reverse, be copied or extracted by the London papers.

One final, and very interesting, group (which would probably repay further study) is the French papers, which were always interested in him. They reported interesting speeches in the British parliament, and they also reviewed his novels. In 1844 de Tocqueville even invited him to be foreign correspondent for his paper, *Le Commerce.* Unfortunately, he wrote to de Tocqueville, he was too busy in England then to accept. [31 Aug. 1844] He did write, later on, in 1848, for a strange French-language weekly, *Le Spectateur de Londres,* funded in England by Metternich and run by one of Metternich's secret agents, Georg Klindworth. (Disraeli would later put Klindworth on his own political payroll in the 1850s.) [29 Aug. 1848]

On the broad scale, these make up the 'journals of every school of politics' and 'every district' which he describes in the memorandum. As illustration of his method, our paper will look at some individual instances in the *Letters*—both amusing and instructive—about his day-to-day interaction with the papers. We have chosen four—*The Times, The Morning Chronicle,* and *The Morning Post*—and from the provinces, the appropriately-named *Shropshire Conservative.*

To begin with, it is quite remarkable that, at the beginning of the decade, he was able to get coverage at all, since papers normally did not bother much with backbenchers. What he did have was good relations with

editors—probably from his leader-writing days. At *The Times,* he was friendly with the editor, John Delane, and with the proprietors, the two John Walters (father and son). At *The Morning Post,* he knew Charles Michele, who had also been its editor in the 1830s. In Shrewsbury, his constituency from 1841-47, he became friendly during the 1841 election with the editor of *The Shropshire Conservative,* T.J. Ouseley, a man whose loyalty is best demonstrated by his refusal in 1845 to be bought away from Disraeli when the Peelites came calling with offers of Government advertising for his paper. [1399A (11 Apr. 1845)] All three of these papers were Conservative; but (as he stated in his memorandum) he also managed coverage in the hostile press. With *The Morning Chronicle,* which was, until 1848, a Whig paper largely controlled by Palmerston, he cultivated the proprietor, Sir John Easthope (who dropped his "h"s and was dubbed disparagingly by Dickens, "the Barrow Knight").[4] [1456 (21 Dec. 1845), 1460 (11 Jan. 1846)]

He also took care to co-operate with the Parliamentary reporters. Several letters accompany passages from his speeches sent up by request to reporters in the Gallery. [1289X (29 Mar. 1843), 2 July 1849] With the chief parliamentary reporter for *The Times,* J. F. Neilson, he co-operated on at least one out-of-town occasion so that Neilson was able to get copy to London in time for next day's issue [1503 (4 Aug. 1846)]; he also rehearsed speeches to Neilson beforehand.[5]

All this meant that when he made an important speech, he was able to ask for the coverage he wanted. Before a speech on the Consular Service in 1842, he told his wife, Mary Anne: "I shall write this evening to the Times to secure a good report." [1221 (5 Mar. 1842)] Afterwards, he was generally pleased: "The Times Report, with the exception of the first half column, is a good report. Many a happy sarcasm & airy turn is lost, but the order of the general statements & correctness of the facts is remarkable." [1224 (9 Mar. 1842)] Later, he ordered for a Parliamentary friend "a couple of copies of the No. of Hansard April 23—in [which] there is a capital report of the 'Consular statement.'" [1244 (21 May 1842)] (Which may have been "capital" because Disraeli had corrected it; many MPs took this opportunity to "improve" the reports; and we know he did this too, and recommended to Hansard the best newspaper report to use.) [30 Mar. 1849]

Similarly, before an extremely important speech in February 1846, in which he would outline his protectionist principles, he could write to Easthope: "I intend to speak to night about ten o'ck, & if you will have the kindness to give directions that I shall be well reported, you wd. oblige very much." [1472 (20 Feb. 1846)] As a result, *The Morning Chronicle* gave him no less than six columns of accurate report (valuable enough in a friendly paper, like *The Times,* which also gave him six columns, but even more so in a hostile one); it was only partly undercut by the caustic leader which accompanied it: "Mr. Disraeli is a man of too much cleverness to be in earnest on all this, but he suffers himself to be allured by the glitter of heading a party."[6]

Perhaps the best example of his management of coverage is that for an even more important speech, his summary of the Parliamentary session in August 1848. It was a crucial time. The Protectionist faction was still leaderless; and it was his chance to make an impact, which he did with a devastating critique of the Whigs' inefficiency. In preparation, he wrote to Delane on 25 August to secure one of his best reporters; then the date was suddenly changed, and he wrote again on the 26th. [26 Aug. 1848] Greville the diarist sneered that it was "a sort of advertisement that the great actor would take his benefit," but it was sound planning. This was an occasion when, he fully realised, he was "speaking to the country."[7]

After his speech, which lasted three hours, he went straight to Delane's office to oversee the printing. "God knows," he wrote to Mary Anne, "how long & how often I shall be there—as the speech must be 8 columns at least. I shall however come home & dine at *8* even if I have to go, as I expect again." [30 Aug. 1848] (He added: "Write to Lewis [the news agent] & order 6 'Times' for tomorrow.") The personal supervision was worthwhile. A few days later he wrote to his sister: "I am sorry you read the 'Morning Herald' [which] was certainly . . . nonsense almost unrivalled. However I have no cause to complain of the reporters: the Version of the 'Times,' [which] now sells 40,000 copies a day is almost verbatim. . . . The success is universal. I never knew a greater parliamentary *coup.* The country papers teem with articles. . . . " [4 Sept. 1848]

When a report originated in the provinces, he was equally careful. In August 1844, for example, he had to make an unplanned visit to Shrewsbury to meet the electors, who were understandably alarmed by his growing independence from the party. On 28 August, three hours before he was to make a speech to them, he found out that the meeting would be reported by *The Shropshire Conservative.* In some trepidation, he wrote to Mary Anne: "I have now withdrawn to my bedroom . . . where I hope to collect my thoughts a little, as I did not count on this reporting. [It] rather annoys me, as it will be in all the London papers: & I must be careful." [1371 (28 Aug. 1844)]

He *was* careful. In the speech which he finally made, he argued that he had attacked Peel out of principle, not out of disappointment at not being given office: "Sir Robert Peel knows me too well," he claimed, "to think for a moment that any pecuniary circumstances influence my conduct," and went on to his famous conclusion: "I was his supporter when in adversity—in

prosperity I will not be his slave." The fact that we *have* this text, however, is due to *The Shropshire Conservative* and the care with which he instructed T.J. Ouseley in a letter the next day. He took the trouble to enclose the text of two crucial passages, to make sure that they were not omitted. The first passage concerned his remarks 'on the "Condition of England" and his trenchant analysis of the causes of recent unrest in the country: "one half of the population of the country," he said, "was overworked and the other half underpaid. Hence the fearful diminution of the term of human life in Lancashire; hence the fires of Suffolk, the two causes producing the same result, the degradation of the species." It was a point he had made before, and it would be the basis of his "two nations" theme in *Sybil,* the novel he was about to begin; and it was important to remind readers in London as well as tradespeople in Shrewsbury that he had been a consistent champion of the poor, against what he saw as the misguided social policies of the Conservatives under Peel.

The second passage was equally important to get right, the refuting of the charges of self-interest. He told Ouseley to be particularly careful here: "Remember the end. In his adversity I was his supporter; in his prosperity I will not be his slave." [1372 (29 Aug. 1844)]

The care was rewarded. *The Shropshire Conservative* of 31 August carried a lengthy report; and it was copied by both *The Times* (on 2 Sept.) and *The Morning Post* (on 3 Sept.). His attention to detail in the provinces had ensured that a declaration of principle made on a local stage went at once to Peel and his supporters in London. *The Morning Post* told its London readers: "Differing from Mr. Disraeli on some points, and blaming him on others, we believe we speak the sentiments of most honest men, when we say that no doubt can be cast upon the purity of the Hon. Gentleman's motives in the course which he has pursued since he entered Parliament."

This kind of personal management was not confined to parliamentary reports. On one occasion, he used his influence with *The Times* to alter completely their reviews of one of his novels. The first *Times* review of *Coningsby* appeared on 11 May 1844, and was rather perfunctory. On that day Delane wrote to him that he would arrange for a second notice which would "do more credit to the paper and more justice to your work." Unfortunately, it did neither. We do not know who the reviewer was—Delane said he was a man "with plenty of political experience"—but his review was puzzlingly hostile. The opinions in the book, he wrote, would "be offensive to some, and unintelligible to more."

In the meantime, the anti-Conservative *Morning Chronicle* had done better than this, with a generally favourable review by Thackeray, and Disraeli complained stiffly, in almost identical letters to Delane and Walter. "Considering the influence of *The Times,* and the generally understood sympathy of its columns with many of the topics treated in **Coningsby,** the review is one calculated to do the work very great injury." Modern authors suffering a bad review would envy him the result. Walter wrote back, agreed with him, and promised: "I will do what I can that your immortality shall start as soon as possible." Not one, but three, more articles appeared. They were generally much more enthusiastic, and concluded more positively that **Coningsby** outlined in "the progress of an individual mind the operation of causes which are . . . acting on the educated youth of England." [1345, 1346 (15 May 1844)] (In fact, they showed such understanding of the novel's ideas that we cannot rule out some participation by Disraeli himself!)

The said "educated youth of England" were themselves also acting, by assisting in the spread of his opinions. He encouraged both Smythe and Manners in their literary efforts and both also published books in 1844. More relevant to our topic, however, is a sort of writing school which he seems to have run for his followers at the beginning of 1845. The evidence that can be deciphered from Smythe's infuriatingly tiny handwriting suggests that Disraeli had in mind articles for the press. Typically, Smythe seems not to have been totally diligent. On one occasion he wrote, "I have not been working alack"; on another: "I am sticking horribly, but shall nevertheless bring my quota." He seems eventually to have been successful: "To day I wrote two Articles, and both began with *you:* but *they* cut out your name and the citation . . . from Sybil." [1434 (23 Aug. 1845)]

Some of the results seem to have appeared in a monthly (again, a journal which would repay more study). *The Oxford and Cambridge Review* outlasted Young England, but it began precisely when, in July 1845, *The Times* (under Walter Sr.) withdrew its support from the group. Disraeli does not seem himself to have written overtly for it; but his sister calls it "your young Review" and its early numbers were what one can only call incestuous. The first number had an anonymous review of **Sybil** (which turned out to be by Manners) and a long, sympathetic review of six books of poems by Young Englanders; the second had an article on Lord Grey, which was in fact by Smythe and which took care to mention Disraeli by name. The third had a review of a new edition of Disraeli's **Contarini Fleming** and **Alroy.** And so it went.

The *Review* continued to publish long articles on Young England, and later on Protectionism. The initial excitement, however, did not last, and the Young Englanders, instead of capitalising on it, went off on holiday. Manner's contribution dwindled to articles on the Corn

Laws and travel pieces which are virtual transcriptions from his diaries. Disraeli remarked plaintively, "So much for Dandies being Critics." [1434 (23 Aug. 1845)]

Smythe's debt to Disraeli, however, proved useful. Unlike T.J. Ouseley, Smythe was bought by the Peelites in 1846, lured away from Disraeli by the Under Secretaryship for Foreign Affairs (a wholly appropriate post). [1455 (17 Dec. 1845)] *The Morning Chronicle* (which had been Whig) was purchased in 1848 from Easthope as a Peelite organ, and Smythe joined it as a leader-writer. All the articles in *The Morning Chronicle* are, of course, anonymous, but certain allusions, as well as style, seem to allow some identification of Smythe's authorship. Certainly, Disraeli got praise from the *Chronicle* which, considering his opposition to Peel, he might not otherwise have expected. Its leader of 31 Aug. 1848, for example, praising his summary of the session, is probably by Smythe. On 29 August he had written to Disraeli hinting that he would be writing just such an article and pointing out: "You may not be sorry for one word of homage from one who looks back to 43 and 44." [31 August 1848] As well, its terms of reference draw closely on **Coningsby,** particularly in its discussion of the "Venetian" principles of party government which **Coningsby** had criticized.

Again, on 16 December 1848, *The Morning Chronicle* ran a major article which must have helped Disraeli's standing when it proclaimed him *de facto* leader of the Protectionists in the Commons: "He is their only man of genius . . . the only speaker of their party who rescues their doctrines from contempt." It then provocatively turned on him the very question with which he had ended **Coningsby,** asking of the hero . . ."'What will be his fate? Will he maintain, in august assemblies and high places the great truths which in study and solitude he has embraced? or [and here the *The Morning Chronicle* text changes to italics for emphasis] *will his skilled intelligence subside into being the adroit tool of a corrupt party?*'" It was an appropriate question for the point at which Disraeli now stood, and perhaps only Smythe, the original for Coningsby, could have asked it. [20 Dec. 1848]

And what of Disraeli's own writing for the press at this time? One real problem here is, of course, the anonymity of newspaper leaders and articles; even the archives of *The Times* do not identify their writers until the 1850s; and we are continually frustrated by lack of other evidence in firmly ascribing to Disraeli pieces which, from their style and content, seem to be his.

From 1-17 April 1845, he wrote a series of 10 leaders in *The Times,* condemning Peel as party leader in terms reminiscent of some of Disraeli's speeches. [1399 (5 Apr. 1835)] The leaders were brilliant, savage and witty: for example, his piece on the passivity of the Conservatives (not unlike his later comparison of the Whigs to a "row of extinct volcanoes"). On this occasion, he compares them to a Greek chorus which never acts, only looks on: "On either side the vista that conducts to the altar of the State stands a venerable row. Clean, sleek, pious, and resigned, they resemble the victim that bleeds before them [that is, the country under Peel]. Such are the two moieties of the Conservative party. While they are chanting some solemn form of altercation, profaner hands are doing the work of the day."[8] Beneath the rhetoric and beneath the personal attacks lay a deep concern: "A serious question is beginning to occupy the public mind. It is this:—By what sort of political morality is the country to be governed? It has, in its day, been governed by mere brute force. . . . The sword and the gallows settled perplexities. . . . The Premier is the author of a new policy, beyond the example of his predecessors, and it is only fair to add, without a parallel among his contemporaries. He governs by deception. . . . Such is the political morality of a new *regime*—a morality not of force, nor of corruption, but of fraud and disguise."[9]

We think he probably wrote others of this kind closer to the time of Peel's resignation on 29 June 1846; certainly his triumphant note of that day emphasises what had been done through the written word: "All 'Coningsby' & 'Young England' the general exclamation here. Everyone says [the Government] were fairly written down." [1499 (29 June 1846)]

For *The Morning Post,* after Peel's resignation, he seems to have written parts of a series of long political letters in late 1846 and early 1847 published under the heading "The Past, the Present, and the Future," and signed "Phocion." The letters actively promoted the Protectionists as the true Conservative party and attacked the Peelites as dangerously ineffectual. [1530 (26 Dec. 1846)] Not all the pieces in this series bear Disraeli's stamp but some undoubtedly do. This, for example, from 18 November 1846: "Where are the El Dorados promised by Free Trade to our commerce? Where are those piled-up stores, those bursting granaries . . . ? Where are those continuous shipments from Odessa and the Baltic? Where the great Cereal Armada that was to chase hunger from the land . . . ?"

As modern readers, though, we may be most astonished at some newspaper coverage of Disraeli's campaigning in the 1847 election. This is because it involved his reporting his own election meetings—anonymously, of course. Here again, there was a good political reason behind the apparent brazenness. Buckinghamshire was a new constituency for Disraeli, and there were strong movements against him during the campaign. His own press contributions were one way of countering the opposition he faced. On 15 June, at the height of canvassing, he wrote to Michele of *The Morning Post:* "Just arrived. I send you a slight sketch of a very animated scene this morning." [1569] On 17 June, under "election intelligence," there indeed appeared in *The Morning Post* a description of an election appearance by Disraeli at Leighton Buzzard. Not surprisingly, it praised his campaigning, and had particularly good things to say about his speech, airily describing his rural hearers as "several hundreds" and claiming that he had "completely electrified his audience . . . with so much fire and humour that the farmers became enthusiastic."

He tried the same tactic with *The Times.* On 9 June 1847, Delane sent down one of his best reporters to cover a Bucks election meeting. Perhaps thinking to save him trouble for the next one on 12 June, Disraeli wrote to him on 10 June: "1000 thanks for your ever vigilant kindness. The art: in the Times did me great service. With your permission, [which] I shall assume if I do not hear to the contrary, I will myself report the meeting at Buckingham on Saturday, & let you have it at the office on Sunday night." [10 June 1847] He actually did send in a report (again anonymously). But nothing appeared in *The Times,* and he wrote again, enquiring about the fate of his piece, though with a marked change of tone. Diplomatically, he supposed it to have been mislaid: "I don't, for a moment, presume to question the propriety of its insertion or non-appearance." He then humbly asked Delane about coverage for another meeting on 19 June: "If you shd. think what I say there not unworthy of reporting, I shd be obliged & glad." [14 June 1847]

Humility was rewarded. In *The Times* of 21 June appears a two-column account of the meeting, marked (perhaps in rebuke?) "From our Own Reporter." He could do that kind of thing with *The Morning Post,* but not with *The Times.*

By the time of his assuming Protectionist leadership in 1849, Disraeli could not quite yet assert, as he had put it in his 1842 memorandum, that his ideas had "become the voice of a nation." But, largely thanks to his careful management of the press which carried those ideas, he was well on his way. Only two years into the next decade, he would be the Chancellor of the Exchequer (even if only briefly) in a Conservative government made up of those who shared his political opinions.

Finally, the press reaction to his rise in the 1840s even included *Punch* (which was at this time one of the periodicals with whom he had *least* influence.) [1340 (14 Mar. 1844)] *Punch* found him newsworthy from its very earliest numbers in 1841, even when it saw him only as a wordy novelist. In the new Parliament, it thought, "Ben D'Israeli" would move, but only "for a return of all the hard words in Johnson's Dictionary" (28 Aug. 1841). It was harking back to his dandy days when it made fun of him as "the Hebrew Adonis" (11 Dec. 1841), but even then it knew enough about him to be able to give a very respectable parody of his speaking style (2 Oct. 1841). Its respect grew along with its coverage, as when (on 12 Apr. 1845) describing the boxing match between Disraeli, the "Shrewsbury Slasher," and Peel, "Pawky Bob," it acknowledged that Disraeli had got the best of it. By the end of the decade, it mixed real admiration with its irreverence. "Up gits the best man the Tories have to their backs—I mean, in course, their Upper Benjamin. I'm told all was so silent, you might have heard Peel's courage drop. Well, Disreally made hisself up to speak—took his persition! And I can liken that young man on the floor o' the House, to nothin but a penknife of a hundred blades—and every blade open— . . . Yes; Disreally, the Penknife of a Hundred Blades—the Porkipine with steel quills!" [10 Feb. 1849] And when in 1849 Disraeli was at least leader (albeit of the Opposition) in the Commons, it acknowledged his position, even as it undercut him, when it announced under "Good News for Government": "It is not probable that any firm stand against Her Majesty's Ministers will be made in the House of Commons. The head of the Opposition, it is understood, is decidedly Dizzy." [*Ibid.*]

Notes

[1] *Benjamin Disraeli: Letters,* edited M.G. Wiebe, J.B. Conacher, J.P. Matthews and Mary S. Millar III and IV (U of Toronto P, 1987, 1989) V (in press) 23 October 1849. All subsequent quotations from Disraeli's letters are from this edition and are cited in the text. Published letters are referred to by number and date; unpublished letters (to appear in Volume V, in press) by date only. References to appendixes are by Volume number and appendix number.

[2] Donald Read *Peel and the Victorians* (Oxford: Basil Blackwell, 1987).

[3] For more details on parliamentary reporting, see John M. Robson *What Did He Say? Editing Nineteenth-Century Speeches from Hansard and the Newspapers* (University of Lethbridge, 1988).

[4] *The Letters of Charles Dickens* ed Madeline House, Graham Storey, Kathleen Tillotson (Oxford: Clarendon Press, 1974) III 359.

[5] William Flavelle Monypenny and George Earle Buckle *The Life of Benjamin Disraeli Earl of Beaconsfield* (London: John Murray, 1914) III 5.

[6] *The Morning Chronicle* 21 Feb. 1846.

[7] Charles Greville *The Greville Memoirs 1814-1860* ed Lytton Strachey and Roger Fulford (London: Macmillan, 1938) VI 105.

[8] *The Times* 7 Apr. 1845.

[9] *The Times* 16 Apr. 1845.

FURTHER READING

Bibliography

Stewart, R. W. *Benjamin Disraeli: A List of Writings by Him, and Writings about Him, with Notes.* Metuchen, N. J.: The Scarecrow Press, 1972, 278 p.

> In addition to a bibliography of Disraeli's published writings, includes a list of early bibliographies of Disraeli's work and a chronological compilation of his speeches.

Biography

Blake, Robert. *Disraeli.* London: Eyre and Spottiswoode, 1966, 819 p.

> Acclaimed biography stressing Disraeli's personality and its influence on his novels.

Bloomfield, Paul. *Disraeli,* rev. ed. Writers and Their Work: No. 138. Published for the British Council by Longman Group, 1970, 44 p.

> Presents a brief critical overview of Disraeli's life and career.

Bradford, Sarah. *Disraeli.* London: Weidenfeld and Nicolson, 1982, 432 p.

> Explores recently discovered materials relating to Disraeli's private life, in an attempt to more fully understand Disraeli's political career.

Braun, Thom. *Disraeli the Novelist.* London: George Allen & Unwin, 1981, 149 p.

> Traces the development of Disraeli's writing career.

Davis, Richard W. *Disraeli.* Boston: Little, Brown and Co., 1976, 231 p.

> Emphasizes Disraeli's political career.

Monypenny, William Flavelle, and George Earle Buckle. *The Life of Benjamin Disraeli, Earl of Beaconsfield.* 6 vols. New York: Macmillan, 1910-20.

> Definitive biography of Disraeli.

Ridley, Jane. *The Young Disraeli.* London: Sinclair-Stevenson, 1995, 406 p.

> Studies Disraeli's life through 1846.

Criticism

Bewley, Marius. "Towards Reading Disraeli." *Prose* 4 (1972): 5-23.

> Discusses how Disraeli's political career informed his fiction, defending the author against charges that he lacked a sense of history and that his novels were excessively theatrical.

Bodenheimer, Rosemarie. "Politics and the Recovery of Story." In *The Politics of Story in Victorian Social Fiction,* pp. 166-230. Ithaca, N.Y.: Cornell University Press, 1988.

> Examines Disraeli's *Sybil* in a study of how "the shape and movement of narrative" in mid-Victorian novels expresses a response to social change.

Engel, Elliot, and King, Margaret F. "Benjamin Disraeli." In *The Victorian Novel before Victoria: British Fiction during the Reign of William IV, 1830-37,* pp. 61-86. London: Macmillan, 1984.

> Asserts that Disraeli's novels of the 1830s were "at best interesting failures" due to the author's "inability to create a realistic structure onto which his Romanticism could be effectively grafted."

Matthews, John. "Literature and Politics: A Disraelian View." *English Studies in Canada* X, No. 2 (June 1984): 172-87.

> Provides an overview of Disraeli's early novels in an examination of the author's view of the political process.

McCabe, Bernard. "Benjamin Disraeli." In *Minor British Novelists,* edited by Charles Alva Hoyt, pp. 79-97. Carbondale and Edwardsville: Southern Illinois University Press, 1967.

> Evaluates Disraeli's literary career, acknowledging his achievement in making the novel "something intelligently concerned with the spirit of the age."

McCully, Michael. "Beyond 'The Convent and the Cottage': A Reconsideration of Disraeli's *Sybil.*" *CLA Journal* XXIX, No. 3 (March 1986): 318-35.

> Analyzes the development of the title character in *Sybil,* concluding that Disraeli "can be credited with considerable success in bringing his principles to life in her character."

Mitchell, Paul. "The Initiation Motif in Benjamin Disraeli's *Coningsby.*" *The Southern Quarterly* IX, No. 2 (January 1971): 223-30.

> Asserts that Coningsby's initiation into adulthood and into the world of politics provides structure and unity in the novel.

Modder, Montagu Frank. "The Alien Patriot in Disraeli's Novels." *The London Quarterly and Holborn Review* 3, series 6 (July 1934): 363-72.

> Explores how Disraeli's novels reflect both his status as a Jewish member of English society and his pride in his heritage.

Oppenheimer, Franz M. "Survival and Ascendancy." *The American Scholar* 61, No. 3 (Summer 1992): 446-52.

> Surveys Disraeli's career, includes excerpts from his private correspondence, and briefly discusses his political trilogy.

Rosa, Matthew Whiting. "Disraeli." In his *The Silver-Fork School: Novels of Fashion Preceding "Vanity Fair,"* pp. 99-115. New York: Columbia University Press, 1936.

> Discusses Disraeli's prose works from *Vivian Grey* through *Coningsby* as examples of the fashionable novel.

Smith, Sheila, ed. *Mr. Disraeli's Readers.* Nottingham: Sisson and Parker Ltd., 1966, 65 p.

> Excerpts a number of letters written to Disraeli in an effort to explore the contemporary critical response to *Sybil.*

Stafford, William. "Romantic Elitism in the Thought of Benjamin Disraeli." *Literature and History* 6, No. 1 (Spring 1980): 43-58.

> Argues that Disraeli's political ideas were informed by Byronic romanticism.

Weeks, Richard G., Jr. "Disraeli as Political Egoist: A Literary and Historical Investigation." *Journal of British Studies* 28, No. 4 (October 1989): 387-410.

> Contends that Disraeli's novels demonstrate the development of his "peculiar psychology, his consuming sense of ambition, and his romantic Young England vision."

> **Additional coverage of Disraeli's life and career is contained in the following sources published by The Gale Group:** *Dictionary of Literary Biography, Vol. 21: Victorian Novelists before 1885,* **and** *Dictionary of Literary Biography, Vol. 55: Victorian Prose Writers before 1867.*

"The Minister's Black Veil"

Nathaniel Hawthorne

American novelist, short story writer, and essayist.

The following entry presents criticism on Hawthorne's short story "The Minister's Black Veil." For a discussion of Hawthorne's complete career, see *NCLC*, Volumes 2 and 39.

INTRODUCTION

"The Minister's Black Veil" (1836) is one of Hawthorne's best known and most respected short stories. First published in the *Token,* the story is also included in Hawthorne's first collection of short stories, *Twice Told Tales* (1837). On the basis of his efforts in such early stories as "The Minister's Black Veil," which was singled out by critics, Hawthorne earned critical praise and began to establish himself as an American author of repute. Known for its ambiguous and dark tone, the story recounts the tale of a minister so consumed with human sin and duplicity that he dons a veil to hide his face and manifest the spiritual veils that all humans wear. The reasons for the minister's actions and their implications are never fully explained, leaving readers to ponder Hawthorne's meaning. As in such works as "Young Goodman Brown" (1835) and *The Scarlet Letter* (1850), Hawthorne employed the settings and themes that are characteristic of his fiction: a Puritan New England setting, a fascination with the secret sins of humanity, the transformation of an object into a symbol, a dark, somber tone, and a reliance on ambiguity.

Biography

Hawthorne was born into a prominent New England family in Salem, Massachusetts, in July, 1804. His rich family heritage and the leading role his ancestors played in American history shaped Hawthorne's philosophy and writing. His first American ancestor, William Hathorne (the author added a "w" to his name in his youth), arrived in 1630; later, he was involved in the persecution of Shakers. Subsequent family members included John Hathorne, a judge in the Salem Witch Trials of 1692, and Daniel Hathorne, a well-known and respected privateer during the American Revolution. Raised in New England, steeped in his Puritan heritage, and troubled by his ancestors' role in the persecution of others, Hawthorne focused on these themes throughout his life. The author spent his youth in Salem and among his maternal relatives in

Maine, where his family moved in 1818. Breaking with the seafaring tradition of his father's family, Hawthorne attended Bowdoin College in the early to mid 1820s and decided to become a writer. He met with little success for many years and so loathed his self-published and anonymous novel *Fanshawe* (1828) that he attempted to destroy every copy. However, building on the success and critical attention he was beginning to garner from the publication of stories in magazines during the 1830s, he published a collection of short stories and essays entitled *Twice-Told Tales.* The book was ignored by the public and did not earn Hawthorne a profit until its third edition. However, the stories were a great success among critics, including Edgar Allan Poe and Henry Wadsworth Longfellow. Hawthorne finally overcame his financial troubles when he published *The Scarlet Letter,* a novel which has its roots in his earlier writings about Puritan America. After Hawthorne's critical and popular success with *The House of the Seven Gables* (1851), his work began to decline. Upon his death in 1864, Hawthorne had fundamentally altered American literature, serving as the first author to combine a distinctive American voice and historical setting with universal themes of suffering and guilt. Critics cite his work as both reflecting American heritage and timeless.

Plot and Major Characters

"The Minister's Black Veil" is narrated by an unnamed Puritan parishioner in Milford congregation where the title character has lived and preached through the first half of the eighteenth century. The narrator recounts with sympathy and objectivity the story of how the minister, Mr. Hooper, at thirty years of age first donned a veil and how his congregation reacted to this gesture. While the narrator ponders the events, he offers no explanation for why Mr. Hooper took such an extreme action nor what it means. The story opens with the appearance of Mr. Hooper before his congregation on the Sunday morning on which he first wears the piece of black crepe, which in double folds conceals his upper face, particularly his eyes. The events of the first day comprise approximately two-fifths of the story. The congregation is alarmed and shocked by the veil, but the covering seems to lend the minister a new power over them, as seen by the effect of his sermon on the topic of secret sins. The congregation senses that he has entered their hearts and viewed the secrets they hide there. Following the afternoon service, Hooper officiates at the funeral of a young woman. A mourner states that she saw the corpse shudder upon seeing under the veil to the now-covered face of the minister, while another woman describes seeing the minister and the dead young woman standing hand in hand after the funeral. At a wedding which follows the funeral, Hooper's veil casts a somber tone over the normally joyous event. Hooper himself, upon seeing his reflection, is so frightened by it that he spills the wine and departs. Members of the church attempt to ask the minister to remove the veil; however, in its presence they are unable to speak of it. Only Hooper's fiancee, Elizabeth, is not frightened of it. She confronts Hooper, asking what it means and if he will remove it at least once so she can see his face again. Hooper provides her with a mysterious answer which is incomprehensible to her, and although he begs her not to leave him, he insists that he cannot remove the veil for anyone. The narrator describes Hooper's life from then on: revered and possessing a special power over those in moral anguish but cut off from the fellowship of the community and forever alone. The story concludes with the death of Hooper, tended by a devoted Elizabeth. As Hooper is dying, a young minister asks Hooper to remove his veil once before he dies, but Hooper rebukes him, declaring that everyone around him is wearing a veil—all humans wear a veil of darkness. The minister is buried in the veil.

Major Themes

In "The Minister's Black Veil" Hawthorne established the traits for which his fiction would be known. The book is set in Puritan New England and focuses on the particular ideology and theology of the time period. At the heart of The Great Awakening, the Puritans were consumed with the idea of the pervasiveness of sin, believing that all humans sin continuously and that even most church-attending Christians would not enter heaven. However, Hawthorne, living in a later period, objected to such an extreme preoccupation with sin, and while he believed in original sin, he thought that it was tempered by humanity's capacity to do good. In such a setting, Hooper flourishes as a symbol to his parishioners of their own transgressions and the uncertainty of their ultimate fate. As is Mr. Hooper, Hawthorne was fascinated by the idea of secrets, sins which in their isolation destroyed the sinner. The author developed this theme further in *The Scarlet Letter*. In addition, Hawthorne built his story on the effect which an object has on an individual and the community. The veil is transformed from an object into a symbol, significant in its black color and in its ability to shroud and hide. Hawthorne employed the veil to represent the secret, sinful nature of humans, who hide unappealing aspects of themselves behind a veneer of respectability. This is a device he further developed in *The Scarlet Letter*. Throughout his career, Hawthorne advanced an ambiguous view of life, presenting topics from many perspectives, focusing on all possible meanings rather than providing definitive answers. Scholars agree that "The Minister's Black Veil" is Hawthorne's most ambiguous story, seemingly providing several different, even conflicting explanations for the minister's actions and the congregation's reaction.

Critical Reception

"The Minister's Black Veil" is one of Hawthorne's most ambiguous stories and one of the most contentious works in American literature. The fact that Hawthorne did not provide a conclusive and comprehensive explanation of Hooper's motivations and intentions has led critics to engage in over a century of debate, resulting in many varied theories. Some scholars, such as Austin Warren and Leland Schubert, have focused on Hooper's motivations for donning the veil, reflecting upon the terrible sin Hooper must have committed to drive him to such an extreme action. Edgar Allan Poe has argued that Hooper had committed a sexual sin against the woman whose funeral Hooper conducted on the first day. Robert D. Crie has asserted that Hooper fears women and uses the veil as a means to shield himself from sexual encounters. Other scholars have found that the focus of the story is not on what motivates Hooper to wear the veil, but the effect the covering has on the minister and his congregation. Still other commentators discuss the importance of the veil as a symbol of the sin of humanity, noting its black color. Focusing on the tale's ecclesiastic setting and subject, many scholars have considered it in light of Biblical references. The results range from William Bysshe Stein's comparison of Paul's writings about veils in II Corinthians, to Gilbert P. Voigt's theories on the relevance of Old Testament prophets. In contrast, other critics such as George Monteiro and Nicholas Canaday, Jr. have viewed Hooper as a demonic figure who defies God's will. Despite the controversy over the meaning of the story, critics have generally agreed that the story is successful. And still other scholars have proposed that ambiguity is the point of the story. Neal Frank Doubleday has stated: "Discussion of Hawthorne's work should never proceed . . . as if his characteristic ambiguity were not ambiguity really, but a sort of puzzle set for critical acumen to solve. Hawthorne's ambiguity is one of his ways of representing his pervasive sense of mystery, a kind of humility in him." While a few critics, such as Edgar Allan Poe, have found that the story is confusing and fails to achieve its potential, most scholars have praised it as an example of Hawthorne's finest work. For instance, Robert E. Morsberger has declared that the power of the story is Hawthorne's transcendence of the Puritan setting to create a tale which is enduring and timeless and still relevant to today's reader.

CRITICISM

Richard Harter Fogle (essay date 1952)

SOURCE: "The Minister's Black Veil," in *Hawthorne's Fiction: The Light and the Dark,* University of Oklahoma Press, 1952, pp. 33-40.

[*In the following essay, Fogle argues that Hawthorne failed to achieve the full potential of "The Minister's Black Veil."*]

Hawthorne's characteristic fusion of surface simplicity and underlying complexity is perhaps nowhere more clearly evident than in **"The Minister's Black Veil,"** a brief, highly typical, and thoroughly successful story. It is subtitled "A Parable," and the outer meaning of the parable is abundantly clear. An apparently blameless minister inexplicably dons a black veil and wears it throughout his lifetime, despite many well-meant pleas to cast it off. On his deathbed he reveals its secret and its justification:

> What, but the mystery which it obscurely typifies, has made this piece of crape so awful? When the friend shows his inmost heart to his friend; the lover to his best beloved; when man does not vainly shrink from the eye of his Creator, loathsomely treasuring up the secret of his sin; then deem me a monster, for the symbol beneath which I have lived, and die! I look around me, and, lo! on every visage a Black Veil!

The moral is impressive; but as a proposition it is not difficult to grasp, however it may wind and reverberate within the deeps of the imagination. The veil as the visible symbol of secret sin was suggested by Hawthorne's reading in New England history and legend. The veil's solid actuality has the effect of isolating the minister from human society, which unhappy result presumably differs only in degree from the self-isolation of every living soul. The minister is Everyman, bearing his lonely fate in order to demonstrate a tragic truth.

The moral is explicit and orthodox. The explicit statement, however, leads to more than a single possibility. The self-imposed martyrdom of Father Hooper must correspond with some deep necessity of his nature. He who isolates himself in the outward fact must already have performed the deed in spirit. The act of donning the veil has in it something of caprice; it is entirely out of proportion to any obvious necessity or benefit. By it the minister forfeits the affection of his congregation, the chance of human love and marriage, and the sympathy of society in general—and to what end? No note of triumph sounds for him. With remorseless consistency, Hawthorne pursues him even into the grave.

> Still veiled, they laid him in his coffin, and a veiled corpse they bore him to the grave. The grass of many years has sprung up and withered on that grave, the burial-stone is moss-grown, and good Mr. Hooper's face is dust; but awful still is the thought that it mouldered beneath the Black Veil!

One may feel that the veil is less representative of mankind than of the eccentricity of the minister himself, who severs himself from men either through perverse pride or through some other obscure and tragic compulsion. His preoccupation with sin has blunted his perceptions of the normal and the good, which lie as ready to his hand as evil. In rejecting the love of his betrothed, Elizabeth, he casts away a gift of inestimable value in order to satisfy a wild obsession.

If we continue with this reading of the story, we shall take Elizabeth to exemplify the normal and well-ordered human being, as Mr. Hooper represents the abnormal, who has lost the power of seeing life steadily and whole. The "calm energy" of her character, her "direct simplicity," contrasts with the "gentle, but unconquerable obstinacy" of the minister, whom her good counsel fails to persuade, and with his infatuated love of mystification. Hawthorne inherited the psychology, but not the theology nor the morality of his Puritan ancestors; and Elizabeth is more likely to represent his ideal than is the gloomy and sin-crazed Hooper.

Which, then, of these two interpretations shall we accept? Both, I believe—they are both in the story.

Either presents its difficulties. If we take **"The Minister's Black Veil"** at its face value as a homily on secret sin, we are confronted with the apparent disproportion between the act and its causes. The minister himself is to outward gaze the gentlest and least sinful of men; and we have no vivid sense of that presence of Evil which would necessitate so heroic an object lesson. But if we wholly accede to the second interpretation, which makes the steady view of life, the *aurea mediocritas,* the highest good, then the tone and emphasis of the story remain to be explained. It is too deeply gloomy and intense to harmonize fully with such a moral, which should demand a certain dry sparkle and lightness.

This ambivalence of meaning is realized in ambiguity, which occurs with unusual frequency in **"The Minister's Black Veil."** Here its most marked effect is to maintain a balance between subjective and objective in the portrait of the minister, to invite us inside his character while excluding us from any final certainty about it, and, of course, to preserve the objectivity of the narrator, who simultaneously offers and reserves his judgment. Thus, for example, we do not quite know what Mr. Hooper saw through the veil, "which entirely concealed his features, except the mouth and chin, but *probably* did not intercept his sight, further than to give a darkened aspect to all living and inanimate things." The word "probably" bars us from certainty on the point. Again, as the minister preaches for the first time from beneath the veil, it "lay heavily on his uplifted countenance. Did he seek to hide it from the dread Being whom he was addressing?" Hawthorne proposes the question, but does not answer it.

Pressed by Elizabeth to expound the meaning of the veil, Mr. Hooper will reply only darkly. "'If it be a sign of mourning,'" says he, "'I, perhaps, like most other mortals, have sorrows dark enough to be typified by a black veil.'" When she further relates the scandalous whispers in the village that he hides his face from consciousness of secret sin, he will not deny the imputation. "'If I hide my face for sorrow, there is cause enough,'" he merely replies; "'and if I cover it for secret sin, what mortal might not do the same?'" Hawthorne holds out the suggestion that the veil is a penance for an actual and serious crime, while at the same time permitting no real grounds for it. The vulgar interpret the meaning vulgarly, the complacent complacently, and men of good will regretfully. The calm good sense of Elizabeth forces her to regard the veil as the emblem of a tragic but unbased obsession. She believes at first that "'there is nothing terrible in this piece of crape'" but at length yields to its influence, not from a dread of the veil itself, but of what the veil tells her of her lover's state of mind.

The mystery of the veil is hidden to the end among these artfully contrived ambiguities. As Elizabeth leaves him, "Mr. Hooper smiled to think that only a material emblem had separated him from happiness, though the horrors, which it shadowed forth, must be drawn darkly between the fondest of lovers." It is confusing to have the symbol detached from its meaning in this fashion; and the passage calls up another consideration. If the veil alone has separated the minister from happiness, what are we to do with "the horrors, which it shadowed forth?" Surely it is they which shut him off from earthly good. The effect is at once to assert and to cast doubt on the reality of what the veil portrays but also hides. And the smile itself, shining dimly from beneath the black cloth, emphasizes in its self-irony the ambiguity of the minister's character.

The veil has varying effects on different minds and different levels of society. To those "who claimed a superiority to popular prejudice," it is merely "an eccentric whim." In the multitude it occasions either impertinence or superstitious dread, reactions equally grievous to its unhappy wearer. It is whispered that the veil is the obscure intimation of a horrible crime; and there are hints of supernatural forces:

> Thus, from beneath the black veil, there rolled a cloud into the sunshine, *an ambiguity of sin or sorrow,* which enveloped the poor minister, so that love or sympathy could never reach him. *It was said* that ghost and fiend consorted with him there. With self-shudderings and outward terrors, he walked continually in its shadow, groping darkly within his own soul, or gazing through a medium that saddened the whole world. Even the lawless wind, *it was believed,* respected his dreadful secret, and never blew aside the veil. But still good Mr. Hooper sadly smiled at the pale visages of the worldly throng as he passed by.

In one respect, however, the veil makes Mr. Hooper a more efficient clergyman, for it allows him to "sympathize with all dark affections." His words are imbued with its gloomy power, and he can bring sinners to the light denied to him. Yet here as well the effects of the veil are ambiguous. His converts regard the minister with dread, not with love or joy, even though they owe their redemption to him. "Dying sinners cried aloud for Mr. Hooper, and would not yield their breath till he appeared; though ever, as he stooped to whisper consolation, they shuddered at the veiled face so near their own." Hawthorne summarizes the twofold influence of the veil in a climactic ambiguity which embodies its dualism in a series of antitheses: "In this manner Mr. Hooper spent a long life, irreproachable in outward act, yet shrouded in dismal suspicions; kind and loving, though unloved, and dimly feared; a man apart from men, shunned in their health and joy, but ever summoned to their aid in mortal anguish."

This dubiety persists in the final scene at the deathbed, despite the explicit pronouncement with which the scene ends. As the minister lies dying, the veil still rests upon his face, stirred slightly by his faint breath.

> All through life that piece of crape had hung between him and the world; it had separated him from cheerful brotherhood and woman's love, and kept him in that saddest of all prisons, his own heart; and still it lay upon his face, as if to deepen the gloom of his darksome chamber, and shade him from the sunshine of eternity.

If, however, the veil is emblematic of the common plight of man, why should it isolate its wearer with a poignancy unfelt by other men and leave him lonely and alone? We have no sense in the story that all men feel as does Mr. Hooper; they are portrayed, in fact, as a cohesive band, united if only in dread of the fearful veil. Even the minister's colleague, praying by his bedside, rather cruelly misunderstands its significance. Or, on the other hand, is it possible that we can go further afield and determine that the message of the veil *is* representative and universal: that the failure to recognize it is simply the last and most chilling proof of man's imprisonment within himself? If this latter interpretation is the true one, we must conclude that Hawthorne's emphasis upon the problem as embodied in Mr. Hooper has made it impossible for him to deal with it in other characters. To achieve unity of composition his canvas can contain only one important figure. In order to present the tragic isolation of one man, Hawthorne is obliged to consider society as a solid group arrayed against his hero, ignoring for the time being the fact that this hero is Everyman.

We conclude, then, without arriving at a clear decision about the meaning of the tale, but with a sense of depths unplumbed, of rich potentialities not fully realized. The discrepancies between the two interpretations which have been outlined here must go unreconciled. Their mutual presence can, I think, be satisfactorily explained in two ways—one psychological, and one aesthetic—separable, and yet closely related. In the first place, these discrepancies represent the faculties of Hawthorne's own psychology, the heart and the head. His heart, his imagination, the inherited bent of his Puritan ancestry—all his instincts, in short—bind him in sympathy with the possessed minister, who broods over the vague and bottomless abyss of Evil. But his head, his intellect, is with the calm and steady-minded Elizabeth, who is unable to look upon the minister's vow as other than a sad but groundless whim. The ancestral Hawthorne stands beside the nineteenth-century Hawthorne in **"The Minister's Black Veil,"** and their voices do not wholly harmonize.

Second, Hawthorne does not force a reconciliation which he has not, in Keats's words, "proved upon his pulses." Having chosen the symbol of the black veil and invented an action for it, he refrains from pushing the reader to a single conclusion. The minister himself believes the veil to be an emblem of the secret sin that poisons the souls of all mankind, but we are not compelled to accept his reading of the matter. We may, if we like, consider it rather a veil upon his understanding, whose gloomy shade conceals from the eyes behind it as much as it discloses. As it casts its shadow over the bright and various colors of the material world—colors distinct to every unhandicapped observer—so does it darken the vision of the spiritual eye.

The imagination, however, playing freely over the theme, will not content itself to remain within the limits of any single meaning. Beneath the explicit statement, the clear and simple outline of the tale, lie the irony of the minister's smile and the ambiguity of almost every incident. In **"The Minister's Black Veil"** the moral constitutes the framework; but it is merely an element of the completed structure.

Nicholas Canaday, Jr. (essay date 1967)

SOURCE: "Hawthorne's Minister and the Veiling Deceptions of Self," in *Studies in Short Fiction,* Vol. IV, No. 2, Winter, 1967, pp. 135-42.

[*In the following essay, Canaday argues that "The Minister's Black Veil" is not about secret sin but is instead about the sin of pride.*]

Critics have treated the sin of the Reverend Mr. Hooper in **"The Minister's Black Veil"** with a kind of tentativeness not observed in the general critical view of many of Hawthorne's other major characters.[1] That the author's severe moral judgment of Mr. Hooper has never been sufficiently emphasized may be owing not alone to the subtlety of the portrait but also to the brevity of the tale and to the limited cast of characters. The result is that Mr. Hooper is seen in less breadth, though not less depth, than, for example, Arthur Dimmesdale. The rich tapestry of *The Scarlet Letter* pictures complexities of the human soul that can only be suggested in the tale.

"The Minister's Black Veil" has a more exclusively theological base than *The Scarlet Letter,* and thus while it gains in profundity, it loses a measure of universality. In this tale, Hawthorne focuses on man's hypocrisy, specifically that extension of hypocrisy that Reinhold Niebuhr terms the "veiling deceptions" of self.[2] The self as deceiver is constantly engaged in a desperate effort to deceive others with a veil of pretension—whether, indeed, a pretension to respectability, goodness, or even holiness—so that the self as deceiver may gain an ally against the self as deceived. Inevitably the ally of public respect can only be a temporary assuagement of anguish, scarcely of use to the self in believing a deception that the self—as author of the deception—cannot itself believe. This veil of pretension is the result of human hypocrisy, and Mr. Hooper has seen this fact of spiritual life in the members of his congregation and within himself before the tale begins. Upon this general theological base rests the allegory of Mr. Hooper's career.[3]

Yet the broad theological assumption is not the focus of Hawthorne's allegory. It is Mr. Hooper's act of donning the veil, with its ethical and theological results, that is of central thematic concern. Mr. Hooper's awareness of the veiling deceptions of all men has put him in a state of tension that he finds unbearable, and Hawthorne is dramatizing the unhappy results that ensue when Mr. Hooper attempts to ease the tension in the wrong way. Having seen the futility of achieving public respect when self-respect is lacking, Mr. Hooper's response is satanic, motivated by despair and pride.[4] Since it is man's fate to wear a veil, he determines that his will be a real one. With diabolical irony, he mocks himself and his God. Mr. Hooper puts on a real veil to represent (to his congregation, ultimately) the veiling deceptions of all humans and to serve notice (to his God) that he both understands and dares to resent his human condition. Pride is the chief motivation for his act. His veil is visible and tangible and thus superior to the veils all men wear. And so that he will remain intellectually superior to others, pride demands that he merely hint at the meaning of the emblem during his lifetime, reveal it as he expires. He correctly anticipates the consternation his act will cause.[5] The act results in an increasing isolation from fellow man and a growing inhumanity, even cruelty, toward others. Viewed theologically, the results are even more disastrous: the veiling is a conscious and willful act that not only strengthens his pride but also, because it gives him what he believes is a new and superior perspective on human life, results in still another self-deception.

The immediate response of Mr. Hooper's congregation on that first Sunday he wears the veil is one of amazement and confusion. The veil is a barrier between them and their pastor, and his isolation begins at this point. As he prays, the minister's new isolation from God is also revealed: "Did he seek to hide it [his countenance] from the dread Being whom he was addressing?"[6] An estrangement begins here and persists throughout Mr. Hooper's life. One notes that the life of Hester Prynne in *The Scarlet Letter* parallels his in this regard. Her spiritual isolation continues to the end of her life, but like Mr. Hooper she is re-integrated into the community life within a relatively brief time. He becomes by the end of his life the revered Father Hooper. What Hawthorne writes about him applies with equal accuracy to Hester: "Mr. Hooper spent a long life, irreproachable in outward act, yet shrouded in dismal suspicions; kind and loving, though unloved, and dimly feared; a man apart from men, shunned in their health and joy, but ever summoned to their aid in mortal anguish" (I, 66). Both characters redeem themselves in the eyes of mankind, though there are similar reservations in each case; and after their early aberration the townspeople give both a special place in the life of the community, the differences arising solely from Mr. Hooper's position as a clergyman, though even here Hester's role as nurse and confidante is parallel. But as with Hester it is the outward act that is irreproachable; inside there is prideful superiority. Hawthorne's comment on the acceptance of Hester by the people also may serve as a gloss on the status of the venerable Father Hooper: "Society was inclined to show its former victim a more benign countenance than she cared to be favored with, or, perchance, than she deserved." (v, 196)

Mr. Hooper's sermon on the Sunday he first wears the black veil takes secret sin as its subject. The choice of the subject matter does not indicate that he has in mind a specific secret sin of his own, but rather reflects his concern on this momentous day with the veils of deception by which men in general hide their sins and keep them secret. Hawthorne describes the sermon in general terms: "The subject had reference to secret sin, and those sad mysteries which we hide from our nearest and dearest, and would fain conceal from our own consciousness, even forgetting that the Omniscient can detect them" (I, 55). The phrase "would fain conceal from our own consciousness" reveals Hawthorne's understanding of the tension between the self as deceiver and the self as deceived, and the "forgetting that the Omniscient can detect" the sins is, of course, only a momentary forgetting. In short, Mr. Hooper's sermon is motivated and informed by an insight that he has had into the nature of all men by the simple device of examining himself. Unfortunately, the import of the sermon is obscured by the black veil. The effect of the sermon is great, but it is due to the veil and not to the words; its effect is emotional and not intellectual. Mr. Hooper has found a new power to move his congregation, but it is made clear throughout the tale that they never understand him. Something "in the sentiment of the discourse itself, or in the imagination of the auditors" (*Ibid.*), now moves his congregation. The black veil affords his sermon a powerful emotional aura but at the same time obscures its essential meaning.

The obscurity is deliberate and effective. As if to re-emphasize the function of the black veil as barrier to effective communication, Hawthorne puts the final comment on Mr. Hooper's appearance in the mouth of the self-confessed "sober-minded" man of the village, typically the physician. This sage observes: "Something must surely be amiss with Mr. Hooper's intellects" (I, 57). The physician is speaking about the minister's act of donning the veil, and that he makes no reference to the sermon itself indicates that even the more intellectual members of the community have responded only emotionally.

When Mr. Hooper disappears into the parsonage at the end of his first veiled appearance in church, "a sad smile gleamed faintly from beneath the black veil" (I, 56). At this point one might take the smile to indicate fondness; it is soon revealed as diabolical. The melancholy smile is referred to seven more times during the course of the tale: once when he receives the delegation of parishioners, three times in the important central scene with Elizabeth, once as he contemplates the rumors that the veil has given him supernatural powers, once on his deathbed just before he pronounces his final moralizing statement about the veils of men in general, and finally as it lingers on his corpse lying in the coffin. The import of this smile, which is condescending and self-satisfied, is crucial as a symbol of his spiritual pride. Roger Chillingworth's smile of self-irony, mentioned twice in the opening scene of *The Scarlet Letter,* and the constant presence of the same smile during his first interview with Hester in Chapter IV are an effective gloss on Mr. Hooper's smile. Hawthorne describes Chillingworth's smile as "a smile of dark and self-relying intelligence" (v, 97). Therefore, I do not agree with the reading of Thomas F. Walsh that Mr. Hooper's smile is ambiguous in the sense that it "betokens the minister's tenuous ties with his fellow men and his shaky hold on his own sanity."[7] Walsh bases his reading on the *smile-light* association, the smile frequently gleaming or glimmering in contrast to the enveloping blackness of the veil. But again we may profitably go to *The Scarlet Letter* in order to understand this imagery. Hawthorne does something very similar when at the end of the novel he describes the meaning of the heraldic device of the tombstone: the "sombre" legend is "relieved by one ever-glowing point of light gloomier than the shadow" (v, 312). Viewed theologically, the scarlet of passion is gloomier than its Puritan environment, just as Mr. Hooper's smile, though a glimmer of light, is gloomier than the black veil. Hawthorne seems fond of this paradox.

At the moments when he smiles, Mr. Hooper is deceiving himself into believing that he has resolved the tension of his warring self. In the first instance he is bidding farewell to his congregation, proudly perceiving the consternation he has wrought. An ambiguity is possible here: it could be sympathy. But in the second instance a delegation of parishioners has assembled "to make the black veil a subject of friendly remonstrance" (I, 60). Yet the black veil itself intimidates them, and Mr. Hooper speaks not a word. In this tense scene some overt word of sympathy from their pastor is what they require, but they perceive only the melancholy smile. This and later references to the smile consistently indicate Mr. Hooper's pride in a new superiority he feels over ordinary human beings because of his black veil. The view from behind the veil gives Mr. Hooper what he believes to be an absolute perspective on life, but central to Hawthorne's allegory is the author's recognition that finite man can never achieve such a view. The act of donning the veil has thus resulted in further sin: the failure of Mr. Hooper to recognize the finiteness in his new perspective, the pride that accompanies this lack of recognition, and the cruelty that accompanies the pride.

Mr. Hooper's first call to pastoral duty after he has donned the black veil occurs that first Sunday afternoon when he must officiate at the funeral service of a young lady. This scene serves to show the increasing isolation of Mr. Hooper from his flock and affords him the opportunity to hint further at the meaning of the black veil. As he bends over the corpse and his features are momentarily disclosed by the swinging veil, did the corpse shudder? Hawthorne points out that only one person, "a superstitious old woman" (I, 58), so testified. This detail simply reinforces the idea of the emotional response that the veil has engendered in the people. And the people are impressed by his prayer: "The people trembled, though they but darkly understood him when he prayed that they, and himself, and all of mortal race, might be ready, as he trusted this young maiden had been, for the dreadful hour that should snatch the veil from their faces" (*Ibid.*). Again the impression the prayer makes is emotional; they tremble, but they understand only darkly. The universal significance of the veil is only hinted, and there is pride in Mr. Hooper's gnostical attitude.

The wedding scene that follows the same night is the last episode of the first day. The funeral had been a time of grief; now there is a time of joy. At the funeral, Mr. Hooper did nothing to assuage the grief of his parishioners, as his pastoral duty would require; and at the wedding he effectively spoils the joy of the occasion. Hawthorne links these two scenes, putting them in close proximity, in order to show Mr. Hooper's inhumanity in the widest possible spectrum of normal relationships to his congregation. The whisper that "the maiden who had been buried a few hours before was come from her grave to be married" (I, 59) reflects once again the emotional impact of the black veil while at the same time showing how the joy of the wedding was dispelled by Mr. Hooper's presence. When the minister catches a glimpse of his own veil in the wine glass, he shudders with horror, spills the wine, and rushes away. From that moment "the black veil involved his own spirit in the horror with which it overwhelmed all others" (*Ibid.*). Essentially this is a moment when Mr. Hooper sees that he has redoubled his own sin, a moment of self-transcendence when he sees both the sinful nature of the act and the results of it.

Once having established the conflict between Mr. Hooper and his congregation resulting from the wearing of the veil, Hawthorne next turns to a more personal and intimate relationship, that between the minister and his intended bride. It is with Elizabeth that Hawthorne shows the black veil to have its most serious consequences: the violation of a human heart. As Elizabeth comes to him, she is the "one person in the village unappalled by the awe with which the black veil has impressed all beside herself" (I, 61). She asks him to put aside his veil and, failing that, to tell her why he wears it. His smile glimmers faintly as he answers: "There is an hour to come . . . when all of us shall cast aside our veils" (*Ibid.*). Such an answer is unintelligible to Elizabeth, although it hints again at the veiling deceptions of all mankind. Mr. Hooper's pride demands that he do no more than hint. That he smiles before he gives the answer warns the reader that he will be deceptive. Elizabeth then asks him to explain his words, and he replies that "this veil is a type and symbol" (I, 62). Even in that explanation he reveals his pride. The veil is typical of the veils that all men wear and (in his mind) superior because it is a conscious, concrete embodiment of this veiling impulse. So it becomes also, in more general terms and unrecognized by Mr. Hooper, a symbol of the pride of the evil will. Elizabeth, misunderstanding because deliberately misled, assumes it to be a symbol of some grievous and secret affliction. "If it be a sign of mourning," Mr. Hooper continues, "I, perhaps, like most other mortals, have sorrows dark enough to be typified by a black veil" (*Ibid.*). The *if* clause deliberately deceives, as does his statement that follows, again preceded by the same smile: "If I hide my face for sorrow, there is cause enough, . . . and if I cover it for secret sin, what mortal might not do the same?" (*Ibid.*). His real reason is contained in none of these speculations.

Elizabeth represents the norm of human wholeness and love in the story. Her love even transcends the human when it becomes self-sacrificing. In character she is the superior of Mr. Hooper: "Though of a firmer character than his own, the tears rolled down her cheeks" (I, 63). Finally, the "terrors" (*Ibid.*) of the black veil overcome her, and she cannot speak. Her response is stronger than that of the others (terror, not horror) because she is closer to this man; and in a flash of insight she sees the veil truly as a symbol of his own weakness and sin, a symptom of a deep spiritual disease. Her response contains understanding as well as strong emotion. She will not speak of this response, though he specifically asks her how she is affected, and the minister momentarily despairs in his loneliness. After this brief moment of self-transcendence, however, he soon smiles again "to think that only a material emblem had separated him from happiness, though the horrors which it shadowed forth, must be drawn darkly between the fondest of lovers" (I, 63-64).

Again he is secretly pleased with the effect of the black veil, failing to see in his ignorance that Elizabeth fears for him and that it is his sin, not his emblem, that has in fact separated him from happiness.

Mr. Hooper spends the rest of his life isolated from human love and sympathy, though Elizabeth remains faithful through all of his life and at the end nurses him on his deathbed. His antipathy to mirrors or the reflecting surface of water becomes well known. He is frightened when he himself sees the black veil. And the antipathy "was what gave plausibility to the whispers, that Mr. Hooper's conscience tortured him for some great crime too horrible to be entirely concealed, or otherwise than so obscurely intimated" (I, 64-65). But this reason is founded only on rumor. Mr. Hooper is frightened not because of a secret sin in his past but because the veil, when he can see its reflection, reminds him of the awful sin embodied in the act of donning the veil. Now he becomes a more effective preacher: he has more power. What this means is that he has a new power to evoke an emotional response of horror in his congregation that they in their ignorance mistake for a powerful spirituality. At the end of the tale Hawthorne summarizes the results of Mr. Hooper's act: "All through life that piece of crape had hung between him and the world: it had separated him from cheerful brotherhood and woman's love, and kept him in the saddest of all prisons, his own heart." (I, 67)

At the end of his life Mr. Hooper pridefully reveals his so-called motive for donning the black veil, that it typifies the veiling deceptions of all men. In his famous comment on this story, Poe rightly calls this speech "the moral put into the mouth of the dying minister" and correctly sees that this overt moral is not "the true import of the narrative."[8] Yet the true import escapes Poe. Hawthorne is not stressing secret sin in this tale, especially sexual sin as Poe suggests. Rather he is exploring the sin of pride with its demoniac pretensions and inhuman results. The misguided minister, aware of the finiteness of the human condition, yet daring to resent it, seeks to compensate for it and thus to overcome it. With satanic irony Mr. Hooper dons the veil in order to gain an absolute perspective on life. The final irony is Hawthorne's, for whom the veil must symbolize the imperfect human vision, which, because of the finiteness of the human condition, sees only darkly.

Notes

1 An excellent summary of the criticism of this tale is provided by E. Earle Stibitz, "Ironic Unity in Hawthorne's 'The Minister's Black Veil,'" *American Literature,* XXXIV (May 1962), 183-184. Not included is the reading of Robert W. Cochran, "Hawthorne's Choice: The Veil or the Jaundiced Eye," *College English,* XXIII (February 1962), 342-346, which sees Mr.

Hooper as achieving a steady acceptance of life and the ultimate in human knowledge. Cochran's reading, which he correctly describes as at sharp variance with the consensus, is, I believe, mistaken.

2 *The Nature and Destiny of Man* (New York, 1946), p. 207.

3 Mr. Hooper has an awareness, before the beginning of the story, that Arthur Dimmesdale achieves only near the end of *The Scarlet Letter.* Dimmesdale's act of stripping away all veiling deception and revealing his naked self to the people and to God cannot renew a debilitated body, but it restores the spiritual vitality of his soul.

4 William B. Stein, "The Parable of the Antichrist in 'The Minister's Black Veil,'" *American Literature,* XXVII (November 1955), 390, correctly points to the satanic denial of love in the minister's act, but I believe that Mr. Hooper sees more than merely "a shadow of his own veil" (p. 392) on the faces of his people.

5 In the central chapter of *The Scarlet Letter,* "The Minister's Vigil," we observe Arthur Dimmesdale on the scaffold at midnight having a vision of how it would be should he remain there until morning. He too is thinking of the consternation he would create among his parishioners. Each minister is concerned with his public image even as he proclaims his own sin; and because of the element of pride unmistakably present, we know that true repentance is still in the future.

6 *The Complete Works of Nathaniel Hawthorne,* George P. Lathrop, ed. (Boston, 1883), I, 54. All subsequent page references to this edition will be made parenthetically in my text.

7 "Hawthorne: Mr. Hooper's 'Affable Weakness,'" *Modern Language Notes,* LXXIV (May 1959), 406. E. E. Stibitz, with whose previously cited essay I am in general agreement, accepts Walsh's assumption of ambiguity but stresses its ironic element.

8 *The Works of Edgar Allan Poe,* John H. Ingram, ed. (London, 1899), IV, 218.

Robert D. Crie (essay date 1967)

SOURCE: "'The Minister's Black Veil': Mr. Hooper's Symbolic Fig Leaf," in *Literature and Psychology,* Vol. XVII, No. 4, 1967, pp. 211-18.

[*In the essay below, Crie first provides an overview of the critical theories regarding Hooper's reasons for wearing the veil, then argues that it serves to protect the minister from women, whom he fears.*]

Then the eyes of both were opened, and they knew that they were naked; and they sewed fig leaves together and made themselves aprons.

—Gen. iii.7.

Nathaniel Hawthorne's short story, **"The Minister's Black Veil,"** first published in the *Token* (1836), and later in **Twice Told Tales** (1837), relates how an apparently innocent minister inexplicably covers his face with a black veil which he wears throughout his lifetime, despite the pleas of many people that he cast it off. Critical interpretations of the story vary, but the approaches taken may be divided into five categories.

(1) The veil indicates that the good minister is guilty of some crime, some secret sin which he harbors in his soul. This interpretation, held by such critics as William Bysshe Stein, Richard Harter Fogle, Millicent Bell, Edgar Allan Poe, Darrel Abel, R. B. Browne, Marden J. Clark, and Harry Levin, would seem to be the most popular one, although no critic can suggest satisfactorily what the secret sin is.[1]

(2) The veil symbolizes man's natural bent toward a withdrawal from life into a self-imposed isolation, into a realm of concentrated introspection for the sake of personal insight and knowledge. Such a contention might at first seem valid, for Mr. Hooper becomes a more effective clergyman and a greater source of comfort to the suffering after he dons the veil. But exactly how a withdrawal from life produces adequately compensating benefits is left unexplained by those critics who hold this view: Hyatt Waggoner, Newton Arvin, R. W. B. Lewis, Carl Van Doren, Robert W. Cochran.[2]

(3) Another group of critics, including Neal F. Doubleday, Terence Martin, Randall Stewart, and E. E. Stibitz, see the black veil as a symbol pointing up the basic hyprocrisy of all men, for as the minister wears a literal veil which hides his face, so all men wear figurative veils to hide their real selves.[3]

(4) Still other critics (Henry Seidel Canby, Thomas Walsh) view the wearing of the veil as a sadistic or masochistic practice. By his wearing of it, he harms others as well as himself.[4]

(5) A final group of critics see the veil as a psychological symbol, but only in an incomplete and limited sense. Arlin Turner stresses that Hawthorne's "study was human nature" and his concern "mainly psychological," but Mr. Turner supplies no details. Richard P. Adams feels that Hawthorne, "like Freud," was "much interested in what is now called the 'Oedipus Complex,'" and he notes that such themes as "incest, parricide, and fear of castration . . . appear in both men's work," but he does not expand his statement and he makes no detailed study of specific tales. Adams does

admit that three themes in Hawthorne—"the young man's attraction to a sexually potent woman, his struggle to free himself from . . . a fatherly man, and his achievement of, or his failure to achieve adult status"—"are precisely those with which modern psychoanalysis has been most deeply concerned," but again he names no characters who evidence such traits. Rather, he leaves the reader to draw his own conclusions. The only critic who comes close to what seems to be the most reasonable explanation for the veil is Rudolph Von Abele, although he, too, stops short of a full and complete discussion of all the implications. Attempting to interpret Hawthorne's writings in terms of Hawthorne's biography, Mr. Von Abele stresses that Hawthorne was "haunted . . . by the image of the sexually attractive woman in whose atmosphere men become strangely ineffectual." His contention is that Hawthorne feared sex, deriving no "pleasure in the play of physical love," and choosing to equate the three terms "dirt," "excrement," and "sex." Such an equation is most obvious, says Von Abele, when one reads his love letters to Sophia Peabody written during their courtship.[5] Speaking generally, Mr. Von Abele mentions Hawthorne's "womb-dwellers" who are "sexually crippled," and he hints that "the veil worn by Father Hooper . . . is a case in point" (see Von Abele, pp. 29, 104), but he hesitates to say more. He thus suggests (by implication) that the veil is a psychological hiding place behind which Father Hooper dwells because he doubts his manhood. But does Mr. Hooper don the veil because it is an effective hiding place? Does he fear the responsibilities of manhood which a normal life would thrust upon him? Can he achieve a measure of peace by "taking the veil"? Such questions Mr. Von Abele never directly asks nor answers, but he does lay open the way for the reader to discover a more reasonable explanation for the veil than has been previously suggested.

A good place to begin a detailed study is with the subtitle, "A Parable." What is a parable, and what bearing does this subtitle have on the story? Technically, a parable is any short narrative which is used to convey moral instruction. The most obvious associations are the Biblical parables, and one thinks immediately of the ewe lamb (II Sam. xii.1-4), the prodigal son (Luke xv.11-32), or the lost sheep (Matt. xviii.11-14). Sometimes the meaning of the parable is explained (as in the case of the "sower who went forth to sow" [Matt. xiii.3-23]), but more often only hints as to its meaning are given, the hearers interpreting for themselves. Such an approach is Hawthorne's. He tells a story subtitled "A Parable" without explaining its meaning, but he tells it in such a way that the informed reader should have little trouble understanding his point.

Several of Hawthorne's notebook entries cast light on the meaning. In an entry dated 1836 the following idea occurs: "An essay on the misery of being always under a mask. A veil may be needful, but never a mask. Instances of people who wear masks . . . and never take them off even in the most familiar moments."[6] Another entry, this one noted by Julian Hawthorne, reports: "Miss Rebecca Pennell says that . . . she used to see a certain old Orthodox minister . . . [who] looked so much unlike everybody else, that it never occurred to her that he was a man, but some . . . sort of contrivance."[7]

The fact that Hawthorne here is not writing a realistic story but an allegory or a "parable" is important. **"The Minister's Black Veil"** is not realistic, for one cannot imagine a minister donning a black veil as part of his clerical garb, or a congregation retaining a minister who wore such a thing. Rather, Hawthorne seems to be doing the same here as in *The House of the Seven Gables,* for as he suggests in the Preface to that book, a certain advantage exists in writing a Romance instead of a Novel, such as permitting an author the "right to present . . . truth under circumstances . . . of the author's own choosing or creation." Yet he uses the word "truth," a significant choice. Thus the story, while not bound by any conception of "minute fidelity," does seek to present reality. Hawthorne discusses this intermingling of truth and imagination also in his Preface to *Twice Told Tales,* of which this story is part. Here he suggests that "even in what purports to be pictures of actual life we have allegory," implying that the minister's veil is a real veil, but also more than a veil.

All of the interpretations mentioned above see the veil as a symbol, but that symbol demands closer examination. In the usual sense, a veil is merely a length of cloth worn to cover the head and shoulders, and sometimes, especially in eastern countries, to cover the face. The term also suggests the "outer covering of a nun's headdress," or the "cloistered life of a nun." Veils are worn for protection or ornament, and they hide or obscure things. "Vale," a term pronounced the same way but spelled differently, suggests a further meaning. Here the idea is of a valley or a dale, the word deriving from *valere,* "to be strong," and akin to *wield.* Mr. Hooper indeed dons his veil as a protection from the world (now it may no longer see his face), and as the symbol of his withdrawal from the world (he has "taken the veil"). As a result he lives withdrawn in a kind of valley or dale experience apart, cut off, protected. Hawthorne is very fond of the veil image, and uses it often in his fiction, especially in *The House of the Seven Gables*[8] and in *The Blithedale Romance.*[9] Hyatt Waggoner believes that Hawthorne uses veils to indicate changes in attitudes, and he uses *The Blithedale Romance* as evidence. "As the years darkened around Coverdale," notes Mr. Waggoner, he sees "the meaning of the veil changing from that which hides a truth one wants to know to that which hides a reality one fears to know." Richard Harter Fogle says much the same thing when he points up a relationship to the veil symbol in Shelley's poetry, the piercing of which brings knowledge, but not always desired blessings.[10] Does Mr. Hooper wear the veil to hide a reality he fears to know, his own inadequacy? We know when Mr. Hooper dons the veil, but as yet why he put it on and what it signifies remain mysteries.

In 1837, as has already been pointed out, Hawthorne published **"The Minister's Black Veil"** as one story in his *Twice Told Tales* collection. Interestingly, and one feels not accidentally, the story appeared in a significant spot in the collection, sandwiched between **"The Wedding Knell,"** a mysterious tale which presents a bridegroom in his shroud, wedding bells which sound like a funeral knell, and speeches such as this: "Come, my bride, . . . the hearse is ready. . . . Let us be married, and then to our coffins" (ed. Pearce, p. 20); and one of Hawthorne's most realistic works dealing with sexual relationships between man and woman, **"The Maypole of Merrymount."** Five years after the publication of *Twice Told Tales,* Hawthorne married Sophia Peabody, this in spite of his ambivalent attitude toward marriage. In **"Earth's Holocaust"** he seems to urge the abolition of marriage; in **"The Canterbury Pilgrims"** he stresses the disappointments of marriage; in *The Blithedale Romance,* chapter six, he suggests that marriage often has a deleterious effect on women's manners, and in chapter twenty-two, he hints that marriages are often prompted both by despair and by hope; in *Fanshaw* (chap. 4) he treats of marriage for money. It is also interesting that the man chosen to wear the veil in this story is a minister, one of that class toward which Hawthorne seemed to show much hatred.[11] One sees a certain reluctance on Hawthorne's part to view ministers as anything but bloodless, spineless creatures, standing somewhere between the marriage-death image of **"The Wedding Knell"** and the frustrations implied in the maypole experience. Is it possible that the Reverend Mr. Hooper dons the veil to protect himself from the demands of manhood, of marriage, of sex?[12] The suggestions of such a conclusion are abundant in the story. For here Hawthorne has chosen to use veiled sexual overtones, in vocabulary and in actions, to hint at the fact that the minister wears his veil as an escape from the responsibilities of his manhood.

The story opens with definite sexual overtones: the sexton "stood . . . pulling . . . the bell-rope," the old people "came stooping," the "children with bright faces, tripped merrily," and "spruce bachelors looked sidelong at the pretty maidens" (p. 123).[13] The day is right for a love experience. But when Mr. Hooper appears, his face veiled, the parishioners are astonished. Now the minister is not Mr. Hooper, but only "the semblance of Mr. Hooper" (p. 123), only a non-material essence hidden behind a veil. Mr. Hooper, a man "of about thirty, though still a bachelor" (p. 124), may well don the veil at this time because he fears to face responsibilities. Not only has he ceased to be his true self ("the semblance" hinting at some type of mutilation), but he wears a black (dead) cloth "swathed about his forehead, and hanging down over his face" (p. 124). The veil, in its shape and color, suggests a fig-leaf-shaped loin cloth hiding the bright visage of the young minister. He has chosen to forsake the world at an age when his powers of manhood are at their greatest ("thirty"), and he has taken the way of a symbolic mutilation experience. He walks about in a way "customary with abstracted men" (p. 124), suggesting that a part of him ("abstracted") has been taken away (*abstrahere,* "to draw away"). His parishioners, "wonderstruck" by his appearance, cannot "really feel as if . . . Mr. Hooper's face was behind that . . . crape" (p. 124). If they cannot feel that his face is there, where has it gone? Has it symbolically been lost? Also, crape (or "crepe" as it is now commonly spelled) is a death symbol, the cloth usually worn on a hat or a sleeve as a sign of mourning. If Hawthorne is not trying to suggest mutilation, why does he so carefully use terms indicative of such a thing? One old woman in the congregation, well past her prime in life, does not like the veil, calling the minister "something awful" ("awful" may be used here in its usual meaning of "terrible," or Hawthorne may have in mind the historical meaning, "full of awe"), while Goodman Gray (a male commentator) feels that his minister "has gone mad" (p. 124). Although Hawthorne is careful to note the general "perturbation" of the congregation, he singles out one "white-haired great grandsire" for special consideration. As Mr. Hooper enters the church, he bows to this one man (and to no other person), who is visibly moved by the veil. The reverence due to an obvious "father-figure" is, perhaps, joined with a suggestion of identification with one who has passed the age of potential fatherhood.

Hawthorne, of course, never states openly what he means the veil to symbolize, but his choice of words to treat of it bears investigation. The veil is first called a "mysterious emblem" (p. 125), and is then treated in terms strangely akin to the sexual. As the minister preached, the veil "shook with his measured breath." It "threw its obscurity" out over the listeners. When he ceased, "the veil lay heavily on his uplifted countenance." And Hawthorne asks a question strangely reminiscent of the reason that Adam and Eve "sewed fig leaves together": "Did he seek to hide it from the dread Being whom he was addressing?" The effect both of his appearance and apparently of his words was so great, Hawthorne notes, that "more than one woman of delicate nerves was forced to leave the meeting-house" (p. 125). The minister's first sermon from beneath the veil is heavy in voyeuristic overtones, for not only is the topic "secret sin," but each listener feels as if the minister has "crept upon" him and "discovered" his "hoarded iniquity of deed or thought" (pp. 125-126). The longer the congregation listen, the more sexually suggestive become the words used to describe their reactions. They seem to feel that "a stranger's visage," not Mr. Hooper's, is under the veil, though "the form" is Hooper's. They hurry out of the service with "indecorous confusion" and "pentup amazement," a few of the faithful intimating that "they could penetrate the mystery" (p. 125). The effect of the veil on the minister himself is also worth noting. Wearing the veil, he seems "ghostlike from head to foot," and one woman suggests to her husband that now the minister might be "afraid to be alone with himself," to which her husband responds, "Men sometimes are" (p. 127).

Three not accidental and not unrelated events occur on the first day that the minister wears his veil. He first preaches the sermon on secret sin just mentioned. Then he conducts a funeral, at which a most interesting thing happens. As the minister is bending over the coffin (which contains the corpse of a young "maiden"), the veil swings out, revealing his hidden face to the corpse. At that moment the corpse "slightly shuddered, rustling the shroud and muslin cap" (p. 127). The "dead maiden" has seen beneath the veil; she has peeped under the figleaf. The result is so shocking (and only two witnesses observe the event—the impotent minister and "a superstitious old woman") that even a dead body seems to react. One mourner, after the ceremony, notes that perhaps during the ceremony "the minister and the maiden's spirit were walking hand in hand" (p. 128). If both the girl and the minister are dead (the girl physically, the minister sexually and emotionally), that is not hard to believe. Finally, he performs a wedding, joining "in wedlock the handsomest couple" in the village. Hawthorne is careful at this point to suggest that the minister's veil can "portend nothing but evil to the wedding" (p. 128). A wedding brings hopes of sexual fulfillment and physical delight, but the veiled minister can bring only "evil" if his veil is suggestive of mutilation, for such a suggestion has no place in a wedding ceremony. Furthermore, when the minister attempts to drink a glass of wine after the ceremony, his own reflection in a looking glass frightens him, causing him to spill the wine. Thus he is never permitted to taste the wine, a symbol of revelry. Because Bacchus (Dionysus), the god of wine and fertility, has no sympathy with emasculation, the minister may hardly be allowed to partake of a bacchanalian potion.

Several other items in the story are worth noting, insofar as they bear on this idea. The "imitative little imp" who mimicks the minister by wearing a black handkerchief has not yet reached puberty; the minister suffers from a "painful . . . degree of self-distrust" (p. 129), a hint that he doubts his own

masculinity; when the church committee calls on him to inquire about the veil, the crape seems "to hang down before his heart" (protecting him), and the committee (robust men that they are) cannot communicate with him (they are "speechless" in his presence) (p. 130); as a result of the veil, the minister becomes "a very efficient clergyman," but one who lives "a man apart from men," only being summoned in times of "mortal anguish" (pp. 133-134), a kind of sexless angel of mercy, necessary but apart; it is the minister's "customary" habit to "walk at sunset to the burial ground" (p. 133), a practice he had apparently always engaged in, but hardly one indicating an active life in the world of men; as the years go by, he acquires the title "Father Hooper" (p. 134), although he is neither a celibate priest nor an actual father. The title is thus ironic in one sense (he was never an earthly father, having fled from such, and at his death he had no "natural connections" or kin), and factual in another. He does become a man apart, a sexless doer of good deeds, a kind of unreal or Platonic essence of goodness.

Mr. Hooper has retired from the active world of men into a sexless world of his own creating, and even his "plighted" cannot enter it. Elizabeth does feel, however, that "it should be her privilege to know what the black veil concealed" (after all, she thinks she will be his wife!), but she is never "overawed" by it. The multitude may be frightened and awestruck by its solemnity, but to Elizabeth it is nothing "but a double fold of crape." She does not fear it as an object, for she says "there is nothing terrible in this piece of crape"; she does, however, fear it as a symbol of something greater than itself: "it hides a face which I am always glad to look upon" (p. 130). The only horror which the piece of crape has for this womanly woman is the fear of sexual denial, a fear which the minister only increases when he tells her, "this veil is a type and a symbol, and I am bound to wear it ever, . . . in light and darkness, in solitude and before the gaze of multitudes, and as with strangers, so with my familiar friends. No mortal eye will see it withdrawn" (p. 131). Two items in this speech are worth noting: the minister must wear it to hide his private self (his face) from the gaze of others, and he must wear it to hide himself (his mutilation?) from himself.[14] Lest Elizabeth take any hope that she might have a part in the veil's removal, Mr. Hooper adds, "even you, Elizabeth, can never come behind it" (p. 131).

The minister's own explanation for the veil suggests two ideas: he hides his face, he says, "for sorrow" or "for secret sin" (p. 131). Mutilation, especially self-inflicted physically or emotionally, would be a cause for sorrow, and the deliberate harming of one's body is sin, as Paul suggests: "Know ye not that ye are the temple of God. . . . If any man defile the temple of

God, him shall God destroy; for the temple of God is holy, which temple ye are" (I Cor. iii.16-17). Thus if the minister has harmed his own physical body, he might, as a man of religion, see a reason for hiding his face. But in this case his "sorrow" or "secret sin" is not, as some critics would have us believe, a moral sin, but merely a self-inflicted sexual annihilation.[15] That Elizabeth seems to understand the full impact of his words in terms of her own life is obvious when we note that she is so overwhelmingly moved "the tears rolled down her cheeks" (p. 132). Furthermore, Elizabeth remains unmarried all of her life (has she too "taken the veil"?), and we discover her nursing the minister in his dying hours, perhaps to guarantee that his veil, his symbolic figleaf, may remain intact and unmoved. For even as he lay dying, the minister "still showed an awful solicitude lest the black veil should slip aside," but Hawthorne reminds us, if such should happen, faithful Elizabeth, "with averted eyes" (of course!) "would have covered that aged face" (p. 135), perhaps protecting herself from a curse similar to the one which fell upon Ham when he saw his father Noah's nakedness (Gen. ix.20-27). Thus the veil, which "had separated him from cheerful brotherhood and woman's love" (p. 135), remains intact even to the time of his interment, protecting him from the prying eyes of his fellows.

Here endeth the reading of the lesson ("parable"), but is such an explanation psychologically defensible? Are behavioral patterns such as the minister's common to men? Seemingly they are, for Norris Yates suggests that a clear relationship exists between Hawthorne's use of masks and the "medieval Dance of Death," showing an unconscious death wish, while Martin Grotjahn argues that the man who had "lost his face" had also lost his individuality, for he had become a nobody.[16]

Mr. Hooper's black veil: what then does it symbolize? Is it, as some have suggested, a public declaration of a secret sin? Is it a symbolic statement of man's natural bent toward isolation? Is it a way for the minister to point up graphically the basic hypocrisy of all men? Is it a sadistic practice engaged in by a tortured individual seeking to impose his own misery upon others? Or is it a symbolic way for Hawthorne to show a psychological conflict existing in the minister's soul, a basic dependence upon, yet fear of women? A careful rereading of the story will admit the possibility of all five interpretations, but should point up the final possibility (the psychological conflict due to sexual maladjustment) which most satisfactorily provides a solution to the mystery of the black veil, the minister's symbolic fig leaf.

Notes

1 Stein, "The Parable of the Antichrist in 'The Minister's Black Veil,'" *American Literature,* XXVII, 392 (Nov,

1955); Fogle, *Hawthorne's Fiction: The Light and the Dark* (Norman, Okla., 1954), p.6; Bell, *Hawthorne's View of the Artist* (New York, 1962), p. 68; Poe, "Nathaniel Hawthorne: Twice Told Tales," in *Complete Works* (New York, 1902), VII, 348; Abel, *American Literature* (Great Neck, N. Y., 1963), II, 193, 197; Browne, "The Oft-Told Twice Told Tales; Their Folklore Motifs," *Southern Folklore Quarterly,* XXII, 75 (June, 1958); Clark, "The Wages of Sin in Hawthorne." *Brigham Young Univ. Studies,* I. 21-36 (Winter, 1959); Levin, *The Power of Blackness* (New York, 1958), pp. 17, 42, 46.

2 Waggoner, *Hawthorne: A Critical Study* (Cambridge, Mass., 1955), p. 187; Arvin, *Hawthorne* (New York, 1961), p. 59; Lewis, "The Return Into Time: Hawthorne," in *The American Adam* (Chicago, 1955), p. 115; VanDoren, in *DAB* s. v. "Hawthorne, Nathaniel"; Cochran, "Hawthorne's Choice: The Veil or the Jaundiced Eye," *College English,* XXIII, 344-345 (1962).

3 Doubleday, "Hawthorne's Inferno," *College English,* I, 658-663 (1940); Martin, *Nathaniel Hawthorne* (New York, 1965), pp. 53, 81-85, 119; Stewart, *The American Notebooks* (New Haven, Conn., 1932), p. xiviii; see also Mr. Stewart's comments in *Nathaniel Hawthorne: A Biography* (New Haven, Conn., 1948), pp. 256-259; Stibitz, "Ironic Unity in Hawthorne's The Minister's Black Veil.'" *American Literature,* XXXIV, 182-190 (May, 1962).

4 Canby, "Hawthorne and Melville," in *Classic Americans* (New York, 1959), pp. 229-240, 245, 248; Walsh, "Hawthorne: Mr. Hooper's 'Affable Weakness,'" *Modern Language Notes,* LXXIV, 404 (May, 1959).

5 Turner, *Nathaniel Hawthorne: An Introduction and Interpretation* (New York, 1961), p. 64; Adams, "Hawthorne's Provincial Tales," *New England Quarterly,* XXX, 52 (1957); Von Abele, *The Death of the Artist* (The Hague, Holland, 1955), p. 7.

6 Stewart, *The American Notebooks,* p. 35.

7 *Nathaniel Hawthorne and His Wife* (Boston, 1886), I, 493.

8 Phoebe, as a result of living with Hepzibah and Clifford in the House, felt that "a veil was beginning to be muffled about her," cutting her off from the world (New York, 1961), p. 187.

9 The "veiled lady" who plays so important a role in this novel is mysterious yet sexually attractive (see chaps. 1 and 13), and she speaks of being "a sad and lonely prisoner, in a bondage which is worse to me than death." When Theodore flings her veil upwards, he catches a glimpse of her "virgin lips" and of a "pale,

lovely face" (New York, 1958), pp. 130-131. Also, late in the book after Zenobia has been rejected by Hollingsworth, She says to Coverdale, "When you next hear of Zenobia, her face will be behind the black veil" (p. 232); Zenobia, of course, is referring to the fact that she will kill herself by drowning and will next be seen only as a corpse.

[10] Waggoner, *Hawthorne: A Critical Study,* p. 186; Fogle, "Nathaniel Hawthorne," in *Eight American Writers,* ed. Norman Foerster and Robert P. Falk (New York, 1963), p. 623. One might examine Shelley's "The Revolt of Islam" in this connection.

[11] Julian Hawthorne, I. 107. Hawthorne, writing to his mother from Salem, March 13, 1821, says: "I have not yet concluded what profession I shall have. The being a minister is of course out of the question. I should not think that even you could desire me to choose so dull a way of life. . . . I was not born to vegetate forever . . . to live and die as *calm and tranquil as—a puddle of water*" ([italic] face mine).

[Ed. note: footnote number 12 is missing from original.]

[13] All page references to the story are given in parentheses and refer to *Selected Tales and Sketches,* ed. Hyatt H. Waggoner (New York, 1956).

[14] Psychoanalysts, on the basis of dream analysis, have discovered an unconscious relationship between the face and the genitals. See Sigmund Freud, *Collected Papers,* ed. Ernest Jones (New York, 1959), IV, 84, 92, 96; and Freud, *The Basic Writings,* ed. A. A. Brill (New York, 1938), pp. 388, 565, 568.

[15] See Bruno Bettelheim, "Ritual Surgery," in *Symbolic Wounds* (New York, 1962), pp. 90-108, for possible implications.

[16] Yates, "Ritual and Reality: Mask and Dance Motifs in Hawthorne's Fiction," *Philological Quarterly,* XXXIV, 56 (1955); Grotjahn, *Beyond Laughter* (New York, 1957), p. 184.

W.B. Carnochan (essay date 1969)

SOURCE: "'The Minister's Black Veil': Symbol, Meaning, and the Context of Hawthorne's Art," in *Nineteenth-Century Fiction,* Vol. 24, No. 2, September, 1969, pp. 182-92.

[*In the essay below, Carnochan discusses the role of the veil both to conceal and to represent concealment.*]

"The Minister's Black Veil," one of Hawthorne's early tales (1836), has a reputation as one of his best.

It has had less attention than, say, **"Rappaccini's Daughter"** or **"My Kinsman, Major Molineux,"** no doubt because it is in some ways less problematic and is a less bravura piece than are they. Still the story presents its own kind of difficulties, and there is no critical unanimity among its readers. On one view the Reverend Mr. Hooper is a saintly figure, calling his people to repentance in the manner of an old testament prophet;[1] on another view he is a victim of monomaniac obsession, one of Hawthorne's unpardonable sinners or, even, a type of antichrist.[2] Between these extremes, opinion shades off to a less monochromatic center.[3] But interpretation of the story generally rests on some moral assessment or explanation of the minister's symbolic self-veiling. The mystery is conceived as one to be *solved,* just as Poe conceived it when he argued that the minister had committed a "crime of dark dye" against the "young lady" whose burial is described.[4] What Poe calls a defect—"that to the rabble its exquisite skill will be *caviare*"—he surely thinks a virtue: he is happy in the discovery of concealed evidence, from which he infers a romantic solution more congenial to his taste than the merely generalized didacticism of the "moral" that the minister pronounces at his death. I shall argue, to the contrary, that neither solutions, like Poe's, nor moral estimates, like many a critic's and even the minister's own, are essential.[5] The story, I believe, is concerned above all with the veil as a symbolic object, pointing toward questions that cluster about the notion of a symbol itself. Beside these questions the moral character of the minister who wears the veil is relatively a minor matter.

If so, this early story has a more important place than it is usually given in Hawthorne's canon: like *The Scarlet Letter*—which is *about* the letter of its title, just as this story is about the veil—**"The Minister's Black Veil"** has to do with the materials of Hawthorne's own art in proportion as it has to do with the nature of symbolic meaning. Thinking about this story, we need to remember all the while the abortive history of Hawthorne's last romances and the altogether desolate end of his literary life—where we get, as Hyatt H. Waggoner has said, "no merely technical failure, and no turning to new subjects that he did not know how to handle, but a failure at the very center, a failure of meaning."[6] This failure of meaning is a failure of the symbolic process: the relationship, always for Hawthorne a difficult matter, between symbol and reference breaks down entirely, and the course of his artistic life can be roughly plotted in terms of this disintegration.[7] **"The Minister's Black Veil"** stakes out the ground on which Hawthorne was to struggle with the angel of destruction.

Even to ask the bald question, "What does the veil stand for?" implies the difficulty of giving any answer. Perhaps it is just as well, however, to frame the question in a way that makes the difficulties apparent. In any case, the Hawthornian business of false leads and doubtful clarifications is under way from the very start of the tale. In an introductory note, we hear about "another clergyman in New England, Mr. Joseph Moody, of York, Maine, who died about eighty years since" and who "made himself remarkable by the same eccentricity that is here related of the Reverend Mr. Hooper." Then, still with an air of being helpful and direct, Hawthorne offers what seem to be distinctions: "In his case [Moody's], however, the symbol had a different import. In early life he had accidentally killed a beloved friend; and from that day till the hour of his death, he hid his face from men." But what sort of distinctions are these? And how precisely are Moody and Hooper different cases? The explanation, on a closer look, turns out not to be an explanation at all. Of what is Mr. Moody's veil a "symbol"? Grief, surely; but we do not know the "accidental" means by which he killed his friend, nor do we know except in a general way why he hid his face from men. We are faced with an "ambiguity of sin or sorrow," as much as in Hooper's case. Hawthorne's note—like the veil itself—obscures as much as it reveals. Still, despite the falseness of its reassurance, there is something of the genuine in it, too; it is in keeping, as I want to show, with the whole point of the tale that Hooper's mysterious veil has a counterpart in reality. Here again it is like the scarlet letter with its counterpart that Hawthorne finds in the custom house and is at such pains to be precise about ("By an accurate measurement, each limb proved to be precisely three inches and a quarter in length" [V, 50]). Each fictional symbol is attached to a fact in the real world.

We can try another question, a little less blatant: what does Hooper's veil stand for in its own context? Because the minister's dying speech sounds a dominant note, or seems to, it is easy to go there first of all:

> When the friend shows his inmost heart to his friend; the lover to his best beloved; when man does not vainly shrink from the eye of his Creator, loathsomely treasuring up the secret of his sin; then deem me a monster, for the symbol beneath which I have lived, and die! I look around me, and, lo! on every visage a Black Veil!

Coming as it does at the end, this looks like summary and conclusion. But that is as deceptive as the authoritative air of the opening footnote. If we throw caution aside and take this last pronouncement as conclusive, the story is that parable of hidden guilt which it is usually supposed to be—and also, I think, a less interesting story than it really is. Hooper's final piety, his deathbed utterance with its implied confession, all this needs to be taken dramatically—as a formal setpiece—and with the reservations appropriate to so pat a gesture. It is the end, or almost the end, of the story—but

not the whole of it. We need not, in fact cannot, let it go as a drama of clandestine sin. Granted that Hawthorne was concerned, deeply so, with that theme; but here it is concealment and mystery, not guilt, that concerns him most, and that makes the difference.

The very nature of the veil itself is to avert explicit statements of what it stands for, or at least to throw them immediately in doubt. It is not just that "the meaning of the symbol is ambiguous"; that would tell us little we did not always know. Rather the strange quality of the veil is that not only does it conceal what is behind it, it is a sign of that concealment; it both symbolizes and generates what is symbolized, is its own symbol—and, in its self-containment, is in one sense beyond interpretation, i.e., beyond any rendering in referential terms. But to "mean" is a function of the human, to "be" a function of the divine; a symbol, humanly speaking, implies something symbolized that is not only itself. So the veil, creating meaning and simultaneously hiding it, invites speculation and resists it. No one ever dares ask Hooper why he wears the veil. The deputation from the church, sent to "deal with Mr. Hooper about the mystery"— how obviously inappropriate is the commercial dealing with mystery—never comes to the point: "Were the veil but cast aside, they might speak freely of it, but not till then." Because the meaning of the veil consists only in what is hidden, meaning is lost in the very act of revelation. It is in this that the veil serves as "type" and "symbol" of types and symbols in their general nature. As language gives a meaning to experience but also comes between the subject and any direct perception or re-creation of that experience, so does the veil. "In a Symbol," says Carlyle (as Professor Teufelsdröckh), "there is concealment and yet revelation."[8] Hooper's veil embodies the paradox.

In this setting the common Hawthornian tactic that F. O. Matthiessen calls "the device of multiple choice" and Yvor Winters "the formula of alternative possibilities"[9] works to special advantage. The tactic is uncomplicated: merely that of offering several explanations of events or symbolic circumstances and apparently leaving the reader, according to his own lights, to accept the one that suits him best. "The reader may choose," says Hawthorne, among the several theories proposed to explain the mark (if there was one) "imprinted" in the Reverend Mr. Dimmesdale's flesh (V, 305-306). But the formula is really designed to prevent, not to encourage, speculation. We are intended *not* to choose; it is difficult to suppose that Donatello has furry ears, but it is damaging to suppose that he doesn't. And, by the same token, it is damaging to limit the extensions of the veil to this one or to that. It is not one veil but every veil. It is the glass through which we see darkly; Hooper appears in the pulpit *face to face* [my emphasis] with his congregation, except for"—a grim irony—"the black veil." Elsewhere it is associated with the darkness of night that obscures the visible world, or with "the veil that shuts in time from eternity." Sometimes it turns Hooper away from the mirrors of self-knowledge: "In truth, his own antipathy to the veil was known to be so great, that he never willingly passed before a mirror, nor stooped to drink at a still fountain, lest, in its peaceful bosom, he should be affrighted by himself." He resists the last knowledge that he is hidden even from himself. But, still elsewhere, the veil itself becomes a magic mirror, reversing the world of normal experience in its transfiguring presence: the funeral of the young woman is transformed to a marriage ("I had a fancy," says one observer—giving Poe the lead he was looking for—"that the minister and the maiden's spirit were walking hand in hand"), and the "cold fingers" and "death-like paleness" of a bride at her wedding change the ceremony into a dance of death. For the veil all things are possible; its extensions come naturally from its primary character as a symbol of symbols, hence capable of all their protean changes. If we cannot eliminate the human fact of reference, still we need not commit ourselves to other versions of the absolute and insist on singleness of reference; since a single correspondence cannot be finally established, that way lies either delusion or skepticism and despair.

To insist on a single meaning or explanation is in fact to be like the townspeople of the story, who speculate upon the reasons for Mr. Hooper's veil: "A few shook their sagacious heads, intimating that they could penetrate the mystery; while one or two affirmed that there was no mystery at all, but only that Mr. Hooper's eyes were so weakened by the midnight lamp, as to require a shade." In this case we are specifically not asked to choose—the technique has not yet crystallized into a "formula" of alternative possibilities—and we do well to profit from the absence of advice. The alternatives available are each intended to be unacceptable: on one hand, to be identified with the "sagacious" few who think they can penetrate the mystery; on the other, to deny the mystery altogether. Either choice is self-defeating. But "sagacious" readers have not been wanting.

In truth, however, they have better reasons than any we have seen so far. Misguided prying into the mystery by "all the busybodies and impertinent people in the parish" is one thing; the case of Elizabeth, betrothed to Mr. Hooper, looks more doubtful. Her plea that Hooper take off the veil and reveal his secret to her is a sympathetic one; probably it is her presence that accounts for the view of Hooper as a malevolent spirit: "As his plighted wife, it should be her privilege to know what the black veil concealed." The scene that follows between Elizabeth and Hooper is a strange one, however. To her request that he "lift the veil but once," he answers that it cannot be. The feeling aimed at seems to be that the veil in literal fact *cannot* be re-

moved; it is not, we are made to think, a volitional matter. But Elizabeth bids Hooper farewell, and the strangeness is especially in Hooper's response: "But, even amid his grief, Mr. Hooper smiled to think that only a material emblem had separated him from happiness, though the horrors, which it shadowed forth, must be drawn darkly between the fondest of lovers." On one hand it is "only a material emblem," on the other it seems to be everything; but symbol and thing symbolized, however (other than itself) that may be interpreted, are felt as concordant with one another. And there seems to lie the motive for Elizabeth's reappearance to nurse Hooper at his death—"no hired handmaiden of death, but one whose calm affection had endured thus long in secrecy, in solitude, amid the chill of age, and would not perish, even at the dying hour." The long endurance of a "calm affection" comes unexpectedly after Elizabeth's abrupt farewell in the earlier scene; the assertion of fidelity in the presence of mystery is no easy one for Hawthorne to make, and the narrative lacks cohesion at the point of greatest strain. An assertion, nonetheless, there is: to keep faith is to accept the fact of human meaning behind the veil—even though that meaning, in the nature of things, is hidden to the eye.

But the phantom lure of knowing the unknowable is not so easily set aside. Mr. Hooper's veil and the efforts—Elizabeth's well-intentioned ones, the townspeople's vulgar and impertinent ones—to discover what lies behind it anticipate the veils and masks and efforts to "penetrate their mystery" that are so important in Hawthorne's later fiction. They make a large subject, beyond the reach of this paper.[10] Also beyond the reach of this paper are the details of Hawthorne's decline. But this generalization may be risked: it is the possibility of faith—by that I mean a habit of mind more crucial than any specifically religious belief, the failure of which is sometimes supposed to account for Hawthorne's fate as an artist—that is for him ever more in doubt. The vain hope of lifting the veil and the fears of what might be found there (or, really, what might not be found there) become obsessive and, in the long run, paralyzing to the imagination. A brief and very selective glance ahead will throw a last light on Mr. Hooper's story. Elizabeth, in her enduring affection, is an image of what Hawthorne would, but in the event could not, be.

A good place to look first is Zenobia's legend, in *Blithedale,* of the veiled lady—that odd amalgam of folklore and pure Gothic claptrap ("undeniable nonsense," says Coverdale, "but not necessarily the worse for that")—where the situation is identical, in its essentials, with that of **"The Minister's Black Veil."** The outcome has changed, however, and the Gothic terrors are real enough as things, this time, are forced to their conclusion. The prying Theodore refuses to kiss the lady unless he see her face unveiled; she rebukes him for coming "not in holy faith" but in "scornful scepticism and idle curiosity"; he lifts the veil, still fearing lest he kiss "the lips of a dead girl, or the jaws of a skeleton, or the grinning cavity of a monster's mouth," and the lady vanishes. If Hooper's story and Elizabeth's good faith intimate the presence of meanings behind the veil, even diabolic meanings, Zenobia's fable raises another possibility that is more sinister: "But what, in good sooth, had become of the Veiled Lady? Had all her existence been comprehended within that mysterious veil, and was she now annihilated?" (V, 442; 448; 449) The fears that are buried deep and never (unless, we shall see, at the very end) allowed to emerge in **"The Minister's Black Veil"** are explicit here: that existence is comprehended only in veils and masks, liable to annihilation and revealing then the nothingness behind them.

These fears are the stuff of nightmare, and the carnival scene at the end of *The Marble Faun,* where the masks of the revellers are not just veils that conceal but grotesque images that haunt and mock the observer, marks another critical point on the long downward line. Kenyon, waiting information about Hilda, clings desperately to a lamppost lest he be swept away by the crowd (the allegory is plain enough) and searches the faces about him: "He looked at each mask,—harlequin, ape, bulbous-headed monster, or anything that was absurdest,—not knowing but that the messenger might come, even in such fantastic guise. . . . At times, his disquietude took a hopeful aspect; and he fancied that Hilda might come by, her own sweet self, in some shy disguise which the instinct of his love would be sure to penetrate." To observers on a balcony above the crowd, detached epicurean spectators of the chaos, Kenyon's search for the messenger (intelligence and meaning) and for Hilda (love and requital) makes him ludicrous. His behavior looks "unutterably absurd" as he pores "into this whirlpool of nonsense so earnestly, in quest of what was to make his life dark or bright." The moral of the nightmare scene: "Earnest people, who try to get a reality out of human existence, are necessarily absurd in the view of the revellers and masqueraders." They are absurd because perhaps no "reality" is to be "gotten out" of human existence at all. But then comes the extraordinary sequel, in which the strength of doubt is compensated by an extravagance of rhetoric and event, marking a conviction, surely, that it is now a case of all or nothing. A shower of confetti makes Kenyon look upward to the balcony where he sees the priest to whom Hilda has made confession. He fails to associate him with Hilda, looks back to the crowd, and is immediately struck from one side by a cauliflower, from the other by "a single rose-bud, so fresh that it seemed that moment gathered. It flew from the opposite balcony, smote gently on his lips, and fell into his hand. He looked upward, and beheld the face of his lost Hilda!" (VI, 508; 510) The laugh-

ing epicurean gods are replaced by Hilda in her white domino; memories of the ridiculous cauliflower, cancelled out by the mystical rose.

Unintentionally funny as the scene may in some ways be, the urgency of it all is underlined by the tortuous and unsatisfying explanation of events that Hawthorne "reluctantly" added to his romance. He has failed, he thinks, "in throwing about this Romance the kind of atmosphere essential to the effect at which he aimed." That is, he has failed to avert questions on the order of: had Donatello furry ears? "As respects all who ask such questions, the book is, to that extent, a failure." But he goes on, even so, to "throw light upon several matters in which some of his readers appear to feel an interest," and he admits that "he was himself troubled with a curiosity similar to that which he has just deprecated on the part of his readers." This is disastrous, for here is poor Hawthorne as an unspiritualized Paul Pry, a meddling and impotent questioner who cries out finally "with intense earnestness," "Did Donatello's ears resemble those of the Faun of Praxiteles?" and gets the only possible answer: "'I know, but may not tell,' replied Kenyon, smiling mysteriously. 'On that point, at all events, there shall be not one word of explanation.'" (VI, 522; 523; 527) Of course the failure to strike a balance between romance and reality might be set down as a failure of craftsmanship, just as Hawthorne seems to prefer, so dark is the alternative. But in fact all relationships have been shattered—between romance and reality, symbol and reference, cause and effect. For one thing Hawthorne has failed to establish adequate connections between events and failed equally to establish conditions in which these connections could be accepted as present, though concealed. Elizabeth's reappearance at the close of **"The Minister's Black Veil,"** though a little startling, is psychologically plausible—and nothing at all like Hilda's miraculous incarnation on the balcony, an assertion of meaning that is felt only as an isolated event, one with no antecedent cause. For another thing Hawthorne has failed to endow Donatello's ears with the symbolic range, the manifold possibilities of reference, that he imparted to Hooper's veil. Even for Hawthorne, it seems, Donatello's ears require somehow to be one thing or another, to be furry or not; indeed the symbol here has dwindled into a thing. And Hawthorne never had much confidence in "mere" things.

The case of Donatello's ears brings us very close to the last, unfinished fragments where the nature of the disease is defined by symbols or things—who is really to say?—that point nowhere. This is Winters' diagnosis: "We have the symbolic footprint, the symbolic spider, the symbolic elixirs and poisons, but we have not that of which they are symbolic."[11] Or to put it another way: Hawthorne has no assurance that symbols are symbolic of something, and that in turn is to say (with Waggoner) that meanings have failed. Perhaps symbols are no more than things; events, perhaps without explanations; the present, without an identifiable past. In Hawthorne's futile search, while he was in England, for the facts of his own ancestry, he had found that the veil separating him from his origins could not be lifted. He would not have missed the typological possibilities of his failure. It was as though (an American neurosis) he had no origins at all.

From this bleak vantage, we can look back to **"The Minister's Black Veil,"** now in a fuller perspective. Despite Elizabeth's fidelity and despite the wan hope in that "faint, sad smile, so often there, [that] seemed to glimmer from its obscurity, and linger on Father Hooper's lips" as he dies, no one is likely to mistake the mood of the tale. Elizabeth's affection, revealed so late, scarcely relieves the gloom, and the last word is still the veil: "The grass of many years has sprung up and withered on that grave, the burial stone is moss-grown, and good Mr. Hooper's face is dust; but awful is still the thought that it mouldered beneath the Black Veil!" The veil survives the changes of time after its meanings have turned to dust. Acceptance was not Hawthorne's lot, nor was the unreflective life, whose matter-of-factness he sometimes catches sight of with a touch of longing and reproduces here in the accents of the village, at the beginning of the tale:

> "Are you sure it is our parson?" inquired Goodman Gray of the sexton.

> "Of a certainty it is good Mr. Hooper," replied the sexton. "He was to have exchanged pulpits with Parson Shute, of Westbury; but Parson Shute sent to excuse himself yesterday, being to preach a funeral sermon."

"Certainty" is for the unthoughtful, acceptance for the faithful; for Hawthorne, there will be only the gathering pressure of questions not to be answered and meanings not to be found. In its fine rhetorical adjustment of means to ends, **The Minister's Black Veil"** is among Hawthorne's best stories; in mood and substance it is grimly prophetic of what was to come.

Notes

[1] See Gilbert P. Voigt, "The Meaning of 'The Minister's Black Veil,'" *College English,* XIII (March 1952), 337-338; also Robert W. Cochran, "Hawthorne's Choice: The Veil or the Jaundiced Eye," *College English,* XXIII (Feb. 1962), 342-346. "The Reverend Mr. Hooper," says Cochran, "has been permitted to cross over beyond the veil of mystery to achieve the ultimate in human knowledge" (p. 345).

[2] See E. Earle Stibitz, "Ironic Unity in Hawthorne's 'The Minister's Black Veil,'" *American Literature,* XXXIV (May 1962), 182-190; William Bysshe Stein, "The Parable of the Antichrist in 'The Minister's Black Veil,'" *American Literature,* XXVII (Nov. 1955), 386-392; also Nicholas Canaday, Jr., "Hawthorne's Minister and the Veiling Deceptions of Self," *Studies in Short Fiction,* IV (Winter 1967), 135-142; and Frederick C. Crews, *The Sins of the Fathers: Hawthorne's Psychological Themes* (New York, 1966), pp. 106-111.

[3] E.g., R. H. Fogle, "'An Ambiguity of Sin or Sorrow,'" *New England Quarterly,* XXI (Sept. 1948), 342-349.

[4] *The Works of Edgar Allan Poe,* ed. John H. Ingram (London, 1901), IV, 218. For "The Minister's Black Veil," see *The Complete Works of Nathaniel Hawthorne,* ed. George Parsons Lathrop (Boston, 1883), I, 52-69. Quotations from Hawthorne's works are identified in the text by volume and page reference to this edition.

[5] George Monteiro comes near my sense of the story by emphasizing Hawthorne's recurrent use of the word "mystery"; *Explicator,* XXII (Oct. 1963), no. 9. So does Frederick W. Turner, III, who says that the veil is "to be interpreted as ignorance or that which divides men from the true knowledge of things"; *Studies in Short Fiction,* V (Winter 1968), 187.

[6] *Hawthorne: A Critical Study* (rev. ed.; Cambridge, Mass., 1963), p. 236.

[7] Rudolph von Abele has done so in *The Death of the Artist: A Study of Hawthorne's Disintegration* (The Hague, 1955). His argument in part is this: "My contention here is that so far as Hawthorne failed to work by the method of presenting things as 'lived experience,' he failed completely, which in practice means that he failed almost every time his symbolism was overt and deliberate" (p. 19). He thinks "The Minister's Black Veil" a success, essentially because it is "realistic": "Hawthorne sometimes resorted to symbols that required no rationalization to be seen in a normative naturalist context. The veil worn by Father Hooper in 'The Minister's Black Veil' is a case in point, and an interesting one. The only problem in connection with it is of motivation, but this problem is satisfactorily solved on a number of different levels—Hawthorne's, Hooper's, the reader's. The gesture may be eccentric, but it is not miraculous, and it is not explained away" (p. 29).

[8] *Sartor Resartus,* ed. Charles Frederick Harrold (New York, 1937), p. 219.

[9] Matthiessen, *American Renaissance* (New York, 1941), p. 276; Winters, *Maule's Curse* (Norfolk, Conn., 1938), p. 18.

[10] The subject becomes even more far-reaching as soon as one looks to other writers contemporary with Hawthorne. Robert Edward Goodfriend raises some of the issues in a master's thesis, "Transformation of the Gothic: A Study of the Veil in the Works of Poe, Hawthorne and Melville" (Stanford, 1965).

[11] P. 19.

Raymond Benoit (essay date 1971)

SOURCE: "Hawthorne's Psychology of Death: 'The Minister's Black Veil,'" in *Studies in Short Fiction,* Vol. VIII, No. 4, Fall, 1971, pp. 553-60.

[*In the essay below, Benoit traces the existential philosophy in "The Minister's Black Veil," arguing that Hooper represents the freedom of accepting human finitude.*]

Straightforward analyses of Hawthorne are hard to come by for the simple reason that he was not straightforward; he was fully aware that the world of human affairs is indeed a round one. More often than otherwise, enigmas rather than answers—or enigmas that are answers—confront the reader of his fiction: the red letter on the black field at the end of *The Scarlet Letter,* the Pantheon in *The Marble Faun,* the man with the red and black face who startles Robin in **"My Kinsman, Major Molineux,"** or the minister's veil. It is no anachronism to say that he seems to set himself squarely against any Great Society by calling attention through visual symbols to something negative at the center of human existence. Alfred Kazin had this in mind when he wrote in *The New York Review of Books* of what he called Hawthorne's ghost sense: "As a storyteller, choosing to represent psychic situations rather than to explain them, Hawthorne found himself suggesting uncertainties where there had always been God's truth, drawing shadows and hinting at abysses where there had always been clarity, straining to find images of the imponderable, the blackness and the vagueness, even the horror that waits in what he called 'the dim region beyond the daylight of our perfect consciousness.'"[1] Indeed; with such an emphasis Hawthorne stands to Emerson as Kierkegaard to Hegel: their fiction and philosophy remind the essentialists of existence by reminding them of death and of the limitations of theory in the face of death. Hawthorne stresses the dimensional, and is a pioneer of that movement towards the concrete that we call existentialism. He does not muse lovingly upon the bric-a-brac in his parlor or the goods for sale in Hepzibah's cent-shop for nothing: like Hemingway he also fears abstraction and its attendant disorder. In significance, the cent-shop is not far from the camp in "Big Two-Hearted River": heaven and hell like war and civilization might be problematic, but selling gingerbread men and making flapjacks are certain.

Further studies of Hawthorne may very well go in this direction. The themes of existentialism are there: the relationship between faith and science, the danger of abstraction, the limitations of reason in the face of human finitude, the conflict between the genuine and the false self, and the notion of truth as subjective. His works, in fact, re-examine the concept of truth. They show powerfully that truth is not a matter of the intellect's judging correctly (Plato's view), but of the whole man's experiencing concretely (Kierkegaard's view)—Hester and Dimmesdale, Hepzibah and Clifford, Miriam and Donatello. Perhaps the person who learns this distinction most painfully is Hollingsworth in *The Blithedale Romance,* who comes to know only through Zenobia's death that he owes homage to the Furies as well as to Apollo. But it takes her death to make him realize this, to make him realize that man's aspirations are shot through and through with his limitations, and that these limitations are integral to being a man, to being at all. Similarly, the eighteenth chapter of *The House of the Seven Gables* is a masterful presentation of what it means to live. The picture of Judge Pyncheon alone and dead in the house dramatizes, paradoxically, that he was dead as a person while he lived as a social power and financial success. In long and macabre paragraphs Hawthorne depicts the civic functions that the Judge would be attending at the moment if he were alive. The contrast, however, is not between death and life but between two kinds of death, each as real as the other. The whole episode recalls "The Death of Ivan Ilyich," and it is just as important in the history of changing thought. Hawthorne's fiction does define what it means to be. The play of light and dark images that we find in his work should be read from this angle, and not as opposite emotions jousting for supremacy in Hawthorne himself. The idea of a divided Hawthorne shrouded in Puritanic gloom but dedicated to nineteenth-century normalcy arises from a basic failure to grasp what he shows about human nature. Fully to be for him means to see non-being in the center of being.

The widespread misinterpretation of this emphasis on "the blackness and the vagueness" stems possibly from an important early story and even from its title, **"The Minister's Black Veil"** (1836). It is one of the richest Hawthorne wrote and one of the least understood because it deals with a mood that has only recently been defined for us—the mood of anxiety. If we can understand that mood and this story, then it seems to me that we will be in a better position to understand that Hawthorne's works draw shadows and hint at abysses for reasons often other than those we have accepted.

The plot is simple enough. A minister, about thirty, appears one Sunday morning wearing a black veil "which entirely concealed his features, except the mouth and chin, but probably did not intercept his sight, farther than to give a darkened aspect to all living and inanimate things."[2] No one understands why he wears it, though it is "a type and a symbol" that affects all who see it, including his betrothed, Elizabeth, who leaves him when he will not lift the veil for her. After a long life as "a man apart from men, shunned in their health and joy, but ever summoned to their aid in mortal anguish," he dies and is buried still wearing the veil. Since the tale has the subtitle "A Parable," presumably it is meant to teach a lesson. Many have been puzzled, however, by the meaning of the lesson. Professor R. H. Fogle explains that if Mr. Hooper's story is a homily on secret sin "we have no vivid sense of that presence of Evil which would necessitate so heroic an object lesson." On the other hand, if the parable presents the normal view of life as the highest good that Elizabeth exemplifies by contrast, "then the tone and emphasis of the story remain to be explained. It is too deeply gloomy and intense to harmonize fully with such a moral. . . . "[3] He concludes that both interpretations should be accepted "but with a sense of depths unplumbed, of rich potentialities not fully realized."[4]

The tale embodies a variation on a common theme in Hawthorne, the separation of the head from the heart—not of Hawthorne's own, though, as Professor Fogle suggests, and not even of Mr. Hooper's, but indeed of all the people in the story other than Mr. Hooper. They, not he, live half lives. The parable is about them in their relation to and reaction against the black veil: they shun it or poke fun at it and fall back upon habit and diversion and each other to protect themselves from the knowledge that each and every one of them also wears a black veil—the seed of dissolution and death. Mr. Hooper's dying words confirm his life as an individual in the face of the paradoxically deathlike "circle of pale spectators" around him who have never lived because they have never taken to heart what he tries again to reveal: "I look around me, and lo! on every visage a Black Veil!" Refusing such knowledge, not one has been defined, as Mr. Hooper has, through what Martin Heidegger in *Being and Time* calls "an impassioned *freedom towards death*—a freedom which has been released from the Illusions of the 'they,' and which is factical, certain of itself, and anxious."[5] It is just potentiality that the tale does realize. The depth that Hawthorne plumbs is man's potentiality for non-being. The major character is this pervasive mood whose warp and woof is at once medieval and existential. In other words, by emphasizing the fragility of life in a medieval way, the tale also existentially demonstrates the defining value of the moment. Normalcy, in any case, is certainly not the highest good in the story; nor is it an evil; it is simply an escape. The basic contrast, then, is not between a damning isolation and a saving sympathy, but between death and life, or more exactly between death-in-life and life-in-death: between living without death that leads to general existence—to no real existence at all; and living with death that leads to particular and meaningful existence through a sense of one's uniqueness that only death reveals.

The structure of the tale emphasizes this difference. It consists of a series of contrasts between a solitary and kind Mr. Hooper and the dependent, spiteful townspeople; and between a wedding that stresses relationship and reliance on the one hand, and a funeral that proves a radical isolation on the other. The first paragraph plants the seed for the contrasts that the tale explores:

> The sexton stood up in the porch of Milford meeting-house pulling lustily at the bell rope. The old people of the village came stooping along the street. Children with bright faces, tript merrily beside their parents, or mimicked a graver gait, in the conscious dignity of their Sunday clothes. Spruce bachelors looked sidelong at the pretty maidens, and fancied that the Sabbath sunshine made them prettier than on weekdays. When the throng had mostly streamed into the porch, the sexton began to toll the bell, keeping his eye on the Reverend Mr. Hooper's door. The first glimpse of the clergyman's figure, was the signal for the bell to cease its summons.

The ringing of the bell gathers under one roof a cross-section of all periods of life: children, bachelors and maidens, parents, the old. The meetinghouse becomes a symbolic center of the life of the community of Milford and by implication of the course of life. Mr. Hooper, parson of the community, is also the presiding minister of the dance of life, the caretaker and overseer of its whole progress from beginning to end. As we learn shortly, it is the end of that progress that accounts for his peculiar appearance with the black veil. Death has become personal for him, and it is that relationship he exemplifies to the startled and unsettled "throng." Goodman Gray—a carefully chosen name of no identity—asks the sexton whether "it is our parson," and he replies that it certainly is "good Mr. Hooper." The question and answer are perfectly natural, but the rest of the story reveals that they function to intimate early the crucial difference between existing generally ("our parson") and existing specifically ("good Mr. Hooper") that the tale will reveal. Overnight the minister has become a person. The sexton continues that the minister was to have exchanged pulpits with Parson Shute but that the Reverend Shute had "sent to excuse himself . . . to preach a funeral sermon." Whatever Mr. Hooper was the day before, he is now different, and the only intervening explanation we have is Reverend Shute's innocent excuse. Like the dialogue between Goodman Gray and the sexton, this too gathers a significance from the rest of the story which it does not initially seem to have. Funerals have finally caught up with good Mr. Hooper, and with them an ascending knowledge that the child with the bright face is father of the stooping old man, that life is bound up with death, and that man cannot be free to fulfill himself without this knowledge. The rest of his own life becomes an action homily with this threefold import.

The subsequent contrasts between the people and Mr. Hooper confirm that this is what has occurred. The people expend considerable effort to avoid what he knows, and they pay the very high price of remaining bound to the general. Mr. Hooper, though, becomes a more effective parson because he has become a more individual human being. In the following passage, for example, the ritualistic dignity of Mr. Hooper's exit contrasts with the "indecorous confusion" of the nameless crowd whose action is criticized through carefully wrought description and through grammatical difference from the last sentence whose subject is Mr. Hooper. Only in the last sentence does the predicate come first, with the main clause decorated on either side by parenthetical elements that serve to enclose and elevate the subject along with the stately rhythm of the three strongly accented monosyllables "forth came good":

> At the close of the services, the people hurried out with indecorous confusion, eager to communicate their pent-up amazement, and conscious of lighter spirits, the moment they lost sight of the black veil. Some gathered in little circles, huddled closely together, with their mouths all whispering in the centre; some went homeward alone, wrapt in silent meditation; some talked loudly, and profaned the Sabbath-day with ostentatious laughter. A few shook their sagacious heads, intimating that they could penetrate the mystery; while one or two affirmed that there was no mystery at all, but only that Mr. Hooper's eyes were so weakened by the midnight lamp, as to require a shade. After a brief interval, forth came good Mr. Hooper also, in the rear of his flock.

More is at work here than the device of multiple choice that F. O. Matthiessen noted in Hawthorne. Different responses are recorded with a vengeance that is clear from the funnel-like construction whose tone is less and less critical as the view narrows from the general to the more particular, from "mouths all whispering," through "some" to the "few," then to "one or two," and finally to Mr. Hooper when the tone is entirely favorable. There can be little doubt, at least syntactically, that Mr. Hooper is the shepherd. Also it is certain who the sheep are.

Mankind cannot stand very much reality; and since Mr. Hooper is too real, the throng begins to retaliate for this intrusion on its illusory safety. No one wants to see himself alone, and it is that prospect which

Mr. Hooper literally personifies: "But with the multitude, good Mr. Hooper was irreparably a bugbear. He could not walk the street with any peace of mind, so conscious was he that the gentle and timid would turn aside to avoid him, and that others would make it a point of hardihood to throw themselves in his way. The impertinence of the latter class compelled him to give up his customary walk, at sunset, to the burial-ground; for when he leaned pensively over the gate, there would always be faces behind the grave-stones, peeping at his black veil." There is no mystery about the veil at all, or only insofar as it visualizes a mystery—death. About that it could not be clearer. The ghoulish irony of the "others" who hide behind grave-stones to catch a glimpse of the veil is certainly intentional. Such irony also boomerangs on the people who whisper that Mr. Hooper has a tortured conscience for some great crime, and that ghosts and fiends consort with him in the graveyard: "But still good Mr. Hooper sadly smiled at the pale visages of the worldly throng as he passed by." The point is not that people project their own sins and fears onto Mr. Hooper—though they do—but rather more importantly they project their own sins and fears to hide from an even deeper truth, not the truth that they are sinners but the truth which their pale visages verify—death is in them too. (Sin here is a euphemism.) And as a result, the being they do have is not genuine at all, but ersatz. Their being is what Heidegger calls "Being-along-side" and "Being-with." From the catalyst of Parson Shute's excuse, by contrast, Hawthorne represents a psychic situation in Mr. Hooper that Heidegger later explained:

> Death does not just "belong" to one's own Dasein [human existence] in an undifferentiated way; death *lays claim* to it as an *individual* Dasein. The non-relational character of death, as understood in anticipation, individualizes Dasein down to itself. This individualizing is a way in which the "there" is disclosed for existence. It makes manifest that all Being-along-side the things with which we concern ourselves, and all Being-with Others, will fail us when our ownmost potentiality-for-Being is the issue. Dasein can be *authentically itself* only if it makes this possible for itself of its own accord.[6]

Mr. Hooper has made this possible for himself, as externalized by the black veil. Through contrasts and ironies, the people are found wanting in life because they shun the personal character of death.

The tragedy of the townspeople is that they do anticipate the non-relational character of death ("there was a feeling of dread, neither plainly confessed nor carefully concealed") but they still choose to cohere and to move as one; each possible identity continues submerged "in the everydayness of the they-self."[7] When they send a deputation "to deal with Mr. Hooper about the mystery, before it should grow into a scandal," the deputies can only sit and gaze "speechless, confused, and shrinking uneasily. . . . " They return "abashed to their constituents, pronouncing the matter too weighty to be handled, except by a council of the churches, if, indeed, it might not require a general synod." The lightsome quality of the tone does not hide a faint disgust: the constituents send the deputies, who suggest a council which might in turn call a synod. In defense they move centrifugally away into larger and more general bodies from the particularity of each that the death-veil asseverates.

The juxtaposition of the funeral and the wedding has the same dramatic function. The wedding comes in the same evening of the Sunday that Mr. Hooper first wears the veil. Here the handsomest couple in Milford are united to be-with; but earlier, in the afternoon, a young woman's funeral underscores how being is one's own finally, whether with others or with things or not. The non-relational character of death cannot be escaped, nor should it be. The wedding is the one ceremony that most emphasizes relationship and mutual dependence, and therefore it is purposely intertwined with references and images from the earlier funeral to dramatically highlight the story's parable: "The bridal pair stood up before the minister. But the bride's cold fingers quivered in the tremulous hand of the bridegroom, and her deathlike paleness caused a whisper, that the maiden who had been buried a few hours before, was come from her grave to be married. If ever another wedding were so dismal, it was that famous one, where they tolled the wedding knell." Contrast is not enough. It must be shown how death resides in the very celebration of life in order to make that celebration authentic.

In a genuine way Mr. Hooper performs the same service that the ancient mariner does for the wedding-guest. The effect that the veil has on Elizabeth, for one, is just as thorough: it imparts the ghost-sense to her, reveals the nightmare Life-in-Death. Hawthorne could not have chosen a better symbol than the black veil, for when people look at it they see exactly what it means—Nothing. It is this fact of finitude which he stresses early here that clarifies the later ambiguities, for it is the fact of finitude, as William C. Barrett has written in *Irrational Man*, that "brings us to the center of man, where positive and negative existence coincide and interpenetrate to such an extent that a man's strength coincides with his pathos, his vision with his blindness, his truth with his untruth, his being with his non-being. And if human finitude is not understood, neither is the nature of man."[8] In the text of St. Paul, unless a man die in Christ he cannot be born again, Hawthorne's Puritanism and existentialism coincide. Unless a man die in one sense, he cannot become a better man because in another more fundamental sense he cannot become a man at all. How well Hawthorne

understood that and understood human nature is clear from his uncompromising depiction of human finitude in **"The Minister's Black Veil."** To understand his later works we have to see early here that his power of blackness adds up to something quite other than gloom. That is the lesson that "young and zealous" Reverend Clark, who buries Mr. Hooper, will presumably learn as time goes by for him, too.

Notes

[1] "The Ghost Sense," October 24, 1968, p. 26.

[2] *Great Short Works of Hawthorne,* ed. Frederick C. Crews (New York: Harper and Row, 1967), p. 286.

[3] *Hawthorne's Fiction: The Light & the Dark* (Norman: University of Oklahoma, 1965), p. 35.

[4] *Ibid.,* p. 39.

[5] Trans. John Macquarrie and Edward Robinson (New York: Harper, 1962), p. 311.

[6] *Ibid.,* p. 308.

[7] *Ibid.,* p. 307.

[8] Garden City: Doubleday, 1962, p. 290.

Neal Frank Doubleday (essay date 1972)

SOURCE: "The Masterpieces in *Twice-Told Tales,*" in *Hawthorne's Early Tales, A Critical Study,* Duke University Press, 1972, pp. 159-81.

[*In the following excerpt, Doubleday argues that "The Minister's Black Veil" is a straightforward allegory of humankind's sinful nature and that critics should accept Hawthorne's ambiguity as purposeful.*]

Since Hawthorne included **"The Minister's Black Veil: A Parable"** in the first edition of *Twice-Told Tales,* he apparently did not think it a difficult tale—rather one that "may be understood and felt by anybody who will give himself the trouble to read it." Yet his critics have by no means agreed about its purport; and although we do not ordinarily think of a parable having multiple meanings, this tale has been read in very different fashions. Since it was first printed in 1835 in *The Token* for 1836, it seems not to have been one of the pieces for the projected "Story-Teller" volume, and it may have been written not long before its first printing.

"The Minister's Black Veil" has two kinds of importance in Hawthorne's development. He uses American materials in the tale, but he uses them to his own purposes; the tale stands in considerable contrast to, say, **"The Gray Champion,"** first printed in the same year. In the second place, the tale is an early example of Hawthorne's way of "turning different sides of the same dark idea to the reader's eye,"[18] exploring its every nuance, exhausting its suggestion. This is the technique that distinguishes *The Scarlet Letter* and seems less satisfactory in the other three romances. We see something of it in other tales, notably in **"The Birthmark,"** but it appears in no marked fashion earlier than **"The Minister's Black Veil."** One looks far to find a comparable success in this technique in other writers: Tolstoy's *The Death of Ivan Ilych* is one; perhaps Albert Camus' *The Fall* is another. But a writer attempting this persistent and minute manipulation of an idea risks an intolerable repetitousness that he can avoid only through finish of style and perfection of pattern. Hawthorne achieves both in **"The Minister's Black Veil."**

Since the minister preaches an election sermon during Governor Belcher's administration (1730-1741), years after he had put on his black veil, the time of the action is fixed as the first part of the eighteenth century. The narrator of the tale seems a citizen of Milford; we may suppose him in the latter part of his life a deacon in Mr. Hooper's church. He has been acquainted with Mr. Hooper through the many years the tale spans and, with one exception, he reports only what he could have heard and seen, and, of course, his inferences therefrom. And even the interview between Mr. Hooper and his fiancée he might have known through some account of it by Elizabeth. Throughout his story he considers the meaning of what he has to tell, and by implication invites the reader to consider it with him. He emerges clearly: a likable, shrewd man who views Mr. Hooper and his parishioners sympathetically or, on occasion, with a wry amusement. He moves his story with remarkable skill from the time Mr. Hooper was "about thirty" through his "long life."

The narrator begins with an account of Mr. Hooper's congregation gathering on a Sunday morning in their various ages and conditions, for all are to be affected by the mysteries of the veil he has donned for the first time. The account of this first Sunday occupies about two-fifths of the narrative. It includes the Sunday morning service, the funeral of a young lady following the afternoon service, and an evening wedding—the rituals for what is really important in human experience. The next day Mr. Hooper's parishioners talk of little but his black veil, and their preoccupation with the veil grows so that at length it is "found expedient to send a deputation of the church, in order to deal with Mr. Hooper about the mystery." The narrator's amused remark about its result is a fine touch: the deputies pronounce the matter "too weighty to be handled, except by a council of the churches, if, indeed, it might not require a general synod."

When the deputies have failed, Elizabeth endeavors to discover the secret of the veil. Her interview with Mr. Hooper is directly reported at some length. But if we are to suppose that Elizabeth has been able "to penetrate the mystery of the black veil" (and there is a suggestion that she has), we must suppose that she has not communicated her knowledge to the narrator, and he moves into summary narrative with a single sentence of transition: "From that time no attempts were made to remove Mr. Hooper's black veil, or, by a direct appeal, to discover the secret which it was supposed to hide."

The summary narrative records what is commonly thought and said about Mr. Hooper and his veil, and it is often interpretive, but it leaves the mystery unresolved. It brings us—at long last, as we feel under its spell—to Mr. Hooper's deathbed. The illusion of elapsing time is complete; the adroit transitions sustain our feeling of continuity and wholeness. When the narrator has recorded what is said to Mr. Hooper at his deathbed and what Mr. Hooper replies, he has done, we feel, all he can toward his and our understanding of the veil his clergyman has felt himself bound to wear through almost a lifetime.

Hawthorne doubtless assumed that Mr. Hooper's deathbed speech would be accepted as a sufficient interpretation of the tale—had he not, it is most unlikely that he would have included **"The Minister's Black Veil"** in *Twice-Told Tales.* When the clergyman attending Mr. Hooper pleads that he remove his veil, and then insists that he do so, Mr. Hooper gathers his last strength to say what he had meant by the symbol he had worn so long:

> Why do you tremble at me alone? Tremble also at each other! Have men avoided me, and women shown no pity, and children screamed and fled, only for my black veil? What, but the mystery which it obscurely typifies, has made this piece of crape so awful? When the friend shows his inmost heart to his friend; the lover to his best beloved; when man does not vainly shrink from the eye of his Creator, loathsomely treasuring up the secret of his sin; then deem me a monster, for the symbol beneath which I have lived, and die! I look around me, and, lo! on every visage a Black Veil!

So far as Mr. Hooper is an allegorical figure, he seems to have interpreted his own significance.

Hawthorne's note to the tale indicates its inception and seems to suggest the direction of its interpretation:

> Another clergyman in New England, Mr. Joseph Moody, of York, Maine, who died about eighty years since, made himself remarkable by the same eccentricity that is here related of the Reverend Mr. Hooper. In his case, however, the symbol had

a different import. In early life he had accidentally killed a beloved friend; and from that day till the hour of his own death, he hid his face from men.

As *The Scarlet Letter* seems to have had its inception in Hawthorne's reflection on the spiritual result of an enforced and continual confession by the wearing of a symbol, so, in something the same way, **"The Minister's Black Veil"** seems to stem from speculation about the spiritual import of a symbol of concealment voluntarily worn. And since the Reverend Mr. Moody wore his veil as a self-imposed penance and Mr. Hooper's veil has "a different import," Hawthorne seems to be saying that the reader's primary concern need not be to identify the nature of some guilt in the minister. But that has often enough been the concern of critics of the tale.

Edgar Allan Poe's interpretation of the tale in his 1842 review of *Twice-Told Tales* may be the first effort on the part of a critic to identify Mr. Hooper's guilt:

> **"The Minister's Black Veil"** is a masterly composition, of which the sole defect is that to the rabble its exquisite skill will be *caviare*. *The obvious* meaning of this article will be found to smother its insinuated one. The *moral* put into the mouth of the dying minister will be supposed to convey the *true* import of the narrative; and that a crime of dark dye (having reference to the "young lady") has been committed, is a point which only minds congenial with that of the author will perceive.

Poe has apparently seized upon a preternatural suggestion the narrator records without assenting to it—a suggestion such as we learn to expect from Hawthorne. At the funeral of the young lady, as the minister bends over the coffin and his black veil hangs straight from his forehead, he hastily pulls it back, as if he feared the corpse might see his face. A witness affirms that at this moment "the corpse had slightly shuddered." "A superstitious old woman," the narrator remarks amusedly, "was the only witness of this prodigy." Another preternatural suggestion seems to point in a different direction. As the mourners are leaving, a woman who had looked back at Mr. Hooper remarks, "I had a fancy that the minister and the maiden's spirit were walking hand in hand." Her husband confesses to the same fancy, but it is a fancy that hardly suggests "a crime of dark dye."

Nevertheless Poe points to a problem: there is an ambiguity in the tale that does not depend upon half-playful preternatural suggestion. The narrator speaks of "an ambiguity of sin or sorrow, which enveloped the poor minister"; and when Elizabeth warns Mr. Hooper that "there may be whispers that you hide your face under the consciousness of secret sin," he answers, "If I hide my face for sorrow, there is cause enough, and if I

cover it for secret sin, what mortal might not do the same?" Even his dying speech does not preclude his having treasured up "the secret of his sin"; nor does anything the narrator says preclude it.

It is perhaps no wonder, then, that writers on the tale have tried to identify some sort of guilt or guilt feeling in the minister. Of late it has been insisted that it is a guilt Mr. Hooper—or perhaps Hawthorne himself—does not consciously recognize.[19] The tale seems to invite such attempts, but they run into trouble.

Discussion of Hawthorne's work should never proceed, it seems to me, as if his characteristic ambiguity were not ambiguity really, but a sort of puzzle set for critical acumen to solve. Hawthorne's ambiguity is one of his ways of representing his pervasive sense of mystery, a kind of humility in him. Even in a children's story, **"The Minotaur,"** he remarks that "the heart of any ordinary man . . . is ten times as great a mystery as the labyrinth of Crete." He will not presume to solve the mystery, nor can he forget it. If one reads a Hawthorne tale recognizing the ambiguity, but accepting it as really ambiguous, he is reading the tale, it is safe to say, as Hawthorne intended it to be read, and to that extent reading it well.

This consideration applies in a special way to **"The Minister's Black Veil."** The narrator does not know what the veil conceals, and it conceals perhaps a "dreadful secret." A reading of the tale that disclosed the secret—could it do so—either as a sinful act or a psychological quirk would destroy the impressiveness of the symbol, destroy the very quality for which the tale exists. From time to time a "faint, sad smile" glimmers or flickers on Mr. Hooper's lips, but always in the same context, always when some one or more of his fellowmen seek an explanation of the veil. It is as if he smiles in the realization that what the questioners seek to know is at once simpler and far more complex than they can think. That faint smile lingers yet.

The central concern of the tale, indeed, is not the minister but the effect of the black veil on all of Milford. The narrator records its effect on the minister, on his ministry, on his fiancee, on the deputation of the church, on the officials who listen to his election day sermon, on the citizens of Milford, down to the "imitative little imp" who covers his face and is, as the narrator thinks the minister may be, "affrighted by himself." By the effect of the veil, Mr. Hooper becomes "a man of awful power over souls that were in agony for sin." Dying sinners shudder at the veil, but will not yield their breath without its wearer. The gloom of the veil enables him "to sympathize with all dark affections." And the veil has its effect not because Mr. Hooper's fellows do not recognize its meaning as a symbol, but because they do recognize it. "What," the minister asks at last, "but the mystery which it obscurely typifies, has made this piece of crape so awful?"

The citizens of Milford recognize, as everyone at least in some of his experience recognizes, how far alone each man and woman is. They do not put their recognition into words; few of us have been able to say what all mankind know. Sometimes a poet has said it for us; Matthew Arnold in "To Marguerite" has. And in a poem by Hawthorne's contemporary, Christopher Pearse Cranch, there seems almost an echo of Hawthorne's tale:

> We are spirits clad in veils;
>   Man by man was never seen;
> All our deep communing fails
>   To remove the shadowy screen.
>
> Heart to heart was never known;
>   Mind with mind did never meet;
> We are columns left alone
>   Of a temple once complete.

Of this human burden Mr. Hooper has vowed to make himself, and does make himself, the "type and symbol." **"The Minister's Black Veil"** is a parable just in its representation of that burden.

If the tale is read as a parable, it touches us nearly. "Always the struggle of the human soul," Don Marquis once wrote, "is to break through the barriers of silence and distance into companionship. Friendship, lust, love, art, religion—we rush into them pleading, fighting, clamoring for the touch of spirit laid against our spirit." If the tale is read as a parable, some passages become, not indications of a morbid condition in Mr. Hooper, but allegorical representations of human need. "It is but a mortal veil—it is not for eternity!" the minister says to Elizabeth. "O! you know not how lonely I am, and how frightened, to be alone behind my black veil."

To neglect what Poe calls "the *moral* put into the mouth of the dying minister" is to neglect what the narrative has proceeded toward. The "ambiguity of sin or sorrow, which enveloped the poor minister," is an ambiguity in his person and his past; his last words concern us all, and they are unambiguous. An interpretation of the tale that disregards or depreciates its next-to-last paragraph is rather like an interpretation of Robert Frost's "Desert Places" which should disregard the last stanza of the poem. And such interpretation of the tale neglects Hawthorne's preoccupation with the need of men for their fellows and, therefore, obscures the place of **"The Minister's Black Veil"** in a pattern that his takes make.

"The Minister's Black Veil" has also an important relationship to *The Scarlet Letter;* it becomes part of the fabric of the romance and a means to the development of the character of the Reverend Mr. Dimmesdale. Mr. Hooper, Sir Leslie Stephen remarks, is "a kind of symbolic prophecy of Dimmesdale"; but more than that, Dimmesdale has attributes nearly identical with some of those of Mr. Hooper. The narrator of the tale assures us that the black veil had made its wearer "a very efficient clergyman": converts and dying sinners both found in him a peculiar spiritual power. Now the clerical efficiency of Mr. Dimmesdale is of the same kind as that of Mr. Hooper. Both, set apart from their parishioners, have yet by a secret sharing with them a special insight. Mr. Hooper inspires in his people a strange mixture of dread, confidence, and dependence. Mr. Dimmesdale has a power denied to the "true saintly fathers" among his brother clergy of reaching common men, "of addressing the whole human brotherhood in the heart's native language." We are strangely reminded of Mr. Hooper's "ambiguity of sin or sorrow" when the narrator in the romance says of Mr. Dimmesdale:

> The burden, whatever it might be, of crime or anguish, beneath which it was his doom to totter . . . gave him sympathies so intimate with the sinful brotherhood of mankind; so that his heart vibrated in unison with theirs, and received their pain into itself, and sent its own throb of pain through a thousand other hearts, in gushes of sad, persuasive eloquence. Oftenest persuasive, but sometimes terrible! The people knew not the power that moved them thus. [chap. 11]

The gloom of the black veil enables Mr. Hooper "to sympathize with all dark affections"; Dimmesdale has "sympathies so intimate with the sinful brotherhood of mankind." Mr. Hooper has "an awful power" over souls in agony for sin; Dimmesdale's eloquence is "sometimes terrible." We cannot suppose Hawthorne unconscious of Dimmesdale's spiritual descent from Mr. Hooper.

Nor can we suppose Hawthorne unconscious of another return to **"The Minister's Black Veil"** in the romance. In the last chapter the narrator presents us with a version of Dimmesdale's career and death quite different from that of the central narrative, but one which is like a new version of **"The Minister's Black Veil"** in little. Some of Dimmesdale's parishioners reject entirely any idea of his guilt with Hester, and deny that his dying words acknowledge or imply it; he has, they believe, "made the manner of his death a parable, in order to impress on his admirers the mighty and mournful lesson, that, in the view of Infinite Purity, we are sinners all alike." As Mr. Dimmesdale's loyal parishioners see him, he has, like Mr. Hooper—but to use the words of "Fancy's Show Box"—claimed "his brotherhood, even with the guiltiest." . . .

Notes

[18] The quoted expression is from a letter of Hawthorne's to James T. Fields concerning *The Scarlet Letter*. See Fields, p. 51.

[19] Here is a selection of recent interpretations: William Bysshe Stein, "The Parable of the Antichrist in 'The Minister's Black Veil,'" *American Literature* 27 (1955): 386-92; Thomas F. Walsh, Jr., "Hawthorne: Mr. Hooper's 'Affable Weakness,'" *Modern Language Notes* 74 (1959): 404-6; E. Earle Stibitz, "Ironic Unity in Hawthorne's 'The Minister's Black Veil,'" *American Literature* 34 (1962): 182-90; Frederick C. Crews, *The Sins of the Fathers* (New York, 1966), pp. 106-111. . . .

Robert E. Morsberger (essay date 1973)

SOURCE: "'The Minister's Black Veil': Shrouded in a Blackness, Ten Times Black," in *The New England Quarterly,* Vol. XLVI, No. 3, September, 1973, pp. 454-63.

[*In the following essay, Morsberger interprets "The Minister's Black Veil" in the context of Hawthorne's and the Puritans' theology.*]

As a chronicler of New England colonial history, Hawthorne can be said to have created in considerable measure the legend of our Puritan past. Yet there are a good many dramatic episodes and individuals that he only touched on obliquely if at all: the Plymouth plantation, the trials and exile of Roger Williams and Anne Hutchinson (his biographical sketch of the latter consists merely of several frozen tableaux), the Pequot War, the actual trials at Salem for witchcraft, and the Great Awakening. Jonathan Edwards, in some ways the greatest Puritan of them all, never appears in any of Hawthorne's fiction, though the "Surprising Conversions," bizarre behavior, and spiritual crises of the Great Awakening in Northhampton could have provided suitably dramatic material for his fiction, as could the expulsion of Edwards from his parish, and his exile as missionary to the Stockbridge Indians. None of this did Hawthorne deal with directly.

Yet, in a way, one of his greatest Puritan tales, **"The Minister's Black Veil,"** presents the sort of spiritual tension seen in much introspective Puritan literature and perhaps best dramatized in the life and work of Edwards. Set during Edwards' lifetime in the first half of the eighteenth century, the story of the Reverend Mr. Hooper of Milford was, superficially, suggested by the case of Joseph Moody, a clergyman of York, Maine, who wore until his death a black veil to symbolize his having accidentally killed a friend. This guilt for a specific if unintentional sinful act resembles **"Roger Malvin's Burial"** more than it does **"The Minister's Black Veil,"** which deals more generally with Puritan melancholy. In **"The Old Manse,"** Hawthorne noted, "a clergyman,— a man not estranged from human life, yet enveloped in the midst of it with a veil woven of intermingled gloom and brightness." In Father Hooper's case, there is no brightness, only the gloomy estrangement caused by the veil.

It is a mistake to concentrate too much on the veil itself. Aside from Mr. Moody, no one wore such a veil, and the possessor of it is merely an eccentric. But as Ahab tells Starbuck, "All visible objects, man, are but as pasteboard masks. . . . If man will strike, strike through the mask!"[1] D. H. Lawrence's statement about Hawthorne, that "You *must* look through the surfaces of American art, and see the inner diabolism of the symbolic meaning. Otherwise it is all mere childishness,"[2] is particularly applicable to **"The Minister's Black Veil."**

If, then, Hawthorne's tale is to have more significance than simply a curiosity piece about a uniquely obsessed clergyman, what broader meaning does it imply?

Father Hooper himself explains that the veil is a symbol of sin but refuses to answer whether it represents a specific act committed or a general awareness of sinful humanity: "If I hide my face for sorrow, there is cause enough . . . and if I cover it for secret sin, what mortal might not do the same." This is practically a paraphrase of the statement in Thomas Shepherd's *The Sincere Convert* (1641), that " . . . no unregenerate man, though he go never so far, let him do never so much, but he lives in some one sin or other, secret or open, little or great."[3] The concept of secret sin could link the tale to Dimmesdale, Reuben Bourne, or to an apprehensive criminal like Raskolnikov. But *The Scarlet Letter* and **"Roger Malvin's Burial"** between them deal quite adequately with the psychological consequences of secret sin; the impact of **"The Minister's Black Veil"** is the suggestion that it may stand more broadly for a profound sense of blighted human nature.

As in **"Young Goodman Brown,"** Hawthorne is critical of the Puritans' excessive preoccupation with sin, a consequence of their doctrine of total depravity, which Hawthorne rejected. Melville wrote that Hawthorne's effects often come from a sense of Original Sin, but original sin is not total and is balanced by a human capacity for goodness and compassion. For most Christians, Christ came "to redeem the sins of the whole world"; whereas rigid Calvinism maintained that all of mankind deserves damnation and most of mankind will obtain it—all but God's few elect, who are chosen for the unearned grace that comes from limited atonement by Christ, so limited that according to Thomas Shepherd, "most of them that live in the church shall perish."[4] It is this kind of monomaniac obsession with sin that is signified by Hooper's black veil.

Hooper need not have committed any specific sin; for the hardened Puritan, his humanity was sinful enough, and he wore it the way a medieval penitent would his hair shirt. Anything less than absolute perfection was absolute corruption. The saintly John Bunyan, who called himself *The Chief of Sinners*, wrote:

> . . . I saw that I wanted a perfect righteousness to present me without fault before God, and this righteousness was nowhere to be found, but in the person of Jesus Christ.

> But my original and inward pollution, that, that was my plague and my affliction; that, I say, at a dreadful rate, always putting forth itself within me; that I had the guilt of, to amazement; by reason of that, I was more loathsome in my own eyes than was a toad; and I thought I was so in God's eyes too; . . . I thought none but the devil himself could equalise me for inward wickedness and pollution of mind. I fell, therefore, at the sight of my own vileness, deeply into despair; for I concluded that this condition that I was in could not stand with a state of grace. Sure, thought I, I am forsaken of God. . . . [5]

Steeped in Bunyan, Hawthorne would no doubt be familiar with this and similar passages, which are symptomatic of what William James called "the sick soul." But Bunyan also recognized forgiveness and "was in hopes that my sin was not unpardonable. . . . "[6] Hooper, on the other hand, leaves out the prospect of Christian forgiveness. Or if God can forgive him (Hooper tells Elizabeth they may be together in heaven), he can meanwhile not forgive himself.

Though the black veil creates an estrangement between himself and the community, it does make him peculiarly effective as a minister, and the first sermon he preaches after wearing the mask has an impact like Jonathan Edwards' "Sinners in the Hands of an Angry God," preached at Enfield during the height of the Great Awakening. Edwards' pulpitry was like that of Hooper, whom Hawthorne describes as "a good preacher, but not an energetic one; he strove to win his people heavenward, by mild, persuasive influences, rather than to drive them thither by the thunders of the Word." But as at Enfield, the members of Hooper's congregation "felt as if the preacher had crept upon them, behind his awful veil, and discovered their hoarded iniquity of deed or thought." In Edwards' sermon, "There is reason to think, that there are many in this congregation now hearing this discourse, that will actually be the subjects of this very misery to all eternity. We know not who they are, or in what seats they sit, or what thoughts they now have. . . . And

it would be no wonder if some persons, that now sit here, in some seats of this meeting-house, in health, quiet and secure, should be there before tomorrow morning."[7] As Bunyan found himself "more loathsome . . . than was a toad" in both his eyes and God's, so Edwards proclaimed; "The God that holds you over the pit of hell, much as one holds a spider, or some loathsome insect over the fire, abhors you, and is dreadfully provoked. . . . "[8]

Edwards, even after his conversion, ordination, and sense of "divine things" and "inward sweetness," resembled Hooper in his gloom:

> Often, since I lived in this town, I have had very affecting views of my own sinfulness and vileness; . . . I have had a vastly greater sense of my own wickedness, and the badness of my own heart, than ever I had before my conversion. It has often appeared to me, that if God should mark iniquity against me, I should appear the very worst of all mankind; . . . My wickedness, as I am in myself, has long appeared to me perfectly ineffable, and swallowing up all thought and imagination; like an infinite deluge, or mountains over my head. I know not how to express better what my sins appear to me to be, than by heaping infinite upon infinite, and multiplying infinite by infinite. . . . When I look into my heart, and take a view of my wickedness, it looks like an abyss infinitely deeper than hell. And it appears to me, that were it not for free grace, . . . I should appear sunk down in my sins below hell itself; far beyond the sight of every thing, but the eye of sovereign grace, that can pierce even down to such a depth.[9]

There was no reason for Edwards, Bunyan, or Hooper to feel this way. Far from being depraved criminals, they led exemplary lives; their wallowing in self-accusing guilt is a kind of spiritual masochism. They were not guilty of the catalogue of colonial crimes that the devil discloses to Goodman Brown, let alone of such horrors as the Inquisition, the butchery of the Thirty Years' War, the sanctimonious slaughter carried out by the Covenanters, or the nightmare of the Middle Passage (to confine oneself to history up to Edwards' time), let alone the atrocities of subsequent history. Samuel Sewall and Cotton Mather, partly responsible for the death of twenty innocent people at Salem, had more reason for remorse; but Mather seems never to have felt it, and Sewall, though he made public confession of his error, continued to live affirmatively. But Hooper has vowed never to remove the veil, and Edwards wrote, "I have greatly longed of late, for a broken heart, and to lie low before God; and, when I ask for humility, I cannot bear the thoughts of being no more humble than other Christians. It seems to me, that though their degrees of humility may be suitable for them, yet it would be a vile self-exaltation to me, not to be the lowest in humility of all mankind."[10]

There is an extremism in this unreasonable self-abasement that is a spiritual flagellation and may be an inverted pride. Edwards had no justification to consider himself the worst of mankind. Yet his spiritual state in such passages can be matched by that of other Puritan writers, John Winthrop and Michael Wigglesworth among them, and it is such a state that is signified by the black veil.

It need not indicate any specific crime; for sin is not an act but a condition, exaggerated by the Puritans to the concept of total depravity. Writing of "the dusky, overshadowed conscience of the Puritans," Henry James noted, "This darkening cloud was no essential part of the nature of the individual; it stood fixed in the general moral heaven under which he grew up and looked at life. It projected from above, from outside, a black patch over his spirit, and it was for him to do what he could with the black patch."[11] Bunyan and Edwards freed themselves from the slough of despond and praised the mercy and love of God more than they chronicled their unworthiness and His wrath, but Hooper remains adamant.

In his insistence on publicly dramatizing the symbol of sin, he drags the judgment of God down to the level of village gossip, as does Dimmesdale in *The Scarlet Letter.* God may know all, but that is no reason why the villagers must understand and judge. Secret sin is hidden not from God but from man. Yet such concealment does isolate the sinner, as Dimmesdale and Reuben Bourne discovered to their sorrow, and this is why Hawthorne so strongly admired the Catholic rite of confession and absolution. Yet as Pascal wrote:

> Is it not true that we hate truth and those who tell it us, and that we like them to be deceived in our favor, and prefer to be esteemed by them as being other than what we are in fact? One proof of this makes me shudder. The Catholic religion does not bind us to confess our sins indiscriminately to everybody; it allows them to remain hidden from all other men save one, to whom she bids us reveal the innermost recesses of our heart, and show ourselves as we are. There is only this one man in the world whom she orders us to undeceive, and she binds him to an inviolable secrecy, which makes this knowledge to him as if it were not. Can we imagine anything more charitable and pleasant? And yet the corruption of man is such that he finds even this law harsh; and it is one of the main reasons which has caused a great part of Europe to rebel against the Church.[12]

Hooper, of course, in confessing all confesses nothing specific, with the result that his wearing the veil accuses everyone as much as himself. His presence is a *memento mori,* and therefore his parishioners shun him. His veil does, however, make him "a very efficient clergyman" by enabling him "to sympathize with all dark affections," a consequence confirmed by a French melancholiac who found that "the experience has made me sympathetic with the morbid feelings of others ever since."[13] Those who desperately request Hooper's ministry are those afflicted by an "agony for sin."

Such agony is real enough, and not only during the seventeenth and eighteenth centuries. Despite its period setting, **"The Minister's Black Veil"** is not merely a historical reconstruction but a story of enduring relevance. To concentrate too much on the setting and on the veil itself rather than on the motivating forces behind it is to make it merely a curiosity piece, like the episode of the student at Oregon State University in the mid-1960's, who attended class shrouded in a black bag.

The veil is merely the external emblem of that condition that William James, in *The Varieties of Religious Experience,* labels "The Sick Soul." For victims of such profound melancholia, "evil is no mere relation of the subject to particular outer things, but something more radical and general, a wrongness or vice in his essential nature."[14] As an example that resembles Father Hooper, James quotes Henry Alline, an evangelist of the early nineteenth century, who confessed, "My sins seemed to be laid open; so that I thought that every one I saw knew them . . . yea sometimes it seemed to me as if every one was pointing me out as the most guilty wretch upon earth. I had now so great a sense of the vanity and emptiness of all things here below, that I knew the whole world could not possibly make me happy. . . . "[15] James examines numerous cases of such pathological and private depression, which he labels *anhedonia,* observing, "For this extremity of pessimism to be reached, something more is needed than observation of life and reflection upon death. The individual must in his own person become the prey of a pathological melancholy."[16]

Father Hooper may seem more outwardly subdued than these cases, for the detached narrator does not lead us into his mind; his voice is muted, and his motives remain hidden behind the mask; he has little dialogue, but twice when he speaks, it is in desperation. Pleading with his betrothed Elizabeth to remain with him, he cries, "Oh! you know not how lonely I am, and how frightened, to be alone behind my black veil. Do not leave me in this miserable obscurity for ever!" And on his deathbed, in final agony more of spirit than of body, he lashes out at his parishioners to "Tremble also at each other!" and denounces their sin when "men avoided me, and women [have] shown no pity, and children screamed and fled. . . . I look around me, and, lo! on every visage a Black Veil!"

If so, the fault is largely his own, for the story can also be seen as a case of the contagion of sin. In his morbid obsession with depravity, Father Hooper becomes guilty of something akin to Hawthorne's Unpardonable Sin, except that his preoccupation is more emotional than intellectual, though it is derived from Calvinist ideology. For the sake of it, and in his obsessive insistence on wearing the veil, he is as much guilty of driving away the companionship of his congregation as they are of reacting with ostracism. The isolation is a mutual act, for he admits, "This dismal shade must separate me from the world; even you, Elizabeth, can never come behind it." If therefore she rejects him as a husband, he drives her to it. The veil is a useless gesture—worse, since it corrupts others by its contagious presence.

William James calls excessive preoccupation with evil a disease; "Repentance, according to . . . healthy-minded Christians, means *getting away from* the sin, not groaning and writhing over its commission," and he quotes Spinoza's statement that "gnawings of conscience" are "deleterious and evil passions" forming "a particular kind of sadness. . . . "[17] What is missing in Father Hooper's flawed Christianity is forgiveness. This is also a factor missing in rigidly predestinarian Calvinism, according to which everyone deserves damnation, most of mankind will experience damnation, and the grace of God through Christ is a limited atonement reserved only for the arbitrarily chosen "elect." Even Jonathan Edwards conceded that as a youth he had "been full of objections against the doctrine of God's sovereignty, in choosing whom He would to eternal life, and rejecting whom He pleased; leaving them eternally to perish, and be everlastingly tormented in hell."[18] Edwards finally brought himself around to accepting this doctrine, "But never could give an account, how, or by what means, I was thus convinced";[19] one of his sermons is entitled "The Justification of God in the Damnation of Sinners." Despite this, Edwards was enough of a Christian to focus primarily on the love and mercy of Christ; yet all too often, as in Wigglesworth's "The Day of Doom," the Calvinist Christ appears as a hanging judge, God the Father emerges as the sort of tyrannical adversary Captain Ahab defies, and God the Holy Ghost becomes (in Phyllis McGinley's words) "The Holy Terror."

Yet Puritans could also "Confess Jehovah Thankfully"; and some, like Edward Taylor, were rhapsodic over the love God showed man through the Incarnation and Atonement. Hester Prynne says to Dimmesdale, "Heaven would show mercy . . . hadst thou but the strength to take advantage of it."[20] In his inability or refusal to do so, Father Hooper lets his sin become a spiritual pride. He concedes that "I . . . like most other mortals, have sorrows dark enough to be typified by a black veil." If so, why should he single himself out except from perverse pride or a deep disease of spirit. Presumably all Christian ministers recog-

nize sin in themselves, but they do not act as Hooper did. John Bunyan and Jonathan Edwards did not wear a black veil. St. Peter himself is said to have denounced Christ thrice before the crucifixion; yet not only did he not wear a black veil, but he accepted forgiveness and became the chief of the apostles. Ultimately, Hooper seems like Marlowe's Doctor Faustus, who cries that his sins are so great as to be beyond the power of God's redemption.

In his bleak despair, Hooper also resembles the Beatrice Cenci, of whom Hawthorne has Hilda say in *The Marble Faun,* "She knows that her sorrow is so strange and so immense that she ought to be solitary forever . . ."[21] and like Donatello, of whom Kenyon reflects, " . . . he finds it too horrible to be uttered, and fancies himself the only mortal that ever felt the anguish of remorse."[22] Yet Kenyon lectures Donatello, " . . . you do not know what is requisite for your spiritual growth, seeking, as you do, to keep your soul perpetually in the unwholesome region of remorse. It was needful for you to pass through that dark valley, but it is infinitely dangerous to linger there too long; there is poison in the atmosphere, when we sit down and brood in it, instead of girding up our loins to press onward."[23]

Here, Kenyon can be considered the author's spokesman, for Hawthorne's friend Hillard wrote of him, "There was nothing morbid in his character or temperament. He was, indeed, much the reverse of morbid."[24] And in *Fanshawe,* Hawthorne condemned the "joy of grief" in which "a man becomes a haunter of death-beds, a tormentor of afflicted hearts, and a follower of funerals."[25]

In his final words, Father Hooper exclaims, "When the friend shows his inmost heart to his friend; the lover to his best beloved; when man does not vainly shrink from the eye of his Creator, loathsomely treasuring up the secret of his sin; then deem me a monster, for the symbol beneath which I have lived, and die!" Likewise, Pascal confessed: "Human life is . . . only a perpetual illusion; . . . Man is then only disguise, falsehood, and hypocrisy, both in himself and in regard to others. He does not wish any one to tell him the truth; he avoids telling it to others, and all these dispositions, so removed from justice and reason, have a natural root in his heart."[26] To this extent, Father Hooper may be right; yet as Graham Greene says, echoing Scripture, the unpardonable sin is despair.

Notes

[1] Herman Melville, *Moby-Dick,* Charles Feidelson, Jr., editor (Indianapolis, 1964), 220.

[2] D. H. Lawrence, *Studies in Classic American Literature,* in *The Shock of Recognition,* Edmund Wilson, editor (New York, 1955), 984.

[3] Thomas Shepherd, *The Sincere Convert,* in *American Thought and Writing, The Colonial Period,* Russel B. Nye and Norman S. Grabo, editors (Boston, 1965), 1, 96.

[4] Shepherd, *The Sincere Convert,* 92.

[5] John Bunyan, *Grace Abounding and The Life and Death of Mr. Badman* (London and New York, 1956), 28.

[6] Bunyan, *Grace Abounding . . . ,* 59.

[7] Jonathan Edwards, *Representative Selections,* Clarence H. Faust and Thomas H. Johnson, editors (New York, 1935), 169-170.

[8] Edwards, *Representative Selections,* 164.

[9] Edwards, *Representative Selections,* 69-70.

[10] Edwards, *Representative Selections,* 70-71.

[11] Henry James, *Hawthorne,* in *The Shock of Recognition,* Edmund Wilson, editor (New York, 1955), 470.

[12] Blaise Pascal, *Pensees,* W. F. Trotter, translator (London and New York, 1954), 31-32.

[13] William James, *The Varieties of Religious Experience* (New York, n.d.), 158.

[14] James, *Varieties of Religious Experience,* 132.

[15] James, *Varieties of Religious Experience,* 156.

[16] James, *Varieties of Religious Experience,* 142.

[17] James, *Varieties of Religious Experience,* 126.

[18] Edwards, *Representative Selections,* 58.

[19] Edwards, *Representative Selections,* 58.

[20] Nathaniel Hawthorne, *The Complete Novels and Selected Tales,* Norman Holmes Pearson, editor (New York, 1937), 201.

[21] Hawthorne, *The Complete Novels . . . ,* 627.

[22] Hawthorne, *The Complete Novels . . . ,* 741.

[23] Hawthorne, *The Complete Novels . . . ,* 747.

[24] *The Atlantic Monthly,* XXVI, 257 (Sept., 1870).

[25] Hawthorne, *The Complete Novels . . . ,* 71.

[26] Pascal, *Pensées,* 32-33.

Michael J. Colacurcio (essay date 1984)

SOURCE: "The True Sight of Sin: Parson Hooper and the Power of Blackness," in *The Province of Piety: Moral History in Hawthorne's Early Tales,* Harvard University Press, 1984, pp. 314-85.

[In the following excerpt, Colacurcio explores the "moral history" as well as the religious context of "The Minister's Black Veil."]

The case of Parson Hooper is more difficult than that of Goodman Brown—arguably it is the most difficult of all Hawthorne's cases of Puritan conscience.[1] On the one hand, "intrinsically," the text itself seems to thwart interpretation, as if neither Hooper *nor* Hawthorne quite understood the "ambiguity of sin or sorrow" in which he became enveloped. Rationalists might suspect obscurantism, and theorists discover indeterminacy; but perhaps the old ("New") critics were right, for once, to protest that the tendency to explain everything is simply wrong-headed; that, unlike the Emersonian universe, a Hawthorne text cannot be counted on to answer all the questions it raises.[2] And, on the other hand, "extrinsic" or "contextual" aids to interpretation have been hard to come by. The "fact" that Hooper once preached before Governor Belcher (1730-1741) has been noticed, but it has produced neither a shock of critical recognition nor a flood of historical commentary. To be sure, many critics regard the tale as "historical," but they have been unable to "place" Hooper in any significant stretch of Puritan history.[3]

Perhaps, therefore, **"The Minister's Black Veil"** should be thought of not only as the most ambiguous but also as the most nominal of Hawthorne's tales of the Puritans, not at all an analysis of motivation and behavior under the pressures of some well-defined historical moment, but only a generalized evocation of some putative psychological essence, such as "Puritan Subjectivity." Or, perhaps, even more radically, it represents the terminus toward which Hawthorne's other fictional researches were all along tending, the point where specific events altogether failed to embody his "deeper" meanings. Or perhaps we missed something.

At the outset, then, the task of interpretation is double: not only to grasp, if we can, some intuition of the approximate depth and drift of Hooper's meaning, but also to inquire whether his career of exacerbated subjectivity contains any clues to a principle of historical representation. Only if we fail in the first should our bottom line read "ambiguity." And only if we fail in the second will we be forced to seek the magical rescue of modernism—whether the personal obsession with sex and solipsism or the more properly authorial compulsion to play with the self-reference of all signs.[4] Both these meta-problems lurk here, of course, at least as ominously as they do in the darkness which surrounds the highlighting of any text. And we can always explore them, whenever we conclude the old laws no longer apply. But if we are patient we may yet discover **"The Minister's Black Veil"** as a model of Hawthorne's "moral history" at its most complex and demanding.

1

At first glance Hooper's difficulties appear deep indeed. Though attempts to link him to Dimmesdale in terms of specific guilt are probably misdirected, Hooper does seem a "forestudy" of intense introspection and privateness. And surely Hooper is a more challenging "figure," if not a more fully developed "character," than Goodman Brown, having seen or felt things beyond the range of that Average Sensual Puritan. If we cannot accept the critical judgment that Hooper succeeds just where Brown fails, still it is from Hooper's level of consciousness that we most effectively sound the depths of Brown's shallows.[5] Hooper's tone is, *almost* everywhere, milder, sadder, wiser; his style less declamatory and sophomoric. Surely he is the deepest of Hawthorne's early Puritan figures. For once, it almost seems, Hawthorne has given us an adequately complex, if not entirely sympathetic, presentation of the psychological equivalent of Puritan separatism.

And yet Hooper's career reveals distressing similarities to that of Richard Digby. However complicated, ambiguous, modern, and adequate may be Hooper's understanding, his *fate* seems identical to that of Hawthorne's crudest Puritan *figura*. Indeed it seems likely that **"The Man of Adamant"** was written after **"The Minister's Black Veil,"** as something of a simple gloss on a meaning that had somehow got too complicated.[6] Perhaps the paradox will bear a little inspection.

The outline of Digby's moral progress is, we recall, very simple: his sense of being unique separates him from the community; the separation is hardened by his refusal of the graces not only of a woman's love but indeed of all natural influences; thus alienated, he damns himself to stony solipsism. Stated thus generally, the outline will also work for the moral career of Hooper. And surely the image of him, at the end of his life, as a "dark old man" who has effectively severed all his former (indeed all natural) ties with the community is an evocation of the Digby syndrome. The clear suggestion about Hooper is that he loses all chance for human communion when his veil prevents the consummation of his marriage to Elizabeth and causes his congregation to suspend their invitations to Sunday dinner. From a "structural" point of view, **"The Man of Adamant"** and **"The Minister's Black Veil"** are the same story. Their essential action is identical: a self-regarding protagonist confirms his potentially solipsistic separation by refusing natural graces. The Digby "mytheme." Period.

Still—says the less strict voice of a more semantic (and potentially historical) interpretation—once all this has been observed, a number of important qualifications spring to mind. Granted that in these two stories (as in so many others) Hawthorne is generally at pains to "deplore all attempts to step aside" from "the common highway of life,"[7] nevertheless the particular deployment of meaning is really quite different. Hooper's initial "separating" insight does not seem morally arrogant; indeed nothing could seem further from Digby's belief in the uniqueness of his own salvation than Hooper's sense that *all* men treasure up secret guilt. Further, the "amiable" Mr. Hooper seems far less simply hostile to other people: he tries, in his way, to share his insight with them; and his refusal of the gracious Elizabeth seems infinitely more ambivalent than Digby's hysterical rejection of the angelic Mary Goffe. Indeed one might argue that Hooper is separated because no one else can come up to his standard of honesty or level of moral apprehension; that he merely suffers the fate of any prophet whose message is too profoundly true for the majority of his hearers to accept. And, however complete his isolation, metaphysically considered, he does continue to minister to the community, from behind his veil and smile.

Clearly all these differences are significant. In one sense our response to Hooper may depend on whether we concentrate on the shape of the essential action or choose to immerse ourselves in all the psychological particulars. But however we choose, it would be both sentimental and critically naive to ignore altogether the features of Digby behind the veil of Hooper. Because there is, evidently, something of that "purest" of the Puritans in Hooper, not even his Dimmesdalean sensitivity can save him. Worlds beyond Goodman Brown in point of perception and moral logic, he is still (somehow) not at all beyond the simplistic absolutism of Digby. And not at all beyond Puritanism.

Which brings us to our second preliminary consideration—Hooper's historical meaning, his possible significance as "representative" Puritan. And here, where particularities may be supposed to matter most, details of doctrinal difference may count for more than outlines of structural similarity. If, in the one view, Hooper already seems a relatively complicated case of the Puritan as Separatist, he may yet appear as a particularly subtle example of the imaginative recovery and symbolic representation of the authentically Puritan "true sight" of sin.

Evidently Hooper avoids the vulgar errors of Puritan epistemology. First of all, he does not make the paranoid distinction between his own moral case and that of everybody else. Quite the reverse. If anything, he feels himself (like Jonathan Edwards) the very worst of sinners. More technically, of course, it may be truer to say that, far more than anybody else, he simply sees his own sin "clearly" and "convictingly." Following the explicit instructions of somebody like Thomas Hooker, let us say, he has grasped the root fact of his own pervasive and interior sinfulness "not in the appearance and paint of it but in the power of it; not . . . in the notion and conceit only, but . . . with Application."[8] Thus Hooper may indeed *be* different. He may, as a sort of Puritan hero of consciousness, *see* more than anyone else about the dark mysteries of the Secret Sinful Self. But ultimately, as he sees things, all men *are* in the same condition of being trapped behind a veil of sinful subjectivity, and all should be able to see themselves in exactly the same terrifying way. Accordingly, therefore, Hooper sees nothing so plainly as the deceptiveness of all moral appearances. To judge by any such appearances is, in his severely Puritan view, to live by social compromises rather than by the knowledge of reality as it stands in the mind of God, the only true Searcher of Hearts. And, Puritan fashion, he evidently refuses to live by any less absolute standard.

Thus Hooper's career can fairly be said to begin where Brown's ends: the sadly smiling minister seems to know there is no human way to tell whether saint or witch lurks behind the veil of human subjectivity. Perhaps he even realizes that in most ways there is *no* difference. Yet the insight does not save him. Having exposed the theory of visible sanctity for the easy presumption it most assuredly is, and having confronted his not-very-Puritan congregation with the laxity of their eighteenth-century premises and perceptions, he seems himself to become obsessed with the very idea of the pervasiveness and ineluctability of human moral secretness. Because all social intercourse is based on some compromise, he effectively rejects it altogether. Or at least he loses it. The man who will accept nothing less than God's truth, and who finds that such truth is embodied in no human institution and validates no human relationship, is evidently doomed to solipsism and rejection of life as utterly as is Goodman Brown. Or as Richard Digby, the separatist paradigm of them both.

This thematic formulation of **"The Minister's Black Veil"** takes us closer to the provincial heart of American Puritanism than does any other Hawthorne tale. The normal, social assumption of that historic creed, so plainly on trial in **"Young Goodman Brown,"** is that once putative Christians have learned to put aside all moral, theological, and ecclesiological compromises, the result will be a Church of Saints separated out from a World of Sinners; that in grace the ability to distinguish the Kingdom of Light from the Kingdom of

Darkness approaches certainty as a sort of asymptotic limit. And this Hawthornean discovery would seem in many ways to be the defining rationale of Puritan experience as we now most usefully understand it. But the case of Parson Hooper reminds us that there is probably a deeper premise still, of which visible sanctity is only one not-quite-necessary application. That far-more-absolutist premise touches the human possibility and religious necessity of discovering, under the aspect of depravity, and of communicating, through the medium of symbol, some fundamental truth about the moral status of the human Self as such. And some such premise is evidently on trial in **"The Minister's Black Veil."**

Probably it is this very "essential" character of Hooper's experience that has made it seem unnecessary to locate any proximate context for his revealing-and-concealing action of self-veiling. To those critics concerned with the Romantic and modern problem of subjectivity itself, the import has seemed clear enough. On Hawthorne's more historical critics Hooper's words and actions have simply imposed themselves—as an ultimate and paradigmatic Puritan gesture, however unique in literature or absurd under the aspect of Governor Belcher. And for certain purposes it probably is enough to know the moral geography and mythic sequence: beyond Goodman Brown and on his way to being Dimmesdale, Hooper is nevertheless, in his absolutism, still a Digby-figure.

Yet Hooper is not quite an archetype. And the way to discover this is to place his experience in the New England of the 1730's and 1740's. Hooper "flourishes," it turns out, during precisely those crucial years of the "Great Awakening." Once we take this historical fact seriously, everything begins to make a much fuller and firmer sense. Hooper, we are expected to see, is an "awakened Puritan," living in the midst of decent and common-sensical but not spiritually illuminated Yankees. Most simply: Hooper somehow recovers or "revives" an older insight into the problem of sin and the self; thereupon, he forces his hapless congregation to the limits of their slackened, eighteenth-century consciences. In doing so he presents himself to us as the figure of Hawthorne's Puritan par excellence, the prophetic preacher of "the true sight of sin."

What follows as a result of his awakening insight and prophetic gesture is significant indeed. Although Hawthorne never emphasizes sociology, the alienation of Hooper from a significant number of his parishioners provides a classic image of the social dynamics of the phenomenon historians have come to call "Revivalism and Separatism in New England."[9] It also tells us much about the schizophrenic split that seemed to occur in the collective American consciousness in the eighteenth century, with Edwards on one side and Franklin on the other—New England contemporaries who seem to us to have lived in different universes. Startling as it may seem to critics who have thought of Hooper's career primarily as a proof text for Hawthorne's obsessive involvement in Puritan gloom, or Romantic subjectivity, or Victorian sexual fear, or Existentialist absurdity, or Modern artistic alienation, there really is more historically disciplined observation about the exact moral causes of specific social effects in **"The Minister's Black Veil"** than in **"The Gentle Boy"** or **"Young Goodman Brown."** To be sure, we get no shouting or swooning, and very little hint of itinerant preaching and intracongregational bitterness; just as, elsewhere, we get nothing about accusations, trials, and executions. But we do get an absolutely firm sense of the relation between a heightened spiritual awareness and the disruption of ordinary affairs.

Nevertheless, the emphasis is primarily on the meaning of Hooper's own troubled but instructive career. Puritanism, we are thus permitted to see, *is* awakening: in essence its peculiar style of "piety" is nothing but an expanded consciousness of the self under the aspect of hidden but pervasive "sin." As such it is a far from trivial form of moral intelligence. Indeed it may look like the highest form of Truth itself. In the very next moment, however, or in the order of praxis, all sorts of difficulties begin to appear. A sinful self can be a True Self only For Itself—or in the sight of God. And so the problem of what follows practically, at the level of community, from the Puritan consciousness of sin becomes the source of a whole new range of ambiguities which that consciousness itself has no power to resolve. Sin separates. Absolute sin separates absolutely. Granted that God may forgive any man, still no one else can know for certain that He has; so that this side of the Last Judgment all human communities are compromises. And Hooper is unwilling to compromise his insight.

Hooper is no self-righteous, sectarian "Pope in his own Parish." But it is hard to believe that his arch-Puritan solution to the problem of sin and community is a very happy one. After a long career of mild and indulgent alienation, his final hour is strident as well as gloomy, and Hawthorne is careful to carve "no hopeful verse upon his tombstone." All his honesty and all his insight are not enough, apparently, to save him from the terrible loneliness of solitary sainthood.[10]

2

"The Minister's Black Veil" opens with an image of the integrity of ordinary life—the natural goodness of which only a very strict Puritan would deny, but from which Hooper is about to exile himself. The vision of the sunshine of natural benevolence and illumination falling "peacefully on the cottages and fields" might appall Richard Digby, but it is supposed to appeal to the ordinary reader. And even more reassuring is the human scene this Sabbath morning:

> The sexton stood in the porch of Milford meeting-house, pulling lustily at the bell-rope. The old people of the village came stooping along the street. Children, with bright faces, tripped merrily behind their parents, or mimicked a graver gait, in the conscious dignity of their Sunday clothes. Spruce bachelors looked sidelong at pretty maidens, and fancied that the Sabbath sunshine made them prettier than on weekdays. (37)[11]

As in a well-composed picture, everything is very satisfactory. Everybody is there (except, at this point, Hooper) in a setting that seems solid, suitable, and sufficient to the purpose; it seems good to be alive in God's world, going to an act of common celebration, on the day which the Lord has made. What, in such a world, could possibly be wrong?

Nothing very drastic, surely. Endicott himself might be hard pressed to find a fault. To be sure, this eighteenth-century congregation is not noticeably "Puritan" according to Hawthorne's sense. They seem to treat the Sabbath as something of an innocent holiday, a thing Hawthorne believed it never was in the sterner seventeenth century. But no one will suppose that this dignified and decorous group will move from divine service to an afternoon of "sports and pastimes": Puritan solidarity and bourgeois domesticity have overcome too utterly for anything like that. The people's sense of natural pleasure carries with it no hint of "mirth" or "jollity," and the idea of revelry, debauchery, or conscious debasement is, here, simply incredible. And besides, there is no Endicott-narrator to protest that there is no such thing as natural experience which is "merely innocent," or as a "thing indifferent"; and no holidays that are not really holy days. So what could be wrong?

A strict Sabbatarian might worry about the new clothes and the mild flirtatiousness of the young. Jonathan Edwards, for example, in his *Faithful Narrative of Surprising Conversions,* makes such youthful worldliness almost as telling a sign of a people's unconverted state as a subtle and silent creeping Arminianism.[12] But our narrator is not nearly so scrupulous: he finds the Sabbath being "profaned" only later when, ironically, loud talk and "ostentatious laughter" try to dispel the gloomy shock of Hooper's prophetic gesture and searching sermon (40). And our own first impression is likely to be either personal relief or historical tolerance: by this time (the late 1720's or early 1730's) the strict piety of the original Puritans has simply worn off. The Puritan Sabbath is still observed, no doubt. But the congregation does not seem to be expecting either a Jeremiad or a stiff, Hooker-like, preparationist sermon on the nature and effects of sin; and their reaction to their minister's veil suggests that they have grown unaccustomed to unwonted displays of deep or eccentric piety. This congregation is, quite clearly, "backslidden"; but who are we to lament that? Or to imagine that Hawthorne himself is not "fervently" thankful for being so many steps "further from them in the march of ages"? Religion in New England, we are likely to conclude, has merely the status of religion anywhere else, and pending some deeper insight we sense nothing particularly wrong with this. God is still in His heaven; but in His world He lets His people be.

If there is any loaded word in the first paragraph, any hint of a meaning that runs subtly counter to the dominant impression of natural integrity, it is of course "conscious." The "conscious dignity" of the children is the only verbal clue we have to the fact that the story is ultimately about kinds and degrees of consciousness. And by the standards implied in Hooper's donning of the symbolic veil, a heightened consciousness is not a distinguishing mark of this particular eighteenth-century congregation.

We are not told what generally occupies the minds of the middle-aged and elderly persons of this unawakened "Milford," but we should not be surprised if they seem determined to take things as they appear in the light of common sense. Perhaps the height of their consciousness will not be far above the child-like awareness of the change of clothes from Saturday to Sunday, or the adolescent sense that the glory of the divine work and week is a certain *je ne sais quoi* enhancement of maidenly charm. One begins to sound like a Puritan to say so, perhaps, but it is not evident that the sacred and the secular stand in quite so simple a relation. And perhaps there are more (terrifying) things in heaven and earth than have been naturally stored up in the provincial mind of Massachusetts and Connecticut.

And so we quickly discover. Although everyone is deeply disturbed by the sudden alteration in Hooper's natural appearance, feeling that by hiding his face "he has changed himself into something awful" (38), still the attempts to deal with his symbolic meaning are primitive indeed. Some hardheaded individuals think him simply mad behind his veil; and the local physician, a "sober-minded man," even puts this *simpliste* verdict in a jargon typical of an easy Enlightenment: "Something must surely be amiss with Mr. Hooper's intellects" (41). The idea that the problem might concern his *soul* has evidently not occurred to him. Others among this group of Yankee interpreters shake their "sagacious" heads and, anticipating the acumen of Edgar Poe, "penetrate the mystery" and solve it in the obvious moralistic way. Still others, perhaps the most hard-headed of all, affirm that "there [is] no mystery"; it is merely that "Mr. Hooper's eyes were so weakened

by the midnight lamp, as to require a shade" (40-41). Generalized, the spiritual prescription appropriate to such a diagnosis might translate as follows: when emerging from the Dark Night of the Soul, wear sunglasses. (Isn't that Saint John of the Cross behind those Foster Grants?)

But if there is almost certainly more of deep religious awe concealed and trying to reveal itself behind Hooper's veil-as-symbol, still the hard-heads may not be entirely wrong. As anyone who has ever thought about the problem of "the Light and the Dark" in Hawthorne's fiction can easily understand, Hooper's eyes may indeed have become sensitive to "the light." We simply have to be more careful than anyone in the tale about the difference between cause and effect, and between literal and spiritual-metaphorical statements. This latter is not always easy to do in a world where, as Edwards and Emerson agree, all our words for spiritual realities are drawn from natural appearances. Or in the works of a writer whose subtle play with our opposing tendencies to literalistic reduction and allegorical overextension is such that we often find ourselves constructing spiritual interpretations before ever settling what literally happens. And especially in a tale where the narrator—himself neither speculative mystic nor hermeneutical theorist—does not always know enough to keep things straight.[13]

Literally, of course, the veil does serve "to give a darkened aspect to all living and inanimate things" (38). But this is obviously not the cause of Hooper's problem. His sight of the corporeal world through a veil, darkly, is (we must suppose) only an after-image of his insight into the nature of some spiritual reality. And, obviously, it is this insight, and not the veil, which throws the significant "obscurity between him and the holy page, as he [reads] the Scriptures" (39). So understood, his veil is nothing but the metaphor for his awakened Puritanism which, if truly revived rather than merely inherited, might indeed amount to somewhat more than the "gloom" so easily diagnosed by popular romancers and Unitarians. With them, Hawthorne has recognized that a temperamental bias to the negative might be the significant legacy of Puritanism; and that for a certain number of generations no great harm is done in saying it was. But the case is at least thinkable in which somebody, somehow, by some grace of insight or imagination, actually recovers or revives the authentic thing in all its original power. True revivals are just as possible as valid history. And doubtlessly both of these things are happening here: Hawthorne has re-created a moment in which somebody has become sensitive to the light because he has had a genuine Puritan glimpse of the dark. To come up to Hawthorne's own standard of judgment, we must imagine that Hooper may really know something. Puritans may actually see something which their liberal historians do not.

It is impossible to recover the specificities of Hooper's first veiled sermon: the narrator is in our way. Perhaps he does not know the precise heads of doctrine and application Hooper employed; or perhaps he is uninterested in such details. Possibly he assumes that a theologically literate audience can instantly supply the details from its own experience, either of sermons or of the personal consciousness of sin. Or possibly he assumes the reader will be interested primarily in the domestic sociology of the case and will only be embarrassed by too precise an attention to the gloomy formulations of a gothic theology. Certainly Hawthorne himself must have felt a queer mixture of those last two motives, as he designed a tale which might divide and elect its audience much like a converting sermon itself. But in any case, the reader may clear his own conscience of the charge of obscurantism or reductionism only if he tries to follow Hooper as deep as he may possibly be thought to have gone.

About the affective power of Hooper's performance there is no doubt or disagreement. On this first day no one seems to understand or approve what is being expressed, but no one is left complacent. Just after the event some may try to laugh it off or explain it away, but even our rationalistic physician is eventually led to reflect that men sometimes are "afraid to be alone with [themselves]." And at the sermon itself no one evades the "subtle power [that] was breathed into his words": "Each member of the congregation, the most innocent girl, and the man of hardened breast, felt as if the preacher had crept upon them, behind his awful veil, and discovered their hoarded iniquity of deed or thought. Many spread their clasped hands on their bosom" (40). No one shrieks or swoons or stands up to confess sin and profess repentance, but "more than one woman of delicate nerves was forced to leave the meeting-house" (39); and in every way it is hard to miss the suggestion that this sermon, delivered in the mild manner of a Jonathan Edwards (rather than in the more rampant and inflammatory style of a Whitefield) is in fact a piece of conversion rhetoric.[14]

It is no wonder the congregation does not like it: it is designed to remind them that beneath all their own sunny and smiling Sunday appearances, they are, in their secret deeds, or at least in their silent life of thought, wish, desire, fantasy, and motive, *simply* sinners. And such sin—if the truth of it be told—alienates man from God by smiting at His essence; and from every one of his fellows by making his whole outward appearance of decency, decorum, domesticity, and natural virtue a sham and a lie. The wonder is that, eventually, in the world we are given, it makes any converts at all. Or that the whole congregation does not officially declare Hooper mad (as a whole town later declares a simi-

larly motived Roderick Ellison) and apply to a "council of the churches" or perhaps even a "general synod" (45), not merely to inquire into the meaning of the veil, but to petition his removal from his pastoral office. Or that the majority of them do not simply pick up and remove themselves from Hooper's ministry to another, remoter part of New England. Such things happened, repeatedly, in just such a world, at just such a time. And for no more serious cause: the revivalist reminder that the radical and pervasive but secret sinfulness of all human beings must be known, in its power, and with application, before individuals or societies can ever be true. That, I take it, is nothing but the Puritan-Evangelical theory of "a Christian America."

The other surprising thing is that our narrator, given his limitations or biases, comes as close as he does to naming and correctly interpreting Hooper's real theme. He seems to approach about as near as a merely "notional" Christian may get; and in a studiedly general way, he is actually quite expansive: "The subject had reference to secret sin, and those sad mysteries which we hide from our nearest and dearest, and would fain conceal from our own consciousness, even forgetting that the Omniscient can detect them" (40). To go any further than this the narrator would have himself to adopt the language and the attitudes of the Evangelical Christian. This he is manifestly unable or unwilling to do: the indirection of his "had reference" utterly betrays the "objectivity" of his approach to the subject.[15] And any further explicit analysis of "the true sight of sin" would turn the story from a species of moral history into a form of preaching. And that function would violate the skepticism required by Hawthorne's historical calling and imposed by his own ironical narration.

We are given just this much, together with a few more hints of precisely the same purport later: Hooper recovers the Puritan sight of a kind of sinfulness so subtle and "original" that only God and the Awakened Self can see it, but so pervasive as to effect a total alienation of the family of man. This is supposed to be enough, even apart from the original context of **"The Story Teller,"** where a Methodist preacher of the "new birth" is struggling with whatever soul may be possessed by an irresponsible man of letters who is running away from his evangelical-Puritan upbringing.[16] If we require more, we may be convicting ourselves of an "obtuse secularism" not much different from the sort displayed in the story itself. Anyone who cannot find that Hawthorne was profoundly interested in Puritan history as such, and particularly (though skeptically) in the problematic effects of the struggle between sin and grace therein revealed, is going to have trouble with Parson Hooper.

3

But granting, for the moment, some such thematic interest, where does this historical placement leave us in the internal attempt to decide between the claims of the self-exiled Hooper and his newly alienated congregation? How are we to evaluate Hooper's newly acquired consciousness of sin? And what can be said on behalf of the congregation's stubborn but not particularly hardened inability (or unwillingness—in classic Puritan theory they are exactly the same thing) to take Hooper's converting insight into their own hearts and lives? Can we locate any significant tipping of the balance between Puritan Consciousness and Ordinary Life? Or, at very least, can we define the limits of Hawthorne's ambivalences and of the story's famous ambiguity with any precision drawn from an historical understanding of the issue?

In fact the balance is fairly delicate. On one side the congregation would obviously prefer to see matters return to normal. They would like to get the mystery cleared up, once and for all. They wish, understandably, to put an end to the upset and go on with their lives in the world; and in the Church. Someone might accuse them of adding willful complacency to their constitutional obtuseness, but probably we should not. We must assume that, left alone, their lives would continue to have the same inherent satisfactoriness suggested by the first paragraph. Surely life in eighteenth-century New England might go on as "unterribly" as Robert Frost says it does in most American times and places. Given adequate moral leisure, somebody might even invent the street light. But, obviously, Hooper's continuing prophecy is effectively designed to prevent any such reassuring outcome. A newly awakened man, Hooper intends what preparationist preachers always intend toward their audience: to keep their "Conscience under an arrest, so that it cannot make an escape from the Evidence and Authority of it, so that there is no way, but either to obey the Rule of it, or else be condemned by it."[17] Between such a minister and his congregation there cannot be the simple peace of ordinariness as usual. And if the danger on the one side is the shallow trap of natural self-satisfaction, on the other looms the deeper pitfall of spiritual self-obsession.

As mild mannered as ever, Hooper's new sermons all get tinged "more darkly than usual." His veil has not blinded him to things as they naturally are; neither does it cause him to hallucinate, like some madly inspired enthusiast. His darkened optic has merely afforded him a vision of the world he lacked before. Natural men and women, bright and healthy as they may continue outwardly to appear, now seem all fallen. "Spruce bachelors" and "pretty maidens" abroad in the natural world on an innocent Sabbath are revealed as the sinners they "truly" are, in the sight of the Calvin-

ist God, even if their conscience should trouble them with no glaringly "actual" sin. And the hopeful Scriptures now seem just as truly a Book of Sorrows.

Some conversion has brought what Thomas Hooker called "a strange and a sudden alteration" into Hooper's world; it has varied "the price and the value of things and persons beyond imagination." He now judges "not by outward appearances as is the guise of men of corrupt minds, but upon experience, that which [he has] found and felt in [his] own heart . . . and cannot but see so and judge so of others." By some process which the story does not explore—but which may indeed have to do with "the midnight lamp" not of eye-straining study but of truly illuminating self-examination—he has come to glimpse not only the vanity of the natural world but the fallenness effectively masked by human appearances. Unlike his abidingly natural congregation, Hooper will not now live by appearances or judge according to nature but will measure existence absolutely. No more than Saint Paul will he judge "humanly." His world may or may not be "well amended," but clearly it is "strangely altered."[18] And his conscious design is to produce the same revolutionary change in the subjective "worlds" of as many of his hearers as possible.

And eventually, as we are told, he is not entirely unsuccessful. Though he immediately alienates Squire Saunders, totally balks and baffles the congregational deputation sent to inquire about the meaning of his strange new prophecy, sadly instructs but does not make a convert (or a wife) of Elizabeth, makes himself generally a "bugbear" to the multitude and alternately a fright or mockery to children, and finally defies the extreme unctuousness of the well-meaning (though clearly obtuse) brother-minister who attends him at his deathbed, his reputation and his record of accomplishment as an occasional cause of conversion experience must be regarded as impressive. And we must take this aspect of Hooper's career somewhat seriously if we are to adjust the balance accurately.

The narrator, as our structural sense ought to inform us, has constructed the story so as to give a whole series of dramatic instances of the humanly unfortunate consequences of Hooper's conversionist calling: amply illustrated are the domestic penalties attendant upon a career of Puritan Prophecy. But he has reduced the "Christian History" of Hooper's achievements to a bare list, compressed into a simple paragraph near the end of the story. Still, the list of specifics is fairly long. And, more cogently, the generalization which introduces it contains one phrase so telling that it must be regarded as an index to the complexity of the author's own ironic estimate: "Among all its bad influences, the black veil had *the one desirable effect,* of making its wearer a very efficient clergyman" (49, my italics). Critics have suggested that "efficient" here is "not very flattering." Perhaps it is not, though it does seem to be a technical term in the official jargon of revivalists, rather like "experimental" in the lexicon of piety associated with the "Application of Redemption."[19] But in any case the more significant irony informs the idea of "the one desirable effect": what is easily taken as a scarcely flattering concession may more literally be read as *somebody's* trenchant assertion that the only good Hooper ever did, amidst so much that seems humanly bad, is the only spiritual good desirable, the only true good there ever could be. Though Hooper may smile ironically at the disruptions and alienations he produces, he himself evidently considers it all a world well lost. And so might anybody else who is completely convinced that salvation lies on the other side of a true sight of sin.

That class of persons includes, pre-eminently, all of Hooper's converts. To "souls that were in agony for sin," as everyone in the way of "preparation for salvation" must always be, according to the orthodoxy of New Puritanism, his "awful power" is both necessary and, in the outcome, a positive good. What true religion without "awe"? And, false sympathy and sentiment aside, what "efficient" exposure of human self-deception and pretense without the "power" to destroy self-defense? True, each of Hooper's converts has once regarded him with "a dread peculiar to themselves," but how else will the anxious soul regard an agency intending nothing less than the death of its old consciousness, its old self? What wonder if before Hooper could bring his converts "to celestial light" they must first be with him "behind the black veil" (49)? With authentic Puritanism it is never otherwise: without an awful "conviction" of sin, nothing else follows. Only a flagrant antinomianism or a pathetic liberalism would teach that the good news of salvation comes before (or independent of) the bad news of sin. Spiritually considered, Hooper's "veil" is utterly orthodox; the response of his converts, perfectly according to the established morphology.

Equally intelligible are Hooper's other accomplishments as authentic reinventor of the Puritan consciousness. He ministers effectively to dying sinners and to all who are overtaken by "dark affections." He profoundly affects many itinerant visitors who have come "long distances to attend services at his church": in Hawthorne's ironic revision of the classic formula, they came to "gaze" and stayed to "quake." And finally—in the detail expressly designed to tell us very literally and precisely where we are, in case the whole spiritual outline of the awakening situation is still unclear to us—he gives an election sermon "during Governor Belcher's administration" (spanning the years of Edwards' first revivals at Northampton and of Whitefield's first great tour of

America) which convinces the legislators to enact measures favorable to the "piety of our earliest ancestral sway" (49).

To a certain extent, therefore, what can be said for Hooper is whatever our religious sensitivies tell us must be said on behalf of revivals or awakenings. That they have socially disruptive effects on the daily lives and weekly church-going habits of people of ordinary human decency and virtue is scarcely news: that truism has been perfectly obvious to everyone, at least since Edwards defined "the distinguishing marks of a work of the spirit" and defended its importance in spite of a far more grotesque display of human craziness than has found its way into **"The Minister's Black Veil."** The true definition of "confusion," Edwards argues, is the disruption of means that are known to lead to man's proper and highest end.[20] And since, on Puritan premise, natural life and ordinary consciousness lead only to the "vanity" of Ecclesiastes, or the "corruption" of Augustine, or the "self-love" of Calvin, then evidently natural life and ordinary consciousness ought to be broken up. Calvinist salvation is not natural life but a New Birth. The New Birth is not natural consciousness but conversion. And conversion begins in the consciousness of the self under the aspect of "sin"—or, rather, that habitual ("Calvinistic") sinfulness which is as "secret" to the natural man himself as it is to the outside view of the casual observer.

To see the question in proper perspective, then, the reader must get beyond the anti-evangelical bias of the narrator and imagine that Hooper's "one desirable effect" *might* be a very important one indeed. To fail of this imaginative recognition is to trivialize the whole case. To call Hooper simply crazy (or pridefully self-deluded, or a false prophet, or an antichrist) would be much like taking the views of Charles Chauncey, at face value, as an adequate account of the whole meaning of the Great Awakening. Even if we should judge that Hooper's way of salvation is ultimately a falsehood and a delusion, we must yet allow for its moral seriousness and psychological power.[21]

But of course we can scarcely stop there; for the story's final judgment does seem to be against Hooper. Even with the narrator unmasked, the story will scarcely read otherwise. And if it did, we should hardly trust our own judgment: given Hawthorne's own clear-enough rejection of Puritan orthodoxy—in both its ancestral, inherited, "gloomy" form at Salem and its more current, revived, "powerful" embodiment at Bowdoin—where should we locate his sudden conversion? Or why should we imagine Hawthorne would sponsor in art what he evaded in life? Or endorse in **"The Minister's Black Veil"** what he exposed in **"The Gentle Boy"?** With some assurance, then, we turn to the case against Hooper, still hoping to strike some uneven balance. We must be sensitive enough, both to history and to the terrors of the spiritual life, to "throw in something, somehow like Original Sin." But perhaps we should not throw out everything else.[22]

What tips the balance against Hooper is some sense of his too-powerful partialness. To come to terms with him we need to take seriously the idea (of Hooker and Edwards and other such "formidable Christians") that natural man needs to have his consciousness renewed and his world turned upside down, and that there may indeed be a form of divine wisdom that will always appear as folly to the world. But even as we do, we begin to sense that Hooper himself may have taken these ideas *too* seriously, if that were somehow possible. Or that he has somehow crossed over the fine line which divides the needful "wisdom that is woe" from a more extreme "woe that is madness." Probably it is some such thought which helps us get things back in perspective, and to come to terms with Hawthorne himself.

Surely the balance is not restored by any powerfully positive and dramatically realized counterimage of moral heroism or spiritual insight which close analysis may yet discover in Hooper's congregation. Indeed, to look beneath their explicitly unawakened naiveté for some major revelation of truth or virtue, buried in their collective or "catholic" wisdom, is probably to misconstrue Hawthorne's commitment to the sanative power of the ordinary, precisely as such.[23] It is, by definition, simply ordinary: without categorical understanding, and insusceptible of interpretative revaluation, it simply is whatever it is, savable or damnable in those terms alone. It is once-born. Or, if that generalization seems too wide, at least it would be a thankless task to enter a special plea for the other-than-ordinary character of the persons with whom we see Hooper having to deal. As if by some predestinating decree, they remain simply unawakened. Or, alternately, they may be obeying some romantic law that the plain people should not mean but be. In any case, the really heightened consciousness remains pretty much the sole possession of the minister. Hooper alone has looked on subjectivity bare.

To be sure, Elizabeth seems the sanest intelligence in the story. And in her interview with her "plighted" husband she comes close to meeting Hooper (in our behalf) on his own ground. And her own long life of single devotion to the self-exiled bachelor-minister may well strike us as more truly selfless than Hooper's tormented career as delegated minister to the haunted mind. Still, we see so little of her that only a premature investment in the values of domestic sentiment can cause us to elevate her to the stature of an ideal spiritual role-model. Theologically, and in relation to Hooper, she may figure as a rejected natural grace. But literarily, and to us, she is no "heroine," only the jilted but ever-faithful girl-next-door. And around

her, filling up the definition of the community she most sympathetically represents, are ranged only versions of that invincible moral ignorance which simply *cannot* take Hooper's point with the power of subjective application.

Hooper's converts we never directly see. About the efficacy and human satisfactoriness of his cure of those souls "in agony for sin," who become the proper object of his ministry, nothing definitive can be said. Though the "experimental" details of their religious experiences may run to considerable length in the pages of *The Christian History*—the official record of the historic revival with which Hooper's fictional career is associated—they are simply not in this "narrative" in any effective way. Fair or not, all we are given is the sick-soul psychology of Hooper himself, to be measured against the once-born naiveté of persons who seem, by and large, not to sense the presence of disease anywhere but in the "intellects" of their spiritual physician; and in relation to the disruptions produced, in Hooper's own ordinary life and in theirs. But even when we have compensated for this narrative bias, by granting the authentic existence of a significant class of New-Light Hooperites in this incorrigibly Old-Light world, it is hard to feel that what is gained quite compensates for what has been lost.

Obviously we must be wary of resting our case against Hooper solely on the disruptions produced by his doctrine or style of prophecy. On the one hand, emotionally, our personal recoil probably does not spring from that source primarily. And, on the other, our intellectual objections would be vulnerable to Edwards' famous reply that *of course* the Spirit will break up the patterns of the ordinary in favor of the "true." We might yet clear ourselves by rejoining that there are limits of decorum not to be violated by *any* agency; that certain universal folkways, having a sort of sacramental efficacy, can be defended on grounds other than rationalistic prejudice or affective attenuation. But, far more simply, what leads us to the deeper source of our feelings about the tragic failure of Hooper's career, and indeed of his life, is a precisely Edwardsean question about the true nature of his spiritual achievements. What, we should ask ourself, are the "fruits" of Hooper's own conversion?[24]

One obvious and fairly telling "sign" is that Hooper's spiritual life does not seem to grow or advance. From his initial donning of the black veil straight through to his final deathbed speech, his insight bears only repetition. It may deepen, but it does not lead on to anything else. Indeed it seems to trap him. It is as if he were in the *midst* of some very profound and important process but unable to move on to its saving completion. For him at least the fruits of the Puritan consciousness of sin are identically that consciousness. A form of awareness everywhere defined and evaluated as "preparatory" seems here to begin and end with itself.[25] The spectacle is not pleasant, nor is the prospect hopeful. What may, as process, look like a necessary step in a saving progress or as an important stage along life's way comes to appear, as an end in itself, not true spiritual health but a very desperate form of spiritual insanity. So that—to say the least—Hooper's last state may be not better than his first.

The individual reader may or may not believe that man as such is sick in his being and radically in need of a spiritual cure. And critics will no doubt continue to suggest various estimates of Hawthorne's own precise relation to evangelical orthodoxy. But few of us, I suspect, are willing to grant that *any* salvation is exempt from the general rule that a cure must not be worse than its relative disease. And it may prove hard to resist making the appropriate application of that maxim to Hooper, who cannot seem to move beyond the tragic human implications of the true sight of sin.

The other sign that all is not well in the spiritual case of the Reverend Mr. Hooper is at once more obvious and more subtle in its implications. Surely some deep spiritual dis-ease is manifesting itself in his obsession with *the veil itself,* the mere external symbol by which he has sought to express the spiritual import of his insight. His jealous guarding of the outward appearance of a veil which hides his individual face becomes as important to him as the universal fact of a sinfulness which prevents spirits in deepest communion from ever adequately revealing their inmost hearts and minds. Hooper develops a kind of symbolic literalism which actually resembles the congregation's own persistent reduction of his message to its medium, except that theirs is naive and his compulsive. It is almost as if—like certain literary critics who want all symbolic works to be about the function of symbols, or indeed all literary works to be about their own literariness—Hooper has got trapped in the epistemology of his chosen career. Or, more to the story's Puritan point, as if some Jonathan Edwards had suddenly become more interested in the metaphors of his "rhetoric of sensation" than in the moral psychology of sin and grace.[26]

Eventually, of course, we may wish to ask·why Hawthorne would have imagined such an exaggeration or mystification of the "merely" literary to occur in the midst of the American eighteenth century, whose common-sense philosophy is not noticeably indebted to Heidegger; just as, indeed, we must eventually face all the widest implications of Hooper's symbolic and subjective self-entrapment. But to leap at once to such considerations is to pass too quickly through the historical surface of Hawthorne's tale of the revival of Puritan consciousness. Almost certainly it is to misread the tale's precise referent; and very likely it is to involve ourselves in yet an-

other species of Hooper's own problem, which the story exists to identify rather than to spread. Much nearer Hawthorne's starting point would be some observation about the Puritan source and moral dimension of Hooper's obsessive self-reference.

In these terms Hooper's insistence on the importance of his own veil is merely the sign of a deeper moral problem still, his perpetual and finally self-convicting insistence on his own exemplariness, in spite of the explicitly universal character of his express doctrine. In his attempt to make a symbolic prophecy about the sinfulness of absolutely *every* person's secret or subjective life, he seems forced to use his own self as exemplum. To the person well acquainted with all the various genres of Puritan writing, Hooper's life-long experiment with "Auto-Machia" may seem simply inevitable, as indeed Hawthorne intends Hooper's effort to be widely representative of a major effort of the Puritan consciousness. And there is no doubt that such a project can often be productive of great literary results: we scarcely need the example of Whitman to remind us that, given adequate standards of genuine personal frankness, usually mixed with at least a modicum of self-mockery, self-reference is the very stuff of modern literature. But neither should we need to be reminded that the first-person exemplum everywhere tends to spread out and take over the whole psychological field; and that when such a thing actually happens, heroic honesty may turn into something much less admirable. If we need any reminder, it is identically the one which **"The Minister's Black Veil"** exists to give—namely, that such a thing might happen in a Puritan world as easily as anywhere else; or, more perceptively, that it is precisely there that such things predictably began to happen.[27]

Thus the case of Hooper stands primarily as Hawthorne's figure of that potentially exhaustive and incipiently solipsistic sort of self-reference into which a powerfully heightened or Puritan or even "true" sight of sin can be discovered all ironically to lead. And the likelihood appears especially great in a common-sense world whose sociology no longer reflects that level of consciousness and whose established mode of discourse has lost touch with the symbolic idiom on which such a consciousness would seem to depend. In such a world one does not have to be a self-congratulating bigot of the Digby variety to end up utterly alone, irrecoverably lost in the cave of self-hood. Rather the reverse: the more one insists on the absolutely universal application of one's own perfectly subjective discovery of sin, the more isolated one becomes. The irony of such an unlooked-for outcome might well provoke, in an appropriately situated person, a sad smile. And surely an adequately instructed critic might sympathize with such a smile, even if it were tinged with a trace of self-pity. But if the sadly humorous recognition of the penalties of divine wisdom should turn into an hysterical rejection of the compensatory good of all merely relative human palliatives, then one may pardonably decide that salvation is to be sought elsewhere.

And so, even when we grant that Hooper's dark illumination has afforded him—or, more accurately, has been identical with—a revived sight of sinful human subjectivity, we are still required to wonder if he has not stopped short of some other "light beyond."[28] In possessing so absolutely the Truth of the Self, he has somehow lost the Good of the Other. A partial conversion, surely. Or if it should turn out that the "preparatory" insight into the radical alienation of the Self is the ultimate knowledge available to the human point of view, then we may still conclude that such ultimates are too true to be useful. . . .

Notes

[1] In treating Hooper as a "case of conscience," I invoke the example of Austin Warren; see *The New England Conscience* (Ann Arbor: University of Michigan Press, 1966), pp. 132-142.

[2] For the classic view of unresolvable ambiguity in "The Minister's Black Veil" (MBV), see Richard Harter Fogle, *Hawthorne's Fiction* (Norman: University of Oklahoma Press, 1952), pp. 33-40.

[3] The most meaningful comment on the sermon before Belcher is the brief reference by Glenn C. Altschuler in "The Puritan Dilemma in MBV," *American Transcendental Quarterly,* 24 (1974), 25-27. The "fact" is also mentioned by Michael Davitt Bell, *Hawthorne and the Historical Romance of New England* (Princeton, N. J.: Princeton University Press, 1971), p. 68; and Neal Frank Doubleday, *Hawthorne's Early Tales* (Durham, N.C.: Duke University Press, 1972), p. 171. For other generally "historical" interpretations, see Robert H. Fossum, *Hawthorne's Inviolable Circle* (Deland, Fla.: Everett/Edwards, 1972), pp. 56-59; Harry B. Henderson, *Versions of the Past* (New York: Oxford, 1974), pp. 101, 109; and Robert E. Morsberger, "MBV: Shrouded in Blackness, Ten Times Black," *New England Quarterly,* 46 (1973), 454-462. For explicit rejections of significant "historicity," see Raymond Benoit, "Hawthorne's Psychology of Death," *Studies in Short Fiction,* 8 (1971), 553-560; and Nina Baym, *The Shape of Hawthorne's Career* (Ithaca, N.Y.: Cornell University Press, 1976), p. 58.

[4] For the psychoanalytic reading of MBV, see Frederick Crews, *Sins of the Fathers* (New York: Oxford, 1966), pp. 106-111; for the outlines of a semiological approach, see W. B. Carnochan, "MBV: Symbol, Meaning, and the Context of Hawthorne's Art," *Nineteenth-Century Fiction,* 24 (1969), 182-192.

[5] The "knowing" view of Hooper as guilty of some explicit (probably) sexual crime drives from Poe's (widely reprinted) review of *Twice-told Tales.* For a carefully guarded comparison with Dimmesdale, see Doubleday, *Early Tales,* pp. 177-178. And for the classic case *for* Hooper (as against Brown), see Robert W. Cochran, "Hawthorne's Choice: The Veil or the Jaundiced Eye," *College English,* 23 (1962), 342-346.

[6] The similarity between Digby and Hooper is well established in the criticism. For their relative status as images of "the Puritan," see Michael Bell, *Historical Romance,* pp. 64-68. For their similarity as Romantic "egoists," see Millicent Bell, *Hawthorne's View of the Artist* (New York: New York University Press, 1962), pp. 23-24. And for Digby as the "grotesque" version of Hawthorne's sexual "escapists," see Crews, *Sins,* pp. 114-116. MBV was first published in *The Token* for 1836 and was almost certainly part of "The Story Teller" as it existed in 1834; "The Man of Adamant" appeared in *The Token* for 1837.

[7] Baym, *Shape,* p. 55.

[8] Hooker, *The Application of Redemption;* quoted from Perry Miller and Thomas H. Johnson, ed., *The Puritans* (New York: Harper and Row, 1963), p. 292.

[9] Cf. C. C. Goen, *Revivalism and Separatism in New England, 1740-1800* (New Haven, Conn.: Yale University Press, 1962), esp. pp. 1-114; and, a bit less specifically, Edwin Scott Gaustad, *The Great Awakening in New England* (New York: Harper and Row, 1957), pp. 102-125.

[10] Fogle's premise of radical ambiguity has found relatively few supporters; it has seemed necessary to decide. Against Hooper, see W. B. Stein, "The Parable of Antichrist in MBV," *American Literature,* 27 (1955), 386-392; E. E. Stibitz, "Ironic Unity in Hawthorne's MBV," *American Literature,* 34 (1962), 182-190; and Nicholas Canaday, Jr., "Hawthorne's Minister and the Veiling Deceptions of Self," *Studies in Short Fiction,* 4 (1967), 135-142. In favor, see Benoit, "Psychology of Death"; Cochran, "Hawthorne's Choice"; G. P. Voight, "The Meaning of MBV," *College English,* 13 (1952), 337-338; Victor Strandberg, "The Artist's Black Veil," *New England Quarterly,* 41 (1968), 567-574; and G. A. Santangelo, "The Absurdity of MBV," *Pacific Coast Philology,* 5 (1970), 61-66.

[11] All citations from the text of MBV refer to *Twice-told Tales* (Columbus: Ohio State University Press, 1974).

[12] See *Faithful Narrative,* in C. C. Goen, ed., *The Great Awakening* (New Haven, Conn.: Yale University Press, 1972), pp. 144-149. And for the more general relevance

of Edwards (as well as of Bunyan and Shepard), see Morsberger, "Shrowded in Blackness."

[13] Evidently something like a "Puritan" problem lies behind our own critical tendency to disregard the literal in Hawthorne; see David Levin, "Shadows of Doubt," *American Literature,* 34 (1962), 344-352.

[14] The creator of the flamboyant Awakening "style" was Whitefield rather than Edwards. Even the famous "imagistic" "Sinners in the Hands of an Angry God" was delivered by Edwards in monotone, with "his eyes fixed on the bell-rope;" the upset came from the auditors. See Perry Miller, *Jonathan Edwards* (New York: William Sloane, 1949), pp. 145-146.

[15] The narrator may be confusing "secret sin" with the related but secondary problem of other "sad mysteries"; but the theologically literate reader should not do so. The primary sense of "secret sin" should clearly be Clavin's sense of sinfulness rooted in our nature which we (while unregenerate) are unaware of. For Puritans, this should all be an "open secret"; and confusion on this point marks the narrator's (or the critic's) loss of touch with the Calvinist idiom.

[16] Cf. "Passages from a Relinquished Work," published in the *New England Magazine* (December 1834). The bibliographical argument for the inclusion of MBV within the projected "Story Teller" was first advanced by Seymour Gross, "Four Possible Additions to Hawthorne's 'Story Teller,'" *Papers of the Bibliographical Society of America,* 51 (1957), 90-95. The argument has been rejected by Doubleday (*Early Tales,* p. 170) and Baym (*Shape,* p. 40); but the tale's narrative peculiarities would seem to support inclusion. For the most complete discussions of "The Story Teller," see Nelson F. Adkins, "The Early Projected Works of Nathaniel Hawthorne," *Papers of the Bibliographical Society of America,* 39 (1945), 119-155; and Alfred Weber, *Die Entwicklung der Rahmenerzählungen Nathaniel Hawthornes* (Berlin: Erich Schmidt, 1973), pp. 142-307.

[17] Thomas Hooker, *Application of Redemption;* quoted from Miller and Johnson, *Puritans,* p. 305.

[18] Quoted from Miller and Johnson, *Puritans,* p. 312.

[19] For the innocent response to "efficient," see Stibitz, "Ironic Unity," p. 189. The official status of the word may be inferred from Joseph Tracy's favorable characterization of Edwards as "perhaps the most efficient preacher in New England"; see *A History of the Revival of Religion* (Boston: Tappan and Dennet, 1842), p. 214. For Hawthorne's interest in revivalist phenomena, see Frank Shuffleton, "Nathaniel Hawthorne and the Revival Movement," *American Transcendental Quarterly,* 44 (1979), 311-323.

[20] See *Distinguishing Marks,* in Goen, *Great Awakening,* pp. 266-267.

[21] The critics *most* hostile to Hooper are Stein and Stibitz (see note 10).

[22] Accepting the Melvillean hint, we may yet stop short of the argument which would make Hawthorne himself a latter-day Puritan whose system emphasizes sin but omits grace; see Austin Warren, "Introduction," *Nathaniel Hawthorne* (Cincinnati: American Book Co., 1934), pp. xix-xxi.

[23] Lying in wait for those who overvalue the commonplace in Hawthorne is (still) Frederick Crews. His arguments answer not only a simplistic theology like that of Edward Wagenknecht in *Nathaniel Hawthorne* (New York: Oxford, 1961), pp. 172-201, but also the sort of truistic moralism associated with Chester E. Eisenger's "Hawthorne as Champion of the Middle Way," *New England Quarterly,* 27 (1954), 27-52.

[24] Hooper might conceivably pass the test of the *Religious Affections:* his consciousness is arguably "spiritual," and his outwardly irreproachable life agrees well enough with Edwards' "neonomian" Twelfth Sign, which insists on "Christian practice." But the relevant standard might be in the earlier *Faithful Narrative:* Hooper would not seem to possess that "holy repose of soul" which marks the last stage in Edwards' simplified morphology; and the unrelieved blackness (or monochromatic grayness) of his veiled vision might associate him with those unregenerate men who would discuss the precise hue of salvation knowing only the "names of colors" (see Goen, *Awakening,* pp. 173-174).

[25] It is as if Hooper had experienced Thomas Shepard's preparatory phases of "conviction," "compunction," and "humiliation," without going on to "faith," with its "privileges" of "justification," "reconciliation," and "adoption"; see *The Sound Believer,* in J. A. Albro, ed., *The Works of Thomas Shepard* (Boston: Doctrinal Tract and Book Society, 1853), I, 115-284.

[26] Perry Miller himself seems always flirting with the temptation to regard Edwards as primarily "literary": see not only his *Edwards* (1949) but also "The Rhetoric of Sensation," in *Errand into the Wilderness* (Cambridge: Harvard University Press, 1956); and "Introduction," *Images or Shadows of Divine Things* (New Haven, Conn.: Yale University Press, 1948).

[27] Cf. Sacvan Bercovitch, *The Puritan Origins of the American Self* (New Haven, Conn.: Yale University Press, 1975), esp. pp. 1-34.

[28] Though some critics have, undeniably, worked too simply with the positive or affirmative values in

Hawthorne, the problem itself remains valid and important; and a book like Leonard J. Fick's *The Light Beyond* (Westminster, Md.: Newman Press, 1955) does not *entirely* collapse under the attack of Frederick Crews.

Edgar A. Dryden (essay date 1993)

SOURCE: "Through a Glass Darkly: 'The Minister's Black Veil' as Parable," in *New Essays on Hawthorne's Major Tales,* edited by Millicent Bell, Cambridge University Press, 1993, pp. 133-50.

[*In the following essay, Dryden considers "The Minister's Black Veil" as a fictitious parable rather than a fictionalized historic event.*]

As a self-designated "romance-writer"[1] (149) Hawthorne was fascinated by the theoretical implications of the generic mark; the problem of generic designations, which is a central concern in his prefaces, appears even more explicitly in subtitled designations as in *The Scarlet Letter: A Romance* or **"The Minister's Black Veil: A Parable,"** the generic denomination I intend to explore in this essay. What exactly does it mean to say that **"The Minister's Black Veil"** is a parable? What is the relation between the title and subtitle? To what extent can the subtitle be seen as an interpretive clue to the reader that will allow him or her to place the text within a contextual order by establishing a set of generic expectations? These preliminary questions are complicated by the fact that the subtitle marking the story as parable is itself marked by a footnote giving the reader Hawthorne's historical "source" for the account of Parson Hooper.[2]

> Another clergyman in New England, Mr. Joseph Moody, of York, Maine, who died about eighty years since, made himself remarkable by the same eccentricity that is here related of the Reverend Mr. Hooper. In his case, however, the symbol had a different import. In early life he had accidentally killed a beloved friend; and from that day till the hour of his own death, he had hid his face from men. (371)

The curious relation between the story's subtitle and the footnote that purports to explain it offers a fitting entrance to the shadowy world of **"The Minister's Black Veil."** In parables as in fables we usually find "'statements of fact, which do not even pretend to be historical, used as vehicles for the exhibition of a general truth.'"[3] And yet Hawthorne asks us to see Mr. Hooper as an historical figure or at least to view him as the literary copy of a historical original whose eccentricity is the source that will partially explain the eccentricity of the fictional character.[4] In the case of Mr. Moody the "import" of the symbolic veil is clear:

It is the sign of the shame and guilt he feels at having "accidentally killed a beloved friend." In the case of Mr. Hooper, however, the reasons for his donning the veil remain "unaccountable" (372), and it becomes a "material emblem" (379-80) whose meaning remains to the end obscure. In both cases the crucial relationship is that between figural connotation and literal reference, a relationship that seems clear and uncomplicated in the case of the historical Mr. Moody but aberrant and threatening for the fictional Mr. Hooper, whose life is radically disturbed by the horrible irony that "only a material emblem had separated him from happiness" (379-80). One could say that the space that separates Reverend Hooper's "simple piece of crape" (373) from the "mystery which it obscurely typifies" (384) is analogous to that which distances the historical Mr. Moody from the fictional character who in some obscure way represents him. This ironic distance is marked in the story by the "faint, sad smile" that "glimmer[s] from [the] obscurity" (383) of the "double fold of crape" (378), a smile that is Hooper's only response to all questions as to his motives for putting it on. And those motives certainly seem obscure. The narrator, like Hooper, offers no specific explanation for the character's unaccountable behavior, although the generic mark inscribed by the story's subtitle suggests that Hooper's actions may have a scriptural or institutional precedent that may be more helpful than the factual one suggested by the footnote. And indeed the Bible seems to suggest several possibilities.[5]

When Moses returns to the children of Israel after spending forty days and forty nights in the presence of God "the skin of his face shone; and they were afraid to come nigh him" (Exodus 34:30) until Moses "put a vail on his face" (Exodus 34:33), a "vail" that he removes when he enters the tabernacle to speak with the Lord. This act of veiling, like that of the Reverend Mr. Hooper, becomes the object of an elaborate figural reading, as in Paul's letters to the Corinthians.

> But if the ministration of death, written *and* engraven in stones, was glorious, so that the children of Israel could not steadfastly behold the face of Moses for the glory of his countenance; which *glory* was to be done away:
>
> How shall not the ministration of the spirit be rather glorious? . . .
>
> For if that which is done away *was* glorious, much more that which remaineth *is* glorious.
>
> Seeing then that we have such hope, we use great plainness of speech:
>
> And not as Moses, *which* put a vail over his face, that the children of Israel could not steadfastly look to the end of that which is abolished:
>
> But their minds were blinded: for until this day remaineth the same vail untaken away in the reading of the old testament; which *vail* is done away in Christ.

But even unto this day, when Moses is read, the vail is upon their heart.

Nevertheless when it shall turn to the Lord, the vail shall be taken away.

Now the Lord is that Spirit: and where the Spirit of the Lord *is,* there *is* liberty.

But we all, with open face beholding as in a glass the glory of the Lord, are changed into the same image from glory to glory, *even* as by the Spirit of the Lord.

II Corinthians 3:7-18

This passage concludes the complex figure of reading and writing that structures the third chapter of II Corinthians, a figure that turns on the distinction between the spirit and the letter: *"Forasmuch as ye are* manifestly declared to be the epistle of Christ ministered by us, written not with ink but with the spirit of the living God; and not in tables of stone, but in the fleshy tables of the heart" (3:3). According to a nineteenth-century commentary of the sort Hawthorne would have known, St. Paul was the

ministering pen or other instrument of writing as well as the ministering bearer and presenter of the letter. "Not with ink" stands in contrast to the letters of commendation which "some" at Corinth (v. 1) used. *Ink* is also used here to include all outward materials for writing, such as the Sinaitic tables of stone were. These, however were not written with ink, but "graven" by the "finger of God" (Exodus 31.18; 32.16). Christ's epistle (his believing members converted by St. Paul) is better still: it is written not merely with the *finger,* but with the *"Spirit of the Living God,"* it is not the "ministration of death" as the law, but the *"living* Spirit" that "giveth life."[6]

Paul contrasts the clearness and fearlessness of the Apostolic teachings with the concealment and indirection of the Old Testament. And in doing so he

passes from the literal fact to the truth symbolized by it, the blindness of Jews and Judaizers to the ultimate end of the law: stating that Moses *put on the veil that they might not look steadfastly at* (Romans 10.4) *the end of that* (law) *which* (like Moses' glory) *is done away.* Not that *Moses* had this *purpose;* but often God attributes to His prophets the purpose which he has himself. Because the Jews *would not see,* God judicially gave them up *so as not to see.* The glory of Moses' face is antitypically Christ's glory shining behind the veil of legal ordinances. The veil which has been taken off to the believer is left on to the unbelieving Jew, so that he should not see. . . . He stops short at the letter of the law, not seeing the end of it. The evangelical glory of the law, like the shining of Moses' face, cannot be borne by a carnal people, and therefore remains veiled to them until the spirit come to take away the veil. (Jamieson, vol. 2, p. 305)

And when that occurs "Christians, a contrasted with the Jews who have a *veil* on their hearts, answering to Moses' veil on his face," will stand with open face "changed into His image by beholding Him" (Jamieson, vol. 2, p. 305).

As this commentary suggests, figural reading such as Paul's is itself a form of veiling that requires in its turn careful interpretation. When he figures himself as an instrument of writing and the lives of his converts as epistles from Christ able to be read by all men, he is speaking parabolically, and the parables in both the Old and New Testaments are dark sayings where one thing is expressed in terms of something else so that it demands attention and insight, sometimes an actual explanation (Smith, vol. 3, p. 2328). Associated with the dark sayings of rabbinic teachings, parables are linked with those things "darkly announced under the ancient economy, and during that period darkly understood, but fully published under the Gospel" (Jamieson, vol. 2, p. 43). But Christ's decision to adopt the parabolic mode complicates this distinction by calling attention to the generic resemblance between the form of his teaching and that of the rabbis.

The parable was made the intrument for teaching the young disciple to discern the treasures of wisdom of which the "accursed multitude" was ignorant. The teaching of our Lord at the commencement of his ministry was, in every way, the opposite of this. The Sermon on the Mount may be taken as the type of the "words of Grace" which he spake, "not as the scribes." Beatitudes, laws, promises were uttered distinctly, not indeed without similitudes, but with similitudes that explained themselves. So for some months he taught in synagogues and on the sea-shore of Galilee, as he had before taught in Jerusalem, and as yet without a parable. But then there comes a change. His direct teaching was met with scorn, unbelief, hardness, and He seems for a time to abandon it for that which took the form of parables. The question of the disciples (Matt. xiii. 10) implies that they were astonished. Their master was no longer proclaiming the Gospel of the kingdom as before. He was falling back into one at least of the forms of Rabbinic teaching. . . . He was speaking to the multitude in the parables and dark sayings which the Rabbis reserved for their chosen disciples. . . . He had chosen this form of teaching because the people were spiritually blind and deaf . . . and in order that they might remain so. . . . Men have set themselves against the truth, and therefore it is hid from their eyes, presented to them in forms in which it is not easy for them to recognize it. To the inner circle of the chosen it is given to know the mysteries of the kingdom of God. To those who are without, all these things are done in parables. (Smith, vol. 3, pp. 2328-9)

Biblical parables, in short, are veils that serve the double purpose of revealing and concealing, making manifest through their figural drapery and mysteries of the kingdom to those capable of knowing and relishing them and providing some temporary fictitious entertainment to those insensible to spiritual things. In this sense, parabolic, figurative language like the "double VEIL" that shrouds the Holy of Holies in the tabernacle, is a "dread symbol of *separation between God and guilty men*" (Jamieson, vol. 2, p. 61). It withdraws the light from those who love darkness and protects the truth from scoffers, but through the process of interpretation offers the possibility of direct access to divine presence. Those "who ask the meaning of the parable, will not rest till the teacher has explained it, are led step by step to the laws of interpretation, so that they can understand all parables, and then pass into the higher region in which parables arc no longer necessary, but all things are spoken plainly" (Smith, vol. 3, p. 2329).

This happy crossing between literal and figural, between seeing and being, between the Old and the New Testaments, that the biblical text enacts is short-circuited in Hawthorne's parable which dramatizes a collision between literal reference and illustrative significance. The story opens with a description of communal life in a "real" town (Milford, Connecticut) where there seems to be a perfect solidarity of signs and meanings.

> The sexton stood in the porch of Milford meeting-house, pulling lustily at the bell-rope. The old people of the village came stooping along the street. Children, with bright faces, tript merrily beside their parents, or mimicked a graver gait, in the conscious dignity of their Sunday clothes. Spruce bachelors looked sidelong at pretty maidens, and fancied that the Sabbath sunshine made them prettier than on week-days. When the throng had mostly streamed into the porch, the sexton began to toll the bell, keeping his eye on the Reverend Mr. Hooper's door. The first glimpse of the clergyman's figure was the signal for the bell to cease its summons. (371)

Here is a world characterized by its smooth, untroubled surface, the result of the easy familiarity of the happily conventional, a world whose contents may be assumed to be unambiguously *given*. The behavior of the people is as natural and fitting as the sunshine that illuminates their faces; and the figure of their clergyman whose arrival they await seems equally to confirm the shared awareness of a given, common humanity. A "gentlemanly person . . . dressed with due clerical neatness," he is, with one exception, entirely unremarkable. But that "one thing remarkable in his appearance" is enough to disturb the untroubled surface of the community by making him "strange" (371) and "unaccountable" (372). He has put on a black veil that seems to consist of "two folds of crape, which entirely concealed his features, except the mouth and chin, but probably did not inter-

cept his sight, farther than to give a darkened aspect to all living and inanimate things" (372). The most immediate and drastic effects of this "simple piece of crape" (373), however, have nothing to do with the way it changes the minister's view of the world. Rather they result from the fact that it defamiliarizes him for his parishioners: "'I can't really feel as if good Mr. Hooper's face was behind that piece of crape,' said the sexton. 'I don't like it,' muttered an old woman, as she hobbled into the meeting-house. 'He has changed himself into something awful, only by hiding his face'" (372).

> "How strange," said a lady, "that a simple black veil, such as any woman might wear on her bonnet, should become such a terrible thing on Mr. Hooper's face!" "Something must surely be amiss with Mr. Hooper's intellects," observed her husband. . . . "But the strangest part of the affair is the effect of this vagary even on a soberminded man like myself. The black veil, though it covers only our pastor's face, throws its influence over his whole person, and makes him ghostlike from head to foot." (374)

Apparently the "horrible black veil['s]" (376) awful "influence" (374) derives from the fact that, in covering the face, it radically disfigures or defaces, making the minister an object of both morbid, idle curiosity and peculiar dread.

> His converts always regarded him with a dread peculiar to themselves, affirming, though but figuratively, that, before he brought them to celestial light, they had been with him behind the black veil. . . . Dying sinners cried aloud for Mr. Hooper, and would not yield their breath till he appeared; though ever, as he stooped to whisper consolation, they shuddered at the veiled face so near their own. Such were the terrors of the black veil, even when Death had bared his visage! Strangers came long distances to attend service at his church, with the mere idle curiosity of gazing at his figure, because it was forbidden them to behold his face. (381)

The effect of the veil is to make Hooper visible as being veiled, to substitute for a "face to face" (373) relationship one where the other is perceived "through a glass, darkly" (I Corinthians 13:12) or enigmatically, that is to say, figuratively. On the one hand the story insists on the literalness of the veil, that it is simply a physical object (one "cause" of Hooper's sad, ironic smile is the recognition that "only a material emblem had separated him from happiness" [379-80]) whereas on the other, as the above passage suggests, it becomes a figure for trope itself. Once Hooper uses it to cover his face the double piece of crape can never again be simply its innocent existential self, for as a covering it becomes part of a system of preestablished relationships, a system of figures invoked by the story's subtitle, which points us to a world where material objects stand for something other than themselves. When his coverts assert "though but figuratively" that they have been behind the black veil they point to the process of comparison and substitution, the chain of figures, that controls a system of representation. Or to put the point another way: In the act of veiling his own face Hooper reminds us of the ways in which we give a face even to mute and senseless "Death" by incorporating it into the metaphoric chain of veiling and unveiling that energizes the story.

Indeed one could say that the veiled Hooper (a disfigured figure) is an uncanny appearance, in the real world, of a figure, and as such he disturbs the normal assumptions that govern the relationship between the literal and figural. The initial effect of his veiled figure is to confuse, destabilize, and obscure. There is a "rustling" and "shuffling" among his congregation "greatly at variance with that hushed repose which should attend the entrance of the minister," and the veil throws its "obscurity between him and the holy page, as he read the Scriptures" (373). "A subtle power was breathed into his words" (373), but it is a power that darkens rather than enlightens. "The people trembled, though they but darkly understood him, when he prayed that they, and himself, and all of mortal race, might be ready, as he trusted this young maiden had been, for the dreadful hour that should snatch the veil from their faces" (375). Hooper is speaking figuratively here and doing so within a well established scriptural tradition, but the literal veil that covers his face prevents a traditional, untroubled response to his words. And his parishioners' reaction is echoed by the reader's when Hooper on his death bed "snatched both his hands from beneath the bed-clothes, and pressed them strongly on the black veil" in response to Reverend Mr. Clark's plea: "'Before the veil of eternity be lifted, let me cast aside this black veil from your face'" (383). In these two examples the relationship between the literal and figural veils, as well as that between the acts of "snatching," is not a symmetrical one, and the lack of symmetry obscures the meaning of both even as it encourages further figuration. Plain, unadorned, nonfigurative speech becomes impossible— "It was remarkable that, of all the busy-bodies and impertinent people in the parish, not one ventured to put the plain question to Mr. Hooper wherefore he did this thing" (377)—even between the Reverend Hooper and his "plighted wife" (378).

> "No," said she aloud, and smiling, "there is nothing terrible in this piece of crape, except that it hides a face which I am always glad to look upon. Come, good sir, let the sun shine from behind the cloud. First lay aside your black veil: then tell me why you put it on."
>
> Mr Hooper's smile glimmered faintly.

> "There is an hour to come," said he, "when all of us shall cast aside our veils. Take it not amiss, beloved friend, if I wear this piece of crape till then."
>
> "Your words are a mystery too," returned the young lady. "Take away the veil from them, at least."
>
> "Elizabeth, I will," said he, "as far as my vow may suffer me. Know, then, this veil is a type and a symbol, and I am bound to wear it ever." (378)

With her eyes "fixed . . . steadfastly upon the veil" and "unappalled by the awe with which [it] had impressed all beside herself," Elizabeth is determined to see only what is there: "a double fold of crape" (378). But not even her "direct simplicity" can break the spell of the veil, for she too immediately is caught up in the system of figures that it generates. And her figure of speech—"let the sun shine from behind the cloud"—entangles her language and perception in the knot of analogies that complicates the narrative logic of **"The Minister's Black Veil"**: Veil is to face as cloud is to sun, as night is to day, as time is to eternity, as body is to spirit, as words are to truth, and, most disturbingly perhaps, as face is to self. Many of the complexities of these associations must be put aside to be gathered up later, but it is important to note at this point that the focus is now on the problem of words and their meanings. Hooper's words like his face are veiled in the sense that they are figurative or parabolic expressions, public utterances that are the exoteric expression of an esoteric message. When he is asked by Elizabeth to unveil them, he does so by asserting the figural nature of the "piece of crape" but refusing to specify its meaning. The result is that she too is now enveloped by the veil's "terrors" despite Hooper's assurance that it is only a "material emblem" (380).

> "Have patience with me, Elizabeth!" cried he, passionately. "Do not desert me, though this veil must be between us here on earth. Be mine, and hereafter there shall be no veil over my face, no darkness between our souls! It is but a mortal veil—it is not for eternity! Oh! you know not now how lonely I am, and how frightened to be alone behind my black veil. Do not leave me in my miserable obscurity for ever!"
>
> "Lift the veil but once, and look me in the face," said she.
>
> "Never! It cannot be!" replied Mr. Hooper.
>
> "Then farewell!" said Elizabeth. (379)

The impasse here is the result of a sort of erosion of the distinction between literal and figural modes on which significance depends. Both Elizabeth and Hooper insist on the literal or material aspects of the veil, but neither of them is able to focus exclusively on it as a physical object. It is as if the "piece of crape" is always already figurative and thwarts all attempts firmly to fix its referential status. This sense of figurative excess is strengthened if the textual context is enlarged to include Hawthorne's other writings, for the veil is a figure that assumes a major structuring role in his world. As I have argued elsewhere, the question of the nature of the writer's identity is a central one for Hawthorne.[7] For him the relation between a writer's personal identity and the form of its manifestation to the world is a part of the larger problem of the relation between a human being's inner and social beings. More than most writers he is fascinated by the ways in which a writer's work is at once a veil that he wears and a manifestation of his most intimate concerns. The metaphorics of veiling do not creep into his text unreflectively. A "cloudy veil stretches over the abyss of my nature,"[8] he writes to Sophia, and most of his characters figuratively veil themselves in one way or another albeit without inspiring the dread that the Reverend Hooper does. Holgrave, for example, "habitually masked whatever lay near his heart" by his "New England reserve" (610), and Zenobia's pseudonymity is "a sort of mask in which she comes before the world, retaining all the privileges of privacy—a contrivance . . . like the white drapery of the Veiled Lady, only a little more transparent" (637).

As author, Hawthorne is as fond of veils as are his characters. His fascination with pseudonyms is well known—he used at different times M. de l'Aubépine, Oberon, and Ashley Allen Royce—and he published many of his early sketches either anonymously or under the signature of Nathaniel Hawthorne, having inserted a "w" in his family name at college. Fiction for him is a way of "opening an intercourse with the world" (1152) only in the sense that it is an appeal to "sensibilities . . . such as are diffused among us all. So far as I am a man of really individual attributes, I veil my face" (1147). Not even the apparently autobiographical figure of the prefaces can be taken as an unveiled version of the author. The writer's "external habits, his abode, his casual associates" are veils that "hide the man, instead of displaying him" (1154-5), and his characters too are veils or disguises that he wears. Coverdale, for example, as the "most extensively autobiographical character in Hawthorne's fiction"[9] is at once a manifestation of Hawthorne and a distortion that alters that manifestation. Hence in **"The Custom House"** he writes that "we may prate of circumstances that lie around us, and even of ourself, but still keep the inmost Me behind its veil" (121). The "veil" in this case is precisely that of figure, for the author ("keeping up the metaphor of the political guillotine") first asks that the sketch be

> considered as the POSTHUMOUS PAPERS OF A DECAPITATED SURVEYOR . . . and if too autobiographical for a modest person to publish in his lifetime, will be readily excused in a gentleman

who writes from beyond the grave. Peace be with all the world! My blessings on my friends! My forgiveness to my enemies! For I am in the realm of quiet! (156)

But as he announces the freedom that his "figurative self" enjoys, he reminds us that the "real human being with his head safely on his shoulders . . . had opened a long-disused writing desk and was again a literary man" (155-6). To be a "literary man," however, is also to wear the veil of figure. The narrator of **"The Custom House"** cannot be present in his own person but must appear as the "representative" (127) of others who are absent: his ancestors, his "ancient predecessor, Mr. Surveyor Pue" (156), even an earlier version of himself, a "scribbler of bygone days" (157). Substituting for self-presence, according to the "law of literary propriety" is the figure of a "literary man," a "romance writer" (149), and this figurative self, the self given by the act of language, is the only one locatable in Hawthorne's text. That self is always a veiled self, for it is an "I" or a subject represented by its signs or markers.

Thus, when Hooper dons his black veil his literal action repeats a biblical and literary figure but in a way that disturbs its status as a convention. His insistence that the veil is simultaneously literal and figural (a "material emblem" [380]) generates the uncanny wavering of a double reading that contaminates and breaks down the symmetrical chiasmus between the material and the emblematic. This disturbing wavering is most apparent in the associations between the veil and death, for death, since it cannot be experienced sensuously or psychologically, has to be expressed figuratively. The "hour" of death is the "dreadful hour that should snatch the veil from [our] faces" (375), and when the "veil of eternity [is] lifted" (383), "Death [bares] his visage" (381) and holds us in his "arms" (383). To speak of death as apocalyptic in the etymological sense of revelation or unveiling is to speak biblically and to anticipate that moment when all things are spoken plainly without the veil of similitude, but to give death a face and body is to figure or refigure it and to imply a necessary dependency on figurative language that defaces at the same time that it gives a face.

> While his auditors shrank from one another, in mutual affright, Father Hooper fell back upon his pillow, a veiled corpse, with a faint smile lingering on the lips. Still veiled, they laid him in his coffin, and a veiled corpse they bore him to the grave. The grass of many years has sprung up and withered on that grave, the burial-stone is moss-grown, and good Mr. Hooper's face is dust; but awful is still the thought that it mouldered beneath the Black Veil! (384)

This passage is about a literal corpse, not about a figure for death or a figural representation of death. But the corpse is a veiled corpse, and as such it disrupts our conception of the literal as opposed to the figural by disturbing the system of analogies that energizes the text. When the veiled corpse is inserted in the chain of figures—veil is to face as body is to soul, as face is to self, as letter is to spirit, as veil is to corpse—the corpse occupies the position that face, soul, self, and spirit do in the system of analogies and disturbs the symmetrical structure of that system. When the corpse takes the place of the living body, the veil becomes the veil of a veil, the covering of a covering; it introduces the possibility that the face, the self, the spirit, the soul are figures. What is terrifyingly awful is the thought that veil and face decay together, for that thought reveals the literal as effaced figure and suggests that language works to cover up such effacements. To be told that Mr. Hooper's face turns to dust beneath the veil is to be reminded of the fact that Hooper's "pale-faced congregation was almost as fearful a sight to the minister, as his black veil to them" (373). Their "pale visages," it appears, remind him of the "visage" of "Death" (381), for he is forced "to give up his customary walk, at sunset, to the burial ground," because "there would always be faces behind the gravestones, peeping at his black veil. A fable went the rounds, that the stare of the dead people drove him thence" (380). The human face here no less than the sunset is a figure for death, the figure that fills the blank about which nothing can be said literally.

The human countenance, then, like the parable cannot be taken at face value, and therefore our situation as readers of **"The Minister's Black Veil"** is allegorically expressed by the situation of the characters in the story.[10] We, like Father Hooper's congregation, are denied a "face to face" (39) relation with the author who remains concealed behind the veil of the text, and he, like Hooper, insists at one and the same time on the text's material and emblematic status. Like *The Scarlet Letter,* **"The Minister's Black Veil"** is, on the one hand, "putatively historical . . . based on a reconstructed literal past" and yet on the other, it presents its actualities as signs or emblems[11] that signify something other than themselves and hence require interpretive action from a reader. In this sense Hawthorne's texts, like Christ's parables, seem to consist of a manifest carnal sense for the uninitiated outsider and a latent spiritual one available to the insider who has the benefit of special eye-opening knowledge and who therefore understands that the story cannot be taken at face value.[12] This certainly is the way Melville reads Hawthorne.

> The truth seems to be, that like many other geniuses, this Man of Mosses takes a great delight in hoodwinking the world. . . . But with whatever motive, playful or profound, Nathaniel Hawthorne has chosen to entitle his pieces in the manner he has, it is certain, that

some of them are directly calculated to deceive—egregiously deceive—the superficial skimmer of pages.

Still, as Melville's essay suggests, it is not easy to articulate what the "eagle-eyed reader" sees in the text that is as "deep as Dante" except to say that it is a "direct and unqualified manifestation" of Hawthorne's "blackness,"[13] a response not unlike that of Father Hooper's congregation to his black veil. In a curious way Hawthorne's text appears to turn insiders into outsiders, as Christ's parables seem to do in Mark's rather severe account of them. Kermode points out that Mark uses "mystery" as a synonym for "parable" and implies that the stories are dark riddles that not even the disciples, the most privileged interpreters, can answer (Kermode, 46). In this sense the parable as a genre seems remarkably similar to Romance as Hawthorne defines it in his prefaces. Romance for Hawthorne offers a mode of communication that maintains a tension between the hidden and the shown, thereby insuring that something will always remain in reserve, either as an unformulated thought shaded by language or in the form of a veiled figure whose meaning is not explicitly signified. Consider, for example, Hawthorne's description of Dimmesdale's confession in "The Revelation of the Scarlet Letter": "With a convulsive motion he tore away the ministerial band from before his breast. It was revealed! But it were irreverent to describe that revelation" (338). Like the "multitude" with its "strange, deep voice of awe and wonder, which could not as yet find utterance, save in the murmur" that follows Dimmesdale's "final word" (339), the narrator finds it difficult directly to say what he sees, perhaps because what he sees remains shaded by the veil of figure even in the "mid-day sunshine" (341). Dimmesdale himself suggests as much when, after insisting that Hester's scarlet letter "with all its mysterious horror . . . is but the shadow of what he bears on his own breast," goes on to say that "his own red stigma, is no more than the type of what has seared his inmost heart" (338). No wonder then that "there was more than one account of what had been witnessed on the scaffold."

> It is singular, nevertheless, that certain persons, who were spectators of the whole scene, and professed never once to have removed their eyes from the Reverend Dimmesdale, denied that there was any mark whatever on his breast, more than on a new-born infant's. Neither, by their report, had his dying words acknowledged, nor even remotely implied, any, the slightest connection, on his part, with the guilt for which Hester Prynne had so long worn the scarlet letter. According to these highly respectable witnesses, the minister, conscious that he was dying,—conscious, also, that the reverence of the multitude placed him already among saints and angels,—had desired, by yielding up his breath in the arms of that fallen woman, to express to the

world how utterly nugatory is the choicest of man's own righteousness. After exhausting life in his efforts for mankind's spiritual good, he had made the manner of his death a parable, in order to impress upon his admirers the mighty and mournful lesson, that, in the view of Infinite Purity, we are sinner all alike. It was to teach them, that the holiest among us has but attained so far above his fellows as to discern more clearly the Mercy which looks down, and repudiate more utterly the phantom of human merit, which would look aspiringly upward. (340-1)

This "version of Mr. Dimmesdale's story" (341) suggests how seeing for Hawthorne is always interpretation in the sense that what is seen inevitably is taken as a sign standing for something else as in the case of a hieroglyph or a parable. And the meanings or "morals" which these signs "press upon us" must be "put . . . into . . . sentence[s]" (341) that become in their turn perplexing. Hence the "curious investigator" (the reader) who "perplex[es] himself with the purport" of the "semblance of an engraved escutcheon" carved on the "simple slab of slate" (345) marking the graves of Hester and Dimmesdale merely echoes the reactions of the "men of rank and dignity" who witness Dimmesdale's confession and are "perplexed as to the purport of what they saw" (336). This aspect of the human situation appears most clearly in the face of death (in Dimmesdale's "dying words" and in Hooper's "veiled corpse") for since death is nothing, our anguished anticipation of it, our attempt to articulate our relation to it, is necessarily oblique and parabolic.

For Hawthorne, then, the generic mark is not so much the sign of an aesthetic and/or historical category as it is a sort of epitaphic inscription that becomes a figure for story as such, that "Faery Land" realm inhabited by ghostlike presences that have a "propriety of their own" (633). Ordinary words like Hooper's veiled face "are a mystery" (378) because they are defamiliarized, detached from their referential function, from a present moment and a living "I," and hence presuppose as well as record the fact of death—in the case of **"The Minister's Black Veil"** that of the historical original, "Mr. Joseph Moody of York, Maine, who died about eighty years since" (371), that of Parson Hooper, Moody's fictional representation, and, finally, that of the author. Romance and parable are names for "Posthumous papers," fictional products of one "who writes from beyond the grave" (156), speaking monuments whose words like those inscribed on Hester and Dimmesdale's tombstone serve only to "perplex" the reader who is always the last surviving consciousness.

Notes

1 All references to Hawthorne's fiction will be to the following editions: Nathaniel Hawthorne, *Novels,* ed.

Millicent Bell (New York: The Library of America, 1983); *Tales and Sketches,* ed. Roy Harvey Pearce (New York: The Library of America, 1982).

2 For a discussion of the Reverend Moody of York, Maine, and his relation to Hawthorne's story, see J. Hillis Miller, "Literature and History: The Example of Hawthorne's 'The Minister's Black Veil,'" *Bulletin of the American Academy of Arts and Sciences* 41 (Feb. 1988), 20-1, and especially Frederick Newberry, "The Biblical Veil: Sources and Typology in Hawthorne's 'The Minister's Black Veil,'" *Texas Studies in Language and Literature* 31 (Summer 1989), 171-83.

3 William Smith, *Dictionary of the Bible,* ed. H. B. Hackett (New York: Hurd and Houghton, 1871), vol 1, p. 807. I am using Smith's and other nineteenth-century works of biblical scholarship with the assumption that they will reflect Hawthorne's understanding of parable. Hereafter cited in the text as Smith.

4 This tension between historical and figural meaning is reflected in recent commentary on Hawthorne's story, which is seen, on the one hand, as the representation of a particular historical moment in the evolution of New England Puritanism (Michael Colacurcio, *The Province of Piety: Moral History in Hawthorne's Early Tales* [Cambridge: Harvard University Press, 1984], pp. 314-85, and Newberry, cited above, 169-95) and, on the other, as an expression of a linguistic turn in humanistic studies that concedes that language can no longer be understood as simply a medium for the representation of a reality outside itself (Miller, cited above, 15-31, and J. Hillis Miller, "The Profession of English: An Exchange," *ADE Bulletin* 88 [Winter 1987], 41-8). My own reading resembles Miller's rhetorical one (I am especially indebted to his discussion of the trope of prosopopoeia in Hawthorne's text) but differs from his in suggesting that the generic mark offers at least a partial solution to the story's hermeneutical difficulties.

5 For two useful but different treatments of the biblical context of Hawthorne's story see Judy McCarthy, "'The Minister's Black Veil': The Concealing Moses and the Holy of Holies," *Studies in Short Fiction* 24 (Spring 1987), 131-8, and Newberry, cited above. Newberry's account is an especially suggestive one, but his reading differs from mine in seeing the story as a criticism of Father Hooper because his veil "divides mortals from one another and from God, and . . . finally amounts to a profound anachronism whose emphasis on the age of Old Adam essentially renounces the availability of redemption through Christ's only historical appearance" (189).

6 Robert Jamieson, A. R. Fausset, and David Brown, *A Commentary, Critical and Explanatory on the Old and*

New Testaments, 2 vols. (Philadelphia: S. S. Scranton & Co., 1872), vol. 2, p. 304. Hereafter cited in the text as Jamieson.

[7] Edgar Dryden, *Nathaniel Hawthrone: The Poetics of Enchantment* (Ithaca and London: Cornell University Press, 1977).

[8] Nathaniel Hawthorne, *The Letters 1813-1843, The Centenary Edition of the Works of Nathaniel Hawthorne,* eds. William Charvat, Roy Harvey Pearce, and Claude Simpson (Columbus: Ohio State University Press), vol. 15, p. 612.

[9] Arlin Turner, "Introduction," Nathaniel Hawthorne, *The Blithedale Romance* (New York: W. W. Norton, 1958), p. 23.

[10] On this point see Miller, "Literature and History," 45-6.

[11] Millicent Bell, "The Obliquity of Signs: *The Scarlet Letter,*" *Massachusetts Review* (Spring 1982), 10.

[12] I am indebted here to Frank Kermode's discussion of parable in *The Genesis of Secrecy* (Cambridge: Harvard University Press, 1979), p. 4. Hereafter cited in the text as Kermode.

[13] Herman Melville, *The Piazza Tales and Other Prose Pieces 1839-1860,* eds. Harrison Hayford, Alma A. MacDougall, and G. Thomas Tanselle (Evanston: Northwestern University Press, 1987), vol. 9, pp. 250-1.

FURTHER READING

Criticism

Altschuler, Glenn C. "The Puritan Dilemma in 'The Minister's Black Veil.'" *American Transcendental Quarterly Journal of New England Writers,* Supplement. No. 24 (Fall 1974): 25-7.
> Considers Puritan ideology, particularly The Great Awakening, as an explanation for the meaning of "The Minister's Black Veil."

Martin, Terence. "Six Tales." In *Nathaniel Hawthorne: Revised Edition,* edited by Lewis Leary, pp. 72-104. Boston: Twayne Publishers, 1983.
> Considers Hawthorne's literary structure in "The Minister's Black Veil," stressing the importance of the veil as a metaphor.

Monteiro, George. "The Full Particulars of the Minister's Behavior—According to Hale." *The Nathaniel Hawthorne Journal* 2 (1972): 173-82.
> After a brief introduction by Monteiro, reprints the 1889 fictionalized re-telling of "The Minister's Black Veil" by minister and author Edward Everett Hale (1822-1909).

———. "Hawthorne's 'The Minister's Black Veil.'" *The Explicator* XXII, No. 2 (October 1963): item 9.
> Analyzes Hawthorne's use of the word "mystery" to establish the Biblical context for Hooper's actions.

Stein, William Bysshe. "The Parable of the Antichrist in 'The Minister's Black Veil.'" *American Literature* 27, No. 3 (November 1995): 386-92.
> Compares "The Minister's Black Veil" to St. Paul's writings in *II Corinthians,* arguing that Hooper represents a man separated from the will of God.

Turner, Frederick W., III. "Hawthorne's Black Veil." *Studies in Short Fiction* V, No. 2 (Winter 1968): 186-7.
> Suggests that the veil represents man's ignorance about the nature of sin.

Voigt, Gilbert P. "The Meaning of 'The Minister's Black Veil'." *College English* 13, No. 6 (March 1952): 337-8.
> Likens Hooper to an Old Testament prophet whose physical act both reflects the shortcomings of his people and serves to shock them into changing their sinful ways.

Walsh, Thomas F. "Hawthorne: Mr. Hooper's 'Affable Weakness'." *Modern Language Notes* LXXIV, No. 5 (May 1959): 404-06.
> Offers a psychological profile of Hooper as "a man whose mistaken notions about the nature of evil prompt him to attempt the salvation of his fellow men by a method which seriously endangers his own salvation: the donning of the black veil."

Sarah Winnemucca

1844?-1891

(Born Thocmetony; also known as Sarah Winnemucca Hopkins) American political activist and autobiographer.

INTRODUCTION

An outspoken advocate of Native American rights, Winnemucca is principally remembered for her *Life Among the Piutes: Their Wrongs and Claims* (1883), considered the first autobiography by a Native American woman. A member of the Paiute tribe, Winnemucca rose to a level of public notoriety while conducting a series of American lecture tours in which she criticized unfair federal acquisition of native lands and the harsh treatment of Indians forced to live on reservations. Since her death, Winnemucca has also been acknowledged for her support of Native American education and espousal of the peaceful coexistence of whites and Native Americans.

Biographical Information

Winnemucca—whose name in her native Northern Pauite language was Thocmetony, meaning "shell flower"—was born in approximately 1844 on Paiute land near Humboldt Lake in what is now Nevada. Her grandfather, Truckee, was a Paiute chieftain, although not chief of the entire Paiute tribe as Winnemucca would later claim. As a child, Winnemucca learned Spanish and English through her close contact with several white families in California and Nevada. She was schooled briefly at the Convent of Notre Dame in San Jose during her teens, but was otherwise largely self taught. Acting on behalf of the Paiute, she traveled to Fort McDermit in 1866 to persuade the United States military to put an end to white aggression against her tribe. Shortly thereafter, a segment of the Paiute were resettled to a reservation at Malheur, Oregon. In the ensuing years, Winnemucca was frequently engaged as a military interpreter and liaison to the Paiute, a capacity she served when hostilities between U. S. armed forces and the Paiute, Bannock, and Shoshoni people erupted in the Bannock War of 1878. The conflict ended with the indefinite relocation of Paiute prisoners to the Yakima reservation in Washington State. Winnemucca, meanwhile, spoke out publicly in a number of lectures designed to raise awareness of inhumane practices demonstrated by government agents and missionaries on the reservation. She traveled to Washington, D. C. to obtain the Paiute release from Yakima, a plea that was authorized, but never initiated. In 1882, she married a dissolute mili-

tary officer, Lieutenant Lewis H. Hopkins, in what was the last of her four relatively brief and ill-fated marriages to white men. In 1883, Winnemucca began a lengthy lecture tour of New England, and again denounced U. S. government policy toward Native Americans. While speaking in Boston she formed a friendship with Elizabeth Palmer Peabody, an educator, and her sister Mary Mann. Both women encouraged Winnemucca in her political activities, prompting her to write *Life Among the Piutes* and providing her with financial and editorial assistance. Winnemucca used some of the profits from her lectures and the sale of her book to establish a school for Paiute children in 1884. After the school was closed in 1887, Winnemucca relocated to Henry's Lake, Idaho where she died of tuberculosis on 17 October, 1891.

Major Works

Life Among the Piutes: Their Wrongs and Claims recounts the years 1844 to 1883, beginning with Winnemucca's early involvement in the volatile relations between

Native Americans and whites during this period. The narrative opens with the violent invasion of Paiute lands (occupying what is now western Nevada) by whites in the 1840s. As the volume proceeds, Winnemucca recalls her younger years as a domestic, the death of her grandfather, chief Truckee, in 1860 during the Pyramid Lake War, and her appointment as Pauite language interpreter at Fort McDermit. She describes the 1865 massacre of her family, including her father Old Winnemucca—an experience that left her as tribal leader—in the increasingly harsh tone that characterizes the remainder of the autobiography. Further sections of the work criticize the brutality of the missionary W. V. Rinehart of the Malheur Agency in Oregon, and describe Winnemucca's intercession on behalf of her tribe during the Bannock War. The final portion of *Life Among the Piutes* details the forced march of surrendered Paiutes from Malheur to the Yakima Reservation some 350 miles away in January of 1879.

Critical Reception

Critics have acknowledged that during her lifetime Winnemucca endeavored to overturn negative stereotypes of Native Americans through her lectures, stage appearances, and autobiography. A thoroughgoing advocate of peace, she portrayed the brutality of white aggression toward Indians and sought in her *Life Among the Piutes* to adapt the romantic rhetoric of the "noble savage" by characterizing herself as an enlightened woman warrior. In the years since her death, Winnemucca has come to represent the struggles of Native American women in the nineteenth century, while her autobiography has continued to be read and studied as an important cultural document. In the latter half of the twentieth century, critics have principally focused on the work's evocative style and the nature and extent of its literary influences, considering it a blend of elements from romance, slave narrative, and Paiute oral tradition. Of *Life Among the Piutes,* Kathleen Mullen Sands has written: "It is Winnemucca's verve, her certainty of the epic nature of her life, her absolute dedication, despite enormous personal sacrifice, and her genteelly Victorian use of language that work in concert to move the reader and convince the audience of the justice of Indian rights even a century after its first publication."

PRINCIPAL WORKS

"The Pah-Utes" (essay) 1882

Life Among the Piutes: Their Wrongs and Claims (autobiography) 1883

CRITICISM

Catherine S. Fowler (essay date 1976)

SOURCE: "Sarah Winnemucca: Northern Paiute, ca. 1844-1891," in *American Indian Intellectuals,* edited by Margot Liberty, West Publishing Co., 1976, pp. 32-42.

[*In the following essay, Fowler offers an ethnological study of Winnemucca as a figure who attempted to assimilate with white culture.*]

Sarah Winnemucca is a historical figure whose life and works have had more direct impact on the course of 19th century United States Indian policy than on the discipline of anthropology. In the latter half of the 19th century, she wrote a book (Hopkins 1883: *Life Among the Piutes: Their Wrongs and Claims*) and at least one article (Winnemucca 1882) detailing the harried course of Northern Paiute-White relations to that time. She also lectured extensively in the far West and in the East on reservation conditions, inequities in federal Indian policy and government agent corruption. Her book and speeches lent direct support to the passage of the controversial "lands in severalty" legislation, then before the Congress. Sarah Winnemucca also established and operated for two years her own school for Northern Paiute children near Lovelock, Nevada—an early attempt at self-determination in Indian education.

Sarah Winnemucca is a controversial figure, and herein lies some of her historical interest. Robert Heizer (1960:3) suggests that her "selfless motives and tremendous energies and high purpose make her a person to admire in the history of our far West." Omer Stewart (1939:129) on the other hand, described her as "ambitious, educated . . . , trying to attain self-aggrandizement by exalting her father." Sarah's ethnographic and ethnohistoric contributions are rarely cited by Great Basin ethnographers beyond some cursory statement to the effect that she wrote a book that was probably little read in her native state of Nevada.

In this paper, I will briefly examine the life of Sarah Winnemucca, some of the controversy that surrounds her and some of her ethnohistoric and ethnographic contributions. The events of her life suggest clearly some of the motives that led her to speak for Indian rights at a time when a Native American *woman* would hardly be respected for doing so. I would like to suggest in the light of 20th century ethnohistoric and ethnographic hindsight that Sarah's position on assimilation, perhaps more than any other single factor, has led scholars, and to a certain degree her own people, to diminish her contributions to Native American scholarship.

Sarah Winnemucca was born about 1844 near the Sink of the Humboldt River, in what is now western Nevada. She came from a family that from the time of first contact with Whites had advocated peaceful coexistence—a position that did not gain the members favor among all segments of the Northern Paiute population. Sarah's maternal grandfather, Truckee, had been favorably disposed toward early explorers, and settlers, interpreting their advent as the reuniting of the Northern Paiutes with their lost White brothers and sisters, as foretold in the Northern Paiute creation cycle (Hopkins 1883:6). Truckee served as a guide to various emigrant parties traversing the Sierra, fought in California with John C. Fremont in his Mexican campaigns and continually befriended White families and individuals throughout northern Nevada and California. There is good evidence that Truckee and several other Northern Paiutes spent as many as half of the years between 1842 and 1860, the year of his death, in the settlements of California. He spoke both Spanish and English in addition to his native Northern Paiute, making him an effective go-between when present in Nevada. He also continually related the wonders of developing California to his people. Sarah (Hopkins 1883:18) describes how she and some of her people learned to sing what she later identified as soldiers' roll calls and the Star Spangled Banner long before they could understand the words.

Sarah's father, Old Winnemucca, was also generally on the side of peace and coexistence, although several specific events from the mid 1860's through the 1870's made him cautious and wary. During this time, partly as a result of the massacre of members of his band on the shores of Mud Lake in 1865 (Hopkins 1883:77; Angel 1881:170), Winnemucca became sullen and withdrawn, choosing a path of avoidance rather than accommodation. Sarah continually stressed that her father was "chief" of all the Paiutes, a point of controversy for latter-day ethnographers and ethnohistorians.

Sarah's brother, Naches, also acted as a go-between in relations between Indians and Whites in western nevada. Naches was convinced of the utility of agriculture and for several years operated a cooperative farm on 160 acres of land near Lovelock, Nevada. He obtained the land partly through cash purchase and partly by convincing railroad magnate Leland Stanford that he intended to put the land to good use. (The land was a railroad section.)

Thus, the Winnemuccas were what would be labeled today "White-men's Indians" at least from outward appearances. However, there is also a strong current of self-determination that runs through their attitudes and activities that is less often stressed. Again, hindsight may clarify this position as we proceed.

When Sarah was approximately 10 years of age, she and her mother and siblings spent part of a year with Truckee near San Jose, California. She describes in detail in her book (Hopkins 1883:27 ff.) her impressions of this strange land, its strange goods, and even stranger people. She had an almost pathological fear of Whites as a child, in spite of her grandfather's continual reassurances concerning their kindly nature and good intentions. She was greatly impressed by the material possessions and wealth of the foreigners, attributing their success to industry in agriculture and ranching.

In 1858, Sarah and her sister went to live in the home of Major William Ormsby in Carson Valley. She learned English rapidly under these circumstances (Hopkins 1883:58). In 1860, upon the death-bed request of Truckee, Sarah and her sister were returned to friends in California and there entered a school run by the Sisters of Charity in San Jose. They were there only a short while when pressure from the local White citizenry forced their removal. Upon her return to Nevada, Sarah continued her education on her own while working as a domestic in and around Virginia City. One newspaper (Helena Daily Herald 11/4/1891) account notes that she spent a goodly portion of her meager earnings on books, a reasonably scarce commodity on the frontier at the time. She states candidly, however, that she always had trouble with reading (Hopkins 1883:58).

Sarah began to take an active interest in Indian affairs in 1866, when with her brother, Naches, she was requested to go to Fort McDermitt to discuss scattered depredations in the region. They were also requested by the army to try to convince Old Winnemucca and his band to come to Fort McDermitt to be settled on a reservation. At this time, Sarah began a series of run-ins with agents in the vicinity over a number of inequities, including the meager provisions being given the people. She spoke openly against the policy of the agent at Pyramid Lake, which required that the people turn over 2/3 of their produce and then feed themselves and take their next year's seed from the remainder. Sarah's hostilities extended to the missionaries who by this time were taking over agent positions in the Indian Service. She notes that these "so-called Christians" were mainly concerned with money and had few truly benevolent feelings toward the people. She vividly describes the issue of clothing to the Shoshones near Battle Mountain by Colonel Dodge, on which occasion she acted as interpreter:

> Oh such an issue! It was enough to make a doll laugh. A family numbering eight persons got two blankets, three shirts, no dress goods. Some got a fishhook and a line; some got one and a half yards of flannel, red and blue.
>
> . . . In the morning some of the men went around with only one leg dressed in red flannel. . . . And this man called himself a Christian, too. (Hopkins 1883:86-7)

In the ensuing years to 1875, Sarah worked periodically as an interpreter for the military at Ft. McDermitt and Camp Harney. She remained convinced throughout her life that her people fared better under the military than the Indian Bureau. In fact, a subtle, but interesting picture of the value of being "prisoners" of the military can be drawn from her accounts. At one point, for example, Old Winnemucca even pleaded with the commander at Ft. McDermitt that he and his band be taken prisoners instead of being sent to Malheur Reservation (Hopkins 1883:121). Regular rations, clothing of better quality, and protection from White depredations far outweighed the inconvenience of confinement.

There was to be one notable exception to Sarah's rule about agents, and the association with him was of major importance in her life. His name was Samuel Parrish, recently appointed agent at Malheur, Oregon. Parrish offered Sarah a position as interpreter in 1875, and later a post as teacher's aid. He immediately put the people to work at agriculture, with the following admonition:

> I have not come here to do nothing; I have no time to throw away. I have come to show you how to work, and work we must. I am not like the man who has just left you. I can't kneel down and pray for sugar and flour and potatoes to rain down as he did. I am a bad man; but I will teach you all how to work, so you can do for your selves by-and-by . . . I will build a school house and my brother's wife will teach your children how to read like the White children. I want 3 young men to learn to be blacksmiths and 3 to learn to be carpenters. I want to teach you all to do like White people. (Hopkins 1883:1060)

Parrish kept his promises and the first year the agricultural venture was a success. The people kept all of the produce for themselves with the exception of items sold to Parrish and his employees. Unlike previous agents, Parrish paid for his needs at a labor rate of one dollar per day per man. His staff did likewise.

But all came to naught in the following year when Parrish was dismissed—he was not a good Christian—and replaced by William Rinehart. Rinehart's policies precipitated trouble almost from the beginning. Most importantly, he changed Parrish's policy on land and labor. He also discharged Sarah when she reported his misdeeds to the military, an action for which she did not blame him.

In his opening speech to the people at Malheur, Rinehart stated clearly that "the land you are living on is government land. If you do well and are willing to work for the government, the government will give you work" (Hopkins 1883). Egan, spokesman for one group of Paiutes on the reservation answered:

> Our father, we cannot read; we do not understand anything; we don't want the Big Father in Washington to fool with us. We are men, not children. He sends one man to say one thing and another to say something else. The man who just left us told us the land was ours, and what we do on it was ours. And you say it is government land and not ours. You may be right. We love money as well as you. It is a great deal of money to pay. There are a great many of us and when we work, we all work. (Hopkins 1883:124)

Not understanding Rinehart's labor policy, and expecting that work done would bring one dollar per day per man, everyone reported for work and then for pay. Rinehart's answer came not in cash, but in issues, labeled conveniently, "blankets - $6, coats - $5, pants - $5, shoes - $3," etc. The Bannock War of 1878 was in part an aftermath of troubles that began at Malheur. Angry and bitter Paiute farmers were easily encouraged to join Bannock hostiles, and they left the reservation *en masse*.

During the Bannock War, Sarah again went to work for the military as an interpreter in the command of General Oliver Otis Howard. Howard⸱ described her conduct during the campaign as excellent, and "especially compassionate to women and children who were brought in as prisoners" (Howard 1883:1). Sarah remained for several months at Vancouver Barracks and later at Yakima Reservation where the Paiute prisoners were detained, working as an interpreter and teacher. Yakima was a nightmare of overcrowding, abject poverty and intertribal hostilities. There was barely enough support for the Yakima, let alone 534 Paiute aliens (Wilber 1879).

With the cessation of hostilities, Sarah's position was abolished. At that time, she began to lecture in San Francisco and in Nevada, dramatizing the problems at Malheur and Yakima, and pleading for the return of Leggins' band of Paiutes unjustly detained at Yakima. She spoke against Indian agents and called specifically for the resignation of Rinehart and the restoration of Malheur to the people. On November 25, 1879, she delivered her first lecture at Platt's Hall in San Francisco. According to newspaper accounts of the lecture, she was attired in native dress and spoke eloquently and without notes. According to the account in the *San Francisco Call:*

> There was little left of the redoubtable Christian agent when she finished him. She described him as having a right arm longer than his left, and while beckoning them to be kind and good and honest with one hand, the other was busy grabbing behind their backs. She wound up with a summary of Mr. Rineharts character with a bit of mischievous sarchasm that brought down the house. (Daily Silver State 11/28/79)

Word of Sarah's success on the lecture platform spread, and it was only a month before she and Naches, along with Old Winnemucca and Captain Jim were summoned to Washington to meet with various government officials. After several rounds of discussion, they succeeded in obtaining a document from then Secretary of the Interior, Carl Schurz, granting the release of Leggins' band at Yakima, and specifying that they and other Paiutes who so wished were free to return to the Malheur reservation,

> "whereupon, at this their primeval home, they and others heretofore entitled, are to have lands allotted to them in severalty at the rate of one-hundred and sixty acres to each head of a family, and each adult male. Such lands they are to cultivate for their own benefit. As soon as enabled to do so, this department is to give to the Indians patents for each tract of land conveying to each occupant the fee-simple in the lot he occupies." (Hopkins 1883:224)

With an apparent victory won, Sarah and the three men returned to Nevada, where they waited at Lovelock for supplies to help the people go to Malheur (it was February, the dead of winter). They did not come. After a perilous ride to Yakima, Sarah also found that the agent there would provide neither provisions nor an escort for Leggins' band to go to Malheur (Wilber 1880). The grant by the Secretary of the Interior was for nothing, as it provided no basic support.

Also at this time, largely at the instigation of Rinehart, an intensive campaign to discredit Sarah ethically and morally was begun. Files in the Office of Indian Affairs (United States Bureau of Indian Affairs 1965), brought together under the title, "The Case of Sarah Winnemucca," contain many damaging letters. She did retain a few staunch supporters, however, among them General Howard and several citizens of Lovelock. In all fairness to her detractors, Sarah was short tempered, particularly in the context of offenses to her people, and she was known to take a drink and to scream and swear on occasion. She also had three husbands, two of them White men.

In 1883, Sarah went East on a lecture tour. On May 9, she appeared in Boston before an audience consisting of General Howard, and several other military figures (Daily Mountain Democrat 3/9/1883). She again spoke of the corruption of the agents, misappropriations, poor government policies and the missionaries. At the end of her speech, a letter from Senator Henry Dawes, currently sponsoring the "Lands in Severalty" legislation before the congress, was read to the effect that he was "in perfect accord with the object of the meeting, which was looking at the abolishing of the so-called Indian Agents." Mr. Dawes' plan to grant Indians title to their lands in severalty, which in effect would accomplish this end, must have seemed inspired.

Between April, 1883, and August, 1884, Sarah gave nearly 300 lectures from Boston and New York to Baltimore and Washington D.C. From newspaper accounts, the lectures were well received. Sarah spoke continually of inequities and called for restoration of lands in severalty to the Paiutes. While in Boston, she became fast friends with Elizabeth Palmer Peabody, noted pioneer in kindergarten education and her sister, Mary Tyler Mann, widow of Horace Mann. Under their direction, she also spoke in the homes of Ralph Waldo Emerson, John Greenleaf Whittier and those of several distinguished congressmen, among them Senator Dawes. Sarah also completed her book at this time, through the encouragement and under the editorship of Mary Mann. She earned many supporters and at the same time, her lectures and book lent support to the passage of SB48, the "Lands in Severalty" bill. Its eastern advocates found their shining example of the effects of education and self-determination in Sarah. There is, in fact, more than a hint of usuary in their efforts on Sarah's behalf. She wanted the restoration of lands at Malheur. They favored general allotment. In the concluding note to Sarah's book, Mary Mann states that the plan was to present the following petition to the Congress in the hope that it "will help to shape aright the new Indian policy, by means of the discussion it will receive" (Hopkins 1883:247).

Then follows the text of a petition requesting the grant of lands in severalty to the Paiute at Malheur Reservation, where "they may enjoy said lands without losing their tribal relations, so essential to their happiness and good character, and where their citizenship, implied in this distribution of land, will defend them from the encroachments of the white settlers, so detrimental to their interests and their virtues" (Hopkins 1883:247).

Although the general lands in severalty legislation finally passed both houses of Congress in 1887, the grant of lands at Malheur apparently died in the Committee of Indian Affairs. On at least six occasions from December, 1883, to April, 1884, petitions with previous text and more than 4,000 signatures were presented to the Congress personally by Sarah and other delegates (Congressional Record 1883-1884). But Malheur was already in the hands of White squatters and little action seemed possible.

Discouraged, Sarah returned to Nevada in August of 1884 to begin preparations for founding her own school for Paiute children with the partial financial support of Miss Peabody and with money earned from the sale of her book and her lectures. The school was to be at Pyramid Lake, but contrary to promises made to Sarah and Elizabeth Peabody by the Commissioner of Indian Affairs (Peabody 1884) the position of teacher was given to the agent's wife. To raise money on her own to build the school on Naches' farm near Lovelock, Sarah again went on a lecture tour, speaking in Reno, Carson City and San Francisco. In a lecture delivered in San Francisco in February, 1885, Sarah proposed her most novel solution to the Indian problem. She stated that:

> if she had the wealth of several whom she named, she would place all the Indians of Nevada on the ships in the harbor, take them to New York and land them there as immigrants, that they might be received with open arms, blessed with the blessings of universal suffrage, and thus placed beyond the necessity of reservation help and out of reach of the Indian agents. (Daily Silver State 2/6/1885)

With great financial difficulty, Sarah succeeded in operating her school for a little over two years. In a published report of the school's first year, Elizabeth Peabody (1886) summarizes Sarah Winnemucca's "practical solution to the Indian problem" as one involving Indian controlled education, Indians' right to run their own lives, and the full privileges of owning land in severalty. Naches' farm and Sarah's school are used repeatedly as examples. The second annual report (Peabody 1887) pleads for funds to carry on this "new departure." Funds were not forthcoming, and in ill health and despondent over marital problems, Sarah was forced to close the school in 1887. Soon thereafter, she went to Henry's Lake, Idaho, to be with her sister. She died there in 1891.

Sarah Winnemucca's desire to see lands issued in severalty to the Paiute without inducing the effects of tribal disintegration was not realized in her lifetime. And, by 1895, the effects of the passage of the general allotment legislation in 1887 were already apparent. Dawes himself, in the Proceedings of the Lake Mohonk Conference of the Friends of the Indian (1896), conceded that clauses he had to add for political reasons allowing the sale of surplus lands once allotments were made, as well as the assignment of allotments on poor lands by unscrupulous agents, had already taken their toll. Dawes (1896:49) states: "The law has fallen among thieves and there are not enough good Samaritans to take care of it." Sarah's "so-called Christians" had won again.

Sarah Winnemucca's known publications include her book (Hopkins 1883) and one article titled **"The Pah-Utes"** (Winnemucca 1882). The latter may have been an excerpt from one of her speeches. Sarah's book is principally an autobiographical and historical account of the period 1844 through 1883, while her article is essentially a statement on pre-contact ethnography. The coverage of cultural data in Sarah's article parallels in many ways the ethnographic paradigm in early anthropology. She provides data on Northern Paiute subsistence patterns, trade, shamanism, puberty observances, courting and marriage customs, death and burial practices, and more. Some of these topics are also given expanded treatment in her book. Sarah's description of antelope charming and hunting is particularly detailed,

perhaps because her father, Old Winnemucca, had antelope power and she witnessed the procedure several times (Hopkins 1883:55 ff.).

Both Sarah's book and her article also contain valuable data on her perceptions of the cultural and attitudinal changes she felt were occurring during this period. For example, she suggests that less stability exists in Northern Paiute marriages than existed formerly:

> They take a woman now without much ado, as white people do, and leave them oftener than of old . . . an indulgence taken advantage of to abandon an old wife and secure a younger one. They argue that it is better for them to do so than to leave their young women for the temptation of white men. (Hopkins 1882:255)

In another example, she notes that native doctors are beginning to "know their value," to have more political power and to extract money fees from patients in emulation of White doctors. There are numerous suggestions of other changes as well.

Subtle courtesies, assumptions and values are also portrayed in Sarah's materials. For example, she speaks of always making a place for a weary guest to sit, making a fire to warm him or her and offering the person something to eat (Hopkins 1883:12). She also describes the decision-making process by which everyone gets an opportunity to speak and think about matters before deciding on an issue (ibid., 27). Differences in values held by Whites and Paiutes are also discussed; for example, Sarah's attempt to make Old Winnemucca understand that it is often the sincere custom of Whites to give gifts to friends when they depart. Old Winnemucca was very hesitant to take Agent Sam Parrish's gifts when Parrish was relieved at Malheur because they would be painful reminders of his absence. Similarly, Old Winnemucca reasoned, one keeps nothing that belongs to the dead (ibid., 52). In another passage, Sarah also explains to the people the peculiar White custom of hanging clothes on a line to dry. This did not mean, she adds, that they were being thrown away and were free for the taking. Indians had been shot in Virginia city for "stealing" laundry (ibid., 120).

From all accounts, Sarah's speeches also contained considerable ethnographic material. In fact, one might speculate that perhaps more was known about Northern Paiute ethnography by the general public in the 1880's partly through Sarah's efforts than has been known at any time since.

One of the most interesting features of Sarah's book, and, I suspect one of the most important for interpreting it, is its narrative style. Her tale is told with numerous quotes from participants, although, quite obviously by reconstruction. I suspect that this may be the same quotative style that is a major feature of Northern Paiute narratives. Sarah's book is, perhaps, her narrative tale, her view of the history of her family and the difficulties of her people—her ethnohistory. As such, from our point of view, it contains some errors of historical fact (although considering the many names and dates, and the amount of detail, it is remarkably accurate). In line with this reasoning, it is interesting to compare Sarah's account with those by other authors in the same period. Examples of the detail she gives: 1) a thorough description of the townsite of Genoa, Nevada, with the location of houses and businesses and the names of occupants; and 2) an account of the supposed murder of two White men, McMullen and Mac Williams in 1858 at the hands of the Washoe. The former is verified by early plat maps of the settlement. Thompson and West's account (Angel 1881:334) of the latter lists their names as McMarlin and Williams and the date as 1857. From the academic perspective, her book lacks the balance of historical evaluation that scholarly models would suggest. However, placed in the more appropriate context of Northern Paiute oral tradition, her account would be balanced by those of other narrators—a context that it loses in print. Accusations of bias and error may result from attempts to judge her work according to another model.

The book's narrative style, as well as some of its ethnographic subtleties, lead me to conclude that while some of Sarah's contemporaries questioned the fact, the book is primarily her effort and not that of Mary Mann. Although Mann undoubtedly edited the book for sentence structure, spelling and punctuation, as she freely states in her preface, it could only be Sarah's detractors that would suggest that she were not capable of the achievement. There are enough of Sarah's original letters, as well as the testimony of her speeches, to demonstrate that she had good command of English. Sentences in her letters do contain errors in spelling and punctuation. They are also frequently conjoined. But on the whole, her letters are generally well written. Internal features in the book, like the conjoining tendency, and a number of what I suspect are "pronunciation spellings," like "Acotrass" for "Alcatraz," "Carochel" for "Churchill" and "shut off the postles" for "shoot off the pistols" indicate that Mann may not have caught everything. However, in the absence of a manuscript for either book or article, we cannot be sure of the nature and extent of author/editor collaboration.

In conclusion, Sarah Winnemucca attempted through accommodation and selective assimilation to bridge the gap between two cultures. She was firmly convinced that with education, agricultural land and freedom from outside intervention, the Paiutes could and should manage their own lives. She was not shy and retiring as might have been her prescribed behaviour given her identity. She was a fighter, quick to learn, and an astute observer of the customs of the Whites as well as those of her own people. In one sense, she is Stewart's

(1939:129) ambitious, educated and self seeking woman. In another she is also Heizer's (1960:3) person of "selfless motives, tremendous energies and high purpose, making her a person to be admired in the history of our far West."

Works Cited

Angel, Myron, ed. *History of Nevada, With Illustrations and Biographical Sketches of Its Prominent Men and Pioneers.* Oakland, Calif.: Thompson and West. [1881]

Congressional Record. *Petitions Presented.* Congressional Record, Dec. 10, 1883; Dec. 14, 1883; Jan. 17, 1884; Jan. 24, 1884; March 10, 1884; April 9, 1884. Washington. [1883-1884]

Dawes, Henry L. *The Severalty Law. Proceedings of the Thirteenth Annual Meeting of the Lake Mohonk Conference of the Friends of the Indian,* 1895, p. 48-52. Boston: The Lake Mohonk Conference. [1896]

Heizer, Robert F. *Notes on Some Paviotso Personalities and Material Culture.* Nevada State Museum Anthropological Papers, No. 2. [1960]

Hopkins, Sarah Winnemucca. *Life Among the Piutes: Their Wrongs and Claims.* Boston: Cupples, Upham and Co. [1883]

Howard, Oliver O. "Letter, To Whom It May Concern," April 3, 1883. In *Life Among the Piutes: Their Wrongs and Claims,* by Sarah Winnemucca Hopkins, p. 249. Boston: Cupples, Upham and Co. [1883]

Peabody, Elizabeth P. "Letter, to Commissioner of Indian Affairs," April 10, 1884. National Archives, RG-75, Washington. [1844]

————. *Sarah Winnemucca's Practical Solution of the Indian Problem: A Letter to Dr. Lyman Abbot of the "Christian Union."* Cambridge: John Wilson and Son. [1886]

————. *The Piutes: Second Report of the Model School of Sarah Winnemucca 1886-87.* Cambridge: John Wilson and Son. [1887]

Stewart, Omer C. *The Northern Paiute Bands.* University of California Anthropological Records, Vol. 2, No. 3, pp. 127-149. [1939]

United States Bureau of Indian Affairs. The Case of Sarah Winnemucca. "Special Files of the Office of Indian Affairs, 1807-1904," No. 268. National Archives Microfilm Publication, No. 574. Washington. [1965]

Wilber, James H. "Letter, to Commissioner of Indian Affairs," January 30, 1879. In *Letters Received by the*

Office of Indian Affairs, 1824-81: Washington Superintendency. [1879] National Archives Microfilm Publications, No. 234. Washington.

————. "Letter, to Commissioner of Indian Affairs, June 29, 1880." In *Letters Received by the Office of Indian Affairs, 1824-81: Washington Superintendency.* National Archives Microfilm Publications, No. 234. Washington. [1880]

Winnemucca, Sarah. "The Pah-Utes." The Californian, 6:252-6. [1882]

A. LaVonne Brown Ruoff (essay date 1987)

SOURCE: "Western American Indian Writers, 1854-1960," in *A Literary History of the American West,* Texas Christian University Press, 1987, pp. 1038-57.

[*In the following excerpt, Ruoff discusses the influence of Winnemucca's autobiography* Life among the Piutes: Their Wrongs and Claims.]

Hostile government policies and public attitudes created a climate generally unfavorable to the development of Indian literature [in the mid-1800s]. . . . White audiences were far more interested in reading the accounts of explorers, settlers, and gold miners who conquered the West than they were in reading of Indian suffering brought about by this conquest. In 1883, however, the voice of the vanquished tribes of the far West was heard when the fiery Sarah Winnemucca Hopkins (Thocmetony; ca. 1844-91) strode across the lecture platforms of America to castigate whites for their unchristian treatment of her people, the Paiutes. With the publication of *Life Among the Piutes; Their Wrongs and Claims* (1883),[1] Winnemucca became the first Indian woman writer of personal and tribal history. Born near the Sink of the Humboldt River in Nevada, Winnemucca was the granddaughter of Truckee, whom she claimed was chief of all the Paiutes, and daughter of Old Winnemucca, who succeeded his father as chief. Because Winnemucca and her family followed Truckee's policy of peaceful co-existence with whites, she spent much of her life serving as a liaison between the Paiutes and whites in her people's native Nevada and in Oregon, where they moved to escape white encroachment on their Pyramid Lake Reservation. After the end of the Bannock War of 1878, in which many Paiutes participated after leaving the Malheur Reservation in Oregon, Winnemucca accompanied her father and her brother Naches to Washington, D.C., to obtain from Secretary of the Interior Carl Schurz permission for the Paiutes to return to the Oregon reservation. Unfortunately, the government provided neither supplies nor transportation for the tribe's return.

Winnemucca's disillusionment with federal Indian policy and with its agents aroused her to take the Paiute cause to the public. Encouraged by the success of her first lecture in San Francisco in 1879, she toured the East delivering more than three hundred lectures. Both her lectures and her book *Life Among the Piutes* strongly supported the General Allotment Act, then under consideration by Congress.[2] By the time the bill was passed in 1887, much of the land on the Malheur Reservation to be allotted to the Paiutes had already been seized by whites. Winnemucca, who earlier had witnessed white seizure of lands at the Pyramid Lake Reservation, lost faith in the power and desire of the government to protect Indian land. Consequently, in 1884, she returned to Nevada to found a school for Paiute children that was located on her brother's farm near Lovelock. Forced by ill health and lack of funds to abandon the school in 1887, she died four years later.

Life Among the Piutes is among the most imaginative personal and tribal histories of the nineteenth century. Winnemucca uses the narrative technique of mixing personal experience and tribal ethnography and the authenticating device of including letters from well-known whites to document her moral character and achievements, both methods used by earlier Indian autobiographers. But whereas these writers made conversion to Christianity and the spiritual journey central to their narratives, Winnemucca never alludes to these. Her central theme is Indian-white relations, a secondary theme in the narratives of earlier writers. The impact of white contact on Paiute life is depicted through Winnemucca's descriptions of her experiences as a child and adult. Especially moving is her description of her terror when as a small child she was buried alive temporarily by her parents to hide her from whites, who were reputed to be cannibals. Winnemucca reveals far more of her childhood and of her adult personality than do earlier writers. Both in her valuable Paiute ethnography and in her exciting accounts of her service as a liaison between Paiutes and whites, Winnemucca emphasizes the roles played by women in traditional Paiute culture and by Winnemucca herself in achieving peace for her people. Her own role was unusual for any woman in her day. Her daring exploits as she raced back and forth between enemy lines, risking rape by white males or murder by hostile whites and Indians, rival those of the heroines of the dime Westerns of the period.

Winnemucca's style is particularly effective because she dramatizes important episodes. Margot Liberty suggests that Winnemucca's recreation of dialogue derives from the quotative style of Northern Paiute narratives.[3] The technique enables Winnemucca to dramatize scenes in which she successfully confronts government officials about their unjust treatment of her people. She displays considerable narrative skill in her dramatization of her grandfather Truckee's death in 1859, in which she weaves together the threads of autobiography, ethnography, and Indian-white relations that dominate the book. She also uses her considerable oratorical power to arouse the sympathy of her audience, demonstrated in her final exhortation for justice for Indian people: "For shame! for shame! You dare to cry out Liberty, when you hold us in places against our will, driving us from place to place as if we were beasts. . . . Oh, my dear readers, talk for us, and if the white people will treat us like human beings, we will behave like a people; but if we are treated by white savages as if we are savages, we are relentless and desperate; yet no more so than any other badly treated people. Oh, dear friends, I am pleading for God and for humanity."[4] Winnemucca's *Life Among the Piutes* was the only book she ever published. However, in 1882, the year before this volume appeared, she published an article on Paiute ethnography entitled **"The Pah-Utes,"** which appeared in *The Californian.*

By the time Winnemucca wrote her personal narrative, the spiritual confession and missionary reminiscence, which so strongly influenced the personal narratives of eastern and midwestern Indian writers, were no longer dominant. The Plains Indians, who were prolific writers of autobiographies, followed Winnemucca's lead in describing life before and after the coming of the white man and the forced settlement of Indians on reservations. The Plains writers forcefully depict the cultural changes faced by their people, particularly by their children sent away from their families to distant schools run by whites who deprived the children of their Indian names, languages, religions, and customs. Their autobiographies and those by writers of other western tribes, most of which appeared from the early 1900s through the 1930s, are valuable contributions to our knowledge of the impact on Indian people of the conquest of the West. They are also important contributions to the literary history of the local color movement and of regional writing. . . .

Notes

[1] The standard spelling of *Paiute* is followed rather than Winnemucca's various spellings of *Piute* or *Pah-Ute*. Research for this chapter was supported by a research grant from the National Endowment for the Humanities.

[2] The General Allotment Act of 1887 was designed to break up Indian reservations—a goal supported by both reformers and opportunists. Under this act, Indians who took their land in severalty became citizens of the United States and were subject to all its obligations. Far from turning Indians into prosperous owners of private land, though, the Allotment Act introduced an era in which Indians lost their land by fraud and by force. By 1934, 60 percent of the land owned by Indians in 1887 had passed out of their control. See Wilcomb E. Washburn, *The Indian in America* (New York: Harper and Row, 1975), pp. 242-43.

[3] "Sarah Winnemucca," in *American Indian Intellectuals:* 1976 Proceedings of the American Ethnological Society, ed. Margot Liberty (St. Paul, Minnesota: West, 1978), pp. 40-41.

[4] Sarah Winnemucca, *Life Among the Piutes* (New York: Putnam, 1883), pp. 243-44. Rpt. Bishop, Calif.: Sierra Media, 1969.

H. David Brumble III (essay date 1988)

SOURCE: "The Preliterate Traditions at Work: White Bull, Two Leggings, and Sarah Winnemucca," in *American Indian Autobiography,* University of California Press, 1988, pp. 48-71.

[*In the following excerpt, Brumble contends that Winnemucca was not aware of contemporary literary models in her writing of* Life among the Piutes, *but rather adapted Paiute oral conventions to the persuasion of white audiences.*]

Sarah Winnemucca was born probably in 1844.[11] . . .

By the time she reached adulthood . . . Winnemucca had experienced a wide range of what late-nineteenth-century America had to offer. As a young child she had lived with a stone-age, hunter-gatherer people; by the time she was twenty she had made her stage debut, acting in Indian tableaux vivants and interpreting for her father in his attempts to explain the Paiutes to the good burghers of Virginia City. By twenty-four she was a figure of some influence in the Great Basin, serving as the Army's emissary to recalcitrant bands of Paiutes and Bannocks, to win them to the reservations. In 1870, when a letter she had written on the plight of the Paiutes was published by *Harper's Weekly,* she became one of the darlings of the eastern Indian enthusiasts. In 1881 she headed East on a speaking tour, spending most of her time in Boston, where she became the especial friend of Elizabeth Palmer Peabody (the woman who published the works of the Transcendentalists) and her sister, Mrs. Horace Mann. It was Mrs. Mann who edited Winnemucca's autobiography, and Elizabeth Peabody who published it. Winnemucca delivered lectures in the homes of Emerson and John Greenleaf Whittier (Fowler, 1978:38).

When her life is described in this way, we might expect that her autobiography would be like that of the educated Indian autobiographers. In a forthcoming article LaVonne Ruoff, for example, asks us to consider Winnemucca along with two other early, literate Indian autobiographers, William Apes and George Copway.[12] Copway, indeed, was very widely read. Ruoff argues that *Life among the Piutes* should be understood in the light of contemporary literary trends and types, such as the captivity narratives and the slave narratives. She points to a number of features which *Life among the Piutes* has in common with such narratives: some sexual violence, for example, and lots of daring adventures. But probably Ruoff is telling us more about Winnemucca's audience than about what might have influenced Winnemucca in writing her autobiography. I think it is unlikely that Winnemucca herself was familiar with such literature; indeed, aside from the hymns she quotes occasionally, it is unlikely that Winnemucca was much aware of literary influences at all.

In fact, it is not at all clear just how literate Winnemucca was. She was certainly a fluent *speaker* of English, as numerous newspaper accounts of her lectures and interviews attest.[13] She was employed as an interpreter on many occasions. And there is little reason to doubt that she did, herself, write *Life among the Piutes.* But her editor, Mrs. Horace Mann, had this to say in a letter to a friend about Winnemucca's manuscript:

> I wish you could see her manuscript as a matter of curiosity. I don't think the English language ever got such treatment before. I have to recur to her sometimes to know what a word is, as spelling is an unknown quantity to her. . . . She often takes syllables off of words & adds them or rather prefixes them to other words, but the story is heart-breaking, and told with a simplicity & eloquence that cannot be described. (In Canfield, 1983:203)

The book allows us to see some of this for ourselves. As Catherine Fowler has noticed, some of Winnemucca's "pronunciation spellings" slipped past Mann's editorial eye: "Acotrass" for "Alcatraz," "Carochel" for "Churchill," and even "shut off the postles" for "shot off the pistols" (1978:40). Now, this is exactly what we would expect of one who was a fluent speaker, but an infrequent reader—as those of us who read undergraduate writing know to our cost. Winnemucca herself candidly confirms this. She recalls reading a four-line letter: "It took me some time to read it, as I was [at age 24] very poor, indeed, at reading writing; and I assure you, my dear readers, I am not much better now" (82). And what little is known of her education seems to indicate that she had virtually no formal schooling (Canfield, 1983:30-31; Fowler, 1978:35). According to her own account in *Life among the Piutes,* she had just three weeks at a convent school in San Jose before a group of anxious parents convinced the pious sisters that it was unseemly that their white and delightsome daughters be educated in the company of an Indian (70).

One must be careful not to overstate this. Winnemucca could read; and she carried on a remarkable correspondence, some of which, in fact, was published, once in *Harper's,* as we have seen, and more often in local newspapers. And, of course, Canfield and Fowler may just possibly be wrong in their estimation of Winnemucca's education.[14] But given what they tell us, given Mann's

letter, and given what Winnemucca herself tells us in *Life among the Piutes,* it does seem that we should not simply *assume* the degree of literacy and the breadth of reading which Ruoff's argument would require of Winnemucca. *Life among the Piutes* probably was not influenced by written captivity or slave narratives.

Winnemucca's autobiography does, on the other hand, seem to owe a good deal to preliterate autobiographical traditions. Consider how different Winnemucca's autobiography is from other early autobiographies by literate Indians. William Apes (1829), George Copway (1847), Charles Alexander Eastman (1902, 1916), and Joseph Griffis (1915) all made the journey Winnemucca made, from the tribal world to the white world. The autobiographies of Apes and Copway have at their center their conversion to Christianity. Eastman and Griffis . . . saw themselves as embodiments of Social Darwinist ideas about the progression of the races. All four of these men wrote autobiography in such a way as to describe an individual self and to account for just how that self came to be. Their autobiographies describe certain clear turning points. Had Eastman not been taken away from the Santee Sioux by his father and sent to school, he would not have become the man he became. Had Apes not found Christianity, he would have remained in a state of sin. In this way, at least, all four are typical modern autobiographers in the Western tradition.

Winnemucca has virtually nothing to say in *Life among the Piutes* about turning points. Her biographer, Canfield, on the other hand, quite reasonably does include a chapter entitled "The Turning Point." The turning points are there for Western eyes to see; Winnemucca saw her life differently.

And she is again unlike modern, Western autobiographers in that she is unconcerned about self-definition. In 1870 a Sacramento reporter sought her out in a Paiute village:

> She said: I am glad to see you, although I have not now a parlor to ask you into except the one made by nature for all. I like this Indian life tolerably well; however, my only object in staying with these people is that I may do them good. I would rather be with my people, but not live as they live. I was not raised so; . . . my happiest life has been spent in Santa Clara while at school and living among the whites. (In Canfield, 1983:65)

The choices here seem to have little to do with the question of self-definition. Winnemucca enjoys living a comfortable life in the cities; when she can live in a house, she gladly does so. When she must live in a brush nobee, she is not unwilling to do so. She knows how to live in the Paiute way. She stays with her people, however, not because of a fervent love of their ways—she certainly does not stay with them because of her love of the Nevada landscape,[15] say, or roots, or rabbit's flesh. She stays, rather, out of a sense of obligation. Winnemucca did remember some of the Paiute rituals fondly, and she may be exaggerating her altruism a bit. But this passage does seem to suggest that Winnemucca did not see the choice between the Paiute and the white way as having to do with self-definition. Eastman, Griffis, and Luther Standing Bear, on the other hand, were concerned to work out an explicit sense of who they were in relation to the two worlds they knew. Their autobiographies suggest in many ways that, in moving from prereservation Indian life to the white world, they were passing over a great divide. They speak as from a great distance of the "superstitions" of their people. Eastman and Standing Bear, especially, describe the prereservation Sioux as being simple and "childlike."

Winnemucca does not seem to see any such fundamental difference between her Indian people and the whites. Certainly she is aware of different customs; she is outraged at how dishonest the whites are, and she contrasts this with the honesty of her own people; she realizes that her people have to learn a great deal in order to become self-supporting farmers, but she nowhere suggests that there are *essential* differences. Indeed, the point of her chapter on "Domestic and Social Moralities" would seem to be that the Paiutes are *not* essentially different from whites: they are "taught to love everybody"; their women are *not* allowed to marry "until they have come to womanhood"; and, says Winnemucca, "We have a republic as well as you. The council-tent is our Congress." All of this is a part of the book's argument that the Paiutes ought to be granted land in severalty and full rights of citizenship.

Quite aside from this line of argument, Winnemucca just does not seem to see differences beyond differences in customs. Indian agent Henry Douglas wrote of Winnemucca that "She conforms readily to civilized customs, and will as readily join in an Indian dance" (Canfield, 1983:62). He would probably not have been surprised to find that she has nothing to say in *Life among the Piutes* about her conversion to Christianity; nothing, either, about a moment when she decided that, really, she preferred the white to the Paiute way. She spent time among whites; she spent time among the Paiutes. In reading her book *we* may see implicit in some of her experiences features of a cultural identity crisis, but she seems herself not to have thought about her life in this way.

In many ways she is like White Bull and Two Leggings. Like those two warriors, she seems mainly concerned to set down her *deeds*. And I think she is like them, too, in conceiving of herself as something like the sum total of her deeds. Like White Bull and Two Leggings, she assumes that she may rise in the regard of her tribe by telling her deeds; and like Two Leggings

she realizes that the written word may allow her to rise in the regard of a much larger tribe. At one point Winnemucca is explaining the position of women in the tribe:

> [The women] are always interested in what their husbands are doing and thinking about. And they take some part even in the wars. They are always near at hand when fighting is going on, ready to snatch their husbands up and carry them off if wounded or killed. One splendid woman . . . went out on the battle-field after her uncle was killed, and went into the front ranks and cheered the men on. Her uncle's horse was dressed in a splendid robe made of eagles' feathers and she snatched it off and swung it in the face of the enemy . . . ; and she staid and took her uncle's place, as brave as any of the men. (53)

Winnemucca wants to be remembered in this way, as a woman who was brave as any man, as a woman who did great things. She recalls leading a detail of soldiers to rescue her father and his band of Paiutes from the hostile Bannocks, for example. Her relish of this memory is nearly palpable: "we have come with you," she remembers the soldiers saying, "and [we] are at your command. Whatever you say we will follow you" (156). She talks about these soldiers as "my men," her "boys" (155). Later she says,

> This was the hardest work I ever did for the government in all my life . . . having been in the saddle night and day; distance about two hundred and twenty-three miles. Yes, I went for the government when the officers could not get an Indian man or white man to go for love or money. I, only an Indian woman, went and saved my father and his people. (164)

Clearly, she is telling something like a coup tale. And she remembers her father's praise of her before the Paiutes:

> Oh, yes! my child's name is so far beyond yours; none of you can ever come up to hers. Her name is everywhere and everyone praises her. Oh! how thankful I feel that it is my own child who has saved so many lives. . . . Now hereafter we will look on her as our chieftain, for none of us are worthy of being chief but her, and all I can say to you is to send her to the wars and you stay and do women's work, and talk as women do. (193)

Bataille and Sands claim that Winnemucca's autobiography is "heavily biased by her acculturated and Christianized point of view" (1984:21). A good Methodist—and Winnemucca was a Methodist—should recognize vanity in such passages, all vanity. White Bull, I think, would be puzzled by such a response. And Two Leggings? Every sinew of his being yearned to hear just such praise. He would—he did—quite literally kill to hear such words. Winnemucca is trying to establish her standing, trying to establish just how it is that she ought to be regarded, just as did Two Leggings and White Bull. In many ways, *Life among the Piutes* assumes an audience with Paiute habits of mind, not Christian. She is what she has accomplished; like White Bull and Two Leggings—and Achilles—she is the sum of her reputation. And so the maintenance of her reputation is of great importance to Winnemucca.

Like White Bull and Two Leggings, her first education was in a shame culture rather than a guilt culture. It should not surprise us, then, that she is concerned with self-vindication. . . . [W]hen Nathaniel accused Don Talayesva of being a Two-Heart, his defense took the form of a detailed recounting of the events related to the charge and a detailed countercharge, urging that his accuser is himself a Two-Heart. Talayesva makes his case persuasive by bringing into his account details and events that it had never occurred to his accuser to mention. Much of *Life among the Piutes* works according to this pattern. Winnemucca remembers many such scenes in her book. At one point, for example, a Captain Jerome bade them come talk with him, since the Indian agent, Newgent, had accused the Paiutes of killing two white men:

> We went like the wind, never stopping until we got there. The officer met us. I told him everything from the first beginning of the trouble. I told him that the agent sold some powder to an Indian, and that his own men had killed the Indian. I told him how brother and I went to him and asked him and his men to go away, as we had heard that our people were going to kill him. I told him that he talked bad to brother and me, because we went to tell him of it. I told this to the officer right before the agent. The agent did not have anything to say, and then the officer asked my brother what he knew about it. (83)

This is typical of Paiute responses to accusations in the book. Does this seem merely "natural," universally human? I think not—at least not in Winnemucca's view. The whites in her book respond to accusations very differently. For example, the Paiutes had a great deal of trouble with another agent, Rinehart. Once they charged him and his cronies with stealing their government-issue clothing: "You are all wearing the clothes that we fools thought belonged to us." Rinehart's response?

> He turned round . . . and said, "If you don't like the way I do, you can all leave here. I am not going to be fooled with by you. I never allow a white man to talk to me like that. (126)

Nearly every Paiute answer to an accusation is "autobiographical" or "historical": "No, no—in fact, I (or we) did this, and then this happened, and then I (or we) did thus, whereupon you did such a thing."[16] The white people in the book, on the other hand, never

respond to charges "autobiographically." They reply with dismissals, flat denials, and, especially, with assertions of authority. Another agent, Wilbur, simply refused, repeatedly, to speak with a Paiute delegation at all: "You are talking against me all the time, and if you don't look out I will have you put in irons and in prison" (239). Winnemucca's Paiutes even had an explanation for such behavior. After yet another promise had been broken, Winnemucca recalls,

> My uncle, Captain John, rose and spoke, saying, "My dear people, I have lived many years with white people . . . and I have known a great many of them. I have never known one of them to do what they promised. I think they mean it just at the time, but I tell you they are very forgetful. It seems to me, sometimes, that their memory is not good, and since I have understood them, if they say they will do so and so for me, I would say to them, now or never. . . . They are a weak people." (225)

The weakness has to do with memory. Small wonder, then, that all of Winnemucca's Paiutes use autobiographical-historical self-vindications, while the whites, in their weakness, must rely simply upon authority. In this book it is the Indians who have the memory that history requires. Indeed, Winnemucca's whole book may be seen as an extended self-vindication, as an attempt to defend her own reputation and that of her family and her tribe:

> 1. The Paiutes would have rescued the Donner party (the famous party that tried to make it over the Donner Pass too late in the season; they ended up eating one another) but they were *afraid* to approach too closely, because the members of this same party had wantonly burned the winter stores of the Paiutes on their way to the Donner Pass. (13)

> 2. She includes a whole chapter on the moral education of the Paiutes, which seems designed to demonstrate that they are not "savages," contrary to white assertions. (45-57)

> 3. The Paiutes are not "revengeful." (54)

> 4. "There is nothing cruel about [the Paiutes]. They never scalped a human being." (54)

> 5. "The chiefs do not live in idleness." They are poor because they feel it is their responsibility to give to the poor. (54)

> 6. She responds to a particular charge that "bloodthirsty savages" killed "innocent" white men. (71)

Among many other examples that might be adduced are the letters appended to the book, twenty-seven letters (!) bearing witness to Winnemucca's good character and important work. (Witnesses, it seems, are at least as important to Winnemucca as they are to White Bull and Two Leggings.) Just as part of Talayesva's response to Nathaniel was an attack upon his attacker, so Winnemucca sometimes attacks the whites (and other detractors):

1. The Paiutes were "less barbarous" before they fell under the influence of the whites. (10)

2. "There were very bad men there. Sometimes they would throw ropes over our women, and do fearful things to them." (228)

3. The "citizens" who follow the army are forever urging the extermination of the Paiutes, but when a battle is at hand, they fall to the rear, until the battle is over, whereupon they commence their looting. (177)

Examples could be multiplied; the broken promises alone would require a sizable list. But I would not wish to be misunderstood: I am not claiming that only a Paiute could have conceived of autobiography as a way to answer slander. My point is that we do not have to look to contemporary literary models to explain the form of *Life among the Piutes.* Indians of many tribes were answering their accusers with autobiographical narratives long before the Paiutes came into contact with the white man.

This does leave the question of the book's narrative polish. We may talk about ways in which the conception of self implicit in the book is closer to that which we find in White Bull's *Personal Narrative* than it is to the conception of self that is usual in the autobiographies of literate moderns, but these are differences we must teach ourselves to notice. If I am right about the book, Ruoff is wrong not at all because she is an insensitive reader, but rather because Winnemucca was so good at adapting Paiute oral conventions to the uses of the pen and to the entertainment and persuasion of white audiences. In this, of course, she had a good deal of practice before she ever sat down to write *Life among the Piutes.*

Winnemucca first appeared on stage in 1864, in Virginia City.[17] In that same year she appeared at the Metropolitan Theater in San Francisco. In these early performances she acted in tableaux vivants: "The Indian Camp," "The Camp Fire," "The Message of War," "The War Council," "The War Dance," "The Capture of a Bannock Spy," "Scalping the Prisoner," and others. She also interpreted her father's brief speeches on these occasions. Her father evidently undertook these exercises in Indian stereotyping in order to get money for his people (Canfield, 1983:41). But these experiences put Winnemucca before the public eye, and they must have given her an immediate sense of what she might accomplish with an audience. With her command of English, she soon became an important spokesperson for her people not only in their negotiations with agents and army, then, but also on the lecture platform.

She was evidently an effective lecturer. Even a reporter who doubted her personal morality could write that "she speaks with force and decision, and talks eloquently of her people" (Canfield, 1983:163). Another San Francisco reporter described one of her lectures:

San Francisco was treated to the most novel entertainment it has ever known, last evening, in the shape of an address by Sarah, daughter of Chief Winnemucca. . . . The Princess wore a short buckskin dress, the skirt bordered with fringe and embroidery. . . . On her head she wore a proud head dress of eagle's feathers. . . . The lecture was unlike anything ever before heard in the civilized world—eloquent, pathetic, tragical at times; at others her quaint anecdotes, sarcasms and wonderful mimicry surprised the audience again and again into bursts of laughter and rounds of applause. *There was no set lecture from written manuscript, but a spontaneous flow of eloquence.* Nature's child spoke in natural, unconstrained language, accompanied by gestures that were scarcely ever surpassed by any actress on the stage. . . . [T]he Indian girl walked upon the stage in an easy, unembarrassed manner, and entered at once upon the story of her race. (In Canfield, 1983:163-164)

Perhaps Secretary of the Interior Carl Schurz bore the most convincing testimony as to her power to move an audience: he did everything he could to keep her from lecturing while she was seeking justice in Washington. He knew that her subjects would have been the evils of "the Indian Ring" and the wrongs of the Paiutes.

Much of *Life among the Piutes: Their Wrongs and Claims* must have had its original in one of her lectures. By the time she came to write it down, she would have delivered her tale, in parts, on many occasions, and she would have had a lively sense of how white audiences had responded to this version of a particular episode, and how they had responded to the other version of the same episode. Again, we need not assume that Winnemucca was at all aware of literary models.

Winnemucca's autobiography is far from White Bull's in some ways. She had learned a good deal about her white audience. She also works self-consciously with analogies in ways White Bull does not. For example, she tells a tale from the mythic history of her people. At one time the Paiutes' neighbors were cannibals. The Paiutes did everything they could to avoid war even with these "barbrians"; when finally they did rise up and smite these neighbors, they did so out of necessity. The tale serves, then, not only as a refutation of the charge that the Paiutes are "bloodthirsty savages";

it also suggests a neat historical analogue for one of the first groups of whites the Paiutes came to know—the Donner party. Winnemucca's work is "connected" in ways that White Bull's certainly is not. But Winnemucca's book is like White Bull's in that it is essentially an oral performance put down in writing.[18]

In her conception of her self, too, and in her conception of what it means to tell the story of one's life, she was not far from White Bull and Two Leggings. Eastman and Griffis felt a great gulf to open up between themselves and the Indians they had "left behind." They became full-time participants in the modern world, however much they may have yearned with a part of their being for the old life. Sarah Winnemucca, however much she may have preferred the comforts of a California house to the dirt and draft of a Paiute reed shelter, never seems to have felt such a distance between herself and her people. For all her acquaintance with the Transcendentalists, for all her Indian activism, Winnemucca retained an essentially tribal sense of self.

Notes

[11] Canfield's (1983) biography of Sarah Winnemucca is essential reading for anyone interested in *Life among the Piutes.* Fowler (1978) is also helpful, especially for her arguments about the authorship and style of the book.

[12] While I do take issue with some of what Ruoff has to say about Winnemucca, her essay is a very helpful introduction to three early autobiographers who have otherwise received scant attention. Ruoff places Apes in relation to early American pietistic autobiography, and she is able to tell us a great deal about the life of Copway, who seems to have been a more deeply troubled man than his autobiographical writings would suggest.

[13] Canfield (1983:88, 164) includes a good sampling of these.

[14] Canfield and Fowler both warn us that it is difficult to know just how literate Winnemucca was. One newspaper man reported in 1891 that Winnemucca "spent a goodly portion of her meager earnings on books" (Fowler, 1978:58). See also the manuscript letter reproduced in Canfield (1983:66) that is virtually free of errors. But it is not at all difficult to imagine Winnemucca seeking out assistance from friendly whites when she had an important letter to write—just as she had Mann's help in writing her book.

[15] N. Scott Momaday has written so evocatively about landscape and self-definition that he has inspired a good deal of nonsense. Bataille and Sands, for example, go so far as to assert that one of the "basic characteristics" oral Indian literature "shares" with American Indian women's autobiography is the "concern with

landscape" (1984:3). In fact, of course, one could easily find many autobiographical narratives by Indian men *and* women and hundreds of transcriptions of oral performances by Indians which do not mention landscape at all.

[16] See, e.g., *Life among the Piutes:* 142, 166, 190-191, 235.

[17] All that follows relating to Winnemucca's stage career comes from Canfield (1983).

[18] She probably had already set some of her stories down in writing, in letters to supporters and in letters written to appeal to various authorities. See, e.g., the passage where Bannock Jack, realizing that Winnemucca "can talk on paper," asks her to write down all that he will tell her about certain injustices that his band has suffered. He then asks her to send it to "our Great Father in Washington" (142-143).

A. LaVonne Brown Ruoff (essay date 1990)

SOURCE: "Three Nineteenth-Century American Indian Autobiographers," in *Redefining American Literary History,* edited by A. LaVonne Brown Ruoff and Jerry W. Ward, Jr., The Modern Language Association of America, 1990, pp. 251-69.

[*In the following excerpt, Ruoff evaluates* Life among the Piutes *by comparing it to other American Indian autobiographies and slave narratives of the same period.*]

One of the few Indian autobiographies published during the last half of the nineteenth century was Sarah Winnemucca's *Life among the Piutes.* The fiery Winnemucca (Thocmetony; Paiute; 1844-91) was the first Indian woman writer of personal and tribal history. Like the slave narrators of the second half of the century, Winnemucca abandons the strongly Christian flavor of earlier personal narratives; unlike [William] Apes and [George] Copway, she does not pattern her narrative after spiritual confessions and missionary reminiscences. Her emphasis on personal experience as part of the ethnohistory of her tribe owes more to tribal narrative traditions than to religious ones. Further, her life history is considerably more militant than theirs.

Winnemucca's *Life among the Piutes* also differs from typical women's autobiographies. In *A Poetics of Women's Autobiography,* Sidonie Smith comments that women autobiographers deal with two stories. On the one hand, the woman autobiographer "engages in the fiction of selfhood that constitutes the discourse of man and that conveys by the way a vision of the fabricating power of male subjectivity." On the other hand, because the story of man is not exactly her story, woman's "relationship to the empowering figure of male selfhood is inevitably problematic." Matters are further complicated by the fact that she must also "engage the fictions of selfhood that constitute the idea of woman and that specify the parameters of female subjectivity, including woman's problematic relationship to language, desire, power, and meaning." This leads Smith to conclude that because the ideology of gender makes woman's life history a nonstory, the ideal woman is "self-effacing rather than self-promoting" and her "natural" story shapes itself "not around the public, heroic life but around the fluid, circumstantial, contingent responsiveness to others that, according to patriarchal ideology, characterizes the life of women but not autobiography" (50).

Smith notes that when the autobiographer is a woman of color or of the working class, she faces even more complex imbroglios of male-female figures:

> Here identities of race and class, sometimes even of nationality, intersect and confound those of gender. As a result, she is doubly or triply the subject of other people's representations, turned again and again in stories that reflect and promote certain forms of selfhood identified with class, race, and nationality as well as with sex. In every case, moreover, she remains marginalized in that she finds herself resident on the margins of discourse, always removed from the center of power within the culture she inhabits. (51)[17]

Although marginalized within the dominant society because of her racial heritage, Winnemucca played a central role in her tribe. Born near the sink of the Humboldt River in Nevada, she was the granddaughter of Truckee, who, Winnemucca claimed, was chief of all the Paiutes, and the daughter of Old Winnemucca, who succeeded his father as chief. Because she and her family followed Truckee's policy of peaceful coexistence with whites, Winnemucca spent much of her life as a liaison between Paiutes and whites.[18] As such she became a courageous and eloquent spokeswoman for her people, pleading the Paiute cause before government officials and the general public. Far from being marginalized, Winnemucca's role as advocate made her the mightiest word warrior of her tribe. In "Indian Women's Personal Narrative," Kathleen Mullen Sands concludes that Winnemucca portrays herself in opposing roles in her autobiography: male and female, private and public: "She not only presents herself as a warrior for Indian justice, but she also develops a portrait of a child terrified by white power who, toward the end of her narrative, has become a dedicated teacher of Indian pupils—a version of motherhood" (ms. 19). In *American Indian Autobiography,* Brumble perceptively argues that *Life among the Piutes* is a kind of coup tale in which Winnemucca records her deeds in order to establish how she ought to be regarded, as have such Indian men as Two Leggings and White Bull (65-66).

Life among the Piutes covers the period from Winnemucca's birth to 1883, four decades that roughly encompass the first contacts between whites and Paiutes, through their many conflicts with whites, resettlements, and negotiations to receive justice from the federal government. After the discovery of gold in California, in 1849, pressures increased on the tribe as hordes of emigrants passed through Paiute territory on their way to the California goldfields, Idaho ore deposits, or Oregon timber. Winnemucca's disillusionment with federal Indian policy and with its agents aroused her to take the Paiute cause to the public. Encouraged by the success of her first lecture in San Francisco in 1879, she toured the East, delivering more than three hundred speeches. In Boston, she was befriended by Elizabeth Palmer Peabody, well known for her support of kindergarten education, and by her sister Mary Tyler Mann, widow of Horace. Through their intercession, Winnemucca was invited to speak in the homes of such distinguished Bostonians as Ralph Waldo Emerson, John Greenleaf Whittier, and Senator Henry L. Dawes. Enthusiastic response to her lectures and support from Mary Mann led Winnemucca to write *Life among the Piutes,* a blend of autobiography, ethnography, and history of Paiute-white relations between 1844 and 1883. Both in her lectures and in her book, Winnemucca staunchly supported the General Allotment Act, sponsored by Senator Dawes, under which Indians would be allotted tribal lands in severalty.[19]

In the book, Winnemucca combines the authenticating devices and narrative techniques of earlier Indian autobiographies with dramatic re-creations of episodes from her own and her family's personal experiences, a combination that makes the book one of the most colorful personal and tribal histories of the nineteenth century. Like Apes and Copway, Winnemucca is careful to validate her narrative. Her editor, Mary Mann, emphatically states in the "Editor's Preface" that her own "editing has consisted in copying the original manuscript in correct orthography and punctuation, with occasional emendations by the author" (ii). Winnemucca appends many documents attesting to her high moral character and to her services as an interpreter and intermediary for the government. In fact, such documents were necessary not only to establish her credibility as someone capable of writing a true account of her own life and history of her tribe but also to defend herself against scurrilous attacks on her virtue and honesty. For example, *The Council Fire and Arbitrator,* a monthly journal supposedly devoted to "civilization" and the "rights of American Indians," publicized accusations that Major William V. Rinehart, an agent whom Winnemucca harshly criticized, had sent to prejudice officials against her on her first trip to Washington: "She is notorious for her untruthfulness as to be wholly unreliable. She is known . . . to have been a common camp follower, consorting with common soldiers" (qtd. in Canfield 204). To combat such libels, Winnemucca published tributes from Brevet Major General Oliver Howard and other high-ranking officers with whom she served. Although such authenticating devices are common in slave narratives, Brumble also links her use of them to the oral traditions of self-vindication in American Indian personal narratives (*Autobiography* 69).

Unlike Apes and Copway, Winnemucca does not make the spiritual journey a central element in her narrative. She also departs from their example by being much more critical of white hypocrisy; her critical tone parallels that of post-Civil War slave narrators. In fact, her central theme is Indian-white relations, a secondary theme in the narratives by Apes and Copway. The emphasis is clear in the organization of the narrative. Part 1 consists of a single chapter on the background of her family and on the impact of white migration on Paiute life after 1844. Part 2, also composed of only one chapter, describes the domestic and social moralities of the Paiutes and provides ethnographic information about the tribe. The six chapters of part 3 are devoted to the conflicts between the Paiutes and whites from 1860 to 1883, as the Indians struggled to retain their native land, were moved from one reservation to another, and attempted to gain allotments on the Malheur agency in Oregon.

Life among the Piutes is more personalized than the autobiographies of Apes and Copway, a trend in slave narratives after the 1850s as well. The work contains a detailed account of Winnemucca's childhood, stressing, in particular, her strong attachment to her grandfather, Truckee, and her intense fear of white men, who reminded her of owls. Although she provides little information about herself as an adolescent and adult, Winnemucca reveals far more of her adult personality than Apes and Copway. The sensitive side of her nature is illustrated in her anguish when she must tell the Paiutes that they will be forced to move in midwinter to the Yakima agency—despite government assurances at the end of the Bannock War that the tribe would not be relocated. Her anguish is deepened by her realization that the Paiutes will say that she lied. Wishing that this were her last day in "this cruel world," Winnemucca questions the motives of a president who would force the weakened Paiutes to travel through freezing cold and deep snows to Yakima: "Oh what can the President be thinking about? Oh, tell me, what is he? Is he man or beast? Yes, he must be a beast; if he has no feeling for my people, surely he ought to have some for the soldiers" (204, 205).

The personal characteristics Winnemucca most consistently demonstrates are courage and stamina, particularly in her account of her role in the Bannock War. Her exploits rival those of the western adventure tales and recall the harrowing experiences of the heroines of captivity and slave narratives. Between 13 and 15 June 1878, Winnemucca rode 223 miles, on horseback and by wagon, between the Indian and army lines, in danger both from the warring Bannocks and from whites eager to kill her for helping the Paiutes.

Winnemucca is acutely conscious that the role she played in Paiute-white relations was unusual for a woman. In addition to the dangers encountered by any emissary passing between enemy lines, Winnemucca and her sister Mattie, who often accompanied her, faced the threat of rape. Warned by her cousin that whites had been lassoing Paiute women and doing "fearful" things to them, Winnemucca asserted: "If such an outrageous thing is to happen to me, it will not be done by one man or two, while there are two women with knives, for I know what an Indian can do. She can never be outraged by one man; but she may by two" (228). That Winnemucca was prepared to defend herself is illustrated by the incident in which she and her sister were forced by circumstances to share one room overnight with eight cowboys. Touched by one of them during the night, Winnemucca jumped up, punched the offender in the face, and warned: "Go away, or I will cut you to pieces, you mean man!" The startled culprit fled before she could carry out her threat (231).

Winnemucca's narrow escapes titillated the reading public's taste for both the imminence of sexuality and the triumph of virtue. The literary descendants of Pamela were expected to die rather than face dishonor, a fate they usually managed to escape. Sexual violence was a staple of both captivity and slave narratives. The women in captivity narratives trusted to their God to deliver them from the danger of rape or servitude as the captive wives of "heathen savages." If such narratives convinced whites of the innate cruelty of nonwhites, the slave narratives reminded whites of their own brutality. The degradation of slave women at the hands of masters provided the writers of slave narratives with the opportunity to demonstrate how the slave system destroyed the morality of blacks and whites.[20] Unlike the heroines of sentimental literature or of captivity and slave narratives, Winnemucca is not a victim but rather an independent woman determined to fight off her attackers. Her strength of character, as well as a fast horse and sharp knife, enable her to achieve victories denied to her literary sisters. They also distinguish her life history from the less dramatic accounts by other women autobiographers.

The description of the impact of white migration into Paiute territory provides a dramatic backdrop for Winnemucca's discussions of tribal beliefs and customs, which reflect the oral tradition of linking personal narrative to a family, clan, and tribal context. Her detailed accounts of the roles played by girls and women represent a subject receiving little emphasis in nineteenth-century autobiographies and ethnographies. Her description of the Paiute councils is an eloquent reminder that Indian women in traditional cultures had political power that was denied to white women in the "civilized" society: "The women know as much as the men do and their advice is often asked. We have a republic as well as you. The council-tent is our Congress, and anybody can speak who has anything to say, women and all. . . . If women would go into your Congress, I think justice would soon be done to the Indians" (53). Like Copway, Winnemucca stresses the importance of dreams in tribal culture. She vividly illustrates the Paiutes' belief in the truth of dreams when she describes how her father gathered his people to tell them that his vision foretold their destruction by whites. The incident also demonstrates the tribe's process of making decisions by consensus, when its members agree to follow his advice to retreat to the mountains.

In the longest section of *Life among the Piutes,* chronicling the tribe's relations with whites in the 1860s and 1870s, Indian agents got rich, Winnemucca charges, by starting their own stores and then bringing in cattlemen to pay them a dollar a head to graze their cattle on reservation land. Winnemucca bitterly attacks Major Rinehart, the agent at the Malheur reservation, and the Rev. James H. Wilbur, agent of the Yakima reservation in Washington, to which the Paiutes were sent.

Stylistically, *Life among the Piutes* is the most interesting of the three autobiographies, primarily because its author effectively dramatizes key episodes. Carolyn S. Fowler suggests that Winnemucca's re-creation of dialogue derives from the quotative style of Northern Paiute narratives (40). Dramatizing scenes and reproducing dialogue enable Winnemucca to strengthen her attacks against her adversaries by including the testimony of witnesses. The technique emphasizes, as well, the influence of the performance aspects of storytelling in native oral traditions. Examples of her narrative skill occur in the scene in which her grandfather calls his people together to retell the Paiute origin myth (6-7) and in her dramatization of Truckee's death, in 1859, in which she weaves together the threads of autobiography, ethnography, and Indian-white relations that dominate the book. Truckee's final speeches express his love for his family, his wish that his granddaughters be sent to a convent school, and his concern for good relations between Paiutes and whites. The author eloquently describes her grief at his passing: "I could not speak. I felt the world growing cold; everything seemed dark. The great light had gone out. I had father, mother, brothers, and sisters; it seemed I would rather lose all of them than my poor grandpa" (69). Her grief was shared by the Paiutes, who gathered from near and far for his deathwatch and funeral.

Like Apes and Copway, Winnemucca uses oratorical power to great effect in arousing the sympathy of her audience. One of the best examples of this style is her final exhortation:

For shame! for shame! You dare to cry out Liberty, when you hold us in places against our will, driving us from place to place as if we were beasts. Ah, there is one thing you cannot say of the Indian. You call him savage, and everything that is bad, but one; but, thanks be to God, I am so proud to say that my people have never outraged your women, or have even insulted them by looks or words. . . . Oh, my dear readers, talk for us, and if the white people will treat us like human beings, we will behave like a people; but if we are treated by white savages as if we are savages, we are relentless and desperate; yet no more so than any other badly treated people. Oh, dear friends, I am pleading for God and for humanity. (243-44)

Life among the Piutes is the only book Winnemucca ever published. In 1882, the year before her book appeared, she published an article on Paiute ethnography, "The Pah-Utes," in *The Californian.* Despite her acute observations of Paiute life, her skillful storytelling, and her often eloquent style, Winnemucca did not continue her career as a writer. In 1884, she returned to her brother Naches's farm near Lovelock, Nevada, to establish a school for Paiute children. Ill health, despondence over marital difficulties, and lack of money forced her to abandon the school in 1887. Four years later she died. . . .

Notes

[17] S. Smith gives an excellent summary of the theoretical approaches to autobiography in her chapter "Autobiography Criticism and the Problematics of Gender" (*Poetics* 3-43). See also Jelinek, "Introduction: Women's Autobiography and the Male Tradition" in *Women's Autobiography* (1-20). As Sands points out, in "Indian Women's Personal Narrative," books on women's autobiography have not dealt with American Indian life histories. One of the few books to treat this topic is Bataille and Sands.

[18] For a full-length biography, see Canfield. Additional biographical information is contained in articles by Brimlow; C. Fowler; P. Stewart.

[19] The General Allotment Act of 1887 was designed to end the reservation system. Under the act, supported by both reformers and opportunists, Indians who took their land in severalty became citizens of the United States and were subject to all its obligations. Although the act was passed to enable Indians to become prosperous landowners, the measure instead ushered in an era in which Indians lost their land by fraud and force. By 1934, sixty percent of the land owned by Indians in 1887 had passed from their control. See Washburn, *The Indian in America* 242-43. For an Indian view of the impact of allotment, see D'Arcy McNickle (Cree-Salish), *Native American Tribalism* 80-85, 91-92, an excellent source for the history of Indian-white relations in the twentieth century.

[20] F. S. Foster 132, 58. Harriet A. Brent Jacobs (Linda Brent) treats the theme of sexual harassment in *Incidents in the Life of a Slave Girl* (1861). Elizabeth Keckley's *Behind the Scenes* (1868) treats this theme briefly.

In *American Indian Autobiography,* Brumble concludes that *Life among the Piutes* was probably not influenced by written captivity or slave narratives. Brumble, whose comments are based on a draft of my essay, asserts that "we should not simply *assume* the degree of literacy and breadth of reading which Ruoff's argument would require of Winnemucca" (61, 63, 69). He believes that the elements of sexual violence and daring adventures in Winnemucca's autobiography that I point out as present in captivity and slave narratives "tell us more about Winnemucca's audience than about what might have influenced Winnemucca in writing her autobiography" (61).

Brumble misinterprets the thrust of my argument, which is that Winnemucca's and Copway's autobiographies in particular reflect a complex blend of influences: Native American oral traditions and popular literary forms. This does not suggest that Apes, Copway, or Winnemucca, all of whom had very little education, read widely in the genres whose forms and themes may be reflected in their work. We simply do not know what or how much they read. Such parallels may well reflect other kinds of influences. All three were skilled and experienced platform speakers who developed dramatic presentations of their life histories to convince their audiences of the virtues and values of their native cultures and to horrify their listeners with vivid descriptions of the suffering that whites inflicted on American Indians. To gain the attention of their audiences, they structured their narratives to reflect not only native oral traditions but also the forms and themes to which their readers would respond. The presence of aspects of popular literature in their autobiographies may reflect the narrators' responses to their non-Indian audiences, spouses, friends, and editors. Consequently, these parallels may well mirror the taste of the age rather than the literary background of the narrators.

William C. Strange (essay date 1991)

SOURCE: "Story, Take Me Home; Instances of Resonance in Sarah Winnemucca Hopkins' *Life Among the Piutes*," in *Entering the 90s: The North American Experience,* edited by Thomas E. Schirer, Lake Superior State University Press, 1991, pp. 184-94.

[*In the following essay, Strange considers Winnemucca's* Life among the Piutes *as a work filled with personal resonances.*]

Life Among the Piutes: Their Wrongs and Claims

was published in Boston in 1883, "edited by Mrs. Horace Mann," as its title page announced, and "printed for the author," Sarah Winnemucca Hopkins (p. 1). Editor and author had met while Sarah was working hard in the east as a controversial and increasingly popular lecturer who staged herself as Princess Sarah in fringed buckskins and beads with a golden crown on her head and at her waist a velvet wampum bag with a cupid worked on it. She had to dress up in order to draw the crowds and dollars she needed to support her cause, herself and the drunken consumptive who was the last of her husbands, Lt. Lewis H. Hopkins of Virginia. It is not a promising pair this title page offers—a Bostonian editor sure of her ways and an author who has distanced herself from her people by her marriage, by her stagey practice and by aristocratic pretensions far beyond any that Paiute society would have recognized. However, this author had a powerful story to tell and the editor who took her up, the good sense to get out of its way. Mary Mann corrected her manuscript but added nothing of her own, aside from a one page preface and a handful of short footnotes. "I wish you could see her manuscript," she wrote to a friend. "I don't think the English language ever got such a treatment before. I have to recur to her sometimes to know what a word is, as spelling is an unknown quantity to her . . . , but the story is heart-breaking and told with a simplicity & eloquence that cannot be described . . ." (Canfield, 1983, p. 203). Sarah Winnemucca Hopkins might not have been able to spell, but she came to Mary Mann fluent in at least four languages and with something worth saying in all of them. Ten years after her book was published she was dead, buried in a still-unmarked grave in Idaho, but then what name belongs there? *Sarah,* alone, seems so demeaning. *Hopkins* was a hindrance more than a helpmate to an already burdened woman. And *Winnemucca,* "The Giver," was her father's name, not her family's. In what follows, I will call her *Sarah.* In Hebrew it means "Princess," and for her public self, at least, that is what she wanted to be.

I. Resonance: Facts Felt Along the Bone.

Forty years take the Northern Paiute, or the Numa as they called themselves, from first contact to near annihilation, and Sarah Winnemucca Hopkins lives through them all. Because of her work as an interpreter—occasionally for agents, who seldom could stomach her honesty for long, more often for the U.S. Army who came to know and value that honesty and the courage that went with it—Sarah was exactly where she needed to be to observe and to record her people's distress, and she writes of it with the accuracy and passion of a skilled investigative reporter. If it's facts you want, she gives them to you. She can list by name, rank, and office every soldier on General Howard's staff during the Bannock war though she spent scant time among them. She identifies each agent who has cheated her people and specifies exactly how he went about his greedy business. She names each Paiute who has turned against his own kind: Numana or Captain Dave who became the complaisant interpreter a succession of agents at Pyramid Lake required; her cousin Jarry, made desperate by his blindness and willing as interpreter to say and do whatever Major Reinhart, agent at Malheur, required of him; the chief Oytes who betrayed into Bannock captivity any Paiute who would not follow him into the Bannock war. She can come right to the point when she wants to without blunting it with too much detail—"The only way the cattlemen and farmers get to make money is to start an Indian war, so that the troops may come and buy their beef, cattle, horses, and grain. The settlers get fat by it" (Hopkins, 1883, p. 78). "There were no Custers among the officers in Nevada" (Hopkins, 1883, p. 178). And she can fix a complex swirling event such as the dizzy confusion of the Bannock war with the stark clarity of a single image like a photographer on the field of battle at My Lai or Bensonhurst. The Paiute were caught in an absurd trap during the Bannock war: pursued by the army because they weren't on their reservation, held captive by the Bannock and their allies because they wanted to be. Kafka could have dreamed it in its gruesome stupidity. "Poor Egan, who was not for war, was most shamefully murdered by the Umatilla Indians." Though a Paiute leader, Egan was born among the Cayuse, near neighbors of the Umatilla. "He was cut in pieces by them, and his head taken to the officers, and Dr. Fitzgerald boiled it to get the skull to keep" (Hopkins, 1883, p. 182). Poor Egan, indeed. What better emblem for the Bannock war than that savaged and sanitized skull, and Sarah's pen remembers to record it.

Yet I think we are leaving something out if we read her book only for her facts, her analyses and comments, her sharp images. There is a kind of resonance in this book that takes it beyond fact, indictment, or photograph. Let me illustrate what I mean. Sarah is describing the first time that her grandfather, Captain Truckee, talks with a party of emigrants, to offer them his friendship and his aid and to receive friendship in return.

> During their stay my grandfather and some of his people called upon them, and they all shook hands, and when our white brothers were going away they gave my grandfather a white tin plate. Oh, what a time they had over that beautiful gift,—it was so bright! They say that after they left, my grandfather called for his people to come together, and he then showed them the beautiful gift which he had received from his white brothers. Everybody was so pleased; nothing like it was ever seen in our country before. My grandfather thought so much of it that he bored holes in it and fastened it on his head, and wore it as his hat. (Hopkins, 1883, p. 8)

Old Truckee with a plate on his head may seem to pale into insignificance beside Egan's skull, for the skull makes its grizzly sense with no opportunity for mistaking it

while Truckee's hat seems to make no sense at all. It is foolishness, and we laugh at it as Truckee will learn to do. But what understanding preceded this misunderstanding and let him to commit it in the first place? Surely, Truckee must have recognized something in the plate that made the bright gift meaningful, even powerful, before it became simply table ware.

On the northern edge of the Paiute country, actually in a kind of overlapping boundary zone where Klamath, Modoc and Paiute all meet, there is a distinctive run to petroglyph sites consisting of panels covered almost entirely with concentric circles. Today, the handsomest of them is located in southeastern Oregon just above the California-Nevada borders in a dry streambed known locally as Paradise Creek. At one point the walls of the creek bed open and soften a bit, and a small ledge of rock breaks through its eastern bank. About twenty feet long and twelve or fifteen high, this formation cups at its center a smooth rockface covered with a remarkable variety of concentric circles. Some are quite large relative to the rest, others are small. Some are made up of only one circle inside another, some of two or three, and some contain not another circle but a fully pecked disk. Some have been touched so recently that traces of white or red paint linger on their edges, and some have nearly vanished as natural repatination has drawn them back into the stone. Paradise Creek is a remarkable place that feels very like paradise if one is lucky enough to come upon it burning in the afternoon sun, but what does it have to do with reading Sarah Winnemucca Hopkins?

Let me be very careful about what I claim here. I cannot argue that old Truckee's people worked these circles. I cannot even date them. And most certainly I cannot say what it is that they mean though no one standing in front of them can deny their meaning and power. But I do know that these panels with nothing but concentric circles on them are unique among the petroglyphs of the region; that they seem to mark a special place, a boundary zone where Klamath, Modoc and Paiute met; and that some of them look very like a tin plate! Consider what emerges from all this tentativeness. Precisely in that narrow stretch of frontier where northern Paiute lands butt upon their strongest and strangest neighbors someone has worked, and continued working close to our century as the daubs of paint reveal, a series of petroglyph sites made up on only concentric circles. Precisely at that moment when Truckee meets the strangers he has for two or more years been trying to meet, he is given by them a bright object with concentric circles worked upon it. Even if the Paradise Creek petroglyphs were as puzzling to Truckee as they are to us, they demonstrate that a tin plate need be neither unfamiliar nor meaningless to Truckee in his own terms. Considered as a design object and in the context in which he receives it, the plate is another concentric circle offered or announced between strangers, and this short scene that seems so foolish now may have been resonant to the Paiute with Truckee's attempt to find his own meaning in the newness he has been offered.

In fact, it is just this possibility of resonance that reading Sarah as if she were only a reporter of simple fact blinds us to. Any American author could have drawn up an accounting of the crimes committed upon her people and of their claims for justice. But wrongs and claims are her subtitle, the American side of the ledger, while life among the Paiute is a different matter of resonances actively sought for and recognized by a people who were more than the passive victims of a terrible newness and strangeness. Persons important to Sarah are defined in her book not just by the wrongs they suffer, which would subordinate them to the culture that invades them, but also by the way they understand these wrongs within their own experience even as they learn to endure them. *Life Among the Piutes* is not a catalogue of outrages but a story of Paiute intelligences trying to take the world again and make it their own. Let me describe something of what it feels like to learn to read her book for these resonances.

II. Character: A Grandfather's Story.

As a girl, before she became Sarah Winnemucca the chief's daughter or married Lieutenant Hopkins, Sarah was Thocmetony, "Shell-flower." We do not know her grandfather's Paiute name. John Frémont, the young soldier-explorer he chose to fight beside in the Bear Flag Rebellion, called him Captain Truckee: *Captain,* the title given to any Paiute that Americans wished to recognize or to install as a leader they could deal with; and *Truckee,* a Paiute word meaning *copesetic, all right, hot damn.* The coinage is nearly Dickensian and singularly appropriate to what we will learn of this generous old man: Thocmetony and Captain Truckee, a girl and her grandfather. The most important resonances in the book, its principle adaptive strategies, cluster in direct opposition around these two figures. They are the points of its compass rose. They define the crux of its moral dilemma.

With Captain Truckee these resonances are most direct. He knows what settlers are before he ever sees them, and he is just as certain what his response to them must be. In her first chapter Sarah describes her grandfather calling his people together to tell them a story they already know. He summons his people, and tells them this tradition:

> "In the beginning of the world there were only four, two girls and two boys. Our forefather and mother were only two, and we are their children. You all know that a great while ago there was a happy family in this world. One girl and one boy were dark and the others were white. For ,a time they got along together without quarrelling, but soon they disagreed, and there was trouble . . . our father took the dark boy and girl, and the white boy and girl, and asked

> them, 'Why are you so cruel to each other?' They hung their heads down and would not speak . . . He said, 'Depart from each other, you cruel children;—go across the mighty ocean and do not seek each other's lives.'

> " . . . And by-and-by the dark children grew into a large nation; and we believe it is the one we belong to, and that the nation that sprung from the white children will some time send some one to meet us and heal all the old trouble. Now, the white people we saw a few days ago must certainly be our white brothers, and I want to welcome them. I want to love them as I love all of you." (Hopkins, 1883, pp. 6-7)

The tradition of the quarrelling children that Truckee invokes here was extremely popular among the Paiute. At least one version, usually more, can be found in most any collection of Paiute narrative materials. These alternate versions reveal two suggestive facts about Truckee's re-telling of the tradition. First, he is extremely careful as to how much of the story he allows himself to remember. Second, again and again his people, especially his granddaughter, remind him of what he leaves out of the story by insisting upon these forgotten or ignored resonances within their own lives. In effect, Truckee hears only part of this most basic Paiute creation myth echoing in his experience of contact with whites while the rest of the Numa hear another part that is not nearly so comforting in what it implies.

The myth is too long and too varied to permit a detailed retelling of it, but even a quick account will show what Captain Truckee leaves out. I have assembled what follows from nine different tellings of the creation story collected and published from as early as 1873 to as late as 1980 (Fowler and Fowler, 1971; Kelly, 1938; Ramsey, 1977; Walker, 1980; Liljeblad, 1986). The story falls into three sections:

Attack of the Cannibals.

A number of Indians are playing the hand game. They are in one camp and a single woman is in another, or they are indoors and the woman outside; either way she is emphatically not of them. She hears the cannibal coming—Nümüzoho, people pounder, is its name—and she tries to warn the others; but they are so obsessed with their gambling that they ignore her. Nümüzoho kills all of them just by looking at them, leaving only the woman and a baby who has been sleeping on the ground behind the gamblers or hidden in a basket with the woman. The cannibal leaves; she takes the baby and flees for both their lives.

What we seem to have in this first section of the myth is a congerie of a social beings, most obviously with the cannibals but also in the woman who is always outside and alone, and perhaps in the baby forgotten in the heat of the game. Only the gamblers have a camp,

Sarah Winnemucca, standing, Chief Winnemucca, seated, Natchez, standing, Captain Jim, seated.

a house, a society that accepts them, and for the moment they are oblivious to anyone or anything not in their game, and vulnerable as a consequence. With a fine Dantean justice the cannibal taunts their blindness and kills them with the flash of his own hungry eye: "'Shut your eyes dry' they all sat still without closing their eyes. Cannibal just looked and went away. He killed them just by looking at them . . ." (Kelly, 1938, p. 366). When a society closes its eyes to all but its own concerns, when the game becomes a form of blindness, then comes the time of the cannibals and, if we are lucky, of that saving remnant who may learn to see anew. This part of the story seems packed with meanings that Truckee could have used, but he will have none of them. It is the same with the second section.

Adventures on the Road.

There are three adventures here. First, the woman is overtaken by the same or another cannibal and saves herself only by distracting him with a baby he then devours. Some tellers soften this unpleasantness by having Nümühozo find the baby on his own and bait a trap for the woman with its crying; in other versions she tells Nümühozo where this better food than she is has been buried. Second, after her escape the woman is given food and shelter by an older woman often identified as the grandmother of the cannibals. She conceals the fugitive from her own children and sends her on her way with instructions not to meddle with anything she finds on the road. Sometimes, the old woman is Beaver who sends the young woman to her sister Gopher for these instructions, and it is their brother Rat who must rescue her again when she ignores them. Always, their charity stands in sharp contract to the glassy eyes of the gamesters. Society is beginning to happen again; a people and a world are being made anew.

This summary may seem excessively moralizing, but isn't this a most moral progress, permitting the woman to learn just what she must know to found a new people in a difficult land? Watch out for cannibals; they usually are somewhere on the edges of things. Do unto others, etc. . . . , or you risk becoming Nümüzoho yourself. It is not nice to meddle with Mother Nature; unless you have good reason, leave her heads and her baskets where she put them by the road. Now the woman is ready for a family of her own. Once again, it is quite remarkable how little of the tradition he invokes Truckee actually is willing or able to use. Do unto others . . . Surely, that's the lesson Truckee wanted to teach, but why doesn't he hear it here in this part of the story? Creation as education and growth in a woman's journey is something he chooses to ignore.

The Contentious Children.

Finally, we get to the part of the story Truckee rests his understanding upon. Unfortunately, this section of the myth is the most difficult to summarize both because this is more variation here in simple details of plot than ever there was before and because the whole notion of journey is translated within this last section into a quite different dimension. All versions agree that after her adventures on the road the woman escapes the cannibals and finds her man and they marry. By means of womb or miraculous water bottle, in the fullness of time or magically day by day, this couple has four children, who fight incessantly among themselves until, in anger and despair, the father drives the children out, sending them far apart and setting out himself, sometimes with his wife, sometimes telling her she will not see him again until she dies. The children are left behind in Stillwater and in Lovelock, two towns in Nevada, or as the Pit River tribe and Paiutes, or just as warring Indians. Sometimes, one pair of them is white as Truckee claims. The mother is left sorrowing for the family she has lost, alone as she was at the beginning, but in the course of the story she has become Numü pa-a, First Mother of the Paiutes, and her husband has revealed himself as Nu-min-a, their Spirit Father who will greet them in the "Land of the Sunny South" (Fowler, 1971, p. 242) when they die.

This would seem a most cyclical notion of history, spinning order out of contention and back again, except that the final leg of this journey breaks time's round and takes the angry father and the grieving mother quite literally off any conventional map. In the most carefully localized version of the story that I have seen (Walker, pp. 165-170), the parents start out from their courting ground on Job's Peak in central Nevada; travel less than twenty miles southeast to Chalk Mountain leaving a pass and a series of springs behind them; turn due east on what is now US 50 through West Gate, Middle Gate and East Gate; and in not quite ten miles come to a large body of water where none is on the map! They walk over it as if it were land, rest for a while on a white mountain without a name but apparently somewhere in the Toiyabe or Simpson Park Range, and then the clouds open upon a beautiful green valley that could be their endless home. Like Oedipus and Colonus their journey begins in a named precinct. Thebes or the Nevadan equivalent, but ends with Nu-min-a and his wife striding off of our maps and out of our simple being. Other versions report this startling turn even more movingly than the one I have just described. For example, in Kelly (1938), who collects five different versions of the story, the father always abandons the mother to this life while he goes alone sometimes "to the other sides of the clouds" (p. 368) or to the ocean and walks over it "as if it were ice" (p. 370) or south on the people's trail, the Milky Way (p. 372). Always we start before time and end beyond it; and in between we make a most moral transit along the Paiute way.

It is amazing to see how much of this story Truckee chooses not to apply to his own circumstances. Even in the part that he tells much is lost. By making the tradition of the contentious children black and white, pun intended, Truckee offers his people a known world and clear moral imperatives with one hand while with the other he cuts them and the story loose from all that careful anchoring of their imaginations in the details of a known landscape in the Nu-mü tu-wip, the people's home. Most painfully, he drives out all of the story's mystery, substituting for it the simple facts of a geography lesson learned from Captain John Frémont.

Just look at the ocean that the Paiute mother and father walk across, the ocean that isn't there on any of our maps. For Tuckee it is simply ocean and conveniently not there so he can put it somewhere else by making it into the ocean the white pair of children must cross in their attempt to get back to their darker brothers in the Numü tu-wip. He gives the story a distinctly European twist so that he can make use of it to make sense of Europeans, and that is a desperate stratagem that rests more on his own disposition than Paiute tradition. He is after all, Captain Truckee, Captain All's Right.

What alternatives are there to his convenient misplacing of ocean? This ocean could remain just what the story makes it when it is told in place, the ghost of an ocean. After all, much of the central Nevada landscape consists of the basins and beachlines of a great inland sea that leaves its traces but is no longer there. Or ocean in the story might even be a memory of a time when water did lap these dusty shores. It seems unlikely that an oral tradition could remember so far back into the geological past, but Jarold Ramsay has pointed out that one of the most popular Paiute stories may display just such a long remembering. "The Theft of Pine Nuts" tells of Coyote stealing pine nuts for the Paiute from a people who live in the North behind an insurmountable wall of ice. Ramsey comments "The Detail of the Ice Wall is strange—if, as seems likely, Indians were in southwest Oregon at the end of the past period of heavy glaciations, could a tribal memory of the glaciers account for this detail?" (1977, p. 284).

Another suggestive fact of the Nevada landscape also may bring this doubtful ocean back where the myth says it belongs. After they have crossed the ocean that isn't there and climbed the nameless white mountain, Nu-min-a keeps on climbing into the clouds. Hickison summit lies about where this white mountain and green valley ought to be. If it is where the Paiute father steps off this world leaving his wife behind, someone has marked this holy place with an extensive series of petroglyphs. The most striking of them seems a clear reminder of all that the father abandons. There are vulva forms carved everywhere in Paiute country, all over Nevada and Northeastern California, but none are quite so monumental as the one found at Hickison Summit. Is it a memorial to Numü pa? If so, it is one more indication that the landscape, the face of Numü twip, keeps prompting Truckee with more of his story than he is willing to tell.

But one does not need to take a trip to Nevada or even to the library to begin to hear those parts of the story that Truckee winces from. Sarah's book is full of such reminders, and they fall pointedly into place within the Paiute creation myth. Truckee looks only at the end of the story so that he may claim the emigrants as his lost white brothers. His people insist upon the beginning of the story and see them as Nümüzoho, the cannibal who is always there in their dreams. This identification receives fearful support from the plight of the Donner party. "Our mothers told us that the whites were killing everybody and eating them. So we were all afraid of them" (Hopkins, 1983, p. 11). "'Surely they don't eat people?' 'Yes they do eat people, because they ate each other up in the mountains last winter' (Hopkins, 1883, p. 15)." Sarah will go on to focus the full force of the Numa's rejection of Truckee's resonance into the girl she was, Thocmetony, his granddaughter and then to derive herself from their argument. Thocmetony and Truckee add up. Their sum is Princess Sarah.

However, adding Thocmetony to Truckee and deriving Princess Sarah from them . . . Well, had we but world enough and time. We don't Hence, this short report must tease with an instance of a resonance too often ignored, in hopes that future readers of *Life Among the Piutes* will try to hear more of it when they pick it up.

References

Canfield, G.W. (1983). *Sarah Winnemucca of the Northern Paiutes*. Norman and London: University of Oklahoma Press.

Fowler, D.D. & Fowler, C.S. (Eds.). (1971). *Anthropology of the Numa: John Wesley Powell's Manuscripts on the Numic Peoples of Western North America, 1868-1880*. (Smithsonian Contributions to Anthropology Number 14). Washington, D.C.: Smithsonian Institution Press.

Hopkins, S.W. (1883). *Life Among the Piutes: Their Wrongs and Claims*. New York: G.P. Putnam's Sons. In (1969) M.R. Harrington, R. & A. Johnson (Eds.), Reproduction of *Life Among the Piutes: Their Wrongs and Claims*. Bishop Ca. Chalfant Press.

Kelly, I.T. (1938). Northern Paiute Tales. *The Journal of American Folklore,* 51, 363-438.

Ramsey, Jarold. (1977). *Coyote Was Going There: Indian Literature of the Oregon Country,* Seattle and London: University of Washington Press.

Liljeblad, S. (1986). Oral tradition: Content and style of verbal arts. In W.C. Sturtevant (General Ed.) &

W.L. D'Azevedo (Volume Ed.), *Handbook of North American Indians:* Vol. 11. Great Basin (pp. 641-659). Washington: Smithsonian Institution.

Walker, D.E., Jr. (1980). *Myths of Idaho Indians.* Moscow: The University Press of Idaho.

Kathleen Mullen Sands (essay date 1992)

SOURCE: "Indian Women's Personal Narrative: Voices Past and Present," in *American Women's Autobiography: Fea(s)ts of Memory,* edited by Margo Culley, University of Wisconsin Press, 1992, pp. 268-94.

[*In the following excerpt, Sands examines the intent and technique of Winnemucca's* Life among the Piutes: Their Wrongs and Claims.]

One of the earliest written autobiographies by an American Indian is Sarah Winnemucca Hopkins' *Life among the Piutes: Their Wrongs and Claims,* published in 1883. As the title suggests, this autobiography is not only a personal narrative, but also a cultural history of the Northern Paiute tribe from early contact with whites to the 1880s, and a plea for an end to unjust treatment of her people.

Thocmentony (translated Shell Flower), as she was named when she was born, probably in 1844, in the vicinity of Humboldt Lake in present-day northern Nevada, was the granddaughter of Truckee "who had been a guide to early emigrants crossing the Great Basin" and leader of the Numa, as the Northern Paiutes called themselves (Canfield 4). She was the daughter of Winnemucca, an important antelope shaman who became the leader and spokesman for his tribe upon Truckee's death. Sarah Winnemucca was born into an important family at a time of rapid and bewildering change for her people.

Her first encounter with whites was filled with terror. Stories of cannibalism in the doomed Donner party had filtered into the tribe and become the basis of stories of fierce whites who would eat Numas (Hopkins 11), so Thocmentony did not believe her grandfather's story about the tradition of the white men as prophesied benevolent lost brothers of the Numa (Canfield 6). Frightened by the approach of a party of whites, Thocmentony's mother buried Thocmentony and her cousin to the neck and hid them under sagebrush, leaving them there all day until she could safely return to uncover them. The trauma of this event stayed with the child, making her fearful and timid, especially after one of her uncles was killed by a party of whites (Hopkins 20). She was especially terrified when her grandfather insisted that his daughter and granddaughter and other kinsmen accompany him to California. During the journey, gifts of sugar from white settlers

and the kind nursing of a white woman when Thocmentony became ill with poison oak finally dissolved her fear of "the owls," as the Numa called white people because of their bearded faces and light eyes (Hopkins 11-32). In fact, she was so thoroughly taken with her nurse she claims in her autobiography that this incident made her "come to love the white people" (Hopkins 33). By 1858, in fact, Sarah and her sister were living with a white family and learning English rapidly (Hopkins 58). The timid little girl who had been mute, too afraid even to speak her native language around whites, was finding her voice and would soon become an interpreter for negotiations between the army and her people though she was only an adolescent. Her skill as a translator and her position as a member of the most prominent family in the tribe brought her to the very center of her tribe's negotiations with Indian agents and army officers and rapidly led to her role as spokeswoman for her people to white society in western towns and cities and eventually as a lecturer and lobbyist for Indian causes in the eastern United States.

Sarah Winnemucca, as she became known to whites, wrote her autobiography to reach a wider audience than her lectures could in order to convince the white world that her people were not bloodthirsty savages but decent people willing to coexist peacefully with the growing white population in their traditional homeland (now western Nevada, southeastern Oregon, and northeastern California), if only the injustices and corruption of Indian policy could be redressed.

In Elizabeth Palmer Peabody and Mary Mann, the widow of Horace Mann, Sarah Winnemucca found loyal support; Peabody found her lecturing engagements and Mann volunteered to edit Sarah's book, which she quickly found to be quite a task. Writing about the narrative of this self-educated Indian woman, Mann says:

> I wish you could see her manuscript as a matter of curiosity. I don't think the English language ever got such treatment before. I have to recur to her sometimes to know what a word is, as spelling is an unknown quantity to her. . . . She often takes syllables off of words & adds them or rather prefixes them to other words, but the story is heart-breaking, and told with simplicity & eloquence that cannot be described, for it is not high-faluting eloquence, tho' sometimes it lapses into verse (and quite poetical verse too). I was always considered fanatical about Indians, but I have a wholly new conception of them now, and we civilized people may well stand abashed before their purity of life & their truthfulness. (Canfield 201)

Mann's enthusiasm for the project did not fade despite Sarah's unorthodox writing; in fact, she aided in defraying publication costs by getting subscriptions to underwrite printing. Mann's comments on the project are particularly useful because they verify that Sarah

Winnemucca composed her autobiography with relatively little help from Mann, who writes in the preface, "My editing has consisted in copying the original manuscript in correct orthography and punctuation, with occasional emendations by the author, of a book which is an heroic act on the part of the writer" (Hopkins 3).

Sarah Winnemucca's personal narrative fits poorly into the genre of women's autobiography as reminiscence; rather, because of the very public nature of her life, it corresponds more accurately to the memoir style of male autobiography. That her mentors were active in the transcendentalist movement and that she had become quite sophisticated in eastern society suggest that she may well have been deliberately modeling Victorian male autobiographies, though that must remain purely speculation, since no records exist of literary influences on her text. The political nature of her authorial intent must also be taken into account, and so must the nature of her life experience. A pivotal figure in the relations of her tribe with the military and bureaucratic agencies of the United States government,[12] she acted as a scout for the U.S. Army under General Howard's command in the Bannock War (Canfield 141). In the appendix to her autobiography, a letter written in 1878, by R. F. Bernard, a cavalry captain, verifies her role:

> This is to certify that Sara Winnemucca has rendered most valuable services during the operations of this year against the hostile Bannock and Piute Indians. About the commencement of hostilities, she went for me from my camp to that of the hostiles, distant about a hundred miles, and returned bringing exceedingly valuable information concerning their number, location, intentions, etc., and she also succeeded in getting her father, the Piute chief Winnemucca, with many of his band, to leave the enemy and go to Camp McDermit, Nevada, where they remained during the summer campaign. (Hopkins 259)

Sarah's version of these events is considerably more dramatic:

> This was the hardest work I ever did for the government in all my life,—the whole round trip, from 10 o'clock June 13 up to June 15, arriving back at 5:30 P.M., having been in the saddle night and day; distance, about two hundred and twenty-three miles. Yes, I went for the government when the officers could not get an Indian man or a white man to go for love or money. I, only an Indian woman, went and saved my father and his people. (Hopkins 164)

Her vision of herself as a warrior woman dominates this summary and interpretation of her actions. She presents herself as a hero, brave beyond either Indian or white males, yet speaks of herself as "only" an Indian woman, a dramatic contrast that indicates her awareness of her readership who certainly would not expect such bravery of a "squaw."

Winnemucca does not, however, reject the Euro-American stereotype of "princess"; she allows herself to be billed as "Princess Sarah Winnemucca of the Piutes" for her lectures (Canfield 200), perhaps in this case deliberately using the stereotype of exotic royalty to work for her cause.

Sarah Winnemucca is a very self-conscious narrator. At work here are "strategies by which the author seeks to explain or justify her current sense of herself, a need which might be especially strong in a woman who feels herself moving into uncharted waters . . ." (Chevigny 83). She writes her narrative directly to her audience, frequently addressing them in the second person and using genteel language as when she describes the traditional flower festival among her people:

> Oh, with what eagerness we girls used to watch every spring for the time when we could meet with our hearts' delight, the young men, whom in civilized life you call beaux. We would all go in company to see if the flowers we were named for were yet in bloom, for almost all the girls are named for flowers. (Hopkins 46)

Note the term "civilized." It is hard to believe that she sees white society as more civilized than her own; she frequently chastises whites for their perfidy in dealing with Indians and portrays her people as trustworthy, gentle, clean, hospitable, and above all, moral—far superior to the corrupt agents who steal their food rations and keep the income from tribal farming for their own enrichment. It is clear who she thinks is really civilized, but she knows how to play her audience and uses her "only an Indian woman" pose to gain sympathy for her cause, just as she uses the image of the exotic "princess" to fill a lecture hall.

Winnemucca takes considerable pains to give details of traditional life, especially the training of young men and women for adult roles as spouses and parents. In her chapter entitled "Domestic and Social Moralities" she also makes it clear that women have power within her tribe. She writes:

> The women know as much as the men do, and their advice is often asked. We have a republic as well as you. The council-tent is our Congress, and anybody can speak who has anything to say, women and all. (Hopkins 53)

She continues, giving an account of a woman who takes her fallen uncle's place in battle. Winnemucca, herself, of course, remains the ultimate warrior of her tribe, risking her life to rescue her people and also fighting for her people in the council tents, lecture halls, and even the halls of Congress and of the White House itself, yet maintaining the demeanor of a humble Indian woman when it suits her need for audience reception. Adroit at two techniques, she uses a conventional autobiographical form for her time, and she manipulates her status as an Indian woman in her own favor. She has it both ways—male and female, private and public. Not only does she present herself as a warrior for Indian justice, but she also develops a portrait of a child terrified by white power who, toward the end of her narrative, has become a dedicated teacher of Indian pupils—a version of motherhood.

The fact that she is a woman is a great asset for her in reaching her audience. Male Indian warriors may threaten; look at Geronimo, Sitting Bull, etc., but a woman as warrior, in alliance with the U.S. Army and her own people, is safe—a powerful yet acceptable image, not so very different from Pocahontas after all, especially considering she has a white man for a husband. She ironically fits all the conventions already well established in the American mind and thus gains reader acceptance despite her strident accusations of injustice toward her people. Winnemucca does call very public attention to herself, not so much by writing her autobiography as by appearing as the "princess" in full buckskin dress before audiences on both Pacific and Atlantic coasts, speaking out to whites on behalf of Indians, pointing out the misuse of Indian women by white men, accusing whites of lying to Indians. She also calls attention to herself in her own tribe. As interpreter between tribe and whites, she is particularly vulnerable to criticism if things do not go as promised, if blankets and food are not delivered as scheduled, or land settlements she negotiated in Washington are not implemented. She is an easy scapegoat among her people, and as a highly unconventional representative of Indian women in white society, is also open to scrutiny and occasional barbs, particularly about her liaisons with white men, including two marriages. The first marriage to a drunken gambler who wasted her meager resources was disastrous, and the second, to Louis Hopkins, was stormy and unconventional. In part, the autobiography defends her against gossip about her private life and criticism of her public life; it is a rationale—but clearly not an apology—for the unusual thrust of her life in a period of Victorian sensibilities in white society and confusing social change in tribal society. Sarah Winnemucca's autobiography explains her public life and makes a case for her integrity as a Northern Paiute woman working for understanding and cooperation between tribal people and the dominant society.

The reliability of the Winnemucca text, as with all autobiographical texts, is suspect particularly because she uses her life story to promote the cause of her own personal integrity and the broader cause of tribal justice—she has axes to grind. It is also suspect at another level. Included in the text, in fact dominant in it, lengthy speeches and dialogues highly unlikely to have been remembered and written verbatim are presented in the conventional forms of quoted monologue and dialogue, and thus purport to be accurate. These techniques suggest a considerable use of poetic license, recollections edited with political as well as artistic intent in mind, other voices played through the voice of the narrator, noticeably in the narrator's narrative style. The text is not a polyphony; only the single voice of Winnemucca actually narrates dramatic events and characters. She creates speeches by her grandfather to move a white audience to admire him and the nature of tribal culture. Sarah's dialogues with military officers, white settlers, her family, and others enhance her own stature and her case for justice toward the Paiutes. In the name of justice, she sees manipulation of the past as fair. Her "fictions," as Geertz would put it, however suspect, make the autobiography far livelier than it would be without such dramatic devices.

Sarah Winnemucca places herself at the center of every event and action in the autobiography, from her description of her terror at the first contact with whites, where, actually, she is only a bit player, to her daring rescue of her father and his band, where she is indeed center stage, to her negotiations with congressmen and cabinet members. It is Winnemucca's verve, her certainty of the epic nature of her life, her absolute dedication, despite enormous personal sacrifice, and her genteelly Victorian use of language that work in concert to move the reader and convince the audience of the justice of Indian rights even a century after its first publication. . . .

Notes

[12] Several biographers call Sarah Winnemucca Hopkins a chief; one, by Dorothy Nafus Morrison, is titled *Chief Sarah: Sarah Winnemucca's Fight for Indian Rights.* As a spokesperson, negotiator, and warrior, she does, in fact, fill the role of a chief though she never bore the title; however in one speech, her father said, "Now hereafter we will look on her as our chieftain, for none of us are worthy of being chief but her" (193), or at least in her autobiography she reports that that is what he said.

Works Cited

Canfield, Gae Whitney. *Sarah Winnemucca of the Northern Paiutes.* Norman, University of Oklahoma Press, 1931.

Chevigny, Bell Gale. "Daughters Writing: Toward a Theory of Women's Biography." *Feminist Studies,* 9/1 (1983), 79-102.

Geertz, Clifford. *The Interpretation of Cultures.* New York: Basic Books, 1973.

Hopkins, Sarah Winnemucca. *Life among the Piutes: Their Wrongs and Claims.* Boston: Printed for the Author, 1883. Photographically reproduced by Chalfant Press, Bishop, CA, 1969.

Brigitte Georgi-Findlay (essay date 1993)

SOURCE: "The Frontiers of Native American Women's Writing: Sarah Winnemucca's *Life among the Piutes*," in *New Voices in Native American Literary Criticism,* edited by Arnold Krupat, Smithsonian Institution Press, 1993, pp. 222-52.

[In the following excerpt, Georgi-Findlay explores Winnemucca's Life among the Piutes *as it presents the role of gender in Indian-white relations.]*

The study of the history, literature, and popular mythology of American westward expansion and the frontier West has, during the past decades, undergone some crucial reconsideration, if not revision, through the inclusion of two new angles of vision: the focus on the tribal people dispossessed by the westward movement and, more recently, on the largely ignored and for a long time invisible participation of women in this move west. These two relatively new fields of study, it would appear, do not have much in common with each other—except, of course, for their combined efforts to rewrite previously excluded groups of people as presences and agents into American history and literature. Thus it should not come as a surprise that both areas have kept rather aloof from each other and have only recently approached each other in studies focusing on Native American women. Both areas of study, however, may be made profitable for each other also in the reconsideration of the frontier experience in American literature and culture, from which both Native American and female voices have long been absent. Focusing on one of the first autobiographical narratives written by a Native American woman, Sarah Winnemucca Hopkins's **Life among the Piutes: Their wrongs and claims** (1883),[1] I aim at such a reconsideration of the frontier experience from the female and the Native American point of view, by drawing on some of the critical questions raised by both fields of study.

Historical research on the American frontier has tended to view westward expansion as a predominantly male activity, and studies dealing with the "popular mythology of the frontier"[2] have defined it as a cultural idea almost exclusively linked to and shaped by male concerns, although admittedly assigning women an important symbolic presence.[3] Both have for a long time based their evidence on texts written by white men. However, recent historical research, mostly undertaken by women, has established women's presence on the various western frontiers on the basis of their published and private writings in the form of travel narratives, memoirs, diaries, and letters.[4] In their writings, these westering women have recorded their encounters with native women—sometimes expressing unconcealed racism and ethnocentrism, sometimes full of fear and distrust, and sometimes with a refreshing openness and willingness to understand the "other," as represented by tribal cultures and people, in a way that leaves us wondering about the impact of these encounters on tribal women, both on a cultural as well as an interpersonal level. One of the main problems in the study of the female experience of the frontier is, of course, the problem of written evidence. Researchers have so far mostly focused on the experience of Euroamerican middle-class women for the obvious reason that these more or less educated women furnished the largest part of the written material on the female frontier. During the 1980s, however, large retrieval efforts have resulted in the recovery and establishment of an ever increasing store of women's texts on the frontiers, which has also multiplied the complexity of perspectives.[5] Aware of the immense variety of women's experience, researchers increasingly emphasize the need to consider the impact of many cultures when studying women and call for a "new multicultural framework."[6] Of course, the admittedly problematic text status and limited amount of the material which is available to study the experiences especially of Native American women, consisting to a large degree of originally oral narratives and raising serious questions of authorship, have prevented researchers so far from taking a closer look at native women's texts. However, studies on Native American autobiographies on the one hand, and of women's autobiographies on the other hand, have already developed methodological approaches to the interpretation of these difficult texts.[7] As a matter of fact, it is remarkable that the studies of both Native American and women's autobiographies deal with similar difficulties and often come up with similar conclusions. Here I only want to point to the questions of authorship and voice, the role of the "framing" of texts through prefaces, appendixes, and generic conventions, to the special circumstances of text production, distribution, and reception, as well as to the issues of power and authority surrounding editor-narrator relations. Both areas of study often come to the conclusion that the characteristics identified as generic to the American autobiography are largely based on the study of texts by male white Americans; both often contend that the concept of self-projected in the "master texts" of the American autobiography informs neither—or only marginally—the autobiographical narratives of tribal people nor those of women.[8]

While researchers on the female frontier have recently called for a multicultural framework in the study of women's experiences of the western frontiers, Native American studies, both anthropological and literary, have begun to focus on Native American women and to put emphasis on the construction and role of gender in North American tribal cultures.[9] Although the studies of Native American literature have come to acknowledge the prominence of contemporary native women writers and the important thematic and formal role of gender in contemporary Native American literary works,[10] they have not considered well enough the role of gender in earlier Native American literature. These literary expressions of Native Americans in the eighteenth and nineteenth centuries have been interpreted mainly in the context of political Indian-white relations, of acculturation and assimilation, an approach which is of course fully legitimized by the circumstances surrounding and motivating the production of these early texts.[11] I would argue, however, that we have not considered well enough the role of gender in the history of Indian-white relations, of cultural contact, colonization, and assimilation—especially in the interpretation of the texts written, authored or coauthored, or narrated by Native American women. Shouldn't we wonder whether the experience and process of assimilation is different for native women than for native men?[12] How did cultural contact, colonization, and change affect tribal women? How did it affect their views of themselves as tribal persons and as women, and how did they express these views in their autobiographical narratives?[13] And how did these women place themselves within the changing world of the western frontiers? These, I would suggest, are the questions that may add new angles of vision to the study of early native women's texts.

One of the first autobiographical texts written by a Native American woman, Sarah Winnemucca Hopkins's *Life among the Piutes,* seems to me to be a case in point, since it demonstrates the need for an interpretation that is sensitive to the complex role of gender and gender relations in the narrator's appeal for the vindication of her people's rights. In the following I want to suggest that this text may be read in more than one context. It may be read, of course, as a Native American autobiographical narrative that incorporates a political message. Yet, I would argue, it is not only a political statement on Indian-white power relations toward the end of the nineteenth century, but is itself shaped by the realities of sexual politics in Indian-white relations. At the same time, it may be read as an example of women's writing on the western frontier, a reading which is suggested by the fact that the text is anthologized in collections of western women's writing.[14] Sarah Winnemucca was born, as she states in her autobiographical narrative, "somewhere near 1844" near the sink of the Humboldt River in what is now western Nevada. She came from a Northern Paiute[15] family that from the time of first contact with whites had advocated peaceful coexistence. Her maternal grandfather Truckee, who she claimed was the chief of all the Paiutes, welcomed early explorers and settlers and served as a guide to various emigrant parties traveling to California. He had fought in California with John C. Frémont in his Mexican campaigns and befriended white families and individuals throughout northern Nevada and California. Sarah's father, Old Winnemucca, succeeded Truckee as chief.[16]

By the time she reached adulthood, Sarah Winnemucca was in the public eye as an "Indian Princess"[17] and a spokeswoman of the Paiute tribe. At the age of twenty, she appeared on stage with her family, acting in Indian *tableaux vivants* and interpreting for her father in his attempts to mediate between the Paiutes and the citizens of Virginia City. At twenty-four she was a figure of some prominence and influence, serving as a liaison between the Paiutes and the whites in her people's native Nevada and in Oregon, where they were assigned to the Malheur Reservation, soon living lives of poverty dependent on the whims of an Indian agent. During the Bannock War of 1878 she acted in the controversial role of the army's emissary to recalcitrant bands of Paiutes and Bannocks, bringing them onto the reservations. Already in 1870, a letter she had written on the plight of the Paiutes was published by *Harper's Weekly,* attracting the attention of eastern Indian reformers particularly after its republication in the appendix of Helen Hunt Jackson's *A Century of Dishonor* (1881). After the Bannock War, Sarah accompanied her father and her brother Natchez to Washington to talk to President Hayes and to obtain from secretary of the interior Carl Schurz permission for the Paiutes to return to the Malheur Reservation in Oregon, after they had been crowded onto the Yakima Reservation in Washington. The government, however, provided neither supplies nor transportation for the tribe's return. Disillusioned with federal Indian policy and its agents, Sarah started taking the Paiute cause to the public. Encouraged by the success of her first lecture in San Francisco in 1879, she went east on a lecture tour. Giving nearly three hundred talks between April 1883 and August 1884, from Boston and New York to Baltimore and Washington, she exposed inequities in federal Indian policy and the corruption of federal Indian agents and called for the restoration of lands in severalty to the Paiutes. In Boston she met Elizabeth Palmer Peabody, the promoter of kindergarten education and publisher of the works of the transcendentalists, and her sister Mary Mann, who took up the Paiutes' cause.[18] Under their direction, she also spoke in the homes of Ralph Waldo Emerson, John Greenleaf Whittier, and those of congressmen, among them Senator Henry Dawes.[19] Evidently encouraged by the two women, Sarah Winnemucca, now Mrs. Hopkins, wrote her autobiographical book *Life among the Piutes,* which was edited by Mary Mann and published in 1883 by Elizabeth Palmer Peabody. This book, which contains the text of a petition requesting the grant of lands in severalty to the Paiutes at Malheur Reservation, is together with her lectures generally claimed to have lent support to the passage of the General Allotment Act, also known as the Dawes Act, in 1887.[20]

Consequently, Bernd C. Peyer has read Sarah Winnemucca's autobiography, together with other autobiographical texts of the period, as a political text in the context of Indian-white political relations in the last quarter of the nineteenth century. In his reading, these texts reflect changes of the time both in federal Indian policy and in the public interest in Indian affairs. Thus the lessened focus on the religious conversion experience, which had been so prominent in earlier autobiographical works, is explained by the secularization of Indian education, which no longer aims predominantly at the education and training of preachers. At the same time, the end of any major Native American military resistance by 1890 at the latest and the confinement of tribes on reservations gave rise to a scholarly and humanist interest in the history and fate of Native Americans, which, together with the founding of numerous organizations of "friends," created a greater market for Native American literature with an emphasis on traditional life. Thus, Peyer argues, the works written by Native Americans during this period, among them that of Sarah Winnemucca, include much more ethnohistorical detail and, as the situation on the reservations quickly became unbearable, turn more and more critical of the conquering society.[21]

In a similar fashion, A. LaVonne Brown Ruoff notes that Winnemucca's text, unlike the earlier autobiographies of William Apes and George Copway, is not influenced by religious autobiographies, and that its central theme is not the conversion experience, but Indian-white relations.[22] Contradicting Bernd Peyer, however, she contends that hostile government policies and public attitudes created a climate generally unfavorable to the development of Native American literature during this period. White audiences, she argues, were far more interested in reading the accounts of the explorers, settlers, and gold miners who conquered the West than they were in reading of Native American suffering brought about by this conquest.[23] This would suggest that Native American literature of the time had, so to speak, to compete with western literature. Yet, although Ruoff discovers allusions to dime-novel westerns in Winnemucca's text, she does not elaborate further on this interesting intertextual aspect and on the whole seems to privilege a reading of the autobiography as a political statement supporting the General Allotment Act. In another publication Ruoff argues that **Life among the Piutes** should be understood in the light of contemporary literary trends and types, such as the captivity narratives and the slave narratives. She points to a number of features that the text has in common with such narratives, such as some sexual violence and lots of daring adventures.[24] In reaction to this argument, H. David Brumble regards it as unlikely that Winnemucca herself was familiar with such literature. He asks that we "not simply *assume* the degree of literacy and the breadth of reading which Ruoff's argument would require of Winnemucca"[25] and argues that Winnemucca's autobiography was not influenced by written captivity or slave narratives, but seems instead to owe a good deal to preliterate autobiographical traditions. He proposes to look at Winnemucca instead as a well-experienced *speaker* who adapted Paiute oral conventions to the uses of the pen and to the

entertainment and persuasion of white audiences. By the time she came to write her narrative down, he argues, Winnemucca would have delivered it, in parts, on many occasions, and she would have had a lively sense of how white audiences had responded to the various versions of particular episodes. Thus we need not assume that Winnemucca was at all aware of literary models, but we have to take into account that she had learned a great deal about her white audience.[26]

My reading of **Life among the Piutes** sustains Peyer's and Ruoff's interpretations of the autobiography as a text of some political impact in the area of Indian policy, although I cannot fully follow the connections Peyer draws between changes in federal Indian policy and the impact of these changes on the content and style of Native American literature in the last quarter of the nineteenth century. As the title suggests, the work may be identified as both autobiographical and ethnographic. In it Winnemucca tells the story of Indian dispossession and legal incapacitation, exemplified in the case of her tribe, the Northern Paiutes. Its publication may be seen as a sign of increasing humanitarian concern among eastern reformers for the plight of Native Americans, and also of changes in the federal Indian policy leading to the Dawes Act of 1887. Moreover, H. David Brumble's reading of the text as following a preliterate autobiographical tradition seems to be a convincing explanation for the striking differences distinguishing it from both the earlier and later Native American autobiographies of William Apes (1829), George Copway (1847), Charles Eastman (1902, 1916), and Joseph Griffis (1915). These differences consist, for instance, in the absence of turning points or conversion experiences as well as in Winnemucca's reference to her actions as solely motivated by the service to her people. As Brumble suggests, she seems mainly concerned with setting down her deeds, assuming, with other male Native autobiographers, that she may rise in the regard of her tribe by the telling of these deeds, thus implicitly assuming an audience with Paiute habits of mind, not Christian.[27] From this vantage point, he comes to the conclusion that "for all her acquaintance with the Transcendentalists, for all her Indian activism, Winnemucca retained an essentially tribal sense of self,"[28] an interpretation that justly contradicts Bataille's and Sands's claim that Winnemucca's autobiography is "heavily biased by her acculturated and Christianized point of view."[29] Although it supports his interpretation in many of its main arguments, my reading of the text will try to expand its focus by pointing to another one of its dimensions which has so far not been considered. Concurring with Brumble's thesis that Winnemucca was less aware of literary models than of the potential response of her white—and potentially tribal—audience to her speeches, I want to suggest that Winnemucca's identity as a woman and the way her womanhood is, so to speak, "incorporated" into her text, form an important part of Winnemucca's dialogue with her public that should not be underestimated. I would even go so far as to suggest that the very fact that Winnemucca was a woman was crucial in the public reception of her person, her lectures, and her book by a contemporary audience.[30] A reading of the text from this perspective, however, will necessarily lead to a modification of Brumble's suggestion that Sarah Winnemucca retained an essentially tribal self throughout her autobiographical narrative.

When I reread Winnemucca's *Life among the Piutes* in terms of what it might reveal about being a Native American woman in the transitional culture of the frontier West, I was appalled at the sense of personal pain, yet also of personal pride, pervading the text; but I was also surprised at the way this woman had written herself, or possibly, had been written into the text. What difference did it make, I wondered, that the author of this bitter attack on the reservation system was a woman, and a Native American woman at that? Hers is a distressing story that aims at her audience's emotional commitment and concern. That the author is a woman seems to be part of this effect; that the editor is a woman is evidence of the fact, of which a contemporary public doubtless had been aware, that toward the end of the nineteenth century women played an important part in the reform movements of the time, and particularly in the Indian reform movement, where women's organizations in fact had initially formulated policies that were later endorsed by other groups and adopted by the government.[31]

Although most critics note Sarah Winnemucca's exceptional position as the female public voice of her tribe, none of them has considered the implications of this exceptionalism in the text itself. In his preface to the 1969 reprint of the text, M. R. Harrington remarks that "not often has an Indian woman been allowed to become so vocal and to bring the history of her people before the public." Ruoff as well notes this exceptionalism and points to Winnemucca's emphasis on the roles played by women in achieving peace for her people, yet does not go beyond relating the narrative of Winnemucca's daring exploits to the western dime novels featuring adventurous heroines.[32] Peyer points to Winnemucca's position as the first major female Native American writer, and Fowler argues that the events of Winnemucca's life suggest clearly some of the motives that led her to speak for Indian rights at a time when a Native American *woman* would hardly be respected for doing so.[33] Only Brumble registers Winnemucca's own explanation of the position of women in the tribe and draws the conclusion that "Winnemucca wants to be remembered in this way, as a woman who was brave as any man, as a woman who did great things."[34] I would go even father and argue that the female presence of Sarah Winnemucca in her text extends this traditional tribal role by incorporating references to concepts

of Victorian womanhood, and is thus in fact much more ambiguous than Brumble suggests.[35]

The reports on Sarah Winnemucca's public appearances support the idea that she was aware of the effect she had on her public in the romantic role of the "Indian Princess," a role certainly not entirely of her own making.[36] In a similar fashion, she seems to capitalize on this romantic public image in her lectures and her autobiographical narrative for the purpose of winning her audience's sympathy for her tribe. However, in *Life among the Piutes* this self-stylization as an Indian princess takes on exactly the paradoxical quality of the image of the Indian woman in American culture, which Rayna Green had stressed: Sarah faces what Green describes as the basic crux of the Native American woman, the impossibility "to be seen as real . . . As some abstract, noble Princess tied to 'America' and to sacrificial zeal, she has power as a symbol. As the Squaw, a depersonalized object of scornful convenience, she is powerless."[37] Linked to the main narrative dealing with the story of her tribe, we discover a subtext of personal defense, which has led Brumble to read the text as "an extended self-vindication, as an attempt to defend her own reputation and that of her family and her tribe," relating it to a preliterate, tribal conception of autobiography "as a way to answer slander," and arguing that "Indians of many tribes were answering their accusers with autobiographical narratives long before the Paiutes came into contact with the white man."[38] As a matter of fact, Winnemucca's own person is at times so overwhelmingly present in the narrative of her tribe's plight that we might be tempted to read the text as an enterprise of self-aggrandizement in the tradition of the male American autobiography—an enterprise that, to my knowledge, no American woman had undertaken so far. It also seems to be no coincidence that, as Catherine S. Fowler has pointed out, Winnemucca emerges in the works of cultural anthropologists as a controversial figure, a woman with two faces.[39] Considering the fact that she is writing against the silencing of Native American tribal voices in the context of a paternalistic federal Indian policy, her focus on her own person may of course be seen as a strategy of authentication, of claiming authority and representativity as a spokeswoman of her tribe. And yet what distinguishes Sarah's strategy of claiming authority from other native authors' strategies, say, for instance, from that of Charles Eastman, is not only the absence of the discourse of conversion, but also the awareness, ever present in her text, that this claim of authority is in a problematic way tied to issues of gender. I would argue therefore that the subtext of personal defense implies that Winnemucca had to defend herself against attacks particularly aimed at her as a woman. This becomes especially clear when we consider the framework of the book, which is provided not only by a foreword of the editor, but also by an appendix—a well-known and important textual device in the publication of Native American autobiographies as well as of slave narratives—that includes affidavits testifying to the respectable and reliable character of Sarah Winnemucca Hopkins, and thus implying, although rather subtly and unobtrusively, that her respectability must somehow have been questioned. Read against this framework, the issues of sexuality and morality written into the text take on a new meaning: what is negotiated in her presentation of Indian-white relations is not only the issue of the dispossession of tribal land, an issue a white audience dedicated to the rhetoric of national westward expansion would not have espoused without restrictions, but also the outrageous issues of sexual violence and miscegenation revealed in the violation of native women's bodies by white men.

The personal attacks against Sarah Winnemucca, as they are indirectly referred to in the affidavits in the book's appendix, seem even tame compared to the press reports and letters written about Sarah and sent to officials in Washington: Sarah is described as nothing less than a prostitute, an easy woman, a common camp follower.[40] Now we begin to identify the voices Sarah must implicitly have been writing against: those who disclaim her authority as a political spokeswoman by disclaiming her respectability as a woman, by exposing the woman who speaks and acts in public as a "public woman,"[41] by putting the Native American "princess" in her negative stereotypical place as savage woman, as "squaw," a promiscuous consort lacking "civilized" womanly virtue and restraint. As a matter of fact, even today's critics feel compelled to apologize for Sarah Winnemucca's supposedly unwomanly habits.[42] If we take further into consideration that Sarah reportedly had to defend herself against other Native women's insults as well as that her book was written during a lecture tour in the East, encouraged by, edited, and promoted by women active in or affiliated with various reform movements known for their concern for morality, domesticity, and the integrity of the family, we may assume the high importance this issue of respectability—and, implicitly, of sexuality, seduction, and slandered virtue—must have had in the production, promotion, and reception of the text.[43]

Life among the Piutes is apparently the result of a collaboration, or rather, of a dialogue of voices, female and male, eastern and western, Indian and white. Yet it is not the collaboration of a tribal person with one of the increasing numbers of anthropologists, as will be the case with many of the Native American autobiographies produced in the first decades of the twentieth century, which were informed by the scientific concerns of the young discipline of cultural anthropology.[44] It is a collaboration between women of two cultures. Arnold Krupat has suggested that "to see the Indian autobiography as a ground on which two cultures meet is to see it as the textual equivalent of the frontier."[45] In this sense, Winnemucca's *Life* could be

read as a textual equivalent of a woman's frontier which is defined by the boundaries and reciprocal relationships between her native culture on the one hand and both eastern and western cultures on the other hand.

In her preface, Mary Mann describes the book as "an heroic act on the part of the writer," and as "the first outbreak of the American Indian in human literature, [which] has a single aim—to *tell the truth* as it lies in the heart and mind of a true patriot, and one whose knowledge of the two races gives her an opportunity of comparing them justly." She describes the motivation of Sarah Winnemucca, who is, in view of the attacks upon her respectability, significantly referred to as Mrs. Hopkins, to write the book: "Finding that in extemporaneous speech she could only speak at one time of a few points, she determined to write out the most important part of what she wished to say." She draws attention to the importance of the book at a particular historical instance: "At this moment, when the United States seems waking up to their duty to the original possessors of our immense territory, it is of the first importance to hear what only an Indian *and an Indian woman* [my emphasis] can tell." Why should it be of the first importance, at that particular historical moment, to hear what only an Indian woman can tell? Because, I would suggest, Indian reform is regarded, at this historical moment, as a domain which is of particular concern to women. The book is thus placed in a feminine discourse which assumes moral responsibility in the realm of political reform.

Mary Mann further informs her readers that the writing of the book was Sarah's "own deep impulse, and the dying charge given her by her father, the truly parental chief of his beloved tribe." Sarah Winnemucca herself will, in her narrative, legitimize her own role as spokeswoman with her family position as granddaughter of Truckee, whom she introduces as chief of the entire Paiute nation[46] and as daughter of Winnemucca, whom she describes as the legitimate successor of Truckee. Thus she suggests that her authority is based on kinship and relation: she is spokeswoman first by way of relation, and only secondarily by way of education. The idea is also underlined by her devaluation of her educational training. In this she distinguishes herself from other authors of Native American autobiographies who present themselves as educated Christians.

Mary Mann describes her own editing as "copying the original manuscript in correct orthography and punctuation, with occasional emendation by the author." The final version of the text is credited as Sarah's own: "In fighting with her literary deficiencies she loses some of the fervid eloquence which her extraordinary command of the English language enables her to utter, but I am confident that no one would desire that her own original words should be altered." To a friend, however, Mary Mann had confided that she had found the work of editing the manuscript rather difficult, which suggests not only that she may have interfered in the original text more than she cared to admit in her preface, but also that she may have realized the oral dimension of Sarah's written text:

> I wish you could see her manuscript as a matter of curiosity. I don't think the English language ever got such a treatment before. I have to recur to her sometimes to know what a word is, as spelling is an unknown quantity to her, as you mathematicians would express it. She often takes syllables off of words & adds them or rather prefixes them to other words, but the story is heart-breaking, and told with a simplicity & eloquence that cannot be described, for it is not high-faluting eloquence, tho' sometimes it lapses into verse (and quite poetical verse too). I was always considered fanatical about Indians, but I have a wholly new conception of them now, and we civilized people may well stand abashed before their purity of life & their truthfulness.[47]

Sarah Winnemucca's *Life among the Piutes* is arranged in eight chapters, following in general a linear chronology of events from her childhood to the present in 1882-83. As a child she witnesses the first encounters between Paiutes and white people in the 1840s and 1850s and the impact of the westward movement on the overland trails on tribal life. Retrospectively, she describes the first coming of white people as the central event of her childhood, the event that marks the beginning of the story of her life, and that—as in many other Native autobiographical narratives—is seen prophesied in visions and dreams.[48] Thus she puts herself in the position of both tribal historian and autobiographical narrator. From the beginning of her text, she uses direct speech and dialogue as narrative devices, which give the text an extraordinary vividness and preserve a sense of the oral quality of her narration; at the same time they add a dramatic element to her story, especially in the rendering of speeches. The purpose of this first chapter is clearly to establish the peaceful intent of the Paiutes in their relations with whites, revising the idea of hostile savages promoted by bloodcurdling tales of emigrant trains attacked by Paiute bands in the years of increasing emigration to California. As a matter of fact, the coming of the emigrant trains every summer lends a structure and repetitive rhythmic pattern to the narrative, which reproduces the movement of white people closing in upon the migratory Paiutes from all sides. The Paiutes' frontier, the encounter with a foreign people on the territory they call their homeland, of course does not resemble the Turnerian concept of *the* American frontier. Although the Paiutes are reaching out to welcome the strangers, they are encircled and finally expelled from their homeland. . . .

At the end of the narrative, Sarah Winnemucca is a woman in between, attacked from all sides—a woman desperately alone, yet trying to assume a collective voice. As if she had given up her own voice as speaker, and deferred the talking to her readers, she now appeals to them in the name of all tribes:

> Hear our pitiful cry to you, sweep away the agency system; give us homes to live in, for God's sake and for humanity's sake. I left my poor people in despair, I knew I had so many against me . . . I see that all who say they are working for Indians are against me. (243)

And she goes on to appeal not only to her readers' national values, but also to their sense of morality. Again she speaks as part of a group, of Indians confronting whites:

> For shame! for shame! You dare to cry out Liberty, when you hold us in places against our will, driving us from place to place as if we were beasts. Ah, there is one thing you cannot say of the Indian. You call him savage, and everything that is bad but one; but, thanks be to God, I am so proud to say that my people have never outraged your women, or have even insulted them by looks or words. Can you say the same of the negroes or the whites? They do commit some most horrible outrages on your women, but you do not drive them round like dogs. Oh, my dear readers, talk for us, and if the white people will treat us like human beings, we will behave like a people; but if we are treated by white savages as if we are savages, we are relentless and desperate; yet not more so than any other badly treated people. Oh, dear friends, I am pleading for God and for humanity. (244)

And thus ends her autobiographical narrative: "Finding it impossible to do any thing for my people I did not return to Yakima, but after I left Vancouver Barracks I went to my sister in Montana. After my marriage to Mr. Hopkins I visited my people once more at Pyramid Lake Reservation, and they urged me again to come to the East and talk for them, and so I have come" (246).

Appended to the main text is a note by the editor asking readers to sign the petition made by Sarah Winnemucca to the next Congress, asking to restore Malheur Reservation in severalty to the Paiutes, and to let the portion of Paiutes removed to Yakima return to Malheur. The language of the petition reveals its link to a female rhetoric of domesticity:

> And especially do we petition for the return of that portion of the tribe arbitrarily removed from the Malheur Reservation . . . in which removal families were ruthlessly separated, and have never ceased to pine for husbands, wives, and children, which restoration was pledged to them by the Secretary of the Interior in 1880, but has not been fulfilled. (247)

Mary Mann finally draws attention to the last three pages of the appendix, which will show that the friends of the agents she criticizes are active to discredit her; but it has been ascertained that every definite charge made to the Indian office has no better endorsement than the name of Reinhard, who is characterized, to my personal knowledge, by some of the army officers who have known of his proceedings, as "a thoroughly wicked and unscrupulous man." (248)[63]

The appendix is not only commented on by the editor, but also held together by Sarah's voice who finally places her text within the context of a campaign aimed at discrediting her as a spokes*woman:*

> I know now, from the highest authority, that the government was deceived by the agent, Renehart, who said the Indians would not stay at the Malheur Reservation. After being driven away by starvation, after having had every promise broken, falsehoods were told about them and *there was no one to take their part but a woman. Every one knows what a woman must suffer who undertakes to act against bad men. My reputation has been assailed, and it is done so cunningly that I cannot prove it to be unjust. I can only protest that it is unjust, and say that wherever I have been known, I have been believed and trusted.* . . . Those who have maligned me have not known me. It is true that my people sometimes distrust me, but that is because words have been put into my mouth which have turned out to be nothing but idle wind. Promises have been made to me in high places that have not been kept, and I have had to suffer for this in the loss of my people's confidence. (258)

Sarah Winnemucca Hopkins's *Life among the Piutes* has answered many of my initial questions about the role of gender in Indian-white relations and about the way cultural contact affected Native American women's lives. Indian-white relations, as they emerge in Sarah's narrative, are highly charged with the issues of sexual violence and sexual stereotyping. Sarah herself uses her text to fight against stereotypical images of Native American women, and although she draws on the image of the Indian princess, it mainly serves as a legitimizing strategy to underline her authority as spokeswoman. Her narrative represents the attempt of a Native American woman to become real as a woman beyond stereotypes. It also counters the image of Sarah as the "fallen woman" by depicting her relationship with her sister-in-law and other women, and by presenting her, also through the voice of her editor, as part of a female community. Acculturation, however, is a double-edged sword in Sarah's narrative, as ambiguous as the image of Sarah's personality which emerges in this text. As the product of an encounter between female voices, East and West, white and Indian, the narrative presents a rather complex concept of the woman and tribal person. By referring to the role of women in the political affairs of the Paiute

band, and by emphasizing the absence of the separation of female and male spheres in the tribe, Sarah Winnemucca draws authority for her public role as spokeswoman from both this position of women within the tribe and from her kinship position as daughter and granddaughter of chiefs. Placing her life story within the context of the story of her tribe, she takes on the various roles of peacemaker, interpreter, helper of both whites and Paiutes, as scout, chieftain, and woman warrior, thus legitimizing her public role with role models which are apparently in accord with Paiute concepts of womanhood. Her acts of heroism and self-reliance thus have their roots in her conception of her Native American womanhood.

On the other hand, Sarah Winnemucca draws upon images of genteel Victorian womanhood by presenting herself, within the context of feminine respectability, as a lady in appearance and manners, distancing herself from the image of the erotic or even lewd Native American "squaw." Yet whenever she emphasizes her own morality and modesty, she explains their rationale by pointing to her Paiute upbringing, and it is the voice of the editor that relates principles of Paiute womanhood to those of white respectable womanhood. When Sarah Winnemucca is seen crying, she cries over the plight of her people, which of course may have a special effect on her audience since it shows her as a sensitive woman. However, references to other aspects of "true womanhood," such as piety, submissiveness, and domesticity, are significantly lacking. Sarah Winnemucca does not present herself as a religious woman. Neither does she claim for herself a "civilizing" influence on her people. References to these aspects of ideal white womanhood are, however, contained in her remarks on white women which underline her own arguments by valuing genteel army wives and kind pioneer women over rough frontier women and immoral Indian agents' wives. Although Sarah hints at her domestic work for white women in Nevada and Oregon, there are no references to herself as a domestic woman. The idea, or rather the ideology, of "domestic feminism" so often elaborated on in the literature on white nineteenth-century women is only appealed to in references to her people's search for a permanent home where families can be reunited. She herself presents herself rather as a working woman who, although proud of her achievements, describes them as acts of necessity and duty.

Sarah Winnemucca's narrative exemplifies the necessity for a multicultural framework in the study of women's experience, which so far has focused predominantly on white middle-class women—a framework that should also allow for an analysis that takes class into account. What is presented in Sarah Winnemucca's *Life among the Piutes,* is the image of a complex personality who draws her strength from a cultural encounter whose negative impact, in the form of the white control of Native

American lives, is at the center of her story. How far Sarah had control over her own narrative in the encounter with her editor and publisher, still remains to be debated. Nevertheless, although the nature of these women's collaboration still needs to be investigated more thoroughly, I would venture the thesis that this text is very much Sarah's own in the sense that she can present the complexity of her situation, both as a mouthpiece of many voices, and as a woman who is forced to find her own voice in order to defend her personal dignity. Sarah Winnemucca emerges, on the one hand, as an individual who has to defend her reputation as a modest and respectable Native American woman against both white and Indian voices, a woman who stands alone under attacks from various sides. On the other hand, she transgresses the boundaries imposed on white respectable womanhood. We see her as a tribal person committed to her people through bonds of love and kinship, drawing strength for her heroic deeds from an allegedly tribal, or rather Indian, role model of the woman warrior. It is her gender which, in the eyes of both her supporters and her attackers, singles her out. She has spoken out both as a daughter and a Paiute spokesperson, never claiming a voice of her own. But she was most vulnerable and alone when she had to find her own voice as a woman between two worlds.

Notes

I would like to thank Eve Keitel for her thoughtful reading of this article's various drafts.

[1] Hopkins (1969).

[2] The term has been used by Slotkin (1973).

[3] Slotkin (1973) shows how women have been used as the motive behind male manipulation and destruction of both the natural world and the indigenous inhabitants of the frontier. Women are symbolically present in the popular mythology of the frontier as civilizing maternal forces from whom men flee into the wilderness or as legitimation for the conquest of Indian land.

[4] See Jeffrey (1979); Faragher (1979); Schlissel (1982); Myres (1982); Riley (1988). The only major work dealing with the imaginative constructs women have projected onto the western frontiers in their literary writings is Kolodny (1984). A textual study of women's private writings has been undertaken by Hampsten (1982). Articles of an interdisciplinary sort on western women have been collected in Armitage and Jameson (1987) and Norwood and Monk (1987).

[5] See Riley (1985:83-84).

[6] See Jensen and Miller (1980:185). See also DuBois and Ruiz (1990). Riley (1984:xvi) has examined the relation-

ship between white women and Native Americans, taking as her basis the diaries and letters of westering women. Yet she puts no special focus on the relations between white and Native American women. The perspective of her study is "that of white history rather than white-Indian or Indian history." Myres (1982) has included Native American women's perspectives, based on a reading of oral and written sources. The articles included in Myres (1982) and Norwood and Monk (1987) demonstrate this growing concern for a multicultural framework in the study of western women.

[7] On Native American autobiography see Krupat (1985); Brumble (1988); Sands (1982:55-65); Theisz (1981:65-80). On women's autobiography and personal narratives, see Personal Narratives Group (1989); Hoffmann and Culley (1985); Brodzki and Schenck (1988); Buss (1989:1-17).

[8] Krupat (1985:31) has argued that the principle constituting the Native American autobiography as a genre is the principle of "original bicultural composite composition." Krupat (1989:133-134, 141, 149) refines this definition by describing the model of the Native American autobiography as a dialogic model of the self. In their introduction, Brodzki and Schenck (1988:2) state that "the implicit attitude toward the masculine representative self . . . is reflective . . . of a generic exclusivity in the critical treatment of autobiography, rendering this model inadequate for a theory of women's autobiography." They regard "self-definition in relation to significant others" (Brodzki and Schenck 1988:8) as the most pervasive characteristic of the female autobiography.

[9] See Albers and Medicine (1983); Green (1983); Powers (1986); Liberty (1982:10-19); Mathes (1980:20-25). See also Williams (1986).

[10] See the literary criticism on Silko's novel *Ceremony,* for example, Herzog (1985: 25-36); Rubenstein (1987); Allen (1986:118-126).

[11] See Peyer (1981:1-12; 386-402).

[12] This issue is discussed in Armitage and Jameson (1987:51ff). Various papers in this collection, particularly those by Kirk and Smith, explore whether gender has an impact on intercultural relationships, and whether women and men view people of different cultures differently.

[13] The value of an interpretation of Native American women's life stories for an understanding of the complexities of cultural contact and change is increasingly acknowledged. One of the first works analyzing these life stories was Bataille and Sands (1984).

Carr's (1988:131-153) excellent essay on native women's life stories of the twentieth century, which has profited from recent research in both feminist and poststructuralist theory, demonstrates the fruitfulness of an approach that is sensitive to the textuality and the special "framing" of these texts.

[14] See Fischer (1977); Luchetti (1982); Moynihan, Armitage, and Dichamp (1990).

[15] In the historical and anthropological literature, there are many variations for the spelling of *Paiute*. I have used the popular blanket term *Paiute* throughout the text, except in direct quotations.

[16] See Hopkins (1969:5), chaps. 1-4; Fowler (1978:33-42); Ruoff (1982:151-152).

[17] The term *Indian Princess* occurs very often in the literature on Sarah Winnemucca. Gehm (1975) uses the term rather uncritically, without being aware of the ideological implications of this stereotype. Green (1975:698-714) has explored how the paradoxical but positive image of the Indian Princess, "exotic and sexual, yet maternal and contradictorily virginal" (Green 1975:709-710), is paired with the negative image of the Indian Squaw in the national imagination. Both the native woman's "nobility as a Princess and her savagery as a Squaw are defined in terms of her relationships with male figures" (Green 1975:703), either as exotic helper and guide, whose "sexuality can be hinted at but never realized" (Green 1975:711) or as real woman and sexual partner, in which case the positive image is converted into a negative one.

[18] Peabody's letters of the years 1883-1887 show how Sarah and the Paiute case figure prominently in the old lady's correspondence before her death in 1894. See Ronda (1984:esp. 397-398, 414-415, 439-440, 442-443).

[19] For these biographical details, see Canfield (1983).

[20] See Fowler (1978:38); Brumble (1988:61); Ruoff (1982:151).

[21] See Peyer (1981:6, 392).

[22] See Ruoff (1987:1041).

[23] See Ruoff (1987:1040).

[24] See Ruoff (1990). I am relying here on Brumble's interpretation of Ruoff's article, since I have not yet been able to locate the publication.

[25] See Brumble (1988:63).

[26] See Brumble (1988:69-71).

[27] See Brumble (1988:65-66).

[28] See Brumble (1988:71).

[29] See Bataille and Sands (1984:21).

[30] This argument is partially supported by Canfield's biography of Sarah Winnemucca, which is an invaluable source on the reception of her lectures, since it collects evidence from both the eastern and the western contemporary press. Although she is concerned mainly with the accurate historical compilation of the "facts" of a life gathered from various sources, and does not consider the textual implications of her sources, Canfield (1983) provides a fascinating reconstruction of the life of Sarah Winnemucca.

[31] See Mathes (1990:15-16, csp. 14).

[32] See Ruoff (1987:1041).

[33] See Peyer (1981:392); Fowler (1978:33).

[34] See Brumble (1988:65).

[35] Much of the scholarship on nineteenth-century women's history is based on the assumption that women's lives, particularly among the emerging bourgeoisie in the first half of the nineteenth century, were lived in a separate domestic "sphere," on which basis they were able to claim a kind of social power distinct from that of men. Reified in prescriptive literature, realized in daily life, and ritualized in female collectivities, this "woman's sphere" came to be seen as the foundation of women's culture and community within the Victorian middle class. See Hewitt (1990:1-14). Welter (1966:151-174) has first identified the construction of a new ideology of gender that defined the "true woman" as pious, pure, domestic, and submissive. Other formative works on Victorian womanhood are Cott (1977); Smith-Rosenberg (1975:1-29).

[36] Note the way Sarah appears as the "Indian Princess' in De Quille (1947:11-12, 201-202).

[37] See Green (1975:713).

[38] See Brumble (1988:68, 69).

[39] See Fowler (1978:33): "Robert Heizer (1960:3) suggests that her 'selfless motives and tremendous energies and high purpose make her a person to admire in the history of our far West.' Omer Stewart (1939:129) on the other hand, described her as 'ambitious, educated, . . . trying to attain self-aggrandizement by exalting her father.'"

[40] See Canfield (1983:172ff) where she quotes affidavits to Washington, signed by nine gentlemen of Can-

yon City: "That this woman has been several times married, but that by reason of her adulterous and drunken habits, neither squawmen nor Indians would long live with her, that in addition to her character of Harlot and drunkard, she merits and possesses that of a notorious liar and malicious schemer [sic]."

[41] Ryan (1990:48-94) discusses this double bind of women who began to claim the public, political arena for themselves in Victorian America.

[42] See Fowler (1978:37): "In all fairness to her detractors, Sarah was short tempered, particularly in the context of offenses to her people, and she was known to take a drink and to scream and swear on occasion. She also had three husbands, two of them White men."

[43] Note especially the titles of Peabody's and Mann's publications that emphasize the "moral" as a key term, although it might have had a different significance for nineteenth-century readers than for a twentieth-century audience. See Peabody and Mann (1870); Peabody (1874).

[44] See Krupat (1985:33).

[45] See Krupat (1985:33).

[46] See Hopkins (1969:5); further references to the autobiography will appear in the text.

[47] Quoted in Canfield (1983:203).

[48] See the autobiography of Black Hawk (1964); see also *Co-ge-we-a, the Half-Blood* (Mourning Dove 1927).

[63] Peabody (1874:415) emphasized the same in a letter she wrote to the editor of the *Boston Daily Advertiser* in 1883: "Now I want to tell you how she has been misrepresented in some quarters—& how every thing has been thoroughly investigated & every thing is perfectly right about her. She has shared our bed & board for months this last summer and fall. I want the Daily Advertiser to recognize her & her cause—& think you will agree." One can imagine how important the support of this woman must have been for Sarah Winnemucca Hopkins at this difficult time in her life.

References

Albers, Patricia, and Beatrice Medicine. 1983. *The Hidden Half: Studies of Plains Indian Women.* Washington, D.C.: University Press of America.

Allen, Paula Gunn, ed. 1982. *Studies in American Indian Literature.* New York: Modern Language Association.

———. 1986. *The Sacred Hoop: Recovering the Feminine in American Indian Traditions.* Boston: Beacon Press.

Armitage, Susan, and Elizabeth Jameson, eds. 1989. *The Women's West.* Norman and London: University of Oklahoma Press.

Bataille, Gretchen, and Kathleen Sands. 1984. *American Indian Women: Telling Their Lives.* Lincoln and London: University of Nebraska Press.

Black Hawk. 1964. *Black Hawk: An Autobiography.* Edited by Donald Jackson. Urbana: University of Illinois Press.

Brimlow, George F. 1952. "The Life of Sarah Winnemucca: The Formative Years." *Oregon Historical Quarterly,* June 2:103-134.

Brodzki, Bella, and Celeste Schenck, eds. 1988. *Life/Lines: Theorizing Women's Autobiography.* Ithaca and London: Cornell University Press.

Brumble, H. David. 1988. *American Indian Autobiography.* Berkeley: University of California Press.

Buss, Helen M. 1989. "'The Dear Domestic Circle': Frameworks of the Literary Study of Women's Personal Narratives in Archival Collections." *Studies in Canadian Fiction* 1-17.

Canfield, Gae Whitney. 1983. *Sarah Winnemucca of the Northern Paiutes.* Norman: University of Oklahoma Press.

Carr, Helen. 1988. "In Other Words: Native American Women's Autobiography." In *Life/Lines,* edited by Bella Brodzki and Celeste Schenck, 131-153. Ithaca and London: Cornell University Press.

Cott, Nancy. *The Bonds of Womanhood: 'Women's Sphere' in New England, 1780-1835.* New Haven: Yale University Press.

De Quille, Dan (William Wright). 1947 [1876]. *The Big Bonanza.* New York: Knopf.

DuBois, Carol, and Vicki L. Ruiz, eds. 1990. *Unequal Sisters: A Multicultural Reader in U.S. Women's History.* New York and London: Routledge.

Faragher, John Mack. 1979. *Women and Men on the Overland Trail.* New Haven and London: Yale University Press.

Fischer, Christiane, ed. 1977. *Let Them Speak for Themselves: Women in the American West.* Hamden, Conn.: Shoestring Press.

Fowler, Catherine S. 1978. "Sarah Winnemucca, Northern Paiute, 1844-1891." In *American Indian Intellectuals,* edited by Margot Liberty, 33-42. St. Paul: West Publishing.

Gehm, Katherine. 1975. *Sarah Winnemucca: Most Extraordinary Woman of the Paiute Nation.* Phoenix: O'Sullivan.

Green, Rayna. 1975. "The Pocahontas Perplex: The Image of Indian Women in American Culture." *The Massachusetts Review,* Autumn 16:698-714.

————. 1980. "Native American Women." *Signs,* Winter 6:248-267.

————. 1983. *Native American Women: A Contextual Bibliography.* Bloomington: Indiana University Press.

Hampsten, Elizabeth. 1982. *Read This Only to Yourself: The Private Writings of Midwestern Women, 1880-1910.* Bloomington: Indiana University Press.

Herzog, Kristin. 1985. "Feeling Man and Thinking Woman: Gender in Silko's *Ceremony.*" *MELUS,* Spring 12:1:25-36.

Hewitt, Nancy A. 1990. "Beyond the Search for Sisterhood: American Women's History in the 1980s." In *Unequal Sisters,* edited by Carol DuBois and Vicki L. Ruiz, 1-14. New York and London: Routledge.

Hoffmann, Leonore, and Margo Culley, eds. 1985. *Women's Personal Narratives: Essays in Criticism and Pedagogy.* New York: Modern Language Association.

Hopkins, Sarah Winnemucca. 1969 [1883]. *Life among the Piutes: Their Wrongs and Claims.* Edited by Mrs. Horace Mann. Bishop, Calif.: Sierra Media.

Jeffrey, Julie Roy. 1979. *Frontier Women: The Trans-Mississippi West 1840-1880.* New York: Hill and Wang.

Jensen, Joan, and Darlis A. Miller. 1980. "The Gentle Tamers Revisited: New Approaches to the History of Women in the American West." *Pacific Historical Review* 49:2:173-212.

Kolodny, Annette. 1984. *The Land Before Her: Fantasy and Experience of the American Frontiers, 1630-1860.* Chapel Hill and London: University of North Carolina Press.

Krupat, Arnold. 1985. *For Those Who Come After: A Study of Native American Autobiography.* Berkeley: University of California Press.

————. 1989. *The Voice in the Margin: Native American Literature and the Canon.* Berkeley: University of California Press.

Liberty, Margot. 1982. "Hell Came with Horses: Plains Indian Women in the Equestrian Era." *Montana, The Magazine of Western History,* Summer 32:10-19.

Luchetti, Cathy, in collaboration with Carol Olwell. 1982. *Women of the West.* St. George, Ut.: Antelope Island Press.

Mann, Mary Tyler, and Elizabeth Palmer Peabody. 1870. *Moral Culture of Infancy and Kindergarten Guide.* New York: Schenterhorn.

Mathes, Valerie Sherer. 1980. "American Indian Women and the Catholic Church." *North Dakota History,* Fall 20-25.

————. 1990. *Helen Hunt Jackson and Her Indian Reform Legacy.* Austin: University of Texas Press.

Mourning Dove (Hum-ishu-ma). 1929. *Co-ge-we-a, The Half-Blood: A Depiction of the Great Montana Cattle Range,* as told to Sho-pow-tan. Boston: Four Seas.

Moynihan, Ruth B., Susan Armitage, and Christiane Fischer Dichamp, eds. 1990. *So Much to Be Done: Women Settlers on the Mining and Ranching Frontier.* Lincoln and London: University of Nebraska Press.

Myres, Sandra L. 1982. *Westering Women and the Frontier Experience, 1800-1915.* Albuquerque: University of New Mexico Press.

Norwood, Vera, and Janice Monk, eds. 1987. *The Desert Is No Lady: Southwestern Landscapes in Women's Writing and Art.* New Haven and London: Yale University Press.

Peabody, Elizabeth Palmer. 1874. *Record of Mr. Alcott's School, Exemplifying the Principles and Methods of Moral Culture.* 3d ed. Boston: Roberts Brothers.

Personal Narratives Group, ed. 1989. *Interpreting Women's Lives: Feminist Theory and Personal Narratives.* Bloomington: Indiana University Press.

Peyer, Bernd C. 1981. "Autobiographical Works Written by Native Americans." *Amerikastudien/American Studies* 26:3/4:386-402.

————. 1981. "The Importance of Native American Authors." *American Indian Culture and Research Journal* 5:3:1-12.

Powers, Marla. 1986. *Oglala Women: Myth, Ritual, and Reality*. Chicago: University of Chicago Press.

Riley, Glenda. 1984. *Women and Indians on the Frontier, 1825-1915*. Albuquerque: University of New Mexico Press.

———. 1985. "Women on the Great Plains: Recent Developments in Research." *Great Plains Quarterly* 5:2:81-92.

———. 1988. *The Female Frontier: A Comparative View of Women on the Prairie and Plains*. Lawrence: University Press of Kansas.

Ronda, Bruce A., ed. 1984. *Letters of Elizabeth Palmer Peabody: American Renaissance Woman*. Middletown, Conn.: Wesleyan University Press.

Rubenstein, Roberta. 1987. *Boundaries of the Self: Gender, Culture, Fiction*. Urbana and Chicago: University of Illinois Press.

Ruoff, A. LaVonne Brown. 1982. "Old Traditions and New Forms." In *Studies in American Indian Literature*, edited by Paula Gunn Allen, 147-168. New York: Modern Language Association.

———. 1987. "Western American Indian Writers, 1854-1960." In *A Literary History of the American West*, edited by The Western Literature Association, 1038-1057. Fort Worth: Texas Christian University Press.

———. 1990. "Nineteenth-Century American Indian Autobiographers: William Apes, George Copway, and Sarah Winnemucca." In *Redefining American Literary History*, edited by A. LaVonne Ruoff and Jerry Ward. New York: Modern Language Association.

Ryan, Mary. 1990. *Women in Public: Between Banners and Ballots, 1825-1880*. Baltimore: Johns Hopkins Press.

Sands, Kathleen Mullen. 1982. "American Indian Autobiography," in *Studies in American Indian Literature*, edited by Paula Gunn Allen, 55-65. New York: Modern Language Association.

Schlissel, Lillian. 1982. *Women's Diaries of the Westward Journey*. New York: Schocken Books.

Schlissel, Lillian, Vicki L. Ruiz, and Janice Monk, eds. 1988. *Western Women: Their Land, Their Lives*. Albuquerque: University of New Mexico Press.

Slotkin, Richard. 1973. *Regeneration through Violence: The Mythology of the American Frontier, 1600-1860*. Middletown, Conn.: Wesleyan University Press.

Smith-Rosenberg, Carroll. 1975. "The Female World of Love and Ritual: Relations between Women in Nineteenth-Century America." *Signs,* Autumn 1:1-29.

Stoller, Marianne L. 1987. "Peregrians with Many Visions: Hispanic Women Artists of New Mexico, Southern Colorado, and Texas." In *The Desert Is No Lady,* edited by Vera Norwood and Janice Monk, 125-145. New Haven and London: Yale University Press.

Theisz, R. D. 1981. "The Critical Collaboration: Introductions as a Gateway to the Study of Native American Bi-Autobiography." *American Culture and Research Journal* 5:1:65-80.

Williams, Walter L. 1986. *The Spirit and the Flesh: Sexual Diversity in American Indian Culture*. Boston: Beacon Press.

FURTHER READING

Bibliography

Hardy, Gayle J. "Sarah Winnemucca (1844?-1891)." In *American Women Civil Rights Activists: Bibliographies of 68 Leaders, 1825-1992,* pp. 414-20. Jefferson, N. C.: McFarland & Company, Inc., 1993.

Bibliography of primary and secondary sources preceded by a brief biographical introduction.

Biography

Canfield, Gae Whitney. *Sarah Winnemucca of the Northern Paiutes*. Norman: University of Oklahoma Press, 1983, 306 p.

Comprehensive biography of Winnemucca.

Howard, O. O. "Famous Indian Chiefs." *St. Nicholas* XXXV, No. 9 (July 1908): 815-22.

Includes a laudatory biographical sketch of Winnemucca.

Morrison, Dorothy Nafus. *Chief Sarah: Sarah Winnemucca's Fight for Indian Rights*. New York: Atheneum, 1980, 170 p.

Biography based in large part upon Winnemucca's *Life among the Piutes*.

Ohrn, Deborah Gore. "Sarah Winnemucca." In *Herstory: Women Who Changed the World,* edited by Ruth Ashby and Deborah Gore Ohrn, pp. 135-37. New York: Viking, 1995.

Considers Winnemucca "an eloquent defender of the rights of Native Americans."

Richey, Elinor. "Sagebrush Princess With a Cause: Sarah Winnemucca's Lifelong Crusade for Paiute Indian Rights." *The American West* XII, No. 6 (November 1975): 30-33, 57-63.

Recounts Winnemucca's exploits with the United States Indian Bureau on behalf of the Paiute.

Criticism

Scherer, Joanna Cohan. "The Public Faces of Sarah Winnemucca." *Cultural Anthropology* 3, No. 2 (May 1988): 178-204.

Study of Winnemucca's manipulation of her public persona which principally employs pictorial evidence.

Scholten, Pat Creech. "Exploitation of Ethos: Sarah Winnemucca and Bright Eyes on the Lecture Tour." *Western Journal of Speech Communication* 41, No. 4 (Fall 1977): 233-44.

Examines the rhetorical strategies used by Winnemucca, and by another Native American woman, Bright Eyes, to undermine public stereotypes of Indians in the eastern United States.

Nineteenth-Century Literature Criticism

Cumulative Indexes
Volumes 1-79

How to Use This Index

20/1631
See Upward, Allen
A/C Cross
See Lawrence, T(homas) E(dward)
Abasiyanik, Sait Faik 1906-1954
See Sait Faik
See also CA 123
Abbey, Edward 1927-1989 **CLC 36, 59**
See also CA 45-48; 128; CANR 2, 41; MTCW
2
Abbott, Lee K(ittredge) 1947- .... **CLC 48**
See also CA 124; CANR 51; DLB 130
Abe, Kobo 1924-1993 **CLC 8, 22, 53, 81; DAM NOV**
See also CA 65-68; 140; CANR 24, 60; DLB
182; MTCW 1, 2
Abelard, Peter c. 1079-c. 1142
CMLC 11
See also DLB 115, 208
Abell, Kjeld 1901-1961 **CLC 15**
See also CA 111
Abish, Walter 1931- **CLC 22**
See also CA 101; CANR 37; DLB 130
Abrahams, Peter (Henry) 1919- **CLC 4**
See also BW 1; CA 57-60; CANR 26; DLB 117;
MTCW 1, 2
Abrams, M(eyer) H(oward) 1912- **CLC 24**
See also CA 57-60; CANR 13, 33; DLB 67
Abse, Dannie 1923- **CLC 7, 29; DAB; DAM POET**
See also CA 53-56; CAAS 1; CANR 4, 46, 74;
DLB 27; MTCW 1
Achebe, (Albert) Chinua(lumogu) 1930- **CLC 1, 3, 5, 7, 11, 26, 51, 75; BLC 1; DA; DAB; DAC; DAM MST, MULT, NOV; WLC**
See also AAYA 15; BW 2, 3; CA 1-4R; CANR
6, 26, 47; CLR 20; DLB 117; MAICYA;
MTCW 1, 2; SATA 38, 40; SATA-Brief 38
Acker, Kathy 1948-1997 **CLC 45, 111**
See also CA 117; 122; 162; CANR 55
Ackroyd, Peter 1949- **CLC 34, 52**
See also CA 123; 127; CANR 51, 74; DLB 155;
INT 127; MTCW 1
Acorn, Milton 1923- **CLC 15; DAC**
See also CA 103; DLB 53; INT 103
Adamov, Arthur 1908-1970 **CLC 4, 25; DAM DRAM**
See also CA 17-18; 25-28R; CAP 2; MTCW 1
Adams, Alice (Boyd) 1926- **CLC 6, 13, 46; SSC 24**
See also CA 81-84; CANR 26, 53, 75; DLBY
86; INT CANR-26; MTCW 1, 2
Adams, Andy 1859-1935 **TCLC 56**
See also YABC 1
Adams, Brooks 1848-1927 **TCLC 80**
See also CA 123; DLB 47

Adams, Douglas (Noel) 1952- **CLC 27, 60; DAM POP**
See also AAYA 4; BEST 89:3; CA 106; CANR
34, 64; DLBY 83; JRDA; MTCW 1
Adams, Francis 1862-1893 .... **NCLC 33**
Adams, Henry (Brooks) 1838-1918 **TCLC 4, 52; DA; DAB; DAC; DAM MST**
See also CA 104; 133; CANR 77; DLB 12, 47,
189; MTCW 1
Adams, Richard (George) 1920- **CLC 4, 5, 18; DAM NOV**
See also AAYA 16; AITN 1, 2; CA 49-52;
CANR 3, 35; CLR 20; JRDA; MAICYA;
MTCW 1, 2; SATA 7, 69
Adamson, Joy(-Friederike Victoria) 1910-1980 **CLC 17**
See also CA 69-72; 93-96; CANR 22; MTCW
1; SATA 11; SATA-Obit 22
Adcock, Fleur 1934- .... **CLC 41**
See also CA 25-28R; CAAS 23; CANR 11, 34,
69; DLB 40
Addams, Charles (Samuel) 1912-1988 **CLC 30**
See also CA 61-64; 126; CANR 12, 79
Addams, Jane 1860-1945 .... **TCLC 76**
Addison, Joseph 1672-1719 .... **LC 18**
See also CDBLB 1660-1789; DLB 101
Adler, Alfred (F.) 1870-1937 .... **TCLC 61**
See also CA 119; 159
Adler, C(arole) S(chwerdtfeger) 1932- .. **CLC 35**
See also AAYA 4; CA 89-92; CANR 19, 40;
JRDA; MAICYA; SAAS 15; SATA 26, 63,
102
Adler, Renata 1938- .... **CLC 8, 31**
See also CA 49-52; CANR 5, 22, 52; MTCW 1
Ady, Endre 1877-1919 .... **TCLC 11**
See also CA 107
A.E. 1867-1935 .... **TCLC 3, 10**
See also Russell, George William
Aeschylus 525B.C.-456B.C. ..**CMLC 11; DA; DAB; DAC; DAM DRAM, MST; DC 8; WLCS**
See also DLB 176
Aesop 620(?)B.C.-564(?)B.C. .... **CMLC 24**
See also CLR 14; MAICYA; SATA 64
Affable Hawk
See MacCarthy, Sir(Charles Otto) Desmond
Africa, Ben
See Bosman, Herman Charles
Afton, Effie
See Harper, Frances Ellen Watkins
Agapida, Fray Antonio
See Irving, Washington
Agee, James (Rufus) 1909-1955 **TCLC 1, 19; DAM NOV**
See also AITN 1; CA 108; 148; CDALB 1941-
1968; DLB 2, 26, 152; MTCW 1
Aghill, Gordon

See Silverberg, Robert
Agnon, S(hmuel) Y(osef Halevi) 1888-1970
CLC 4, 8, 14; SSC 30
See also CA 17-18; 25-28R; CANR 60; CAP 2;
MTCW 1, 2
Agrippa von Nettesheim, Henry Cornelius
1486-1535 .... **LC 27**
Aherne, Owen
See Cassill, R(onald) V(erlin)
Ai 1947- .... **CLC 4, 14, 69**
See also CA 85-88; CAAS 13; CANR 70; DLB
120
Aickman, Robert (Fordyce) 1914-1981 **CLC 57**
See also CA 5-8R; CANR 3, 72
Aiken, Conrad (Potter) 1889-1973 **CLC 1, 3, 5, 10, 52; DAM NOV, POET; PC 26; SSC 9**
See also CA 5-8R; 45-48; CANR 4, 60; CDALB
1929-1941; DLB 9, 45, 102; MTCW 1, 2;
SATA 3, 30
Aiken, Joan (Delano) 1924- .... **CLC 35**
See also AAYA 1, 25; CA 9-12R; CANR 4, 23,
34, 64; CLR 1, 19; DLB 161; JRDA;
MAICYA; MTCW 1; SAAS 1; SATA 2, 30,
73
Ainsworth, William Harrison 1805-1882
NCLC 13
See also DLB 21; SATA 24
Aitmatov, Chingiz (Torekulovich) 1928- **CLC 71**
See also CA 103; CANR 38; MTCW 1; SATA
56
Akers, Floyd
See Baum, L(yman) Frank
Akhmadulina, Bella Akhatovna 1937- **CLC 53; DAM POET**
See also CA 65-68
Akhmatova, Anna 1888-1966 **CLC 11, 25, 64; DAM POET; PC 2**
See also CA 19-20; 25-28R; CANR 35; CAP 1;
MTCW 1, 2
Aksakov, Sergei Timofeyvich 1791-1859
NCLC 2
See also DLB 198
Aksenov, Vassily
See Aksyonov, Vassily (Pavlovich)
Akst, Daniel 1956- .... **CLC 109**
See also CA 161
Aksyonov, Vassily (Pavlovich) 1932- **CLC 22, 37, 101**
See also CA 53-56; CANR 12, 48, 77
Akutagawa, Ryunosuke 1892-1927 **TCLC 16**
See also CA 117; 154
Alain 1868-1951 .... **TCLC 41**
See also CA 163
Alain-Fournier .... **TCLC 6**
See also Fournier, Henri Alban
See also DLB 65
Alarcon, Pedro Antonio de 1833-1891 **NCLC 1**

DAM DRAM
See also AITN 1; CA 21-24R; CANR 32; DLB 7

Anderson, Sherwood 1876-1941 **TCLC 1, 10, 24; DA; DAB; DAC; DAM MST, NOV; SSC 1; WLC**
See also AAYA 30; CA 104; 121; CANR 61; CDALB 1917-1929; DLB 4, 9, 86; DLBD 1; MTCW 1, 2

Andier, Pierre
See Desnos, Robert

Andouard
See Giraudoux, (Hippolyte) Jean

Andrade, Carlos Drummond de .... **CLC 18**
See also Drummond de Andrade, Carlos

Andrade, Mario de 1893-1945 .... **TCLC 43**

Andreae, Johann V(alentin) 1586-1654 **LC 32**
See also DLB 164

Andreas-Salome, Lou 1861-1937 ... **TCLC 56**
See also DLB 66

Andress, Lesley
See Sanders, Lawrence

Andrewes, Lancelot 1555-1626 .... **LC 5**
See also DLB 151, 172

Andrews, Cicily Fairfield
See West, Rebecca

Andrews, Elton V.
See Pohl, Frederik

Andreyev, Leonid (Nikolaevich) 1871-1919 **TCLC 3**
See also CA 104

Andric, Ivo 1892-1975 .... **CLC 8**
See also CA 81-84; 57-60; CANR 43, 60; DLB 147; MTCW 1

Androvar
See Prado (Calvo), Pedro

Angelique, Pierre
See Bataille, Georges

Angell, Roger 1920- .... **CLC 26**
See also CA 57-60; CANR 13, 44, 70; DLB 171, 185

Angelou, Maya 1928-**CLC 12, 35, 64, 77; BLC 1; DA; DAB; DAC; DAM MST, MULT, POET, POP; WLCS**
See also AAYA 7, 20; BW 2, 3; CA 65-68; CANR 19, 42, 65; CDALBS; CLR 53; DLB 38; MTCW 1, 2; SATA 49

Anna Comnena 1083-1153 .... **CMLC 25**

Annensky, Innokenty (Fyodorovich) 1856-1909 **TCLC 14**
See also CA 110; 155

Annunzio, Gabriele d'
See D'Annunzio, Gabriele

Anodos
See Coleridge, Mary E(lizabeth)

Anon, Charles Robert
See Pessoa, Fernando (Antonio Nogueira)

Anouilh, Jean (Marie Lucien Pierre) 1910-1987 **CLC 1, 3, 8, 13, 40, 50; DAM DRAM; DC 8**
See also CA 17-20R; 123; CANR 32; MTCW 1, 2

Anthony, Florence
See Ai

Anthony, John
See Ciardi, John (Anthony)

Anthony, Peter
See Shaffer, Anthony (Joshua); Shaffer, Peter (Levin)

Anthony, Piers 1934- ..... **CLC 35; DAM POP**
See also AAYA 11; CA 21-24R; CANR 28, 56, 73; DLB 8; MTCW 1, 2; SAAS 22; SATA 84

Anthony, Susan B(rownell) 1916-1991**TCLC 84**

See also CA 89-92; 134

Antoine, Marc
See Proust, (Valentin-Louis-George-Eugene-) Marcel

Antoninus, Brother
See Everson, William (Oliver)

Antonioni, Michelangelo 1912- .... **CLC 20**
See also CA 73-76; CANR 45, 77

Antschel, Paul 1920-1970
See Celan, Paul
See also CA 85-88; CANR 33, 61; MTCW 1

Anwar, Chairil 1922-1949 .... **TCLC 22**
See also CA 121

Apess, William 1798-1839(?)**NCLC 73; DAM MULT**
See also DLB 175; NNAL

Apollinaire, Guillaume 1880-1918**TCLC 3, 8, 51; DAM POET; PC 7**
See also Kostrowitzki, Wilhelm Apollinaris de
See also CA 152; MTCW 1

Appelfeld, Aharon 1932- .... **CLC 23, 47**
See also CA 112; 133

Apple, Max (Isaac) 1941- .... **CLC 9, 33**
See also CA 81-84; CANR 19, 54; DLB 130

Appleman, Philip (Dean) 1926- ....**CLC 51**
See also CA 13-16R; CAAS 18; CANR 6, 29, 56

Appleton, Lawrence
See Lovecraft, H(oward) P(hillips)

Apteryx
See Eliot, T(homas) S(tearns)

Apuleius, (Lucius Madaurensis) 125(?)-175(?) **CMLC 1**
See also DLB 211

Aquin, Hubert 1929-1977 .... **CLC 15**
See also CA 105; DLB 53

Aquinas, Thomas 1224(?)-1274 ..... **CMLC 33**
See also DLB 115

Aragon, Louis 1897-1982 ..**CLC 3, 22; DAM NOV, POET**
See also CA 69-72; 108; CANR 28, 71; DLB 72; MTCW 1, 2

Arany, Janos 1817-1882 .... **NCLC 34**

Aranyos, Kakay
See Mikszath, Kalman

Arbuthnot, John 1667-1735 .... **LC 1**
See also DLB 101

Archer, Herbert Winslow
See Mencken, H(enry) L(ouis)

Archer, Jeffrey (Howard) 1940- ..... **CLC 28; DAM POP**
See also AAYA 16; BEST 89:3; CA 77-80; CANR 22, 52; INT CANR-22

Archer, Jules 1915- ....**CLC 12**
See also CA 9-12R; CANR 6, 69; SAAS 5; SATA 4, 85

Archer, Lee
See Ellison, Harlan (Jay)

Arden, John 1930-**CLC 6, 13, 15; DAM DRAM**
See also CA 13-16R; CAAS 4; CANR 31, 65, 67; DLB 13; MTCW 1

Arenas, Reinaldo 1943-1990 . **CLC 41; DAM MULT; HLC**
See also CA 124; 128; 133; CANR 73; DLB 145; HW 1; MTCW 1

Arendt, Hannah 1906-1975 .... **CLC 66, 98**
See also CA 17-20R; 61-64; CANR 26, 60; MTCW 1, 2

Aretino, Pietro 1492-1556 .... **LC 12**

Arghezi, Tudor 1880-1967 ....**CLC 80**
See also Theodorescu, Ion N.
See also CA 167

Arguedas, Jose Maria 1911-1969**CLC 10, 18;**

HLCS 1
See also CA 89-92; CANR 73; DLB 113; HW 1

Argueta, Manlio 1936- .... **CLC 31**
See also CA 131; CANR 73; DLB 145; HW 1

Ariosto, Ludovico 1474-1533 .... **LC 6**

Aristides
See Epstein, Joseph

Aristophanes 450B.C.-385B.C.**CMLC 4; DA; DAB; DAC; DAM DRAM, MST; DC 2; WLCS**
See also DLB 176

Aristotle 384B.C.-322B.C. ... **CMLC 31; DA; DAB; DAC; DAM MST; WLCS**
See also DLB 176

Arlt, Roberto (Godofredo Christophersen) 1900-1942 ....**TCLC 29; DAM MULT; HLC**
See also CA 123; 131; CANR 67; HW 1, 2

Armah, Ayi Kwei 1939- . **CLC 5, 33; BLC 1; DAM MULT, POET**
See also BW 1; CA 61-64; CANR 21, 64; DLB 117; MTCW 1

Armatrading, Joan 1950- .... **CLC 17**
See also CA 114

Arnette, Robert
See Silverberg, Robert

Arnim, Achim von (Ludwig Joachim von Arnim) 1781-1831 ...... **NCLC 5; SSC 29**
See also DLB 90

Arnim, Bettina von 1785-1859 .... **NCLC 38**
See also DLB 90

Arnold, Matthew 1822-1888**NCLC 6, 29; DA; DAB; DAC; DAM MST, POET; PC 5; WLC**
See also CDBLB 1832-1890; DLB 32, 57

Arnold, Thomas 1795-1842 .... **NCLC 18**
See also DLB 55

Arnow, Harriette (Louisa) Simpson 1908-1986 **CLC 2, 7, 18**
See also CA 9-12R; 118; CANR 14; DLB 6; MTCW 1, 2; SATA 42; SATA-Obit 47

Arouet, Francois-Marie
See Voltaire

Arp, Hans
See Arp, Jean

Arp, Jean 1887-1966 .... **CLC 5**
See also CA 81-84; 25-28R; CANR 42, 77

Arrabal
See Arrabal, Fernando

Arrabal, Fernando 1932-.... **CLC 2, 9, 18, 58**
See also CA 9-12R; CANR 15

Arrick, Fran .... **CLC 30**
See also Gaberman, Judie Angell

Artaud, Antonin (Marie Joseph) 1896-1948 **TCLC 3, 36; DAM DRAM**
See also CA 104; 149; MTCW 1

Arthur, Ruth M(abel) 1905-1979 ...... **CLC 12**
See also CA 9-12R; 85-88; CANR 4; SATA 7, 26

Artsybashev, Mikhail (Petrovich) 1878-1927 **TCLC 31**
See also CA 170

Arundel, Honor (Morfydd) 1919-1973**CLC 17**
See also CA 21-22; 41-44R; CAP 2; CLR 35; SATA 4; SATA-Obit 24

Arzner, Dorothy 1897-1979 ....**CLC 98**

Asch, Sholem 1880-1957 .... **TCLC 3**
See also CA 105

Ash, Shalom
See Asch, Sholem

Ashbery, John (Lawrence) 1927-**CLC 2, 3, 4, 6, 9, 13, 15, 25, 41, 77; DAM POET; PC 26**
See also CA 5-8R; CANR 9, 37, 66; DLB 5,

165; DLBY 81; INT CANR-9; MTCW 1, 2
Ashdown, Clifford
    See Freeman, R(ichard) Austin
Ashe, Gordon
    See Creasey, John
Ashton-Warner, Sylvia (Constance) 1908-1984
    CLC 19
    See also CA 69-72; 112; CANR 29; MTCW 1,
    2
Asimov, Isaac 1920-1992 CLC 1, 3, 9, 19, 26,
    76, 92; DAM POP
    See also AAYA 13; BEST 90:2; CA 1-4R; 137;
    CANR 2, 19, 36, 60; CLR 12; DLB 8; DLBY
    92; INT CANR-19; JRDA; MAICYA;
    MTCW 1, 2; SATA 1, 26, 74
Assis, Joaquim Maria Machado de
    See Machado de Assis, Joaquim Maria
Astley, Thea (Beatrice May) 1925- .. CLC 41
    See also CA 65-68; CANR 11, 43, 78
Aston, James
    See White, T(erence) H(anbury)
Asturias, Miguel Angel 1899-1974 CLC 3, 8,
    13; DAM MULT, NOV; HLC
    See also CA 25-28; 49-52; CANR 32; CAP 2;
    DLB 113; HW 1; MTCW 1, 2
Atares, Carlos Saura
    See Saura (Atares), Carlos
Atheling, William
    See Pound, Ezra (Weston Loomis)
Atheling, William, Jr.
    See Blish, James (Benjamin)
Atherton, Gertrude (Franklin Horn) 1857-1948
    TCLC 2
    See also CA 104; 155; DLB 9, 78, 186
Atherton, Lucius
    See Masters, Edgar Lee
Atkins, Jack
    See Harris, Mark
Atkinson, Kate .... CLC 99
    See also CA 166
Attaway, William (Alexander) 1911-1986CLC
    92; BLC 1; DAM MULT
    See also BW 2, 3; CA 143; DLB 76
Atticus
    See Fleming, Ian (Lancaster); Wilson, (Thomas)
    Woodrow
Atwood, Margaret (Eleanor) 1939-CLC 2, 3,
    4, 8, 13, 15, 25, 44, 84; DA; DAB; DAC;
    DAM MST, NOV, POET; PC 8; SSC 2;
    WLC
    See also AAYA 12; BEST 89:2; CA 49-52;
    CANR 3, 24, 33, 59; DLB 53; INT CANR-
    24; MTCW 1, 2; SATA 50
Aubigny, Pierre d'
    See Mencken, H(enry) L(ouis)
Aubin, Penelope 1685-1731(?).............. LC 9
    See also DLB 39
Auchincloss, Louis (Stanton) 1917-CLC 4, 6,
    9, 18, 45; DAM NOV; SSC 22
    See also CA 1-4R; CANR 6, 29, 55; DLB 2;
    DLBY 80; INT CANR-29; MTCW 1
Auden, W(ystan) H(ugh) 1907-1973CLC 1, 2,
    3, 4, 6, 9, 11, 14, 43; DA; DAB; DAC; DAM
    DRAM, MST, POET; PC 1; WLC
    See also AAYA 18; CA 9-12R; 45-48; CANR
    5, 61; CDBLB 1914-1945; DLB 10, 20;
    MTCW 1, 2
Audiberti, Jacques 1900-1965CLC 38; DAM
    DRAM
    See also CA 25-28R
Audubon, John James 1785-1851 .. NCLC 47
Auel, Jean M(arie) 1936-CLC 31, 107; DAM
    POP

See also AAYA 7; BEST 90:4; CA 103; CANR
    21, 64; INT CANR-21; SATA 91
Auerbach, Erich 1892-1957 .... TCLC 43
    See also CA 118; 155
Augier, Emile 1820-1889................. NCLC 31
    See also DLB 192
August, John
    See De Voto, Bernard (Augustine)
Augustine 354-430CMLC 6; DA; DAB; DAC;
    DAM MST; WLCS
    See also DLB 115
Aurelius
    See Bourne, Randolph S(illiman)
Aurobindo, Sri
    See Ghose, Aurabinda
Austen, Jane 1775-1817 NCLC 1, 13, 19, 33,
    51; DA; DAB; DAC; DAM MST, NOV;
    WLC
    See also AAYA 19; CDBLB 1789-1832; DLB
    116
Auster, Paul 1947- ....CLC 47
    See also CA 69-72; CANR 23, 52, 75; MTCW
    1
Austin, Frank
    See Faust, Frederick (Schiller)
Austin, Mary (Hunter) 1868-1934 . TCLC 25
    See also CA 109; DLB 9, 78, 206
Autran Dourado, Waldomiro
    See Dourado, (Waldomiro Freitas) Autran
Averroes 1126-1198 .... CMLC 7
    See also DLB 115
Avicenna 980-1037 .... CMLC 16
    See also DLB 115
Avison, Margaret 1918- CLC 2, 4, 97; DAC;
    DAM POET
    See also CA 17-20R; DLB 53; MTCW 1
Axton, David
    See Koontz, Dean R(ay)
Ayckbourn, Alan 1939- CLC 5, 8, 18, 33, 74;
    DAB; DAM DRAM
    See also CA 21-24R; CANR 31, 59; DLB 13;
    MTCW 1, 2
Aydy, Catherine
    See Tennant, Emma (Christina)
Ayme, Marcel (Andre) 1902-1967 ..... CLC 11
    See also CA 89-92; CANR 67; CLR 25; DLB
    72; SATA 91
Ayrton, Michael 1921-1975 .... CLC 7
    See also CA 5-8R; 61-64; CANR 9, 21
Azorin .... CLC 11
    See also Martinez Ruiz, Jose
Azuela, Mariano 1873-1952 . TCLC 3; DAM
    MULT; HLC
    See also CA 104; 131; CANR 81; HW 1, 2;
    MTCW 1, 2
Baastad, Babbis Friis
    See Friis-Baastad, Babbis Ellinor
Bab
    See Gilbert, W(illiam) S(chwenck)
Babbis, Eleanor
    See Friis-Baastad, Babbis Ellinor
Babel, Isaac
    See Babel, Isaak (Emmanuilovich)
Babel, Isaak (Emmanuilovich) 1894-1941(?)
    TCLC 2, 13; SSC 16
    See also CA 104; 155; MTCW 1
Babits, Mihaly 1883-1941 .... TCLC 14
    See also CA 114
Babur 1483-1530 .... LC 18
Bacchelli, Riccardo 1891-1985 .... CLC 19
    See also CA 29-32R; 117
Bach, Richard (David) 1936- CLC 14; DAM
    NOV, POP

See also AITN 1; BEST 89:2; CA 9-12R; CANR
    18; MTCW 1; SATA 13
Bachman, Richard
    See King, Stephen (Edwin)
Bachmann, Ingeborg 1926-1973 ...... CLC 69
    See also CA 93-96; 45-48; CANR 69; DLB 85
Bacon, Francis 1561-1626 .... LC 18, 32
    See also CDBLB Before 1660; DLB 151
Bacon, Roger 1214(?)-1292 .... CMLC 14
    See also DLB 115
Bacovia, George .... TCLC 24
    See also Vasiliu, Gheorghe
Badanes, Jerome 1937- .... CLC 59
Bagehot, Walter 1826-1877 .... NCLC 10
    See also DLB 55
Bagnold, Enid 1889-1981 ...... CLC 25; DAM
    DRAM
    See also CA 5-8R; 103; CANR 5, 40; DLB 13,
    160, 191; MAICYA; SATA 1, 25
Bagritsky, Eduard 1895-1934 .... TCLC 60
Bagrjana, Elisaveta
    See Belcheva, Elisaveta
Bagryana, Elisaveta .... CLC 10
    See also Belcheva, Elisaveta
    See also DLB 147
Bailey, Paul 1937- .... CLC 45
    See also CA 21-24R; CANR 16, 62; DLB 14
Baillie, Joanna 1762-1851 .... NCLC 71
    See also DLB 93
Bainbridge, Beryl (Margaret) 1933-CLC 4, 5,
    8, 10, 14, 18, 22, 62; DAM NOV
    See also CA 21-24R; CANR 24, 55, 75; DLB
    14; MTCW 1, 2
Baker, Elliott 1922- ....CLC 8
    See also CA 45-48; CANR 2, 63
Baker, Jean H. .... TCLC 3, 10
    See also Russell, George William
Baker, Nicholson 1957- . CLC 61; DAM POP
    See also CA 135; CANR 63
Baker, Ray Stannard 1870-1946 .... TCLC 47
    See also CA 118
Baker, Russell (Wayne) 1925- .... CLC 31
    See also BEST 89:4; CA 57-60; CANR 11, 41,
    59; MTCW 1, 2
Bakhtin, M.
    See Bakhtin, Mikhail Mikhailovich
Bakhtin, M. M.
    See Bakhtin, Mikhail Mikhailovich
Bakhtin, Mikhail
    See Bakhtin, Mikhail Mikhailovich
Bakhtin, Mikhail Mikhailovich 1895-1975
    CLC 83
    See also CA 128; 113
Bakshi, Ralph 1938(?)-..................... CLC 26
    See also CA 112; 138
Bakunin, Mikhail (Alexandrovich) 1814-1876
    NCLC 25, 58
Baldwin, James (Arthur) 1924-1987CLC 1, 2,
    3, 4, 5, 8, 13, 15, 17, 42, 50, 67, 90; BLC 1;
    DA; DAB; DAC; DAM MST, MULT, NOV,
    POP; DC 1; SSC 10, 33; WLC
    See also AAYA 4; BW 1; CA 1-4R; 124; CABS
    1; CANR 3, 24; CDALB 1941-1968; DLB
    2, 7, 33; DLBY 87; MTCW 1, 2; SATA 9;
    SATA-Obit 54
Ballard, J(ames) G(raham) 1930-CLC 3, 6, 14,
    36; DAM NOV, POP; SSC 1
    See also AAYA 3; CA 5-8R; CANR 15, 39, 65;
    DLB 14, 207; MTCW 1, 2; SATA 93
Balmont, Konstantin (Dmitriyevich) 1867-1943
    TCLC 11
    See also CA 109; 155
Baltausis, Vincas

Beardsley, Aubrey 1872-1898 .... **NCLC 6**

Beattie, Ann 1947-**CLC 8, 13, 18, 40, 63; DAM NOV, POP; SSC 11**
See also BEST 90:2; CA 81-84; CANR 53, 73; DLBY 82; MTCW 1, 2

Beattie, James 1735-1803 .... **NCLC 25**
See also DLB 109

Beauchamp, Kathleen Mansfield 1888-1923
See Mansfield, Katherine
See also CA 104; 134; DA; DAC; DAM MST; MTCW 2

Beaumarchais, Pierre-Augustin Caron de 1732-1799 .... **DC 4**
See also DAM DRAM

Beaumont, Francis 1584(?)-1616**LC 33; DC 6**
See also CDBLB Before 1660; DLB 58, 121

Beauvoir, Simone (Lucie Ernestine Marie Bertrand) de 1908-1986 **CLC 1, 2, 4, 8, 14, 31, 44, 50, 71; DA; DAB; DAC; DAM MST, NOV; SSC 35; WLC**
See also CA 9-12R; 118; CANR 28, 61; DLB 72; DLBY 86; MTCW 1, 2

Becker, Carl (Lotus) 1873-1945 ..... **TCLC 63**
See also CA 157; DLB 17

Becker, Jurek 1937-1997 .... **CLC 7, 19**
See also CA 85-88; 157; CANR 60; DLB 75

Becker, Walter 1950- .... **CLC 26**

Beckett, Samuel (Barclay) 1906-1989**CLC 1, 2, 3, 4, 6, 9, 10, 11, 14, 18, 29, 57, 59, 83; DA; DAB; DAC; DAM DRAM, MST, NOV; SSC 16; WLC**
See also CA 5-8R; 130; CANR 33, 61; CDBLB 1945-1960; DLB 13, 15; DLBY 90; MTCW 1, 2

Beckford, William 1760-1844 .... **NCLC 16**
See also DLB 39

Beckman, Gunnel 1910- .... **CLC 26**
See also CA 33-36R; CANR 15; CLR 25; MAICYA; SAAS 9; SATA 6

Becque, Henri 1837-1899 .... **NCLC 3**
See also DLB 192

Beddoes, Thomas Lovell 1803-1849 **NCLC 3**
See also DLB 96

Bede c. 673-735 .... **CMLC 20**
See also DLB 146

Bedford, Donald F.
See Fearing, Kenneth (Flexner)

Beecher, Catharine Esther 1800-1878 **N C L C 30**
See also DLB 1

Beecher, John 1904-1980 .... **CLC 6**
See also AITN 1; CA 5-8R; 105; CANR 8

Beer, Johann 1655-1700 .... **LC 5**
See also DLB 168

Beer, Patricia 1924- .... **CLC 58**
See also CA 61-64; CANR 13, 46; DLB 40

Beerbohm, Max
See Beerbohm, (Henry) Max(imilian)

Beerbohm, (Henry) Max(imilian) 1872-1956 **TCLC 1, 24**
See also CA 104; 154; CANR 79; DLB 34, 100

Beer-Hofmann, Richard 1866-1945**TCLC 60**
See also CA 160; DLB 81

Begiebing, Robert J(ohn) · 1946- .... **CLC 70**
See also CA 122; CANR 40

Behan, Brendan 1923-1964 **CLC 1, 8, 11, 15, 79; DAM DRAM**
See also CA 73-76; CANR 33; CDBLB 1945-1960; DLB 13; MTCW 1, 2

Behn, Aphra 1640(?)-1689 **LC 1, 30, 42; DA; DAB; DAC; DAM DRAM, MST, NOV, POET; DC 4; PC 13; WLC**
See also DLB 39, 80, 131

Behrman, S(amuel) N(athaniel) 1893-1973 **CLC 40**
See also CA 13-16; 45-48; CAP 1; DLB 7, 44

Belasco, David 1853-1931 .... **TCLC 3**
See also CA 104; 168; DLB 7

Belcheva, Elisaveta 1893- .... **CLC 10**
See also Bagryana, Elisaveta

Beldone, Phil "Cheech"
See Ellison, Harlan (Jay)

Beleno
See Azuela, Mariano

Belinski, Vissarion Grigoryevich 1811-1848 **NCLC 5**
See also DLB 198

Belitt, Ben 1911- .... **CLC 22**
See also CA 13-16R; CAAS 4; CANR 7, 77; DLB 5

Bell, Gertrude (Margaret Lowthian) 1868-1926 **TCLC 67**
See also CA 167; DLB 174

Bell, J. Freeman
See Zangwill, Israel

Bell, James Madison 1826-1902 ... **TCLC 43; BLC 1; DAM MULT**
See also BW 1; CA 122; 124; DLB 50

Bell, Madison Smartt 1957- ..... **CLC 41, 102**
See also CA 111; CANR 28, 54, 73; MTCW 1

Bell, Marvin (Hartley) 1937-**CLC 8, 31; DAM POET**
See also CA 21-24R; CAAS 14; CANR 59; DLB 5; MTCW 1

Bell, W. L. D.
See Mencken, H(enry) L(ouis)

Bellamy, Atwood C.
See Mencken, H(enry) L(ouis)

Bellamy, Edward 1850-1898 .... **NCLC 4**
See also DLB 12

Bellin, Edward J.
See Kuttner, Henry

Belloc, (Joseph) Hilaire (Pierre Sebastien Rene Swanton) 1870-1953 **TCLC 7, 18; DAM POET; PC 24**
See also CA 106; 152; DLB 19, 100, 141, 174; MTCW 1; YABC 1

Belloc, Joseph Peter Rene Hilaire
See Belloc, (Joseph) Hilaire (Pierre Sebastien Rene Swanton)

Belloc, Joseph Pierre Hilaire
See Belloc, (Joseph) Hilaire (Pierre Sebastien Rene Swanton)

Belloc, M. A.
See Lowndes, Marie Adelaide (Belloc)

Bellow, Saul 1915-**CLC 1, 2, 3, 6, 8, 10, 13, 15, 25, 33, 34, 63, 79; DA; DAB; DAC; DAM MST, NOV, POP; SSC 14; WLC**
See also AITN 2; BEST 89:3; CA 5-8R; CABS 1; CANR 29, 53; CDALB 1941-1968; DLB 2, 28; DLBD 3; DLBY 82; MTCW 1, 2

Belser, Reimond Karel Maria de 1929-
See Ruyslinck, Ward
See also CA 152

Bely, Andrey .... **TCLC 7; PC 11**
See also Bugayev, Boris Nikolayevich
See also MTCW 1

Belyi, Andrei
See Bugayev, Boris Nikolayevich

Benary, Margot
See Benary-Isbert, Margot

Benary-Isbert, Margot 1889-1979 ....**CLC 12**
See also CA 5-8R; 89-92; CANR 4, 72; CLR 12; MAICYA; SATA 2; SATA-Obit 21

Benavente (y Martinez), Jacinto 1866-1954 **TCLC 3; DAM DRAM, MULT; HLCS 1**

See also CA 106; 131; CANR 81; HW 1, 2; MTCW 1, 2

Benchley, Peter (Bradford) 1940-. **CLC 4, 8; DAM NOV, POP**
See also AAYA 14; AITN 2; CA 17-20R; CANR 12, 35, 66; MTCW 1, 2; SATA 3, 89

Benchley, Robert (Charles) 1889-1945**T C L C 1, 55**
See also CA 105; 153; DLB 11

Benda, Julien 1867-1956 .... **TCLC 60**
See also CA 120; 154

Benedict, Ruth (Fulton) 1887-1948 **TCLC 60**
See also CA 158

Benedict, Saint c. 480-c. 547 .... **CMLC 29**

Benedikt, Michael 1935- .... **CLC 4, 14**
See also CA 13-16R; CANR 7; DLB 5

Benet, Juan 1927- .... **CLC 28**
See also CA 143

Benet, Stephen Vincent 1898-1943 .**TCLC 7; DAM POET; SSC 10**
See also CA 104; 152; DLB 4, 48, 102; DLBY 97; MTCW 1; YABC 1

Benet, William Rose 1886-1950 ... **TCLC 28; DAM POET**
See also CA 118; 152; DLB 45

Benford, Gregory (Albert) 1941- ..... **CLC 52**
See also CA 69-72; 175; CAAE 175; CAAS 27; CANR 12, 24, 49; DLBY 82

Bengtsson, Frans (Gunnar) 1894-1954**T C L C 48**
See also CA 170

Benjamin, David
See Slavitt, David R(ytman)

Benjamin, Lois
See Gould, Lois

Benjamin, Walter 1892-1940 .... **TCLC 39**
See also CA 164

Benn, Gottfried 1886-1956 .... **TCLC 3**
See also CA 106; 153; DLB 56

Bennett, Alan 1934-**CLC 45, 77; DAB; DAM MST**
See also CA 103; CANR 35, 55; MTCW 1, 2

Bennett, (Enoch) Arnold 1867-1931**TCLC 5, 20**
See also CA 106; 155; CDBLB 1890-1914; DLB 10, 34, 98, 135; MTCW 2

Bennett, Elizabeth
See Mitchell, Margaret (Munnerlyn)

Bennett, George Harold 1930-
See Bennett, Hal
See also BW 1; CA 97-100

Bennett, Hal .... **CLC 5**
See also Bennett, George Harold
See also DLB 33

Bennett, Jay 1912- .... **CLC 35**
See also AAYA 10; CA 69-72; CANR 11, 42, 79; JRDA; SAAS 4; SATA 41, 87; SATA-Brief 27

Bennett, Louise (Simone) 1919-**CLC 28; BLC 1; DAM MULT**
See also BW 2, 3; CA 151; DLB 117

Benson, E(dward) F(rederic) 1867-1940 **TCLC 27**
See also CA 114; 157; DLB 135, 153

Benson, Jackson J. 1930- .... **CLC 34**
See also CA 25-28R; DLB 111

Benson, Sally 1900-1972 .... **CLC 17**
See also CA 19-20; 37-40R; CAP 1; SATA 1, 35; SATA-Obit 27

Benson, Stella 1892-1933 .... **TCLC 17**
See also CA 117; 155; DLB 36, 162

Bentham, Jeremy 1748-1832 .... **NCLC 38**
See also DLB 107, 158

Bentley, E(dmund) C(lerihew) 1875-1956
  TCLC 12
    See also CA 108; DLB 70
Bentley, Eric (Russell) 1916- .... **CLC 24**
    See also CA 5-8R; CANR 6, 67; INT CANR-6
Beranger, Pierre Jean de 1780-1857 **NCLC 34**
Berdyaev, Nicolas
    See Berdyaev, Nikolai (Aleksandrovich)
Berdyaev, Nikolai (Aleksandrovich) 1874-1948
  TCLC 67
    See also CA 120; 157
Berdyayev, Nikolai (Aleksandrovich)
    See Berdyaev, Nikolai (Aleksandrovich)
Berendt, John (Lawrence) 1939- ..... **CLC 86**
    See also CA 146; CANR 75; MTCW 1
Beresford, J(ohn) D(avys) 1873-1947 . **T C L C
  81**
    See also CA 112; 155; DLB 162, 178, 197
Bergelson, David 1884-1952 .... **TCLC 81**
Berger, Colonel
    See Malraux, (Georges-)Andre
Berger, John (Peter) 1926- .... **CLC 2, 19**
    See also CA 81-84; CANR 51, 78; DLB 14, 207
Berger, Melvin H. 1927- .... **CLC 12**
    See also CA 5-8R; CANR 4; CLR 32; SAAS 2;
    SATA 5, 88
Berger, Thomas (Louis) 1924- **CLC 3, 5, 8, 11,
  18, 38; DAM NOV**
    See also CA 1-4R; CANR 5, 28, 51; DLB 2;
    DLBY 80; INT CANR-28; MTCW 1, 2
Bergman, (Ernst) Ingmar 1918- **CLC 16, 72**
    See also CA 81-84; CANR 33, 70; MTCW 2
Bergson, Henri(-Louis) 1859-1941 **TCLC 32**
    See also CA 164
Bergstein, Eleanor 1938- .... **CLC 4**
    See also CA 53-56; CANR 5
Berkoff, Steven 1937- .... **CLC 56**
    See also CA 104; CANR 72
Bermant, Chaim (Icyk) 1929- .... **CLC 40**
    See also CA 57-60; CANR 6, 31, 57
Bern, Victoria
    See Fisher, M(ary) F(rances) K(ennedy)
Bernanos, (Paul Louis) Georges 1888-1948
  TCLC 3
    See also CA 104; 130; DLB 72
Bernard, April 1956- .... **CLC 59**
    See also CA 131
Berne, Victoria
    See Fisher, M(ary) F(rances) K(ennedy)
Bernhard, Thomas 1931-1989 **CLC 3, 32, 61**
    See also CA 85-88; 127; CANR 32, 57; DLB
    85, 124; MTCW 1
Bernhardt, Sarah (Henriette Rosine) 1844-1923
  TCLC 75
    See also CA 157
Berriault, Gina 1926- . **CLC 54, 109; SSC 30**
    See also CA 116; 129; CANR 66; DLB 130
Berrigan, Daniel 1921- .... **CLC 4**
    See also CA 33-36R; CAAS 1; CANR 11, 43,
    78; DLB 5
Berrigan, Edmund Joseph Michael, Jr. 1934-
  1983
    See Berrigan, Ted
    See also CA 61-64; 110; CANR 14
Berrigan, Ted .... **CLC 37**
    See also Berrigan, Edmund Joseph Michael, Jr.
    See also DLB 5, 169
Berry, Charles Edward Anderson 1931-
    See Berry, Chuck
    See also CA 115
Berry, Chuck .... **CLC 17**
    See also Berry, Charles Edward Anderson
Berry, Jonas

    See Ashbery, John (Lawrence)
Berry, Wendell (Erdman) 1934- **CLC 4, 6, 8,
  27, 46; DAM POET**
    See also AITN 1; CA 73-76; CANR 50, 73; DLB
    5, 6; MTCW 1
Berryman, John 1914-1972 **CLC 1, 2, 3, 4, 6, 8,
  10, 13, 25, 62; DAM POET**
    See also CA 13-16; 33-36R; CABS 2; CANR
    35; CAP 1; CDALB 1941-1968; DLB 48;
    MTCW 1, 2
Bertolucci, Bernardo 1940- .... **CLC 16**
    See also CA 106
Berton, Pierre (Francis Demarigny) 1920-
  CLC 104
    See also CA 1-4R; CANR 2, 56; DLB 68; SATA
    99
Bertrand, Aloysius 1807-1841 .... **NCLC 31**
Bertran de Born c. 1140-1215 .... **CMLC 5**
Besant, Annie (Wood) 1847-1933 .... **TCLC 9**
    See also CA 105
Bessie, Alvah 1904-1985 .... **CLC 23**
    See also CA 5-8R; 116; CANR 2, 80; DLB 26
Bethlen, T. D.
    See Silverberg, Robert
Beti, Mongo ... **CLC 27; BLC 1; DAM MULT**
    See also Biyidi, Alexandre
    See also CANR 79
Betjeman, John 1906-1984 **CLC 2, 6, 10, 34,
  43; DAB; DAM MST, POET**
    See also CA 9-12R; 112; CANR 33, 56; CDBLB
    1945-1960; DLB 20; DLBY 84; MTCW 1,
    2
Bettelheim, Bruno 1903-1990 .... **CLC 79**
    See also CA 81-84; 131; CANR 23, 61; MTCW
    1, 2
Betti, Ugo 1892-1953 .... **TCLC 5**
    See also CA 104; 155
Betts, Doris (Waugh) 1932- ...... **CLC 3, 6, 28**
    See also CA 13-16R; CANR 9, 66, 77; DLBY
    82; INT CANR-9
Bevan, Alistair
    See Roberts, Keith (John Kingston)
Bey, Pilaff
    See Douglas, (George) Norman
Bialik, Chaim Nachman 1873-1934 **TCLC 25**
    See also CA 170
Bickerstaff, Isaac
    See Swift, Jonathan
Bidart, Frank 1939- .... **CLC 33**
    See also CA 140
Bienek, Horst 1930- .... **CLC 7, 11**
    See also CA 73-76; DLB 75
Bierce, Ambrose (Gwinett) 1842-1914(?)
  **TCLC 1, 7, 44; DA; DAC; DAM MST; SSC
  9; WLC**
    See also CA 104; 139; CANR 78; CDALB
    1865-1917; DLB 11, 12, 23, 71, 74, 186
Biggers, Earl Derr 1884-1933 .... **TCLC 65**
    See also CA 108; 153
Billings, Josh
    See Shaw, Henry Wheeler
Billington, (Lady) Rachel (Mary) 1942- **C L C
  43**
    See also AITN 2; CA 33-36R; CANR 44
Binyon, T(imothy) J(ohn) 1936- .... **CLC 34**
    See also CA 111; CANR 28
Bioy Casares, Adolfo 1914-1999 **CLC 4, 8, 13,
  88; DAM MULT; HLC; SSC 17**
    See also CA 29-32R; 177; CANR 19, 43, 66;
    DLB 113; HW 1, 2; MTCW 1, 2
Bird, Cordwainer
    See Ellison, Harlan (Jay)
Bird, Robert Montgomery 1806-1854 **NCLC 1**

    See also DLB 202
Birkerts, Sven 1951- .... **CLC 116**
    See also CA 128; 133; 176; CAAS 29; INT 133
Birney, (Alfred) Earle 1904-1995 **CLC 1, 4, 6,
  11; DAC; DAM MST, POET**
    See also CA 1-4R; CANR 5, 20; DLB 88;
    MTCW 1
Biruni, al 973-1048(?) .... **CMLC 28**
Bishop, Elizabeth 1911-1979 **CLC 1, 4, 9, 13,
  15, 32; DA; DAC; DAM MST, POET; PC
  3**
    See also CA 5-8R; 89-92; CABS 2; CANR 26,
    61; CDALB 1968-1988; DLB 5, 169;
    MTCW 1, 2; SATA-Obit 24
Bishop, John 1935- .... **CLC 10**
    See also CA 105
Bissett, Bill 1939- .... **CLC 18; PC 14**
    See also CA 69-72; CAAS 19; CANR 15; DLB
    53; MTCW 1
Bissoondath, Neil (Devindra) 1955- **CLC 120;
  DAC**
    See also CA 136
Bitov, Andrei (Georgievich) 1937- .... **CLC 57**
    See also CA 142
Biyidi, Alexandre 1932-
    See Beti, Mongo
    See also BW 1, 3; CA 114; 124; CANR 81;
    MTCW 1, 2
Bjarme, Brynjolf
    See Ibsen, Henrik (Johan)
Bjoernson, Bjoernstjerne (Martinius) 1832-
  1910 .... **TCLC 7, 37**
    See also CA 104
Black, Robert
    See Holdstock, Robert P.
Blackburn, Paul 1926-1971 .... **CLC 9, 43**
    See also CA 81-84; 33-36R; CANR 34; DLB
    16; DLBY 81
Black Elk 1863-1950 **TCLC 33; DAM MULT**
    See also CA 144; MTCW 1; NNAL
Black Hobart
    See Sanders, (James) Ed(ward)
Blacklin, Malcolm
    See Chambers, Aidan
Blackmore, R(ichard) D(oddridge) 1825-1900
  TCLC 27
    See also CA 120; DLB 18
Blackmur, R(ichard) P(almer) 1904-1965
  CLC 2, 24
    See also CA 11-12; 25-28R; CANR 71; CAP 1;
    DLB 63
Black Tarantula
    See Acker, Kathy
Blackwood, Algernon (Henry) 1869-1951
  TCLC 5
    See also CA 105; 150; DLB 153, 156, 178
Blackwood, Caroline 1931-1996 **CLC 6, 9, 100**
    See also CA 85-88; 151; CANR 32, 61, 65; DLB
    14, 207; MTCW 1
Blade, Alexander
    See Hamilton, Edmond; Silverberg, Robert
Blaga, Lucian 1895-1961 .... **CLC 75**
    See also CA 157
Blair, Eric (Arthur) 1903-1950
    See Orwell, George
    See also CA 104; 132; DA; DAB; DAC; DAM
    MST, NOV; MTCW 1, 2; SATA 29
Blair, Hugh 1718-1800 .... **NCLC 75**
Blais, Marie-Claire 1939- **CLC 2, 4, 6, 13, 22;
  DAC; DAM MST**
    See also CA 21-24R; CAAS 4; CANR 38, 75;
    DLB 53; MTCW 1, 2
Blaise, Clark 1940- .... **CLC 29**

Burns, Tex
  See L'Amour, Louis (Dearborn)
Burnshaw, Stanley 1906- .... **CLC 3, 13, 44**
  See also CA 9-12R; DLB 48; DLBY 97
Burr, Anne 1937- ....**CLC 6**
  See also CA 25-28R
Burroughs, Edgar Rice 1875-1950 . **TCLC 2,
    32; DAM NOV**
  See also AAYA 11; CA 104; 132; DLB 8;
    MTCW 1, 2; SATA 41
Burroughs, William S(eward) 1914-1997**CLC
    1, 2, 5, 15, 22, 42, 75, 109; DA; DAB; DAC;
    DAM MST, NOV, POP; WLC**
  See also AITN 2; CA 9-12R; 160; CANR 20,
    52; DLB 2, 8, 16, 152; DLBY 81, 97; MTCW
    1, 2
Burton, SirRichard F(rancis) 1821-1890
    NCLC 42
  See also DLB 55, 166, 184
Busch, Frederick 1941- ..... **CLC 7, 10, 18, 47**
  See also CA 33-36R; CAAS 1; CANR 45, 73;
    DLB 6
Bush, Ronald 1946- .... **CLC 34**
  See also CA 136
Bustos, F(rancisco)
  See Borges, Jorge Luis
Bustos Domecq, H(onorio)
  See Bioy Casares, Adolfo; Borges, Jorge Luis
Butler, Octavia E(stelle) 1947- **CLC 38, 121;
    BLCS; DAM MULT, POP**
  See also AAYA 18; BW 2, 3; CA 73-76; CANR
    12, 24, 38, 73; DLB 33; MTCW 1, 2; SATA
    84
Butler, Robert Olen (Jr.) 1945-**CLC 81; DAM
    POP**
  See also CA 112; CANR 66; DLB 173; INT 112;
    MTCW 1
Butler, Samuel 1612-1680 .... **LC 16, 43**
  See also DLB 101, 126
Butler, Samuel 1835-1902 . **TCLC 1, 33; DA;
    DAB; DAC; DAM MST, NOV; WLC**
  See also CA 143; CDBLB 1890-1914; DLB 18,
    57, 174
Butler, Walter C.
  See Faust, Frederick (Schiller)
Butor, Michel (Marie Francois) 1926-**CLC 1,
    3, 8, 11, 15**
  See also CA 9-12R; CANR 33, 66; DLB 83;
    MTCW 1, 2
Butts, Mary 1892(?)-1937 .... **TCLC 77**
  See also CA 148
Buzo, Alexander (John) 1944- .... **CLC 61**
  See also CA 97-100; CANR 17, 39, 69
Buzzati, Dino 1906-1972 .... **CLC 36**
  See also CA 160; 33-36R; DLB 177
Byars, Betsy (Cromer) 1928-............ **CLC 35**
  See also AAYA 19; CA 33-36R; CANR 18, 36,
    57; CLR 1, 16; DLB 52; INT CANR-18;
    JRDA; MAICYA; MTCW 1; SAAS 1; SATA
    4, 46, 80; SATA-Essay 108
Byatt, A(ntonia) S(usan Drabble) 1936- **C L C
    19, 65; DAM NOV, POP**
  See also CA 13-16R; CANR 13, 33, 50, 75;
    DLB 14, 194; MTCW 1, 2
Byrne, David 1952- .... **CLC 26**
  See also CA 127
Byrne, John Keyes 1926-
  See Leonard, Hugh
  See also CA 102; CANR 78; INT 102
Byron, George Gordon (Noel) 1788-1824
    **NCLC 2, 12; DA; DAB; DAC; DAM MST,
    POET; PC 16; WLC**
  See also CDBLB 1789-1832; DLB 96, 110

Byron, Robert 1905-1941 .... **TCLC 67**
  See also CA 160; DLB 195
C. 3. 3.
  See Wilde, Oscar
Caballero, Fernan 1796-1877 ....**NCLC 10**
Cabell, Branch
  See Cabell, James Branch
Cabell, James Branch 1879-1958 .... **TCLC 6**
  See also CA 105; 152; DLB 9, 78; MTCW 1
Cable, George Washington 1844-1925 **T C L C
    4; SSC 4**
  See also CA 104; 155; DLB 12, 74; DLBD 13
Cabral de Melo Neto, Joao 1920- ... **CLC 76;
    DAM MULT**
  See also CA 151
Cabrera Infante, G(uillermo) 1929-**CLC 5, 25,
    45, 120; DAM MULT; HLC**
  See also CA 85-88; CANR 29, 65; DLB 113;
    HW 1, 2; MTCW 1, 2
Cade, Toni
  See Bambara, Toni Cade
Cadmus and Harmonia
  See Buchan, John
Caedmon fl. 658-680 .... **CMLC 7**
  See also DLB 146
Caeiro, Alberto
  See Pessoa, Fernando (Antonio Nogueira)
Cage, John (Milton, Jr.) 1912-1992 ..**CLC 41**
  See also CA 13-16R; 169; CANR 9, 78; DLB
    193; INT CANR-9
Cahan, Abraham 1860-1951 .... **TCLC 71**
  See also CA 108; 154; DLB 9, 25, 28
Cain, G.
  See Cabrera Infante, G(uillermo)
Cain, Guillermo
  See Cabrera Infante, G(uillermo)
Cain, James M(allahan) 1892-1977**CLC 3, 11,
    28**
  See also AITN 1; CA 17-20R; 73-76; CANR 8,
    34, 61; MTCW 1
Caine, Mark
  See Raphael, Frederic (Michael)
Calasso, Roberto 1941- .... **CLC 81**
  See also CA 143
Calderon de la Barca, Pedro 1600-1681 ..**L C
    23; DC 3; HLCS 1**
Caldwell, Erskine (Preston) 1903-1987**CLC 1,
    8, 14, 50, 60; DAM NOV; SSC 19**
  See also AITN 1; CA 1-4R; 121; CAAS 1;
    CANR 2, 33; DLB 9, 86; MTCW 1, 2
Caldwell, (Janet Miriam) Taylor (Holland)
    1900-1985**CLC 2, 28, 39; DAM NOV, POP**
  See also CA 5-8R; 116; CANR 5; DLBD 17
Calhoun, John Caldwell 1782-1850**NCLC 15**
  See also DLB 3
Calisher, Hortense 1911-**CLC 2, 4, 8, 38; DAM
    NOV; SSC 15**
  See also CA 1-4R; CANR 1, 22, 67; DLB 2;
    INT CANR-22; MTCW 1, 2
Callaghan, Morley Edward 1903-1990**CLC 3,
    14, 41, 65; DAC; DAM MST**
  See also CA 9-12R; 132; CANR 33, 73; DLB
    68; MTCW 1, 2
Callimachus c. 305B.C.-c. 240B.C. **CMLC 18**
  See also DLB 176
Calvin, John 1509-1564 .... **LC 37**
Calvino, Italo 1923-1985**CLC 5, 8, 11, 22, 33,
    39, 73; DAM NOV; SSC 3**
  See also CA 85-88; 116; CANR 23, 61; DLB
    196; MTCW 1, 2
Cameron, Carey 1952- .... **CLC 59**
  See also CA 135
Cameron, Peter 1959- .... **CLC 44**

  See also CA 125; CANR 50
Campana, Dino 1885-1932 .... **TCLC 20**
  See also CA 117; DLB 114
Campanella, Tommaso 1568-1639 ...... **LC 32**
Campbell, John W(ood, Jr.) 1910-1971 **C L C
    32**
  See also CA 21-22; 29-32R; CANR 34; CAP 2;
    DLB 8; MTCW 1
Campbell, Joseph 1904-1987............. **CLC 69**
  See also AAYA 3; BEST 89:2; CA 1-4R; 124;
    CANR 3, 28, 61; MTCW 1, 2
Campbell, Maria 1940-................**CLC 85; DAC**
  See also CA 102; CANR 54; NNAL
Campbell, (John) Ramsey 1946-**CLC 42; SSC
    19**
  See also CA 57-60; CANR 7; INT CANR-7
Campbell, (Ignatius) Roy (Dunnachie) 1901-
    1957 .... **TCLC 5**
  See also CA 104; 155; DLB 20; MTCW 2
Campbell, Thomas 1777-1844 ....**NCLC 19**
  See also DLB 93; 144
Campbell, Wilfred .... **TCLC 9**
  See also Campbell, William
Campbell, William 1858(?)-1918
  See Campbell, Wilfred
  See also CA 106; DLB 92
Campion, Jane ....**CLC 95**
  See also CA 138
Campos, Alvaro de
  See Pessoa, Fernando (Antonio Nogueira)
Camus, Albert 1913-1960**CLC 1, 2, 4, 9, 11, 14,
    32, 63, 69; DA; DAB; DAC; DAM DRAM,
    MST, NOV; DC 2; SSC 9; WLC**
  See also CA 89-92; DLB 72; MTCW 1, 2
Canby, Vincent 1924-................................**CLC 13**
  See also CA 81-84
Cancale
  See Desnos, Robert
Canetti, Elias 1905-1994**CLC 3, 14, 25, 75, 86**
  See also CA 21-24R; 146; CANR 23, 61, 79;
    DLB 85, 124; MTCW 1, 2
Canfield, Dorothea F.
  See Fisher, Dorothy (Frances) Canfield
Canfield, Dorothea Frances
  See Fisher, Dorothy (Frances) Canfield
Canfield, Dorothy
  See Fisher, Dorothy (Frances) Canfield
Canin, Ethan 1960- ....**CLC 55**
  See also CA 131; 135
Cannon, Curt
  See Hunter, Evan
Cao, Lan 1961- .... **CLC 109**
  See also CA 165
Cape, Judith
  See Page, P(atricia) K(athleen)
Capek, Karel 1890-1938 ... **TCLC 6, 37; DA;
    DAB; DAC; DAM DRAM, MST, NOV; DC
    1; WLC**
  See also CA 104; 140; MTCW 1
Capote, Truman 1924-1984**CLC 1, 3, 8, 13, 19,
    34, 38, 58; DA; DAB; DAC; DAM MST,
    NOV, POP; SSC 2; WLC**
  See also CA 5-8R; 113; CANR 18, 62; CDALB
    1941-1968; DLB 2, 185; DLBY 80, 84;
    MTCW 1, 2; SATA 91
Capra, Frank 1897-1991 ....**CLC 16**
  See also CA 61-64; 135
Caputo, Philip 1941- ....**CLC 32**
  See also CA 73-76; CANR 40
Caragiale, Ion Luca 1852-1912 ...... **TCLC 76**
  See also CA 157
Card, Orson Scott 1951-**CLC 44, 47, 50; DAM
    POP**

See also CA 110

Challans, Mary 1905-1983
See Renault, Mary
See also CA 81-84; 111; CANR 74; MTCW 2;
SATA 23; SATA-Obit 36

Challis, George
See Faust, Frederick (Schiller)

Chambers, Aidan 1934- .... **CLC 35**
See also AAYA 27; CA 25-28R; CANR 12, 31,
58; JRDA; MAICYA; SAAS 12; SATA 1, 69,
108

Chambers, James 1948-
See Cliff, Jimmy
See also CA 124

Chambers, Jessie
See Lawrence, D(avid) H(erbert Richards)

Chambers, Robert W(illiam) 1865-1933
TCLC 41
See also CA 165; DLB 202; SATA 107

Chandler, Raymond (Thornton) 1888-1959
TCLC 1, 7; SSC 23
See also AAYA 25; CA 104; 129; CANR 60;
CDALB 1929-1941; DLBD 6; MTCW 1, 2

Chang, Eileen 1920-1995 .... **SSC 28**
See also CA 166

Chang, Jung 1952- .... **CLC 71**
See also CA 142

Chang Ai-Ling
See Chang, Eileen

Channing, William Ellery 1780-1842 . **NCLC
17**
See also DLB 1, 59

Chao, Patricia 1955- .... **CLC 119**
See also CA 163

Chaplin, Charles Spencer 1889-1977 **CLC 16**
See also Chaplin, Charlie
See also CA 81-84; 73-76

Chaplin, Charlie
See Chaplin, Charles Spencer
See also DLB 44

Chapman, George 1559(?)-1634 **LC 22; DAM
DRAM**
See also DLB 62, 121

Chapman, Graham 1941-1989 .... **CLC 21**
See also Monty Python
See also CA 116; 129; CANR 35

Chapman, John Jay 1862-1933 .... **TCLC 7**
See also CA 104

Chapman, Lee
See Bradley, Marion Zimmer

Chapman, Walker
See Silverberg, Robert

Chappell, Fred (Davis) 1936- ..... **CLC 40, 78**
See also CA 5-8R; CAAS 4; CANR 8, 33, 67;
DLB 6, 105

Char, Rene(-Emile) 1907-1988 **CLC 9, 11, 14,
55; DAM POET**
See also CA 13-16R; 124; CANR 32; MTCW
1, 2

Charby, Jay
See Ellison, Harlan (Jay)

Chardin, Pierre Teilhard de
See Teilhard de Chardin, (Marie Joseph) Pierre

Charles I 1600-1649 .... **LC 13**

Charriere, Isabelle de 1740-1805 ..**NCLC 66**

Charyn, Jerome 1937- .... **CLC 5, 8, 18**
See also CA 5-8R; CAAS 1; CANR 7, 61;
DLBY 83; MTCW 1

Chase, Mary (Coyle) 1907-1981 .... **DC 1**
See also CA 77-80; 105; SATA 17; SATA-Obit
29

Chase, Mary Ellen 1887-1973 .... **CLC 2**
See also CA 13-16; 41-44R; CAP 1; SATA 10

Chase, Nicholas
See Hyde, Anthony

Chateaubriand, Francois Rene de 1768-1848
NCLC 3
See also DLB 119

Chatterje, Sarat Chandra 1876-1936(?)
See Chatterji, Saratchandra
See also CA 109

Chatterji, Bankim Chandra 1838-1894 **NCLC
19**

Chatterji, Saratchandra .... **TCLC 13**
See also Chatterje, Sarat Chandra

Chatterton, Thomas 1752-1770 . **LC 3; DAM
POET**
See also DLB 109

Chatwin, (Charles) Bruce 1940-1989 **CLC 28,
57, 59; DAM POP**
See also AAYA 4; BEST 90:1; CA 85-88; 127;
DLB 194, 204

Chaucer, Daniel
See Ford, Ford Madox

Chaucer, Geoffrey 1340(?)-1400 **LC 17; DA;
DAB; DAC; DAM MST, POET; PC 19;
WLCS**
See also CDBLB Before 1660; DLB 146

Chaviaras, Strates 1935-
See Haviaras, Stratis
See also CA 105

Chayefsky, Paddy .... **CLC 23**
See also Chayefsky, Sidney
See also DLB 7, 44; DLBY 81

Chayefsky, Sidney 1923-1981
See Chayefsky, Paddy
See also CA 9-12R; 104; CANR 18; DAM
DRAM

Chedid, Andree 1920- .... **CLC 47**
See also CA 145

Cheever, John 1912-1982 **CLC 3, 7, 8, 11, 15,
25, 64; DA; DAB; DAC; DAM MST, NOV,
POP; SSC 1; WLC**
See also CA 5-8R; 106; CABS 1; CANR 5, 27,
76; CDALB 1941-1968; DLB 2, 102; DLBY
80, 82; INT CANR-5; MTCW 1, 2

Cheever, Susan 1943- .... **CLC 18, 48**
See also CA 103; CANR 27, 51; DLBY 82; INT
CANR-27

Chekhonte, Antosha
See Chekhov, Anton (Pavlovich)

Chekhov, Anton (Pavlovich) 1860-1904 **TCLC
3, 10, 31, 55; DA; DAB; DAC; DAM
DRAM, MST; DC 9; SSC 2, 28; WLC**
See also CA 104; 124; SATA 90

Chernyshevsky, Nikolay Gavrilovich 1828-1889
NCLC 1

Cherry, Carolyn Janice 1942-
See Cherryh, C. J.
See also CA 65-68; CANR 10

Cherryh, C. J. .... **CLC 35**
See also Cherry, Carolyn Janice
See also AAYA 24; DLBY 80; SATA 93

Chesnutt, Charles W(addell) 1858-1932
TCLC 5, 39; BLC 1; DAM MULT; SSC 7
See also BW 1, 3; CA 106; 125; CANR 76; DLB
12, 50, 78; MTCW 1, 2

Chester, Alfred 1929(?)-1971 .... **CLC 49**
See also CA 33-36R; DLB 130

Chesterton, G(ilbert) K(eith) 1874-1936
TCLC 1, 6, 64; DAM NOV, POET; SSC 1
See also CA 104; 132; CANR 73; CDBLB
1914-1945; DLB 10, 19, 34, 70, 98, 149,
178; MTCW 1, 2; SATA 27

Chiang, Pin-chin 1904-1986
See Ding Ling

See also CA 118

Ch'ien Chung-shu 1910- .... **CLC 22**
See also CA 130; CANR 73; MTCW 1, 2

Child, L. Maria
See Child, Lydia Maria

Child, Lydia Maria 1802-1880 ... **NCLC 6, 73**
See also DLB 1, 74; SATA 67

Child, Mrs.
See Child, Lydia Maria

Child, Philip 1898-1978 .... **CLC 19, 68**
See also CA 13-14; CAP 1; SATA 47

Childers, (Robert) Erskine 1870-1922 **TCLC
65**
See also CA 113; 153; DLB 70

Childress, Alice 1920-1994 **CLC 12, 15, 86, 96;
BLC 1; DAM DRAM, MULT, NOV; DC 4**
See also AAYA 8; BW 2, 3; CA 45-48; 146;
CANR 3, 27, 50, 74; CLR 14; DLB 7, 38;
JRDA; MAICYA; MTCW 1, 2; SATA 7, 48,
81

Chin, Frank (Chew, Jr.) 1940- .... **DC 7**
See also CA 33-36R; CANR 71; DAM MULT;
DLB 206

Chislett, (Margaret) Anne 1943- ...... **CLC 34**
See also CA 151

Chitty, Thomas Willes 1926- .... **CLC 11**
See also Hinde, Thomas
See also CA 5-8R

Chivers, Thomas Holley 1809-1858 **NCLC 49**
See also DLB 3

Choi, Susan .... **CLC 119**

Chomette, Rene Lucien 1898-1981
See Clair, Rene
See also CA 103

Chopin, Kate **TCLC 5, 14; DA; DAB; SSC 8;
WLCS**
See also Chopin, Katherine
See also CDALB 1865-1917; DLB 12, 78

Chopin, Katherine 1851-1904
See Chopin, Kate
See also CA 104; 122; DAC; DAM MST, NOV

Chretien de Troyes c. 12th cent. - .. **CMLC 10**
See also DLB 208

Christie
See Ichikawa, Kon

Christie, Agatha (Mary Clarissa) 1890-1976
**CLC 1, 6, 8, 12, 39, 48, 110; DAB; DAC;
DAM NOV**
See also AAYA 9; AITN 1, 2; CA 17-20R; 61-
64; CANR 10, 37; CDBLB 1914-1945; DLB
13, 77; MTCW 1, 2; SATA 36

Christie, (Ann) Philippa
See Pearce, Philippa
See also CA 5-8R; CANR 4

Christine de Pizan 1365(?)-1431(?) ...... **LC 9**
See also DLB 208

Chubb, Elmer
See Masters, Edgar Lee

Chulkov, Mikhail Dmitrievich 1743-1792 **LC 2**
See also DLB 150

Churchill, Caryl 1938- ..... **CLC 31, 55; DC 5**
See also CA 102; CANR 22, 46; DLB 13;
MTCW 1

Churchill, Charles 1731-1764 .... **LC 3**
See also DLB 109

Chute, Carolyn 1947- .... **CLC 39**
See also CA 123

Ciardi, John (Anthony) 1916-1986 . **CLC 10,
40, 44; DAM POET**
See also CA 5-8R; 118; CAAS 2; CANR 5, 33;
CLR 19; DLB 5; DLBY 86; INT CANR-5;
MAICYA; MTCW 1, 2; SAAS 26; SATA 1,
65; SATA-Obit 46

51; DAM DRAM
See also AITN 1; CA 17-18; 41-44R; CANR
35; CAP 2; CDBLB 1914-1945; DLB 10;
MTCW 1, 2
Cowley, Abraham 1618-1667 .... LC 43
See also DLB 131, 151
Cowley, Malcolm 1898-1989 .... CLC 39
See also CA 5-8R; 128; CANR 3, 55; DLB 4,
48; DLBY 81, 89; MTCW 1, 2
Cowper, William 1731-1800 . NCLC 8; DAM
POET
See also DLB 104, 109
Cox, William Trevor 1928- .... CLC 9, 14, 71;
DAM NOV
See also Trevor, William
See also CA 9-12R; CANR 4, 37, 55, 76; DLB
14; INT CANR-37; MTCW 1, 2
Coyne, P. J.
See Masters, Hilary
Cozzens, James Gould 1903-1978 CLC 1, 4, 11,
92
See also CA 9-12R; 81-84; CANR 19; CDALB
1941-1968; DLB 9; DLBD 2; DLBY 84, 97;
MTCW 1, 2
Crabbe, George 1754-1832 .... NCLC 26
See also DLB 93
Craddock, Charles Egbert
See Murfree, Mary Noailles
Craig, A. A.
See Anderson, Poul (William)
Craik, Dinah Maria (Mulock) 1826-1887
NCLC 38
See also DLB 35, 163; MAICYA; SATA 34
Cram, Ralph Adams 1863-1942 ..... TCLC 45
See also CA 160
Crane, (Harold) Hart 1899-1932 TCLC 2, 5,
80; DA; DAB; DAC; DAM MST, POET;
PC 3; WLC
See also CA 104; 127; CDALB 1917-1929;
DLB 4, 48; MTCW 1, 2
Crane, R(onald) S(almon) 1886-1967 CLC 27
See also CA 85-88; DLB 63
Crane, Stephen (Townley) 1871-1900 TCLC
11, 17, 32; DA; DAB; DAC; DAM MST,
NOV, POET; SSC 7; WLC
See also AAYA 21; CA 109; 140; CDALB 1865-
1917; DLB 12, 54, 78; YABC 2
Cranshaw, Stanley
See Fisher, Dorothy (Frances) Canfield
Crase, Douglas 1944- .... CLC 58
See also CA 106
Crashaw, Richard 1612(?)-1649 .... LC 24
See also DLB 126
Craven, Margaret 1901-1980 . CLC 17; DAC
See also CA 103
Crawford, F(rancis) Marion 1854-1909 TCLC
10
See also CA 107; 168; DLB 71
Crawford, Isabella Valancy 1850-1887 N C L C
12
See also DLB 92
Crayon, Geoffrey
See Irving, Washington
Creasey, John 1908-1973 .... CLC 11
See also CA 5-8R; 41-44R; CANR 8, 59; DLB
77; MTCW 1
Crebillon, Claude Prosper Jolyot de (fils) 1707-
1777 .... LC 1, 28
Credo
See Creasey, John
Credo, Alvaro J. de
See Prado (Calvo), Pedro
Creeley, Robert (White) 1926- CLC 1, 2, 4, 8,

11, 15, 36, 78; DAM POET
See also CA 1-4R; CAAS 10; CANR 23, 43;
DLB 5, 16, 169; DLBD 17; MTCW 1, 2
Crews, Harry (Eugene) 1935- CLC 6, 23, 49
See also AITN 1; CA 25-28R; CANR 20, 57;
DLB 6, 143, 185; MTCW 1, 2
Crichton, (John) Michael 1942- CLC 2, 6, 54,
90; DAM NOV, POP
See also AAYA 10; AITN 2; CA 25-28R; CANR
13, 40, 54, 76; DLBY 81; INT CANR-13;
JRDA; MTCW 1, 2; SATA 9, 88
Crispin, Edmund ....CLC 22
See also Montgomery, (Robert) Bruce
See also DLB 87
Cristofer, Michael 1945(?)- .... CLC 28; DAM
DRAM
See also CA 110; 152; DLB 7
Croce, Benedetto 1866-1952 .... TCLC 37
See also CA 120; 155
Crockett, David 1786-1836 .... NCLC 8
See also DLB 3, 11
Crockett, Davy
See Crockett, David
Crofts, Freeman Wills 1879-1957 .. TCLC 55
See also CA 115; DLB 77
Croker, John Wilson 1780-1857 ..... NCLC 10
See also DLB 110
Crommelynck, Fernand 1885-1970 .. CLC 75
See also CA 89-92
Cromwell, Oliver 1599-1658 .... LC 43
Cronin, A(rchibald) J(oseph) 1896-1981 C L C
32
See also CA 1-4R; 102; CANR 5; DLB 191;
SATA 47; SATA-Obit 25
Cross, Amanda
See Heilbrun, Carolyn G(old)
Crothers, Rachel 1878(?)-1958 ...... TCLC 19
See also CA 113; DLB 7
Crovcs, Hal
See Traven, B.
Crow Dog, Mary (Ellen) (?)- .... CLC 93
See also Brave Bird, Mary
See also CA 154
Crowfield, Christopher
See Stowe, Harriet (Elizabeth) Beecher
Crowley, Aleister .... TCLC 7
See also Crowley, Edward Alexander
Crowley, Edward Alexander 1875-1947
See Crowley, Aleister
See also CA 104
Crowley, John 1942- .... CLC 57
See also CA 61-64; CANR 43; DLBY 82; SATA
65
Crud
See Crumb, R(obert)
Crumarums
See Crumb, R(obert)
Crumb, R(obert) 1943- .... CLC 17
See also CA 106
Crumbum
See Crumb, R(obert)
Crumski
See Crumb, R(obert)
Crum the Bum
See Crumb, R(obert)
Crunk
See Crumb, R(obert)
Crustt
See Crumb, R(obert)
Cryer, Gretchen (Kiger) 1935- .... CLC 21
See also CA 114; 123
Csath, Geza 1887-1919 .... TCLC 13
See also CA 111

Cudlip, David R(ockwell) 1933- .... CLC 34
See also CA 177
Cullen, Countee 1903-1946 TCLC 4, 37; BLC
1; DA; DAC; DAM MST, MULT, POET;
PC 20; WLCS
See also BW 1; CA 108; 124; CDALB 1917-
1929; DLB 4, 48, 51; MTCW 1, 2; SATA 18
Cum, R.
See Crumb, R(obert)
Cummings, Bruce F(rederick) 1889-1919
See Barbellion, W. N. P.
See also CA 123
Cummings, E(dward) E(stlin) 1894-1962 CLC
1, 3, 8, 12, 15, 68; DA; DAB; DAC; DAM
MST, POET; PC 5; WLC
See also CA 73-76; CANR 31; CDALB 1929-
1941; DLB 4, 48; MTCW 1, 2
Cunha, Euclides (Rodrigues Pimenta) da 1866-
1909 .... TCLC 24
See also CA 123
Cunningham, E. V.
See Fast, Howard (Melvin)
Cunningham, J(ames) V(incent) 1911-1985
CLC 3, 31
See also CA 1-4R; 115; CANR 1, 72; DLB 5
Cunningham, Julia (Woolfolk) 1916- CLC 12
See also CA 9-12R; CANR 4, 19, 36; JRDA;
MAICYA; SAAS 2; SATA 1, 26
Cunningham, Michael 1952- .... CLC 34
See also CA 136
Cunninghame Graham, R(obert) B(ontine)
1852-1936 .... TCLC 19
See also Graham, R(obert) B(ontine)
Cunninghame
See also CA 119; DLB 98
Currie, Ellen 19(?)- .... CLC 44
Curtin, Philip
See Lowndes, Marie Adelaide (Belloc)
Curtis, Price
See Ellison, Harlan (Jay)
Cutrate, Joe
See Spiegelman, Art
Cynewulf c. 770-c. 840 .... CMLC 23
Czaczkes, Shmuel Yosef
See Agnon, S(hmuel) Y(osef Halevi)
Dabrowska, Maria (Szumska) 1889-1965 CLC
15
See also CA 106
Dabydeen, David 1955- .... CLC 34
See also BW 1; CA 125; CANR 56
Dacey, Philip 1939- .... CLC 51
See also CA 37-40R; CAAS 17; CANR 14, 32,
64; DLB 105
Dagerman, Stig (Halvard) 1923-1954 T C L C
17
See also CA 117; 155
Dahl, Roald 1916-1990 CLC 1, 6, 18, 79; DAB;
DAC; DAM MST, NOV, POP
See also AAYA 15; CA 1-4R; 133; CANR 6,
32, 37, 62; CLR 1, 7, 41; DLB 139; JRDA;
MAICYA; MTCW 1, 2; SATA 1, 26, 73;
SATA-Obit 65
Dahlberg, Edward 1900-1977 .. CLC 1, 7, 14
See also CA 9-12R; 69-72; CANR 31, 62; DLB
48; MTCW 1
Daitch, Susan 1954- .... CLC 103
See also CA 161
Dale, Colin ....TCLC 18
See also Lawrence, T(homas) E(dward)
Dale, George E.
See Asimov, Isaac
Daly, Elizabeth 1878-1967 .... CLC 52
See also CA 23-24; 25-28R; CANR 60; CAP 2

```

**Daly, Maureen** 1921- ......... **CLC 17**
See also AAYA 5; CANR 37; JRDA; MAICYA; SAAS 1; SATA 2
**Damas, Leon-Gontran** 1912-1978 .... **CLC 84**
See also BW 1; CA 125; 73-76
**Dana, Richard Henry Sr.** 1787-1879 **NCLC 53**
**Daniel, Samuel** 1562(?)-1619 ............. **LC 24**
See also DLB 62
**Daniels, Brett**
See Adler, Renata
**Dannay, Frederic** 1905-1982 . **CLC 11; DAM POP**
See also Queen, Ellery
See also CA 1-4R; 107; CANR 1, 39; DLB 137; MTCW 1
**D'Annunzio, Gabriele** 1863-1938 **TCLC 6, 40**
See also CA 104; 155
**Danois, N. le**
See Gourmont, Remy (-Marie-Charles) de
**Dante** 1265-1321 .... **CMLC 3, 18; DA; DAB; DAC; DAM MST, POET; PC 21; WLCS**
**d'Antibes, Germain**
See Simenon, Georges (Jacques Christian)
**Danticat, Edwidge** 1969- ............ **CLC 94**
See also AAYA 29; CA 152; CANR 73; MTCW 1
**Danvers, Dennis** 1947- ........... **CLC 70**
**Danziger, Paula** 1944- ............ **CLC 21**
See also AAYA 4; CA 112; 115; CANR 37; CLR 20; JRDA; MAICYA; SATA 36, 63, 102; SATA-Brief 30
**Da Ponte, Lorenzo** 1749-1838 ........ **NCLC 50**
**Dario, Ruben** 1867-1916 ....... **TCLC 4; DAM MULT; HLC; PC 15**
See also CA 131; CANR 81; HW 1, 2; MTCW 1, 2
**Darley, George** 1795-1846 ............ **NCLC 2**
See also DLB 96
**Darrow, Clarence (Seward)** 1857-1938 **TCLC 81**
See also CA 164
**Darwin, Charles** 1809-1882 ........... **NCLC 57**
See also DLB 57, 166
**Daryush, Elizabeth** 1887-1977 ..... **CLC 6, 19**
See also CA 49-52; CANR 3, 81; DLB 20
**Dasgupta, Surendranath** 1887-1952 **TCLC 81**
See also CA 157
**Dashwood, Edmee Elizabeth Monica de la Pasture** 1890-1943
See Delafield, E. M.
See also CA 119; 154
**Daudet, (Louis Marie) Alphonse** 1840-1897 **NCLC 1**
See also DLB 123
**Daumal, Rene** 1908-1944 ............... **TCLC 14**
See also CA 114
**Davenant, William** 1606-1668 ............ **LC 13**
See also DLB 58, 126
**Davenport, Guy (Mattison, Jr.)** 1927- **CLC 6, 14, 38; SSC 16**
See also CA 33-36R; CANR 23, 73; DLB 130
**Davidson, Avram (James)** 1923-1993
See Queen, Ellery
See also CA 101; 171; CANR 26; DLB 8
**Davidson, Donald (Grady)** 1893-1968 **CLC 2, 13, 19**
See also CA 5-8R; 25-28R; CANR 4; DLB 45
**Davidson, Hugh**
See Hamilton, Edmond
**Davidson, John** 1857-1909 ............. **TCLC 24**
See also CA 118; DLB 19
**Davidson, Sara** 1943- .......... **CLC 9**
See also CA 81-84; CANR 44, 68; DLB 185

**Davie, Donald (Alfred)** 1922-1995 **CLC 5, 8, 10, 31**
See also CA 1-4R; 149; CAAS 3; CANR 1, 44; DLB 27; MTCW 1
**Davies, Ray(mond Douglas)** 1944- .... **CLC 21**
See also CA 116; 146
**Davies, Rhys** 1901-1978 ................... **CLC 23**
See also CA 9-12R; 81-84; CANR 4; DLB 139, 191
**Davies, (William) Robertson** 1913-1995 **C L C 2, 7, 13, 25, 42, 75, 91; DA; DAB; DAC; DAM MST, NOV, POP; WLC**
See also BEST 89:2; CA 33-36R; 150; CANR 17, 42; DLB 68; INT CANR-17; MTCW 1, 2
**Davies, W(illiam) H(enry)** 1871-1940 **TCLC 5**
See also CA 104; DLB 19, 174
**Davies, Walter C.**
See Kornbluth, C(yril) M.
**Davis, Angela (Yvonne)** 1944- **CLC 77; DAM MULT**
See also BW 2, 3; CA 57-60; CANR 10, 81
**Davis, B. Lynch**
See Bioy Casares, Adolfo; Borges, Jorge Luis
**Davis, B. Lynch**
See Bioy Casares, Adolfo
**Davis, Harold Lenoir** 1894-1960 ...... **CLC 49**
See also CA 89-92; DLB 9, 206
**Davis, Rebecca (Blaine) Harding** 1831-1910 **TCLC 6**
See also CA 104; DLB 74
**Davis, Richard Harding** 1864-1916 **TCLC 24**
See also CA 114; DLB 12, 23, 78, 79, 189; DLBD 13
**Davison, Frank Dalby** 1893-1970 ..... **CLC 15**
See also CA 116
**Davison, Lawrence H.**
See Lawrence, D(avid) H(erbert Richards)
**Davison, Peter (Hubert)** 1928- .......... **CLC 28**
See also CA 9-12R; CAAS 4; CANR 3, 43; DLB 5
**Davys, Mary** 1674-1732 ................. **LC 1, 46**
See also DLB 39
**Dawson, Fielding** 1930- ....................... **CLC 6**
See also CA 85-88; DLB 130
**Dawson, Peter**
See Faust, Frederick (Schiller)
**Day, Clarence (Shepard, Jr.)** 1874-1935 **TCLC 25**
See also CA 108; DLB 11
**Day, Thomas** 1748-1789 ...................... **LC 1**
See also DLB 39; YABC 1
**Day Lewis, C(ecil)** 1904-1972 . **CLC 1, 6, 10; DAM POET; PC 11**
See also Blake, Nicholas
See also CA 13-16; 33-36R; CANR 34; CAP 1; DLB 15, 20; MTCW 1, 2
**Dazai Osamu** 1909-1948 ................. **TCLC 11**
See also Tsushima, Shuji
See also CA 164; DLB 182
**de Andrade, Carlos Drummond** 1892-1945
See Drummond de Andrade, Carlos
**Deane, Norman**
See Creasey, John
**de Beauvoir, Simone (Lucie Ernestine Marie Bertrand)**
See Beauvoir, Simone (Lucie Ernestine Marie Bertrand) de
**de Beer, P.**
See Bosman, Herman Charles
**de Brissac, Malcolm**
See Dickinson, Peter (Malcolm)
**de Chardin, Pierre Teilhard**

See Teilhard de Chardin, (Marie Joseph) Pierre
**Dee, John** 1527-1608 ............ **LC 20**
**Deer, Sandra** 1940- ............. **CLC 45**
**De Ferrari, Gabriella** 1941- ............. **CLC 65**
See also CA 146
**Defoe, Daniel** 1660(?)-1731 ..... **LC 1, 42; DA; DAB; DAC; DAM MST, NOV; WLC**
See also AAYA 27; CDBLB 1660-1789; DLB 39, 95, 101; JRDA; MAICYA; SATA 22
**de Gourmont, Remy(-Marie-Charles)**
See Gourmont, Remy (-Marie-Charles) de
**de Hartog, Jan** 1914- ............... **CLC 19**
See also CA 1-4R; CANR 1
**de Hostos, E. M.**
See Hostos (y Bonilla), Eugenio Maria de
**de Hostos, Eugenio M.**
See Hostos (y Bonilla), Eugenio Maria de
**Deighton, Len** .............. **CLC 4, 7, 22, 46**
See also Deighton, Leonard Cyril
See also AAYA 6; BEST 89:2; CDBLB 1960 to Present; DLB 87
**Deighton, Leonard Cyril** 1929-
See Deighton, Len
See also CA 9-12R; CANR 19, 33, 68; DAM NOV, POP; MTCW 1, 2
**Dekker, Thomas** 1572(?)-1632 .. **LC 22; DAM DRAM**
See also CDBLB Before 1660; DLB 62, 172
**Delafield, E. M.** 1890-1943 ............. **TCLC 61**
See also Dashwood, Edmee Elizabeth Monica de la Pasture
See also DLB 34
**de la Mare, Walter (John)** 1873-1956 **TCLC 4, 53; DAB; DAC; DAM MST, POET; SSC 14; WLC**
See also CA 163; CDBLB 1914-1945; CLR 23; DLB 162; MTCW 1; SATA 16
**Delaney, Franey**
See O'Hara, John (Henry)
**Delaney, Shelagh** 1939- **CLC 29; DAM DRAM**
See also CA 17-20R; CANR 30, 67; CDBLB 1960 to Present; DLB 13; MTCW 1
**Delany, Mary (Granville Pendarves)** 1700-1788 **LC 12**
**Delany, Samuel R(ay, Jr.)** 1942- **CLC 8, 14, 38; BLC 1; DAM MULT**
See also AAYA 24; BW 2, 3; CA 81-84; CANR 27, 43; DLB 8, 33; MTCW 1, 2
**De La Ramee, (Marie) Louise** 1839-1908
See Ouida
See also SATA 20
**de la Roche, Mazo** 1879-1961 ........... **CLC 14**
See also CA 85-88; CANR 30; DLB 68; SATA 64
**De La Salle, Innocent**
See Hartmann, Sadakichi
**Delbanco, Nicholas (Franklin)** 1942- **CLC 6, 13**
See also CA 17-20R; CAAS 2; CANR 29, 55; DLB 6
**del Castillo, Michel** 1933- ................. **CLC 38**
See also CA 109; CANR 77
**Deledda, Grazia (Cosima)** 1875(?)-1936 **TCLC 23**
See also CA 123
**Delibes, Miguel** .............................. **CLC 8, 18**
See also Delibes Setien, Miguel
**Delibes Setien, Miguel** 1920-
See Delibes, Miguel
See also CA 45-48; CANR 1, 32; HW 1; MTCW 1
**DeLillo, Don** 1936- **CLC 8, 10, 13, 27, 39, 54, 76; DAM NOV, POP**
```

See also BEST 89:1; CA 81-84; CANR 21, 76;
DLB 6, 173; MTCW 1, 2
de Lisser, H. G.
See De Lisser, H(erbert) G(eorge)
See also DLB 117
De Lisser, H(erbert) G(eorge) 1878-1944
TCLC 12
See also de Lisser, H. G.
See also BW 2; CA 109; 152
Deloney, Thomas 1560(?)-1600 .... **LC 41**
See also DLB 167
Deloria, Vine (Victor), Jr. 1933- ..... **CLC 21;**
DAM MULT
See also CA 53-56; CANR 5, 20, 48; DLB 175;
MTCW 1; NNAL; SATA 21
Del Vecchio, John M(ichael) 1947- .. **CLC 29**
See also CA 110; DLBD 9
de Man, Paul (Adolph Michel) 1919-1983
CLC 55
See also CA 128; 111; CANR 61; DLB 67;
MTCW 1, 2
De Marinis, Rick 1934- .... **CLC 54**
See also CA 57-60; CAAS 24; CANR 9, 25, 50
Dembry, R. Emmet
See Murfree, Mary Noailles
Demby, William 1922-**CLC 53; BLC 1; DAM**
MULT
See also BW 1, 3; CA 81-84; CANR 81; DLB
33
de Menton, Francisco
See Chin, Frank (Chew, Jr.)
Demijohn, Thom
See Disch, Thomas M(ichael)
de Montherlant, Henry (Milon)
See Montherlant, Henry (Milon) de
Demosthenes 384B.C.-322B.C. ...... **CMLC 13**
See also DLB 176
de Natale, Francine
See Malzberg, Barry N(athaniel)
Denby, Edwin (Orr) 1903-1983 .... **CLC 48**
See also CA 138; 110
Denis, Julio
See Cortazar, Julio
Denmark, Harrison
See Zelazny, Roger (Joseph)
Dennis, John 1658-1734 .... **LC 11**
See also DLB 101
Dennis, Nigel (Forbes) 1912-1989 .... **CLC 8**
See also CA 25-28R; 129; DLB 13, 15; MTCW
1
Dent, Lester 1904(?)-1959 .... **TCLC 72**
See also CA 112; 161
De Palma, Brian (Russell) 1940- ...... **CLC 20**
See also CA 109
De Quincey, Thomas 1785-1859 ...... **NCLC 4**
See also CDBLB 1789-1832; DLB 110; 144
Deren, Eleanora 1908(?)-1961
See Deren, Maya
See also CA 111
Deren, Maya 1917-1961 .... **CLC 16, 102**
See also Deren, Eleanora
Derleth, August (William) 1909-1971**CLC 31**
See also CA 1-4R; 29-32R; CANR 4; DLB 9;
DLBD 17; SATA 5
Der Nister 1884-1950 .... **TCLC 56**
de Routisie, Albert
See Aragon, Louis
Derrida, Jacques 1930- .... **CLC 24, 87**
See also CA 124; 127; CANR 76; MTCW 1
Derry Down Derry
See Lear, Edward
Dersonnes, Jacques
See Simenon, Georges (Jacques Christian)

Desai, Anita 1937-**CLC 19, 37, 97; DAB; DAM**
NOV
See also CA 81-84; CANR 33, 53; MTCW 1,
2; SATA 63
Desai, Kiran 1971-........................... **CLC 119**
See also CA 171
de Saint-Luc, Jean
See Glassco, John
de Saint Roman, Arnaud
See Aragon, Louis
Descartes, Rene 1596-1650 .... **LC 20, 35**
De Sica, Vittorio 1901(?)-1974 .... **CLC 20**
See also CA 117
Desnos, Robert 1900-1945 .... **TCLC 22**
See also CA 121; 151
Destouches, Louis-Ferdinand 1894-1961**C L C**
9, 15
See also Celine, Louis-Ferdinand
See also CA 85-88; CANR 28; MTCW 1
de Tolignac, Gaston
See Griffith, D(avid Lewelyn) W(ark)
Deutsch, Babette 1895-1982 .... **CLC 18**
See also CA 1-4R; 108; CANR 4, 79; DLB 45;
SATA 1; SATA-Obit 33
Devenant, William 1606-1649 .... **LC 13**
Devkota, Laxmiprasad 1909-1959 . **TCLC 23**
See also CA 123
De Voto, Bernard (Augustine) 1897-1955
TCLC 29
See also CA 113; 160; DLB 9
De Vries, Peter 1910-1993 **CLC 1, 2, 3, 7, 10,**
28, 46; DAM NOV
See also CA 17-20R; 142; CANR 41; DLB 6;
DLBY 82; MTCW 1, 2
Dewey, John 1859-1952 .... **TCLC 95**
See also CA 114; 170
Dexter, John
See Bradley, Marion Zimmer
Dexter, Martin
See Faust, Frederick (Schiller)
Dexter, Pete 1943- ... **CLC 34, 55; DAM POP**
See also BEST 89:2; CA 127; 131; INT 131;
MTCW 1
Diamano, Silmang
See Senghor, Leopold Sedar
Diamond, Neil 1941-........................**CLC 30**
See also CA 108
Diaz del Castillo, Bernal 1496-1584 .. **LC 31;**
HLCS 1
di Bassetto, Corno
See Shaw, George Bernard
Dick, Philip K(indred) 1928-1982**CLC 10, 30,**
72; DAM NOV, POP
See also AAYA 24; CA 49-52; 106; CANR 2,
16; DLB 8; MTCW 1, 2
Dickens, Charles (John Huffam) 1812-1870
NCLC 3, 8, 18, 26, 37, 50; DA; DAB; DAC;
DAM MST, NOV; SSC 17; WLC
See also AAYA 23; CDBLB 1832-1890; DLB
21, 55, 70, 159, 166; JRDA; MAICYA; SATA
15
Dickey, James (Lafayette) 1923-1997 **CLC 1,**
2, 4, 7, 10, 15, 47, 109; DAM NOV, POET,
POP
See also AITN 1, 2; CA 9-12R; 156; CABS 2;
CANR 10, 48, 61; CDALB 1968-1988; DLB
5, 193; DLBD 7; DLBY 82, 93, 96, 97, 98;
INT CANR-10; MTCW 1, 2
Dickey, William 1928-1994 .... **CLC 3, 28**
See also CA 9-12R; 145; CANR 24, 79; DLB 5
Dickinson, Charles 1951-.................**CLC 49**
See also CA 128
Dickinson, Emily (Elizabeth) 1830-1886

NCLC 21, 77; DA; DAB; DAC; DAM
MST, POET; PC 1; WLC
See also AAYA 22; CDALB 1865-1917; DLB
1; SATA 29
Dickinson, Peter (Malcolm) 1927-**CLC 12, 35**
See also AAYA 9; CA 41-44R; CANR 31, 58;
CLR 29; DLB 87, 161; JRDA; MAICYA;
SATA 5, 62, 95
Dickson, Carr
See Carr, John Dickson
Dickson, Carter
See Carr, John Dickson
Diderot, Denis 1713-1784 .... **LC 26**
Didion, Joan 1934-**CLC 1, 3, 8, 14, 32; DAM**
NOV
See also AITN 1; CA 5-8R; CANR 14, 52, 76;
CDALB 1968-1988; DLB 2, 173, 185;
DLBY 81, 86; MTCW 1, 2
Dietrich, Robert
See Hunt, E(verette) Howard, (Jr.)
Difusa, Pati
See Almodovar, Pedro
Dillard, Annie 1945-...**CLC 9, 60, 115; DAM**
NOV
See also AAYA 6; CA 49-52; CANR 3, 43, 62;
DLBY 80; MTCW 1, 2; SATA 10
Dillard, R(ichard) H(enry) W(ilde) 1937-
CLC 5
See also CA 21-24R; CAAS 7; CANR 10; DLB
5
Dillon, Eilis 1920-1994 .... **CLC 17**
See also CA 9-12R; 147; CAAS 3; CANR 4,
38, 78; CLR 26; MAICYA; SATA 2, 74;
SATA-Essay 105; SATA-Obit 83
Dimont, Penelope
See Mortimer, Penelope (Ruth)
Dinesen, Isak .... **CLC 10, 29, 95; SSC 7**
See also Blixen, Karen (Christentze Dinesen)
See also MTCW 1
Ding Ling .... **CLC 68**
See also Chiang, Pin-chin
Diphusa, Patty
See Almodovar, Pedro
Disch, Thomas M(ichael) 1940- ... **CLC 7, 36**
See also AAYA 17; CA 21-24R; CAAS 4;
CANR 17, 36, 54; CLR 18; DLB 8;
MAICYA; MTCW 1, 2; SAAS 15; SATA 92
Disch, Tom
See Disch, Thomas M(ichael)
d'Isly, Georges
See Simenon, Georges (Jacques Christian)
Disraeli, Benjamin 1804-1881**NCLC 2, 39, 79**
See also DLB 21, 55
Ditcum, Steve
See Crumb, R(obert)
Dixon, Paige
See Corcoran, Barbara
Dixon, Stephen 1936- .... **CLC 52; SSC 16**
See also CA 89-92; CANR 17, 40, 54; DLB 130
Doak, Annie
See Dillard, Annie
Dobell, Sydney Thompson 1824-1874 **N C L C**
43
See also DLB 32
Doblin, Alfred .... **TCLC 13**
See also Doeblin, Alfred
Dobrolyubov, Nikolai Alexandrovich 1836-1861
NCLC 5
Dobson, Austin 1840-1921 .... **TCLC 79**
See also DLB 35; 144
Dobyns, Stephen 1941-.....................**CLC 37**
See also CA 45-48; CANR 2, 18
Doctorow, E(dgar) L(aurence) 1931- **CLC 6,**

11, 15, 18, 37, 44, 65, 113; DAM NOV, POP
See also AAYA 22; AITN 2; BEST 89:3; CA 45-48; CANR 2, 33, 51, 76; CDALB 1968-1988; DLB 2, 28, 173; DLBY 80; MTCW 1, 2

Dodgson, Charles Lutwidge 1832-1898
See Carroll, Lewis
See also CLR 2; DA; DAB; DAC; DAM MST, NOV, POET; MAICYA; SATA 100; YABC 2

Dodson, Owen (Vincent) 1914-1983 **CLC 79; BLC 1; DAM MULT**
See also BW 1; CA 65-68; 110; CANR 24; DLB 76

Doeblin, Alfred 1878-1957 .... **TCLC 13**
See also Doblin, Alfred
See also CA 110; 141; DLB 66

Doerr, Harriet 1910- .... **CLC 34**
See also CA 117; 122; CANR 47; INT 122

Domecq, H(onorio Bustos)
See Bioy Casares, Adolfo

Domecq, H(onorio) Bustos
See Bioy Casares, Adolfo; Borges, Jorge Luis

Domini, Rey
See Lorde, Audre (Geraldine)

Dominique
See Proust, (Valentin-Louis-George-Eugene-) Marcel

Don, A
See Stephen, SirLeslie

Donaldson, Stephen R. 1947- **CLC 46; DAM POP**
See also CA 89-92; CANR 13, 55; INT CANR-13

Donleavy, J(ames) P(atrick) 1926-**CLC 1, 4, 6, 10, 45**
See also AITN 2; CA 9-12R; CANR 24, 49, 62, 80; DLB 6, 173; INT CANR-24; MTCW 1, 2

Donne, John 1572-1631**LC 10, 24; DA; DAB; DAC; DAM MST, POET; PC 1; WLC**
See also CDBLB Before 1660; DLB 121, 151

Donnell, David 1939(?)- .... **CLC 34**

Donoghue, P. S.
See Hunt, E(verette) Howard, (Jr.)

Donoso (Yanez), Jose 1924-1996**CLC 4, 8, 11, 32, 99; DAM MULT; HLC; SSC 34**
See also CA 81-84; 155; CANR 32, 73; DLB 113; HW 1, 2; MTCW 1, 2

Donovan, John 1928-1992 .... **CLC 35**
See also AAYA 20; CA 97-100; 137; CLR 3; MAICYA; SATA 72; SATA-Brief 29

Don Roberto
See Cunninghame Graham, R(obert) B(ontine)

Doolittle, Hilda 1886-1961**CLC 3, 8, 14, 31, 34, 73; DA; DAC; DAM MST, POET; PC 5; WLC**
See also H. D.
See also CA 97-100; CANR 35; DLB 4, 45; MTCW 1, 2

Dorfman, Ariel 1942- ...... **CLC 48, 77; DAM MULT; HLC**
See also CA 124; 130; CANR 67, 70; HW 1, 2; INT 130

Dorn, Edward (Merton) 1929- ... **CLC 10, 18**
See also CA 93-96; CANR 42, 79; DLB 5; INT 93-96

Dorris, Michael (Anthony) 1945-1997 ..**C L C 109; DAM MULT, NOV**
See also AAYA 20; BEST 90:1; CA 102; 157; CANR 19, 46, 75; CLR 58; DLB 175; MTCW 2; NNAL; SATA 75; SATA-Obit 94

Dorris, Michael A.
See Dorris, Michael (Anthony)

Dorsan, Luc
See Simenon, Georges (Jacques Christian)

Dorsange, Jean
See Simenon, Georges (Jacques Christian)

Dos Passos, John (Roderigo) 1896-1970 **C L C 1, 4, 8, 11, 15, 25, 34, 82; DA; DAB; DAC; DAM MST, NOV; WLC**
See also CA 1-4R; 29-32R; CANR 3; CDALB 1929-1941; DLB 4, 9; DLBD 1, 15; DLBY 96; MTCW 1, 2

Dossage, Jean
See Simenon, Georges (Jacques Christian)

Dostoevsky, Fedor Mikhailovich 1821-1881 **NCLC 2, 7, 21, 33, 43; DA; DAB; DAC; DAM MST, NOV; SSC 2, 33; WLC**

Doughty, Charles M(ontagu) 1843-1926 **TCLC 27**
See also CA 115; DLB 19, 57, 174

Douglas, Ellen ....**CLC 73**
See also Haxton, Josephine Ayres; Williamson, Ellen Douglas

Douglas, Gavin 1475(?)-1522 .... **LC 20**
See also DLB 132

Douglas, George
See Brown, George Douglas

Douglas, Keith (Castellain) 1920-1944**T C L C 40**
See also CA 160; DLB 27

Douglas, Leonard
See Bradbury, Ray (Douglas)

Douglas, Michael
See Crichton, (John) Michael

Douglas, (George) Norman 1868-1952**T C L C 68**
See also CA 119; 157; DLB 34, 195

Douglas, William
See Brown, George Douglas

Douglass, Frederick 1817(?)-1895**NCLC 7, 55; BLC 1; DA; DAC; DAM MST, MULT; WLC**
See also CDALB 1640-1865; DLB 1, 43, 50, 79; SATA 29

Dourado, (Waldomiro Freitas) Autran 1926-**CLC 23, 60**
See also CA 25-28R; CANR 34, 81; DLB 145; HW 2

Dourado, Waldomiro Autran
See Dourado, (Waldomiro Freitas) Autran

Dove, Rita (Frances) 1952-**CLC 50, 81; BLCS; DAM MULT, POET; PC 6**
See also BW 2; CA 109; CAAS 19; CANR 27, 42, 68, 76; CDALBS; DLB 120; MTCW 1

Doveglion
See Villa, Jose Garcia

Dowell, Coleman 1925-1985 .... **CLC 60**
See also CA 25-28R; 117; CANR 10; DLB 130

Dowson, Ernest (Christopher) 1867-1900 **TCLC 4**
See also CA 105; 150; DLB 19, 135

Doyle, A. Conan
See Doyle, Arthur Conan

Doyle, Arthur Conan 1859-1930**TCLC 7; DA; DAB; DAC; DAM MST, NOV; SSC 12; WLC**
See also AAYA 14; CA 104; 122; CDBLB 1890-1914; DLB 18, 70, 156, 178; MTCW 1, 2; SATA 24

Doyle, Conan
See Doyle, Arthur Conan

Doyle, John
See Graves, Robert (von Ranke)

Doyle, Roddy 1958(?)- ....**CLC 81**
See also AAYA 14; CA 143; CANR 73; DLB 194

Doyle, Sir A. Conan
See Doyle, Arthur Conan

Doyle, Sir Arthur Conan
See Doyle, Arthur Conan

Dr. A
See Asimov, Isaac; Silverstein, Alvin

Drabble, Margaret 1939-**CLC 2, 3, 5, 8, 10, 22, 53; DAB; DAC; DAM MST, NOV, POP**
See also CA 13-16R; CANR 18, 35, 63; CDBLB 1960 to Present; DLB 14, 155; MTCW 1, 2; SATA 48

Drapier, M. B.
See Swift, Jonathan

Drayham, James
See Mencken, H(enry) L(ouis)

Drayton, Michael 1563-1631 ......**LC 8; DAM POET**
See also DLB 121

Dreadstone, Carl
See Campbell, (John) Ramsey

Dreiser, Theodore (Herman Albert) 1871-1945 **TCLC 10, 18, 35, 83; DA; DAC; DAM MST, NOV; SSC 30; WLC**
See also CA 106; 132; CDALB 1865-1917; DLB 9, 12, 102, 137; DLBD 1; MTCW 1, 2

Drexler, Rosalyn 1926- .... **CLC 2, 6**
See also CA 81-84; CANR 68

Dreyer, Carl Theodor 1889-1968 ......**CLC 16**
See also CA 116

Drieu la Rochelle, Pierre(-Eugene) 1893-1945 **TCLC 21**
See also CA 117; DLB 72

Drinkwater, John 1882-1937 .... **TCLC 57**
See also CA 109; 149; DLB 10, 19, 149

Drop Shot
See Cable, George Washington

Droste-Hulshoff, Annette Freiin von 1797-1848 **NCLC 3**
See also DLB 133

Drummond, Walter
See Silverberg, Robert

Drummond, William Henry 1854-1907**T C L C 25**
See also CA 160; DLB 92

Drummond de Andrade, Carlos 1902-1987 **CLC 18**
See also Andrade, Carlos Drummond de
See also CA 132; 123

Drury, Allen (Stuart) 1918-1998 ....**CLC 37**
See also CA 57-60; 170; CANR 18, 52; INT CANR-18

Dryden, John 1631-1700**LC 3, 21; DA; DAB; DAC; DAM DRAM, MST, POET; DC 3; PC 25; WLC**
See also CDBLB 1660-1789; DLB 80, 101, 131

Duberman, Martin (Bauml) 1930-......**CLC 8**
See also CA 1-4R; CANR 2, 63

Dubie, Norman (Evans) 1945- ....**CLC 36**
See also CA 69-72; CANR 12; DLB 120

Du Bois, W(illiam) E(dward) B(urghardt) 1868-1963 ..**CLC 1, 2, 13, 64, 96; BLC 1; DA; DAC; DAM MST, MULT, NOV; WLC**
See also BW 1, 3; CA 85-88; CANR 34; CDALB 1865-1917; DLB 47, 50, 91; MTCW 1, 2; SATA 42

Dubus, Andre 1936-1999**CLC 13, 36, 97; SSC 15**
See also CA 21-24R; 177; CANR 17; DLB 130; INT CANR-17

Duca Minimo
See D'Annunzio, Gabriele

Ducharme, Rejean 1941- ....**CLC 74**

See also BEST 90:4; CA 73-76; CANR 16, 37, 62; MTCW 1, 2
Eich, Guenter 1907-1972 .... **CLC 15**
See also CA 111; 93-96; DLB 69, 124
Eichendorff, Joseph Freiherr von 1788-1857 **NCLC 8**
See also DLB 90
Eigner, Larry .... **CLC 9**
See also Eigner, Laurence (Joel)
See also CAAS 23; DLB 5
Eigner, Laurence (Joel) 1927-1996
See Eigner, Larry
See also CA 9-12R; 151; CANR 6; DLB 193
Einstein, Albert 1879-1955 .... **TCLC 65**
See also CA 121; 133; MTCW 1, 2
Eiseley, Loren Corey 1907-1977 .... **CLC 7**
See also AAYA 5; CA 1-4R; 73-76; CANR 6; DLBD 17
Eisenstadt, Jill 1963- .... **CLC 50**
See also CA 140
Eisenstein, Sergei (Mikhailovich) 1898-1948 **TCLC 57**
See also CA 114; 149
Eisner, Simon
See Kornbluth, C(yril) M.
Ekeloef, (Bengt) Gunnar 1907-1968 **CLC 27; DAM POET; PC 23**
See also CA 123; 25-28R
Ekelof, (Bengt) Gunnar
See Ekeloef, (Bengt) Gunnar
Ekelund, Vilhelm 1880-1949 .... **TCLC 75**
Ekwensi, C. O. D.
See Ekwensi, Cyprian (Odiatu Duaka)
Ekwensi, Cyprian (Odiatu Duaka) 1921-**CLC 4; BLC 1; DAM MULT**
See also BW 2, 3; CA 29-32R; CANR 18, 42, 74; DLB 117; MTCW 1, 2; SATA 66
Elaine .... **TCLC 18**
See also Leverson, Ada
El Crummo
See Crumb, R(obert)
Elder, Lonne III 1931-1996 .... **DC 8**
See also BLC 1; BW 1, 3; CA 81-84; 152; CANR 25; DAM MULT; DLB 7, 38, 44
Elia
See Lamb, Charles
Eliade, Mircea 1907-1986 .... **CLC 19**
See also CA 65-68; 119; CANR 30, 62; MTCW 1
Eliot, A. D.
See Jewett, (Theodora) Sarah Orne
Eliot, Alice
See Jewett, (Theodora) Sarah Orne
Eliot, Dan
See Silverberg, Robert
Eliot, George 1819-1880 **NCLC 4, 13, 23, 41, 49; DA; DAB; DAC; DAM MST, NOV; PC 20; WLC**
See also CDBLB 1832-1890; DLB 21, 35, 55
Eliot, John 1604-1690 .... **LC 5**
See also DLB 24
Eliot, T(homas) S(tearns) 1888-1965**CLC 1, 2, 3, 6, 9, 10, 13, 15, 24, 34, 41, 55, 57, 113; DA; DAB; DAC; DAM DRAM, MST, POET; PC 5; WLC**
See also AAYA 28; CA 5-8R; 25-28R; CANR 41; CDALB 1929-1941; DLB 7, 10, 45, 63; DLBY 88; MTCW 1, 2
Elizabeth 1866-1941 .... **TCLC 41**
Elkin, Stanley L(awrence) 1930-1995 **CLC 4, 6, 9, 14, 27, 51, 91; DAM NOV, POP; SSC 12**
See also CA 9-12R; 148; CANR 8, 46; DLB 2,

28; DLBY 80; INT CANR-8; MTCW 1, 2
Elledge, Scott .... **CLC 34**
Elliot, Don
See Silverberg, Robert
Elliott, Don
See Silverberg, Robert
Elliott, George P(aul) 1918-1980 .... **CLC 2**
See also CA 1-4R; 97-100; CANR 2
Elliott, Janice 1931- .... **CLC 47**
See also CA 13-16R; CANR 8, 29; DLB 14
Elliott, Sumner Locke 1917-1991 ..... **CLC 38**
See also CA 5-8R; 134; CANR 2, 21
Elliott, William
See Bradbury, Ray (Douglas)
Ellis, A. E. .... **CLC 7**
Ellis, Alice Thomas .... **CLC 40**
See also Haycraft, Anna
See also DLB 194; MTCW 1
Ellis, Bret Easton 1964-**CLC 39, 71, 117; DAM POP**
See also AAYA 2; CA 118; 123; CANR 51, 74; INT 123; MTCW 1
Ellis, (Henry) Havelock 1859-1939 **TCLC 14**
See also CA 109; 169; DLB 190
Ellis, Landon
See Ellison, Harlan (Jay)
Ellis, Trey 1962- .... **CLC 55**
See also CA 146
Ellison, Harlan (Jay) 1934- ... **CLC 1, 13, 42; DAM POP; SSC 14**
See also AAYA 29; CA 5-8R; CANR 5, 46; DLB 8; INT CANR-5; MTCW 1, 2
Ellison, Ralph (Waldo) 1914-1994 **CLC 1, 3, 11, 54, 86, 114; BLC 1; DA; DAB; DAC; DAM MST, MULT, NOV; SSC 26; WLC**
See also AAYA 19; BW 1, 3; CA 9-12R; 145; CANR 24, 53; CDALB 1941-1968; DLB 2, 76; DLBY 94; MTCW 1, 2
Ellmann, Lucy (Elizabeth) 1956- ...... **CLC 61**
See also CA 128
Ellmann, Richard (David) 1918-1987**CLC 50**
See also BEST 89:2; CA 1-4R; 122; CANR 2, 28, 61; DLB 103; DLBY 87; MTCW 1, 2
Elman, Richard (Martin) 1934-1997 **CLC 19**
See also CA 17-20R; 163; CAAS 3; CANR 47
Elron
See Hubbard, L(afayette) Ron(ald)
Eluard, Paul .... **TCLC 7, 41**
See also Grindel, Eugene
Elyot, Sir Thomas 1490(?)-1546 .... **LC 11**
Elytis, Odysseus 1911-1996 **CLC 15, 49, 100; DAM POET; PC 21**
See also CA 102; 151; MTCW 1, 2
Emecheta, (Florence Onye) Buchi 1944-**C L C 14, 48; BLC 2; DAM MULT**
See also BW 2, 3; CA 81-84; CANR 27, 81; DLB 117; MTCW 1, 2; SATA 66
Emerson, Mary Moody 1774-1863 **NCLC 66**
Emerson, Ralph Waldo 1803-1882 .**NCLC 1, 38; DA; DAB; DAC; DAM MST, POET; PC 18; WLC**
See also CDALB 1640-1865; DLB 1, 59, 73
Eminescu, Mihail 1850-1889 .... **NCLC 33**
Empson, William 1906-1984**CLC 3, 8, 19, 33, 34**
See also CA 17-20R; 112; CANR 31, 61; DLB 20; MTCW 1, 2
Enchi, Fumiko (Ueda) 1905-1986 ..... **CLC 31**
See also CA 129; 121; DLB 182
Ende, Michael (Andreas Helmuth) 1929-1995 **CLC 31**
See also CA 118; 124; 149; CANR 36; CLR 14; DLB 75; MAICYA; SATA 61; SATA-

Brief 42; SATA-Obit 86
Endo, Shusaku 1923-1996 **CLC 7, 14, 19, 54, 99; DAM NOV**
See also CA 29-32R; 153; CANR 21, 54; DLB 182; MTCW 1, 2
Engel, Marian 1933-1985 .... **CLC 36**
See also CA 25-28R; CANR 12; DLB 53; INT CANR-12
Engelhardt, Frederick
See Hubbard, L(afayette) Ron(ald)
Enright, D(ennis) J(oseph) 1920-**CLC 4, 8, 31**
See also CA 1-4R; CANR 1, 42; DLB 27; SATA 25
Enzensberger, Hans Magnus 1929- ..**CLC 43**
See also CA 116; 119
Ephron, Nora 1941- .... **CLC 17, 31**
See also AITN 2; CA 65-68; CANR 12, 39
Epicurus 341B.C.-270B.C. .... **CMLC 21**
See also DLB 176
Epsilon
See Betjeman, John
Epstein, Daniel Mark 1948- .... **CLC 7**
See also CA 49-52; CANR 2, 53
Epstein, Jacob 1956- .... **CLC 19**
See also CA 114
Epstein, Jean 1897-1953 .... **TCLC 92**
Epstein, Joseph 1937- .... **CLC 39**
See also CA 112; 119; CANR 50, 65
Epstein, Leslie 1938- .... **CLC 27**
See also CA 73-76; CAAS 12; CANR 23, 69
Equiano, Olaudah 1745(?)-1797 **LC 16; BLC 2; DAM MULT**
See also DLB 37, 50
ER .... **TCLC 33**
See also CA 160; DLB 85
Erasmus, Desiderius 1469(?)-1536 ..... **LC 16**
Erdman, Paul E(mil) 1932- .... **CLC 25**
See also AITN 1; CA 61-64; CANR 13, 43
Erdrich, Louise 1954-**CLC 39, 54, 120; DAM MULT, NOV, POP**
See also AAYA 10; BEST 89:1; CA 114; CANR 41, 62; CDALBS; DLB 152, 175, 206; MTCW 1; NNAL; SATA 94
Erenburg, Ilya (Grigoryevich)
See Ehrenburg, Ilya (Grigoryevich)
Erickson, Stephen Michael 1950-
See Erickson, Steve
See also CA 129
Erickson, Steve 1950- .... **CLC 64**
See also Erickson, Stephen Michael
See also CANR 60, 68
Ericson, Walter
See Fast, Howard (Melvin)
Eriksson, Buntel
See Bergman, (Ernst) Ingmar
Ernaux, Annie 1940- .... **CLC 88**
See also CA 147
Erskine, John 1879-1951 .... **TCLC 84**
See also CA 112; 159; DLB 9, 102
Eschenbach, Wolfram von
See Wolfram von Eschenbach
Eseki, Bruno
See Mphahlele, Ezekiel
Esenin, Sergei (Alexandrovich) 1895-1925 **TCLC 4**
See also CA 104
Eshleman, Clayton 1935- .... **CLC 7**
See also CA 33-36R; CAAS 6; DLB 5
Espriella, Don Manuel Alvarez
See Southey, Robert
Espriu, Salvador 1913-1985 .... **CLC 9**
See also CA 154; 115; DLB 134
Espronceda, Jose de 1808-1842 ..... **NCLC 39**

Esse, James
See Stephens, James
Esterbrook, Tom
See Hubbard, L(afayette) Ron(ald)
Estleman, Loren D. 1952-**CLC 48; DAM NOV, POP**
See also AAYA 27; CA 85-88; CANR 27, 74; INT CANR-27; MTCW 1, 2
Euclid 306B.C.-283B.C. .... **CMLC 25**
Eugenides, Jeffrey 1960(?)- .... **CLC 81**
See also CA 144
Euripides c. 485B.C.-406B.C.**CMLC 23; DA; DAB; DAC; DAM DRAM, MST; DC 4; WLCS**
See also DLB 176
Evan, Evin
See Faust, Frederick (Schiller)
Evans, Caradoc 1878-1945 .... **TCLC 85**
Evans, Evan
See Faust, Frederick (Schiller)
Evans, Marian
See Eliot, George
Evans, Mary Ann
See Eliot, George
Evarts, Esther
See Benson, Sally
Everett, Percival L. 1956- .... **CLC 57**
See also BW 2; CA 129
Everson, R(onald) G(ilmour) 1903-. **CLC 27**
See also CA 17-20R; DLB 88
Everson, William (Oliver) 1912-1994 **CLC 1, 5, 14**
See also CA 9-12R; 145; CANR 20; DLB 212; MTCW 1
Evtushenko, Evgenii Aleksandrovich
See Yevtushenko, Yevgeny (Alexandrovich)
Ewart, Gavin (Buchanan) 1916-1995**CLC 13, 46**
See also CA 89-92; 150; CANR 17, 46; DLB 40; MTCW 1
Ewers, Hanns Heinz 1871-1943 ..... **TCLC 12**
See also CA 109; 149
Ewing, Frederick R.
See Sturgeon, Theodore (Hamilton)
Exley, Frederick (Earl) 1929-1992 **CLC 6, 11**
See also AITN 2; CA 81-84; 138; DLB 143; DLBY 81
Eynhardt, Guillermo
See Quiroga, Horacio (Sylvestre)
Ezekiel, Nissim 1924- .... **CLC 61**
See also CA 61-64
Ezekiel, Tish O'Dowd 1943- .... **CLC 34**
See also CA 129
Fadeyev, A.
See Bulgya, Alexander Alexandrovich
Fadeyev, Alexander .... **TCLC 53**
See also Bulgya, Alexander Alexandrovich
Fagen, Donald 1948- .... **CLC 26**
Fainzilberg, Ilya Arnoldovich 1897-1937
See Ilf, Ilya
See also CA 120; 165
Fair, Ronald L. 1932- .... **CLC 18**
See also BW 1; CA 69-72; CANR 25; DLB 33
Fairbairn, Roger
See Carr, John Dickson
Fairbairns, Zoe (Ann) 1948- .... **CLC 32**
See also CA 103; CANR 21
Falco, Gian
See Papini, Giovanni
Falconer, James
See Kirkup, James
Falconer, Kenneth
See Kornbluth, C(yril) M.

Falkland, Samuel
See Heijermans, Herman
Fallaci, Oriana 1930- .... **CLC 11, 110**
See also CA 77-80; CANR 15, 58; MTCW 1
Faludy, George 1913- .... **CLC 42**
See also CA 21-24R
Faludy, Gyoergy
See Faludy, George
Fanon, Frantz 1925-1961 .. **CLC 74; BLC 2; DAM MULT**
See also BW 1; CA 116; 89-92
Fanshawe, Ann 1625-1680 .... **LC 11**
Fante, John (Thomas) 1911-1983 ..... **CLC 60**
See also CA 69-72; 109; CANR 23; DLB 130; DLBY 83
Farah, Nuruddin 1945-**CLC 53; BLC 2; DAM MULT**
See also BW 2, 3; CA 106; CANR 81; DLB 125
Fargue, Leon-Paul 1876(?)-1947 ... **TCLC 11**
See also CA 109
Farigoule, Louis
See Romains, Jules
Farina, Richard 1936(?)-1966 .... **CLC 9**
See also CA 81-84; 25-28R
Farley, Walter (Lorimer) 1915-1989 **CLC 17**
See also CA 17-20R; CANR 8, 29; DLB 22; JRDA; MAICYA; SATA 2, 43
Farmer, Philip Jose 1918- .... **CLC 1, 19**
See also AAYA 28; CA 1-4R; CANR 4, 35; DLB 8; MTCW 1; SATA 93
Farquhar, George 1677-1707 ...**LC 21; DAM DRAM**
See also DLB 84
Farrell, J(ames) G(ordon) 1935-1979 **CLC 6**
See also CA 73-76; 89-92; CANR 36; DLB 14; MTCW 1
Farrell, James T(homas) 1904-1979**CLC 1, 4, 8, 11, 66; SSC 28**
See also CA 5-8R; 89-92; CANR 9, 61; DLB 4, 9, 86; DLBD 2; MTCW 1, 2
Farren, Richard J.
See Betjeman, John
Farren, Richard M.
See Betjeman, John
Fassbinder, Rainer Werner 1946-1982**CLC 20**
See also CA 93-96; 106; CANR 31
Fast, Howard (Melvin) 1914- **CLC 23; DAM NOV**
See also AAYA 16; CA 1-4R; CAAS 18; CANR 1, 33, 54, 75; DLB 9; INT CANR-33; MTCW 1; SATA 7; SATA-Essay 107
Faulcon, Robert
See Holdstock, Robert P.
Faulkner, William (Cuthbert) 1897-1962**CLC 1, 3, 6, 8, 9, 11, 14, 18, 28, 52, 68; DA; DAB; DAC; DAM MST, NOV; SSC 1, 35; WLC**
See also AAYA 7; CA 81-84; CANR 33; CDALB 1929-1941; DLB 9, 11, 44, 102; DLBD 2; DLBY 86, 97; MTCW 1, 2
Fauset, Jessie Redmon 1884(?)-1961**CLC 19, 54; BLC 2; DAM MULT**
See also BW 1; CA 109; DLB 51
Faust, Frederick (Schiller) 1892-1944(?) **TCLC 49; DAM POP**
See also CA 108; 152
Faust, Irvin 1924- .... **CLC 8**
See also CA 33-36R; CANR 28, 67; DLB 2, 28; DLBY 80
Fawkes, Guy
See Benchley, Robert (Charles)
Fearing, Kenneth (Flexner) 1902-1961 .**CLC 51**

See also CA 93-96; CANR 59; DLB 9
Fecamps, Elise
See Creasey, John
Federman, Raymond 1928- .... **CLC 6, 47**
See also CA 17-20R; CAAS 8; CANR 10, 43; DLBY 80
Federspiel, J(uerg) F. 1931- .... **CLC 42**
See also CA 146
Feiffer, Jules (Ralph) 1929- ..... **CLC 2, 8, 64; DAM DRAM**
See also AAYA 3; CA 17-20R; CANR 30, 59; DLB 7, 44; INT CANR-30; MTCW 1; SATA 8, 61
Feige, Hermann Albert Otto Maximilian
See Traven, B.
Feinberg, David B. 1956-1994 .... **CLC 59**
See also CA 135; 147
Feinstein, Elaine 1930- .... **CLC 36**
See also CA 69-72; CAAS 1; CANR 31, 68; DLB 14, 40; MTCW 1
Feldman, Irving (Mordecai) 1928- ..... **CLC 7**
See also CA 1-4R; CANR 1; DLB 169
Felix-Tchicaya, Gerald
See Tchicaya, Gerald Felix
Fellini, Federico 1920-1993 .... **CLC 16, 85**
See also CA 65-68; 143; CANR 33
Felsen, Henry Gregor 1916- .... **CLC 17**
See also CA 1-4R; CANR 1; SAAS 2; SATA 1
Fenno, Jack
See Calisher, Hortense
Fenollosa, Ernest (Francisco) 1853-1908 **TCLC 91**
Fenton, James Martin 1949- .... **CLC 32**
See also CA 102; DLB 40
Ferber, Edna 1887-1968 .... **CLC 18, 93**
See also AITN 1; CA 5-8R; 25-28R; CANR 68; DLB 9, 28, 86; MTCW 1, 2; SATA 7
Ferguson, Helen
See Kavan, Anna
Ferguson, Samuel 1810-1886 .... **NCLC 33**
See also DLB 32
Fergusson, Robert 1750-1774 .... **LC 29**
See also DLB 109
Ferling, Lawrence
See Ferlinghetti, Lawrence (Monsanto)
Ferlinghetti, Lawrence (Monsanto) 1919(?)-**CLC 2, 6, 10, 27, 111; DAM POET; PC 1**
See also CA 5-8R; CANR 3, 41, 73; CDALB 1941-1968; DLB 5, 16; MTCW 1, 2
Fernandez, Vicente Garcia Huidobro
See Huidobro Fernandez, Vicente Garcia
Ferrer, Gabriel (Francisco Victor) Miro
See Miro (Ferrer), Gabriel (Francisco Victor)
Ferrier, Susan (Edmonstone) 1782-1854 **NCLC 8**
See also DLB 116
Ferrigno, Robert 1948(?)- .... **CLC 65**
See also CA 140
Ferron, Jacques 1921-1985 ....**CLC 94; DAC**
See also CA 117; 129; DLB 60
Feuchtwanger, Lion 1884-1958 .... **TCLC 3**
See also CA 104; DLB 66
Feuillet, Octave 1821-1890 .... **NCLC 45**
See also DLB 192
Feydeau, Georges (Leon Jules Marie) 1862-1921 .... **TCLC 22; DAM DRAM**
See also CA 113; 152; DLB 192
Fichte, Johann Gottlieb 1762-1814 **NCLC 62**
See also DLB 90
Ficino, Marsilio 1433-1499 .... **LC 12**
Fiedeler, Hans
See Doeblin, Alfred
Fiedler, Leslie A(aron) 1917- . **CLC 4, 13, 24**

See also CA 9-12R; CANR 7, 63; DLB 28, 67;
    MTCW 1, 2
Field, Andrew 1938- .... **CLC 44**
    See also CA 97-100; CANR 25
Field, Eugene 1850-1895 .... **NCLC 3**
    See also DLB 23, 42, 140; DLBD 13; MAICYA;
    SATA 16
Field, Gans T.
    See Wellman, Manly Wade
Field, Michael 1915-1971 .... **TCLC 43**
    See also CA 29-32R
Field, Peter
    See Hobson, Laura Z(ametkin)
Fielding, Henry 1707-1754 ..... **LC 1, 46; DA;**
    DAB; DAC; DAM DRAM, MST, NOV;
    WLC
    See also CDBLB 1660-1789; DLB 39, 84, 101
Fielding, Sarah 1710-1768 .... **LC 1, 44**
    See also DLB 39
Fields, W. C. 1880-1946 .... **TCLC 80**
    See also DLB 44
Fierstein, Harvey (Forbes) 1954- .... **CLC 33;**
    DAM DRAM, POP
    See also CA 123; 129
Figes, Eva 1932- .... **CLC 31**
    See also CA 53-56; CANR 4, 44; DLB 14
Finch, Anne 1661-1720 .... **LC 3; PC 21**
    See also DLB 95
Finch, Robert (Duer Claydon) 1900- **CLC 18**
    See also CA 57-60; CANR 9, 24, 49; DLB 88
Findley, Timothy 1930- . **CLC 27, 102; DAC;**
    DAM MST
    See also CA 25-28R; CANR 12, 42, 69; DLB
    53
Fink, William
    See Mencken, H(enry) L(ouis)
Firbank, Louis 1942-
    See Reed, Lou
    See also CA 117
Firbank, (Arthur Annesley) Ronald 1886-1926
    TCLC 1
    See also CA 104; 177; DLB 36
Fisher, Dorothy (Frances) Canfield 1879-1958
    TCLC 87
    See also CA 114; 136; CANR 80; DLB 9, 102;
    MAICYA; YABC 1
Fisher, M(ary) F(rances) K(ennedy) 1908-1992
    CLC 76, 87
    See also CA 77-80; 138; CANR 44; MTCW 1
Fisher, Roy 1930- .... **CLC 25**
    See also CA 81-84; CAAS 10; CANR 16; DLB
    40
Fisher, Rudolph 1897-1934 **TCLC 11; BLC 2;**
    DAM MULT; SSC 25
    See also BW 1, 3; CA 107; 124; CANR 80; DLB
    51, 102
Fisher, Vardis (Alvero) 1895-1968 ...... **CLC 7**
    See also CA 5-8R; 25-28R; CANR 68; DLB 9,
    206
Fiske, Tarleton
    See Bloch, Robert (Albert)
Fitch, Clarke
    See Sinclair, Upton (Beall)
Fitch, John IV
    See Cormier, Robert (Edmund)
Fitzgerald, Captain Hugh
    See Baum, L(yman) Frank
FitzGerald, Edward 1809-1883 .... **NCLC 9**
    See also DLB 32
Fitzgerald, F(rancis) Scott (Key) 1896-1940
    TCLC 1, 6, 14, 28, 55; DA; DAB; DAC;
    DAM MST, NOV; SSC 6, 31; WLC
    See also AAYA 24; AITN 1; CA 110; 123;

CDALB 1917-1929; DLB 4, 9, 86; DLBD 1,
    15, 16; DLBY 81, 96; MTCW 1, 2
Fitzgerald, Penelope 1916- ... **CLC 19, 51, 61**
    See also CA 85-88; CAAS 10; CANR 56; DLB
    14, 194; MTCW 2
Fitzgerald, Robert (Stuart) 1910-1985 **CLC 39**
    See also CA 1-4R; 114; CANR 1; DLBY 80
FitzGerald, Robert D(avid) 1902-1987 **CLC 19**
    See also CA 17-20R
Fitzgerald, Zelda (Sayre) 1900-1948 **TCLC 52**
    See also CA 117; 126; DLBY 84
Flanagan, Thomas (James Bonner) 1923-
    CLC 25, 52
    See also CA 108; CANR 55; DLBY 80; INT
    108; MTCW 1
Flaubert, Gustave 1821-1880 **NCLC 2, 10, 19,**
    62, 66; DA; DAB; DAC; DAM MST, NOV;
    SSC 11; WLC
    See also DLB 119
Flecker, Herman Elroy
    See Flecker, (Herman) James Elroy
Flecker, (Herman) James Elroy 1884-1915
    TCLC 43
    See also CA 109; 150; DLB 10, 19
Fleming, Ian (Lancaster) 1908-1964 . **CLC 3,**
    30; DAM POP
    See also AAYA 26; CA 5-8R; CANR 59;
    CDBLB 1945-1960; DLB 87, 201; MTCW
    1, 2; SATA 9
Fleming, Thomas (James) 1927- .... **CLC 37**
    See also CA 5-8R; CANR 10; INT CANR-10;
    SATA 8
Fletcher, John 1579-1625 .... **LC 33; DC 6**
    See also CDBLB Before 1660; DLB 58
Fletcher, John Gould 1886-1950 .... **TCLC 35**
    See also CA 107; 167; DLB 4, 45
Fleur, Paul
    See Pohl, Frederik
Flooglebuckle, Al
    See Spiegelman, Art
Flying Officer X
    See Bates, H(erbert) E(rnest)
Fo, Dario 1926- **CLC 32, 109; DAM DRAM;**
    DC 10
    See also CA 116; 128; CANR 68; DLBY 97;
    MTCW 1, 2
Fogarty, Jonathan Titulescu Esq.
    See Farrell, James T(homas)
Folke, Will
    See Bloch, Robert (Albert)
Follett, Ken(neth Martin) 1949- ..... **CLC 18;**
    DAM NOV, POP
    See also AAYA 6; BEST 89:4; CA 81-84; CANR
    13, 33, 54; DLB 87; DLBY 81; INT CANR-
    33; MTCW 1
Fontane, Theodor 1819-1898 .... **NCLC 26**
    See also DLB 129
Foote, Horton 1916- **CLC 51, 91; DAM DRAM**
    See also CA 73-76; CANR 34, 51; DLB 26; INT
    CANR-34
Foote, Shelby 1916- **CLC 75; DAM NOV, POP**
    See also CA 5-8R; CANR 3, 45, 74; DLB 2,
    17; MTCW 2
Forbes, Esther 1891-1967 .... **CLC 12**
    See also AAYA 17; CA 13-14; 25-28R; CAP 1;
    CLR 27; DLB 22; JRDA; MAICYA; SATA
    2, 100
Forche, Carolyn (Louise) 1950- **CLC 25, 83,**
    86; DAM POET; PC 10
    See also CA 109; 117; CANR 50, 74; DLB 5,
    193; INT 117; MTCW 1
Ford, Elbur
    See Hibbert, Eleanor Alice Burford

Ford, Ford Madox 1873-1939 **TCLC 1, 15, 39,**
    57; DAM NOV
    See also CA 104; 132; CANR 74; CDBLB
    1914-1945; DLB 162; MTCW 1, 2
Ford, Henry 1863-1947 .... **TCLC 73**
    See also CA 115; 148
Ford, John 1586-(?) .... **DC 8**
    See also CDBLB Before 1660; DAM DRAM;
    DLB 58
Ford, John 1895-1973 .... **CLC 16**
    See also CA 45-48
Ford, Richard 1944- .... **CLC 46, 99**
    See also CA 69-72; CANR 11, 47; MTCW 1
Ford, Webster
    See Masters, Edgar Lee
Foreman, Richard 1937- .... **CLC 50**
    See also CA 65-68; CANR 32, 63
Forester, C(ecil) S(cott) 1899-1966 ... **CLC 35**
    See also CA 73-76; 25-28R; DLB 191; SATA
    13
Forez
    See Mauriac, Francois (Charles)
Forman, James Douglas 1932- .... **CLC 21**
    See also AAYA 17; CA 9-12R; CANR 4, 19,
    42; JRDA; MAICYA; SATA 8, 70
Fornes, Maria Irene 1930- **CLC 39, 61; DC 10;**
    HLCS 1
    See also CA 25-28R; CANR 28, 81; DLB 7;
    HW 1, 2; INT CANR-28; MTCW 1
Forrest, Leon (Richard) 1937-1997 .. **CLC 4;**
    BLCS
    See also BW 2; CA 89-92; 162; CAAS 7; CANR
    25, 52; DLB 33
Forster, E(dward) M(organ) 1879-1970 **C L C**
    1, 2, 3, 4, 9, 10, 13, 15, 22, 45, 77; DA; DAB;
    DAC; DAM MST, NOV; SSC 27; WLC
    See also AAYA 2; CA 13-14; 25-28R; CANR
    45; CAP 1; CDBLB 1914-1945; DLB 34, 98,
    162, 178, 195; DLBD 10; MTCW 1, 2; SATA
    57
Forster, John 1812-1876 .... **NCLC 11**
    See also DLB 144, 184
Forsyth, Frederick 1938- **CLC 2, 5, 36; DAM**
    NOV, POP
    See also BEST 89:4; CA 85-88; CANR 38, 62;
    DLB 87; MTCW 1, 2
Forten, Charlotte L. .... **TCLC 16; BLC 2**
    See also Grimke, Charlotte L(ottie) Forten
    See also DLB 50
Foscolo, Ugo 1778-1827 .... **NCLC 8**
Fosse, Bob ....**CLC 20**
    See also Fosse, Robert Louis
Fosse, Robert Louis 1927-1987
    See Fosse, Bob
    See also CA 110; 123
Foster, Stephen Collins 1826-1864 **NCLC 26**
Foucault, Michel 1926-1984 . **CLC 31, 34, 69**
    See also CA 105; 113; CANR 34; MTCW 1, 2
Fouque, Friedrich (Heinrich Karl) de la Motte
    1777-1843 .... **NCLC 2**
    See also DLB 90
Fourier, Charles 1772-1837 .... **NCLC 51**
Fournier, Henri Alban 1886-1914
    See Alain-Fournier
    See also CA 104
Fournier, Pierre 1916- .... **CLC 11**
    See also Gascar, Pierre
    See also CA 89-92; CANR 16, 40
Fowles, John (Philip) 1926- **CLC 1, 2, 3, 4, 6,**
    9, 10, 15, 33, 87; DAB; DAC; DAM MST;
    SSC 33
    See also CA 5-8R; CANR 25, 71; CDBLB 1960
    to Present; DLB 14, 139, 207; MTCW 1, 2;

MAICYA; SATA 4, 68

Gallico, Paul (William) 1897-1976 ..... **CLC 2**
See also AITN 1; CA 5-8R; 69-72; CANR 23;
DLB 9, 171; MAICYA; SATA 13

Gallo, Max Louis 1932- .... **CLC 95**
See also CA 85-88

Gallois, Lucien
See Desnos, Robert

Gallup, Ralph
See Whitemore, Hugh (John)

Galsworthy, John 1867-1933 **TCLC 1, 45; DA;
DAB; DAC; DAM DRAM, MST, NOV;
SSC 22; WLC**
See also CA 104; 141; CANR 75; CDBLB
1890-1914; DLB 10, 34, 98, 162; DLBD 16;
MTCW 1

Galt, John 1779-1839 .... **NCLC 1**
See also DLB 99, 116, 159

Galvin, James 1951- .... **CLC 38**
See also CA 108; CANR 26

Gamboa, Federico 1864-1939 .... **TCLC 36**
See also CA 167; HW 2

Gandhi, M. K.
See Gandhi, Mohandas Karamchand

Gandhi, Mahatma
See Gandhi, Mohandas Karamchand

Gandhi, Mohandas Karamchand 1869-1948
TCLC 59; DAM MULT
See also CA 121; 132; MTCW 1, 2

Gann, Ernest Kellogg 1910-1991 ..... **CLC 23**
See also AITN 1; CA 1-4R; 136; CANR 1

Garcia, Cristina 1958- .... **CLC 76**
See also CA 141; CANR 73; HW 2

Garcia Lorca, Federico 1898-1936 **TCLC 1, 7,
49; DA; DAB; DAC; DAM DRAM, MST,
MULT, POET; DC 2; HLC; PC 3; WLC**
See also CA 104; 131; CANR 81; DLB 108;
HW 1, 2; MTCW 1, 2

Garcia Marquez, Gabriel (Jose) 1928- **CLC 2,
3, 8, 10, 15, 27, 47, 55, 68; DA; DAB; DAC;
DAM MST, MULT, NOV, POP; HLC; SSC
8; WLC**
See also AAYA 3; BEST 89:1, 90:4; CA 33-
36R; CANR 10, 28, 50, 75; DLB 113; HW
1, 2; MTCW 1, 2

Gard, Janice
See Latham, Jean Lee

Gard, Roger Martin du
See Martin du Gard, Roger

Gardam, Jane 1928- .... **CLC 43**
See also CA 49-52; CANR 2, 18, 33, 54; CLR
12; DLB 14, 161; MAICYA; MTCW 1;
SAAS 9; SATA 39, 76; SATA-Brief 28

Gardner, Herb(ert) 1934- .... **CLC 44**
See also CA 149

Gardner, John (Champlin), Jr. 1933-1982
**CLC 2, 3, 5, 7, 8, 10, 18, 28, 34; DAM NOV,
POP; SSC 7**
See also AITN 1; CA 65-68; 107; CANR 33,
73; CDALBS; DLB 2; DLBY 82; MTCW 1;
SATA 40; SATA-Obit 31

Gardner, John (Edmund) 1926- **CLC 30; DAM
POP**
See also CA 103; CANR 15, 69; MTCW 1

Gardner, Miriam
See Bradley, Marion Zimmer

Gardner, Noel
See Kuttner, Henry

Gardons, S. S.
See Snodgrass, W(illiam) D(e Witt)

Garfield, Leon 1921-1996 .... **CLC 12**
See also AAYA 8; CA 17-20R; 152; CANR 38,
41, 78; CLR 21; DLB 161; JRDA; MAICYA;

SATA 1, 32, 76; SATA-Obit 90

Garland, (Hannibal) Hamlin 1860-1940
TCLC 3; SSC 18
See also CA 104; DLB 12, 71, 78, 186

Garneau, (Hector de) Saint-Denys 1912-1943
TCLC 13
See also CA 111; DLB 88

Garner, Alan 1934- **CLC 17; DAB; DAM POP**
See also AAYA 18; CA 73-76; CANR 15, 64;
CLR 20; DLB 161; MAICYA; MTCW 1, 2;
SATA 18, 69; SATA-Essay 108

Garner, Hugh 1913-1979 .... **CLC 13**
See also CA 69-72; CANR 31; DLB 68

Garnett, David 1892-1981 .... **CLC 3**
See also CA 5-8R; 103; CANR 17, 79; DLB
34; MTCW 2

Garos, Stephanie
See Katz, Steve

Garrett, George (Palmer) 1929- **CLC 3, 11, 51;
SSC 30**
See also CA 1-4R; CAAS 5; CANR 1, 42, 67;
DLB 2, 5, 130, 152; DLBY 83

Garrick, David 1717-1779 .... **LC 15; DAM
DRAM**
See also DLB 84

Garrigue, Jean 1914-1972 .... **CLC 2, 8**
See also CA 5-8R; 37-40R; CANR 20

Garrison, Frederick
See Sinclair, Upton (Beall)

Garth, Will
See Hamilton, Edmond; Kuttner, Henry

Garvey, Marcus (Moziah, Jr.) 1887-1940
TCLC 41; BLC 2; DAM MULT
See also BW 1; CA 120; 124; CANR 79

Gary, Romain .... **CLC 25**
See also Kacew, Romain
See also DLB 83

Gascar, Pierre .... **CLC 11**
See also Fournier, Pierre

Gascoyne, David (Emery) 1916- .... **CLC 45**
See also CA 65-68; CANR 10, 28, 54; DLB 20;
MTCW 1

Gaskell, Elizabeth Cleghorn 1810-1865 **NCLC
70; DAB; DAM MST; SSC 25**
See also CDBLB 1832-1890; DLB 21, 144, 159

Gass, William H(oward) 1924- **CLC 1, 2, 8, 11,
15, 39; SSC 12**
See also CA 17-20R; CANR 30, 71; DLB 2;
MTCW 1, 2

Gasset, Jose Ortega y
See Ortega y Gasset, Jose

Gates, Henry Louis, Jr. 1950- **CLC 65; BLCS;
DAM MULT**
See also BW 2, 3; CA 109; CANR 25, 53, 75;
DLB 67; MTCW 1

Gautier, Theophile 1811-1872 .. **NCLC 1, 59;
DAM POET; PC 18; SSC 20**
See also DLB 119

Gawsworth, John
See Bates, H(erbert) E(rnest)

Gay, John 1685-1732 ... **LC 49; DAM DRAM**
See also DLB 84, 95

Gay, Oliver
See Gogarty, Oliver St. John

Gaye, Marvin (Penze) 1939-1984 ..... **CLC 26**
See also CA 112

Gebler, Carlo (Ernest) 1954- .... **CLC 39**
See also CA 119; 133

Gee, Maggie (Mary) 1948- .... **CLC 57**
See also CA 130; DLB 207

Gee, Maurice (Gough) 1931- .... **CLC 29**
See also CA 97-100; CANR 67; CLR 56; SATA
46, 101

Gelbart, Larry (Simon) 1923- .... **CLC 21, 61**
See also CA 73-76; CANR 45

Gelber, Jack 1932- .... **CLC 1, 6, 14, 79**
See also CA 1-4R; CANR 2; DLB 7

Gellhorn, Martha (Ellis) 1908-1998 **CLC 14,
60**
See also CA 77-80; 164; CANR 44; DLBY 82,
98

Genet, Jean 1910-1986 **CLC 1, 2, 5, 10, 14, 44,
46; DAM DRAM**
See also CA 13-16R; CANR 18; DLB 72;
DLBY 86; MTCW 1, 2

Gent, Peter 1942- .... **CLC 29**
See also AITN 1; CA 89-92; DLBY 82

Gentlewoman in New England, A
See Bradstreet, Anne

Gentlewoman in Those Parts, A
See Bradstreet, Anne

George, Jean Craighead 1919- .... **CLC 35**
See also AAYA 8; CA 5-8R; CANR 25; CLR 1;
DLB 52; JRDA; MAICYA; SATA 2, 68

George, Stefan (Anton) 1868-1933 **TCLC 2, 14**
See also CA 104

Georges, Georges Martin
See Simenon, Georges (Jacques Christian)

Gerhardi, William Alexander
See Gerhardie, William Alexander

Gerhardie, William Alexander 1895-1977
CLC 5
See also CA 25-28R; 73-76; CANR 18; DLB
36

Gerstler, Amy 1956- .... **CLC 70**
See also CA 146

Gertler, T. .... **CLC 34**
See also CA 116; 121; INT 121

Ghalib .... **NCLC 39, 78**
See also Ghalib, Hsadullah Khan

Ghalib, Hsadullah Khan 1797-1869
See Ghalib
See also DAM POET

Ghelderode, Michel de 1898-1962 **CLC 6, 11;
DAM DRAM**
See also CA 85-88; CANR 40, 77

Ghiselin, Brewster 1903- .... **CLC 23**
See also CA 13-16R; CAAS 10; CANR 13

Ghose, Aurabinda 1872-1950 .... **TCLC 63**
See also CA 163

Ghose, Zulfikar 1935- .... **CLC 42**
See also CA 65-68; CANR 67

Ghosh, Amitav 1956- .... **CLC 44**
See also CA 147; CANR 80

Giacosa, Giuseppe 1847-1906 .... **TCLC 7**
See also CA 104

Gibb, Lee
See Waterhouse, Keith (Spencer)

Gibbon, Lewis Grassic .... **TCLC 4**
See also Mitchell, James Leslie

Gibbons, Kaye 1960- **CLC 50, 88; DAM POP**
See also CA 151; CANR 75; MTCW 1

Gibran, Kahlil 1883-1931 . **TCLC 1, 9; DAM
POET, POP; PC 9**
See also CA 104; 150; MTCW 2

Gibran, Khalil
See Gibran, Kahlil

Gibson, William 1914- .. **CLC 23; DA; DAB;
DAC; DAM DRAM, MST**
See also CA 9-12R; CANR 9, 42, 75; DLB 7;
MTCW 1; SATA 66

Gibson, William (Ford) 1948- ... **CLC 39, 63;
DAM POP**
See also AAYA 12; CA 126; 133; CANR 52;
MTCW 1

Gide, Andre (Paul Guillaume) 1869-1951

Gordon, Mary (Catherine) 1949-**CLC 13, 22**
    See also CA 102; CANR 44; DLB 6; DLBY
    81; INT 102; MTCW 1
Gordon, N. J.
    See Bosman, Herman Charles
Gordon, Sol 1923- .... **CLC 26**
    See also CA 53-56; CANR 4; SATA 11
Gordone, Charles 1925-1995**CLC 1, 4; DAM
    DRAM; DC 8**
    See also BW 1, 3; CA 93-96; 150; CANR 55;
    DLB 7; INT 93-96; MTCW 1
Gore, Catherine 1800-1861 .... **NCLC 65**
    See also DLB 116
Gorenko, Anna Andreevna
    See Akhmatova, Anna
Gorky, Maxim 1868-1936**TCLC 8; DAB; SSC
    28; WLC**
    See also Peshkov, Alexei Maximovich
    See also MTCW 2
Goryan, Sirak
    See Saroyan, William
Gosse, Edmund (William) 1849-1928**TCLC 28**
    See also CA 117; DLB 57, 144, 184
Gotlieb, Phyllis Fay (Bloom) 1926- . **CLC 18**
    See also CA 13-16R; CANR 7; DLB 88
Gottesman, S. D.
    See Kornbluth, C(yril) M.; Pohl, Frederik
Gottfried von Strassburg fl. c. 1210-. **C M L C
    10**
    See also DLB 138
Gould, Lois .... **CLC 4, 10**
    See also CA 77-80; CANR 29; MTCW 1
Gourmont, Remy (-Marie-Charles) de 1858-
    1915 .... **TCLC 17**
    See also CA 109; 150; MTCW 2
Govier, Katherine 1948- .... **CLC 51**
    See also CA 101; CANR 18, 40
Goyen, (Charles) William 1915-1983**CLC 5, 8,
    14, 40**
    See also AITN 2; CA 5-8R; 110; CANR 6, 71;
    DLB 2; DLBY 83; INT CANR-6
Goytisolo, Juan 1931- . **CLC 5, 10, 23; DAM
    MULT; HLC**
    See also CA 85-88; CANR 32, 61; HW 1, 2;
    MTCW 1, 2
Gozzano, Guido 1883-1916 .... **PC 10**
    See also CA 154; DLB 114
Gozzi, (Conte) Carlo 1720-1806 .... **NCLC 23**
Grabbe, Christian Dietrich 1801-1836**N C L C
    2**
    See also DLB 133
Grace, Patricia Frances 1937- .... **CLC 56**
    See also CA 176
Gracian y Morales, Baltasar 1601-1658**LC 15**
Gracq, Julien .... **CLC 11, 48**
    See also Poirier, Louis
    See also DLB 83
Grade, Chaim 1910-1982 .... **CLC 10**
    See also CA 93-96; 107
Graduate of Oxford, A
    See Ruskin, John
Grafton, Garth
    See Duncan, Sara Jeannette
Graham, John
    See Phillips, David Graham
Graham, Jorie 1951- .... **CLC 48, 118**
    See also CA 111; CANR 63; DLB 120
Graham, R(obert) B(ontine) Cunninghame
    See Cunninghame Graham, R(obert) B(ontine)
    See also DLB 98, 135, 174
Graham, Robert
    See Haldeman, Joe (William)
Graham, Tom

    See Lewis, (Harry) Sinclair
Graham, W(illiam) S(ydney) 1918-1986**C L C
    29**
    See also CA 73-76; 118; DLB 20
Graham, Winston (Mawdsley) 1910- **CLC 23**
    See also CA 49-52; CANR 2, 22, 45, 66; DLB
    77
Grahame, Kenneth 1859-1932**TCLC 64; DAB**
    See also CA 108; 136; CANR 80; CLR 5; DLB
    34, 141, 178; MAICYA; MTCW 2; SATA
    100; YABC 1
Granovsky, Timofei Nikolaevich 1813-1855
    NCLC 75
    See also DLB 198
Grant, Skeeter
    See Spiegelman, Art
Granville-Barker, Harley 1877-1946**TCLC 2;
    DAM DRAM**
    See also Barker, Harley Granville
    See also CA 104
Grass, Guenter (Wilhelm) 1927-**CLC 1, 2, 4, 6,
    11, 15, 22, 32, 49, 88; DA; DAB; DAC;
    DAM MST, NOV; WLC**
    See also CA 13-16R; CANR 20, 75; DLB 75,
    124; MTCW 1, 2
Gratton, Thomas
    See Hulme, T(homas) E(rnest)
Grau, Shirley Ann 1929- ..**CLC 4, 9; SSC 15**
    See also CA 89-92; CANR 22, 69; DLB 2; INT
    CANR-22; MTCW 1
Gravel, Fern
    See Hall, James Norman
Graver, Elizabeth 1964- .... **CLC 70**
    See also CA 135; CANR 71
Graves, Richard Perceval 1945- .... **CLC 44**
    See also CA 65-68; CANR 9, 26, 51
Graves, Robert (von Ranke) 1895-1985 **C L C
    1, 2, 6, 11, 39, 44, 45; DAB; DAC; DAM
    MST, POET; PC 6**
    See also CA 5-8R; 117; CANR 5, 36; CDBLB
    1914-1945; DLB 20, 100, 191; DLBD 18;
    DLBY 85; MTCW 1, 2; SATA 45
Graves, Valerie
    See Bradley, Marion Zimmer
Gray, Alasdair (James) 1934- .... **CLC 41**
    See also CA 126; CANR 47, 69; DLB 194; INT
    126; MTCW 1, 2
Gray, Amlin 1946- .... **CLC 29**
    See also CA 138
Gray, Francine du Plessix 1930- ..... **CLC 22;
    DAM NOV**
    See also BEST 90:3; CA 61-64; CAAS 2;
    CANR 11, 33, 75, 81; INT CANR-11;
    MTCW 1, 2
Gray, John (Henry) 1866-1934 ...... **TCLC 19**
    See also CA 119; 162
Gray, Simon (James Holliday) 1936- **CLC 9,
    14, 36**
    See also AITN 1; CA 21-24R; CAAS 3; CANR
    32, 69; DLB 13; MTCW 1
Gray, Spalding 1941-**CLC 49, 112; DAM POP;
    DC 7**
    See also CA 128; CANR 74; MTCW 2
Gray, Thomas 1716-1771**LC 4, 40; DA; DAB;
    DAC; DAM MST; PC 2; WLC**
    See also CDBLB 1660-1789; DLB 109
Grayson, David
    See Baker, Ray Stannard
Grayson, Richard (A.) 1951- .... **CLC 38**
    See also CA 85-88; CANR 14, 31, 57
Greeley, Andrew M(oran) 1928- ..... **CLC 28;
    DAM POP**
    See also CA 5-8R; CAAS 7; CANR 7, 43, 69;

    MTCW 1, 2
Green, Anna Katharine 1846-1935 **TCLC 63**
    See also CA 112; 159; DLB 202
Green, Brian
    See Card, Orson Scott
Green, Hannah
    See Greenberg, Joanne (Goldenberg)
Green, Hannah 1927(?)-1996 .... **CLC 3**
    See also CA 73-76; CANR 59
Green, Henry 1905-1973 .... **CLC 2, 13, 97**
    See also Yorke, Henry Vincent
    See also CA 175; DLB 15
Green, Julian (Hartridge) 1900-1998
    See Green, Julien
    See also CA 21-24R; 169; CANR 33; DLB 4,
    72; MTCW 1
Green, Julien .... **CLC 3, 11, 77**
    See also Green, Julian (Hartridge)
    See also MTCW 2
Green, Paul (Eliot) 1894-1981**CLC 25; DAM
    DRAM**
    See also AITN 1; CA 5-8R; 103; CANR 3; DLB
    7, 9; DLBY 81
Greenberg, Ivan 1908-1973
    See Rahv, Philip
    See also CA 85-88
Greenberg, Joanne (Goldenberg) 1932- **C L C
    7, 30**
    See also AAYA 12; CA 5-8R; CANR 14, 32,
    69; SATA 25
Greenberg, Richard 1959(?)- .... **CLC 57**
    See also CA 138
Greene, Bette 1934- .... **CLC 30**
    See also AAYA 7; CA 53-56; CANR 4; CLR 2;
    JRDA; MAICYA; SAAS 16; SATA 8, 102
Greene, Gael .... **CLC 8**
    See also CA 13-16R; CANR 10
Greene, Graham (Henry) 1904-1991**CLC 1, 3,
    6, 9, 14, 18, 27, 37, 70, 72; DA; DAB; DAC;
    DAM MST, NOV; SSC 29; WLC**
    See also AITN 2; CA 13-16R; 133; CANR 35,
    61; CDBLB 1945-1960; DLB 13, 15, 77,
    100, 162, 201, 204; DLBY 91; MTCW 1, 2;
    SATA 20
Greene, Robert 1558-1592 .... **LC 41**
    See also DLB 62, 167
Greer, Richard
    See Silverberg, Robert
Greer, Arthur 1923- .... **CLC 9**
    See also CA 25-28R; CAAS 10; CANR 11;
    SATA 36
Gregor, Lee
    See Pohl, Frederik
Gregory, Isabella Augusta (Persse) 1852-1932
    TCLC 1
    See also CA 104; DLB 10
Gregory, J. Dennis
    See Williams, John A(lfred)
Grendon, Stephen
    See Derleth, August (William)
Grenville, Kate 1950- .... **CLC 61**
    See also CA 118; CANR 53
Grenville, Pelham
    See Wodehouse, P(elham) G(renville)
Greve, Felix Paul (Berthold Friedrich) 1879-
    1948
    See Grove, Frederick Philip
    See also CA 104; 141, 175; CANR 79; DAC;
    DAM MST
Grey, Zane 1872-1939 .. **TCLC 6; DAM POP**
    See also CA 104; 132; DLB 212; MTCW 1, 2
Grieg, (Johan) Nordahl (Brun) 1902-1943
    TCLC 10

Author Index

Hasegawa Tatsunosuke
See Futabatei, Shimei
Hasek, Jaroslav (Matej Frantisek) 1883-1923
TCLC 4
See also CA 104; 129; MTCW 1, 2
Hass, Robert 1941- ... CLC 18, 39, 99; PC 16
See also CA 111; CANR 30, 50, 71; DLB 105,
206; SATA 94
Hastings, Hudson
See Kuttner, Henry
Hastings, Selina .... CLC 44
Hathorne, John 1641-1717 .... LC 38
Hatteras, Amelia
See Mencken, H(enry) L(ouis)
Hatteras, Owen .... TCLC 18
See also Mencken, H(enry) L(ouis); Nathan,
George Jean
Hauptmann, Gerhart (Johann Robert) 1862-
1946 .... TCLC 4; DAM DRAM
See also CA 104; 153; DLB 66, 118
Havel, Vaclav 1936- ... CLC 25, 58, 65; DAM
DRAM; DC 6
See also CA 104; CANR 36, 63; MTCW 1, 2
Haviaras, Stratis .... CLC 33
See also Chaviaras, Strates
Hawes, Stephen 1475(?)-1523(?) .... LC 17
See also DLB 132
Hawkes, John (Clendennin Burne, Jr.) 1925-
1998 .. CLC 1, 2, 3, 4, 7, 9, 14, 15, 27, 49
See also CA 1-4R; 167; CANR 2, 47, 64; DLB
2, 7; DLBY 80, 98; MTCW 1, 2
Hawking, S. W.
See Hawking, Stephen W(illiam)
Hawking, Stephen W(illiam) 1942- CLC 63,
105
See also AAYA 13; BEST 89:1; CA 126; 129;
CANR 48; MTCW 2
Hawkins, Anthony Hope
See Hope, Anthony
Hawthorne, Julian 1846-1934 .... TCLC 25
See also CA 165
Hawthorne, Nathaniel 1804-1864 NCLC 39;
DA; DAB; DAC; DAM MST, NOV; SSC
3, 29; WLC
See also AAYA 18; CDALB 1640-1865; DLB
1, 74; YABC 2
Haxton, Josephine Ayres 1921-
See Douglas, Ellen
See also CA 115; CANR 41
Hayaseca y Eizaguirre, Jorge
See Echegaray (y Eizaguirre), Jose (Maria
Waldo)
Hayashi, Fumiko 1904-1951 .... TCLC 27
See also CA 161; DLB 180
Haycraft, Anna
See Ellis, Alice Thomas
See also CA 122; MTCW 2
Hayden, Robert E(arl) 1913-1980 CLC 5, 9,
14, 37; BLC 2; DA; DAC; DAM MST,
MULT, POET; PC 6
See also BW 1, 3; CA 69-72; 97-100; CABS 2;
CANR 24, 75; CDALB 1941-1968; DLB 5,
76; MTCW 1, 2; SATA 19; SATA-Obit 26
Hayford, J(oseph) E(phraim) Casely
See Casely-Hayford, J(oseph) E(phraim)
Hayman, Ronald 1932- .... CLC 44
See also CA 25-28R; CANR 18, 50; DLB 155
Haywood, Eliza (Fowler) 1693(?)-1756 LC 1,
44
See also DLB 39
Hazlitt, William 1778-1830 .... NCLC 29
See also DLB 110, 158
Hazzard, Shirley 1931- .... CLC 18

See also CA 9-12R; CANR 4, 70; DLBY 82;
MTCW 1
Head, Bessie 1937-1986 CLC 25, 67; BLC 2;
DAM MULT
See also BW 2, 3; CA 29-32R; 119; CANR 25;
DLB 117; MTCW 1, 2
Headon, (Nicky) Topper 1956(?)- ..... CLC 30
Heaney, Seamus (Justin) 1939- CLC 5, 7, 14,
25, 37, 74, 91; DAB; DAM POET; PC 18;
WLCS
See also CA 85-88; CANR 25, 48, 75; CDBLB
1960 to Present; DLB 40; DLBY 95; MTCW
1, 2
Hearn, (Patricio) Lafcadio (Tessima Carlos)
1850-1904 .... TCLC 9
See also CA 105; 166; DLB 12, 78, 189
Hearne, Vicki 1946- .... CLC 56
See also CA 139
Hearon, Shelby 1931- .... CLC 63
See also AITN 2; CA 25-28R; CANR 18, 48
Heat-Moon, William Least .... CLC 29
See also Trogdon, William (Lewis)
See also AAYA 9
Hebbel, Friedrich 1813-1863 NCLC 43; DAM
DRAM
See also DLB 129
Hebert, Anne 1916- CLC 4, 13, 29; DAC; DAM
MST, POET
See also CA 85-88; CANR 69; DLB 68; MTCW
1, 2
Hecht, Anthony (Evan) 1923- CLC 8, 13, 19;
DAM POET
See also CA 9-12R; CANR 6; DLB 5, 169
Hecht, Ben 1894-1964 .... CLC 8
See also CA 85-88; DLB 7, 9, 25, 26, 28, 86
Hedayat, Sadeq 1903-1951 .... TCLC 21
See also CA 120
Hegel, Georg Wilhelm Friedrich 1770-1831
NCLC 46
See also DLB 90
Heidegger, Martin 1889-1976 .... CLC 24
See also CA 81-84; 65-68; CANR 34; MTCW
1, 2
Heidenstam, (Carl Gustaf) Verner von 1859-
1940 .... TCLC 5
See also CA 104
Heifner, Jack 1946- .... CLC 11
See also CA 105; CANR 47
Heijermans, Herman 1864-1924 .... TCLC 24
See also CA 123
Heilbrun, Carolyn G(old) 1926- .... CLC 25
See also CA 45-48; CANR 1, 28, 58
Heine, Heinrich 1797-1856 NCLC 4, 54; PC 25
See also DLB 90
Heinemann, Larry (Curtiss) 1944- ... CLC 50
See also CA 110; CAAS 21; CANR 31, 81;
DLBD 9; INT CANR-31
Heiney, Donald (William) 1921-1993
See Harris, MacDonald
See also CA 1-4R; 142; CANR 3, 58
Heinlein, Robert A(nson) 1907-1988 CLC 1, 3,
8, 14, 26, 55; DAM POP
See also AAYA 17; CA 1-4R; 125; CANR 1,
20, 53; DLB 8; JRDA; MAICYA; MTCW 1,
2; SATA 9, 69; SATA-Obit 56
Helforth, John
See Doolittle, Hilda
Hellenhofferu, Vojtech Kapristian z
See Hasek, Jaroslav (Matej Frantisek)
Heller, Joseph 1923- CLC 1, 3, 5, 8, 11, 36, 63;
DA; DAB; DAC; DAM MST, NOV, POP;
WLC
See also AAYA 24; AITN 1; CA 5-8R; CABS

1; CANR 8, 42, 66; DLB 2, 28; DLBY 80;
INT CANR-8; MTCW 1, 2
Hellman, Lillian (Florence) 1906-1984 CLC 2,
4, 8, 14, 18, 34, 44, 52; DAM DRAM; DC 1
See also AITN 1, 2; CA 13-16R; 112; CANR
33; DLB 7; DLBY 84; MTCW 1, 2
Helprin, Mark 1947- CLC 7, 10, 22, 32; DAM
NOV, POP
See also CA 81-84; CANR 47, 64; CDALBS;
DLBY 85; MTCW 1, 2
Helvetius, Claude-Adrien 1715-1771 . LC 26
Helyar, Jane Penelope Josephine 1933-
See Poole, Josephine
See also CA 21-24R; CANR 10, 26; SATA 82
Hemans, Felicia 1793-1835 .... NCLC 71
See also DLB 96
Hemingway, Ernest (Miller) 1899-1961 C L C
1, 3, 6, 8, 10, 13, 19, 30, 34, 39, 41, 44, 50,
61, 80; DA; DAB; DAC; DAM MST, NOV;
SSC 1, 25; WLC
See also AAYA 19; CA 77-80; CANR 34;
CDALB 1917-1929; DLB 4, 9, 102, 210;
DLBD 1, 15, 16; DLBY 81, 87, 96, 98;
MTCW 1, 2
Hempel, Amy 1951- .... CLC 39
See also CA 118; 137; CANR 70; MTCW 2
Henderson, F. C.
See Mencken, H(enry) L(ouis)
Henderson, Sylvia
See Ashton-Warner, Sylvia (Constance)
Henderson, Zenna (Chlarson) 1917-1983 S S C
29
See also CA 1-4R; 133; CANR 1; DLB 8; SATA
5
Henkin, Joshua .... CLC 119
See also CA 161
Henley, Beth .... CLC 23; DC 6
See also Henley, Elizabeth Becker
See also CABS 3; DLBY 86
Henley, Elizabeth Becker 1952-
See Henley, Beth
See also CA 107; CANR 32, 73; DAM DRAM,
MST; MTCW 1, 2
Henley, William Ernest 1849-1903 .. TCLC 8
See also CA 105; DLB 19
Hennissart, Martha
See Lathen, Emma
See also CA 85-88; CANR 64
Henry, O. .... TCLC 1, 19; SSC 5; WLC
See also Porter, William Sydney
Henry, Patrick 1736-1799 .... LC 25
Henryson, Robert 1430(?)-1506(?) ..... LC 20
See also DLB 146
Henry VIII 1491-1547 .... LC 10
See also DLB 132
Henschke, Alfred
See Klabund
Hentoff, Nat(han Irving) 1925- .... CLC 26
See also AAYA 4; CA 1-4R; CAAS 6; CANR
5, 25, 77; CLR 1, 52; INT CANR-25; JRDA;
MAICYA; SATA 42, 69; SATA-Brief 27
Heppenstall, (John) Rayner 1911-1981 . C L C
10
See also CA 1-4R; 103; CANR 29
Heraclitus c. 540B.C.-c. 450B.C. .... CMLC 22
See also DLB 176
Herbert, Frank (Patrick) 1920-1986 CLC 12,
23, 35, 44, 85; DAM POP
See also AAYA 21; CA 53-56; 118; CANR 5,
43; CDALBS; DLB 8; INT CANR-5; MTCW
1, 2; SATA 9, 37; SATA-Obit 47
Herbert, George 1593-1633 ..... LC 24; DAB;
DAM POET; PC 4

Hogarth, Emmett
See Polonsky, Abraham (Lincoln)

Hogg, James 1770-1835 .... **NCLC 4**
See also DLB 93, 116, 159

Holbach, Paul Henri Thiry Baron 1723-1789
LC 14

Holberg, Ludvig 1684-1754 .... **LC 6**

Holden, Ursula 1921- .... **CLC 18**
See also CA 101; CAAS 8; CANR 22

Holderlin, (Johann Christian) Friedrich 1770-
1843 .... **NCLC 16; PC 4**

Holdstock, Robert
See Holdstock, Robert P.

Holdstock, Robert P. 1948- .... **CLC 39**
See also CA 131; CANR 81

Holland, Isabelle 1920- .... **CLC 21**
See also AAYA 11; CA 21-24R; CANR 10, 25,
47; CLR 57; JRDA; MAICYA; SATA 8, 70,
SATA-Essay 103

Holland, Marcus
See Caldwell, (Janet Miriam) Taylor (Holland)

Hollander, John 1929- .... **CLC 2, 5, 8, 14**
See also CA 1-4R; CANR 1, 52; DLB 5; SATA
13

Hollander, Paul
See Silverberg, Robert

Holleran, Andrew 1943(?)- .... **CLC 38**
See also CA 144

Hollinghurst, Alan 1954- .... **CLC 55, 91**
See also CA 114; DLB 207

Hollis, Jim
See Summers, Hollis (Spurgeon, Jr.)

Holly, Buddy 1936-1959 .... **TCLC 65**

Holmes, Gordon
See Shiel, M(atthew) P(hipps)

Holmes, John
See Souster, (Holmes) Raymond

Holmes, John Clellon 1926-1988 ..... **CLC 56**
See also CA 9-12R; 125; CANR 4; DLB 16

Holmes, Oliver Wendell, Jr. 1841-1935**TCLC
77**
See also CA 114

Holmes, Oliver Wendell 1809-1894**NCLC 14**
See also CDALB 1640-1865; DLB 1, 189;
SATA 34

Holmes, Raymond
See Souster, (Holmes) Raymond

Holt, Victoria
See Hibbert, Eleanor Alice Burford

Holub, Miroslav 1923-1998 ....**CLC 4**
See also CA 21-24R; 169; CANR 10

Homer c. 8th cent. B.C.- ... **CMLC 1, 16; DA;
DAB; DAC; DAM MST, POET; PC 23;
WLCS**
See also DLB 176

Hongo, Garrett Kaoru 1951- .... **PC 23**
See also CA 133; CAAS 22; DLB 120

Honig, Edwin 1919- ....**CLC 33**
See also CA 5-8R; CAAS 8; CANR 4, 45; DLB
5

Hood, Hugh (John Blagdon) 1928-**CLC 15, 28**
See also CA 49-52; CAAS 17; CANR 1, 33;
DLB 53

Hood, Thomas 1799-1845 .... **NCLC 16**
See also DLB 96

Hooker, (Peter) Jeremy 1941- .... **CLC 43**
See also CA 77-80; CANR 22; DLB 40

hooks, bell .... **CLC 94; BLCS**
See also Watkins, Gloria
See also MTCW 2

Hope, A(lec) D(erwent) 1907- ...... **CLC 3, 51**
See also CA 21-24R; CANR 33, 74; MTCW 1,
2

Hope, Anthony 1863-1933 .... **TCLC 83**
See also CA 157; DLB 153, 156

Hope, Brian
See Creasey, John

Hope, Christopher (David Tully) 1944- **C L C
52**
See also CA 106; CANR 47; SATA 62

Hopkins, Gerard Manley 1844-1889 .. **N C L C
17; DA; DAB; DAC; DAM MST, POET;
PC 15; WLC**
See also CDBLB 1890-1914; DLB 35, 57

Hopkins, John (Richard) 1931-1998 ..**CLC 4**
See also CA 85-88; 169

Hopkins, Pauline Elizabeth 1859-1930**T C L C
28; BLC 2; DAM MULT**
See also BW 2, 3; CA 141; DLB 50

Hopkinson, Francis 1737-1791 .... **LC 25**
See also DLB 31

Hopley-Woolrich, Cornell George 1903-1968
See Woolrich, Cornell
See also CA 13-14; CANR 58; CAP 1; MTCW
2

Horatio
See Proust, (Valentin-Louis-George-Eugene-)
Marcel

Horgan, Paul (George Vincent O'Shaughnessy)
1903-1995 .... **CLC 9, 53; DAM NOV**
See also CA 13-16R; 147; CANR 9, 35; DLB
212; DLBY 85; INT CANR-9; MTCW 1, 2;
SATA 13; SATA-Obit 84

Horn, Peter
See Kuttner, Henry

Hornem, Horace Esq.
See Byron, George Gordon (Noel)

**Horney, Karen (Clementine Theodore
Danielsen)** 1885-1952 .... **TCLC 71**
See also CA 114; 165

Hornung, E(rnest) W(illiam) 1866-1921
TCLC 59
See also CA 108; 160; DLB 70

Horovitz, Israel (Arthur) 1939-**CLC 56; DAM
DRAM**
See also CA 33-36R; CANR 46, 59; DLB 7

Horvath, Odon von
See Horvath, Oedoen von
See also DLB 85, 124

Horvath, Oedoen von 1901-1938 ... **TCLC 45**
See also Horvath, Odon von
See also CA 118

Horwitz, Julius 1920-1986 ....**CLC 14**
See also CA 9-12R; 119; CANR 12

Hospital, Janette Turner 1942- ....**CLC 42**
See also CA 108; CANR 48

Hostos, E. M. de
See Hostos (y Bonilla), Eugenio Maria de

Hostos, Eugenio M. de
See Hostos (y Bonilla), Eugenio Maria de

Hostos, Eugenio Maria
See Hostos (y Bonilla), Eugenio Maria de

Hostos (y Bonilla), Eugenio Maria de 1839-
1903 .... **TCLC 24**
See also CA 123; 131; HW 1

Houdini
See Lovecraft, H(oward) P(hillips)

Hougan, Carolyn 1943- ....**CLC 34**
See also CA 139

Household, Geoffrey (Edward West) 1900-1988
CLC 11
See also CA 77-80; 126; CANR 58; DLB 87;
SATA 14; SATA-Obit 59

Housman, A(lfred) E(dward) 1859-1936
**TCLC 1, 10; DA; DAB; DAC; DAM MST,
POET; PC 2; WLCS**

See also CA 104; 125; DLB 19; MTCW 1, 2

Housman, Laurence 1865-1959 .... **TCLC 7**
See also CA 106; 155; DLB 10; SATA 25

Howard, Elizabeth Jane 1923- ..... **CLC 7, 29**
See also CA 5-8R; CANR 8, 62

Howard, Maureen 1930- .... **CLC 5, 14, 46**
See also CA 53-56; CANR 31, 75; DLBY 83;
INT CANR-31; MTCW 1, 2

Howard, Richard 1929- .... **CLC 7, 10, 47**
See also AITN 1; CA 85-88; CANR 25, 80; DLB
5; INT CANR-25

Howard, Robert E(rvin) 1906-1936 **TCLC 8**
See also CA 105; 157

Howard, Warren F.
See Pohl, Frederik

Howe, Fanny (Quincy) 1940- .... **CLC 47**
See also CA 117; CAAS 27; CANR 70; SATA-
Brief 52

Howe, Irving 1920-1993 .... **CLC 85**
See also CA 9-12R; 141; CANR 21, 50; DLB
67; MTCW 1, 2

Howe, Julia Ward 1819-1910 .... **TCLC 21**
See also CA 117; DLB 1, 189

Howe, Susan 1937- .... **CLC 72**
See also CA 160; DLB 120

Howe, Tina 1937- .... **CLC 48**
See also CA 109

Howell, James 1594(?)-1666 .... **LC 13**
See also DLB 151

Howells, W. D.
See Howells, William Dean

Howells, William D.
See Howells, William Dean

Howells, William Dean 1837-1920**TCLC 7, 17,
41**
See also CA 104; 134; CDALB 1865-1917;
DLB 12, 64, 74, 79, 189; MTCW 2

Howes, Barbara 1914-1996 .... **CLC 15**
See also CA 9-12R; 151; CAAS 3; CANR 53;
SATA 5

Hrabal, Bohumil 1914-1997 .... **CLC 13, 67**
See also CA 106; 156; CAAS 12; CANR 57

Hroswitha of Gandersheim c. 935-c. 1002
CMLC 29
See also DLB 148

Hsun, Lu
See Lu Hsun

Hubbard, L(afayette) Ron(ald) 1911-1986
CLC 43; DAM POP
See also CA 77-80; 118; CANR 52; MTCW 2

Huch, Ricarda (Octavia) 1864-1947**TCLC 13**
See also CA 111; DLB 66

Huddle, David 1942- .... **CLC 49**
See also CA 57-60; CAAS 20; DLB 130

Hudson, Jeffrey
See Crichton, (John) Michael

Hudson, W(illiam) H(enry) 1841-1922 **T C L C
29**
See also CA 115; DLB 98, 153, 174; SATA 35

Hueffer, Ford Madox
See Ford, Ford Madox

Hughart, Barry 1934- .... **CLC 39**
See also CA 137

Hughes, Colin
See Creasey, John

Hughes, David (John) 1930- .... **CLC 48**
See also CA 116; 129; DLB 14

Hughes, Edward James
See Hughes, Ted
See also DAM MST, POET

Hughes, (James) Langston 1902-1967**CLC 1,
5, 10, 15, 35, 44, 108; BLC 2; DA; DAB;
DAC; DAM DRAM, MST, MULT, POET;**

DC 3; PC 1; SSC 6; WLC
See also AAYA 12; BW 1, 3; CA 1-4R; 25-28R;
CANR 1, 34; CDALB 1929-1941; CLR 17;
DLB 4, 7, 48, 51, 86; JRDA; MAICYA;
MTCW 1, 2; SATA 4, 33

Hughes, Richard (Arthur Warren) 1900-1976
CLC 1, 11; DAM NOV
See also CA 5-8R; 65-68; CANR 4; DLB 15,
161; MTCW 1; SATA 8; SATA-Obit 25

Hughes, Ted 1930-1998 .. **CLC 2, 4, 9, 14, 37,
119; DAB; DAC; PC 7**
See also Hughes, Edward James
See also CA 1-4R; 171; CANR 1, 33, 66; CLR
3; DLB 40, 161; MAICYA; MTCW 1, 2;
SATA 49; SATA-Brief 27; SATA-Obit 107

Hugo, Richard F(ranklin) 1923-1982 **CLC 6,
18, 32; DAM POET**
See also CA 49-52; 108; CANR 3; DLB 5, 206

Hugo, Victor (Marie) 1802-1885 **NCLC 3, 10,
21; DA; DAB; DAC; DAM DRAM, MST,
NOV, POET; PC 17; WLC**
See also AAYA 28; DLB 119, 192; SATA 47

Huidobro, Vicente
See Huidobro Fernandez, Vicente Garcia

Huidobro Fernandez, Vicente Garcia 1893-
1948 .... **TCLC 31**
See also CA 131; HW 1

Hulme, Keri 1947- .... **CLC 39**
See also CA 125; CANR 69; INT 125

Hulme, T(homas) E(rnest) 1883-1917 **TCLC
21**
See also CA 117; DLB 19

Hume, David 1711-1776 .... **LC 7**
See also DLB 104

Humphrey, William 1924-1997 .... **CLC 45**
See also CA 77-80; 160; CANR 68; DLB 212

Humphreys, Emyr Owen 1919- .... **CLC 47**
See also CA 5-8R; CANR 3, 24; DLB 15

Humphreys, Josephine 1945- ..... **CLC 34, 57**
See also CA 121; 127; INT 127

Huneker, James Gibbons 1857-1921 **TCLC 65**
See also DLB 71

Hungerford, Pixie
See Brinsmead, H(esba) F(ay)

Hunt, E(verette) Howard, (Jr.) 1918- . **CLC 3**
See also AITN 1; CA 45-48; CANR 2, 47

Hunt, Kyle
See Creasey, John

Hunt, (James Henry) Leigh 1784-1859 **NCLC
1, 70; DAM POET**
See also DLB 96, 110, 144

Hunt, Marsha 1946- .... **CLC 70**
See also BW 2, 3; CA 143; CANR 79

Hunt, Violet 1866(?)-1942 .... **TCLC 53**
See also DLB 162, 197

Hunter, E. Waldo
See Sturgeon, Theodore (Hamilton)

Hunter, Evan 1926- . **CLC 11, 31; DAM POP**
See also CA 5-8R; CANR 5, 38, 62; DLBY 82;
INT CANR-5; MTCW 1; SATA 25

Hunter, Kristin (Eggleston) 1931- ... **CLC 35**
See also AITN 1; BW 1; CA 13-16R; CANR
13; CLR 3; DLB 33; INT CANR-13;
MAICYA; SAAS 10; SATA 12

Hunter, Mollie 1922- .... **CLC 21**
See also McIlwraith, Maureen Mollie Hunter
See also AAYA 13; CANR 37, 78; CLR 25; DLB
161; JRDA; MAICYA; SAAS 7; SATA 54,
106

Hunter, Robert (?)-1734 .... **LC 7**

Hurston, Zora Neale 1903-1960 **CLC 7, 30, 61;
BLC 2; DA; DAC; DAM MST, MULT,
NOV; SSC 4; WLCS**

See also AAYA 15; BW 1, 3; CA 85-88; CANR
61; CDALBS; DLB 51, 86; MTCW 1, 2

Huston, John (Marcellus) 1906-1987 **CLC 20**
See also CA 73-76; 123; CANR 34; DLB 26

Hustvedt, Siri 1955- .... **CLC 76**
See also CA 137

Hutten, Ulrich von 1488-1523 .... **LC 16**
See also DLB 179

Huxley, Aldous (Leonard) 1894-1963 **CLC 1,
3, 4, 5, 8, 11, 18, 35, 79; DA; DAB; DAC;
DAM MST, NOV; WLC**
See also AAYA 11; CA 85-88; CANR 44;
CDBLB 1914-1945; DLB 36, 100, 162, 195;
MTCW 1, 2; SATA 63

Huxley, T(homas) H(enry) 1825-1895 **NCLC
67**
See also DLB 57

Huysmans, Joris-Karl 1848-1907 **TCLC 7, 69**
See also CA 104; 165; DLB 123

Hwang, David Henry 1957- ... **CLC 55; DAM
DRAM; DC 4**
See also CA 127; 132; CANR 76; DLB 212;
INT 132; MTCW 2

Hyde, Anthony 1946- .... **CLC 42**
See also CA 136

Hyde, Margaret O(ldroyd) 1917- ..... **CLC 21**
See also CA 1-4R; CANR 1, 36; CLR 23; JRDA;
MAICYA; SAAS 8; SATA 1, 42, 76

Hynes, James 1956(?)- .... **CLC 65**
See also CA 164

Ian, Janis 1951- .... **CLC 21**
See also CA 105

Ibanez, Vicente Blasco
See Blasco Ibanez, Vicente

Ibarguengoitla, Jorge 1928-1983 ...... **CLC 37**
See also CA 124; 113; HW 1

Ibsen, Henrik (Johan) 1828-1906 **TCLC 2, 8,
16, 37, 52; DA; DAB; DAC; DAM DRAM,
MST; DC 2; WLC**
See also CA 104; 141

Ibuse, Masuji 1898-1993 .... **CLC 22**
See also CA 127; 141; DLB 180

Ichikawa, Kon 1915- .... **CLC 20**
See also CA 121

Idle, Eric 1943- .... **CLC 21**
See also Monty Python
See also CA 116; CANR 35

Ignatow, David 1914-1997 .. **CLC 4, 7, 14, 40**
See also CA 9-12R; 162; CAAS 3; CANR 31,
57; DLB 5

Ihimaera, Witi 1944- .... **CLC 46**
See also CA 77-80

Ilf, Ilya .... **TCLC 21**
See also Fainzilberg, Ilya Arnoldovich

Illyes, Gyula 1902-1983 .... **PC 16**
See also CA 114; 109

Immermann, Karl (Lebrecht) 1796-1840
NCLC 4, 49
See also DLB 133

Ince, Thomas H. 1882-1924 .... **TCLC 89**

Inchbald, Elizabeth 1753-1821 ...... **NCLC 62**
See also DLB 39, 89

Inclan, Ramon (Maria) del Valle
See Valle-Inclan, Ramon (Maria) del

Infante, G(uillermo) Cabrera
See Cabrera Infante, G(uillermo)

Ingalls, Rachel (Holmes) 1940- .... **CLC 42**
See also CA 123; 127

Ingamells, Reginald Charles
See Ingamells, Rex

Ingamells, Rex 1913-1955 .... **TCLC 35**
See also CA 167

Inge, William (Motter) 1913-1973 **CLC 1, 8,**

19; DAM DRAM
See also CA 9-12R; CDALB 1941-1968; DLB
7; MTCW 1, 2

Ingelow, Jean 1820-1897 .... **NCLC 39**
See also DLB 35, 163; SATA 33

Ingram, Willis J.
See Harris, Mark

Innaurato, Albert (F.) 1948(?)- .. **CLC 21, 60**
See also CA 115; 122; CANR 78; INT 122

Innes, Michael
See Stewart, J(ohn) I(nnes) M(ackintosh)

Innis, Harold Adams 1894-1952 .... **TCLC 77**
See also DLB 88

Ionesco, Eugene 1909-1994 **CLC 1, 4, 6, 9, 11,
15, 41, 86; DA; DAB; DAC; DAM DRAM,
MST; WLC**
See also CA 9-12R; 144; CANR 55; MTCW 1,
2; SATA 7; SATA-Obit 79

Iqbal, Muhammad 1873-1938 .... **TCLC 28**

Ireland, Patrick
See O'Doherty, Brian

Iron, Ralph
See Schreiner, Olive (Emilie Albertina)

Irving, John (Winslow) 1942- **CLC 13, 23, 38,
112; DAM NOV, POP**
See also AAYA 8; BEST 89:3; CA 25-28R;
CANR 28, 73; DLB 6; DLBY 82; MTCW 1,
2

Irving, Washington 1783-1859 . **NCLC 2, 19;
DA; DAB; DAC; DAM MST; SSC 2; WLC**
See also CDALB 1640-1865; DLB 3, 11, 30,
59, 73, 74, 186; YABC 2

Irwin, P. K.
See Page, P(atricia) K(athleen)

Isaacs, Jorge Ricardo 1837-1895 ... **NCLC 70**

Isaacs, Susan 1943- .... **CLC 32; DAM POP**
See also BEST 89:1; CA 89-92; CANR 20, 41,
65; INT CANR-20; MTCW 1, 2

Isherwood, Christopher (William Bradshaw)
1904-1986 ... **CLC 1, 9, 11, 14, 44; DAM
DRAM, NOV**
See also CA 13-16R; 117; CANR 35; DLB 15,
195; DLBY 86; MTCW 1, 2

Ishiguro, Kazuo 1954- ... **CLC 27, 56, 59, 110;
DAM NOV**
See also BEST 90:2; CA 120; CANR 49; DLB
194; MTCW 1, 2

Ishikawa, Hakuhin
See Ishikawa, Takuboku

Ishikawa, Takuboku 1886(?)-1912 **TCLC 15;
DAM POET; PC 10**
See also CA 113; 153

Iskander, Fazil 1929- .... **CLC 47**
See also CA 102

Isler, Alan (David) 1934- .... **CLC 91**
See also CA 156

Ivan IV 1530-1584 .... **LC 17**

Ivanov, Vyacheslav Ivanovich 1866-1949
TCLC 33
See also CA 122

Ivask, Ivar Vidrik 1927-1992 .... **CLC 14**
See also CA 37-40R; 139; CANR 24

Ives, Morgan
See Bradley, Marion Zimmer

Izumi Shikibu c. 973-c. 1034 .... **CMLC 33**

J. R. S.
See Gogarty, Oliver St. John

Jabran, Kahlil
See Gibran, Kahlil

Jabran, Khalil
See Gibran, Kahlil

Jackson, Daniel
See Wingrove, David (John)

See also CA 85-88; DLB 14

Jolley, (Monica) Elizabeth 1923-**CLC 46; SSC 19**
See also CA 127; CAAS 13; CANR 59

Jones, Arthur Llewellyn 1863-1947
See Machen, Arthur
See also CA 104

Jones, D(ouglas) G(ordon) 1929- ..... **CLC 10**
See also CA 29-32R; CANR 13; DLB 53

Jones, David (Michael) 1895-1974**CLC 2, 4, 7, 13, 42**
See also CA 9-12R; 53-56; CANR 28; CDBLB 1945-1960; DLB 20, 100; MTCW 1

Jones, David Robert 1947-
See Bowie, David
See also CA 103

Jones, Diana Wynne 1934- .... **CLC 26**
See also AAYA 12; CA 49-52; CANR 4, 26, 56; CLR 23; DLB 161; JRDA; MAICYA; SAAS 7; SATA 9, 70, 108

Jones, Edward P. 1950-...................... **CLC 76**
See also BW 2, 3; CA 142; CANR 79

Jones, Gayl 1949- ... **CLC 6, 9; BLC 2; DAM MULT**
See also BW 2, 3; CA 77-80; CANR 27, 66; DLB 33; MTCW 1, 2

Jones, James 1921-1977 ...... **CLC 1, 3, 10, 39**
See also AITN 1, 2; CA 1-4R; 69-72; CANR 6; DLB 2, 143; DLBD 17; DLBY 98; MTCW 1

Jones, John J.
See Lovecraft, H(oward) P(hillips)

Jones, LeRoi .... **CLC 1, 2, 3, 5, 10, 14**
See also Baraka, Amiri
See also MTCW 2

Jones, Louis B. 1953- .... **CLC 65**
See also CA 141; CANR 73

Jones, Madison (Percy, Jr.) 1925-.......**CLC 4**
See also CA 13-16R; CAAS 11; CANR 7, 54; DLB 152

Jones, Mervyn 1922- .... **CLC 10, 52**
See also CA 45-48; CAAS 5; CANR 1; MTCW 1

Jones, Mick 1956(?)- .... **CLC 30**

Jones, Nettie (Pearl) 1941- .... **CLC 34**
See also BW 2; CA 137; CAAS 20

Jones, Preston 1936-1979 .... **CLC 10**
See also CA 73-76; 89-92; DLB 7

Jones, Robert F(rancis) 1934-.............**CLC 7**
See also CA 49-52; CANR 2, 61

Jones, Rod 1953-................................ **CLC 50**
See also CA 128

Jones, Terence Graham Parry 1942- **CLC 21**
See Jones, Terry; Monty Python
See also CA 112; 116; CANR 35; INT 116

Jones, Terry
See Jones, Terence Graham Parry
See also SATA 67; SATA-Brief 51

Jones, Thom 1945(?)- .... **CLC 81**
See also CA 157

Jong, Erica 1942- **CLC 4, 6, 8, 18, 83; DAM NOV, POP**
See also AITN 1; BEST 90:2; CA 73-76; CANR 26, 52, 75; DLB 2, 5, 28, 152; INT CANR-26; MTCW 1, 2

Jonson, Ben(jamin) 1572(?)-1637 .. **LC 6, 33; DA; DAB; DAC; DAM DRAM, MST, POET; DC 4; PC 17; WLC**
See also CDBLB Before 1660; DLB 62, 121

Jordan, June 1936-**CLC 5, 11, 23, 114; BLCS; DAM MULT, POET**
See also AAYA 2; BW 2, 3; CA 33-36R; CANR 25, 70; CLR 10; DLB 38; MAICYA; MTCW 1; SATA 4

Jordan, Neil (Patrick) 1950- .... **CLC 110**
See also CA 124; 130; CANR 54; INT 130

Jordan, Pat(rick M.) 1941-................. **CLC 37**
See also CA 33-36R

Jorgensen, Ivar
See Ellison, Harlan (Jay)

Jorgenson, Ivar
See Silverberg, Robert

Josephus, Flavius c. 37-100 .... **CMLC 13**

Josipovici, Gabriel 1940- .... **CLC 6, 43**
See also CA 37-40R; CAAS 8; CANR 47; DLB 14

Joubert, Joseph 1754-1824 .... **NCLC 9**

Jouve, Pierre Jean 1887-1976 .... **CLC 47**
See also CA 65-68

Jovine, Francesco 1902-1950 .... **TCLC 79**

Joyce, James (Augustine Aloysius) 1882-1941 **TCLC 3, 8, 16, 35, 52; DA; DAB; DAC; DAM MST, NOV, POET; PC 22; SSC 3, 26; WLC**
See also CA 104; 126; CDBLB 1914-1945; DLB 10, 19, 36, 162; MTCW 1, 2

Jozsef, Attila 1905-1937 .... **TCLC 22**
See also CA 116

Juana Ines de la Cruz 1651(?)-1695 .... **LC 5; HLCS 1; PC 24**

Judd, Cyril
See Kornbluth, C(yril) M.; Pohl, Frederik

Julian of Norwich 1342(?)-1416(?) .... **LC 6**
See also DLB 146

Junger, Sebastian 1962- .... **CLC 109**
See also AAYA 28; CA 165

Juniper, Alex
See Hospital, Janette Turner

Junius
See Luxemburg, Rosa

Just, Ward (Swift) 1935-............... **CLC 4, 27**
See also CA 25-28R; CANR 32; INT CANR-32

Justice, Donald (Rodney) 1925- .. **CLC 6, 19, 102; DAM POET**
See also CA 5-8R; CANR 26, 54, 74; DLBY 83; INT CANR-26; MTCW 2

Juvenal c. 60-c. 13 .... **CMLC 8**
See also Juvenalis, Decimus Junius
See also DLB 211

Juvenalis, Decimus Junius 55(?)-c. 127(?)
See Juvenal

Juvenis
See Bourne, Randolph S(illiman)

Kacew, Romain 1914-1980
See Gary, Romain
See also CA 108; 102

Kadare, Ismail 1936-..........................**CLC 52**
See also CA 161

Kadohata, Cynthia .... **CLC 59**
See also CA 140

Kafka, Franz 1883-1924**TCLC 2, 6, 13, 29, 47, 53; DA; DAB; DAC; DAM MST, NOV; SSC 5, 29, 35; WLC**
See also CA 105; 126; DLB 81; MTCW 1, 2

Kahanovitsch, Pinkhes
See Der Nister

Kahn, Roger 1927- .... **CLC 30**
See also CA 25-28R; CANR 44, 69; DLB 171; SATA 37

Kain, Saul
See Sassoon, Siegfried (Lorraine)

Kaiser, Georg 1878-1945 .... **TCLC 9**
See also CA 106; DLB 124

Kaletski, Alexander 1946- .... **CLC 39**
See also CA 118; 143

Kalidasa fl. c. 400-.............. **CMLC 9; PC 22**

Kallman, Chester (Simon) 1921-1975 **CLC 2**
See also CA 45-48; 53-56; CANR 3

Kaminsky, Melvin 1926-
See Brooks, Mel
See also CA 65-68; CANR 16

Kaminsky, Stuart M(elvin) 1934- ..... **CLC 59**
See also CA 73-76; CANR 29, 53

Kandinsky, Wassily 1866-1944 ...... **TCLC 92**
See also CA 118; 155

Kane, Francis
See Robbins, Harold

Kane, Paul
See Simon, Paul (Frederick)

Kane, Wilson
See Bloch, Robert (Albert)

Kanin, Garson 1912-1999 ....**CLC 22**
See also AITN 1; CA 5-8R; 177; CANR 7, 78; DLB 7

Kaniuk, Yoram 1930- ....**CLC 19**
See also CA 134

Kant, Immanuel 1724-1804 ..... **NCLC 27, 67**
See also DLB 94

Kantor, MacKinlay 1904-1977 ....**CLC 7**
See also CA 61-64; 73-76; CANR 60, 63; DLB 9, 102; MTCW 2

Kaplan, David Michael 1946- ....**CLC 50**

Kaplan, James 1951-...........................**CLC 59**
See also CA 135

Karageorge, Michael
See Anderson, Poul (William)

Karamzin, Nikolai Mikhailovich 1766-1826 **NCLC 3**
See also DLB 150

Karapanou, Margarita 1946- ....**CLC 13**
See also CA 101

Karinthy, Frigyes 1887-1938 ....**TCLC 47**
See also CA 170

Karl, Frederick R(obert) 1927-.........**CLC 34**
See also CA 5-8R; CANR 3, 44

Kastel, Warren
See Silverberg, Robert

Kataev, Evgeny Petrovich 1903-1942
See Petrov, Evgeny
See also CA 120

Kataphusin
See Ruskin, John

Katz, Steve 1935-...............................**CLC 47**
See also CA 25-28R; CAAS 14, 64; CANR 12; DLBY 83

Kauffman, Janet 1945- ....**CLC 42**
See also CA 117; CANR 43; DLBY 86

Kaufman, Bob (Garnell) 1925-1986 .**CLC 49**
See also BW 1; CA 41-44R; 118; CANR 22; DLB 16, 41

Kaufman, George S. 1889-1961**CLC 38; DAM DRAM**
See also CA 108; 93-96; DLB 7; INT 108; MTCW 2

Kaufman, Sue .... **CLC 3, 8**
See also Barondess, Sue K(aufman)

Kavafis, Konstantinos Petrou 1863-1933
See Cavafy, C(onstantine) P(eter)
See also CA 104

Kavan, Anna 1901-1968 .... **CLC 5, 13, 82**
See also CA 5-8R; CANR 6, 57; MTCW 1

Kavanagh, Dan
See Barnes, Julian (Patrick)

Kavanagh, Julie 1952- .... **CLC 119**
See also CA 163

Kavanagh, Patrick (Joseph) 1904-1967 **C L C 22**
See also CA 123; 25-28R; DLB 15, 20; MTCW 1

See also CA 115

Martinez Sierra, Maria (de la O'LeJarraga)
1874-1974 .... **TCLC 6**
See also CA 115

Martinsen, Martin
See Follett, Ken(neth Martin)

Martinson, Harry (Edmund) 1904-1978**C L C
14**
See also CA 77-80; CANR 34

Marut, Ret
See Traven, B.

Marut, Robert
See Traven, B.

Marvell, Andrew 1621-1678 ... **LC 4, 43; DA;
DAB; DAC; DAM MST, POET; PC 10;
WLC**
See also CDBLB 1660-1789; DLB 131

Marx, Karl (Heinrich) 1818-1883 . **NCLC 17**
See also DLB 129

Masaoka Shiki .... **TCLC 18**
See also Masaoka Tsunenori

Masaoka Tsunenori 1867-1902
See Masaoka Shiki
See also CA 117

Masefield, John (Edward) 1878-1967**CLC 11,
47; DAM POET**
See also CA 19-20; 25-28R; CANR 33; CAP 2;
CDBLB 1890-1914; DLB 10, 19, 153, 160;
MTCW 1, 2; SATA 19

Maso, Carole 19(?)- .... **CLC 44**
See also CA 170

Mason, Bobbie Ann 1940-**CLC 28, 43, 82; SSC
4**
See also AAYA 5; CA 53-56; CANR 11, 31,
58; CDALBS; DLB 173; DLBY 87; INT
CANR-31; MTCW 1, 2

Mason, Ernst
See Pohl, Frederik

Mason, Lee W.
See Malzberg, Barry N(athaniel)

Mason, Nick 1945- .... **CLC 35**

Mason, Tally
See Derleth, August (William)

Mass, William
See Gibson, William

Master Lao
See Lao Tzu

Masters, Edgar Lee 1868-1950 **TCLC 2, 25;
DA; DAC; DAM MST, POET; PC 1;
WLCS**
See also CA 104; 133; CDALB 1865-1917;
DLB 54; MTCW 1, 2

Masters, Hilary 1928- .... **CLC 48**
See also CA 25-28R; CANR 13, 47

Mastrosimone, William 19(?)- .... **CLC 36**

Mathe, Albert
See Camus, Albert

Mather, Cotton 1663-1728 .... **LC 38**
See also CDALB 1640-1865; DLB 24, 30, 140

Mather, Increase 1639-1723 .... **LC 38**
See also DLB 24

Matheson, Richard Burton 1926- .... **CLC 37**
See also CA 97-100; DLB 8, 44; INT 97-100

Mathews, Harry 1930- .... **CLC 6, 52**
See also CA 21-24R; CAAS 6; CANR 18, 40

Mathews, John Joseph 1894-1979 .. **CLC 84;
DAM MULT**
See also CA 19-20; 142; CANR 45; CAP 2;
DLB 175; NNAL

Mathias, Roland (Glyn) 1915- .... **CLC 45**
See also CA 97-100; CANR 19, 41; DLB 27

Matsuo Basho 1644-1694 .... **PC 3**
See also DAM POET

Mattheson, Rodney
See Creasey, John

Matthews, Brander 1852-1929 .... **TCLC 95**
See also DLB 71, 78; DLBD 13

Matthews, Greg 1949- .... **CLC 45**
See also CA 135

Matthews, William (Procter, III) 1942-1997
CLC 40
See also CA 29-32R; 162; CAAS 18; CANR
12, 57; DLB 5

Matthias, John (Edward) 1941- .... **CLC 9**
See also CA 33-36R; CANR 56

Matthiessen, Peter 1927-**CLC 5, 7, 11, 32, 64;
DAM NOV**
See also AAYA 6; BEST 90:4; CA 9-12R;
CANR 21, 50, 73; DLB 6, 173; MTCW 1, 2;
SATA 27

Maturin, Charles Robert 1780(?)-1824**NCLC
6**
See also DLB 178

Matute (Ausejo), Ana Maria 1925- .. **CLC 11**
See also CA 89-92; MTCW 1

Maugham, W. S.
See Maugham, W(illiam) Somerset

Maugham, W(illiam) Somerset 1874-1965
**CLC 1, 11, 15, 67, 93; DA; DAB; DAC;
DAM DRAM, MST, NOV; SSC 8; WLC**
See also CA 5-8R; 25-28R; CANR 40; CDBLB
1914-1945; DLB 10, 36, 77, 100, 162, 195;
MTCW 1, 2; SATA 54

Maugham, William Somerset
See Maugham, W(illiam) Somerset

Maupassant, (Henri Rene Albert) Guy de 1850-
1893**NCLC 1, 42; DA; DAB; DAC; DAM
MST; SSC 1; WLC**
See also DLB 123

Maupin, Armistead 1944-**CLC 95; DAM POP**
See also CA 125; 130; CANR 58; INT 130;
MTCW 2

Maurhut, Richard
See Traven, B.

Mauriac, Claude 1914-1996 .... **CLC 9**
See also CA 89-92; 152; DLB 83

Mauriac, Francois (Charles) 1885-1970 **C L C
4, 9, 56; SSC 24**
See also CA 25-28; CAP 2; DLB 65; MTCW 1,
2

Mavor, Osborne Henry 1888-1951
See Bridie, James
See also CA 104

Maxwell, William (Keepers, Jr.) 1908-**CLC 19**
See also CA 93-96; CANR 54; DLBY 80; INT
93-96

May, Elaine 1932- .... **CLC 16**
See also CA 124; 142; DLB 44

Mayakovski, Vladimir (Vladimirovich) 1893-
1930 .... **TCLC 4, 18**
See also CA 104; 158; MTCW 2

Mayhew, Henry 1812-1887 .... **NCLC 31**
See also DLB 18, 55, 190

Mayle, Peter 1939(?)- .... **CLC 89**
See also CA 139; CANR 64

Maynard, Joyce 1953- .... **CLC 23**
See also CA 111; 129; CANR 64

Mayne, William (James Carter) 1928-**CLC 12**
See also AAYA 20; CA 9-12R; CANR 37, 80;
CLR 25; JRDA; MAICYA; SAAS 11; SATA
6, 68

Mayo, Jim
See L'Amour, Louis (Dearborn)

Maysles, Albert 1926- .... **CLC 16**
See also CA 29-32R

Maysles, David 1932- .... **CLC 16**

Mazer, Norma Fox 1931- .... **CLC 26**
See also AAYA 5; CA 69-72; CANR 12, 32,
66; CLR 23; JRDA; MAICYA; SAAS 1;
SATA 24, 67, 105

Mazzini, Guiseppe 1805-1872 .... **NCLC 34**

McAuley, James Phillip 1917-1976 . **CLC 45**
See also CA 97-100

McBain, Ed
See Hunter, Evan

McBrien, William Augustine 1930- . **CLC 44**
See also CA 107

McCaffrey, Anne (Inez) 1926-**CLC 17; DAM
NOV, POP**
See also AAYA 6; AITN 2; BEST 89:2; CA 25-
28R; CANR 15, 35, 55; CLR 49; DLB 8;
JRDA; MAICYA; MTCW 1, 2; SAAS 11;
SATA 8, 70

McCall, Nathan 1955(?)- .... **CLC 86**
See also BW 3; CA 146

McCann, Arthur
See Campbell, John W(ood, Jr.)

McCann, Edson
See Pohl, Frederik

McCarthy, Charles, Jr. 1933-
See McCarthy, Cormac
See also CANR 42, 69; DAM POP; MTCW 2

McCarthy, Cormac 1933- **CLC 4, 57, 59, 101**
See also McCarthy, Charles, Jr.
See also DLB 6, 143; MTCW 2

McCarthy, Mary (Therese) 1912-1989**CLC 1,
3, 5, 14, 24, 39, 59; SSC 24**
See also CA 5-8R; 129; CANR 16, 50, 64; DLB
2; DLBY 81; INT CANR-16; MTCW 1, 2

McCartney, (James) Paul 1942-. **CLC 12, 35**
See also CA 146

McCauley, Stephen (D.) 1955- .... **CLC 50**
See also CA 141

McClure, Michael (Thomas) 1932-**CLC 6, 10**
See also CA 21-24R; CANR 17, 46, 77; DLB
16

McCorkle, Jill (Collins) 1958- .... **CLC 51**
See also CA 121; DLBY 87

McCourt, Frank 1930- .... **CLC 109**
See also CA 157

McCourt, James 1941- .... **CLC 5**
See also CA 57-60

McCourt, Malachy 1932- .... **CLC 119**

McCoy, Horace (Stanley) 1897-1955**TCLC 28**
See also CA 108; 155; DLB 9

McCrae, John 1872-1918 .... **TCLC 12**
See also CA 109; DLB 92

McCreigh, James
See Pohl, Frederik

McCullers, (Lula) Carson (Smith) 1917-1967
**CLC 1, 4, 10, 12, 48, 100; DA; DAB; DAC;
DAM MST, NOV; SSC 9, 24; WLC**
See also AAYA 21; CA 5-8R; 25-28R; CABS
1, 3; CANR 18; CDALB 1941-1968; DLB
2, 7, 173; MTCW 1, 2; SATA 27

McCulloch, John Tyler
See Burroughs, Edgar Rice

McCullough, Colleen 1938(?)- **CLC 27, 107;
DAM NOV, POP**
See also CA 81-84; CANR 17, 46, 67; MTCW
1, 2

McDermott, Alice 1953- .... **CLC 90**
See also CA 109; CANR 40

McElroy, Joseph 1930- .... **CLC 5, 47**
See also CA 17-20R

McEwan, Ian (Russell) 1948- .... **CLC 13, 66;
DAM NOV**
See also BEST 90:4; CA 61-64; CANR 14, 41,
69; DLB 14, 194; MTCW 1, 2

McFadden, David 1940- .... **CLC 48**
See also CA 104; DLB 60; INT 104
McFarland, Dennis 1950- .... **CLC 65**
See also CA 165
McGahern, John 1934-**CLC 5, 9, 48; SSC 17**
See also CA 17-20R; CANR 29, 68; DLB 14;
MTCW 1
McGinley, Patrick (Anthony) 1937- **CLC 41**
See also CA 120; 127; CANR 56; INT 127
McGinley, Phyllis 1905-1978 .... **CLC 14**
See also CA 9-12R; 77-80; CANR 19; DLB 11,
48; SATA 2, 44; SATA-Obit 24
McGinniss, Joe 1942- .... **CLC 32**
See also AITN 2; BEST 89:2; CA 25-28R;
CANR 26, 70; DLB 185; INT CANR-26
McGivern, Maureen Daly
See Daly, Maureen
McGrath, Patrick 1950- .... **CLC 55**
See also CA 136; CANR 65
McGrath, Thomas (Matthew) 1916-1990**CLC
28, 59; DAM POET**
See also CA 9-12R; 132; CANR 6, 33; MTCW
1; SATA 41; SATA-Obit 66
McGuane, Thomas (Francis III) 1939-**CLC 3,
7, 18, 45**
See also AITN 2; CA 49-52; CANR 5, 24, 49;
DLB 2, 212; DLBY 80; INT CANR-24;
MTCW 1
McGuckian, Medbh 1950- ..... **CLC 48; DAM
POET; PC 27**
See also CA 143; DLB 40
McHale, Tom 1942(?)-1982 .... **CLC 3, 5**
See also AITN 1; CA 77-80; 106
McIlvanney, William 1936- .... **CLC 42**
See also CA 25-28R; CANR 61; DLB 14, 207
McIlwraith, Maureen Mollie Hunter
See Hunter, Mollie
See also SATA 2
McInerney, Jay 1955-**CLC 34, 112; DAM POP**
See also AAYA 18; CA 116; 123; CANR 45,
68; INT 123; MTCW 2
McIntyre, Vonda N(eel) 1948- .... **CLC 18**
See also CA 81-84; CANR 17, 34, 69; MTCW
1
McKay, Claude**TCLC 7, 41; BLC 3; DAB; PC
2**
See also McKay, Festus Claudius
See also DLB 4, 45, 51, 117
McKay, Festus Claudius 1889-1948
See McKay, Claude
See also BW 1, 3; CA 104; 124; CANR 73; DA;
DAC; DAM MST, MULT, NOV, POET;
MTCW 1, 2; WLC
McKuen, Rod 1933- .... **CLC 1, 3**
See also AITN 1; CA 41-44R; CANR 40
McLoughlin, R. B.
See Mencken, H(enry) L(ouis)
McLuhan, (Herbert) Marshall 1911-1980
CLC 37, 83
See also CA 9-12R; 102; CANR 12, 34, 61;
DLB 88; INT CANR-12; MTCW 1, 2
McMillan, Terry (L.) 1951- **CLC 50, 61, 112;
BLCS; DAM MULT, NOV, POP**
See also AAYA 21; BW 2, 3; CA 140; CANR
60; MTCW 2
McMurtry, Larry (Jeff) 1936-**CLC 2, 3, 7, 11,
27, 44; DAM NOV, POP**
See also AAYA 15; AITN 2; BEST 89:2; CA 5-
8R; CANR 19, 43, 64; CDALB 1968-1988;
DLB 2, 143; DLBY 80, 87; MTCW 1, 2
McNally, T. M. 1961- .... **CLC 82**
McNally, Terrence 1939- ... **CLC 4, 7, 41, 91;
DAM DRAM**

See also CA 45-48; CANR 2, 56; DLB 7;
MTCW 2
McNamer, Deirdre 1950- .... **CLC 70**
McNeal, Tom .... **CLC 119**
McNeile, Herman Cyril 1888-1937
See Sapper
See also DLB 77
McNickle, (William) D'Arcy 1904-1977 **C L C
89; DAM MULT**
See also CA 9-12R; 85-88; CANR 5, 45; DLB
175, 212; NNAL; SATA-Obit 22
McPhee, John (Angus) 1931- .... **CLC 36**
See also BEST 90:1; CA 65-68; CANR 20, 46,
64, 69; DLB 185; MTCW 1, 2
McPherson, James Alan 1943- .. **CLC 19, 77;
BLCS**
See also BW 1, 3; CA 25-28R; CAAS 17;
CANR 24, 74; DLB 38; MTCW 1, 2
McPherson, William (Alexander) 1933- **C L C
34**
See also CA 69-72; CANR 28; INT CANR-28
Mead, George Herbert 1873-1958 . **TCLC 89**
Mead, Margaret 1901-1978 .... **CLC 37**
See also AITN 1; CA 1-4R; 81-84; CANR 4;
MTCW 1, 2; SATA-Obit 20
Meaker, Marijane (Agnes) 1927-
See Kerr, M. E.
See also CA 107; CANR 37, 63; INT 107;
JRDA; MAICYA; MTCW 1; SATA 20, 61,
99
Medoff, Mark (Howard) 1940- ... **CLC 6, 23;
DAM DRAM**
See also AITN 1; CA 53-56; CANR 5, DLB 7;
INT CANR-5
Medvedev, P. N.
See Bakhtin, Mikhail Mikhailovich
Meged, Aharon
See Megged, Aharon
Meged, Aron
See Megged, Aharon
Megged, Aharon 1920- .... **CLC 9**
See also CA 49-52; CAAS 13; CANR 1
Mehta, Ved (Parkash) 1934- .... **CLC 37**
See also CA 1-4R; CANR 2, 23, 69; MTCW 1
Melanter
See Blackmore, R(ichard) D(oddridge)
Melies, Georges 1861-1938 .... **TCLC 81**
Melikow, Loris
See Hofmannsthal, Hugo von
Melmoth, Sebastian
See Wilde, Oscar
Meltzer, Milton 1915- .... **CLC 26**
See also AAYA 8; CA 13-16R; CANR 38; CLR
13; DLB 61; JRDA; MAICYA; SAAS 1;
SATA 1, 50, 80
Melville, Herman 1819-1891**NCLC 3, 12, 29,
45, 49; DA; DAB; DAC; DAM MST, NOV;
SSC 1, 17; WLC**
See also AAYA 25; CDALB 1640-1865; DLB
3, 74; SATA 59
Menander c. 342B.C.-c. 292B.C. ... **CMLC 9;
DAM DRAM; DC 3**
See also DLB 176
Mencken, H(enry) L(ouis) 1880-1956 **T C L C
13**
See also CA 105; 125; CDALB 1917-1929;
DLB 11, 29, 63, 137; MTCW 1, 2
Mendelsohn, Jane 1965(?)- .... **CLC 99**
See also CA 154
Mercer, David 1928-1980**CLC 5; DAM DRAM**
See also CA 9-12R; 102; CANR 23; DLB 13;
MTCW 1
Merchant, Paul

See Ellison, Harlan (Jay)
Meredith, George 1828-1909 . **TCLC 17, 43;
DAM POET**
See also CA 117; 153; CANR 80; CDBLB 1832-
1890; DLB 18, 35, 57, 159
Meredith, William (Morris) 1919-**CLC 4, 13,
22, 55; DAM POET**
See also CA 9-12R; CAAS 14; CANR 6, 40;
DLB 5
Merezhkovsky, Dmitry Sergeyevich 1865-1941
TCLC 29
See also CA 169
Merimee, Prosper 1803-1870**NCLC 6, 65; SSC
7**
See also DLB 119, 192
Merkin, Daphne 1954- .... **CLC 44**
See also CA 123
Merlin, Arthur
See Blish, James (Benjamin)
Merrill, James (Ingram) 1926-1995**CLC 2, 3,
6, 8, 13, 18, 34, 91; DAM POET**
See also CA 13-16R; 147; CANR 10, 49, 63;
DLB 5, 165; INT CANR-10;
MTCW 1, 2
Merriman, Alex
See Silverberg, Robert
Merriman, Brian 1747-1805 .... **NCLC 70**
Merritt, E. B.
See Waddington, Miriam
Merton, Thomas 1915-1968**CLC 1, 3, 11, 34,
83; PC 10**
See also CA 5-8R; 25-28R; CANR 22, 53; DLB
48; DLBY 81; MTCW 1, 2
Merwin, W(illiam) S(tanley) 1927- **CLC 1, 2,
3, 5, 8, 13, 18, 45, 88; DAM POET**
See also CA 13-16R; CANR 15, 51; DLB 5,
169; INT CANR-15; MTCW 1, 2
Metcalf, John 1938- .... **CLC 37**
See also CA 113; DLB 60
Metcalf, Suzanne
See Baum, L(yman) Frank
Mew, Charlotte (Mary) 1870-1928 .. **TCLC 8**
See also CA 105; DLB 19, 135
Mewshaw, Michael 1943- .... **CLC 9**
See also CA 53-56; CANR 7, 47; DLBY 80
Meyer, June
See Jordan, June
Meyer, Lynn
See Slavitt, David R(ytman)
Meyer-Meyrink, Gustav 1868-1932
See Meyrink, Gustav
See also CA 117
Meyers, Jeffrey 1939- .... **CLC 39**
See also CA 73-76; CANR 54; DLB 111
Meynell, Alice (Christina Gertrude Thompson)
1847-1922 .... **TCLC 6**
See also CA 104; 177; DLB 19, 98
Meyrink, Gustav .... **TCLC 21**
See also Meyer-Meyrink, Gustav
See also DLB 81
Michaels, Leonard 1933- **CLC 6, 25; SSC 16**
See also CA 61-64; CANR 21, 62; DLB 130;
MTCW 1
Michaux, Henri 1899-1984 .... **CLC 8, 19**
See also CA 85-88; 114
Micheaux, Oscar (Devereaux) 1884-1951
TCLC 76
See also BW 3; CA 174, DLB 50
Michelangelo 1475-1564 .... **LC 12**
Michelet, Jules 1798-1874 .... **NCLC 31**
Michels, Robert 1876-1936............. **TCLC 88**
Michener, James A(lbert) 1907(?)-1997 **C L C
1, 5, 11, 29, 60, 109; DAM NOV, POP**

CLC 8, 19; DAM DRAM
See also CA 85-88; 37-40R; DLB 72; MTCW
1
Monty Python
See Chapman, Graham; Cleese, John
(Marwood); Gilliam, Terry (Vance); Idle,
Eric; Jones, Terence Graham Parry; Palin,
Michael (Edward)
See also AAYA 7
Moodie, Susanna (Strickland) 1803-1885
NCLC 14
See also DLB 99
Mooney, Edward 1951-
See Mooney, Ted
See also CA 130
Mooney, Ted .... **CLC 25**
See also Mooney, Edward
Moorcock, Michael (John) 1939- **CLC 5, 27, 58**
See also Bradbury, Edward P.
See also AAYA 26; CA 45-48; CAAS 5; CANR
2, 17, 38, 64; DLB 14; MTCW 1, 2; SATA
93
Moore, Brian 1921-1999 **CLC 1, 3, 5, 7, 8, 19,**
32, 90; DAB; DAC; DAM MST
See also CA 1-4R; 174; CANR 1, 25, 42, 63;
MTCW 1, 2
Moore, Edward
See Muir, Edwin
Moore, G. E. 1873-1958 .... **TCLC 89**
Moore, George Augustus 1852-1933 **TCLC 7;**
SSC 19
See also CA 104; 177; DLB 10, 18, 57, 135
Moore, Lorrie .... **CLC 39, 45, 68**
See also Moore, Marie Lorena
Moore, Marianne (Craig) 1887-1972 **CLC 1, 2,**
4, 8, 10, 13, 19, 47; DA; DAB; DAC; DAM
MST, POET; PC 4; WLCS
See also CA 1-4R; 33-36R; CANR 3, 61;
CDALB 1929-1941; DLB 45; DLBD 7;
MTCW 1, 2; SATA 20
Moore, Marie Lorena 1957-
See Moore, Lorrie
See also CA 116; CANR 39
Moore, Thomas 1779-1852 .... **NCLC 6**
See also DLB 96, 144
Morand, Paul 1888-1976 .... **CLC 41; SSC 22**
See also CA 69-72; DLB 65
Morante, Elsa 1918-1985 .... **CLC 8, 47**
See also CA 85-88; 117; CANR 35; DLB 177;
MTCW 1, 2
Moravia, Alberto 1907-1990 **CLC 2, 7, 11, 27,**
46; SSC 26
See also Pincherle, Alberto
See also DLB 177; MTCW 2
More, Hannah 1745-1833 .... **NCLC 27**
See also DLB 107, 109, 116, 158
More, Henry 1614-1687 .... **LC 9**
See also DLB 126
More, Sir Thomas 1478-1535 .... **LC 10, 32**
Moreas, Jean .... **TCLC 18**
See also Papadiamantopoulos, Johannes
Morgan, Berry 1919- .... **CLC 6**
See also CA 49-52; DLB 6·
Morgan, Claire
See Highsmith, (Mary) Patricia
Morgan, Edwin (George) 1920- .... **CLC 31**
See also CA 5-8R; CANR 3, 43; DLB 27
Morgan, (George) Frederick 1922- . **CLC 23**
See also CA 17-20R; CANR 21
Morgan, Harriet
See Mencken, H(enry) L(ouis)
Morgan, Jane
See Cooper, James Fenimore

Morgan, Janet 1945- .... **CLC 39**
See also CA 65-68
Morgan, Lady 1776(?)-1859 .... **NCLC 29**
See also DLB 116, 158
Morgan, Robin (Evonne) 1941- .... **CLC 2**
See also CA 69-72; CANR 29, 68; MTCW 1;
SATA 80
Morgan, Scott
See Kuttner, Henry
Morgan, Seth 1949(?)-1990 .... **CLC 65**
See also CA 132
Morgenstern, Christian 1871-1914 . **TCLC 8**
See also CA 105
Morgenstern, S.
See Goldman, William (W.)
Moricz, Zsigmond 1879-1942 .... **TCLC 33**
See also CA 165
Morike, Eduard (Friedrich) 1804-1875 **NCLC**
10
See also DLB 133
Moritz, Karl Philipp 1756-1793 .... **LC 2**
See also DLB 94
Morland, Peter Henry
See Faust, Frederick (Schiller)
Morley, Christopher (Darlington) 1890-1957
TCLC 87
See also CA 112; DLB 9
Morren, Theophil
See Hofmannsthal, Hugo von
Morris, Bill 1952- .... **CLC 76**
Morris, Julian
See West, Morris L(anglo)
Morris, Steveland Judkins 1950(?)-
See Wonder, Stevie
See also CA 111
Morris, William 1834-1896 .... **NCLC 4**
See also CDBLB 1832-1890; DLB 18, 35, 57,
156, 178, 184
Morris, Wright 1910-1998 **CLC 1, 3, 7, 18, 37**
See also CA 9-12R; 167; CANR 21, 81; DLB
2, 206; DLBY 81; MTCW 1, 2
Morrison, Arthur 1863-1945 .... **TCLC 72**
See also CA 120; 157; DLB 70, 135, 197
Morrison, Chloe Anthony Wofford
See Morrison, Toni
Morrison, James Douglas 1943-1971
See Morrison, Jim
See also CA 73-76; CANR 40
Morrison, Jim .... **CLC 17**
See also Morrison, James Douglas
Morrison, Toni 1931- **CLC 4, 10, 22, 55, 81, 87;**
BLC 3; DA; DAB; DAC; DAM MST,
MULT, NOV, POP
See also AAYA 1, 22; BW 2, 3; CA 29-32R;
CANR 27, 42, 67; CDALB 1968-1988; DLB
6, 33, 143; DLBY 81; MTCW 1, 2; SATA 57
Morrison, Van 1945- .... **CLC 21**
See also CA 116; 168
Morrissy, Mary 1958- .... **CLC 99**
Mortimer, John (Clifford) 1923- **CLC 28, 43;**
DAM DRAM, POP
See also CA 13-16R; CANR 21, 69; CDBLB
1960 to Present; DLB 13; INT CANR-21;
MTCW 1, 2
Mortimer, Penelope (Ruth) 1918- .... **CLC 5**
See also CA 57-60; CANR 45
Morton, Anthony
See Creasey, John
Mosca, Gaetano 1858-1941 .... **TCLC 75**
Mosher, Howard Frank 1943- .... **CLC 62**
See also CA 139; CANR 65
Mosley, Nicholas 1923- .... **CLC 43, 70**
See also CA 69-72; CANR 41, 60; DLB 14, 207

Mosley, Walter 1952- **CLC 97; BLCS; DAM**
MULT, POP
See also AAYA 17; BW 2; CA 142; CANR 57;
MTCW 2
Moss, Howard 1922-1987 **CLC 7, 14, 45, 50;**
DAM POET
See also CA 1-4R; 123; CANR 1, 44; DLB 5
Mossgiel, Rab
See Burns, Robert
Motion, Andrew (Peter) 1952- .... **CLC 47**
See also CA 146; DLB 40
Motley, Willard (Francis) 1909-1965 **CLC 18**
See also BW 1; CA 117; 106; DLB 76, 143
Motoori, Norinaga 1730-1801 .... **NCLC 45**
Mott, Michael (Charles Alston) 1930- **CLC 15,**
34
See also CA 5-8R; CAAS 7; CANR 7, 29
Mountain Wolf Woman 1884-1960 ... **CLC 92**
See also CA 144; NNAL
Moure, Erin 1955- .... **CLC 88**
See also CA 113; DLB 60
Mowat, Farley (McGill) 1921- **CLC 26; DAC;**
DAM MST
See also AAYA 1; CA 1-4R; CANR 4, 24, 42,
68; CLR 20; DLB 68; INT CANR-24; JRDA;
MAICYA; MTCW 1, 2; SATA 3, 55
Mowatt, Anna Cora 1819-1870 ...... **NCLC 74**
Moyers, Bill 1934- .... **CLC 74**
See also AITN 2; CA 61-64; CANR 31, 52
Mphahlele, Es'kia
See Mphahlele, Ezekiel
See also DLB 125
Mphahlele, Ezekiel 1919- .. **CLC 25; BLC 3;**
DAM MULT
See also Mphahlele, Es'kia
See also BW 2, 3; CA 81-84; CANR 26, 76;
MTCW 2
Mqhayi, S(amuel) E(dward) K(rune Loliwe)
1875-1945 **TCLC 25; BLC 3; DAM MULT**
See also CA 153
Mrozek, Slawomir 1930- .... **CLC 3, 13**
See also CA 13-16R; CAAS 10; CANR 29;
MTCW 1
Mrs. Belloc-Lowndes
See Lowndes, Marie Adelaide (Belloc)
Mtwa, Percy (?)- .... **CLC 47**
Mueller, Lisel 1924- .... **CLC 13, 51**
See also CA 93-96; DLB 105
Muir, Edwin 1887-1959 .... **TCLC 2, 87**
See also CA 104; DLB 20, 100, 191
Muir, John 1838-1914 .... **TCLC 28**
See also CA 165; DLB 186
Mujica Lainez, Manuel 1910-1984 ... **CLC 31**
See also Lainez, Manuel Mujica
See also CA 81-84; 112; CANR 32; HW 1
Mukherjee, Bharati 1940- **CLC 53, 115; DAM**
NOV
See also BEST 89:2; CA 107; CANR 45, 72;
DLB 60; MTCW 1, 2
Muldoon, Paul 1951- **CLC 32, 72; DAM POET**
See also CA 113; 129; CANR 52; DLB 40; INT
129
Mulisch, Harry 1927- .... **CLC 42**
See also CA 9-12R; CANR 6, 26, 56
Mull, Martin 1943- .... **CLC 17**
See also CA 105
Muller, Wilhelm .... **NCLC 73**
Mulock, Dinah Maria
See Craik, Dinah Maria (Mulock)
Munford, Robert 1737(?)-1783 .... **LC 5**
See also DLB 31
Mungo, Raymond 1946- .... **CLC 72**
See also CA 49-52; CANR 2

See also DLB 166
Nik. T. O.
See Annensky, Innokenty (Fyodorovich)
Nin, Anais 1903-1977 **CLC 1, 4, 8, 11, 14, 60; DAM NOV, POP; SSC 10**
See also AITN 2; CA 13-16R; 69-72; CANR 22, 53; DLB 2, 4, 152; MTCW 1, 2
Nishida, Kitaro 1870-1945 .... **TCLC 83**
Nishiwaki, Junzaburo 1894-1982 .... **PC 15**
See also CA 107
Nissenson, Hugh 1933- .... **CLC 4, 9**
See also CA 17-20R; CANR 27; DLB 28
Niven, Larry ....**CLC 8**
See also Niven, Laurence Van Cott
See also AAYA 27; DLB 8
Niven, Laurence Van Cott 1938-
See Niven, Larry
See also CA 21-24R; CAAS 12; CANR 14, 44, 66; DAM POP; MTCW 1, 2; SATA 95
Nixon, Agnes Eckhardt 1927- .... **CLC 21**
See also CA 110
Nizan, Paul 1905-1940 .... **TCLC 40**
See also CA 161; DLB 72
Nkosi, Lewis 1936- ... **CLC 45; BLC 3; DAM MULT**
See also BW 1, 3; CA 65-68; CANR 27, 81; DLB 157
Nodier, (Jean) Charles (Emmanuel) 1780-1844 **NCLC 19**
See also DLB 119
Noguchi, Yone 1875-1947 .... **TCLC 80**
Nolan, Christopher 1965- .... **CLC 58**
See also CA 111
Noon, Jeff 1957-................................ **CLC 91**
See also CA 148
Norden, Charles
See Durrell, Lawrence (George)
Nordhoff, Charles (Bernard) 1887-1947 **TCLC 23**
See also CA 108; DLB 9; SATA 23
Norfolk, Lawrence 1963- .... **CLC 76**
See also CA 144
Norman, Marsha 1947-**CLC 28; DAM DRAM; DC 8**
See also CA 105; CABS 3; CANR 41; DLBY 84
Normyx
See Douglas, (George) Norman
Norris, Frank 1870-1902 .... **SSC 28**
See also Norris, (Benjamin) Frank(lin, Jr.)
See also CDALB 1865-1917; DLB 12, 71, 186
Norris, (Benjamin) Frank(lin, Jr.) 1870-1902 **TCLC 24**
See also Norris, Frank
See also CA 110; 160
Norris, Leslie 1921- .... **CLC 14**
See also CA 11-12; CANR 14; CAP 1; DLB 27
North, Andrew
See Norton, Andre
North, Anthony
See Koontz, Dean R(ay)
North, Captain George
See Stevenson, Robert Louis (Balfour)
North, Milou
See Erdrich, Louise
Northrup, B. A.
See Hubbard, L(afayette) Ron(ald)
North Staffs
See Hulme, T(homas) E(rnest)
Norton, Alice Mary
See Norton, Andre
See also MAICYA; SATA 1, 43
Norton, Andre 1912- .... **CLC 12**

See also Norton, Alice Mary
See also AAYA 14; CA 1-4R; CANR 68; CLR 50; DLB 8, 52; JRDA; MTCW 1; SATA 91
Norton, Caroline 1808-1877 .... **NCLC 47**
See also DLB 21, 159, 199
Norway, Nevil Shute 1899-1960
See Shute, Nevil
See also CA 102; 93-96; MTCW 2
Norwid, Cyprian Kamil 1821-1883 **NCLC 17**
Nosille, Nabrah
See Ellison, Harlan (Jay)
Nossack, Hans Erich 1901-1978 .... **CLC 6**
See also CA 93-96; 85-88; DLB 69
Nostradamus 1503-1566 .... **LC 27**
Nosu, Chuji
See Ozu, Yasujiro
Notenburg, Eleanora (Genrikhovna) von
See Guro, Elena
Nova, Craig 1945- .... **CLC 7, 31**
See also CA 45-48; CANR 2, 53
Novak, Joseph
See Kosinski, Jerzy (Nikodem)
Novalis 1772-1801 .... **NCLC 13**
See also DLB 90
Novis, Emile
See Weil, Simone (Adolphine)
Nowlan, Alden (Albert) 1933-1983 . **CLC 15; DAC; DAM MST**
See also CA 9-12R; CANR 5; DLB 53
Noyes, Alfred 1880-1958 ...... **TCLC 7; PC 27**
See also CA 104; DLB 20
Nunn, Kem ....**CLC 34**
See also CA 159
Nye, Robert 1939-... **CLC 13, 42; DAM NOV**
See also CA 33-36R; CANR 29, 67; DLB 14; MTCW 1; SATA 6
Nyro, Laura 1947- .... **CLC 17**
Oates, Joyce Carol 1938-**CLC 1, 2, 3, 6, 9, 11, 15, 19, 33, 52, 108; DA; DAB; DAC; DAM MST, NOV, POP; SSC 6; WLC**
See also AAYA 15; AITN 1; BEST 89:2; CA 5-8R; CANR 25, 45, 74; CDALB 1968-1988; DLB 2, 5, 130; DLBY 81; INT CANR-25; MTCW 1, 2
O'Brien, Darcy 1939-1998 .... **CLC 11**
See also CA 21-24R; 167; CANR 8, 59
O'Brien, E. G.
See Clarke, Arthur C(harles)
O'Brien, Edna 1936- **CLC 3, 5, 8, 13, 36, 65, 116; DAM NOV; SSC 10**
See also CA 1-4R; CANR 6, 41, 65; CDBLB 1960 to Present; DLB 14; MTCW 1, 2
O'Brien, Fitz-James 1828-1862 ..... **NCLC 21**
See also DLB 74
O'Brien, Flann .... **CLC 1, 4, 5, 7, 10, 47**
See also O Nuallain, Brian
O'Brien, Richard 1942- .... **CLC 17**
See also CA 124
O'Brien, (William) Tim(othy) 1946- .**CLC 7, 19, 40, 103; DAM POP**
See also AAYA 16; CA 85-88; CANR 40, 58; CDALBS; DLB 152; DLBD 9; DLBY 80; MTCW 2
Obstfelder, Sigbjoern 1866-1900 ... **TCLC 23**
See also CA 123
O'Casey, Sean 1880-1964**CLC 1, 5, 9, 11, 15, 88; DAB; DAC; DAM DRAM, MST; WLCS**
See also CA 89-92; CANR 62; CDBLB 1914-1945; DLB 10; MTCW 1, 2
O'Cathasaigh, Sean
See O'Casey, Sean
Ochs, Phil 1940-1976 .... **CLC 17**

See also CA 65-68
O'Connor, Edwin (Greene) 1918-1968**CLC 14**
See also CA 93-96; 25-28R
O'Connor, (Mary) Flannery 1925-1964 **C L C 1, 2, 3, 6, 10, 13, 15, 21, 66, 104; DA; DAB; DAC; DAM MST, NOV; SSC 1, 23; WLC**
See also AAYA 7; CA 1-4R; CANR 3, 41; CDALB 1941-1968; DLB 2, 152; DLBD 12; DLBY 80; MTCW 1, 2
O'Connor, Frank .... **CLC 23; SSC 5**
See also O'Donovan, Michael John
See also DLB 162
O'Dell, Scott 1898-1989 .... **CLC 30**
See also AAYA 3; CA 61-64; 129; CANR 12, 30; CLR 1, 16; DLB 52; JRDA; MAICYA; SATA 12, 60
Odets, Clifford 1906-1963**CLC 2, 28, 98; DAM DRAM; DC 6**
See also CA 85-88; CANR 62; DLB 7, 26; MTCW 1, 2
O'Doherty, Brian 1934- .... **CLC 76**
See also CA 105
O'Donnell, K. M.
See Malzberg, Barry N(athaniel)
O'Donnell, Lawrence
See Kuttner, Henry
O'Donovan, Michael John 1903-1966**CLC 14**
See also O'Connor, Frank
See also CA 93-96
Oe, Kenzaburo 1935- **CLC 10, 36, 86; DAM NOV; SSC 20**
See also CA 97-100; CANR 36, 50, 74; DLB 182; DLBY 94; MTCW 1, 2
O'Faolain, Julia 1932- .... **CLC 6, 19, 47, 108**
See also CA 81-84; CAAS 2; CANR 12, 61; DLB 14; MTCW 1
O'Faolain, Sean 1900-1991 **CLC 1, 7, 14, 32, 70; SSC 13**
See also CA 61-64; 134; CANR 12, 66; DLB 15, 162; MTCW 1, 2
O'Flaherty, Liam 1896-1984**CLC 5, 34; SSC 6**
See also CA 101; 113; CANR 35; DLB 36, 162; DLBY 84; MTCW 1, 2
Ogilvy, Gavin
See Barrie, J(ames) M(atthew)
O'Grady, Standish (James) 1846-1928**T C L C 5**
See also CA 104; 157
O'Grady, Timothy 1951- .... **CLC 59**
See also CA 138
O'Hara, Frank 1926-1966 . **CLC 2, 5, 13, 78; DAM POET**
See also CA 9-12R; 25-28R; CANR 33; DLB 5, 16, 193; MTCW 1, 2
O'Hara, John (Henry) 1905-1970**CLC 1, 2, 3, 6, 11, 42; DAM NOV; SSC 15**
See also CA 5-8R; 25-28R; CANR 31, 60; CDALB 1929-1941; DLB 9, 86; DLBD 2; MTCW 1, 2
O Hehir, Diana 1922- ....**CLC 41**
See also CA 93-96
Okigbo, Christopher (Ifenayichukwu) 1932-1967 **CLC 25, 84; BLC 3; DAM MULT, POET; PC 7**
See also BW 1, 3; CA 77-80; CANR 74; DLB 125; MTCW 1, 2
Okri, Ben 1959- ....**CLC 87**
See also BW 2, 3; CA 130; 138; CANR 65; DLB 157; INT 138; MTCW 2
Olds, Sharon 1942-.... **CLC 32, 39, 85; DAM POET; PC 22**
See also CA 101; CANR 18, 41, 66; DLB 120; MTCW 2

Park, Jordan
  See Kornbluth, C(yril) M.; Pohl, Frederik
Park, Robert E(zra) 1864-1944 ...... **TCLC 73**
  See also CA 122; 165
Parker, Bert
  See Ellison, Harlan (Jay)
Parker, Dorothy (Rothschild) 1893-1967**C L C
  15, 68; DAM POET; SSC 2**
  See also CA 19-20; 25-28R; CAP 2; DLB 11,
  45, 86; MTCW 1, 2
Parker, Robert B(rown) 1932-**CLC 27; DAM
  NOV, POP**
  See also AAYA 28; BEST 89:4; CA 49-52;
  CANR 1, 26, 52; INT CANR-26; MTCW 1
Parkin, Frank 1940- .... **CLC 43**
  See also CA 147
Parkman, Francis, Jr. 1823-1893 ... **NCLC 12**
  See also DLB 1, 30, 186
Parks, Gordon (Alexander Buchanan) 1912-
  CLC 1, 16; BLC 3; DAM MULT
  See also AITN 2; BW 2, 3; CA 41-44R; CANR
  26, 66; DLB 33; MTCW 2; SATA 8, 108
Parmenides c. 515B.C.-c. 450B.C. **CMLC 22**
  See also DLB 176
Parnell, Thomas 1679-1718 .... **LC 3**
  See also DLB 94
Parra, Nicanor 1914- ...... **CLC 2, 102; DAM
  MULT; HLC**
  See also CA 85-88; CANR 32; HW 1; MTCW
  1
Parrish, Mary Frances
  See Fisher, M(ary) F(rances) K(ennedy)
Parson
  See Coleridge, Samuel Taylor
Parson Lot
  See Kingsley, Charles
Partridge, Anthony
  See Oppenheim, E(dward) Phillips
Pascal, Blaise 1623-1662 .... **LC 35**
Pascoli, Giovanni 1855-1912 .... **TCLC 45**
  See also CA 170
Pasolini, Pier Paolo 1922-1975 . **CLC 20, 37,
  106; PC 17**
  See also CA 93-96; 61-64; CANR 63; DLB 128,
  177; MTCW 1
Pasquini
  See Silone, Ignazio
Pastan, Linda (Olenik) 1932- **CLC 27; DAM
  POET**
  See also CA 61-64; CANR 18, 40, 61; DLB 5
Pasternak, Boris (Leonidovich) 1890-1960
  **CLC 7, 10, 18, 63; DA; DAB; DAC; DAM
  MST, NOV, POET; PC 6; SSC 31; WLC**
  See also CA 127; 116; MTCW 1, 2
Patchen, Kenneth 1911-1972 ... **CLC 1, 2, 18;
  DAM POET**
  See also CA 1-4R; 33-36R; CANR 3, 35; DLB
  16, 48; MTCW 1
Pater, Walter (Horatio) 1839-1894 .. **NCLC 7**
  See also CDBLB 1832-1890; DLB 57, 156
Paterson, A(ndrew) B(arton) 1864-1941
  TCLC 32
  See also CA 155; SATA 97
Paterson, Katherine (Womeldorf) 1932-**C L C
  12, 30**
  See also AAYA 1; CA 21-24R; CANR 28, 59;
  CLR 7, 50; DLB 52; JRDA; MAICYA;
  MTCW 1; SATA 13, 53, 92
Patmore, Coventry Kersey Dighton 1823-1896
  NCLC 9
  See also DLB 35, 98
Paton, Alan (Stewart) 1903-1988 **CLC 4, 10,
  25, 55, 106; DA; DAB; DAC; DAM MST,

NOV; WLC**
  See also AAYA 26; CA 13-16; 125; CANR 22;
  CAP 1; DLBD 17; MTCW 1, 2; SATA 11;
  SATA-Obit 56
Paton Walsh, Gillian 1937-
  See Walsh, Jill Paton
  See also CANR 38; JRDA; MAICYA; SAAS 3;
  SATA 4, 72, 109
Patton, George S. 1885-1945 .... **TCLC 79**
Paulding, James Kirke 1778-1860 ... **NCLC 2**
  See also DLB 3, 59, 74
Paulin, Thomas Neilson 1949-
  See Paulin, Tom
  See also CA 123; 128
Paulin, Tom ....**CLC 37**
  See also Paulin, Thomas Neilson
  See also DLB 40
Paustovsky, Konstantin (Georgievich) 1892-
  1968 ....**CLC 40**
  See also CA 93-96; 25-28R
Pavese, Cesare 1908-1950 ... **TCLC 3; PC 13;
  SSC 19**
  See also CA 104; 169; DLB 128, 177
Pavic, Milorad 1929- ....**CLC 60**
  See also CA 136; DLB 181
Pavlov, Ivan Petrovich 1849-1936 . **TCLC 91**
  See also CA 118
Payne, Alan
  See Jakes, John (William)
Paz, Gil
  See Lugones, Leopoldo
Paz, Octavio 1914-1998**CLC 3, 4, 6, 10, 19, 51,
  65, 119; DA; DAB; DAC; DAM MST,
  MULT, POET; HLC; PC 1; WLC**
  See also CA 73-76; 165; CANR 32, 65; DLBY
  90, 98; HW 1, 2; MTCW 1, 2
p'Bitek, Okot 1931-1982 .... **CLC 96; BLC 3;
  DAM MULT**
  See also BW 2, 3; CA 124; 107; DLB 125;
  MTCW 1, 2
Peacock, Molly 1947- ....**CLC 60**
  See also CA 103; CAAS 21; CANR 52; DLB
  120
Peacock, Thomas Love 1785-1866 . **NCLC 22**
  See also DLB 96, 116
Peake, Mervyn 1911-1968 .... **CLC 7, 54**
  See also CA 5-8R; 25-28R; CANR 3; DLB 15,
  160; MTCW 1; SATA 23
Pearce, Philippa ....**CLC 21**
  See also Christie, (Ann) Philippa
  See also CLR 9; DLB 161; MAICYA; SATA 1,
  67
Pearl, Eric
  See Elman, Richard (Martin)
Pearson, T(homas) R(eid) 1956- ....**CLC 39**
  See also CA 120; 130; INT 130
Peck, Dale 1967- ....**CLC 81**
  See also CA 146; CANR 72
Peck, John 1941- ....**CLC 3**
  See also CA 49-52; CANR 3
Peck, Richard (Wayne) 1934- ....**CLC 21**
  See also AAYA 1, 24; CA 85-88; CANR 19,
  38; CLR 15; INT CANR-19; JRDA;
  MAICYA; SAAS 2; SATA 18, 55, 97
Peck, Robert Newton 1928- ..... **CLC 17; DA;
  DAC; DAM MST**
  See also AAYA 3; CA 81-84; CANR 31, 63;
  CLR 45; JRDA; MAICYA; SAAS 1; SATA
  21, 62; SATA-Essay 108
Peckinpah, (David) Sam(uel) 1925-1984**C L C
  20**
  See also CA 109; 114
Pedersen, Knut 1859-1952

See Hamsun, Knut
  See also CA 104; 119; CANR 63; MTCW 1, 2
Peeslake, Gaffer
  See Durrell, Lawrence (George)
Peguy, Charles Pierre 1873-1914 ... **TCLC 10**
  See also CA 107
Peirce, Charles Sanders 1839-1914 **TCLC 81**
Pena, Ramon del Valle y
  See Valle-Inclan, Ramon (Maria) del
Pendennis, Arthur Esquir
  See Thackeray, William Makepeace
Penn, William 1644-1718 .... **LC 25**
  See also DLB 24
PEPECE
  See Prado (Calvo), Pedro
Pepys, Samuel 1633-1703 **LC 11; DA; DAB;
  DAC; DAM MST; WLC**
  See also CDBLB 1660-1789; DLB 101
Percy, Walker 1916-1990**CLC 2, 3, 6, 8, 14, 18,
  47, 65; DAM NOV, POP**
  See also CA 1-4R; 131; CANR 1, 23, 64; DLB
  2; DLBY 80, 90; MTCW 1, 2
Percy, William Alexander 1885-1942**TCLC 84**
  See also CA 163; MTCW 2
Perec, Georges 1936-1982 .... **CLC 56, 116**
  See also CA 141; DLB 83
Pereda (y Sanchez de Porrua), Jose Maria de
  1833-1906 .... **TCLC 16**
  See also CA 117
Pereda y Porrua, Jose Maria de
  See Pereda (y Sanchez de Porrua), Jose Maria
  de
Peregoy, George Weems
  See Mencken, H(enry) L(ouis)
Perelman, S(idney) J(oseph) 1904-1979 **C L C
  3, 5, 9, 15, 23, 44, 49; DAM DRAM; SSC
  32**
  See also AITN 1, 2; CA 73-76; 89-92; CANR
  18; DLB 11, 44; MTCW 1, 2
Peret, Benjamin 1899-1959 .... **TCLC 20**
  See also CA 117
Peretz, Isaac Loeb 1851(?)-1915 .. **TCLC 16;
  SSC 26**
  See also CA 109
Peretz, Yitzkhok Leibush
  See Peretz, Isaac Loeb
Perez Galdos, Benito 1843-1920 .. **TCLC 27;
  HLCS 2**
  See also CA 125; 153; HW 1
Perrault, Charles 1628-1703 .... **LC 2**
  See also MAICYA; SATA 25
Perry, Brighton
  See Sherwood, Robert E(mmet)
Perse, St.-John
  See Leger, (Marie-Rene Auguste) Alexis Saint-
  Leger
Perutz, Leo(pold) 1882-1957 .... **TCLC 60**
  See also CA 147; DLB 81
Peseenz, Tulio F.
  See Lopez y Fuentes, Gregorio
Pesetsky, Bette 1932- ....**CLC 28**
  See also CA 133; DLB 130
Peshkov, Alexei Maximovich 1868-1936
  See Gorky, Maxim
  See also CA 105; 141; DA; DAC; DAM DRAM,
  MST, NOV; MTCW 2
Pessoa, Fernando (Antonio Nogueira) 1888-
  1935**TCLC 27; DAM MULT; HLC; PC 20**
  See also CA 125
Peterkin, Julia Mood 1880-1961 .... **CLC 31**
  See also CA 102; DLB 9
Peters, Joan K(aren) 1945- ....**CLC 39**
  See also CA 158

TCLC 21
See also CA 112

Porter, Katherine Anne 1890-1980**CLC 1, 3, 7, 10, 13, 15, 27, 101; DA; DAB; DAC; DAM MST, NOV; SSC 4, 31**
See also AITN 2; CA 1-4R; 101; CANR 1, 65; CDALBS; DLB 4, 9, 102; DLBD 12; DLBY 80; MTCW 1, 2; SATA 39; SATA-Obit 23

Porter, Peter (Neville Frederick) 1929-**CLC 5, 13, 33**
See also CA 85-88; DLB 40

Porter, William Sydney 1862-1910
See Henry, O.
See also CA 104; 131; CDALB 1865-1917; DA; DAB; DAC; DAM MST; DLB 12, 78, 79; MTCW 1, 2; YABC 2

Portillo (y Pacheco), Jose Lopez
See Lopez Portillo (y Pacheco), Jose

Post, Melville Davisson 1869-1930 **TCLC 39**
See also CA 110

Potok, Chaim 1929- .... **CLC 2, 7, 14, 26, 112; DAM NOV**
See also AAYA 15; AITN 1, 2; CA 17-20R; CANR 19, 35, 64; DLB 28, 152; INT CANR-19; MTCW 1, 2; SATA 33, 106

Potter, (Helen) Beatrix 1866-1943
See Webb, (Martha) Beatrice (Potter)
See also MAICYA; MTCW 2

Potter, Dennis (Christopher George) 1935-1994 **CLC 58, 86**
See also CA 107; 145; CANR 33, 61; MTCW 1

Pound, Ezra (Weston Loomis) 1885-1972**CLC 1, 2, 3, 4, 5, 7, 10, 13, 18, 34, 48, 50, 112; DA; DAB; DAC; DAM MST, POET; PC 4; WLC**
See also CA 5-8R; 37-40R; CANR 40; CDALB 1917-1929; DLB 4, 45, 63; DLBD 15; MTCW 1, 2

Povod, Reinaldo 1959-1994 .... **CLC 44**
See also CA 136; 146

Powell, Adam Clayton, Jr. 1908-1972**CLC 89; BLC 3; DAM MULT**
See also BW 1, 3; CA 102; 33-36R

Powell, Anthony (Dymoke) 1905-**CLC 1, 3, 7, 9, 10, 31**
See also CA 1-4R; CANR 1, 32, 62; CDBLB 1945-1960; DLB 15; MTCW 1, 2

Powell, Dawn 1897-1965.................. **CLC 66**
See also CA 5-8R; DLBY 97

Powell, Padgett 1952-........................ **CLC 34**
See also CA 126; CANR 63

Power, Susan 1961- .... **CLC 91**

Powers, J(ames) F(arl) 1917-**CLC 1, 4, 8, 57; SSC 4**
See also CA 1-4R; CANR 2, 61; DLB 130; MTCW 1

Powers, John J(ames) 1945-
See Powers, John R.
See also CA 69-72

Powers, John R. .... **CLC 66**
See also Powers, John J(ames)

Powers, Richard (S.) 1957-............... **CLC 93**
See also CA 148; CANR 80

Pownall, David 1938- .... **CLC 10**
See also CA 89-92; CAAS 18; CANR 49; DLB 14

Powys, John Cowper 1872-1963**CLC 7, 9, 15, 46**
See also CA 85-88; DLB 15; MTCW 1, 2

Powys, T(heodore) F(rancis) 1875-1953 **TCLC 9**
See also CA 106; DLB 36, 162

Prado (Calvo), Pedro 1886-1952 .... **TCLC 75**

See also CA 131; HW 1

Prager, Emily 1952- .... **CLC 56**

Pratt, E(dwin) J(ohn) 1883(?)-1964 **CLC 19; DAC; DAM POET**
See also CA 141; 93-96; CANR 77; DLB 92

Premchand .... **TCLC 21**
See also Srivastava, Dhanpat Rai

Preussler, Otfried 1923- .... **CLC 17**
See also CA 77-80; SATA 24

Prevert, Jacques (Henri Marie) 1900-1977 **CLC 15**
See also CA 77-80; 69-72; CANR 29, 61; MTCW 1; SATA-Obit 30

Prevost, Abbe (Antoine Francois) 1697-1763 **LC 1**

Price, (Edward) Reynolds 1933-**CLC 3, 6, 13, 43, 50, 63; DAM NOV; SSC 22**
See also CA 1-4R; CANR 1, 37, 57; DLB 2; INT CANR-37

Price, Richard 1949- .... **CLC 6, 12**
See also CA 49-52; CANR 3; DLBY 81

Prichard, Katharine Susannah 1883-1969 **CLC 46**
See also CA 11-12; CANR 33; CAP 1; MTCW 1; SATA 66

Priestley, J(ohn) B(oynton) 1894-1984**CLC 2, 5, 9, 34; DAM DRAM, NOV**
See also CA 9-12R; 113; CANR 33; CDBLB 1914-1945; DLB 10, 34, 77, 100, 139; DLBY 84; MTCW 1, 2

Prince 1958(?)- .... **CLC 35**

Prince, F(rank) T(empleton) 1912-... **CLC 22**
See also CA 101; CANR 43, 79; DLB 20

Prince Kropotkin
See Kropotkin, Peter (Alekseevich)

Prior, Matthew 1664-1721 .... **LC 4**
See also DLB 95

Prishvin, Mikhail 1873-1954 .... **TCLC 75**

Pritchard, William H(arrison) 1932- **CLC 34**
See also CA 65-68; CANR 23; DLB 111

Pritchett, V(ictor) S(awdon) 1900-1997 **C L C 5, 13, 15, 41; DAM NOV; SSC 14**
See also CA 61-64; 157; CANR 31, 63; DLB 15, 139; MTCW 1, 2

Private 19022
See Manning, Frederic

Probst, Mark 1925- .... **CLC 59**
See also CA 130

Prokosch, Frederic 1908-1989 ..... **CLC 4, 48**
See also CA 73-76; 128; DLB 48; MTCW 2

Propertius, Sextus c. 50B.C.-c. 16B.C.**C M L C 32**
See also DLB 211

Prophet, The
See Dreiser, Theodore (Herman Albert)

Prose, Francine 1947- .... **CLC 45**
See also CA 109; 112; CANR 46; SATA 101

Proudhon
See Cunha, Euclides (Rodrigues Pimenta) da

Proulx, Annie
See Proulx, E(dna) Annie

Proulx, E(dna) Annie 1935-... **CLC 81; DAM POP**
See also CA 145; CANR 65; MTCW 2

Proust, (Valentin-Louis-George-Eugene-) Marcel 1871-1922 **TCLC 7, 13, 33; DA; DAB; DAC; DAM MST, NOV; WLC**
See also CA 104; 120; DLB 65; MTCW 1, 2

Prowler, Harley
See Masters, Edgar Lee

Prus, Boleslaw 1845-1912 .... **TCLC 48**

Pryor, Richard (Franklin Lenox Thomas) 1940- **CLC 26**

See also CA 122; 152

Przybyszewski, Stanislaw 1868-1927**TCLC 36**
See also CA 160; DLB 66

Pteleon
See Grieve, C(hristopher) M(urray)
See also DAM POET

Puckett, Lute
See Masters, Edgar Lee

Puig, Manuel 1932-1990**CLC 3, 5, 10, 28, 65; DAM MULT; HLC**
See also CA 45-48; CANR 2, 32, 63; DLB 113; HW 1, 2; MTCW 1, 2

Pulitzer, Joseph 1847-1911 .... **TCLC 76**
See also CA 114; DLB 23

Purdy, A(lfred) W(ellington) 1918-**CLC 3, 6, 14, 50; DAC; DAM MST, POET**
See also CA 81-84; CAAS 17; CANR 42, 66; DLB 88

Purdy, James (Amos) 1923-**CLC 2, 4, 10, 28, 52**
See also CA 33-36R; CAAS 1; CANR 19, 51; DLB 2; INT CANR-19; MTCW 1

Pure, Simon
See Swinnerton, Frank Arthur

Pushkin, Alexander (Sergeyevich) 1799-1837 **NCLC 3, 27; DA; DAB; DAC; DAM DRAM, MST, POET; PC 10; SSC 27; WLC**
See also DLB 205; SATA 61

P'u Sung-ling 1640-1715........**LC 49; SSC 31**

Putnam, Arthur Lee
See Alger, Horatio, Jr.

Puzo, Mario 1920-1999 **CLC 1, 2, 6, 36, 107; DAM NOV, POP**
See also CA 65-68; CANR 4, 42, 65; DLB 6; MTCW 1, 2

Pygge, Edward
See Barnes, Julian (Patrick)

Pyle, Ernest Taylor 1900-1945
See Pyle, Ernie
See also CA 115; 160

Pyle, Ernie 1900-1945 .... **TCLC 75**
See also Pyle, Ernest Taylor
See also DLB 29; MTCW 2

Pyle, Howard 1853-1911 .... **TCLC 81**
See also CA 109; 137; CLR 22; DLB 42, 188; DLBD 13; MAICYA; SATA 16, 100

Pym, Barbara (Mary Crampton) 1913-1980 **CLC 13, 19, 37, 111**
See also CA 13-14; 97-100; CANR 13, 34; CAP 1; DLB 14, 207; DLBY 87; MTCW 1, 2

Pynchon, Thomas (Ruggles, Jr.) 1937-**CLC 2, 3, 6, 9, 11, 18, 33, 62, 72; DA; DAB; DAC; DAM MST, NOV, POP; SSC 14; WLC**
See also BEST 90:2; CA 17-20R; CANR 22, 46, 73; DLB 2, 173; MTCW 1, 2

Pythagoras c. 570B.C.-c. 500B.C. . **CMLC 22**
See also DLB 176

Q
See Quiller-Couch, SirArthur (Thomas)

Qian Zhongshu
See Ch'ien Chung-shu

Qroll
See Dagerman, Stig (Halvard)

Quarrington, Paul (Lewis) 1953-.......**CLC 65**
See also CA 129; CANR 62

Quasimodo, Salvatore 1901-1968 ..... **CLC 10**
See also CA 13-16; 25-28R; CAP 1; DLB 114; MTCW 1

Quay, Stephen 1947- ....**CLC 95**

Quay, Timothy 1947- ....**CLC 95**

Queen, Ellery ....**CLC 3, 11**
See also Dannay, Frederic; Davidson, Avram

See also AAYA 26; CA 126; SATA 109
Robinson, Lloyd
See Silverberg, Robert
Robinson, Marilynne 1944- .... **CLC 25**
See also CA 116; CANR 80; DLB 206
Robinson, Smokey .... **CLC 21**
See also Robinson, William, Jr.
Robinson, William, Jr. 1940-
See Robinson, Smokey
See also CA 116
Robison, Mary 1949- .... **CLC 42, 98**
See also CA 113; 116; DLB 130; INT 116
Rod, Edouard 1857-1910 .... **TCLC 52**
Roddenberry, Eugene Wesley 1921-1991
See Roddenberry, Gene
See also CA 110; 135; CANR 37; SATA 45;
SATA-Obit 69
Roddenberry, Gene .... **CLC 17**
See also Roddenberry, Eugene Wesley
See also AAYA 5; SATA-Obit 69
Rodgers, Mary 1931- .... **CLC 12**
See also CA 49-52; CANR 8, 55; CLR 20; INT
CANR-8; JRDA; MAICYA; SATA 8
Rodgers, W(illiam) R(obert) 1909-1969**CLC 7**
See also CA 85-88; DLB 20
Rodman, Eric
See Silverberg, Robert
Rodman, Howard 1920(?)-1985 .... **CLC 65**
See also CA 118
Rodman, Maia
See Wojciechowska, Maia (Teresa)
Rodriguez, Claudio 1934- .... **CLC 10**
See also DLB 134
Roelvaag, O(le) E(dvart) 1876-1931**TCLC 17**
See also CA 117; 171; DLB 9
Roethke, Theodore (Huebner) 1908-1963**CLC**
1, 3, 8, 11, 19, 46, 101; DAM POET; PC 15
See also CA 81-84; CABS 2; CDALB 1941-
1968; DLB 5, 206; MTCW 1, 2
Rogers, Samuel 1763-1855 .... **NCLC 69**
See also DLB 93
Rogers, Thomas Hunton 1927- .... **CLC 57**
See also CA 89-92; INT 89-92
Rogers, Will(iam Penn Adair) 1879-1935
TCLC 8, 71; DAM MULT
See also CA 105; 144; DLB 11; MTCW 2;
NNAL
Rogin, Gilbert 1929- .... **CLC 18**
See also CA 65-68; CANR 15
Rohan, Koda .... **TCLC 22**
See also Koda Shigeyuki
Rohlfs, Anna Katharine Green
See Green, Anna Katharine
Rohmer, Eric .... **CLC 16**
See also Scherer, Jean-Marie Maurice
Rohmer, Sax .... **TCLC 28**
See also Ward, Arthur Henry Sarsfield
See also DLB 70
Roiphe, Anne (Richardson) 1935- . **CLC 3, 9**
See also CA 89-92; CANR 45, 73; DLBY 80;
INT 89-92
Rojas, Fernando de 1465-1541**LC 23; HLCS 1**
Rolfe, Frederick (William Serafino Austin
Lewis Mary) 1860-1913 .... **TCLC 12**
See also CA 107; DLB 34, 156
Rolland, Romain 1866-1944 .... **TCLC 23**
See also CA 118; DLB 65
Rolle, Richard c. 1300-c. 1349 ...... **CMLC 21**
See also DLB 146
Rolvaag, O(le) E(dvart)
See Roelvaag, O(le) E(dvart)
Romain Arnaud, Saint
See Aragon, Louis

Romains, Jules 1885-1972 .... **CLC 7**
See also CA 85-88; CANR 34; DLB 65; MTCW
1
Romero, Jose Ruben 1890-1952 ..... **TCLC 14**
See also CA 114; 131; HW 1
Ronsard, Pierre de 1524-1585 ... **LC 6; PC 11**
Rooke, Leon 1934- .. **CLC 25, 34; DAM POP**
See also CA 25-28R; CANR 23, 53
Roosevelt, Franklin Delano 1882-1945**T C L C**
93
See also CA 116; 173
Roosevelt, Theodore 1858-1919 ..... **TCLC 69**
See also CA 115; 170; DLB 47, 186
Roper, William 1498-1578 .... **LC 10**
Roquelaure, A. N.
See Rice, Anne
Rosa, Joao Guimaraes 1908-1967 .. **CLC 23;**
HLCS 1
See also CA 89-92; DLB 113
Rose, Wendy 1948-**CLC 85; DAM MULT; PC**
13
See also CA 53-56; CANR 5, 51; DLB 175;
NNAL; SATA 12
Rosen, R. D.
See Rosen, Richard (Dean)
Rosen, Richard (Dean) 1949- .... **CLC 39**
See also CA 77-80; CANR 62; INT CANR-30
Rosenberg, Isaac 1890-1918 .... **TCLC 12**
See also CA 107; DLB 20
Rosenblatt, Joe .... **CLC 15**
See also Rosenblatt, Joseph
Rosenblatt, Joseph 1933-
See Rosenblatt, Joe
See also CA 89-92; INT 89-92
Rosenfeld, Samuel
See Tzara, Tristan
Rosenstock, Sami
See Tzara, Tristan
Rosenstock, Samuel
See Tzara, Tristan
Rosenthal, M(acha) L(ouis) 1917-1996 . **C L C**
28
See also CA 1-4R; 152; CAAS 6; CANR 4, 51;
DLB 5; SATA 59
Ross, Barnaby
See Dannay, Frederic
Ross, Bernard L.
See Follett, Ken(neth Martin)
Ross, J. H.
See Lawrence, T(homas) E(dward)
Ross, John Hume
See Lawrence, T(homas) E(dward)
Ross, Martin
See Martin, Violet Florence
See also DLB 135
Ross, (James) Sinclair 1908-1996 ... **CLC 13;**
DAC; DAM MST; SSC 24
See also CA 73-76; CANR 81; DLB 88
Rossetti, Christina (Georgina) 1830-1894
NCLC 2, 50, 66; DA; DAB; DAC; DAM
MST, POET; PC 7; WLC
See also DLB 35, 163; MAICYA; SATA 20
Rossetti, Dante Gabriel 1828-1882 . **NCLC 4,**
77; DA; DAB; DAC; DAM MST, POET;
WLC
See also CDBLB 1832-1890; DLB 35
Rossner, Judith (Perelman) 1935-**CLC 6, 9, 29**
See also AITN 2; BEST 90:3; CA 17-20R;
CANR 18, 51, 73; DLB 6; INT CANR-18;
MTCW 1, 2
Rostand, Edmond (Eugene Alexis) 1868-1918
TCLC 6, 37; DA; DAB; DAC; DAM
DRAM, MST; DC 10

See also CA 104; 126; DLB 192; MTCW 1
Roth, Henry 1906-1995 ..... **CLC 2, 6, 11, 104**
See also CA 11-12; 149; CANR 38, 63; CAP 1;
DLB 28; MTCW 1, 2
Roth, Philip (Milton) 1933-**CLC 1, 2, 3, 4, 6, 9,**
15, 22, 31, 47, 66, 86, 119; DA; DAB; DAC;
DAM MST, NOV, POP; SSC 26; WLC
See also BEST 90:3; CA 1-4R; CANR 1, 22,
36, 55; CDALB 1968-1988; DLB 2, 28, 173;
DLBY 82; MTCW 1, 2
Rothenberg, Jerome 1931- .... **CLC 6, 57**
See also CA 45-48; CANR 1; DLB 5, 193
Roumain, Jacques (Jean Baptiste) 1907-1944
TCLC 19; BLC 3; DAM MULT
See also BW 1; CA 117; 125
Rourke, Constance (Mayfield) 1885-1941
TCLC 12
See also CA 107; YABC 1
Rousseau, Jean-Baptiste 1671-1741 ..... **LC 9**
Rousseau, Jean-Jacques 1712-1778**LC 14, 36;**
DA; DAB; DAC; DAM MST; WLC
Roussel, Raymond 1877-1933 .... **TCLC 20**
See also CA 117
Rovit, Earl (Herbert) 1927- .... **CLC 7**
See also CA 5-8R; CANR 12
Rowe, Elizabeth Singer 1674-1737 ..... **LC 44**
See also DLB 39, 95
Rowe, Nicholas 1674-1718 .... **LC 8**
See also DLB 84
Rowley, Ames Dorrance
See Lovecraft, H(oward) P(hillips)
Rowson, Susanna Haswell 1762(?)-1824
NCLC 5, 69
See also DLB 37, 200
Roy, Arundhati 1960(?)- .... **CLC 109**
See also CA 163; DLBY 97
Roy, Gabrielle 1909-1983 **CLC 10, 14; DAB;**
DAC; DAM MST
See also CA 53-56; 110; CANR 5, 61; DLB 68;
MTCW 1; SATA 104
Royko, Mike 1932-1997 .... **CLC 109**
See also CA 89-92; 157; CANR 26
Rozewicz, Tadeusz 1921- ... **CLC 9, 23; DAM**
POET
See also CA 108; CANR 36, 66; MTCW 1, 2
Ruark, Gibbons 1941- .... **CLC 3**
See also CA 33-36R; CAAS 23; CANR 14, 31,
57; DLB 120
Rubens, Bernice (Ruth) 1923- .... **CLC 19, 31**
See also CA 25-28R; CANR 33, 65; DLB 14,
207; MTCW 1
Rubin, Harold
See Robbins, Harold
Rudkin, (James) David 1936- .... **CLC 14**
See also CA 89-92; DLB 13
Rudnik, Raphael 1933- .... **CLC 7**
See also CA 29-32R
Ruffian, M.
See Hasek, Jaroslav (Matej Frantisek)
Ruiz, Jose Martinez .... **CLC 11**
See also Martinez Ruiz, Jose
Rukeyser, Muriel 1913-1980**CLC 6, 10, 15, 27;**
DAM POET; PC 12
See also CA 5-8R; 93-96; CANR 26, 60; DLB
48; MTCW 1, 2; SATA-Obit 22
Rule, Jane (Vance) 1931- .... **CLC 27**
See also CA 25-28R; CAAS 18; CANR 12; DLB
60
Rulfo, Juan 1918-1986 .... **CLC 8, 80; DAM**
MULT; HLC; SSC 25
See also CA 85-88; 118; CANR 26; DLB 113;
HW 1, 2; MTCW 1, 2
Rumi, Jalal al-Din 1297-1373 .... **CMLC 20**

Sebastian, Lee
See Silverberg, Robert
Sebastian Owl
See Thompson, Hunter S(tockton)
Sebestyen, Ouida 1924- .... **CLC 30**
See also AAYA 8; CA 107; CANR 40; CLR 17; JRDA; MAICYA; SAAS 10; SATA 39
Secundus, H. Scriblerus
See Fielding, Henry
Sedges, John
See Buck, Pearl S(ydenstricker)
Sedgwick, Catharine Maria 1789-1867 **N C L C 19**
See also DLB 1, 74
Seelye, John (Douglas) 1931- .... **CLC 7**
See also CA 97-100; CANR 70; INT 97-100
Seferiades, Giorgos Stylianou 1900-1971
See Seferis, George
See also CA 5-8R; 33-36R; CANR 5, 36; MTCW 1
Seferis, George .... **CLC 5, 11**
See also Seferiades, Giorgos Stylianou
Segal, Erich (Wolf) 1937- ..**CLC 3, 10; DAM POP**
See also BEST 89:1; CA 25-28R; CANR 20, 36, 65; DLBY 86; INT CANR-20; MTCW 1
Seger, Bob 1945- .... **CLC 35**
Seghers, Anna ....**CLC 7**
See also Radvanyi, Netty
See also DLB 69
Seidel, Frederick (Lewis) 1936- .... **CLC 18**
See also CA 13-16R; CANR 8; DLBY 84
Seifert, Jaroslav 1901-1986 .. **CLC 34, 44, 93**
See also CA 127; MTCW 1, 2
Sei Shonagon c. 966-1017(?) .... **CMLC 6**
Séjour, Victor 1817-1874 .... **DC 10**
See also DLB 50
Sejour Marcou et Ferrand, Juan Victor
See Séjour, Victor
Selby, Hubert, Jr. 1928- **CLC 1, 2, 4, 8; SSC 20**
See also CA 13-16R; CANR 33; DLB 2
Selzer, Richard 1928- .... **CLC 74**
See also CA 65-68; CANR 14
Sembene, Ousmane
See Ousmane, Sembene
Senancour, Etienne Pivert de 1770-1846 **NCLC 16**
See also DLB 119
Sender, Ramon (Jose) 1902-1982**CLC 8; DAM MULT; HLC**
See also CA 5-8R; 105; CANR 8; HW 1; MTCW 1
Seneca, Lucius Annaeus c. 1-c. 65 **CMLC 6; DAM DRAM; DC 5**
See also DLB 211
Senghor, Leopold Sedar 1906- **CLC 54; BLC 3; DAM MULT, POET; PC 25**
See also BW 2, 3; CA 116; 125; CANR 47, 74; MTCW 1, 2
Senna, Danzy 1970- .... **CLC 119**
See also CA 169
Serling, (Edward) Rod(man) 1924-1975**C L C 30**
See also AAYA 14; AITN 1; CA 162; 57-60; DLB 26
Serna, Ramon Gomez de la
See Gomez de la Serna, Ramon
Serpieres
See Guillevic, (Eugene)
Service, Robert
See Service, Robert W(illiam)
See also DAB; DLB 92
Service, Robert W(illiam) 1874(?)-1958**TCLC**

15; **DA; DAC; DAM MST, POET; WLC**
See also Service, Robert
See also CA 115; 140; SATA 20
Seth, Vikram 1952-**CLC 43, 90; DAM MULT**
See also CA 121; 127; CANR 50, 74; DLB 120; INT 127; MTCW 2
Seton, Cynthia Propper 1926-1982 ..**CLC 27**
See also CA 5-8R; 108; CANR 7
Seton, Ernest (Evan) Thompson 1860-1946 **TCLC 31**
See also CA 109; CLR 59; DLB 92; DLBD 13; JRDA; SATA 18
Seton-Thompson, Ernest
See Seton, Ernest (Evan) Thompson
Settle, Mary Lee 1918- .... **CLC 19, 61**
See also CA 89-92; CAAS 1; CANR 44; DLB 6; INT 89-92
Seuphor, Michel
See Arp, Jean
Sevigne, Marie (de Rabutin-Chantal) Marquise de 1626-1696 .... **LC 11**
Sewall, Samuel 1652-1730 .... **LC 38**
See also DLB 24
Sexton, Anne (Harvey) 1928-1974**CLC 2, 4, 6, 8, 10, 15, 53; DA; DAB; DAC; DAM MST, POET; PC 2; WLC**
See also CA 1-4R; 53-56; CABS 2; CANR 3, 36; CDALB 1941-1968; DLB 5, 169; MTCW 1, 2; SATA 10
Shaara, Jeff 1952- .... **CLC 119**
See also CA 163
Shaara, Michael (Joseph, Jr.) 1929-1988**C L C 15; DAM POP**
See also AITN 1; CA 102; 125; CANR 52; DLBY 83
Shackleton, C. C.
See Aldiss, Brian W(ilson)
Shacochis, Bob ....**CLC 39**
See also Shacochis, Robert G.
Shacochis, Robert G. 1951-
See Shacochis, Bob
See also CA 119; 124; INT 124
Shaffer, Anthony (Joshua) 1926- .... **CLC 19; DAM DRAM**
See also CA 110; 116; DLB 13
Shaffer, Peter (Levin) 1926-**CLC 5, 14, 18, 37, 60; DAB; DAM DRAM, MST; DC 7**
See also CA 25-28R; CANR 25, 47, 74; CDBLB 1960 to Present; DLB 13; MTCW 1, 2
Shakey, Bernard
See Young, Neil
Shalamov, Varlam (Tikhonovich) 1907(?)-1982 **CLC 18**
See also CA 129; 105
Shamlu, Ahmad 1925- .... **CLC 10**
Shammas, Anton 1951- .... **CLC 55**
Shange, Ntozake 1948-**CLC 8, 25, 38, 74; BLC 3; DAM DRAM, MULT; DC 3**
See also AAYA 9; BW 2; CA 85-88; CABS 3; CANR 27, 48, 74; DLB 38; MTCW 1, 2
Shanley, John Patrick 1950- .... **CLC 75**
See also CA 128; 133
Shapcott, Thomas W(illiam) 1935- ... **CLC 38**
See also CA 69-72; CANR 49
Shapiro, Jane .... **CLC 76**
Shapiro, Karl (Jay) 1913-**CLC 4, 8, 15, 53; PC 25**
See also CA 1-4R; CAAS 6; CANR 1, 36, 66; DLB 48; MTCW 1, 2
Sharp, William 1855-1905 .... **TCLC 39**
See also CA 160; DLB 156
Sharpe, Thomas Ridley 1928-
See Sharpe, Tom

See also CA 114; 122; INT 122
Sharpe, Tom ....**CLC 36**
See also Sharpe, Thomas Ridley
See also DLB 14
Shaw, Bernard .... **TCLC 45**
See also Shaw, George Bernard
See also BW 1; MTCW 2
Shaw, G. Bernard
See Shaw, George Bernard
Shaw, George Bernard 1856-1950**TCLC 3, 9, 21; DA; DAB; DAC; DAM DRAM, MST; WLC**
See also Shaw, Bernard
See also CA 104; 128; CDBLB 1914-1945; DLB 10, 57, 190; MTCW 1, 2
Shaw, Henry Wheeler 1818-1885 ..**NCLC 15**
See also DLB 11
Shaw, Irwin 1913-1984 **CLC 7, 23, 34; DAM DRAM, POP**
See also AITN 1; CA 13-16R; 112; CANR 21; CDALB 1941-1968; DLB 6, 102; DLBY 84; MTCW 1, 21
Shaw, Robert 1927-1978 .... **CLC 5**
See also AITN 1; CA 1-4R; 81-84; CANR 4; DLB 13, 14
Shaw, T. E.
See Lawrence, T(homas) E(dward)
Shawn, Wallace 1943- .... **CLC 41**
See also CA 112
Shea, Lisa 1953- .... **CLC 86**
See also CA 147
Sheed, Wilfrid (John Joseph) 1930-**CLC 2, 4, 10, 53**
See also CA 65-68; CANR 30, 66; DLB 6; MTCW 1, 2
Sheldon, Alice Hastings Bradley 1915(?)-1987
See Tiptree, James, Jr.
See also CA 108; 122; CANR 34; INT 108; MTCW 1
Sheldon, John
See Bloch, Robert (Albert)
Shelley, Mary Wollstonecraft (Godwin) 1797-1851**NCLC 14, 59; DA; DAB; DAC; DAM MST, NOV; WLC**
See also AAYA 20; CDBLB 1789-1832; DLB 110, 116, 159, 178; SATA 29
Shelley, Percy Bysshe 1792-1822 . **NCLC 18; DA; DAB; DAC; DAM MST, POET; PC 14; WLC**
See also CDBLB 1789-1832; DLB 96, 110, 158
Shepard, Jim 1956- .... **CLC 36**
See also CA 137; CANR 59; SATA 90
Shepard, Lucius 1947- .... **CLC 34**
See also CA 128; 141; CANR 81
Shepard, Sam 1943-**CLC 4, 6, 17, 34, 41, 44; DAM DRAM; DC 5**
See also AAYA 1; CA 69-72; CABS 3; CANR 22; DLB 7, 212; MTCW 1, 2
Shepherd, Michael
See Ludlum, Robert
Sherburne, Zoa (Lillian Morin) 1912-1995 **CLC 30**
See also AAYA 13; CA 1-4R; 176; CANR 3, 37; MAICYA; SAAS 18; SATA 3
Sheridan, Frances 1724-1766 .... **LC 7**
See also DLB 39, 84
Sheridan, Richard Brinsley 1751-1816**N C L C 5; DA; DAB; DAC; DAM DRAM, MST; DC 1; WLC**
See also CDBLB 1660-1789; DLB 89
Sherman, Jonathan Marc .... **CLC 55**
Sherman, Martin 1941(?)- .... **CLC 19**
See also CA 116; 123

34
See also DLB 57, 144

Symons, Arthur 1865-1945 .... **TCLC 11**
See also CA 107; DLB 19, 57, 149

Symons, Julian (Gustave) 1912-1994 **CLC 2, 14, 32**
See also CA 49-52; 147; CAAS 3; CANR 3, 33, 59; DLB 87, 155; DLBY 92; MTCW 1

Synge, (Edmund) J(ohn) M(illington) 1871-1909 .. **TCLC 6, 37; DAM DRAM; DC 2**
See also CA 104; 141; CDBLB 1890-1914; DLB 10, 19

Syruc, J.
See Milosz, Czeslaw

Szirtes, George 1948- .... **CLC 46**
See also CA 109; CANR 27, 61

Szymborska, Wislawa 1923- .... **CLC 99**
See also CA 154; DLBY 96; MTCW 2

T. O., Nik
See Annensky, Innokenty (Fyodorovich)

Tabori, George 1914- .... **CLC 19**
See also CA 49-52; CANR 4, 69

Tagore, Rabindranath 1861-1941**TCLC 3, 53; DAM DRAM, POET; PC 8**
See also CA 104; 120; MTCW 1, 2

Taine, Hippolyte Adolphe 1828-1893 . **N C L C 15**

Talese, Gay 1932- .... **CLC 37**
See also AITN 1; CA 1-4R; CANR 9, 58; DLB 185; INT CANR-9; MTCW 1, 2

Tallent, Elizabeth (Ann) 1954- .... **CLC 45**
See also CA 117; CANR 72; DLB 130

Tally, Ted 1952- .... **CLC 42**
See also CA 120; 124; INT 124

Talvik, Heiti 1904-1947 .... **TCLC 87**

Tamayo y Baus, Manuel 1829-1898 . **NCLC 1**

Tammsaare, A(nton) H(ansen) 1878-1940 **TCLC 27**
See also CA 164

Tam'si, Tchicaya U
See Tchicaya, Gerald Felix

Tan, Amy (Ruth) 1952- . **CLC 59, 120; DAM MULT, NOV, POP**
See also AAYA 9; BEST 89:3; CA 136; CANR 54; CDALBS; DLB 173; MTCW 2; SATA 75

Tandem, Felix
See Spitteler, Carl (Friedrich Georg)

Tanizaki, Jun'ichiro 1886-1965**CLC 8, 14, 28; SSC 21**
See also CA 93-96; 25-28R; DLB 180; MTCW 2

Tanner, William
See Amis, Kingsley (William)

Tao Lao
See Storni, Alfonsina

Tarassoff, Lev
See Troyat, Henri

Tarbell, Ida M(inerva) 1857-1944 . **TCLC 40**
See also CA 122; DLB 47

Tarkington, (Newton) Booth 1869-1946**TCLC 9**
See also CA 110; 143; DLB 9, 102; MTCW 2; SATA 17

Tarkovsky, Andrei (Arsenyevich) 1932-1986 **CLC 75**
See also CA 127

Tartt, Donna 1964(?)- .... **CLC 76**
See also CA 142

Tasso, Torquato 1544-1595 .... **LC 5**

Tate, (John Orley) Allen 1899-1979**CLC 2, 4, 6, 9, 11, 14, 24**
See also CA 5-8R; 85-88; CANR 32; DLB 4,

45, 63; DLBD 17; MTCW 1, 2

Tate, Ellalice
See Hibbert, Eleanor Alice Burford

Tate, James (Vincent) 1943- ..... **CLC 2, 6, 25**
See also CA 21-24R; CANR 29, 57; DLB 5, 169

Tavel, Ronald 1940- .... **CLC 6**
See also CA 21-24R; CANR 33

Taylor, C(ecil) P(hilip) 1929-1981 ....**CLC 27**
See also CA 25-28R; 105; CANR 47

Taylor, Edward 1642(?)-1729 ..... **LC 11; DA; DAB; DAC; DAM MST, POET**
See also DLB 24

Taylor, Eleanor Ross 1920- .... **CLC 5**
See also CA 81-84; CANR 70

Taylor, Elizabeth 1912-1975 ..... **CLC 2, 4, 29**
See also CA 13-16R; CANR 9, 70; DLB 139; MTCW 1; SATA 13

Taylor, Frederick Winslow 1856-1915 **T C L C 76**

Taylor, Henry (Splawn) 1942- ....**CLC 44**
See also CA 33-36R; CAAS 7; CANR 31; DLB 5

Taylor, Kamala (Purnaiya) 1924-
See Markandaya, Kamala
See also CA 77-80

Taylor, Mildred D. ....**CLC 21**
See also AAYA 10; BW 1; CA 85-88; CANR 25; CLR 9, 59; DLB 52; JRDA; MAICYA; SAAS 5; SATA 15, 70

Taylor, Peter (Hillsman) 1917-1994**CLC 1, 4, 18, 37, 44, 50, 71; SSC 10**
See also CA 13-16R; 147; CANR 9, 50; DLBY 81, 94; INT CANR-9; MTCW 1, 2

Taylor, Robert Lewis 1912-1998 ....**CLC 14**
See also CA 1-4R; 170; CANR 3, 64; SATA 10

Tchekhov, Anton
See Chekhov, Anton (Pavlovich)

Tchicaya, Gerald Felix 1931-1988 . **CLC 101**
See also CA 129; 125; CANR 81

Tchicaya U Tam'si
See Tchicaya, Gerald Felix

Teasdale, Sara 1884-1933 .... **TCLC 4**
See also CA 104; 163; DLB 45; SATA 32

Tegner, Esaias 1782-1846 .... **NCLC 2**

Teilhard de Chardin, (Marie Joseph) Pierre 1881-1955 .... **TCLC 9**
See also CA 105

Temple, Ann
See Mortimer, Penelope (Ruth)

Tennant, Emma (Christina) 1937-**CLC 13, 52**
See also CA 65-68; CAAS 9; CANR 10, 38, 59; DLB 14

Tenneshaw, S. M.
See Silverberg, Robert

Tennyson, Alfred 1809-1892 .. **NCLC 30, 65; DA; DAB; DAC; DAM MST, POET; PC 6; WLC**
See also CDBLB 1832-1890; DLB 32

Teran, Lisa St. Aubin de ....**CLC 36**
See also St. Aubin de Teran, Lisa

Terence c. 184B.C.-c. 159B.C.**CMLC 14; DC 7**
See also DLB 211

Teresa de Jesus, St. 1515-1582 .... **LC 18**

Terkel, Louis 1912-
See Terkel, Studs
See also CA 57-60; CANR 18, 45, 67; MTCW 1, 2

Terkel, Studs ....**CLC 38**
See also Terkel, Louis
See also AITN 1; MTCW 2

Terry, C. V.
See Slaughter, Frank G(ill)

Terry, Megan 1932- .... **CLC 19**
See also CA 77-80; CABS 3; CANR 43; DLB 7

Tertullian c. 155-c. 245 .... **CMLC 29**

Tertz, Abram
See Sinyavsky, Andrei (Donatevich)

Tesich, Steve 1943(?)-1996 .... **CLC 40, 69**
See also CA 105; 152; DLBY 83

Tesla, Nikola 1856-1943 .... **TCLC 88**

Teternikov, Fyodor Kuzmich 1863-1927
See Sologub, Fyodor
See also CA 104

Tevis, Walter 1928-1984 .... **CLC 42**
See also CA 113

Tey, Josephine .... **TCLC 14**
See also Mackintosh, Elizabeth
See also DLB 77

Thackeray, William Makepeace 1811-1863 **NCLC 5, 14, 22, 43; DA; DAB; DAC; DAM MST, NOV; WLC**
See also CDBLB 1832-1890; DLB 21, 55, 159, 163; SATA 23

Thakura, Ravindranatha
See Tagore, Rabindranath

Tharoor, Shashi 1956- .... **CLC 70**
See also CA 141

Thelwell, Michael Miles 1939- .... **CLC 22**
See also BW 2; CA 101

Theobald, Lewis, Jr.
See Lovecraft, H(oward) P(hillips)

Theodorescu, Ion N. 1880-1967
See Arghezi, Tudor
See also CA 116

Theriault, Yves 1915-1983 .... **CLC 79; DAC; DAM MST**
See also CA 102; DLB 88

Theroux, Alexander (Louis) 1939-**CLC 2, 25**
See also CA 85-88; CANR 20, 63

Theroux, Paul (Edward) 1941- **CLC 5, 8, 11, 15, 28, 46; DAM POP**
See also AAYA 28; BEST 89:4; CA 33-36R; CANR 20, 45, 74; CDALBS; DLB 2; MTCW 1, 2; SATA 44, 109

Thesen, Sharon 1946- .... **CLC 56**
See also CA 163

Thevenin, Denis
See Duhamel, Georges

Thibault, Jacques Anatole Francois 1844-1924
See France, Anatole
See also CA 106; 127; DAM NOV; MTCW 1, 2

Thiele, Colin (Milton) 1920- .... **CLC 17**
See also CA 29-32R; CANR 12, 28, 53; CLR 27; MAICYA; SAAS 2; SATA 14, 72

Thomas, Audrey (Callahan) 1935-**CLC 7, 13, 37, 107; SSC 20**
See also AITN 2; CA 21-24R; CAAS 19; CANR 36, 58; DLB 60; M1CW 1

Thomas, D(onald) M(ichael) 1935-. **CLC 13, 22, 31**
See also CA 61-64; CAAS 11; CANR 17, 45, 75; CDBLB 1960 to Present; DLB 40, 207; INT CANR-17; MTCW 1, 2

Thomas, Dylan (Marlais) 1914-1953**TCLC 1, 8, 45; DA; DAB; DAC; DAM DRAM, MST, POET; PC 2; SSC 3; WLC**
See also CA 104; 120; CANR 65; CDBLB 1945-1960; DLB 13, 20, 139; MTCW 1, 2; SATA 60

Thomas, (Philip) Edward 1878-1917 . **T C L C 10; DAM POET**
See also CA 106; 153; DLB 98

Thomas, Joyce Carol 1938- .... **CLC 35**
See also AAYA 12; BW 2, 3; CA 113; 116;

See also CA 9-12R; CANR 7, 38, 60; DLB 5

Van Dyne, Edith
See Baum, L(yman) Frank

van Itallie, Jean-Claude 1936- .... **CLC 3**
See also CA 45-48; CAAS 2; CANR 1, 48; DLB 7

van Ostaijen, Paul 1896-1928 .... **TCLC 33**
See also CA 163

Van Peebles, Melvin 1932- . **CLC 2, 20; DAM MULT**
See also BW 2, 3; CA 85-88; CANR 27, 67

Vansittart, Peter 1920- .... **CLC 42**
See also CA 1-4R; CANR 3, 49

Van Vechten, Carl 1880-1964 .... **CLC 33**
See also CA 89-92; DLB 4, 9, 51

Van Vogt, A(lfred) E(lton) 1912- .... **CLC 1**
See also CA 21-24R; CANR 28; DLB 8; SATA 14

Varda, Agnes 1928- .... **CLC 16**
See also CA 116; 122

Vargas Llosa, (Jorge) Mario (Pedro) 1936-
CLC 3, 6, 9, 10, 15, 31, 42, 85; DA; DAB; DAC; DAM MST, MULT, NOV; HLC
See also CA 73-76; CANR 18, 32, 42, 67; DLB 145; HW 1, 2; MTCW 1, 2

Vasiliu, Gheorghe 1881-1957
See Bacovia, George
See also CA 123

Vassa, Gustavus
See Equiano, Olaudah

Vassilikos, Vassilis 1933- .... **CLC 4, 8**
See also CA 81-84; CANR 75

Vaughan, Henry 1621-1695 .... **LC 27**
See also DLB 131

Vaughn, Stephanie .... **CLC 62**

Vazov, Ivan (Minchov) 1850-1921 . **TCLC 25**
See also CA 121; 167; DLB 147

Veblen, Thorstein B(unde) 1857-1929 **T C L C 31**
See also CA 115; 165

Vega, Lope de 1562-1635 ..... **LC 23; HLCS 2**

Venison, Alfred
See Pound, Ezra (Weston Loomis)

Verdi, Marie de
See Mencken, H(enry) L(ouis)

Verdu, Matilde
See Cela, Camilo Jose

Verga, Giovanni (Carmelo) 1840-1922 **T C L C 3; SSC 21**
See also CA 104; 123

Vergil 70B.C.-19B.C. ..... **CMLC 9; DA; DAB; DAC; DAM MST, POET; PC 12; WLCS**
See also Virgil

Verhaeren, Emile (Adolphe Gustave) 1855-1916 **TCLC 12**
See also CA 109

Verlaine, Paul (Marie) 1844-1896 **NCLC 2, 51; DAM POET; PC 2**

Verne, Jules (Gabriel) 1828-1905 **TCLC 6, 52**
See also AAYA 16; CA 110; 131; DLB 123; JRDA; MAICYA; SATA 21

Very, Jones 1813-1880 .... **NCLC 9**
See also DLB 1

Vesaas, Tarjei 1897-1970 .... **CLC 48**
See also CA 29-32R

Vialis, Gaston
See Simenon, Georges (Jacques Christian)

Vian, Boris 1920-1959 .... **TCLC 9**
See also CA 106; 164; DLB 72; MTCW 2

Viaud, (Louis Marie) Julien 1850-1923
See Loti, Pierre
See also CA 107

Vicar, Henry

See Felsen, Henry Gregor

Vicker, Angus
See Felsen, Henry Gregor

Vidal, Gore 1925- **CLC 2, 4, 6, 8, 10, 22, 33, 72; DAM NOV, POP**
See also AITN 1; BEST 90:2; CA 5-8R; CANR 13, 45, 65; CDALBS; DLB 6, 152; INT CANR-13; MTCW 1, 2

Viereck, Peter (Robert Edwin) 1916- **CLC 4; PC 27**
See also CA 1-4R; CANR 1, 47; DLB 5

Vigny, Alfred (Victor) de 1797-1863 **NCLC 7; DAM POET; PC 26**
See also DLB 119, 192

Vilakazi, Benedict Wallet 1906-1947 **TCLC 37**
See also CA 168

Villa, Jose Garcia 1904-1997 .... **PC 22**
See also CA 25-28R; CANR 12

Villaurrutia, Xavier 1903-1950 ...... **TCLC 80**
See also HW 1

Villiers de l'Isle Adam, Jean Marie Mathias Philippe Auguste, Comte de 1838-1889 **NCLC 3; SSC 14**
See also DLB 123

Villon, Francois 1431-1463(?) .... **PC 13**
See also DLB 208

Vinci, Leonardo da 1452-1519 .... **LC 12**

Vine, Barbara .... **CLC 50**
See also Rendell, Ruth (Barbara)
See also BEST 90:4

Vinge, Joan (Carol) D(ennison) 1948- **CLC 30; SSC 24**
See also CA 93-96; CANR 72; SATA 36

Violis, G.
See Simenon, Georges (Jacques Christian)

Virgil 70B.C.-19B.C.
See Vergil
See also DLB 211

Visconti, Luchino 1906-1976 .... **CLC 16**
See also CA 81-84; 65-68; CANR 39

Vittorini, Elio 1908-1966 .... **CLC 6, 9, 14**
See also CA 133; 25-28R

Vivekananda, Swami 1863-1902 .... **TCLC 88**

Vizenor, Gerald Robert 1934- **CLC 103; DAM MULT**
See also CA 13-16R; CAAS 22; CANR 5, 21, 44, 67; DLB 175; MTCW 2; NNAL

Vizinczey, Stephen 1933- .... **CLC 40**
See also CA 128; INT 128

Vliet, R(ussell) G(ordon) 1929-1984 . **CLC 22**
See also CA 37-40R; 112; CANR 18

Vogau, Boris Andreyevich 1894-1937(?)
See Pilnyak, Boris
See also CA 123

Vogel, Paula A(nne) 1951- .... **CLC 76**
See also CA 108

Voigt, Cynthia 1942- .... **CLC 30**
See also AAYA 3, 30; CA 106; CANR 18, 37, 40; CLR 13, 48; INT CANR-18; JRDA; MAICYA; SATA 48, 79; SATA-Brief 33

Voigt, Ellen Bryant 1943- .... **CLC 54**
See also CA 69-72; CANR 11, 29, 55; DLB 120

Voinovich, Vladimir (Nikolaevich) 1932- **C L C 10, 49**
See also CA 81-84; CAAS 12; CANR 33, 67; MTCW 1

Vollmann, William T. 1959- .. **CLC 89; DAM NOV, POP**
See also CA 134; CANR 67; MTCW 2

Voloshinov, V. N.
See Bakhtin, Mikhail Mikhailovich

Voltaire 1694-1778 **LC 14; DA; DAB; DAC; DAM DRAM, MST; SSC 12; WLC**

von Aschendrof, BaronIgnatz
See Ford, Ford Madox

von Daeniken, Erich 1935- .... **CLC 30**
See also AITN 1; CA 37-40R; CANR 17, 44

von Daniken, Erich
See von Daeniken, Erich

von Heidenstam, (Carl Gustaf) Verner
See Heidenstam, (Carl Gustaf) Verner von

von Heyse, Paul (Johann Ludwig)
See Heyse, Paul (Johann Ludwig von)

von Hofmannsthal, Hugo
See Hofmannsthal, Hugo von

von Horvath, Odon
See Horvath, Oedoen von

von Horvath, Oedoen
See Horvath, Oedoen von

von Liliencron, (Friedrich Adolf Axel) Detlev
See Liliencron, (Friedrich Adolf Axel) Detlev von

Vonnegut, Kurt, Jr. 1922- **CLC 1, 2, 3, 4, 5, 8, 12, 22, 40, 60, 111; DA; DAB; DAC; DAM MST, NOV, POP; SSC 8; WLC**
See also AAYA 6; AITN 1; BEST 90:4; CA 1-4R; CANR 1, 25, 49, 75; CDALB 1968-1988; DLB 2, 8, 152; DLBD 3; DLBY 80; MTCW 1, 2

Von Rachen, Kurt
See Hubbard, L(afayette) Ron(ald)

von Rezzori (d'Arezzo), Gregor
See Rezzori (d'Arezzo), Gregor von

von Sternberg, Josef
See Sternberg, Josef von

Vorster, Gordon 1924- .... **CLC 34**
See also CA 133

Vosce, Trudie
See Ozick, Cynthia

Voznesensky, Andrei (Andreievich) 1933- **CLC 1, 15, 57; DAM POET**
See also CA 89-92; CANR 37; MTCW 1

Waddington, Miriam 1917- .... **CLC 28**
See also CA 21-24R; CANR 12, 30; DLB 68

Wagman, Fredrica 1937- .... **CLC 7**
See also CA 97-100; INT 97-100

Wagner, Linda W.
See Wagner-Martin, Linda (C.)

Wagner, Linda Welshimer
See Wagner-Martin, Linda (C.)

Wagner, Richard 1813-1883 .... **NCLC 9**
See also DLB 129

Wagner-Martin, Linda (C.) 1936- .... **CLC 50**
See also CA 159

Wagoner, David (Russell) 1926- **CLC 3, 5, 15**
See also CA 1-4R; CAAS 3; CANR 2, 71; DLB 5; SATA 14

Wah, Fred(erick James) 1939- .... **CLC 44**
See also CA 107; 141; DLB 60

Wahloo, Per 1926-1975 .... **CLC 7**
See also CA 61-64; CANR 73

Wahloo, Peter
See Wahloo, Per

Wain, John (Barrington) 1925-1994 . **CLC 2, 11, 15, 46**
See also CA 5-8R; 145; CAAS 4; CANR 23, 54; CDBLB 1960 to Present; DLB 15, 27, 139, 155; MTCW 1, 2

Wajda, Andrzej 1926- .... **CLC 16**
See also CA 102

Wakefield, Dan 1932- .... **CLC 7**
See also CA 21-24R; CAAS 7

Wakoski, Diane 1937- . **CLC 2, 4, 7, 9, 11, 40; DAM POET; PC 15**
See also CA 13-16R; CAAS 1; CANR 9, 60; DLB 5; INT CANR-9; MTCW 2

See also CA 13-16R; DLB 16

Wiesel, Elie(zer) 1928- **CLC 3, 5, 11, 37; DA; DAB; DAC; DAM MST, NOV; WLCS**
See also AAYA 7; AITN 1; CA 5-8R; CAAS 4; CANR 8, 40, 65; CDALBS; DLB 83; DLBY 87; INT CANR-8; MTCW 1, 2; SATA 56

Wiggins, Marianne 1947- .... **CLC 57**
See also BEST 89:3; CA 130; CANR 60

Wight, James Alfred 1916-1995
See Herriot, James
See also CA 77-80; SATA 55; SATA-Brief 44

Wilbur, Richard (Purdy) 1921-**CLC 3, 6, 9, 14, 53, 110; DA; DAB; DAC; DAM MST, POET**
See also CA 1-4R; CABS 2; CANR 2, 29, 76; CDALBS; DLB 5, 169; INT CANR-29; MTCW 1, 2; SATA 9, 108

Wild, Peter 1940- .... **CLC 14**
See also CA 37-40R; DLB 5

Wilde, Oscar 1854(?)-1900**TCLC 1, 8, 23, 41; DA; DAB; DAC; DAM DRAM, MST, NOV; SSC 11; WLC**
See also CA 104; 119; CDBLB 1890-1914; DLB 10, 19, 34, 57, 141, 156, 190; SATA 24

Wilder, Billy .... **CLC 20**
See also Wilder, Samuel
See also DLB 26

Wilder, Samuel 1906-
See Wilder, Billy
See also CA 89-92

Wilder, Thornton (Niven) 1897-1975**CLC 1, 5, 6, 10, 15, 35, 82; DA; DAB; DAC; DAM DRAM, MST, NOV; DC 1; WLC**
See also AAYA 29; AITN 2; CA 13-16R; 61-64; CANR 40; CDALBS; DLB 4, 7, 9; DLBY 97; MTCW 1, 2

Wilding, Michael 1942-..................... **CLC 73**
See also CA 104; CANR 24, 49

Wiley, Richard 1944- .... **CLC 44**
See also CA 121; 129; CANR 71

Wilhelm, Kate .... **CLC 7**
See also Wilhelm, Katie Gertrude
See also AAYA 20; CAAS 5; DLB 8; INT CANR-17

Wilhelm, Katie Gertrude 1928-
See Wilhelm, Kate
See also CA 37-40R; CANR 17, 36, 60; MTCW 1

Wilkins, Mary
See Freeman, Mary Eleanor Wilkins

Willard, Nancy 1936- .... **CLC 7, 37**
See also CA 89-92; CANR 10, 39, 68; CLR 5; DLB 5, 52; MAICYA; MTCW 1; SATA 37, 71; SATA-Brief 30

William of Ockham 1285-1347 ..... **CMLC 32**

Williams, Ben Ames 1889-1953 ...... **TCLC 89**
See also DLB 102

Williams, C(harles) K(enneth) 1936-**CLC 33, 56; DAM POET**
See also CA 37-40R; CAAS 26; CANR 57; DLB 5

Williams, Charles
See Collier, James L(incoln)

Williams, Charles (Walter Stansby) 1886-1945 **TCLC 1, 11**
See also CA 104; 163; DLB 100, 153

Williams, (George) Emlyn 1905-1987**CLC 15; DAM DRAM**
See also CA 104; 123; CANR 36; DLB 10, 77; MTCW 1

Williams, Hank 1923-1953 .... **TCLC 81**

Williams, Hugo 1942-........................ **CLC 42**
See also CA 17-20R; CANR 45; DLB 40

Williams, J. Walker
See Wodehouse, P(elham) G(renville)

Williams, John A(lfred) 1925-**CLC 5, 13; BLC 3; DAM MULT**
See also BW 2, 3; CA 53-56; CAAS 3; CANR 6, 26, 51; DLB 2, 33; INT CANR-6

Williams, Jonathan (Chamberlain) 1929-**CLC 13**
See also CA 9-12R; CAAS 12; CANR 8; DLB 5

Williams, Joy 1944-............................**CLC 31**
See also CA 41-44R; CANR 22, 48

Williams, Norman 1952- ....**CLC 39**
See also CA 118

Williams, Sherley Anne 1944-**CLC 89; BLC 3; DAM MULT, POET**
See also BW 2, 3; CA 73-76; CANR 25; DLB 41; INT CANR-25; SATA 78

Williams, Shirley
See Williams, Sherley Anne

Williams, Tennessee 1911-1983**CLC 1, 2, 5, 7, 8, 11, 15, 19, 30, 39, 45, 71, 111; DA; DAB; DAC; DAM DRAM, MST; DC 4; WLC**
See also AITN 1, 2; CA 5-8R; 108; CABS 3; CANR 31; CDALB 1941-1968; DLB 7; DLBD 4; DLBY 83; MTCW 1, 2

Williams, Thomas (Alonzo) 1926-1990**CLC 14**
See also CA 1-4R; 132; CANR 2

Williams, William C.
See Williams, William Carlos

Williams, William Carlos 1883-1963**CLC 1, 2, 5, 9, 13, 22, 42, 67; DA; DAB; DAC; DAM MST, POET; PC 7; SSC 31**
See also CA 89-92; CANR 34; CDALB 1917-1929; DLB 4, 16, 54, 86; MTCW 1, 2

Williamson, David (Keith) 1942- ...... **CLC 56**
See also CA 103; CANR 41

Williamson, Ellen Douglas 1905-1984
See Douglas, Ellen
See also CA 17-20R; 114; CANR 39

Williamson, Jack ....**CLC 29**
See also Williamson, John Stewart
See also CAAS 8; DLB 8

Williamson, John Stewart 1908-
See Williamson, Jack
See also CA 17-20R; CANR 23, 70

Willie, Frederick
See Lovecraft, H(oward) P(hillips)

Willingham, Calder (Baynard, Jr.) 1922-1995 **CLC 5, 51**
See also CA 5-8R; 147; CANR 3; DLB 2, 44; MTCW 1

Willis, Charles
See Clarke, Arthur C(harles)

Willis, Fingal O'Flahertie
See Wilde, Oscar

Willy
See Colette, (Sidonie-Gabrielle)

Willy, Colette
See Colette, (Sidonie-Gabrielle)

Wilson, A(ndrew) N(orman) 1950- ...**CLC 33**
See also CA 112; 122; DLB 14, 155, 194; MTCW 2

Wilson, Angus (Frank Johnstone) 1913-1991 **CLC 2, 3, 5, 25, 34; SSC 21**
See also CA 5-8R; 134; CANR 21; DLB 15, 139, 155; MTCW 1, 2

Wilson, August 1945- ... **CLC 39, 50, 63, 118; BLC 3; DA; DAB; DAC; DAM DRAM, MST, MULT; DC 2; WLCS**
See also AAYA 16; BW 2, 3; CA 115; 122; CANR 42, 54, 76; MTCW 1, 2

Wilson, Brian 1942- ....**CLC 12**

Wilson, Colin 1931- .... **CLC 3, 14**
See also CA 1-4R; CAAS 5; CANR 1, 22, 33, 77; DLB 14, 194; MTCW 1

Wilson, Dirk
See Pohl, Frederik

Wilson, Edmund 1895-1972**CLC 1, 2, 3, 8, 24**
See also CA 1-4R; 37-40R; CANR 1, 46; DLB 63; MTCW 1, 2

Wilson, Ethel Davis (Bryant) 1888(?)-1980 **CLC 13; DAC; DAM POET**
See also CA 102; DLB 68; MTCW 1

Wilson, John 1785-1854 .... **NCLC 5**

Wilson, John (Anthony) Burgess 1917-1993
See Burgess, Anthony
See also CA 1-4R; 143; CANR 2, 46; DAC; DAM NOV; MTCW 1, 2

Wilson, Lanford 1937- **CLC 7, 14, 36; DAM DRAM**
See also CA 17-20R; CABS 3; CANR 45; DLB 7

Wilson, Robert M. 1944- .... **CLC 7, 9**
See also CA 49-52; CANR 2, 41; MTCW 1

Wilson, Robert McLiam 1964-......... **CLC 59**
See also CA 132

Wilson, Sloan 1920-............................ **CLC 32**
See also CA 1-4R; CANR 1, 44

Wilson, Snoo 1948-............................. **CLC 33**
See also CA 69-72

Wilson, William S(mith) 1932- .... **CLC 49**
See also CA 81-84

Wilson, (Thomas) Woodrow 1856-1924**TCLC 79**
See also CA 166; DLB 47

Winchilsea, Anne (Kingsmill) Finch Counte 1661-1720
See Finch, Anne

Windham, Basil
See Wodehouse, P(elham) G(renville)

Wingrove, David (John) 1954- .... **CLC 68**
See also CA 133

Winnemucca, Sarah 1844-1891 ..... **NCLC 79**

Wintergreen, Jane
See Duncan, Sara Jeannette

Winters, Janet Lewis .... **CLC 41**
See also Lewis, Janet
See also DLBY 87

Winters, (Arthur) Yvor 1900-1968 **CLC 4, 8, 32**
See also CA 11-12; 25-28R; CAP 1; DLB 48; MTCW 1

Winterson, Jeanette 1959-**CLC 64; DAM POP**
See also CA 136; CANR 58; DLB 207; MTCW 2

Winthrop, John 1588-1649 .... **LC 31**
See also DLB 24, 30

Wirth, Louis 1897-1952 .... **TCLC 92**

Wiseman, Frederick 1930-............... **CLC 20**
See also CA 159

Wister, Owen 1860-1938 .... **TCLC 21**
See also CA 108; 162; DLB 9, 78, 186; SATA 62

Witkacy
See Witkiewicz, Stanislaw Ignacy

Witkiewicz, Stanislaw Ignacy 1885-1939 **TCLC 8**
See also CA 105; 162

Wittgenstein, Ludwig (Josef Johann) 1889-1951 **TCLC 59**
See also CA 113; 164; MTCW 2

Wittig, Monique 1935(?)-................. **CLC 22**
See also CA 116; 135; DLB 83

Wittlin, Jozef 1896-1976 .... **CLC 25**
See also CA 49-52; 65-68; CANR 3

Wodehouse, P(elham) G(renville) 1881-1975
**CLC 1, 2, 5, 10, 22; DAB; DAC; DAM
NOV; SSC 2**
See also AITN 2; CA 45-48; 57-60; CANR 3,
33; CDBLB 1914-1945; DLB 34, 162;
MTCW 1, 2; SATA 22

Woiwode, L.
See Woiwode, Larry (Alfred)

Woiwode, Larry (Alfred) 1941- ... **CLC 6, 10**
See also CA 73-76; CANR 16; DLB 6; INT
CANR-16

Wojciechowska, Maia (Teresa) 1927-**CLC 26**
See also AAYA 8; CA 9-12R; CANR 4, 41; CLR
1; JRDA; MAICYA; SAAS 1; SATA 1, 28,
83; SATA-Essay 104

Wolf, Christa 1929- .... **CLC 14, 29, 58**
See also CA 85-88; CANR 45; DLB 75; MTCW
1

Wolfe, Gene (Rodman) 1931- **CLC 25; DAM
POP**
See also CA 57-60; CAAS 9; CANR 6, 32, 60;
DLB 8; MTCW 2

Wolfe, George C. 1954- .... **CLC 49; BLCS**
See also CA 149

Wolfe, Thomas (Clayton) 1900-1938**TCLC 4,
13, 29, 61; DA; DAB; DAC; DAM MST,
NOV; SSC 33; WLC**
See also CA 104; 132; CDALB 1929-1941;
DLB 9, 102; DLBD 2, 16; DLBY 85, 97;
MTCW 1, 2

Wolfe, Thomas Kennerly, Jr. 1930-
See Wolfe, Tom
See also CA 13-16R; CANR 9, 33, 70; DAM
POP; DLB 185; INT CANR-9; MTCW 1, 2

Wolfe, Tom .... **CLC 1, 2, 9, 15, 35, 51**
See also Wolfe, Thomas Kennerly, Jr.
See also AAYA 8; AITN 2; BEST 89:1; DLB
152

Wolff, Geoffrey (Ansell) 1937- .... **CLC 41**
See also CA 29-32R; CANR 29, 43, 78

Wolff, Sonia
See Levitin, Sonia (Wolff)

Wolff, Tobias (Jonathan Ansell) 1945-.. **C L C
39, 64**
See also AAYA 16; BEST 90:2; CA 114; 117;
CAAS 22; CANR 54, 76; DLB 130; INT 117;
MTCW 2

Wolfram von Eschenbach c. 1170-c. 1220
CMLC 5
See also DLB 138

Wolitzer, Hilma 1930- .... **CLC 17**
See also CA 65-68; CANR 18, 40; INT CANR-
18; SATA 31

Wollstonecraft, Mary 1759-1797 .... **LC 5, 50**
See also CDBLB 1789-1832; DLB 39, 104, 158

Wonder, Stevie .... **CLC 12**
See also Morris, Steveland Judkins

Wong, Jade Snow 1922- .... **CLC 17**
See also CA 109

Woodberry, George Edward 1855-1930
TCLC 73
See also CA 165; DLB 71, 103

Woodcott, Keith
See Brunner, John (Kilian Houston)

Woodruff, Robert W.
See Mencken, H(enry) L(ouis)

Woolf, (Adeline) Virginia 1882-1941**TCLC 1,
5, 20, 43, 56; DA; DAB; DAC; DAM MST,
NOV; SSC 7; WLC**
See also Woolf, Virginia Adeline
See also CA 104; 130; CANR 64; CDBLB
1914-1945; DLB 36, 100, 162; DLBD 10;
MTCW 1

Woolf, Virginia Adeline
See Woolf, (Adeline) Virginia
See also MTCW 2

Woollcott, Alexander (Humphreys) 1887-1943
TCLC 5
See also CA 105; 161; DLB 29

Woolrich, Cornell 1903-1968 .... **CLC 77**
See also Hopley-Woolrich, Cornell George

Wordsworth, Dorothy 1771-1855 .. **NCLC 25**
See also DLB 107

Wordsworth, William 1770-1850 .. **NCLC 12,
38; DA; DAB; DAC; DAM MST, POET;
PC 4; WLC**
See also CDBLB 1789-1832; DLB 93, 107

Wouk, Herman 1915-**CLC 1, 9, 38; DAM NOV,
POP**
See also CA 5-8R; CANR 6, 33, 67; CDALBS;
DLBY 82; INT CANR-6; MTCW 1, 2

Wright, Charles (Penzel, Jr.) 1935-**CLC 6, 13,
28, 119**
See also CA 29-32R; CAAS 7; CANR 23, 36,
62; DLB 165; DLBY 82; MTCW 1, 2

Wright, Charles Stevenson 1932- ... **CLC 49;
BLC 3; DAM MULT, POET**
See also BW 1; CA 9-12R; CANR 26; DLB 33

Wright, Frances 1795-1852 .... **NCLC 74**
See also DLB 73

Wright, Frank Lloyd 1867-1959 .... **TCLC 95**
See also CA 174

Wright, Jack R.
See Harris, Mark

Wright, James (Arlington) 1927-1980**CLC 3,
5, 10, 28; DAM POET**
See also AITN 2; CA 49-52; 97-100; CANR 4,
34, 64; CDALBS; DLB 5, 169; MTCW 1, 2

Wright, Judith (Arandell) 1915- **CLC 11, 53;
PC 14**
See also CA 13-16R; CANR 31, 76; MTCW 1,
2; SATA 14

Wright, L(aurali) R. 1939- .... **CLC 44**
See also CA 138

Wright, Richard (Nathaniel) 1908-1960 **C L C
1, 3, 4, 9, 14, 21, 48, 74; BLC 3; DA; DAB;
DAC; DAM MST, MULT, NOV; SSC 2;
WLC**
See also AAYA 5; BW 1; CA 108; CANR 64;
CDALB 1929-1941; DLB 76, 102; DLBD
2; MTCW 1, 2

Wright, Richard B(ruce) 1937- .... **CLC 6**
See also CA 85-88; DLB 53

Wright, Rick 1945- .... **CLC 35**

Wright, Rowland
See Wells, Carolyn

Wright, Stephen 1946- .... **CLC 33**

Wright, Willard Huntington 1888-1939
See Van Dine, S. S.
See also CA 115; DLBD 16

Wright, William 1930- .... **CLC 44**
See also CA 53-56; CANR 7, 23

Wroth, LadyMary 1587-1653(?) .... **LC 30**
See also DLB 121

Wu Ch'eng-en 1500(?)-1582(?) .... **LC 7**

Wu Ching-tzu 1701-1754 .... **LC 2**

Wurlitzer, Rudolph 1938(?)- .... **CLC 2, 4, 15**
See also CA 85-88; DLB 173

Wyatt, Thomas c. 1503-1542 .... **PC 27**
See also DLB 132

Wycherley, William 1641-1715**LC 8, 21; DAM
DRAM**
See also CDBLB 1660-1789; DLB 80

Wylie, Elinor (Morton Hoyt) 1885-1928
TCLC 8; PC 23
See also CA 105; 162; DLB 9, 45

Wylie, Philip (Gordon) 1902-1971 .... **CLC 43**
See also CA 21-22; 33-36R; CAP 2; DLB 9

Wyndham, John .... **CLC 19**
See also Harris, John (Wyndham Parkes Lucas)
Beynon

Wyss, Johann David Von 1743-1818**NCLC 10**
See also JRDA; MAICYA; SATA 29; SATA-
Brief 27

Xenophon c. 430B.C.-c. 354B.C. ... **CMLC 17**
See also DLB 176

Yakumo Koizumi
See Hearn, (Patricio) Lafcadio (Tessima Carlos)

Yamamoto, Hisaye 1921-**SSC 34; DAM MULT**

Yanez, Jose Donoso
See Donoso (Yanez), Jose

Yanovsky, Basile S.
See Yanovsky, V(assily) S(emenovich)

Yanovsky, V(assily) S(emenovich) 1906-1989
CLC 2, 18
See also CA 97-100; 129

Yates, Richard 1926-1992 .... **CLC 7, 8, 23**
See also CA 5-8R; 139; CANR 10, 43; DLB 2;
DLBY 81, 92; INT CANR-10

Yeats, W. B.
See Yeats, William Butler

Yeats, William Butler 1865-1939**TCLC 1, 11,
18, 31, 93; DA; DAB; DAC; DAM DRAM,
MST, POET; PC 20; WLC**
See also CA 104; 127; CANR 45; CDBLB
1890-1914; DLB 10, 19, 98, 156; MTCW 1,
2

Yehoshua, A(braham) B. 1936- .. **CLC 13, 31**
See also CA 33-36R; CANR 43

Yep, Laurence Michael 1948-............ **CLC 35**
See also AAYA 5; CA 49-52; CANR 1, 46; CLR
3, 17, 54; DLB 52; JRDA; MAICYA; SATA
7, 69

Yerby, Frank G(arvin) 1916-1991 **CLC 1, 7,
22; BLC 3; DAM MULT**
See also BW 1, 3; CA 9-12R; 136; CANR 16,
52; DLB 76; INT CANR-16; MTCW 1

Yesenin, Sergei Alexandrovich
See Esenin, Sergei (Alexandrovich)

Yevtushenko, Yevgeny (Alexandrovich) 1933-
CLC 1, 3, 13, 26, 51; DAM POET
See also CA 81-84; CANR 33, 54; MTCW 1

Yezierska, Anzia 1885(?)-1970 .... **CLC 46**
See also CA 126; 89-92; DLB 28; MTCW 1

Yglesias, Helen 1915- .... **CLC 7, 22**
See also CA 37-40R; CAAS 20; CANR 15, 65;
INT CANR-15; MTCW 1

Yokomitsu Riichi 1898-1947 .... **TCLC 47**
See also CA 170

Yonge, Charlotte (Mary) 1823-1901**TCLC 48**
See also CA 109; 163; DLB 18, 163; SATA 17

York, Jeremy
See Creasey, John

York, Simon
See Heinlein, Robert A(nson)

Yorke, Henry Vincent 1905-1974 ...... **CLC 13**
See also Green, Henry
See also CA 85-88; 49-52

Yosano Akiko 1878-1942 .... **TCLC 59; PC 11**
See also CA 161

Yoshimoto, Banana .... **CLC 84**
See also Yoshimoto, Mahoko

Yoshimoto, Mahoko 1964-
See Yoshimoto, Banana
See also CA 144

Young, Al(bert James) 1939-**CLC 19; BLC 3;
DAM MULT**
See also BW 2, 3; CA 29-32R; CANR 26, 65;
DLB 33

Literary Criticism Series
Cumulative Topic Index

This index lists all topic entries in Gale's *Classical and Medieval Literature Criticism, Contemporary Literary Criticism, Literature Criticism from 1400 to 1800, Nineteenth-Century Literature Criticism,* and *Twentieth-Century Literary Criticism.*

Topic Index

Topic Index

Topic Index

NCLC Cumulative Nationality Index

Nationality Index

NCLC-79 Title Index

ISBN 0-7876-3150-7